Java™ Late Objects Version

HOW TO PROGRAM

EIGHTH EDITION

Deitel® Ser

How To Program Series

Java How to Program, 8/E

Java How to Program, Late Objects Version, 8/E

C++ How to Program, 6/E

C How to Program, 5/E

Internet & World Wide Web How to Program, 4/E

Visual Basic® 2008 How to Program

Visual C#® 2008 How to Program, 3/E

Visual C++® 2008 How to Program, 2/E

Small Java™ How to Program, 6/E

Small C++ How to Program, 5/E

Simply Series

Simply C++: An Application-Driven Tutorial Approach

Simply Java™ Programming: An Application-Driven Tutorial Approach

Simply C#: An Application-Driven Tutorial Approach

Simply Visual Basic® 2008, 3/E: An Application-Driven Tutorial Approach

CourseSmart Web Books

www.deitel.com/books/CourseSmart.html

C++ How to Program, 5/E & 6/E

Java How to Program, 6/E, 7/E & 8/E

Simply C++: An Application-Driven Tutorial Approach

Simply Visual Basic 2008: An Application-Driven Tutorial Approach, 3/E

Small C++ How to Program, 5/E

Small Java How to Program, 6/E

Visual Basic 2008 How to Program

Visual C# 2008 How to Program, 3/E

ies Page

Deitel® Developer Series

AJAX, Rich Internet Applications and
  Web Development for Programmers

C++ for Programmers

C# 2008 for Programmers, 3/E

Java for Programmers

Javascript for Programmers

LiveLessons Video Learning Products
www.deitel.com/books/LiveLessons/

Java Fundamentals Parts 1 and 2

C# Fundamentals Parts 1 and 2

C++ Fundamentals Parts 1 and 2

JavaScript Fundamentals Parts 1 and 2

To receive updates on Deitel publications, Resource Centers, training courses, partner offers and more, please register for the free *Deitel® Buzz Online* e-mail newsletter at:

www.deitel.com/newsletter/subscribe.html

follow us on Twitter®

@deitel

and join the Deitel & Associates group on Facebook®

www.facebook.com/group.php?gid=38765799996

To communicate with the authors, send e-mail to:

deitel@deitel.com

For information on government and corporate *Dive-Into® Series* on-site seminars offered by Deitel & Associates, Inc. worldwide, visit:

www.deitel.com/training/

or write to

deitel@deitel.com

For continuing updates on Prentice Hall/Deitel publications visit:

www.deitel.com
www.pearsonhighered.com/deitel

Check out our Resource Centers for valuable web resources that will help you master Java, other important programming languages, software and Internet- and web-related topics:

www.deitel.com/ResourceCenters.html

Library of Congress Cataloging-in-Publication Data
On file

Vice President and Editorial Director, ECS: **Marcia J. Horton**
Editor-in-Chief, Computer Science: **Michael Hirsch**
Associate Editor: **Carole Snyder**
Supervisor/Editorial Assistant: **Dolores Mars**
Director of Team-Based Project Management: **Vince O'Brien**
Senior Managing Editor: **Scott Disanno**
Managing Editor: **Robert Engelhardt**
A/V Production Editor: **Greg Dulles**
Art Director: **Kristine Carney**
Cover Design: **Abbey S. Deitel, Harvey M. Deitel, Francesco Santalucia, Kristine Carney**
Interior Design: **Harvey M. Deitel, Kristine Carney**
Manufacturing Manager: **Alexis Heydt-Long**
Manufacturing Buyer: **Lisa McDowell**
Director of Marketing: **Margaret Waples**
Marketing Manager: **Erin Davis**

© 2010 by Pearson Education, Inc.
Upper Saddle River, New Jersey 07458

The authors and publisher of this book have used their best efforts in preparing this book. These efforts include the development, research, and testing of the theories and programs to determine their effectiveness. The authors and publisher make no warranty of any kind, expressed or implied, with regard to these programs or to the documentation contained in this book. The authors and publisher shall not be liable in any event for incidental or consequential damages in connection with, or arising out of, the furnishing, performance, or use of these programs.

Many of the designations used by manufacturers and sellers to distinguish their products are claimed as trademarks and registered trademarks. Where those designations appear in this book, and Prentice Hall and the authors were aware of a trademark claim, the designations have been printed in initial caps or all caps. All product names mentioned remain trademarks or registered trademarks of their respective owners.

Printed in the United States of America

10 9 8 7 6 5 4 3 2 1

ISBN-10: 0-13-612371-6

ISBN-13: 978-0-13-612371-2

Pearson Education Ltd., *London*
Pearson Education Australia Pty. Ltd., *Sydney*
Pearson Education Singapore, Pte. Ltd.
Pearson Education North Asia Ltd., *Hong Kong*
Pearson Education Canada, Inc., *Toronto*
Pearson Educación de Mexico, S.A. de C.V.
Pearson Education–Japan, *Tokyo*
Pearson Education Malaysia, Pte. Ltd.
Pearson Education, Inc., *Upper Saddle River, New Jersey*

Java™ Late Objects Version

HOW TO PROGRAM

EIGHTH EDITION

Paul Deitel
Deitel & Associates, Inc.

Harvey Deitel
Deitel & Associates, Inc.

PEARSON
Prentice Hall

Upper Saddle River, New Jersey 07458

Trademarks

In memory of

Kristen Nygaard, co-inventor of Simula, the world's first object-oriented programming language.

Paul and Harvey Deitel

Deitel Resource Centers

Our Resource Centers focus on the vast amounts of free content available online. Find resources, downloads, tutorials, documentation, books, e-books, journals, articles, blogs, RSS feeds and more on many of today's hottest programming and technology topics. For the most up-to-date list of our Resource Centers, visit:

> www.deitel.com/ResourceCenters.html

Let us know what other Resource Centers you'd like to see! Also, please register for the free *Deitel® Buzz Online* e-mail newsletter at:

> www.deitel.com/newsletter/subscribe.html

Computer Science
Functional Programming
Regular Expressions

Programming
ASP.NET 3.5
Adobe Flex
Ajax
Apex
ASP.NET Ajax
ASP.NET
C
C++
C++ Boost Libraries
C++ Game Programming
C#
Code Search Engines and Code Sites
Computer Game Programming
CSS 2.1
Dojo
Facebook Developer Platform
Flash 9
Functional Programming
Java
Java Certification and Assessment Testing
Java Design Patterns
Java EE 5
Java SE 6
Java SE 7 (Dolphin) Resource Center
JavaFX
JavaScript
JSON
Microsoft LINQ
Microsoft Popfly
.NET
.NET 3.0
.NET 3.5
OpenGL
Perl
PHP
Programming Projects
Python
Regular Expressions
Ruby
Ruby on Rails

Silverlight
UML
Visual Basic
Visual C++
Visual Studio Team System
Web 3D Technologies
Web Services
Windows Presentation Foundation
XHTML
XML

Games and Game Programming
Computer Game Programming
Computer Games
Mobile Gaming
Sudoku

Internet Business
Affiliate Programs
Competitive Analysis
Facebook Social Ads
Google AdSense
Google Analytics
Google Services
Internet Advertising
Internet Business Initiative
Internet Public Relations
Link Building
Location-Based Services
Online Lead Generation
Podcasting
Search Engine Optimization
Selling Digital Content
Sitemaps
Web Analytics
Website Monetization
YouTube and AdSense

Java
Java
Java Certification and Assessment Testing
Java Design Patterns
Java EE 5

Java SE 6
Java SE 7 (Dolphin) Resource Center
JavaFX

Microsoft
ASP.NET
ASP.NET 3.5
ASP.NET Ajax
C#
DotNetNuke (DNN)
Internet Explorer 7 (IE7)
Microsoft LINQ
.NET
.NET 3.0
.NET 3.5
SharePoint
Silverlight
Visual Basic
Visual C++
Visual Studio Team System
Windows Presentation Foundation
Windows Vista
Microsoft Popfly

Open Source & LAMP Stack
Apache
DotNetNuke (DNN)
Eclipse
Firefox
Linux
MySQL
Open Source
Perl
PHP
Python
Ruby

Software
Apache
DotNetNuke (DNN)
Eclipse
Firefox
Internet Explorer 7 (IE7)
Linux
MySQL
Open Source

Search Engines
SharePoint
Skype
Web Servers
Wikis
Windows Vista

Web 2.0
Alert Services
Attention Economy
Blogging
Building Web Communities
Community Generated Content
Facebook Developer Platform
Facebook Social Ads
Google Base
Google Video
Google Web Toolkit (GWT)
Internet Video
Joost
Location-Based Services
Mashups
Microformats
Recommender Systems
RSS
Social Graph
Social Media
Social Networking
Software as a Service (SaaS)
Virtual Worlds
Web 2.0
Web 3.0
Widgets

Dive Into® Web 2.0 eBook
Web 2 eBook

Other Topics
Computer Games
Computing Jobs
Gadgets and Gizmos
Ring Tones
Sudoku

Contents

Chapters 26–31 and Appendices H–Q are web-based PDF documents available from the book's Companion Website (www.pearsonhighered.com/deitel).

12 ATM Case Study, Part 1: Object-Oriented Design with the UML   484

13 ATM Case Study Part 2: Implementing an Object-Oriented Design   525

14 GUI Components: Part 1   563

15 Graphics and Java 2D™ 648

16 Strings, Characters and Regular Expressions 689

17   Files, Streams and Object Serialization   719

18   Recursion   756

19   Searching, Sorting and Big O   789

23 Applets and Java Web Start 932

24 Multimedia: Applets and Applications 958

25 GUI Components: Part 2 991

Chapters on the Web   1036

Chapters 26–31 are available as web-based PDF documents. See page 1036 for details.

29 JavaServer™ Faces Web Applications CXC

30 Ajax-Enabled JavaServer™ Faces Web Applications **CCLVI**

31 Web Services **CCLXXXVI**

A   Operator Precedence Chart   1037

B   ASCII Character Set   1039

C   Keywords and Reserved Words   1040

D   Primitive Types   1041

E   Using the Java API Documentation   1042

F   Using the Debugger   1050

G   Formatted Output   1067

Appendices on the Web   1090

Appendices H–Q are available as web-based PDF documents. See page 1090 for details.

H   Number Systems   CCCLIV

I   GroupLayout   CCCLXVII

J   Java Desktop Integration Components (JDIC)   CCCLXXIX

K   Mashups   CCCLXXXV

Live in fragments no longer, only connect.
—Edgar Morgan Foster

Welcome to the Java programming language and *Java How to Program, Late Objects Version, Eighth Edition*! This book is appropriate for introductory-level programming courses (commonly known as CS1 and CS2). It also provides substantial depth for those who already know how to program and want to learn Java.

At the heart of this book is the Deitel signature "live-code approach." Concepts are presented in the context of complete working Java programs, rather than using code snippets. Each code example is immediately followed by one or more sample executions. All the source code is available at www.deitel.com/books/jhtp8LOV/.

Motivation for *Java How to Program, Late Objects Version, 8/e*

There are several approaches for teaching first courses in Java programming. The two most popular are the *late objects approach* and the *early objects approach*. To meet these diverse needs, we have published two versions of this book:

- *Java How to Program, Late Objects Version, 8/e*, and
- *Java How to Program, 8/e* (which offers an early objects approach).

The key difference between these two editions is the order in which topics are presented in Chapters 1–7. The books have virtually identical content from Chapters 8 to 31. In *Java How to Program, Late Objects Version, 8/e*, Chapters 26–31 are available only in PDF format at the book's companion website.

Chapters 1–6 in *Java How to Program, Late Objects Version, 8/e*, form the core of a pure-procedural programming CS1 course that covers operators, data types, input/output, control statements, methods, arrays, strings and files. Instructors who want to introduce *some* object-oriented programming in a first course can include a portion of the next several chapters.

New Features

If you've seen the seventh edition of *Java How to Program*, you might wonder how this book differs. Besides the organizational changes previously mentioned, here are updates we've made for *Java How to Program, Late Objects Version, 8/e*:

- We updated the book to the latest version of Java Standard Edition 6.
- We added the Making a Difference exercises set to help you discover how you can make a difference in the world in which you live. We encourage you to associate computers and the Internet with solving problems that really matter to individuals, communities, countries and the world. These new exercises will encourage

you to think critically as you explore complex social issues. Approach these issues in the context of your own values, politics and beliefs. Many of the new exercises require you to do research on the web and weave the results into your problem-solving process. There are more than 30 Making a Difference exercises throughout the book on subjects including global warming, population growth, gender neutrality, computerization of health records, alternative tax plans, hybrid vehicles, accessibility for people with disabilities and more. A complete list of Making a Difference exercises is available at

www.deitel.com/books/JHTP8LOV/

- We refreshed the book's interior design in a manner that graphically organizes, clarifies and highlights the information and enhances the book's pedagogy.

- We reinforced our object-oriented programming pedagogy, paying careful attention to the guidance of the college instructors on our review teams to ensure that we got the conceptual level right. The treatment of OOP is clear and accessible. We introduce the basic concepts and terminology of object technology in Chapter 1—this section can be deferred to the beginning of Chapter 7 by instructors who wish to teach pure procedural programming in the early chapters. You'll develop your first *customized* classes and objects in Chapter 7.

- We reordered several chapters to facilitate teaching the book in modules. The chapter dependency chart (page xxxii) shows the new modularization.

- We've added many links to the online Java documentation and the Deitel Java-related Resource Centers available at www.deitel.com/ResourceCenters.html.

- Chapter 6 now covers class Arrays—which contains methods for performing common array manipulations, such as searching and sorting an array's contents—and class ArrayList—which implements a dynamically resizable array-like data structure. This follows our philosophy of *using existing classes before learning how to define your own classes*.

- We introduce string and file processing at the end of Chapter 6. This enables instructors to teach these topics early in a first course if they wish. We cover these topics in more depth in Chapters 16 and 17, respectively.

- We've replaced all uses of StringTokenizer with the preferred String method split, which uses Java's robust regular-expression processing capabilities. Class StringTokenizer is still discussed, primarily for backward compatibility with legacy code.

- We reordered our presentation of data structures. We now begin with generic class ArrayList in Chapter 6 (this section can be deferred to Chapter 7) enabling students to understand basic collections and generics concepts early in the book. Our later data structures discussions provide a deeper treatment of generic collections, showing how to use the built-in collections of the Java API. We then show how to implement custom generic methods and classes. Finally, we show how to build custom generic data structures.

- We tuned the *optional* Object-Oriented Design/UML 2 automated teller machine (ATM) case study and reorganized it into two optional chapters (12 and 13) that present the ATM's design and complete code implementation. The

ATM is a nice business example that students relate to. In our experience, teaching these two chapters as a unit helps students tie together many of the object-oriented concepts they learn in Chapters 7–10. A key concept in object-oriented programming is the interactions among objects. In most programming textbooks, the code examples create and use one or two objects. The ATM gives students the opportunity to study interactions of *many* objects that provide the functionality of a substantial system. Chapters 12 and 13 provide complete solutions to *all* of their exercises.

- We added coverage of Java Web Start and the Java Network Launch Protocol (JNLP), which enable *both* applets *and* applications to be launched via a web browser. In addition, the user can install them as shortcuts on the desktop to execute them in the future without revisiting the website. Programs can also request the user's permission to access local system resources such as files—enabling you to develop more robust applets and applications that execute safely using Java's sandbox security model, which applies to downloaded code.

- We now introduce class `BigInteger` for arbitrarily large integer values in Chapter 18.

- The chapter terminology sections now include the page number of each key term's defining occurrence.

Other Features

Other features of *Java How to Program, Late Objects Version, 8/e*, include:

- We audited the presentation against the ACM/IEEE curriculum recommendations and the Computer Science Advanced Placement Examination.

- The classes and objects presentation features class `Time`, class `Employee` and `other` class case studies, some of which weave their way through multiple sections and chapters, gradually introducing deeper OO concepts.

- Instructors teaching introductory courses have a broad choice of the amount of GUI and graphics to cover—from none, to an optional eight-brief-sections introductory sequence spread over the early chapters, to a deep treatment in Chapters 14, 15, 23, 24 and 25, and Appendix J. (See the section Optional GUI and Graphics Track for more information.)

- Our object-oriented programming and design presentations use the *UML™ (Unified Modeling Language™)*—the industry-standard graphical language for modeling object-oriented systems.

- We provide several substantial object-oriented web programming case studies, mostly for use in second programming courses and by professionals.

- Chapter 28 covers JDBC 4 and uses the Java DB/Apache Derby and MySQL database management systems. The chapter features an OO case study on developing a database-driven address book that demonstrates prepared statements and JDBC 4's automatic driver discovery.

- Chapters 29 and 30 introduce JavaServer Faces (JSF) technology and use it with Netbeans 6.5 to build web applications quickly and easily. Chapter 29 includes examples on building web application GUIs, handling events, validating forms and session tracking. Chapter 30 discusses developing Ajax-enabled web applications, using JavaServer Faces technology. The chapter features a database-driven multitier web address book application that allows users to add and search for contacts. This Ajax-enabled application gives the reader a nice sense of Web 2.0 software development. The application uses Ajax-enabled JSF components to implement "type ahead" capability that suggests contact names as the user types a name to locate.

- Chapter 31 uses a tools-based approach to creating and consuming SOAP- *and* REST-based web services. Case studies include developing blackjack and airline reservation web services.

- We use a new tools-based approach for rapidly developing web applications; all the tools are available free for download.

- We provide 100+ Resource Centers (www.deitel.com/resourcecenters.html) to support our academic and professional readers. Their topics include Java SE 6, Java, Java Assessment and Certification, Java Design Patterns, Java EE 5, Code Search Engines and Code Sites, Game Programming, Programming Projects and many more. Sign up at www.deitel.com/newsletter/subscribe.html for the free *Deitel® Buzz Online* e-mail newsletter—each week we announce our latest Resource Center(s) and include other items of interest to our readers.

- We discuss key software engineering community concepts, such as Web 2.0, Ajax, SaaS (Software as a Service), web services, open-source software, design patterns, mashups, refactoring, agile software development and more.

- We reworked Chapter 26 [special thanks to Brian Goetz and Joseph Bowbeer— co-authors of *Java Concurrency in Practice*, Addison-Wesley, 2006].

- We discuss the SwingWorker class for developing multithreaded user interfaces.

- We discuss the GroupLayout layout manager in the context of the GUI design tool in the NetBeans IDE.

- We present JTable sorting and filtering capabilities which allow the user to re-sort the data in a JTable and filter it by regular expressions.

- We discuss the StringBuilder class, which performs better than StringBuffer in non-threaded applications.

- We present annotations, which greatly reduce the amount of code you have to write to build applications.

Optional GUI and Graphics Track

In *Java How to Program, Late Objects Version, 8/e*, students learn how to *create their own classes* starting in Chapter 7. The optional sections of the GUI and Graphics Track give students the opportunity to *create objects of existing classes* and do interesting things with them *before* the students attempt to create their own customized classes. The optional sections are:

- Section 2.9: Using Dialog Boxes
- Section 3.14: Creating Simple Drawings

- Section 4.10: Drawing Rectangles and Ovals
- Section 5.13: Colors and Filled Shapes
- Section 6.20: Drawing Arcs
- Section 8.16: Using Objects with Graphics
- Section 9.8: Displaying Text and Images Using Labels
- Section 10.8: Drawing with Polymorphism

Instructors who are teaching *pure procedural programming* in the first course can skip them. Instructors teaching the first course with *some* object-oriented programming have several options. They can defer the GUI and Graphics Track sections from Chapters 2–6 until after Chapter 7. Or they can avoid these sections altogether and simply cover the treatment of GUI and graphics that begins in Chapter 14.

Optional Case Study: Designing an Object-Oriented ATM

The UML 2 has become the preferred graphical modeling language for designing object-oriented systems. We use industry standard UML activity diagrams (in preference to the older flowcharts) to demonstrate the flow of control in each of Java's control statements, and we use UML class diagrams to visually represent classes and their inheritance relationships.

The optional Software Engineering Case Study in Chapters 12 and 13 presents a carefully paced introduction to object-oriented design using the UML—we design and fully implement the software for a simple automated teller machine (ATM). The case study has been reviewed by academics and industry professionals, including leaders in the field from Rational (the creators of the UML; Rational is now part of IBM) and the Object Management Group (an industry group now responsible for evolving the UML).

This case study helps prepare you for the kinds of substantial projects you'll encounter in industry. We employ a carefully developed, incremental object-oriented design process to produce a UML 2 model for the ATM system. From this design, we produce a substantial working Java implementation using key object-oriented programming concepts, including classes, objects, encapsulation, visibility, composition, inheritance and polymorphism.

We introduce a concise subset of the UML 2, then guide you through the design process. The case study is not an exercise—it's an end-to-end learning experience that concludes with a detailed walkthrough of the complete Java code.

At the end of Chapter 1, we introduce some basic concepts and terminology of OOD. In Chapter 12, we consider more substantial design issues, as we undertake a challenging problem with the techniques of OOD. We analyze a typical requirements document that specifies a system to be built, determine the objects needed to implement that system, determine the attributes these objects need to have, determine the behaviors these objects need to exhibit, and specify how the objects must interact with one another to meet the system requirements. In Chapter 13, we include a complete Java code implementation of the object-oriented system that we designed in Chapter 12.

Dependency Chart

The chart on the next page shows the dependencies among the chapters to help instructors plan their syllabi. *Java How to Program, Late Objects Version, 8/e* is appropriate for a variety of programming courses at various levels, most notably CS1 and CS2 courses and

**Chapter Dependency
Chart**

[*Note:* Arrows pointing into a
chapter indicate that chapter's
dependencies. Some chapters
have multiple dependencies.]

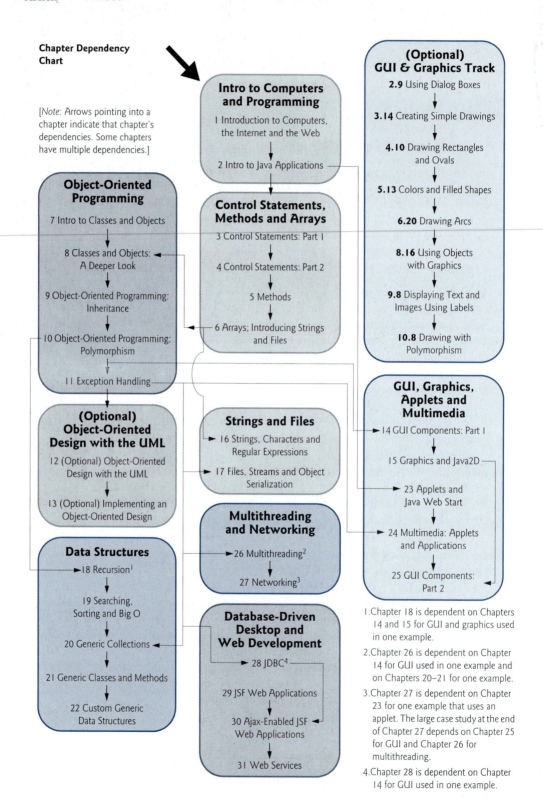

**Intro to Computers
and Programming**

1 Introduction to Computers,
the Internet and the Web

2 Intro to Java Applications

**(Optional)
GUI & Graphics Track**

2.9 Using Dialog Boxes

3.14 Creating Simple Drawings

4.10 Drawing Rectangles
and Ovals

5.13 Colors and Filled Shapes

6.20 Drawing Arcs

8.16 Using Objects
with Graphics

9.8 Displaying Text and
Images Using Labels

10.8 Drawing with
Polymorphism

**Object-Oriented
Programming**

7 Intro to Classes and Objects

8 Classes and Objects:
A Deeper Look

9 Object-Oriented Programming:
Inheritance

10 Object-Oriented Programming:
Polymorphism

11 Exception Handling

**Control Statements,
Methods and Arrays**

3 Control Statements: Part 1

4 Control Statements: Part 2

5 Methods

6 Arrays; Introducing Strings
and Files

**(Optional)
Object-Oriented
Design with the UML**

12 (Optional) Object-Oriented
Design with the UML

13 (Optional) Implementing an
Object-Oriented Design

Strings and Files

16 Strings, Characters and
Regular Expressions

17 Files, Streams and Object
Serialization

**GUI, Graphics,
Applets and
Multimedia**

14 GUI Components: Part 1

15 Graphics and Java2D

23 Applets and
Java Web Start

24 Multimedia: Applets
and Applications

25 GUI Components:
Part 2

Data Structures

18 Recursion[1]

19 Searching,
Sorting and Big O

20 Generic Collections

21 Generic Classes and Methods

22 Custom Generic
Data Structures

**Multithreading
and Networking**

26 Multithreading[2]

27 Networking[3]

**Database-Driven
Desktop and
Web Development**

28 JDBC[4]

29 JSF Web Applications

30 Ajax-Enabled JSF
Web Applications

31 Web Services

1. Chapter 18 is dependent on Chapters
14 and 15 for GUI and graphics used
in one example.

2. Chapter 26 is dependent on Chapter
14 for GUI used in one example and
on Chapters 20–21 for one example.

3. Chapter 27 is dependent on Chapter
23 for one example that uses an
applet. The large case study at the end
of Chapter 27 depends on Chapter 25
for GUI and Chapter 26 for
multithreading.

4. Chapter 28 is dependent on Chapter
14 for GUI used in one example.

introductory course sequences in related disciplines. The book has a convenient modular organization.

Introduction to Computers and Programming

Chapters 1–2 discuss computers, the Internet, the web, then introduce the basics of Java programming, including input/output, arithmetic operators and decision making.

Control Statements, Methods and Arrays

Chapters 3–6 form a clear introduction to procedural programming in Java, covering data types, operators, control statements, methods, arrays, and introducing strings and files. This is the non-object-oriented core of the book's late objects approach.

Object-Oriented Programming

Chapters 7–11 provide a solid introduction to object-oriented programming, covering classes, objects, inheritance, polymorphism, interfaces and exceptions.

(Optional) Object-Oriented Design with the UML

Optional Chapters 12–13 form an accessible introduction to object-oriented design with the UML.

GUI, Graphics, Applets and Multimedia

The GUI and Graphics Track (optional sections in Chapters 2–6 and 8–10) and Chapters 14, 15, 23, 24 and 25 form a substantial GUI, graphics and multimedia sequence.

Strings and Files

Chapters 16–17 continue our coverage of string and file processing that begins in Chapter 6.

Data Structures

Chapters 18–22 form a nice data-structures sequence, including recursion, searching, sorting, using generic collections, defining generic methods and classes, and building custom generic data structures.

Multithreading and Networking

Chapters 26–27 form a solid introduction to multithreading and Internet networking.

Database-Driven Desktop and Web Development

Chapters 28–31 form a database-intensive web development sequence, including coverage of JDBC, JavaServer Faces (JSF), Ajax and web services.

Teaching Approach

Java How to Program, Late Objects Version, 8/e, contains a rich collection of examples. The book concentrates on the principles of good software engineering and stresses program clarity. We teach by example. We are educators who teach leading-edge programming languages and software-related topics in academic, government, military and industry classrooms worldwide.

Live-Code Approach. Java How to Program, Late Objects Version, 8/e, is loaded with "live-code" examples. By this we mean that most new concepts are presented in the context of complete working Java applications, followed immediately by one or more actual executions showing program inputs and outputs.

Syntax Shading. For readability, we syntax shade all the Java code, similar to the way most Java integrated-development environments and code editors syntax color code. Our syntax-shading conventions are as follows:

```
comments appear like this
keywords appear like this
errors appear like this
constants and literal values appear like this
all other code appears in black
```

Code Highlighting. We place gray rectangles around key code segments.

Using Fonts for Emphasis. We place the key terms and the index's page reference for each defining occurrence in bold blue text for easier reference. We emphasize on-screen components in the **bold Helvetica** font (e.g., the **File** menu) and emphasize Java program text in the Lucida font (for example, int x = 5;).

Web Access. All of the source-code examples are available for download from:

```
www.deitel.com/books/jhtp8LOV
```

Quotations. Each chapter begins with quotations. We hope that you enjoy relating these to the chapter material.

Objectives. The quotes are followed by a list of chapter objectives.

Illustrations/Figures. Abundant charts, tables, line drawings, programs and program output are included. We model the flow of control in control statements with UML activity diagrams. UML class diagrams model the fields, constructors and methods of classes. We use six major UML diagram types in the optional OOD/UML 2 ATM case study in Chapters 12 and 13.

Programming Tips. We include programming tips to help you focus on important aspects of program development. These tips and practices represent the best we've gleaned from a combined seven decades of programming and teaching experience.

Good Programming Practice

The Good Programming Practices *call attention to techniques that will help you produce programs that are clearer, more understandable and more maintainable.*

Common Programming Error

Pointing out these Common Programming Errors *reduces the likelihood that you'll make them.*

Error-Prevention Tip

These tips contain suggestions for exposing bugs and removing them from your programs; many describe aspects of Java that prevent bugs from getting into programs in the first place.

Performance Tip

These tips highlight opportunities for making your programs run faster or minimizing the amount of memory that they occupy.

Portability Tip

The Portability Tips *help you write code that will run on a variety of platforms.*

Software Engineering Observation

The Software Engineering Observations *highlight architectural and design issues that affect the construction of software systems, especially large-scale systems.*

Look-and-Feel Observation

The Look-and-Feel Observations *highlight graphical-user-interface conventions. These observations help you design attractive, user-friendly graphical user interfaces that conform to industry norms.*

Wrap-Up Section. Each chapter ends with a "wrap-up" section that recaps the chapter content and transitions to the next chapter.

Summary Bullets. Each chapter ends with additional pedagogical devices. We present a section-by-section, bullet-list-style summary of the chapter.

Terminology. We include an alphabetized list of the important terms defined in each chapter with the page number of the term's defining occurrence.

Self-Review Exercises and Answers. Extensive self-review exercises *and* answers are included for self-study. All of the exercises in the optional ATM case study are fully solved.

Exercises. Each chapter concludes with a substantial set of exercises, including simple recall of important terminology and concepts; identifying the errors in code samples; writing individual program statements; writing small portions of methods and Java classes; writing complete methods, Java classes and programs; and building major projects. Instructors can use these exercises to form homework assignments, short quizzes, major examinations and term projects. [*NOTE:* **Please do not write to us requesting access to the Pearson Instructor's Resource Center which contains the book's instructor supplements, including the exercise solutions. Access is limited strictly to college instructors teaching from the book. Instructors may obtain access only through their Pearson representatives.**] Be sure to check out our Programming Projects Resource Center (`www.deitel.com/ProgrammingProjects/`) for lots of additional exercise and project possibilities.

Thousands of Index Entries. We have included an extensive index, which is especially useful when you use the book as a reference. Defining occurrences of key terms are highlighted with a bold, blue page number.

Student Resources

Many Java development tools are available for purchase, but you need none of these to get started with Java. For Windows systems, all the software you'll need for this book is available free for download from the web or on the accompanying CD. For other platforms, all the software you'll need for this book is generally available free for download from the web. We wrote most of the examples using the free Java Standard Edition Development Kit (JDK) 6. The current JDK version (and separately its documentation) can be downloaded from Sun's Java website `java.sun.com/javase/downloads/index.jsp`. Mac OS X users can download Java from `developer.apple.com/java`. In several chapters, we also used the Netbeans IDE. Netbeans is available as a bundle with the JDK from the preceding Sun Java website, or you can download it separately from `www.netbeans.org/downloads/index.html`. The Eclipse IDE can be downloaded from `www.eclipse.org/downloads/`. MySQL can be downloaded from `dev.mysql.com/downloads/`, and MySQL Connector/J from `dev.mysql.com/downloads/connector/j/5.1.html`. You can find additional resources and software downloads in our Java SE 6 Resource Center at:

> `www.deitel.com/JavaSE6Mustang/`

The CD that accompanies the book contains versions of the following software packages for use on Microsoft® Windows®:

- Java™ SE Development Kit (JDK) 6 Update 11—which was used to create and test all the programs in the book

- Eclipse IDE for Java EE Developers 3.4.1

- NetBeans™ IDE Version 6.5 All Bundle

- MySQL® 5.0 Community Server version 5.0.67

- MySQL Connector/J version 5.1.7

Netbeans and Eclipse are integrated development environments (IDEs) for developing all types of Java applications. MySQL and MySQL Connector/J are provided for the database applications in Chapters 28–31. All of these tools are downloadable for other platforms also, as we discuss in Before You Begin, after this Preface.

Companion Website

We include a set of free, web-based student supplements to the book—the Companion Website—available with new books purchased from Pearson (see the scratch card at the front of the book). The Companion Website includes video walkthroughs (called *Video Notes*) of all the code examples in Chapters 2–11 and some of the code examples in Chapters 14 and 17, solutions to about half of the exercises in the book, and a lab manual. For more information about the Companion Website, please visit

> `www.pearsonhighered.com/deitel/`

Instructors may want to explicitly weave *Video Notes* assignments into their syllabi.

CourseSmart Web Books

Today's students and instructors have increasing demands on their time and money. Pearson has responded to that need by offering digital texts and course materials online through CourseSmart. CourseSmart allows faculty to review course materials online saving time and costs. It is also environmentally sound and offers students a high-quality digital version of the text for as much as 50% off the cost of a print copy of the text. Students receive the same content offered in the print textbook enhanced by search, note-taking, and printing tools. For more information, visit `www.coursesmart.com`.

Instructor Supplements

The following supplements are available to qualified instructors only through Pearson Education's Instructor Resource Center (www.pearsonhighered.com/irc):

- *Solutions Manual* with solutions to most of the end-of-chapter exercises and Lab Manual exercises
- *Test Item File* of multiple-choice questions (approximately two per book section)
- Customizable PowerPoint® slides containing all the code and figures in the text, plus bulleted items that summarize the key points in the text

If you are not already a registered faculty member, contact your Pearson representative or visit www.pearsonhighered.com/educator/replocator/.

Computer Science AP Courses

Java How to Program, Late Objects Version, 8/e, is a suitable textbook for teaching AP Computer Science classes and for preparing students to take the AP exam.

Deitel® Buzz Online Free E-mail Newsletter

The *Deitel® Buzz Online* e-mail newsletter will keep you posted about issues related to *Java How to Program, Late Objects Version, 8/e*. It also includes commentary on industry trends and developments, links to free articles and resources from our published books and upcoming publications, product-release schedules, errata, challenges, anecdotes, information on our corporate instructor-led training courses and more. To subscribe, visit

```
www.deitel.com/newsletter/subscribe.html
```

The Deitel Online Resource Centers

Our website www.deitel.com provides more than 100 Resource Centers on various topics including programming languages, software development, Web 2.0, Internet business and open-source projects—see the list of Resource Centers in the first few pages of this book and visit www.deitel.com/ResourceCenters.html. The Resource Centers evolve out of the research we do to support our publications and business endeavors. We've found many exceptional resources online, including tutorials, documentation, software downloads, articles, blogs, podcasts, videos, code samples, books, e-books and more—most of them are free. Each week we announce our latest Resource Centers in our newsletter, the *Deitel® Buzz Online*. Some of the Resource Centers you might find helpful while studying this book are Java SE 6, Java, Java Assessment and Certification, Java Design Patterns, Java EE 5, Code Search Engines and Code Sites, Game Programming and Programming Projects.

Follow Deitel on Twitter and Facebook

To receive updates on Deitel publications, Resource Centers, training courses, partner offers and more, follow us on Twitter®

```
@deitel
```

and join the Deitel & Associates group on Facebook®

```
www.facebook.com/group.php?gid=38765799996
```

Acknowledgments

It's a pleasure to acknowledge the efforts of people whose names do not appear on the cover, but whose hard work, cooperation, friendship and understanding were crucial to the book's production. Many people at Deitel & Associates, Inc., devoted long hours to this project—thanks especially to Abbey Deitel and Barbara Deitel.

We would also like to thank the participants of our Honors Internship Program who contributed to this new edition—Nicholas Doiron, an Electrical and Computer Engineering major at Carnegie Mellon University; and Matthew Pearson, a Computer Science major at Cornell University.

We are fortunate to have worked on this project with the talented and dedicated team of publishing professionals at Pearson. We appreciate the extraordinary efforts of Marcia Horton, Editorial Director of Pearson's Engineering and Computer Science Division, and Michael Hirsch, Editor-in-Chief of Computer Science. Carole Snyder and Dolores Mars did an extraordinary job recruiting the book's review team and managing the review process. Francesco Santalucia (an independent artist) and Kristine Carney of Pearson did a wonderful job designing the book's cover—we provided the concept, and they made it happen. Scott Disanno and Robert Engelhardt did a marvelous job managing the book's production. Our marketing manager Erin Davis and her boss Margaret Waples did a great job marketing the book through academic and professional channels.

Reviewers

We wish to acknowledge the efforts of our reviewers. Adhering to a tight time schedule, they scrutinized the text and the programs and provided countless suggestions for improving the accuracy and completeness of the presentation:

Academic Reviewers:

- William E. Duncan (Louisiana State University)
- Diana Franklin (University of California, Santa Barbara)
- Edward F. Gehringer (North Carolina State University)
- Ric Heishman (George Mason University)
- Patty Kraft (San Diego State University)
- Manjeet Rege, Ph.D. (Rochester Institute of Technology)
- Tim Margush (University of Akron)
- Sue McFarland Metzger (Villanova University)
- Shyamal Mitra (The University of Texas at Austin)
- Susan Rodger (Duke University)
- Amr Sabry (Indiana University)
- Monica Sweat (Georgia Tech)

Sun Microsystems Reviewers:

- Lance Andersen
- Soundararajan Angusamy
- Lawrence Prem Kumar
- Simon Ritter

- Sang Shin
- Alexander Zuev

Other Industry Reviewers:

- Joseph Bowbeer (Consultant)
- Peter Pilgrim (Lloyds TSB)
- José Antonio González Seco (Parliament of Andalusia)
- S. Sivakumar (Astra Infotech Private Limited)
- Raghavan "Rags" Srinivas (Intuit)
- Vinod Varma (Astra Infotech Private Limited)

Well, there you have it! Java is a powerful programming language that will help you write programs quickly and effectively. It scales nicely into the realm of enterprise systems development to help organizations build their business-critical and mission-critical information systems. As you read the book, we'd sincerely appreciate your comments, criticisms, corrections and suggestions for improving the text. Please address all correspondence to:

```
deitel@deitel.com
```

We'll respond promptly, and post corrections and clarifications on:

```
www.deitel.com/books/jhtp8LOV/
```

We hope you enjoy reading *Java How to Program, Late Objects Version, 8/e*, as much as we enjoyed writing it!

Paul J. Deitel
Dr. Harvey M. Deitel

About the Authors

Paul J. Deitel, CEO and Chief Technical Officer of Deitel & Associates, Inc., is a graduate of MIT's Sloan School of Management, where he studied Information Technology. He holds the Java Certified Programmer and Java Certified Developer certifications and has been designated by Sun Microsystems as a Java Champion. Through Deitel & Associates, Inc., he has delivered Java, C, C++, C#, Visual Basic and Internet programming courses to industry clients, including Cisco, IBM, Sun Microsystems, Dell, Lucent Technologies, Fidelity, NASA at the Kennedy Space Center, the National Severe Storm Laboratory, White Sands Missile Range, Rogue Wave Software, Boeing, SunGard Higher Education, Stratus, Cambridge Technology Partners, Open Environment Corporation, One Wave, Hyperion Software, Adra Systems, Entergy, CableData Systems, Nortel Networks, Puma, iRobot, Invensys and many more. He has also lectured on Java and C++ for the Boston Chapter of the Association for Computing Machinery. He and his co-author, Dr. Harvey M. Deitel, are the world's best-selling programming-language textbook authors.

Dr. Harvey M. Deitel, Chairman and Chief Strategy Officer of Deitel & Associates, Inc., has 48 years of academic and industry experience in the computer field. Dr. Deitel earned B.S. and M.S. degrees from MIT and a Ph.D. from Boston University. He has 20 years of college teaching experience, including earning tenure and serving as the Chairman of the Computer Science Department at Boston College before founding Deitel & Associates, Inc., with his son, Paul J. Deitel. He and Paul are the co-authors of dozens of books and multimedia packages and they are writing many more. With translations published in Traditional Chinese, Simplified Chinese, Japanese, German, Russian, Spanish, Korean, French, Polish, Italian, Portuguese, Greek, Urdu and Turkish, the Deitels' texts have earned international recognition. Dr. Deitel has delivered hundreds of professional seminars to major corporations, academic institutions, government organizations and the military.

About Deitel & Associates, Inc.

Deitel & Associates, Inc., is an internationally recognized corporate training and authoring organization specializing in computer programming languages, Internet and web software technology, object-technology education and Internet business development. The company provides instructor-led courses delivered at client sites worldwide on major programming languages and platforms, such as Java™, C++, C, Visual C#®, Visual Basic®, Visual C++®, XML®, Python®, object technology, Internet and web programming, and a growing list of additional programming and software-development-related courses. The founders of Deitel & Associates, Inc., are Paul J. Deitel and Dr. Harvey M. Deitel. The company's clients include many of the world's largest companies, government agencies, branches of the military, and academic institutions. Through its 33-year publishing partnership with Prentice Hall/Pearson, Deitel & Associates, Inc., publishes leading-edge programming textbooks, professional books, interactive multimedia *Cyber Classrooms*, *LiveLessons* DVD-based and web-based video courses, and e-content for popular course-management systems. Deitel & Associates, Inc., and the authors can be reached via e-mail at:

```
deitel@deitel.com
```

To learn more about Deitel & Associates, Inc., its publications and its *Dive Into*® *Series* Corporate Training curriculum delivered at client locations worldwide, visit:

```
www.deitel.com/training/
```

and subscribe to the free *Deitel*® *Buzz Online* e-mail newsletter at:

```
www.deitel.com/newsletter/subscribe.html
```

Individuals wishing to purchase Deitel books, and *LiveLessons* DVD and web-based training courses can do so through www.deitel.com. Bulk orders by corporations, the government, the military and academic institutions should be placed directly with Pearson. For more information, visit www.prenhall.com/mischtm/support.html#order.

Check out the growing list of online Deitel Resource Centers at:

```
www.deitel.com/resourcecenters.html
```

Before You Begin

This section contains information you should review before using this book and instructions to ensure that your computer is set up properly for use with this book. We'll post updates (if any) to this Before You Begin section on the book's website:

www.deitel.com/books/jhtp8LOV/

Font and Naming Conventions

We use fonts to distinguish between on-screen components (such as menu names and menu items) and Java code or commands. Our convention is to emphasize on-screen components in a sans-serif bold Helvetica font (for example, **File** menu) and to emphasize Java code and commands in a sans-serif Lucida font (for example, System.out.println()).

Software and Hardware System Requirements

The interface to the contents of the CD that accompanies this book is designed to start automatically through the AUTORUN.EXE file (the CD is for use on Microsoft® Windows® systems). If a startup screen does not appear when you insert the CD into your computer, double click the welcome.htm file to launch the CD's interface, or refer to the file readme.txt on the CD. On the welcome.htm page, click the **Software** link at the bottom of the page to view the software and hardware system requirements. Please read these requirements carefully before installing the software on the CD.

The CD that accompanies *Java How to Program, Late Objects Version, 8/e* contains versions of the following software packages for use on Microsoft Windows:

- Java™ SE Development Kit (JDK) 6 Update 11—which was used to create and test all the programs in the book
- Eclipse IDE for Java EE Developers 3.4.1
- NetBeans™ IDE Version 6.5 All Bundle
- MySQL® 5.0 Community Server/v5.0.67
- MySQL Connector/J Version 5.1.7

Netbeans and Eclipse are integrated development environments (IDEs) for developing all types of Java applications. MySQL and MySQL Connector/J are provided for the database applications in Chapters 28–31. All of these tools are downloadable for other platforms as well, which we discuss in the next section.

Installing the Software

The CD includes the software required to compile and execute the examples in *Java How to Program, Late Objects Version, 8/e* on the Windows platform. For other platforms, you can download the software. Mac OS X users can learn about using Java on a Mac at

```
developer.apple.com/java/
```

Linux users can get the latest Java SE Development Kit from

```
java.sun.com/javase/downloads/index.jsp
```

Installation Instructions and Installers

On the left side of the CD's software and hardware requirements page there are links to the installation instructions for each software package for the Windows operating system. Each installation-instructions page contains a link to the corresponding software package's installer. You can also launch these installers directly from the CD's `software` folder. Follow the installation instructions carefully for each software package. Before you can run the applications in *Java How to Program, Late Objects Version, 8/e* or build your own applications, you must install the Java Standard Edition Development Kit (JDK) 6 or a Java development tool, such as the NetBeans (which requires the JDK) or Eclipse integrated development environments (IDEs). NetBeans is required for Chapters 29–31. Eclipse is optional for use with this book. We provide videos to help you get started with NetBeans and Eclipse at

```
www.deitel.com/books/jhtp8LOV/
```

These videos discuss:

- creating single-file programs
- creating multi-file programs
- how the IDEs manage files, directories and Java packages
- using the debugger
- and using third party Java libraries

Downloads for Other Platforms

The software on the CD is also available for other platforms:

- Netbeans bundled with the JDK: `java.sun.com/javase/downloads/index.jsp`
- Netbeans without the JDK bundle: `www.netbeans.org/downloads/index.html`
- Eclipse: `www.eclipse.org/downloads/`
- MySQL Community Edition: `dev.mysql.com/downloads/`
- MySQL Connector/J: `dev.mysql.com/downloads/connector/j/5.1.html`.

Obtaining the Code Examples

You can download the examples for *Java How to Program, Late Objects Version, 8/e*, from:

```
www.deitel.com/books/jhtp8LOV/
```

If you're not already registered at our website, go to www.deitel.com and click the **Register** link below our logo in the upper-left corner of the page. Fill in your information. There is no charge to register, and we do not share your information with anyone. We send you only account-management e-mails unless you register separately for our free *Deitel® Buzz Online* e-mail newsletter at www.deitel.com/newsletter/subscribe.html. After registering, you'll receive a confirmation e-mail with your verification code. *You'll need this code to sign in at www.deitel.com for the first time.* Configure your e-mail client to allow e-mails from deitel.com to ensure that the confirmation e-mail is not filtered as junk mail.

Next, go to www.deitel.com and sign in using the **Login** link below our logo in the upper-left corner of the page. Go to www.deitel.com/books/jhtp8LOV/. Click the **Examples** link to download the Examples.zip file to your computer. Write down the location where you choose to save the file on your computer.

We assume the examples are located at C:\Examples on your computer. Extract the contents of Examples.zip using a tool such as WinZip (www.winzip.com) or the built-in capabilities of Windows XP and Windows Vista (or a similar tool on other platforms).

Setting the PATH Environment Variable

The PATH environment variable on your computer designates which directories the computer searches when looking for applications, such as the applications that enable you to compile and run your Java applications (called javac and java, respectively). *Carefully follow the installation instructions for Java on your platform to ensure that you set the PATH environment variable correctly.*

If you do not set the PATH variable correctly, when you use the JDK's tools, you'll receive a message like:

```
'java' is not recognized as an internal or external command,
operable program or batch file.
```

In this case, go back to the installation instructions for setting the PATH and recheck your steps. If you've downloaded a newer version of the JDK, you may need to change the name of the JDK's installation directory in the PATH variable.

Setting the CLASSPATH Environment Variable

If you attempt to run a Java program and receive a message like

```
Exception in thread "main" java.lang.NoClassDefFoundError: YourClass
```

then your system has a CLASSPATH environment variable that must be modified. To fix the preceding error, follow the steps in setting the PATH environment variable, locate the CLASSPATH variable, then edit the variable's value to include the local directory—typically represented as a dot (.). On Windows add

```
.;
```

at the beginning of the CLASSPATH's value (with no spaces before or after these characters). On other platforms, replace the semicolon with the appropriate path separator characters—often a colon (:)

Java's New Nimbus Look-and-Feel

As of Java SE 6 update 10, Java comes bundled with a new, elegant, cross-platform look-and-feel known as Nimbus. For programs with graphical user interfaces, we've configured our systems to use Nimbus as the default look-and-feel.

To set Nimbus as the default for all Java applications, you must create a text file named `swing.properties` in the `lib` folder of both your JDK installation folder and your JRE installation folder. Place the following line of code in the file:

```
swing.defaultlaf=com.sun.java.swing.plaf.nimbus.NimbusLookAndFeel
```

For more information on locating these installation folders visit `java.sun.com/javase/6/webnotes/install/index.html`. [*Note:* In addition to the standalone JRE, there is a JRE nested in your JDK's installation folder. If you are using an IDE that depends on the JDK (e.g., NetBeans), you may also need to place the `swing.properties` file in the nested `jre` folder's `lib` folder.]

You are now ready to begin your Java studies with *Java How to Program, Late Objects Version, 8/e*. We hope you enjoy the book!

Introduction to Computers, the Internet and the Web

Objectives

In this chapter you'll learn:

- Basic hardware, software and networking concepts.
- The types of programming languages and which are most widely used.
- A typical Java program-development environment.
- Java's role in developing distributed client/server networking applications.
- The history of the Internet and the World Wide Web through Web 2.0.
- Some key recent software technologies.

1.1 Introduction

Welcome to Java—a powerful computer programming language that is fun for novices to learn and appropriate for experienced programmers to use in building substantial enterprise information systems. *Java How to Program, Late Objects Version, Eighth Edition*, is an effective learning tool for each of these audiences. [From this point forward, we'll refer to this book simply as *Java How to Program.*]

Pedagogy

The core of the book emphasizes achieving program *clarity* through the proven techniques of *structured programming* and *object-oriented programming*. Nonprogrammers will learn programming the right way from the beginning. The presentation is clear, straightforward and abundantly illustrated. It includes hundreds of Java programs and shows the outputs produced when they're run on a computer. We teach Java features in the context of complete working programs—we call this the live-code approach. The example programs can be downloaded from www.deitel.com/books/jhtp8LOV/ or www.pearsonhighered.com/deitel—see the Before You Begin section after the Preface for more information.

Fundamentals

The early chapters introduce the fundamentals of computers, computer programming and the Java programming language, providing a solid foundation for the deeper treatment of Java in the later chapters. Experienced programmers tend to read the early chapters quickly and find the treatment of Java in the later chapters rigorous and challenging.

Most people are familiar with the exciting tasks computers perform. Using this book, you'll learn to write instructions commanding computers to perform those tasks. Software (i.e., the instructions you write) controls hardware (i.e., computers). Java, developed by Sun Microsystems, is one of today's most popular languages for developing software.

Evolution of Computing and Programming

Computer use is increasing in almost every field of endeavor. Computing costs are dropping dramatically, owing to rapid developments in both hardware and software technologies. Computers that might have filled large rooms and cost millions of dollars decades ago can now be inscribed on silicon chips smaller than a fingernail, costing perhaps a few dollars each. Fortunately, silicon is one of the most abundant materials on earth—it's an ingredient in common sand. Silicon-chip technology has made computing so economical that more than a billion general-purpose computers are in use worldwide, helping people in business, industry and government and in their personal lives. The number could easily double in the next few years.

Over the years, many programmers learned the methodology called structured programming. You'll learn structured programming and an exciting newer methodology, object-oriented programming. Why do we teach both? Object orientation is the key programming methodology used by programmers today. You'll create and work with many software objects in this text. But you'll discover that their internal structure is often built using structured-programming techniques. Also, the logic of manipulating objects is occasionally expressed with structured programming.

Language of Choice for Networked Applications

Java has become the language of choice for implementing Internet-based applications and software for devices that communicate over a network. Stereos and other devices in homes are often networked together by Java technology. There are now *billions* of Java-enabled mobile phones and handheld devices! Java is the preferred language for meeting many organizations' enterprisewide programming needs.

Java has evolved so rapidly that this eighth edition of *Java How to Program*—based on **Java Standard Edition (Java SE)** 6, Update 11—was published just 13 years after the first edition. Java is used in such a broad spectrum of applications that it has two other editions. The **Java Enterprise Edition (Java EE)** is geared toward developing large-scale, distributed networking applications and web-based applications—we discuss several Java EE features later in the book. The **Java Micro Edition (Java ME)** is geared toward developing applications for small, memory-constrained devices, such as cell phones, pagers and PDAs.

Staying in Touch with the Authors

If you'd like to communicate with us, please send e-mail to `deitel@deitel.com`. We'll respond promptly. To keep up to date with Java developments at Deitel & Associates, register for our free e-mail newsletter, the *Deitel® Buzz Online,* at

> `www.deitel.com/newsletter/subscribe.html`

For lots of additional Java material, visit our growing list of Java Resource Centers at `www.deitel.com/ResourceCenters.html`. We hope that you'll enjoy learning with *Java How to Program.*

1.2 Computers: Hardware and Software

A computer is a device that can perform computations and make logical decisions phenomenally faster than human beings can. Many of today's personal computers can perform billions of calculations in one second. A person operating a calculator could not perform that many calculations in a lifetime. (Points to ponder: How would you know whether the person added that many numbers correctly? How would you know whether the computer added the numbers correctly?) **Supercomputers** are already performing *quadrillions (thousands of trillions)* of instructions per second! To put that in perspective, a quadrillion-instruction-per-second computer can perform more than 100,000 calculations per second for every person on the planet!

Computers process **data** under the control of sets of instructions called **computer programs**. These programs guide the computer through orderly sets of actions specified by people called **computer programmers**.

A computer consists of various devices referred to as **hardware** (e.g., the keyboard, screen, mouse, disks, memory, DVD, CD-ROM and processing units). The programs that run on a computer are referred to as **software**. Hardware costs have been declining dramatically in recent years, to the point that personal computers have become a commodity. Beginning in Chapter 7, Introduction to Classes and Objects, you'll learn proven methodologies that can reduce software-development costs—object-oriented programming and (in our optional Software Engineering Case Study in Chapters 12–13) object-oriented design.

1.3 Computer Organization

Regardless of differences in physical appearance, virtually every computer may be envisioned as divided into various **logical units** or sections:

1. *Input unit*. This "receiving" section obtains information (data and computer programs) from **input devices** and places it at the disposal of the other units so that it can be processed. Most information is entered into computers through keyboards and mouse devices. Information also can be entered in many other ways, including by speaking to your computer, scanning images and barcodes, reading from secondary storage devices (like hard drives, CD drives, DVD drives and USB drives—also called "thumb drives") and having your computer receive information from the Internet (such as when you download videos from YouTube™, e-books from Amazon, and the like).

2. *Output unit*. This "shipping" section takes information that the computer has processed and places it on various **output devices** to make it available for use outside the computer. Most information that is output from computers today is displayed on screens, printed on paper, played on audio players (such as Apple's popular iPods), or used to control other devices. Computers also can output their information to networks, such as the Internet.

3. *Memory unit*. This rapid-access, relatively low-capacity "warehouse" section retains information that has been entered through the input unit, making it immediately available for processing when needed. The memory unit also retains processed information until it can be placed on output devices by the output unit. Information in the memory unit is **volatile**—it's typically lost when the computer's power is turned off. The memory unit is often called either **memory** or **primary memory**.

4. *Arithmetic and logic unit (ALU)*. This "manufacturing" section performs calculations, such as addition, subtraction, multiplication and division. It also contains the decision mechanisms that allow the computer, for example, to compare two

items from the memory unit to determine whether they're equal. In today's systems, the ALU is usually implemented as part of the next logical unit, the CPU.

5. *Central processing unit (CPU).* This "administrative" section coordinates and supervises the operation of the other sections. The CPU tells the input unit when information should be read into the memory unit, tells the ALU when information from the memory unit should be used in calculations and tells the output unit when to send information from the memory unit to certain output devices. Many of today's computers have multiple CPUs and, hence, can perform many operations simultaneously—such computers are called **multiprocessors.** A **multicore processor** implements multiprocessing on a single integrated circuit chip—for example a dual-core processor has two CPUs and a quad-core processor has four CPUs.

6. *Secondary storage unit.* This is the long-term, high-capacity "warehousing" section. Programs or data not actively being used by the other units normally are placed on secondary storage devices (e.g., your hard drive) until they're needed again, possibly hours, days, months or even years later. Therefore, information on secondary storage devices is said to be **persistent**—it is preserved even when the computer's power is turned off. Secondary storage information takes much longer to access than information in primary memory, but the cost per unit of secondary storage is much less than that of primary memory. Examples of secondary storage devices include CDs, DVDs and flash drives (sometimes called memory sticks), which can hold hundreds of millions to billions of characters.

1.4 Early Operating Systems

Early computers could perform only one **job** or **task** at a time. This is often called single-user **batch processing** and was the norm in the 1950s. The computer ran a single program while processing data in groups or **batches**. Users generally submitted their jobs to a computer center on decks of punched cards and often waited hours or even days before printouts were returned to their desks.

Software **operating systems** were developed to make using computers more convenient. Early operating systems smoothed and speeded up the transition between jobs, increasing the amount of work, or **throughput**, computers could process in a given time.

As computers became more powerful, it became evident that single-user batch processing was inefficient, because so much time was spent waiting for slow input/output devices to complete their tasks. The idea was conceived that many jobs or tasks could *share* the resources of the computer to achieve better utilization. This is called **multiprogramming**. Multiprogramming involves the simultaneous operation of many jobs that are competing to share the computer's resources.

In the 1960s, several groups in industry and the universities pioneered **timesharing** operating systems. Timesharing is a special case of multiprogramming in which users access the computer through terminals, typically devices with keyboards and screens. Dozens or even hundreds of users share the computer at once. The computer actually does not run all the jobs simultaneously. Rather, it runs a small portion of one user's job, then moves on to service the next user, perhaps providing service to each user several times per second. Thus, the users' programs *appear* to be running simultaneously. An advantage of timesharing is that user requests receive almost immediate responses.

1.5 Personal, Distributed and Client/Server Computing

In 1977, Apple Computer popularized **personal computing**. Computers became so economical that people could buy them for their own personal or business use. In 1981, IBM, the world's largest computer vendor, introduced the IBM Personal Computer. This quickly legitimized personal computing in business, industry and government organizations.

These computers were "standalone" units—people transported disks back and forth between them to share information (a mode of transfer often called "sneakernet"). Although early personal computers were not powerful enough to support several simultaneous users, these machines could be linked together in computer networks, sometimes over telephone lines and sometimes in **local area networks (LANs)** within an organization. This led to the phenomenon of **distributed computing**, in which an organization's computing, instead of being performed only at some central installation, is distributed over networks to the sites where the organization's work is performed. Personal computers were powerful enough to handle the computing requirements of individual users as well as the basic communications tasks of passing information between computers electronically.

Information is shared easily across computer networks, where computers called **servers** store data that may be used by **client** computers distributed throughout the network—hence the term **client/server computing**. Java has become widely used for writing software for computer networking and for distributed client/server applications. Popular operating systems, such as Linux, Apple's Mac OS X (pronounced "O-S ten") and Microsoft Windows, provide the kinds of capabilities needed today.

1.6 The Internet and the World Wide Web

The **Internet**—a global network of computers—has its roots in the 1960s, when funding was supplied by the U.S. Department of Defense. Originally designed to connect the main computer systems of about a dozen universities and research organizations, the Internet today is accessible by billions of computers and computer-controlled devices worldwide.

With the introduction of the **World Wide Web**—which allows computer users to locate and view multimedia-based documents on almost any subject over the Internet—the Internet has exploded into one of the world's premier communication mechanisms.

In the past, most computer applications ran on computers that were not connected to one another. Today's applications can be written to communicate among the world's computers. The Internet, by mixing computing and communications technologies, makes people's work easier. It makes information instantly and conveniently accessible worldwide. It enables individuals and local small businesses to get worldwide exposure. It's changing the way business is done. People can search for the best prices on virtually any product or service. Special-interest communities can stay in touch with one another. Researchers can be made instantly aware of the latest breakthroughs.

Java How to Program presents programming techniques that allow Java applications to use the Internet and the web to interact with other applications. These capabilities and others allow you to develop the kind of enterprise-level distributed applications that are used in industry today. Java applications can be written to execute portably on every major type of computer, greatly reducing the time and cost of systems development.

1.7 Machine Languages, Assembly Languages and High-Level Languages

Programmers write instructions in various programming languages, some directly understandable by computers and others requiring intermediate translation steps. Hundreds of such languages are in use today. These may be divided into three general types:

1. Machine languages

2. Assembly languages

3. High-level languages

Any computer can directly understand only its own machine language. This is the computer's "natural language," defined by its hardware design. Machine languages generally consist of strings of numbers (ultimately reduced to 1s and 0s) that instruct computers to perform their most elementary operations one at a time. Machine languages are machine dependent (a particular machine language can be used on only one type of computer). Such languages are cumbersome for humans. For example, here is a section of an early machine-language program that adds overtime pay to base pay and stores the result in gross pay:

```
+1300042774
+1400593419
+1200274027
```

Programming in machine-language was simply too slow and tedious a process for most programmers. Instead of using the strings of numbers that computers could directly understand, programmers began using Englishlike abbreviations to represent elementary operations. These abbreviations formed the basis of assembly languages. Translator programs called assemblers were developed to convert early assembly-language programs to machine language at computer speeds. The following section of an assembly-language program also adds overtime pay to base pay and stores the result in gross pay:

```
load     basepay
add      overpay
store    grosspay
```

Although such code is clearer to humans, it's incomprehensible to computers until translated to machine language.

Computer usage increased rapidly with the advent of assembly languages, but programmers still had to use many instructions to accomplish even the simplest tasks. To speed the programming process, high-level languages were developed in which single statements could be written to accomplish substantial tasks. Translator programs called compilers convert high-level language programs into machine language. High-level languages allow you to write instructions that look almost like everyday English and contain commonly used mathematical notations. A payroll program written in a high-level language might contain a statement such as

```
grossPay = basePay + overTimePay
```

From the programmer's standpoint, high-level languages are preferable to machine and assembly languages. C, C++, Microsoft's .NET languages (e.g., Visual Basic, Visual C++ and C#) are among the most widely used high-level programming languages; Java is by far *the* most widely used.

Compiling a high-level language program into machine language can take a considerable amount of computer time. Interpreter programs were developed to execute high-level language programs directly (without the delay of compilation), although slower than compiled programs run. We'll say more about how interpreters work in Section 1.13, where you'll learn that Java uses a clever mixture of compilation and interpretation to ultimately run programs. Exercises 6.30–6.32 (in the Special Section: Building Your Own Computer) guide you through the process of building an interpreter program.

1.8 History of C and C++

Java evolved from C++, which evolved from C, which evolved from BCPL and B. BCPL was developed in 1967 by Martin Richards as a language for writing operating-systems software and compilers. Ken Thompson modeled many features in his language B after their counterparts in BCPL, using B to create early versions of the UNIX operating system at Bell Laboratories in 1970.

C—originally implemented in 1972—was evolved from B by Dennis Ritchie at Bell Laboratories. It initially became widely known as the UNIX operating system's development language. Today, most of the code for general-purpose operating systems (e.g., those found in notebooks, desktops, workstations and small servers) is written in C or C++.

C++, an extension of C, was developed by Bjarne Stroustrup in the early 1980s at Bell Laboratories. C++ provides a number of features that "spruce up" the C language, but more important, it provides capabilities for *object-oriented programming* (discussed in more detail in Section 1.16 and throughout this book). C++ is a hybrid language—it's possible to program in either a C-like style, an object-oriented style or both.

Building software quickly, correctly and economically remains an elusive goal at a time when demands for new and more powerful software are soaring. *Objects*, or more precisely—as we'll see in Section 1.16—the classes objects come from, are essentially reusable software components. There are date objects, time objects, audio objects, video objects, automobile objects, people objects and so on. In fact, almost any noun can be represented as a software object in terms of attributes (e.g., name, color and size) and behaviors (e.g., calculating, moving and communicating). Software developers are discovering that using a modular, object-oriented design and implementation approach can make software-development groups much more productive than was possible with earlier popular techniques like structured programming. Object-oriented programs are often easier to understand, correct and modify. Java is the world's most widely used object-oriented programming language.

1.9 History of Java

The microprocessor revolution's most important contribution to date is that it made possible the development of personal computers, which now number more than a billion worldwide. Personal computers have profoundly affected people's lives and the ways organizations conduct and manage their business.

Microprocessors are having a profound impact in intelligent consumer-electronic devices. Recognizing this, Sun Microsystems in 1991 funded an internal corporate research project, which resulted in a C++-based language that its creator, James Gosling, called Oak after an oak tree outside his window at Sun. It was later discovered that there already was a computer language by that name. When a group of Sun people visited a local coffee shop, the name Java was suggested, and it stuck.

The research project ran into some difficulties. The marketplace for intelligent consumer-electronic devices was not developing as quickly as Sun had anticipated. By sheer good fortune, the web exploded in popularity in 1993, and Sun saw the potential of using Java to add dynamic content, such as interactivity and animations, to web pages. This breathed new life into the project.

Sun formally announced Java at an industry conference in May 1995. Java garnered the attention of the business community because of the phenomenal interest in the web. Java is now used to develop large-scale enterprise applications, to enhance the functionality of web servers (the computers that provide the content we see in our web browsers), to provide applications for consumer devices (e.g., cell phones, pagers and personal digital assistants) and for many other purposes.

1.10 Java Class Libraries

Java programs consist of pieces called classes. Classes include pieces called methods that perform tasks and return information when the tasks complete. You can create each piece you need to form your Java programs. However, most Java programmers take advantage of the rich collections of existing classes in the Java class libraries, which are also known as the Java APIs (Application Programming Interfaces). Thus, there are really two aspects to learning the Java "world." The first is the Java language itself, so that you can program your own classes; the second is the classes in the extensive Java class libraries. Throughout this book we discuss many preexisting Java API classes. To download the Java API documentation, go to java.sun.com/javase/downloads/, scroll down to the **Additional Resources** section and click the **Download** button to the right of **Java SE 6 Documentation**.

Software Engineering Observation 1.1
Use a building-block approach to creating your programs. Avoid reinventing the wheel— use existing pieces wherever possible. This software reuse is a key benefit of object-oriented programming.

We include many Software Engineering Observations throughout the book to explain concepts that affect and improve the overall architecture and quality of software systems. We also highlight other kinds of tips, including:

- Good Programming Practices (to help you write programs that are clearer, more understandable, more maintainable and easier to test and debug—i.e., remove programming errors),

- Common Programming Errors (problems to watch out for and avoid),

- Performance Tips (techniques for writing programs that run faster and use less memory),

- Portability Tips (techniques to help you write programs that can run, with little or no modification, on a variety of computers—these tips also include general observations about how Java achieves its high degree of portability),

- Error-Prevention Tips (techniques for removing bugs from your programs and, more important, techniques for writing bug-free programs in the first place) and

- **Look-and-Feel Observations** (techniques to help you design the "look" and "feel" of your applications' user interfaces for appearance and ease of use).

Many of these are only guidelines. You'll, no doubt, develop your own preferred programming style.

> **Software Engineering Observation 1.2**
> *When programming in Java, you'll typically use the following building blocks: classes and methods from class libraries, classes and methods you create yourself and classes and methods that others create and make available to you.*

The advantage of creating your own classes and methods is that you know exactly how they work and you can examine the Java code. The disadvantage is the time-consuming and potentially complex effort that's required.

> **Performance Tip 1.1**
> *Using Java API classes and methods instead of writing your own versions can improve program performance, because they're carefully written to perform efficiently. This technique also shortens program development time.*

> **Portability Tip 1.1**
> *Using classes and methods from the Java API instead of writing your own improves program portability, because they're included in every Java implementation.*

1.11 Fortran, COBOL, Pascal and Ada

Hundreds of high-level languages have been developed, but only a few have achieved broad acceptance. **Fortran** (FORmula TRANslator) was developed by IBM Corporation in the mid-1950s to be used for scientific and engineering applications that require complex mathematical computations. Fortran is still widely used in engineering applications.

COBOL (COmmon Business Oriented Language) was developed in the late 1950s by computer manufacturers, the U.S. government and industrial computer users. COBOL is used for commercial applications that require precise and efficient manipulation of large amounts of data. Much business software is still programmed in COBOL.

During the 1960s, many large software-development efforts encountered severe difficulties. Software deliveries were typically late, costs greatly exceeded budgets and the finished products were unreliable. People began to realize that software development was a far more complex activity than they had imagined. Research in the 1960s resulted in the evolution of **structured programming**—a disciplined approach to writing programs that are clearer, easier to test and debug and easier to modify than large programs produced with previous techniques.

One of the more tangible results of this research was the development of the Pascal programming language by Professor Niklaus Wirth in 1971. Named after the seventeenth-century mathematician and philosopher Blaise Pascal, it was designed for teaching structured programming in academic environments and rapidly became the preferred programming language in most colleges.

The **Ada** programming language was developed under the sponsorship of the U.S. Department of Defense (DOD) during the 1970s and early 1980s. The DOD wanted a single language that would fill most of its needs. The Ada language was named after Lady

Ada Lovelace, daughter of the poet Lord Byron. Lady Lovelace is credited with writing the world's first computer program in the early 1800s (for the Analytical Engine mechanical computing device designed by Charles Babbage). One important capability of Ada, called **multitasking**, allows programmers to specify that many activities in a program are to occur in parallel. Java, through a technique called *multithreading* (which we discuss in Chapter 26), also enables programmers to write programs with parallel activities.

1.12 BASIC, Visual Basic, Visual C++, C# and .NET

The **BASIC** (Beginner's All-Purpose Symbolic Instruction Code) programming language was developed in the mid-1960s at Dartmouth College as a means of writing simple programs. BASIC's primary purpose was to familiarize novices with programming techniques.

Microsoft's **Visual Basic** language was introduced in the early 1990s to simplify the development of Microsoft Windows applications and is one of the world's most popular programming languages.

Microsoft's latest development tools are part of its corporatewide strategy for integrating the Internet and the web into computer applications. This strategy is implemented in Microsoft's **.NET platform**, which provides developers with the capabilities they need to create and run computer applications that can execute on computers distributed across the Internet. Microsoft's three primary programming languages are Visual Basic (based on the original BASIC), **Visual C++** (based on C++) and **C#** (based on C++ and Java, and developed expressly for the .NET platform). Developers using .NET can write software components in the language they're most familiar with, then form applications by combining those components with others written in any .NET language.

1.13 Typical Java Development Environment

We now explain the commonly used steps in creating and executing a Java application using a Java development environment (illustrated in Fig. 1.1).

Java programs normally go through five phases—edit, compile, load, verify and execute. We discuss these phases in the context of the Java SE Development Kit 6 (JDK6) from Sun Microsystems, Inc. You can download the most up-to-date JDK and its documentation from `java.sun.com/javase/downloads/`. *Carefully follow the installation instructions for the JDK provided in the Before You Begin section of this book to ensure that you set up your computer properly to compile and execute Java programs.* You may also want to visit Sun's New to Java Center at:

```
java.sun.com/new2java/
```

[*Note:* This website provides installation instructions for Windows, Linux and Mac OS X. If you are not using one of these operating systems, refer to the documentation for your system's Java environment or ask your instructor how to accomplish these tasks based on your computer's operating system. If you encounter a problem with this link or any others referenced in this book, please check `www.deitel.com/books/jhtp8LOV/` for errata and please notify us by e-mail at `deitel@deitel.com`.]

Phase 1: Creating a Program
Phase 1 consists of editing a file with an **editor program** (normally known simply as an **editor**). You type a Java program (typically referred to as **source code**) using the editor,

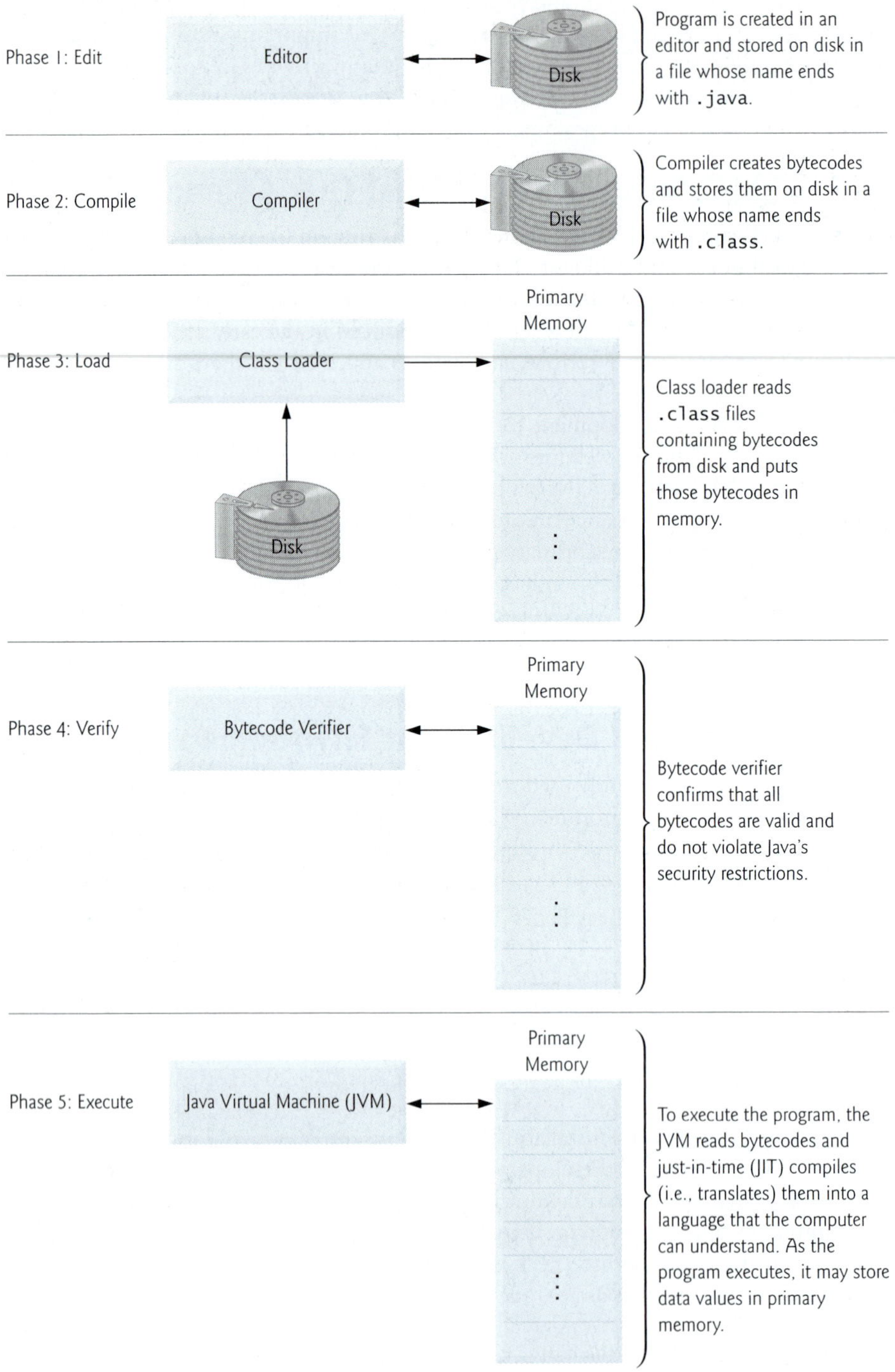

Phase 1: Edit

Editor ⟷ Disk

Program is created in an editor and stored on disk in a file whose name ends with `.java`.

Phase 2: Compile

Compiler ⟷ Disk

Compiler creates bytecodes and stores them on disk in a file whose name ends with `.class`.

Phase 3: Load

Class Loader → Primary Memory

Disk

Class loader reads `.class` files containing bytecodes from disk and puts those bytecodes in memory.

Phase 4: Verify

Bytecode Verifier ⟷ Primary Memory

Bytecode verifier confirms that all bytecodes are valid and do not violate Java's security restrictions.

Phase 5: Execute

Java Virtual Machine (JVM) ⟷ Primary Memory

To execute the program, the JVM reads bytecodes and just-in-time (JIT) compiles (i.e., translates) them into a language that the computer can understand. As the program executes, it may store data values in primary memory.

Fig. 1.1 | Typical Java development environment.

make any necessary corrections and save the program on a secondary storage device, such as your hard drive. A file name ending with the **.java extension** indicates that the file contains Java source code. We assume that you know how to edit a file.

Two editors widely used on Linux systems are vi and emacs. On Windows, Notepad will suffice. Many freeware and shareware editors are also available online, including Edit-Plus (www.editplus.com), TextPad (www.textpad.com) and jEdit (www.jedit.org).

For organizations that develop substantial information systems, **integrated development environments (IDEs)** are available from many major software suppliers. IDEs provide tools that support the software-development process, including editors for writing and editing programs and debuggers for locating **logic errors**—errors that cause programs to execute incorrectly. Popular IDEs include Eclipse (www.eclipse.org), NetBeans (www.netbeans.org), JBuilder (www.codegear.com), JCreator (www.jcreator.com), BlueJ (www.bluej.org) and jGRASP (www.jgrasp.org).

Phase 2: Compiling a Java Program into Bytecodes

In Phase 2, you use the command **javac** (the **Java compiler**) to **compile** a program. For example, to compile a program called Welcome.java, you'd type

```
javac Welcome.java
```

in the command window of your system (i.e., the **Command Prompt** in Windows, the **shell prompt** in Linux or the **Terminal application** in Mac OS X). If the program compiles, the compiler produces a **.class** file called Welcome.class that contains the compiled version of the program.

The Java compiler translates Java source code into **bytecodes** that represent the tasks to execute in the execution phase (Phase 5). Bytecodes are executed by the **Java Virtual Machine (JVM)**—a part of the JDK and the foundation of the Java platform. A **virtual machine (VM)** is a software application that simulates a computer but hides the underlying operating system and hardware from the programs that interact with it. If the same VM is implemented on many computer platforms, applications that it executes can be used on all those platforms. The JVM is one of the most widely used virtual machines. Microsoft's .NET uses a similar virtual-machine architecture.

Unlike machine language, which is dependent on specific computer hardware, bytecodes are platform independent—they do not depend on a particular hardware platform. So, Java's bytecodes are **portable**—without recompiling the source code, the same bytecodes can execute on any platform containing a JVM that understands the version of Java in which the bytecodes were compiled. The JVM is invoked by the **java** command. For example, to execute a Java application called Welcome, you'd type the command

```
java Welcome
```

in a command window to invoke the JVM, which would then initiate the steps necessary to execute the application. This begins Phase 3.

Phase 3: Loading a Program into Memory

In Phase 3, the JVM places the program in memory to execute it—this is known as **loading**. The JVM's **class loader** takes the .class files containing the program's bytecodes and transfers them to primary memory. The class loader also loads any of the .class files provided by Java that your program uses. The .class files can be loaded from a disk on your system or over a network (e.g., your local college or company network, or the Internet).

Phase 4: Bytecode Verification

In Phase 4, as the classes are loaded, the bytecode verifier examines their bytecodes to ensure that they're valid and do not violate Java's security restrictions. Java enforces strong security to make sure that Java programs arriving over the network do not damage your files or your system (as computer viruses and worms might).

Phase 5: Execution

In Phase 5, the JVM executes the program's bytecodes, thus performing the actions specified by the program. In early Java versions, the JVM was simply an interpreter for Java bytecodes. This caused most Java programs to execute slowly, because the JVM would interpret and execute one bytecode at a time. Today's JVMs typically execute bytecodes using a combination of interpretation and so-called just-in-time (JIT) compilation. In this process, the JVM analyzes the bytecodes as they're interpreted, searching for hot spots—parts of the bytecodes that execute frequently. For these parts, a just-in-time (JIT) compiler—known as the Java HotSpot compiler—translates the bytecodes into the underlying computer's machine language. When the JVM encounters these compiled parts again, the faster machine-language code executes. Thus Java programs actually go through two compilation phases—one in which source code is translated into bytecodes (for portability across JVMs on different computer platforms) and a second in which, during execution, the bytecodes are translated into machine language for the actual computer on which the program executes.

Problems That May Occur at Execution Time

Programs might not work on the first try. Each of the preceding phases can fail because of various errors that we'll discuss throughout this book. For example, an executing program might try to divide by zero (an illegal operation for whole-number arithmetic in Java). This would cause the Java program to display an error message. If this occurred, you'd have to return to the edit phase, make the necessary corrections and proceed through the remaining phases again to determine that the corrections fixed the problem(s). [*Note:* Most programs in Java input or output data. When we say that a program displays a message, we normally mean that it displays that message on your computer's screen. Messages and other data may be output to other devices, such as disks and hardcopy printers, or even to a network for transmission to other computers.]

Common Programming Error 1.1

Errors such as division by zero occur as a program runs, so they're called runtime errors or execution-time errors. Fatal runtime errors cause programs to terminate immediately without having successfully performed their tasks. Nonfatal runtime errors allow programs to run to completion, often producing incorrect results.

1.14 Notes about Java and *Java How to Program*

Java is a powerful programming language. Experienced programmers sometimes take pride in creating weird, contorted, convoluted usage of a language. This is a poor programming practice. It makes programs more difficult to read, more likely to behave strangely, more difficult to test and debug, and more difficult to adapt to changing requirements. This book stresses *clarity*. The following is our first Good Programming Practice tip.

Good Programming Practice 1.1

Write your Java programs in a simple and straightforward manner. This is sometimes referred to as KIS ("keep it simple"). Do not "stretch" the language by trying bizarre usages.

You've heard that Java is a portable language and that programs written in Java can run on many different computers. In general, *portability is an elusive goal.*

Portability Tip 1.2

Although it's easier to write portable programs in Java than in most other programming languages, differences between compilers, JVMs and computers can make portability difficult to achieve. Simply writing programs in Java does not guarantee portability.

Error-Prevention Tip 1.1

Always test your Java programs on all systems on which you intend to run them, to ensure that they'll work correctly for their intended audiences.

You can find a web-based version of the Java API documentation at java.sun.com/javase/6/docs/api/index.html, or you can download this documentation to your own computer from java.sun.com/javase/downloads/. For additional technical details on many aspects of Java development, visit java.sun.com/reference/docs/index.html.

Good Programming Practice 1.2

Read the documentation for the version of Java you're using. Refer to it frequently to be sure you're aware of the rich collection of Java features and are using them correctly.

1.15 Test-Driving a Java Application

In this section, you'll run and interact with your first Java application. You'll begin by running an ATM application that simulates the transactions that take place when you use an ATM machine (e.g., withdrawing money, making deposits and checking your account balances). You'll learn how to build this application in the optional, object-oriented case study included in Chapters 12–13. Figure 1.10 at the end of this section suggests other interesting applications that you may also want to test-drive. For the purpose of this section, we assume you're running Microsoft Windows.[1]

In the following steps, you'll run the application and perform various transactions. The elements and functionality you see here are typical of what you'll learn to program in this book. [*Note:* We use fonts to distinguish between features you see on a screen (e.g., the **Command Prompt**) and elements that are not directly related to a screen. Our convention is to emphasize screen features like titles and menus (e.g., the **File** menu) in a semibold **sans-serif Helvetica** font and to emphasize nonscreen elements, such as file names or input (e.g., ProgramName.java) in a sans-serif Lucida font. As you've already noticed, the defining occurrence of each key term in the text is set in bold blue. In the figures in this section, we highlight the user input required by each step and point out significant parts of the application. To make these features more visible, we've changed the background color of the **Command Prompt** windows to white and the foreground color to black.]

---

1. At www.deitel.com/books/jhtp8LOV/, we provide a Linux version of this test-drive. We also provide links to videos that help you get started with several popular integrated development environments (IDEs), including Eclipse and NetBeans.

1. ***Checking your setup.*** Read the Before You Begin section of the book to confirm that you've set up Java properly on your computer and that you've copied the book's examples to your hard drive.

2. ***Locating the completed application.*** Open a **Command Prompt** window. This can be done by selecting **Start > All Programs > Accessories > Command Prompt**. Change to the ATM application directory by typing cd C:\examples\ch01\ATM, then press *Enter* (Fig. 1.2). The command cd is used to change directories.

Using the **cd** command to
change directories

File location of the ATM application

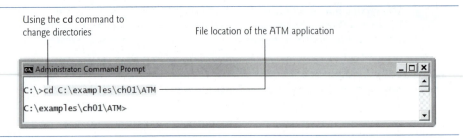

Fig. 1.2 | Opening a **Command Prompt** and changing directories.

3. ***Running the ATM application.*** Type the command java ATMCaseStudy (Fig. 1.3) and press *Enter*. Recall that the java command, followed by the name of the application's .class file (in this case, ATMCaseStudy), executes the application. Specifying the .class extension when using the java command results in an error. [*Note:* Java commands are case sensitive. It's important to type the name of this application with a capital A, T and M in "ATM," a capital C in "Case" and a capital S in "Study." Otherwise, the application will not execute.] If you receive the error message, "Exception in thread "main" java.lang.NoClass-DefFoundError: ATMCaseStudy," your system has a CLASSPATH problem. Please refer to the Before You Begin section of the book for instructions to help you fix this problem.

Fig. 1.3 | Using the java command to execute the ATM application.

4. ***Entering an account number.*** When the application first executes, it displays a "Welcome!" greeting and prompts you for an account number. Type 12345 at the "Please enter your account number:" prompt (Fig. 1.4) and press *Enter*.

5. ***Entering a PIN.*** Once a valid account number is entered, the application displays the prompt "Enter your PIN:". Type "54321" as your valid PIN (Personal Identification Number) and press *Enter*. The ATM main menu containing a list of options will be displayed (Fig. 1.5).

6. ***Viewing the account balance.*** Select option 1, "View my balance", from the ATM menu (Fig. 1.6). The application then displays two numbers—the Avail-

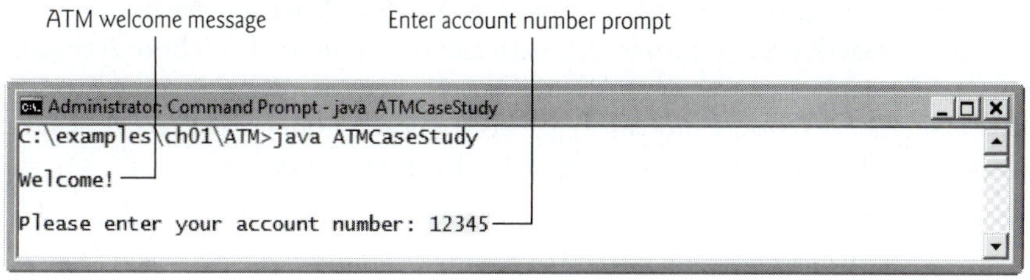

ATM welcome message   Enter account number prompt

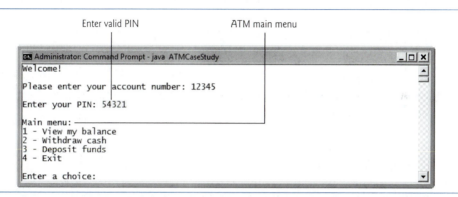

Fig. 1.4 | Prompting the user for an account number.

Enter valid PIN   ATM main menu

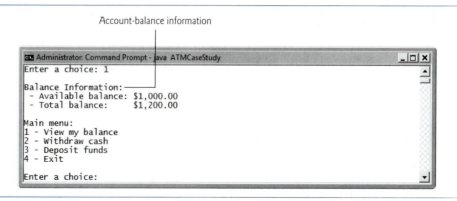

Fig. 1.5 | Entering a valid PIN number and displaying the ATM application's main menu.

able balance ($1000.00) and the Total balance ($1200.00). The available balance is the maximum amount of money in your account which is available for withdrawal at a given time. In some cases, certain funds, such as recent deposits, are not immediately available for the user to withdraw, so the available balance may be less than the total balance, as it is here. After the account-balance information is shown, the application's main menu is displayed again.

Account-balance information

```
Administrator: Command Prompt - java ATMCaseStudy          _ □ ×
Enter a choice: 1

Balance Information:
 - Available balance: $1,000.00
 - Total balance:     $1,200.00

Main menu:
1 - View my balance
2 - Withdraw cash
3 - Deposit funds
4 - Exit

Enter a choice:
```

Fig. 1.6 | ATM application displaying user account-balance information.

7. **Withdrawing money from the account.** Select option 2, "Withdraw cash", from the application menu. You're then presented (Fig. 1.7) with a list of dollar

amounts (e.g., 20, 40, 60, 100 and 200). You are also given the option to cancel the transaction and return to the main menu. Withdraw $100 by selecting option 4. The application displays "Please take your cash now." and returns to the main menu. [*Note:* Unfortunately, this application only *simulates* the behavior of a real ATM and thus does not actually dispense money.]

ATM withdrawal menu

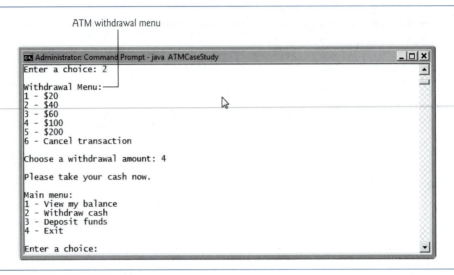

Fig. 1.7 | Withdrawing money from the account and returning to the main menu.

8. *Confirming that the account information has been updated.* From the main menu, select option 1 again to view your current account balance (Fig. 1.8). Note that both the available balance and the total balance have been updated to reflect your withdrawal transaction.

Confirming updated account-balance
information after withdrawal transaction

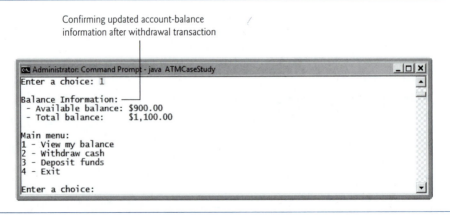

Fig. 1.8 | Checking the new balance.

9. *Ending the transaction.* To end your current ATM session, select option 4, "Exit" from the main menu (Fig. 1.9). The ATM will exit the system and display a good-

bye message to the user. The application will then return to its original prompt, asking for the next user's account number.

ATM goodbye message   Account-number prompt for next user

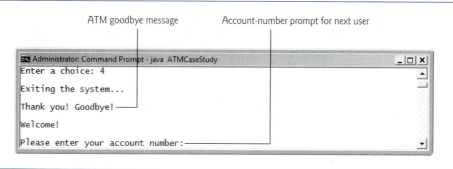

Fig. 1.9 | Ending an ATM transaction session.

10. *Exiting the ATM application and closing the* **Command Prompt** *window.* Most applications provide an option to exit and return to the **Command Prompt** directory from which the application was run. A real ATM does not provide a user with the option to turn off the ATM machine. Rather, when a user has completed all desired transactions and chosen the menu option to exit, the ATM resets itself and displays a prompt for the next user's account number. As Fig. 1.9 illustrates, the ATM application here behaves similarly. Choosing the menu option to exit ends only the current user's ATM session, not the entire ATM application. To actually exit the ATM application, click the close (**x**) button in the upper-right corner of the **Command Prompt** window. Closing the window causes the running application to terminate.

Java How to Program *Applications to Test-Drive*

Figure 1.10 lists a few of the hundreds of applications found in the book's examples and exercises. These programs introduce many of the powerful and fun features of Java. Run these programs to see more of the types of applications you'll learn how to build in this book. The examples folder for this chapter contains all the files required to run each application. Simply type the commands listed in Fig. 1.10 in a **Command Prompt** window.

Application name	Chapter location	Commands to run
Tic-Tac-Toe	Chapter 8	`cd C:\examples\ch01\Tic-Tac-Toe` `java TicTacToeTest`
Guessing Game	Chapter 14	`cd C:\examples\ch01\GuessGame` `java GuessGame`
Logo Animator	Chapter 24	`cd C:\examples\ch01\LogoAnimator` `java LogoAnimator`
Bouncing Ball	Chapter 26	`cd C:\examples\ch01\BouncingBall` `java BouncingBall`

Fig. 1.10 | Additional applications to test-drive.

1.16 Introduction to Object Technology and the UML

Now we introduce object orientation, a natural way of thinking about the world and writing computer programs. Optional Chapters 12–13 present a carefully paced introduction to object-oriented design. Our goal here is to help you develop an object-oriented way of thinking and to introduce you to the **Unified Modeling Language™ (UML™)**—a graphical language that allows people who design software systems to use an industry-standard notation to represent them. In this section, we introduce object-oriented concepts and terminology. Chapters 12–13 present an object-oriented design and implementation of the software for a simple automated teller machine (ATM). Sections 12.2–12.7

- analyze a typical requirements document that describes a software system (the ATM) to be built
- determine the objects required to implement that system
- determine the attributes the objects will have
- determine the behaviors these objects will exhibit
- specify how the objects interact with one another to meet the system requirements.

Sections 13.2–13.3 modify and enhance the design presented in Sections 12.2–12.7. Section 13.4 contains a complete, working Java implementation of the object-oriented ATM software system.

You'll experience a concise, yet solid introduction to object-oriented design with the UML. Also, you'll sharpen your code-reading skills by touring the complete, carefully written and well-documented Java implementation of the ATM in Section 13.4.

Basic Object-Technology Concepts

We begin our introduction to object orientation with some key terminology. Everywhere you look in the real world you see **objects**—people, animals, plants, cars, planes, buildings, computers and so on. Humans think in terms of objects. Telephones, houses, traffic lights, microwave ovens and water coolers are just a few more objects. Computer programs, such as the Java programs you'll read in this book and the ones you'll write, are composed of lots of interacting software objects.

We sometimes divide objects into two categories: animate and inanimate. Animate objects are "alive" in some sense—they move around and do things. Inanimate objects, on the other hand, do not move on their own. Objects of both types, however, have some things in common. They all have **attributes** (e.g., size, shape, color and weight), and they all exhibit **behaviors** (e.g., a ball rolls, bounces, inflates and deflates; a baby cries, sleeps, crawls, walks and blinks; a car accelerates, brakes and turns; a towel absorbs water). We'll study the kinds of attributes and behaviors that software objects have.

Humans learn about existing objects by studying their attributes and observing their behaviors. Different objects can have similar attributes and can exhibit similar behaviors. Comparisons can be made, for example, between babies and adults and between humans and chimpanzees.

Object-oriented design (OOD) models software in terms similar to those that people use to describe real-world objects. It takes advantage of **class** relationships, where objects of a certain class, such as a class of vehicles, have the same characteristics—cars, trucks, little red wagons and roller skates have much in common. OOD also takes advantage of inheritance relationships, where new classes of objects are derived by absorbing characteristics of existing classes and adding unique characteristics of their own. An object of class "convertible" certainly has the characteristics of the more general class "automobile," but more specifically, the roof goes up and down.

Object-oriented design provides a natural and intuitive way to view the software design process—namely, modeling objects by their attributes and behaviors, just as we describe real-world objects. OOD also models communication between objects. Just as people send messages to one another (e.g., a sergeant commands a soldier to stand at attention), objects also communicate via messages. A bank-account object may receive a message to decrease its balance by a certain amount because the customer has withdrawn that amount of money.

OOD encapsulates (i.e., wraps) attributes and operations (behaviors) into objects—an object's attributes and operations are intimately tied together. Objects have the property of information hiding. This means that objects may know how to communicate with one another across well-defined interfaces, but normally they're not allowed to know how other objects are implemented—implementation details are hidden within the objects themselves. We can drive a car effectively, for instance, without knowing the details of how engines, transmissions, brakes and exhaust systems work internally—as long as we know how to use the accelerator pedal, the brake pedal, the wheel and so on. Information hiding, as we'll see, is crucial to good software engineering.

Languages like Java are object oriented. Programming in such a language, called object-oriented programming (OOP), allows you to implement an object-oriented design as a working system. Languages like C, on the other hand, are procedural, so programming tends to be action oriented. In C, the unit of programming is the function. Groups of actions that perform some common task are formed into functions, and functions are grouped to form programs. In Java, the unit of programming is the class from which objects are eventually instantiated (created). Java classes contain methods (which implement operations and are similar to functions in C) as well as fields (which implement attributes).

Java programmers concentrate on creating classes. Each class contains fields and the set of methods that manipulate the fields and provide services to clients (i.e., other classes that use the class). The programmer uses existing classes as the building blocks for constructing new classes.

Classes are to objects as blueprints are to houses. Just as we can build many houses from one blueprint, we can instantiate (create) many objects from one class. You cannot cook meals in the kitchen of a blueprint; you can cook meals in the kitchen of a house.

Classes can have relationships with other classes. For example, in an object-oriented design of a bank, the "bank teller" class needs to relate to the "customer" class, the "cash drawer" class, the "safe" class, and so on. These relationships are called associations.

Packaging software as classes makes it possible for future software systems to reuse the classes. Groups of related classes are often packaged as reusable components. Just as realtors often say that the three most important factors affecting the price of real estate are "location, location and location," people in the software community often say that the three most important factors affecting the future of software development are "reuse, reuse and reuse." Reuse of existing classes when building new classes and programs saves time and effort. Reuse also helps you build more reliable and effective systems, because existing classes and components often have gone through extensive testing, debugging and performance tuning.

With object technology, you can build much of the software you'll need by combining classes, just as automobile manufacturers combine interchangeable parts. Each new class you create will have the potential to become a "software asset" that you and other programmers can use to speed and enhance the quality of future software-development efforts.

Introduction to Object-Oriented Analysis and Design (OOAD)

Soon you'll be writing programs in Java. How will you create the code for your programs? Perhaps, like many programmers, you'll simply turn on your computer and start typing. This approach may work for small programs (like the ones we present in the early chapters of the book), but what if you were asked to create a software system to control thousands of automated teller machines for a major bank? Or suppose you were asked to work on a team of 1,000 software developers building the next U.S. air traffic control system? For projects so large and complex, you should not simply sit down and start writing programs.

To create the best solutions, you should follow a detailed process for **analyzing** your project's **requirements** (i.e., determining *what* the system is supposed to do) and developing a **design** that satisfies them (i.e., deciding *how* the system should do it). Ideally, you'd go through this process and carefully review the design (or have your design reviewed by other software professionals) before writing any code. If this process involves analyzing and designing your system from an object-oriented point of view, it's called an **object-oriented analysis and design (OOAD) process**. Experienced programmers know that analysis and design can save many hours by helping them to avoid an ill-planned system-development approach that has to be abandoned part way through its implementation, possibly wasting considerable time, money and effort.

OOAD is the generic term for the process of analyzing a problem and developing an approach for solving it. Small problems like the ones discussed in these first few chapters do not require an exhaustive OOAD process. It may be sufficient to write **pseudocode** before we begin writing Java code. Pseudocode is an informal means of expressing program logic. It's not actually a programming language, but we can use it as a kind of outline to guide us as we write our code. We introduce pseudocode in Chapter 3.

As problems and the groups of people solving them increase in size, OOAD methods become more appropriate than pseudocode. Ideally, a group should agree on a strictly defined process for solving its problem and a uniform way of communicating the results of that process to one another. Although many different OOAD processes exist, a single graphical language for communicating the results of *any* OOAD process has come into wide use. This language, known as the Unified Modeling Language (UML), was developed in the mid-1990s under the initial direction of three software methodologists—Grady Booch, James Rumbaugh and Ivar Jacobson.

History of the UML

In the 1980s, increasing numbers of organizations began using OOP to build their applications, and a need developed for a standard OOAD process. Many methodologists—including Booch, Rumbaugh and Jacobson—individually produced and promoted separate processes to satisfy this need. Each process had its own notation, or "language" (in the form of graphical diagrams), to convey the results of analysis and design.

By the early 1990s, different organizations, and even divisions within the same organization, were using their own unique processes and notations. At the same time, these organizations also wanted to use software tools that would support their particular processes. Software vendors found it difficult and costly to provide tools for so many processes. A standard notation and standard processes were needed.

In 1994, James Rumbaugh joined Grady Booch at Rational Software Corporation (now a division of IBM), and the two began working to unify their popular processes. They soon were joined by Ivar Jacobson. In 1996, the group released early versions of the UML to the software engineering community and requested feedback. Around the same time, an organization known as the **Object Management Group™ (OMG™)** invited submissions for a common modeling language. The OMG (www.omg.org) is a nonprofit organization that promotes the standardization of object-oriented technologies by issuing guidelines and specifications, such as the UML. Several corporations—among them HP, IBM, Microsoft, Oracle and Rational Software—had already recognized the need for a common modeling language. In response to the OMG's request for proposals, these companies formed **UML Partners**—the consortium that developed the UML version 1.1 and submitted it to the OMG. The OMG accepted the proposal and, in 1997, assumed responsibility for the continuing maintenance and revision of the UML. We present UML 2 terminology and notation throughout this book.

What Is the UML?

The UML is now the most widely used graphical representation scheme for modeling object-oriented systems. It has indeed unified the various popular notational schemes. Those who design systems use the language (in the form of diagrams) to model their systems.

An attractive feature of the UML is its flexibility. It is **extensible** (i.e., capable of being enhanced with new features) and is independent of any particular OOAD process. UML modelers are free to use various processes in designing systems, but all developers can now express their designs with one standard set of graphical notations.

The UML is a complex, feature-rich graphical language. We present our first UML diagrams in Chapters 3 and 4. In our (optional) ATM Software Engineering Case Study in Chapters 12–13 we present a simple, concise subset of the UML's features. We then use this subset to guide you through a first design experience with the UML, intended for novice object-oriented programmers in first- or second-semester programming courses. For more information about the UML, visit our UML Resource Center at www.deitel.com/UML/.

Section 1.16 Self-Review Exercises

1.1   List three examples of real-world objects that we did not mention. For each object, list several attributes and behaviors.

1.2   Pseudocode is _____.
   a)   another term for OOAD
   b)   a programming language used to display UML diagrams
   c)   an informal means of expressing program logic
   d)   a graphical representation scheme for modeling object-oriented systems

1.3   The UML is used primarily to _____.
   a)   test object-oriented systems
   b)   design object-oriented systems
   c)   implement object-oriented systems
   d)   Both a and b

Answers to Section 1.16 Self-Review Exercises

1.1   [*Note:* Answers may vary.] a) A television's attributes include the size of the screen, the number of colors it can display, its current channel and its current volume. A television turns on and off, changes channels, displays video and plays sounds. b) A coffee maker's attributes include the maximum volume of water it can hold, the time required to brew a pot of coffee and the temperature of the heating plate under the coffee pot. A coffee maker turns on and off, brews coffee and heats coffee. c) A turtle's attributes include its age, the size of its shell and its weight. A turtle walks, retreats into its shell, emerges from its shell and eats vegetation.

1.2   c.

1.3   b.

1.17 Web 2.0

The web literally exploded in the mid-to-late 1990s, but the "dot com" economic bust brought hard times in the early 2000s. The resurgence that began in 2004 or so has been named Web 2.0. The first Web 2.0 Conference was held in 2004. A year into its life, the term "Web 2.0" garnered about 10 million hits on the Google search engine, growing to 60 million a year later. Google is widely regarded as the signature company of Web 2.0. Some others are Craigslist (free classified listings), Flickr (photo sharing), del.icio.us (social bookmarking), YouTube (video sharing), MySpace and FaceBook (social networking), Twitter (social messaging), Salesforce (business software offered as online services), Second Life (a virtual world), Skype (Internet telephony) and Wikipedia (a free online encyclopedia).

At Deitel & Associates, we launched our Web 2.0-based Internet Business Initiative in 2005. We research the key technologies of Web 2.0 and use them to build Internet businesses. We share our research in the form of Resource Centers at `www.deitel.com/resourcecenters.html`. Each week, we announce the latest Resource Centers in our newsletter, the *Deitel® Buzz Online* (`www.deitel.com/newsletter/subscribe.html`). Each lists many links to mostly free content and software on the Internet.

Chapter 31 presents a substantial treatment of web services. One common use of web services is for mashups—an applications-development methodology in which you can rapidly develop powerful and intriguing applications by combining complementary web services and other forms of information feeds of two or more organizations. A popular mashup is `www.housingmaps.com`, which combines the real estate listings provided by `www.craigslist.org` with the mapping capabilities of Google Maps to offer maps that show the locations of real estate listings in a given area.

Ajax is one of the premier Web 2.0 technologies. Though the term's use exploded in 2005, it just names a group of technologies and programming techniques that have been in use since the late 1990s. Ajax helps Internet-based applications perform like desktop applications—a difficult task, given that such applications suffer transmission delays as data is shuttled back and forth between your computer and other computers on the Internet. Using Ajax, applications like Google Maps have achieved excellent performance and approach the look-and-feel of desktop applications. Although we don't discuss "raw" Ajax programming (which is quite complex) in this text, we do show in Chapter 30 how to build Ajax-enabled applications using JavaServer Faces (JSF) Ajax-enabled components.

Blogs are websites (currently 100+ million of them) that are like online diaries, with the most recent entries appearing first. Bloggers quickly post their opinions about news, product releases, political candidates, controversial issues, and just about everything else. The collection of all blogs and the blogging community is called the blogosphere and is becoming increasingly influential. Technorati and Google Blog Search are two of the popular blog search engines.

RSS feeds enable sites to push information to subscribers. A common use of RSS feeds is to deliver the latest blog postings to people who subscribe to blogs.

Web 3.0 is another name for the next generation of the web, also called the Semantic Web. Web 1.0 was almost purely HTML-based. Web 2.0 is making increasing use of XML, especially in technologies like RSS feeds and web services. Web 3.0 will make deep use of XML, creating a "web of meaning." If you're a student looking for a great research paper or thesis topic, or an entrepreneur looking for business opportunities, check out our Web 3.0 Resource Center.

To follow the latest developments in Web 2.0, read `www.techcrunch.com` and `www.slashdot.org` and check out the growing list of Internet- and web-related Resource Centers at `www.deitel.com/resourcecenters.html`.

1.18 Software Technologies

In this section, we discuss a number of software engineering buzzwords that you'll hear in the software-development community. We've created Resource Centers on most of these topics, with more on the way.

Agile Software Development is a set of methodologies that try to get software implemented quickly using fewer resources than previous methodologies. Check out the Agile Alliance (`www.agilealliance.org`) and the Agile Manifesto (`www.agilemanifesto.org`).

Refactoring involves reworking code to make it clearer and easier to maintain while preserving its functionality. It's widely employed with agile development methodologies. Many refactoring tools are available to do major portions of the reworking automatically.

Design patterns are proven architectures for constructing flexible and maintainable object-oriented software (see Appendix Q). The field of design patterns tries to enumerate those recurring patterns, encouraging software designers to reuse them to develop better-quality software with less time, money and effort.

Game programming is a fun and challenging career for software developers. The computer game business is already larger than the first-run movie business. College courses and even majors are now devoted to the sophisticated techniques used in game programming. Check out our Game Programming and Programming Projects Resource Centers.

Open-source software is a software-development style that departs from the proprietary development that dominated software's early years. With open-source development, individuals and companies contribute their efforts in developing, maintaining and evolving software in exchange for the right to use that software for their own purposes, typically at no charge. Open-source code generally gets scrutinized by a much larger audience than proprietary software, so errors often get removed faster. Open-source also encourages more innovation. Sun has open-sourced the Sun implementation of the Java Development Kit. Some organizations you'll hear a lot about in the open-source community are the Eclipse Foundation (the Eclipse IDE is popular for Java software development), the Mozilla Foundation (creators of the Firefox web browser), the Apache Software Foundation (creators of the Apache web server) and SourceForge (which provides the tools for managing open-source projects and currently has over 100,000 open-source projects under development).

Linux is an open-source operating system and one of the greatest successes of the open-source movement. **MySQL** is an open-source database management system. **PHP** is the most popular open-source server-side Internet "scripting" language for developing Internet-based applications. **LAMP** is an acronym for the set of open-source technologies that many developers used to build web applications—it stands for Linux, Apache, MySQL and PHP (or Perl or Python—two other languages used for similar purposes).

Ruby on Rails combines the scripting language Ruby with the Rails web application framework developed by the company 37Signals. Their book, *Getting Real*, is a must read for today's web application developers; read it free at `gettingreal.37signals.com/toc.php`. Many Ruby on Rails developers have reported significant productivity gains over using other languages when developing database-intensive web applications.

Software has generally been viewed as a product; most software still is offered this way. If you want to run an application, you buy a software package from a software vendor. You then install that software on your computer and run it as needed. As new versions of the software appear, you upgrade your software, often at significant expense. This process can become cumbersome for organizations with tens of thousands of systems that must be maintained on a diverse array of computer equipment. With **Software as a Service (SAAS)** the software runs on servers elsewhere on the Internet. When such servers are updated, all clients worldwide see the new capabilities; no local installation is needed. You access the service through a browser. Browsers are quite portable, so you can run the same applications on different kinds of computers from anywhere in the world. Salesforce.com, Google, and Microsoft's Office Live and Windows Live all offer SAAS.

1.19 Wrap-Up

This chapter introduced basic hardware, software and communications concepts and basic object-technology concepts, including classes, objects, attributes, behaviors, encapsulation and inheritance. We discussed the different types of programming languages and which specific languages are most widely used. You learned the steps for creating and executing a Java application using Sun's JDK 6. The chapter explored the history of the Internet and the World Wide Web up to the Web 2.0 phenomenon, and Java's role in developing distributed client/server applications for the Internet and the web. You also learned about the history and purpose of the UML—the industry-standard graphical language for modeling object-oriented software systems. You "test-drove" one or more sample Java applications similar to those you'll learn to program in this book. We discussed a number of important recent software technologies.

In Chapter 2, you'll create your first Java applications. You'll see examples that show how programs display messages and obtain information from the user at the keyboard for processing. You'll use Java's primitive data types and arithmetic operators. You'll use Java's equality and relational operators to write simple decision-making statements. We'll analyze and explain each example to help you ease into Java programming.

1.20 Web Resources

This section lists many sites that will be useful to you as you learn Java. The sites include Java resources, Java development tools for students and professionals, and our own websites where you can find downloads and resources associated with this book.

Deitel & Associates Websites

www.deitel.com

Contains updates, corrections and additional resources for all Deitel publications.

www.deitel.com/newsletter/subscribe.html

Subscribe to the free *Deitel® Buzz Online* e-mail newsletter to follow the Deitel & Associates publishing program, including updates and errata to this book.

www.deitel.com/books/jhtp8LOV/

The Deitel & Associates site for *Java How to Program, Late Objects Version, Eighth Edition*. Here you'll find links to the book's examples and other resources.

www.deitel.com/books/jhtp8/

The Deitel & Associates site for *Java How to Program, Early Objects Version, Eighth Edition*.

Deitel Java and Related Resource Centers

www.deitel.com/Java/

Our Java Resource Center focuses on the enormous amount of Java free content available online. Start your search here for tools, integrated development environments (IDEs), resources, downloads, tutorials, documentation, books, e-books, journals, articles, blogs and more that will help you develop Java applications.

www.deitel.com/JavaSE6Mustang/

Our Java SE 6 (Mustang) Resource Center is your guide to the latest release of Java. The site includes the best resources we found online to help you get started with Java SE 6 development.

www.deitel.com/CodeSearchEngines/

Our Code Search Engines and Code Sites Resource Center includes resources developers use to find source code online.

www.deitel.com/ProgrammingProjects/

Our Programming Projects Resource Center is your online guide to great ideas for student programming projects.

Editors and Integrated Development Environments

www.eclipse.org

The Eclipse development environment can be used to develop code in any programming language. You can download the environment and several Java plug-ins to develop your Java programs.

www.netbeans.org

The NetBeans IDE is one of the most widely used, freely distributed Java development tools.

www.blueJ.org

BlueJ is a free tool designed to help teach object-oriented Java to new programmers.

www.jgrasp.org

jGRASP is a "lighter weight" integrated development environment that was developed at Auburn University. The tool also displays visual representations of Java programs to aid comprehension.

www.jcreator.com

JCreator is a popular Java IDE. JCreator Lite Edition is available as a free download. A 30-day trial version of JCreator Pro Edition is also available.

www.textpad.com

TextPad is an editor that also enables you to compile and run your Java programs.

www.editplus.com

EditPlus is an editor that can be configured to compile and run your Java programs.

www.jedit.org

jEdit is an editor that is written in Java and can be used with many programming languages.

Summary

Section 1.1 Introduction
- Java has become the language of choice for implementing Internet-based applications and software for devices that communicate over a network.
- Java Enterprise Edition (Java EE) is geared toward developing large-scale, distributed networking applications and web-based applications.
- Java Micro Edition (Java ME) is geared toward developing applications for small, memory-constrained devices, such as cell phones, pagers and PDAs.

Section 1.2 Computers: Hardware and Software
- A computer is a device that can perform computations and make logical decisions phenomenally faster than human beings can.
- Computers process data under the control of sets of instructions called computer programs. Programs guide computers through actions specified by people called computer programmers.
- A computer consists of various devices referred to as hardware. The programs that run on a computer are referred to as software.

Section 1.3 Computer Organization
- Virtually every computer may be envisioned as divided into six logical units or sections.
- The input unit obtains information from input devices and places this information at the disposal of the other units so that it can be processed.
- The output unit takes information that the computer has processed and places it on various output devices to make it available for use outside the computer.
- The memory unit is the rapid-access, relatively low-capacity "warehouse" section of the computer. It retains information that has been entered through the input unit, making it immediately available for processing when needed. It also retains processed information until it can be placed on output devices by the output unit.
- The arithmetic and logic unit (ALU) is responsible for performing calculations (such as addition, subtraction, multiplication and division) and making decisions.
- The central processing unit (CPU) coordinates and supervises the operation of the other sections. The CPU tells the input unit when information should be read into the memory unit, tells the ALU when information from the memory unit should be used in calculations and tells the output unit when to send information from the memory unit to certain output devices.
- Multiprocessors have multiple CPUs and, hence, can perform many operations simultaneously.
- A multi-core processor implements multiprocessing on a single integrated circuit chip—for example a dual-core processor has two CPUs and a quad-core processor has four CPUs.
- The secondary storage unit is the long-term, high-capacity "warehousing" section of the computer. Programs or data not actively being used by the other units normally are placed on secondary storage devices until they're needed again.

Section 1.4 Early Operating Systems
- Early computers could perform only one job or task at a time.
- Operating systems were developed to make using computers more convenient.
- Multiprogramming involves the simultaneous operation of many jobs.
- With timesharing, the computer runs a small portion of one user's job, then moves on to service the next user, perhaps providing service to each user several times per second.

Section 1.5 Personal, Distributed and Client/Server Computing

- In 1977, Apple Computer popularized personal computing.
- In 1981, IBM, the world's largest computer vendor, introduced the IBM Personal Computer, which quickly legitimized personal computing in business, industry and government.
- In distributed computing, instead of being performed only at a central computer, computing is distributed over networks to the sites where the organization's work is performed.
- Servers store data that may be used by client computers distributed throughout the network, hence the term client/server computing.
- Java has become widely used for writing software for computer networking and for distributed client/server applications.

Section 1.6 The Internet and the World Wide Web

- The Internet is accessible by more than a billion computers and computer-controlled devices.
- With the introduction of the World Wide Web the Internet has exploded into one of the world's premier communication mechanisms.

Section 1.7 Machine Languages, Assembly Languages and High-Level Languages

- Any computer can directly understand only its own machine language.
- Machine language is the "natural language" of a computer.
- Machine languages generally consist of strings of numbers (ultimately reduced to 1s and 0s) that instruct computers to perform their most elementary operations one at a time.
- Machine languages are machine dependent.
- Programmers began using Englishlike abbreviations to represent elementary operations. These abbreviations formed the basis of assembly languages.
- Translator programs called assemblers were developed to convert early assembly-language programs to machine language at computer speeds.
- To speed the programming process, high-level languages were developed in which single statements could be written to accomplish substantial tasks.
- Translator programs called compilers convert high-level language programs into machine language.
- High-level languages allow you to write instructions that look almost like everyday English and contain commonly used mathematical notations.
- Java is by far the most widely used high-level language.
- Compiling a high-level language program into machine language can take a considerable amount of computer time. Interpreter programs were developed to execute high-level language programs directly (without the delay of compilation), although slower than compiled programs run.

Section 1.8 History of C and C++

- Java evolved from C++, which evolved from C, which evolved from BCPL and B.
- The C language was developed by Dennis Ritchie at Bell Laboratories. It initially became widely known as the development language of the UNIX operating system.
- C++, an extension of C, was developed by Bjarne Stroustrup in the early 1980s at Bell Laboratories. C++ provides a number of features that "spruce up" the C language, and capabilities for object-oriented programming.

Section 1.9 History of Java

- Java is used to develop large-scale enterprise applications, to enhance the functionality of web servers, to provide applications for consumer devices and for many other purposes.

- Java programs consist of pieces called classes. Classes include pieces called methods that perform tasks and return information when the tasks are completed.

Section 1.10 Java Class Libraries
- Most Java programmers take advantage of the rich collections of existing classes in the Java class libraries, also known as the Java APIs (Application Programming Interfaces).
- The advantage of creating your own classes and methods is that you know how they work and can examine the code. The disadvantage is the time-consuming and potentially complex effort.

Section 1.11 Fortran, COBOL, Pascal and Ada
- Fortran (FORmula TRANslator) was developed by IBM Corporation in the mid-1950s for use in scientific and engineering applications that require complex mathematical computations.
- COBOL (COmmon Business Oriented Language) is used for commercial applications that require precise and efficient manipulation of large amounts of data.
- Research in the 1960s resulted in structured programming—an approach to writing programs that are clearer, and easier to test, debug and modify than those produced with earlier techniques.
- Pascal was designed for teaching structured programming in academic environments and rapidly became the preferred programming language in most colleges.
- The Ada programming language was developed under the sponsorship of the U.S. Department of Defense (DOD) to fill most of its needs. An Ada capability called multitasking allows programmers to specify that activities are to occur in parallel. Java, through a technique called *multithreading*, also enables programmers to write programs with parallel activities.

Section 1.12 BASIC, Visual Basic, Visual C++, C# and .NET
- BASIC was developed in the mid-1960s for writing simple programs.
- Microsoft's Visual Basic language simplifies the development of Windows applications.
- Microsoft's .NET platform integrates the Internet and the web into computer applications.

Section 1.13 Typical Java Development Environment
- Java programs normally go through five phases—edit, compile, load, verify and execute.
- Phase 1 consists of editing a file with an editor. You type a program using the editor, make corrections and save the program on a secondary storage device, such as your hard drive.
- A file name ending with the `.java` extension indicates that the file contains Java source code.
- Integrated development environments (IDEs) provide tools that support software development, including editors for writing and editing programs and debuggers for locating logic errors.
- In Phase 2, the programmer uses the command `javac` to compile a program.
- If a program compiles, the compiler produces a `.class` file that contains the compiled program.
- The Java compiler translates Java source code into bytecodes that represent the tasks to be executed. Bytecodes are executed by the Java Virtual Machine (JVM).
- In Phase 3, loading, the class loader takes the `.class` files containing the program's bytecodes and transfers them to primary memory.
- In Phase 4, as the classes are loaded, the bytecode verifier examines their bytecodes to ensure that they're valid and do not violate Java's security restrictions.
- In Phase 5, the JVM executes the program's bytecodes.

Section 1.14 Notes about Java and Java How to Program
- Portability is an elusive goal. Simply writing programs in Java does not guarantee portability.

Section 1.15 Test-Driving a Java Application
- In this section, you ran and interacted with your first Java application.

Section 1.16 Introduction to Object Technology and the UML
- The Unified Modeling Language (UML) is a graphical language that allows people who build systems to represent their object-oriented designs in a common notation.
- Object-oriented design (OOD) models software components in terms of real-world objects.
- Objects have the property of information hiding—objects of one class are normally not allowed to know how objects of other classes are implemented.
- Object-oriented programming (OOP) implements object-oriented designs.
- Java programmers concentrate on creating their own user-defined types called classes. Each class contains data as well as methods that manipulate that data and provide services to clients.
- The data components of a class are attributes or fields; the operation components are methods.
- Classes can have relationships with other classes; these relationships are called associations.
- Packaging software as classes makes it possible for future software systems to reuse the classes.
- An instance of a class is called an object.
- The process of analyzing and designing a system from an object-oriented point of view is called object-oriented analysis and design (OOAD).

Section 1.17 Web 2.0
- The resurgence of the web that began in 2004 or so has been named Web 2.0.
- Mashups enable you to rapidly develop powerful and intriguing applications by combining complementary web services and other forms of information feeds of two or more organizations.
- Ajax helps Internet-based applications perform like desktop applications—a difficult task, given that such applications suffer transmission delays as data is shuttled back and forth between your computer and other computers on the Internet.
- Blogs are websites that are like online diaries, with the most recent entries appearing first.
- RSS feeds enable sites to push information to subscribers.
- Web 3.0 is another name for the next generation of the web, also called the Semantic Web. Web 3.0 will make deep use of XML, creating a "web of meaning."

Section 1.18 Software Technologies
- Agile Software Development is a set of methodologies that try to get software implemented quickly using fewer resources than previous methodologies.
- Refactoring involves reworking code to make it clearer and easier to maintain while preserving its functionality.
- Design patterns are proven architectures for constructing flexible and maintainable object-oriented software.
- Game programming is a fun and challenging career for software developers. College courses and even majors are devoted to the sophisticated software techniques used in game programming.
- With open-source development, individuals and companies contribute their efforts in developing, maintaining and evolving software in exchange for the right to use that software for their own purposes, typically at no charge. Open-source code generally gets scrutinized by a much larger audience than proprietary software, so errors often get removed faster. Open-source also encourages more innovation.

- Linux is an open-source operating system and one of the greatest successes of the open-source movement. MySQL is an open-source database management system. PHP is the most popular open-source server-side Internet "scripting" language for developing Internet-based applications. LAMP is an acronym for the set of open-source technologies that many developers used to build web applications—it stands for Linux, Apache, MySQL and PHP (or Perl or Python—two other languages used for similar purposes).

- Ruby on Rails combines the scripting language Ruby with the Rails web application framework developed by the company 37Signals. Many Ruby on Rails developers have reported productivity gains over using other languages when developing database-intensive web applications.

- With Software as a Service (SAAS) the software runs on servers elsewhere on the Internet. You access the service through a browser. Browsers are quite portable, so you can run the same applications on different kinds of computers from anywhere in the world.

Terminology

Self-Review Exercises

1.1   Fill in the blanks in each of the following statements:

   a)   The company that popularized personal computing was _____.

   b)   The computer that made personal computing legitimate in business and industry was the _____.

   c)   Computers process data under the control of sets of instructions called _____.

d) The key logical units of the computer are the _____, _____, _____, _____, _____ and _____.

e) The three types of languages discussed in the chapter are _____, _____ and _____.

f) The programs that translate high-level language programs into machine language are called _____.

g) The _____ allows computer users to locate and view multimedia-based documents on almost any subject over the Internet.

h) _____ allows a Java program to perform multiple activities in parallel.

1.2 Fill in the blanks in each of the following sentences about the Java environment:

a) The _____ command from the JDK executes a Java application.

b) The _____ command from the JDK compiles a Java program.

c) A Java program file must end with the _____ file extension.

d) When a Java program is compiled, the file produced by the compiler ends with the _____ file extension.

e) The file produced by the Java compiler contains _____ that are executed by the Java Virtual Machine.

1.3 Fill in the blanks in each of the following statements (based on Section 1.16):

a) Objects have the property of _____—although objects may know how to communicate with one another across well-defined interfaces, they normally are not allowed to know how other objects are implemented.

b) Java programmers concentrate on creating _____, which contain fields and the set of methods that manipulate those fields and provide services to clients.

c) Classes can have relationships called _____ with other classes.

d) The process of analyzing and designing a system from an object-oriented point of view is called _____.

e) OOD takes advantage of _____ relationships, where new classes of objects are derived by absorbing characteristics of existing classes, then adding unique characteristics of their own.

f) _____ is a graphical language that allows people who design software systems to use an industry-standard notation to represent them.

g) The size, shape, color and weight of an object are considered _____ of the object's class.

Answers to Self-Review Exercises

1.1   a) Apple. b) IBM Personal Computer. c) programs. d) input unit, output unit, memory unit, central processing unit, arithmetic and logic unit, secondary storage unit. e) machine languages, assembly languages, high-level languages. f) compilers. g) World Wide Web. h) Multithreading.

1.2   a) java. b) javac. c) .java. d) .class. e) bytecodes.

1.3   a) information hiding. b) classes. c) associations. d) object-oriented analysis and design (OOAD). e) inheritance. f) The Unified Modeling Language (UML). g) attributes.

Exercises

1.4   Categorize each of the following items as either hardware or software:

a) CPU

b) Java compiler

c) JVM

d) input unit

e) editor

1.5 Fill in the blanks in each of the following statements:

a) The logical unit of the computer that receives information from outside the computer for use by the computer is the _____.

b) The process of instructing the computer to solve a problem is called _____.

c) _____ is a type of computer language that uses Englishlike abbreviations for machine-language instructions.

d) _____ is a logical unit of the computer that sends information which has already been processed by the computer to various devices so that it may be used outside the computer.

e) _____ and _____ are logical units of the computer that retain information.

f) _____ is a logical unit of the computer that performs calculations.

g) _____ is a logical unit of the computer that makes logical decisions.

h) _____ languages are most convenient to the programmer for writing programs quickly and easily.

i) The only language a computer can directly understand is that computer's _____.

j) _____ is a logical unit of the computer that coordinates the activities of all the other logical units.

1.6 What is the difference between fatal errors and nonfatal errors? Why might you prefer to experience a fatal rather than a nonfatal error?

1.7 Fill in the blanks in each of the following statements:

a) _____ is now used to develop large-scale enterprise applications, to enhance the functionality of web servers, to provide applications for consumer devices and for many other purposes.

b) _____ was designed specifically for the .NET platform to enable programmers to migrate easily to .NET.

c) _____ initially became widely known as the development language of the UNIX operating system.

d) _____ was developed at Dartmouth College in the mid-1960s as a means of writing simple programs.

e) _____ was developed by IBM Corporation in the mid-1950s to be used for scientific and engineering applications that require complex mathematical computations.

f) _____ is used for commercial applications that require precise and efficient manipulation of large amounts of data.

g) The _____ programming language was developed by Bjarne Stroustrup in the early 1980s at Bell Laboratories.

1.8 Fill in the blanks in each of the following statements:

a) Java programs normally go through five phases—_____, _____, _____, _____ and _____.

b) A(n) _____ provides many tools that support the software-development process, such as editors for writing and editing programs, debuggers for locating logic errors in programs, and many other features.

c) The command `java` invokes the _____, which executes Java programs.

d) A(n) _____ is a software application that simulates a computer, but hides the underlying operating system and hardware from the programs that interact with it.

e) A(n) _____ program can run on multiple platforms.

f) The _____ takes the `.class` files containing the program's bytecodes and transfers them to primary memory.

g) The _____ examines bytecodes to ensure that they're valid.

1.9 Explain the two compilation phases of Java programs.

1.10 You are probably wearing on your wrist one of the world's most common types of objects—a watch. Discuss how each of the following terms and concepts applies to the notion of a watch: object, attributes, behaviors, class, inheritance (consider, for example, an alarm clock), abstraction, modeling, messages, encapsulation, interface and information hiding.

Making a Difference

1.11 *(Test Drive: Carbon Footprint Calculator)* Some scientists believe that carbon emissions, especially from the burning of fossil fuels, contribute significantly to global warming and that this can be combatted if individuals take steps to limit their use of carbon-based fuels. Organizations and individuals are increasingly concerned about their "carbon footprints." Websites such as TerraPass

    www.terrapass.com/carbon-footprint-calculator/

and Carbon Footprint

    www.carbonfootprint.com/calculator.aspx

provide carbon footprint calculators. Test drive these calculators to determine your carbon footprint. Exercises in later chapters will ask you to program your own carbon footprint calculator. To prepare for this, research the formulas for calculating carbon footprints.

1.12 *(Test Drive: Body Mass Index Calculator)* By recent estimates, two-thirds of the people in the United States are overweight and about half of those are obese. This causes significant increases in illnesses such as diabetes and heart disease. To determine whether a person is overweight or obese, you can use a measure called the body mass index (BMI). The United States Department of Health and Human Services provides a BMI calculator at www.nhlbisupport.com/bmi/. Use it to calculate your own BMI. An exercise in Chapter 2 will ask you to program your own BMI calculator. To prepare for this, research the formulas for calculating BMI.

1.13 *(Attributes of Hybrid Vehicles)* In this chapter you learned the basics of classes. Now you'll begin "fleshing out" aspects of a class called "Hybrid Vehicle." Hybrid vehicles are becoming increasingly popular, because they often get much better mileage than purely gasoline-powered vehicles. Browse the web and study the features of four or five of today's popular hybrid cars, then list as many of their hybrid-related attributes as you can. For example, common attributes include city-miles-per-gallon and highway-miles-per-gallon. Also list the attributes of the batteries (type, weight, etc.).

1.14 *(Gender Neutrality)* Many people want to eliminate sexism in all forms of communication. You've been asked to create a program that can process a paragraph of text and replace gender-specific words with gender-neutral ones. Assuming that you've been given a list of gender-specific words and their gender-neutral replacements (e.g., replace "wife" by "spouse," "man" by "person," "daughter" by "child" and so on), explain the procedure you'd use to read through a paragraph of text and manually perform these replacements. How might your procedure generate a strange term like "woperchild," which is actually listed in the Urban Dictionary (www.urbandictionary.com)? In Chapter 3, you'll learn that a more formal term for "procedure" is "algorithm," and that an algorithm specifies the *steps* to be performed and the *order* in which to perform them.

Introduction to Java Applications

What's in a name?
That which we call a rose
By any other name would
smell as sweet.
—William Shakespeare

When faced with a decision, I
always ask, "What would be the
most fun?"
—Peggy Walker

"Take some more tea," the
March Hare said to Alice, very
earnestly. "I've had nothing
yet," Alice replied in an
offended tone: "so I can't take
more." "You mean you can't
take less," said the Hatter: "It's
very easy to take more than
nothing."
—Lewis Carroll

Objectives

In this chapter you'll learn:

- To write simple Java applications.

- To use input and output statements.

- Java's primitive types.

- Basic memory concepts.

- To use arithmetic operators.

- The precedence of arithmetic operators.

- To write decision-making statements.

- To use relational and equality operators.

2.1 Introduction

In this chapter, we introduce Java application programming with simple programs to get you started with building Java programs. We begin with several examples that display messages on the screen, then demonstrate a program that obtains two numbers from a user, calculates their sum and displays the result. You'll learn how to perform arithmetic calculations and save their results for later use. The last example demonstrates decision making by showing you how to compare numbers, then display messages based on the comparison results. This chapter uses the tools from the JDK to compile and run programs. We've also posted videos at www.deitel.com/books/jhtp8LOV/ to help you get started with the popular Eclipse and NetBeans integrated development environments.

2.2 Our First Program in Java: Printing a Line of Text

A Java **application** is a computer program that executes when you use the **java command** to launch the Java Virtual Machine (JVM). Let's consider a simple application that displays a line of text. (Later in this section we'll discuss how to compile and run an application.) The program and its output are shown in Fig. 2.1. The output appears in the box at the end of the program. The program illustrates several important Java language features. Each program we present includes line numbers, which are not part of actual Java programs. We'll soon see that line 9 does the real work of the program—displaying the phrase Welcome to Java Programming! on the screen.

```
1   // Fig. 2.1: Welcome1.java
2   // Text-printing program.
3
4   public class Welcome1
5   {
6      // main method begins execution of Java application
7      public static void main( String[] args )
8      {
9         System.out.println( "Welcome to Java Programming!" );
10     } // end method main
11  } // end class Welcome1
```

```
Welcome to Java Programming!
```

Fig. 2.1 | Text-printing program.

Commenting Your Programs
Line 1

```
// Fig. 2.1: Welcome1.java
```

begins with **//**, indicating that the line is a **comment**. You insert comments to **document programs** and improve their readability. The Java compiler ignores comments, so they do not cause the computer to perform any action when the program is run. By convention, we begin every program with a comment indicating the figure number and file name.

A comment that begins with // is an **end-of-line comment**—it terminates at the end of the line on which it appears. An end-of-line comment also can begin in the middle of a line and continue until the end of that line (as in lines 10 and 11). Another kind of comment, called a **traditional comment**, can be spread over several lines as in

```
/* This is a traditional comment. It
   can be split over multiple lines */
```

This type of comment begins with **/*** and ends with ***/**. All text between the delimiters is ignored by the compiler. Java incorporated traditional comments and end-of-line comments from the C and C++ programming languages, respectively. In this book, we use only // comments.

Java also provides **Javadoc comments** that are delimited by **/**** and ***/**. As with traditional comments, all text between the Javadoc comment delimiters is ignored by the compiler. Javadoc comments enable you to embed program documentation directly in your programs. Such comments are the preferred Java documenting format in industry. The **javadoc utility program** (part of the Java SE Development Kit) reads Javadoc comments and uses them to prepare your program's documentation in HTML format. We demonstrate Javadoc comments and the javadoc utility in Appendix M, Creating Documentation with javadoc.

Line 2

```
// Text-printing program.
```

is a comment that describes the purpose of the program.

Common Programming Error 2.1

Forgetting one of the delimiters of a traditional or Javadoc comment is a syntax error. The syntax of a programming language specifies the rules for creating proper programs in that language, similar to how a natural language's grammar rules specify sentence structure. A syntax error occurs when the compiler encounters code that violates Java's language rules (i.e., its syntax). In this case, the compiler issues an error message and prevents your program from compiling. Syntax errors are also called compiler errors, compile-time errors or compilation errors, because the compiler detects them during the compilation phase.

Good Programming Practice 2.1

Some organizations require every program to begin with a comment that states the program's purpose and mentions the author, date and time when the program was last modified.

Using Blank Lines
Line 3 is a blank line. Blank lines and space characters make programs easier to read. Together, blank lines, spaces and tabs are known as **white space** (or whitespace). White space is ignored by the compiler.

Good Programming Practice 2.2

Use blank lines and spaces to enhance program readability.

Declaring a Class
Line 4

```
public class Welcome1
```

begins a **class declaration** for class `Welcome1`. Every Java program consists of at least one class that you (the programmer) define. These are known as **programmer-defined classes**. The **class keyword** introduces a class declaration and is immediately followed by the **class name** (`Welcome1`). **Keywords** (sometimes called **reserved words**) are reserved for use by Java and are always spelled with all lowercase letters. The complete list of keywords is shown in Appendix C.

By convention, class names begin with a capital letter and capitalize the first letter of each word they include (e.g., `SampleClassName`). A class name is an **identifier**—a series of characters consisting of letters, digits, underscores (_) and dollar signs ($) that does not begin with a digit and does not contain spaces. Some valid identifiers are `Welcome1`, `$value`, `_value`, `m_inputField1` and `button7`. The name `7button` is not a valid identifier because it begins with a digit, and the name `input field` is not a valid identifier because it contains a space. Normally, an identifier that does not begin with a capital letter is not a class name. Java is **case sensitive**—uppercase and lowercase letters are distinct—so `a1` and `A1` are different (but both valid) identifiers.

Good Programming Practice 2.3

By convention, begin each class name identifier with a capital letter and start each subsequent word in the identifier with a capital letter.

Common Programming Error 2.2

Java is case sensitive. Not using the proper uppercase and lowercase letters for an identifier normally causes a compilation error.

In Chapters 2–6, every class we define begins with the **public** keyword. For now, we simply require this keyword. For our application, the file name is `Welcome1.java`. You'll learn more about `public` and non-`public` classes in Chapter 8.

Common Programming Error 2.3

A `public` class must be placed in a file that has the same name as the class (in terms of both spelling and capitalization) plus the `.java` extension; otherwise, a compilation error occurs. For example, `public class Welcome` must be placed in a file named `Welcome.java`.

A **left brace** (at line 5 in this program), `{`, begins the **body** of every class declaration. A corresponding **right brace** (at line 11), `}`, must end each class declaration. Note that lines 6–10 are indented. This indentation is one of the spacing conventions mentioned earlier.

Error-Prevention Tip 2.1

When you type an opening left brace, `{`, immediately type the closing right brace, `}`, then reposition the cursor between the braces and indent to begin typing the body. This practice helps prevent errors due to missing braces. Many IDEs insert the braces for you.

Good Programming Practice 2.4

Indent the entire body of each class declaration one "level" between the left brace and the right brace that delimit the body of the class. This format emphasizes the class declaration's structure and makes it easier to read.

Good Programming Practice 2.5

Many IDEs insert indentation for you in all the right places. The Tab key may also be used to create indents, but tab stops vary among text editors. We recommend three spaces per indent.

Common Programming Error 2.4

It's a syntax error if braces do not occur in matching pairs.

Declaring a Method
Line 6

```
// main method begins execution of Java application
```

is an end-of-line comment indicating the purpose of lines 7–10 of the program. Line 7

```
public static void main( String[] args )
```

is the starting point of every Java application. The **parentheses** after the identifier main indicate that it's a program building block called a **method**. Java class declarations normally contain one or more methods. For a Java application, one of the methods must be called main and must be defined as shown in line 7; otherwise, the JVM will not execute the application. Methods perform tasks and can return information when they complete their tasks. Keyword **void** indicates that this method will not return any information. Later, we'll see how a method can return information. For now, simply mimic main's first line in your Java applications. In line 7, the String[] args in parentheses is a required part of the method main's declaration. We discuss this in Chapter 6.

The left brace in line 8 begins the **body of the method declaration**. A corresponding right brace must end the method declaration's body (line 10). Note that line 9 in the method body is indented between the braces.

Good Programming Practice 2.6

Indent the entire body of each method declaration one "level" between the braces that define the body of the method. This makes the structure of the method stand out and makes the method declaration easier to read.

Performing Output with `System.out.println`
Line 9

```
System.out.println( "Welcome to Java Programming!" );
```

instructs the computer to perform an action—namely, to print the **string** of characters contained between the double quotation marks (but not the quotation marks themselves). A string is sometimes called a **character string** or a **string literal**. White-space characters in strings are not ignored by the compiler. Strings cannot span multiple lines of code.

The **System.out** object is known as the **standard output object**. It allows Java applications to display strings in the **command window** from which the Java application executes. In recent versions of Microsoft Windows, the command window is the **Command Prompt**. In UNIX/Linux/Mac OS X, the command window is called a **terminal window** or a **shell**. Many programmers refer to the command window simply as the **command line**.

Method **System.out.println** displays (or prints) a line of text in the command window. The string in the parentheses in line 9 is the **argument** to the method. When System.out.println completes its task, it positions the output cursor (the location where the next character will be displayed) at the beginning of the next line in the command window. (This is similar to when you press the *Enter* key while typing in a text editor—the cursor appears at the beginning of the next line in the document.)

The entire line 9, including System.out.println, the argument "Welcome to Java Programming!" in the parentheses and the **semicolon** (;), is called a **statement**. Most statements end with a semicolon. When the statement in line 9 executes, it displays Welcome to Java Programming! in the command window. A method typically contains one or more statements that perform the method's task.

Common Programming Error 2.5
When a semicolon is required to end a statement, omitting the semicolon is a syntax error.

Error-Prevention Tip 2.2
When learning how to program, sometimes it's helpful to "break" a working program so you can familiarize yourself with the compiler's syntax-error messages. These messages do not always state the exact problem in the code. When you encounter such syntax-error messages, you'll have an idea of what caused the error. [Try removing a semicolon or brace from the program of Fig. 2.1, then recompile the program to see the error messages generated by the omission.]

Error-Prevention Tip 2.3
When the compiler reports a syntax error, the error may not be on the line indicated by the error message. First, check the line for which the error was reported. If that line does not contain syntax errors, check several preceding lines.

Using End-of-Line Comments on Right Braces for Readability
We include an end-of-line comment after a closing brace that ends a method declaration and after a closing brace that ends a class declaration. For example, line 10

```
} // end method main
```

indicates the closing brace of method main, and line 11

```
} // end class Welcome1
```

indicates the closing brace of class Welcome1. Each comment indicates the method or class that the right brace terminates.

Good Programming Practice 2.7
To improve program readability, follow the closing brace of a method body or class declaration with a comment indicating the method or class declaration to which the brace belongs.

Compiling and Executing Your First Java Application

We're now ready to compile and execute our program. We assume you're using the Sun Microsystems' Java SE Development Kit (JDK) 6 Update 10 (or higher), not an IDE. Our Java Resource Centers at www.deitel.com/ResourceCenters.html provide links to tutorials that help you get started with several popular Java development tools, including Net-Beans™, Eclipse™ and others. We've also posted NetBeans and Eclipse videos at www.deitel.com/books/jhtp8LOV/ to help you get started using these popular IDEs.

To prepare to compile the program, open a command window and change to the directory where the program is stored. Many operating systems use the command cd to change directories. For example,

```
cd c:\examples\ch02\fig02_01
```

changes to the fig02_01 directory on Windows. The command

```
cd ~/examples/ch02/fig02_01
```

changes to the fig02_01 directory on UNIX/Linux/Max OS X.

To compile the program, type

```
javac Welcome1.java
```

If the program contains no syntax errors, the preceding command creates a new file called Welcome1.class (known as the **class file** for Welcome1) containing the platform-independent Java bytecodes that represent our application. When we use the java command to execute the application on a given platform, these bytecodes will be translated by the JVM into instructions that are understood by the underlying operating system.

Error-Prevention Tip 2.4

When attempting to compile a program, if you receive a message such as "bad command or filename," "javac: command not found" or "'javac' is not recognized as an internal or external command, operable program or batch file," then your Java software was not installed properly. If you are using the JDK, this indicates that the system's PATH environment variable was not set properly. Please carefully review the installation instructions in the Before You Begin section of this book. On some systems, after correcting the PATH, you may need to reboot your computer or open a new command window for these settings to take effect.

Error-Prevention Tip 2.5

Each syntax-error message contains the file name and line number where the error occurred. For example, Welcome1.java:6 indicates that an error occurred in the file Welcome1.java at line 6. The remainder of the error message provides information about the syntax error.

Error-Prevention Tip 2.6

The compiler error message "class Welcome1 is public, should be declared in a file named Welcome1.java" indicates that the file name does not exactly match the name of the public class in the file or that you typed the class name incorrectly when compiling the class.

Figure 2.2 shows the program of Fig. 2.1 executing in a Microsoft® Windows Vista® **Command Prompt** window. To execute the program, type java Welcome1. This launches the JVM, which loads the `.class` file for class `Welcome1`. Note that the `.class` file-name extension is omitted from the preceding command; otherwise, the JVM will not execute the program. The JVM calls method `main`. Next, the statement at line 9 of `main` displays `"Welcome to Java Programming!"` [*Note:* Many environments show command prompts with black backgrounds and white text. We adjusted these settings in our environment to make our screen captures more readable.]

Fig. 2.2 | Executing Welcome1 from the **Command Prompt**.

Error-Prevention Tip 2.7
When attempting to run a Java program, if you receive a message such as "`Exception in thread "main" java.lang.NoClassDefFoundError: Welcome1`," your CLASSPATH environment variable has not been set properly. Please carefully review the installation instructions in the Before You Begin section of this book. On some systems, you may need to reboot your computer or open a new command window after configuring the CLASSPATH.

2.3 Modifying Our First Java Program

In this section, we modify the example in Fig. 2.1 to print text on one line by using multiple statements and to print text on several lines by using a single statement.

Displaying a Single Line of Text with Multiple Statements
`Welcome to Java Programming!` can be displayed several ways. Class `Welcome2`, shown in Fig. 2.3, uses two statements to produce the same output as that shown in Fig. 2.1. From this point forward, we highlight the new and key features in each code listing, as shown in lines 9–10 of this program.

The program is similar to Fig. 2.1, so we discuss only the changes here. Line 2

```
// Printing a line of text with multiple statements.
```

is an end-of-line comment stating the purpose of this program. Line 4 begins the `Welcome2` class declaration. Lines 9–10 of method `main`

```
System.out.print( "Welcome to " );
System.out.println( "Java Programming!" );
```

display one line of text in the command window. The first statement uses `System.out`'s method `print` to display a string. Unlike `println`, after displaying its argument, `print` does not position the output cursor at the beginning of the next line in the command

```
1   // Fig. 2.3: Welcome2.java
2   // Printing a line of text with multiple statements.
3
4   public class Welcome2
5   {
6      // main method begins execution of Java application
7      public static void main( String[] args )
8      {
9         System.out.print( "Welcome to " );
10        System.out.println( "Java Programming!" );
11     } // end method main
12  } // end class Welcome2
```

```
Welcome to Java Programming!
```

Fig. 2.3 | Printing a line of text with multiple statements.

window—the next character the program displays will appear immediately after the last character that print displays. Thus, line 10 positions the first character in its argument (the letter "J") immediately after the last character that line 9 displays (the space character before the string's closing double-quote character). Each print or println statement resumes displaying characters from where the last print or println statement stopped displaying characters.

Displaying Multiple Lines of Text with a Single Statement

A single statement can display multiple lines by using newline characters, which indicate to System.out's print and println methods when to position the output cursor at the beginning of the next line in the command window. Like blank lines, space characters and tab characters, newline characters are white-space characters. Figure 2.4 outputs four lines of text, using newline characters to determine when to begin each new line. Most of the program is identical to those in Fig. 2.1 and Fig. 2.3, so we discuss only the changes here.

```
1   // Fig. 2.4: Welcome3.java
2   // Printing multiple lines of text with a single statement.
3
4   public class Welcome3
5   {
6      // main method begins execution of Java application
7      public static void main( String[] args )
8      {
9         System.out.println( "Welcome\nto\nJava\nProgramming!" );
10     } // end method main
11  } // end class Welcome3
```

```
Welcome
to
Java
Programming!
```

Fig. 2.4 | Printing multiple lines of text with a single statement.

Line 2

```
// Printing multiple lines of text with a single statement.
```

is a comment stating the program's purpose. Line 4 begins the `Welcome3` class declaration.
Line 9

```
System.out.println( "Welcome\nto\nJava\nProgramming!" );
```

displays four separate lines of text in the command window. Normally, the characters in a string are displayed exactly as they appear in the double quotes. Note, however, that the two characters \ and n (repeated three times in the statement) do not appear on the screen. The **backslash** (\) is called an **escape character**. It indicates to `System.out`'s `print` and `println` methods that a "special character" is to be output. When a backslash appears in a string of characters, Java combines the next character with the backslash to form an **escape sequence**. The escape sequence \n represents the newline character. When a newline character appears in a string being output with `System.out`, the newline character causes the screen's output cursor to move to the beginning of the next line in the command window. Figure 2.5 lists several common escape sequences and describes how they affect the display of characters in the command window. For the complete list of escape sequences, visit `java.sun.com/docs/books/jls/third_edition/html/lexical.html#3.10.6`.

Escape sequence	Description
\n	Newline. Position the screen cursor at the beginning of the next line.
\t	Horizontal tab. Move the screen cursor to the next tab stop.
\r	Carriage return. Position the screen cursor at the beginning of the current line—do not advance to the next line. Any characters output after the carriage return overwrite the characters previously output on that line.
\\	Backslash. Used to print a backslash character.
\"	Double quote. Used to print a double-quote character. For example, `System.out.println( "\"in quotes\"" );` displays `"in quotes"`

Fig. 2.5 | Some common escape sequences.

2.4 Displaying Text with `printf`

The **`System.out.printf`** method (`f` means "formatted") displays formatted data. Figure 2.6 uses this method to output the strings `"Welcome to"` and `"Java Programming!"`.
Lines 9–10

```
System.out.printf( "%s\n%s\n",
    "Welcome to", "Java Programming!" );
```

call method `System.out.printf` to display the program's output. The method call specifies three arguments. When a method requires multiple arguments, the arguments are placed in a **comma-separated list**.

```
1   // Fig. 2.6: Welcome4.java
2   // Displaying multiple lines with method System.out.printf.
3
4   public class Welcome4
5   {
6      // main method begins execution of Java application
7      public static void main( String[] args )
8      {
9         System.out.printf( "%s\n%s\n",
10            "Welcome to", "Java Programming!" );
11     } // end method main
12  } // end class Welcome4
```

```
Welcome to
Java Programming!
```

Fig. 2.6 | Displaying multiple lines with method `System.out.printf`.

Good Programming Practice 2.8
Place a space after each comma (,) in an argument list to make programs more readable.

Lines 9–10 represent only one statement. Java allows large statements to be split over many lines. We indent line 10 to indicate that it's a continuation of line 9. Note that you cannot split a statement in the middle of an identifier or in the middle of a string.

Common Programming Error 2.6
Splitting a statement in the middle of an identifier or a string is a syntax error.

Method `printf`'s first argument is a **format string** that may consist of **fixed text** and **format specifiers**. Fixed text is output by `printf` just as it would be by `print` or `println`. Each format specifier is a placeholder for a value and specifies the type of data to output. Format specifiers also may include optional formatting information.

Format specifiers begin with a percent sign (%) and are followed by a character that represents the data type. For example, the format specifier **%s** is a placeholder for a string. The format string in line 9 specifies that `printf` should output two strings, each followed by a newline character. At the first format specifier's position, `printf` substitutes the value of the first argument after the format string. At each subsequent format specifier's position, `printf` substitutes the value of the next argument in the argument list. So this example substitutes "Welcome to" for the first %s and "Java Programming!" for the second %s. The output shows that two lines of text are displayed.

We introduce various formatting features as they're needed throughout the book. Appendix G presents the details of formatting output with `printf`.

2.5 Another Application: Adding Integers

Our next application reads (or inputs) two **integers** (whole numbers, like –22, 7, 0 and 1024) typed by a user at the keyboard, computes the sum of the values and displays the result. This program must keep track of the numbers supplied by the user for the calculation later in the program. Programs remember numbers and other data in the computer's memory and access that data through program elements called variables. The program of Fig. 2.7 demonstrates these concepts. In the sample output, we use bold text to identify the user's input (i.e., **45** and **72**).

```java
1   // Fig. 2.7: Addition.java
2   // Addition program that displays the sum of two numbers.
3   import java.util.Scanner; // program uses class Scanner
4
5   public class Addition
6   {
7      // main method begins execution of Java application
8      public static void main( String[] args )
9      {
10        // create a Scanner to obtain input from the command window
11        Scanner input = new Scanner( System.in );
12
13        int number1; // first number to add
14        int number2; // second number to add
15        int sum; // sum of number1 and number2
16
17        System.out.print( "Enter first integer: " ); // prompt
18        number1 = input.nextInt(); // read first number from user
19
20        System.out.print( "Enter second integer: " ); // prompt
21        number2 = input.nextInt(); // read second number from user
22
23        sum = number1 + number2; // add numbers, then store total in sum
24
25        System.out.printf( "Sum is %d\n", sum ); // display sum
26     } // end method main
27  } // end class Addition
```

```
Enter first integer: 45
Enter second integer: 72
Sum is 117
```

Fig. 2.7 | Addition program that displays the sum of two numbers.

Lines 1–2

```java
// Fig. 2.7: Addition.java
// Addition program that displays the sum of two numbers.
```

state the figure number, file name and purpose of the program. Line 3

```java
import java.util.Scanner; // program uses class Scanner
```

is an **import declaration** that helps the compiler locate a class that is used in this program. A great strength of Java is its rich set of predefined classes that you can reuse rather than "reinventing the wheel." These classes are grouped into **packages**—named groups of related classes—and are collectively referred to as the **Java class library**, or the **Java Application Programming Interface (Java API)**. You use import declarations to identify the predefined classes used in a Java program. The import declaration in line 3 indicates that this example uses Java's predefined Scanner class (discussed shortly) from package **java.util**.

Common Programming Error 2.7

All import declarations must appear before the first class declaration in the file. Placing an import declaration inside a class declaration's body or after a class declaration is a syntax error.

Error-Prevention Tip 2.8

Forgetting to include an import declaration for a class used in your program typically results in a compilation error containing a message such as "cannot find symbol." When this occurs, check that you provided the proper import declarations and that the names in the import declarations are spelled correctly, including proper use of uppercase and lowercase letters.

Line 5

```
public class Addition
```

begins the declaration of class `Addition`. The file name for this `public` class must be `Addition.java`. Remember that the body of each class declaration starts with an opening left brace (line 6) and ends with a closing right brace (line 27).

The application begins execution with method `main` (lines 8–26). The left brace (line 9) marks the beginning of `main`'s body, and the corresponding right brace (line 26) marks the end of `main`'s body. Note that method `main` is indented one level in the body of class `Addition` and that the code in the body of `main` is indented another level for readability.

Line 11

```
Scanner input = new Scanner( System.in );
```

is a **variable declaration statement** that specifies the name (`input`) and type (`Scanner`) of a variable that is used in this program. A variable is a location in the computer's memory where a value can be stored for use later in a program. All Java variables must be declared with a **name** and a **type** before they can be used. A variable's name enables the program to access the value of the variable in memory. A variable's name can be any valid identifier. (Identifier naming requirements are given in Section 2.2.) A variable's type specifies what kind of information is stored at that location in memory. Like other statements, declaration statements end with a semicolon (;).

The declaration in line 11 specifies that the variable named `input` is of type `Scanner`. A **Scanner** enables a program to read data (e.g., numbers) for use in a program. The data can come from many sources, such as the user at the keyboard or a file on disk. Before using a `Scanner`, you must create it and specify the source of the data.

The equals sign (=) in line 11 indicates that `Scanner` variable `input` should be **initialized** (i.e., prepared for use in the program) in its declaration with the result of the expression new `Scanner(System.in)` to the right of the equals sign. This expression uses the **new** keyword to create a `Scanner` object that reads characters typed by the user at the keyboard. The **standard input object**, **System.in**, enables applications to read bytes of information typed by the user. The `Scanner` object translates these bytes into types (like `int`s) that can be used in a program.

The variable declaration statements at lines 13–15

```
int number1; // first number to add
int number2; // second number to add
int sum; // sum of number1 and number2
```

declare that variables `number1`, `number2` and `sum` hold data of type **int**—they can hold integer values (whole numbers such as 72, –1127 and 0). These variables are not yet initialized. The range of values for an `int` is –2,147,483,648 to +2,147,483,647. [*Note:* Actual `int` values may not contain commas.] We'll soon discuss types **float** and **double**, for holding real numbers, and type **char**, for holding character data. Real numbers contain decimal points, such as 3.4, 0.0 and –11.19. Variables of type char represent individual characters, such as an uppercase letter (e.g., A), a digit (e.g., 7), a special character (e.g., * or %) or an escape sequence (e.g., the newline character, \n). The types `int`, `float`, `double` and `char` are called **primitive types**. Primitive-type names are keywords and must appear in all lowercase letters. Appendix D summarizes the characteristics of the eight primitive types (`boolean`, `byte`, `char`, `short`, `int`, `long`, `float` and `double`).

Several variables of the same type may be declared in one declaration with the variable names separated by commas (i.e., a comma-separated list of variable names). For example, lines 13–15 can also be written as a single statement as follows:

```
int number1, // first number to add
    number2, // second number to add
    sum; // sum of number1 and number2
```

Good Programming Practice 2.9

Declare each variable on a separate line. This format allows a descriptive comment to be easily inserted next to each declaration.

Good Programming Practice 2.10

Choosing meaningful variable names helps a program to be self-documenting (i.e., one can understand the program simply by reading it rather than by reading manuals or viewing an excessive number of comments).

Good Programming Practice 2.11

By convention, variable-name identifiers begin with a lowercase letter, and every word in the name after the first word begins with a capital letter. For example, variable-name identifier `firstNumber` starts its second word, `Number`, with a capital N.

Line 17

```
System.out.print( "Enter first integer: " ); // prompt
```

uses `System.out.print` to display the message `"Enter first integer: "`. This message is called a **prompt** because it directs the user to take a specific action. We used method `print` here rather than `println` so that the user's input appears on the same line as the prompt. Recall from Section 2.2 that identifiers starting with capital letters typically represent class names. So, `System` is a class. Class `System` is part of package **java.lang**. Notice that class `System` is not imported with an `import` declaration at the beginning of the program.

Software Engineering Observation 2.1

By default, package `java.lang` is imported in every Java program; thus, classes in `java.lang` are the only ones in the Java API that do not require an `import` declaration.

Line 18

```
number1 = input.nextInt(); // read first number from user
```

uses Scanner object input's nextInt method to obtain an integer from the user at the keyboard. At this point the program waits for the user to type the number and press the *Enter* key to submit the number to the program.

Our program assumes that the user enters a valid integer value. If not, a runtime error will occur and the program will terminate. Chapter 11, Exception Handling, discusses how to make your programs more robust by enabling them to handle such errors. This helps make your program fault tolerant.

In line 18, the result of the call to method nextInt (an int value) is placed in variable number1 by using the **assignment operator, =**. The statement is read as "number1 gets the value of input.nextInt()." Operator = is called a **binary operator**, because it has two **operands**—number1 and the result of the method call input.nextInt(). This statement is called an assignment statement because it assigns a value to a variable. Everything to the right of the assignment operator, =, is evaluated before the assignment is performed.

Good Programming Practice 2.12
Place spaces on either side of a binary operator to make it stand out and make the program more readable.

Line 20

```
System.out.print( "Enter second integer: " ); // prompt
```

prompts the user to input the second integer.
Line 21

```
number2 = input.nextInt(); // read second number from user
```

reads the second integer and assigns it to variable number2.
Line 23

```
sum = number1 + number2; // add numbers then store total in sum
```

is an assignment statement that calculates the sum of the variables number1 and number2 then assigns the result to variable sum by using the assignment operator, =. The statement is read as "sum gets the value of number1 + number2." In general, calculations are performed in assignment statements. When the program encounters the addition operation, it uses the values stored in the variables number1 and number2 to perform the calculation. In the preceding statement, the addition operator is a binary operator—its two operands are the variables number1 and number2. Portions of statements that contain calculations are called **expressions**. In fact, an expression is any portion of a statement that has a value associated with it. For example, the value of the expression number1 + number2 is the sum of the numbers. Similarly, the value of the expression input.nextInt() is the integer typed by the user.

After the calculation has been performed, line 25

```
System.out.printf( "Sum is %d\n", sum ); // display sum
```

uses method System.out.printf to display the sum. The format specifier **%d** is a placeholder for an int value (in this case the value of sum)—the letter d stands for "decimal integer." Note that other than the %d format specifier, the remaining characters in the format string are all fixed text. So method printf displays "Sum is ", followed by the value of sum (in the position of the %d format specifier) and a newline.

Note that calculations can also be performed inside `printf` statements. We could have combined the statements at lines 23 and 25 into the statement

```
System.out.printf( "Sum is %d\n", ( number1 + number2 ) );
```

The parentheses around the expression `number1 + number2` are not required—they're included to emphasize that the value of the entire expression is output in the position of the `%d` format specifier.

Java API Documentation
For each new Java API class we use, we indicate the package in which it's located. This information helps you locate descriptions of each package and class in the Java API documentation. A web-based version of this documentation can be found at

```
java.sun.com/javase/6/docs/api/
```

You can download this documentation from

```
java.sun.com/javase/downloads
```

Appendix E shows how to use this documentation.

2.6 Memory Concepts
Variable names such as `number1`, `number2` and `sum` actually correspond to locations in the computer's memory. Every variable has a **name**, a **type**, a **size** (in bytes) and a **value**.

In the addition program of Fig. 2.7, when the following statement (line 18) executes:

```
number1 = input.nextInt(); // read first number from user
```

the number typed by the user is placed into a memory location corresponding to the name `number1`. Suppose that the user enters 45. The computer places that integer value into location `number1` (Fig. 2.8), replacing the previous value (if any) in that location. The previous value is lost.

number1	45

Fig. 2.8 | Memory location showing the name and value of variable `number1`.

When the statement (line 21)

```
number2 = input.nextInt(); // read second number from user
```

executes, suppose that the user enters 72. The computer places that integer value into location `number2`. The memory now appears as shown in Fig. 2.9.

number1	45
number2	72

Fig. 2.9 | Memory locations after storing values for `number1` and `number2`.

After the program of Fig. 2.7 obtains values for `number1` and `number2`, it adds the values and places the total into variable `sum`. The statement (line 23)

```
sum = number1 + number2; // add numbers, then store total in sum
```

performs the addition, then replaces any previous value in `sum`. After `sum` has been calculated, memory appears as shown in Fig. 2.10. Note that the values of `number1` and `number2` appear exactly as they did before they were used in the calculation of `sum`. These values were used, but not destroyed, as the computer performed the calculation. Thus, when a value is read from a memory location, the process is nondestructive.

number1	45
number2	72
sum	117

Fig. 2.10 | Memory locations after storing the sum of `number1` and `number2`.

2.7 Arithmetic

Most programs perform arithmetic calculations. The **arithmetic operators** are summarized in Fig. 2.11. Note the use of various special symbols not used in algebra. The **asterisk** (*) indicates multiplication, and the percent sign (%) is the **remainder operator**, which we'll discuss shortly. The arithmetic operators are binary operators because they each operate on two operands. For example, the expression `f + 7` contains the binary operator + and the two operands `f` and `7`.

Java operation	Operator	Algebraic expression	Java expression
Addition	+	$f + 7$	`f + 7`
Subtraction	–	$p - c$	`p - c`
Multiplication	*	bm	`b * m`
Division	/	x/y or $\frac{x}{y}$ or $x \div y$	`x / y`
Remainder	%	$r \bmod s$	`r % s`

Fig. 2.11 | Arithmetic operators.

Integer division yields an integer quotient—for example, the expression `7 / 4` evaluates to `1`, and the expression `17 / 5` evaluates to `3`. Any fractional part in integer division is simply discarded (i.e., truncated)—no rounding occurs. Java provides the remainder operator, `%`, which yields the remainder after division. The expression `x % y` yields the remainder after `x` is divided by `y`. Thus, `7 % 4` yields `3`, and `17 % 5` yields `2`. This operator is most commonly used with integer operands but can also be used with other arithmetic types. In this chapter's exercises and in later chapters, we consider several interesting applications of the remainder operator, such as determining whether one number is a multiple of another.

Arithmetic Expressions in Straight-Line Form
Arithmetic expressions in Java must be written in **straight-line form** to facilitate entering programs into the computer. Thus, expressions such as "a divided by b" must be written as a / b, so that all constants, variables and operators appear in a straight line. The following algebraic notation is generally not acceptable to compilers:

$$\frac{a}{b}$$

Parentheses for Grouping Subexpressions
Parentheses are used to group terms in Java expressions in the same manner as in algebraic expressions. For example, to multiply a times the quantity b + c, we write

    a * (b + c)

If an expression contains **nested parentheses**, such as

    ((a + b) * c)

the expression in the innermost set of parentheses (a + b in this case) is evaluated first.

Rules of Operator Precedence
Java applies the operators in arithmetic expressions in a precise sequence determined by the following **rules of operator precedence**, which are generally the same as those followed in algebra (Fig. 2.12):

1. Multiplication, division and remainder operations are applied first. If an expression contains several such operations, they're applied from left to right. Multiplication, division and remainder operators have the same level of precedence.

2. Addition and subtraction operations are applied next. If an expression contains several such operations, the operators are applied from left to right. Addition and subtraction operators have the same level of precedence.

These rules enable Java to apply operators in the correct order.[1] When we say that operators are applied from left to right, we are referring to their **associativity**. Some operators associate from right to left. Figure 2.12 summarizes these rules of operator precedence. A complete precedence chart is included in Appendix A.

Operator(s)	Operation(s)	Order of evaluation (precedence)
* / %	Multiplication Division Remainder	Evaluated first. If there are several operators of this type, they're evaluated from left to right.
+ -	Addition Subtraction	Evaluated next. If there are several operators of this type, they're evaluated from left to right.
=	Assignment	Evaluated last.

Fig. 2.12 | Precedence of arithmetic operators.

1. We use simple examples to explain the order of evaluation of expressions. Subtle issues occur in the more complex expressions you'll encounter later in the book. For more information on order of evaluation, see Chapter 15 of *The Java™ Language Specification* (java.sun.com/docs/books/jls/).

Sample Algebraic and Java Expressions

Now let's consider several expressions in light of the rules of operator precedence. Each example lists an algebraic expression and its Java equivalent. The following is an example of an arithmetic mean (average) of five terms:

Algebra:$m = \dfrac{a + b + c + d + e}{5}$

*Java:*m = (a + b + c + d + e) / 5;

The parentheses are required because division has higher precedence than addition. The entire quantity (a + b + c + d + e) is to be divided by 5. If the parentheses are erroneously omitted, we obtain a + b + c + d + e / 5, which evaluates as

$$a + b + c + d + \frac{e}{5}$$

The following is an example of the equation of a straight line:

Algebra:$y = mx + b$

Java: y = m * x + b;

No parentheses are required. The multiplication operator is applied first because multiplication has a higher precedence than addition. The assignment occurs last because it has a lower precedence than multiplication or addition.

The following example contains remainder (%), multiplication, division, addition and subtraction operations:

Algebra: $z = pr\%q + w/x - y$

Java: z = p * r % q + w / x - y;

         ⑥   ①   ②   ④   ③   ⑤

The circled numbers under the statement indicate the order in which Java applies the operators. The *, % and / operations are evaluated first in left-to-right order (i.e., they associate from left to right), because they have higher precedence than + and -. The + and - operations are evaluated next. These operations are also applied from left to right. The assignment (=) operaton is evaluated last.

Evaluation of a Second-Degree Polynomial

To develop a better understanding of the rules of operator precedence, consider the evaluation of an assignment expression that includes a second-degree polynomial $ax^2 + bx + c$:

y = a * x * x + b * x + c;

       ⑥   ①   ②   ④   ③   ⑤

In this statement, the multiplication operations are evaluated first in left-to-right order (i.e., they associate from left to right), because they have higher precedence than addition. The addition operations are evaluated next and are applied from left to right. There is no arithmetic operator for exponentiation in Java, so x^2 is represented as x * x. Section 4.4 shows an alternative for performing exponentiation. Suppose that a, b, c and x in the preceding second-degree polynomial are initialized (given values) as follows: a = 2, b = 3, c = 7 and x = 5. Figure 2.13 illustrates the order in which the operators are applied.

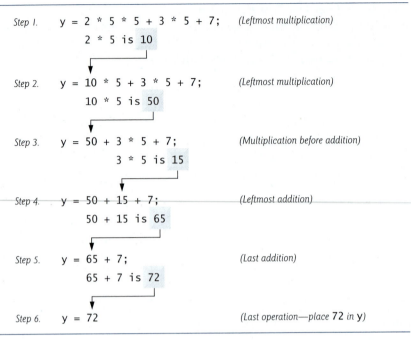

Step 1.   `y = 2 * 5 * 5 + 3 * 5 + 7;`   *(Leftmost multiplication)*

          `2 * 5 is 10`

Step 2.   `y = 10 * 5 + 3 * 5 + 7;`   *(Leftmost multiplication)*

          `10 * 5 is 50`

Step 3.   `y = 50 + 3 * 5 + 7;`   *(Multiplication before addition)*

          `3 * 5 is 15`

Step 4.   `y = 50 + 15 + 7;`   *(Leftmost addition)*

          `50 + 15 is 65`

Step 5.   `y = 65 + 7;`   *(Last addition)*

          `65 + 7 is 72`

Step 6.   `y = 72`   *(Last operation—place 72 in y)*

Fig. 2.13 | Order in which a second-degree polynomial is evaluated.

As in algebra, it's acceptable to place **redundant parentheses** (unnecessary parentheses) in an expression to make the expression clearer. For example, the preceding statement might be parenthesized as follows:

```
y = ( a * x * x ) + ( b * x ) + c;
```

Good Programming Practice 2.13
Using redundant parentheses in complex arithmetic expressions can make them easier to read.

2.8 Decision Making: Equality and Relational Operators

A **condition** is an expression that can be **true** or **false**. This section introduces Java's **if selection statement** that allows a program to make a **decision** based on a condition's value. For example, the condition "grade is greater than or equal to 60" determines whether a student passed a test. If the condition in an if statement is true, the body of the if statement executes. If the condition is false, the body does not execute. We'll see an example shortly.

Conditions in if statements can be formed by using the **equality operators** (== and !=) and **relational operators** (>, <, >= and <=) summarized in Fig. 2.14. Both equality operators have the same level of precedence, which is lower than that of the relational operators. The equality operators associate from left to right. The relational operators all have the same level of precedence and also associate from left to right.

Fig. 2.15 uses six if statements to compare two integers input by the user. If the condition in any of these if statements is true, the output statement associated with that if

Standard algebraic equality or relational operator	Java equality or relational operator	Sample Java condition	Meaning of Java condition
Equality operators			
=	==	x == y	x is equal to y
≠	!=	x != y	x is not equal to y
Relational operators			
>	>	x > y	x is greater than y
<	<	x < y	x is less than y
≥	>=	x >= y	x is greater than or equal to y
≤	<=	x <= y	x is less than or equal to y

Fig. 2.14 | Equality and relational operators.

statement executes; otherwise, the statement is skipped. The program uses a Scanner to input the two integers from the user and store them in variables number1 and number2. Then the program compares the numbers and displays the results of the comparisons that are true. We show three sample outputs.

```
1   // Fig. 2.15: Comparison.java
2   // Compare integers using if statements, relational operators
3   // and equality operators.
4   import java.util.Scanner; // program uses class Scanner
5
6   public class Comparison
7   {
8      // main method begins execution of Java application
9      public static void main( String[] args )
10     {
11        // create Scanner to obtain input from command window
12        Scanner input = new Scanner( System.in );
13
14        int number1; // first number to compare
15        int number2; // second number to compare
16
17        System.out.print( "Enter first integer: " ); // prompt
18        number1 = input.nextInt(); // read first number from user
19
20        System.out.print( "Enter second integer: " ); // prompt
21        number2 = input.nextInt(); // read second number from user
22
23        if ( number1 == number2 )
24           System.out.printf( "%d == %d\n", number1, number2 );
25
26        if ( number1 != number2 )
27           System.out.printf( "%d != %d\n", number1, number2 );
28
```

Fig. 2.15 | Compare integers using if statements, relational operators and equality operators. (Part 1 of 2.)

```
29        if ( number1 < number2 )
30           System.out.printf( "%d < %d\n", number1, number2 );
31
32        if ( number1 > number2 )
33           System.out.printf( "%d > %d\n", number1, number2 );
34
35        if ( number1 <= number2 )
36           System.out.printf( "%d <= %d\n", number1, number2 );
37
38        if ( number1 >= number2 )
39           System.out.printf( "%d >= %d\n", number1, number2 );
40     } // end method main
41  } // end class Comparison
```

```
Enter first integer: 777
Enter second integer: 777
777 == 777
777 <= 777
777 >= 777
```

```
Enter first integer: 1000
Enter second integer: 2000
1000 != 2000
1000 < 2000
1000 <= 2000
```

```
Enter first integer: 2000
Enter second integer: 1000
2000 != 1000
2000 > 1000
2000 >= 1000
```

Fig. 2.15 | Compare integers using `if` statements, relational operators and equality operators. (Part 2 of 2.)

The declaration of class `Comparison` begins at line 6

```
public class Comparison
```

The class's `main` method (lines 9–40) begins the execution of the program. Line 12

```
Scanner input = new Scanner( System.in );
```

declares Scanner variable `input` and assigns it a Scanner that inputs data from the standard input (i.e., the keyboard).

Lines 14–15

```
int number1; // first number to compare
int number2; // second number to compare
```

declare the `int` variables used to store the values input from the user.

Lines 17–18

```
System.out.print( "Enter first integer: " ); // prompt
number1 = input.nextInt(); // read first number from user
```

prompt the user to enter the first integer and input the value, respectively. The input value is stored in variable `number1`.

Lines 20–21

```
System.out.print( "Enter second integer: " ); // prompt
number2 = input.nextInt(); // read second number from user
```

prompt the user to enter the second integer and input the value, respectively. The input value is stored in variable `number2`.

Lines 23–24

```
if ( number1 == number2 )
    System.out.printf( "%d == %d\n", number1, number2 );
```

compare the values of `number1` and `number2` to determine whether they're equal. An `if` statement always begins with keyword `if`, followed by a condition in parentheses. An `if` statement expects one statement in its body, but may contain multiple statements if they're enclosed in a set of braces (`{}`). The indentation of the body statement shown here is not required, but it improves the program's readability by emphasizing that the statement in line 24 is part of the `if` statement that begins at line 23. Line 24 executes only if the numbers stored in variables `number1` and `number2` are equal (i.e., the condition is true). The `if` statements in lines 26–27, 29–30, 32–33, 35–36 and 38–39 compare `number1` and `number2` with the operators `!=`, `<`, `>`, `<=` and `>=`, respectively. If the condition in any of the `if` statements is true, the corresponding body statement executes.

Common Programming Error 2.8

Forgetting the left and/or right parentheses for the condition in an `if` statement is a syntax error—the parentheses are required.

Common Programming Error 2.9

Confusing the equality operator, `==`, with the assignment operator, `=`, can cause a logic error or a syntax error. The equality operator should be read as "is equal to," and the assignment operator should be read as "gets" or "gets the value of." To avoid confusion, some people read the equality operator as "double equals" or "equals equals."

Good Programming Practice 2.14

Placing only one statement per line in a program enhances program readability.

Note that there is no semicolon (`;`) at the end of the first line of each `if` statement. Such a semicolon would result in a logic error at execution time. For example,

```
if ( number1 == number2 ); // logic error
    System.out.printf( "%d == %d\n", number1, number2 );
```

would actually be interpreted by Java as

```
if ( number1 == number2 )
    ; // empty statement
System.out.printf( "%d == %d\n", number1, number2 );
```

where the semicolon on the line by itself—called the **empty statement**—is the statement to execute if the condition in the `if` statement is true. When the empty statement executes, no task is performed in the program. The program then continues with the output statement, which always executes, regardless of whether the condition is true or false, because the output statement is not part of the if statement.

Common Programming Error 2.10

Placing a semicolon immediately after the right parenthesis of the condition in an if statement is normally a logic error.

Note the use of white space in Fig. 2.15. Recall that white space is normally ignored by the compiler. So, statements may be split over several lines and may be spaced according to your preferences without affecting the meaning of a program. It's incorrect to split identifiers and strings. Ideally, statements should be kept small, but this is not always possible.

Good Programming Practice 2.15

A lengthy statement can be spread over several lines. If a single statement must be split across lines, choose breaking points that make sense, such as after a comma in a comma-separated list, or after an operator in a lengthy expression. If a statement is split across two or more lines, indent all subsequent lines until the end of the statement.

Figure 2.16 shows the operators discussed so far in decreasing order of precedence. All these operators, with the exception of the assignment operator, =, associate from left to right. Addition is left associative, so an expression like x + y + z is evaluated as if it had been written as (x + y) + z. The assignment operator, =, associates from right to left, so an expression like x = y = 0 is evaluated as if it had been written as x = (y = 0), which first assigns the value 0 to variable y, then assigns the result of that assignment, 0, to x.

Operators				Associativity	Type
*	/	%		left to right	multiplicative
+	−			left to right	additive
<	<=	>	>=	left to right	relational
==	!=			left to right	equality
=				right to left	assignment

Fig. 2.16 | Precedence and associativity of operators discussed.

Good Programming Practice 2.16

Refer to the operator precedence chart (Appendix A) when writing expressions containing many operators. Confirm that the operations in the expression are performed in the order you expect. If you are uncertain about the order of evaluation in a complex expression, use parentheses to force the order, exactly as you'd do in algebraic expressions.

2.9 (Optional) GUI and Graphics Case Study: Using Dialog Boxes

This optional case study is designed for those who want to begin learning Java's powerful capabilities for creating graphical user interfaces (GUIs) and graphics early in the book, before the main discussions of these topics in Chapter 14, GUI Components: Part 1, Chapter 15, Graphics and Java 2D™, and Chapter 25, GUI Components: Part 2.

The GUI and Graphics Case Study appears in 10 brief sections (see Fig. 2.17). Each section introduces several new concepts and provides examples with screen captures that show sample interactions and results. In the first few sections, you'll create your first graphical applications. In subsequent sections, you'll create an application that draws a variety of shapes. When we formally introduce GUIs in Chapter 14, we use the mouse to choose exactly which shapes to draw and where to draw them. In Chapter 15, we add capabilities of the Java 2D graphics API to draw the shapes with different line thicknesses and fills. We hope you find this case study informative and entertaining.

Location	Title—Exercise(s)
Section 2.4	Using Dialog Boxes—Basic input and output with dialog boxes
Section 3.14	Creating Simple Drawings—Displaying and drawing lines on the screen
Section 4.10	Drawing Rectangles and Ovals—Using shapes to represent data
Section 5.13	Colors and Filled Shapes—Drawing a bull's-eye and random graphics
Section 6.20	Drawing Arcs—Drawing spirals with arcs
Section 8.16	Using Objects with Graphics—Storing shapes as objects
Section 9.8	Displaying Text and Images Using Labels—Providing status information
Section 10.8	Drawing with Polymorphism—Identifying the similarities between shapes
Exercise 14.17	Expanding the Interface—Using GUI components and event handling
Exercise 15.31	Adding Java 2D—Using the Java 2D API to enhance drawings

Fig. 2.17 | Summary of the GUI and Graphics Case Study in each chapter.

Displaying Text in a Dialog Box

The programs presented thus far display output in the command window. Many applications use windows or **dialog boxes** (also called **dialogs**) to display output. Web browsers such as Mozilla Firefox and Microsoft Internet Explorer display web pages in their own windows. E-mail programs allow you to type and read messages in a window. Typically, dialog boxes are windows in which programs display important messages to users. Class **JOptionPane** provides prebuilt dialog boxes that enable programs to display windows containing messages—such windows are called **message dialogs**. Figure 2.18 displays the String "Welcome\nto\nJava" in a message dialog.

```
1   // Fig. 2.18: Dialog1.java
2   // Printing multiple lines in dialog box.
3   import javax.swing.JOptionPane; // import class JOptionPane
4
5   public class Dialog1
6   {
7      public static void main( String[] args )
8      {
9         // display a dialog with a message
10        JOptionPane.showMessageDialog( null, "Welcome\nto\nJava" );
11     } // end main
12  } // end class Dialog1
```

Fig. 2.18 | Using JOptionPane to display multiple lines in a dialog box. (Part 1 of 2.)

Fig. 2.18 | Using JOptionPane to display multiple lines in a dialog box. (Part 2 of 2.)

Line 3 indicates that the program uses class JOptionPane from package **javax.swing**. This package contains many classes that help you create **graphical user interfaces (GUIs)**. **GUI components** facilitate data entry by a program's user and presentation of outputs to the user. Line 10 calls JOptionPane method **showMessageDialog** to display a dialog box containing a message. The method requires two arguments. The first helps the Java application determine where to position the dialog box. A dialog is typically displayed from a GUI application with its own window. The first argument refers to that window (known as the parent window) and causes the dialog to appear centered over the application's window. If the first argument is null, the dialog box is displayed at the center of your screen. The second argument is the String to display in the dialog box.

Introducing static Methods

JOptionPane method showMessageDialog is a so-called **static method**. Such methods often define frequently used tasks. For example, many programs display dialog boxes, and the code to do this is the same each time. Rather than requiring you to "reinvent the wheel" and create code to display a dialog, the designers of class JOptionPane declared a static method that performs this task for you. A static method is typically called by using its class name followed by a **dot separator** (.) and the method name, as in

ClassName.*methodName*(*arguments*)

Notice that you do not create an object of class JOptionPane to use its static method showMessageDialog. Chapter 5 discusses static methods in more detail.

Entering Text in a Dialog

Figure 2.19 uses another predefined JOptionPane dialog called an **input dialog** that allows the user to enter data into a program. The program asks for the user's name, and responds with a message dialog containing a greeting and the name that the user entered.

```
1   // Fig. 2.19: NameDialog.java
2   // Basic input with a dialog box.
3   import javax.swing.JOptionPane;
4
5   public class NameDialog
6   {
7      public static void main( String[] args )
8      {
9         // prompt user to enter name
10        String name =
11           JOptionPane.showInputDialog( "What is your name?" );
```

Fig. 2.19 | Obtaining user input from a dialog. (Part 1 of 2.)

```
12
13          // create the message
14          String message =
15             String.format( "Welcome, %s, to Java Programming!", name );
16
17          // display the message to welcome the user by name
18          JOptionPane.showMessageDialog( null, message );
19       } // end main
20    } // end class NameDialog
```

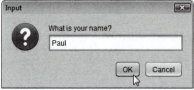 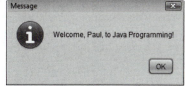

Fig. 2.19 | Obtaining user input from a dialog. (Part 2 of 2.)

Lines 10–11 use JOptionPane method **showInputDialog** to display an input dialog containing a prompt and a **text field** in which the user can enter text. Method showInputDialog's argument is the prompt that indicates what the user should enter. The user types characters in the text field, then clicks the **OK** button or presses the *Enter* key to return the String to the program. Method showInputDialog (line 11) returns a String containing the characters typed by the user. We store the String in variable name (line 10). [*Note:* If you press the dialog's **Cancel** button or press the *Esc* key, the method returns null and the program displays the word "null" as the name.]

Lines 14–15 use static String method **format** to return a String containing a greeting with the user's name. Method format works like method System.out.printf, except that format returns the formatted String rather than displaying it in a command window. Line 18 displays the greeting in a message dialog, just as we did in Fig. 2.18.

GUI and Graphics Case Study Exercise

2.1   Modify the addition program in Fig. 2.7 to use dialog-based input and output with the methods of class JOptionPane. Since method showInputDialog returns a String, you must convert the String the user enters to an int for use in calculations, as in as in

```
int value =
   Integer.parseInt( JOptionPane.showInputDialog( "Enter an integer:" ) );
```

The Integer class's static method parseInt takes a String argument representing an integer (e.g., the result of JOptionPane.showInputDialog) and returns the value as an int. Method parseInt is a static method of class Integer (from package java.lang). Note that if the String does not contain a valid integer, the program will terminate with an error.

2.10 Wrap-Up

You learned many important features of Java in this chapter, including displaying data on the screen in a **Command Prompt**, inputting data from the keyboard, performing calculations with arithmetic operators and making decisions with the if statement and the relational and equality operators. The applications presented here were meant to introduce you to basic programming concepts. In the next chapter we begin our introduction to control statements, which specify the order in which a program's actions are performed. Control statements are the building blocks that allow you to specify the logic required for methods to perform their tasks.

Summary

Section 2.2 Our First Program in Java: Printing a Line of Text

- A Java application is a computer program that executes when you use the java command to launch the JVM.
- Comments document programs and improve their readability. They're ignored by the compiler.
- A comment that begins with // is called an end-of-line comment—it terminates at the end of the line on which it appears.
- Traditional comments can be spread over several lines and are delimited by /* and */.
- Javadoc comments, delimited by /** and */, enable you to embed program documentation in your code. The javadoc utility program generates HTML pages based on these comments.
- A syntax error occurs when the compiler encounters code that violates Java's language rules. This is similar to a grammar error in a natural language.
- Blank lines, space characters and tab characters are known as white space. White space makes programs easier to read and is ignored by the compiler.
- Every program that you create consists of at least one programmer-defined class.
- Keywords are reserved for use by Java and are always spelled with all lowercase letters.
- Keyword class introduces a class declaration and is immediately followed by the class name.
- By convention, all class names in Java begin with a capital letter and capitalize the first letter of each word they include (e.g., SampleClassName).
- A Java class name is an identifier—a series of characters consisting of letters, digits, underscores (_) and dollar signs ($) that does not begin with a digit and does not contain spaces.
- Java is case sensitive—that is, uppercase and lowercase letters are distinct.
- The body of every class declaration is delimited by braces, { and }.
- A public class declaration must be saved in a file with the same name as the class followed by the ".java" file-name extension.
- Method main is the starting point of every Java application and must begin with

```
public static void main( String[] args )
```

otherwise, the JVM will not execute the application.

- Methods perform tasks and return information when they complete their tasks. Keyword void indicates that a method will perform a task but will not return any information.
- Statements instruct the computer to perform actions.
- A string in double quotes is sometimes called a character string or a string literal.
- The standard output object (System.out) displays characters in the command window.
- Method System.out.println displays its argument in the command window followed by a newline character to position the output cursor to the beginning of the next line.
- You compile a program with the command javac. If the program contains no syntax errors, a class file containing the Java bytecodes that represent the application is created. These bytecodes are interpreted by the JVM when we execute the program.
- To run an application, type java followed by the name of the class that contains main.

Section 2.3 Modifying Our First Java Program

- `System.out.print` displays its argument and positions the output cursor immediately after the last character displayed.
- A backslash (\) in a string is an escape character. Java combines the next character with the backslash to form an escape sequence. The escape sequence \n represents the newline character.

Section 2.4 Displaying Text with `printf`

- `System.out.printf` method (f means "formatted") displays formatted data.
- Method `printf`'s first argument is a format string that may consist of fixed text and format specifiers. Each format specifier is a placeholder for a value and specifies the type of data to output.
- Format specifiers begin with `%` and are followed by a character that represents the data type.
- The format specifier `%s` is a placeholder for a string. Each format specifier is replaced with the value of the corresponding argument that appears after the format string.

Section 2.5 Another Application: Adding Integers

- An `import` declaration helps the compiler locate a class that is used in a program.
- Java's rich set of predefined classes are grouped into packages—named groups of classes. These are referred to as the Java class library, or the Java Application Programming Interface (Java API).
- A variable is a location in the computer's memory where a value can be stored for use later in a program. All variables must be declared with a name and a type before they can be used.
- A variable's name enables the program to access the value of the variable in memory.
- A `Scanner` (package `java.util`) enables a program to read data for use in a program.
- Variables should be initialized to prepare them for use in a program.
- The expression `new Scanner( System.in )` creates a `Scanner` that reads from the standard input object (`System.in`)—normally the keyboard.
- Data type `int` is used to declare variables that will hold integer values. The range of values for an `int` is –2,147,483,648 to +2,147,483,647.
- Types `float` and `double` specify real numbers with decimal points, such as `3.4` and `–11.19`.
- Variables of type `char` represent individual characters, such as an uppercase letter (e.g., A), a digit (e.g., 7), a special character (e.g., * or %) or an escape sequence (e.g., newline, \n).
- Types such as `int`, `float`, `double` and `char` are primitive types. Primitive-type names are keywords; thus, they must appear in all lowercase letters.
- A prompt directs the user to take a specific action.
- `Scanner` method `nextInt` obtains an integer for use in a program.
- The assignment operator, `=`, enables the program to give a value to a variable. Operator `=` is called a binary operator because it has two operands.
- Portions of statements that have values are called expressions.
- The format specifier `%d` is a placeholder for an `int` value.

Section 2.6 Memory Concepts

- Variable names correspond to locations in the computer's memory. Every variable has a name, a type, a size and a value.
- A value that is placed in a memory location replaces the location's previous value, which is lost.

Section 2.7 Arithmetic

- The arithmetic operators are +, -, * (multiplication), / (division) and % (remainder).

- Integer division yields an integer quotient.

- The remainder operator, %, yields the remainder after division.

- Arithmetic expressions must be written in straight-line form.

- If an expression contains nested parentheses, the innermost set of parentheses is evaluated first.

- Java applies the operators in arithmetic expressions in a precise sequence determined by the rules of operator precedence.

- When we say that operators are applied from left to right, we are referring to their associativity. Some operators associate from right to left.

- Redundant parentheses in an expression can make an expression clearer.

Section 2.8 Decision Making: Equality and Relational Operators

- The if statement makes a decision based on a condition's value (true or false).

- Conditions in if statements can be formed by using the equality (== and !=) and relational (>, <, >= and <=) operators.

- An if statement begins with keyword if followed by a condition in parentheses and expects one statement in its body.

- The empty statement is a statement that does not perform a task.

Terminology

!= ("is not equal to") operator 56
%d format specifier 51
%s format specifier 47
< ("less than") operator 56
<= ("less than or equal to") operator 56
== ("is equal to") operator 56
> ("greater than") operator 56
>= ("greater than or equal to") operator 56
addition operator (+) 53
application 38
argument 42
arithmetic operators (*, /, %, + and -) 53
assignment operator (=) 51
associativity of operators 54
asterisk (*) 53
backslash (\) escape character 46
binary operator 51
body of a class declaration 40
body of a method declaration 41
case sensitive 40
cd 43
char primitive type 50
character string 41
class declaration 40
class file 43
class keyword 40
class name 40
comma-separated list 46
command line 42
command window 42

comment 39
compilation error 39
compile-time error 39
compiler error 39
condition 56
decision 56
division operator (/) 53
document programs 39
dot separator (.) 62
double primitive type 50
empty statement (;) 59
end-of-line comment (//) 39
equality operators 56
escape character 46
escape sequence 46
expression 51
false keyword 56
fixed text in a format string 47
float primitive type 50
format specifier 47
format string 47
identifier 40
if statement 56
import declaration 48
initialize a variable in a declaration 49
initialized 49
int (integer) primitive type 50
integer 47
integer division 53
Java Application Programming Interface 48

Self-Review Exercises

2.1   Fill in the blanks in each of the following statements:
   a) A(n) _____ begins the body of every method, and a(n) _____ ends the body of every method.
   b) The _____ statement is used to make decisions.
   c) _____ begins an end-of-line comment.
   d) _____, _____ and _____ are called white space.
   e) _____ are reserved for use by Java.
   f) Java applications begin execution at method _____.
   g) Methods _____, _____ and _____ display information in a command window.

2.2   State whether each of the following is *true* or *false*. If *false*, explain why.
   a) Comments cause the computer to print the text after the // on the screen when the program executes.
   b) All variables must be given a type when they are declared.
   c) Java considers the variables number and NuMbEr to be identical.
   d) The remainder operator (%) can be used only with integer operands.
   e) The arithmetic operators *, /, %, + and - all have the same level of precedence.

2.3   Write statements to accomplish each of the following tasks:
   a) Declare variables c, thisIsAVariable, q76354 and number to be of type int.
   b) Prompt the user to enter an integer.

  c) Input an integer and assign the result to int variable value. Assume Scanner variable input can be used to read a value from the keyboard.

  d) Print "This is a Java program" on one line in the command window. Use method System.out.println.

  e) Print "This is a Java program" on two lines in the command window. The first line should end with Java. Use method System.out.println.

  f) Print "This is a Java program" on two lines in the command window. The first line should end with Java. Use method System.out.printf and two %s format specifiers.

  g) If the variable number is not equal to 7, display "The variable number is not equal to 7".

2.4 Identify and correct the errors in each of the following statements:

  a) if (c < 7);
    System.out.println("c is less than 7");

  b) if (c => 7)
    System.out.println("c is equal to or greater than 7");

2.5 Write declarations, statements or comments that accomplish each of the following tasks:

  a) State that a program will calculate the product of three integers.

  b) Create a Scanner called input that reads values from the standard input.

  c) Declare the variables x, y, z and result to be of type int.

  d) Prompt the user to enter the first integer.

  e) Read the first integer from the user and store it in the variable x.

  f) Prompt the user to enter the second integer.

  g) Read the second integer from the user and store it in the variable y.

  h) Prompt the user to enter the third integer.

  i) Read the third integer from the user and store it in the variable z.

  j) Compute the product of the three integers contained in variables x, y and z, and assign the result to the variable result.

  k) Display the message "Product is" followed by the value of the variable result.

2.6 Using the statements you wrote in Exercise 2.5, write a complete program that calculates and prints the product of three integers.

Answers to Self-Review Exercises

2.1 a) left brace ({), right brace (}). b) if. c) //. d) Space characters, newlines and tabs. e) Keywords. f) main. g) System.out.print, System.out.println and System.out.printf.

2.2 a) False. Comments do not cause any action to be performed when the program executes. They're used to document programs and improve their readability.

  b) True.

  c) False. Java is case sensitive, so these variables are distinct.

  d) False. The remainder operator can also be used with noninteger operands in Java.

  e) False. The operators *, / and % are on the same level of precedence, and the operators + and - are on a lower level of precedence.

2.3 a) int c, thisIsAVariable, q76354, number;
    or
    int c;
    int thisIsAVariable;
    int q76354;
    int number;

  b) System.out.print("Enter an integer: ");

  c) value = input.nextInt();

  d) System.out.println("This is a Java program");

e) `System.out.println( "This is a Java\nprogram" );`

f) `System.out.printf( "%s\n%s\n", "This is a Java", "program" );`

g) `if ( number != 7 )`
   `System.out.println( "The variable number is not equal to 7" );`

2.4   a) Error: Semicolon after the right parenthesis of the condition (c < 7) in the `if`.
   Correction: Remove the semicolon after the right parenthesis. [*Note:* As a result, the output statement will execute regardless of whether the condition in the `if` is true.]

   b) Error: The relational operator => is incorrect. Correction: Change => to >=.

2.5   a) `// Calculate the product of three integers`

   b) `Scanner input = new Scanner( System.in );`

   c) `int x, y, z, result;`
   or
   `int x;`
   `int y;`
   `int z;`
   `int result;`

   d) `System.out.print( "Enter first integer: " );`

   e) `x = input.nextInt();`

   f) `System.out.print( "Enter second integer: " );`

   g) `y = input.nextInt();`

   h) `System.out.print( "Enter third integer: " );`

   i) `z = input.nextInt();`

   j) `result = x * y * z;`

   k) `System.out.printf( "Product is %d\n", result );`

2.6   The solution to Self-Review Exercise 2.6 is as follows:

```
1    // Ex. 2.6: Product.java
2    // Calculate the product of three integers.
3    import java.util.Scanner; // program uses Scanner
4
5    public class Product
6    {
7       public static void main( String[] args )
8       {
9          // create Scanner to obtain input from command window
10         Scanner input = new Scanner( System.in );
11
12         int x; // first number input by user
13         int y; // second number input by user
14         int z; // third number input by user
15         int result; // product of numbers
16
17         System.out.print( "Enter first integer: " ); // prompt for input
18         x = input.nextInt(); // read first integer
19
20         System.out.print( "Enter second integer: " ); // prompt for input
21         y = input.nextInt(); // read second integer
22
23         System.out.print( "Enter third integer: " ); // prompt for input
24         z = input.nextInt(); // read third integer
25
26         result = x * y * z; // calculate product of numbers
27         System.out.printf( "Product is %d\n", result );
28      } // end method main
29   } // end class Product
```

```
Enter first integer: 10
Enter second integer: 20
Enter third integer: 30
Product is 6000
```

Exercises

2.7 Fill in the blanks in each of the following statements:
  a) _____ are used to document a program and improve its readability.
  b) A decision can be made in a Java program with a(n) _____.
  c) Calculations are normally performed by _____ statements.
  d) The arithmetic operators with the same precedence as multiplication are _____ and _____.
  e) When parentheses in an arithmetic expression are nested, the _____ set of parentheses is evaluated first.
  f) A location in the computer's memory that may contain different values at various times throughout the execution of a program is called a(n) _____.

2.8 Write Java statements that accomplish each of the following tasks:
  a) Display the message "Enter an integer: ", leaving the cursor on the same line.
  b) Assign the product of variables b and c to variable a.
  c) State that a program performs a sample payroll calculation (i.e., use text that helps to document a program).

2.9 State whether each of the following is *true* or *false*. If *false*, explain why.
  a) Java operators are evaluated from left to right.
  b) The following are all valid variable names: _under_bar_, m928134, t5, j7, her_sales$, his_$account_total, a, b$, c, z and z2.
  c) A valid Java arithmetic expression with no parentheses is evaluated from left to right.
  d) The following are all invalid variable names: 3g, 87, 67h2, h22 and 2h.

2.10 Assuming that x = 2 and y = 3, what does each of the following statements display?
  a) System.out.printf("x = %d\n", x);
  b) System.out.printf("Value of %d + %d is %d\n", x, x, (x + x));
  c) System.out.printf("x =");
  d) System.out.printf("%d = %d\n", (x + y), (y + x));

2.11 Which of the following Java statements contain variables whose values are modified?
  a) p = i + j + k + 7;
  b) System.out.println("variables whose values are modified");
  c) System.out.println("a = 5");
  d) value = input.nextInt();

2.12 Given that $y = ax^3 + 7$, which of the following are correct Java statements for this equation?
  a) y = a * x * x * x + 7;
  b) y = a * x * x * (x + 7);
  c) y = (a * x) * x * (x + 7);
  d) y = (a * x) * x * x + 7;
  e) y = a * (x * x * x) + 7;
  f) y = a * x * (x * x + 7);

2.13 State the order of evaluation of the operators in each of the following Java statements, and show the value of x after each statement is performed:
  a) x = 7 + 3 * 6 / 2 - 1;
  b) x = 2 % 2 + 2 * 2 - 2 / 2;
  c) x = (3 * 9 * (3 + (9 * 3 / (3))));

2.14   Write an application that displays the numbers 1 to 4 on the same line, with each pair of adjacent numbers separated by one space. Write the program using the following techniques:

   a) Use one `System.out.println` statement.
   b) Use four `System.out.print` statements.
   c) Use one `System.out.printf` statement.

2.15   *(Arithmetic)* Write an application that asks the user to enter two integers, obtains them from the user and prints their sum, product, difference and quotient (division). Use the techniques shown in Fig. 2.7.

2.16   *(Comparing Integers)* Write an application that asks the user to enter two integers, obtains them from the user and displays the larger number followed by the words `"is larger"`. If the numbers are equal, print the message `"These numbers are equal"`. Use the techniques shown in Fig. 2.15.

2.17   *(Arithmetic, Smallest and Largest)* Write an application that inputs three integers from the user and displays the sum, average, product, smallest and largest of the numbers. Use the techniques shown in Fig. 2.15. [*Note:* The calculation of the average in this exercise should result in an integer representation of the average. So, if the sum of the values is 7, the average should be 2, not 2.3333....]

2.18   *(Displaying Shapes with Asterisks)* Write an application that displays a box, an oval, an arrow and a diamond using asterisks (*), as follows:

```
*********        ***           *              *
*       *       *   *         ***            * *
*       *      *     *       *****           *   *
*       *      *     *         *           *     *
*       *      *     *         *          *       *
*       *      *     *         *           *     *
*       *      *     *         *            *   *
*       *       *   *          *             * *
*********        ***           *              *
```

2.19   What does the following code print?

```
System.out.println( "*\n**\n***\n****\n*****" );
```

2.20   What does the following code print?

```
System.out.println( "*" );
System.out.println( "***" );
System.out.println( "*****" );
System.out.println( "****" );
System.out.println( "**" );
```

2.21   What does the following code print?

```
System.out.print( "*" );
System.out.print( "***" );
System.out.print( "*****" );
System.out.print( "****" );
System.out.println( "**" );
```

2.22   What does the following code print?

```
System.out.print( "*" );
System.out.println( "***" );
System.out.println( "*****" );
System.out.print( "****" );
System.out.println( "**" );
```

2.23   What does the following code print?

```
System.out.printf( "%s\n%s\n%s\n", "*", "***", "*****" );
```

2.24 *(Largest and Smallest Integers)* Write an application that reads five integers, and determines and prints the largest and smallest integers in the group. Use only the programming techniques you learned in this chapter.

2.25 *(Odd or Even)* Write an application that reads an integer and determines and prints whether it's odd or even. [*Hint:* Use the remainder operator. An even number is a multiple of 2. Any multiple of 2 leaves a remainder of 0 when divided by 2.]

2.26 *(Multiples)* Write an application that reads two integers, determines whether the first is a multiple of the second and prints the result. [*Hint:* Use the remainder operator.]

2.27 *(Checkerboard Pattern of Asterisks)* Write an application that displays a checkerboard pattern, as follows:

```
* * * * * * * *
 * * * * * * * *
* * * * * * * *
 * * * * * * * *
* * * * * * * *
 * * * * * * * *
* * * * * * * *
 * * * * * * * *
```

2.28 *(Diameter, Circumference and Area of a Circle)* Here's a peek ahead. In this chapter, you learned about integers and the type int. Java can also represent floating-point numbers that contain decimal points, such as 3.14159. Write an application that inputs from the user the radius of a circle as an integer and prints the circle's diameter, circumference and area using the floating-point value 3.14159 for π. Use the techniques shown in Fig. 2.7. [*Note:* You may also use the predefined constant Math.PI for the value of π. This constant is more precise than the value 3.14159. Class Math is defined in package java.lang. Classes in that package are imported automatically, so you do not need to import class Math to use it.] Use the following formulas (r is the radius):

$$diameter = 2r$$
$$circumference = 2\pi r$$
$$area = \pi r^2$$

Do not store the results of each calculation in a variable. Rather, specify each calculation as the value that will be output in a System.out.printf statement. Note that the values produced by the circumference and area calculations are floating-point numbers. Such values can be output with the format specifier %f in a System.out.printf statement. You'll learn more about floating-point numbers in Chapter 3.

2.29 *(Integer Value of a Character)* Here's another peek ahead. In this chapter, you learned about integers and the type int. Java can also represent uppercase letters, lowercase letters and a considerable variety of special symbols. Every character has a corresponding integer representation. The set of characters a computer uses together with the corresponding integer representations for those characters is called that computer's character set. You can indicate a character value in a program simply by enclosing that character in single quotes, as in 'A'.

You can determine a character's integer equivalent by preceding that character with (int), as in

```
(int) 'A'
```

This form is called a cast operator. (You'll learn about cast operators in Chapter 3.) The following statement outputs a character and its integer equivalent:

```
System.out.printf(
    "The character %c has the value %d\n", 'A', ( (int) 'A' ) );
```

When the preceding statement executes, it displays the character A and the value 65 (from the Unicode® character set) as part of the string. Note that the format specifier %c is a placeholder for a character (in this case, the character 'A').

Using statements similar to the one shown earlier in this exercise, write an application that displays the integer equivalents of some uppercase letters, lowercase letters, digits and special symbols. Display the integer equivalents of the following: A B C a b c 0 1 2 $ * + / and the blank character.

2.30   *(Separating the Digits in an Integer)* Write an application that inputs one number consisting of five digits from the user, separates the number into its individual digits and prints the digits separated from one another by three spaces each. For example, if the user types in the number 42339, the program should print

```
4    2    3    3    9
```

Assume that the user enters the correct number of digits. What happens when you execute the program and type a number with more than five digits? What happens when you execute the program and type a number with fewer than five digits? [*Hint:* It's possible to do this exercise with the techniques you learned in this chapter. You'll need to use both division and remainder operations to "pick off" each digit.]

2.31   *(Table of Squares and Cubes)* Using only the programming techniques you learned in this chapter, write an application that calculates the squares and cubes of the numbers from 0 to 10 and prints the resulting values in table format, as shown below. [*Note:* This program does not require any input from the user.]

```
number   square   cube
0        0        0
1        1        1
2        4        8
3        9        27
4        16       64
5        25       125
6        36       216
7        49       343
8        64       512
9        81       729
10       100      1000
```

2.32   *(Negative, Positive and Zero Values)* Write a program that inputs five numbers and determines and prints the number of negative numbers input, the number of positive numbers input and the number of zeros input.

Making a Difference

2.33   *(Body Mass Index Calculator)* We introduced the body mass index (BMI) calculator in Exercise 1.12. The formulas for calculating BMI are

$$BMI = \frac{weightInPounds \times 703}{heightInInches \times heightInInches}$$

or

$$BMI = \frac{weightInKilograms}{heightInMeters \times heightInMeters}$$

Create a BMI calculator application that reads the user's weight in pounds and height in inches (or, if you prefer, the user's weight in kilograms and height in meters), then calculates and displays the user's body mass index. Also, the application should display the following information from the Department of Health and Human Services/National Institutes of Health so the user can evaluate his/her BMI:

```
BMI VALUES
Underweight: less than 18.5
Normal:      between 18.5 and 24.9
Overweight:  between 25 and 29.9
Obese:       30 or greater
```

[*Note:* In this chapter, you learned to use the int type to represent whole numbers. The BMI calculations when done with int values will both produce whole-number results. In Chapter 3 you'll learn to use the double type to represent numbers with decimal points. When the BMI calculations are performed with doubles, they'll both produce numbers with decimal points—these are called "floating-point" numbers.]

2.34 *(World Population Growth Calculator)* Use the web to determine the current world population and the annual world population growth rate. Write an application that inputs these values, then displays the estimated world population after one, two, three, four and five years.

2.35 *(Car-Pool Savings Calculator)* Research several car-pooling websites. Create an application that calculates your daily driving cost, so that you can estimate how much money could be saved by car pooling, which also has other advantages such as reducing carbon emissions and reducing traffic congestion. The application should input the following information and display the user's cost per day of driving to work:

   a) Total miles driven per day.
   b) Cost per gallon of gasoline.
   c) Average miles per gallon.
   d) Parking fees per day.
   e) Tolls per day.

Control Statements: Part I

Let's all move one place on.
—Lewis Carroll

The wheel is come full circle.
—William Shakespeare

How many apples fell on Newton's head before he took the hint!
—Robert Frost

All the evolution we know of proceeds from the vague to the definite.
—Charles Sanders Peirce

Objectives

In this chapter you'll learn:

- To use basic problem-solving techniques.

- To develop algorithms through the process of top-down, stepwise refinement using pseudocode.

- To use the `if` and `if...else` statements to choose among alternative actions.

- To use the `while` statement to execute statements in a program repeatedly.

- To use counter-controlled repetition and sentinel-controlled repetition.

- To use the compound assignment, increment and decrement operators.

3.1 Introduction

Before writing a program to solve a problem, you should have a thorough understanding of the problem and a carefully planned approach to solving it. When writing a program, you also should understand the types of building blocks that are available and employ proven program-construction techniques. In this chapter and in Chapter 4, Control Statements: Part 2, we discuss these issues in our presentation of the theory and principles of structured programming. As you'll see in Chapter 7 and the remainder of the book, the concepts presented here are crucial in building classes and manipulating objects.

In this chapter, we introduce Java's `if`, `if...else` and `while` statements, three of the building blocks that allow you to specify the logic required for methods to perform their tasks. One example uses control statements to calculate the average of a set of student grades. Another example demonstrates additional ways to combine control statements to solve a similar problem. We introduce Java's compound assignment, increment and decrement operators. Finally, we discuss the portability of Java's primitive types.

3.2 Algorithms

Any computing problem can be solved by executing a series of actions in a specific order. A procedure for solving a problem in terms of

1. the **actions** to execute and

2. the **order** in which these actions execute

is called an **algorithm**. The following example demonstrates that correctly specifying the order in which the actions execute is important.

Consider the "rise-and-shine algorithm" followed by one executive for getting out of bed and going to work: (1) Get out of bed; (2) take off pajamas; (3) take a shower; (4) get dressed; (5) eat breakfast; (6) carpool to work. This routine gets the executive to work well prepared to make critical decisions. Suppose that the same steps are performed in a slightly different order: (1) Get out of bed; (2) take off pajamas; (3) get dressed; (4) take a shower; (5) eat breakfast; (6) carpool to work. In this case, our executive shows up for work soaking wet. Specifying the order in which statements (actions) execute in a program is called **program control**. This chapter investigates program control using Java's **control statements**.

3.3 Pseudocode

Pseudocode is an informal language that helps you develop algorithms without having to worry about the strict details of Java language syntax. The pseudocode we present is particularly useful for developing algorithms that will be converted to structured portions of Java programs. Pseudocode is similar to everyday English—it's convenient and user friendly, but it's not an actual computer programming language. You'll see an algorithm written in pseudocode in Fig. 3.5.

Pseudocode does not execute on computers. Rather, it helps you "think out" a program before attempting to write it in a programming language, such as Java. This chapter provides several examples of how to use pseudocode to develop Java programs.

The style of pseudocode we present consists purely of characters, so you can type pseudocode conveniently, using any text-editor program. A carefully prepared pseudocode program can easily be converted to a corresponding Java program.

Pseudocode normally describes only statements representing the actions that occur after you convert a program from pseudocode to Java and the program is run on a computer. Such actions might include input, output or calculations. We typically do not include variable declarations in our pseudocode, but some programmers choose to list variables and mention their purposes at the beginning of their pseudocode.

3.4 Control Structures

Normally, statements in a program are executed one after the other in the order in which they're written. This process is called **sequential execution**. Various Java statements, which we'll soon discuss, enable you to specify that the next statement to execute is not necessarily the next one in sequence. This is called **transfer of control**.

During the 1960s, it became clear that the indiscriminate use of transfers of control was the root of much difficulty experienced by software development groups. The blame was pointed at the **goto statement** (widely used in most programming languages of the time), which allows the programmer to specify a transfer of control to one of a wide range of destinations in a program. The term **structured programming** became almost synonymous with "goto elimination." [*Note:* Java does not have a goto statement; however, the word goto is reserved by Java and cannot be used as an identifier in programs.]

The research of Bohm and Jacopini[1] had demonstrated that programs could be written *without* any goto statements. The challenge of the era for programmers was to shift their styles to "goto-less programming." Not until the 1970s did most programmers start taking structured programming seriously. The results were impressive. Software development groups reported shorter development times, more frequent on-time delivery of systems and more frequent within-budget completion of software projects. The key to these successes was that structured programs were clearer, easier to debug and modify, and more likely to be bug free in the first place.

Bohm and Jacopini's work demonstrated that all programs could be written in terms of only three control structures—the **sequence structure**, the **selection structure** and the **repetition structure**. When we introduce Java's control structure implementations, we'll refer to them in the terminology of the *Java Language Specification* as "control statements."

---

1. Bohm, C., and G. Jacopini, "Flow Diagrams, Turing Machines, and Languages with Only Two Formation Rules," *Communications of the ACM*, Vol. 9, No. 5, May 1966, pp. 336–371.

Sequence Structure in Java

The sequence structure is built into Java. Unless directed otherwise, the computer executes Java statements one after the other in the order in which they're written—that is, in sequence. The **activity diagram** in Fig. 3.1 illustrates a typical sequence structure in which two calculations are performed in order. Java lets you have as many actions as you want in a sequence structure. As we'll soon see, anywhere a single action may be placed, we may place several actions in sequence.

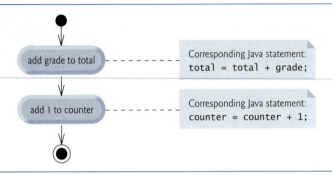

Fig. 3.1 | Sequence structure activity diagram.

A UML activity diagram models the **workflow** (also called the **activity**) of a portion of a software system. Such workflows may include a portion of an algorithm, like the sequence structure in Fig. 3.1. Activity diagrams are composed of symbols, such as **action-state symbols** (rectangles with their left and right sides replaced with outward arcs), **diamonds** and **small circles**. These symbols are connected by **transition arrows**, which represent the flow of the activity—that is, the order in which the actions should occur.

Like pseudocode, activity diagrams help you develop and represent algorithms, although many programmers prefer pseudocode. Activity diagrams clearly show how control structures operate. We use the UML in this chapter and Chapter 4 to show control flow in control statements. In Chapters 12–13, we use the UML in an optional real-world automated-teller machine object-oriented design and implementation case study.

Consider the sequence structure activity diagram in Fig. 3.1. It contains two **action states** that represent actions to perform. Each action state contains an **action expression**—for example, "add grade to total" or "add 1 to counter"—that specifies a particular action to perform. Other actions might include calculations or input/output operations. The arrows in the activity diagram represent **transitions**, which indicate the order in which the actions represented by the action states occur. The program that implements the activities illustrated by the diagram in Fig. 3.1 first adds grade to total, then adds 1 to counter.

The **solid circle** at the top of the activity diagram represents the **initial state**—the beginning of the workflow before the program performs the modeled actions. The **solid circle surrounded by a hollow circle** that appears at the bottom of the diagram represents the **final state**—the end of the workflow after the program performs its actions.

Figure 3.1 also includes rectangles with the upper-right corners folded over. These are UML **notes** (like comments in Java)—explanatory remarks that describe the purpose of symbols in the diagram. Figure 3.1 uses UML notes to show the Java code associated with each action state. A **dotted line** connects each note with the element it describes. Activity diagrams normally do not show the Java code that implements the activity. We do this here to illustrate how the diagram relates to Java code. For more information on the UML, see our optional object-oriented design and implementation case study (Chapters 12–13), our UML Resource Center at www.deitel.com/UML or visit www.uml.org.

Selection Statements in Java

Java has three types of **selection statements** (discussed in this chapter and Chapter 4). The if statement either performs (selects) an action, if a condition is true, or skips it, if the condition is false. The if...else statement performs an action if a condition is true and performs a different action if the condition is false. The switch statement (Chapter 4) performs one of many different actions, depending on the value of an expression.

The if statement is a **single-selection statement** because it selects or ignores a single action (or, as we'll soon see, a single group of actions). The if...else statement is called a **double-selection statement** because it selects between two different actions (or groups of actions). The switch statement is called a **multiple-selection statement** because it selects among many different actions (or groups of actions).

Repetition Statements in Java

Java provides three **repetition statements** (also called **looping statements**) that enable programs to perform statements repeatedly as long as a condition (called the **loop-continuation condition**) remains true. The repetition statements are the while, do...while and for statements. (Chapter 4 presents the do...while and for statements.) The while and for statements perform the action (or group of actions) in their bodies zero or more times—if the loop-continuation condition is initially false, the action (or group of actions) will not execute. The do...while statement performs the action (or group of actions) in its body one or more times. The words if, else, switch, while, do and for are Java keywords. A complete list of Java keywords appears in Appendix C.

Summary of Control Statements in Java

Java has only three kinds of control structures, which from this point forward we refer to as control statements—the sequence statement, selection statements (three types) and repetition statements (three types). Every program is formed by combining as many of these statements as is appropriate for the algorithm the program implements. We can model each control statement as an activity diagram. Like Fig. 3.1, each diagram contains an initial state and a final state that represent a control statement's entry point and exit point, respectively. **Single-entry/single-exit control statements** make it easy to build programs—we simply connect the exit point of one to the entry point of the next. We call this **control-statement stacking**. We'll learn that there is only one other way in which control statements may be connected—**control-statement nesting**—in which one control statement appears inside another. Thus, algorithms in Java programs are constructed from only three kinds of control statements, combined in only two ways. This is the essence of simplicity.

3.5 if Single-Selection Statement

Programs use selection statements to choose among alternative courses of action. For example, suppose that the passing grade on an exam is 60. The pseudocode statement

If student's grade is greater than or equal to 60
   Print "Passed"

determines whether the condition "student's grade is greater than or equal to 60" is true. If so, "Passed" is printed, and the next pseudocode statement in order is "performed." (Remember, pseudocode is not a real programming language.) If the condition is false, the *Print* statement is ignored, and the next pseudocode statement in order is performed. The indentation of the second line of this selection statement is optional, but recommended, because it emphasizes the inherent structure of structured programs.

The preceding pseudocode *If* statement may be written in Java as

```java
if ( studentGrade >= 60 )
    System.out.println( "Passed" );
```

Note that the Java code corresponds closely to the pseudocode. This is one of the properties of pseudocode that makes it such a useful program development tool.

Figure 3.2 illustrates the single-selection if statement. This figure contains the most important symbol in an activity diagram—the diamond, or **decision symbol**, which indicates that a decision is to be made. The workflow continues along a path determined by the symbol's associated **guard conditions**, which can be true or false. Each transition arrow emerging from a decision symbol has a guard condition (specified in square brackets next to the arrow). If a guard condition is true, the workflow enters the action state to which the transition arrow points. In Fig. 3.2, if the grade is greater than or equal to 60, the program prints "Passed," then transitions to the activity's final state. If the grade is less than 60, the program immediately transitions to the final state without displaying a message.

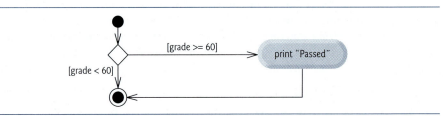

Fig. 3.2 | if single-selection statement UML activity diagram.

The if statement is a single-entry/single-exit control statement. We'll see that the activity diagrams for the remaining control statements also contain initial states, transition arrows, action states that indicate actions to perform, decision symbols (with associated guard conditions) that indicate decisions to be made, and final states.

Envision seven bins, each containing only one type of Java control statement. The control statements are all empty. Your task is to assemble a program from as many of each type of control statement as the algorithm demands, combining them in only two possible ways (stacking or nesting), then filling in the action states and decisions with action expressions and guard conditions appropriate for the algorithm. We'll discuss the variety of ways in which actions and decisions can be written.

3.6 if...else Double-Selection Statement

The if single-selection statement performs an indicated action only when the condition is true; otherwise, the action is skipped. The **if...else double-selection statement** allows you to specify an action to perform when the condition is true and a different action when the condition is false. For example, the pseudocode statement

> *If student's grade is greater than or equal to 60*
>   *Print "Passed"*
> *Else*
>   *Print "Failed"*

prints "Passed" if the student's grade is greater than or equal to 60, but prints "Failed" if it's less than 60. In either case, after printing occurs, the next pseudocode statement in sequence is "performed."

The preceding *If...Else* pseudocode statement can be written in Java as

```java
if ( grade >= 60 )
    System.out.println( "Passed" );
else
    System.out.println( "Failed" );
```

Note that the body of the else is also indented. Whatever indentation convention you choose should be applied consistently throughout your programs.

Good Programming Practice 3.1
Indent both body statements of an if...else statement.

Good Programming Practice 3.2
If there are several levels of indentation, each level should be indented the same additional amount of space.

Figure 3.3 illustrates the flow of control in the if...else statement. Once again, the symbols in the UML activity diagram (besides the initial state, transition arrows and final state) represent action states and decisions.

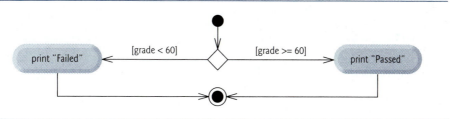

Fig. 3.3 | if...else double-selection statement UML activity diagram.

Conditional Operator (?:)

Java provides the **conditional operator** (**?:**) that can be used in place of an if...else statement. This is Java's only **ternary operator** (operator that takes three operands). Together, the operands and the ?: symbol form a **conditional expression**. The first operand (to the left of the ?) is a **boolean expression** (i.e., a condition that evaluates to a boolean value—**true** or **false**), the second operand (between the ? and :) is the value of the conditional expression if the boolean expression is true and the third operand (to the right of the :) is the value of the conditional expression if the boolean expression evaluates to false. For example, the statement

```java
System.out.println( studentGrade >= 60 ? "Passed" : "Failed" );
```

prints the value of println's conditional-expression argument. The conditional expression in this statement evaluates to the string "Passed" if the boolean expression student-Grade >= 60 is true and to the string "Failed" if it is false. Thus, this statement with the conditional operator performs essentially the same function as the if...else statement shown earlier in this section. The precedence of the conditional operator is low, so the entire conditional expression is normally placed in parentheses. We'll see that conditional expressions can be used in some situations where if...else statements cannot.

Good Programming Practice 3.3

Conditional expressions are more difficult to read than if...else statements and should be used to replace only simple if...else statements that choose between two values.

Nested *if...else* Statements

A program can test multiple cases by placing if...else statements inside other if...else statements to create **nested if...else statements**. For example, the following pseudocode represents a nested if...else that prints A for exam grades greater than or equal to 90, B for grades 80 to 89, C for grades 70 to 79, D for grades 60 to 69 and F for all other grades:

> *If student's grade is greater than or equal to 90*
>   *Print "A"*
> *else*
>   *If student's grade is greater than or equal to 80*
>   *Print "B"*
>   *else*
>   *If student's grade is greater than or equal to 70*
>   *Print "C"*
>   *else*
>   *If student's grade is greater than or equal to 60*
>   *Print "D"*
>   *else*
>   *Print "F"*

This pseudocode may be written in Java as

```java
if ( studentGrade >= 90 )
   System.out.println( "A" );
else
   if ( studentGrade >= 80 )
      System.out.println( "B" );
   else
      if ( studentGrade >= 70 )
         System.out.println( "C" );
      else
         if ( studentGrade >= 60 )
            System.out.println( "D" );
         else
            System.out.println( "F" );
```

If variable studentGrade is greater than or equal to 90, the first four conditions in the nested if...else statement will be true, but only the statement in the if part of the first if...else statement will execute. After that statement executes, the else part of the "outermost" if...else statement is skipped. Most Java programmers prefer to write the preceding nested if...else statement as

```java
if ( studentGrade >= 90 )
   System.out.println( "A" );
else if ( studentGrade >= 80 )
   System.out.println( "B" );
else if ( studentGrade >= 70 )
   System.out.println( "C" );
else if ( studentGrade >= 60 )
   System.out.println( "D" );
else
   System.out.println( "F" );
```

The two forms are identical except for the spacing and indentation, which the compiler ignores. The latter form is popular because it avoids deep indentation of the code to the right. Such indentation often leaves little room on a line of source code, forcing lines to be split.

Dangling-else Problem

The Java compiler always associates an else with the immediately preceding if unless told to do otherwise by the placement of braces ({ and }). This behavior can lead to what is referred to as the **dangling-else problem**. For example,

```java
if ( x > 5 )
   if ( y > 5 )
       System.out.println( "x and y are > 5" );
   else
       System.out.println( "x is <= 5" );
```

appears to indicate that if x is greater than 5, the nested if statement determines whether y is also greater than 5. If so, the string "x and y are > 5" is output. Otherwise, it appears that if x is not greater than 5, the else part of the if...else outputs the string "x is <= 5". Beware! This nested if...else statement does not execute as it appears. The compiler actually interprets the statement as

```java
if ( x > 5 )
   if ( y > 5 )
       System.out.println( "x and y are > 5" );
   else
       System.out.println( "x is <= 5" );
```

in which the body of the first if is a nested if...else. The outer if statement tests whether x is greater than 5. If so, execution continues by testing whether y is also greater than 5. If the second condition is true, the proper string—"x and y are > 5"—is displayed. However, if the second condition is false, the string "x is <= 5" is displayed, even though we know that x is greater than 5. Equally bad, if the outer if statement's condition is false, the inner if...else is skipped and nothing is displayed. To force the nested if...else statement to execute as it was originally intended, you write it as follows:

```java
if ( x > 5 )
{
   if ( y > 5 )
       System.out.println( "x and y are > 5" );
}
else
   System.out.println( "x is <= 5" );
```

The braces indicate that the second if is in the body of the first and that the else is associated with the *first* if. Exercises 3.27–3.28 investigate the dangling-else problem further.

Blocks

The if statement normally expects only one statement in its body. To include several statements in the body of an if (or the body of an else for an if...else statement), enclose the statements in braces. Statements contained in a pair of braces form a **block**. A block can be placed anywhere in a program that a single statement can be placed.

The following example includes a block in the else part of an if...else statement:

```
if ( grade >= 60 )
    System.out.println( "Passed" );
else
{
    System.out.println( "Failed" );
    System.out.println( "You must take this course again." );
}
```

In this case, if grade is less than 60, the program executes both statements in the body of the else and prints

```
Failed.
You must take this course again.
```

Note the braces surrounding the two statements in the else clause. These braces are important. Without the braces, the statement

```
System.out.println( "You must take this course again." );
```

would be outside the body of the else part of the if...else statement and would execute *regardless* of whether the grade was less than 60.

Syntax errors (e.g., omitting a brace in a block) are caught by the compiler. A **logic error** (e.g., omitting both braces in a block) has its effect at execution time. A **fatal logic error** causes a program to fail and terminate prematurely. A **nonfatal logic error** allows a program to continue executing but causes it to produce incorrect results.

Common Programming Error 3.1

Forgetting one or both of the braces that delimit a block can lead to syntax or logic errors.

Good Programming Practice 3.4

Always using braces in an if...else (or other) control statement helps prevent their accidental omission, especially when adding statements to the if part or the else part at a later time. To avoid omitting one or both of the braces, type the beginning and ending braces of blocks before typing the individual statements within the braces.

Just as a block can be placed anywhere a single statement can be placed, it's also possible to have an empty statement. Recall from Section 2.8 that the empty statement is represented by placing a semicolon (;) where a statement would normally be.

Common Programming Error 3.2

Placing a semicolon after the condition in an if or if...else statement leads to a logic error in single-selection if statements and a syntax error in double-selection if...else statements (when the if-part contains an actual body statement).

3.7 `while` Repetition Statement

A **repetition** (or **looping**) **statement** allows you to specify that a program should repeat an action while some condition remains true. The pseudocode statement

> *While there are more items on my shopping list*
> *Purchase next item and cross it off my list*

describes the repetition that occurs during a shopping trip. The condition "there are more items on my shopping list" may be true or false. If it's true, then the action "Purchase next item and cross it off my list" is performed. This action will be performed repeatedly while the condition remains true. The statement(s) contained in the *While* repetition statement constitute its body, which may be a single statement or a block. Eventually, the condition will become false (when the last item on the shopping list has been purchased and crossed off). At this point, the repetition terminates, and the first statement after the repetition statement executes.

As an example of Java's **while repetition statement**, consider a program segment designed to find the first power of 3 larger than 100. Suppose that the `int` variable `product` is initialized to 3. When the following `while` statement finishes executing, `product` contains the result:

```
while ( product <= 100 )
    product = 3 * product;
```

When this `while` statement begins execution, the value of variable `product` is 3. Each iteration of the `while` statement multiplies `product` by 3, so `product` takes on the values 9, 27, 81 and 243 successively. When variable `product` becomes 243, the `while`-statement condition—`product <= 100`—becomes false. This terminates the repetition, so the final value of `product` is 243. At this point, program execution continues with the next statement after the `while` statement.

Common Programming Error 3.3

Not providing, in the body of a `while` statement, an action that eventually causes the condition in the `while` to become false normally results in a logic error called an infinite loop (the loop never terminates).

The UML activity diagram in Fig. 3.4 illustrates the flow of control in the preceding `while` statement. Once again, the symbols in the diagram (besides the initial state, transition arrows, a final state and three notes) represent an action state and a decision. This diagram also introduces the UML's **merge symbol**. The UML represents both the merge symbol and the decision symbol as diamonds. The merge symbol joins two flows of activity into one. In this diagram, the merge symbol joins the transitions from the initial state and from the action state, so they both flow into the decision that determines whether the loop should begin (or continue) executing. The decision and merge symbols can be distinguished by the number of "incoming" and "outgoing" transition arrows. A decision symbol has one transition arrow pointing to the diamond and two or more pointing out from it to indicate possible transitions from that point. In addition, each transition arrow pointing out of a decision symbol has a guard condition next to it. A merge symbol has two or more transition arrows pointing to the diamond and only one pointing from the diamond, to indicate multiple activity flows merging to continue the activity. None of the transition arrows associated with a merge symbol has a guard condition.

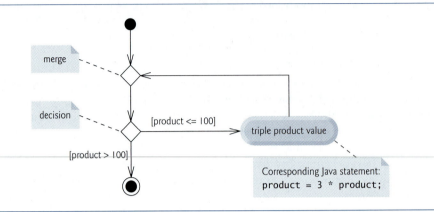

Fig. 3.4 | `while` repetition statement UML activity diagram.

Figure 3.4 clearly shows the repetition of the `while` statement discussed earlier in this section. The transition arrow emerging from the action state points back to the merge, from which program flow transitions back to the decision that is tested at the beginning of each iteration of the loop. The loop continues to execute until the guard condition `product > 100` becomes true. Then the `while` statement exits (reaches its final state), and control passes to the next statement in sequence in the program.

3.8 Formulating Algorithms: Counter-Controlled Repetition

To illustrate how algorithms are developed, we solve two variations of a problem that averages student grades. Consider the following problem statement:

> *A class of ten students took a quiz. The grades (integers in the range 0 to 100) for this quiz are available to you. Determine the class average on the quiz.*

The class average is equal to the sum of the grades divided by the number of students. The algorithm for solving this problem on a computer must input each grade, keep track of the total of all grades input, perform the averaging calculation and print the result.

Pseudocode Algorithm with Counter-Controlled Repetition
Let's use pseudocode to list the actions to execute and specify the order in which they should execute. We use **counter-controlled repetition** to input the grades one at a time. This technique uses a variable called a **counter** (or **control variable**) to control the number of times a set of statements will execute. Counter-controlled repetition is often called **definite repetition**, because the number of repetitions is known before the loop begins executing. In this example, repetition terminates when the counter exceeds 10. This section presents a fully developed pseudocode algorithm (Fig. 3.5) and a corresponding Java program (Fig. 3.6) that implements the algorithm. In Section 3.9, we demonstrate how to use pseudocode to develop such an algorithm from scratch.

Software Engineering Observation 3.1

Experience has shown that the most difficult part of solving a problem on a computer is developing the algorithm for the solution. Once a correct algorithm has been specified, producing a working Java program from the algorithm is usually straightforward.

Note the references in the algorithm of Fig. 3.5 to a total and a counter. A **total** is a variable used to accumulate the sum of several values. A counter is a variable used to count—in this case, the grade counter indicates which of the 10 grades is about to be entered by the user. Variables used to store totals are normally initialized to zero before being used in a program.

```
 1   Set total to zero
 2   Set grade counter to one
 3
 4   While grade counter is less than or equal to ten
 5       Prompt the user to enter the next grade
 6       Input the next grade
 7       Add the grade into the total
 8       Add one to the grade counter
 9
10   Set the class average to the total divided by ten
11   Print the class average
```

Fig. 3.5 | Pseudocode algorithm that uses counter-controlled repetition to solve the class-average problem.

Implementing Counter-Controlled Repetition

In Fig. 3.6, method main (lines 7–36) implements the class-averaging algorithm described by the pseudocode in Fig. 3.5—it allows the user to enter 10 grades, then calculates and displays the average.

```java
 1   // Fig. 3.6: ClassAverage.java
 2   // Counter-controlled repetition: Class-average problem.
 3   import java.util.Scanner; // program uses class Scanner
 4
 5   public class ClassAverage
 6   {
 7      public static void main( String[] args )
 8      {
 9         // create Scanner to obtain input from command window
10         Scanner input = new Scanner( System.in );
11
12         int total; // sum of grades entered by user
13         int gradeCounter; // number of the grade to be entered next
14         int grade; // grade value entered by user
15         int average; // average of grades
16
```

Fig. 3.6 | Counter-controlled repetition: Class-average problem. (Part 1 of 2.)

```
17          // initialization phase
18          total = 0; // initialize total
19          gradeCounter = 1; // initialize loop counter
20
21          // processing phase
22          while ( gradeCounter <= 10 ) // loop 10 times
23          {
24              System.out.print( "Enter grade: " ); // prompt
25              grade = input.nextInt(); // input next grade
26              total = total + grade; // add grade to total
27              gradeCounter = gradeCounter + 1; // increment counter by 1
28          } // end while
29
30          // termination phase
31          average = total / 10; // integer division yields integer result
32
33          // display total and average of grades
34          System.out.printf( "\nTotal of all 10 grades is %d\n", total );
35          System.out.printf( "Class average is %d\n", average );
36      } // end main
37  } // end class ClassAverage
```

```
Enter grade: 67
Enter grade: 78
Enter grade: 89
Enter grade: 67
Enter grade: 87
Enter grade: 98
Enter grade: 93
Enter grade: 85
Enter grade: 82
Enter grade: 100

Total of all 10 grades is 846
Class average is 84
```

Fig. 3.6 | Counter-controlled repetition: Class-average problem. (Part 2 of 2.)

Line 10 declares and initializes Scanner variable input, which is used to read values entered by the user. Lines 12–15 declare variables total, gradeCounter, grade and average to be of type int. Variable grade stores the user input. Variables declared in the body of a particular method (such as main) are known as **local variables** and can be used only in that method. When that method terminates, the values of its local variables are lost. In Chapter 5, you'll create programs that contain multiple method declarations, each with their own local variables.

Note that the declarations (in lines 12–15) appear in the body of method main. Variables declared in a method body are local variables and can be used only from the line of their declaration to the closing right brace of the method declaration. A local variable's declaration must appear before the variable is used in that method. A local variable cannot be accessed outside the method in which it's declared.

The assignments (in lines 18–19) initialize total to 0 and gradeCounter to 1. Note that these initializations occur before the variables are used in calculations. Variables grade and average (for the user input and calculated average, respectively) need not be initialized here—their values will be assigned as they're input or calculated later in the method.

Common Programming Error 3.4

Using the value of a local variable before it's initialized results in a compilation error. All local variables must be initialized before their values are used in expressions.

Error-Prevention Tip 3.1

Initialize each counter and total, either in its declaration or in an assignment statement. Totals are normally initialized to 0. Counters are normally initialized to 0 or 1, depending on how they're used (we'll show examples of when to use 0 and when to use 1).

Line 22 indicates that the while statement should continue looping (also called **iterating**) as long as gradeCounter's value is less than or equal to 10. While this condition remains true, the while statement repeatedly executes the statements (lines 24–27) between the braces that delimit its body.

Line 24 displays the prompt "Enter grade: ". Line 25 reads the grade entered by the user and assigns it to variable grade. Then line 26 adds the new grade entered by the user to the total and assigns the result to total, which replaces its previous value.

Line 27 adds 1 to gradeCounter to indicate that the program has processed a grade and is ready to input the next grade from the user. Incrementing gradeCounter eventually causes it to exceed 10. Then the loop terminates, because its condition (line 22) becomes false.

When the loop terminates, line 31 performs the averaging calculation and assigns its result to the variable average. Line 34 uses System.out's printf method to display the text "Total of all 10 grades is " followed by variable total's value. Line 35 then uses printf to display the text "Class average is " followed by variable average's value.

Notes on Integer Division and Truncation

The averaging calculation performed by method main produces an integer result. The program's output indicates that the sum of the grade values in the sample execution is 846, which, when divided by 10, should yield the real number 84.6—also called a floating-point number (i.e., a number with a decimal point). However, the result of the calculation total / 10 (line 31 of Fig. 3.6) is the integer 84, because total and 10 are both integers. Dividing two integers results in **integer division**—any fractional part of the calculation is lost (i.e., **truncated**). In the next section we'll see how to obtain a floating-point result from the averaging calculation.

Common Programming Error 3.5

Assuming that integer division rounds (rather than truncates) can lead to incorrect results. For example, 7 ÷ 4, which yields 1.75 in conventional arithmetic, truncates to 1 in integer arithmetic, rather than rounding to 2.

3.9 Formulating Algorithms: Sentinel-Controlled Repetition

Let's generalize Section 3.8's class-average problem. Consider the following problem:

> *Develop a class-averaging program that processes grades for an arbitrary number of students each time it is run.*

In the previous class-average example, the problem statement specified the number of students, so the number of grades (10) was known in advance. In this example, no indication is given of how many grades the user will enter during the program's execution. The program must process an arbitrary number of grades. How can it determine when to stop the input of grades? How will it know when to calculate and print the class average?

One way to solve this problem is to use a special value called a **sentinel value** (also called a **signal value**, a **dummy value** or a **flag value**) to indicate "end of data entry." The user enters grades until all legitimate grades have been entered. The user then types the sentinel value to indicate that no more grades will be entered. **Sentinel-controlled repetition** is often called **indefinite repetition** because the number of repetitions is not known before the loop begins executing.

Clearly, a sentinel value must be chosen that cannot be confused with an acceptable input value. Grades on a quiz are nonnegative integers, so –1 is an acceptable sentinel value for this problem. Thus, a run of the class-average program might process a stream of inputs such as 95, 96, 75, 74, 89 and –1. The program would then compute and print the class average for the grades 95, 96, 75, 74 and 89; since –1 is the sentinel value, it should not enter into the averaging calculation.

Common Programming Error 3.6

Choosing a sentinel value that is also a legitimate data value is a logic error.

Developing the Pseudocode Algorithm with Top-Down, Stepwise Refinement:
The Top and First Refinement
We approach this class-average program with a technique called **top-down, stepwise refinement**, which is essential to the development of well-structured programs. We begin with a pseudocode representation of the **top**—a single statement that conveys the overall function of the program:

Determine the class average for the quiz

The top is, in effect, a *complete* representation of a program. Unfortunately, the top rarely conveys sufficient detail from which to write a Java program. So we now begin the refinement process. We divide the top into a series of smaller tasks and list these in the order in which they'll be performed. This results in the following **first refinement**:

Initialize variables
Input, sum and count the quiz grades
Calculate and print the class average

This refinement uses only the sequence structure—the steps listed should execute in order, one after the other.

Software Engineering Observation 3.2

Each refinement, as well as the top itself, is a complete specification of the algorithm—only the level of detail varies.

Software Engineering Observation 3.3

Many programs can be divided logically into three phases: an initialization phase that initializes the variables; a processing phase that inputs data values and adjusts program variables accordingly; and a termination phase that calculates and outputs the final results.

Proceeding to the Second Refinement

The preceding Software Engineering Observation is often all you need for the first refinement in the top-down process. To proceed to the next level of refinement—that is, the **second refinement**—we commit to specific variables. In this example, we need a running total of the numbers, a count of how many numbers have been processed, a variable to receive the value of each grade as it's input by the user and a variable to hold the calculated average. The pseudocode statement

> *Initialize variables*

can be refined as follows:

> *Initialize total to zero*
> *Initialize counter to zero*

Only the variables *total* and *counter* need to be initialized before they're used. The variables *average* and *grade* (for the calculated average and the user input, respectively) need not be initialized, because their values will be replaced as they're calculated or input.

The pseudocode statement

> *Input, sum and count the quiz grades*

requires a repetition structure (i.e., a loop) that successively inputs each grade. We do not know in advance how many grades are to be processed, so we'll use sentinel-controlled repetition. The user enters grades one at a time. After entering the last grade, the user enters the sentinel value. The program tests for the sentinel value after each grade is input and terminates the loop when the user enters the sentinel value. The second refinement of the preceding pseudocode statement is then

> *Prompt the user to enter the first grade*
> *Input the first grade (possibly the sentinel)*
>
> *While the user has not yet entered the sentinel*
>   *Add this grade into the running total*
>   *Add one to the grade counter*
>   *Prompt the user to enter the next grade*
>   *Input the next grade (possibly the sentinel)*

In pseudocode, we do not use braces around the statements that form the body of the *While* structure. We simply indent the statements under the *While* to show that they belong to the *While*. Again, pseudocode is only an informal program development aid.

The pseudocode statement

> *Calculate and print the class average*

can be refined as follows:

> *If the counter is not equal to zero*
>   *Set the average to the total divided by the counter*
>   *Print the average*
> *else*
>   *Print "No grades were entered"*

We are careful here to test for the possibility of division by zero—a logic error that, if undetected, would cause the program to fail or produce invalid output. The complete second refinement of the pseudocode for the class-average problem is shown in Fig. 3.7.

Error-Prevention Tip 3.2

When performing division by an expression whose value could be zero, test for this and handle it (e.g., print an error message) rather than allow the error to occur.

```
 1   Initialize total to zero
 2   Initialize counter to zero
 3
 4   Prompt the user to enter the first grade
 5   Input the first grade (possibly the sentinel)
 6
 7   While the user has not yet entered the sentinel
 8       Add this grade into the running total
 9       Add one to the grade counter
10       Prompt the user to enter the next grade
11       Input the next grade (possibly the sentinel)
12
13   If the counter is not equal to zero
14       Set the average to the total divided by the counter
15       Print the average
16   else
17       Print "No grades were entered"
```

Fig. 3.7 | Class-average problem pseudocode algorithm with sentinel-controlled repetition.

In Fig. 3.5 and Fig. 3.7, we include blank lines and indentation in the pseudocode to make it more readable. The blank lines separate the algorithms into their phases and set off control statements; the indentation emphasizes the bodies of the control statements.

The pseudocode algorithm in Fig. 3.7 solves the more general class-average problem. This algorithm was developed after two refinements. Sometimes more are needed.

Software Engineering Observation 3.4

Terminate the top-down, stepwise refinement process when you've specified the pseudocode algorithm in sufficient detail for you to convert the pseudocode to Java. Normally, implementing the Java program is then straightforward.

Software Engineering Observation 3.5

Some programmers do not use program development tools like pseudocode. They feel that their ultimate goal is to solve the problem on a computer and that writing pseudocode merely delays the production of final outputs. Although this may work for simple and familiar problems, it can lead to serious errors and delays in large, complex projects.

Implementing Sentinel-Controlled Repetition

In Fig. 3.8, method main (lines 7–51) implements the pseudocode algorithm of Fig. 3.7. Although each grade is an integer, the averaging calculation is likely to produce a number with a decimal point—in other words, a real (i.e., floating-point) number. The type int cannot represent such a number, so this class uses type double to do so.

In this example, we see that control statements may be stacked on top of one another (in sequence). The while statement (lines 27–35) is followed in sequence by an if...else statement (lines 39–50). Much of the code in this program is identical to that in Fig. 3.6, so we concentrate on the new concepts.

```java
1   // Fig. 3.8: ClassAverage.java
2   // Sentinel-controlled repetition: Class-average problem.
3   import java.util.Scanner; // program uses class Scanner
4
5   public class ClassAverage
6   {
7      public static void main( String[] args )
8      {
9         // create Scanner to obtain input from command window
10        Scanner input = new Scanner( System.in );
11
12        int total; // sum of grades
13        int gradeCounter; // number of grades entered
14        int grade; // grade value
15        double average; // number with decimal point for average
16
17        // initialization phase
18        total = 0; // initialize total
19        gradeCounter = 0; // initialize loop counter
20
21        // processing phase
22        // prompt for input and read grade from user
23        System.out.print( "Enter grade or -1 to quit: " );
24        grade = input.nextInt();
25
26        // loop until sentinel value read from user
27        while ( grade != -1 )
28        {
29           total = total + grade; // add grade to total
30           gradeCounter = gradeCounter + 1; // increment counter
31
32           // prompt for input and read next grade from user
33           System.out.print( "Enter grade or -1 to quit: " );
34           grade = input.nextInt();
35        } // end while
36
37        // termination phase
38        // if user entered at least one grade...
39        if ( gradeCounter != 0 )
40        {
41           // calculate average of all grades entered
42           average = (double) total / gradeCounter;
43
44           // display total and average (with two digits of precision)
45           System.out.printf( "\nTotal of the %d grades entered is %d\n",
46              gradeCounter, total );
```

Fig. 3.8 | Sentinel-controlled repetition: Class-average problem. (Part 1 of 2.)

```
47              System.out.printf( "Class average is %.2f\n", average );
48         } // end if
49         else // no grades were entered, so output appropriate message
50              System.out.println( "No grades were entered" );
51     } // end main
52  } // end class ClassAverage
```

```
Enter grade or -1 to quit: 97
Enter grade or -1 to quit: 88
Enter grade or -1 to quit: 72
Enter grade or -1 to quit: -1

Total of the 3 grades entered is 257
Class average is 85.67
```

Fig. 3.8 | Sentinel-controlled repetition: Class-average problem. (Part 2 of 2.)

Floating-Point Number Precision and Memory Requirements

Most averages are not whole numbers (e.g., 0, −22 and 1024). For this reason, we calculate the class average in this example as a **floating-point number** (i.e., a number with a decimal point, such as 7.33, 0.0975 or 1000.12345). Java provides two primitive types for storing floating-point numbers in memory—float and double. The primary difference between them is that double variables can store numbers with larger magnitude and finer detail (i.e., more digits to the right of the decimal point—also known as the number's **precision**) than float variables.

Variables of type **float** represent **single-precision floating-point numbers** and can represent up to seven significant digits. Variables of type **double** represent **double-precision floating-point numbers**. These require twice as much memory as float variables and provide 15 significant digits—approximately double the precision of float variables. For the range of values required by most programs, variables of type float should suffice, but you can use double to "play it safe." In some applications, even variables of type double will be inadequate. Most programmers represent floating-point numbers with type double. In fact, Java treats all floating-point numbers you type in a program's source code (such as 7.33 and 0.0975) as double values by default. Such values in the source code are known as **floating-point literals**. See Appendix D, Primitive Types, for the ranges of values for floats and doubles.

Although floating-point numbers are not always 100% precise, they have numerous applications. For example, when we speak of a "normal" body temperature of 98.6, we do not need to be precise to a large number of digits. When we read the temperature on a thermometer as 98.6, it may actually be 98.5999473210643. Calling this number simply 98.6 is fine for most applications involving body temperatures. Owing to the imprecise nature of floating-point numbers, type double is preferred over type float, because double variables can represent floating-point numbers more accurately. For this reason, we primarily use type double throughout the book. For precise floating-point numbers, Java provides class BigDecimal (package java.math).

Floating-point numbers also arise as a result of division, such as in this example's class-average calculation. In conventional arithmetic, when we divide 10 by 3, the result is 3.3333333…, with the sequence of 3s repeating infinitely. The computer allocates only a fixed amount of space to hold such a value, so clearly the stored floating-point value can be only an approximation.

Common Programming Error 3.7

Using floating-point numbers in a manner that assumes they're represented precisely can lead to incorrect results.

Program Logic for Sentinel-Controlled Repetition vs. Counter-Controlled Repetition
Line 15 (Fig. 3.8) declares `double` variable `average`, which allows us to store the class average as a floating-point number. Line 19 initializes `gradeCounter` to 0, because no grades have been entered yet. Remember that this program uses sentinel-controlled repetition to input the grades. To keep an accurate record of the number of grades entered, the program increments `gradeCounter` only when the user enters a valid grade.

Compare the program logic for sentinel-controlled repetition in this application with that for counter-controlled repetition in Fig. 3.6. In counter-controlled repetition, each iteration of the `while` statement (e.g., lines 22–28 of Fig. 3.6) reads a value from the user, for the specified number of iterations. In sentinel-controlled repetition, the program reads the first value (lines 23–24 of Fig. 3.8) before reaching the `while`. This value determines whether the program's flow of control should enter the body of the `while`. If the condition of the `while` is false, the user entered the sentinel value, so the body of the `while` does not execute (i.e., no grades were entered). If, on the other hand, the condition is true, the body begins execution, line 29 adds the `grade` value to the `total` and line 30 increments `grade-Counter`. Then lines 33–34 in the loop body input the next value from the user. Next, program control reaches the closing right brace of the loop body at line 35, so execution continues with the test of the `while`'s condition (line 27). The condition uses the most recent `grade` input by the user to determine whether the loop body should execute again. Note that the value of variable `grade` is always input from the user immediately before the program tests the `while` condition. This allows the program to determine whether the value just input is the sentinel value *before* the program processes that value (i.e., adds it to the `total`). If the sentinel value is input, the loop terminates, and the program does not add –1 to the `total`.

Good Programming Practice 3.5

In a sentinel-controlled loop, the prompts requesting data should remind the user of the sentinel.

After the loop terminates, the `if...else` statement at lines 39–50 executes. The condition at line 39 determines whether any grades were input. If none were input, the `else` part (lines 49–50) of the `if...else` statement executes and displays the message `"No grades were entered"` and the method returns control to the calling method.

Notice the `while` statement's block in Fig. 3.8 (lines 28–35). Without the braces, the loop would consider its body to be only the first statement, which adds the `grade` to the `total`. The last three statements in the block would fall outside the loop body, causing the computer to interpret the code incorrectly as follows:

```
while ( grade != -1 )
    total = total + grade; // add grade to total
gradeCounter = gradeCounter + 1; // increment counter

// prompt for input and read next grade from user
System.out.print( "Enter grade or -1 to quit: " );
grade = input.nextInt();
```

The preceding code would cause an infinite loop in the program if the user did not input the sentinel -1 at line 24 (before the `while` statement).

Common Programming Error 3.8

Omitting the braces that delimit a block can lead to logic errors, such as infinite loops. To prevent this problem, some programmers enclose the body of every control statement in braces, even if the body contains only a single statement.

Explicitly and Implicitly Converting Between Primitive Types

If at least one grade was entered, line 42 of Fig. 3.8 calculates the average of the grades. Recall from Fig. 3.6 that integer division yields an integer result. Even though variable average is declared as a `double` (line 15), the calculation

```
average = total / gradeCounter;
```

loses the fractional part of the quotient before the result of the division is assigned to average. This occurs because `total` and `gradeCounter` are both integers, and integer division yields an integer result. To perform a floating-point calculation with integer values, we must temporarily treat these values as floating-point numbers for use in the calculation. Java provides the **unary cast operator** to accomplish this task. Line 42 uses the **(double)** cast operator—a unary operator—to create a *temporary* floating-point copy of its operand `total` (which appears to the right of the operator). Using a cast operator in this manner is called **explicit conversion** or **type cast**. The value stored in `total` is still an integer.

The calculation now consists of a floating-point value (the temporary `double` version of `total`) divided by the integer `gradeCounter`. Java knows how to evaluate only arithmetic expressions in which the operands' types are identical. To ensure that the operands are of the same type, Java performs an operation called **promotion** (or **implicit conversion**) on selected operands. For example, in an expression containing values of the types `int` and `double`, the `int` values are promoted to `double` values for use in the expression. In this example, the value of `gradeCounter` is promoted to type `double`, then the floating-point division is performed and the result of the calculation is assigned to `average`. As long as the `(double)` cast operator is applied to any variable in the calculation, the calculation will yield a `double` result. Later in this chapter, we discuss all the primitive types. You'll learn more about the promotion rules in Section 5.7.

Common Programming Error 3.9

A cast operator can be used to convert between primitive numeric types, such as `int` and `double`. Casting to the wrong type may cause compilation errors.

Cast operators are available for any type. The cast operator is formed by placing parentheses around the name of a type. The operator is a **unary operator** (i.e., an operator that takes only one operand). Java also supports unary versions of the plus (+) and minus (–) operators, so you can write expressions like –7 or +5. Cast operators associate from right to left and have the same precedence as other unary operators, such as unary + and unary –. This precedence is one level higher than that of the **multiplicative operators** *, / and %. (See the operator precedence chart in Appendix A.) We indicate the cast operator with the notation (*type*) in our precedence charts, to indicate that any type name can be used to form a cast operator.

Line 47 displays the class average. In this example, we use `printf` to display the class average rounded to the nearest hundredth. The format specifier `%f` in `printf`'s format control string (line 47) is used to output values of type `float` or `double`. The `.2` between `%` and `f` represents the number of decimal places (2) that should be output to the right of the decimal point in the floating-point number—also known as the number's **precision**. Any floating-point value output with `%.2f` will be rounded to the hundredths position—for example, 123.457 would be rounded to 123.46, 27.333 would be rounded to 27.33 and 123.455 would be rounded to 123.46. The three grades entered during the sample execution (Fig. 3.8) total 257, which yields the average 85.666666.... Method `printf` uses the precision in the format specifier to round the value to the specified number of digits. In this program, the average is rounded to the hundredths position and the average is displayed as `85.67`.

3.10 Formulating Algorithms: Nested Control Statements

For the next example, we once again formulate an algorithm by using pseudocode and top-down, stepwise refinement, and write a corresponding Java program. We've seen that control statements can be stacked on top of one another (in sequence). In this case study, we examine the only other structured way control statements can be connected—namely, by **nesting** one control statement within another.

Consider the following problem statement:

A college offers a course that prepares students for the state licensing exam for real estate brokers. Last year, ten of the students who completed this course took the exam. The college wants to know how well its students did on the exam. You've been asked to write a program to summarize the results. You've been given a list of these 10 students. Next to each name is written a 1 if the student passed the exam or a 2 if the student failed.

Your program should analyze the results of the exam as follows:

1. *Input each test result (i.e., a 1 or a 2). Display the message "Enter result" on the screen each time the program requests another test result.*

2. *Count the number of test results of each type.*

3. *Display a summary of the test results, indicating the number of students who passed and the number who failed.*

4. *If more than eight students passed the exam, print the message "Bonus to instructor!"*

After reading the problem statement carefully, we make the following observations:

1. The program must process test results for 10 students. A counter-controlled loop can be used, because the number of test results is known in advance.

2. Each test result has a numeric value—either a 1 or a 2. Each time it reads a test result, the program must determine whether it is a 1 or a 2. We test for a 1 in our algorithm. If the number is not a 1, we assume that it's a 2. (Exercise 3.24 considers the consequences of this assumption.)

3. Two counters are used to keep track of the exam results—one to count the number of students who passed the exam and one to count the number who failed.

4. After the program has processed all the results, it must decide whether more than eight students passed the exam.

Let's proceed with top-down, stepwise refinement. We begin with a pseudocode representation of the top:

Analyze exam results and decide whether tuition should be raised

Once again, the top is a *complete* representation of the program, but several refinements are likely to be needed before the pseudocode can evolve naturally into a Java program.

Our first refinement is

Initialize variables
Input the 10 exam results, and count passes and failures
Print a summary of the exam results and decide whether tuition should be raised

Here, too, even though we have a complete representation of the entire program, further refinement is necessary. We now commit to specific variables. Counters are needed to record the passes and failures, a counter will be used to control the looping process and a variable is needed to store the user input. The variable in which the user input will be stored is not initialized at the start of the algorithm, because its value is read from the user during each iteration of the loop.

The pseudocode statement

Initialize variables

can be refined as follows:

Initialize passes to zero
Initialize failures to zero
Initialize student counter to one

Notice that only the counters are initialized at the start of the algorithm.

The pseudocode statement

Input the 10 exam results, and count passes and failures

requires a loop that successively inputs the result of each exam. We know in advance that there are precisely 10 exam results, so counter-controlled looping is appropriate. Inside the loop (i.e., nested within the loop), a double-selection structure will determine whether each exam result is a pass or a failure and will increment the appropriate counter. The refinement of the preceding pseudocode statement is then

While student counter is less than or equal to 10
Prompt the user to enter the next exam result
Input the next exam result

If the student passed
Add one to passes
Else
Add one to failures

Add one to student counter

We use blank lines to isolate the *If...Else* control structure, which improves readability.

The pseudocode statement

Print a summary of the exam results and decide whether tuition should be raised

can be refined as follows:

> *Print the number of passes*
> *Print the number of failures*
>
> *If more than eight students passed*
> *Print "Bonus to instructor!"*

Complete Second Refinement of Pseudocode and Conversion to Class `Analysis`

The complete second refinement appears in Fig. 3.9. Notice that blank lines are also used to set off the *While* structure for program readability. This pseudocode is now sufficiently refined for conversion to Java.

1	*Initialize passes to zero*
2	*Initialize failures to zero*
3	*Initialize student counter to one*
4	
5	*While student counter is less than or equal to 10*
6	*Prompt the user to enter the next exam result*
7	*Input the next exam result*
8	
9	*If the student passed*
10	*Add one to passes*
11	*Else*
12	*Add one to failures*
13	
14	*Add one to student counter*
15	
16	*Print the number of passes*
17	*Print the number of failures*
18	
19	*If more than eight students passed*
20	*Print "Bonus to instructor!"*

Fig. 3.9 | Pseudocode for examination-results problem.

The Java class that implements the pseudocode algorithm and two sample executions are shown in Fig. 3.10. Lines 13–16 of `main` declare the variables that are used to process the examination results. Several of these declarations use Java's ability to incorporate variable initialization into declarations (`passes` is assigned 0, `failures` 0 and `studentCounter` 1). Looping programs may require initialization at the beginning of each repetition—normally performed by assignment statements rather than in declarations.

Error-Prevention Tip 3.3

Initializing local variables when they're declared helps you avoid any compilation errors that might arise from attempts to use uninitialized variables. While Java does not require that local-variable initializations be incorporated into declarations, it does require that local variables be initialized before their values are used in an expression.

The `while` statement (lines 19–33) loops 10 times. During each iteration, the loop inputs and processes one exam result. Notice that the `if...else` statement (lines 26–29) for processing each result is nested in the `while` statement. If the `result` is 1, the `if...else` statement increments `passes`; otherwise, it assumes the `result` is 2 and increments `failures`. Line 32 increments `studentCounter` before the loop condition is tested again at line 19. After 10 values have been input, the loop terminates and line 36 displays the number of passes and `failures`. The `if` statement at lines 39–40 determines whether more than eight students passed the exam and, if so, outputs the message "Bonus to instructor!".

```
1    // Fig. 3.10: Analysis.java
2    // Analysis of examination results.
3    import java.util.Scanner; // class uses class Scanner
4
5    public class Analysis
6    {
7       public static void main( String[] args )
8       {
9          // create Scanner to obtain input from command window
10         Scanner input = new Scanner( System.in );
11
12         // initializing variables in declarations
13         int passes = 0; // number of passes
14         int failures = 0; // number of failures
15         int studentCounter = 1; // student counter
16         int result; // one exam result (obtains value from user)
17
18         // process 10 students using counter-controlled loop
19         while ( studentCounter <= 10 )
20         {
21            // prompt user for input and obtain value from user
22            System.out.print( "Enter result (1 = pass, 2 = fail): " );
23            result = input.nextInt();
24
25            // if...else nested in while
26            if ( result == 1 )          // if result 1,
27               passes = passes + 1;     // increment passes;
28            else                        // else result is not 1, so
29               failures = failures + 1; // increment failures
30
31            // increment studentCounter so loop eventually terminates
32            studentCounter = studentCounter + 1;
33         } // end while
34
35         // termination phase; prepare and display results
36         System.out.printf( "Passed: %d\nFailed: %d\n", passes, failures );
37
38         // determine whether more than 8 students passed
39         if ( passes > 8 )
40            System.out.println( "Bonus to instructor!" );
41      } // end main
42   } // end class Analysis
```

Fig. 3.10 | Nested control structures: Examination-results problem. (Part 1 of 2.)

```
Enter result (1 = pass, 2 = fail): 1
Enter result (1 = pass, 2 = fail): 2
Enter result (1 = pass, 2 = fail): 1
Enter result (1 = pass, 2 = fail): 1
Enter result (1 = pass, 2 = fail): 1
Enter result (1 = pass, 2 = fail): 1
Enter result (1 = pass, 2 = fail): 1
Enter result (1 = pass, 2 = fail): 1
Enter result (1 = pass, 2 = fail): 1
Enter result (1 = pass, 2 = fail): 1
Passed: 9
Failed: 1
Bonus to instructor!
```

```
Enter result (1 = pass, 2 = fail): 1
Enter result (1 = pass, 2 = fail): 2
Enter result (1 = pass, 2 = fail): 1
Enter result (1 = pass, 2 = fail): 2
Enter result (1 = pass, 2 = fail): 1
Enter result (1 = pass, 2 = fail): 2
Enter result (1 = pass, 2 = fail): 2
Enter result (1 = pass, 2 = fail): 1
Enter result (1 = pass, 2 = fail): 1
Enter result (1 = pass, 2 = fail): 1
Passed: 6
Failed: 4
```

Fig. 3.10 | Nested control structures: Examination-results problem. (Part 2 of 2.)

Figure 3.10 shows the input and output from two sample executions of the program. During the first sample execution, the condition at line 39 of method main is true—more than eight students passed the exam, so the program outputs a message indicating that the instructor should receive a bonus.

3.11 Compound Assignment Operators

The **compound assignment operators** abbreviate assignment expressions. Statements like

> *variable* = *variable operator expression*;

where *operator* is one of the binary operators +, -, *, / or % (or others we discuss later in the text) can be written in the form

> *variable operator= expression*;

For example, you can abbreviate the statement

```
c = c + 3;
```

with the **addition compound assignment operator**, +=, as

```
c += 3;
```

The += operator adds the value of the expression on its right to the value of the variable on its left and stores the result in the variable on the left of the operator. Thus, the assignment expression c += 3 adds 3 to c. Figure 3.11 shows the arithmetic compound assignment operators, sample expressions using the operators and explanations of what the operators do.

Assignment operator	Sample expression	Explanation	Assigns
Assume: int c = 3, d = 5, e = 4, f = 6, g = 12;			
+=	c += 7	c = c + 7	10 to c
-=	d -= 4	d = d - 4	1 to d
*=	e *= 5	e = e * 5	20 to e
/=	f /= 3	f = f / 3	2 to f
%=	g %= 9	g = g % 9	3 to g

Fig. 3.11 | Arithmetic compound assignment operators.

3.12 Increment and Decrement Operators

Java provides two unary operators for adding 1 to or subtracting 1 from the value of a numeric variable. These are the unary **increment operator**, **++**, and the unary **decrement operator**, **--**, which are summarized in Fig. 3.12. A program can increment by 1 the value of a variable called c using the increment operator, ++, rather than the expression c = c + 1 or c += 1. An increment or decrement operator that is prefixed to (placed before) a variable is referred to as the **prefix increment** or **prefix decrement operator**, respectively. An increment or decrement operator that is postfixed to (placed after) a variable is referred to as the **postfix increment** or **postfix decrement operator**, respectively.

Operator	Operator name	Sample expression	Explanation
++	prefix increment	++a	Increment a by 1, then use the new value of a in the expression in which a resides.
++	postfix increment	a++	Use the current value of a in the expression in which a resides, then increment a by 1.
--	prefix decrement	--b	Decrement b by 1, then use the new value of b in the expression in which b resides.
--	postfix decrement	b--	Use the current value of b in the expression in which b resides, then decrement b by 1.

Fig. 3.12 | Increment and decrement operators.

Using the prefix increment (or decrement) operator to add (or subtract) 1 from a variable is known as **preincrementing** (or **predecrementing**) the variable. Preincrementing (or predecrementing) a variable causes the variable to be incremented (decremented) by 1;

then the new value of the variable is used in the expression in which it appears. Using the postfix increment (or decrement) operator to add (or subtract) 1 from a variable is known as **postincrementing** (or **postdecrementing**) the variable. This causes the current value of the variable to be used in the expression in which it appears; then the variable's value is incremented (decremented) by 1.

Good Programming Practice 3.6

Unlike binary operators, the unary increment and decrement operators should be placed next to their operands, with no intervening spaces.

Figure 3.13 demonstrates the difference between the prefix increment and postfix increment versions of the ++ increment operator. The decrement operator (--) works similarly.

```java
1   // Fig. 3.13: Increment.java
2   // Prefix increment and postfix increment operators.
3
4   public class Increment
5   {
6      public static void main( String[] args )
7      {
8         int c;
9
10        // demonstrate postfix increment operator
11        c = 5; // assign 5 to c
12        System.out.println( c );    // prints 5
13        System.out.println( c++ ); // prints 5 then postincrements
14        System.out.println( c );    // prints 6
15
16        System.out.println(); // skip a line
17
18        // demonstrate prefix increment operator
19        c = 5; // assign 5 to c
20        System.out.println( c );    // prints 5
21        System.out.println( ++c ); // preincrements then prints 6
22        System.out.println( c );    // prints 6
23     } // end main
24  } // end class Increment
```

```
5
5
6

5
6
6
```

Fig. 3.13 | Preincrementing and postincrementing.

Line 11 initializes the variable c to 5, and line 12 outputs c's initial value. Line 13 outputs the value of the expression c++. This expression postincrements the variable c, so c's original value (5) is output, then c's value is incremented (to 6). Thus, line 13 outputs c's initial value (5) again. Line 14 outputs c's new value (6) to prove that the variable's value was indeed incremented in line 13.

Line 19 resets c's value to 5, and line 20 outputs c's value. Line 21 outputs the value of the expression ++c. This expression preincrements c, so its value is incremented; then the new value (6) is output. Line 22 outputs c's value again to show that the value of c is still 6 after line 21 executes.

The arithmetic compound assignment operators and the increment and decrement operators can be used to simplify program statements. For example, the three assignment statements in Fig. 3.10 (lines 27, 29 and 32)

```
passes = passes + 1;
failures = failures + 1;
studentCounter = studentCounter + 1;
```

can be written more concisely with compound assignment operators as

```
passes += 1;
failures += 1;
studentCounter += 1;
```

with prefix increment operators as

```
++passes;
++failures;
++studentCounter;
```

or with postfix increment operators as

```
passes++;
failures++;
studentCounter++;
```

When incrementing or decrementing a variable in a statement by itself, the prefix increment and postfix increment forms have the same effect, and the prefix decrement and postfix decrement forms have the same effect. It's only when a variable appears in the context of a larger expression that preincrementing and postincrementing the variable have different effects (and similarly for predecrementing and postdecrementing).

Common Programming Error 3.10

Attempting to use the increment or decrement operator on an expression other than one to which a value can be assigned is a syntax error. For example, writing ++(x + 1) is a syntax error, because (x + 1) is not a variable.

Figure 3.14 shows the precedence and associativity of the operators we've introduced. They're shown from top to bottom in decreasing order of precedence. The second column describes the associativity of the operators at each level of precedence. The conditional operator (?:); the unary operators increment (++), decrement (--), plus (+) and minus (-); the cast operators and the assignment operators =, +=, -=, *=, /= and %= associate from right to left. All the other operators in the operator precedence chart in Fig. 3.14 associate from left to right. The third column lists the type of each group of operators.

Operators						Associativity	Type
++	--					right to left	unary postfix
++	--	+	-	(*type*)		right to left	unary prefix
*	/	%				left to right	multiplicative
+	-					left to right	additive
<	<=	>	>=			left to right	relational
==	!=					left to right	equality
?:						right to left	conditional
=	+=	-=	*=	/=	%=	right to left	assignment

Fig. 3.14 | Precedence and associativity of the operators discussed so far.

3.13 Primitive Types

The table in Appendix D lists the eight primitive types in Java. Like its predecessor languages C and C++, Java requires all variables to have a type. For this reason, Java is referred to as a **strongly typed language**.

In C and C++, programmers frequently have to write separate versions of programs to support different computer platforms, because the primitive types are not guaranteed to be identical from computer to computer. For example, an int value on one machine might be represented by 16 bits (2 bytes) of memory, and on another machine by 32 bits (4 bytes) of memory. In Java, int values are always 32 bits (4 bytes).

Portability Tip 3.1
The primitive types in Java are portable across all computer platforms that support Java.

Each type in Appendix D is listed with its size in bits (there are eight bits to a byte) and its range of values. Because the designers of Java want to ensure portability, they use internationally recognized standards for both character formats (Unicode; for more information, visit www.unicode.org) and floating-point numbers (IEEE 754; for more information, visit grouper.ieee.org/groups/754/).

3.14 (Optional) GUI and Graphics Case Study: Creating Simple Drawings

An appealing feature of Java is its graphics support, which enables you to visually enhance your applications. This section introduces one of Java's graphical capabilities—drawing lines. It also covers the basics of creating a window to display a drawing on the computer screen.

Java's Coordinate System
To draw in Java, you must understand Java's **coordinate system** (Fig. 3.15), a scheme for identifying points on the screen. By default, the upper-left corner of a GUI component has the coordinates (0, 0). A coordinate pair is composed of an *x*-coordinate (the **horizontal coordinate**) and a *y*-coordinate (the **vertical coordinate**). The *x*-coordinate is the hor-

izontal location moving from left to right. The *y*-coordinate is the vertical location moving from top to bottom. The *x-axis* describes every horizontal coordinate, and the *y-axis* every vertical coordinate.

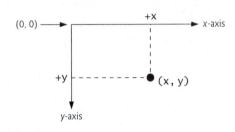

Fig. 3.15 | Java coordinate system. Units are measured in pixels.

Coordinates indicate where graphics should be displayed on a screen. Coordinate units are measured in **pixels.** The term pixel stands for "picture element." A pixel is a display monitor's smallest unit of resolution.

First Drawing Application

Our first drawing application (Fig. 3.16) simply draws two lines. Lines 10–23 of class `DrawPanel` perform the actual drawing, and the `main` method (lines 25–39) creates a window to display the drawing. The `import` statements in lines 3–5 allow us to use class `Graphics` (from package `java.awt`), which provides various methods for drawing text and shapes onto the screen, class `JPanel` (from package `javax.swing`), which provides an area on which we can draw, and class `JFrame`, which provides a window in which we can display our drawing.

```
1   // Fig. 3.16: DrawPanel.java
2   // Using drawLine to connect the corners of a panel.
3   import java.awt.Graphics;
4   import javax.swing.JPanel;
5   import javax.swing.JFrame;
6
7   public class DrawPanel extends JPanel
8   {
9      // draws an X from the corners of the panel
10     public void paintComponent( Graphics g )
11     {
12        // call paintComponent to ensure the panel displays correctly
13        super.paintComponent( g );
14
15        int width = getWidth(); // total width
16        int height = getHeight(); // total height
17
18        // draw a line from the upper-left to the lower-right
19        g.drawLine( 0, 0, width, height );
20
```

Fig. 3.16 | Using `drawLine` to connect the corners of a panel. (Part 1 of 2.)

```
21              // draw a line from the lower-left to the upper-right
22              g.drawLine( 0, height, width, 0 );
23          } // end method paintComponent
24
25          public static void main( String[] args )
26          {
27              // create a panel that contains our drawing
28              DrawPanel panel = new DrawPanel();
29
30              // create a new frame to hold the panel
31              JFrame application = new JFrame();
32
33              // set the frame to exit when it is closed
34              application.setDefaultCloseOperation( JFrame.EXIT_ON_CLOSE );
35
36              application.add( panel ); // add the panel to the frame
37              application.setSize( 250, 250 ); // set the size of the frame
38              application.setVisible( true ); // make the frame visible
39          } // end main
40      } // end class DrawPanel
```

(a) Window shown at its original size (250 by 250 pixels) when you first execute the program

(b) Window shown after using the mouse to resize it

Fig. 3.16 | Using drawLine to connect the corners of a panel. (Part 2 of 2.)

Line 7 uses the keyword **extends** to indicate that class DrawPanel is an enhanced type of JPanel. The keyword extends represents a so-called inheritance relationship in which our new class DrawPanel begins with the existing capabilities of class JPanel. The class from which DrawPanel **inherits**, JPanel, appears to the right of keyword extends. We can then customize JPanel's capabilities with new features—in this example, we add the ability to draw two lines along the panel's diagonals. Inheritance is explained in detail in Chapter 9. For now, you should mimic our DrawPanel class when creating your own graphics programs. Our goal is to get you comfortable with using objects and drawing some nifty graphics.

Method *paintComponent*
Every JPanel, including our DrawPanel, has a **paintComponent** method (lines 10–23), which the system automatically calls every time it needs to display the JPanel—just like the main method is called automatically when we execute a Java application. Method paintComponent must be declared as shown in line 10—otherwise, the system will not call it. This method is called automatically when a JPanel is first displayed on the screen, when it's covered then uncovered by a window on the screen and when the window in which it appears is resized. Method paintComponent requires one argument, a Graphics object, that is provided by the system when it calls paintComponent.

The first statement (line 13) in every `paintComponent` method you create must be

```
super.paintComponent( g );
```

which ensures that the panel is properly rendered before we begin drawing on it. For now write this statement as you see it. We explain the use of `super` in Section 9.4. Next, lines 15–16 call methods that class `DrawPanel` inherits from `JPanel`. Methods `getWidth` and `getHeight` return the `JPanel`'s width and height, respectively. Lines 15–16 store these values in the local variables `width` and `height`. Finally, lines 19 and 22 use the `Graphics` variable `g` to call method `drawLine` to draw the two lines. Method `drawLine` draws a line between two points represented by its four arguments. The first two arguments are the *x*- and *y*-coordinates for one endpoint, and the last two arguments are the coordinates for the other endpoint. Line 19 draws a line between the upper-left and lower-right corners of the panel. Line 22 draws a line between the lower-left and upper-right corners of the panel. If you use the mouse to resize the window, the lines will scale accordingly, because the draw-Line arguments are based on the panel's current `width` and `height`. *Resizing the window causes the system to call* `paintComponent` *to redraw the DrawPanel's contents.*

Method main

To display the `DrawPanel` on the screen, you must place it in a window. You create a window with an object of class `JFrame`. Line 28 in `main` creates a `DrawPanel` object, which contains our drawing, and line 31 creates a new `JFrame` that can hold and display our panel. Line 34 calls `JFrame` method `setDefaultCloseOperation` and passes it the argument `JFrame.EXIT_ON_CLOSE` to indicate that the application should terminate when the user closes the window. Line 36 uses class `JFrame`'s **add method** to attach the `DrawPanel` to the `JFrame` so that the `DrawPanel` will be displayed when the `JFrame` is displayed. Line 37 sets the size of the `JFrame`. Method **setSize** takes two parameters that represent the width and height of the `JFrame`, respectively. Finally, line 38 displays the `JFrame` by calling its **set-Visible method** with the argument `true`. When the `JFrame` is displayed, the `DrawPanel`'s `paintComponent` method (lines 10–23) is called automatically, and the two lines are drawn. Try resizing the window to see that the lines always draw based on the window's current width and height.

GUI and Graphics Case Study Exercises

3.1 Using loops and control statements to draw lines can lead to many interesting designs.

   a) Create the design in the left screen capture of Fig. 3.17. This design draws lines from the top-left corner, fanning them out until they cover the upper-left half of the panel. One approach is to divide the width and height into an equal number of steps (we found 15 steps worked well). The first endpoint of a line will always be in the top-left corner (0, 0). The second endpoint can be found by starting at the bottom-left corner and moving up one vertical step and right one horizontal step. Draw a line between the two endpoints. Continue moving up and to the right one step to find each successive endpoint. The figure should scale accordingly as you resize the window.

   b) Modify your answer in part (a) to have lines fan out from all four corners, as shown in the right screen capture of Fig. 3.17. Lines from opposite corners should intersect along the middle.

3.2 Figure 3.18 displays two additional designs created using `while` loops and `drawLine`.

   a) Create the design in the left screen capture of Fig. 3.18. Begin by dividing each edge into an equal number of increments (we chose 15 again). The first line starts in the top-

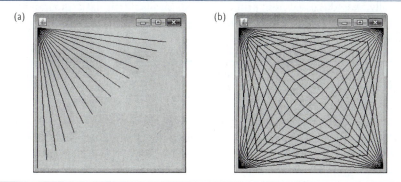

Fig. 3.17 | Lines fanning from a corner.

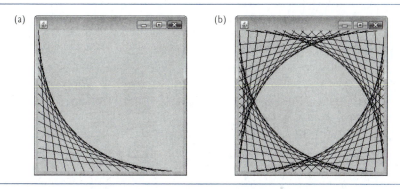

Fig. 3.18 | Line art with loops and `drawLine`.

left corner and ends one step right on the bottom edge. For each successive line, move down one increment on the left edge and right one increment on the bottom edge. Continue drawing lines until you reach the bottom-right corner. The figure should scale as you resize the window so that the endpoints always touch the edges.

b) Modify your answer in part (a) to mirror the design in all four corners, as shown in the right screen capture of Fig. 3.18.

3.15 Wrap-Up

This chapter demonstrated how to construct an algorithm (i.e., an approach to solving a problem), then how to refine the algorithm through several phases of pseudocode development, resulting in Java code that can be executed as part of a method. We showed how to use top-down, stepwise refinement to plan out the specific actions that a method must perform and the order in which the method must perform these actions.

Only three types of control statements—sequence, selection and repetition—are needed to develop any problem-solving algorithm. Specifically, we demonstrated the `if` single-selection statement, the `if...else` double-selection statement and the `while` repetition statement. We used control-statement stacking to total and compute the average of a set of student grades with counter- and sentinel-controlled repetition, and we used control-statement nesting to analyze and make decisions based on a set of exam results. We introduced Java's compound assignment operators and its increment and decrement operators. Finally, we discussed the primitive types available to Java programmers. In Chapter 4, we continue our discussion of control statements, introducing the `for`, `do...while` and `switch` statements.

Summary

Section 3.1 Introduction
- Before writing a program to solve a problem, you must have a thorough understanding of the problem and a carefully planned approach to solving it. You must also understand the building blocks that are available and to employ proven program-construction techniques.

Section 3.2 Algorithms
- Any computing problem can be solved by executing a series of actions in a specific order.
- A procedure for solving a problem in terms of the actions to execute and the order in which they execute is called an algorithm.
- Specifying the order in which statements execute in a program is called program control.

Section 3.3 Pseudocode
- Pseudocode is an informal language that helps programmers develop algorithms without having to worry about the strict details of Java language syntax.
- Pseudocode is similar to everyday English—it's convenient and user friendly, but it's not an actual computer programming language.
- Pseudocode helps you "think out" a program before attempting to write it in a programming language, such as Java.
- Carefully prepared pseudocode can easily be converted to a corresponding Java program.

Section 3.4 Control Structures
- Normally, statements in a program are executed one after the other in the order in which they're written. This process is called sequential execution.
- Various Java statements enable the programmer to specify that the next statement to execute is not necessarily the next one in sequence. This is called transfer of control.
- Bohm and Jacopini demonstrated that all programs could be written in terms of only three control structures—the sequence structure, the selection structure and the repetition structure.
- The term "control structures" comes from the field of computer science. The *Java Language Specification* refers to "control structures" as "control statements."
- The sequence structure is built into Java. Unless directed otherwise, the computer executes Java statements one after the other in the order in which they're written—that is, in sequence.
- Anywhere a single action may be placed, several actions may be placed in sequence.
- Activity diagrams are part of the UML. An activity diagram models the workflow (also called the activity) of a portion of a software system.
- Activity diagrams are composed of symbols—such as action-state symbols, diamonds and small circles—that are connected by transition arrows, which represent the flow of the activity.
- Action states contain action expressions that specify particular actions to perform.
- The arrows in an activity diagram represent transitions, which indicate the order in which the actions represented by the action states occur.
- The solid circle located at the top of an activity diagram represents the activity's initial state—the beginning of the workflow before the program performs the modeled actions.

- The solid circle surrounded by a hollow circle that appears at the bottom of the diagram represents the final state—the end of the workflow after the program performs its actions.
- Rectangles with their upper-right corners folded over are UML notes—explanatory remarks that describe the purpose of symbols in the diagram.
- Java has three types of selection statements.
- The if single-selection statement selects or ignores a single action or a single group of actions.
- The if...else double-selection statement selects between two actions or groups of actions.
- The switch statement is called a multiple-selection statement because it selects among many different actions or groups of actions.
- Java provides the while, do...while and for repetition (looping) statements that enable programs to perform statements repeatedly as long as a loop-continuation condition remains true.
- The while and for statements perform the action(s) in their bodies zero or more times—if the loop-continuation condition is initially false, the action(s) will not execute. The do...while statement performs the action(s) in its body one or more times.
- The words if, else, switch, while, do and for are Java keywords. Keywords cannot be used as identifiers, such as variable names.
- Every program is formed by combining as many sequence, selection and repetition statements as is appropriate for the algorithm the program implements.
- Single-entry/single-exit control statements are attached to one another by connecting the exit point of one to the entry point of the next. This is known as control-statement stacking.
- A control statement may also be nested inside another control statement.

Section 3.5 if Single-Selection Statement
- Programs use selection statements to choose among alternative courses of action.
- The single-selection if statement's activity diagram contains the diamond symbol, which indicates that a decision is to be made. The workflow follows a path determined by the symbol's associated guard conditions. If a guard condition is true, the workflow enters the action state to which the corresponding transition arrow points.
- The if statement is a single-entry/single-exit control statement.

Section 3.6 if...else Double-Selection Statement
- The if single-selection statement performs an indicated action only when the condition is true.
- The if...else double-selection statement performs one action when the condition is true and a different action when the condition is false.
- The conditional operator (?:) is Java's only ternary operator—it takes three operands. Together, the operands and the ?: symbol form a conditional expression.
- A program can test multiple cases with nested if...else statements.
- The Java compiler associates an else with the immediately preceding if unless told to do otherwise by the placement of braces.
- The if statement expects one statement in its body. To include several statements in the body of an if (or the body of an else for an if...else statement), enclose the statements in braces.
- A block of statements can be placed anywhere in a program that a single statement can be placed.
- A logic error has its effect at execution time. A fatal logic error causes a program to fail and terminate prematurely. A nonfatal logic error allows a program to continue executing, but causes the program to produce incorrect results.

- Just as a block can be placed anywhere a single statement can be placed, you can also use an empty statement, represented by placing a semicolon (;) where a statement would normally be.

Section 3.7 `while` Repetition Statement
- The `while` repetition statement allows the programmer to specify that a program should repeat an action while some condition remains true.
- The UML's merge symbol joins two flows of activity into one.
- The decision and merge symbols can be distinguished by the number of "incoming" and "outgoing" transition arrows. A decision symbol has one transition arrow pointing to the diamond and two or more transition arrows pointing out from the diamond to indicate possible transitions from that point. Each transition arrow pointing out of a decision symbol has a guard condition. A merge symbol has two or more transition arrows pointing to the diamond and only one transition arrow pointing from the diamond, to indicate multiple activity flows merging to continue the activity. None of the transition arrows associated with a merge symbol has a guard condition.

Section 3.8 Formulating Algorithms: Counter-Controlled Repetition
- Counter-controlled repetition uses a variable called a counter (or control variable) to control the number of times a set of statements execute.
- Counter-controlled repetition is often called definite repetition, because the number of repetitions is known before the loop begins executing.
- A total is a variable used to accumulate the sum of several values. Variables used to store totals are normally initialized to zero before being used in a program.
- A local variable's declaration must appear before the variable is used in that method. A local variable cannot be accessed outside the method in which it's declared.
- Dividing two integers results in integer division—the calculation's fractional part is truncated.

Section 3.9 Formulating Algorithms: Sentinel-Controlled Repetition
- In sentinel-controlled repetition, a special value called a sentinel value (also called a signal value, a dummy value or a flag value) is used to indicate "end of data entry."
- A sentinel value must be chosen that cannot be confused with an acceptable input value.
- Top-down, stepwise refinement is essential to the development of well-structured programs.
- A floating-point number is a number with a decimal point, such as 7.33, 0.0975 or 1000.12345. Java provides two primitive types for storing floating-point numbers in memory—`float` and `double`. The primary difference between these types is that `double` variables can store numbers with larger magnitude and finer detail (known as the number's precision) than `float` variables.
- Variables of type `float` represent single-precision floating-point numbers and have seven significant digits. Variables of type `double` represent double-precision floating-point numbers. These require twice as much memory as `float` variables and provide 15 significant digits—approximately double the precision of `float` variables.
- Floating-point literals are of type `double` by default.
- The format specifier `%f` is used to output values of type `float` or `double`. The format specifier `%.2f` specifies that two digits of precision should be output to the right of the decimal point in the floating-point number.
- Division by zero is a logic error.
- To perform a floating-point calculation with integer values, cast one of the integers to type `double`.
- Java knows how to evaluate only arithmetic expressions in which the operands' types are identical. To ensure this, Java performs an operation called promotion on selected operands.
- The unary cast operator is formed by placing parentheses around the name of a type.

Section 3.11 Compound Assignment Operators
- The compound assignment operators abbreviate assignment expressions. Statements of the form

    variable = variable operator expression;

    where *operator* is one of the binary operators +, -, *, / or %, can be written in the form

    variable operator= expression;

- The += operator adds the value of the expression on the right of the operator to the value of the variable on the left of the operator and stores the result in the variable on the left of the operator.

Section 3.12 Increment and Decrement Operators
- The unary increment operator, ++, and the unary decrement operator, --, add 1 to or subtract 1 from the value of a numeric variable.
- An increment or decrement operator that is prefixed to a variable is the prefix increment or prefix decrement operator, respectively. An increment or decrement operator that is postfixed to a variable is the postfix increment or postfix decrement operator, respectively.
- Using the prefix increment or decrement operator to add or subtract 1 is known as preincrementing or predecrementing, respectively.
- Preincrementing or predecrementing a variable causes the variable to be incremented or decremented by 1; then the new value of the variable is used in the expression in which it appears.
- Using the postfix increment or decrement operator to add or subtract 1 is known as postincrementing or postdecrementing, respectively.
- Postincrementing or postdecrementing the variable causes its value to be used in the expression in which it appears; then the variable's value is incremented or decremented by 1.
- When incrementing or decrementing a variable in a statement by itself, the prefix and postfix increment have the same effect, and the prefix and postfix decrement have the same effect.

Section 3.13 Primitive Types
- Java requires all variables to have a type. Thus, Java is referred to as a strongly typed language.
- Java uses Unicode characters and IEEE 754 floating-point numbers.

Terminology

Self-Review Exercises

3.1 Fill in the blanks in each of the following statements:

a) All programs can be written in terms of three types of control structures: _____, _____ and _____.

b) The _____ statement is used to execute one action when a condition is true and another when that condition is false.

c) Repeating a set of instructions a specific number of times is called _____ repetition.

d) When it's not known in advance how many times a set of statements will be repeated, a(n) _____ value can be used to terminate the repetition.

e) The _____ structure is built into Java—by default, statements execute in the order they appear.

f) Java is a(n) _____ language—it requires all variables to have a type.

g) If the increment operator is _____ to a variable, first the variable is incremented by 1, then its new value is used in the expression.

h) Primitive types _____ and _____ store floating-point numbers.

i) Variables of type double represent _____ floating-point numbers.

j) A(n) _____ is a number with a decimal point, such as 7.33, 0.0975 or 1000.12345.

k) Variables of type float represent _____ floating-point numbers.

l) The format specifier _____ is used to output values of type float or double.

3.2 State whether each of the following is *true* or *false*. If *false*, explain why.

a) An algorithm is a procedure for solving a problem in terms of the actions to execute and the order in which they execute.

b) A set of statements contained within a pair of parentheses is called a block.

c) A selection statement specifies that an action is to be repeated while some condition remains true.

d) A nested control statement appears in the body of another control statement.

e) Java provides the arithmetic compound assignment operators +=, -=, *=, /= and %= for abbreviating assignment expressions.

f) The primitive types (boolean, char, byte, short, int, long, float and double) are portable across only Windows platforms.

g) Specifying the order in which statements (actions) execute in a program is called program control.

h) The unary cast operator (double) creates a temporary integer copy of its operand.

i) Instance variables of type boolean are given the value true by default.

j) Pseudocode helps a programmer think out a program before attempting to write it in a programming language.

k) Floating-point values that appear in source code are known as floating-point literals and are type float by default.

3.3 Write four different Java statements that each add 1 to integer variable x.

3.4 Write Java statements to accomplish each of the following tasks:

a) Use one statement to assign the sum of x and y to z, then increment x by 1.

b) Test whether variable count is greater than 10. If it is, print "Count is greater than 10".

c) Use one statement to decrement the variable x by 1, then subtract it from variable total and store the result in variable total.

d) Calculate the remainder after q is divided by divisor, and assign the result to q. Write this statement in two different ways.

3.5 Write a Java statement to accomplish each of the following tasks:

a) Declare variables sum and x to be of type int.

b) Assign 1 to variable x.

c) Assign 0 to variable sum.

d) Add variable x to variable sum, and assign the result to variable sum.

e) Print "The sum is: ", followed by the value of variable sum.

3.6 Combine the statements that you wrote in Exercise 3.5 into a Java application that calculates and prints the sum of the integers from 1 to 10. Use a while statement to loop through the calculation and increment statements. The loop should terminate when the value of x becomes 11.

3.7 Determine the value of the variables in the statement product *= x++; after the calculation is performed. Assume that all variables are type int and initially have the value 5.

3.8   Identify and correct the errors in each of the following sets of code:

a)
```
while ( c <= 5 )
{
    product *= c;
    ++c;
```

b)
```
if ( gender == 1 )
    System.out.println( "Woman" );
else;
    System.out.println( "Man" );
```

3.9   What is wrong with the following `while` statement?

```
while ( z >= 0 )
    sum += z;
```

Answers to Self-Review Exercises

3.1   a) sequence, selection, repetition. b) `if...else`. c) counter-controlled (or definite). d) sentinel, signal, flag or dummy. e) sequence. f) strongly typed. g) prefixed. h) `float`, `double`. i) double-precision. j) floating-point number. k) single-precision. l) `%f`.

3.2   a) True. b) False. A set of statements contained within a pair of braces ({ and }) is called a block. c) False. A repetition statement specifies that an action is to be repeated while some condition remains true. d) True. e) True. f) False. The primitive types (`boolean`, `char`, `byte`, `short`, `int`, `long`, `float` and `double`) are portable across all computer platforms that support Java. g) True. h) False. The unary cast operator `(double)` creates a temporary floating-point copy of its operand. i) False. Instance variables of type `boolean` are given the value `false` by default. j) True. k) False. Such literals are of type `double` by default.

3.3
```
x = x + 1;
x += 1;
++x;
x++;
```

3.4   a) `z = x++ + y;`

b)
```
if ( count > 10 )
    System.out.println( "Count is greater than 10" );
```

c) `total -= --x;`

d)
```
q %= divisor;
q = q % divisor;
```

3.5   a)
```
int sum;
int x;
```

b) `x = 1;`

c) `sum = 0;`

d) `sum += x; or sum = sum + x;`

e) `System.out.printf( "The sum is: %d\n", sum );`

3.6   The program is as follows:

```
1   // Exercise 3.6: Calculate.java
2   // Calculate the sum of the integers from 1 to 10
3   public class Calculate
4   {
5       public static void main( String[] args )
6       {
```

```
 7          int sum;
 8          int x;
 9
10          x = 1;   // initialize x to 1 for counting
11          sum = 0; // initialize sum to 0 for totaling
12
13          while ( x <= 10 ) // while x is less than or equal to 10
14          {
15             sum += x; // add x to sum
16             ++x; // increment x
17          } // end while
18
19          System.out.printf( "The sum is: %d\n", sum );
20       } // end main
21    } // end class Calculate
```

```
The sum is: 55
```

3.7   product = 25, x = 6

3.8   a) Error: The closing right brace of the while statement's body is missing.
           Correction: Add a closing right brace after the statement ++c;.
       b) Error: The semicolon after else results in a logic error. The second output statement
           will always be executed.
           Correction: Remove the semicolon after else.

3.9   The value of the variable z is never changed in the while statement. Therefore, if the loop-
continuation condition (z >= 0) is true, an infinite loop is created. To prevent an infinite loop from
occurring, z must be decremented so that it eventually becomes less than 0.

Exercises

3.10   Compare and contrast the if single-selection statement and the while repetition statement.
How are these two statements similar? How are they different?

3.11   Explain what happens when a Java program attempts to divide one integer by another.
What happens to the fractional part of the calculation? How can a programmer avoid that outcome?

3.12   Describe the two ways in which control statements can be combined.

3.13   What type of repetition would be appropriate for calculating the sum of the first 100 positive integers? What type of repetition would be appropriate for calculating the sum of an arbitrary
number of positive integers? Briefly describe how each of these tasks could be performed.

3.14   What is the difference between preincrementing and postincrementing a variable?

3.15   Identify and correct the errors in each of the following pieces of code. [*Note:* There may be
more than one error in each piece of code.]

```
a)  if ( age >= 65 );
        System.out.println( "Age is greater than or equal to 65" );
    else
        System.out.println( "Age is less than 65 )";
b)  int x = 1, total;
    while ( x <= 10 )
    {
        total += x;
        ++x;
    }
```

```
    c)  while ( x <= 100 )
            total += x;
            ++x;
    d)  while ( y > 0 )
        {
            System.out.println( y );
            ++y;
```

3.16   What does the following program print?

```
 1   // Exercise 3.16: Mystery.java
 2   public class Mystery
 3   {
 4      public static void main( String[] args )
 5      {
 6         int y;
 7         int x = 1;
 8         int total = 0;
 9
10         while ( x <= 10 )
11         {
12            y = x * x;
13            System.out.println( y );
14            total += y;
15            ++x;
16         } // end while
17
18         System.out.printf( "Total is %d\n", total );
19      } // end main
20   } // end class Mystery
```

For Exercise 3.17 through Exercise 3.20, perform each of the following steps:
   a) Read the problem statement.
   b) Formulate the algorithm using pseudocode and top-down, stepwise refinement.
   c) Write a Java program.
   d) Test, debug and execute the Java program.
   e) Process three complete sets of data.

3.17   *(Gas Mileage)* Drivers are concerned with the mileage their automobiles get. One driver has kept track of several tankfuls of gasoline by recording the miles driven and gallons used for each tankful. Develop a Java application that will input the miles driven and gallons used (both as integers) for each tankful. The program should calculate and display the miles per gallon obtained for each tankful and print the combined miles per gallon obtained for all tankfuls up to this point. All averaging calculations should produce floating-point results. Use class Scanner and sentinel-controlled repetition to obtain the data from the user.

3.18   *(Credit Limit Calculator)* Develop a Java application that determines whether any of several department-store customers has exceeded the credit limit on a charge account. For each customer, the following facts are available:
   a) account number
   b) balance at the beginning of the month
   c) total of all items charged by the customer this month
   d) total of all credits applied to the customer's account this month
   e) allowed credit limit.

The program should input all these facts as integers, calculate the new balance (= *beginning balance + charges – credits*), display the new balance and determine whether the new balance exceeds the customer's credit limit. For those customers whose credit limit is exceeded, the program should display the message "Credit limit exceeded".

3.19 *(Sales Commission Calculator)* A large company pays its salespeople on a commission basis. The salespeople receive $200 per week plus 9% of their gross sales for that week. For example, a salesperson who sells $5000 worth of merchandise in a week receives $200 plus 9% of $5000, or a total of $650. You've been supplied with a list of the items sold by each salesperson. The values of these items are as follows:

Item	Value
1	239.99
2	129.75
3	99.95
4	350.89

Develop a Java application that inputs one salesperson's items sold for last week and calculates and displays that salesperson's earnings. There is no limit to the number of items that can be sold.

3.20 *(Salary Calculator)* Develop a Java application that determines the gross pay for each of three employees. The company pays straight time for the first 40 hours worked by each employee and time and a half for all hours worked in excess of 40. You are given a list of the employees, their number of hours worked last week and their hourly rates. Your program should input this information for each employee, then determine and display the employee's gross pay. Use class Scanner to input the data.

3.21 *(Find the Largest Number)* The process of finding the largest value is used frequently in computer applications. For example, a program that determines the winner of a sales contest would input the number of units sold by each salesperson. The salesperson who sells the most units wins the contest. Write a pseudocode program, then a Java application that inputs a series of 10 integers and determines and prints the largest integer. Your program should use at least the following three variables:

    a) counter: A counter to count to 10 (i.e., to keep track of how many numbers have been input and to determine when all 10 numbers have been processed).
    b) number: The integer most recently input by the user.
    c) largest: The largest number found so far.

3.22 *(Tabular Output)* Write a Java application that uses looping to print the following table of values:

N	10*N	100*N	1000*N
1	10	100	1000
2	20	200	2000
3	30	300	3000
4	40	400	4000
5	50	500	5000

3.23 *(Find the Two Largest Numbers)* Using an approach similar to that for Exercise 3.21, find the *two* largest values of the 10 values entered. [*Note:* You may input each number only once.]

3.24 *(Validating User Input)* Modify the program in Fig. 3.10 to validate its inputs. For any input, if the value entered is other than 1 or 2, keep looping until the user enters a correct value.

3.25 What does the following program print?

```
1   // Exercise 3.25: Mystery2.java
2   public class Mystery2
3   {
4      public static void main( String[] args )
5      {
6         int count = 1;
```

```
 7          while ( count <= 10 )
 8          {
 9             System.out.println( count % 2 == 1 ? "*****" : "++++++++" );
10             ++count;
11          } // end while
12       } // end main
13    } // end class Mystery2
```

3.26   What does the following program print?

```
 1    // Exercise 3.26: Mystery3.java
 2    public class Mystery3
 3    {
 4       public static void main( String[] args )
 5       {
 6          int row = 10;
 7          int column;
 8
 9          while ( row >= 1 )
10          {
11             column = 1;
12
13             while ( column <= 10 )
14             {
15                System.out.print( row % 2 == 1 ? "<" : ">" );
16                ++column;
17             } // end while
18
19             --row;
20             System.out.println();
21          } // end while
22       } // end main
23    } // end class Mystery3
```

3.27   *(Dangling-else Problem)* Determine the output for each of the given sets of code when x is 9 and y is 11 and when x is 11 and y is 9. Note that the compiler ignores the indentation in a Java program. Also, the Java compiler always associates an else with the immediately preceding if unless told to do otherwise by the placement of braces ({}). On first glance, the programmer may not be sure which if a particular else matches—this situation is referred to as the "dangling-else problem." We've eliminated the indentation from the following code to make the problem more challenging. [*Hint:* Apply the indentation conventions you've learned.]

a)
```
if ( x < 10 )
if ( y > 10 )
System.out.println( "*****" );
else
System.out.println( "#####" );
System.out.println( "$$$$$" );
```

b)
```
if ( x < 10 )
{
if ( y > 10 )
System.out.println( "*****" );
}
else
{
System.out.println( "#####" );
System.out.println( "$$$$$" );
}
```

3.28 *(Another Dangling-else Problem)* Modify the given code to produce the output shown in each part of the problem. Use proper indentation techniques. Make no changes other than inserting braces and changing the indentation of the code. The compiler ignores indentation in a Java program. We've eliminated the indentation from the given code to make the problem more challenging. [*Note:* It's possible that no modification is necessary for some of the parts.]

```java
if ( y == 8 )
if ( x == 5 )
System.out.println( "@@@@@" );
else
System.out.println( "#####" );
System.out.println( "$$$$$" );
System.out.println( "&&&&&" );
```

a) Assuming that x = 5 and y = 8, the following output is produced:

```
@@@@@
$$$$$
&&&&&
```

b) Assuming that x = 5 and y = 8, the following output is produced:

```
@@@@@
```

c) Assuming that x = 5 and y = 8, the following output is produced:

```
@@@@@
&&&&&
```

d) Assuming that x = 5 and y = 7, the following output is produced. [*Note:* The last three output statements after the else are all part of a block.]

```
#####
$$$$$
&&&&&
```

3.29 *(Square of Asterisks)* Write an application that prompts the user to enter the size of the side of a square, then displays a hollow square of that size made of asterisks. Your program should work for squares of all side lengths between 1 and 20.

3.30 *(Palindromes)* A palindrome is a sequence of characters that reads the same backward as forward. For example, each of the following five-digit integers is a palindrome: 12321, 55555, 45554 and 11611. Write an application that reads in a five-digit integer and determines whether it's a palindrome. If the number is not five digits long, display an error message and allow the user to enter a new value.

3.31 *(Printing the Decimal Equivalent of a Binary Number)* Write an application that inputs an integer containing only 0s and 1s (i.e., a binary integer) and prints its decimal equivalent. [*Hint:* Use the remainder and division operators to pick off the binary number's digits one at a time, from right to left. In the decimal number system, the rightmost digit has a positional value of 1 and the next digit to the left a positional value of 10, then 100, then 1000, and so on. The decimal number 234 can be interpreted as $4 * 1 + 3 * 10 + 2 * 100$. In the binary number system, the rightmost digit has a positional value of 1, the next digit to the left a positional value of 2, then 4, then 8, and so on. The decimal equivalent of binary 1101 is $1 * 1 + 0 * 2 + 1 * 4 + 1 * 8$, or $1 + 0 + 4 + 8$ or, 13.]

3.32 *(Checkerboard Pattern of Asterisks)* Write an application that uses only the output statements

```java
System.out.print( "* " );
System.out.print( "  " );
System.out.println();
```

to display the checkerboard pattern that follows. Note that a `System.out.println` method call with no arguments causes the program to output a single newline character. [*Hint:* Repetition statements are required.]

```
* * * * * * * *
 * * * * * * * *
* * * * * * * *
 * * * * * * * *
* * * * * * * *
 * * * * * * * *
* * * * * * * *
 * * * * * * * *
```

3.33 *(Multiples of 2 with an Infinite Loop)* Write an application that keeps displaying in the command window the multiples of the integer 2—namely, 2, 4, 8, 16, 32, 64, and so on. Your loop should not terminate (i.e., it should create an infinite loop). What happens when you run this program?

3.34 What is wrong with the following statement? Provide the correct statement to add one to the sum of x and y.

```
System.out.println( ++(x + y) );
```

3.35 *(Sides of a Triangle)* Write an application that reads three nonzero values entered by the user and determines and prints whether they could represent the sides of a triangle.

3.36 *(Sides of a Right Triangle)* Write an application that reads three nonzero integers and determines and prints whether they could represent the sides of a right triangle.

3.37 *(Factorial)* The factorial of a nonnegative integer n is written as $n!$ (pronounced "n factorial") and is defined as follows:

$$n! = n \cdot (n-1) \cdot (n-2) \cdot \ldots \cdot 1 \quad \text{(for values of } n \text{ greater than or equal to 1)}$$

and

$$n! = 1 \quad \text{(for } n = 0\text{)}$$

For example, $5! = 5 \cdot 4 \cdot 3 \cdot 2 \cdot 1$, which is 120.

a) Write an application that reads a nonnegative integer and computes and prints its factorial.

b) Write an application that estimates the value of the mathematical constant e by using the following formula. Allow the user to enter the number of terms to calculate.

$$e = 1 + \frac{1}{1!} + \frac{1}{2!} + \frac{1}{3!} + \ldots$$

c) Write an application that computes the value of e^x by using the following formula. Allow the user to enter the number of terms to calculate.

$$e^x = 1 + \frac{x}{1!} + \frac{x^2}{2!} + \frac{x^3}{3!} + \ldots$$

Making a Difference

3.38 *(Enforcing Privacy with Cryptography)* The explosive growth of Internet communications and data storage on Internet-connected computers has greatly increased privacy concerns. The field of cryptography is concerned with coding data to make it difficult (and hopefully—with the most advanced schemes—impossible) for unauthorized users to read. In this exercise you'll investigate a simple scheme for encrypting and decrypting data. A company that wants to send data over the Internet has asked you to write a program that will encrypt it so that it may be transmitted more securely. All the data is transmitted as four-digit integers. Your application should read a four-digit integer entered by the user and encrypt it as follows: Replace each digit with the result of adding 7 to the digit and getting the remainder after dividing the new value by 10. Then swap the first digit with the third, and swap the second digit with the fourth. Then print the encrypted integer. Write a separate application that inputs an encrypted four-digit integer and decrypts it (by reversing the encryption scheme) to form the original number. [*Optional reading project:* Research "public key cryptography" in general and the PGP (Pretty Good Privacy) specific public key scheme. You may also want to investigate the RSA scheme, which is widely used in industrial-strength applications.]

3.39   *(World Population Growth)* World population has grown considerably over the centuries. Continued growth could eventually challenge the limits of breathable air, drinkable water, arable cropland and other limited resources. There is evidence that growth has been slowing in recent years and that world population could peak some time this century, then start to decline.

For this exercise, research world population growth issues online. *Be sure to investigate various viewpoints.* Get estimates for the current world population and its growth rate (the percentage by which it is likely to increase this year). Write a program that calculates world population growth each year for the next 75 years, *using the simplifying assumption that the current growth rate will stay constant.* Print the results in a table. The first column should display the year from year 1 to year 75. The second column should display the anticipated world population at the end of that year. The third column should display the numerical increase in the world population that would occur that year. Using your results, determine the year in which the population would be double what it is today, if this year's growth rate were to persist.

4

Control Statements: Part 2

Not everything that can be counted counts, and not every thing that counts can be counted.
—Albert Einstein

Who can control his fate?
—William Shakespeare

The used key is always bright.
—Benjamin Franklin

Intelligence ... is the faculty of making artificial objects, especially tools to make tools.
—Henri Bergson

Objectives

In this chapter you'll learn:

- The essentials of counter-controlled repetition.

- To use the **for** and **do...while** statements to execute statements in a program repeatedly.

- To understand multiple selection using the **switch** statement.

- To use the **break** and **continue** statements to alter the flow of control.

- To use the logical operators to form complex conditional expressions in control statements.

4.1 Introduction

This chapter continues our presentation of structured programming theory and principles by introducing all but one of Java's remaining control statements. We demonstrate Java's for, do...while and `switch` statements. Through a series of short examples using while and for, we explore the essentials of counter-controlled repetition. We use a `switch` statement to count the number of A, B, C, D and F grade equivalents in a set of numeric grades entered by the user. We introduce the `break` and `continue` program-control statements. We discuss Java's logical operators, which enable you to use more complex conditional expressions in control statements. Finally, we summarize Java's control statements and the proven problem-solving techniques presented in this chapter and Chapter 3.

4.2 Essentials of Counter-Controlled Repetition

This section uses the `while` repetition statement introduced in Chapter 3 to formalize the elements required to perform counter-controlled repetition. Counter-controlled repetition requires

1. a **control variable** (or loop counter)

2. the **initial value** of the control variable

3. the **increment** (or **decrement**) by which the control variable is modified each time through the loop (also known as **each iteration of the loop**)

4. the **loop-continuation condition** that determines if looping should continue.

To see these elements of counter-controlled repetition, consider the application of Fig. 4.1, which uses a loop to display the numbers from 1 through 10.

```
1  // Fig. 4.1: WhileCounter.java
2  // Counter-controlled repetition with the while repetition statement.
3
4  public class WhileCounter
5  {
6     public static void main( String[] args )
7     {
```

Fig. 4.1 | Counter-controlled repetition with the while repetition statement. (Part 1 of 2.)

```
 8          int counter = 1; // declare and initialize control variable
 9
10          while ( counter <= 10 ) // loop-continuation condition
11          {
12             System.out.printf( "%d  ", counter );
13             ++counter; // increment control variable by 1
14          } // end while
15
16          System.out.println(); // output a newline
17       } // end main
18    } // end class WhileCounter
```

```
1  2  3  4  5  6  7  8  9  10
```

Fig. 4.1 | Counter-controlled repetition with the `while` repetition statement. (Part 2 of 2.)

In Fig. 4.1, the elements of counter-controlled repetition are defined in lines 8, 10 and 13. Line 8 declares the control variable (`counter`) as an `int`, reserves space for it in memory and sets its initial value to 1. Variable `counter` could also have been declared and initialized with the following local-variable declaration and assignment statements:

```
int counter; // declare counter
counter = 1; // initialize counter to 1
```

Line 12 displays control variable `counter`'s value during each iteration of the loop. Line 13 increments the control variable by 1 for each iteration of the loop. The loop-continuation condition in the `while` (line 10) tests whether the value of the control variable is less than or equal to 10 (the final value for which the condition is `true`). Note that the program performs the body of this `while` even when the control variable is 10. The loop terminates when the control variable exceeds 10 (i.e., `counter` becomes 11).

Common Programming Error 4.1

Because floating-point values may be approximate, controlling loops with floating-point variables may result in imprecise counter values and inaccurate termination tests.

Error-Prevention Tip 4.1

Use integers to control counting loops.

Good Programming Practice 4.1

Place blank lines above and below repetition and selection control statements, and indent the statement bodies to enhance readability.

The program in Fig. 4.1 can be made more concise by initializing `counter` to 0 in line 8 and preincrementing `counter` in the `while` condition as follows:

```
while ( ++counter <= 10 ) // loop-continuation condition
   System.out.printf( "%d  ", counter );
```

This code saves a statement (and eliminates the need for braces around the loop's body), because the `while` condition performs the increment before testing the condition. (Recall from Section 3.12 that the precedence of ++ is higher than that of <=.) Writing such condensed code takes practice; might make code more difficult to read, debug, modify and maintain; and typically should be avoided.

Software Engineering Observation 4.1

"Keep it simple" is good advice for most of the code you'll write.

4.3 for Repetition Statement

Section 4.2 presented the essentials of counter-controlled repetition. The while statement can be used to implement any counter-controlled loop. Java also provides the **for repetition statement**, which specifies the counter-controlled-repetition details in a single line of code. Figure 4.2 reimplements the application of Fig. 4.1 using for.

```
1   // Fig. 4.2: ForCounter.java
2   // Counter-controlled repetition with the for repetition statement.
3
4   public class ForCounter
5   {
6      public static void main( String[] args )
7      {
8         // for statement header includes initialization,
9         // loop-continuation condition and increment
10        for ( int counter = 1; counter <= 10; counter++ )
11           System.out.printf( "%d   ", counter );
12
13        System.out.println(); // output a newline
14     } // end main
15  } // end class ForCounter
```

```
1  2  3  4  5  6  7  8  9  10
```

Fig. 4.2 | Counter-controlled repetition with the for repetition statement.

The application's main method operates as follows: When the for statement (lines 10–11) begins executing, the control variable counter is declared and initialized to 1. (Recall from Section 4.2 that the first two elements of counter-controlled repetition are the control variable and its initial value.) Next, the program checks the loop-continuation condition, counter <= 10, which is between the two required semicolons. Because the initial value of counter is 1, the condition initially is true. Therefore, the body statement (line 11) displays control variable counter's value, namely 1. After executing the loop's body, the program increments counter in the expression counter++, which appears to the right of the second semicolon. Then the loop-continuation test is performed again to determine whether the program should continue with the next iteration of the loop. At this point, the control-variable value is 2, so the condition is still true (the final value is not exceeded)—thus, the program performs the body statement again (i.e., the next iteration of the loop). This process continues until the numbers 1 through 10 have been displayed and the counter's value becomes 11, causing the loop-continuation test to fail and repetition to terminate (at line 10, after 10 repetitions of the loop body). Then the program performs the first statement after the for—in this case, line 13.

Note that Fig. 4.2 uses (in line 10) the loop-continuation condition `counter <= 10`. If you incorrectly specified `counter < 10` as the condition, the loop would iterate only nine times. This is a common logic error called an **off-by-one error**.

Common Programming Error 4.2

Using an incorrect relational operator or an incorrect final value of a loop counter in the loop-continuation condition of a repetition statement can cause an off-by-one error.

Error-Prevention Tip 4.2

Using the final value in the condition of a while *or* for *statement and using the <= relational operator helps avoid off-by-one errors. For a loop that prints the values 1 to 10, the loop-continuation condition should be* counter <= 10 *rather than* counter < 10 *(which causes an off-by-one error) or* counter < 11 *(which is correct). Many programmers prefer so-called zero-based counting, in which to count 10 times,* counter *would be initialized to zero and the loop-continuation test would be* counter < 10.

Figure 4.3 takes a closer look at the `for` statement in Fig. 4.2. The `for`'s first line (including the keyword `for` and everything in parentheses after `for`)—line 10 in Fig. 4.2—is sometimes called the **for statement header**. Note that the `for` header "does it all"—it specifies each item needed for counter-controlled repetition with a control variable. If there is more than one statement in the body of the `for`, braces are required to define the body of the loop.

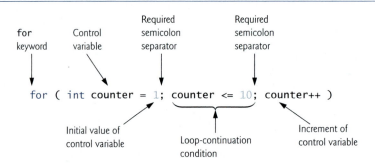

Fig. 4.3 | for statement header components.

The general format of the `for` statement is

> **for** (*initialization*; *loopContinuationCondition*; *increment*)
>   *statement*

where the *initialization* expression names the loop's control variable and optionally provides its initial value, *loopContinuationCondition* determines whether the loop should continue executing and *increment* modifies the control variable's value (possibly an increment or decrement), so that the loop-continuation condition eventually becomes false. The two semicolons in the `for` header are required.

Common Programming Error 4.3

Using commas instead of the two required semicolons in a for header is a syntax error.

In most cases, the `for` statement can be represented with an equivalent `while` statement as follows:

```
initialization;
while ( loopContinuationCondition )
{
    statement
    increment;
}
```

In Section 4.7, we show a case in which a `for` statement cannot be represented with an equivalent `while` statement.

Typically, `for` statements are used for counter-controlled repetition and `while` statements for sentinel-controlled repetition. However, `while` and `for` can each be used for either repetition type.

If the *initialization* expression in the `for` header declares the control variable (i.e., the control variable's type is specified before the variable name, as in Fig. 4.2), the control variable can be used only in that `for` statement—it will not exist outside it. This restricted use is known as the variable's **scope**. The scope of a variable defines where it can be used in a program. For example, a local variable can be used only in the method that declares it and only from the point of declaration through the end of the method. Scope is discussed in detail in Chapter 5, Methods.

Common Programming Error 4.4

When a `for` statement's control variable is declared in the initialization section of the `for`'s header, using the control variable after the `for`'s body is a compilation error.

All three expressions in a `for` header are optional. If the *loopContinuationCondition* is omitted, Java assumes that the loop-continuation condition is always true, thus creating an infinite loop. You might omit the *initialization* expression if the program initializes the control variable before the loop. You might omit the *increment* expression if the program calculates the increment with statements in the loop's body or if no increment is needed. The increment expression in a `for` acts as if it were a standalone statement at the end of the `for`'s body. Therefore, the expressions

```
counter = counter + 1
counter += 1
++counter
counter++
```

are equivalent increment expressions in a `for` statement. Many programmers prefer counter++ because it's concise and because a `for` loop evaluates its increment expression after its body executes. Therefore, the postfix increment form seems more natural. In this case, the variable being incremented does not appear in a larger expression, so preincrementing and postincrementing actually have the same effect.

Performance Tip 4.1

There is a slight performance advantage to preincrementing, but if you choose to post-increment because it seems more natural (as in a `for` header), optimizing compilers will typically generate Java bytecode that uses the more efficient form anyway. So you should use the idiom with which you feel most comfortable in these situations.

Common Programming Error 4.5

Placing a semicolon immediately to the right of the right parenthesis of a for *header makes that* for'*s body an empty statement. This is normally a logic error.*

Error-Prevention Tip 4.3

Infinite loops occur when the loop-continuation condition in a repetition statement never becomes false. *To prevent this situation in a counter-controlled loop, ensure that the control variable is incremented (or decremented) during each iteration of the loop. In a sentinel-controlled loop, ensure that the sentinel value is able to be input.*

The initialization, loop-continuation condition and increment portions of a for statement can contain arithmetic expressions. For example, assume that x = 2 and y = 10. If x and y are not modified in the body of the loop, the statement

```
for ( int j = x; j <= 4 * x * y; j += y / x )
```

is equivalent to the statement

```
for ( int j = 2; j <= 80; j += 5 )
```

The increment of a for statement may also be negative, in which case it's really a decrement, and the loop counts downward.

If the loop-continuation condition is initially false, the program does not execute the for statement's body. Instead, execution proceeds with the statement following the for.

Programs frequently display the control-variable value or use it in calculations in the loop body, but this use is not required. The control variable is commonly used to control repetition without being mentioned in the body of the for.

Error-Prevention Tip 4.4

Although the value of the control variable can be changed in the body of a for *loop, avoid doing so, because this practice can lead to subtle errors.*

The for statement's UML activity diagram is similar to that of the while statement (Fig. 3.4). Figure 4.4 shows the activity diagram of the for statement in Fig. 4.2. The diagram makes it clear that initialization occurs *once* before the loop-continuation test is evaluated the first time, and that incrementing occurs *each* time through the loop after the body statement executes.

4.4 Examples Using the for Statement

The following examples show techniques for varying the control variable in a for statement. In each case, we write the appropriate for header. Note the change in the relational operator for loops that decrement the control variable.

a) Vary the control variable from 1 to 100 in increments of 1.

```
for ( int i = 1; i <= 100; i++ )
```

b) Vary the control variable from 100 to 1 in decrements of 1.

```
for ( int i = 100; i >= 1; i-- )
```

c) Vary the control variable from 7 to 77 in increments of 7.

```
for ( int i = 7; i <= 77; i += 7 )
```

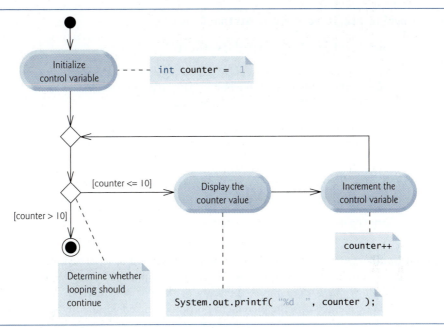

Fig. 4.4 | UML activity diagram for the for statement in Fig. 4.2.

d) Vary the control variable from 20 to 2 in decrements of 2.

```
for ( int i = 20; i >= 2; i -= 2 )
```

e) Vary the control variable over the values 2, 5, 8, 11, 14, 17, 20.

```
for ( int i = 2; i <= 20; i += 3 )
```

f) Vary the control variable over the values 99, 88, 77, 66, 55, 44, 33, 22, 11, 0.

```
for ( int i = 99; i >= 0; i -= 11 )
```

Common Programming Error 4.6

Using an incorrect relational operator in the loop-continuation condition of a loop that counts downward (e.g., using i <= 1 instead of i >= 1 in a loop counting down to 1) is usually a logic error.

Application: Summing the Even Integers from 2 to 20

We now consider two sample applications that demonstrate simple uses of for. The application in Fig. 4.5 uses a for statement to sum the even integers from 2 to 20 and store the result in an int variable called total.

```
1   // Fig. 4.5: Sum.java
2   // Summing integers with the for statement.
3
4   public class Sum
5   {
```

Fig. 4.5 | Summing integers with the for statement. (Part 1 of 2.)

```
6       public static void main( String[] args )
7       {
8          int total = 0; // initialize total
9
10         // total even integers from 2 through 20
11         for ( int number = 2; number <= 20; number += 2 )
12            total += number;
13
14         System.out.printf( "Sum is %d\n", total ); // display results
15      } // end main
16   } // end class Sum
```

```
Sum is 110
```

Fig. 4.5 | Summing integers with the for statement. (Part 2 of 2.)

The *initialization* and *increment* expressions can be comma-separated lists that enable you to use multiple initialization expressions or multiple increment expressions. For example, *although this is discouraged*, the body of the for statement in lines 11–12 of Fig. 4.5 could be merged into the increment portion of the for header by using a comma as follows:

```
for ( int number = 2; number <= 20; total += number, number += 2 )
    ; // empty statement
```

Good Programming Practice 4.2

For readability limit the size of control-statement headers to a single line if possible.

Application: Compound-Interest Calculations

The next application uses the for statement to compute compound interest. Consider the following problem:

> *A person invests $1000 in a savings account yielding 5% interest. Assuming that all the interest is left on deposit, calculate and print the amount of money in the account at the end of each year for 10 years. Use the following formula to determine the amounts:*
>
> $$a = p\,(1 + r)^n$$
>
> *where*
>
> > p is the original amount invested (i.e., the principal)
> > r is the annual interest rate (e.g., use 0.05 for 5%)
> > n is the number of years
> > a is the amount on deposit at the end of the nth year.

The solution to this problem (Fig. 4.6) involves a loop that performs the indicated calculation for each of the 10 years the money remains on deposit. Lines 8–10 in method main declare double variables amount, principal and rate, and initialize principal to 1000.0 and rate to 0.05. Java treats floating-point constants like 1000.0 and 0.05 as type double. Similarly, Java treats whole-number constants like 7 and -22 as type int.

```
1   // Fig. 4.6: Interest.java
2   // Compound-interest calculations with for.
3
4   public class Interest
5   {
6      public static void main( String[] args )
7      {
8         double amount; // amount on deposit at end of each year
9         double principal = 1000.0; // initial amount before interest
10        double rate = 0.05; // interest rate
11
12        // display headers
13        System.out.printf( "%s%20s\n", "Year", "Amount on deposit" );
14
15        // calculate amount on deposit for each of ten years
16        for ( int year = 1; year <= 10; year++ )
17        {
18           // calculate new amount for specified year
19           amount = principal * Math.pow( 1.0 + rate, year );
20
21           // display the year and the amount
22           System.out.printf( "%4d%,20.2f\n", year, amount );
23        } // end for
24     } // end main
25  } // end class Interest
```

```
Year     Amount on deposit
   1            1,050.00
   2            1,102.50
   3            1,157.63
   4            1,215.51
   5            1,276.28
   6            1,340.10
   7            1,407.10
   8            1,477.46
   9            1,551.33
  10            1,628.89
```

Fig. 4.6 | Compound-interest calculations with for.

Formatting Strings with Field Widths and Justification

Line 13 outputs the headers for this application's two columns of output. The first column displays the year, and the second column the amount on deposit at the end of that year. Note that we use the format specifier %20s to output the String "Amount on Deposit". The integer 20 between the % and the conversion character s indicates that the value output should be displayed with a **field width** of 20—that is, printf displays the value with at least 20 character positions. If the value to be output is less than 20 character positions wide (17 characters in this example), the value is **right justified** in the field by default. If the year value to be output were more than four character positions wide, the field width would be extended to the right to accommodate the entire value—this would push the amount field to the right, upsetting the neat columns of our tabular output. To indicate that values should be output **left justified**, simply precede the field width with the **minus sign (–) formatting flag** (e.g., %-20s).

Performing the Interest Calculations
The for statement (lines 16–23) executes its body 10 times, varying control variable year from 1 to 10 in increments of 1. This loop terminates when control variable year becomes 11. (Note that year represents *n* in the problem statement.)

Classes provide methods that perform common tasks on objects. In fact, most methods must be called on a specific object. For example, to output text in Fig. 4.6, line 13 calls method printf on the System.out object. Many classes also provide methods that perform common tasks and do not require objects. These are called static methods. For example, Java does not include an exponentiation operator, so the designers of Java's Math class defined static method pow for raising a value to a power. You can call a static method by specifying the class name followed by a dot (.) and the method name, as in

ClassName.*methodName*(*arguments*)

In Chapter 5, you'll learn how to implement static methods in your own classes.

We use static method **pow** of class **Math** to perform the compound-interest calculation in Fig. 4.6. Math.pow(*x*, *y*) calculates the value of *x* raised to the *y*^th power. The method receives two double arguments and returns a double value. Line 19 performs the calculation $a = p(1 + r)^n$, where *a* is amount, *p* is principal, *r* is rate and *n* is year. Note that the Math class is defined in package java.lang, which is imported automatically, so you do not need to import class Math to use it.

Note that the body of the for statement contains the calculation 1.0 + rate, which appears as an argument to the Math.pow method. In fact, this calculation produces the same result each time through the loop, so repeating it every iteration of the loop is wasteful.

Performance Tip 4.2
In loops, avoid calculations for which the result never changes—such calculations should typically be placed before the loop. [Note: Many of today's sophisticated optimizing compilers will place such calculations outside loops in the compiled code.]

Formatting Floating-Point Numbers
After each calculation, line 22 outputs the year and the amount on deposit at the end of that year. The year is output in a field width of four characters (as specified by %4d). The amount is output as a floating-point number with the format specifier %,20.2f. The **comma (,) formatting flag** indicates that the floating-point value should be output with a **grouping separator**. The actual separator used is specific to the user's locale (i.e., country). For example, in the United States, the number will be output using commas to separate every three digits and a decimal point to separate the fractional part of the number, as in 1,234.45. The number 20 in the format specification indicates that the value should be output right justified in a field width of 20 characters. The .2 specifies the formatted number's precision—in this case, the number is rounded to the nearest hundredth and output with two digits to the right of the decimal point.

A Warning about Displaying Rounded Values
We declared variables amount, principal and rate to be of type double in this example. We are dealing with fractional parts of dollars and thus need a type that allows decimal points in its values. Unfortunately, floating-point numbers can cause trouble. Here is a simple explanation of what can go wrong when using double (or float) to represent dollar

amounts (assuming that dollar amounts are displayed with two digits to the right of the decimal point): Two `double` dollar amounts stored in the machine could be 14.234 (which would normally be rounded to 14.23 for display purposes) and 18.673 (which would normally be rounded to 18.67 for display purposes). When these amounts are added, they produce the internal sum 32.907, which would normally be rounded to 32.91 for display purposes. Thus, your output could appear as

```
     14.23
  + 18.67
  -------
     32.91
```

but a person adding the individual numbers as displayed would expect the sum to be 32.90. You've been warned!

Error-Prevention Tip 4.5

Do not use variables of type double *(or* float*) to perform precise monetary calculations. The imprecision of floating-point numbers can cause errors. In the exercises, you'll learn how to use integers to perform precise monetary calculations. Java also provides class* java.math.BigDecimal *to perform precise monetary calculations. For more information, see* java.sun.com/javase/6/docs/api/java/math/BigDecimal.html.

4.5 do...while Repetition Statement

The **do...while repetition statement** is similar to the `while` statement. In the `while`, the program tests the loop-continuation condition at the beginning of the loop, before executing the loop's body; if the condition is false, the body never executes. The do...while statement tests the loop-continuation condition *after* executing the loop's body; therefore, the body always executes at least once. When a do...while statement terminates, execution continues with the next statement in sequence. Figure 4.7 uses a do...while (lines 10–14) to output the numbers 1–10.

```java
1   // Fig. 4.7: DoWhileTest.java
2   // do...while repetition statement.
3
4   public class DoWhileTest
5   {
6      public static void main( String[] args )
7      {
8         int counter = 1; // initialize counter
9
10        do
11        {
12           System.out.printf( "%d  ", counter );
13           ++counter;
14        } while ( counter <= 10 ); // end do...while
15
16        System.out.println(); // outputs a newline
17     } // end main
18  } // end class DoWhileTest
```

Fig. 4.7 | do...while repetition statement. (Part 1 of 2.)

1	2	3	4	5	6	7	8	9	10

Fig. 4.7 | do...while repetition statement. (Part 2 of 2.)

Line 8 declares and initializes control variable counter. Upon entering the do...while statement, line 12 outputs counter's value and line 13 increments counter. Then the program evaluates the loop-continuation test at the bottom of the loop (line 14). If the condition is true, the loop continues from the first body statement in the do...while (line 12). If the condition is false, the loop terminates and the program continues with the next statement after the loop.

Figure 4.8 contains the UML activity diagram for the do...while statement. This diagram makes it clear that the loop-continuation condition is not evaluated until after the loop performs the action state at least once. Compare this activity diagram with that of the while statement (Fig. 3.4).

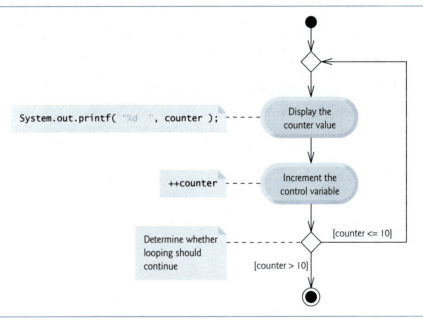

Fig. 4.8 | do...while repetition statement UML activity diagram.

It isn't necessary to use braces in the do...while repetition statement if there's only one statement in the body. However, most programmers include the braces, to avoid confusion between the while and do...while statements. For example,

```
while ( condition )
```

is normally the first line of a while statement. A do...while statement with no braces around a single-statement body appears as:

```
do
    statement
while ( condition );
```

which can be confusing. A reader may misinterpret the last line—while(*condition*);— as a while statement containing an empty statement (the semicolon by itself). Thus, the do...while statement with one body statement is usually written as follows:

```
do
{
    statement
} while ( condition );
```

Good Programming Practice 4.3

Always include braces in a do...while statement, even if they're not necessary. This helps eliminate ambiguity between the while statement and a do...while statement containing only one statement.

4.6 switch Multiple-Selection Statement

Chapter 3 discussed the if single-selection statement and the if...else double-selection statement. The **switch multiple-selection statement** performs different actions based on the possible values of a **constant integral expression** of type byte, short, int or char.

Using a switch Statement to Count A, B, C, D and F Grades

Figure 4.9 calculates the class average of a set of numeric grades entered by the user, and uses a switch statement to determine whether each grade is the equivalent of an A, B, C, D or F and to increment the appropriate grade counter. The program also displays a summary of the number of students who received each grade.

```
1   // Fig. 4.9: LetterGrades.java
2   // LetterGrades class uses switch statement to count letter grades.
3   import java.util.Scanner; // program uses class Scanner
4
5   public class LetterGrades
6   {
7      public static void main( String[] args )
8      {
9         int total = 0; // sum of grades
10        int gradeCounter = 0; // number of grades entered
11        int aCount = 0; // count of A grades
12        int bCount = 0; // count of B grades
13        int cCount = 0; // count of C grades
14        int dCount = 0; // count of D grades
15        int fCount = 0; // count of F grades
16        int grade; // grade entered by user
17
18        Scanner input = new Scanner( System.in );
19
20        System.out.printf( "%s\n%s\n   %s\n   %s\n",
21           "Enter the integer grades in the range 0-100.",
22           "Type the end-of-file indicator to terminate input:",
23           "On UNIX/Linux/Mac OS X type <Ctrl> d then press Enter",
24           "On Windows type <Ctrl> z then press Enter" );
25
```

Fig. 4.9 | LetterGrades class uses switch statement to count letter grades. (Part 1 of 3.)

```
26          // loop until user enters the end-of-file indicator
27          while ( input.hasNext() )
28          {
29             grade = input.nextInt(); // read grade
30             total += grade; // add grade to total
31             ++gradeCounter; // increment number of grades
32
33             //  increment appropriate letter-grade counter
34             switch ( grade / 10 )
35             {
36                case 9:  // grade was between 90
37                case 10: // and 100, inclusive
38                   ++aCount; // increment aCount
39                   break; // necessary to exit switch
40
41                case 8: // grade was between 80 and 89
42                   ++bCount; // increment bCount
43                   break; // exit switch
44
45                case 7: // grade was between 70 and 79
46                   ++cCount; // increment cCount
47                   break; // exit switch
48
49                case 6: // grade was between 60 and 69
50                   ++dCount; // increment dCount
51                   break; // exit switch
52
53                default: // grade was less than 60
54                   ++fCount; // increment fCount
55                   break; // optional; will exit switch anyway
56             } // end switch
57          } // end while
58
59          // display grade report
60          System.out.println( "\nGrade Report:" );
61
62          // if user entered at least one grade...
63          if ( gradeCounter != 0 )
64          {
65             // calculate average of all grades entered
66             double average = (double) total / gradeCounter;
67
68             // output summary of results
69             System.out.printf( "Total of the %d grades entered is %d\n",
70                gradeCounter, total );
71             System.out.printf( "Class average is %.2f\n", average );
72             System.out.printf( "%s\n%s%d\n%s%d\n%s%d\n%s%d\n%s%d\n",
73                "Number of students who received each grade:",
74                "A: ", aCount,    // display number of A grades
75                "B: ", bCount,    // display number of B grades
76                "C: ", cCount,    // display number of C grades
77                "D: ", dCount,    // display number of D grades
78                "F: ", fCount );  // display number of F grades
79          } // end if
```

Fig. 4.9 | LetterGrades class uses switch statement to count letter grades. (Part 2 of 3.)

```
80              else // no grades were entered, so output appropriate message
81                  System.out.println( "No grades were entered" );
82          } // end main
83      } // end class LetterGrades
```

```
Enter the integer grades in the range 0-100.
Type the end-of-file indicator to terminate input:
   On UNIX/Linux/Mac OS X type <Ctrl> d then press Enter
   On Windows type <Ctrl> z then press Enter
99
92
45
57
63
71
76
85
90
100
^Z

Grade Report:
Total of the 10 grades entered is 778
Class average is 77.80
Number of students who received each grade:
A: 4
B: 1
C: 2
D: 1
F: 2
```

Fig. 4.9 | LetterGrades class uses switch statement to count letter grades. (Part 3 of 3.)

Like earlier versions of the class-average program, the main method of class Letter-Grades (Fig. 4.9) declares instance variables total (line 9) and gradeCounter (line 10) to keep track of the sum of the grades entered by the user and the number of grades entered, respectively. Lines 11–15 declare counter variables for each grade category. Note that the variables in lines 9–15 are explicitly initialized to 0.

Method main has two key parts. Lines 27–57 read an arbitrary number of integer grades from the user using sentinel-controlled repetition, update instance variables total and gradeCounter, and increment an appropriate letter-grade counter for each grade entered. Lines 60–81 output a report containing the total of all grades entered, the average of the grades and the number of students who received each letter grade. Let's examine these parts in more detail.

Reading Grades from the User

Line 16 declares variable grade, which will store the user's input. Lines 20–24 prompt the user to enter integer grades and to type the end-of-file indicator to terminate the input. The **end-of-file indicator** is a system-dependent keystroke combination which the user enters to indicate that there is no more data to input. In Chapter 6, Arrays; Introducing Strings and Files, we'll see how the end-of-file indicator is used when a program reads its input from a file.

On UNIX/Linux/Mac OS X systems, end-of-file is entered by typing the sequence

> *<Ctrl> d*

on a line by itself. This notation means to simultaneously press both the *Ctrl* key and the *d* key. On Windows systems, end-of-file can be entered by typing

> *<Ctrl> z*

[*Note:* On some systems, you must press *Enter* after typing the end-of-file key sequence. Also, Windows typically displays the characters ^Z on the screen when the end-of-file indicator is typed, as is shown in the output of Fig. 4.9.]

Portability Tip 4.1
The keystroke combinations for entering end-of-file are system dependent.

The `while` statement (lines 27–57) obtains the user input. The condition at line 27 calls `Scanner` method **`hasNext`** to determine whether there is more data to input. This method returns the `boolean` value `true` if there is more data; otherwise, it returns `false`. The returned value is then used as the value of the condition in the `while` statement. As long as the end-of-file indicator has not been typed, method `hasNext` will return `true`.

Line 29 inputs a grade value from the user. Line 30 uses the += operator to add `grade` to `total`. Line 31 increments `gradeCounter`. These variables are used to compute the average of the grades. Lines 34–56 use a `switch` statement to increment the appropriate letter-grade counter based on the numeric grade entered.

Summarizing the Letter Grades

The `switch` statement (lines 34–56) determines which counter to increment. We assume that the user enters a valid grade in the range 0–100. A grade in the range 90–100 represents A, 80–89 represents B, 70–79 represents C, 60–69 represents D and 0–59 represents F. The `switch` statement consists of a block that contains a sequence of **case labels** and an optional **default case**. These are used in this example to determine which counter to increment based on the grade.

When the flow of control reaches the `switch`, the program evaluates the expression in the parentheses (`grade / 10`) following keyword `switch`. This is the `switch`'s **controlling expression**. The program compares the controlling expression's value (which must evaluate to an integral value of type `byte`, `char`, `short` or `int`) with each `case` label. The controlling expression in line 34 performs integer division, which truncates the fractional part of the result. Thus, when we divide a value from 0 to 100 by 10, the result is always a value from 0 to 10. We use several of these values in our `case` labels. For example, if the user enters the integer 85, the controlling expression evaluates to 8. The `switch` compares 8 with each `case` label. If a match occurs (`case 8:` at line 41), the program executes that `case`'s statements. For the integer 8, line 42 increments bCount, because a grade in the 80s is a B. The **break statement** (line 43) causes program control to proceed with the first statement after the `switch`—in this program, we reach the end of the `while` loop, so control returns to the loop-continuation condition in line 34 to determine whether the loop should continue executing.

The cases in our `switch` explicitly test for the values 10, 9, 8, 7 and 6. Note the cases at lines 36–37 that test for the values 9 and 10 (both of which represent the grade A). Listing cases consecutively in this manner with no statements between them enables the cases to perform the same set of statements—when the controlling expression evaluates to 9 or 10, the statements in lines 38–39 will execute. The switch statement does not provide a mechanism for testing ranges of values, so every value you need to test must be listed in a separate case label. Note that each case can have multiple statements. The switch statement differs from other control statements in that it does not require braces around multiple statements in a case.

Without break statements, each time a match occurs in the switch, the statements for that case and subsequent cases execute until a break statement or the end of the switch is encountered. This is often referred to as "falling through" to the statements in subsequent cases. (This feature is perfect for writing a concise program that displays the iterative song "The Twelve Days of Christmas" in Exercise 4.29.)

Common Programming Error 4.7

Forgetting a break statement when one is needed in a switch is a logic error.

If no match occurs between the controlling expression's value and a case label, the default case (lines 53–55) executes. We use the default case in this example to process all controlling-expression values that are less than 6—that is, all failing grades. If no match occurs and the switch does not contain a default case, program control simply continues with the first statement after the switch.

Displaying the Grade Report

Lines 60–81 output a report based on the grades entered (as shown in the input/output window in Fig. 4.9). Line 63 determines whether the user entered at least one grade—this helps us avoid dividing by zero. If so, line 66 calculates the average of the grades. Lines 69–78 then output the total of all the grades, the class average and the number of students who received each letter grade. If no grades were entered, line 81 outputs an appropriate message. The output in Fig. 4.9 shows a sample grade report based on 10 grades.

switch Statement UML Activity Diagram

Figure 4.10 shows the UML activity diagram for the general switch statement. Most switch statements use a break in each case to terminate the switch statement after processing the case. Figure 4.10 emphasizes this by including break statements in the activity diagram. The diagram makes it clear that the break statement at the end of a case causes control to exit the switch statement immediately.

The break statement is not required for the switch's last case (or the optional default case, when it appears last), because execution continues with the next statement after the switch.

Software Engineering Observation 4.2

Provide a default case in switch statements. Including a default case focuses you on the need to process exceptional conditions.

Good Programming Practice 4.4

Although each case and the default case in a switch can occur in any order, place the default case last. When the default case is listed last, the break for that case is not required.

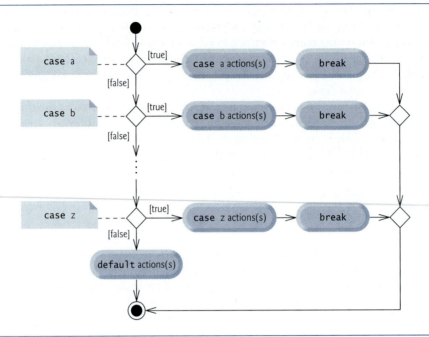

Fig. 4.10 | switch multiple-selection statement UML activity diagram with break statements.

Notes on the Expression in Each *case* of a *switch*

When using the switch statement, remember that each case must contain a constant integral expression—that is, any combination of integer constants that evaluates to a constant integer value (e.g., –7, 0 or 221). An integer constant is simply an integer value. In addition, you can use **character constants**—specific characters in single quotes, such as 'A', '7' or '$'—which represent the integer values of characters. (Appendix B shows the integer values of the characters in the ASCII character set, which is a subset of the Unicode character set used by Java.)

The expression in each case can also be a **constant variable**—a variable that contains a value which does not change for the entire program. Such a variable is declared with keyword final, which is discussed in Chapter 5. Java has a feature called enumerations, which we also present in Chapter 5. Enumeration constants can also be used in case labels. In Chapter 10, Object-Oriented Programming: Polymorphism, we present a more elegant way to implement switch logic—we use a technique called polymorphism to create programs that are often clearer, easier to maintain and easier to extend than programs using switch logic.

4.7 break and continue Statements

In addition to selection and repetition statements, Java provides statements break and **continue** (presented in this section and Appendix O) to alter the flow of control. The preceding section showed how break can be used to terminate a switch statement's execution. This section discusses how to use break in repetition statements.

break *Statement*

The break statement, when executed in a while, for, do...while or switch, causes immediate exit from that statement. Execution continues with the first statement after the control statement. Common uses of the break statement are to escape early from a loop or to skip the remainder of a switch (as in Fig. 4.9). Figure 4.11 demonstrates a break statement exiting a for.

```java
1   // Fig. 4.11: BreakTest.java
2   // break statement exiting a for statement.
3   public class BreakTest
4   {
5      public static void main( String[] args )
6      {
7         int count; // control variable also used after loop terminates
8
9         for ( count = 1; count <= 10; count++ ) // loop 10 times
10        {
11           if ( count == 5 ) // if count is 5,
12              break;          // terminate loop
13
14           System.out.printf( "%d ", count );
15        } // end for
16
17        System.out.printf( "\nBroke out of loop at count = %d\n", count );
18     } // end main
19  } // end class BreakTest
```

```
1 2 3 4
Broke out of loop at count = 5
```

Fig. 4.11 | break statement exiting a for statement.

When the if statement nested at line 11 in the for statement (lines 9–15) detects that count is 5, the break statement at line 12 executes. This terminates the for statement, and the program proceeds to line 17 (immediately after the for statement), which displays a message indicating the value of the control variable when the loop terminated. The loop fully executes its body only four times instead of 10.

continue *Statement*

The continue statement, when executed in a while, for or do...while, skips the remaining statements in the loop body and proceeds with the next iteration of the loop. In while and do...while statements, the program evaluates the loop-continuation test immediately after the continue statement executes. In a for statement, the increment expression executes, then the program evaluates the loop-continuation test.

Figure 4.12 uses the continue statement to skip the statement at line 12 when the nested if (line 9) determines that count's value is 5. When the continue statement executes, program control continues with the increment of the control variable in the for statement (line 7).

```java
1  // Fig. 4.12: ContinueTest.java
2  // continue statement terminating an iteration of a for statement.
3  public class ContinueTest
4  {
5     public static void main( String[] args )
6     {
7        for ( int count = 1; count <= 10; count++ ) // loop 10 times
8        {
9           if ( count == 5 ) // if count is 5,
10             continue; // skip remaining code in loop
11
12          System.out.printf( "%d ", count );
13       } // end for
14
15       System.out.println( "\nUsed continue to skip printing 5" );
16    } // end main
17 } // end class ContinueTest
```

```
1 2 3 4 6 7 8 9 10
Used continue to skip printing 5
```

Fig. 4.12 | continue statement terminating an iteration of a for statement.

In Section 4.3, we stated that while could be used in most cases in place of for. This is not the case when the increment expression in the while follows a continue statement. In this case, the increment does not execute before the program evaluates the repetition-continuation condition, so the while does not execute in the same manner as the for.

Software Engineering Observation 4.3

Some programmers feel that break and continue violate structured programming. Since the same effects are achievable with structured programming techniques, these programmers do not use break or continue.

Software Engineering Observation 4.4

There is a tension between achieving quality software engineering and achieving the best-performing software. Often, one of these goals is achieved at the expense of the other. For all but the most performance-intensive situations, apply the following rule of thumb: First, make your code simple and correct; then make it fast and small, but only if necessary.

4.8 Logical Operators

The if, if...else, while, do...while and for statements each require a condition to determine how to continue a program's flow of control. So far, we've studied only simple conditions, such as count <= 10, number != sentinelValue and total > 1000. Simple conditions are expressed in terms of the relational operators >, <, >= and <= and the equality operators == and !=, and each expression tests only one condition. To test multiple conditions in the process of making a decision, we performed these tests in separate statements or in nested if or if...else statements. Sometimes, control statements require more complex conditions to determine a program's flow of control.

Java's **logical operators** enable you to form more complex conditions by combining simple conditions. The logical operators are && (conditional AND), || (conditional OR), & (boolean logical AND), | (boolean logical inclusive OR), ∧ (boolean logical exclusive OR) and ! (logical NOT). [*Note:* The &, | and ∧ operators are also bitwise operators when they're applied to integral operands. We discuss the bitwise operators in Appendix N.]

Conditional AND (&&) Operator

Suppose we wish to ensure at some point in a program that two conditions are *both* true before we choose a certain path of execution. In this case, we can use the && (**conditional AND**) operator, as follows:

```
if ( gender == FEMALE && age >= 65 )
    ++seniorFemales;
```

This if statement contains two simple conditions. The condition gender == FEMALE compares variable gender to the constant FEMALE to determine whether a person is female. The condition age >= 65 might be evaluated to determine whether a person is a senior citizen. The if statement considers the combined condition

```
gender == FEMALE && age >= 65
```

which is true if and only if both simple conditions are true. In this case, the if statement's body increments seniorFemales by 1. If either or both of the simple conditions are false, the program skips the increment. Some programmers find that the preceding combined condition is more readable when redundant parentheses are added, as in:

```
( gender == FEMALE ) && ( age >= 65 )
```

The table in Fig. 4.13 summarizes the && operator. The table shows all four possible combinations of false and true values for *expression1* and *expression2*. Such tables are called **truth tables**. Java evaluates to false or true all expressions that include relational operators, equality operators or logical operators.

expression1	expression2	expression1 && expression2
false	false	false
false	true	false
true	false	false
true	true	true

Fig. 4.13 | && (conditional AND) operator truth table.

Conditional OR (||) Operator

Now suppose we wish to ensure that either *or* both of two conditions are true before we choose a certain path of execution. In this case, we use the || (**conditional OR**) operator, as in the following program segment:

```
if ( ( semesterAverage >= 90 ) || ( finalExam >= 90 ) )
    System.out.println ( "Student grade is A" );
```

This statement also contains two simple conditions. The condition semesterAverage >= 90 evaluates to determine whether the student deserves an A in the course because of a solid performance throughout the semester. The condition `finalExam >= 90` evaluates to determine whether the student deserves an A in the course because of an outstanding performance on the final exam. The `if` statement then considers the combined condition

`( semesterAverage >= 90 ) || ( finalExam >= 90 )`

and awards the student an A if either or both of the simple conditions are true. The only time the message `"Student grade is A"` is *not* printed is when both of the simple conditions are false. Figure 4.14 is a truth table for operator conditional OR (`||`). Operator `&&` has a higher precedence than operator `||`. Both operators associate from left to right.

expression1	expression2	expression1 || expression2
false	false	false
false	true	true
true	false	true
true	true	true

Fig. 4.14 | `||` (conditional OR) operator truth table.

Short-Circuit Evaluation of Complex Conditions

The parts of an expression containing `&&` or `||` operators are evaluated only until it's known whether the condition is true or false. Thus, evaluation of the expression

`( gender == FEMALE ) && ( age >= 65 )`

stops immediately if `gender` is not equal to `FEMALE` (i.e., the entire expression is `false`) and continues if `gender` *is* equal to `FEMALE` (i.e., the entire expression could still be `true` if the condition `age >= 65` is true). This feature of conditional AND and conditional OR expressions is called **short-circuit evaluation**.

Common Programming Error 4.8

In expressions using operator &&, a condition—we'll call this the dependent condition—may require another condition to be true for the evaluation of the dependent condition to be meaningful. In this case, the dependent condition should be placed after the other condition, or an error might occur. For example, in the expression (i != 0) && (10 / i == 2), the second condition must appear after the first condition, or a divide-by-zero error might occur.

Boolean Logical AND (&) and Boolean Logical Inclusive OR (|) Operators

The **boolean logical AND (&)** and **boolean logical inclusive OR (|)** operators are identical to the `&&` and `||` operators, except that the `&` and `|` operators *always* evaluate both of their operands (i.e., they do not perform short-circuit evaluation). So, the expression

`( gender == 1 ) & ( age >= 65 )`

evaluates `age >= 65` regardless of whether `gender` is equal to 1. This is useful if the right operand of the boolean logical AND or boolean logical inclusive OR operator has a required **side effect**—a modification of a variable's value. For example, the expression

`( birthday == true ) | ( ++age >= 65 )`

guarantees that the condition ++age >= 65 will be evaluated. Thus, the variable age is incremented, regardless of whether the overall expression is true or false.

Error-Prevention Tip 4.6

For clarity, avoid expressions with side effects in conditions. The side effects may look clever, but they can make it harder to understand code and can lead to subtle logic errors.

Boolean Logical Exclusive OR (^)

A simple condition containing the **boolean logical exclusive OR** (^) operator is true *if and only if one of its operands is* true *and the other is* false. If both are true or both are false, the entire condition is false. Figure 4.15 is a truth table for the boolean logical exclusive OR operator (^). This operator is guaranteed to evaluate both of its operands.

expression1	expression2	expression1 ^ expression2
false	false	false
false	true	true
true	false	true
true	true	false

Fig. 4.15 | ^ (boolean logical exclusive OR) operator truth table.

Logical Negation (!) Operator

The ! (**logical NOT**, also called **logical negation** or **logical complement**) operator "reverses" a condition's meaning. Unlike the binary logical operators &&, ||, &, | and ^, which combine two conditions, the unary logical negation operator has only a single condition as an operand. The operator is placed before a condition to choose a path of execution if the original condition (without the logical negation operator) is false, as in

```
if ( ! ( grade == sentinelValue ) )
    System.out.printf( "The next grade is %d\n", grade );
```

which executes the printf call only if grade is not equal to sentinelValue. The parentheses around the condition grade == sentinelValue are needed because the logical negation operator has a higher precedence than the equality operator.

You can avoid using logical negation by expressing the condition with an appropriate relational or equality operator. For example, the previous statement may also be written as:

```
if ( grade != sentinelValue )
    System.out.printf( "The next grade is %d\n", grade );
```

This flexibility can help you express a condition in a more convenient manner. Figure 4.16 is a truth table for the logical negation operator.

expression	!expression
false	true
true	false

Fig. 4.16 | ! (logical negation, or logical NOT) operator truth table.

Logical Operators Example

Figure 4.17 produces the truth tables discussed in this section. The output shows the boolean expression that was evaluated and its result. Note that we used the **%b format specifier** to display the word "true" or the word "false" based on a boolean expression's value. Lines 9–13 produce the truth table for &&. Lines 16–20 produce the truth table for ||. Lines 23–27 produce the truth table for &. Lines 30–35 produce the truth table for |. Lines 38–43 produce the truth table for ^. Lines 46–47 produce the truth table for !.

```
 1   // Fig. 4.17: LogicalOperators.java
 2   // Logical operators.
 3
 4   public class LogicalOperators
 5   {
 6      public static void main( String[] args )
 7      {
 8         // create truth table for && (conditional AND) operator
 9         System.out.printf( "%s\n%s: %b\n%s: %b\n%s: %b\n%s: %b\n\n",
10            "Conditional AND (&&)", "false && false", ( false && false ),
11            "false && true", ( false && true ),
12            "true && false", ( true && false ),
13            "true && true", ( true && true ) );
14
15         // create truth table for || (conditional OR) operator
16         System.out.printf( "%s\n%s: %b\n%s: %b\n%s: %b\n%s: %b\n\n",
17            "Conditional OR (||)", "false || false", ( false || false ),
18            "false || true", ( false || true ),
19            "true || false", ( true || false ),
20            "true || true", ( true || true ) );
21
22         // create truth table for & (boolean logical AND) operator
23         System.out.printf( "%s\n%s: %b\n%s: %b\n%s: %b\n%s: %b\n\n",
24            "Boolean logical AND (&)", "false & false", ( false & false ),
25            "false & true", ( false & true ),
26            "true & false", ( true & false ),
27            "true & true", ( true & true ) );
28
29         // create truth table for | (boolean logical inclusive OR) operator
30         System.out.printf( "%s\n%s: %b\n%s: %b\n%s: %b\n%s: %b\n\n",
31            "Boolean logical inclusive OR (|)",
32            "false | false", ( false | false ),
33            "false | true", ( false | true ),
34            "true | false", ( true | false ),
35            "true | true", ( true | true ) );
36
37         // create truth table for ^ (boolean logical exclusive OR) operator
38         System.out.printf( "%s\n%s: %b\n%s: %b\n%s: %b\n%s: %b\n\n",
39            "Boolean logical exclusive OR (^)",
40            "false ^ false", ( false ^ false ),
41            "false ^ true", ( false ^ true ),
42            "true ^ false", ( true ^ false ),
43            "true ^ true", ( true ^ true ) );
44
```

Fig. 4.17 | Logical operators. (Part 1 of 2.)

```
45        // create truth table for ! (logical negation) operator
46        System.out.printf( "%s\n%s: %b\n%s: %b\n", "Logical NOT (!)",
47           "!false", ( !false ), "!true", ( !true ) );
48     } // end main
49  } // end class LogicalOperators
```

```
Conditional AND (&&)
false && false: false
false && true: false
true && false: false
true && true: true

Conditional OR (||)
false || false: false
false || true: true
true || false: true
true || true: true

Boolean logical AND (&)
false & false: false
false & true: false
true & false: false
true & true: true

Boolean logical inclusive OR (|)
false | false: false
false | true: true
true | false: true
true | true: true

Boolean logical exclusive OR (^)
false ^ false: false
false ^ true: true
true ^ false: true
true ^ true: false

Logical NOT (!)
!false: true
!true: false
```

Fig. 4.17 | Logical operators. (Part 2 of 2.)

Figure 4.18 shows the precedence and associativity of the Java operators introduced so far. The operators are shown from top to bottom in decreasing order of precedence.

Operators	Associativity	Type
++ --	right to left	unary postfix
++ -- + - ! (*type*)	right to left	unary prefix
* / %	left to right	multiplicative
+ -	left to right	additive
< <= > >=	left to right	relational
== !=	left to right	equality

Fig. 4.18 | Precedence/associativity of the operators discussed so far. (Part 1 of 2.)

Operators	Associativity	Type
&	left to right	boolean logical AND
^	left to right	boolean logical exclusive OR
|	left to right	boolean logical inclusive OR
&&	left to right	conditional AND
||	left to right	conditional OR
?:	right to left	conditional
= += -= *= /= %=	right to left	assignment

Fig. 4.18 | Precedence/associativity of the operators discussed so far. (Part 2 of 2.)

4.9 Structured Programming Summary

Just as architects design buildings by employing the collective wisdom of their profession, so should programmers design programs. Our field is much younger than architecture, and our collective wisdom is considerably sparser. We've learned that structured programming produces programs that are easier than unstructured programs to understand, test, debug, modify and even prove correct in a mathematical sense.

Figure 4.19 uses UML activity diagrams to summarize Java's control statements. The initial and final states indicate the single entry point and the single exit point of each control statement. Arbitrarily connecting individual symbols in an activity diagram can lead to unstructured programs. Therefore, the programming profession has chosen a limited set of control statements that can be combined in only two simple ways to build structured programs.

For simplicity, Java includes only single-entry/single-exit control statements—there is only one way to enter and only one way to exit each control statement. Connecting control statements in sequence to form structured programs is simple. The final state of one control statement is connected to the initial state of the next—that is, the control statements are placed one after another in a program in sequence. We call this control-statement stacking. The rules for forming structured programs also allow for control statements to be nested.

Figure 4.20 shows the rules for forming structured programs. The rules assume that action states may be used to indicate any action. The rules also assume that we begin with the simplest activity diagram (Fig. 4.21) consisting of only an initial state, an action state, a final state and transition arrows.

Applying the rules in Fig. 4.20 always results in a properly structured activity diagram with a neat, building-block appearance. For example, repeatedly applying rule 2 to the simplest activity diagram results in an activity diagram containing many action states in sequence (Fig. 4.22). Rule 2 generates a stack of control statements, so let's call rule 2 the **stacking rule**. [*Note:* The vertical dashed lines in Fig. 4.22 are not part of the UML. We use them to separate the four activity diagrams that demonstrate rule 2 of Fig. 4.20 being applied.]

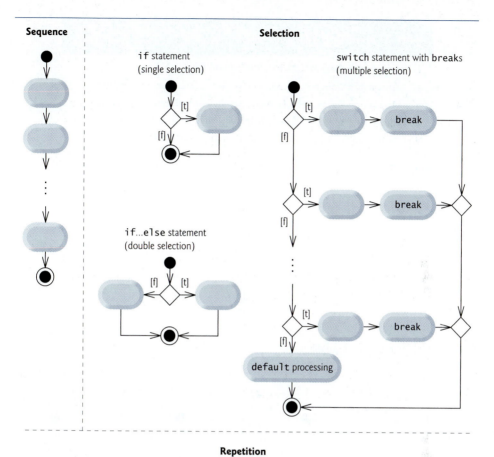

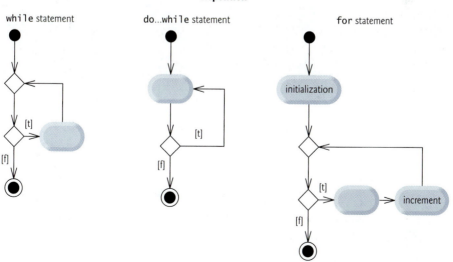

Fig. 4.19 | Java's single-entry/single-exit sequence, selection and repetition statements.

> ### Rules for forming structured programs
>
> 1. Begin with the simplest activity diagram (Fig. 4.21).
> 2. Any action state can be replaced by two action states in sequence.
> 3. Any action state can be replaced by any control statement (sequence of action states, if, if...else, switch, while, do...while or for).
> 4. Rules 2 and 3 can be applied as often as you like and in any order.

Fig. 4.20 | Rules for forming structured programs.

Fig. 4.21 | Simplest activity diagram.

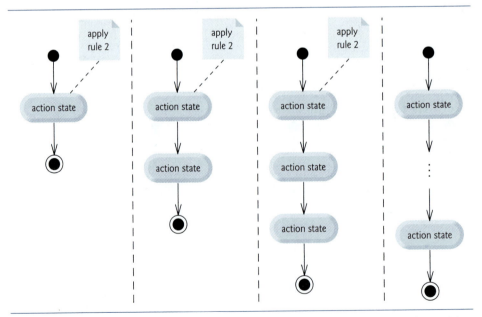

Fig. 4.22 | Repeatedly applying the stacking rule (rule 2) of Fig. 4.20 to the simplest activity diagram.

Rule 3 is called the **nesting rule**. Repeatedly applying rule 3 to the simplest activity diagram results in an activity diagram with neatly nested control statements. For example, in Fig. 4.23, the action state in the simplest activity diagram is replaced with a double-selection (if...else) statement. Then rule 3 is applied again to the action states in the double-selection statement, replacing each with a double-selection statement. The dashed action-state symbol around each double-selection statement represents the action state that was replaced. [*Note:* The dashed arrows and dashed action-state symbols shown in Fig. 4.23 are not part of the UML. They're used here to illustrate that any action state can be replaced with a control statement.]

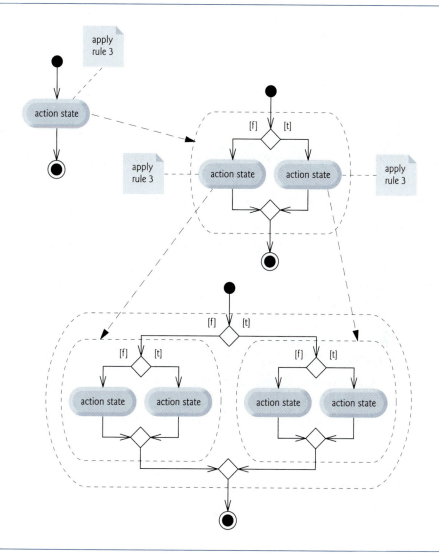

Fig. 4.23 | Repeatedly applying the nesting rule (rule 3) of Fig. 4.20 to the simplest activity diagram.

Rule 4 generates larger, more involved and more deeply nested statements. The diagrams that emerge from applying the rules in Fig. 4.20 constitute the set of all possible structured activity diagrams and hence the set of all possible structured programs. The beauty of the structured approach is that we use only seven simple single-entry/single-exit control statements and assemble them in only two simple ways.

If the rules in Fig. 4.20 are followed, an "unstructured' activity diagram (like the one in Fig. 4.24) cannot be created. If you are uncertain about whether a particular diagram is structured, apply the rules of Fig. 4.20 in reverse to reduce the diagram to the simplest activity diagram. If you can reduce it, the original diagram is structured; otherwise, it's not.

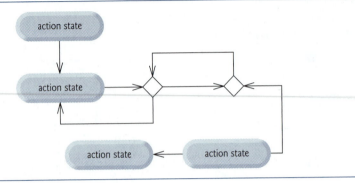

Fig. 4.24 | "Unstructured" activity diagram.

Structured programming promotes simplicity. Bohm and Jacopini have given us the result that only three forms of control are needed to implement an algorithm:

- Sequence
- Selection
- Repetition

The sequence structure is trivial. Simply list the statements to execute in the order in which they should execute. Selection is implemented in one of three ways:

- `if` statement (single selection)
- `if...else` statement (double selection)
- `switch` statement (multiple selection)

In fact, it's straightforward to prove that the simple `if` statement is sufficient to provide any form of selection—everything that can be done with the `if...else` statement and the `switch` statement can be implemented by combining `if` statements (although perhaps not as clearly and efficiently).

Repetition is implemented in one of three ways:

- `while` statement
- `do...while` statement
- `for` statement

[*Note:* There is a fourth repetition statement—the enhanced `for` statement—that we discuss in Section 6.6.] It's straightforward to prove that the `while` statement is sufficient to provide any form of repetition. Everything that can be done with `do...while` and `for` can be done with the `while` statement (although perhaps not as conveniently).

Combining these results illustrates that any form of control ever needed in a Java program can be expressed in terms of

- sequence
- `if` statement (selection)
- `while` statement (repetition)

and that these can be combined in only two ways—stacking and nesting. Indeed, structured programming is the essence of simplicity.

4.10 (Optional) GUI and Graphics Case Study: Drawing Rectangles and Ovals

Our next program (Fig. 4.25) demonstrates drawing rectangles and ovals, using the Graphics methods **drawRect** and **drawOval**, respectively. Method paintComponent (lines 10–21) performs the actual drawing. Remember, the first statement in every paintComponent method must be a call to super.paintComponent, as in line 12. Lines 14–20 loop 10 times to draw 10 rectangles and 10 ovals.

```java
 1   // Fig. 4.25: Shapes.java
 2   // Demonstrates drawing different shapes.
 3   import java.awt.Graphics;
 4   import javax.swing.JPanel;
 5   import javax.swing.JFrame;
 6
 7   public class Shapes extends JPanel
 8   {
 9      // draws a cascade of shapes starting from the top-left corner
10      public void paintComponent( Graphics g )
11      {
12         super.paintComponent( g );
13
14         for ( int i = 0; i < 10; i++ )
15         {
16            g.drawRect( 10 + i * 10, 10 + i * 10,
17               50 + i * 10, 50 + i * 10 );
18            g.drawOval( 240 + i * 10, 10 + i * 10,
19               50 + i * 10, 50 + i * 10 );
20         } // end for
21      } // end method paintComponent
22
23      public static void main( String[] args )
24      {
25         Shapes panel = new Shapes(); // create the panel
26         JFrame application = new JFrame(); // creates a new JFrame
27
28         application.setDefaultCloseOperation( JFrame.EXIT_ON_CLOSE );
29         application.add( panel ); // add the panel to the frame
30         application.setSize( 500, 290 ); // set the desired size
31         application.setVisible( true ); // show the frame
32      } // end main
33   } // end class Shapes
```

Fig. 4.25 | Drawing a cascade of shapes based on the user's choice. (Part 1 of 2.)

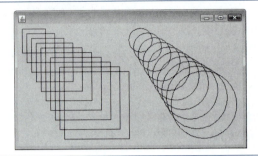

Fig. 4.25 | Drawing a cascade of shapes based on the user's choice. (Part 2 of 2.)

Lines 16–17 call Graphics method drawRect, which requires four arguments. The first two represent the *x*- and *y*-coordinates of the upper-left corner of the rectangle; the next two represent the rectangle's width and height. In this example, we start at a position 10 pixels down and 10 pixels right of the top-left corner, and every iteration of the loop moves the upper-left corner another 10 pixels down and to the right. The width and the height of the rectangle start at 50 pixels and increase by 10 pixels in each iteration.

Lines 18–19 in the loop draw ovals. Method drawOval creates an imaginary rectangle called a **bounding rectangle** and places inside it an oval that touches the midpoints of all four sides. The method's four arguments represent the *x*- and *y*-coordinates of the upper-left corner of the bounding rectangle and the bounding rectangle's width and height. The values passed to drawOval in this example are exactly the same as those passed to drawRect in lines 16–17, except that the first oval's bounding box has an *x*-coordinate that starts 240 pixels from the left side of the panel. Since the width and height of the bounding rectangle are identical in this example, lines 18–19 draw a circle. As an exercise, modify the program to draw both rectangles and ovals with the same arguments. This will allow you to see how each oval touches all four sides of the corresponding rectangle.

Line 25 in main creates a Shapes object. Lines 26–31 perform the standard operations that create and set up a window in this case study—create a frame, set it to exit the application when closed, add the drawing to the frame, set the frame size and make it visible.

GUI and Graphics Case Study Exercises

4.1 Draw 12 concentric circles in the center of a JPanel (Fig. 4.26). The innermost circle should have a radius of 10 pixels, and each successive circle should have a radius 10 pixels larger than

Fig. 4.26 | Drawing concentric circles.

the previous one. Begin by finding the center of the JPanel. To get the upper-left corner of a circle, move up one radius and to the left one radius from the center. The width and height of the bounding rectangle are both the same as the circle's diameter (i.e., twice the radius).

4.11 Wrap-Up

In this chapter, we completed our introduction to Java's control statements, which enable you to control the flow of execution in methods. Chapter 3 discussed Java's if, if...else and while statements. The current chapter demonstrated the for, do...while and switch control statements. We showed that any algorithm can be developed using combinations of the sequence structure (i.e., statements listed in the order in which they should execute), the three types of selection statements—if, if...else and switch—and the three types of repetition statements—while, do...while and for. In this chapter and Chapter 3, we discussed how you can combine these building blocks to utilize proven program-construction and problem-solving techniques. This chapter also introduced Java's logical operators, which enable you to use more complex conditional expressions in control statements.

Chapter 3 and Chapter 4 introduced the types of control statements that you can use to specify program logic. In Chapter 5, we examine methods in depth.

Summary

Section 4.2 Essentials of Counter-Controlled Repetition
- Counter-controlled repetition requires a control variable (or loop counter), the initial value of the control variable, the increment (or decrement) by which the control variable is modified each time through the loop (also known as each iteration of the loop) and the loop-continuation condition that determines whether looping should continue.
- You can declare a variable and initialize it in the same statement.

Section 4.3 *for Repetition Statement*
- The while statement can be used to implement any counter-controlled loop.
- The for statement specifies the details of counter-controlled repetition in a single line of code.
- When the for statement begins executing, its control variable is declared and initialized. Next, the program checks the loop-continuation condition. If the condition is initially true, the body executes. After executing the loop's body, the increment expression executes. Then the loop-continuation test is performed again to determine whether the program should continue with the next iteration of the loop.
- The general format of the for statement is

      for (*initialization*; *loopContinuationCondition*; *increment*)
          statement

where the *initialization* expression names the loop's control variable and provides its initial value, *loopContinuationCondition* determines whether the loop should continue executing and *increment* modifies the control variable's value, so that the loop-continuation condition eventually becomes false. The two semicolons in the for header are required.

- Most `for` statements can be represented with equivalent `while` statements as follows:

  initialization;
  `while` (*loopContinuationCondition*)
  {
      statement
      increment;
  }

- Typically, `for` statements are used for counter-controlled repetition and `while` statements for sentinel-controlled repetition.

- If the *initialization* expression in the `for` header declares the control variable, the control variable can be used only in that `for` statement—it will not exist outside the `for` statement.

- The expressions in a `for` header are optional. If the *loopContinuationCondition* is omitted, Java assumes that it's always true, thus creating an infinite loop. You might omit the *initialization* expression if the control variable is initialized before the loop. You might omit the *increment* expression if the increment is calculated with statements in the loop's body or if no increment is needed.

- The increment expression in a `for` acts as if it's a standalone statement at the end of the `for`'s body.

- A `for` statement can count downward by using a negative increment (i.e., a decrement).

- If the loop-continuation condition is initially `false`, the program does not execute the `for` statement's body. Instead, execution proceeds with the statement following the `for`.

Section 4.4 Examples Using the `for` Statement
- Java treats floating-point constants like `1000.0` and `0.05` as type `double`. Similarly, Java treats whole-number constants like `7` and `-22` as type `int`.

- The format specifier `%4s` outputs a `String` in a field width of 4—that is, `printf` displays the value with at least 4 character positions. If the value to be output is less than 4 character positions wide, the value is right justified in the field by default. If the value is greater than 4 character positions wide, the field width expands to accommodate the appropriate number of characters. To left justify the value, use a negative integer to specify the field width.

- `Math.pow(x, y)` calculates the value of x raised to the yth power. The method receives two `double` arguments and returns a `double` value.

- The comma (`,`) formatting flag in a format specifier (e.g., `%,20.2f`) indicates that a floating-point value should be output with a grouping separator. The actual separator used is specific to the user's locale (i.e., country). In the United States, the number will have commas separating every three digits and a decimal point separating the fractional part of the number, as in 1,234.45.

- The `.` in a format specifier (e.g., `%,20.2f`) indicates that the integer to its right is the number's precision.

Section 4.5 do…while Repetition Statement
- The `do…while` statement is similar to the `while` statement. In the `while`, the program tests the loop-continuation condition at the beginning of the loop, before executing its body; if the condition is false, the body never executes. The `do…while` statement tests the loop-continuation condition *after* executing the loop's body; therefore, the body always executes at least once.

- It's not necessary to use braces in the `do…while` repetition statement if there is only one statement in the body. Most programmers include the braces, to avoid confusion between the `while` and `do…while` statements.

Section 4.6 switch Multiple-Selection Statement
- The `switch` statement performs different actions based on the possible values of a constant integral expression (i.e., a constant value of type `byte`, `short`, `int` or `char`, but not `long`).

- The end-of-file indicator is a system-dependent keystroke combination that terminates user input. On UNIX/Linux/Mac OS X systems, end-of-file is entered by typing the sequence *<Ctrl> d* on a line by itself. This notation means to simultaneously press both the *Ctrl* key and the *d* key. On Windows systems, enter end-of-file by typing *<Ctrl> z*.

- `Scanner` method `hasNext` determines whether there is more data to input. This method returns the `boolean` value `true` if there is more data; otherwise, it returns `false`. As long as the end-of-file indicator has not been typed, method `hasNext` will return `true`.

- The `switch` statement consists of a block that contains a sequence of `case` labels and an optional `default` case.

- When the flow of control reaches a `switch`, the program evaluates the `switch`'s controlling expression and compares its value with each `case` label. If a match occurs, the program executes the statements for that `case`.

- Listing cases consecutively with no statements between them enables the cases to perform the same set of statements.

- Every value you wish to test in a `switch` must be listed in a separate `case` label.

- Each `case` can have multiple statements, and these are not required to be placed in braces.

- Without `break` statements, each time a match occurs in the `switch`, the statements for that case and subsequent cases execute until a `break` statement or the end of the `switch` is encountered.

- If no match occurs between the controlling expression's value and a `case` label, the optional `default` case executes. If no match occurs and the `switch` does not contain a `default` case, program control simply continues with the first statement after the `switch`.

Section 4.7 **break** *and* `continue` *Statements*

- The `break` statement, when executed in a `while`, `for`, `do...while` or `switch`, causes immediate exit from that statement. Execution continues with the first statement after the control statement.

- The `continue` statement, when executed in a `while`, `for` or `do...while`, skips the remaining statements in the loop body and proceeds with the next iteration of the loop. In `while` and `do...while` statements, the program evaluates the loop-continuation test immediately. In a `for` statement, the increment expression executes, then the program evaluates the loop-continuation test.

Section 4.8 *Logical Operators*

- Simple conditions are expressed in terms of the relational operators >, <, >= and <= and the equality operators == and !=, and each expression tests only one condition.

- Logical operators enable you to form more complex conditions by combining simple conditions. The logical operators are && (conditional AND), || (conditional OR), & (boolean logical AND), | (boolean logical inclusive OR), ∧ (boolean logical exclusive OR) and ! (logical NOT).

- To ensure that two conditions are *both* true, use the && (conditional AND) operator. If either or both of the simple conditions are false, the entire expression is false.

- To ensure that either *or* both of two conditions are true, use the || (conditional OR) operator, which evaluates to true if either or both of its simple conditions are true.

- A condition using && or || operators uses short-circuit evaluation—they're evaluated only until it's known whether the condition is true or false.

- The boolean logical AND (&) and boolean logical inclusive OR (|) operators work identically to the && (conditional AND) and || (conditional OR) operators, but always evaluate both operands.

- A simple condition containing the boolean logical exclusive OR (∧) operator is `true` *if and only if one of its operands is* `true` *and the other is* `false`. If both operands are `true` or both are `false`, the entire condition is `false`. This operator is also guaranteed to evaluate both of its operands.

- The unary ! (logical NOT) operator "reverses" the value of a condition.

Terminology

^, boolean logical exclusive OR operator 147	end-of-file indicator 139
!, logical NOT operator (also called logical negation or logical complement) 147	field width (formatted output) 133
	for repetition statement 127
&, boolean logical AND operator 146	for statement header 128
&&, conditional AND operator 145	grouping separator (formatted output) 134
%b format specifier 148	hasNext method of class Scanner 140
|, boolean logical inclusive OR operator 146	increment a control variable 125
||, conditional OR operator 145	initial value of a control variable 125
boolean logical AND (&) operator 146	iteration of a loop 125
boolean logical exclusive OR (^) operator 147	left justified (formatted output) 133
boolean logical inclusive OR (|) operator 146	logical NOT (!) operator (also called logical negation or logical complement) 147
break statement 140	
case label 140	logical operators 145
character constant 142	loop-continuation condition 125
comma (,) formatting flag (formatted output) 134	minus sign (-) formatting flag (formatted output) 133
conditional AND (&&) operator 145	nesting rule (control statements) 152
conditional OR (||) operator 145	off-by-one error 128
constant integral expression 137	pow method of class Math 134
constant variable 142	right justified (formatted output) 133
continue statement 142	scope of a variable 129
control variable 125	short-circuit evaluation 146
controlling expression of a switch 140	side effect of an expression 146
decrement a control variable 125	stacking rule (control statements) 150
default case in a switch 140	switch multiple-selection statement 137
do...while repetition statement 135	truth table 145

Self-Review Exercises

4.1 Fill in the blanks in each of the following statements:

a) Typically, _____ statements are used for counter-controlled repetition and _____ statements for sentinel-controlled repetition.

b) The do...while statement tests the loop-continuation condition _____ executing the loop's body; therefore, the body always executes at least once.

c) The _____ statement selects among multiple actions based on the possible values of an integer variable or expression.

d) The _____ statement, when executed in a repetition statement, skips the remaining statements in the loop body and proceeds with the next iteration of the loop.

e) The _____ operator can be used to ensure that two conditions are *both* true before choosing a certain path of execution.

f) If the loop-continuation condition in a for header is initially _____, the program does not execute the for statement's body.

g) Methods that perform common tasks and do not require objects are called _____ methods.

4.2 State whether each of the following is *true* or *false*. If *false*, explain why.

a) The default case is required in the switch selection statement.

b) The break statement is required in the last case of a switch selection statement.

c) The expression ((x > y) && (a < b)) is true if either x > y is true or a < b is true.

d) An expression containing the || operator is true if either or both of its operands are true.

e) The comma (,) formatting flag in a format specifier (e.g., %,20.2f) indicates that a value should be output with a thousands separator.

f) To test for a range of values in a switch statement, use a hyphen (-) between the start and end values of the range in a case label.

g) Listing cases consecutively with no statements between them enables the cases to perform the same set of statements.

4.3   Write a Java statement or a set of Java statements to accomplish each of the following tasks:

a) Sum the odd integers between 1 and 99, using a for statement. Assume that the integer variables sum and count have been declared.

b) Calculate the value of 2.5 raised to the power of 3, using the pow method.

c) Print the integers from 1 to 20, using a while loop and the counter variable i. Assume that the variable i has been declared, but not initialized. Print only five integers per line. [*Hint:* Use the calculation i % 5. When the value of this expression is 0, print a newline character; otherwise, print a tab character. Assume that this code is an application. Use the System.out.println() method to output the newline character, and use the System.out.print('\t') method to output the tab character.]

d) Repeat part (c), using a for statement.

4.4   Find the error in each of the following code segments, and explain how to correct it:

a)
```java
i = 1;

while ( i <= 10 );
    i++;
}
```

b)
```java
for ( k = 0.1; k != 1.0; k += 0.1 )
    System.out.println( k );
```

c)
```java
switch ( n )
{
    case 1:
        System.out.println( "The number is 1" );
    case 2:
        System.out.println( "The number is 2" );
        break;
    default:
        System.out.println( "The number is not 1 or 2" );
        break;
}
```

d) The following code should print the values 1 to 10:
```java
n = 1;
while ( n < 10 )
    System.out.println( n++ );
```

Answers to Self-Review Exercises

4.1   a) for, while. b) after. c) switch. d) continue. e) && (conditional AND). f) false. g) static.

4.2   a) False. The default case is optional. If no default action is needed, then there is no need for a default case. b) False. The break statement is used to exit the switch statement. The break statement is not required for the last case in a switch statement. c) False. Both of the relational expressions must be true for the entire expression to be true when using the && operator. d) True. e) True. f) False. The switch statement does not provide a mechanism for testing ranges of values, so every value that must be tested should be listed in a separate case label. g) True.

4.3   a) ```
sum = 0;
for (count = 1; count <= 99; count += 2)
    sum += count;
```
   b)  ```
double result = Math.pow( 2.5, 3 );
```
   c) ```
i = 1;

while (i <= 20)
{
   System.out.print(i);

   if (i % 5 == 0)
      System.out.println();
   else
      System.out.print('\t');

   ++i;
}
```
   d)  ```
for ( i = 1; i <= 20; i++ )
{
   System.out.print( i );

   if ( i % 5 == 0 )
      System.out.println();
   else
      System.out.print( '\t' );
}
```

4.4   a) Error: The semicolon after the `while` header causes an infinite loop, and there is a missing left brace.
Correction: Replace the semicolon by a {, or remove both the ; and the }.
   b) Error: Using a floating-point number to control a `for` statement may not work, because floating-point numbers are represented only approximately by most computers.
Correction: Use an integer, and perform the proper calculation in order to get the values you desire:

```
for ( k = 1; k != 10; k++ )
   System.out.println( (double) k / 10 );
```

   c) Error: The missing code is the `break` statement in the statements for the first case.
Correction: Add a `break` statement at the end of the statements for the first case. Note that this omission is not necessarily an error if you want the statement of `case 2:` to execute every time the `case 1:` statement executes.
   d) Error: An improper relational operator is used in the `while`'s continuation condition.
Correction: Use <= rather than <, or change 10 to 11.

Exercises

4.5   Describe the four basic elements of counter-controlled repetition.

4.6   Compare and contrast the `while` and `for` repetition statements.

4.7   Discuss a situation in which it would be more appropriate to use a do...while statement than a `while` statement. Explain why.

4.8   Compare and contrast the `break` and `continue` statements.

4.9   Find and correct the error(s) in each of the following segments of code:

a) ```
For (i = 100, i >= 1, i++)
    System.out.println(i);
```

b) The following code should print whether integer value is odd or even:

```
switch ( value % 2 )
{
    case 0:
        System.out.println( "Even integer" );

    case 1:
        System.out.println( "Odd integer" );
}
```

c) The following code should output the odd integers from 19 to 1:

```
for ( i = 19; i >= 1; i += 2 )
    System.out.println( i );
```

d) The following code should output the even integers from 2 to 100:

```
counter = 2;

do
{
    System.out.println( counter );
    counter += 2;
} While ( counter < 100 );
```

4.10   What does the following program do?

```
1   // Exercise 4.10: Printing.java
2   public class Printing
3   {
4      public static void main( String[] args )
5      {
6         for ( int i = 1; i <= 10; i++ )
7         {
8            for ( int j = 1; j <= 5; j++ )
9               System.out.print( '@' );
10
11           System.out.println();
12        } // end outer for
13     } // end main
14  } // end class Printing
```

4.11   *(Find the Smallest Value)* Write an application that finds the smallest of several integers. Assume that the first value read specifies the number of values to input from the user.

4.12   *(Calculating the Product of Odd Integers)* Write an application that calculates the product of the odd integers from 1 to 15.

4.13   *(Factorials)* *Factorials* are used frequently in probability problems. The factorial of a positive integer *n* (written *n*! and pronounced "*n* factorial") is equal to the product of the positive integers from 1 to *n*. Write an application that calculates the factorials of 1 through 20. Use type long. Display the results in tabular format. What difficulty might prevent you from calculating the factorial of 100?
```

4.14 *(Modified Compound Interest Program)* Modify the compound-interest application of Fig. 4.6 to repeat its steps for interest rates of 5%, 6%, 7%, 8%, 9% and 10%. Use a for loop to vary the interest rate.

4.15 *(Triangle Printing Program)* Write an application that displays the following patterns separately, one below the other. Use for loops to generate the patterns. All asterisks (*) should be printed by a single statement of the form System.out.print('*'); which causes the asterisks to print side by side. A statement of the form System.out.println(); can be used to move to the next line. A statement of the form System.out.print(' '); can be used to display a space for the last two patterns. There should be no other output statements in the program. [*Hint:* The last two patterns require that each line begin with an appropriate number of blank spaces.]

```
(a)              (b)              (c)              (d)
*                **********       **********                *
**               *********         *********               **
***              ********           ********              ***
****             *******             *******             ****
*****            ******               ******            *****
******           *****                 *****           ******
*******          ****                   ****          *******
********         ***                     ***         ********
*********        **                       **        *********
**********       *                         *       **********
```

4.16 *(Bar Chart Printing Program)* One interesting application of computers is to display graphs and bar charts. Write an application that reads five numbers between 1 and 30. For each number that is read, your program should display the same number of adjacent asterisks. For example, if your program reads the number 7, it should display *******. Display the bars of asterisks *after* you read all five numbers.

4.17 *(Calculating Sales)* An online retailer sells five products whose retail prices are as follows: Product 1, $2.98; product 2, $4.50; product 3, $9.98; product 4, $4.49 and product 5, $6.87. Write an application that reads a series of pairs of numbers as follows:
a) product number
b) quantity sold

Your program should use a switch statement to determine the retail price for each product. It should calculate and display the total retail value of all products sold. Use a sentinel-controlled loop to determine when the program should stop looping and display the final results.

4.18 *(Modified Compound Interest Program)* Modify the application in Fig. 4.6 to use only integers to calculate the compound interest. [*Hint:* Treat all monetary amounts as integral numbers of pennies. Then break the result into its dollars and cents portions by using the division and remainder operations, respectively. Insert a period between the dollars and the cents portions.]

4.19 Assume that i = 1, j = 2, k = 3 and m = 2. What does each of the following statements print?
a) System.out.println(i == 1);
b) System.out.println(j == 3);
c) System.out.println((i >= 1) && (j < 4));
d) System.out.println((m <= 99) & (k < m));
e) System.out.println((j >= i) || (k == m));
f) System.out.println((k + m < j) | (3 - j >= k));
g) System.out.println(!(k > m));

4.20 *(Calculating the Value of π)* Calculate the value of π from the infinite series

$$\pi = 4 - \frac{4}{3} + \frac{4}{5} - \frac{4}{7} + \frac{4}{9} - \frac{4}{11} + \cdots$$

Print a table that shows the value of π approximated by computing the first 200,000 terms of this series. How many terms do you have to use before you first get a value that begins with 3.14159?

4.21 *(Pythagorean Triples)* A right triangle can have sides whose lengths are all integers. The set of three integer values for the lengths of the sides of a right triangle is called a Pythagorean triple. The lengths of the three sides must satisfy the relationship that the sum of the squares of two of the sides is equal to the square of the hypotenuse. Write an application that displays a table of the Pythagorean triples for side1, side2 and the hypotenuse, all no larger than 500. Use a triple-nested for loop that tries all possibilities. This method is an example of "brute-force" computing. You'll learn in more advanced computer science courses that for many interesting problems there is no known algorithmic approach other than using sheer brute force.

4.22 *(Modified Triangle Printing Program)* Modify Exercise 4.15 to combine your code from the four separate triangles of asterisks such that all four patterns print side by side. [*Hint:* Make clever use of nested for loops.]

4.23 *(De Morgan's Laws)* In this chapter, we discussed the logical operators &&, &, ||, |, ^ and !. De Morgan's laws can sometimes make it more convenient for us to express a logical expression. These laws state that the expression !(*condition1* && *condition2*) is logically equivalent to the expression (!*condition1* || !*condition2*). Also, the expression !(*condition1* || *condition2*) is logically equivalent to the expression (!*condition1* && !*condition2*). Use De Morgan's laws to write equivalent expressions for each of the following, then write an application to show that both the original expression and the new expression in each case produce the same value:

a) !(x < 5) && !(y >= 7)
b) !(a == b) || !(g != 5)
c) !((x <= 8) && (y > 4))
d) !((i > 4) || (j <= 6))

4.24 *(Diamond Printing Program)* Write an application that prints the following diamond shape. You may use output statements that print a single asterisk (*), a single space or a single newline character. Maximize your use of repetition (with nested for statements), and minimize the number of output statements.

```
    *
   ***
  *****
 *******
*********
 *******
  *****
   ***
    *
```

4.25 *(Modified Diamond Printing Program)* Modify the application you wrote in Exercise 4.24 to read an odd number in the range 1 to 19 to specify the number of rows in the diamond. Your program should then display a diamond of the appropriate size.

4.26 *(Structured Equivalent of **break** Statement)* A criticism of the break statement and the continue statement is that each is unstructured. Actually, these statements can always be replaced by structured statements, although doing so can be awkward. Describe in general how you'd remove any break statement from a loop in a program and replace it with some structured equivalent. [*Hint:* The break statement exits a loop from the body of the loop. The other way to exit is by failing the loop-continuation test. Consider using in the loop-continuation test a second test that indicates "early exit because of a 'break' condition."] Use the technique you develop here to remove the break statement from the application in Fig. 4.11.

4.27 What does the following program segment do?

```
for ( i = 1; i <= 5; i++ )
{
   for ( j = 1; j <= 3; j++ )
   {
      for ( k = 1; k <= 4; k++ )
         System.out.print( '*' );

      System.out.println();
   } // end inner for

   System.out.println();
} // end outer for
```

4.28 *(Structured Equivalent of* **continue** *Statement)* Describe in general how you'd remove any continue statement from a loop in a program and replace it with some structured equivalent. Use the technique you develop here to remove the continue statement from the program in Fig. 4.12.

4.29 *("The Twelve Days of Christmas" Song)* Write an application that uses repetition and switch statements to print the song "The Twelve Days of Christmas." One switch statement should be used to print the day ("first," "second," and so on). A separate switch statement should be used to print the remainder of each verse. Visit the website en.wikipedia.org/wiki/The_Twelve_Days_of_Christmas_(song) for the lyrics of the song.

Making a Difference

4.30 *(Global Warming Facts Quiz)* The controversial issue of global warming has been widely publicized by the film *An Inconvenient Truth*, featuring former Vice President Al Gore. Mr. Gore and a U.N. network of scientists, the Intergovernmental Panel on Climate Change, shared the 2007 Nobel Peace Prize in recognition of "their efforts to build up and disseminate greater knowledge about man-made climate change." Research *both* sides of the global warming issue online (you might want to search for phrases like "global warming skeptics"). Create a five-question multiple-choice quiz on global warming, each question having four possible answers (numbered 1–4). Be objective and try to fairly represent both sides of the issue. Next, write an application that administers the quiz, calculates the number of correct answers (zero through five) and returns a message to the user. If the user correctly answers five questions, print "Excellent"; if four, print "Very good"; if three or fewer, print "Time to brush up on your knowledge of global warming," and include a list of some of the websites where you found your facts.

4.31 *(Tax Plan Alternatives; The "FairTax")* There are many proposals to make taxation fairer. Check out the FairTax initiative in the United States at

```
www.fairtax.org/site/PageServer?pagename=calculator
```

Research how the proposed FairTax works. One suggestion is to eliminate income taxes and most other taxes in favor of a 23% consumption tax on all products and services that you buy. Some FairTax opponents question the 23% figure and say that because of the way the tax is calculated, it would be more accurate to say the rate is 30%—check this carefully. Write a program that prompts the user to enter expenses in various expense categories they have (e.g., housing, food, clothing, transportation, education, health care, vacations), then prints the estimated FairTax that person would pay.

Methods

5

The greatest invention of the nineteenth century was the invention of the method of invention.
—Alfred North Whitehead

Call me Ishmael.
—Herman Melville

When you call me that, smile!
—Owen Wister

Answer me in one word.
—William Shakespeare

O! call back yesterday, bid time return.
—William Shakespeare

Objectives

In this chapter you'll learn:

- How to declare your own methods and call them.

- To use common **Math** methods from the Java API.

- How the method call/return mechanism is supported by the method-call stack and activation records.

- How to use random-number generation to implement game-playing applications.

- How the visibility of declarations is limited to specific regions of programs.

- What method overloading is and how to create overloaded methods.

5.1 Introduction

Experience has shown that the best way to develop and maintain a large program is to construct it from small, simple pieces, or modules. This technique is called divide and conquer. In this chapter, you'll learn how to declare and use methods to facilitate the design, implementation, operation and maintenance of large programs.

Previously, you've called methods on specific objects—for example, method `nextInt` on `Scanner` objects and methods `printf` and `println` on the `System.out` object. You'll see that it's possible for certain methods, called `static` methods, to be called without the need for an object of the class to exist. You'll learn how to declare `static` methods, then call them from other methods (such as `main`). You'll also learn how Java is able to keep track of which method is currently executing, how local variables of methods are maintained in memory and how a method knows where to return after it completes its task.

We'll take a brief diversion into simulation techniques with random-number generation and develop a version of the casino dice game called craps that uses most of the programming techniques you've used to this point in the book. In addition, you'll learn how to declare values that cannot change (i.e., constants) in your programs.

Many of the classes you'll use or create will have more than one method of the same name. This technique, called overloading, is used to implement methods that perform similar tasks for arguments of different types or for different numbers of arguments.

We continue discussing methods in Chapter 7, Introduction to Classes and Objects, where you'll declare your own classes, create objects of those classes and invoke their methods. We discuss methods further in Chapter 18, Recursion. Recursion provides an intriguing way of thinking about methods and algorithms. If you're interested in studying recursion immediately, you can read Sections 18.1–18.7 after reading this chapter.

5.2 Program Modules in Java

Three kinds of modules exist in Java—methods, classes and packages. Java programs are written by combining new methods and classes that you write with predefined methods and classes available in the Java Application Programming Interface (also referred to as the Java API or Java class library) and in various other class libraries. Related classes are typically grouped into packages so that they can be imported into programs and reused. You'll learn how to group your own classes into packages in Chapter 8. The Java API provides a rich collection of predefined classes that contain methods for performing common mathematical calculations, string manipulations, character manipulations, input/output operations, database operations, networking operations, file processing, error checking and many other useful tasks.

Software Engineering Observation 5.1

Familiarize yourself with the rich collection of classes and methods provided by the Java API (java.sun.com/javase/6/docs/api/). In Section 5.8, we present an overview of several common packages. In Appendix E, we explain how to navigate the Java API documentation. Don't reinvent the wheel. When possible, reuse Java API classes and methods. This reduces program development time and avoids introducing programming errors.

Methods (called functions or procedures in some other languages) help you modularize a program by separating its tasks into self-contained units. You've declared a `main` method in every program you've written. The `main` method is special in that it is called once to begin a program's execution. When you create other methods, the statements in the method bodies are written only once, are hidden from other methods and can be reused from several locations in a program.

One motivation for modularizing a program into methods is the divide-and-conquer approach, which makes program development more manageable by constructing programs from small, simple pieces. Another is software reusability—using existing methods as building blocks to create new programs. Often, you can create programs mostly from standardized methods rather than by building customized code. For example, in earlier programs, we did not define how to read data values from the keyboard—Java provides these capabilities in class `Scanner`. A third motivation is that dividing a program into meaningful methods makes the program easier to debug and maintain.

Software Engineering Observation 5.2

To promote software reusability, every method should be limited to performing a single, well-defined task, and the name of the method should express that task effectively.

Error-Prevention Tip 5.1

A method that performs one task is easier to test and debug than one that performs many tasks.

Software Engineering Observation 5.3

If you cannot choose a concise name that expresses a method's task, your method might be attempting to perform too many tasks. Break such a method into several smaller methods.

A method is invoked by a method call, and when the called method completes its task, it either returns a result or simply returns control to the caller. An analogy to this program structure is the hierarchical form of management (Fig. 5.1). A boss (the caller) asks a worker (the called method) to perform a task and report back (return) the results after completing the task. The boss method does not know how the worker method performs its designated tasks. The worker may also call other worker methods, unbeknown to the boss. This "hiding" of implementation details promotes good software engineering. Figure 5.1 shows the boss method communicating with several worker methods in a hierarchical manner. The boss method divides its responsibilities among the various worker methods. Note that worker1 acts as a "boss method" to worker4 and worker5.

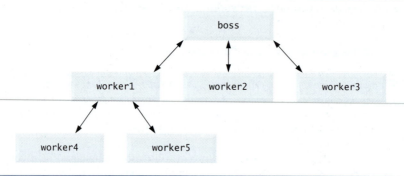

Fig. 5.1 | Hierarchical boss-method/worker-method relationship.

5.3 static Methods, static Fields and Class Math

Most methods execute in response to method calls on specific objects, but this is not always the case. Sometimes a method performs a task that does not depend on the contents of any object. Such a method applies to the class in which it's declared as a whole and is known as a static method or a **class method**. It's common for classes to contain convenient static methods to perform common tasks. For example, recall that we used static method pow of class Math to raise a value to a power in Fig. 4.6. To declare a method as static, place the keyword static before the return type in the method's declaration. You can call any static method by specifying the name of the class in which the method is declared, followed by a dot (.) and the method name, as in

> *ClassName*.*methodName*(*arguments*)

We use various Math class methods here to present the concept of static methods. Class Math provides a collection of methods that enable you to perform common mathematical calculations. For example, you can calculate the square root of 900.0 with the static method call

> Math.sqrt(900.0)

The preceding expression returns 30.0. Method sqrt takes an argument of type double and returns a result of type double. To output the value of the preceding method call in the command window, you might write the statement

> System.out.println(Math.sqrt(900.0));

In this statement, the value that sqrt returns becomes the argument to method println. Note that there was no need to create a Math object before calling method sqrt. *All* Math class methods are static—therefore, each is called by preceding the name of the method with the class name Math and the dot (.) separator.

Software Engineering Observation 5.4

Class Math *is part of the* java.lang *package, which is implicitly imported by the compiler, so it's not necessary to import class* Math *to use its methods.*

Method arguments may be constants, variables or expressions. If c = 13.0, d = 3.0 and f = 4.0, then the statement

```
System.out.println( Math.sqrt( c + d * f ) );
```

calculates and prints the square root of 13.0 + 3.0 * 4.0 = 25.0—namely, 5.0. Figure 5.2 summarizes several Math class methods. In the figure, *x* and *y* are of type double.

Method	Description	Example
abs(*x*)	absolute value of *x*	abs(23.7) is 23.7 abs(0.0) is 0.0 abs(-23.7) is 23.7
ceil(*x*)	rounds *x* to the smallest integer not less than *x*	ceil(9.2) is 10.0 ceil(-9.8) is -9.0
cos(*x*)	trigonometric cosine of *x* (*x* in radians)	cos(0.0) is 1.0
exp(*x*)	exponential method e^x	exp(1.0) is 2.71828 exp(2.0) is 7.38906
floor(*x*)	rounds *x* to the largest integer not greater than *x*	floor(9.2) is 9.0 floor(-9.8) is -10.0
log(*x*)	natural logarithm of *x* (base *e*)	log(Math.E) is 1.0 log(Math.E * Math.E) is 2.0
max(*x*, *y*)	larger value of *x* and *y*	max(2.3, 12.7) is 12.7 max(-2.3, -12.7) is -2.3
min(*x*, *y*)	smaller value of *x* and *y*	min(2.3, 12.7) is 2.3 min(-2.3, -12.7) is -12.7
pow(*x*, *y*)	*x* raised to the power *y* (i.e., x^y)	pow(2.0, 7.0) is 128.0 pow(9.0, 0.5) is 3.0
sin(*x*)	trigonometric sine of *x* (*x* in radians)	sin(0.0) is 0.0
sqrt(*x*)	square root of *x*	sqrt(900.0) is 30.0
tan(*x*)	trigonometric tangent of *x* (*x* in radians)	tan(0.0) is 0.0

Fig. 5.2 | Math class methods.

Math Class Constants PI and E

Class Math declares two fields that represent commonly used mathematical constants— **Math.PI** and **Math.E**. Math.PI (3.141592653589793) is the ratio of a circle's circumference to its diameter. Math.E (2.718281828459045) is the base value for natural logarithms (calculated with static Math method log). These fields are declared in class Math with the modifiers public, final and static. Making them public allows you to use these fields in your own classes. Any field declared with keyword **final** is constant—its value cannot change after the field is initialized. PI and E are declared final because their values never change. Making these fields static allows them to be accessed via the class name Math and a dot (.) separator, just like class Math's methods. Such static fields are also known as class variables. You'll learn more about static fields in Section 8.11.

Why Is Method *main* Declared *static*?

Why must main be declared static? When you execute the Java Virtual Machine (JVM) with the java command, the JVM attempts to invoke the main method of the class you specify. Declaring main as static allows the JVM to invoke main without creating an object of the class. When you execute your application, you specify its class name as an argument to the command java, as in

> java *ClassName argument1 argument2 ...*

The JVM loads the class specified by *ClassName* and uses that class name to invoke method main. In the preceding command, *ClassName* is a command-line argument to the JVM that tells it which class to execute. Following the *ClassName*, you can also specify a list of Strings (separated by spaces) as command-line arguments that the JVM will pass to your application. Such arguments might be used to specify options (e.g., a file name) to run the application. As you'll learn in Chapter 6, your application can access those command-line arguments and use them to customize the application.

5.4 Declaring Methods

So far, each class we declared contained one method named main. Class MaximumFinder (Fig. 5.3) has two methods—main (lines 8–25) and maximum (lines 28–41). The maximum method determines and returns the largest of three double values. Recall that main is a special method that is always called automatically by the Java Virtual Machine (JVM) when you execute an application. Most methods do not get called automatically. As you'll soon see, you must call method maximum explicitly to tell it to perform its task. We begin our discussion with method maximum's declaration.

```
 1   // Fig. 5.3: MaximumFinder.java
 2   // Programmer-declared method maximum with three double parameters.
 3   import java.util.Scanner;
 4
 5   public class MaximumFinder
 6   {
 7      // application starting point
 8      public static void main( String[] args )
 9      {
10         // create Scanner for input from command window
11         Scanner input = new Scanner( System.in );
12
13         // prompt for and input three floating-point values
14         System.out.print(
15            "Enter three floating-point values separated by spaces: " );
16         double number1 = input.nextDouble(); // read first double
17         double number2 = input.nextDouble(); // read second double
18         double number3 = input.nextDouble(); // read third double
19
```

Fig. 5.3 | Programmer-declared method maximum with three double parameters. (Part 1 of 2.)

```
20          // determine the maximum value
21          double result = maximum( number1, number2, number3 );
22
23          // display maximum value
24          System.out.println( "Maximum is: " + result );
25       } // end main
26
27       // returns the maximum of its three double parameters
28       public static double maximum( double x, double y, double z )
29       {
30          double maximumValue = x; // assume x is the largest to start
31
32          // determine whether y is greater than maximumValue
33          if ( y > maximumValue )
34             maximumValue = y;
35
36          // determine whether z is greater than maximumValue
37          if ( z > maximumValue )
38             maximumValue = z;
39
40          return maximumValue;
41       } // end method maximum
42    } // end class MaximumFinder
```

```
Enter three floating-point values separated by spaces: 9.35 2.74 5.1
Maximum is: 9.35
```

```
Enter three floating-point values separated by spaces: 5.8 12.45 8.32
Maximum is: 12.45
```

```
Enter three floating-point values separated by spaces: 6.46 4.12 10.54
Maximum is: 10.54
```

Fig. 5.3 | Programmer-declared method `maximum` with three `double` parameters. (Part 2 of 2.)

The public and static Keywords

Method `maximum`'s declaration begins with keywords `public` to indicate that the method is "available to the public"—it can be called from methods of other classes. The keyword `static` enables the `main` method (another `static` method) to call `maximum` as shown in line 21 without qualifying the method name with the class name `MaximumFinder`—`static` methods in the same class can call each other directly. Any other class that uses `maximum` must fully qualify the method name with the class name. The examples in this chapter and the next begin every method declaration with the keywords `public` and `static`. (You'll learn about non-`public` and non-`static` methods in Chapter 7.)

The Return Type

After keywords `public` and `static` is the method's **return type**, which specifies the type of data the method returns (i.e., gives back) after performing its task. For example, when you go to an automated teller machine (ATM) and request your account balance, you expect the ATM to give you back a value that represents your balance. Similarly, when a statement calls method `maximum` in this example, the statement expects to receive back the largest of the three values. The return type `double` indicates that this method will perform a task then return a `double` value to the **calling method** (i.e., `main` in this example). You've already used methods that return information—for example, in Chapter 2 you used `Scanner` method `nextInt` to input an integer typed by the user at the keyboard. When `nextInt` reads a value from the user, it returns that value for use in the program. In some cases, you'll define methods that perform a task but will *not* return any information. Such methods use the return type `void`.

The Method Name and Parameters

The method name, `maximum`, follows the return type. By convention, method names begin with a lowercase first letter and subsequent words in the name begin with a capital letter (e.g., `nextInt`). The parentheses after the method name indicate that this is a method. If the parentheses are empty, the method does not require additional information to perform its task. For a method that does require additional information to perform its task, the method can require one or more **parameters** that represent that additional information. Parameters are defined in a comma-separated **parameter list**, which is located in the parentheses that follow the method name. Each parameter must specify a type and an identifier. In this case, method `maximum` requires three parameters of type `double`, which we've named `x`, `y` and `z`. A method's parameters are considered to be local variables of that method and can be used only in that method's body.

Common Programming Error 5.1

Declaring method parameters of the same type as `float x, y` *instead of* `float x, float y` *is a syntax error—a type is required for each parameter in the parameter list.*

A method call supplies values—called arguments—for each of the method's parameters. For example, the method `System.out.println` requires an argument that specifies the data to output in a command window. Similarly, to make a deposit into a bank account, a `deposit` method specifies a parameter that represents the deposit amount. When the `deposit` method is called, an argument value representing the deposit amount is assigned to the method's parameter. The method then makes a deposit of that amount.

The Method Body

Collectively, the elements in line 28 are often referred to as the **method header**. The method header is always followed by the method's body, which is delimited by left and right braces, as in lines 29 and 41. A method's body contains one or more statements that perform the method's task. To determine the maximum value, we begin with the assumption that parameter `x` contains the largest value, so line 30 declares local variable `maximumValue` and initializes it with the value of parameter `x`. Of course, it's possible that parameter `y` or `z` contains the actual largest value, so we must compare each of these values with `maximumValue`. The `if` statement at lines 33–34 determines whether `y` is greater than `maximumValue`. If so, line 34 assigns `y` to `maximumValue`. The `if` statement at lines 37–38 determines whether `z` is greater than `maximumValue`. If so, line 38 assigns `z` to `maximumValue`. At this point the largest of the three values resides in `maximumValue`, so line 40 uses the **return** statement to return that value to the point in the program from which `maximum` was called.

When program control returns to that point, `maximum`'s parameters x, y and z no longer exist in memory.

Method `main` and Calling Method `maximum`
Lines 14–18 in `main` prompt the user to enter three `double` values, then read them from the user via `Scanner` method **`nextDouble`**, which returns the user input as a `double` value. Line 21 calls (or invokes) method `maximum` to determine the largest of the three values that are passed to `maximum` as arguments.

When `maximum` is called, its *parameters* x, y and z are initialized with copies of the values in the *arguments* `number1`, `number2` and `number3`, respectively. There must be one argument in the method call for each parameter in the method declaration. Also, each argument must be "consistent with" the corresponding parameter's type. For example, a parameter of type `double` can receive values like 7.35, 22 or –0.03456, but not `String`s like `"hello"` nor the `boolean` values `true` or `false`. Section 5.7 discusses the argument types that can be provided in a method call for each parameter of a primitive type.

When method `maximum` returns the result to line 21, the program assigns `maximum`'s return value to `main`'s local variable `result`. Then line 24 outputs the maximum value. At the end of this section, we'll discuss the use of operator + in line 24.

Common Programming Error 5.2
A compilation error occurs if the number of arguments in a method call does not match the number of parameters in the method declaration.

Common Programming Error 5.3
A compilation error occurs if the type of any argument in a method call is not consistent with the type of the corresponding parameter in the method declaration.

Implementing Method `maximum` by Reusing Method `Math.max`
The entire body of our maximum method could also be implemented with two calls to `Math.max`, as follows:

```
return Math.max( x, Math.max( y, z ) );
```

The first call to `Math.max` specifies arguments x and `Math.max(y, z)`. Before any method can be called, its arguments must be evaluated to determine their values. If an argument is a method call, the method call must be performed to determine its return value. So, in the preceding statement, `Math.max(y, z)` is evaluated to determine the maximum of y and z. Then the result is passed as the second argument to the other call to `Math.max`, which returns the larger of its two arguments. This is a good example of software reuse—we find the largest of three values by reusing `Math.max`, which finds the largest of two values. Note how concise this code is compared to lines 30–40 of Fig. 5.3.

Assembling Strings with String Concatenation
Java allows you to assemble `String`s into larger `String`s by using operators + or +=. This is known as **string concatenation**. When both operands of operator + are `String`s, operator + creates a new `String` in which the characters of the right operand are placed at the end of those in the left operand—e.g., the expression `"hello " + "there"` creates the `String` `"hello there"`.

In line 24 of Fig. 5.3, the expression "Maximum is: " + result uses operator + with operands of types String and double. Every primitive value and object in Java has a String representation. When one of the + operator's operands is a String, the other is converted to a String, then the two are concatenated. In line 24, the double value is converted to its String representation and placed at the end of the String "Maximum is: ". If there are any trailing zeros in a double value, these will be discarded when the number is converted to a String, for example 9.3500 would be represented as 9.35.

For primitive values used in String concatenation, the primitive values are converted to Strings. If a boolean is concatenated with a String, the boolean is converted to the String "true" or "false". In Chapter 7, you'll learn that all objects have a toString method that returns a String representation of the object. When an object is concatenated with a String, the object's toString method is implicitly called to obtain the String representation of the object.

Programmers sometimes prefer to break large String literals into several smaller Strings and place them on multiple lines of code for readability. In this case, the Strings can be reassembled using concatenation. We discuss the details of Strings in Chapters 6 and 16.

Common Programming Error 5.4

It's a syntax error to break a String literal across lines. If necessary, you can split a String into several smaller Strings and use concatenation to form the desired String.

Common Programming Error 5.5

Confusing the + operator used for string concatenation with the + operator used for addition can lead to strange results. Java evaluates the operands of an operator from left to right. For example, if integer variable y has the value 5, the expression "y + 2 = " + y + 2 results in the string "y + 2 = 52", not "y + 2 = 7", because first the value of y (5) is concatenated to the string "y + 2 = ", then the value 2 is concatenated to the new larger string "y + 2 = 5". The expression "y + 2 = " + (y + 2) produces the desired result "y + 2 = 7".

5.5 Notes on Declaring and Using Methods

There are three ways to call a method:

1. Using a method name by itself to call another method of the same class—such as maximum(number1, number2, number3) in line 21 of Fig. 5.3.

2. Using a variable that represents an object, followed by a dot (.) and the method name to call a method of that object—such as the method call in line 16 of Fig. 5.3, input.nextDouble(), which calls a method of class Scanner from the main method of MaximumFinder.

3. Using the class name and a dot (.) to call a static method of a class—such as Math.sqrt(900.0) in Section 5.3.

There are three ways to return control to the statement that calls a method. If the method does not return a result, control returns when the program flow reaches the method-ending right brace or when the statement

```
return;
```

is executed. If the method returns a result, the statement

> ```
> return expression;
> ```

evaluates the *expression*, then returns the result to the caller.

Common Programming Error 5.6

Declaring a method outside the body of a class declaration or inside the body of another method is a syntax error.

Common Programming Error 5.7

Omitting the return-value-type, *possibly* void, *in a method declaration is a syntax error.*

Common Programming Error 5.8

Placing a semicolon after the right parenthesis enclosing the parameter list of a method declaration is a syntax error.

Common Programming Error 5.9

Redeclaring a parameter as a local variable in the method's body is a compilation error.

Common Programming Error 5.10

Forgetting to return a value from a method that should return a value is a compilation error. If a return type other than void *is specified, the method must contain a* return *statement that returns a value consistent with the method's return type. Returning a value from a method whose return type has been declared* void *is a compilation error.*

5.6 Method-Call Stack and Activation Records

To understand how Java performs method calls, we first need to consider a data structure (i.e., collection of related data items) known as a **stack**. You can think of a stack as analogous to a pile of dishes. When a dish is placed on the pile, it's normally placed at the top (referred to as **pushing** the dish onto the stack). Similarly, when a dish is removed from the pile, it's always removed from the top (referred to as **popping** the dish off the stack). Stacks are known as **last-in, first-out (LIFO) data structures**—the last item pushed (inserted) on the stack is the first item popped (removed) from the stack.

When a program calls a method, the called method must know how to return to its caller, so the return address of the calling method is pushed onto the **program-execution stack** (sometimes referred to as the **method-call stack**). If a series of method calls occurs, the successive return addresses are pushed onto the stack in last-in, first-out order so that each method can return to its caller.

The program-execution stack also contains the memory for the local variables used in each invocation of a method during a program's execution. This data, stored as a portion of the program-execution stack, is known as the **activation record** or **stack frame** of the method call. When a method call is made, the activation record for that method call is pushed onto the program-execution stack. When the method returns to its caller, the activation record for this method call is popped off the stack and those local variables are no longer known to the program.

Of course, the amount of memory in a computer is finite, so only a certain amount of memory can be used to store activation records on the program execution stack. If more method calls occur than can have their activation records stored on the program-execution stack, an error known as a stack overflow occurs.

5.7 Argument Promotion and Casting

Another important feature of method calls is argument promotion—converting an argument's value, if possible, to the type that the method expects to receive in its corresponding parameter. For example, a program can call Math method sqrt with an integer argument even though the method expects to receive a double argument (but, as we'll soon see, not vice versa). The statement

```
System.out.println( Math.sqrt( 4 ) );
```

correctly evaluates Math.sqrt(4) and prints the value 2.0. The method declaration's parameter list causes Java to convert the int value 4 to the double value 4.0 before passing the value to method sqrt. Attempting these conversions may lead to compilation errors if Java's promotion rules are not satisfied. The promotion rules specify which conversions are allowed—that is, which conversions can be performed without losing data. In the sqrt example above, an int is converted to a double without changing its value. However, converting a double to an int truncates the fractional part of the double value—thus, part of the value is lost. Converting large integer types to small integer types (e.g., long to int, or int to short) may also result in changed values.

The promotion rules apply to expressions containing values of two or more primitive types and to primitive-type values passed as arguments to methods. Each value is promoted to the "highest" type in the expression. Actually, the expression uses a temporary copy of each value—the types of the original values remain unchanged. Figure 5.4 lists the primitive types and the types to which each can be promoted. Note that the valid promotions for a given type are always to a type higher in the table. For example, an int can be promoted to the higher types long, float and double.

Type	Valid promotions
double	None
float	double
long	float or double
int	long, float or double
char	int, long, float or double
short	int, long, float or double (but not char)
byte	short, int, long, float or double (but not char)
boolean	None (boolean values are not considered to be numbers in Java)

Fig. 5.4 | Promotions allowed for primitive types.

Converting values to types lower in the table of Fig. 5.4 will result in different values if the lower type cannot represent the value of the higher type (e.g., the int value 2000000 cannot be represented as a short, and any floating-point number with digits after its decimal point cannot be represented in an integer type such as long, int or short). Therefore, in cases where information may be lost due to conversion, the Java compiler requires you to use a cast operator (introduced in Section 3.9) to explicitly force the conversion to occur—otherwise a compilation error occurs. This enables you to "take control" from the compiler. You essentially say, "I know this conversion might cause loss of information, but for my purposes here, that's fine." Suppose method `square` calculates the square of an integer and thus requires an `int` argument. To call `square` with a `double` argument named `doubleValue`, we would be required to write the method call as

```
square( (int) doubleValue )
```

This method call explicitly casts (converts) a *copy* of variable `doubleValue`'s value to an integer for use in method `square`. Thus, if `doubleValue`'s value is `4.5`, the method receives the value 4 and returns 16, not `20.25`.

Common Programming Error 5.11

Converting a primitive-type value to another primitive type may change the value if the new type is not a valid promotion. For example, converting a floating-point value to an integer value may introduce truncation errors (loss of the fractional part) into the result.

5.8 Java API Packages

As you've seen, Java contains many predefined classes that are grouped into categories of related classes called packages. Together, these are known as the Java Application Programming Interface (Java API), or the Java class library. A great strength of Java is the Java API's thousands of classes. Some key Java API packages are described in Fig. 5.5, which represents only a small portion of the reusable components in the Java API.

Package	Description
`java.applet`	The **Java Applet Package** contains a class and several interfaces for creating Java applets—programs that execute in web browsers. Applets are discussed in Chapter 23, Applets and Java Web Start; interfaces are discussed in Chapter 10, Object-Oriented Programming: Polymorphism.)
`java.awt`	The **Java Abstract Window Toolkit Package** contains the classes and interfaces required to create and manipulate GUIs in early versions of Java. In current versions of Java, the Swing GUI components of the `javax.swing` packages are typically used instead. (Some elements of the `java.awt` package are discussed in Chapter 14, GUI Components: Part 1, Chapter 15, Graphics and Java 2D™, and Chapter 25, GUI Components: Part 2.)
`java.awt.event`	The **Java Abstract Window Toolkit Event Package** contains classes and interfaces that enable event handling for GUI components in both the `java.awt` and `javax.swing` packages. (See Chapter 14, GUI Components: Part 1 and Chapter 25, GUI Components: Part 2.)
`java.awt.geom`	The **Java 2D Shapes Package** contains classes and interfaces for working with Java's advanced two-dimensional graphics capabilities. (See Chapter 15, Graphics and Java 2D™.)

Fig. 5.5 | Java API packages (a subset). (Part 1 of 2.)

Package	Description
`java.io`	The **Java Input/Output Package** contains classes and interfaces that enable programs to input and output data. (See Chapter 17, Files, Streams and Object Serialization.)
`java.lang`	The **Java Language Package** contains classes and interfaces (discussed bookwide) that are required by many Java programs. This package is imported by the compiler into all programs.
`java.net`	The **Java Networking Package** contains classes and interfaces that enable programs to communicate via computer networks like the Internet. (See Chapter 27, Networking.)
`java.sql`	The **JDBC Package** contains classes and interfaces for working with databases. (See Chapter 28, Accessing Databases with JDBC.)
`java.text`	The **Java Text Package** contains classes and interfaces that enable programs to manipulate numbers, dates, characters and strings. The package provides internationalization capabilities that enable a program to be customized to locales (e.g., a program may display strings in different languages, based on the user's country).
`java.util`	The **Java Utilities Package** contains utility classes and interfaces that enable such actions as date and time manipulations, random-number processing (class Random, Section 5.9) and the storing and processing of large amounts of data.
`java.util.` `concurrent`	The **Java Concurrency Package** contains utility classes and interfaces for implementing programs that can perform multiple tasks in parallel. (See Chapter 26, Multithreading.)
`javax.media`	The **Java Media Framework Package** contains classes and interfaces for working with Java's multimedia capabilities. (See Chapter 24, Multimedia: Applets and Applications.)
`javax.swing`	The **Java Swing GUI Components Package** contains classes and interfaces for Java's Swing GUI components that provide support for portable GUIs. (See Chapter 14, GUI Components: Part 1 and Chapter 25, GUI Components: Part 2.)
`javax.swing.event`	The **Java Swing Event Package** contains classes and interfaces that enable event handling (e.g., responding to button clicks) for GUI components in package `javax.swing`. (See Chapter 14, GUI Components: Part 1 and Chapter 25, GUI Components: Part 2.)
`javax.xml.ws`	The **JAX-WS Package** contains classes and interfaces for working with web services in Java. (See Chapter 31, Web Services.)

Fig. 5.5 | Java API packages (a subset). (Part 2 of 2.)

The set of packages available in Java SE 6 is quite large. In addition to those summarized in Fig. 5.5, Java SE 6 includes packages for complex graphics, advanced graphical user interfaces, printing, advanced networking, security, database processing, multimedia, accessibility (for people with disabilities), concurrent programming, cryptography, XML processing and more. For an overview of the packages in Java SE 6, visit

`java.sun.com/javase/6/docs/api/overview-summary.html`

You can locate additional information about a predefined Java class's methods in the Java API documentation at java.sun.com/javase/6/docs/api/. When you visit this site, click the **Index** link to see an alphabetical listing of all the classes and methods in the Java API. Locate the class name and click its link to see the online description of the class. Click the **METHOD** link to see a table of the class's methods. Each static method will be listed with the word "static" preceding the method's return type.

5.9 Case Study: Random-Number Generation

We now take a brief diversion into a popular type of programming application—simulation and game playing. In this and the next section, we develop a nicely structured game-playing program with multiple methods. The program uses most of the control statements presented thus far in the book and introduces several new programming concepts.

There is something in the air of a casino that invigorates people—from the high rollers at the plush mahogany-and-felt craps tables to the quarter poppers at the one-armed bandits. It's the element of chance, the possibility that luck will convert a pocketful of money into a mountain of wealth. The element of chance can be introduced in a program via an object of class **Random** (package java.util) or via the static method random of class Math. Objects of class Random can produce random boolean, byte, float, double, int, long and Gaussian values, whereas Math method random can produce only double values in the range $0.0 \leq x < 1.0$, where x is the value returned by method random. In the next several examples, we use objects of class Random to produce random values.

A new random-number generator object can be created as follows:

```
Random randomNumbers = new Random();
```

It can then be used to generate random boolean, byte, float, double, int, long and Gaussian values—we discuss only random int values here. For more information on the Random class, see java.sun.com/javase/6/docs/api/java/util/Random.html.

Consider the following statement:

```
int randomValue = randomNumbers.nextInt();
```

Random method **nextInt** generates a random int value in the range –2,147,483,648 to +2,147,483,647, inclusive. If it truly produces values at random, then every value in the range should have an equal chance (or probability) of being chosen each time nextInt is called. The numbers are actually pseudorandom numbers—a sequence of values produced by a complex mathematical calculation. The calculation uses the current time of day (which, of course, changes constantly) to seed the random-number generator such that each execution of a program yields a different sequence of random values.

The range of values produced directly by method nextInt often differs from the range of values required in a particular Java application. For example, a program that simulates coin tossing might require only 0 for "heads" and 1 for "tails." A program that simulates the rolling of a six-sided die might require random integers in the range 1–6. A program that randomly predicts the next type of spaceship (out of four possibilities) that will fly across the horizon in a video game might require random integers in the range 1–4. For cases like these, class Random provides another version of method nextInt that receives an int argument and returns a value from 0 up to, but not including, the argument's value. For example, for coin tossing, the following statement returns 0 or 1.

```
int randomValue = randomNumbers.nextInt( 2 );
```

Rolling a Six-Sided Die

To demonstrate random numbers, let's develop a program that simulates 20 rolls of a six-sided die and displays the value of each roll. We begin by using `nextInt` to produce random values in the range 0–5, as follows:

```
face = randomNumbers.nextInt( 6 );
```

The argument 6—called the **scaling factor**—represents the number of unique values that `nextInt` should produce (in this case six—0, 1, 2, 3, 4 and 5). This manipulation is called **scaling** the range of values produced by Random method `nextInt`.

A six-sided die has the numbers 1–6 on its faces, not 0–5. So we **shift** the range of numbers produced by adding a **shifting value**—in this case 1—to our previous result, as in

```
face = 1 + randomNumbers.nextInt( 6 );
```

The shifting value (1) specifies the first value in the desired range of random integers. The preceding statement assigns `face` a random integer in the range 1–6.

Figure 5.6 shows two sample outputs which confirm that the preceding calculation produces integers in the range 1–6. Note that each output shows a different sequence of random numbers.

```
1   // Fig. 5.6: RandomIntegers.java
2   // Shifted and scaled random integers.
3   import java.util.Random; // program uses class Random
4
5   public class RandomIntegers
6   {
7      public static void main( String[] args )
8      {
9         Random randomNumbers = new Random(); // random number generator
10        int face; // stores each random integer generated
11
12        // loop 20 times
13        for ( int counter = 1; counter <= 20; counter++ )
14        {
15           // pick random integer from 1 to 6
16           face = 1 + randomNumbers.nextInt( 6 );
17
18           System.out.printf( "%d  ", face ); // display generated value
19
20           // if counter is divisible by 5, start a new line of output
21           if ( counter % 5 == 0 )
22              System.out.println();
23        } // end for
24     } // end main
25  } // end class RandomIntegers
```

```
1  5  3  6  2
5  2  6  5  2
4  4  4  2  6
3  1  6  2  2
```

Fig. 5.6 | Shifted and scaled random integers. (Part 1 of 2.)

```
6  5  4  2  6
1  2  5  1  3
6  3  2  2  1
6  4  2  6  4
```

Fig. 5.6 | Shifted and scaled random integers. (Part 2 of 2.)

Line 3 imports class Random from the java.util package. Line 9 creates the Random object randomNumbers to produce random values. Line 16 executes 20 times in a loop to roll the die. The if statement (lines 21–22) in the loop starts a new line of output after every five numbers.

Rolling a Six-Sided Die 6000 Times
To show that the numbers produced by nextInt occur with approximately equal likelihood, let's simulate 6000 rolls of a die with the application in Fig. 5.7. Each integer from 1 to 6 should appear approximately 1000 times.

```java
1   // Fig. 5.7: RollDie.java
2   // Roll a six-sided die 6000 times.
3   import java.util.Random;
4
5   public class RollDie
6   {
7      public static void main( String[] args )
8      {
9         Random randomNumbers = new Random(); // random number generator
10
11        int frequency1 = 0; // maintains count of 1s rolled
12        int frequency2 = 0; // count of 2s rolled
13        int frequency3 = 0; // count of 3s rolled
14        int frequency4 = 0; // count of 4s rolled
15        int frequency5 = 0; // count of 5s rolled
16        int frequency6 = 0; // count of 6s rolled
17
18        int face; // stores most recently rolled value
19
20        // tally counts for 6000 rolls of a die
21        for ( int roll = 1; roll <= 6000; roll++ )
22        {
23           face = 1 + randomNumbers.nextInt( 6 ); // number from 1 to 6
24
25           // determine roll value 1-6 and increment appropriate counter
26           switch ( face )
27           {
28              case 1:
29                 ++frequency1; // increment the 1s counter
30                 break;
31              case 2:
32                 ++frequency2; // increment the 2s counter
33                 break;
```

Fig. 5.7 | Rolling a six-sided die 6000 times. (Part 1 of 2.)

```
34                    case 3:
35                        ++frequency3; // increment the 3s counter
36                        break;
37                    case 4:
38                        ++frequency4; // increment the 4s counter
39                        break;
40                    case 5:
41                        ++frequency5; // increment the 5s counter
42                        break;
43                    case 6:
44                        ++frequency6; // increment the 6s counter
45                        break; // optional at end of switch
46                } // end switch
47            } // end for
48
49            System.out.println( "Face\tFrequency" ); // output headers
50            System.out.printf( "1\t%d\n2\t%d\n3\t%d\n4\t%d\n5\t%d\n6\t%d\n",
51                frequency1, frequency2, frequency3, frequency4,
52                frequency5, frequency6 );
53        } // end main
54    } // end class RollDie
```

Face	Frequency
1	982
2	1001
3	1015
4	1005
5	1009
6	988

Face	Frequency
1	1029
2	994
3	1017
4	1007
5	972
6	981

Fig. 5.7 | Rolling a six-sided die 6000 times. (Part 2 of 2.)

As the sample outputs show, scaling and shifting the values produced by nextInt enables the program to simulate rolling a six-sided die. The application uses nested control statements (the switch is nested inside the for) to determine the number of times each side of the die appears. The for statement (lines 21–47) iterates 6000 times. During each iteration, line 23 produces a random value from 1 to 6. That value is then used as the controlling expression (line 26) of the switch statement (lines 26–46). Based on the face value, the switch statement increments one of the six counter variables during each iteration of the loop. When we study arrays in Chapter 6, we'll show an elegant way to replace the entire switch statement in this program with a single statement! Note that this switch statement has no default case, because we have a case for every possible die value that the expression in line 23 could produce. Run the program, and observe the results. As you'll see, every time you run this program, it produces different results.

5.9.1 Generalized Scaling and Shifting of Random Numbers

Previously, we simulated the rolling of a six-sided die with the statement

```
face = 1 + randomNumbers.nextInt( 6 );
```

This statement always assigns to variable `face` an integer in the range $1 \leq face \leq 6$. The width of this range (i.e., the number of consecutive integers in the range) is 6, and the starting number in the range is 1. Referring to the preceding statement, we see that the width of the range is determined by the number 6 that is passed as an argument to `Random` method `nextInt`, and the starting number of the range is the number 1 that is added to `randomNumberGenerator.nextInt(6)`. We can generalize this result as

```
number = shiftingValue + randomNumbers.nextInt( scalingFactor );
```

where *shiftingValue* specifies the first number in the desired range of consecutive integers and *scalingFactor* specifies how many numbers are in the range.

It's also possible to choose integers at random from sets of values other than ranges of consecutive integers. For example, to obtain a random value from the sequence 2, 5, 8, 11 and 14, you could use the statement

```
number = 2 + 3 * randomNumbers.nextInt( 5 );
```

In this case, `randomNumberGenerator.nextInt(5)` produces values in the range 0–4. Each value produced is multiplied by 3 to produce a number in the sequence 0, 3, 6, 9 and 12. We add 2 to that value to shift the range of values and obtain a value from the sequence 2, 5, 8, 11 and 14. We can generalize this result as

```
number = shiftingValue +
    differenceBetweenValues * randomNumbers.nextInt( scalingFactor );
```

where *shiftingValue* specifies the first number in the desired range of values, *differenceBetweenValues* represents the constant difference between consecutive numbers in the sequence and *scalingFactor* specifies how many numbers are in the range.

5.9.2 Random-Number Repeatability for Testing and Debugging

Class `Random`'s methods actually generate pseudorandom numbers based on complex mathematical calculations—the sequence of numbers appears to be random. The calculation that produces the numbers uses the time of day as a **seed value** to change the sequence's starting point. Each new `Random` object seeds itself with a value based on the computer system's clock at the time the object is created, enabling each execution of a program to produce a different sequence of random numbers.

When debugging an application, it's sometimes useful to repeat the exact same sequence of pseudorandom numbers during each execution of the program. This repeatability enables you to prove that your application is working for a specific sequence of random numbers before you test the program with different sequences of random numbers. When repeatability is important, you can create a `Random` object as follows:

```
Random randomNumbers = new Random( seedValue );
```

The `seedValue` argument (of type `long`) seeds the random-number calculation. If the same `seedValue` is used every time, the `Random` object produces the same sequence of numbers. You can set a Random object's seed at any time during program execution by calling the object's set method, as in

```
randomNumbers.set( seedValue );
```

Error-Prevention Tip 5.2

While developing a program, create the Random object with a specific seed value to produce a repeatable sequence of numbers each time the program executes. If a logic error occurs, fix the error and test the program again with the same seed value—this allows you to reconstruct the same sequence of numbers that caused the error. Once the logic errors have been removed, create the Random object without using a seed value, causing the Random object to generate a new sequence of random numbers each time the program executes.

5.10 Case Study: A Game of Chance; Introducing Enumerations

A popular game of chance is a dice game known as craps, which is played in casinos and back alleys throughout the world. The rules of the game are straightforward:

> You roll two dice. Each die has six faces, which contain one, two, three, four, five and six spots, respectively. After the dice have come to rest, the sum of the spots on the two upward faces is calculated. If the sum is 7 or 11 on the first throw, you win. If the sum is 2, 3 or 12 on the first throw (called "craps"), you lose (i.e., the "house" wins). If the sum is 4, 5, 6, 8, 9 or 10 on the first throw, that sum becomes your "point." To win, you must continue rolling the dice until you "make your point" (i.e., roll that same point value). You lose by rolling a 7 before making your point.

The application in Fig. 5.8 simulates the game of craps, using methods to implement the game's logic. The main method (lines 21–65) calls the rollDice method (lines 68–81) as necessary to roll the dice and compute their sum. The sample outputs show winning and losing on the first roll, and winning and losing on a subsequent roll.

```java
1   // Fig. 5.8: Craps.java
2   // Craps class simulates the dice game craps.
3   import java.util.Random;
4
5   public class Craps
6   {
7      // create random number generator for use in method rollDice
8      private static final Random randomNumbers = new Random();
9
10     // enumeration with constants that represent the game status
11     private enum Status { CONTINUE, WON, LOST };
12
13     // constants that represent common rolls of the dice
14     private static final int SNAKE_EYES = 2;
15     private static final int TREY = 3;
16     private static final int SEVEN = 7;
17     private static final int YO_LEVEN = 11;
18     private static final int BOX_CARS = 12;
19
```

Fig. 5.8 | Craps class simulates the dice game craps. (Part 1 of 3.)

```
20      // plays one game of craps
21      public static void main( String[] args )
22      {
23          int myPoint = 0; // point if no win or loss on first roll
24          Status gameStatus; // can contain CONTINUE, WON or LOST
25
26          int sumOfDice = rollDice(); // first roll of the dice
27
28          // determine game status and point based on first roll
29          switch ( sumOfDice )
30          {
31              case SEVEN: // win with 7 on first roll
32              case YO_LEVEN: // win with 11 on first roll
33                  gameStatus = Status.WON;
34                  break;
35              case SNAKE_EYES: // lose with 2 on first roll
36              case TREY: // lose with 3 on first roll
37              case BOX_CARS: // lose with 12 on first roll
38                  gameStatus = Status.LOST;
39                  break;
40              default: // did not win or lose, so remember point
41                  gameStatus = Status.CONTINUE; // game is not over
42                  myPoint = sumOfDice; // remember the point
43                  System.out.printf( "Point is %d\n", myPoint );
44                  break; // optional at end of switch
45          } // end switch
46
47          // while game is not complete
48          while ( gameStatus == Status.CONTINUE ) // not WON or LOST
49          {
50              sumOfDice = rollDice(); // roll dice again
51
52              // determine game status
53              if ( sumOfDice == myPoint ) // win by making point
54                  gameStatus = Status.WON;
55              else
56                  if ( sumOfDice == SEVEN ) // lose by rolling 7 before point
57                      gameStatus = Status.LOST;
58          } // end while
59
60          // display won or lost message
61          if ( gameStatus == Status.WON )
62              System.out.println( "Player wins" );
63          else
64              System.out.println( "Player loses" );
65      } // end main
66
67      // roll dice, calculate sum and display results
68      public static int rollDice()
69      {
70          // pick random die values
71          int die1 = 1 + randomNumbers.nextInt( 6 ); // first die roll
72          int die2 = 1 + randomNumbers.nextInt( 6 ); // second die roll
73
```

Fig. 5.8 | Craps class simulates the dice game craps. (Part 2 of 3.)

```
74            int sum = die1 + die2; // sum of die values
75
76            // display results of this roll
77            System.out.printf( "Player rolled %d + %d = %d\n",
78               die1, die2, sum );
79
80            return sum; // return sum of dice
81         } // end method rollDice
82      } // end class Craps
```

```
Player rolled 5 + 6 = 11
Player wins
```

```
Player rolled 1 + 2 = 3
Player loses
```

```
Player rolled 5 + 4 = 9
Point is 9
Player rolled 2 + 2 = 4
Player rolled 2 + 6 = 8
Player rolled 4 + 2 = 6
Player rolled 3 + 6 = 9
Player wins
```

```
Player rolled 2 + 6 = 8
Point is 8
Player rolled 5 + 1 = 6
Player rolled 1 + 6 = 7
Player loses
```

Fig. 5.8 | Craps class simulates the dice game craps. (Part 3 of 3.)

Method rollDice

In the rules of the game, the player must roll two dice on the first roll and must do the
same on all subsequent rolls. We declare method rollDice (lines 68–81) to roll the dice
and compute and print their sum. Method rollDice is declared once, but it's called from
two places (lines 26 and 50) in main, which contains the logic for one complete game of
craps. Method rollDice takes no arguments, so it has an empty parameter list. Each time
it's called, rollDice returns the sum of the dice, so the return type int is indicated in the
method header (line 68). Although lines 71 and 72 look the same (except for the die
names), they do not necessarily produce the same result. Each of these statements produces
a random value in the range 1–6. Note that randomNumbers (used in lines 71–72) is not
declared in the method. Instead it's declared as a private static final variable of the
class and initialized in line 8. This enables us to create one Random object that is reused in
each call to rollDice.

Method main's Local Variables

The game is reasonably involved. The player may win or lose on the first roll, or may win
or lose on any subsequent roll. Method main (lines 21–65) uses local variable myPoint (line
23) to store the "point" if the player does not win or lose on the first roll, local variable

gameStatus (line 24) to keep track of the overall game status and local variable sumOfDice (line 26) to hold the sum of the dice for the most recent roll. Note that myPoint is initialized to 0 to ensure that the application will compile. If you do not initialize myPoint, the compiler issues an error, because myPoint is not assigned a value in every case of the switch statement, and thus the program could try to use myPoint before it is assigned a value. By contrast, gameStatus *is* assigned a value in *every* case of the switch statement—thus, it's guaranteed to be initialized before it's used and does not need to be initialized.

enum *Type* Status

Local variable gameStatus (line 24) is declared to be of a new type called Status (declared at line 11). Type Status is a private member of class Craps, because Status will be used only in that class. Status is a type called an **enumeration**, which, in its simplest form, declares a set of constants represented by identifiers. An enumeration is a special kind of class that is introduced by the keyword **enum** and a type name (in this case, Status). As with classes, braces delimit an enum declaration's body. Inside the braces is a comma-separated list of **enumeration constants**, each representing a unique value. The identifiers in an enum must be unique. (You'll learn more about enumerations in Chapter 8.)

Good Programming Practice 5.1
Use only uppercase letters in the names of enumeration constants. This makes the constants stand out and reminds you that enumeration constants are not variables.

Variables of type Status can be assigned only the three constants declared in the enumeration (line 11) or a compilation error will occur. When the game is won, the program sets local variable gameStatus to Status.WON (lines 33 and 54). When the game is lost, the program sets local variable gameStatus to Status.LOST (lines 38 and 57). Otherwise, the program sets local variable gameStatus to Status.CONTINUE (line 41) to indicate that the game is not over and the dice must be rolled again.

Good Programming Practice 5.2
Using enumeration constants (like Status.WON, Status.LOST and Status.CONTINUE) rather than literal values (such as 0, 1 and 2) makes programs easier to read and maintain.

Logic of the **main** Method

Line 26 in method main calls rollDice, which picks two random values from 1 to 6, displays the values of the first die, the second die and the sum of the dice, and returns the sum. Method main next enters the switch statement at lines 29–45, which uses the sumOfDice value from line 26 to determine whether the game has been won or lost, or whether it should continue with another roll. The sums of the dice that would result in a win or loss on the first roll are declared as public static final int constants in lines 14–18. These are used in the cases of the switch statement. The identifier names use casino parlance for these sums. Note that these constants, like enum constants, are declared with all capital letters by convention, to make them stand out in the program. Lines 31–34 determine whether the player won on the first roll with SEVEN (7) or YO_LEVEN (11). Lines 35–39 determine whether the player lost on the first roll with SNAKE_EYES (2), TREY (3), or BOX_CARS (12). After the first roll, if the game is not over, the default case (lines 40–44) sets gameStatus to Status.CONTINUE, saves sumOfDice in myPoint and displays the point.

If we're still trying to "make our point" (i.e., the game is continuing from a prior roll), lines 48–58 execute. Line 50 rolls the dice again. If sumOfDice matches myPoint (line 53), line 54 sets gameStatus to Status.WON, then the loop terminates because the game is complete. If sumOfDice is SEVEN (line 56), line 57 sets gameStatus to Status.LOST, and the loop terminates because the game is complete. When the game completes, lines 61–64 display a message indicating whether the player won or lost, and the program terminates.

Note the use of the various program-control mechanisms we've discussed. The Craps class uses two methods—main and rollDice (called twice from main)—and the switch, while, if...else and nested if control statements. Note also the use of multiple case labels in the switch statement to execute the same statements for sums of SEVEN and YO_LEVEN (lines 31–32) and for sums of SNAKE_EYES, TREY and BOX_CARS (lines 35–37).

Why Some Constants Are Not Defined as **enum** *Constants*

You might be wondering why we declared the sums of the dice as public final static int constants rather than as enum constants. The answer is that the program must compare the int variable sumOfDice (line 26) to these constants to determine the outcome of each roll. Suppose we were to declare enum Sum containing constants (e.g., Sum.SNAKE_EYES) representing the five sums used in the game, then use these constants in the cases of the switch statement (lines 29–45). Doing so would prevent us from using sumOfDice as the switch statement's controlling expression, because *Java does not allow an int to be compared to an enumeration constant.* To achieve the same functionality as the current program, we would have to use a variable currentSum of type Sum as the switch's controlling expression. Unfortunately, Java does not provide an easy way to convert an int value to a particular enum constant. This could be done with a separate switch statementm but it would be cumbersome and not improve the readability of the program (thus defeating the purpose of using an enum).

5.11 Scope of Declarations

You've seen declarations of various Java entities, such as classes, methods, variables and parameters. Declarations introduce names that can be used to refer to such Java entities. The scope of a declaration is the portion of the program that can refer to the declared entity by its name. Such an entity is said to be "in scope" for that portion of the program. This section introduces several important scope issues. (For more scope information, see the *Java Language Specification, Section 6.3: Scope of a Declaration*, at java.sun.com/docs/books/jls/third_edition/html/names.html#103228.)

The basic scope rules are as follows:

1. The scope of a parameter declaration is the body of the method in which the declaration appears.

2. The scope of a local-variable declaration is from the point at which the declaration appears to the end of that block.

3. The scope of a local-variable declaration that appears in the initialization section of a for statement's header is the body of the for statement and the other expressions in the header.

4. A method or field's scope is the entire body of the class.

Any block may contain variable declarations. If a local variable or parameter in a method has the same name as a field of the class, the field is "hidden" until the block terminates execution—this is called **shadowing**. In Chapter 8, we discuss how to access shadowed fields. The application in Fig. 5.9 demonstrates scoping issues with fields and local variables.

Common Programming Error 5.12

A compilation error occurs when a local variable is declared more than once in a method.

Error-Prevention Tip 5.3

Use different names for fields and local variables to help prevent subtle logic errors that occur when a method is called and a local variable of the method shadows a field in the class.

```java
1   // Fig. 5.9: Scope.java
2   // Scope class demonstrates field and local variable scopes.
3
4   public class Scope
5   {
6      // field that is accessible to all methods of this class
7      private static int x = 1;
8
9      // method main creates and initializes local variable x
10     // and calls methods useLocalVariable and useField
11     public static void main( String[] args )
12     {
13        int x = 5; // method's local variable x shadows field x
14
15        System.out.printf( "local x in method begin is %d\n", x );
16
17        useLocalVariable(); // useLocalVariable has local x
18        useField(); // useField uses class Scope's field x
19        useLocalVariable(); // useLocalVariable reinitializes local x
20        useField(); // class Scope's field x retains its value
21
22        System.out.printf( "\nlocal x in method begin is %d\n", x );
23     } // end method begin
24
25     // create and initialize local variable x during each call
26     public static void useLocalVariable()
27     {
28        int x = 25; // initialized each time useLocalVariable is called
29
30        System.out.printf(
31           "\nlocal x on entering method useLocalVariable is %d\n", x );
32        ++x; // modifies this method's local variable x
33        System.out.printf(
34           "local x before exiting method useLocalVariable is %d\n", x );
35     } // end method useLocalVariable
36
```

Fig. 5.9 | Scope class demonstrating scopes of a field and local variables. (Part 1 of 2.)

```
37      // modify class Scope's field x during each call
38      public static void useField()
39      {
40         System.out.printf(
41            "\nfield x on entering method useField is %d\n", x );
42         x *= 10; // modifies class Scope's field x
43         System.out.printf(
44            "field x before exiting method useField is %d\n", x );
45      } // end method useField
46   } // end class Scope
```

```
local x in method begin is 5

local x on entering method useLocalVariable is 25
local x before exiting method useLocalVariable is 26

field x on entering method useField is 1
field x before exiting method useField is 10

local x on entering method useLocalVariable is 25
local x before exiting method useLocalVariable is 26

field x on entering method useField is 10
field x before exiting method useField is 100

local x in method begin is 5
```

Fig. 5.9 | Scope class demonstrating scopes of a field and local variables. (Part 2 of 2.)

Line 7 declares and initializes the field x to 1. This field is shadowed (hidden) in any block (or method) that declares a local variable named x. Method main (lines 11–23) declares a local variable x (line 13), initializes it to 5 then outputs its value to show that the field x (whose value is 1) is shadowed in method main. The program declares two other methods—useLocalVariable (lines 26–35) and useField (lines 38–45)—that each take no arguments and return no results. Method main calls each method twice (lines 17–20). Method useLocalVariable declares local variable x (line 28). When useLocalVariable is first called (line 17), it creates local variable x and initializes it to 25 (line 28), outputs the value of x (lines 30–31), increments x (line 32) and outputs the value of x again (lines 33–34). When useLocalVariable is called a second time (line 19), it recreates local variable x and re-initializes it to 25, so the output of each useLocalVariable call is identical.

Method useField does not declare any local variables. Therefore, when it refers to x, field x (line 7) of the class is used. When method useField is first called (line 18), it outputs the value (1) of field x (lines 40–41), multiplies the field x by 10 (line 42) and outputs the value (10) of field x again (lines 43–44) before returning. The next time method useField is called (line 20), the field has its modified value (10), so the method outputs 10, then 100. Finally, in method main, the program outputs the value of local variable x again (line 22) to show that none of the method calls modified main's local variable x, because the methods all referred to variables named x in other scopes.

5.12 Method Overloading

Methods of the same name can be declared in the same class, as long as they have different sets of parameters (determined by the number, types and order of the parameters)—this is called **method overloading**. When an overloaded method is called, the Java compiler selects the appropriate method by examining the number, types and order of the arguments in the call. Method overloading is commonly used to create several methods with the same name that perform the same or similar tasks, but on different types or different numbers of arguments. For example, Math methods abs, min and max (summarized in Section 5.3) are overloaded with four versions each:

1. One with two double parameters.

2. One with two float parameters.

3. One with two int parameters.

4. One with two long parameters.

Our next example demonstrates declaring and invoking overloaded methods.

Declaring Overloaded Methods

In our class MethodOverload (Fig. 5.10), we include two overloaded versions of a method called square—one that calculates the square of an int (and returns an int) and one that calculates the square of a double (and returns a double). Although these methods have the same name and similar parameter lists and bodies, think of them simply as *different* methods. It may help to think of the method names as "square of int" and "square of double," respectively.

```java
1   // Fig. 5.10: MethodOverload.java
2   // Overloaded method declarations.
3
4   public class MethodOverload
5   {
6      // test overloaded square methods
7      public static void main( String[] args )
8      {
9         System.out.printf( "Square of integer 7 is %d\n", square( 7 ) );
10        System.out.printf( "Square of double 7.5 is %f\n", square( 7.5 ) );
11     } // end method testOverloadedMethods
12
13     // square method with int argument
14     public static int square( int intValue )
15     {
16        System.out.printf( "\nCalled square with int argument: %d\n",
17           intValue );
18        return intValue * intValue;
19     } // end method square with int argument
20
21     // square method with double argument
22     public static double square( double doubleValue )
23     {
24        System.out.printf( "\nCalled square with double argument: %f\n",
25           doubleValue );
26        return doubleValue * doubleValue;
27     } // end method square with double argument
28  } // end class MethodOverload
```

Fig. 5.10 | Overloaded method declarations. (Part 1 of 2.)

```
Called square with int argument: 7
Square of integer 7 is 49

Called square with double argument: 7.500000
Square of double 7.5 is 56.250000
```

Fig. 5.10 | Overloaded method declarations. (Part 2 of 2.)

In Fig. 5.10, line 9 invokes method `square` with the argument 7. Literal integer values are treated as type `int`, so the method call in line 9 invokes the version of `square` at lines 14–19 that specifies an `int` parameter. Similarly, line 10 invokes method `square` with the argument 7.5. Literal floating-point values are treated as type `double`, so the method call in line 10 invokes the version of `square` at lines 22–27 that specifies a `double` parameter. Each method first outputs a line of text to prove that the proper method was called in each case. Note that the values in lines 10 and 24 are displayed with the format specifier `%f` and that we did not specify a precision in either case. By default, floating-point values are displayed with six digits of precision if the precision is not specified in the format specifier.

Distinguishing Between Overloaded Methods

The compiler distinguishes overloaded methods by their signature—a combination of the method's name and the number, types and order of its parameters. If the compiler looked only at method names during compilation, the code in Fig. 5.10 would be ambiguous—the compiler would not know how to distinguish between the two `square` methods (lines 14–19 and 22–27). Internally, the compiler uses longer method names that include the original method name, the types of each parameter and the exact order of the parameters to determine whether the methods in a class are unique in that class.

For example, in Fig. 5.10, the compiler might use the logical name "square of int" for the `square` method that specifies an `int` parameter and "square of double" for the `square` method that specifies a `double` parameter (the actual names the compiler uses are messier). As another example, if `method1`'s declaration begins as

```
public static void method1( int a, float b )
```

then the compiler might use the logical name "`method1` of `int` and `float`." If the parameters are specified as

```
public static void method1( float a, int b )
```

then the compiler might use the logical name "`method1` of `float` and `int`." Note that the order of the parameter types is important—the compiler considers the preceding two `method1` headers to be distinct.

Return Types of Overloaded Methods

In discussing the logical names of methods used by the compiler, we did not mention the return types of the methods. *Method calls cannot be distinguished by return type.* If you had overloaded methods that differed only by their return types and you called one of the methods in a standalone statement as in:

```
square( 2 );
```

the compiler would not be able to determine the version of the method to call, because the return value is ignored. Figure 5.11 illustrates the compiler errors generated when two methods have the same signature and different return types. Overloaded methods can have different return types if the methods have different parameter lists. Also, overloaded methods need not have the same number of parameters.

Common Programming Error 5.13
Declaring overloaded methods with identical parameter lists is a compilation error regardless of whether the return types are different.

```
 1   // Fig. 5.11: MethodOverloadError.java
 2   // Overloaded methods with identical signatures
 3   // cause compilation errors, even if return types are different.
 4
 5   public class MethodOverloadError
 6   {
 7      // declaration of method square with int argument
 8      public static int square( int x )
 9      {
10         return x * x;
11      }
12
13      // second declaration of method square with int argument
14      // causes compilation error even though return types are different
15      public static double square( int y )
16      {
17         return y * y;
18      }
19   } // end class MethodOverloadError
```

```
MethodOverloadError.java:15: square(int) is already defined in
MethodOverloadError
   public static double square( int y )
                 ^
1 error
```

Fig. 5.11 | Overloaded method declarations with identical signatures cause compilation errors, even if the return types are different.

5.13 (Optional) GUI and Graphics Case Study: Colors and Filled Shapes

Although you can create many interesting designs with just lines and basic shapes, class Graphics provides many more capabilities. The next two features we introduce are colors and filled shapes. Adding color enriches the drawings a user sees on the computer screen. Shapes can be filled with solid colors.

Colors displayed on computer screens are defined by their red, green, and blue components (called RGB values) that have integer values from 0 to 255. The higher the value of a component color, the richer that shade will be in the final color. Java uses class Color in package java.awt to represent colors using their RGB values. For convenience, class Color (java.sun.com/javase/6/docs/api/java/awt/Color.html) contains 13 predefined static Color objects—BLACK, BLUE, CYAN, DARK_GRAY, GRAY, GREEN, LIGHT_GRAY,

MAGENTA, ORANGE, PINK, RED, WHITE and YELLOW. Each can be accessed via the class name and a dot (.) as in Color.RED. You can also create a custom color with a statement of the form:

```
Color c = new Color( redValue, greenValue, blueValue );
```

in which you specify values for the red, green and blue component values.

Graphics methods fillRect and fillOval draw filled rectangles and ovals, respectively. These have the same parameters as drawRect and drawOval; the first two are the coordinates for the upper-left corner of the shape, while the next two determine the width and height. The example in Fig. 5.12 demonstrates colors and filled shapes by drawing and displaying a yellow smiley face on the screen.

```java
1   // Fig. 5.12: DrawSmiley.java
2   // Demonstrates filled shapes.
3   import java.awt.Color;
4   import java.awt.Graphics;
5   import javax.swing.JPanel;
6   import javax.swing.JFrame;
7
8   public class DrawSmiley extends JPanel
9   {
10     public void paintComponent( Graphics g )
11     {
12        super.paintComponent( g );
13
14        // draw the face
15        g.setColor( Color.YELLOW );
16        g.fillOval( 10, 10, 200, 200 );
17
18        // draw the eyes
19        g.setColor( Color.BLACK );
20        g.fillOval( 55, 65, 30, 30 );
21        g.fillOval( 135, 65, 30, 30 );
22
23        // draw the mouth
24        g.fillOval( 50, 110, 120, 60 );
25
26        // "touch up" the mouth into a smile
27        g.setColor( Color.YELLOW );
28        g.fillRect( 50, 110, 120, 30 );
29        g.fillOval( 50, 120, 120, 40 );
30     } // end method paintComponent
31
32     public static void main( String[] args )
33     {
34        DrawSmiley panel = new DrawSmiley(); // create the panel
35        JFrame application = new JFrame(); // creates a new JFrame
36
37        application.setDefaultCloseOperation( JFrame.EXIT_ON_CLOSE );
38        application.add( panel ); // add the panel to the frame
39        application.setSize( 230, 250 ); // set the desired size
```

Fig. 5.12 | Drawing a smiley face using colors and filled shapes. (Part 1 of 2.)

```
40          application.setVisible( true ); // show the frame
41      } // end main
42  } // end class DrawSmiley
```

Fig. 5.12 | Drawing a smiley face using colors and filled shapes. (Part 2 of 2.)

The import statement in lines 3 imports classes Color. Class DrawSmiley uses class Color to specify drawing colors. Line 15 in method paintComponent uses Graphics method setColor to set the current drawing color to Color.YELLOW. Method setColor requires one argument, the Color to set as the drawing color. In this case, we use the pre-defined object Color.YELLOW. Line 16 draws a circle with diameter 200 to represent the face—when the width and height arguments are identical, method fillOval draws a circle. Next, line 19 sets the color to Color.Black, and lines 20–21 draw the eyes. Line 24 draws the mouth as an oval, but this is not quite what we want. To create a happy face, we'll "touch up" the mouth. Line 27 sets the color to Color.YELLOW, so any shapes we draw will blend in with the face. Line 28 draws a rectangle that is half the mouth's height. This "erases" the top half of the mouth, leaving just the bottom half. To create a better smile, line 29 draws another oval to slightly cover the upper portion of the mouth. The main method creates and displays a JFrame containing the drawing. When the JFrame is displayed, the system calls method paintComponent to draw the smiley face.

GUI and Graphics Case Study Exercises

5.1 Using method fillOval, draw a bull's-eye that alternates between two random colors, as in Fig. 5.13. Use a statement like

```
Color color1 = new Color( redValue, greenValue, blueValue );
```

with random arguments to generate random colors.

Fig. 5.13 | A bull's-eye with two alternating, random colors.

5.2   Create a program that draws 10 random filled shapes in random colors, positions and sizes (Fig. 5.14). Method `paintComponent` should contain a loop that iterates 10 times. In each iteration, the loop should determine whether to draw a filled rectangle or an oval, create a random color and choose coordinates and dimensions at random. The coordinates should be chosen based on the panel's width and height. Lengths of sides should be limited to half the width or height of the window.

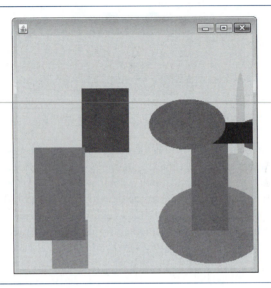

Fig. 5.14 | Randomly generated shapes.

5.14 Wrap-Up

In this chapter, you learned about method declarations and how to call static methods. You learned how to use operators + and += to perform string concatenations. We discussed how the method-call stack and activation records keep track of the methods that have been called and where each method must return to when it completes its task. We also discussed Java's promotion rules for converting implicitly between primitive types and how to perform explicit conversions with cast operators. Next, you learned about some of the commonly used packages in the Java API.

You saw how to declare named constants using both `enum` types and `public static final` variables. You used class `Random` to generate random numbers for simulations. You also learned about the scope of fields and local variables in a class. Finally, you learned that multiple methods in one class can be overloaded by providing methods with the same name and different signatures. Such methods can be used to perform the same or similar tasks using different types or different numbers of parameters.

In Chapter 6, you'll learn how to maintain lists and tables of data in arrays. You'll see a more elegant implementation of the application that rolls a die 6000 times. You'll learn how to access an application's command-line arguments that are passed to method `main` when an application begins execution. You'll study various methods of class `String` for performing `String` manipulations. You'll also write data to and read data from text files on disk.

Summary

Section 5.1 Introduction
- Experience has shown that the best way to develop and maintain a large program is to construct it from small, simple pieces, or modules. This technique is called divide and conquer.

Section 5.2 Program Modules in Java
- Methods are declared within classes. Classes are typically grouped into packages so they can be imported and reused.
- Methods allow you to modularize a program by separating its tasks into self-contained units. The statements in a method are written only once and hidden from other methods.
- Using existing methods as building blocks to create new programs is a form of software reusability that allows you to avoid repeating code within a program.

Section 5.3 `static` Methods, `static` Fields and Class `Math`
- A method call specifies the name of the method to call and provides the arguments that the called method requires to perform its task. When the method call completes, the method returns either a result, or simply control, to its caller.
- A class may contain `static` methods to perform common tasks that do not require an object of the class. Any data a `static` method might require to perform its tasks can be sent to the method as arguments in a method call. A `static` method is called by specifying the name of the class in which the method is declared followed by a dot (`.`) and the method name, as in

    ClassName.*methodName*(*arguments*)

- Class `Math` provides `static` methods for performing common mathematical calculations.
- The constant `Math.PI` (3.141592653589793) is the ratio of a circle's circumference to its diameter. The constant `Math.E` (2.718281828459045) is the base value for natural logarithms (calculated with `static` `Math` method `log`).
- `Math.PI` and `Math.E` are declared with the modifiers `public`, `final` and `static`. Making them `public` allows you to use these fields in your own classes. A field declared with keyword `final` is constant—its value cannot be changed after it's initialized. Both `PI` and `E` are declared `final` because their values never change. Making these fields `static` allows them to be accessed via the class name `Math` and a dot (`.`) separator, just like class `Math`'s methods.
- When you execute the Java Virtual Machine (JVM) with the `java` command, the JVM loads the class you specify and uses that class name to invoke method `main`. You can specify additional command-line arguments that the JVM will pass to your application.

Section 5.4 Declaring Methods
- Unlike `main`, most methods must be called explicitly to tell them to perform their tasks.
- The method's return type specifies the type of data the method returns (i.e., gives back) to the calling method after performing its task.
- In some cases, you'll define methods that perform a task but will *not* return any information. Such methods use the return type `void`.
- By convention, method names begin with a lowercase first letter and subsequent words in the name begin with a capital letter.
- If the parentheses after the method name are empty, the method does not require additional information to perform its task.
- For a method that does require additional information to perform its task, the method can require one or more parameters that represent that additional information.

- Parameters are defined in a comma-separated parameter list, which is located in the parentheses that follow the method name.

- A method's parameters are considered to be local variables of that method and can be used only in that method's body.

- A method call supplies values—called arguments—for each of the method's parameters.

- Collectively, the elements in the first line of a method declaration are often referred to as the method header.

- A method's body contains one or more statements that perform the method's task.

- A return statement is used to return a value to a calling method.

- Scanner method nextDouble returns a double value.

- When a method is called, the program makes a copy of the method's argument values and assigns them to the method's corresponding parameters. When program control returns to the point in the program where the method was called, the method's parameters are removed from memory.

- A method can return at most one value, but the returned value could represent an object that contains many values.

- Variables should be declared as fields of a class only if they're required for use in more than one method of the class or if the program should save their values between calls to the class's methods.

- When a method has more than one parameter, the parameters are specified as a comma-separated list. There must be one argument in the method call for each parameter in the method declaration. Also, each argument must be consistent with the type of the corresponding parameter. If a method does not accept arguments, the parameter list is empty.

- Strings can be concatenated using operator +, which places the characters of the right operand at the end of those in the left operand.

- Every primitive value and object in Java has a String representation. When an object is concatenated with a String, the object is converted to a String, then the two Strings are concatenated.

- If a boolean is concatenated with a String, the word "true" or the word "false" is used to represent the boolean value.

- All objects in Java have a special method named toString that returns a String representation of the object's contents. When an object is concatenated with a String, the JVM implicitly calls the object's toString method to obtain the String representation of the object.

- Programmers sometimes break large String literals into several smaller Strings and place them on multiple lines of code for readability, then reassemble the Strings using concatenation.

Section 5.5 Notes on Declaring and Using Methods

- There are three ways to call a method—using a method name by itself to call another method of the same class; using a variable that represents an object, followed by a dot (.) and the method name to call a method of that object; and using the class name and a dot (.) to call a static method of a class.

- There are three ways to return control to a statement that calls a method. If the method does not return a result, control returns when the program flow reaches the method-ending right brace or when the statement

```
return;
```

is executed. If the method returns a result, the statement

```
return expression;
```

evaluates the *expression*, then immediately returns the resulting value to the caller.

Section 5.6 Method-Call Stack and Activation Records

- Stacks are known as last-in, first-out (LIFO) data structures—the last item pushed (inserted) on the stack is the first item popped (removed) from the stack.

- A called method must know how to return to its caller, so the return address of the calling method is pushed onto the program-execution stack when the method is called. If a series of method calls occurs, the successive return addresses are pushed onto the stack in last-in, first-out order so that the last method to execute will be the first to return to its caller.

- The program-execution stack contains the memory for the local variables used in each invocation of a method during a program's execution. This data is known as the method call's activation record or stack frame. When a method call is made, the activation record for that method call is pushed onto the program-execution stack. When the method returns to its caller, its activation record call is popped off the stack and the local variables are no longer known to the program.

- The amount of memory in a computer is finite, so only a certain amount of memory can be used to store activation records on the program-execution stack. If there are more method calls than can have their activation records stored on the program-execution stack, an error known as a stack overflow occurs. The application will compile correctly, but its execution causes a stack overflow.

Section 5.7 Argument Promotion and Casting

- Argument promotion converts an argument's value to the type that the method expects to receive in its corresponding parameter.

- Promotion rules apply to expressions containing values of two or more primitive types and to primitive-type values passed as arguments to methods. Each value is promoted to the "highest" type in the expression. In cases where information may be lost due to conversion, the Java compiler requires you to use a cast operator to explicitly force the conversion to occur.

Section 5.9 Case Study: Random-Number Generation

- Objects of class Random (package java.util) can produce random int, long, float or double values. Math method random can produce double values in the range $0.0 \leq x < 1.0$, where x is the value returned by method random.

- Random method nextInt generates a random int value in the range –2,147,483,648 to +2,147,483,647. The values returned by nextInt are actually pseudorandom numbers—a sequence of values produced by a complex mathematical calculation. That calculation uses the current time of day to seed the random-number generator such that each execution of a program yields a different sequence of random values.

- Class Random provides another version of method nextInt that receives an int argument and returns a value from 0 up to, but not including, the argument's value.

- Random numbers in a range can be generated with

      number = *shiftingValue* + randomNumbers.nextInt(*scalingFactor*);

  where *shiftingValue* specifies the first number in the desired range of consecutive integers, and *scalingFactor* specifies how many numbers are in the range.

- Random numbers can be chosen from nonconsecutive integer ranges, as in

      number = *shiftingValue* +
          differenceBetweenValues * randomNumbers.nextInt(*scalingFactor*);

  where *shiftingValue* specifies the first number in the range of values, *differenceBetweenValues* represents the difference between consecutive numbers in the sequence and *scalingFactor* specifies how many numbers are in the range.

- For debugging, it's sometimes useful to repeat the sequence of pseudorandom numbers during each program execution. To do so, initialize the Random object with a long integer value. Using the same seed every time the program executes, produces the same sequence of numbers.

Section 5.10 Case Study: A Game of Chance; Introducing Enumerations

- An enumeration is introduced by the keyword enum and a type name. As with any class, braces ({ and }) delimit the body of an enum declaration. Inside the braces is a comma-separated list of enumeration constants, each representing a unique value. The identifiers in an enum must be unique. Variables of an enum type can be assigned only constants of that enum type.
- Constants can also be declared as public final static variables. Such constants are declared with all capital letters by convention to make them stand out in the program.

Section 5.11 Scope of Declarations

- Scope is the portion of the program in which an entity, such as a variable or a method, can be referred to by its name. Such an entity is said to be "in scope" for that portion of the program.
- The scope of a parameter declaration is the body of the method in which the declaration appears.
- The scope of a local-variable declaration is from the point at which the declaration appears to the end of that block.
- The scope of a local-variable declaration that appears in the initialization section of a for statement's header is the body of the for statement and the other expressions in the header.
- The scope of a method or field of a class is the entire body of the class.
- Any block may contain variable declarations. If a local variable or parameter in a method has the same name as a field, the field is shadowed until the block terminates execution.

Section 5.12 Method Overloading

- Java allows several methods of the same name to be declared in a class, as long as the methods have different sets of parameters (determined by the number, order and types of the parameters). This technique is called method overloading.
- Overloaded methods are distinguished by their signatures—combinations of the methods' names and the number, types and order of their parameters. Methods cannot be distinguished by return type.

Terminology

Self-Review Exercises

5.1 Fill in the blanks in each of the following statements:
a) A method is invoked with a(n) _____.
b) A variable known only within the method in which it's declared is called a(n) _____.
c) The _____ statement in a called method can be used to pass the value of an expression back to the calling method.
d) The keyword _____ indicates that a method does not return a value.
e) Data can be added or removed only from the _____ of a stack.
f) Stacks are known as _____ data structures—the last item pushed (inserted) on the stack is the first item popped (removed) from the stack.
g) The three ways to return control from a called method to a caller are _____, _____ and _____.
h) An object of class _____ produces random numbers.
i) The program-execution stack contains the memory for local variables on each invocation of a method during a program's execution. This data, stored as a portion of the program-execution stack, is known as the _____ or _____ of the method call.
j) If there are more method calls than can be stored on the program-execution stack, an error known as a(n) _____ occurs.
k) The _____ of a declaration is the portion of a program that can refer to the entity in the declaration by name.
l) It's possible to have several methods with the same name that each operate on different types or numbers of arguments. This feature is called method _____.
m) The program-execution stack is also referred to as the _____ stack.
n) Scanner method _____ returns a double value.

5.2 For the class Craps in Fig. 5.8, state the scope of each of the following entities:
a) the variable randomNumbers.
b) the variable die1.
c) the method rollDice.
d) the method main.
e) the variable sumOfDice.

5.3 Write an application that tests whether the examples of the Math class method calls shown in Fig. 5.2 actually produce the indicated results.

5.4 Give the method header for each of the following methods:
a) Method hypotenuse, which takes two double-precision, floating-point arguments side1 and side2 and returns a double-precision, floating-point result.
b) Method smallest, which takes three integers x, y and z and returns an integer.
c) Method instructions, which does not take any arguments and does not return a value. [*Note:* Such methods are commonly used to display instructions to a user.]
d) Method intToFloat, which takes an integer argument number and returns a floating-point result.

5.5   Find the error in each of the following program segments. Explain how to correct the error.

a) ```java
void g()
{
    System.out.println("Inside method g");

    void h()
    {
        System.out.println("Inside method h");
    }
}
```

b) ```java
int sum( int x, int y )
{
    int result;
    result = x + y;
}
```

c) ```java
void f(float a)
{
    float a;
    System.out.println(a);
}
```

d) ```java
void product()
{
    int a = 6, b = 5, c = 4, result;
    result = a * b * c;
    System.out.printf( "Result is %d\n", result );
    return result;
}
```

5.6   Write a complete Java application to prompt the user for the double radius of a sphere, and call method sphereVolume to calculate and display the volume of the sphere. Use the following statement to calculate the volume:

```java
double volume = ( 4.0 / 3.0 ) * Math.PI * Math.pow( radius, 3 )
```

Answers to Self-Review Exercises

5.1   a) method call. b) local variable. c) return. d) void. e) top. f) last-in, first-out (LIFO). g) return; or return *expression*; or encountering the closing right brace of a method. h) Random. i) activation record, stack frame. j) stack overflow. k) scope. l) method overloading. m) method call. n) nextDouble.

5.2   a) class body. b) block that defines method rollDice's body. c) class body. d) class body. e) block that defines method main's body.

5.3   The following solution demonstrates the Math class methods in Fig. 5.2:

```java
1   // Exercise 5.3: MathTest.java
2   // Testing the Math class methods.
3
4   public class MathTest
5   {
6       public static void main( String[] args )
7       {
8           System.out.printf( "Math.abs( 23.7 ) = %f\n", Math.abs( 23.7 ) );
9           System.out.printf( "Math.abs( 0.0 ) = %f\n", Math.abs( 0.0 ) );
```

```
10          System.out.printf( "Math.abs( -23.7 ) = %f\n", Math.abs( -23.7 ) );
11          System.out.printf( "Math.ceil( 9.2 ) = %f\n", Math.ceil( 9.2 ) );
12          System.out.printf( "Math.ceil( -9.8 ) = %f\n", Math.ceil( -9.8 ) );
13          System.out.printf( "Math.cos( 0.0 ) = %f\n", Math.cos( 0.0 ) );
14          System.out.printf( "Math.exp( 1.0 ) = %f\n", Math.exp( 1.0 ) );
15          System.out.printf( "Math.exp( 2.0 ) = %f\n", Math.exp( 2.0 ) );
16          System.out.printf( "Math.floor( 9.2 ) = %f\n", Math.floor( 9.2 ) );
17          System.out.printf( "Math.floor( -9.8 ) = %f\n",
18             Math.floor( -9.8 ) );
19          System.out.printf( "Math.log( Math.E ) = %f\n",
20             Math.log( Math.E ) );
21          System.out.printf( "Math.log( Math.E * Math.E ) = %f\n",
22             Math.log( Math.E * Math.E ) );
23          System.out.printf( "Math.max( 2.3, 12.7 ) = %f\n",
24             Math.max( 2.3, 12.7 ) );
25          System.out.printf( "Math.max( -2.3, -12.7 ) = %f\n",
26             Math.max( -2.3, -12.7 ) );
27          System.out.printf( "Math.min( 2.3, 12.7 ) = %f\n",
28             Math.min( 2.3, 12.7 ) );
29          System.out.printf( "Math.min( -2.3, -12.7 ) = %f\n",
30             Math.min( -2.3, -12.7 ) );
31          System.out.printf( "Math.pow( 2.0, 7.0 ) = %f\n",
32             Math.pow( 2.0, 7.0 ) );
33          System.out.printf( "Math.pow( 9.0, 0.5 ) = %f\n",
34             Math.pow( 9.0, 0.5 ) );
35          System.out.printf( "Math.sin( 0.0 ) = %f\n", Math.sin( 0.0 ) );
36          System.out.printf( "Math.sqrt( 900.0 ) = %f\n",
37             Math.sqrt( 900.0 ) );
38          System.out.printf( "Math.tan( 0.0 ) = %f\n", Math.tan( 0.0 ) );
39       } // end main
40    } // end class MathTest
```

```
Math.abs( 23.7 ) = 23.700000
Math.abs( 0.0 ) = 0.000000
Math.abs( -23.7 ) = 23.700000
Math.ceil( 9.2 ) = 10.000000
Math.ceil( -9.8 ) = -9.000000
Math.cos( 0.0 ) = 1.000000
Math.exp( 1.0 ) = 2.718282
Math.exp( 2.0 ) = 7.389056
Math.floor( 9.2 ) = 9.000000
Math.floor( -9.8 ) = -10.000000
Math.log( Math.E ) = 1.000000
Math.log( Math.E * Math.E ) = 2.000000
Math.max( 2.3, 12.7 ) = 12.700000
Math.max( -2.3, -12.7 ) = -2.300000
Math.min( 2.3, 12.7 ) = 2.300000
Math.min( -2.3, -12.7 ) = -12.700000
Math.pow( 2.0, 7.0 ) = 128.000000
Math.pow( 9.0, 0.5 ) = 3.000000
Math.sin( 0.0 ) = 0.000000
Math.sqrt( 900.0 ) = 30.000000
Math.tan( 0.0 ) = 0.000000
```

5.4   a) `double hypotenuse( double side1, double side2 )`
      b) `int smallest( int x, int y, int z )`
      c) `void instructions()`
      d) `float intToFloat( int number )`

5.5   a) Error: Method h is declared within method g.
        Correction: Move the declaration of h outside the declaration of g.

b) Error: The method is supposed to return an integer, but does not.
Correction: Delete the variable `result`, and place the statement

```
return x + y;
```

in the method, or add the following statement at the end of the method body:

```
return result;
```

c) Error: The semicolon after the right parenthesis of the parameter list is incorrect, and the parameter a should not be redeclared in the method.
Correction: Delete the semicolon after the right parenthesis of the parameter list, and delete the declaration `float a;`.

d) Error: The method returns a value when it's not supposed to.
Correction: Change the return type from `void` to `int`.

5.6   The following solution calculates the volume of a sphere, using the radius entered by the user:

```
 1   // Exercise 5.6: Sphere.java
 2   // Calculate the volume of a sphere.
 3   import java.util.Scanner;
 4
 5   public class Sphere
 6   {
 7      // obtain radius from user and display volume of sphere
 8      public static void main( String[] args )
 9      {
10         Scanner input = new Scanner( System.in );
11
12         System.out.print( "Enter radius of sphere: " );
13         double radius = input.nextDouble();
14
15         System.out.printf( "Volume is %f\n", sphereVolume( radius ) );
16      } // end method determineSphereVolume
17
18      // calculate and return sphere volume
19      public static double sphereVolume( double radius )
20      {
21         double volume = ( 4.0 / 3.0 ) * Math.PI * Math.pow( radius, 3 );
22         return volume;
23      } // end method sphereVolume
24   } // end class Sphere
```

```
Enter radius of sphere: 4
Volume is 268.082573
```

Exercises

5.7   What is the value of x after each of the following statements is executed?
a) x = Math.abs(7.5);
b) x = Math.floor(7.5);
c) x = Math.abs(0.0);
d) x = Math.ceil(0.0);
e) x = Math.abs(-6.4);
f) x = Math.ceil(-6.4);
g) x = Math.ceil(-Math.abs(-8 + Math.floor(-5.5)));

5.8   *(Parking Charges)* A parking garage charges a $2.00 minimum fee to park for up to three hours. The garage charges an additional $0.50 per hour for each hour *or part thereof* in excess of three hours. The maximum charge for any given 24-hour period is $10.00. Assume that no car parks for longer than 24 hours at a time. Write an application that calculates and displays the parking charges for each customer who parked in the garage yesterday. You should enter the hours parked for each customer. The program should display the charge for the current customer and should calculate and display the running total of yesterday's receipts. It should use the method `calculateCharges` to determine the charge for each customer.

5.9   *(Rounding Numbers)* `Math.floor` can be used to round values to the nearest integer—e.g.,

```
y = Math.floor( x + 0.5 );
```

will round the number x to the nearest integer and assign the result to y. Write an application that reads `double` values and uses the preceding statement to round each of the numbers to the nearest integer. For each number processed, display both the original number and the rounded number.

5.10   *(Rounding Numbers)* To round numbers to specific decimal places, use a statement like

```
y = Math.floor( x * 10 + 0.5 ) / 10;
```

which rounds x to the tenths position (i.e., the first position to the right of the decimal point), or

```
y = Math.floor( x * 100 + 0.5 ) / 100;
```

which rounds x to the hundredths position (i.e., the second position to the right of the decimal point). Write an application that defines four methods for rounding a number x in various ways:

a) `roundToInteger( number )`
b) `roundToTenths( number )`
c) `roundToHundredths( number )`
d) `roundToThousandths( number )`

For each value read, your program should display the original value, the number rounded to the nearest integer, the number rounded to the nearest tenth, the number rounded to the nearest hundredth and the number rounded to the nearest thousandth.

5.11   Answer each of the following questions:

a) What does it mean to choose numbers "at random"?
b) Why is the `nextInt` method of class `Random` useful for simulating games of chance?
c) Why is it often necessary to scale or shift the values produced by a `Random` object?
d) Why is computerized simulation of real-world situations a useful technique?

5.12   Write statements that assign random integers to the variable *n* in the following ranges:

a) $1 \leq n \leq 2$.
b) $1 \leq n \leq 100$.
c) $0 \leq n \leq 9$.
d) $1000 \leq n \leq 1112$.
e) $-1 \leq n \leq 1$.
f) $-3 \leq n \leq 11$.

5.13   For each of the following sets of integers, write a single statement that will display a number at random from the set:

a) 2, 4, 6, 8, 10.
b) 3, 5, 7, 9, 11.
c) 6, 10, 14, 18, 22.

5.14   *(Exponentiation)* Write a method `integerPower(base, exponent)` that returns the value of

$$base^{\,exponent}$$

For example, `integerPower(3, 4)` calculates 3^4 (or 3 * 3 * 3 * 3). Assume that exponent is a positive, nonzero integer and that base is an integer. Method `integerPower` should use a `for` or `while` statement to control the calculation. Do not use any `Math` class methods. Incorporate this method into an application that reads integer values for base and exponent and performs the calculation with the `integerPower` method.

5.15 *(Hypotenuse Calculations)* Define a method hypotenuse that calculates the hypotenuse of a right triangle when the lengths of the other two sides are given. The method should take two arguments of type double and return the hypotenuse as a double. Incorporate this method into an application that reads values for side1 and side2 and performs the calculation with the hypotenuse method. Use Math methods pow and sqrt to determine the length of the hypotenuse for each of the triangles in Fig. 5.15. [*Note:* Class Math also provides method hypot to perform this calculation.]

Triangle	Side 1	Side 2
1	3.0	4.0
2	5.0	12.0
3	8.0	15.0

Fig. 5.15 | Values for the sides of triangles in Exercise 5.15.

5.16 *(Multiples)* Write a method isMultiple that determines, for a pair of integers, whether the second integer is a multiple of the first. The method should take two integer arguments and return true if the second is a multiple of the first and false otherwise. [*Hint:* Use the remainder operator.] Incorporate this method into an application that inputs a series of pairs of integers (one pair at a time) and determines whether the second value in each pair is a multiple of the first.

5.17 *(Even or Odd)* Write a method isEven that uses the remainder operator (%) to determine whether an integer is even. The method should take an integer argument and return true if the integer is even and false otherwise. Incorporate this method into an application that inputs a sequence of integers (one at a time) and determines whether each is even or odd.

5.18 *(Displaying a Square of Asterisks)* Write a method squareOfAsterisks that displays a solid square (the same number of rows and columns) of asterisks whose side is specified in integer parameter side. For example, if side is 4, the method should display

```
****
****
****
****
```

Incorporate this method into an application that reads an integer value for side from the user and outputs the asterisks with the squareOfAsterisks method.

5.19 *(Displaying a Square of Any Character)* Modify the method created in Exercise 5.18 to receive a second parameter of type char called fillCharacter. Form the square using the char provided as an argument. Thus, if side is 5 and fillCharacter is #, the method should display

```
#####
#####
#####
#####
#####
```

Use the following statement (in which input is a Scanner object) to read a character from the user at the keyboard:

```
char fill = input.next().charAt( 0 );
```

5.20 *(Circle Area)* Write an application that prompts the user for the radius of a circle and uses a method called circleArea to calculate the area of the circle.

5.21 *(Separating Digits)* Write methods that accomplish each of the following tasks:
   a) Calculate the integer part of the quotient when integer a is divided by integer b.
   b) Calculate the integer remainder when integer a is divided by integer b.

    c) Use the methods developed in parts (a) and (b) to write a method `displayDigits` that receives an integer between 1 and 99999 and displays it as a sequence of digits, separating each pair of digits by two spaces. For example, the integer 4562 should appear as

        4 5 6 2

Incorporate the methods into an application that inputs an integer and calls `displayDigits` by passing the method the integer entered. Display the results.

5.22 *(Temperature Conversions)* Implement the following integer methods:
    a) Method `celsius` returns the Celsius equivalent of a Fahrenheit temperature, using the calculation

```
celsius = 5.0 / 9.0 * ( fahrenheit - 32 );
```

    b) Method `fahrenheit` returns the Fahrenheit equivalent of a Celsius temperature, using the calculation

```
fahrenheit = 9.0 / 5.0 * celsius + 32;
```

    c) Use the methods from parts (a) and (b) to write an application that enables the user either to enter a Fahrenheit temperature and display the Celsius equivalent or to enter a Celsius temperature and display the Fahrenheit equivalent.

5.23 *(Find the Minimum)* Write a method `minimum3` that returns the smallest of three floating-point numbers. Use the `Math.min` method to implement `minimum3`. Incorporate the method into an application that reads three values from the user, determines the smallest value and displays the result.

5.24 *(Perfect Numbers)* An integer number is said to be a *perfect number* if its factors, including 1 (but not the number itself), sum to the number. For example, 6 is a perfect number, because 6 = 1 + 2 + 3. Write a method `isPerfect` that determines if parameter `number` is a perfect number. Use this method in an application that displays all the perfect numbers between 1 and 1000. Display the factors of each perfect number to confirm that the number is indeed perfect. Challenge the computing power of your computer by testing numbers much larger than 1000. Display the results.

5.25 *(Prime Numbers)* A positive integer is *prime* if it's divisible by only 1 and itself. For example, 2, 3, 5 and 7 are prime, but 4, 6, 8 and 9 are not. The number 1, by definition, is not prime.
    a) Write a method that determines whether a number is prime.
    b) Use this method in an application that determines and displays all the prime numbers less than 10,000. How many numbers up to 10,000 do you have to test to ensure that you've found all the primes?
    c) Initially, you might think that $n/2$ is the upper limit for which you must test to see whether a number n is prime, but you need only go as high as the square root of n. Rewrite the program, and run it both ways.

5.26 *(Reversing Digits)* Write a method that takes an integer value and returns the number with its digits reversed. For example, given the number 7631, the method should return 1367. Incorporate the method into an application that reads a value from the user and displays the result.

5.27 *(Greatest Common Divisor)* The *greatest common divisor* (*GCD*) of two integers is the largest integer that evenly divides each of the two numbers. Write a method `gcd` that returns the greatest common divisor of two integers. [*Hint:* You might want to use Euclid's algorithm. You can find information about the algorithm at `en.wikipedia.org/wiki/Euclidean_algorithm`.] Incorporate the method into an application that reads two values from the user and displays the result.

5.28 Write a method `qualityPoints` that inputs a student's average and returns 4 if the student's average is 90–100, 3 if the average is 80–89, 2 if the average is 70–79, 1 if the average is 60–69 and 0 if the average is lower than 60. Incorporate the method into an application that reads a value from the user and displays the result.

5.29 *(Coin Tossing)* Write an application that simulates coin tossing. Let the program toss a coin each time the user chooses the "Toss Coin" menu option. Count the number of times each side of the coin appears. Display the results. The program should call a separate method flip that takes no arguments and returns a value from a Coin enum (HEADS and TAILS). [*Note:* If the program realistically simulates coin tossing, each side of the coin should appear approximately half the time.]

5.30 *(Guess the Number)* Write an application that plays "guess the number" as follows: Your program chooses the number to be guessed by selecting a random integer in the range 1 to 1000. The application displays the prompt Guess a number between 1 and 1000. The player inputs a first guess. If the player's guess is incorrect, your program should display Too high. Try again. or Too low. Try again. to help the player "zero in" on the correct answer. The program should prompt the user for the next guess. When the user enters the correct answer, display Congratulations. You guessed the number!, and allow the user to choose whether to play again. [*Note:* The guessing technique employed in this problem is similar to a binary search, which is discussed in Chapter 19, Searching, Sorting and Big O.]

5.31 *(Guess the Number Modification)* Modify the program of Exercise 5.30 to count the number of guesses the player makes. If the number is 10 or fewer, display Either you know the secret or you got lucky! If the player guesses the number in 10 tries, display Aha! You know the secret! If the player makes more than 10 guesses, display You should be able to do better! Why should it take no more than 10 guesses? Well, with each "good guess," the player should be able to eliminate half of the numbers, then half of the remaining numbers, and so on.

5.32 *(Distance Between Points)* Write method distance to calculate the distance between two points (*x1*, *y1*) and (*x2*, *y2*). All numbers and return values should be of type double. Incorporate this method into an application that enables the user to enter the coordinates of the points.

5.33 *(Craps Game Modification)* Modify the craps program of Fig. 5.8 to allow wagering. Initialize variable bankBalance to 1000 dollars. Prompt the player to enter a wager. Check that wager is less than or equal to bankBalance, and if it's not, have the user reenter wager until a valid wager is entered. After a correct wager is entered, run one game of craps. If the player wins, increase bankBalance by wager and display the new bankBalance. If the player loses, decrease bankBalance by wager, display the new bankBalance, check whether bankBalance has become zero and, if so, display the message "Sorry. You busted!" As the game progresses, display various messages to create some "chatter," such as "Oh, you're going for broke, huh?" or "Aw c'mon, take a chance!" or "You're up big. Now's the time to cash in your chips!". Implement the "chatter" as a separate method that randomly chooses the string to display.

5.34 *(Table of Binary, Octal and Hexadecimal Numbers)* Write an application that displays a table of the binary, octal and hexadecimal equivalents of the decimal numbers in the range 1 through 256. If you are not familiar with these number systems, read Appendix H first.

Making a Difference

As computer costs decline, it becomes feasible for every student, regardless of economic circumstance, to have a computer and use it in school. This creates exciting possibilities for improving the educational experience of all students worldwide as suggested by the next five exercises. [*Note:* Check out initiatives such as the One Laptop Per Child Project (www.laptop.org). Also, research "green" laptops—what are some key "going green" characteristics of these devices? Look into the Electronic Product Environmental Assessment Tool (www.epeat.net) which can help you assess the "greenness" of desktops, notebooks and monitors to help you decide which products to purchase.]

5.35 *(Computer-Assisted Instruction)* The use of computers in education is referred to as *computer-assisted instruction (CAI)*. Write a program that will help an elementary school student learn multiplication. Use a Random object to produce two positive one-digit integers. The program should then prompt the user with a question, such as

```
How much is 6 times 7?
```

The student then inputs the answer. Next, the program checks the student's answer. If it's correct, display the message "Very good!" and ask another multiplication question. If the answer is wrong, display the message "No. Please try again." and let the student try the same question repeatedly until the student finally gets it right. A separate method should be used to generate each new question. This method should be called once when the application begins execution and each time the user answers the question correctly.

5.36   *(Computer-Assisted Instruction: Reducing Student Fatigue)* One problem in CAI environments is student fatigue. This can be reduced by varying the computer's responses to hold the student's attention. Modify the program of Exercise 5.35 so that various comments are displayed for each answer as follows:

Possible responses to a correct answer:

```
Very good!
Excellent!
Nice work!
Keep up the good work!
```

Possible responses to an incorrect answer:

```
No. Please try again.
Wrong. Try once more.
Don't give up!
No. Keep trying.
```

Use random-number generation to choose a number from 1 to 4 that will be used to select one of the four appropriate responses to each correct or incorrect answer. Use a switch statement to issue the responses.

5.37   *(Computer-Assisted Instruction: Monitoring Student Performance)* More sophisticated computer-assisted instruction systems monitor the student's performance over a period of time. The decision to begin a new topic is often based on the student's success with previous topics. Modify the program of Exercise 5.36 to count the number of correct and incorrect responses typed by the student. After the student types 10 answers, your program should calculate the percentage that are correct. If the percentage is lower than 75%, display "Please ask your teacher for extra help.", then reset the program so another student can try it. If the percentage is 75% or higher, display "Congratulations, you are ready to go to the next level!", then reset the program so another student can try it.

5.38   *(Computer-Assisted Instruction: Difficulty Levels)* Exercise 5.35 through Exercise 5.37 developed a computer-assisted instruction program to help teach an elementary school student multiplication. Modify the program to allow the user to enter a difficulty level. At a difficulty level of 1, the program should use only single-digit numbers in the problems; at a difficulty level of 2, numbers as large as two digits, and so on.

5.39   *(Computer-Assisted Instruction: Varying the Types of Problems)* Modify the program of Exercise 5.38 to allow the user to pick a type of arithmetic problem to study. An option of 1 means addition problems only, 2 means subtraction problems only, 3 means multiplication problems only, 4 means division problems only and 5 means a random mixture of all these types.

6

Arrays; Introducing Strings and Files

Now go, write it before them in a table, and note it in a book.
—Isaiah 30:8

To go beyond is as wrong as to fall short.
—Confucius

Begin at the beginning, ... and go on till you come to the end: then stop.
—Lewis Carroll

Objectives

In this chapter you'll learn:

- What arrays are.
- To use arrays to manipulate lists and tables of values.
- To use the enhanced **for** statement with arrays.
- To pass arrays to methods.
- To declare and manipulate multidimensional arrays.
- To write variable-length-argument-list methods.
- To read command-line arguments into a program.
- To use the **ArrayList** collection.
- To create and manipulate immutable character-string objects of class **String**.
- To create, read and write update files.

6.1 Introduction

This chapter introduces data structures—collections of related data items. Arrays are data structures consisting of related data items of the same type. Arrays make it convenient to process related groups of values. Arrays remain the same length once they are created, although an array variable may be reassigned such that it refers to a new array of a different length. We study data structures in depth in Chapters 20–22.

After discussing how arrays are declared, created and initialized, we present practical examples that demonstrate common array manipulations. We introduce the enhanced `for` statement, which provides easier access to the data in an array than does the counter-controlled `for` statement presented in Section 4.3. We use arrays to store and analyze student grades from multiple exams. We show how to use variable-length argument lists to create methods that can be called with varying numbers of arguments, and we demonstrate how to process command-line arguments in method `main`. Next, we present some common array manipulations with `static` methods of class `Arrays` from the `java.util` package.

Although commonly used, arrays have limited capabilities. For instance, you must specify an array's size, and if at execution time you wish to modify it, you must create a new array. After discussing arrays, we introduce one of Java's prebuilt data structures from the Java API's collection classes. These offer greater capabilities than traditional arrays. They're reusable, reliable, powerful and efficient and have been designed and tested to ensure quality and performance. We focus on the `ArrayList` collection. `ArrayList`s are similar to arrays but provide additional functionality, such as dynamic resizing—they automatically increase their size at execution time to accommodate additional elements.

Next, we introduce the fundamentals of `String` processing. Class `String` provides capabilities for comparing `String`s, searching for substrings in `String`s and other common manipulations that are appropriate for validating program input, displaying information to users and more. Chapter 16 discusses additional `String`- and character-processing capabilities. Finally, we show how to use files for long-term data retention, after your programs terminate. Data stored in variables and arrays is temporary—it's lost when a local variable goes out of scope or when the program terminates. You'll learn here how to write text to and read text from files on disk; in Chapter 17, we continue this discussion with Java's powerful capabilities for writing objects to and reading objects from files on disk.

6.2 Primitive Types vs. Reference Types

Java's types are divided into primitive types and **reference types**. The primitive types are `boolean`, `byte`, `char`, `short`, `int`, `long`, `float` and `double`. All nonprimitive types are reference types, so classes, which specify the types of objects, are reference types.

Software Engineering Observation 6.1

A variable's declared type (e.g., `int`, `double` or `Scanner`) indicates whether the variable is of a primitive or a reference type. If a variable's type is not one of the eight primitive types, then it's a reference type.

A primitive-type variable can store exactly one value of its declared type at a time. For example, an `int` variable can store one whole number (such as 7) at a time. When another value is assigned to that variable, its initial value is replaced.

Programs use variables of reference types (sometimes called **references**) to store the locations of objects in the computer's memory. Such a variable is said to **refer to an object** in the program. For example, the statement

```
Scanner input = new Scanner( System.in );
```

which you've used in many programs, creates variable `input` which refers to a `Scanner` object. Objects that are referenced may each contain data and methods.

When using an object of another class, a reference to the object is required to **invoke** (i.e., call) its methods. For example, the statement

```
int number = input.nextInt();
```

uses the variable `input` to send messages to the `Scanner` object. These messages are calls to methods (like `nextInt` and `nextDouble`) that enable the program to interact with the `Scanner` object. If the method being invoked requires additional data to perform its task, then the message would include the argument(s) that method requires. Note that primitive-type variables do not refer to objects, so such variables cannot be used to invoke methods.

6.3 Arrays

An array is a group of variables (called **elements** or **components**) containing values that all have the same type. Arrays are objects, so they're considered reference types. As you'll soon see, what we typically think of as an array is actually a reference to an array object in memory. The elements of an array can be either primitive types or reference types (including arrays, as we'll see in Section 6.8). To refer to a particular element in an array, we specify the name of the reference to the array and the position number of the element in the array. The position number of the element is called the element's **index** or **subscript**.

Figure 6.1 shows a logical representation of an integer array called c. This array contains 12 elements. A program refers to any one of these elements with an **array-access expression** that includes the name of the array followed by the index of the particular element in **square brackets ([])**. The first element in every array has **index zero** and is sometimes called the **zeroth element.** Thus, the elements of array c are c[0], c[1], c[2] and so on. The highest index in array c is 11, which is 1 less than 12—the number of elements in the array. Array names follow the same conventions as other variable names.

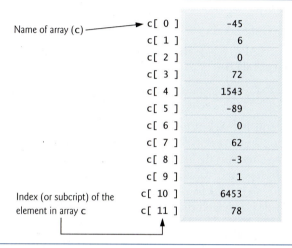

Name of array (c)

c[0]	-45
c[1]	6
c[2]	0
c[3]	72
c[4]	1543
c[5]	-89
c[6]	0
c[7]	62
c[8]	-3
c[9]	1
c[10]	6453
c[11]	78

Index (or subcript) of the element in array c

Fig. 6.1 | A 12-element array.

An index must be a nonnegative integer. A program can use an expression as an index. For example, if we assume that variable a is 5 and variable b is 6, then the statement

```
c[ a + b ] += 2;
```

adds 2 to c[11]. An indexed array name is an array-access expression. Such expressions can be used on the left side of an assignment to place a new value into an array element.

 Common Programming Error 6.1
An index must be an int value or a value of a type that can be promoted to int—namely, byte, short or char, but not long; otherwise, a compilation error occurs.

Let's examine array c in Fig. 6.1 more closely. The **name** of the array is c. Every array object knows its own length and stores it in a **length instance variable**. The expression c.length accesses array c's length field to determine the length of the array. Note that, even though the length instance variable of an array is public, it cannot be changed because it's a final variable. This array's 12 elements are referred to as c[0], c[1], c[2], …, c[11]. The value of c[0] is -45, the value of c[1] is 6, the value of c[2] is 0, the value of c[7] is 62 and the value of c[11] is 78. To calculate the sum of the values contained in the first three elements of array c and store the result in variable sum, we would write

```
sum = c[ 0 ] + c[ 1 ] + c[ 2 ];
```

To divide the value of c[6] by 2 and assign the result to the variable x, we would write

```
x = c[ 6 ] / 2;
```

6.4 Declaring and Creating Arrays

Array objects occupy space in memory. Like other objects, arrays are created with keyword new. To create an array object, you specify the type of the array elements and the number of elements as part of an **array-creation expression** that uses keyword new. Such an expression returns a reference that can be stored in an array variable. The following declaration and array-creation expression create an array object containing 12 int elements and store the array's reference in array variable c:

```
int[] c = new int[ 12 ];
```

This expression can be used to create the array shown in Fig. 6.1. This task also can be performed in two steps as follows:

```
int[] c; // declare the array variable
c = new int[ 12 ]; // create the array; assign to array variable
```

In the declaration, the square brackets following the type indicate that c is a variable that will refer to an array (i.e., the variable will store an array reference). In the assignment statement, the array variable c receives the reference to a new array of 12 int elements. When an array is created, each element of the array receives a default value—zero for the numeric primitive-type elements, false for boolean elements and null for references. As you'll soon see, you can provide nondefault initial element values when you create an array.

Common Programming Error 6.2

In an array declaration, specifying the number of elements in the square brackets of the declaration (e.g., int[12] c;) is a syntax error.

A program can create several arrays in a single declaration. The following declaration reserves 100 elements for b and 27 elements for x:

```
String[] b = new String[ 100 ], x = new String[ 27 ];
```

When type of the array and the square brackets are combined at the beginning of the declaration, all the identifiers in the declaration are array variables. In this case, variables b and x refer to String arrays. For readability, we prefer to declare only one variable per declaration. The preceding declaration is equivalent to:

```
String[] b = new String[ 100 ]; // create array b
String[] x = new String[ 27 ]; // create array x
```

Good Programming Practice 6.1

For readability, declare only one variable per declaration. Keep each declaration on a separate line, and include a comment describing the variable being declared.

When only one variable is declared in each declaration, the square brackets can be placed either after the type or after the array variable name, as in:

```
String b[] = new String[ 100 ]; // create array b
String x[] = new String[ 27 ]; // create array x
```

Common Programming Error 6.3

Declaring multiple array variables in a single declaration can lead to subtle errors. Consider the declaration int[] a, b, c;. If a, b and c should be declared as array variables, then this declaration is correct—placing square brackets directly following the type indicates that all the identifiers in the declaration are array variables. However, if only a is intended to be an array variable, and b and c are intended to be individual int variables, then this declaration is incorrect—the declaration int a[], b, c; would achieve the desired result.

A program can declare arrays of any type. Every element of a primitive-type array contains a value of the array's declared element type. Similarly, in an array of a reference type, every element is a reference to an object of the array's declared element type. For example, every element of an int array is an int value, and every element of a String array is a reference to a String object.

6.5 Examples Using Arrays

This section presents several examples that demonstrate declaring arrays, creating arrays, initializing arrays and manipulating array elements.

Creating and Initializing an Array

The application of Fig. 6.2 uses keyword new to create an array of 10 int elements, which are initially zero (the default for int variables). Line 8 declares array—a reference capable of referring to an array of int elements. Line 10 creates the array object and assigns its reference to variable array. Line 12 outputs the column headings. The first column contains the index (0–9) of each array element, and the second column contains the default value (0) of each array element.

The for statement in lines 15–16 outputs the index number (represented by counter) and the value of each array element (represented by array[counter]). Note that the loop-

```
1   // Fig. 6.2: InitArray.java
2   // Initializing the elements of an array to default values of zero.
3
4   public class InitArray
5   {
6      public static void main( String[] args )
7      {
8         int[] array; // declare array named array
9
10        array = new int[ 10 ]; // create the array object
11
12        System.out.printf( "%s%8s\n", "Index", "Value" ); // column headings
13
14        // output each array element's value
15        for ( int counter = 0; counter < array.length; counter++ )
16           System.out.printf( "%5d%8d\n", counter, array[ counter ] );
17     } // end main
18  } // end class InitArray
```

Fig. 6.2 | Initializing the elements of an array to default values of zero. (Part 1 of 2.)

Index	Value
0	0
1	0
2	0
3	0
4	0
5	0
6	0
7	0
8	0
9	0

Fig. 6.2 | Initializing the elements of an array to default values of zero. (Part 2 of 2.)

control variable `counter` is initially 0—index values start at 0, so using zero-based counting allows the loop to access every element of the array. The `for`'s loop-continuation condition uses the expression `array.length` (line 15) to determine the length of the array. In this example, the length of the array is 10, so the loop continues executing as long as the value of control variable `counter` is less than 10. The highest index value of a 10-element array is 9, so using the less-than operator in the loop-continuation condition guarantees that the loop does not attempt to access an element beyond the end of the array (i.e., during the final iteration of the loop, `counter` is 9). We'll soon see what Java does when it encounters such an out-of-range index at execution time.

Using an Array Initializer

You can create an array and initialize its elements with an **array initializer**—a comma-separated list of expressions (called an **initializer list**) enclosed in braces. In this case, the array length is determined by the number of elements in the initializer list. For example,

```
int[] n = { 10, 20, 30, 40, 50 };
```

creates a five-element array with index values 0–4. Element n[0] is initialized to 10, n[1] is initialized to 20, and so on. When the compiler encounters an array declaration that includes an initializer list, it counts the number of initializers in the list to determine the size of the array, then sets up the appropriate new operation "behind the scenes."

The application in Fig. 6.3 initializes an integer array with 10 values (line 9) and displays the array in tabular format. The code for displaying the array elements (lines 14–15) is identical to that in Fig. 6.2 (lines 15–16).

```
 1   // Fig. 6.3: InitArray.java
 2   // Initializing the elements of an array with an array initializer.
 3
 4   public class InitArray
 5   {
 6      public static void main( String[] args )
 7      {
 8         // initializer list specifies the value for each element
 9         int[] array = { 32, 27, 64, 18, 95, 14, 90, 70, 60, 37 };
10
```

Fig. 6.3 | Initializing the elements of an array with an array initializer. (Part 1 of 2.)

```
11          System.out.printf( "%s%8s\n", "Index", "Value" ); // column headings
12
13          // output each array element's value
14          for ( int counter = 0; counter < array.length; counter++ )
15              System.out.printf( "%5d%8d\n", counter, array[ counter ] );
16      } // end main
17  } // end class InitArray
```

```
Index   Value
    0      32
    1      27
    2      64
    3      18
    4      95
    5      14
    6      90
    7      70
    8      60
    9      37
```

Fig. 6.3 | Initializing the elements of an array with an array initializer. (Part 2 of 2.)

Calculating the Values to Store in an Array

The application in Fig. 6.4 creates a 10-element array and assigns to each element one of the even integers from 2 to 20 (2, 4, 6, ..., 20). Then the application displays the array in tabular format. The for statement at lines 12–13 calculates an array element's value by multiplying the current value of the control variable counter by 2, then adding 2.

```
1   // Fig. 6.4: InitArray.java
2   // Calculating values to be placed into elements of an array.
3
4   public class InitArray
5   {
6      public static void main( String[] args )
7      {
8         final int ARRAY_LENGTH = 10; // declare constant
9         int[] array = new int[ ARRAY_LENGTH ]; // create array
10
11         // calculate value for each array element
12         for ( int counter = 0; counter < array.length; counter++ )
13             array[ counter ] = 2 + 2 * counter;
14
15         System.out.printf( "%s%8s\n", "Index", "Value" ); // column headings
16
17         // output each array element's value
18         for ( int counter = 0; counter < array.length; counter++ )
19             System.out.printf( "%5d%8d\n", counter, array[ counter ] );
20      } // end main
21  } // end class InitArray
```

Fig. 6.4 | Calculating the values to be placed into the elements of an array. (Part 1 of 2.)

```
Index   Value
  0       2
  1       4
  2       6
  3       8
  4      10
  5      12
  6      14
  7      16
  8      18
  9      20
```

Fig. 6.4 | Calculating the values to be placed into the elements of an array. (Part 2 of 2.)

Line 8 uses the modifier `final` to declare the constant variable `ARRAY_LENGTH` with the value 10. Constant variables must be initialized before they're used and cannot be modified thereafter. If you attempt to modify a `final` variable after it's initialized in its declaration (as in line 8), the compiler issues an error message like

> `cannot assign a value to final variable` *variableName*

If an attempt is made to access the value of a `final` variable before it's initialized, the compiler issues an error message like

> `variable` *variableName* `might not have been initialized`

Good Programming Practice 6.2

Constant variables also are called named constants. They often make programs more readable than programs that use literal values (e.g., 10)—a named constant such as `ARRAY_LENGTH` clearly indicates its purpose, whereas a literal value could have different meanings based on its context.

Common Programming Error 6.4

Assigning a value to a constant variable after it has been initialized is a compilation error.

Common Programming Error 6.5

Attempting to use a constant before it's initialized is a compilation error.

Summing the Elements of an Array

Often, the elements of an array represent a series of values to be used in a calculation. If, for example, they represent exam grades, a professor may wish to total the elements of the array and use that sum to calculate the class average for the exam. The example in Fig. 6.13 uses this technique.

Figure 6.5 sums the values contained in a 10-element integer array. The program declares, creates and initializes the array at line 8. The `for` statement performs the calculations. [*Note:* The values supplied as array initializers are often read into a program rather than specified in an initializer list. For example, an application could input the values from a user or from a file on disk (as discussed in Chapter 17, Files, Streams and Object Serialization). Reading the data into a program (rather than "hand coding" it into the program) makes the program more reusable, because it can be used with different sets of data.]

```java
1   // Fig. 6.5: SumArray.java
2   // Computing the sum of the elements of an array.
3
4   public class SumArray
5   {
6      public static void main( String[] args )
7      {
8         int[] array = { 87, 68, 94, 100, 83, 78, 85, 91, 76, 87 };
9         int total = 0;
10
11        // add each element's value to total
12        for ( int counter = 0; counter < array.length; counter++ )
13           total += array[ counter ];
14
15        System.out.printf( "Total of array elements: %d\n", total );
16     } // end main
17  } // end class SumArray
```

```
Total of array elements: 849
```

Fig. 6.5 | Computing the sum of the elements of an array.

Using Bar Charts to Display Array Data Graphically

Many programs present data to users in a graphical manner. For example, numeric values are often displayed as bars in a bar chart. In such a chart, longer bars represent proportionally larger numeric values. One simple way to display numeric data graphically is with a bar chart that shows each numeric value as a bar of asterisks (*).

Professors often like to examine the distribution of grades on an exam. A professor might graph the number of grades in each of several categories to visualize the grade distribution. Suppose the grades on an exam were 87, 68, 94, 100, 83, 78, 85, 91, 76 and 87. Note that they include one grade of 100, two grades in the 90s, four grades in the 80s, two grades in the 70s, one grade in the 60s and no grades below 60. Our next application (Fig. 6.6) stores this grade distribution data in an array of 11 elements, each corresponding to a category of grades. For example, array[0] indicates the number of grades in the range 0–9, array[7] the number of grades in the range 70–79 and array[10] the number of 100 grades. The example in Fig. 6.13 contains code that calculates grade frequencies based on a set of grades. For now, we manually create the array with the given grade frequencies.

```java
1   // Fig. 6.6: BarChart.java
2   // Bar chart printing program.
3
4   public class BarChart
5   {
6      public static void main( String[] args )
7      {
```

Fig. 6.6 | Bar chart printing program. (Part 1 of 2.)

```
8          int[] array = { 0, 0, 0, 0, 0, 0, 1, 2, 4, 2, 1 };
9
10         System.out.println( "Grade distribution:" );
11
12         // for each array element, output a bar of the chart
13         for ( int counter = 0; counter < array.length; counter++ )
14         {
15            // output bar label ( "00-09: ", ..., "90-99: ", "100: " )
16            if ( counter == 10 )
17               System.out.printf( "%5d: ", 100 );
18            else
19               System.out.printf( "%02d-%02d: ",
20                  counter * 10, counter * 10 + 9  );
21
22            // print bar of asterisks
23            for ( int stars = 0; stars < array[ counter ]; stars++ )
24               System.out.print( "*" );
25
26            System.out.println(); // start a new line of output
27         } // end outer for
28      } // end main
29   } // end class BarChart
```

```
Grade distribution:
00-09:
10-19:
20-29:
30-39:
40-49:
50-59:
60-69: *
70-79: **
80-89: ****
90-99: **
  100: *
```

Fig. 6.6 | Bar chart printing program. (Part 2 of 2.)

The application reads the numbers from the array and graphs the information as a bar chart. It displays each grade range followed by a bar of asterisks indicating the number of grades in that range. To label each bar, lines 16–20 output a grade range (e.g., "70-79: ") based on the current value of counter. When counter is 10, line 17 outputs 100 with a field width of 5, followed by a colon and a space, to align the label "100: " with the other bar labels. The nested for statement (lines 23–24) outputs the bars. Note the loop-continuation condition at line 23 (stars < array[counter]). Each time the program reaches the inner for, the loop counts from 0 up to array[counter], thus using a value in array to determine the number of asterisks to display. In this example, no students received a grade below 60, so array[0]–array[5] contain zeroes, and no asterisks are displayed next to the first six grade ranges. In line 19, the format specifier %02d indicates that an int value should be formatted as a field of two digits. The **0 flag** in the format specifier displays a leading 0 for values with fewer digits than the field width (2).

Using the Elements of an Array as Counters

Sometimes, programs use counter variables to summarize data, such as the results of a survey. In Fig. 5.7, we used separate counters in our die-rolling program to track the number of occurrences of each side of a six-sided die as the program rolled the die 6000 times. An array version of this application is shown in Fig. 6.7.

```java
1   // Fig. 6.7: RollDie.java
2   // Die-rolling program using arrays instead of switch.
3   import java.util.Random;
4
5   public class RollDie
6   {
7      public static void main( String[] args )
8      {
9         Random randomNumbers = new Random(); // random number generator
10        int[] frequency = new int[ 7 ]; // array of frequency counters
11
12        // roll die 6000 times; use die value as frequency index
13        for ( int roll = 1; roll <= 6000; roll++ )
14           ++frequency[ 1 + randomNumbers.nextInt( 6 ) ];
15
16        System.out.printf( "%s%10s\n", "Face", "Frequency" );
17
18        // output each array element's value
19        for ( int face = 1; face < frequency.length; face++ )
20           System.out.printf( "%4d%10d\n", face, frequency[ face ] );
21     } // end main
22  } // end class RollDie
```

```
Face Frequency
   1       988
   2       963
   3      1018
   4      1041
   5       978
   6      1012
```

Fig. 6.7 | Die-rolling program using arrays instead of `switch`.

Figure 6.7 uses the array `frequency` (line 10) to count the occurrences of each side of the die. *The single statement in line 14 of this program replaces lines 23–46 of Fig. 5.7.* Line 14 uses the random value to determine which `frequency` element to increment during each iteration of the loop. The calculation in line 14 produces random numbers from 1 to 6, so the array `frequency` must be large enough to store six counters. However, we use a seven-element array in which we ignore `frequency[0]`—it's more logical to have the face value 1 increment `frequency[1]` than `frequency[0]`. Thus, each face value is used as an index for array `frequency`. In line 14, the calculation inside the square brackets evaluates first to determine which element of the array to increment, then the ++ operator adds one to that element. We also replaced lines 50–52 from Fig. 5.7 by looping through array `frequency` to output the results (lines 19–20).

Using Arrays to Analyze Survey Results

Figure 6.8 uses arrays to summarize the results of data collected in a survey:

> *Forty students were asked to rate the quality of the food in the student cafeteria on a scale of 1 to 10 (where 1 means awful and 10 means excellent). Place the 40 responses in an integer array, and summarize the results of the poll.*

This is a typical array-processing application. We wish to summarize the number of responses of each type (i.e., 1 through 10). The array `responses` (lines 9–11) is a 40-element `int` array of the survey responses. We use an 11-element array `frequency` (line 12) to count the number of occurrences of each response (1 to 10). Each element is initialized to zero by default. As in Fig. 6.7, we ignore `frequency[0]`.

```java
1   // Fig. 6.8: StudentPoll.java
2   // Poll analysis program.
3
4   public class StudentPoll
5   {
6      public static void main( String[] args )
7      {
8         // array of survey responses
9         int[] responses = { 1, 2, 6, 4, 8, 5, 9, 7, 8, 10, 1, 6, 3, 8, 6,
10           10, 3, 8, 2, 7, 6, 5, 7, 6, 8, 6, 7, 5, 6, 6, 5, 6, 7, 5, 6,
11           4, 8, 6, 8, 10 };
12        int[] frequency = new int[ 11 ]; // array of frequency counters
13
14        // for each answer, select responses element and use that value
15        // as frequency index to determine element to increment
16        for ( int answer = 0; answer < responses.length; answer++ )
17           ++frequency[ responses[ answer ] ];
18
19        System.out.printf( "%s%10s", "Rating", "Frequency" );
20
21        // output each array element's value
22        for ( int rating = 1; rating < frequency.length; rating++ )
23           System.out.printf( "%d%10d", rating, frequency[ rating ] );
24     } // end main
25   } // end class StudentPoll
```

```
Rating Frequency
    1         2
    2         2
    3         2
    4         2
    5         5
    6        11
    7         5
    8         7
    9         1
   10         3
```

Fig. 6.8 | Poll analysis program.

The `for` loop at lines 16–17 takes the responses one at a time from array `responses` and increments one of the 10 counters in the `frequency` array (`frequency[1]` to frequency[10]). The key statement in the loop is line 17, which increments the appropriate frequency counter, depending on the value of responses[answer].

Let's consider several iterations of the for loop. When control variable answer is 0, the value of responses[answer] is the value of responses[0] (i.e., 1), so the program interprets ++frequency[responses[answer]] as

```
++frequency[ 1 ]
```

which increments the value in array element 1. To evaluate the expression, start with the value in the innermost set of square brackets (answer). Once you know answer's value (which is the value of the loop control variable in line 16), plug it into the expression and evaluate the next outer set of square brackets (i.e., responses[answer], which is a value selected from the responses array in lines 9–11). Then use the resulting value as the index for the frequency array to specify which counter to increment.

When answer is 1, responses[answer] is the value of responses[1] (2), so the program interprets ++frequency[responses[answer]] as

```
++frequency[ 2 ]
```

which increments array element 2.

When answer is 2, responses[answer] is the value of responses[2] (6), so the program interprets ++frequency[responses[answer]] as

```
++frequency[ 6 ]
```

which increments array element 6, and so on. Regardless of the number of responses processed in the survey, the program requires only an 11-element array (ignoring element zero) to summarize the results, because all the response values are between 1 and 10 and the index values for an 11-element array are 0 through 10.

If the data in the responses array had contained invalid values, such as 13, the program would have attempted to add 1 to frequency[13], which is outside the bounds of the array. Java doesn't allow this. When a Java program executes, the JVM checks array indices to ensure that they're greater than or equal to 0 and less than the length of the array—this is called **bounds checking**. If a program uses an invalid index, Java generates a so-called exception to indicate that an error occurred in the program at execution time. A control statement can be used to prevent such an "out-of-bounds" error from occurring. For example, the condition in a control statement could determine whether an index is valid before allowing it to be used in an array-access expression.

Error-Prevention Tip 6.1

An exception indicates that an error has occurred. You often can write code to recover from an exception and continue program execution, rather than abnormally terminating the program. When a program attempts to access an element outside the array bounds, an ArrayIndexOutOfBoundsException *occurs. Exception handling is discussed in Chapter 11.*

Error-Prevention Tip 6.2

When writing code to loop through an array, ensure that the array index is always greater than or equal to 0 and less than the length of the array. The loop-continuation condition should prevent accessing elements outside this range.

6.6 Enhanced for Statement

The enhanced for statement iterates through the elements of an array without using a counter, thus avoiding the possibility of "stepping outside" the array. We show how to use the enhanced for statement with the Java API's prebuilt data structures (called collections) in Section 6.13. The syntax of an enhanced for statement is:

```
for ( parameter : arrayName )
    statement
```

where *parameter* has a type and an identifier (e.g., int number), and *arrayName* is the array through which to iterate. The type of the parameter must be consistent with the type of the elements in the array. As the next example illustrates, the identifier represents successive values in the array on successive iterations of the loop.

Figure 6.9 uses the enhanced for statement (lines 12–13) to sum the integers in an array of student grades. The enhanced for's parameter is of type int, because array contains int values—the loop selects one int value from the array during each iteration. The enhanced for statement iterates through successive values in the array one by one. The statement's header can be read as "for each iteration, assign the next element of array to int variable number, then execute the following statement." Thus, for each iteration, identifier number represents an int value in array.

```
1   // Fig. 6.9: EnhancedForTest.java
2   // Using enhanced for statement to total integers in an array.
3
4   public class EnhancedForTest
5   {
6      public static void main( String[] args )
7      {
8         int[] array = { 87, 68, 94, 100, 83, 78, 85, 91, 76, 87 };
9         int total = 0;
10
11        // add each element's value to total
12        for ( int number : array )
13           total += number;
14
15        System.out.printf( "Total of array elements: %d\n", total );
16     } // end main
17  } // end class EnhancedForTest
```

```
Total of array elements: 849
```

Fig. 6.9 | Using the enhanced for statement to total integers in an array.

Lines 12–13 are equivalent to the following counter-controlled repetition used in lines 12–13 of Fig. 6.5 to total the integers in array:

```
for ( int counter = 0; counter < array.length; counter++ )
    total += array[ counter ];
```

The enhanced for statement simplifies the code for iterating through an array. Note, however, that the enhanced for statement can be used only to obtain array elements—it cannot be used to modify elements. If your program needs to modify elements, use the traditional counter-controlled `for` statement.

The enhanced `for` statement can be used in place of the counter-controlled `for` statement whenever code looping through an array does not require access to the counter indicating the index of the current array element. For example, totaling the integers in an array requires access only to the element values—the index of each element is irrelevant. However, if a program must use a counter for some reason other than simply to loop through an array (e.g., to print an index number next to each array element value, as in the examples earlier in this chapter), use the counter-controlled `for` statement.

6.7 Passing Arrays to Methods

This section demonstrates how to pass arrays and individual array elements as arguments to methods. To pass an array argument to a method, specify the name of the array without any brackets. For example, if array `hourlyTemperatures` is declared as

```
double[] hourlyTemperatures = new double[ 24 ];
```

then the method call

```
modifyArray( hourlyTemperatures );
```

passes the reference of array `hourlyTemperatures` to method `modifyArray`. Every array object "knows" its own length (via its `length` field). Thus, when we pass an array object's reference into a method, we need not pass the array length as an additional argument.

For a method to receive an array reference through a method call, the method's parameter list must specify an array parameter. For example, the method header for method `modifyArray` might be written as

```
void modifyArray( double[] b )
```

indicating that `modifyArray` receives the reference of a `double` array in parameter `b`. The method call passes array `hourlyTemperature`'s reference, so when the called method uses the array variable `b`, it refers to the same array object as `hourlyTemperatures` in the caller.

When a method argument is an entire array or an individual array element of a reference type, the called method receives a copy of the reference. When a method argument is an individual primitive-type array element, the called method receives a copy of the element's value. Such primitive values are called scalars or scalar quantities. To pass an individual array element to a method, use the indexed name of the array element.

Figure 6.10 demonstrates the difference between passing an entire array and passing a primitive-type array element to a method. Notice that `main` invokes `static` methods `modifyArray` (line 19) and `modifyElement` (line 30) directly. Recall from Chapter 5 that a `static` method of a class can invoke other `static` methods of the same class directly.

The enhanced `for` statement at lines 16–17 outputs the five `int` elements of `array`. Line 19 invokes method `modifyArray`, passing `array` as an argument. Method `modifyArray` (lines 36–40) receives a copy of `array`'s reference and uses the reference to multiply each of `array`'s elements by 2. To prove that `array`'s elements were modified, lines 23–24 output the five elements of `array` again. As the output shows, method `modifyArray` doubled the value of each element. Note that we could not use the enhanced `for` statement in lines 38–39 because we are modifying the array's elements.

```java
1   // Fig. 6.10: PassArray.java
2   // Passing arrays and individual array elements to methods.
3
4   public class PassArray
5   {
6      // main creates array and calls modifyArray and modifyElement
7      public static void main( String[] args )
8      {
9         int[] array = { 1, 2, 3, 4, 5 };
10
11        System.out.println(
12           "Effects of passing reference to entire array:\n" +
13           "The values of the original array are:" );
14
15        // output original array elements
16        for ( int value : array )
17           System.out.printf( "   %d", value );
18
19        modifyArray( array ); // pass array reference
20        System.out.println( "\n\nThe values of the modified array are:" );
21
22        // output modified array elements
23        for ( int value : array )
24           System.out.printf( "   %d", value );
25
26        System.out.printf(
27           "\n\nEffects of passing array element value:\n" +
28           "array[3] before modifyElement: %d\n", array[ 3 ] );
29
30        modifyElement( array[ 3 ] ); // attempt to modify array[ 3 ]
31        System.out.printf(
32           "array[3] after modifyElement: %d\n", array[ 3 ] );
33     } // end main
34
35     // multiply each element of an array by 2
36     public static void modifyArray( int[] array2 )
37     {
38        for ( int counter = 0; counter < array2.length; counter++ )
39           array2[ counter ] *= 2;
40     } // end method modifyArray
41
42     // multiply argument by 2
43     public static void modifyElement( int element )
44     {
45        element *= 2;
46        System.out.printf(
47           "Value of element in modifyElement: %d\n", element );
48     } // end method modifyElement
49  } // end class PassArray
```

```
Effects of passing reference to entire array:
The values of the original array are:
   1   2   3   4   5
```

Fig. 6.10 | Passing arrays and individual array elements to methods. (Part 1 of 2.)

```
The values of the modified array are:
   2   4   6   8   10

Effects of passing array element value:
array[3] before modifyElement: 8
Value of element in modifyElement: 16
array[3] after modifyElement: 8
```

Fig. 6.10 | Passing arrays and individual array elements to methods. (Part 2 of 2.)

Figure 6.10 next demonstrates that when a copy of an individual primitive-type array element is passed to a method, modifying the copy in the called method does not affect the original value of that element in the calling method's array. Lines 26–28 output the value of array[3] before invoking method modifyElement. Remember that the value of this element is now 8 after it was modified in the call to modifyArray. Line 30 calls method modifyElement and passes array[3] as an argument. Remember that array[3] is actually one int value (8) in array. Therefore, the program passes a copy of the value of array[3]. Method modifyElement (lines 43–48) multiplies the value received as an argument by 2, stores the result in its parameter element, then outputs the value of element (16). Since method parameters, like local variables, cease to exist when the method in which they're declared completes execution, the method parameter element is destroyed when method modifyElement terminates. When the program returns control to main, lines 31–32 output the unmodified value of array[3] (i.e., 8).

Notes on Passing Arguments to Methods

The preceding example demonstrated how arrays and primitive-type array elements are passed as arguments to methods. We now take a closer look at how arguments in general are passed to methods. Two ways to pass arguments in method calls in many programming languages are **pass-by-value** and **pass-by-reference** (also called **call-by-value** and **call-by-reference**). When an argument is passed by value, a copy of the argument's *value* is passed to the called method. The called method works exclusively with the copy. Changes to the called method's copy do not affect the original variable's value in the caller.

When an argument is passed by reference, the called method can access the argument's value in the caller directly and modify that data, if necessary. Pass-by-reference improves performance by eliminating the need to copy possibly large amounts of data.

Unlike some other languages, Java does not allow programmers to choose pass-by-value or pass-by-reference—all arguments are passed by value. A method call can pass two types of values to a method—copies of primitive values (e.g., values of type int and double) and copies of references to objects. Objects themselves cannot be passed to methods. When a method modifies a primitive-type parameter, changes to the parameter have no effect on the original argument value in the calling method. For example, when line 30 in main of Fig. 6.10 passes array[3] to method modifyElement, the statement in line 45 that doubles the value of parameter element has no effect on the value of array[3] in main. This is also true for reference-type parameters. If you modify a reference-type parameter so that it refers to another object, only the parameter refers to the new object— the reference stored in the caller's variable still refers to the original object.

Although an object's reference is passed by value, a method can still interact with the referenced object by calling its public methods using the copy of the object's reference. Since the reference stored in the parameter is a copy of the reference that was passed as an argument, the parameter in the called method and the argument in the calling method refer to the same object in memory. For example, in Fig. 6.10, both parameter array2 in method modifyArray and variable array in main refer to the same array object in memory. Any changes made using the parameter array2 are carried out on the object that array references in the calling method. In Fig. 6.10, the changes made in modifyArray using array2 affect the contents of the array object referenced by array in main. Thus, with a reference to an object, the called method can manipulate the caller's object directly.

Performance Tip 6.1

Passing arrays by reference makes sense for performance reasons. If arrays were passed by value, a copy of each element would be passed. For large, frequently passed arrays, this would waste time and consume considerable storage for the copies of the arrays.

6.8 Multidimensional Arrays

Multidimensional arrays with two dimensions often represent tables of values consisting of information arranged in rows and columns. To identify a particular table element, we must specify two indices—the first identifies the element's row and the second its column. Arrays that require two indices to identify an element are called **two-dimensional arrays**. (Multidimensional arrays can have more than two dimensions.) Java does not support multidimensional arrays directly, but it does allow you to specify one-dimensional arrays whose elements are one-dimensional arrays, thus achieving the same effect. Figure 6.11 shows a two-dimensional array named a that contains three rows and four columns (i.e., a three-by-four array). In general, an array with *m* rows and *n* columns is called an *m-by-n* **array**.

Every element in array a is identified in Fig. 6.11 by an array-access expression of the form a[row][column]; a is the name of the array, and row and column are the indices that uniquely identify each element in array a by row and column number. Note that the names of the elements in row 0 all have a first index of 0, and the names of the elements in column 3 all have a second index of 3.

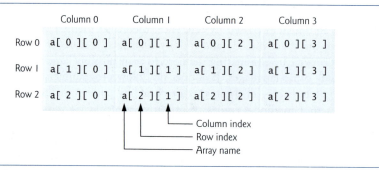

Fig. 6.11 | Two-dimensional array with three rows and four columns.

Arrays of One-Dimensional Arrays

Like one-dimensional arrays, multidimensional arrays can be initialized with array initializers in declarations. A two-dimensional array b with two rows and two columns could be declared and initialized with **nested array initializers** as follows:

```
int[][] b = { { 1, 2 }, { 3, 4 } };
```

The initial values are grouped by row in braces. So 1 and 2 initialize b[0][0] and b[0][1], respectively, and 3 and 4 initialize b[1][0] and b[1][1], respectively. The compiler counts the number of nested array initializers (represented by sets of braces within the outer braces) to determine the number of rows in array b. The compiler counts the initializer values in the nested array initializer for a row to determine the number of columns in that row. As we'll see momentarily, this means that rows can have different lengths.

Multidimensional arrays are maintained as arrays of one-dimensional arrays. Therefore array b in the preceding declaration is actually composed of two separate one-dimensional arrays—one containing the values in the first nested initializer list { 1, 2 } and one containing the values in the second nested initializer list { 3, 4 }. Thus, array b itself is an array of two elements, each a one-dimensional array of int values.

Two-Dimensional Arrays with Rows of Different Lengths

The manner in which multidimensional arrays are represented makes them quite flexible. In fact, the lengths of the rows in array b are not required to be the same. For example,

```
int[][] b = { { 1, 2 }, { 3, 4, 5 } };
```

creates integer array b with two elements (determined by the number of nested array initializers) that represent the rows of the two-dimensional array. Each element of b is a reference to a one-dimensional array of int variables. The int array for row 0 is a one-dimensional array with two elements (1 and 2), and the int array for row 1 is a one-dimensional array with three elements (3, 4 and 5).

Creating Two-Dimensional Arrays with Array-Creation Expressions

A multidimensional array with the same number of columns in every row can be created with an array-creation expression. For example, the following lines declare array b and assign it a reference to a three-by-four array:

```
int[][] b = new int[ 3 ][ 4 ];
```

In this case, we use the literal values 3 and 4 to specify the number of rows and columns, respectively. Programs can also use variables to specify array dimensions, because new creates arrays at execution time—not at compile time. As with one-dimensional arrays, the elements of a multidimensional array are initialized when the array object is created.

A multidimensional array in which each row has a different number of columns can be created as follows:

```
int[][] b = new int[ 2 ][ ];    // create 2 rows
b[ 0 ] = new int[ 5 ]; // create 5 columns for row 0
b[ 1 ] = new int[ 3 ]; // create 3 columns for row 1
```

The preceding statements create a two-dimensional array with two rows. Row 0 has five columns, and row 1 has three columns.

Two-Dimensional Array Example: Displaying Element Values

Figure 6.12 demonstrates initializing two-dimensional arrays with array initializers and using nested for loops to traverse the arrays (i.e., manipulate every element of each array). Class InitArray's main declares two arrays. The declaration of array1 (line 9) uses nested array initializers to initialize the first row to the values 1, 2 and 3, and the second row to the values 4, 5 and 6. The declaration of array2 (line 10) uses nested initializers of different lengths. In this case, the first row is initialized to two elements with the values 1 and 2, respectively. The second row is initialized to one element with the value 3. The third row is initialized to three elements with the values 4, 5 and 6, respectively.

```java
1   // Fig. 6.12: InitArray.java
2   // Initializing two-dimensional arrays.
3
4   public class InitArray
5   {
6      // create and output two-dimensional arrays
7      public static void main( String[] args )
8      {
9         int[][] array1 = { { 1, 2, 3 }, { 4, 5, 6 } };
10        int[][] array2 = { { 1, 2 }, { 3 }, { 4, 5, 6 } };
11
12        System.out.println( "Values in array1 by row are" );
13        outputArray( array1 ); // displays array1 by row
14
15        System.out.println( "\nValues in array2 by row are" );
16        outputArray( array2 ); // displays array2 by row
17     } // end main
18
19     // output rows and columns of a two-dimensional array
20     public static void outputArray( int[][] array )
21     {
22        // loop through array's rows
23        for ( int row = 0; row < array.length; row++ )
24        {
25           // loop through columns of current row
26           for ( int column = 0; column < array[ row ].length; column++ )
27              System.out.printf( "%d  ", array[ row ][ column ] );
28
29           System.out.println(); // start new line of output
30        } // end outer for
31     } // end method outputArray
32  } // end class InitArray
```

```
Values in array1 by row are
1  2  3
4  5  6

Values in array2 by row are
1  2
3
4  5  6
```

Fig. 6.12 | Initializing two-dimensional arrays.

Lines 13 and 16 call method `outputArray` (lines 20–31) to output the elements of `array1` and `array2`, respectively. Method `outputArray`'s parameter—`int[][] array`—indicates that the method receives a two-dimensional array. The for statement (lines 23–30) outputs the rows of a two-dimensional array. In the loop-continuation condition of the outer for statement, the expression `array.length` determines the number of rows in the array. In the inner for statement, the expression `array[row].length` determines the number of columns in the current row of the array. This condition enables the loop to determine the exact number of columns in each row.

Common Multidimensional-Array Manipulations Performed with for Statements

Many common array manipulations use for statements. As an example, the following for statement sets all the elements in row 2 of array a in Fig. 6.11 to zero:

```
for ( int column = 0; column < a[ 2 ].length; column++)
    a[ 2 ][ column ] = 0;
```

We specified row 2; therefore, we know that the first index is always 2 (0 is the first row, and 1 is the second row). This for loop varies only the second index (i.e., the column index). If row 2 of array a contains four elements, then the preceding for statement is equivalent to the assignment statements

```
a[ 2 ][ 0 ] = 0;
a[ 2 ][ 1 ] = 0;
a[ 2 ][ 2 ] = 0;
a[ 2 ][ 3 ] = 0;
```

The following nested for statement totals the values of all the elements in array a:

```
int total = 0;
for ( int row = 0; row < a.length; row++ )
{
    for ( int column = 0; column < a[ row ].length; column++ )
        total += a[ row ][ column ];
} // end outer for
```

These nested for statements total the array elements one row at a time. The outer for statement begins by setting the row index to 0 so that the first row's elements can be totaled by the inner for statement. The outer for then increments row to 1 so that the second row can be totaled. Then, the outer for increments row to 2 so that the third row can be totaled. The variable total can be displayed when the outer for statement terminates. In the next example, we show how to process a two-dimensional array in a similar manner using nested enhanced for statements.

6.9 Case Study: Summarizing Student Exam Grades Using a Two-Dimensional Array

In most semesters, students take several exams. Professors are likely to want to analyze grades across the entire semester, both for a single student and for the class as a whole.

Storing Student Grades in a Two-Dimensional Array in Class GradeBook

Figure 6.13 uses a two-dimensional array gradesArray (lines 8–18) to store the grades of several students on multiple exams. Each row of the array represents a single student's grades for the entire course, and each column represents the grades of all the students who took a particular exam. In this example, we use a ten-by-three array containing 10 students' grades on three exams. The main method passes this array to the class's other static methods to display a report summarizing the students' grades for the semester. Five methods perform array manipulations to process the grades. Method getMinimum (lines 33–51) determines the lowest grade of any student for the semester. Method getMaximum (lines 54–72) determines the highest grade of any student for the semester. Method getAverage (lines 75–85) determines a particular student's semester average. Method `outputBarChart` (lines 88–118) outputs a bar chart of the distribution of all student grades for the semester. Method `outputGrades` (lines 121–145) outputs the two-dimensional array in a tabular format, along with each student's semester average.

```java
1   // Fig. 6.13: SummarizeGrades.java
2   // SummarizeGrades using a two-dimensional array to store grades.
3   public class SummarizeGrades
4   {
5      public static void main( String[] args )
6      {
7         // two-dimensional array of student grades
8         int[][] gradesArray =
9            { { 87, 96, 70 },
10            { 68, 87, 90 },
11            { 94, 100, 90 },
12            { 100, 81, 82 },
13            { 83, 65, 85 },
14            { 78, 87, 65 },
15            { 85, 75, 83 },
16            { 91, 94, 100 },
17            { 76, 72, 84 },
18            { 87, 93, 73 } };
19
20         // output grades array
21         outputGrades( gradesArray );
22
23         // call methods getMinimum and getMaximum
24         System.out.printf( "\n%s %d\n%s %d\n\n",
25            "Lowest grade is", getMinimum( gradesArray ),
26            "Highest grade is", getMaximum( gradesArray ) );
27
28         // output grade distribution chart of all grades on all tests
29         outputBarChart( gradesArray );
30      } // end main
31
32      // find minimum grade
33      public static int getMinimum( int grades[][] )
34      {
35         // assume first element of grades array is smallest
36         int lowGrade = grades[ 0 ][ 0 ];
37
38         // loop through rows of grades array
39         for ( int[] studentGrades : grades )
40         {
41            // loop through columns of current row
42            for ( int grade : studentGrades )
43            {
44               // if grade less than lowGrade, assign it to lowGrade
45               if ( grade < lowGrade )
46                  lowGrade = grade;
47            } // end inner for
48         } // end outer for
```

Fig. 6.13 | SummarizeGrades uses a two-dimensional array to store grades. (Part 1 of 4.)

```
49
50        return lowGrade; // return lowest grade
51     } // end method getMinimum
52
53     // find maximum grade
54     public static int getMaximum( int grades[][] )
55     {
56        // assume first element of grades array is largest
57        int highGrade = grades[ 0 ][ 0 ];
58
59        // loop through rows of grades array
60        for ( int[] studentGrades : grades )
61        {
62           // loop through columns of current row
63           for ( int grade : studentGrades )
64           {
65              // if grade greater than highGrade, assign it to highGrade
66              if ( grade > highGrade )
67                 highGrade = grade;
68           } // end inner for
69        } // end outer for
70
71        return highGrade; // return highest grade
72     } // end method getMaximum
73
74     // determine average grade for particular set of grades
75     public static double getAverage( int[] setOfGrades )
76     {
77        int total = 0; // initialize total
78
79        // sum grades for one student
80        for ( int grade : setOfGrades )
81           total += grade;
82
83        // return average of grades
84        return (double) total / setOfGrades.length;
85     } // end method getAverage
86
87     // output bar chart displaying overall grade distribution
88     public static void outputBarChart( int grades[][] )
89     {
90        System.out.println( "Overall grade distribution:" );
91
92        // stores frequency of grades in each range of 10 grades
93        int[] frequency = new int[ 11 ];
94
95        // for each grade in GradeBook, increment the appropriate frequency
96        for ( int[] studentGrades : grades )
97        {
98           for ( int grade : studentGrades )
99              ++frequency[ grade / 10 ];
100       } // end outer for
101
```

Fig. 6.13 | SummarizeGrades uses a two-dimensional array to store grades. (Part 2 of 4.)

```
102        // for each grade frequency, print bar in chart
103        for ( int count = 0; count < frequency.length; count++ )
104        {
105           // output bar label ( "00-09: ", ..., "90-99: ", "100: " )
106           if ( count == 10 )
107              System.out.printf( "%5d: ", 100 );
108           else
109              System.out.printf( "%02d-%02d: ",
110                 count * 10, count * 10 + 9 );
111
112           // print bar of asterisks
113           for ( int stars = 0; stars < frequency[ count ]; stars++ )
114              System.out.print( "*" );
115
116           System.out.println(); // start a new line of output
117        } // end outer for
118     } // end method outputBarChart
119
120     // output the contents of the grades array
121     public static void outputGrades( int grades[][] )
122     {
123        System.out.println( "The grades are:\n" );
124        System.out.print( "                " ); // align column heads
125
126        // create a column heading for each of the tests
127        for ( int test = 0; test < grades[ 0 ].length; test++ )
128           System.out.printf( "Test %d  ", test + 1 );
129
130        System.out.println( "Average" ); // student average column heading
131
132        // create rows/columns of text representing array grades
133        for ( int student = 0; student < grades.length; student++ )
134        {
135           System.out.printf( "Student %2d", student + 1 );
136
137           for ( int test : grades[ student ] ) // output student's grades
138              System.out.printf( "%8d", test );
139
140           // call method getAverage to calculate student's average grade;
141           // pass row of grades as the argument to getAverage
142           double average = getAverage( grades[ student ] );
143           System.out.printf( "%9.2f\n", average );
144        } // end outer for
145     } // end method outputGrades
146  } // end class SummarizeGrades
```

```
The grades are:

              Test 1  Test 2  Test 3  Average
Student  1       87      96      70    84.33
Student  2       68      87      90    81.67
Student  3       94     100      90    94.67
Student  4      100      81      82    87.67
```

Fig. 6.13 | SummarizeGrades uses a two-dimensional array to store grades. (Part 3 of 4.)

```
Student  5        83       65       85       77.67
Student  6        78       87       65       76.67
Student  7        85       75       83       81.00
Student  8        91       94      100       95.00
Student  9        76       72       84       77.33
Student 10        87       93       73       84.33

Lowest grade is 65
Highest grade is 100

Overall grade distribution:
00-09:
10-19:
20-29:
30-39:
40-49:
50-59:
60-69: ***
70-79: ******
80-89: ************
90-99: *******
  100: ***
```

Fig. 6.13 | SummarizeGrades uses a two-dimensional array to store grades. (Part 4 of 4.)

Methods getMinimum *and* getMaximum

Methods getMinimum, getMaximum, outputBarChart and outputGrades each loop through array grades by using nested for statements—for example, the nested enhanced for statement in method getMinimum (lines 39–48). The outer enhanced for statement iterates through the two-dimensional array grades, assigning successive rows to parameter studentGrades on successive iterations. The square brackets following the parameter name indicate that studentGrades refers to a one-dimensional int array—namely, a row in array grades containing one student's grades. To find the lowest overall grade, the inner for statement compares the elements of the current one-dimensional array student-Grades to variable lowGrade. For example, on the first iteration of the outer for, row 0 of grades is assigned to parameter studentGrades. The inner enhanced for statement then loops through studentGrades and compares each grade value with lowGrade. If a grade is less than lowGrade, lowGrade is set to that grade. On the second iteration of the outer enhanced for statement, row 1 of grades is assigned to studentGrades, and the elements of this row are compared with variable lowGrade. This repeats until all rows of grades have been traversed. When execution of the nested statement is complete, lowGrade contains the lowest grade in the two-dimensional array. Method getMaximum (lines 54–72) works similarly to method getMinimum.

Method outputBarChart

Method outputBarChart (lines 88–118) outputs the overall grade distribution for a whole semester. Line 93 declares and creates array frequency of 11 ints to store the frequency of grades in each grade category. For each grade in array grades, lines 96–100 use nested enhanced for statements to increment the appropriate element of the frequency array. To determine which element to increment, line 99 divides the current grade by 10 using integer division. For example, if grade is 85, line 99 increments frequency[8] to update the count of grades in the range 80–89. Lines 103–117 next display the bar chart (see Fig. 6.13) based on the values in array frequency. Like lines 23–24 of Fig. 6.6, lines 113–114 of Fig. 6.13 use a value in array frequency to determine the number of asterisks to display in each bar.

Method outputGrades

Method outputGrades (lines 121–145) uses nested for statements to output values of the array grades and each student's semester average. The output (Fig. 6.13) shows the result, which resembles the tabular format of a professor's physical grade book. Lines 127–128 print the column headings for each test. We use a counter-controlled for statement here so that we can identify each test with a number. Similarly, the for statement in lines 133–144 first outputs a row label using a counter variable to identify each student (line 135). Although array indices start at 0, lines 128 and 135 output test + 1 and student + 1, respectively, to produce test and student numbers starting at 1 (see Fig. 6.13). The inner for statement (lines 137–138) uses the outer for statement's counter variable student to loop through a specific row of array grades and output each student's test grade. Note that an enhanced for statement can be nested in a counter-controlled for statement, and vice versa. Finally, line 142 obtains each student's semester average by passing the current row of grades (i.e., grades[student]) to method getAverage.

Method getAverage

Method getAverage (lines 75–85) takes one argument—a one-dimensional array of test results for a particular student. When line 142 calls getAverage, the argument is grades[student], which specifies that a particular row of the two-dimensional array grades should be passed to getAverage. For example, based on the array created in Fig. 6.13, the argument grades[1] represents the three values (a one-dimensional array of grades) stored in row 1 of the two-dimensional array grades. Recall that a two-dimensional array is one whose elements are one-dimensional arrays. Method getAverage calculates the sum of the array elements, divides the total by the number of test results and returns the floating-point result as a double value (line 84).

6.10 Variable-Length Argument Lists

With variable-length argument lists, you can create methods that receive an unspecified number of arguments. A type followed by an ellipsis (...) in a method's parameter list indicates that the method receives a variable number of arguments of that particular type. This use of the ellipsis can occur only once in a parameter list, and the ellipsis, together with its type, must be placed at the end of the parameter list. While you can use method overloading and array passing to accomplish much of what is accomplished with variable-length argument lists, using an ellipsis in a method's parameter list is more concise.

Figure 6.14 demonstrates method average (lines 7–16), which receives a variable-length sequence of doubles. Java treats the variable-length argument list as an array of the specified type. Hence, the method body can manipulate the parameter numbers as an array of doubles. Lines 12–13 use the enhanced for loop to walk through the array and calculate the total of the doubles in the array. Line 15 accesses numbers.length to obtain the size of the numbers array for use in the averaging calculation. Lines 29, 31 and 33 in main call method average with two, three and four arguments, respectively. Method average has a variable-length argument list (line 7), so it can average as many `double` arguments as the caller passes. The output shows that each call to method `average` returns the correct value.

Common Programming Error 6.6

Placing an ellipsis indicating a variable-length argument list in the middle of a parameter list is a syntax error. An ellipsis may be placed only at the end of the parameter list.

```
1   // Fig. 6.14: VarargsTest.java
2   // Using variable-length argument lists.
3
4   public class VarargsTest
5   {
6      // calculate average
7      public static double average( double... numbers )
8      {
9         double total = 0.0; // initialize total
10
11        // calculate total using the enhanced for statement
12        for ( double d : numbers )
13           total += d;
14
15        return total / numbers.length;
16     } // end method average
17
18     public static void main( String[] args )
19     {
20        double d1 = 10.0;
21        double d2 = 20.0;
22        double d3 = 30.0;
23        double d4 = 40.0;
24
25        System.out.printf( "d1 = %.1f\nd2 = %.1f\nd3 = %.1f\nd4 = %.1f\n\n",
26           d1, d2, d3, d4 );
27
28        System.out.printf( "Average of d1 and d2 is %.1f\n",
29           average( d1, d2 ) );
30        System.out.printf( "Average of d1, d2 and d3 is %.1f\n",
31           average( d1, d2, d3 ) );
32        System.out.printf( "Average of d1, d2, d3 and d4 is %.1f\n",
33           average( d1, d2, d3, d4 ) );
34     } // end main
35  } // end class VarargsTest
```

```
d1 = 10.0
d2 = 20.0
d3 = 30.0
d4 = 40.0

Average of d1 and d2 is 15.0
Average of d1, d2 and d3 is 20.0
Average of d1, d2, d3 and d4 is 25.0
```

Fig. 6.14 | Using variable-length argument lists.

6.11 Using Command-Line Arguments

On many systems it's possible to pass arguments from the command line (these are known as **command-line arguments**) to an application by including a parameter of type `String[]` (i.e., an array of `String`s) in the parameter list of main, exactly as we've done in every application in the book. By convention, this parameter is named `args`. When an application is executed using the `java` command, Java passes the command-line arguments that appear after the class name in the `java` command to the application's main method as `String`s in the array `args`. The number of command-line arguments is obtained by accessing the array's `length` attribute. For example, the command `"java MyClass a b"` passes two command-line arguments, `a` and `b`, to application `MyClass`. Note that command-line arguments are separated by white space, not commas. When this command executes, `MyClass`'s main method receives the two-element array `args` (i.e., `args.length` is 2) in which `args[0]` contains the `String "a"` and `args[1]` contains the `String "b"`. Common uses of command-line arguments include passing options and file names to applications.

Figure 6.15 uses three command-line arguments to initialize an array. When the program executes, if `args.length` is not 3, the program prints an error message and terminates (lines 9–12). Otherwise, lines 14–32 initialize and display the array based on the values of the command-line arguments.

The command-line arguments become available to main as `String`s in `args`. Line 16 gets `args[0]`—a `String` that specifies the array size—and converts it to an int value that the program uses to create the array in line 17. The `static` method `parseInt` of class `Integer` converts its `String` argument to an int.

```
 1   // Fig. 6.15: InitArray.java
 2   // Initializing an array using command-line arguments.
 3
 4   public class InitArray
 5   {
 6      public static void main( String[] args )
 7      {
 8         // check number of command-line arguments
 9         if ( args.length != 3 )
10            System.out.println(
11               "Error: Please re-enter the entire command, including\n" +
12               "an array size, initial value and increment." );
13         else
14         {
15            // get array size from first command-line argument
16            int arrayLength = Integer.parseInt( args[ 0 ] );
17            int[] array = new int[ arrayLength ]; // create array
18
19            // get initial value and increment from command-line arguments
20            int initialValue = Integer.parseInt( args[ 1 ] );
21            int increment = Integer.parseInt( args[ 2 ] );
22
23            // calculate value for each array element
24            for ( int counter = 0; counter < array.length; counter++ )
25               array[ counter ] = initialValue + increment * counter;
```

Fig. 6.15 | Initializing an array using command-line arguments. (Part 1 of 2.)

```
26
27                 System.out.printf( "%s%8s\n", "Index", "Value" );
28
29             // display array index and value
30             for ( int counter = 0; counter < array.length; counter++ )
31                 System.out.printf( "%5d%8d\n", counter, array[ counter ] );
32         } // end else
33     } // end main
34 } // end class InitArray
```

```
java InitArray
Error: Please re-enter the entire command, including
an array size, initial value and increment.
```

```
java InitArray 5 0 4
Index    Value
    0        0
    1        4
    2        8
    3       12
    4       16
```

```
java InitArray 8 1 2
Index    Value
    0        1
    1        3
    2        5
    3        7
    4        9
    5       11
    6       13
    7       15
```

Fig. 6.15 | Initializing an array using command-line arguments. (Part 2 of 2.)

Lines 20–21 convert the args[1] and args[2] command-line arguments to int values and store them in initialValue and increment, respectively. Lines 24–25 calculate the value for each array element.

The output of the first execution shows that the application received an insufficient number of command-line arguments. The second execution uses command-line arguments 5, 0 and 4 to specify the size of the array (5), the value of the first element (0) and the increment of each value in the array (4), respectively. The corresponding output shows that these values create an array containing the integers 0, 4, 8, 12 and 16. The output from the third execution shows that the command-line arguments 8, 1 and 2 produce an array whose 8 elements are the nonnegative odd integers from 1 to 15.

6.12 Class Arrays

Class **Arrays** helps you avoid reinventing the wheel by providing **static** methods for common array manipulations. These methods include **sort** for sorting an array (i.e., arranging elements into increasing order), **binarySearch** for searching an array (i.e., determining whether an array contains a specific value and, if so, where the value is located), **equals** for comparing arrays and **fill** for placing values into an array. These methods are overloaded for primitive-type arrays and for arrays of objects. Our focus in this section is on using the built-in capabilities provided by the Java API. Chapter 19, Searching, Sorting and Big O, shows how to implement your own sorting and searching algorithms, which are of great interest to computer science researchers and students.

Figure 6.16 uses Arrays methods **sort**, **binarySearch**, **equals** and **fill**, and shows how to copy arrays with class System's static **arraycopy method**. In main, line 11 sorts the elements of array doubleArray. The static method sort of class Arrays orders the array's elements in *ascending* order by default. We discuss how to sort in *descending* order later in the chapter. Overloaded versions of sort allow you to sort a specific range of elements. Lines 12–15 output the sorted array.

```
1   // Fig. 6.16: ArrayManipulations.java
2   // Arrays class methods and System.arraycopy.
3   import java.util.Arrays;
4
5   public class ArrayManipulations
6   {
7      public static void main( String[] args )
8      {
9         // sort doubleArray into ascending order
10        double[] doubleArray = { 8.4, 9.3, 0.2, 7.9, 3.4 };
11        Arrays.sort( doubleArray );
12        System.out.printf( "\ndoubleArray: " );
13
14        for ( double value : doubleArray )
15           System.out.printf( "%.1f ", value );
16
17        // fill 10-element array with 7s
18        int[] filledIntArray = new int[ 10 ];
19        Arrays.fill( filledIntArray, 7 );
20        displayArray( filledIntArray, "filledIntArray" );
21
22        // copy array intArray into array intArrayCopy
23        int[] intArray = { 1, 2, 3, 4, 5, 6 };
24        int[] intArrayCopy = new int[ intArray.length ];
25        System.arraycopy( intArray, 0, intArrayCopy, 0, intArray.length );
26        displayArray( intArray, "intArray" );
27        displayArray( intArrayCopy, "intArrayCopy" );
28
29        // compare intArray and intArrayCopy for equality
30        boolean b = Arrays.equals( intArray, intArrayCopy );
31        System.out.printf( "\n\nintArray %s intArrayCopy\n",
32           ( b ? "==" : "!=" ) );
33
34        // compare intArray and filledIntArray for equality
35        b = Arrays.equals( intArray, filledIntArray );
36        System.out.printf( "intArray %s filledIntArray\n",
37           ( b ? "==" : "!=" ) );
```

Fig. 6.16 | Arrays class methods. (Part 1 of 2.)

```
38
39          // search intArray for the value 5
40          int location = Arrays.binarySearch( intArray, 5 );
41
42          if ( location >= 0 )
43             System.out.printf(
44                "Found 5 at element %d in intArray\n", location );
45          else
46             System.out.println( "5 not found in intArray" );
47
48          // search intArray for the value 8763
49          location = Arrays.binarySearch( intArray, 8763 );
50
51          if ( location >= 0 )
52             System.out.printf(
53                "Found 8763 at element %d in intArray\n", location );
54          else
55             System.out.println( "8763 not found in intArray" );
56       } // end main
57
58       // output values in each array
59       public static void displayArray( int[] array, String description )
60       {
61          System.out.printf( "\n%s: ", description );
62
63          for ( int value : array )
64             System.out.printf( "%d ", value );
65       } // end method displayArray
66    } // end class ArrayManipulations
```

```
doubleArray: 0.2 3.4 7.9 8.4 9.3
filledIntArray: 7 7 7 7 7 7 7 7 7 7
intArray: 1 2 3 4 5 6
intArrayCopy: 1 2 3 4 5 6

intArray == intArrayCopy
intArray != filledIntArray
Found 5 at element 4 in intArray
8763 not found in intArray
```

Fig. 6.16 | Arrays class methods. (Part 2 of 2.)

Line 19 calls static method fill of class Arrays to populate all 10 elements of filledIntArray with 7s. Overloaded versions of fill allow you to populate a specific range of elements with the same value. Line 20 calls our class's displayArray method (declared at lines 59–65) to output the contents of filledIntArray.

Line 25 copies the elements of intArray into intArrayCopy. The first argument (intArray) passed to System method arraycopy is the array from which elements are to be copied. The second argument (0) is the index that specifies the starting point in the range of elements to copy from the array. This value can be any valid array index. The third argument (intArrayCopy) specifies the destination array that will store the copy. The fourth argument (0) specifies the index in the destination array where the first copied element should be stored. The last argument specifies the number of elements to copy from the array in the first argument. In this case, we copy all the elements in the array.

Lines 30 and 35 call static method equals of class Arrays to determine whether all the elements of two arrays are equivalent. If the arrays contain the same elements in the same order, the method returns true; otherwise, it returns false.

Lines 40 and 49 call static method binarySearch of class Arrays to perform a binary search on intArray, using the second argument (5 and 8763, respectively) as the key. If value is found, binarySearch returns the index of the element; otherwise, binary-Search returns a negative value. The negative value returned is based on the search key's insertion point—the index where the key would be inserted in the array if we were performing an insert operation. After binarySearch determines the insertion point, it changes its sign to negative and subtracts 1 to obtain the return value. For example, in Fig. 6.16, the insertion point for the value 8763 is the element with index 6 in the array. Method binarySearch changes the insertion point to −6, subtracts 1 from it and returns the value −7. Subtracting 1 from the insertion point guarantees that method binarySearch returns positive values (>= 0) if and only if the key is found. This return value is useful for inserting elements in a sorted array. Chapter 19 discusses binary searching in detail.

Common Programming Error 6.7

Passing an unsorted array to binarySearch is a logic error—the value returned is undefined.

6.13 Introduction to Collections and Class ArrayList

The Java API provides several predefined data structures, called collections, used to store groups of related objects. These classes provide efficient methods that organize, store and retrieve your data without requiring knowledge of how the data is being stored. This reduces application-development time.

You've used arrays to store sequences of objects. Arrays do not automatically change their size at execution time to accommodate additional elements. The collection class ArrayList<T> (from package java.util) provides a convenient solution to this problem—it can dynamically change its size to accommodate more elements. The T is a placeholder—when declaring a new ArrayList, replace it with the type of elements that you want the ArrayList to hold. This is similar to specifying the type when declaring an array, except that only nonprimitive types can be used with these collection classes. For example,

```
ArrayList< String > list;
```

declares list as an ArrayList collection that can store only Strings. Classes with this kind of placeholder that can be used with any type are called generic classes. Additional generic collection classes and generics are discussed in Chapters 20 and 21, respectively. Figure 6.17 shows some common methods of class ArrayList<T>.

Method	Description
add	Adds an element to the end of the ArrayList.
clear	Removes all the elements from the ArrayList.

Fig. 6.17 | Some methods and properties of class ArrayList<T>. (Part 1 of 2.)

Method	Description
contains	Returns true if the `ArrayList` contains the specified element; otherwise, returns false.
get	Returns the element at the specified index.
indexOf	Returns the index of the first occurrence of the specified element in the `ArrayList`.
remove	Removes the first occurrence of the specified value.
remove	Removes the element at the specified index.
size	Returns the number of elements stored in the `ArrayList`.
trimToSize	Trims the capacity of the `ArrayList` to current number of elements.

Fig. 6.17 | Some methods and properties of class `ArrayList<T>`. (Part 2 of 2.)

Figure 6.18 demonstrates some common `ArrayList` capabilities. Line 10 creates a new empty `ArrayList` of `Strings` with an initial capacity of 10 elements. The capacity indicates how many items the `ArrayList` can hold without growing. `ArrayList` is implemented using an array behind the scenes. When the `ArrayList` grows, it must create a larger internal array and copy each element to the new array. This is a time-consuming operation. It would be inefficient for the `ArrayList` to grow each time an element is added. Instead, it grows only when an element is added *and* the number of elements is equal to the capacity—i.e., there is no space for the new element.

The **add** method adds elements to the `ArrayList` (lines 12–13). The add method with one argument appends its argument to the end of the `ArrayList`. The add method with two arguments inserts a new element at the specified position. The first argument is an index. As with arrays, collection indices start at zero. The second argument is the value that is to insert at that index. All elements at the specified index and above are shifted up by one position. This is usually slower than adding an element to the end of the `ArrayList`.

```java
1   // Fig. 6.18: ArrayListCollection.java
2   // Generic ArrayList collection demonstration.
3   import java.util.ArrayList;
4
5   public class ArrayListCollection
6   {
7      public static void main( String[] args )
8      {
9         // create a new ArrayList of Strings
10        ArrayList< String > items = new ArrayList< String >();
11
12        items.add( "red" ); // append an item to the list
13        items.add( 0, "yellow" ); // insert the value at index 0
14
15        // header
16        System.out.print(
17           "Display list contents with counter-controlled loop:" );
18
```

Fig. 6.18 | Generic `ArrayList<T>` collection demonstration. (Part 1 of 2.)

```
19          // display the colors in the list
20          for ( int i = 0; i < items.size(); i++ )
21             System.out.printf( " %s", items.get( i ) );
22
23          // display colors using foreach in the display method
24          display( items,
25             "\nDisplay list contents with enhanced for statement:" );
26
27          items.add( "green" ); // add "green" to the end of the list
28          items.add( "yellow" ); // add "yellow" to the end of the list
29          display( items, "List with two new elements:" );
30
31          items.remove( "yellow" ); // remove the first "yellow"
32          display( items, "Remove first instance of yellow:" );
33
34          items.remove( 1 ); // remove item at index 1
35          display( items, "Remove second list element (green):" );
36
37          // check if a value is in the List
38          System.out.printf( "\"red\" is %sin the list\n",
39             items.contains( "red" ) ? "": "not " );
40
41          // display number of elements in the List
42          System.out.printf( "Size: %s\n", items.size() );
43       } // end main
44
45       // display the ArrayList's elements on the console
46       public static void display( ArrayList< String > items, String header )
47       {
48          System.out.print( header ); // display header
49
50          // display each element in items
51          for ( String item : items )
52             System.out.printf( " %s", item );
53
54          System.out.println(); // display end of line
55       } // end method display
56    } // end class ArrayListCollection
```

```
Display list contents with counter-controlled loop: yellow red
Display list contents with enhanced for statement: yellow red
List with two new elements: yellow red green yellow
Remove first instance of yellow: red green yellow
Remove second list element (green): red yellow
"red" is in the list
Size: 2
```

Fig. 6.18 | Generic ArrayList<T> collection demonstration. (Part 2 of 2.)

Lines 20–21 display the items in the ArrayList. The **size** method returns the number of elements currently in the ArrayList. ArrayLists method **get** (line 21) obtains the element at a specified index. Lines 24–25 display the elements again by invoking method display (defined at lines 46–55). Lines 27–28 add two more elements to the ArrayList, then line 29 displays the elements again to confirm that the two elements were added to the end of the collection.

The **remove** method is used to remove an element with a specific value (line 31). Note that it removes only the first such element. If no such element is in the `ArrayList`, `remove` does nothing. An overloaded version of the method removes the element at the specified index (line 34). When an element is removed through either of these methods, all elements above that index are shifted down by one.

Line 39 uses the **contains** method to check if an item is in the `ArrayList`. The contains method returns `true` if the element is found in the `ArrayList`, and `false` otherwise. The method compares its argument to each element of the `ArrayList` in order, so using `contains` on a large `ArrayList` is inefficient. Line 42 displays the `ArrayList`'s size.

6.14 Fundamentals of Characters and Strings

Now we introduce Java's string- and character-processing capabilities. The techniques discussed here and in Chapter 16 are appropriate for validating program input, displaying information to users and other text-based manipulations. They're also appropriate for developing text editors, word processors, page-layout software, computerized typesetting systems and other kinds of text-processing software. We've already presented several string-processing capabilities in earlier chapters. This chapter discusses in detail the capabilities of class `String`. Chapter 16 discusses class `StringBuilder` and class `Character` from the `java.lang` package. These classes provide the foundation for string and character manipulation in Java. Chapter 16 also discusses regular expressions that provide applications with powerful capabilities to validate input. The functionality is located in class `String` and classes `Matcher` and `Pattern` from the `java.util.regex` package.

Characters are the fundamental building blocks of Java source programs. Every program is composed of a sequence of characters that—when grouped together meaningfully—are interpreted by the computer as a series of instructions used to accomplish a task. A program may contain **character literals**. A character literal is an integer value represented as a character in single quotes. For example, `'z'` represents the integer value of z, and `'\n'` represents the integer value of newline. The value of a character literal is the integer value of the character in the **Unicode character set**. Appendix B presents the integer equivalents of the characters in the ASCII character set, which is a subset of Unicode (discussed in Appendix L). For detailed information on Unicode, visit `www.unicode.org`.

Recall from Section 2.2 that a string is a sequence of characters treated as a single unit. A string may include letters, digits and various **special characters**, such as +, -, *, / and $. A string is an object of class `String`. **String literals** (stored in memory as `String` objects) are written as a sequence of characters in double quotation marks, as in:

```
"John Q. Doe"              (a name)
"9999 Main Street"         (a street address)
"Waltham, Massachusetts"   (a city and state)
"(201) 555-1212"           (a telephone number)
```

A string may be assigned to a `String` reference. The declaration

```
String color = "blue";
```

initializes `String` variable `color` to refer to a `String` object that contains the string `"blue"`.

Performance Tip 6.2

Java treats all string literals with the same contents as a single `String` object that has many references to it. This conserves memory.

6.15 Class String

Class String is used to represent strings in Java. The next several subsections cover many of class String's capabilities.

6.15.1 Initializing Strings

Class String provides various notations for creating and initializing Strings. After we introduce object orientation in Chapter 7, you'll see that lines 12–15 invoke "constructors" of class String to initialize new String objects. Four of these constructors are demonstrated in the main method of Fig. 6.19.

```java
 1   // Fig. 6.19: StringConstructors.java
 2   // String class constructors.
 3
 4   public class StringConstructors
 5   {
 6      public static void main( String[] args )
 7      {
 8         char[] charArray = { 'b', 'i', 'r', 't', 'h', ' ', 'd', 'a', 'y' };
 9         String s = new String( "hello" );
10
11         // use String constructors
12         String s1 = new String();
13         String s2 = new String( s );
14         String s3 = new String( charArray );
15         String s4 = new String( charArray, 6, 3 );
16
17         System.out.printf(
18            "s1 = %s\ns2 = %s\ns3 = %s\ns4 = %s\n",
19            s1, s2, s3, s4 ); // display strings
20      } // end main
21   } // end class StringConstructors
```

```
s1 =
s2 = hello
s3 = birth day
s4 = day
```

Fig. 6.19 | String class constructors.

Line 12 instantiates a new String using class String's no-argument constructor and assigns its reference to s1. The new String object contains no characters (i.e., the **empty string**, which can also be represented as "") and has a length of 0. Line 13 instantiates a new String object using class String's constructor that takes a String object as an argument and assigns its reference to s2. The new String object contains the same sequence of characters as the String object s that is passed as an argument to the constructor.

Software Engineering Observation 6.2

It's not necessary to copy an existing String object. String objects are immutable—their character contents cannot be changed after they're created, because class String does not provide any methods that allow the contents of a String object to be modified.

Line 14 instantiates a new `String` object and assigns its reference to s3 using class `String`'s constructor that takes a char array as an argument. The new `String` object contains a copy of the characters in the array.

Line 15 instantiates a new `String` object and assigns its reference to s4 using class `String`'s constructor that takes a char array and two integers as arguments. The second argument specifies the starting position (the offset) from which characters in the array are accessed. Remember that the first character is at position 0. The third argument specifies the number of characters (the count) to access in the array. The new `String` object is formed from the accessed characters. If the offset or the count specified as an argument results in accessing an element outside the bounds of the character array, a `StringIndexOutOfBoundsException` is thrown.

Common Programming Error 6.8

Accessing a character outside the bounds of a String (i.e., an index less than 0 or an index greater than or equal to the String's length) results in a StringIndexOutOfBounds-Exception.

6.15.2 String Methods `length`, `charAt` and `getChars`

String methods **length**, **charAt** and **getChars** return the length of a `String`, obtain the character at a specific location in a `String` and retrieve a set of characters from a `String` as a char array, respectively. Figure 6.20 demonstrates each of these methods.

Line 15 uses `String` method `length` to determine the number of characters in `String` s1. Like arrays, `Strings` know their own length. However, unlike arrays, you cannot access a `String`'s length via a `length` field—instead you must call the `String`'s `length` method.

```java
1   // Fig. 6.20: StringMiscellaneous.java
2   // This application demonstrates the length, charAt and getChars
3   // methods of the String class.
4
5   public class StringMiscellaneous
6   {
7      public static void main( String[] args )
8      {
9         String s1 = "hello there";
10        char[] charArray = new char[ 5 ];
11
12        System.out.printf( "s1: %s", s1 );
13
14        // test length method
15        System.out.printf( "\nLength of s1: %d", s1.length() );
16
17        // loop through characters in s1 with charAt and display reversed
18        System.out.print( "\nThe string reversed is: " );
19
20        for ( int count = s1.length() - 1; count >= 0; count-- )
21           System.out.printf( "%c ", s1.charAt( count ) );
22
23        // copy characters from string into charArray
24        s1.getChars( 0, 5, charArray, 0 );
```

Fig. 6.20 | String class character-manipulation methods. (Part 1 of 2.)

```
25          System.out.print( "\nThe character array is: " );
26
27          for ( char character : charArray )
28             System.out.print( character );
29
30          System.out.println();
31       } // end main
32    } // end class StringMiscellaneous
```

```
s1: hello there
Length of s1: 11
The string reversed is: e r e h t   o l l e h
The character array is: hello
```

Fig. 6.20 | String class character-manipulation methods. (Part 2 of 2.)

Lines 20–21 print the characters of the String s1 in reverse order (and separated by spaces). String method charAt (line 21) returns the character at a specific position in the String. Method charAt receives an integer argument that is used as the index and returns the character at that position. Like arrays, the first element of a String is at position 0.

Line 24 uses String method getChars to copy the characters of a String into a character array. The first argument is the starting index in the String from which characters are to be copied. The second argument is the index that is one past the last character to be copied from the String. The third argument is the character array into which the characters are to be copied. The last argument is the starting index where the copied characters are placed in the target character array. Next, lines 27–28 print the char array contents one character at a time.

6.15.3 Comparing Strings

Chapter 19 discusses sorting and searching arrays. Frequently, the information being sorted or searched consists of Strings that must be compared to place them into order or to determine whether a string appears in an array. Class String provides methods for comparing strings, as are demonstrated in the next two examples.

To understand what it means for one string to be greater than or less than another, consider the process of alphabetizing a series of last names. No doubt, you'd place "Jones" before "Smith" because the first letter of "Jones" comes before the first letter of "Smith" in the alphabet. But the alphabet is more than just a list of 26 letters—it's an ordered set of characters. Each letter occurs in a specific position within the set. Z is more than just a letter of the alphabet—it's specifically the twenty-sixth letter of the alphabet.

How does the computer know that one letter comes before another? All characters are represented in the computer as numeric codes (see Appendix B). When the computer compares strings, it actually compares the numeric codes of the characters in the strings.

Figure 6.21 demonstrates String methods equals, equalsIgnoreCase, compareTo and **regionMatches** and using the equality operator == to compare String objects.

The condition at line 17 uses method equals to compare String s1 and the String literal "hello" for equality. Method equals (a method of class Object overridden in String) tests any two objects for equality—the strings contained in the two objects are identical. The method returns true if the contents of the objects are equal, and false otherwise. The preceding condition is true because String s1 was initialized with the String literal "hello". Method equals uses a **lexicographical comparison**—it compares the integer Unicode values (see Appendix L for more information) that represent each character in each String. Thus, if the String "hello" is compared with the string "HELLO", the result is false, because the integer representation of a lowercase letter is different from that of the corresponding uppercase letter.

```java
1   // Fig. 6.21: StringCompare.java
2   // String methods equals, equalsIgnoreCase, compareTo and regionMatches.
3
4   public class StringCompare
5   {
6      public static void main( String[] args )
7      {
8         String s1 = new String( "hello" ); // s1 is a copy of "hello"
9         String s2 = "goodbye";
10        String s3 = "Happy Birthday";
11        String s4 = "happy birthday";
12
13        System.out.printf(
14           "s1 = %s\ns2 = %s\ns3 = %s\ns4 = %s\n\n", s1, s2, s3, s4 );
15
16        // test for equality
17        if ( s1.equals( "hello" ) )  // true
18           System.out.println( "s1 equals \"hello\"" );
19        else
20           System.out.println( "s1 does not equal \"hello\"" );
21
22        // test for equality with ==
23        if ( s1 == "hello" )  // false; they are not the same object
24           System.out.println( "s1 is the same object as \"hello\"" );
25        else
26           System.out.println( "s1 is not the same object as \"hello\"" );
27
28        // test for equality (ignore case)
29        if ( s3.equalsIgnoreCase( s4 ) )  // true
30           System.out.printf( "%s equals %s with case ignored\n", s3, s4 );
31        else
32           System.out.println( "s3 does not equal s4" );
33
34        // test compareTo
35        System.out.printf(
36           "\ns1.compareTo( s2 ) is %d", s1.compareTo( s2 ) );
37        System.out.printf(
38           "\ns2.compareTo( s1 ) is %d", s2.compareTo( s1 ) );
39        System.out.printf(
40           "\ns1.compareTo( s1 ) is %d", s1.compareTo( s1 ) );
41        System.out.printf(
42           "\ns3.compareTo( s4 ) is %d", s3.compareTo( s4 ) );
43        System.out.printf(
44           "\ns4.compareTo( s3 ) is %d\n\n", s4.compareTo( s3 ) );
```

Fig. 6.21 | String methods equals, equalsIgnoreCase, compareTo and regionMatches. (Part 1 of 2.)

```
45
46          // test regionMatches (case sensitive)
47          if ( s3.regionMatches( 0, s4, 0, 5 ) )
48              System.out.println( "First 5 characters of s3 and s4 match" );
49          else
50              System.out.println(
51                  "First 5 characters of s3 and s4 do not match" );
52
53          // test regionMatches (ignore case)
54          if ( s3.regionMatches( true, 0, s4, 0, 5 ) )
55              System.out.println(
56                  "First 5 characters of s3 and s4 match with case ignored" );
57          else
58              System.out.println(
59                  "First 5 characters of s3 and s4 do not match" );
60      } // end main
61   } // end class StringCompare
```

```
s1 = hello
s2 = goodbye
s3 = Happy Birthday
s4 = happy birthday

s1 equals "hello"
s1 is not the same object as "hello"
Happy Birthday equals happy birthday with case ignored

s1.compareTo( s2 ) is 1
s2.compareTo( s1 ) is -1
s1.compareTo( s1 ) is 0
s3.compareTo( s4 ) is -32
s4.compareTo( s3 ) is 32

First 5 characters of s3 and s4 do not match
First 5 characters of s3 and s4 match with case ignored
```

Fig. 6.21 | String methods equals, equalsIgnoreCase, compareTo and regionMatches. (Part 2 of 2.)

The condition at line 23 uses the equality operator == to compare String s1 for equality with the String literal "hello". When primitive-type values are compared with ==, the result is true if both values are identical. When references are compared with ==, the result is true if both references refer to the same object in memory. To compare the actual contents (or state information) of objects for equality, a method must be invoked. In the case of Strings, that method is equals. The preceding condition evaluates to false at line 23 because the reference s1 was initialized with the statement

```
s1 = new String( "hello" );
```

which creates a new String object with a copy of string literal "hello" and assigns the new object to variable s1. If s1 had been initialized with the statement

```
s1 = "hello";
```

which directly assigns the string literal "hello" to variable s1, the condition would be true. Java treats all string literal objects with the same contents as one String object to which there can be many references. Thus, lines 8, 17 and 23 all refer to the same String object "hello" in memory.

> **Common Programming Error 6.9**
> *Comparing references with == can lead to logic errors, because == compares the references to determine whether they refer to the same object, not whether two objects have the same contents. When two identical (but separate) objects are compared with ==, the result will be false. When comparing objects to determine whether they have the same contents, use method equals.*

If you are sorting Strings, you may compare them for equality with method equalsIgnoreCase, which ignores whether the letters in each String are uppercase or lowercase when performing the comparison. Thus, "hello" and "HELLO" compare as equal. Line 29 uses String method equalsIgnoreCase to compare String s3—Happy Birthday—for equality with String s4—happy birthday. The result of this comparison is true because the comparison ignores case sensitivity.

Lines 35–44 use method compareTo to compare Strings. Method compareTo is declared in the Comparable interface and implemented in the String class. Line 36 compares String s1 to String s2. Method compareTo returns 0 if the Strings are equal, a negative number if the String that invokes compareTo is less than the String that is passed as an argument and a positive number if the String that invokes compareTo is greater than the String that is passed as an argument. Method compareTo uses a lexicographical comparison—it compares the numeric values of corresponding characters in each String. (For more information on the exact value returned by the compareTo method, see java.sun.com/javase/6/docs/api/java/lang/String.html.)

The condition at line 47 uses String method regionMatches to compare portions of two Strings for equality. The first argument is the starting index in the String that invokes the method. The second argument is a comparison String. The third argument is the starting index in the comparison String. The last argument is the number of characters to compare between the two Strings. The method returns true only if the specified number of characters are lexicographically equal.

Finally, the condition at line 54 uses a five-argument version of String method regionMatches to compare portions of two Strings for equality. When the first argument is true, the method ignores the case of the characters being compared. The remaining arguments are identical to those described for the four-argument regionMatches method.

String Methods startsWith and endsWith

Figure 6.22 demonstrates String methods **startsWith** and **endsWith**. Method main creates array strings containing "started", "starting", "ended" and "ending". The remainder of method main consists of three for statements that test the elements of the array to determine whether they start with or end with a particular set of characters.

```
1   // Fig. 6.22: StringStartEnd.java
2   // String methods startsWith and endsWith.
3
4   public class StringStartEnd
5   {
```

Fig. 6.22 | String methods startsWith and endsWith. (Part 1 of 2.)

```
 6      public static void main( String[] args )
 7      {
 8          String[] strings = { "started", "starting", "ended", "ending" };
 9
10          // test method startsWith
11          for ( String string : strings )
12          {
13              if ( string.startsWith( "st" ) )
14                  System.out.printf( "\"%s\" starts with \"st\"\n", string );
15          } // end for
16
17          System.out.println();
18
19          // test method startsWith starting from position 2 of string
20          for ( String string : strings )
21          {
22              if ( string.startsWith( "art", 2 ) )
23                  System.out.printf(
24                      "\"%s\" starts with \"art\" at position 2\n", string );
25          } // end for
26
27          System.out.println();
28
29          // test method endsWith
30          for ( String string : strings )
31          {
32              if ( string.endsWith( "ed" ) )
33                  System.out.printf( "\"%s\" ends with \"ed\"\n", string );
34          } // end for
35      } // end main
36  } // end class StringStartEnd
```

```
"started" starts with "st"
"starting" starts with "st"

"started" starts with "art" at position 2
"starting" starts with "art" at position 2

"started" ends with "ed"
"ended" ends with "ed"
```

Fig. 6.22 | String methods startsWith and endsWith. (Part 2 of 2.)

Lines 11–15 use the version of method startsWith that takes a String argument. The condition in the if statement (line 13) determines whether each String in the array starts with the characters "st". If so, the method returns true and the application prints that String. Otherwise, the method returns false and nothing happens.

Lines 20–25 use the startsWith method that takes a String and an integer as arguments. The integer specifies the index at which the comparison should begin in the String. The condition in the if statement (line 22) determines whether each String in the array has the characters "art" beginning with the third character in each String. If so, the method returns true and the application prints the String.

The third for statement (lines 30–34) uses method endsWith, which takes a String argument. The condition at line 32 determines whether each String in the array ends with the characters "ed". If so, the method returns true and the application prints the String.

6.15.4 Locating Characters and Substrings in Strings

Often it's useful to search a string for a character or set of characters. For example, if you are creating your own word processor, you might want to provide a capability for searching through documents. Figure 6.23 demonstrates the many versions of String methods indexOf and lastIndexOf that search for a specified character or substring in a String.

All the searches in this example are performed on the String letters (initialized with "abcdefghijklmabcdefghijklm"). Lines 11–16 use method indexOf to locate the first occurrence of a character in a String. If the method finds the character, it returns the character's index in the String—otherwise, it returns -1. There are two versions of indexOf that search for characters in a String. The expression in line 12 uses the version of method indexOf that takes an integer representation of the character to find. The expression at line 14 uses another version of method indexOf, which takes two integer arguments—the character and the starting index at which the search of the String should begin.

```
1   // Fig. 6.23: StringIndexMethods.java
2   // String searching methods indexOf and lastIndexOf.
3
4   public class StringIndexMethods
5   {
6      public static void main( String[] args )
7      {
8         String letters = "abcdefghijklmabcdefghijklm";
9
10        // test indexOf to locate a character in a string
11        System.out.printf(
12           "'c' is located at index %d\n", letters.indexOf( 'c' ) );
13        System.out.printf(
14           "'a' is located at index %d\n", letters.indexOf( 'a', 1 ) );
15        System.out.printf(
16           "'$' is located at index %d\n\n", letters.indexOf( '$' ) );
17
18        // test lastIndexOf to find a character in a string
19        System.out.printf( "Last 'c' is located at index %d\n",
20           letters.lastIndexOf( 'c' ) );
21        System.out.printf( "Last 'a' is located at index %d\n",
22           letters.lastIndexOf( 'a', 25 ) );
23        System.out.printf( "Last '$' is located at index %d\n\n",
24           letters.lastIndexOf( '$' ) );
25
26        // test indexOf to locate a substring in a string
27        System.out.printf( "\"def\" is located at index %d\n",
28           letters.indexOf( "def" ) );
29        System.out.printf( "\"def\" is located at index %d\n",
30           letters.indexOf( "def", 7 ) );
31        System.out.printf( "\"hello\" is located at index %d\n\n",
32           letters.indexOf( "hello" ) );
```

Fig. 6.23 | String-searching methods indexOf and lastIndexOf. (Part 1 of 2.)

```
33
34          // test lastIndexOf to find a substring in a string
35          System.out.printf( "Last \"def\" is located at index %d\n",
36             letters.lastIndexOf( "def" ) );
37          System.out.printf( "Last \"def\" is located at index %d\n",
38             letters.lastIndexOf( "def", 25 ) );
39          System.out.printf( "Last \"hello\" is located at index %d\n",
40             letters.lastIndexOf( "hello" ) );
41       } // end main
42    } // end class StringIndexMethods
```

```
'c' is located at index 2
'a' is located at index 13
'$' is located at index -1

Last 'c' is located at index 15
Last 'a' is located at index 13
Last '$' is located at index -1

"def" is located at index 3
"def" is located at index 16
"hello" is located at index -1

Last "def" is located at index 16
Last "def" is located at index 16
Last "hello" is located at index -1
```

Fig. 6.23 | String-searching methods `indexOf` and `lastIndexOf`. (Part 2 of 2.)

Lines 19–24 use method `lastIndexOf` to locate the last occurrence of a character in a `String`. The method searches from the end of the `String` toward the beginning. If it finds the character, it returns the character's index in the `String`—otherwise, it returns –1. There are two versions of `lastIndexOf` that search for characters in a `String`. The expression at line 20 uses the version that takes the integer representation of the character. The expression at line 22 uses the version that takes two integer arguments—the integer representation of the character and the index from which to begin searching backward.

Lines 27–40 demonstrate versions of methods `indexOf` and `lastIndexOf` that each take a `String` as the first argument. These versions perform identically to those described earlier except that they search for sequences of characters (or substrings) that are specified by their `String` arguments. If the substring is found, these methods return the index in the `String` of the first character in the substring.

6.15.5 Extracting Substrings from Strings

Class `String` provides two `substring` methods to enable a new `String` object to be created by copying part of an existing `String` object. Each method returns a new `String` object. Both methods are demonstrated in Fig. 6.24.

The expression `letters.substring( 20 )` at line 12 uses the `substring` method that takes one integer argument. The argument specifies the starting index in the original `String letters` from which characters are to be copied. The substring returned contains a copy of the characters from the starting index to the end of the String. Specifying an index outside the bounds of the String causes a **StringIndexOutOfBoundsException**.

```
1   // Fig. 6.24: SubString.java
2   // String class substring methods.
3
4   public class SubString
5   {
6      public static void main( String[] args )
7      {
8         String letters = "abcdefghijklmabcdefghijklm";
9
10        // test substring methods
11        System.out.printf( "Substring from index 20 to end is \"%s\"\n",
12           letters.substring( 20 ) );
13        System.out.printf( "%s \"%s\"\n",
14           "Substring from index 3 up to, but not including 6 is",
15           letters.substring( 3, 6 ) );
16     } // end main
17  } // end class SubString
```

```
Substring from index 20 to end is "hijklm"
Substring from index 3 up to, but not including 6 is "def"
```

Fig. 6.24 | String class substring methods.

Line 15 uses the substring method that takes two integer arguments—the starting index from which to copy characters in the original String and the index one beyond the last character to copy (i.e., copy up to, but not including, that index in the String). The substring returned contains a copy of the specified characters from the original String. An index outside the bounds of the String causes a StringIndexOutOfBoundsException.

6.15.6 Concatenating Strings

String method **concat** (Fig. 6.25) concatenates two String objects and returns a new String object containing the characters from both original Strings. The expression s1.concat(s2) at line 13 forms a String by appending the characters in s2 to the characters in s1. The original Strings to which s1 and s2 refer are not modified.

```
1   // Fig. 6.25: StringConcatenation.java
2   // String method concat.
3
4   public class StringConcatenation
5   {
6      public static void main( String[] args )
7      {
8         String s1 = "Happy ";
9         String s2 = "Birthday";
10
```

Fig. 6.25 | String method concat. (Part 1 of 2.)

```
11          System.out.printf( "s1 = %s\ns2 = %s\n\n",s1, s2 );
12          System.out.printf(
13             "Result of s1.concat( s2 ) = %s\n", s1.concat( s2 ) );
14          System.out.printf( "s1 after concatenation = %s\n", s1 );
15       } // end main
16    } // end class StringConcatenation
```

```
s1 = Happy
s2 = Birthday

Result of s1.concat( s2 ) = Happy Birthday
s1 after concatenation = Happy
```

Fig. 6.25 | String method concat. (Part 2 of 2.)

6.15.7 Miscellaneous String Methods

Class `String` provides several methods that return modified copies of `Strings` or that return character arrays. These methods are demonstrated in the application in Fig. 6.26.

```java
1   // Fig. 6.26: StringMiscellaneous2.java
2   // String methods replace, toLowerCase, toUpperCase, trim and toCharArray.
3
4   public class StringMiscellaneous2
5   {
6      public static void main( String[] args )
7      {
8         String s1 = "hello";
9         String s2 = "GOODBYE";
10        String s3 = "   spaces   ";
11
12        System.out.printf( "s1 = %s\ns2 = %s\ns3 = %s\n\n", s1, s2, s3 );
13
14        // test method replace
15        System.out.printf(
16           "Replace 'l' with 'L' in s1: %s\n\n", s1.replace( 'l', 'L' ) );
17
18        // test toLowerCase and toUpperCase
19        System.out.printf( "s1.toUpperCase() = %s\n", s1.toUpperCase() );
20        System.out.printf( "s2.toLowerCase() = %s\n\n", s2.toLowerCase() );
21
22        // test trim method
23        System.out.printf( "s3 after trim = \"%s\"\n\n", s3.trim() );
24
25        // test toCharArray method
26        char[] charArray = s1.toCharArray();
27        System.out.print( "s1 as a character array = " );
28
29        for ( char character : charArray )
30           System.out.print( character );
31
```

Fig. 6.26 | String methods replace, toLowerCase, toUpperCase, trim and toCharArray. (Part 1 of 2.)

```
32          System.out.println();
33       } // end main
34    } // end class StringMiscellaneous2
```

```
s1 = hello
s2 = GOODBYE
s3 =      spaces

Replace 'l' with 'L' in s1: heLLo

s1.toUpperCase() = HELLO
s2.toLowerCase() = goodbye

s3 after trim = "spaces"

s1 as a character array = hello
```

Fig. 6.26 | String methods replace, toLowerCase, toUpperCase, trim and toCharArray. (Part 2 of 2.)

Line 16 uses String method replace to return a new String object in which every occurrence in s1 of character 'l' (lowercase el) is replaced with character 'L'. Method replace leaves the original String unchanged. If there are no occurrences of the first argument in the String, method replace returns the original String. An overloaded version of method replace enables you to replace substrings rather than individual characters.

Line 19 uses String method **toUpperCase** to generate a new String with uppercase letters where corresponding lowercase letters exist in s1. The method returns a new String object containing the converted String and leaves the original String unchanged. If there are no characters to convert, method toUpperCase returns the original String.

Line 20 uses String method **toLowerCase** to return a new String object with lowercase letters where corresponding uppercase letters exist in s2. The original String remains unchanged. If there are no characters in the original String to convert, toLowerCase returns the original String.

Line 23 uses String method **trim** to generate a new String object that removes all white-space characters that appear at the beginning or end of the String on which trim operates. The method returns a new String object containing the String without leading or trailing white-space. The original String remains unchanged.

Line 26 uses String method **toCharArray** to create a new character array containing a copy of the characters in s1. Lines 29–30 output each char in the array.

6.15.8 String Method valueOf

Every object in Java has a toString method that enables a program to obtain the object's String representation. Unfortunately, this technique cannot be used with primitive types because they do not have methods. Class String provides **static** methods that take an argument of any type and convert it to a String object. Figure 6.27 demonstrates the String class **valueOf** methods.

The expression String.valueOf(charArray) at line 18 uses the character array charArray to create a new String object. The expression String.valueOf(charArray, 3, 3) at line 20 uses a portion of the character array charArray to create a new String object.

The second argument specifies the starting index from which the characters are used. The third argument specifies the number of characters to be used.

```java
1   // Fig. 6.27: StringValueOf.java
2   // String valueOf methods.
3
4   public class StringValueOf
5   {
6      public static void main( String[] args )
7      {
8         char[] charArray = { 'a', 'b', 'c', 'd', 'e', 'f' };
9         boolean booleanValue = true;
10        char characterValue = 'Z';
11        int integerValue = 7;
12        long longValue = 10000000000L; // L suffix indicates long
13        float floatValue = 2.5f; // f indicates that 2.5 is a float
14        double doubleValue = 33.333; // no suffix, double is default
15        Object objectRef = "hello"; // assign string to an Object reference
16
17        System.out.printf(
18           "char array = %s\n", String.valueOf( charArray ) );
19        System.out.printf( "part of char array = %s\n",
20           String.valueOf( charArray, 3, 3 ) );
21        System.out.printf(
22           "boolean = %s\n", String.valueOf( booleanValue ) );
23        System.out.printf(
24           "char = %s\n", String.valueOf( characterValue ) );
25        System.out.printf( "int = %s\n", String.valueOf( integerValue ) );
26        System.out.printf( "long = %s\n", String.valueOf( longValue ) );
27        System.out.printf( "float = %s\n", String.valueOf( floatValue ) );
28        System.out.printf(
29           "double = %s\n", String.valueOf( doubleValue ) );
30        System.out.printf( "Object = %s", String.valueOf( objectRef ) );
31     } // end main
32  } // end class StringValueOf
```

```
char array = abcdef
part of char array = def
boolean = true
char = Z
int = 7
long = 10000000000
float = 2.5
double = 33.333
Object = hello
```

Fig. 6.27 | String valueOf methods.

There are seven other overloaded versions of method valueOf, which take arguments of type boolean, char, int, long, float, double and Object, respectively. These are demonstrated in lines 21–30. Note that the version of valueOf that takes an Object as an argument can do so because all Objects in Java can be converted to Strings.

[*Note:* Lines 12–13 use literal values 10000000000L and 2.5f as the initial values of long variable longValue and float variable floatValue, respectively. By default, Java treats integer literals as type int and floating-point literals as type double. Appending the letter L to the literal 10000000000 and appending letter f to the literal 2.5 indicates to the compiler that 10000000000 should be treated as a long and that 2.5 should be treated as a float. An uppercase L or lowercase l can be used to denote a variable of type long and an uppercase F or lowercase f can be used to denote a variable of type float.]

6.16 Introduction to File Processing

Data stored in variables and arrays is temporary—it's lost when a local variable goes out of scope or when the program terminates. For long-term retention of data, even after the programs that create the data terminate, computers use **files**. You use files every day for tasks such as writing an e-mail or creating a spreadsheet. Computers store files on **secondary storage devices** such as hard disks, optical disks, flash drives and magnetic tapes. Data maintained in files is **persistent data** because it exists beyond the duration of program execution. In this chapter, we explain how Java programs create, update and process files.

A programming language must be capable of file processing to support commercial applications, which typically process massive amounts of persistent data. Here and in Chapter 17, we discuss Java's file-processing and stream input/output features. The term "stream" refers to ordered data that is read from or written to a file. We discuss streams in detail in Section 6.18. File processing is a subset of Java's stream-processing capabilities, which include reading from and writing to memory, files and network connections. In this chapter, we'll introduce text-file-processing concepts that will make you comfortable with using files programmatically. In Chapter 17, we'll provide you with sufficient stream-processing capabilities to support the networking features introduced in Chapter 27.

We begin by discussing the hierarchy of data contained in files and Java's view of files. Next we explain that data can be stored in text files and binary files—and we cover the differences between them. Then we demonstrate creating and manipulating sequential-access text files. Working with text files allows the reader to quickly and easily start manipulating files. As you'll learn in Chapter 17, however, it's difficult to read data from text files back into object form. Fortunately, Java provides ways to write objects to and read objects from files (known as object serialization and deserialization). In Chapter 17, we recreate the sequential-access programs you'll learn here, this time by storing objects in binary files.

6.17 Data Hierarchy

Ultimately, a computer processes data items as combinations of zeros and ones, because it's simple and economical for engineers to build electronic devices that can assume two stable states—one representing 0 and the other representing 1. It's remarkable that the impressive functions performed by computers involve only the most fundamental manipulations of 0s and 1s.

Bits
The smallest data item in a computer can assume the value 0 or the value 1. Such a data item is called a **bit** (short for "binary digit"—a digit that can assume one of two values). Computer circuitry performs various simple bit manipulations, such as examining a bit's value, setting a bit's value and reversing a bit's value (from 1 to 0 or from 0 to 1).

Characters

It's cumbersome for programmers to work with data in the low-level form of bits. Instead, they prefer to work with **decimal digits** (0–9), **letters** (A–Z and a–z), and **special symbols** (e.g., $, @, %, &, *, (,), –, +, ", :, ? and /). Digits, letters and special symbols are known as **characters**. The computer's **character set** is the set of all the characters used to write programs and represent data items. Computers process only 1s and 0s, so a computer's character set represents every character as a pattern of 1s and 0s. Java uses **Unicode** characters that are composed of two **bytes**, each composed of eight bits. Java type **byte** can be used to represent byte data. Unicode contains characters for many of the world's languages. See Appendix L for more information on this character set. See Appendix B for more information on the **ASCII (American Standard Code for Information Interchange)** character set, a popular subset of Unicode that represents uppercase and lowercase letters, digits and various common special characters.

Fields

Just as characters are composed of bits, **fields** are composed of characters or bytes. A field is a group of characters or bytes that conveys meaning. For example, a field consisting of uppercase and lowercase letters can be used to represent a person's name.

Data items processed by computers form a **data hierarchy** that becomes larger and more complex in structure as we progress from bits to characters to fields, and so on.

Records and Files

Typically, several fields compose a **record** (implemented as a class in Java). In a payroll system, for example, the record for an employee might consist of the following fields (possible types for these fields are shown in parentheses):

- Employee identification number (int)
- Name (String)
- Address (String)
- Hourly pay rate (double)
- Number of exemptions claimed (int)
- Year-to-date earnings (int or double)
- Amount of taxes withheld (int or double)

Thus, a record is a group of related fields. In the preceding example, all the fields belong to the same employee. A company might have many employees and thus have a payroll record for each one. A **file** is a group of related records. [*Note:* More generally, a file contains arbitrary data in arbitrary formats. In some operating systems, a file is viewed as nothing more than a collection of bytes—any organization of the bytes in a file (e.g., organizing the data into records) is a view created by the applications programmer.] A company's payroll file normally contains one record per employee. Thus, a payroll file for a small company might contain only 22 records, whereas one for a large company might contain thousands. It's not unusual for a company to have many files, some containing billions, or even trillions, of characters of information. Figure 6.28 illustrates a portion of the data hierarchy.

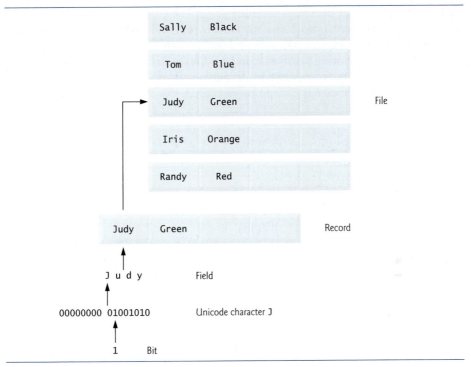

Fig. 6.28 | Data hierarchy.

Record Keys

To facilitate the retrieval of specific records from a file, at least one field in each record is often chosen as a record key. A record key identifies a record as belonging to a particular person or entity and is unique to each record. This field typically is used to search and sort records. In the payroll record described previously, the employee identification number normally would be chosen as the record key.

Sequential Files

There are many ways to organize records in a file. The most common is called a sequential file, in which records are stored in order by the record-key field. For example, a payroll file commonly places records in ascending order by employee identification number.

Databases

Most organizations store data in many different files. Companies might have payroll files, accounts receivable files (listing money due from clients), accounts payable files (listing money due to suppliers), inventory files (listing facts about all the items handled by the business) and many others. Often, a group of related files is called a database. A collection of programs designed to create and manage databases is called a database management system (DBMS). We discuss this topic in Chapter 28, Accessing Databases with JDBC.

6.18 Files and Streams

Java views each file as a sequential stream of bytes (Fig. 6.29). Every operating system provides a mechanism to determine the end of a file, such as an end-of-file marker or a count of the total bytes in the file that is recorded in a system-maintained administrative data structure. A Java program processing a stream of bytes simply receives an indication from the operating system when it reaches the end of the stream—the program does not need to know how the underlying platform represents files or streams. In some cases, the end-of-file indication occurs as an exception. In other cases, the indication is a return value from a method invoked on a stream-processing object.

Fig. 6.29 | Java's view of a file of *n* bytes.

Byte-Based and Character-Based Streams
File streams can be used to input and output data as bytes or characters. Streams that input and output bytes are known as **byte-based streams**, representing data in its binary format. Streams that input and output characters are known as **character-based streams**, representing data as a sequence of characters. For instance, if the value 5 were being stored using a byte-based stream, it would be stored in the binary format of the numeric value 5, or 101. If the value 5 were being stored using a character-based stream, it would be stored in the binary format of the character 5, or 00000000 00110101 (this is the binary representation for the numeric value 53, which indicates the character 5 in the Unicode character set). The difference between the two forms is that the numeric value can be used as an integer in calculations, whereas the character 5 is simply a character that can be used in a string of text, as in "Sarah Miller is 15 years old". Files that are created using byte-based streams are referred to as **binary files**, while files created using character-based streams are referred to as **text files**. Text files can be read by text editors, while binary files are read by programs that understand the specific content of the file and the ordering of that content.

Standard Input, Standard Output and Standard Error Streams
A Java program **opens** a file by creating an object and associating a stream of bytes or characters with it. The classes used to create these objects are discussed shortly. Java can also associate streams with different devices. In fact, Java creates three stream objects that are associated with devices when a Java program begins executing—System.in, System.out and System.err. System.in (the standard input stream object) normally enables a program to input bytes from the keyboard; object System.out (the standard output stream object) normally enables a program to output character data to the screen; and object System.err (the standard error stream object) normally enables a program to output character-based error messages to the screen. Each of these streams can be redirected. For System.in, this capability enables the program to read from a different source. For System.out and System.err, this capability enables the output to be sent to a different location, such as a file on disk. Class System provides methods **setIn**, **setOut** and **setErr** to **redirect** the standard input, output and error streams, respectively.

6.19 Sequential-Access Text Files

In this section, you'll manipulate sequential-access text files in which records are stored in order by the record-key field. You'll learn to create, write data to and read data from sequential-access text files. In Chapter 17, you'll use the techniques you learn here to create an object-oriented credit-inquiry application that can read from a text file and display accounts with credit, zero or debit balances.

6.19.1 Creating a Sequential-Access Text File

Java imposes no structure on a file—concepts such as records do not exist as part of the Java language. Therefore, you must structure files to meet the requirements of your applications. In the following example, we see how to impose a keyed record structure on a file.

The program in Fig. 6.30 creates a simple sequential-access file that might be used in an accounts receivable system to keep track of the amounts owed to a company by its credit clients. For each client, the program obtains from the user an account number and the client's name and balance (i.e., the amount the client owes the company for goods and services received). Each client's data constitutes a "record" for that client. This application uses the account number as the record key—the file will be created and maintained in account-number order. The program assumes that the user enters the records in account-number order. In a comprehensive accounts receivable system (based on sequential-access files), a sorting capability would be provided so that the user could enter the records in any order. The records would then be sorted and written to the file.

```java
1   // Fig. 6.30: CreateTextFile.java
2   // Writing data to a sequential text file with class Formatter.
3   import java.util.Formatter;
4   import java.util.Scanner;
5
6   public class CreateTextFile
7   {
8      public static void main( String[] args ) throws Exception
9      {
10         Formatter output = new Formatter( "clients.txt" ); // open the file
11         Scanner input = new Scanner( System.in ); // reads user input
12
13         int accountNumber; // stores account number
14         String firstName; // stores first name
15         String lastName; // stores last name
16         double balance; // stores account balance
17
18         System.out.printf( "%s\n%s\n%s\n%s\n\n",
19            "To terminate input, type the end-of-file indicator ",
20            "when you are prompted to enter input.",
21            "On UNIX/Linux/Mac OS X type <ctrl> d then press Enter",
22            "On Windows type <ctrl> z then press Enter" );
23
24         System.out.printf( "%s\n%s",
25            "Enter account number (> 0), first name, last name and balance.",
26            "? " );
27
28         while ( input.hasNext() ) // loop until end-of-file indicator
29         {
30            // retrieve data to be output
31            accountNumber = input.nextInt(); // read account number
```

Fig. 6.30 | Writing data to a sequential text file with class `Formatter`. (Part 1 of 2.)

```
32              firstName = input.next(); // read first name
33              lastName = input.next(); // read last name
34              balance = input.nextDouble(); // read balance
35
36              if ( accountNumber > 0 )
37              {
38                  // write new record
39                  output.format( "%d %s %s %.2f\n", accountNumber,
40                      firstName, lastName, balance );
41              } // end if
42              else
43              {
44                  System.out.println(
45                      "Account number must be greater than 0." );
46              } // end else
47
48              System.out.printf( "%s %s\n%s", "Enter account number (>0),",
49                  "first name, last name and balance.", "? " );
50          } // end while
51
52          output.close(); // close file
53      } // end main
54  } // end class CreateTextFile
```

```
To terminate input, type the end-of-file indicator
when you are prompted to enter input.
On UNIX/Linux/Mac OS X type <ctrl> d then press Enter
On Windows type <ctrl> z then press Enter

Enter account number (> 0), first name, last name and balance.
? 100 Bob Jones 24.98
Enter account number (> 0), first name, last name and balance.
? 200 Steve Doe -345.67
Enter account number (> 0), first name, last name and balance.
? 300 Pam White 0.00
Enter account number (> 0), first name, last name and balance.
? 400 Sam Stone -42.16
Enter account number (> 0), first name, last name and balance.
? 500 Sue Rich 224.62
Enter account number (> 0), first name, last name and balance.
? ^Z
```

Fig. 6.30 | Writing data to a sequential text file with class `Formatter`. (Part 2 of 2.)

Class *CreateTextFile*

Now let's examine class `CreateTextFile` (Fig. 6.30). Line 10 declares variable `output` of type `Formatter` (from package `java.util`; imported at line 3). As discussed in Section 6.18, a `Formatter` outputs formatted `Strings`, using the same capabilities as method `System.out.printf`. A `Formatter` can output to various locations, such as the screen or a file, as we do here. Line 10 also creates the `Formatter` object and assigns its reference to variable `output`. The argument in parentheses to the right of `Formatter` is a `String` containing the name and location of the file in which the program will write text. If the location is not specified in the `String`, as is the case here, the JVM assumes that the file is in the directory from which the program was executed. For text files, we use the `.txt` file extension. If the file does not exist, it will be created. If an existing file is opened, its contents are **truncated**—all the data in the file is discarded. At this point the file is open for writing, and the resulting Formatter object can be used to write data to the file.

Line 11 creates a Scanner object for obtaining user input. Lines 13–16 declare the variables in which the program stores the information entered by the user. Lines 18–22 prompt the user to enter the various fields for each record or to enter the end-of-file key sequence when data entry is complete. Figure 6.31 lists the key combinations for entering end-of-file for various computer systems.

Operating system	Key combination
UNIX/Linux/Mac OS X	*<Enter> <Ctrl> d*
Windows	*<Ctrl> z*

Fig. 6.31 | End-of-file key combinations.

Lines 24–26 prompt the user to enter the first record. Line 28 uses Scanner method hasNext to determine whether the end-of-file key combination has been entered. The loop executes until hasNext encounters end-of-file.

Lines 31–34 read and store a record entered by the user. If the account number is greater than 0 (line 36), the record's information is written to clients.txt (lines 39–40) using Formatter method **format,** which uses a format control String to determine the output's format. The method outputs a formatted String to the output destination of the Formatter object—the file clients.txt. The format string "%d %s %s %.2f\n" indicates that the current record will be output to the file as an integer (the account number) followed by a String (the first name), another String (the last name) and a floating-point value (the balance). Each piece of information is separated from the next by a space, and the double value (the balance) is output with two digits to the right of the decimal point (as indicated by the .2 in %.2f). Each record is followed by a newline character (\n). The data in the text file can be viewed with a text editor or retrieved later by a program designed to read the file (Section 6.19.2). Lines 48–49 prompt the user to enter the next record. When the loop terminates, line 52 closes the Formatter object (and thus the file) by simply calling method **close** on output. If method close is not called explicitly, the operating system normally will close the file when program execution terminates—this is an example of operating-system "housekeeping." However, you should always explicitly close a file when it is no longer needed.

Platform-Specific Line-Separator Characters
Lines 39–40 output a line of text followed by a newline (\n). If you use a text editor to open the clients.txt file produced, each record might not display on a separate line. For example, in Notepad (Microsoft Windows), users will see one continuous line of text. This occurs because different platforms use different line-separator characters. On UNIX/Linux/Mac OS X, the line separator is a newline (\n). On Windows, it is a combination of a carriage return and a line feed—represented as \r\n. You can use the %n format specifier in a format control string to output a platform-specific line separator, thus ensuring that the text file can be opened and viewed correctly in a text editor for the platform on which the file was created. Note that the method System.out.println outputs a plat-

form-specific line separator after its argument. Also, note that regardless of the line separator used in a text file, a Java program can still recognize the lines of text and read them.

Possible Runtime Problems

When you programmatically interact with files on disk, there are many potential problems that could occur. For example, security restrictions on the computer could prevent the program from opening a file; if there is something wrong with the disk drive, the computer could have trouble writing information into the file; a program that reads from a file could attempt to open a file that does not exist, and so on. Such problems result in exceptions. An *exception* indicates that a problem occurred during a program's execution. The clause

```
throws Exception
```

in line 10 signifies that there are statements in the `main` method that might cause exceptions. If an exception occurs, the program terminates immediately. As you'll learn in Chapters 11 and 17, certain types of exceptions require you to write code that can deal with these problems; otherwise, your programs won't compile. For simplicity, we use the `throws` clause in line 10 to enable the file processing programs in this chapter to compile. Chapter 11 discusses exception handling in detail and the programs in Chapter 17 use exception-handling extensively.

Sample Data

The sample data we used to test this application is shown in Fig. 6.32. In the sample execution for this program, the user enters information for five accounts, then enters the end-of-file key sequence to signal that data entry is complete. The sample execution does not show how the data records actually appear in the file. In the next section, to verify that the file has been created successfully, we present a program that reads the file and prints its contents. Because this is a text file, you can also verify the information by opening the file in a text editor.

Sample data			
100	Bob	Jones	24.98
200	Steve	Doe	-345.67
300	Pam	White	0.00
400	Sam	Stone	-42.16
500	Sue	Rich	224.62

Fig. 6.32 | Sample data for the program in Fig. 6.30.

6.19.2 Reading Data from a Sequential-Access Text File

We store data in files so that it can be retrieved for processing when needed. Section 6.19.1 demonstrated how to create a text file for sequential access. This section shows how to read data sequentially from a text file using a `Scanner` to read the data from a file rather than the user at the keyboard.

The application in Fig. 6.33 reads records from the file `"clients.txt"` created by the application of Section 6.19.1 and displays the record contents. Note we placed the applications from Figs. 6.30 and 6.33 in the same directory so that they can both access the same clients.txt file, which in each case is assumed to be in the same directory as the application. Section 17.7 demonstrates dialog boxes that enable the user to select files from any location.

```java
1    // Fig. 6.33: ReadTextFile.java
2    // This program reads a text file and displays each record.
3    import java.io.File;
4    import java.util.Scanner;
5
6    public class ReadTextFile
7    {
8       public static void main( String[] args ) throws Exception
9       {
10         // open the text file for reading with a Scanner
11         Scanner input = new Scanner( new File( "clients.txt" ) );
12
13         int accountNumber; // stores account number
14         String firstName; // stores first name
15         String lastName; // stores last name
16         double balance; // stores account balance
17
18         System.out.printf( "%-10s%-12s%-12s%10s\n", "Account",
19            "First Name", "Last Name", "Balance" );
20
21         while ( input.hasNext() )
22         {
23            accountNumber = input.nextInt(); // read account number
24            firstName = input.next(); // read first name
25            lastName = input.next(); // read last name
26            balance = input.nextDouble(); // read balance
27
28            // display record contents
29            System.out.printf( "%-10d%-12s%-12s%10.2f\n",
30               accountNumber, firstName, lastName, balance );
31         } // end while
32
33         input.close(); // close file
34      } // end main
35   } // end class ReadTextFile
```

```
Account   First Name  Last Name    Balance
100       Bob         Jones          24.98
200       Steve       Doe          -345.67
300       Pam         White           0.00
400       Sam         Stone         -42.16
500       Sue         Rich          224.62
```

Fig. 6.33 | Sequential file reading using a Scanner.

Line 13 of Fig. 6.33 creates a Scanner that will be used to read data from the file. There are several ways to initialize a Scanner. When reading data from the user at the keyboard, we initialize a Scanner with the System.in object, which represents a stream that is connected to the keyboard. To read data from a file, you must initialize the Scanner with a **File** object. The argument in the parentheses to the right of Scanner

```
new File( "clients.txt" )
```

indicates that the Scanner should open and read from the file clients.txt located in the directory from which you execute the application. If the file cannot be found, an exception (of type FileNotFoundException) occurs and the program terminates immediately. We show how to handle such exceptions in Chapter 17.

 Common Programming Error 6.10
Initializing a Scanner with a String containing a file name and location creates a Scanner that reads data from that String. rather than from a file of that name and location.

Lines 18–19 display headers for the columns in the application's output. Lines 21–31 read and display records from the file until the end-of-file marker is reached (in which case, method hasNext will return false at line 21). Lines 23–26 use Scanner methods nextInt, next and nextDouble to input an int (the account number), two Strings (the first and last names) and a double value (the balance). Each record is one line of data in the file. If the information in the file is not properly formed (e.g., there is a last name where there should be a balance) or the Scanner is closed before the data is input, an exception occurs and the program terminates immediately. If the program successfully reads a record from the file, the record's information is displayed (lines 29–30). Note in the format string in line 29 that the account number, first name and last name are left justified, while the balance is right justified and output with two digits of precision. Each iteration of the loop inputs one line of text from the text file, which represents one record. Line 33 closes the Scanner.

6.20 (Optional) GUI and Graphics Case Study: Drawing Arcs

Using Java's graphics features, we can create complex drawings that would be tedious to code line by line. In Fig. 6.34, we use arrays and repetition statements to draw a rainbow by using Graphics method fillArc. Drawing arcs in Java is similar to drawing ovals—an arc is simply a section of an oval.

Figure 6.34 begins with the usual import statements for creating drawings (lines 3–6). In method paintComponent, lines 16–17 declare and create two new color constants—VIOLET and INDIGO. The colors of a rainbow are red, orange, yellow, green, blue, indigo and violet—Java has predefined constants only for the first five colors. Lines 21–23 initialize an array with the colors of the rainbow, starting with the innermost arcs first. The array begins with two Color.WHITE elements, which, as you'll soon see, are for drawing the empty arcs at the center of the rainbow.

Line 25 in paintComponent declares local variable radius, which determines the radius of each arc. Local variables centerX and centerY (lines 28–29) determine the location of the midpoint on the base of the rainbow. The loop at lines 32–41 uses control variable counter to count backward from the end of the array, drawing the largest arcs first and placing each successive smaller arc on top of the previous one. Line 35 sets the color to draw the current arc from the array. The reason we have Color.WHITE entries at the beginning of the array is to create the empty arc in the center. Otherwise, the center of the rainbow would just be a solid violet semicircle. [*Note:* You can change the individual colors and the number of entries in the array to create new designs.]

```java
1   // Fig. 6.34: DrawRainbow.java
2   // Demonstrates using colors in an array.
3   import java.awt.Color;
4   import java.awt.Graphics;
5   import javax.swing.JPanel;
6   import javax.swing.JFrame;
7
8   public class DrawRainbow extends JPanel
9   {
10      // draws a rainbow using concentric arcs
11      public void paintComponent( Graphics g )
12      {
13         super.paintComponent( g );
14
15         // define indigo and violet
16         Color VIOLET = new Color( 128, 0, 128 );
17         Color INDIGO = new Color( 75, 0, 130 );
18
19         // colors to use in the rainbow, starting from the innermost
20         // The two white entries result in an empty arc in the center
21         Color[] colors =
22            { Color.WHITE, Color.WHITE, VIOLET, INDIGO, Color.BLUE,
23              Color.GREEN, Color.YELLOW, Color.ORANGE, Color.RED };
24
25         int radius = 20; // radius of an arc
26
27         // draw the rainbow near the bottom-center
28         int centerX = getWidth() / 2;
29         int centerY = getHeight() - 10;
30
31         // draws filled arcs starting with the outermost
32         for ( int counter = colors.length; counter > 0; counter-- )
33         {
34            // set the color for the current arc
35            g.setColor( colors[ counter - 1 ] );
36
37            // fill the arc from 0 to 180 degrees
38            g.fillArc( centerX - counter * radius,
39               centerY - counter * radius,
40               counter * radius * 2, counter * radius * 2, 0, 180 );
41         } // end for
42      } // end method paintComponent
43
44      public static void main( String[] args )
45      {
46         DrawRainbow panel = new DrawRainbow();
47         JFrame application = new JFrame();
48
49         application.setDefaultCloseOperation( JFrame.EXIT_ON_CLOSE );
50         application.add( panel );
51         application.setSize( 400, 250 );
52         application.setVisible( true );
53      } // end main
54   } // end class DrawRainbow
```

Fig. 6.34 | Drawing a rainbow using arcs and an array of colors. (Part 1 of 2.)

Fig. 6.34 | Drawing a rainbow using arcs and an array of colors. (Part 2 of 2.)

The `fillArc` method call at lines 38–40 draws a filled semicircle. Method `fillArc` requires six parameters. The first four represent the bounding rectangle in which the arc will be drawn. The first two of these specify the coordinates for the upper-left corner of the bounding rectangle, and the next two specify its width and height. The fifth parameter is the starting angle on the oval, and the sixth specifies the sweep, or the amount of arc to cover. The starting angle and sweep are measured in degrees, with zero degrees pointing right. A positive sweep draws the arc counterclockwise, while a negative sweep draws the arc clockwise. A method similar to `fillArc` is **drawArc**—it requires the same parameters as `fillArc`, but draws the edge of the arc rather than filling it.

Lines 46–52 create the rainbow and create and set up a JFrame to display the rainbow. Once the program makes the JFrame visible, the system calls the `paintComponent` method to draw the rainbow on the screen.

GUI and Graphics Case Study Exercise

6.1 (*Drawing Spirals*) In this exercise, you'll draw spirals with methods drawLine and drawArc.

a) Draw a square-shaped spiral (as in the left screen capture of Fig. 6.35), centered on the panel, using method drawLine. One technique is to use a loop that increases the line length after drawing every second line. The direction in which to draw the next line should follow a distinct pattern, such as down, left, up, right.

b) Draw a circular spiral (as in the right screen capture of Fig. 6.35), using method drawArc to draw one semicircle at a time. Each successive semicircle should have a larger radius (as specified by the bounding rectangle's width) and should continue drawing where the previous semicircle finished.

Fig. 6.35 | Drawing a spiral using drawLine (left) and drawArc (right).

6.21 Wrap-Up

This chapter began our introduction to data structures, exploring the use of arrays to store data in and retrieve data from lists and tables of values. The chapter examples demonstrated how to declare an array, initialize an array and refer to individual elements of an array. We introduced the enhanced for statement to iterate through arrays. We also illustrated how to pass arrays to methods and how to declare and manipulate multidimensional arrays. Finally, the chapter showed how to write methods that use variable-length argument lists and how to read arguments passed to a program from the command line.

We introduced the ArrayList<T> generic collection, which provides all the functionality and performance of arrays, along with other useful capabilities such as dynamic resizing. We used the add methods to add new items to the end of an ArrayList and to insert items in an ArrayList. The remove method was used to remove the first occurrence of a specified item, and an overloaded version of remove was used to remove an item at a specified index. We used the size method to obtain the number of items in the ArrayList.

We introduced character and String fundamentals and presented String methods for selecting portions of Strings and manipulating Strings. We showed how to write text to and read text from files on disk using classes Formatter and Scanner, respectively.

We continue our coverage of data structures in Chapter 20, Generic Collections, which introduces the Java Collections Framework (also called the Collections API)—Java's predefined set of data structures and algorithms for manipulating them. Chapter 21 presents the topic of generics, which provides the means to create general models of methods and classes that can be declared once, but used with many different data types. Chapter 22, Custom Generic Data Structures, shows how to build dynamic data structures, such as lists, queues, stacks and trees, that can grow and shrink as programs execute.

We've now completed our treatment of Java's non-object-oriented capabilities—control statements, methods, arrays, collections, Strings and files. In Chapters 7–10, we present the core topics of object-oriented programming—classes, objects, inheritance, polymorphism and interfaces. In Chapter 7, you'll learn how to implement your own classes and use objects of those classes in applications.

Summary

Section 6.1 Introduction
- Arrays are data structures consisting of related data items of the same type. Arrays are fixed-length entities—they remain the same length once they're created, although an array variable may be reassigned the reference of a new array of a different length.

Section 6.2 Primitive Types vs. Reference Types
- Types in Java are divided into two categories—primitive types and reference types. The primitive types are boolean, byte, char, short, int, long, float and double. All other types are reference types, so classes, which specify the types of objects, are reference types.
- A primitive-type variable can store exactly one value of its declared type at a time.
- Programs use variables of reference types (called references) to store the location of an object in the computer's memory. Such variables refer to objects in the program.
- A reference to an object is required to invoke an object's methods. A primitive-type variable does not refer to an object and therefore cannot be used to invoke a method.

Section 6.3 Arrays

- An array is a group of variables (called elements or components) containing values that all have the same type. Arrays are objects, so they're considered reference types.

- A program refers to any one of an array's elements with an array-access expression that includes the name of the array followed by the index of the particular element in square brackets ([]).

- The first element in every array has index zero and is sometimes called the zeroth element.

- An index must be a nonnegative integer. A program can use an expression as an index.

- An array object knows its own length and stores this information in a length instance variable.

Section 6.4 Declaring and Creating Arrays

- To create an array object, specify the array's element type and the number of elements as part of an array-creation expression that uses keyword new.

- When an array is created, each element receives a default value—zero for numeric primitive-type elements, false for boolean elements and null for references.

- In an array declaration, the type and the square brackets can be combined at the beginning of the declaration to indicate that all the identifiers in the declaration are array variables.

- Every element of a primitive-type array contains a variable of the array's declared type. Every element of a reference-type array is a reference to an object of the array's declared type.

Section 6.5 Examples Using Arrays

- A program can create an array and initialize its elements with an array initializer.

- Constant variables are declared with keyword final, must be initialized before they're used and cannot be modified thereafter.

- When a Java program executes, the JVM checks array indices to ensure that they're greater than or equal to 0 and less than the array's length. If a program uses an invalid index, Java generates a so-called exception to indicate that an error occurred in the program at execution time.

Section 6.6 Enhanced **for** Statement

- The enhanced for statement allows you to iterate through the elements of an array or a collection without using a counter. The syntax of an enhanced for statement is:

```
for ( parameter : arrayName )
    statement
```

where *parameter* has a type and an identifier (e.g., int number), and *arrayName* is the array through which to iterate.

- The enhanced for statement cannot be used to modify elements in an array. If a program needs to modify elements, use the traditional counter-controlled for statement.

Section 6.7 Passing Arrays to Methods

- When an argument is passed by value, a copy of the argument's value is made and passed to the called method. The called method works exclusively with the copy.

- When an argument is passed by reference, the called method can access the argument's value in the caller directly and possibly modify it.

- Java does not allow programmers to choose between pass-by-value and pass-by-reference—all arguments are passed by value. A method call can pass two types of values to a method—copies of primitive values and copies of references to objects. Although an object's reference is passed by value, a method can still interact with the referenced object by calling its public methods using the copy of the object's reference.

- To pass an object reference to a method, simply specify in the method call the name of the variable that refers to the object.

- When you pass an array or an individual array element of a reference type to a method, the called method receives a copy of the array or element's reference. When you pass an individual element of a primitive type, the called method receives a copy of the element's value.

- To pass an individual array element to a method, use the indexed name of the array as an argument in the method call.

Section 6.8 Multidimensional Arrays

- Multidimensional arrays with two dimensions are often used to represent tables of values consisting of information arranged in rows and columns.

- Arrays that require two indices to identify a particular element are called two-dimensional arrays. An array with *m* rows and *n* columns is called an *m*-by-*n* array. A two-dimensional array can be initialized with an array initializer of the form

      arrayType[][] *arrayName* = { { *row1 initializer* }, { *row2 initializer* }, ... };

- Multidimensional arrays are maintained as arrays of separate one-dimensional arrays. As a result, the lengths of the rows in a two-dimensional array are not required to be the same.

- A multidimensional array with the same number of columns in every row can be created with an array-creation expression of the form

      arrayType[][] *arrayName* = **new** *arrayType*[*numRows*][*numColumns*];

Section 6.10 Variable-Length Argument Lists

- An argument type followed by an ellipsis (...) in a parameter list indicates that the method receives a variable number of arguments of that type. The ellipsis can occur only once in a method's parameter list, and it must be at the end of the parameter list.

- A variable-length argument list is treated as an array within the method body. The number of arguments in the array can be obtained using the array's `length` field.

Section 6.11 Using Command-Line Arguments

- Passing arguments to `main` from the command line is achieved by including a parameter of type `String[]` in the parameter list of `main`. By convention, `main`'s parameter is named `args`.

- Java passes the command-line arguments that appear after the class name in the `java` command to the application's `main` method as `String`s in the array `args`. The number of arguments passed in from the command line is obtained by accessing the array's `length` attribute.

Section 6.12 Class *Arrays*

- Class `Arrays` provides `static` methods that peform common array manipulations, including `sort`, `binarySearch`, `equals` and `fill`.

- Class `System`'s `arraycopy` method enables you to copy the elements of one array into another.

Section 6.13 Introduction to Collections and Class *ArrayList*

- The Java API's collection classes provide efficient methods that organize, store and retrieve data without requiring knowledge of how the data is being stored.

- An `ArrayList<T>` is similar to an array, but can be dynamically resized.

- The `add` method with one argument appends an element to the end of an `ArrayList`.

- The `add` method with two arguments inserts a new element at a specified position in an `ArrayList`.

- The `size` method returns the number of elements currently in an `ArrayList`.

- The `remove` method with a reference to an object as an argument removes the first element that matches the argument's value.

- The remove method with an integer argument removes the element at the specified index and all elements above that index are shifted down by one.
- The contains method returns true if the element is found in the ArrayList, and false otherwise.

Section 6.14 Fundamentals of Characters and Strings
- A character literal's value is its integer value in Unicode. Strings can include letters, digits and special characters such as +, -, *, / and $. A string in Java is an object of class String. String literals are often referred to as String objects and are written in a program in double quotes.

Section 16.15 Class String
- String objects are immutable—after they're created, their character contents cannot be changed.
- String method length returns the number of characters in a String.
- String method charAt returns the character at a specific position.
- String method equals tests for equality. The method returns true if the contents of the Strings are equal, false otherwise. Method equals uses a lexicographical comparison for Strings.
- When primitive-type values are compared with ==, the result is true if both values are identical. When references are compared with ==, the result is true if both refer to the same object.
- Java treats all string literals with the same contents as a single String object.
- String method equalsIgnoreCase performs a case-insensitive string comparison.
- String method compareTo uses a lexicographical comparison and returns 0 if the Strings are equal, a negative number if the string that calls compareTo is less than the argument String and a positive number if the string that calls compareTo is greater than than the argument String.
- String method regionMatches compares portions of two strings for equality.
- String method startsWith determines whether a string starts with the specified characters. String method endsWith determines whether a string ends with the specified characters.
- String method indexOf locates the first occurrence of a character or a substring in a string. String method lastIndexOf locates the last occurrence of a character or a substring in a string.
- String method substring copies and returns part of an existing string object.
- String method concat concatenates two string objects and returns a new string object.
- String method replace returns a new string object that replaces every occurrence in a String of its first character argument with its second character argument.
- String method toUpperCase returns a new string with uppercase letters in the positions where the original string had lowercase letters. String method toLowerCase returns a new string with lowercase letters in the positions where the original string had uppercase letters.
- String method trim returns a new string object in which all white-space characters (e.g., spaces, newlines and tabs) have been removed from the beginning and end of a string.
- String method toCharArray returns a char array containing a copy of the string's characters.
- String class static method valueOf returns its argument converted to a string.

Section 6.16 Introduction to File Processing
- Computers use files for long-term retention of large amounts of persistent data, even after the programs that created the data terminate.
- Computers store files on secondary storage devices such as hard disks.

Section 6.17 Data Hierarchy
- The smallest data item in a computer can assume the value 0 or the value 1 and is called a bit. Ultimately, a computer processes all data items as combinations of 0s and 1s.

- The computer's character set is the set of all characters used to write programs and represent data.
- Characters in Java are Unicode characters composed of two bytes, each composed of eight bits.
- A field is a group of characters or bytes that conveys meaning.
- Data items processed by computers form a data hierarchy that becomes larger and more complex in structure as we progress from bits to characters to fields, and so on.
- Typically, several fields compose a record (implemented as a `class` in Java).
- A record is a group of related fields. A file is a group of related records.
- A record key identifies a record as belonging to a particular person or entity and is unique to each record. Record keys facilitate the retrieval of specific records from a file.
- There are many ways to organize records in a file. The most common is called a sequential file, in which records are stored in order by the record-key field.
- A group of related files is often called a database. A collection of programs designed to create and manage databases is called a database management system (DBMS).

Section 6.18 Files and Streams
- Java views each file as a sequential stream of bytes.
- Every operating system provides a mechanism to determine the end of a file, such as an end-of-file marker or a count of the total bytes in the file.
- Byte-based streams represent data in binary format.
- Character-based streams represent data as sequences of characters.
- Text files (created with character-based streams) can be read by text editors. Binary files (created with byte-based streams) are read by programs that convert the data to a human-readable format.
- Java also can associate streams with different devices. Three stream objects are associated with devices when a Java program begins executing—`System.in`, `System.out` and `System.err`.

Section 6.19 Sequential-Access Text Files
- Java imposes no structure on a file. You must structure files to meet your application's needs.
- To write data to a text file, you can use an object of class `Formatter` and its `format` method. You initialize the `Formatter` with a `String` indicating the name and location of the file on disk.
- To retrieve data sequentially from a file, programs normally start from the beginning of the file and read all the data consecutively until the desired information is found.
- To read data from a text file, you can use an object of class `Scanner` that is initialized with a `File` representing the name and location of the file on disk.

Terminology

Self-Review Exercises

6.1 Fill in the blank(s) in each of the following statements:

a) Lists and tables of values can be stored in _____.

b) An array is a group of _____ (called elements or components) containing values that all have the same _____.

c) The _____ allows programmers to iterate through the elements in an array without using a counter.

d) The number used to refer to a particular array element is called the element's _____.

e) An array that uses two indices is referred to as a(n) _____ array.

f) Use the enhanced for statement _____ to walk through double array numbers.

g) Command-line arguments are stored in _____.

h) Use the expression _____ to receive the total number of arguments in a command line. Assume that command-line arguments are stored in String[] args.

i) Given the command java MyClass test, the first command-line argument is _____.

j) A(n) _____ in the parameter list of a method indicates that the method can receive a variable number of arguments.

k) Ultimately, all data items processed by a computer are reduced to combinations of _____ and _____.

l) The smallest data item a computer can process is called a(n) _____.

m) A(n) _____ can sometimes be viewed as a group of related records.

n) Digits, letters and special symbols are referred to as _____.

o) A database is a group of related _____.

p) Object _____ normally enables a program to output error messages to the screen.

6.2 Determine whether each of the following is *true* or *false*. If *false*, explain why.

a) An array can store many different types of values.

b) An array index should normally be of type float.

c) An individual array element that is passed to a method and modified in that method will contain the modified value when the called method completes execution.

d) Command-line arguments are separated by commas.

e) When String objects are compared using ==, the result is true if the Strings contain the same values.

f) A String can be modified after it's created.

g) You must explicitly create the stream objects System.in, System.out and System.err.

h) Binary files are human readable in a text editor.

i) Class Formatter contains method printf, which enables formatted data to be output to the screen or to a file.

6.3 Perform the following tasks for an array called fractions:

a) Declare a constant ARRAY_SIZE that is initialized to 10.

b) Declare a double array with ARRAY_SIZE elements, and initialize the elements to 0.

c) Refer to array element 4.

d) Assign the value 1.667 to array element 9.

e) Assign the value 3.333 to array element 6.

f) Sum all the elements of the array, using a for statement. Declare the integer variable x as a control variable for the loop.

6.4 Perform the following tasks for an array called table:

a) Declare and create the array as an integer array that has three rows and three columns. Assume that the constant ARRAY_SIZE has been declared to be 3.

b) How many elements does the array contain?

c) Use a for statement to initialize each element of the array to the sum of its indices. Assume that the integer variables x and y are declared as control variables.

6.5 Find and correct the error in each of the following program segments:

a) ```
final int ARRAY_SIZE = 5;
ARRAY_SIZE = 10;
```

b) Assume ```int[] b = new int[ 10 ];```
```
for (int i = 0; i <= b.length; i++)
    b[i] = 1;
```

c) Assume ```int[][] a = { { 1, 2 }, { 3, 4 } };```
```
a[1, 1] = 5;
```
```

Answers to Self-Review Exercises

6.1 a) arrays. b) variables, type. c) enhanced for statement. d) index (or subscript or position number). e) two-dimensional. f) for (double d : numbers). g) an array of Strings, called args by convention. h) args.length. i) test. j) ellipsis (...). k) ones, zeros. l) bit. m) file. n) characters. o) files. p) System.err.

6.2 a) False. An array can store only values of the same type.
   b) False. An array index must be an integer or an integer expression.
   c) For individual primitive-type elements of an array: False. A called method receives and manipulates a copy of the value of such an element, so modifications do not affect the original value. If the reference of an array is passed to a method, however, modifications to the array elements made in the called method are indeed reflected in the original. For individual elements of a reference type: True. A called method receives a copy of the reference of such an element, and changes to the referenced object will be reflected in the original array element.
   d) False. Command-line arguments are separated by white space.
   e) False. String objects are compared using operator == to determine whether they're the same object in memory.
   f) False. String objects are immutable and cannot be modified after they're created. StringBuilder objects can be modified after they're created.
   g) False. These three streams are created for you when a Java application begins executing.
   h) False. Text files are human readable in a text editor. Binary files might be human readable, but only if the bytes in the file represent ASCII characters
   i) False. Class Formatter contains method format, which enables formatted data to be output to the screen or to a file.

6.3 a) `final int ARRAY_SIZE = 10;`
   b) `double[] fractions = new double[ ARRAY_SIZE ];`
   c) `fractions[ 4 ]`
   d) `fractions[ 9 ] = 1.667;`
   e) `fractions[ 6 ] = 3.333;`
   f) `double total = 0.0;`
      `for ( int x = 0; x < fractions.length; x++ )`
      `    total += fractions[ x ];`

6.4 a) `int[][] table = new int[ ARRAY_SIZE ][ ARRAY_SIZE ];`
   b) Nine.
   c) `for ( int x = 0; x < table.length; x++ )`
      `    for ( int y = 0; y < table[ x ].length; y++ )`
      `        table[ x ][ y ] = x + y;`

6.5 a) Error: Assigning a value to a constant after it has been initialized.
      Correction: Assign the correct value to the constant in a `final int ARRAY_SIZE` declaration or declare another variable.
   b) Error: Referencing an array element outside the bounds of the array (b[10]).
      Correction: Change the <= operator to <.
   c) Error: Array indexing is performed incorrectly.
      Correction: Change the statement to a[1][1] = 5;.

Exercises

6.6 Fill in the blanks in each of the following statements:
   a) One-dimensional array p contains four elements. The names of those elements are _____, _____, _____ and _____.

b) Naming an array, stating its type and specifying the number of dimensions in the array is called _____ the array.

c) In a two-dimensional array, the first index identifies the _____ of an element and the second index identifies the _____ of an element.

d) An *m*-by-*n* array contains _____ rows, _____ columns and _____ elements.

e) The name of the element in row 3 and column 5 of array d is _____.

6.7 Determine whether each of the following is *true* or *false*. If *false*, explain why.

a) To refer to a particular location or element within an array, we specify the name of the array and the value of the particular element.

b) An array declaration reserves space for the array.

c) To indicate that 100 locations should be reserved for integer array p, the programmer writes the declaration

```
p[ 100 ];
```

d) An application that initializes the elements of a 15-element array to zero must contain at least one for statement.

e) An application that totals the elements of a two-dimensional array must contain nested for statements.

6.8 Write Java statements to accomplish each of the following tasks:

a) Display the value of element 6 of array f.

b) Initialize each of the five elements of one-dimensional integer array g to 8.

c) Total the 100 elements of floating-point array c.

d) Copy 11-element array a into the first portion of array b, which contains 34 elements.

e) Determine and display the smallest and largest values contained in 99-element floating-point array w.

6.9 Consider a two-by-three integer array t.

a) Write a statement that declares and creates t.

b) How many rows does t have?

c) How many columns does t have?

d) How many elements does t have?

e) Write access expressions for all the elements in row 1 of t.

f) Write access expressions for all the elements in column 2 of t.

g) Write a single statement that sets the element of t in row 0 and column 1 to zero.

h) Write individual statements to initialize each element of t to zero.

i) Write a nested for statement that initializes each element of t to zero.

j) Write a nested for statement that inputs the values for the elements of t from the user.

k) Write a series of statements that determines and displays the smallest value in t.

l) Write a single printf statement that displays the elements of the first row of t.

m) Write a statement that totals the elements of the third column of t. Do not use repetition.

n) Write a series of statements that displays the contents of t in tabular format. List the column indices as headings across the top, and list the row indices at the left of each row.

6.10 *(Sales Commissions)* Use a one-dimensional array to solve the following problem: A company pays its salespeople on a commission basis. The salespeople receive $200 per week plus 9% of their gross sales for that week. For example, a salesperson who grosses $5000 in sales in a week receives $200 plus 9% of $5000, or a total of $650. Write an application (using an array of counters) that determines how many of the salespeople earned salaries in each of the following ranges (assume that each salesperson's salary is truncated to an integer amount):

a) $200–299

b) $300–399

c) $400–499

    d) $500–599
    e) $600–699
    f) $700–799
    g) $800–899
    h) $900–999
    i) $1000 and over

Summarize the results in tabular format.

6.11 Write statements that perform the following one-dimensional-array operations:
    a) Set the 10 elements of integer array `counts` to zero.
    b) Add one to each of the 15 elements of integer array `bonus`.
    c) Display the five values of integer array `bestScores` in column format.

6.12 *(Duplicate Elimination)* Use a one-dimensional array to solve the following problem: Write an application that inputs five numbers, each between 10 and 100, inclusive. As each number is read, display it only if it's not a duplicate of a number already read. Provide for the "worst case," in which all five numbers are different. Use the smallest possible array to solve this problem. Display the complete set of unique values input after the user enters each new value.

6.13 Label the elements of three-by-five two-dimensional array `sales` to indicate the order in which they're set to zero by the following program segment:

```java
for ( int row = 0; row < sales.length; row++ )
{
    for ( int col = 0; col < sales[ row ].length; col++ )
    {
        sales[ row ][ col ] = 0;
    }
}
```

6.14 Write an application that calculates the product of a series of integers that are passed to method `product` using a variable-length argument list. Test your method with several calls, each with a different number of arguments.

6.15 Rewrite Fig. 6.2 so that the size of the array is specified by the first command-line argument. If no command-line argument is supplied, use 10 as the default size of the array.

6.16 Write an application that uses an enhanced `for` statement to sum the `double` values passed by the command-line arguments. [*Hint:* Use the `static` method `parseDouble` of class `Double` to convert a `String` to a `double` value.]

6.17 *(Dice Rolling)* Write an application to simulate the rolling of two dice. The application should use an object of class `Random` once to roll the first die and again to roll the second die. The sum of the two values should then be calculated. Each die can show an integer value from 1 to 6, so the sum of the values will vary from 2 to 12, with 7 being the most frequent sum, and 2 and 12 the least frequent. Figure 6.36 shows the 36 possible combinations of the two dice. Your application should roll the dice 36,000 times. Use a one-dimensional array to tally the number of times each possible sum appears. Display the results in tabular format. Determine whether the totals are reasonable (e.g., there are six ways to roll a 7, so approximately one-sixth of the rolls should be 7).

6.18 *(Game of Craps)* Write an application that runs 1000 games of craps (Fig. 5.8) and answers the following questions:
    a) How many games are won on the first roll, second roll, …, twentieth roll and after the twentieth roll?
    b) How many games are lost on the first roll, second roll, …, twentieth roll and after the twentieth roll?
    c) What are the chances of winning at craps? [*Note:* You should discover that craps is one of the fairest casino games. What do you suppose this means?]

	1	2	3	4	5	6
1	2	3	4	5	6	7
2	3	4	5	6	7	8
3	4	5	6	7	8	9
4	5	6	7	8	9	10
5	6	7	8	9	10	11
6	7	8	9	10	11	12

Fig. 6.36 | The 36 possible sums of two dice.

d) What is the average length of a game of craps?

e) Do the chances of winning improve with the length of the game?

6.19 *(Airline Reservations System)* A small airline has just purchased a computer for its new automated reservations system. You've been asked to develop the new system. You are to write an application to assign seats on each flight of the airline's only plane (capacity: 10 seats).

Your application should display the following alternatives: `Please type 1 for First Class` and `Please type 2 for Economy`. If the user types 1, your application should assign a seat in the first-class section (seats 1–5). If the user types 2, your application should assign a seat in the economy section (seats 6–10). Your application should then display a boarding pass indicating the person's seat number and whether it's in the first-class or economy section of the plane.

Use a one-dimensional array of primitive type `boolean` to represent the seating chart of the plane. Initialize all the elements of the array to `false` to indicate that all the seats are empty. As each seat is assigned, set the corresponding element of the array to `true` to indicate that the seat is no longer available.

Your application should never assign a seat that has already been assigned. When the economy section is full, your application should ask the person if it's acceptable to be placed in the first-class section (and vice versa). If yes, make the appropriate seat assignment. If no, display the message `"Next flight leaves in 3 hours."`

6.20 *(Total Sales)* Use a two-dimensional array to solve the following problem: A company has four salespeople (1 to 4) who sell five different products (1 to 5). Once a day, each salesperson passes in a slip for each type of product sold. Each slip contains the following:

a) The salesperson number

b) The product number

c) The total dollar value of that product sold that day

Thus, each salesperson passes in between 0 and 5 sales slips per day. Assume that the information from all the slips for last month is available. Write an application that will read all this information for last month's sales and summarize the total sales by salesperson and by product. All totals should be stored in the two-dimensional array `sales`. After processing all the information for last month, display the results in tabular format, with each column representing a particular salesperson and each row representing a particular product. Cross-total each row to get the total sales of each product for last month. Cross-total each column to get the total sales by salesperson for last month. Your tabular output should include these cross-totals to the right of the totaled rows and to the bottom of the totaled columns.

6.21 *(Turtle Graphics)* The Logo language made the concept of *turtle graphics* famous. Imagine a mechanical turtle that walks around the room under the control of a Java application. The turtle holds a pen in one of two positions, up or down. While the pen is down, the turtle traces out shapes as it moves, and while the pen is up, the turtle moves about freely without writing anything. In this problem, you'll simulate the operation of the turtle and create a computerized sketchpad.

Use a 20-by-20 array floor that is initialized to zeros. Read commands from an array that contains them. Keep track of the current position of the turtle at all times and whether the pen is currently up or down. Assume that the turtle always starts at position (0, 0) of the floor with its pen up. The set of turtle commands your application must process are shown in Fig. 6.37.

Command	Meaning
1	Pen up
2	Pen down
3	Turn right
4	Turn left
5,10	Move forward 10 spaces (replace 10 for a different number of spaces)
6	Display the 20-by-20 array
9	End of data (sentinel)

Fig. 6.37 | Turtle graphics commands.

Suppose that the turtle is somewhere near the center of the floor. The following "program" would draw and display a 12-by-12 square, leaving the pen in the up position:

```
2
5,12
3
5,12
3
5,12
3
5,12
1
6
9
```

As the turtle moves with the pen down, set the appropriate elements of array floor to 1s. When the 6 command (display the array) is given, wherever there is a 1 in the array, display an asterisk or any character you choose. Wherever there is a 0, display a blank.

Write an application to implement the turtle graphics capabilities discussed here. Write several turtle graphics programs to draw interesting shapes. Add other commands to increase the power of your turtle graphics language.

6.22 *(Knight's Tour)* An interesting puzzler for chess buffs is the Knight's Tour problem, originally proposed by the mathematician Euler. Can the knight piece move around an empty chessboard and touch each of the 64 squares once and only once? We study this intriguing problem in depth here.

The knight makes only L-shaped moves (two spaces in one direction and one space in a perpendicular direction). Thus, as shown in Fig. 6.38, from a square near the middle of an empty chessboard, the knight (labeled K) can make eight different moves (numbered 0 through 7).

a) Draw an eight-by-eight chessboard on a sheet of paper, and attempt a Knight's Tour by hand. Put a 1 in the starting square, a 2 in the second square, a 3 in the third, and so on. Before starting the tour, estimate how far you think you'll get, remembering that a full tour consists of 64 moves. How far did you get? Was this close to your estimate?

b) Now let's develop an application that will move the knight around a chessboard. The board is represented by an eight-by-eight two-dimensional array board. Each square is initialized to zero. We describe each of the eight possible moves in terms of its horizon-

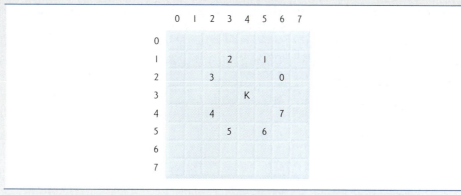

Fig. 6.38 | The eight possible moves of the knight.

tal and vertical components. For example, a move of type 0, as shown in Fig. 6.38, consists of moving two squares horizontally to the right and one square vertically upward. A move of type 2 consists of moving one square horizontally to the left and two squares vertically upward. Horizontal moves to the left and vertical moves upward are indicated with negative numbers. The eight moves may be described by two one-dimensional arrays, horizontal and vertical, as follows:

```
horizontal[ 0 ] = 2      vertical[ 0 ] = -1
horizontal[ 1 ] = 1      vertical[ 1 ] = -2
horizontal[ 2 ] = -1     vertical[ 2 ] = -2
horizontal[ 3 ] = -2     vertical[ 3 ] = -1
horizontal[ 4 ] = -2     vertical[ 4 ] = 1
horizontal[ 5 ] = -1     vertical[ 5 ] = 2
horizontal[ 6 ] = 1      vertical[ 6 ] = 2
horizontal[ 7 ] = 2      vertical[ 7 ] = 1
```

Let the variables currentRow and currentColumn indicate the row and column, respectively, of the knight's current position. To make a move of type moveNumber, where moveNumber is between 0 and 7, your application should use the statements

```
currentRow += vertical[ moveNumber ];
currentColumn += horizontal[ moveNumber ];
```

Write an application to move the knight around the chessboard. Keep a counter that varies from 1 to 64. Record the latest count in each square the knight moves to. Test each potential move to see if the knight has already visited that square. Test every potential move to ensure that the knight does not land off the chessboard. Run the application. How many moves did the knight make?

c) After attempting to write and run a Knight's Tour application, you've probably developed some valuable insights. We'll use these insights to develop a *heuristic* (i.e., a common-sense rule) for moving the knight. Heuristics do not guarantee success, but a carefully developed heuristic greatly improves the chance of success. You may have observed that the outer squares are more troublesome than the squares nearer the center of the board. In fact, the most troublesome or inaccessible squares are the four corners.

Intuition may suggest that you should attempt to move the knight to the most troublesome squares first and leave open those that are easiest to get to, so that when the board gets congested near the end of the tour, there will be a greater chance of success.

We could develop an "accessibility heuristic" by classifying each of the squares according to how accessible it is and always moving the knight (using the knight's L-shaped moves) to the most inaccessible square. We label a two-dimensional array accessibility with numbers indicating from how many squares each particular square is accessible. On a blank chessboard, each of the 16 squares nearest the center is rated as 8, each corner square is rated as 2, and the other squares have accessibility numbers of 3, 4 or 6 as follows:

```
2  3  4  4  4  4  3  2
3  4  6  6  6  6  4  3
4  6  8  8  8  8  6  4
4  6  8  8  8  8  6  4
4  6  8  8  8  8  6  4
4  6  8  8  8  8  6  4
3  4  6  6  6  6  4  3
2  3  4  4  4  4  3  2
```

Write a new version of the Knight's Tour, using the accessibility heuristic. The knight should always move to the square with the lowest accessibility number. In case of a tie, the knight may move to any of the tied squares. Therefore, the tour may begin in any of the four corners. [*Note:* As the knight moves around the chessboard, your application should reduce the accessibility numbers as more squares become occupied. In this way, at any given time during the tour, each available square's accessibility number will remain equal to precisely the number of squares from which that square may be reached.] Run this version of your application. Did you get a full tour? Modify the application to run 64 tours, one starting from each square of the chessboard. How many full tours did you get?

d) Write a version of the Knight's Tour application that, when encountering a tie between two or more squares, decides what square to choose by looking ahead to those squares reachable from the "tied" squares. Your application should move to the tied square for which the next move would arrive at a square with the lowest accessibility number.

6.23   *(Knight's Tour: Brute-Force Approaches)* In part (c) of Exercise 6.22, we developed a solution to the Knight's Tour problem. The approach used, called the "accessibility heuristic," generates many solutions and executes efficiently.

As computers continue to increase in power, we'll be able to solve more problems with sheer computer power and relatively unsophisticated algorithms. This approach is called "brute-force" problem solving.

a) Use random-number generation to enable the knight to walk around the chessboard (in its legitimate L-shaped moves) at random. Your application should run one tour and display the final chessboard. How far did the knight get?

b) Most likely, the application in part (a) produced a relatively short tour. Now modify your application to attempt 1000 tours. Use a one-dimensional array to keep track of the number of tours of each length. When your application finishes attempting the 1000 tours, it should display this information in neat tabular format. What was the best result?

c) Most likely, the application in part (b) gave you some "respectable" tours, but no full tours. Now let your application run until it produces a full tour. [*Caution:* This version of the application could run for hours on a powerful computer.] Once again, keep a table of the number of tours of each length, and display this table when the first full tour is found. How many tours did your application attempt before producing a full tour? How much time did it take?

d) Compare the brute-force version of the Knight's Tour with the accessibility-heuristic version. Which required a more careful study of the problem? Which algorithm was more difficult to develop? Which required more computer power? Could we be certain (in advance) of obtaining a full tour with the accessibility-heuristic approach? Could we be certain (in advance) of obtaining a full tour with the brute-force approach? Argue the pros and cons of brute-force problem solving in general.

6.24   *(Eight Queens)* Another puzzler for chess buffs is the Eight Queens problem, which asks the following: Is it possible to place eight queens on an empty chessboard so that no queen is "attacking" any other (i.e., no two queens are in the same row, in the same column or along the same diagonal)? Use the thinking developed in Exercise 6.22 to formulate a heuristic for solving the Eight Queens problem. Run your application. [*Hint:* It's possible to assign a value to each square of the chessboard to indicate how many squares of an empty chessboard are "eliminated" if a queen is placed in that square. Each of the corners would be assigned the value 22, as demonstrated by Fig. 6.39. Once these "elimination numbers" are placed in all 64 squares, an appropriate heuristic might be as follows: Place the next queen in the square with the smallest elimination number. Why is this strategy intuitively appealing?]

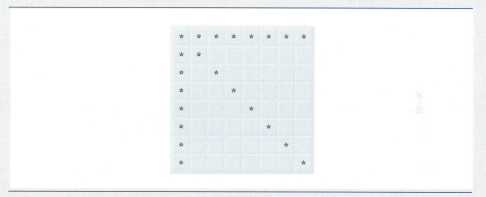

Fig. 6.39 | The 22 squares eliminated by placing a queen in the upper left corner.

6.25   *(Eight Queens: Brute-Force Approaches)* In this exercise, you'll develop several brute-force approaches to solving the Eight Queens problem introduced in Exercise 6.24.

　　　a) Use the random brute-force technique developed in Exercise 6.23 to solve the Eight Queens problem.

　　　b) Use an exhaustive technique (i.e., try all possible combinations of eight queens on the chessboard) to solve the Eight Queens problem.

　　　c) Why might the exhaustive brute-force approach not be appropriate for solving the Knight's Tour problem?

　　　d) Compare and contrast the random brute-force and exhaustive brute-force approaches.

6.26   *(Knight's Tour: Closed-Tour Test)* In the Knight's Tour (Exercise 6.22), a full tour occurs when the knight makes 64 moves, touching each square of the chessboard once and only once. A closed tour occurs when the 64th move is one move away from the square in which the knight started the tour. Modify the application you wrote in Exercise 6.22 to test for a closed tour if a full tour has occurred.

6.27   *(Sieve of Eratosthenes)* A prime number is any integer greater than 1 that is evenly divisible only by itself and 1. The Sieve of Eratosthenes is a method of finding prime numbers. It operates as follows:

　　　a) Create a primitive-type `boolean` array with all elements initialized to `true`. Array elements with prime indices will remain `true`. All other array elements will eventually be set to `false`.

　　　b) Starting with array index 2, determine whether a given element is `true`. If so, loop through the remainder of the array and set to `false` every element whose index is a multiple of the index for the element with value `true`. Then continue the process with the next element with value `true`. For array index 2, all elements beyond element 2 in the array that have indices which are multiples of 2 (indices 4, 6, 8, 10, etc.) will be set to false; for array index 3, all elements beyond element 3 in the array that have indices which are multiples of 3 (indices 6, 9, 12, 15, etc.) will be set to false; and so on.

When this process completes, the array elements that are still true indicate that the index is a prime number. These indices can be displayed. Write an application that uses an array of 1000 elements to determine and display the prime numbers between 2 and 999. Ignore array elements 0 and 1.

6.28   *(Simulation: The Tortoise and the Hare)* In this problem, you'll re-create the classic race of the tortoise and the hare. You'll use random-number generation to develop a simulation of this memorable event.

Our contenders begin the race at square 1 of 70 squares. Each square represents a possible position along the race course. The finish line is at square 70. The first contender to reach or pass square 70 is rewarded with a pail of fresh carrots and lettuce. The course weaves its way up the side of a slippery mountain, so occasionally the contenders lose ground.

A clock ticks once per second. With each tick of the clock, your application should adjust the position of the animals according to the rules in Fig. 6.40. Use variables to keep track of the positions of the animals (i.e., position numbers are 1–70). Start each animal at position 1 (the "starting gate"). If an animal slips left before square 1, move it back to square 1.

Animal	Move type	Percentage of the time	Actual move
Tortoise	Fast plod	50%	3 squares to the right
	Slip	20%	6 squares to the left
	Slow plod	30%	1 square to the right
Hare	Sleep	20%	No move at all
	Big hop	20%	9 squares to the right
	Big slip	10%	12 squares to the left
	Small hop	30%	1 square to the right
	Small slip	20%	2 squares to the left

Fig. 6.40 | Rules for adjusting the positions of the tortoise and the hare.

Generate the percentages in Fig. 6.40 by producing a random integer i in the range $1 \leq i \leq 10$. For the tortoise, perform a "fast plod" when $1 \leq i \leq 5$, a "slip" when $6 \leq i \leq 7$ or a "slow plod" when $8 \leq i \leq 10$. Use a similar technique to move the hare.

Begin the race by displaying

```
BANG !!!!!
AND THEY'RE OFF !!!!!
```

Then, for each tick of the clock (i.e., each repetition of a loop), display a 70-position line showing the letter T in the position of the tortoise and the letter H in the position of the hare. Occasionally, the contenders will land on the same square. In this case, the tortoise bites the hare, and your application should display OUCH!!! beginning at that position. All output positions other than the T, the H or the OUCH!!! (in case of a tie) should be blank.

After each line is displayed, test for whether either animal has reached or passed square 70. If so, display the winner and terminate the simulation. If the tortoise wins, display TORTOISE WINS!!! YAY!!! If the hare wins, display Hare wins. Yuch. If both animals win on the same tick of the clock, you may want to favor the tortoise (the "underdog"), or you may want to display It's a tie. If neither animal wins, perform the loop again to simulate the next tick of the clock. When you are ready to run your application, assemble a group of fans to watch the race. You'll be amazed at how involved your audience gets!

Later in the book, we introduce a number of Java capabilities, such as graphics, images, animation, sound and multithreading. As you study those features, you might enjoy enhancing your tortoise-and-hare contest simulation.

6.29 *(Fibonacci Series)* The Fibonacci series

$$0, 1, 1, 2, 3, 5, 8, 13, 21, \ldots$$

begins with the terms 0 and 1 and has the property that each succeeding term is the sum of the two preceding terms.

a) Write a method `fibonacci( n )` that calculates the nth Fibonacci number. Incorporate this method into an application that enables the user to enter the value of n.

b) Determine the largest Fibonacci number that can be displayed on your system.

c) Modify the application you wrote in part (a) to use `double` instead of `int` to calculate and return Fibonacci numbers, and use this modified application to repeat part (b).

Special Section: Building Your Own Computer

In the next several problems, we take a temporary diversion from the world of high-level language programming to "peel open" a computer and look at its internal structure. We introduce machine-language programming and write several machine-language programs. To make this an especially valuable experience, we then build a computer (through the technique of software-based *simulation*) on which you can execute your machine-language programs.

6.30 *(Machine-Language Programming)* Let's create a computer called the Simpletron. As its name implies, it's a simple, but powerful, machine. The Simpletron runs programs written in the only language it directly understands: Simpletron Machine Language (SML).

The Simpletron contains an *accumulator*—a special register in which information is put before the Simpletron uses that information in calculations or examines it in various ways. All the information in the Simpletron is handled in terms of *words*. A word is a signed four-digit decimal number, such as +3364, −1293, +0007 and −0001. The Simpletron is equipped with a 100-word memory, and these words are referenced by their location numbers 00, 01, ..., 99.

Before running an SML program, we must *load*, or place, the program into memory. The first instruction (or statement) of every SML program is always placed in location 00. The simulator will start executing at this location.

Each instruction written in SML occupies one word of the Simpletron's memory (and hence instructions are signed four-digit decimal numbers). We shall assume that the sign of an SML instruction is always plus, but the sign of a data word may be either plus or minus. Each location in the Simpletron's memory may contain an instruction, a data value used by a program or an unused (and hence undefined) area of memory. The first two digits of each SML instruction are the *operation code* specifying the operation to be performed. SML operation codes are summarized in Fig. 6.41.

Operation code	Meaning
Input/output operations:	
`final int READ = 10;`	Read a word from the keyboard into a specific location in memory.
`final int WRITE = 11;`	Write a word from a specific location in memory to the screen.

Fig. 6.41 | Simpletron Machine Language (SML) operation codes. (Part 1 of 2.)

Operation code	Meaning
Load/store operations:	
`final int LOAD = 20;`	Load a word from a specific location in memory into the accumulator.
`final int STORE = 21;`	Store a word from the accumulator into a specific location in memory.
Arithmetic operations:	
`final int ADD = 30;`	Add a word from a specific location in memory to the word in the accumulator (leave the result in the accumulator).
`final int SUBTRACT = 31;`	Subtract a word from a specific location in memory from the word in the accumulator (leave the result in the accumulator).
`final int DIVIDE = 32;`	Divide a word from a specific location in memory into the word in the accumulator (leave result in the accumulator).
`final int MULTIPLY = 33;`	Multiply a word from a specific location in memory by the word in the accumulator (leave the result in the accumulator).
Transfer-of-control operations:	
`final int BRANCH = 40;`	Branch to a specific location in memory.
`final int BRANCHNEG = 41;`	Branch to a specific location in memory if the accumulator is negative.
`final int BRANCHZERO = 42;`	Branch to a specific location in memory if the accumulator is zero.
`final int HALT = 43;`	Halt. The program has completed its task.

Fig. 6.41 | Simpletron Machine Language (SML) operation codes. (Part 2 of 2.)

The last two digits of an SML instruction are the *operand*—the address of the memory location containing the word to which the operation applies. Let's consider several simple SML programs.

The first SML program (Fig. 6.42) reads two numbers from the keyboard and computes and displays their sum. The instruction +1007 reads the first number from the keyboard and places it into location 07 (which has been initialized to 0). Then instruction +1008 reads the next number into location 08. The *load* instruction, +2007, puts the first number into the accumulator, and the *add* instruction, +3008, adds the second number to the number in the accumulator. *All SML arithmetic instructions leave their results in the accumulator.* The *store* instruction, +2109, places the result back into memory location 09, from which the *write* instruction, +1109, takes the number and displays it (as a signed four-digit decimal number). The *halt* instruction, +4300, terminates execution.

Location	Number	Instruction
00	+1007	(Read A)
01	+1008	(Read B)

Fig. 6.42 | SML program that reads two integers and computes their sum. (Part 1 of 2.)

Location	Number	Instruction
02	+2007	(Load A)
03	+3008	(Add B)
04	+2109	(Store C)
05	+1109	(Write C)
06	+4300	(Halt)
07	+0000	(Variable A)
08	+0000	(Variable B)
09	+0000	(Result C)

Fig. 6.42 | SML program that reads two integers and computes their sum. (Part 2 of 2.)

The second SML program (Fig. 6.43) reads two numbers from the keyboard and determines and displays the larger value. Note the use of the instruction +4107 as a conditional transfer of control, much the same as Java's if statement.

Location	Number	Instruction
00	+1009	(Read A)
01	+1010	(Read B)
02	+2009	(Load A)
03	+3110	(Subtract B)
04	+4107	(Branch negative to 07)
05	+1109	(Write A)
06	+4300	(Halt)
07	+1110	(Write B)
08	+4300	(Halt)
09	+0000	(Variable A)
10	+0000	(Variable B)

Fig. 6.43 | SML program that reads two integers and determines the larger.

Now write SML programs to accomplish each of the following tasks:
a) Use a sentinel-controlled loop to read 10 positive numbers. Compute and display their sum.
b) Use a counter-controlled loop to read seven numbers, some positive and some negative, and compute and display their average.
c) Read a series of numbers, and determine and display the largest number. The first number read indicates how many numbers should be processed.

6.31 *(Computer Simulator)* In this problem, you are going to build your own computer. No, you'll not be soldering components together. Rather, you'll use the powerful technique of *software-based simulation* to create an object-oriented *software model* of the Simpletron of Exercise 6.30. Your Simpletron simulator will turn the computer you are using into a Simpletron, and you'll actually be able to run, test and debug the SML programs you wrote in Exercise 6.30.

When you run your Simpletron simulator, it should begin by displaying:

```
*** Welcome to Simpletron! ***
*** Please enter your program one instruction   ***
*** (or data word) at a time. I will display    ***
*** the location number and a question mark (?) ***
*** You then type the word for that location.   ***
*** Type -99999 to stop entering your program.  ***
```

Your application should simulate the memory of the Simpletron with a one-dimensional array memory that has 100 elements. Now assume that the simulator is running, and let's examine the dialog as we enter the program of Fig. 6.43 (Exercise 6.30):

```
00 ? +1009
01 ? +1010
02 ? +2009
03 ? +3110
04 ? +4107
05 ? +1109
06 ? +4300
07 ? +1110
08 ? +4300
09 ? +0000
10 ? +0000
11 ? -99999
```

Your program should display the memory location followed by a question mark. Each value to the right of a question mark is input by the user. When the sentinel value -99999 is input, the program should display the following:

```
*** Program loading completed ***
*** Program execution begins   ***
```

The SML program has now been placed (or loaded) in array memory. Now the Simpletron executes the SML program. Execution begins with the instruction in location 00 and, as in Java, continues sequentially, unless directed to some other part of the program by a transfer of control.

Use the variable accumulator to represent the accumulator register. Use the variable instructionCounter to keep track of the location in memory that contains the instruction being performed. Use the variable operationCode to indicate the operation currently being performed (i.e., the left two digits of the instruction word). Use the variable operand to indicate the memory location on which the current instruction operates. Thus, operand is the rightmost two digits of the instruction currently being performed. Do not execute instructions directly from memory. Rather, transfer the next instruction to be performed from memory to a variable called instructionRegister. Then "pick off" the left two digits and place them in operationCode, and "pick off" the right two digits and place them in operand. When the Simpletron begins execution, the special registers are all initialized to zero.

Now, let's "walk through" execution of the first SML instruction, +1009 in memory location 00. This procedure is called an *instruction-execution cycle*.

The instructionCounter tells us the location of the next instruction to be performed. We *fetch* the contents of that location from memory by using the Java statement

```
instructionRegister = memory[ instructionCounter ];
```

The operation code and the operand are extracted from the instruction register by the statements

```
operationCode = instructionRegister / 100;
operand = instructionRegister % 100;
```

Now the Simpletron must determine that the operation code is actually a *read* (versus a *write*, a *load*, and so on). A switch differentiates among the 12 operations of SML. In the switch statement, the behavior of various SML instructions is simulated as shown in Fig. 6.44. We discuss branch instructions shortly and leave the others to you.

Instruction	Description
read:	Display the prompt "Enter an integer", then input the integer and store it in location memory[operand].
load:	accumulator = memory[operand];
add:	accumulator += memory[operand];
halt:	This instruction displays the message *** Simpletron execution terminated ***

Fig. 6.44 | Behavior of several SML instructions in the Simpletron.

When the SML program completes execution, the name and contents of each register as well as the complete contents of memory should be displayed. Such a printout is often called a computer dump (no, a computer dump is not a place where old computers go). To help you program your dump method, a sample dump format is shown in Fig. 6.45. Note that a dump after executing a Simpletron program would show the actual values of instructions and data values at the moment execution terminated.

```
REGISTERS:
accumulator          +0000
instructionCounter      00
instructionRegister  +0000
operationCode           00
operand                 00

MEMORY:
        0     1     2     3     4     5     6     7     8     9
 0  +0000 +0000 +0000 +0000 +0000 +0000 +0000 +0000 +0000 +0000
10  +0000 +0000 +0000 +0000 +0000 +0000 +0000 +0000 +0000 +0000
20  +0000 +0000 +0000 +0000 +0000 +0000 +0000 +0000 +0000 +0000
30  +0000 +0000 +0000 +0000 +0000 +0000 +0000 +0000 +0000 +0000
40  +0000 +0000 +0000 +0000 +0000 +0000 +0000 +0000 +0000 +0000
50  +0000 +0000 +0000 +0000 +0000 +0000 +0000 +0000 +0000 +0000
60  +0000 +0000 +0000 +0000 +0000 +0000 +0000 +0000 +0000 +0000
70  +0000 +0000 +0000 +0000 +0000 +0000 +0000 +0000 +0000 +0000
80  +0000 +0000 +0000 +0000 +0000 +0000 +0000 +0000 +0000 +0000
90  +0000 +0000 +0000 +0000 +0000 +0000 +0000 +0000 +0000 +0000
```

Fig. 6.45 | A sample dump.

Let's proceed with the execution of our program's first instruction—namely, the +1009 in location 00. As we've indicated, the switch statement simulates this task by prompting the user to enter a value, reading the value and storing it in memory location memory[operand]. The value is then read into location 09.

At this point, simulation of the first instruction is completed. All that remains is to prepare the Simpletron to execute the next instruction. Since the instruction just performed was not a transfer of control, we need merely increment the instruction-counter register as follows:

```
instructionCounter++;
```

This action completes the simulated execution of the first instruction. The entire process (i.e., the instruction-execution cycle) begins anew with the fetch of the next instruction to execute.

Now let's consider how the branching instructions—the transfers of control—are simulated. All we need to do is adjust the value in the instruction counter appropriately. Therefore, the unconditional branch instruction (40) is simulated within the switch as

```
instructionCounter = operand;
```

The conditional "branch if accumulator is zero" instruction is simulated as

```
if ( accumulator == 0 )
   instructionCounter = operand;
```

At this point, you should implement your Simpletron simulator and run each of the SML programs you wrote in Exercise 6.30. If you desire, you may embellish SML with additional features and provide for these features in your simulator.

Your simulator should check for various types of errors. During the program-loading phase, for example, each number the user types into the Simpletron's memory must be in the range -9999 to +9999. Your simulator should test that each number entered is in this range and, if not, keep prompting the user to re-enter the number until the user enters a correct number.

During the execution phase, your simulator should check for various serious errors, such as attempts to divide by zero, attempts to execute invalid operation codes, and accumulator overflows (i.e., arithmetic operations resulting in values larger than +9999 or smaller than -9999). Such serious errors are called *fatal errors*. When a fatal error is detected, your simulator should display an error message, such as

```
*** Attempt to divide by zero ***
*** Simpletron execution abnormally terminated ***
```

and should display a full computer dump in the format we discussed previously. This treatment will help the user locate the error in the program.

6.32 (*Simpletron Simulator Modifications*) In Exercise 6.31, you wrote a software simulation of a computer that executes programs written in Simpletron Machine Language (SML). In this exercise, we propose several modifications and enhancements to the Simpletron Simulator. In the exercises of Chapter 22, we propose building a compiler that converts programs written in a high-level programming language (a variation of Basic) to Simpletron Machine Language. Some of the following modifications and enhancements may be required to execute the programs produced by the compiler:

a) Extend the Simpletron Simulator's memory to contain 1000 memory locations to enable the Simpletron to handle larger programs.

b) Allow the simulator to perform remainder calculations. This modification requires an additional SML instruction.

c) Allow the simulator to perform exponentiation calculations. This modification requires an additional SML instruction.

d) Modify the simulator to use hexadecimal rather than integer values to represent SML instructions.

e) Modify the simulator to allow output of a newline. This modification requires an additional SML instruction.

f) Modify the simulator to process floating-point values in addition to integer values.

g) Modify the simulator to handle string input. [*Hint:* Each Simpletron word can be divided into two groups, each holding a two-digit integer. Each two-digit integer represents the ASCII (see Appendix B) decimal equivalent of a character. Add a machine-language instruction that will input a string and store the string, beginning at a specific Simpletron memory location. The first half of the word at that location will be a count of the number of characters in the string (i.e., the length of the string). Each succeeding half-word contains one ASCII character expressed as two decimal digits. The machine-language instruction converts each character into its ASCII equivalent and assigns it to a half-word.]

h) Modify the simulator to handle output of strings stored in the format of part (g). [*Hint:* Add a machine-language instruction that will display a string, beginning at a certain Simpletron memory location. The first half of the word at that location is a count of the number of characters in the string (i.e., the length of the string). Each succeeding half-word contains one ASCII character expressed as two decimal digits. The machine-language instruction checks the length and displays the string by translating each two-digit number into its equivalent character.]

6.33 *(Comparing Strings)* Write an application that uses String method compareTo to compare two strings input by the user. Output whether the first string is less than, equal to or greater than the second.

6.34 *(Comparing Portions of Strings)* Write an application that uses String method region-Matches to compare two strings input by the user. The application should input the number of characters to be compared and the starting index of the comparison. The application should state whether the strings are equal. Ignore the case of the characters when performing the comparison.

6.35 *(Displaying Strings in Uppercase and Lowercase)* Write an application that inputs a line of text and outputs the text twice—once in all uppercase letters and once in all lowercase letters.

6.36 *(Searching Strings)* Write an application that inputs a line of text and a search character and uses String method indexOf to determine the number of occurrences of the character in the text.

6.37 *(Searching Strings)* Write an application based on the application in Exercise 6.36 that inputs a line of text and uses String method indexOf to determine the total number of occurrences of each letter of the alphabet in the text. Uppercase and lowercase letters should be counted together. Store the totals for each letter in an array, and print the values in tabular format after the totals have been determined.

6.38 *(Student Poll)* Figure 6.8 contains an array of survey responses that is hard coded into the program. Suppose we wish to process survey results that are stored in a file. This exercise requires two separate programs. First, create an application that prompts the user for survey responses and outputs each response to a file. Use a Formatter to create a file called numbers.txt. Each integer should be written using method format. Then modify the program in Fig. 6.8 to read the survey responses from numbers.txt. The responses should be read from the file by using a Scanner. Use method nextInt to input one integer at a time from the file. The program should continue to read responses until it reaches the end of the file. The results should be output to the text file "output.txt".

Making a Difference

6.39 *(Polling)* The Internet and the web are enabling more people to network, join a cause, voice opinions, and so on. The presidential candidates in 2008 used the Internet intensively to get out their messages and raise money for their campaigns. In this exercise, you'll write a simple polling program that allows users to rate five social-consciousness issues from 1 (least important) to 10 (most important). Pick five causes that are important to you (e.g., political issues, global environmental issues). Use a one-dimensional array topics (of type String) to store the five causes. To summarize the survey responses, use a 5-row, 10-column two-dimensional array responses (of type int), each row corresponding to an element in the topics array. When the program runs, it should ask the user to rate each issue. Have your friends and family respond to the survey. Then have the program display a summary of the results, including:

a) A tabular report with the five topics down the left side and the 10 ratings across the top, listing in each column the number of ratings received for each topic.

b) To the right of each row, show the average of the ratings for that issue.

c) Which issue received the highest point total? Display both the issue and the point total.

d) Which issue received the lowest point total? Display both the issue and the point total.

6.40 *(Cooking with Healthier Ingredients)* Obesity in America is increasing at an alarming rate. Check the map from the Centers for Disease Control and Prevention (CDC) at www.cdc.gov/ nccdphp/dnpa/Obesity/trend/maps/index.htm, which shows obesity trends in the United States over the last 20 years. As obesity increases, so do occurrences of related problems (e.g., heart disease, high blood pressure, high cholesterol, type 2 diabetes). Write a program that helps users choose healthier ingredients when cooking, and helps those allergic to certain foods (e.g., nuts, gluten) find substitutes. The program should read a recipe from a JTextArea and suggest healthier replacements for some of the ingredients. For simplicity, your program should assume the recipe has no abbreviations for measures such as teaspoons, cups, and tablespoons, and uses numerical digits for quantities (e.g., 1 egg, 2 cups) rather than spelling them out (one egg, two cups). Some common substitutions are shown in Fig. 6.46. Your program should display a warning such as, "Always consult your physician before making significant changes to your diet."

Your program should take into consideration that replacements are not always one-for-one. For example, if a cake recipe calls for three eggs, it might reasonably use six egg whites instead. Conversion data for measurements and substitutes can be obtained at websites such as:

```
chinesefood.about.com/od/recipeconversionfaqs/f/usmetricrecipes.htm
www.pioneerthinking.com/eggsub.html
www.gourmetsleuth.com/conversions.htm
```

Your program should consider the user's health concerns, such as high cholesterol, high blood pressure, weight loss, gluten allergy, and so on. For high cholesterol, the program should suggest substitutes for eggs and dairy products; if the user wishes to lose weight, low-calorie substitutes for ingredients such as sugar should be suggested.

Ingredient	Substitution
1 cup sour cream	1 cup yogurt
1 cup milk	1/2 cup evaporated milk and 1/2 cup water
1 teaspoon lemon juice	1/2 teaspoon vinegar
1 cup sugar	1/2 cup honey, 1 cup molasses or 1/4 cup agave nectar
1 cup butter	1 cup margarine or yogurt
1 cup flour	1 cup rye or rice flour
1 cup mayonnaise	1 cup cottage cheese or 1/8 cup mayonnaise and 7/8 cup yogurt
1 egg	2 tablespoons cornstarch, arrowroot flour or potato starch or 2 egg whites or 1/2 large banana (mashed)
1 cup milk	1 cup soy milk
1/4 cup oil	1/4 cup applesauce
white bread	whole-grain bread

Fig. 6.46 | Typical ingredient substitutes.

6.41 *(Spam Scanner)* Spam (or junk e-mail) costs U.S. organizations billions of dollars a year in spam-prevention software, equipment, network resources, bandwidth, and lost productivity. Research online some of the most common spam e-mail messages and words, and check your own junk e-mail folder. Create a list of 30 words and phrases commonly found in spam messages. Write an application in which the user enters an e-mail message in a `JTextArea`. Then, scan the message for each of the 30 keywords or phrases. For each occurrence of one of these within the message, add a point to the message's "spam score." Next, rate the likelihood that the message is spam, based on the number of points it received.

6.42   *(SMS Language)* Short Message Service (SMS) is a communications service that allows sending text messages of 160 or fewer characters between mobile phones. With the proliferation of mobile phone use worldwide, SMS is being used in many developing nations for political purposes (e.g., voicing opinions and opposition), reporting news about natural disasters, and so on. For example, check out `comunica.org/radio2.0/archives/87`. Since the length of SMS messages is limited, SMS Language—abbreviations of common words and phrases in mobile text messages, e-mails, instant messages, etc.—is often used. For example, "in my opinion" is IMO in SMS Language. Research SMS Language online. Write a GUI application in which the user can enter a message using SMS Language, then click a button to translate it into English (or your own language). Also provide a mechanism to translate text written in English (or your own language) into SMS Language. One potential problem is that one SMS abbreviation could expand into a variety of phrases. For example, IMO (as used above) could also stand for "International Maritime Organization," "in memory of," etc.

6.43   *(Phishing Scanner)* Phishing is a form of identity theft in which, in an e-mail, a sender posing as a trustworthy source attempts to acquire private information, such as your user names, passwords, credit-card numbers and social security number. Phishing e-mails claiming to be from popular banks, credit-card companies, auction sites, social networks and online payment services may look quite legitimate. These fraudulent messages often provide links to spoofed (fake) websites where you're asked to enter sensitive information.

Visit McAfee® (`www.mcafee.com/us/threat_center/anti_phishing/phishing_top10.html`), Security Extra (`www.securityextra.com/`), `www.snopes.com` and other websites to find lists of the top phishing scams. Also check out the Anti-Phishing Working Group (`www.antiphishing.org/`), and the FBI's Cyber Investigations website (`www.fbi.gov/cyberinvest/cyberhome.htm`), where you'll find information about the latest scams and how to protect yourself.

Create a list of 30 words, phrases and company names commonly found in phishing messages. Assign a point value to each based on your estimate of its likeliness to be in a phishing message (e.g., one point if it's somewhat likely, two points if moderately likely, or three points if highly likely). Write an application that scans a file of text for these terms and phrases. For each occurrence of a keyword or phrase within the text file, add the assigned point value to the total points for that word or phrase. For each keyword or phrase found, output one line with the word or phrase, the number of occurrences and the point total. Then show the point total for the entire message. Does your program assign a high point total to some actual phishing e-mails you've received? Does it assign a high point total to some legitimate e-mails you've received?

7

Introduction to Classes and Objects

You'll see something new.
Two things. And I call them
Thing One and Thing Two.
—Dr. Theodor Seuss Geisel

Nothing can have value without
being an object of utility.
—Karl Marx

Your public servants serve you
right.
—Adlai E. Stevenson

Knowing how to answer one
who speaks,
To reply to one who sends a
message.
—Amenemope

Objectives

In this chapter you'll learn:

- What classes, objects and instance variables are.

- How to declare a class and use it to create an object.

- How to declare non-`static` methods to implement the class's behaviors.

- How to declare instance variables to implement the class's attributes.

- The differences between instance variables and local variables.

- How to use a constructor to ensure that an object's data is initialized when the object is created.

7.1 Introduction

We introduced the basic terminology and concepts of object-oriented programming in Section 1.16. Typically, the applications you develop in this book will consist of two or more classes, each containing one or more methods. If you become part of a development team in industry, you might work on applications that contain hundreds, or even thousands, of classes. In this chapter, we present a simple framework for organizing object-oriented applications in Java.

First, we motivate the concept of classes with a real-world example. Then we present applications that demonstrate creating and using your own classes. Two of these examples begin developing a grade book class that instructors might use to maintain student test scores. Another example introduces a bank account class that maintains a customer's balance. The last example presents a case study that examines how arrays, classes and objects can help simulate shuffling and dealing playing cards in a card-game application.

7.2 Classes, Objects, Methods and Instance Variables

Let's begin with a simple analogy to help you understand classes and their contents. Suppose you want to drive a car and make it go faster by pressing down on its accelerator pedal. What must happen before you can do this? Well, before you can drive a car, someone has to design it. A car typically begins as engineering drawings, similar to the blueprints used to design a house. These engineering drawings include the design for an accelerator pedal to make the car go faster. The pedal "hides" from the driver the complex mechanisms that actually make the car go faster, just as the brake pedal "hides" the mechanisms that slow the car and the steering wheel "hides" the mechanisms that turn the car. This enables people with little or no knowledge of how engines work to drive a car easily.

Unfortunately, you cannot drive a car's engineering drawings. Before you can drive a car, it must be built from the engineering drawings that describe it. A completed car has an actual accelerator pedal to make the car go faster, but even that's not enough—the car won't accelerate on its own, so the driver must press the accelerator pedal.

Now let's use our car example to introduce the key programming concepts of this section. Performing a task in a program requires a method. The method declaration describes the mechanisms that actually perform its tasks. The method hides from its user the complex tasks that it performs, just as the accelerator pedal of a car hides from the driver the complex mechanisms of making the car go faster. In Java, we begin by creating a program unit called a class to house a method, just as a car's engineering drawings house the design of an accelerator pedal. In a class, you provide one or more methods that are designed to perform the class's tasks. For example, a class that represents a bank account might contain one method to deposit money to an account, another to withdraw money from an account and a third to inquire what the account's current balance is.

Just as you cannot drive an engineering drawing of a car, you cannot "drive" a class. Just as someone has to build a car from its engineering drawings before you can actually drive a car, you must build an object of a class before you can get a program to perform the tasks the class describes how to do. That is one reason Java is known as an object-oriented programming language.

When you drive a car, pressing its gas pedal sends a message to the car to perform a task—that is, make the car go faster. Similarly, you **send messages** to an object—each message is implemented as a method call that tells a method of the object to perform its task.

Thus far, we've used the car analogy to introduce classes, objects and methods. A car, in addition to it's capabilities, also has many attributes, such as its color, the number of doors, the amount of gas in its tank, its current speed and its total miles driven (i.e., its odometer reading). Like the car's capabilities, these attributes are represented as part of a car's design in its engineering diagrams. As you drive a car, these attributes are always associated with the car. Every car maintains its own attributes. For example, each car knows how much gas is in its own gas tank, but not how much is in the tanks of other cars. Similarly, an object has attributes that are carried with the object as it's used in a program. These attributes are specified as part of the object's class. For example, a bank account object has a balance attribute that represents the amount of money in the account. Each bank account object knows the balance in the account it represents, but not the balances of the other accounts in the bank. Attributes are specified by the class's **instance variables**. The remainder of this chapter presents examples that demonstrate the concepts we introduced in the context of the car analogy.

7.3 Declaring a Class and Instantiating an Object of that Class

In many prior examples, you created an object of the existing class `Scanner`, then used that object to read data from the keyboard. In this section, you create a new class, then use it to create an object. We begin with an example that consists of classes `GradeBook` (Fig. 7.1) and `GradeBookTest` (Fig. 7.2). Class `GradeBook` (declared in file `GradeBook.java`) will be used to display a message on the screen (Fig. 7.2) welcoming the instructor to the grade book application. Class `GradeBookTest` (declared in file `GradeBookTest.java`) is an application class in which the `main` method will create and use an object of class `GradeBook`. Such an application class is sometimes called a **test harness**. Each class declaration that begins with keyword `public` must be stored in a file that has the same name as the class and ends with the `.java` file-name extension. Thus, classes `GradeBook` and `GradeBookTest` will be declared in separate files. As we'll discuss, starting in Chapter 8, there are other ways to declare classes.

 Common Programming Error 7.1
Declaring more than one `public` class in the same file is a compilation error.

Software Engineering Observation 7.1

A test harness (or test application) is responsible for creating an object of the class being tested and providing it with data. This data could come from any of several sources. Test data can be placed directly into an array with an array initializer, it can be entered by the user at the keyboard, it can come from a file, or it can come from a network (as you'll see in Chapter 27). After passing this data to the class's constructor to instantiate the object, the test harness should call upon the object to test its methods and manipulate its data. Gathering data in the test harness like this allows the class to manipulate data from several sources.

In earlier chapters, we declared most of an application's variables in main and other methods. Variables declared in the body of a particular method (such as main) are known as local variables and can be used only in that method. When that method terminates, the values of its local variables are lost. Recall from Section 7.2 that an object has attributes that are carried with it as it's used in a program. Such attributes exist before a method is called on an object and after the method completes execution.

A class normally consists of one or more methods that manipulate the attributes that belong to a particular object of the class. Attributes are represented as variables in a class declaration. Such variables are called fields and are declared inside a class declaration but outside the bodies of the class's method declarations. When each object of a class maintains its own copy of an attribute, the field that represents the attribute is also known as an instance variable—each object (instance) of the class has a separate instance of the variable in memory. The example in this section demonstrates a GradeBook class that contains a courseName instance variable to represent a particular GradeBook object's course name.

GradeBook *Class with an Instance Variable, a* set *Method and a* get *Method*

Class GradeBook (Fig. 7.1) maintains the course name as an instance variable so that it can be used or modified at any time during an application's execution. The class contains three methods—setCourseName, getCourseName and displayMessage. Method setCourseName stores a course name in a GradeBook. Method getCourseName obtains a GradeBook's course name. Method displayMessage displays a welcome message that includes the course name; as you'll see, the method obtains the course name by calling another method in the same class—getCourseName.

```
1   // Fig. 7.1: GradeBook.java
2   // GradeBook class that contains a courseName instance variable
3   // and methods to set and get its value.
4
5   public class GradeBook
6   {
7      private String courseName; // course name for this GradeBook
8
9      // method to set the course name
10     public void setCourseName( String name )
11     {
12        courseName = name; // store the course name
13     } // end method setCourseName
14
```

Fig. 7.1 | GradeBook class that contains a courseName instance variable and methods to set and get its value. (Part 1 of 2.)

```
15    // method to retrieve the course name
16    public String getCourseName()
17    {
18        return courseName;
19    } // end method getCourseName
20
21    // display a welcome message to the GradeBook user
22    public void displayMessage()
23    {
24        // calls getCourseName to get the name of
25        // the course this GradeBook represents
26        System.out.printf( "Welcome to the grade book for\n%s!\n",
27            getCourseName() );
28    } // end method displayMessage
29 } // end class GradeBook
```

Fig. 7.1 | GradeBook class that contains a courseName instance variable and methods to set and get its value. (Part 2 of 2.)

The class declaration begins in line 5. The keyword public is an **access modifier**. For now, we'll simply declare every class public. Every class declaration contains keyword class followed immediately by the class's name. Every class's body is enclosed in a pair of left and right braces, as in lines 6 and 29 of class GradeBook.

A typical instructor teaches more than one course, each with its own course name. Line 7 declares that courseName is a variable of type String. Because the variable is declared in the body of the class but outside the bodies of the class's methods (lines 10–13, 16–19 and 22–28), line 7 is a declaration for an instance variable. Every instance (i.e., object) of class GradeBook contains one copy of each instance variable. For example, if there are two GradeBook objects, each object has its own copy of courseName (one per object). A benefit of making courseName an instance variable is that all the methods of the class (in this case, GradeBook) can manipulate any instance variables that appear in the class (in this case, courseName).

Access Modifiers public and private

Most instance-variable declarations are preceded with the keyword private (as in line 7). Like public, keyword **private** is an access modifier. Variables or methods declared with access modifier private are accessible only to methods of the class in which they're declared. Thus, variable courseName can be used *only* in methods setCourseName, getCourseName and displayMessage of (every object of) class GradeBook.

Software Engineering Observation 7.2

Methods declared with access modifier private can be called only by other methods of the class in which the private methods are declared. Such methods are commonly referred to as utility methods or helper methods because they're typically used to support the operation of the class's other methods.

Declaring instance variables with access modifier private is known as **data hiding** or information hiding. When a program creates (instantiates) an object of class GradeBook, variable courseName is encapsulated (hidden) in the object and can be accessed only by methods of the object's class. This prevents courseName from being modified accidentally by a class in another part of the program. In class `GradeBook`, methods `setCourseName` and `getCourseName` manipulate the instance variable `courseName`.

Software Engineering Observation 7.3

Precede each field and method declaration with an access modifier. Generally, instance variables should be declared `private` and methods `public`. (We'll see that it's appropriate to declare certain methods `private`, if they'll be accessed only by other methods of the class.)

Good Programming Practice 7.1

We prefer to list a class's fields first, so that, as you read the code, you see the names and types of the variables before they're used in the class's methods. You can list the class's fields anywhere in the class outside its method declarations, but scattering them tends to lead to hard-to-read code.

Good Programming Practice 7.2

Place a blank line between method declarations to separate the methods and enhance program readability.

Methods *setCourseName and getCourseName*

Method `setCourseName` (lines 10–13) does not return any data when it completes its task, so its return type is `void`. The method receives one parameter—`name`—which represents the course name that will be passed to the method as an argument. Line 12 assigns `name` to instance variable `courseName`. Method `getCourseName` (lines 16–19) does not receive parameters and returns a particular `GradeBook` object's `courseName`. Both method declarations begin with keyword `public` to indicate that these methods are "available to the public"—they can be called from methods of other classes.

Note that the statements in lines 12 and 18 each use `courseName` even though it was not declared in any of the methods. We can use `courseName` in `GradeBook`'s methods because `courseName` is an instance variable of the class. Also note that the order in which methods are declared in a class does not determine when they're called at execution time. So method `getCourseName` could be declared before method `setCourseName`.

Method *displayMessage*

Method `displayMessage` (lines 22–28) is also `public` so it can be called from other classes. This method does not return any data when it completes its task, so its return type is `void`. The method does not receive parameters. Lines 26–27 output a welcome message that includes the value of instance variable `courseName`, which is returned by the call to method `getCourseName` in line 27. Notice that one method of a class (`displayMessage` in this case) can call another method of the same class by using just the method name (`getCourseName` in this case). Once again, we need to create an object of class `GradeBook` and call its methods before the welcome message can be displayed.

A Note about Method Declarations

The methods you declared in earlier chapters were all `static` methods. In this class, the methods are not declared with keyword `static`. A non-`static` method can call any method of the same class directly (i.e., using the method name by itself) and can manipulate any of the class's fields directly. On the other hand, a `static` method can call only other `static` methods of the same class directly and can manipulate only `static` fields in the same class directly. To access the class's non-static members, a static method must use a reference to an object of the class. Recall that static methods relate to a class as a whole, whereas non-static methods are associated with a specific class instance (object) and may manipulate the object's instance variables. Many objects of a class, each with its own copies of the instance variables, may exist at the same time. Suppose a static method were to invoke a non-static method directly. How would the method know which object's instance variables to manipulate? What would happen if no objects of the class existed when the non-static method was invoked? Clearly, this would be problematic. So, Java does not allow a static method to access non-static members of the same class directly.

GradeBookTest *Class That Demonstrates Class* GradeBook

Next, we'd like to use class GradeBook in an application. Class GradeBook cannot execute the application because it does not contain main; if you try to execute GradeBook by typing java GradeBook in the command window, you'll receive an error message like:

```
Exception in thread "main" java.lang.NoSuchMethodError: main
```

This was not a problem in prior examples, because every class you declared had a main method. To fix this problem, we must either declare a separate class that contains a main method or place a main method in class GradeBook. To help you prepare for the larger programs you'll encounter later in this book and in industry, we use a separate class (Grade-BookTest in this example) containing method main to test each new class we create in this chapter. Some programmers refer to such a class as a driver class.

Class GradeBookTest (Fig. 7.2) creates one object of class GradeBook and demonstrates its methods. In this application, we'd like to call class GradeBook's methods to get the initial course name, change the course name and display a welcome message containing the new course name. Typically, you cannot call a method that belongs to another class until you create an object of that class, as shown in line 14. We declare variable myGradeBook with the type GradeBook—the class we declared in Fig. 7.1. Each new class you create becomes a new type that can be used to declare variables and create objects. You can declare new class types as needed; this is one reason why Java is known as an **extensible language**.

```
1   // Fig. 7.2: GradeBookTest.java
2   // Creating and manipulating a GradeBook object.
3   import java.util.Scanner; // program uses Scanner
4
5   public class GradeBookTest
6   {
7      // main method begins program execution
8      public static void main( String[] args )
9      {
10        // create Scanner to obtain input from the command window
11        Scanner input = new Scanner( System.in );
12
13        // create a GradeBook object and assign it to myGradeBook
14        GradeBook myGradeBook = new GradeBook();
15
```

Fig. 7.2 | Creating and manipulating a GradeBook object. (Part 1 of 2.)

```
16        // display initial value of courseName
17        System.out.printf( "Initial course name is: %s\n\n",
18           myGradeBook.getCourseName() );
19
20        // prompt for and read course name
21        System.out.println( "Please enter the course name:" );
22        String theName = input.nextLine(); // read a line of text
23        myGradeBook.setCourseName( theName ); // set the course name
24        System.out.println(); // outputs a blank line
25
26        // display welcome message after specifying course name
27        myGradeBook.displayMessage();
28     } // end main
29  } // end class GradeBookTest
```

```
Initial course name is: null

Please enter the course name:
CS101 Introduction to Java Programming

Welcome to the grade book for
CS101 Introduction to Java Programming!
```

Fig. 7.2 | Creating and manipulating a GradeBook object. (Part 2 of 2.)

Class Instance Creation Expressions

Line 14 creates a GradeBook object and assigns it to local variable myGradeBook. Variable myGradeBook is initialized with the result of the **class instance creation expression** new GradeBook(). Keyword new creates a new object of the class specified to the right of the keyword (i.e., GradeBook). The parentheses to the right of GradeBook are required. As you'll learn in Section 7.4, those parentheses in combination with a class name represent a call to a **constructor**, which is similar to a method but is used only at the time an object is created to initialize the object's data. As you've seen previously, data can be placed in the parentheses to specify initial values for the object's data. For example, line 11 creates a Scanner object and passes the argument System.in to the Scanner class's constructor.

Displaying the Initial Course Name; Default Values for Instance Variables

Just as we can use object System.out to call methods print, printf and println, we can use object myGradeBook to call methods getCourseName, setCourseName and displayMessage. Lines 17–18 display the initial course name by calling the object's getCourseName method and outputting its return value. Note that the first line of the output shows the name "null." Unlike local variables, which are not automatically initialized, every field has a **default initial value**—a value provided by Java when you do not specify the field's initial value. Thus, fields are not required to be explicitly initialized before they're used in a program— unless they must be initialized to values other than their default values. Reference-type instance variables are initialized by default to the value null—a reserved word that represents a "reference to nothing." Primitive-type instance variables of types byte, char, short, int, long, float and double are initialized to 0, and variables of type boolean are initialized to false. You can specify your own initial value for a variable by assigning the variable a value in its declaration. Recall that local variables are *not* initialized by default.

Setting the Course Name

Line 21 prompts the user to enter a course name. Local String variable theName (declared in line 22) is initialized with the course name entered by the user, which is returned by the call to the nextLine method of the Scanner object input. The user types the course name and presses *Enter* to submit the course name to the program. Note that pressing *Enter* inserts a newline character at the end of the characters typed by the user. Method nextLine reads characters typed by the user until the newline character is encountered, then returns a String containing the characters up to, but not including, the newline. The newline character is discarded. Class Scanner also provides a similar method—next—that reads individual words. When the user presses *Enter* after typing input, method next reads characters until a white-space character (such as a space, tab or newline) is encountered, then returns a String containing the characters up to, but not including, the white-space character (which is discarded). All information after the first white-space character is not lost—it can be read by other statements that call the Scanner's methods later in the program.

Line 23 calls object myGradeBook's setCourseName method and supplies theName as the method's argument. When the method is called, the argument's value is assigned to parameter name (line 10, Fig. 7.1) of method setCourseName (lines 10–13, Fig. 7.1). Then the parameter's value is assigned to instance variable courseName (line 12, Fig. 7.1). Line 27 calls object myGradeBook's displayMessage method to display the welcome message containing the course name.

set *and* get *Methods*

A class's private fields can be manipulated only by the class's methods. So a **client of an object**—that is, any class that calls the object's methods—calls the class's public methods to manipulate the private fields of an object of the class. This is why the statements in method main (Fig. 7.2) call the setCourseName, getCourseName and displayMessage methods on a GradeBook object. Classes often provide public methods to allow clients to *set* (i.e., assign values to) or *get* (i.e., obtain the values of) private instance variables. The names of these methods need not begin with *set* or *get*, but this naming convention is recommended and is required for special Java software components called JavaBeans that can simplify programming in many Java integrated development environments (IDEs). The method that *sets* instance variable courseName in this example is called setCourseName, and the method that *gets* the value of courseName is called getCourseName.

Compiling an Application with Multiple Classes

You must compile the classes in Fig. 7.1 and Fig. 7.2 before you can execute the application. First, change to the directory that contains the application's source-code files. Next, type the command

```
javac GradeBook.java GradeBookTest.java
```

to compile both classes at once. If the directory containing the application includes only this application's files, you can compile all the classes in the directory with the command

```
javac *.java
```

The asterisk (*) in *.java indicates that *all* files in the current directory that end with the file-name extension ".java" should be compiled.

GradeBook* UML Class Diagram with an Instance Variable and set *and* get *Methods
Figure 7.3 presents a **UML class diagram** for class GradeBook in Fig. 7.1. Recall from
Section 1.16 that the UML is a graphical language used by programmers to represent object-oriented systems in a standardized manner. In the UML, each class is modeled in a
class diagram as a rectangle with three **compartment**s. The top one contains the name of
the class centered horizontally in boldface type. The middle compartment contains the
class's attributes, which correspond to instance variables in Java. The bottom compartment contains the class's **operations**, which correspond to methods in Java.

GradeBook
– courseName : String
+ setCourseName(name : String) + getCourseName( ) : String + displayMessage( )

Fig. 7.3 | UML class diagram for class GradeBook.

This diagram models class GradeBook's instance variable courseName as an attribute
in the *middle compartment* of the class. The UML represents instance variables as attributes
by listing the attribute name, followed by a colon and the attribute type. The UML type
of attribute courseName is String. Instance variable courseName is private in Java, so the
class diagram lists a minus sign (–) access modifier in front of the corresponding attribute's
name.

Class GradeBook contains three public methods, so the class diagram lists three operations in the *bottom compartment*. The UML models operations by listing the operation
name preceded by an access modifier (in this case + to represent public) and followed by
a set of parentheses. Operation setCourseName has a String parameter called name. The
UML indicates the return type of an operation by placing a colon and the return type after
the parentheses following the operation name. Method getCourseName of class GradeBook
(Fig. 7.1) has a String return type in Java, so the class diagram shows a String return type
in the UML. Note that operations setCourseName and displayMessage do not return
values (i.e., they return void in Java), so the UML class diagram does not specify a return
type after the parentheses of these operations.

Notes on* import *Declarations
Notice the import declaration in Fig. 7.2 (line 3). This indicates to the compiler that the
program uses class Scanner. Why do we need to import class Scanner, but not classes
System, String or GradeBook? Classes System and String are in package java.lang,
which is implicitly imported into every Java program, so all programs can use that package's classes without explicitly importing them. Most other classes you'll use in Java programs must be imported explicitly.

There is a special relationship between classes that are compiled in the same directory
on disk, like classes GradeBook and GradeBookTest. By default, such classes are considered
to be in the same package—known as the **default package**. Classes in the same package are
implicitly imported into the source-code files of other classes in the same package. Thus,

an `import` declaration is not required when one class in a package uses another in the same package—such as when class `GradeBookTest` uses class `GradeBook`.

The `import` declaration in line 3 is not required if we always refer to class `Scanner` as `java.util.Scanner`, which includes the full package name and class name. This is known as the class's **fully qualified class name**. For example, line 12 could be written as

```
java.util.Scanner input = new java.util.Scanner( System.in );
```

Software Engineering Observation 7.4

The Java compiler does not require `import` declarations in a Java source-code file if the fully qualified class name is specified every time a class name is used in the source code. Most Java programmers prefer to use `import` declarations.

7.4 Initializing Objects with Constructors

As mentioned in Section 7.3, when an object of class `GradeBook` (Fig. 7.1) is created, its instance variable `courseName` is initialized to `null` by default. What if you want to provide a course name when you create a `GradeBook` object? Each class you declare can provide a special method called a **constructor** that can be used to initialize an object of a class when the object is created. In fact, Java requires a constructor call for *every* object that is created. Keyword `new` requests memory from the system to store an object, then calls the corresponding class's constructor to initialize the object. The call is indicated by the parentheses after the class name. A constructor *must* have the same name as the class. For example, line 14 of Fig. 7.2 first uses `new` to create a `GradeBook` object. The empty parentheses after "new `GradeBook`" indicate a call to the class's constructor without arguments. By default, the compiler provides a **default constructor** with no parameters in any class that does not explicitly include a constructor. When a class has only the default constructor, its instance variables are initialized to their default values.

When you declare a class, you can provide your own constructor to specify custom initialization for objects of your class. For example, you might want to specify a course name for a `GradeBook` object when the object is created, as in

```
GradeBook myGradeBook =
    new GradeBook( "CS101 Introduction to Java Programming" );
```

In this case, the argument `"CS101 Introduction to Java Programming"` is passed to the `GradeBook` object's constructor and used to initialize the `courseName`. The preceding statement requires that the class provide a constructor with a `String` parameter. Figure 7.4 contains a modified `GradeBook` class with such a constructor.

```
1   // Fig. 7.4: GradeBook.java
2   // GradeBook class with a constructor to initialize the course name.
3
4   public class GradeBook
5   {
6       private String courseName; // course name for this GradeBook
```

Fig. 7.4 | GradeBook class with a constructor to initialize the course name. (Part 1 of 2.)

```
 7
 8      // constructor initializes courseName with String argument
 9      public GradeBook( String name )
10      {
11         courseName = name; // initializes courseName
12      } // end constructor
13
14      // method to set the course name
15      public void setCourseName( String name )
16      {
17         courseName = name; // store the course name
18      } // end method setCourseName
19
20      // method to retrieve the course name
21      public String getCourseName()
22      {
23         return courseName;
24      } // end method getCourseName
25
26      // display a welcome message to the GradeBook user
27      public void displayMessage()
28      {
29         // this statement calls getCourseName to get the
30         // name of the course this GradeBook represents
31         System.out.printf( "Welcome to the grade book for\n%s!\n",
32            getCourseName() );
33      } // end method displayMessage
34   } // end class GradeBook
```

Fig. 7.4 | GradeBook class with a constructor to initialize the course name. (Part 2 of 2.)

Lines 9–12 declare GradeBook's constructor. Like a method, a constructor's parameter list specifies the data it requires to perform its task. When you create a new object (as we'll do in Fig. 7.5), this data is placed in the parentheses that follow the class name. Line 9 indicates that the constructor has a String parameter called name. The name passed to the constructor is assigned to instance variable courseName in line 11.

Figure 7.5 initializes GradeBook objects using the constructor. Lines 11–12 create and initialize the GradeBook object gradeBook1. The GradeBook constructor is called with the argument "CS101 Introduction to Java Programming" to initialize the course name. The class instance creation expression in lines 11–12 returns a reference to the new object, which is assigned to the variable gradeBook1. Lines 13–14 repeat this process, this time passing the argument "CS102 Data Structures in Java" to initialize the course name for gradeBook2. Lines 17–20 use each object's getCourseName method to obtain the course names and show that they were initialized when the objects were created. The output confirms that each GradeBook maintains its own copy of instance variable courseName.

```
1    // Fig. 7.5: GradeBookTest.java
2    // GradeBook constructor used to specify the course name at the
3    // time each GradeBook object is created.
```

Fig. 7.5 | GradeBook constructor used to specify the course name at the time each GradeBook object is created. (Part 1 of 2.)

```
 4
 5    public class GradeBookTest
 6    {
 7       // main method begins program execution
 8       public static void main( String[] args )
 9       {
10          // create GradeBook object
11          GradeBook gradeBook1 = new GradeBook(
12             "CS101 Introduction to Java Programming" );
13          GradeBook gradeBook2 = new GradeBook(
14             "CS102 Data Structures in Java" );
15
16          // display initial value of courseName for each GradeBook
17          System.out.printf( "gradeBook1 course name is: %s\n",
18             gradeBook1.getCourseName() );
19          System.out.printf( "gradeBook2 course name is: %s\n",
20             gradeBook2.getCourseName() );
21       } // end main
22    } // end class GradeBookTest
```

```
gradeBook1 course name is: CS101 Introduction to Java Programming
gradeBook2 course name is: CS102 Data Structures in Java
```

Fig. 7.5 | GradeBook constructor used to specify the course name at the time each GradeBook object is created. (Part 2 of 2.)

An important difference between constructors and methods is that constructors cannot return values, so they cannot specify a return type (not even void). Normally, constructors are declared public. If a class does not include a constructor, the class's instance variables are initialized to their default values. *If you declare any constructors for a class, the Java compiler will not create a default constructor for that class.* Thus, we can no longer create a GradeBook object with new GradeBook() as we did in the earlier examples.

Error-Prevention Tip 7.1

Unless default initialization of your class's instance variables is acceptable, provide a constructor to ensure that your class's instance variables are properly initialized with meaningful values when each new object of your class is created.

Adding the Constructor to Class *GradeBook's* UML Class Diagram

The UML class diagram of Fig. 7.6 models class GradeBook of Fig. 7.4, which has a constructor that has a name parameter of type String. Like operations, the UML models constructors in the third compartment of a class in a class diagram. To distinguish a constructor from a class's operations, the UML requires that the word "constructor" be placed between **guillemets** (« and ») before the constructor's name. It's customary to list constructors before other operations in the third compartment.

Constructors with Multiple Parameters

Sometimes you'll want to initialize objects with multiple pieces of data. Like methods, constructors can specify any number of parameters. For example, Exercise 7.10 asks you

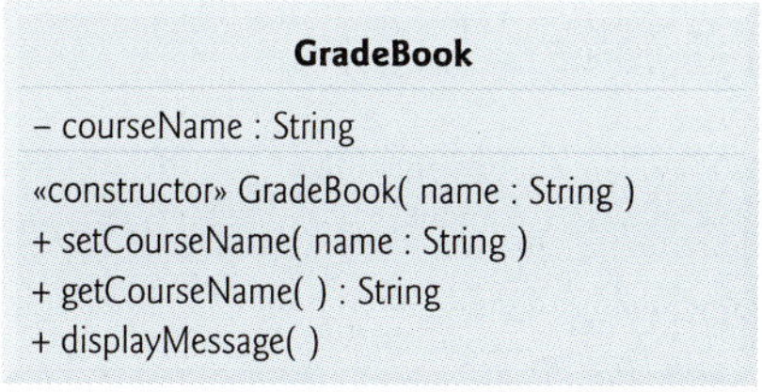

GradeBook
– courseName : String
«constructor» GradeBook(name : String)
+ setCourseName(name : String)
+ getCourseName( ) : String
+ displayMessage( )

Fig. 7.6 | UML class diagram indicating that class GradeBook has a constructor that has a name parameter of UML type String.

to store the course name *and* the instructor's name in a GradeBook object. In this case, the GradeBook's constructor would be modified to receive two Strings, as in

```
public GradeBook( String courseName, String instructorName )
```

and you'd call the GradeBook constructor as follows:

```
GradeBook gradeBook = new GradeBook(
    "CS101 Introduction to Java Programming", "Sue Green" );
```

7.5 Case Study: Account Balances; Validating Constructor Arguments

Our next application (Figs. 7.7–7.8) contains a class named Account (Fig. 7.7) that maintains the balance of a bank account. A typical bank services many accounts, each with its own balance, so line 7 declares an instance variable named balance of type double. Variable balance is an instance variable because it's declared in the body of the class but outside the class's method declarations (lines 10–16, 19–22 and 25–28). Every instance (i.e., object) of class Account contains its own copy of balance.

```
1   // Fig. 7.7: Account.java
2   // Account class with a constructor to validate and
3   // initialize instance variable balance of type double.
4
5   public class Account
6   {
7      private double balance; // instance variable that stores the balance
8
9      // constructor
10     public Account( double initialBalance )
11     {
12        // validate that initialBalance is greater than 0.0;
13        // if it is not, balance is initialized to the default value 0.0
14        if ( initialBalance > 0.0 )
15           balance = initialBalance;
16     } // end Account constructor
17
```

Fig. 7.7 | Account class with a constructor to validate and initialize instance variable balance of type double. (Part I of 2.)

```
18      // credit (add) an amount to the account
19      public void credit( double amount )
20      {
21         balance += amount; // add amount to balance
22      } // end method credit
23
24      // return the account balance
25      public double getBalance()
26      {
27         return balance; // gives the value of balance to the calling method
28      } // end method getBalance
29   } // end class Account
```

Fig. 7.7 | Account class with a constructor to validate and initialize instance variable `balance` of type `double`. (Part 2 of 2.)

Validating the Balance

The class has a constructor and two methods. It's common for someone opening an account to deposit money immediately, so the constructor (lines 10–16) receives a parameter `initialBalance` of type `double` that represents the starting balance. Lines 14–15 validate the constructor argument to ensure that `initialBalance` is greater than `0.0`. If so, `initialBalance`'s value is assigned to instance variable `balance`. Otherwise, `balance` remains at `0.0`—its default initial value.

Methods *credit* and *getBalance*

Method `credit` (lines 19–22) does not return any data when it completes its task, so its return type is `void`. The method receives one parameter named `amount`—a `double` value that will be added to the balance. Line 21 adds `amount` to the current value of `balance`.

Method `getBalance` (lines 25–28) allows clients of the class (i.e., other classes that use this class) to obtain the value of a particular `Account` object's `balance`. The method specifies return type `double` and an empty parameter list.

Once again, note that the statements in lines 15, 21 and 27 use instance variable `balance` even though it was not declared in any of the methods. We can use `balance` in these methods because it's an instance variable of the class.

AccountTest *Class to Use Class* Account

Class `AccountTest` (Fig. 7.8) creates two `Account` objects (lines 10–11) and initializes them with `50.00` and `-7.53`, respectively. Lines 14–17 output the balance in each `Account` by calling the `Account`'s `getBalance` method. When method `getBalance` is called for `account1` from line 15, the value of `account1`'s balance is returned from line 27 of Fig. 7.7 and displayed by the `System.out.printf` statement (Fig. 7.8, lines 14–15). Similarly, when method `getBalance` is called for `account2` from line 17, the value of the `account2`'s balance is returned from line 27 of Fig. 7.7 and displayed by the `System.out.printf` statement (Fig. 7.8, lines 16–17). Note that the balance of `account2` is `0.00`, because the constructor ensured that the account could not begin with a negative balance. The value is output by `printf` with the format specifier `%.2f`.

Line 21 declares local variable `depositAmount` to store each deposit amount entered by the user. Unlike the instance variable `balance` in class `Account`, local variable `deposit-`

Amount in main is *not* initialized to 0.0 by default. However, this variable does not need to be initialized here, because its value will be determined by the user's input.

Line 23 prompts the user to enter a deposit amount for account1. Line 24 obtains the input from the user by calling Scanner object input's nextDouble method, which returns a double value entered by the user. Lines 25–26 display the deposit amount. Line 27 calls

```
1   // Fig. 7.8: AccountTest.java
2   // Manipulating Account objects and validating initializer values.
3   import java.util.Scanner;
4
5   public class AccountTest
6   {
7      // main method begins execution of Java application
8      public static void main( String[] args )
9      {
10        Account account1 = new Account( 50.00 ); // create Account object
11        Account account2 = new Account( -7.53 ); // create Account object
12
13        // display initial balance of each object
14        System.out.printf( "account1 balance: $%.2f\n",
15           account1.getBalance() );
16        System.out.printf( "account2 balance: $%.2f\n\n",
17           account2.getBalance() );
18
19        // create Scanner to obtain input from command window
20        Scanner input = new Scanner( System.in );
21        double depositAmount; // deposit amount read from user
22
23        System.out.print( "Enter deposit amount for account1: " ); // prompt
24        depositAmount = input.nextDouble(); // obtain user input
25        System.out.printf( "\nadding %.2f to account1 balance\n\n",
26           depositAmount );
27        account1.credit( depositAmount ); // add to account1 balance
28
29        // display balances
30        System.out.printf( "account1 balance: $%.2f\n",
31           account1.getBalance() );
32        System.out.printf( "account2 balance: $%.2f\n\n",
33           account2.getBalance() );
34
35        System.out.print( "Enter deposit amount for account2: " ); // prompt
36        depositAmount = input.nextDouble(); // obtain user input
37        System.out.printf( "\nadding %.2f to account2 balance\n\n",
38           depositAmount );
39        account2.credit( depositAmount ); // add to account2 balance
40
41        // display balances
42        System.out.printf( "account1 balance: $%.2f\n",
43           account1.getBalance() );
44        System.out.printf( "account2 balance: $%.2f\n",
45           account2.getBalance() );
46     } // end main
47  } // end class AccountTest
```

Fig. 7.8 | Manipulating Account objects and validating initializer values. (Part 1 of 2.)

```
account1 balance: $50.00
account2 balance: $0.00

Enter deposit amount for account1: 25.53

adding 25.53 to account1 balance

account1 balance: $75.53
account2 balance: $0.00

Enter deposit amount for account2: 123.45

adding 123.45 to account2 balance

account1 balance: $75.53
account2 balance: $123.45
```

Fig. 7.8 | Manipulating Account objects and validating initializer values. (Part 2 of 2.)

object account1's credit method and supplies depositAmount as the method's argument. When the method is called, the argument's value is assigned to parameter amount (line 19 of Fig. 7.7) of method credit (lines 19–22 of Fig. 7.7); then method credit adds that value to the balance (line 21 of Fig. 7.7). Lines 30–33 (Fig. 7.8) output the balances of both Accounts again to show that only account1's balance changed.

Line 35 prompts the user to enter a deposit amount for account2. Line 36 obtains the input from the user by calling Scanner object input's nextDouble method. Lines 37–38 display the deposit amount. Line 39 calls object account2's credit method and supplies depositAmount as the method's argument; then method credit adds that value to the balance. Finally, lines 42–45 output the balances of both Accounts again to show that only account2's balance changed.

UML Class Diagram for Class Account

The UML class diagram in Fig. 7.9 models class Account of Fig. 7.7. The diagram models the private attribute balance with UML type Double to correspond to the class's instance variable balance of Java type double. The diagram models class Account's constructor with a parameter initialBalance of UML type Double in the third compartment of the class. The class's two public methods are modeled as operations in the third compartment as well. The diagram models operation credit with an amount parameter of UML type

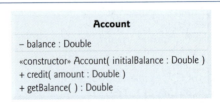

Fig. 7.9 | UML class diagram indicating that class Account has a private balance attribute of UML type Double, a constructor (with a parameter of UML type Double) and two public operations—credit (with an amount parameter of UML type Double) and getBalance (which returns UML type Double).

Double (because the corresponding method has an amount parameter of Java type double) and operation getBalance with a return type of Double (because the corresponding Java method returns a double value).

7.6 Case Study: Card Shuffling and Dealing Simulation

The examples in the chapter thus far have used individual objects of class GradeBook or class Account. In our next example, we manipulate an array of objects. Recall from Section 6.3 that the elements of an array can be either primitive types or reference types. This section uses random-number generation and an array of Card objects, to develop a class that simulates card shuffling and dealing. This class can then be used to implement applications that play specific card games. The exercises at the end of the chapter use the classes developed here to build a simple poker application.

We first develop class Card (Fig. 7.10), which represents a playing card that has a face (e.g., "Ace", "Deuce", "Three", ..., "Jack", "Queen", "King") and a suit (e.g., "Hearts", "Diamonds", "Clubs", "Spades"). Next, we develop the DeckOfCards class (Fig. 7.11), which creates a deck of 52 playing cards in which each element is a Card object. We then build a test application (Fig. 7.12) that demonstrates class DeckOfCards's card shuffling and dealing capabilities.

Class *Card*

Class Card (Fig. 7.10) contains two String instance variables—face and suit—that are used to store references to the face name and suit name for a specific Card. The constructor for the class (lines 10–14) receives two Strings that it uses to initialize face and suit. Method **toString** (lines 17–20) creates a String consisting of the face of the card, the String " of " and the suit of the card. Card's toString method can be invoked explicitly to obtain a string representation of a Card object (e.g., "Ace of Spades"). Actually, all objects have a toString method that returns a String representation of the object. When an object is concatenated with a String or used where a String is expected (e.g., when printf outputs the object as a String using the %s format specifier), the object's toString method is *implicitly* called to obtain the String representation of the object. For this behavior to occur, toString must be declared with the header shown in Fig. 7.10.

```
 1   // Fig. 7.10: Card.java
 2   // Card class represents a playing card.
 3
 4   public class Card
 5   {
 6      private String face; // face of card ("Ace", "Deuce", ...)
 7      private String suit; // suit of card ("Hearts", "Diamonds", ...)
 8
 9      // two-argument constructor initializes card's face and suit
10      public Card( String cardFace, String cardSuit )
11      {
12         face = cardFace; // initialize face of card
13         suit = cardSuit; // initialize suit of card
14      } // end two-argument Card constructor
15
```

Fig. 7.10 | Card class represents a playing card. (Part 1 of 2.)

```
16    // return String representation of Card
17    public String toString()
18    {
19        return face + " of " + suit;
20    } // end method toString
21 } // end class Card
```

Fig. 7.10 | Card class represents a playing card. (Part 2 of 2.)

Class DeckOfCards

Class DeckOfCards (Fig. 7.11) declares as an instance variable a Card array named deck (line 7). Note that an array of a reference type is declared like any other array. Class Deck-OfCards also declares an integer instance variable currentCard (line 8) representing the next Card to be dealt from the deck array and a named constant NUMBER_OF_CARDS (line 9) indicating the number of Cards in the deck (52).

The class's constructor instantiates the deck array (line 20) with NUMBER_OF_CARDS (52) Card elements. When first created, the elements of the deck array are null by default,

```
1    // Fig. 7.11: DeckOfCards.java
2    // DeckOfCards class represents a deck of playing cards.
3    import java.util.Random;
4
5    public class DeckOfCards
6    {
7        private Card[] deck; // array of Card objects
8        private int currentCard; // index of next Card to be dealt
9        private static final int NUMBER_OF_CARDS = 52; // constant # of Cards
10       // random number generator
11       private static final Random randomNumbers = new Random();
12
13       // constructor fills deck of Cards
14       public DeckOfCards()
15       {
16           String[] faces = { "Ace", "Deuce", "Three", "Four", "Five", "Six",
17               "Seven", "Eight", "Nine", "Ten", "Jack", "Queen", "King" };
18           String[] suits = { "Hearts", "Diamonds", "Clubs", "Spades" };
19
20           deck = new Card[ NUMBER_OF_CARDS ]; // create array of Card objects
21           currentCard = 0; // set currentCard so first Card dealt is deck[ 0 ]
22
23           // populate deck with Card objects
24           for ( int count = 0; count < deck.length; count++ )
25               deck[ count ] =
26                   new Card( faces[ count % 13 ], suits[ count / 13 ] );
27       } // end DeckOfCards constructor
28
29       // shuffle deck of Cards with one-pass algorithm
30       public void shuffle()
31       {
32           // after shuffling, dealing should start at deck[ 0 ] again
33           currentCard = 0; // reinitialize currentCard
34
```

Fig. 7.11 | DeckOfCards class represents a deck of playing cards. (Part 1 of 2.)

```
35            // for each Card, pick another random Card and swap them
36            for ( int first = 0; first < deck.length; first++ )
37            {
38                // select a random number between 0 and 51
39                int second = randomNumbers.nextInt( NUMBER_OF_CARDS );
40
41                // swap current Card with randomly selected Card
42                Card temp = deck[ first ];
43                deck[ first ] = deck[ second ];
44                deck[ second ] = temp;
45            } // end for
46        } // end method shuffle
47
48        // deal one Card
49        public Card dealCard()
50        {
51            // determine whether Cards remain to be dealt
52            if ( currentCard < deck.length )
53                return deck[ currentCard++ ]; // return current Card in array
54            else
55                return null; // return null to indicate that all Cards were dealt
56        } // end method dealCard
57    } // end class DeckOfCards
```

Fig. 7.11 | DeckOfCards class represents a deck of playing cards. (Part 2 of 2.)

so the constructor uses a for statement (lines 24–26) to fill the deck array with Cards. The for statement initializes control variable count to 0 and loops while count is less than deck.length, causing count to take on each integer value from 0 to 51 (the indices of the deck array). Each Card is instantiated and initialized with two Strings—one from the faces array (which contains the Strings "Ace" through "King") and one from the suits array (which contains the Strings "Hearts", "Diamonds", "Clubs" and "Spades"). The calculation count % 13 always results in a value from 0 to 12 (the 13 indices of the faces array in lines 16–17), and the calculation count / 13 always results in a value from 0 to 3 (the four indices of the suits array in line 18). When the deck array is initialized, it contains the Cards with faces "Ace" through "King" in order for each suit ("Hearts" then "Diamonds" then "Clubs" then "Spades"). Note that we use arrays of Strings to represent the faces and suits in this example. In Exercise 7.17, we ask you to modify this example to use arrays of enumeration constants to represent the faces and suits.

Method shuffle (lines 30–46) shuffles the Cards in the deck. The method loops through all 52 Cards (array indices 0 to 51). For each Card, a number between 0 and 51 is picked randomly to select another Card. Next, the current Card object and the randomly selected Card object are swapped in the array. This exchange is performed by the three assignments in lines 42–44. The extra variable temp temporarily stores one of the two Card objects being swapped. The swap cannot be performed with only the two statements

```
deck[ first ] = deck[ second ];
deck[ second ] = deck[ first ];
```

If deck[first] is the "Ace" of "Spades" and deck[second] is the "Queen" of "Hearts", after the first assignment, both array elements contain the "Queen" of "Hearts" and the "Ace" of "Spades" is lost—hence, the extra variable temp is needed. After the for loop terminates, the Card objects are randomly ordered. A total of only 52 swaps are made in a single pass of the entire array, and the array of Card objects is shuffled!

Method dealCard (lines 49–56) deals one Card in the array. Recall that currentCard indicates the index of the next Card to be dealt (i.e., the Card at the top of the deck). Thus, line 52 compares currentCard to the length of the deck array. If the deck is not empty (i.e., currentCard is less than 52), line 53 returns the "top" Card and postincrements currentCard to prepare for the next call to dealCard—otherwise, null is returned. Recall that null represents a "reference to nothing."

Shuffling and Dealing Cards
Figure 7.12 demonstrates class DeckOfCards (Fig. 7.11). Line 9 creates a DeckOfCards object named myDeckOfCards. Recall that the DeckOfCards constructor creates the deck with the 52 Card objects in order by suit and face. Line 10 invokes myDeckOfCards's shuffle method to rearrange the Card objects. Lines 13–20 deal all 52 Cards and print them in

```java
 1   // Fig. 7.12: DeckOfCardsTest.java
 2   // Card shuffling and dealing.
 3
 4   public class DeckOfCardsTest
 5   {
 6      // execute application
 7      public static void main( String[] args )
 8      {
 9         DeckOfCards myDeckOfCards = new DeckOfCards(); // create the deck
10         myDeckOfCards.shuffle(); // place Cards in random order
11
12         // print all 52 Cards in the order in which they are dealt
13         for ( int i = 1; i <= 52; i++ )
14         {
15            // deal and display a Card
16            System.out.printf( "%-19s", myDeckOfCards.dealCard() );
17
18            if ( i % 4 == 0 ) // output newline every 4 cards
19               System.out.println();
20         } // end for
21      } // end main
22   } // end class DeckOfCardsTest
```

Six of Spades	Eight of Spades	Six of Clubs	Nine of Hearts
Queen of Hearts	Seven of Clubs	Nine of Spades	King of Hearts
Three of Diamonds	Deuce of Clubs	Ace of Hearts	Ten of Spades
Four of Spades	Ace of Clubs	Seven of Diamonds	Four of Hearts
Three of Clubs	Deuce of Hearts	Five of Spades	Jack of Diamonds
King of Clubs	Ten of Hearts	Three of Hearts	Six of Diamonds
Queen of Clubs	Eight of Diamonds	Deuce of Diamonds	Ten of Diamonds
Three of Spades	King of Diamonds	Nine of Clubs	Six of Hearts
Ace of Spades	Four of Diamonds	Seven of Hearts	Eight of Clubs
Deuce of Spades	Eight of Hearts	Five of Hearts	Queen of Spades
Jack of Hearts	Seven of Spades	Four of Clubs	Nine of Diamonds
Ace of Diamonds	Queen of Diamonds	Five of Clubs	King of Spades
Five of Diamonds	Ten of Clubs	Jack of Spades	Jack of Clubs

Fig. 7.12 | Card shuffling and dealing.

four columns of 13 Cards each. Line 16 deals one Card object by invoking myDeckOf-Cards's dealCard method, then displays the Card left justified in a field of 19 characters. When a Card is output as a String, the Card's toString method (lines 17–20 of Fig. 7.10) is implicitly invoked. Lines 18–19 start a new line after every four Cards.

7.7 Wrap-Up

In this chapter, you learned the basic concepts of classes, objects, methods and instance variables—these will be used in most Java applications you create. In particular, you learned how to declare instance variables of a class to maintain data for each object of the class, and how to declare methods that operate on that data. You learned that instance variables are initialized automatically. You also learned how to use a class's constructor to specify the initial values for an object's instance variables. You saw how the UML can be used to create class diagrams that model the constructors, methods and attributes of classes. Finally, we presented a case study in which we defined two classes to represent a deck of cards, then used those classes to shuffle and deal the cards.

We've now introduced the basic concepts of classes, objects, control statements, methods, arrays and collections. In Chapter 8, we take a deeper look at classes and objects.

Summary

Section 7.2 Classes, Objects, Methods and Instance Variables
- Performing a task in a program requires a method. Inside the method you put the mechanisms that make the method do its tasks.
- A class may contain one or more methods that are designed to perform the class's tasks.
- A method can perform a task and return a result.
- An object has attributes that are carried with the object as it's used in a program. These attributes are specified as part of the object's class. Attributes are specified in classes by fields.

Section 7.3 Declaring a Class and Instantiating an Object of that Class
- Each class declaration that begins with the access modifier public must be stored in a file that has exactly the same name as the class and ends with the .java file-name extension.
- Every class declaration contains keyword class followed immediately by the class's name.
- Every object of a class has its own copy of the class's instance variables.
- private variables and methods are accessible only to the class in which they're declared.
- Declaring instance variables with access modifier private is known as data hiding.
- All the methods of the class can use the fields. A field has a default initial value provided by Java when you do not specify the field's initial value, but a local variable does not.
- A method declaration that begins with keyword public indicates that the method can be called by other classes declared outside the class declaration.
- Classes often provide public methods to allow the class's clients to *set* or *get* private instance variables. By convention, such method names begin with *set* or *get*.
- When you attempt to execute a class, Java looks for the class's main method to begin execution.
- Typically, you cannot call a method of another class until you create an object of that class.
- Class instance creation expressions beginning with keyword new create new objects.
- Scanner method nextLine returns a String up to, but not including, a newline character.

- Scanner method next reads until a white-space character is encountered, then returns a String.
- Class String is in package java.lang, which is imported implicitly into all source-code files.
- Classes that are compiled in the same directory on disk are in the same package and are implicitly imported into the source-code files of other classes in the same package.
- import declarations are not required if you always use fully qualified class names.
- The top compartment in a UML class diagram contains the class's name centered horizontally in boldface. The middle contains the class's attributes, which correspond to fields in Java. The bottom contains the class's operations, which correspond to methods and constructors in Java.
- The UML models operations by listing the operation name followed by a set of parentheses. A plus sign (+) before the name indicates that the operation is public.
- The UML models a parameter of an operation by listing the parameter name, followed by a colon and the parameter type between the parentheses following the operation name.
- The UML has its own data types similar to those of Java. Not all the UML data types have the same names as the corresponding Java types.
- The UML type String corresponds to the Java type String.
- The UML represents instance variables as an attribute name, followed by a colon and the type.
- Private attributes are preceded by a minus sign (–) in the UML.
- The UML indicates an operation's return type by placing a colon and the return type after the parentheses following the operation name.
- UML class diagrams do not specify return types for operations that do not return values.

Section 7.4 Initializing Objects with Constructors
- Keyword new requests memory from the system to store an object, then calls the corresponding class's constructor to initialize the object.
- A constructor can be used to initialize an object of a class when the object is created.
- Constructors can specify parameters but cannot specify return types.
- If a class does not define constructors, the compiler provides a default constructor with no parameters, and the class's instance variables are initialized to their default values.
- Like operations, the UML models constructors in the third compartment of a class diagram. To distinguish a constructor from a class's operations, the UML places the word "constructor" between guillemets (« and ») before the constructor's name.

Section 7.5 Case Study: Account Balances; Validating Constructor Arguments
- The default value for a field of type double is 0.0, and the default value for a field of type int is 0.
- You should validate constructor arguments to ensure that their values are valid before using them to initialize an object's data.

Section 7.6 Case Study: Card Shuffling and Dealing Simulation
- Method toString method is called implicitly when the object is used where a String is expected.

Terminology

access modifier 302
class instance creation expression 305
client of an object 306
compartment 307
constructor 305
data hiding 302

default constructor 308
default initial value 305
default package 308
extensible language 304
fully qualified class name 308
get method 306

Self-Review Exercises

7.1   Fill in the blanks in each of the following:

a) A house is to a blueprint as a(n) _____ is to a class.

b) Each class declaration that begins with keyword _____ must be stored in a file that has exactly the same name as the class and ends with the .java file-name extension.

c) Keyword _____ in a class declaration is followed immediately by the class's name.

d) Keyword _____ requests memory from the system to store an object, then calls the corresponding class's constructor to initialize the object.

e) Each parameter must specify both a(n) _____ and a(n) _____.

f) By default, classes that are compiled in the same directory are considered to be in the same package, known as the _____.

g) When each object of a class maintains its own copy of an attribute, the field that represents the attribute is also known as a(n) _____.

h) Keyword public is an access _____.

i) Scanner method _____ reads characters until a newline character is encountered, then returns those characters as a String.

j) Class String is in package _____.

k) A(n) _____ is not required if you always use a class's fully qualified class name.

7.2   State whether each of the following is *true* or *false*. If *false*, explain why.

a) An import declaration is not required when one class in a package uses another in the same package.

b) Variables or methods declared with access modifier private are accessible only to methods of the class in which they're declared.

c) A primitive-type variable can be used to invoke a method.

d) Variables declared in the body of a particular method are known as instance variables and can be used in all methods of the class.

e) Primitive-type local variables are initialized by default.

f) Reference-type instance variables are initialized by default to the value null.

7.3   What is the difference between a local variable and a field?

Answers to Self-Review Exercises

7.1   a) object. b) public. c) class. d) new. e) type, name. f) default package. g) instance variable. h) modifier. i) nextLine. j) java.lang. k) import declaration.

7.2   a) True. b) True. c) False. A reference to an object is required to invoke an object's methods. d) False. Such variables are called local variables and can be used only in the method in which they're declared. e) False. Primitive-type instance variables are initialized by default. Each local variable must explicitly be assigned a value. f) True.

7.3   A local variable is declared in the body of a method and can be used only from the point at which it is declared through the end of the method declaration. A field is declared in a class, but not in the body of any of the class's methods. Also, fields are accessible to all methods of the class. (We'll see an exception to this in Chapter 8, Classes and Objects: A Deeper Look.)

Exercises

7.4 What is the purpose of keyword new? Explain what happens when you use it.

7.5 What is a default constructor? How are an object's instance variables initialized if a class has only a default constructor?

7.6 Explain the purpose of an instance variable.

7.7 Most classes need to be imported before they can be used in an application. Why is every application allowed to use classes System and String without first importing them?

7.8 Explain how a program could use class Scanner without importing the class.

7.9 Explain why a class might provide a *set* method and a *get* method for an instance variable.

7.10 *(Modified GradeBook Class)* Modify class GradeBook (Fig. 7.4) as follows:
  a) Include a String instance variable that represents the name of the course's instructor.
  b) Provide a *set* method to change the instructor's name and a *get* method to retrieve it.
  c) Modify the constructor to specify two parameters—one for the course name and one for the instructor's name.
  d) Modify method displayMessage to output the welcome message and course name, followed by "This course is presented by: " and the instructor's name.
Use your modified class in a test application that demonstrates the class's new capabilities.

7.11 *(Modified Account Class)* Modify class Account (Fig. 7.7) to provide a method called debit that withdraws money from an Account. Ensure that the debit amount does not exceed the Account's balance. If it does, the balance should be left unchanged and the method should print a message indicating "Debit amount exceeded account balance." Modify class AccountTest (Fig. 7.8) to test method debit.

7.12 *(Invoice Class)* Create a class called Invoice that a hardware store might use to represent an invoice for an item sold at the store. An Invoice should include four pieces of information as instance variables—a part number (type String), a part description (type String), a quantity of the item being purchased (type int) and a price per item (double). Your class should have a constructor that initializes the four instance variables. Provide a *set* and a *get* method for each instance variable. In addition, provide a method named getInvoiceAmount that calculates the invoice amount (i.e., multiplies the quantity by the price per item), then returns the amount as a double value. If the quantity is not positive, it should be set to 0. If the price per item is not positive, it should be set to 0.0. Write a test application named InvoiceTest that demonstrates class Invoice's capabilities.

7.13 *(Employee Class)* Create an Employee class that includes a first name (type String), a last name (type String) and a monthly salary (double) instance variable. Provide a constructor that initializes the three instance variables. Provide a *set* and a *get* method for each instance variable. If the monthly salary is not positive, do not set its value. Write a test application named EmployeeTest that demonstrates class Employee's capabilities. Create two Employee objects and display each object's *yearly* salary. Then give each Employee a 10% raise and display each Employee's yearly salary again.

7.14 *(Date Class)* Create a class called Date that includes three instance variables—a month (type int), a day (type int) and a year (type int). Provide a constructor that initializes the three instance variables and assumes that the values provided are correct. Provide a *set* and a *get* method for each instance variable. Provide a method displayDate that displays the month, day and year separated by forward slashes (/). Write a test application named DateTest that demonstrates class Date's capabilities.

7.15 *(Card Shuffling and Dealing)* Modify the application of Fig. 7.12 to deal a five-card poker hand. Then modify class DeckOfCards of Fig. 7.11 to include methods that determine whether a hand contains
  a) a pair
  b) two pairs
  c) three of a kind (e.g., three jacks)

    d) four of a kind (e.g., four aces)

    e) a flush (i.e., all five cards of the same suit)

    f) a straight (i.e., five cards of consecutive face values)

    g) a full house (i.e., two cards of one face value and three cards of another face value)

[*Hint:* Add methods `getFace` and `getSuit` to class `Card` of Fig. 7.10.]

7.16   *(Card Shuffling and Dealing)* Use the methods developed in Exercise 7.15 to write an application that deals two five-card poker hands, evaluates each hand and determines which is better.

7.17   *(Card Shuffling and Dealing)* Modify the application of Figs. 7.10–7.12 to use `Face` and `Suit` enumerations to represent the faces and suits of the cards. Declare each of these enumerations as a `public` type in its own source-code file. Each `Card` should have a `Face` and a `Suit` instance variable. These should be initialized by the `Card` constructor. In class `DeckOfCards`, create an array of `Faces` that is initialized with the names of the constants in the `Face` enumeration and an array of `Suits` that is initialized with the names of the constants in the `Suit` enumeration. [*Note:* When you output an enumeration constant as a `String`, the name of the constant is displayed.]

Making a Difference

7.18   *(Target-Heart-Rate Calculator)* While exercising, you can use a heart-rate monitor to see that your heart rate stays within a safe range suggested by your trainers and doctors. According to the American Heart Association (AHA) (`www.americanheart.org/presenter.jhtml?identifier=4736`), the formula for calculating your *maximum heart rate* in beats per minute is 220 minus your age in years. Your *target heart rate* is a range that is 50–85% of your maximum heart rate. [*Note:* These formulas are estimates provided by the AHA. Maximum and target heart rates may vary based on the health, fitness and gender of the individual. Always consult a physician or qualified health care professional before beginning or modifying an exercise program.] Create a class called `HeartRates`. The class attributes should include the person's first name, last name and date of birth (consisting of separate attributes for the month, day and year of birth). Your class should have a constructor that receives this data as parameters. For each attribute provide *set* and *get* methods. The class also should include a method that calculates and returns the person's age (in years), a method that calculates and returns the person's maximum heart rate and a method that calculates and returns the person's target heart rate. Write a Java application that prompts for the person's information, instantiates an object of class `HeartRates` and prints the information from that object—including the person's first name, last name and date of birth—then calculates and prints the person's age in (years), maximum heart rate and target-heart-rate range.

7.19   *(Computerization of Health Records)* A health care issue that has been in the news lately is the computerization of health records. This possibility is being approached cautiously because of sensitive privacy and security concerns, among others. [We address such concerns in later exercises.] Computerizing health records could make it easier for patients to share their health profiles and histories among their various health care professionals. This could improve the quality of health care, help avoid drug conflicts and erroneous drug prescriptions, reduce costs and in emergencies, could save lives. In this exercise, you'll design a "starter" `HealthProfile` class for a person. The class attributes should include the person's first name, last name, gender, date of birth (consisting of separate attributes for the month, day and year of birth), height (in inches) and weight (in pounds). Your class should have a constructor that receives this data. For each attribute, provide *set* and *get* methods. The class also should include methods that calculate and return the user's age in years, maximum heart rate and target-heart-rate range (see Exercise 7.18), and body mass index (BMI; see Exercise 2.33). Write a Java application that prompts for the person's information, instantiates an object of class `HealthProfile` for that person and prints the information from that object—including the person's first name, last name, gender, date of birth, height and weight—then calculates and prints the person's age in years, BMI, maximum heart rate and target-heart-rate range. It should also display the "BMI values" chart from Exercise 2.33.

8

Classes and Objects: A Deeper Look

Instead of this absurd division into sexes, they ought to class people as static and dynamic.
—Evelyn Waugh

Is it a world to hide virtues in?
—William Shakespeare

But what, to serve our private ends,
Forbids the cheating of our friends?
—Charles Churchill

This above all: to thine own self be true.
—William Shakespeare

Don't be "consistent," but be simply true.
—Oliver Wendell Holmes, Jr.

Objectives

In this chapter you'll learn:

- Encapsulation and data hiding.
- To use keyword **this**.
- To use **static** variables and methods.
- To import **static** members of a class.
- To use the **enum** type to create sets of constants with unique identifiers.
- To declare **enum** constants with parameters.
- To organize classes in packages to promote reuse.

8.1 Introduction

We now take a deeper look at building classes, controlling access to members of a class and creating constructors. We discuss composition—a capability that allows a class to have references to objects of other classes as members. We reexamine the use of *set* and *get* methods. Recall that Section 5.10 introduced the basic enum type to declare a set of constants. In this chapter, we discuss the relationship between enum types and classes, demonstrating that an enum, like a class, can be declared in its own file with constructors, methods and fields. The chapter also discusses static class members and final instance variables in detail. We investigate issues such as software reusability and encapsulation. Finally, we explain how to organize classes in packages to help manage large applications and promote reuse, then show a special relationship between classes in the same package.

Chapter 9, Object-Oriented Programming: Inheritance, and Chapter 10, Object-Oriented Programming: Polymorphism, introduce two additional key object-oriented programming technologies.

8.2 Time Class Case Study

Our first example consists of two classes—Time1 (Fig. 8.1) and Time1Test (Fig. 8.2). Class Time1 represents the time of day. Class Time1Test is an application class in which the main method creates one object of class Time1 and invokes its methods. These classes must be declared in separate files because they're both public classes. The output of this program appears in Fig. 8.2.

Time1 Class Declaration

Class Time1's private int instance variables hour, minute and second (Fig. 8.1, lines 6–8) represent the time in universal-time format (24-hour clock format in which hours are in the range 0–23). Class Time1 contains public methods setTime (lines 12–17), toUniversalString (lines 20–23) and toString (lines 26–31). These methods are also called the **public services** or the **public interface** that the class provides to its clients.

```
 1   // Fig. 8.1: Time1.java
 2   // Time1 class declaration maintains the time in 24-hour format.
 3
 4   public class Time1
 5   {
 6      private int hour;   // 0 - 23
 7      private int minute; // 0 - 59
 8      private int second; // 0 - 59
 9
10      // set a new time value using universal time; ensure that
11      // the data remains consistent by setting invalid values to zero
12      public void setTime( int h, int m, int s )
13      {
14         hour = ( ( h >= 0 && h < 24 ) ? h : 0 ); // validate hour
15         minute = ( ( m >= 0 && m < 60 ) ? m : 0 ); // validate minute
16         second = ( ( s >= 0 && s < 60 ) ? s : 0 ); // validate second
17      } // end method setTime
18
19      // convert to String in universal-time format (HH:MM:SS)
20      public String toUniversalString()
21      {
22         return String.format( "%02d:%02d:%02d", hour, minute, second );
23      } // end method toUniversalString
24
25      // convert to String in standard-time format (H:MM:SS AM or PM)
26      public String toString()
27      {
28         return String.format( "%d:%02d:%02d %s",
29            ( ( hour == 0 || hour == 12 ) ? 12 : hour % 12 ),
30            minute, second, ( hour < 12 ? "AM" : "PM" ) );
31      } // end method toString
32   } // end class Time1
```

Fig. 8.1 | Time1 class declaration maintains the time in 24-hour format.

Default Constructor

In this example, class Time1 does not declare a constructor, so the class has a default constructor that is supplied by the compiler. Each instance variable implicitly receives the default value 0 for an int. Note that instance variables also can be initialized when they're declared in the class body, using the same initialization syntax as with a local variable.

Method setTime and Maintaining Consistent Data

Method setTime (lines 12–17) is a public method that declares three int parameters and uses them to set the time. A conditional expression tests each argument for validity to determine whether it is in a specified range. For example, the hour value (line 14) must be greater than or equal to 0 and less than 24, because universal-time format represents hours as integers from 0 to 23 (e.g., 1 PM is hour 13 and 11 PM is hour 23; midnight is hour 0 and noon is hour 12). Similarly, minute and second values (lines 15 and 16) must be greater than or equal to 0 and less than 60. Any values outside these ranges are set to zero to ensure that a Time1 object always contains *consistent data*—that is, the object's data values are always kept in range, even if the values provided as arguments to method setTime were *incorrect*. In this example, zero is a consistent value for hour, minute and second. In fact, when you create a Time1 object, its hour, minute and second are all set to zero by default; thus, a Time1 object contains consistent data from the moment it is created.

Correct vs. Consistent Values

It's important to distinguish between a *correct* value and a *consistent* value. A consistent value for minute must be in the range 0 to 59. A correct value for minute in a particular application, such as simply telling time, would be the actual minute at that time of day. Suppose you are setting the time on a watch. If the actual time is 17 minutes after the hour and you accidently set the watch to 19 minutes after, the 19 is a *consistent* value (0 to 59) but not a *correct* value. If you set the watch to 17 minutes after the hour, then 17 is a correct value—and a correct value is *always* a consistent value.

We've designed our setTime method so that when it receives an inconsistent value, it sets the corresponding instance variable to zero. This is certainly a *consistent* value, but it's unlikely to be *correct*. Is there a better approach? We could simply leave the object in its current state, without changing the instance variable. Given that Time objects begin in a consistent state (with hour, minute and second set to zero) and that the setTime method would reject any inconsistent values, the object would always be *guaranteed* to be in a consistent state. Often that state would be the object's last correct state, which some designers feel is superior to setting the instance variables to zero.

Potential Problems

A problem with the approaches discussed so far is that they do not inform the client code of inconsistent values. We could have the setTime return a value such as true if all the values are consistent and false if any of the values are inconsistent. The caller would check the return value, and if it were false, would attempt to set the time again. A problem with this approach is that some Java technologies (such as JavaBeans) require that the *set* methods return void. In Chapter 11, Exception Handling, you'll learn elegant techniques that enable your methods to indicate when inconsistent values are received.

Methods *toUniversalString and toString*

Method toUniversalString (lines 20–23) takes no arguments and returns a String in universal-time format, consisting of two digits each for the hour, minute and second. For example, if the time were 1:30:07 PM, the method would return 13:30:07. Line 22 uses static method **format** of class String to return a String containing the formatted hour, minute and second values, each with two digits and possibly a leading 0 (specified with the 0 flag). Method format is similar to method System.out.printf except that format returns a formatted String rather than displaying it in a command window. The formatted String is returned by method toUniversalString.

Method toString (lines 26–31) takes no arguments and returns a String in standard-time format, consisting of the hour, minute and second values separated by colons and followed by AM or PM (e.g., 1:27:06 PM). Like method toUniversalString, method toString uses static String method format to format the minute and second as two-digit values, with leading zeros if necessary. Line 29 uses a conditional operator (?:) to determine the value for hour in the String—if the hour is 0 or 12 (AM or PM), it appears as 12; otherwise, it appears as a value from 1 to 11. The conditional operator in line 30 determines whether AM or PM will be returned as part of the String.

Recall from Section 5.5 that all objects in Java have a toString method that returns a String representation of the object. We chose to return a String containing the time in standard-time format. Method `toString` can be called implicitly whenever a `Time1` object appears in the code where a `String` is needed, such as the value to output with a `%s` format specifier in a call to `System.out.printf`.

Using Class Time1

As you learned in Chapter 7, each class you declare represents a new type in Java. Therefore, after declaring class `Time1`, we can use it as a type in declarations such as

```
Time1 sunset; // sunset can hold a reference to a Time1 object
```

The `Time1Test` application class (Fig. 8.2) uses class `Time1`. Line 9 declares and creates a `Time1` object and assigns it to local variable `time`. Note that new implicitly invokes class `Time1`'s default constructor, since `Time1` does not declare any constructors. Lines 12–16 output the time first in universal-time format (by invoking `time`'s `toUniversalString` method in line 13), then in standard-time format (by explicitly invoking `time`'s `toString` method in line 15) to confirm that the `Time1` object was initialized properly.

```java
1   // Fig. 8.2: Time1Test.java
2   // Time1 object used in an application.
3
4   public class Time1Test
5   {
6      public static void main( String[] args )
7      {
8         // create and initialize a Time1 object
9         Time1 time = new Time1(); // invokes Time1 constructor
10
11        // output string representations of the time
12        System.out.print( "The initial universal time is: " );
13        System.out.println( time.toUniversalString() );
14        System.out.print( "The initial standard time is: " );
15        System.out.println( time.toString() );
16        System.out.println(); // output a blank line
17
18        // change time and output updated time
19        time.setTime( 13, 27, 6 );
20        System.out.print( "Universal time after setTime is: " );
21        System.out.println( time.toUniversalString() );
22        System.out.print( "Standard time after setTime is: " );
23        System.out.println( time.toString() );
24        System.out.println(); // output a blank line
25
26        // set time with invalid values; output updated time
27        time.setTime( 99, 99, 99 );
28        System.out.println( "After attempting invalid settings:" );
29        System.out.print( "Universal time: " );
30        System.out.println( time.toUniversalString() );
31        System.out.print( "Standard time: " );
32        System.out.println( time.toString() );
33      } // end main
34   } // end class Time1Test
```

Fig. 8.2 | Time1 object used in an application. (Part 1 of 2.)

```
The initial universal time is: 00:00:00
The initial standard time is: 12:00:00 AM

Universal time after setTime is: 13:27:06
Standard time after setTime is: 1:27:06 PM

After attempting invalid settings:
Universal time: 00:00:00
Standard time: 12:00:00 AM
```

Fig. 8.2 | Time1 object used in an application. (Part 2 of 2.)

Line 19 invokes method setTime of the time object to change the time. Then lines 20–24 output the time again in both formats to confirm that it was set correctly.

To illustrate that it maintains the object in a consistent state, line 27 calls method setTime with inconsistent arguments of 99 for the hour, minute and second. Lines 28–32 output the time again in both formats to confirm the object's consistent state, then the program terminates. The last two lines of the output show that the time is reset to midnight—the initial value of a Time1 object—after an attempt to set the time with three out-of-range values.

Notes on the Time1 *Class Declaration*

Consider several issues of class design with respect to class Time1. The instance variables hour, minute and second are each declared private. The actual data representation used within the class is of no concern to the class's clients. For example, it would be perfectly reasonable for Time1 to represent the time internally as the number of seconds since midnight or the number of minutes and seconds since midnight. Clients could use the same public methods and get the same results without being aware of this. (Exercise 8.5 asks you to represent the time in class Time1 as the number of seconds since midnight and show that indeed no change is visible to the clients of the class.)

Software Engineering Observation 8.1

Classes simplify programming, because the client can use only the public methods exposed by the class. Such methods are usually client oriented rather than implementation oriented. Clients are neither aware of, nor involved in, a class's implementation. Clients generally care about what the class does but not how the class does it.

Software Engineering Observation 8.2

Interfaces change less frequently than implementations. When an implementation changes, implementation-dependent code must change accordingly. Hiding the implementation reduces the possibility that other program parts will become dependent on class implementation details.

8.3 Controlling Access to Members

The access modifiers public and private control access to a class's variables and methods. In Chapter 9, we'll introduce the additional access modifier protected. As we stated in Section 8.2, the primary purpose of public methods is to present to the class's clients a view of the services the class provides (the class's public interface). Clients need not be concerned with how the class accomplishes its tasks. For this reason, the class's private variables and private methods (i.e., its implementation details) are not accessible to its clients.

Figure 8.3 demonstrates that `private` class members are not accessible outside the class. Lines 9–11 attempt to access directly the `private` instance variables `hour`, `minute` and `second` of the `Time1` object `time`. When this program is compiled, the compiler generates error messages that these `private` members are not accessible. [*Note:* This program assumes that the `Time1` class from Fig. 8.1 is used.]

 Common Programming Error 8.1

An attempt by a method that is not a member of a class to access a private member of that class is a compilation error.

```
1   // Fig. 8.3: MemberAccessTest.java
2   // Private members of class Time1 are not accessible.
3   public class MemberAccessTest
4   {
5      public static void main( String[] args )
6      {
7         Time1 time = new Time1(); // create and initialize Time1 object
8
9         time.hour = 7; // error: hour has private access in Time1
10        time.minute = 15; // error: minute has private access in Time1
11        time.second = 30; // error: second has private access in Time1
12     } // end main
13  } // end class MemberAccessTest
```

```
MemberAccessTest.java:9: hour has private access in Time1
      time.hour = 7; // error: hour has private access in Time1
          ^
MemberAccessTest.java:10: minute has private access in Time1
      time.minute = 15; // error: minute has private access in Time1
          ^
MemberAccessTest.java:11: second has private access in Time1
      time.second = 30; // error: second has private access in Time1
          ^
3 errors
```

Fig. 8.3 | Private members of class `Time1` are not accessible.

8.4 Referring to the Current Object's Members with the `this` Reference

Every object can access a reference to itself with keyword **this** (sometimes called the **this reference**). When a non-`static` method is called for a particular object, the method's body implicitly uses keyword `this` to refer to the object's instance variables and other methods. This enables the class's code to know which object should be manipulated. As you'll see in Fig. 8.4, you can also use keyword `this` explicitly in a non-`static` method's body. Section 8.5 shows another interesting use of keyword `this`. Section 8.11 explains why keyword `this` cannot be used in a `static` method.

We now demonstrate implicit and explicit use of the `this` reference (Fig. 8.4). Note that this example is the first in which we declare two classes in one file—class `ThisTest` is declared in lines 4–11, and class `SimpleTime` in lines 14–47. We do this to demonstrate that when you compile a .java file containing more than one class, the compiler produces a separate class file with the .class extension for every compiled class. In this case, two separate files are produced—SimpleTime.class and ThisTest.class. When one source-code (.java) file contains multiple class declarations, the compiler places both class files for those classes in the same directory. Note also in Fig.8.4 that only class ThisTest is declared public. A source-code file can contain only one public class—otherwise, a compilation error occurs. Non-public classes can be used only by other classes in the same package. So, in this example, class SimpleTime can be used only by class ThisTest.

```java
1   // Fig. 8.4: ThisTest.java
2   // this used implicitly and explicitly to refer to members of an object.
3
4   public class ThisTest
5   {
6      public static void main( String[] args )
7      {
8         SimpleTime time = new SimpleTime( 15, 30, 19 );
9         System.out.println( time.buildString() );
10      } // end main
11   } // end class ThisTest
12
13   // class SimpleTime demonstrates the "this" reference
14   class SimpleTime
15   {
16      private int hour; // 0-23
17      private int minute; // 0-59
18      private int second; // 0-59
19
20      // if the constructor uses parameter names identical to
21      // instance variable names the "this" reference is
22      // required to distinguish between names
23      public SimpleTime( int hour, int minute, int second )
24      {
25         this.hour = hour; // set "this" object's hour
26         this.minute = minute; // set "this" object's minute
27         this.second = second; // set "this" object's second
28      } // end SimpleTime constructor
29
30      // use explicit and implicit "this" to call toUniversalString
31      public String buildString()
32      {
33         return String.format( "%24s: %s\n%24s: %s",
34            "this.toUniversalString()", this.toUniversalString(),
35            "toUniversalString()", toUniversalString() );
36      } // end method buildString
37
38      // convert to String in universal-time format (HH:MM:SS)
39      public String toUniversalString()
40      {
41         // "this" is not required here to access instance variables,
42         // because method does not have local variables with same
43         // names as instance variables
```

Fig. 8.4 | this used implicitly and explicitly to refer to members of an object. (Part 1 of 2.)

```
44              return String.format( "%02d:%02d:%02d",
45                 this.hour, this.minute, this.second );
46      } // end method toUniversalString
47  } // end class SimpleTime
```

```
this.toUniversalString(): 15:30:19
    toUniversalString(): 15:30:19
```

Fig. 8.4 | this used implicitly and explicitly to refer to members of an object. (Part 2 of 2.)

Class SimpleTime (lines 14–47) declares three private instance variables—hour, minute and second (lines 16–18). The constructor (lines 23–28) receives three int arguments to initialize a SimpleTime object. Note that we used parameter names for the constructor (line 23) that are identical to the class's instance-variable names (lines 16–18). We don't recommend this practice, but we did it here to shadow (hide) the corresponding instance variables so that we could illustrate a case in which explicit use of the this reference is required. If a method contains a local variable with the same name as a field, that method will refer to the local variable rather than the field. In this case, the local variable shadows the field in the method's scope. However, the method can use the this reference to refer to the shadowed field explicitly, as shown on the left sides of the assignments in lines 25–27 for SimpleTime's shadowed instance variables.

Method buildString (lines 31–36) returns a String created by a statement that uses the this reference explicitly and implicitly. Line 34 uses it explicitly to call method toUniversalString. Line 35 it implicitly to call the same method. Note that both lines perform the same task. You typically will not use this explicitly to reference other methods within the current object. Also, note that line 45 in method toUniversalString explicitly uses the this reference to access each instance variable. This is not necessary here, because the method does not have any local variables that shadow the instance variables of the class.

Common Programming Error 8.2

It's often a logic error when a method contains a parameter or local variable that has the same name as a field of the class. In this case, use reference this if you wish to access the field of the class—otherwise, the method parameter or local variable will be referenced.

Error-Prevention Tip 8.1

Avoid method-parameter names or local-variable names that conflict with field names. This helps prevent subtle, hard-to-locate bugs.

Performance Tip 8.1

Java conserves storage by maintaining only one copy of each method per class—this method is invoked by every object of the class. Each object, on the other hand, has its own copy of the class's instance variables (i.e., non-static fields). Each method of the class implicitly uses this to determine the specific object of the class to manipulate.

Application class ThisTest (lines 4–11) demonstrates class SimpleTime. Line 8 creates an instance of class SimpleTime and invokes its constructor. Line 9 invokes the object's buildString method, then displays the results.

8.5 Time Class Case Study: Overloaded Constructors

As you know, you can declare your own constructor to specify how objects of a class should be initialized. Next, we demonstrate a class with several overloaded constructors that enable objects of that class to be initialized in different ways. To overload constructors, simply provide multiple constructor declarations with different signatures. Recall from Section 5.12 that the compiler differentiates signatures by the *number* of parameters, the *types* of the parameters and the *order* of the parameter types in each signature.

Class *Time2* with Overloaded Constructors

The default constructor for class Time1 (Fig. 8.1) initialized hour, minute and second to their default 0 values (which is midnight in universal time). The default constructor does not enable the class's clients to initialize the time with specific nonzero values. Class Time2 (Fig. 8.5) contains five overloaded constructors that provide convenient ways to initialize objects of the new class Time2. Each constructor initializes the object to begin in a consistent state. In this program, four of the constructors invoke a fifth, which in turn calls method setTime to ensure that the value supplied for hour is in the range 0 to 23, and the values for minute and second are each in the range 0 to 59. If a value is out of range, it's set to zero by setTime (once again ensuring that each instance variable remains in a consistent state). The compiler invokes the appropriate constructor by matching the number, types and order of the types of the arguments specified in the constructor call with the number, types and order of the types of the parameters specified in each constructor declaration. Note that class Time2 also provides *set* and *get* methods for each instance variable.

```java
1   // Fig. 8.5: Time2.java
2   // Time2 class declaration with overloaded constructors.
3
4   public class Time2
5   {
6      private int hour; // 0 - 23
7      private int minute; // 0 - 59
8      private int second; // 0 - 59
9
10     // Time2 no-argument constructor: initializes each instance variable
11     // to zero; ensures that Time2 objects start in a consistent state
12     public Time2()
13     {
14        this( 0, 0, 0 ); // invoke Time2 constructor with three arguments
15     } // end Time2 no-argument constructor
16
17     // Time2 constructor: hour supplied, minute and second defaulted to 0
18     public Time2( int h )
19     {
20        this( h, 0, 0 ); // invoke Time2 constructor with three arguments
21     } // end Time2 one-argument constructor
22
23     // Time2 constructor: hour and minute supplied, second defaulted to 0
24     public Time2( int h, int m )
25     {
```

Fig. 8.5 | Time2 class with overloaded constructors. (Part 1 of 3.)

```
26          this( h, m, 0 ); // invoke Time2 constructor with three arguments
27      } // end Time2 two-argument constructor
28
29      // Time2 constructor: hour, minute and second supplied
30      public Time2( int h, int m, int s )
31      {
32          setTime( h, m, s ); // invoke setTime to validate time
33      } // end Time2 three-argument constructor
34
35      // Time2 constructor: another Time2 object supplied
36      public Time2( Time2 time )
37      {
38          // invoke Time2 three-argument constructor
39          this( time.getHour(), time.getMinute(), time.getSecond() );
40      } // end Time2 constructor with a Time2 object argument
41
42      // Set Methods
43      // set a new time value using universal time; ensure that
44      // the data remains consistent by setting invalid values to zero
45      public void setTime( int h, int m, int s )
46      {
47          setHour( h ); // set the hour
48          setMinute( m ); // set the minute
49          setSecond( s ); // set the second
50      } // end method setTime
51
52      // validate and set hour
53      public void setHour( int h )
54      {
55          hour = ( ( h >= 0 && h < 24 ) ? h : 0 );
56      } // end method setHour
57
58      // validate and set minute
59      public void setMinute( int m )
60      {
61          minute = ( ( m >= 0 && m < 60 ) ? m : 0 );
62      } // end method setMinute
63
64      // validate and set second
65      public void setSecond( int s )
66      {
67          second = ( ( s >= 0 && s < 60 ) ? s : 0 );
68      } // end method setSecond
69
70      // Get Methods
71      // get hour value
72      public int getHour()
73      {
74          return hour;
75      } // end method getHour
76
77      // get minute value
78      public int getMinute()
79      {
```

Fig. 8.5 | Time2 class with overloaded constructors. (Part 2 of 3.)

```
80          return minute;
81       } // end method getMinute
82
83       // get second value
84       public int getSecond()
85       {
86          return second;
87       } // end method getSecond
88
89       // convert to String in universal-time format (HH:MM:SS)
90       public String toUniversalString()
91       {
92          return String.format(
93             "%02d:%02d:%02d", getHour(), getMinute(), getSecond() );
94       } // end method toUniversalString
95
96       // convert to String in standard-time format (H:MM:SS AM or PM)
97       public String toString()
98       {
99          return String.format( "%d:%02d:%02d %s",
100            ( (getHour() == 0 || getHour() == 12) ? 12 : getHour() % 12 ),
101            getMinute(), getSecond(), ( getHour() < 12 ? "AM" : "PM" ) );
102      } // end method toString
103   } // end class Time2
```

Fig. 8.5 | Time2 class with overloaded constructors. (Part 3 of 3.)

Class Time2's Constructors

Lines 12–15 declare a so-called **no-argument constructor** that is invoked without arguments. Once you declare any constructors in a class, the compiler will not provide a default constructor. This no-argument constructor ensures that class Time2's clients can create Time2 objects with default values. Such a constructor simply initializes the object as specified in the constructor's body. In the body, we introduce a use of the this reference that is allowed only as the first statement in a constructor's body. Line 14 uses this in method-call syntax to invoke the Time2 constructor that takes three arguments (lines 30–33). The no-argument constructor passes values of 0 for the hour, minute and second to the constructor with three parameters. Using the this reference as shown here is a popular way to reuse initialization code provided by another of the class's constructors rather than defining similar code in the no-argument constructor's body. We use this syntax in four of the five Time2 constructors to make the class easier to maintain and modify. If we need to change how objects of class Time2 are initialized, only the constructor that the class's other constructors call will need to be modified. In fact, even that constructor might not need modification in this example. That constructor simply calls the setTime method to perform the actual initialization, so it's possible that the changes the class might require would be localized to the *set* methods.

Common Programming Error 8.3

It's a syntax error when this is used in a constructor's body to call another constructor of the same class if that call is not the first statement in the constructor. It's also a syntax error when a method attempts to invoke a constructor directly via this.

Lines 18–21 declare a `Time2` constructor with a single `int` parameter representing the hour, which is passed with 0 for the `minute` and `second` to the constructor at lines 30–33. Lines 24–27 declare a `Time2` constructor that receives two `int` parameters representing the hour and `minute`, which are passed with 0 for the `second` to the constructor at lines 30–33. Like the no-argument constructor, each of these constructors invokes the constructor at lines 30–33 to minimize code duplication. Lines 30–33 declare the `Time2` constructor that receives three `int` parameters representing the hour, `minute` and `second`. This constructor calls `setTime` to initialize the instance variables to consistent values.

Common Programming Error 8.4

A constructor can call methods of the class. Be aware that the instance variables might not yet be in a consistent state, because the constructor is in the process of initializing the object. Using instance variables before they have been initialized properly is a logic error.

Lines 36–40 declare a `Time2` constructor that receives a reference to another `Time2` object. In this case, the values from the `Time2` argument are passed to the three-argument constructor at lines 30–33 to initialize the hour, `minute` and `second`. Note that line 39 could have directly accessed the hour, `minute` and `second` values of the constructor's argument `time` with the expressions `time.hour`, `time.minute` and `time.second`—even though hour, `minute` and `second` are declared as `private` variables of class `Time2`. This is due to a special relationship between objects of the same class. We'll see in a moment why it's preferable to use the *get* methods.

Software Engineering Observation 8.3

When one object of a class has a reference to another object of the same class, the first object can access all the second object's data and methods (including those that are `private`).

Notes Regarding Class *Time2's* Set *and* Get *Methods and Constructors*

Note that `Time2`'s *set* and *get* methods are called throughout the class. In particular, method `setTime` calls methods `setHour`, `setMinute` and `setSecond` in lines 47–49, and methods `toUniversalString` and `toString` call methods `getHour`, `getMinute` and `getSecond` in line 93 and lines 100–101, respectively. In each case, these methods could have accessed the class's private data directly without calling the *set* and *get* methods. However, consider changing the representation of the time from three `int` values (requiring 12 bytes of memory) to a single `int` value representing the total number of seconds that have elapsed since midnight (requiring only 4 bytes of memory). If we made such a change, only the bodies of the methods that access the `private` data directly would need to change—in particular, the individual *set* and *get* methods for the hour, `minute` and `second`. There would be no need to modify the bodies of methods `setTime`, `toUniversalString` or `toString` because they do not access the data directly. Designing the class in this manner reduces the likelihood of programming errors when altering the class's implementation.

Similarly, each `Time2` constructor could be written to include a copy of the appropriate statements from methods `setHour`, `setMinute` and `setSecond`. Doing so may be slightly more efficient, because the extra constructor call and call to `setTime` are eliminated. However, duplicating statements in multiple methods or constructors makes changing the class's internal data representation more difficult. Having the `Time2` constructors call the constructor with three arguments (or even call `setTime` directly) requires any changes to the implementation of `setTime` to be made only once. Also, the compiler can optimize programs by removing calls to simple methods and replacing them with the expanded code of their declarations—a technique known as inlining the code, which improves program performance.

Software Engineering Observation 8.4

When implementing a method of a class, use the class's set *and* get *methods to access the class's* private *data. This simplifies code maintenance and reduces the likelihood of errors.*

Using Class Time2's Overloaded Constructors

Class Time2Test (Fig. 8.6) invokes the overloaded Time2 constructors (lines 8–13). Line 8 invokes the no-argument constructor (Fig. 8.5, lines 12–15). Lines 9–13 of the program demonstrate passing arguments to the other Time2 constructors. Line 9 invokes the constructor at lines 18–21 of Fig. 8.5. Line 10 invokes the constructor at lines 24–27 of Fig. 8.5. Lines 11–12 invoke the constructor at lines 30–33 of Fig. 8.5. Line 13 invokes the constructor at lines 36–40 of Fig. 8.5. The application displays the String representation of each Time2 object to confirm that it was initialized properly.

```java
1  // Fig. 8.6: Time2Test.java
2  // Overloaded constructors used to initialize Time2 objects.
3
4  public class Time2Test
5  {
6     public static void main( String[] args )
7     {
8        Time2 t1 = new Time2(); // 00:00:00
9        Time2 t2 = new Time2( 2 ); // 02:00:00
10       Time2 t3 = new Time2( 21, 34 ); // 21:34:00
11       Time2 t4 = new Time2( 12, 25, 42 ); // 12:25:42
12       Time2 t5 = new Time2( 27, 74, 99 ); // 00:00:00
13       Time2 t6 = new Time2( t4 ); // 12:25:42
14
15       System.out.println( "Constructed with:" );
16       System.out.println( "t1: all arguments defaulted" );
17       System.out.printf( "   %s\n", t1.toUniversalString() );
18       System.out.printf( "   %s\n", t1.toString() );
19
20       System.out.println(
21          "t2: hour specified; minute and second defaulted" );
22       System.out.printf( "   %s\n", t2.toUniversalString() );
23       System.out.printf( "   %s\n", t2.toString() );
24
25       System.out.println(
26          "t3: hour and minute specified; second defaulted" );
27       System.out.printf( "   %s\n", t3.toUniversalString() );
28       System.out.printf( "   %s\n", t3.toString() );
29
30       System.out.println( "t4: hour, minute and second specified" );
31       System.out.printf( "   %s\n", t4.toUniversalString() );
32       System.out.printf( "   %s\n", t4.toString() );
33
34       System.out.println( "t5: all invalid values specified" );
```

Fig. 8.6 | Overloaded constructors used to initialize Time2 objects. (Part 1 of 2.)

```
35          System.out.printf( "    %s\n", t5.toUniversalString() );
36          System.out.printf( "    %s\n", t5.toString() );
37
38          System.out.println( "t6: Time2 object t4 specified" );
39          System.out.printf( "    %s\n", t6.toUniversalString() );
40          System.out.printf( "    %s\n", t6.toString() );
41       } // end main
42    } // end class Time2Test
```

```
t1: all arguments defaulted
   00:00:00
   12:00:00 AM
t2: hour specified; minute and second defaulted
   02:00:00
   2:00:00 AM
t3: hour and minute specified; second defaulted
   21:34:00
   9:34:00 PM
t4: hour, minute and second specified
   12:25:42
   12:25:42 PM
t5: all invalid values specified
   00:00:00
   12:00:00 AM
t6: Time2 object t4 specified
   12:25:42
   12:25:42 PM
```

Fig. 8.6 | Overloaded constructors used to initialize `Time2` objects. (Part 2 of 2.)

8.6 Default and No-Argument Constructors

Every class must have at least one constructor. If you do not provide any constructors in a class's declaration, the compiler creates a default constructor that takes no arguments when it's invoked. The default constructor initializes the instance variables to the initial values specified in their declarations or to their default values (zero for primitive numeric types, `false` for `boolean` values and `null` for references). In Section 9.4.1, you'll learn that the default constructor performs another task also.

If your class declares constructors, the compiler will not create a default constructor. In this case, you must declare a no-argument constructor if default initialization is required. Like a default constructor, a no-argument constructor is invoked with empty parentheses. Note that the `Time2` no-argument constructor (lines 12–15 of Fig. 8.5) explicitly initializes a `Time2` object by passing to the three-argument constructor 0 for each parameter. Since 0 is the default value for `int` instance variables, the no-argument constructor in this example could actually be declared with an empty body. In this case, each instance variable would receive its default value when the no-argument constructor was called. If we omit the no-argument constructor, clients of this class would not be able to create a `Time2` object with the expression `new Time2()`.

Common Programming Error 8.5

A compilation error occurs if a program attempts to initialize an object of a class by passing the wrong number or types of arguments to the class's constructor.

Software Engineering Observation 8.5

Java allows other methods of the class besides its constructors to have the same name as the class and to specify return types. Such methods are not constructors and will not be called when an object of the class is instantiated. Java determines which methods are constructors by locating those that have the same name as the class and do not specify a return type.

8.7 Notes on *Set* and *Get* Methods

As you know, a class's `private` fields can be manipulated only by its methods. A typical manipulation might be the adjustment of a customer's bank balance (e.g., a `private` instance variable of a class `BankAccount`) by a method `computeInterest`. Classes often provide `public` methods to allow clients of the class to *set* (i.e., assign values to) or *get* (i.e., obtain the values of) `private` instance variables.

As a naming example, a method that sets instance variable `interestRate` would typically be named `setInterestRate` and a method that gets the `interestRate` would typically be called `getInterestRate`. *Set* methods are also commonly called **mutator methods**, because they typically change an object's state—i.e., modify the values of instance variables. *Get* methods are also commonly called **accessor methods** or **query methods**.

Set *and* Get *Methods vs. `public` Data*

It would seem that providing *set* and *get* capabilities is essentially the same as making the instance variables `public`. This is one of the subtleties that makes Java so desirable for software engineering. A `public` instance variable can be read or written by any method that has a reference to an object that contains that variable. If an instance variable is declared `private`, a `public` *get* method certainly allows other methods to access the it, but the *get* method can control how the client can access it. For example, a *get* method might control the format of the data it returns and thus shield the client code from the actual data representation. A `public` *set* method can—and should—carefully scrutinize attempts to modify the variable's value to ensure that the new value is consistent for that data item. For example, an attempt to *set* the day of the month to 37 would be rejected, an attempt to *set* a person's weight to a negative value would be rejected, and so on. Thus, although *set* and *get* methods provide access to `private` data, the access is restricted by the implementation of the methods. This helps promote good software engineering.

Validity Checking in Set *Methods*

The benefits of data integrity do not follow automatically simply because instance variables are declared `private`—you must provide validity checking. Java enables you to design better programs in a convenient manner. A class's *set* methods could return values indicating that attempts were made to assign invalid data to objects of the class. A client of the class could test the return value of a *set* method to determine whether the client's attempt to modify the object was successful and to take appropriate action. Typically, however, *set* methods have `void` return type and use exception handling to indicate attempts to assign invalid data. We discuss exception handling in detail in Chapter 11.

Software Engineering Observation 8.6

When appropriate, provide `public` methods to change and retrieve the values of `private` instance variables. This architecture helps hide the implementation of a class from its clients, which improves program modifiability.

> ### Error-Prevention Tip 8.2
> *Using* set *and* get *methods helps you create classes that are easier to debug and maintain. If only one method performs a particular task, such as setting the hour in a Time2 object, it's easier to debug and maintain the class. If the hour is not being set properly, the code that actually modifies instance variable hour is localized to one method's body—setHour. Thus, your debugging efforts can be focused on method setHour.*

Predicate Methods

Another common use for accessor methods is to test whether a condition is true or false—such methods are often called **predicate methods.** An example would be class ArrayList's isEmpty method, which returns true if the ArrayList is empty. A program might test isEmpty before attempting to read another item from an ArrayList.

8.8 Composition

A class can have references to objects of other classes as members. This is called **composition** and is sometimes referred to as a *has-a* relationship. For example, an AlarmClock object needs to know the current time and the time when it's supposed to sound its alarm, so it's reasonable to include two references to Time objects in an AlarmClock object.

Our example of composition contains three classes—Date (Fig. 8.7), Employee (Fig. 8.8) and EmployeeTest (Fig. 8.9). Class Date (Fig. 8.7) declares instance variables month, day and year (lines 6–8) to represent a date. The constructor receives three int parameters. Line 14 invokes utility method checkMonth (lines 23–33) to validate the month—an out-of-range value is set to 1 to maintain a consistent state. Line 15 assumes that the value for year is correct and does not validate it. Line 16 invokes utility method checkDay (lines 36–52) to validate the value for day based on the current month and year. Lines 42–43 determine whether the day is correct based on the number of days in the particular month. If the day is not correct, lines 46–47 determine whether the month is February, the day is 29 and the year is a leap year. If lines 42–48 do not return a correct value for day, line 51 returns 1 to maintain the Date in a consistent state. Note that lines 18–19 in the constructor output the this reference as a String. Since this is a reference to the current Date object, the object's toString method (lines 55–58) is called implicitly to obtain the object's String representation.

```
 1   // Fig. 8.7: Date.java
 2   // Date class declaration.
 3
 4   public class Date
 5   {
 6      private int month; // 1-12
 7      private int day; // 1-31 based on month
 8      private int year; // any year
 9
10      // constructor: call checkMonth to confirm proper value for month;
11      // call checkDay to confirm proper value for day
12      public Date( int theMonth, int theDay, int theYear )
13      {
```

Fig. 8.7 | Date class declaration. (Part 1 of 2.)

```
14          month = checkMonth( theMonth ); // validate month
15          year = theYear; // could validate year
16          day = checkDay( theDay ); // validate day
17
18          System.out.printf(
19             "Date object constructor for date %s\n", this );
20       } // end Date constructor
21
22       // utility method to confirm proper month value
23       private int checkMonth( int testMonth )
24       {
25          if ( testMonth > 0 && testMonth <= 12 ) // validate month
26             return testMonth;
27          else // month is invalid
28          {
29             System.out.printf(
30                "Invalid month (%d) set to 1.", testMonth );
31             return 1; // maintain object in consistent state
32          } // end else
33       } // end method checkMonth
34
35       // utility method to confirm proper day value based on month and year
36       private int checkDay( int testDay )
37       {
38          int[] daysPerMonth =
39             { 0, 31, 28, 31, 30, 31, 30, 31, 31, 30, 31, 30, 31 };
40
41          // check if day in range for month
42          if ( testDay > 0 && testDay <= daysPerMonth[ month ] )
43             return testDay;
44
45          // check for leap year
46          if ( month == 2 && testDay == 29 && ( year % 400 == 0 ||
47             ( year % 4 == 0 && year % 100 != 0 ) ) )
48             return testDay;
49
50          System.out.printf( "Invalid day (%d) set to 1.", testDay );
51          return 1;  // maintain object in consistent state
52       } // end method checkDay
53
54       // return a String of the form month/day/year
55       public String toString()
56       {
57          return String.format( "%d/%d/%d", month, day, year );
58       } // end method toString
59    } // end class Date
```

Fig. 8.7 | Date class declaration. (Part 2 of 2.)

Class Employee (Fig. 8.8) has instance variables firstName, lastName, birthDate and hireDate. Members firstName and lastName (lines 6–7) are references to String objects. Members birthDate and hireDate (lines 8–9) are references to Date objects. This demonstrates that a class can have as instance variables references to objects of other classes. The Employee constructor (lines 12–19) takes four parameters—first, last, dateOfBirth and dateOfHire. The objects referenced by the parameters are assigned to the

Employee object's instance variables. Note that when class Employee's toString method is called, it returns a String containing the employee's name and the String representations of the two Date objects. Each of these Strings is obtained with an implicit call to the Date class's toString method.

```
1   // Fig. 8.8: Employee.java
2   // Employee class with references to other objects.
3
4   public class Employee
5   {
6       private String firstName;
7       private String lastName;
8       private Date birthDate;
9       private Date hireDate;
10
11      // constructor to initialize name, birth date and hire date
12      public Employee( String first, String last, Date dateOfBirth,
13         Date dateOfHire )
14      {
15         firstName = first;
16         lastName = last;
17         birthDate = dateOfBirth;
18         hireDate = dateOfHire;
19      } // end Employee constructor
20
21      // convert Employee to String format
22      public String toString()
23      {
24         return String.format( "%s, %s  Hired: %s  Birthday: %s",
25            lastName, firstName, hireDate, birthDate );
26      } // end method toString
27   } // end class Employee
```

Fig. 8.8 | Employee class with references to other objects.

Class EmployeeTest (Fig. 8.9) creates two Date objects (lines 8–9) to represent an Employee's birthday and hire date, respectively. Line 10 creates an Employee and initializes its instance variables by passing to the constructor two Strings (representing the Employee's first and last names) and two Date objects (representing the birthday and hire date). Line 12 implicitly invokes the Employee's toString method to display the values of its instance variables and demonstrate that the object was initialized properly.

```
1   // Fig. 8.9: EmployeeTest.java
2   // Composition demonstration.
3
4   public class EmployeeTest
5   {
6      public static void main( String[] args )
7      {
8         Date birth = new Date( 7, 24, 1949 );
9         Date hire = new Date( 3, 12, 1988 );
```

Fig. 8.9 | Composition demonstration. (Part 1 of 2.)

```
10           Employee employee = new Employee( "Bob", "Blue", birth, hire );
11
12           System.out.println( employee );
13        } // end main
14     } // end class EmployeeTest
```

```
Date object constructor for date 7/24/1949
Date object constructor for date 3/12/1988
Blue, Bob  Hired: 3/12/1988  Birthday: 7/24/1949
```

Fig. 8.9 | Composition demonstration. (Part 2 of 2.)

8.9 Enumerations

In Fig. 5.8 (Craps.java) we introduced the basic enum type, which defines a set of constants represented as unique identifiers. In that program the enum constants represented the game's status. In this section we discuss the relationship between enum types and classes. Like classes, all enum types are reference types. An enum type is declared with an **enum declaration**, which is a comma-separated list of enum constants—the declaration may optionally include other components of traditional classes, such as constructors, fields and methods. Each enum declaration declares an enum class with the following restrictions:

1. enum constants are implicitly final, because they declare constants that shouldn't be modified.

2. enum constants are implicitly static.

3. Any attempt to create an object of an enum type with operator new results in a compilation error.

The enum constants can be used anywhere constants can be used, such as in the case labels of switch statements and to control enhanced for statements.

Figure 8.10 illustrates how to declare instance variables, a constructor and methods in an enum type. The enum declaration (lines 5–37) contains two parts—the enum constants and the other members of the enum type. The first part (lines 8–13) declares six enum constants. Each is optionally followed by arguments which are passed to the **enum constructor** (lines 20–24). Like the constructors you've seen in classes, an enum constructor can specify any number of parameters and can be overloaded. In this example, the enum constructor has two String parameters, hence each enum constant is followed by parentheses containing two String arguments. The second part (lines 16–36) declares the other members of the enum type—two instance variables (lines 16–17), a constructor (lines 20–24) and two methods (lines 27–30 and 33–36).

```
1    // Fig. 8.10: Book.java
2    // Declaring an enum type with constructor and explicit instance fields
3    // and accessors for these fields
```

Fig. 8.10 | Declaring an enum type with constructor and explicit instance fields and accessors for these fields. (Part 1 of 2.)

```
4
5    public enum Book
6    {
7       // declare constants of enum type
8       JHTP( "Java How to Program", "2010" ),
9       CHTP( "C How to Program", "2007" ),
10      IW3HTP( "Internet & World Wide Web How to Program", "2008" ),
11      CPPHTP( "C++ How to Program", "2008" ),
12      VBHTP( "Visual Basic 2008 How to Program", "2009" ),
13      CSHARPHTP( "Visual C# 2008 How to Program", "2009" );
14
15      // instance fields
16      private final String title; // book title
17      private final String copyrightYear; // copyright year
18
19      // enum constructor
20      Book( String bookTitle, String year )
21      {
22         title = bookTitle;
23         copyrightYear = year;
24      } // end enum Book constructor
25
26      // accessor for field title
27      public String getTitle()
28      {
29         return title;
30      } // end method getTitle
31
32      // accessor for field copyrightYear
33      public String getCopyrightYear()
34      {
35         return copyrightYear;
36      } // end method getCopyrightYear
37   } // end enum Book
```

Fig. 8.10 | Declaring an enum type with constructor and explicit instance fields and accessors for these fields. (Part 2 of 2.)

Lines 16–17 declare the instance variables title and copyrightYear. Each enum constant in Book is actually an object of type Book that has its own copy of instance variables title and copyrightYear. The constructor (lines 20–24) takes two String parameters, one that specifies the book's title and one that specifies its copyright year. Lines 22–23 assign these parameters to the instance variables. Lines 27–36 declare two methods, which return the book title and copyright year, respectively.

Figure 8.11 tests the enum type Book and illustrates how to iterate through a range of enum constants. For every enum, the compiler generates the static method **values** (called in line 12) that returns an array of the enum's constants in the order they were declared. Lines 12–14 use the enhanced for statement to display all the constants declared in the enum Book. Line 14 invokes the enum Book's getTitle and getCopyrightYear methods to get the title and copyright year associated with the constant. Note that when an enum constant is converted to a String (e.g., book in line 13), the constant's identifier is used as the String representation (e.g., JHTP for the first enum constant).

```
1   // Fig. 8.11: EnumTest.java
2   // Testing enum type Book.
3   import java.util.EnumSet;
4
5   public class EnumTest
6   {
7      public static void main( String[] args )
8      {
9         System.out.println( "All books:\n" );
10
11        // print all books in enum Book
12        for ( Book book : Book.values() )
13           System.out.printf( "%-10s%-45s%s\n", book,
14              book.getTitle(), book.getCopyrightYear() );
15
16        System.out.println( "\nDisplay a range of enum constants:\n" );
17
18        // print first four books
19        for ( Book book : EnumSet.range( Book.JHTP, Book.CPPHTP ) )
20           System.out.printf( "%-10s%-45s%s\n", book,
21              book.getTitle(), book.getCopyrightYear() );
22     } // end main
23  } // end class EnumTest
```

```
All books:

JHTP       Java How to Program                            2010
CHTP       C How to Program                               2007
IW3HTP     Internet & World Wide Web How to Program       2008
CPPHTP     C++ How to Program                             2008
VBHTP      Visual Basic 2008 How to Program               2009
CSHARPHTP  Visual C# 2008 How to Program                  2009

Display a range of enum constants:

JHTP       Java How to Program                            2010
CHTP       C How to Program                               2007
IW3HTP     Internet & World Wide Web How to Program       2008
CPPHTP     C++ How to Program                             2008
```

Fig. 8.11 | Testing an enum type.

Lines 19–21 use the static method **range** of class **EnumSet** (declared in package java.util) to display a range of the enum Book's constants. Method range takes two parameters—the first and the last enum constants in the range—and returns an EnumSet that contains all the constants between these two constants, inclusive. For example, the expression EnumSet.range(Book.JHTP, Book.CPPHTP) returns an EnumSet containing Book.JHTP, Book.CHTP, Book.IW3HTP and Book.CPPHTP. The enhanced for statement can be used with an EnumSet just as it can with an array, so lines 12–14 use it to display the title and copyright year of every book in the EnumSet. Class EnumSet provides several other static methods for creating sets of enum constants from the same enum type. For more information on class EnumSet, visit java.sun.com/javase/6/docs/api/java/util/EnumSet.html.

Common Programming Error 8.6

In an enum declaration, it's a syntax error to declare enum constants after the enum type's constructors, fields and methods.

8.10 Garbage Collection and Method `finalize`

Every class in Java has the methods of class `Object` (package `java.lang`), one of which is the `finalize` method. This method is rarely used because it can cause performance problems and there is some uncertainty as to whether it will get called. Nevertheless, because `finalize` is part of every class, we discuss it here to help you understand its intended purpose. The complete details of the `finalize` method are beyond the scope of this book, and most programmers should not use it—you'll soon see why. You'll learn more about class `Object` in Chapter 9.

Every object uses system resources, such as memory. We need a disciplined way to give resources back to the system when they're no longer needed; otherwise, "resource leaks" might occur that would prevent them from being reused by your program or possibly by other programs. The JVM performs automatic garbage collection to reclaim the memory occupied by objects that are no longer used. When there are no more references to an object, the object is eligible to be collected. This typically occurs when the JVM executes its garbage collector. So, memory leaks that are common in other languages like C and C++ (because memory is not automatically reclaimed in those languages) are less likely in Java, but some can still happen in subtle ways. Other types of resource leaks can occur. For example, an application may open a file on disk to modify its contents. If it does not close the file, the application must terminate before any other application can use it.

The **finalize method** is called by the garbage collector to perform **termination housekeeping** on an object just before the garbage collector reclaims the object's memory. Method `finalize` does not take parameters and has return type `void`. A problem with method `finalize` is that the garbage collector is not guaranteed to execute at a specified time. In fact, the garbage collector may never execute before a program terminates. Thus, it's unclear if, or when, method `finalize` will be called. For this reason, most programmers should avoid method `finalize`.

Software Engineering Observation 8.7

A class that uses system resources, such as files on disk, should provide a method that programmers can call to release resources when they're no longer needed in a program. Many Java API classes provide `close` or `dispose` methods for this purpose. For example, class `Scanner` (`java.sun.com/javase/6/docs/api/java/util/Scanner.html`) has a `close` method.

8.11 `static` Class Members

Every object has its own copy of all the instance variables of the class. In certain cases, only one copy of a particular variable should be shared by all objects of a class. A **static field**—called a class variable—is used in such cases. A `static` variable represents classwide information—all objects of the class share the same piece of data. The declaration of a `static` variable begins with the keyword `static`.

Let's motivate `static` data with an example. Suppose that we have a video game with `Martian`s and other space creatures. Each `Martian` tends to be brave and willing to attack other space creatures when the Martian is aware that at least four other Martians are present. If fewer than five Martians are present, each of them becomes cowardly. Thus, each Martian needs to know the martianCount. We could endow class Martian with martianCount as an instance variable. If we do this, then every Martian will have a separate copy of the instance variable, and every time we create a new Martian, we'll have to update the instance variable martianCount in every Martian object. This wastes space with the redundant copies, wastes time in updating the separate copies and is error prone. Instead, we declare martianCount to be static, making martianCount classwide data. Every Martian can see the martianCount as if it were an instance variable of class Martian, but only one copy of the static martianCount is maintained. This saves space. We save time by having the Martian constructor increment the static martianCount—there is only one copy, so we do not have to increment separate copies for each Martian object.

Software Engineering Observation 8.8

Use a static variable when all objects of a class must use the same copy of the variable.

Static variables have class scope. We can access a class's public static members through a reference to any object of the class, or by qualifying the member name with the class name and a dot (.), as in Math.random(). A class's private static class members can be accessed by client code only through methods of the class. Actually, static class members exist even when no objects of the class exist—they're available as soon as the class is loaded into memory at execution time. To access a public static member when no objects of the class exist (and even when they do), prefix the class name and a dot (.) to the static member, as in Math.PI. To access a private static member when no objects of the class exist, provide a public static method and call it by qualifying its name with the class name and a dot.

Software Engineering Observation 8.9

Static class variables and methods exist, and can be used, even if no objects of that class have been instantiated.

A static method cannot access non-static class members, because a static method can be called even when no objects of the class have been instantiated. For the same reason, the this reference cannot be used in a static method. The this reference must refer to a specific object of the class, and when a static method is called, there might not be any objects of its class in memory.

Common Programming Error 8.7

A compilation error occurs if a static method calls an instance (non-static) method in the same class by using only the method name. Similarly, a compilation error occurs if a static method attempts to access an instance variable in the same class by using only the variable name.

Common Programming Error 8.8

Referring to this in a static method is a syntax error.

Tracking the Number of Employee Objects That Have Been Created
Our next program declares two classes—Employee (Fig. 8.12) and EmployeeTest
(Fig. 8.13). Class Employee declares private static variable count (Fig. 8.12, line 9) and
public static method getCount (lines 36–39). The static variable count is initialized
to zero in line 9. If a static variable is not initialized, the compiler assigns it a default value—in this case 0, the default value for type int. Variable count maintains a count of the
number of objects of class Employee that have been created so far.

```java
 1   // Fig. 8.12: Employee.java
 2   // Static variable used to maintain a count of the number of
 3   // Employee objects in memory.
 4
 5   public class Employee
 6   {
 7      private String firstName;
 8      private String lastName;
 9      private static int count = 0; // number of Employees created
10
11      // initialize Employee, add 1 to static count and
12      // output String indicating that constructor was called
13      public Employee( String first, String last )
14      {
15         firstName = first;
16         lastName = last;
17
18         ++count;  // increment static count of employees
19         System.out.printf( "Employee constructor: %s %s; count = %d\n",
20            firstName, lastName, count );
21      } // end Employee constructor
22
23      // get first name
24      public String getFirstName()
25      {
26         return firstName;
27      } // end method getFirstName
28
29      // get last name
30      public String getLastName()
31      {
32         return lastName;
33      } // end method getLastName
34
35      // static method to get static count value
36      public static int getCount()
37      {
38         return count;
39      } // end method getCount
40   } // end class Employee
```

Fig. 8.12 | static variable used to maintain a count of the number of Employee objects in
memory.

When Employee objects exist, variable count can be used in any method of an
Employee object—this example increments count in the constructor (line 18). The public

static method getCount (lines 36–39) returns the number of Employee objects that have been created so far. When no objects of class Employee exist, client code can access variable count by calling method getCount via the class name, as in Employee.getCount(). When objects exist, method getCount can also be called via any reference to an Employee object.

Good Programming Practice 8.1

Invoke every static method by using the class name and a dot (.) to emphasize that the method being called is a static method.

EmployeeTest method main (Fig. 8.13) instantiates two Employee objects (lines 13–14). When each Employee object's constructor is invoked, lines 15–16 of Fig. 8.12 assign the Employee's first name and last name to instance variables firstName and lastName. Note that these two statements do not make copies of the original String arguments. Actually, String objects in Java are **immutable**—they cannot be modified after they're created. Therefore, it's safe to have many references to one String object. This is not normally the case for objects of most other classes in Java. If String objects are immutable, you might wonder why are we able to use operators + and += to concatenate String objects. String-concatenation operations actually result in a new Strings object containing the concatenated values. The original String objects are not modified.

```java
1   // Fig. 8.13: EmployeeTest.java
2   // Static member demonstration.
3
4   public class EmployeeTest
5   {
6      public static void main( String[] args )
7      {
8         // show that count is 0 before creating Employees
9         System.out.printf( "Employees before instantiation: %d\n",
10           Employee.getCount() );
11
12        // create two Employees; count should be 2
13        Employee e1 = new Employee( "Susan", "Baker" );
14        Employee e2 = new Employee( "Bob", "Blue" );
15
16        // show that count is 2 after creating two Employees
17        System.out.println( "\nEmployees after instantiation: " );
18        System.out.printf( "via e1.getCount(): %d\n", e1.getCount() );
19        System.out.printf( "via e2.getCount(): %d\n", e2.getCount() );
20        System.out.printf( "via Employee.getCount(): %d\n",
21           Employee.getCount() );
22
23        // get names of Employees
24        System.out.printf( "\nEmployee 1: %s %s\nEmployee 2: %s %s\n",
25           e1.getFirstName(), e1.getLastName(),
26           e2.getFirstName(), e2.getLastName() );
27
28        // in this example, there is only one reference to each Employee,
29        // so the following two statements indicate that these objects
30        // are eligible for garbage collection
```

Fig. 8.13 | static member demonstration. (Part 1 of 2.)

```
31              e1 = null;
32              e2 = null;
33      } // end main
34  } // end class EmployeeTest
```

```
Employees before instantiation: 0
Employee constructor: Susan Baker; count = 1
Employee constructor: Bob Blue; count = 2

Employees after instantiation:
via e1.getCount(): 2
via e2.getCount(): 2
via Employee.getCount(): 2

Employee 1: Susan Baker
Employee 2: Bob Blue
```

Fig. 8.13 | static member demonstration. (Part 2 of 2.)

When main has finished using the two Employee objects, the references e1 and e2 are set to null at lines 31–32. At this point, references e1 and e2 no longer refer to the objects that were instantiated in lines 13–14. The objects become "eligible for garbage collection" because there are no more references to them in the program.

Eventually, the garbage collector might reclaim the memory for these objects (or the operating system will reclaim the memory when the program terminates). The JVM does not guarantee when, or even whether, the garbage collector will execute. When the garbage collector does execute, it's possible that no objects or only a subset of the eligible objects will be collected.

8.12 static Import

In Section 5.3, you learned about the static fields and methods of class Math. We invoked class Math's static fields and methods by preceding each with the class name Math and a dot (.). A **static import** declaration enables you to import the static members of a class or interface so you can access them via their unqualified names in your class—the class name and a dot (.) are not required to use an imported static member.

A static import declaration has two forms—one that imports a particular static member (which is known as single static import) and one that imports all static members of a class (which is known as static import on demand). The following syntax imports a particular static member:

import static *packageName.ClassName.staticMemberName*;

where *packageName* is the package of the class (e.g., java.lang), *ClassName* is the name of the class (e.g., Math) and *staticMemberName* is the name of the static field or method (e.g., PI or abs). The following syntax imports all static members of a class:

import static *packageName.ClassName.**;

where *packageName* is the package of the class (e.g., java.lang) and *ClassName* is the name of the class (e.g., Math). The asterisk (*) indicates that *all* static members of the specified class should be available for use in the class(es) declared in the file. Note that static import declarations import only static class members. Regular import statements should be used to specify the classes used in a program.

Figure 8.14 demonstrates a static import. Line 3 is a static import declaration, which imports all static fields and methods of class Math from package java.lang. Lines 9–12 access the Math class's static field E (line 11) and the static methods sqrt (line 9), ceil (line 10), log (line 11) and cos (line 12) without preceding the field name or method names with class name Math and a dot.

```java
1   // Fig. 8.14: StaticImportTest.java
2   // Static import of Math class methods.
3   import static java.lang.Math.*;
4
5   public class StaticImportTest
6   {
7      public static void main( String[] args )
8      {
9         System.out.printf( "sqrt( 900.0 ) = %.1f\n", sqrt( 900.0 ) );
10        System.out.printf( "ceil( -9.8 ) = %.1f\n", ceil( -9.8 ) );
11        System.out.printf( "log( E ) = %.1f\n", log( E ) );
12        System.out.printf( "cos( 0.0 ) = %.1f\n", cos( 0.0 ) );
13     } // end main
14  } // end class StaticImportTest
```

```
sqrt( 900.0 ) = 30.0
ceil( -9.8 ) = -9.0
log( E ) = 1.0
cos( 0.0 ) = 1.0
```

Fig. 8.14 | Static import of Math class methods.

Common Programming Error 8.9

A compilation error occurs if a program attempts to import from two or more classes static methods that have the same signature or from static fields that have the same name.

8.13 final Instance Variables

The principle of least privilege is fundamental to good software engineering. In the context of an application, it states that code should be granted only the amount of privilege and access that it needs to accomplish its designated task, but no more. This makes your programs more robust by preventing code from accidentally (or maliciously) modifying variable values and calling methods that should not be accessible.

Let's see how this principle applies to instance variables. Some of them need to be modifiable and some do not. You can use the keyword final to specify that a variable is not modifiable (i.e., it's a constant) and that any attempt to modify it is an error. For example,

```java
        private final int INCREMENT;
```

declares a final (constant) instance variable INCREMENT of type int. Although such variables can be initialized when they're declared, this is not required. They can be initialized by each of the class's constructors so that each object of the class has a different value.

Software Engineering Observation 8.10

Declaring an instance variable as final *helps enforce the principle of least privilege. If an instance variable should not be modified, declare it to be* final *to prevent modification.*

Our next example contains two classes—class Increment (Fig. 8.15) and class IncrementTest (Fig. 8.16). Class Increment contains a final int instance variable named INCREMENT (Fig. 8.15, line 7). Note that INCREMENT is not initialized in its declaration, so it must be initialized by the class's constructor (lines 10–13). If the class provided multiple constructors, every one would be required to initialize the final variable. The constructor receives int parameter incrementValue and assigns its value to INCREMENT (line 12). A final variable cannot be modified by assignment after it's initialized. Application class IncrementTest creates an object of class Increment (Fig. 8.16, line 8) and provides as the argument to the constructor the value 5 to be assigned to the constant INCREMENT.

```java
1   // Fig. 8.15: Increment.java
2   // final instance variable in a class.
3
4   public class Increment
5   {
6      private int total = 0; // total of all increments
7      private final int INCREMENT; // constant variable (uninitialized)
8
9      // constructor initializes final instance variable INCREMENT
10     public Increment( int incrementValue )
11     {
12        INCREMENT = incrementValue; // initialize constant variable (once)
13     } // end Increment constructor
14
15     // add INCREMENT to total
16     public void addIncrementToTotal()
17     {
18        total += INCREMENT;
19     } // end method addIncrementToTotal
20
21     // return String representation of an Increment object's data
22     public String toString()
23     {
24        return String.format( "total = %d", total );
25     } // end method toString
26  } // end class Increment
```

Fig. 8.15 | final instance variable in a class.

```java
1   // Fig. 8.16: IncrementTest.java
2   // final variable initialized with a constructor argument.
3
4   public class IncrementTest
5   {
6      public static void main( String[] args )
7      {
```

Fig. 8.16 | final variable initialized with a constructor argument. (Part 1 of 2.)

```
8            Increment value = new Increment( 5 );
9
10           System.out.printf( "Before incrementing: %s\n\n", value );
11
12           for ( int i = 1; i <= 3; i++ )
13           {
14              value.addIncrementToTotal();
15              System.out.printf( "After increment %d: %s\n", i, value );
16           } // end for
17      } // end main
18   } // end class IncrementTest
```

```
Before incrementing: total = 0

After increment 1: total = 5
After increment 2: total = 10
After increment 3: total = 15
```

Fig. 8.16 | final variable initialized with a constructor argument. (Part 2 of 2.)

Common Programming Error 8.10
Attempting to modify a final instance variable after it's initialized is a compilation error.

Error-Prevention Tip 8.3
Attempts to modify a final instance variable are caught at compilation time rather than causing execution-time errors. It's always preferable to get bugs out at compilation time, if possible, rather than allow them to slip through to execution time (where studies have found that repair is often many times more expensive).

Software Engineering Observation 8.11
A final field should also be declared static if it's initialized in its declaration to a value that is the same for all objects of the class. After this initialization, its value can never change. Therefore, we don't need a separate copy of the field for every object of the class. Making the field static enables all objects of the class to share the final field.

If a final variable is not initialized, a compilation error occurs. To demonstrate this, we placed line 12 of Fig. 8.15 in a comment and recompiled the class. Figure 8.17 shows the error message produced by the compiler.

```
Increment.java:13: variable INCREMENT might not have been initialized
   } // end Increment constructor
   ^
1 error
```

Fig. 8.17 | final variable INCREMENT must be initialized.

Common Programming Error 8.11
Not initializing a final instance variable in its declaration or in every constructor of the class yields a compilation error indicating that the variable might not have been initialized.

8.14 Time Class Case Study: Creating Packages

We've seen in almost every example in the text that classes from preexisting libraries, such as the Java API, can be imported into a Java program. Each class in the Java API belongs to a package that contains a group of related classes. These packages are defined once, but can be imported into many programs. As applications become more complex, packages help programmers manage the complexity of application components. Packages also facilitate software reuse by enabling programs to import classes from other packages (as we've done in most examples), rather than copying the classes into each program that uses them. Another benefit of packages is that they provide a convention for unique class names, which helps prevent class-name conflicts (discussed later in this section). This section introduces how to create your own packages.

Steps for Declaring a Reusable Class

Before a class can be imported into multiple applications, it must be placed in a package to make it reusable. Figure 8.18 shows how to specify the package in which a class should be placed. Figure 8.19 shows how to import our packaged class so that it can be used in an application. The steps for creating a reusable class are:

1. Declare a `public` class. If the class is not `public`, it can be used only by other classes in the same package.

2. Choose a unique package name and add a **package** declaration to the source-code file for the reusable class declaration. In each Java source-code file there can be only one `package` declaration, and it must precede all other declarations and statements. Note that comments are not statements, so comments can be placed before a `package` statement in a file. [*Note:* If no `package` statement is provided, the class is placed in the so-called default package and is accessible only to other classes in the default package that are located in the same directory. All prior programs in this book that had two or more classes, used this default package.]

3. Compile the class so that it's placed in the appropriate package directory.

4. Import the reusable class into a program and use the class.

Steps 1 and 2: Creating a **public** Class and Adding the **package** Statement

For *Step 1*, we modify the `public` class `Time1` declared in Fig. 8.1. The new version is shown in Fig. 8.18. No modifications have been made to the implementation of the class, so we'll not discuss its implementation details again here.

For *Step 2*, we add a `package` declaration (line 3) that declares a `package` named `com.deitel.jhtp.ch08`. Placing a `package` declaration at the beginning of a Java source file indicates that the class declared in the file is part of the specified package. Only `package` declarations, `import` declarations and comments can appear outside the braces of a class declaration. A Java source-code file must have the following order:

1. a `package` declaration (if any),

2. `import` declarations (if any), then

3. class declarations.

Only one of the class declarations in a particular file can be `public`. Other classes in the file are placed in the package and can be used only by the other classes in the package. Non-`public` classes are in a package to support the reusable classes in the package.

```
1   // Fig. 8.18: Time1.java
2   // Time1 class declaration maintains the time in 24-hour format.
3   package com.deitel.jhtp.ch08;
4
5   public class Time1
6   {
7      private int hour;   // 0 - 23
8      private int minute; // 0 - 59
9      private int second; // 0 - 59
10
11     // set a new time value using universal time; ensure that
12     // the data remains consistent by setting invalid values to zero
13     public void setTime( int h, int m, int s )
14     {
15        hour   = ( ( h >= 0 && h < 24 ) ? h : 0 ); // validate hour
16        minute = ( ( m >= 0 && m < 60 ) ? m : 0 ); // validate minute
17        second = ( ( s >= 0 && s < 60 ) ? s : 0 ); // validate second
18     } // end method setTime
19
20     // convert to String in universal-time format (HH:MM:SS)
21     public String toUniversalString()
22     {
23        return String.format( "%02d:%02d:%02d", hour, minute, second );
24     } // end method toUniversalString
25
26     // convert to String in standard-time format (H:MM:SS AM or PM)
27     public String toString()
28     {
29        return String.format( "%d:%02d:%02d %s",
30           ( ( hour == 0 || hour == 12 ) ? 12 : hour % 12 ),
31           minute, second, ( hour < 12 ? "AM" : "PM" ) );
32     } // end method toString
33   } // end class Time1
```

Fig. 8.18 | Packaging class Time1 for reuse.

In an effort to provide unique names for every package, Sun Microsystems specifies a convention that you should follow. Every package name should start with your Internet domain name in reverse order. For example, our domain name is deitel.com, so our package names begin with com.deitel. For the domain name *yourcollege*.edu, the package name should begin with edu.*yourcollege*. After the domain name is reversed, you can choose any other names you want for your package. If you are part of a company with many divisions or a university with many schools, you may want to use the name of your division or school as the next name in the package. We chose to use jhtp as the next name in our package name to indicate that this class is from *Java How to Program*. The last name in our package name specifies that this package is for Chapter 8 (ch08).

Step 3: Compiling the Packaged Class

Step 3 is to compile the class so that it's stored in the appropriate package. When a Java file containing a package declaration is compiled, the resulting class file is placed in the directory specified by the declaration. The package declaration in Fig. 8.18 indicates that class Time1 should be placed in the directory

```
com
    deitel
        jhtp
            ch08
```

The directory names in the package declaration specify the exact location of the classes in the package.

When compiling a class in a package, the javac command-line option **-d** causes the javac compiler to create appropriate directories based on the class's package declaration. The option also specifies where the directories should be stored. For example, in a command window, we used the compilation command

```
javac -d . Time1.java
```

to specify that the first directory in our package name should be placed in the current directory. The period (.) after -d in the preceding command represents the current directory on the Windows, UNIX, Linux and Mac OS X operating systems (and several others as well). After execution of the compilation command, the current directory contains a directory called com, com contains a directory called deitel, deitel contains a directory called jhtp and jhtp contains a directory called ch08. In the ch08 directory, you can find the file Time1.class. [*Note:* If you do not use the -d option, then you must copy or move the class file to the appropriate package directory after compiling it.]

The package name is part of the **fully qualified class name**, so the name of class Time1 is actually com.deitel.jhtp.ch08.Time1. You can use this fully qualified name in your programs, or you can import the class and use its **simple name** (the class name by itself— Time1) in the program. If another package also contains a Time1 class, the fully qualified class names can be used to distinguish between the classes in the program and prevent a **name conflict** (also called a **name collision**).

Step 4: Importing the Reusable Class
Once the class is compiled and stored in its package, the class can be imported into programs (*Step 4*). In the Time1PackageTest application of Fig. 8.19, line 3 specifies that class Time1 should be imported for use in class Time1PackageTest. Class Time1PackageTest is in the default package because the class's .java file does not contain a package declaration. Since the two classes are in different packages, the import at line 3 is required so that class Time1PackageTest can use class Time1.

```
1   // Fig. 8.19: Time1PackageTest.java
2   // Time1 object used in an application.
3   import com.deitel.jhtp.ch08.Time1; // import class Time1
4
5   public class Time1PackageTest
6   {
7      public static void main( String[] args )
8      {
9         // create and initialize a Time1 object
10        Time1 time = new Time1(); // calls Time1 constructor
11
12        // output string representations of the time
13        System.out.print( "The initial universal time is: " );
```

Fig. 8.19 | Time1 object used in an application. (Part 1 of 2.)

```
14          System.out.println( time.toUniversalString() );
15          System.out.print( "The initial standard time is: " );
16          System.out.println( time.toString() );
17          System.out.println(); // output a blank line
18
19          // change time and output updated time
20          time.setTime( 13, 27, 6 );
21          System.out.print( "Universal time after setTime is: " );
22          System.out.println( time.toUniversalString() );
23          System.out.print( "Standard time after setTime is: " );
24          System.out.println( time.toString() );
25          System.out.println(); // output a blank line
26
27          // set time with invalid values; output updated time
28          time.setTime( 99, 99, 99 );
29          System.out.println( "After attempting invalid settings:" );
30          System.out.print( "Universal time: " );
31          System.out.println( time.toUniversalString() );
32          System.out.print( "Standard time: " );
33          System.out.println( time.toString() );
34       } // end main
35   } // end class Time1PackageTest
```

```
The initial universal time is: 00:00:00
The initial standard time is: 12:00:00 AM

Universal time after setTime is: 13:27:06
Standard time after setTime is: 1:27:06 PM

After attempting invalid settings:
Universal time: 00:00:00
Standard time: 12:00:00 AM
```

Fig. 8.19 | Time1 object used in an application. (Part 2 of 2.)

Line 3 is known as a **single-type-import declaration**—that is, the import declaration specifies one class to import. When your program uses multiple classes from the same package, you can import those classes with a single import declaration. For example, the import declaration

```
import java.util.*; // import classes from package java.util
```

uses an asterisk (*) at the end of the import declaration to inform the compiler that all public classes from the java.util package are available for use in the program. This is known as a **type-import-on-demand declaration**. Only the classes from package java.util that are used in the program are loaded by the JVM. The preceding import allows you to use the simple name of any class from the java.util package in the program. Throughout this book, we use single-type-import declarations for clarity.

Common Programming Error 8.12

Using the import declaration import java.; causes a compilation error. You must specify the exact name of the package from which you want to import classes.*

Specifying the Classpath During Compilation

When compiling `Time1PackageTest`, javac must locate the `.class` file for `Time1` to ensure that class `Time1PackageTest` uses class `Time1` correctly. The compiler uses a special object called a **class loader** to locate the classes it needs. The class loader begins by searching the standard Java classes that are bundled with the JDK. Then it searches for **optional packages**. Java provides an **extension mechanism** that enables new (optional) packages to be added to Java for development and execution purposes. [*Note:* The extension mechanism is beyond the scope of this book. For more information, visit `java.sun.com/javase/6/docs/technotes/guides/extensions/`.] If the class is not found in the standard Java classes or in the extension classes, the class loader searches the **classpath**, which contains a list of locations in which classes are stored. The classpath consists of a list of directories or **archive files**, each separated by a **directory separator**—a semicolon (;) on Windows or a colon (:) on UNIX/Linux/Mac OS X. Archive files are individual files that contain directories of other files, typically in a compressed format. For example, the standard classes used by your programs are contained in the archive file `rt.jar`, which is installed with the JDK. Archive files normally end with the `.jar` or `.zip` file-name extensions. The directories and archive files specified in the classpath contain the classes you wish to make available to the Java compiler and the JVM.

By default, the classpath consists only of the current directory. However, the classpath can be modified by

1. providing the `-classpath` option to the javac compiler or

2. setting the `CLASSPATH` environment variable (a special variable that you define and the operating system maintains so that applications can search for classes in the specified locations).

For more information on the classpath, visit `java.sun.com/javase/6/docs/technotes/tools/index.html#general`. The section entitled "General Information" contains information on setting the classpath for UNIX/Linux and Windows.

Common Programming Error 8.13

Specifying an explicit classpath eliminates the current directory from the classpath. This prevents classes in the current directory (including packages in the current directory) from loading properly. If classes must be loaded from the current directory, include a dot (.) in the classpath to specify the current directory.

Software Engineering Observation 8.12

In general, it's a better practice to use the `-classpath` option of the compiler, rather than the `CLASSPATH` environment variable, to specify the classpath for a program. This enables each application to have its own classpath.

Error-Prevention Tip 8.4

Specifying the classpath with the `CLASSPATH` environment variable can cause subtle and difficult-to-locate errors in programs that use different versions of the same package.

For Figs. 8.18–8.19, we didn't specify an explicit classpath. Thus, to locate the classes in the `com.deitel.jhtp.ch08` package from this example, the class loader looks in the current directory for the first name in the package—`com`—then navigates the directory structure. Directory `com` contains the subdirectory `deitel`, `deitel` contains the subdirectory jhtp, and jhtp contains subdirectory ch08. In the ch08 directory is the file Time1.class, which is loaded by the class loader to ensure that the class is used properly in our program.

Specifying the Classpath When Executing an Application
When you execute an application, the JVM must be able to locate the .class files of the classes used in that application. Like the compiler, the java command uses a class loader that searches the standard classes and extension classes first, then searches the classpath (the current directory by default). The classpath can be specified explicitly by using either of the techniques discussed for the compiler. As with the compiler, it's better to specify an individual program's classpath via command-line JVM options. You can specify the classpath in the java command via the **-classpath** or **-cp** command-line options, followed by a list of directories or archive files separated by semicolons (;) on Microsoft Windows or by colons (:) on UNIX/Linux/Mac OS X. Again, if classes must be loaded from the current directory, be sure to include a dot (.) in the classpath to specify the current directory.

8.15 Package Access

If no access modifier (public, protected or private—protected is discussed in Chapter 9) is specified for a method or variable when it's declared in a class, the method or variable is considered to have **package access**. In a program that consists of one class declaration, this has no specific effect. However, if a program uses multiple classes from the same package (i.e., a group of related classes), these classes can access each other's package-access members directly through references to objects of the appropriate classes, or in the case of static members through the class name. Package access is rarely used.

The application in Fig. 8.20 demonstrates package access. The application contains two classes in one source-code file—the PackageDataTest application class (lines 5–21) and the PackageData class (lines 24–41). When you compile this program, the compiler produces two separate .class files—PackageDataTest.class and PackageData.class. The compiler places the two .class files in the same directory, so the classes are considered to be part of the same package. Consequently, class PackageDataTest is allowed to modify the package-access data of PackageData objects. Note that you can also place class PackageData (lines 24–41) in a separate source code file. As long as both classes are compiled in the same directory on disk, the package-access relationship will still work.

```
 1   // Fig. 8.20: PackageDataTest.java
 2   // Package-access members of a class are accessible by other classes
 3   // in the same package.
 4
 5   public class PackageDataTest
 6   {
 7      public static void main( String[] args )
 8      {
 9         PackageData packageData = new PackageData();
10
11         // output String representation of packageData
12         System.out.printf( "After instantiation:\n%s\n", packageData );
```

Fig. 8.20 | Package-access members of a class are accessible by other classes in the same package. (Part 1 of 2.)

```
13
14          // change package access data in packageData object
15          packageData.number = 77;
16          packageData.string = "Goodbye";
17
18          // output String representation of packageData
19          System.out.printf( "\nAfter changing values:\n%s\n", packageData );
20       } // end main
21    } // end class PackageDataTest
22
23    // class with package access instance variables
24    class PackageData
25    {
26       int number; // package-access instance variable
27       String string; // package-access instance variable
28
29       // constructor
30       public PackageData()
31       {
32          number = 0;
33          string = "Hello";
34       } // end PackageData constructor
35
36       // return PackageData object String representation
37       public String toString()
38       {
39          return String.format( "number: %d; string: %s", number, string );
40       } // end method toString
41    } // end class PackageData
```

```
After instantiation:
number: 0; string: Hello

After changing values:
number: 77; string: Goodbye
```

Fig. 8.20 | Package-access members of a class are accessible by other classes in the same package. (Part 2 of 2.)

In the `PackageData` class declaration, lines 26–27 declare the instance variables `number` and `string` with no access modifiers—therefore, these are package-access instance variables. The `PackageDataTest` application's `main` method creates an instance of the `PackageData` class (line 9) to demonstrate the ability to modify the `PackageData` instance variables directly (as shown in lines 15–16). The results of the modification can be seen in the output window.

8.16 (Optional) GUI and Graphics Case Study: Using Objects with Graphics

Most of the graphics you've seen to this point did not vary with each program execution. Exercise 5.2 in Section 5.13 asked you to create a program that generated shapes and colors at random. In that exercise, the drawing changed every time the system called paint-

Component to redraw the panel. To create a more consistent drawing that remains the same each time it is drawn, we must store information about the displayed shapes so that we can reproduce them each time the system calls `paintComponent`. To do this, we'll create a set of shape classes that store information about each shape. We'll make these classes "smart" by allowing objects of these classes to draw themselves by using a `Graphics` object.

Class *MyLine*

Figure 8.21 declares class `MyLine`, which has all these capabilities. Class `MyLine` imports `Color` and `Graphics` (lines 3–4). Lines 8–11 declare instance variables for the coordinates needed to draw a line, and line 12 declares the instance variable that stores the color of the line. The constructor at lines 15–22 takes five parameters, one for each instance variable that it initializes. Method `draw` at lines 25–29 requires a `Graphics` object and uses it to draw the line in the proper color and at the proper coordinates.

```java
1   // Fig. 8.21: MyLine.java
2   // Declaration of class MyLine.
3   import java.awt.Color;
4   import java.awt.Graphics;
5
6   public class MyLine
7   {
8      private int x1; // x-coordinate of first endpoint
9      private int y1; // y-coordinate of first endpoint
10     private int x2; // x-coordinate of second endpoint
11     private int y2; // y-coordinate of second endpoint
12     private Color myColor; // color of this shape
13
14     // constructor with input values
15     public MyLine( int x1, int y1, int x2, int y2, Color color )
16     {
17        this.x1 = x1; // set x-coordinate of first endpoint
18        this.y1 = y1; // set y-coordinate of first endpoint
19        this.x2 = x2; // set x-coordinate of second endpoint
20        this.y2 = y2; // set y-coordinate of second endpoint
21        myColor = color; // set the color
22     } // end MyLine constructor
23
24     // Draw the line in the specified color
25     public void draw( Graphics g )
26     {
27        g.setColor( myColor );
28        g.drawLine( x1, y1, x2, y2 );
29     } // end method draw
30  } // end class MyLine
```

Fig. 8.21 | `MyLine` class represents a line.

Class *DrawPanel*

In Fig. 8.22, we declare class `DrawPanel`, which will generate random objects of class `MyLine`. Line 12 declares a `MyLine` array to store the lines to draw. Inside the constructor (lines 15–37), line 17 sets the background color to `Color.WHITE`. Line 19 creates the array with a random length between 5 and 9. The loop at lines 22–36 creates a new MyLine for every element in the array. Lines 25–28 generate random coordinates for each line's end-points, and lines 31–32 generate a random color for the line. Line 35 creates a new MyLine object with the randomly generated values and stores it in the array.

```java
1   // Fig. 8.22: DrawPanel.java
2   // Program that uses class MyLine
3   // to draw random lines.
4   import java.awt.Color;
5   import java.awt.Graphics;
6   import java.util.Random;
7   import javax.swing.JPanel;
8
9   public class DrawPanel extends JPanel
10  {
11     private Random randomNumbers = new Random();
12     private MyLine[] lines; // array of lines
13
14     // constructor, creates a panel with random shapes
15     public DrawPanel()
16     {
17        setBackground( Color.WHITE );
18
19        lines = new MyLine[ 5 + randomNumbers.nextInt( 5 ) ];
20
21        // create lines
22        for ( int count = 0; count < lines.length; count++ )
23        {
24           // generate random coordinates
25           int x1 = randomNumbers.nextInt( 300 );
26           int y1 = randomNumbers.nextInt( 300 );
27           int x2 = randomNumbers.nextInt( 300 );
28           int y2 = randomNumbers.nextInt( 300 );
29
30           // generate a random color
31           Color color = new Color( randomNumbers.nextInt( 256 ),
32              randomNumbers.nextInt( 256 ), randomNumbers.nextInt( 256 ) );
33
34           // add the line to the list of lines to be displayed
35           lines[ count ] = new MyLine( x1, y1, x2, y2, color );
36        } // end for
37     } // end DrawPanel constructor
38
39     // for each shape array, draw the individual shapes
40     public void paintComponent( Graphics g )
41     {
42        super.paintComponent( g );
43
44        // draw the lines
45        for ( MyLine line : lines )
46           line.draw( g );
47     } // end method paintComponent
48  } // end class DrawPanel
```

Fig. 8.22 | Creating random MyLine objects.

Method paintComponent iterates through the MyLine objects in array lines using an enhanced for statement (lines 45–46). Each iteration calls the draw method of the current MyLine object and passes it the Graphics object for drawing on the panel.

Class TestDraw

Class TestDraw in Fig. 8.23 sets up a new window to display our drawing. Since we are setting the coordinates for the lines only once in the constructor, the drawing does not change if paintComponent is called to refresh the drawing on the screen.

```
1   // Fig. 8.23: TestDraw.java
2   // Creating a JFrame to display a DrawPanel.
3   import javax.swing.JFrame;
4
5   public class TestDraw
6   {
7      public static void main( String[] args )
8      {
9         DrawPanel panel = new DrawPanel();
10        JFrame application = new JFrame();
11
12        application.setDefaultCloseOperation( JFrame.EXIT_ON_CLOSE );
13        application.add( panel );
14        application.setSize( 300, 300 );
15        application.setVisible( true );
16     } // end main
17  } // end class TestDraw
```

Fig. 8.23 | Creating a JFrame to display a DrawPanel.

GUI and Graphics Case Study Exercise

8.1   Extend the program in Figs. 8.21–8.23 to randomly draw rectangles and ovals. Create classes MyRectangle and MyOval. Both of these classes should include *x1*, *y1*, *x2*, *y2* coordinates, a color and a boolean flag to determine whether the shape is a filled shape. Declare a constructor in each class with arguments for initializing all the instance variables. To help draw rectangles and ovals, each class should provide methods getUpperLeftX, getUpperLeftY, getWidth and getHeight that calculate the upper-left *x*-coordinate, upper-left *y*-coordinate, width and height, respectively. The upper-left *x*-coordinate is the smaller of the two *x*-coordinate values, the upper-left *y*-coordinate is the smaller of the two *y*-coordinate values, the width is the absolute value of the difference between the two *x*-coordinate values, and the height is the absolute value of the difference between the two *y*-coordinate values.

Class DrawPanel, which extends JPanel and handles the creation of the shapes, should declare three arrays, one for each shape type. The length of each array should be a random number between 1 and 5. The constructor of class DrawPanel will fill each of the arrays with shapes of random position, size, color and fill.

In addition, modify all three shape classes to include the following:

    a) A constructor with no arguments that sets all the coordinates of the shape to 0, the color of the shape to Color.BLACK, and the filled property to false (MyRectangle and MyOval only).

    b) *Set* methods for the instance variables in each class. The methods that set a coordinate value should verify that the argument is greater than or equal to zero before setting the coordinate—if it's not, they should set the coordinate to zero. The constructor should call the *set* methods rather than initialize the local variables directly.

    c) *Get* methods for the instance variables in each class. Method draw should reference the coordinates by the *get* methods rather than access them directly.

8.17 Wrap-Up

In this chapter, we presented additional class concepts. The Time class case study presented a complete class declaration consisting of private data, overloaded public constructors for initialization flexibility, *set* and *get* methods for manipulating the class's data, and methods that returned String representations of a Time object in two different formats. You also learned that every class can declare a toString method that returns a String representation of an object of the class and that method toString can be called implicitly whenever an object of a class appears in the code where a String is expected.

You learned that the this reference is used implicitly in a class's non-static methods to access the class's instance variables and other non-static methods. You also saw explicit uses of the this reference to access the class's members (including shadowed fields) and how to use keyword this in a constructor to call another constructor of the class.

We discussed the differences between default constructors provided by the compiler and no-argument constructors provided by the programmer. You learned that a class can have references to objects of other classes as members—a concept known as composition. You saw the enum class type and learned how it can be used to create a set of constants for use in a program. You learned about Java's garbage-collection capability and how it (unpredictably) reclaims the memory of objects that are no longer used. The chapter explained the motivation for static fields in a class and demonstrated how to declare and use static fields and methods in your own classes. You also learned how to declare and initialize final variables.

You learned how to package your own classes for reuse and how to import those classes into an application. Finally, you learned that fields declared without an access modifier are given package access by default. You saw the relationship between classes in the same package that allows each class in a package to access the package-access members of other classes in the package.

In the next chapter, you'll learn about an important aspect of object-oriented programming in Java—inheritance. You'll see that all classes in Java are related directly or indirectly to the class called Object. You'll also begin to understand how the relationships between classes enable you to build more powerful applications.

Summary

Section 8.2 *Time Class Case Study*

- The public methods of a class are also known as the class's public services or public interface. They present to the class's clients a view of the services the class provides.

- A class's private members are not accessible to the class's clients.

- An object that contains consistent data has data values that are always kept in range.

- A value passed to a method to modify an instance variable is a consistent value if it is in the instance variable's allowed range. A correct value is always a consistent value, but a consistent value is not correct if a method receives an out-of-range value and sets it to a consistent value to maintain the object in a consistent state.

- String class static method format is similar to method System.out.printf except that format returns a formatted String rather than displaying it in a command window.

- All objects in Java have a toString method that returns a String representation of the object. Method toString is called implicitly when an object appears in code where a String is needed.

Section 8.3 *Controlling Access to Members*

- The access modifiers public and private control access to a class's variables and methods.

- The primary purpose of public methods is to present to the class's clients a view of the services the class provides. Clients need not be concerned with how the class accomplishes its tasks.

- A class's private variables and private methods (i.e., its implementation details) are not accessible to its clients.

Section 8.4 *Referring to the Current Object's Members with the* **this** *Reference*

- A non-static method of an object implicitly uses keyword this to refer to the object's instance variables and other methods. Keyword this can also be used explicitly.

- The compiler produces a separate file with the .class extension for every compiled class.

- If a local variable has the same name as a class's field, the local variable shadows the field. You can use the this reference in a method to refer to the shadowed field explicitly.

Section 8.5 *Time Class Case Study: Overloaded Constructors*

- Overloaded constructors enable objects of a class to be initialized in different ways. The compiler differentiates overloaded constructors by their signatures.

- To call one contructor of a class from another of the same class, you can use the this keyword followed by parentheses containing the constructor arguments. Such a constructor call must appear as the first statement in the constructor's body.

Section 8.6 *Default and No-Argument Constructors*

- If no constructors are provided in a class, the compiler creates a default constructor.

- If a class declares constructors, the compiler will not create a default constructor. In this case, you must declare a no-argument constructor if default initialization is required.

Section 8.7 *Notes on* **Set** *and* **Get** *Methods*

- *Set* methods are commonly called mutator methods because they typically change a value. *Get* methods are commonly called accessor methods or query methods. A predicate method tests whether a condition is true or false.

Section 8.8 *Composition*

- A class can have references to objects of other classes as members. This is called composition and is sometimes referred to as a *has-a* relationship.

Section 8.9 Enumerations

- All enum types are reference types. An enum type is declared with an enum declaration, which is a comma-separated list of enum constants. The declaration may optionally include other components of traditional classes, such as constructors, fields and methods.

- enum constants are implicitly final, because they declare constants that should not be modified.

- enum constants are implicitly static.

- Any attempt to create an object of an enum type with operator new results in a compilation error.

- enum constants can be used anywhere constants can be used, such as in the case labels of switch statements and to control enhanced for statements.

- Each enum constant in an enum declaration is optionally followed by arguments which are passed to the enum constructor.

- For every enum, the compiler generates a static method called values that returns an array of the enum's constants in the order in which they were declared.

- EnumSet static method range receives the first and last enum constants in a range and returns an EnumSet that contains all the constants between these two constants, inclusive.

Section 8.10 Garbage Collection and Method `finalize`

- Every class in Java has the methods of class Object, one of which is the finalize method.

- The Java Virtual Machine (JVM) performs automatic garbage collection to reclaim the memory occupied by objects that are no longer in use. When there are no more references to an object, the object is eligible for garbage collection. The memory for such an object can be reclaimed when the JVM executes its garbage collector.

- The finalize method is called by the garbage collector just before it reclaims the object's memory. Method finalize does not take parameters and has return type void.

- The garbage collector may never execute before a program terminates. Thus, it's unclear whether, or when, method finalize will be called.

Section 8.11 `static` Class Members

- A static variable represents classwide information that is shared among all objects of the class.

- Static variables have class scope. A class's public static members can be accessed through a reference to any object of the class, or they can be accessed by qualifying the member name with the class name and a dot (.). Client code can access a class's private static class members only through methods of the class.

- static class members exist as soon as the class is loaded into memory.

- A method declared static cannot access non-static class members, because a static method can be called even when no objects of the class have been instantiated.

- The this reference cannot be used in a static method.

Section 8.12 `static` Import

- A static import declaration enables programmers to refer to imported static members without the class name and a dot (.). A single static import declaration imports one static member, and a static import on demand imports all static members of a class.

Section 8.13 `final` Instance Variables

- In the context of an application, the principle of least privilege states that code should be granted only the amount of privilege and access that the code needs to accomplish its designated task.

- Keyword final specifies that a variable is not modifiable. Such variables must be initialized when they're declared or by each of a class's constructors.

Section 8.14 Time Class Case Study: Creating Packages
- Each class in the Java API belongs to a package that contains a group of related classes. Packages help manage the complexity of application components and facilitate software reuse.
- Packages provide a convention for unique class names that helps prevent class-name conflicts.
- Before a class can be imported into multiple applications, it must be placed in a package. There can be only one package declaration in each Java source-code file, and it must precede all other declarations and statements in the file.
- Every package name should start with your Internet domain name in reverse order. After the domain name is reversed, you can choose any other names you want for your package.
- When compiling a class in a package, the javac command-line option -d specifies where to store the package and causes the compiler to create the package's directories if they do not exist.
- The package name is part of the fully qualified class name. This helps prevent name conflicts.
- A single-type-import declaration specifies one class to import. A type-import-on-demand declaration imports only the classes that the program uses from a particular package.
- The compiler uses a class loader to locate the classes it needs in the classpath. The classpath consists of a list of directories or archive files, each separated by a directory separator.
- The classpath for the compiler and JVM can be specified by providing the -classpath option to the javac or java command, or by setting the CLASSPATH environment variable. If classes must be loaded from the current directory, include a dot (.) in the classpath.

Section 8.15 Package Access
- If no access modifier is specified for a method or variable when it's declared in a class, the method or variable is considered to have package access.

Terminology

accessor method 339
archive file in classpath 358
class loader 358
class variable 346
classpath 358
-classpath command line option to java 359
-classpath command line option to javac 358
CLASSPATH environment variable 358
classwide information 346
composition 340
-cp command line option to java 359
-d compiler option 356
directory separator in classpath 358
enum constructor 343
enum declaration 343
EnumSet class 345
extension mechanism 358
finalize method 346
format method of class String 327
fully qualified class name 356
garbage collection 346
garbage collector 346
has-a relationship 340

immutable object 349
inlining method calls 337
mutator method 339
name collision 356
name conflict 356
no-argument constructor 335
optional package 358
overloaded constructors 333
package access 359
package declaration 354
predicate method 340
principle of least privilege 351
public interface of a class 325
public services of a class 325
query method 339
range method of EnumSet 345
simple name of a class 356
single static import 350
single-type-import declaration 357
static 350
static field 346
static import on demand 350
termination housekeeping 346

this keyword 330   type-import-on-demand declaration 357
this reference 330   values method of an enum 344

Self-Review Exercises

8.1   Fill in the blanks in each of the following statements:
   a) When compiling a class in a package, the javac command-line option _____ speci-
      fies where to store the package and causes the compiler to create the package's directo-
      ries if they do not exist.
   b) String class static method _____ is similar to method System.out.printf, but re-
      turns a formatted String rather than displaying a String in a command window.
   c) If a method contains a local variable with the same name as one of its class's fields, the
      local variable _____ the field in that method's scope.
   d) The _____ method is called by the garbage collector just before it reclaims an object's
      memory.
   e) A(n) _____ declaration specifies one class to import.
   f) If a class declares constructors, the compiler will not create a(n) _____.
   g) An object's _____ method is called implicitly when an object appears in code where
      a String is needed.
   h) *Get* methods are commonly called _____ or _____.
   i) A(n) _____ method tests whether a condition is true or false.
   j) For every enum, the compiler generates a static method called _____ that returns an
      array of the enum's constants in the order in which they were declared.
   k) Composition is sometimes referred to as a(n) _____ relationship.
   l) A(n) _____ declaration contains a comma-separated list of constants.
   m) A(n) _____ variable represents classwide information that is shared by all the objects
      of the class.
   n) A(n) _____ declaration imports one static member.
   o) The _____ states that code should be granted only the amount of privilege and access
      that it needs to accomplish its designated task.
   p) Keyword _____ specifies that a variable is not modifiable.
   q) There can be only one _____ in a Java source-code file, and it must precede all other
      declarations and statements in the file.
   r) A(n) _____ declaration imports only the classes that the program uses from a partic-
      ular package.
   s) The compiler uses a(n) _____ to locate the classes it needs in the classpath.
   t) The classpath for the compiler and JVM can be specified with the _____ option to
      the javac or java command, or by setting the _____ environment variable.
   u) *Set* methods are commonly called _____ because they typically change a value.
   v) A(n) _____ imports all static members of a class.
   w) The public methods of a class are also known as the class's _____ or _____.
   x) In an object, _____ data is data values that is always kept in range.

Answers to Self-Review Exercises

8.1   a) -d. b) format. c) shadows. d) finalize. e) single-type-import. f) default constructor.
g) toString. h) accessor methods, query methods. i) predicate. j) values. k) has-a. l) enum. m) static. n) single static import. o) principle of least privilege. p) final. q) package declaration. r) type-
import-on-demand. s) class loader. t) -classpath, CLASSPATH. u) mutator methods. v) static import on demand. w) public services, public interface. x) consistent.

Exercises

8.2   Explain the notion of package access in Java. Explain the negative aspects of package access.

8.3   What happens when a return type, even void, is specified for a constructor?

8.4   *(Rectangle Class)* Create a class Rectangle with attributes length and width, each of which defaults to 1. Provide methods that calculate the rectangle's perimeter and area. It has *set* and *get* methods for both length and width. The *set* methods should verify that length and width are each floating-point numbers larger than 0.0 and less than 20.0. Write a program to test class Rectangle.

8.5   *(Modifying the Internal Data Representation of a Class)* It would be perfectly reasonable for the Time2 class of Fig. 8.5 to represent the time internally as the number of seconds since midnight rather than the three integer values hour, minute and second. Clients could use the same public methods and get the same results. Modify the Time2 class of Fig. 8.5 to implement the Time2 as the number of seconds since midnight and show that no change is visible to the clients of the class.

8.6   *(Savings Account Class)* Create class SavingsAccount. Use a static variable annualInterestRate to store the annual interest rate for all account holders. Each object of the class contains a private instance variable savingsBalance indicating the amount the saver currently has on deposit. Provide method calculateMonthlyInterest to calculate the monthly interest by multiplying the savingsBalance by annualInterestRate divided by 12—this interest should be added to savingsBalance. Provide a static method modifyInterestRate that sets the annualInterestRate to a new value. Write a program to test class SavingsAccount. Instantiate two savingsAccount objects, saver1 and saver2, with balances of $2000.00 and $3000.00, respectively. Set annualInterestRate to 4%, then calculate the monthly interest for each of 12 months and print the new balances for both savers. Next, set the annualInterestRate to 5%, calculate the next month's interest and print the new balances for both savers.

8.7   *(Enhancing Class Time2)* Modify class Time2 of Fig. 8.5 to include a tick method that increments the time stored in a Time2 object by one second. Provide method incrementMinute to increment the minute by one and method incrementHour to increment the hour by one. The Time2 object should always remain in a consistent state. Write a program that tests the tick method, the incrementMinute method and the incrementHour method to ensure that they work correctly. Be sure to test the following cases:

    a) incrementing into the next minute,

    b) incrementing into the next hour and

    c) incrementing into the next day (i.e., 11:59:59 PM to 12:00:00 AM).

8.8   *(Enhancing Class Date)* Modify class Date of Fig. 8.7 to perform error checking on the initializer values for instance variables month, day and year (currently it validates only the month and day). Provide a method nextDay to increment the day by one. The Date object should remain in a consistent state. Write a program that tests method nextDay in a loop that prints the date during each iteration to illustrate that the method works correctly. Test the following cases:

    a) incrementing into the next month and

    b) incrementing into the next year.

8.9   *(Returning Error Indicators from Methods)* Modify the *set* methods in class Time2 of Fig. 8.5 to return appropriate error values if an attempt is made to set one of the instance variables hour, minute or second of an object of class Time2 to an invalid value. [*Hint:* Use boolean return types on each method.] Write a program that tests these new *set* methods and outputs error messages when incorrect values are supplied.

8.10   Rewrite Fig. 8.14 to use a separate import declaration for each static member of class Math that is used in the example.

8.11 Write an enum type TrafficLight, whose constants (RED, GREEN, YELLOW) take one parameter—the duration of the light. Write a program to test the TrafficLight enum so that it displays the enum constants and their durations.

8.12 *(Complex Numbers)* Create a class called Complex for performing arithmetic with complex numbers. Complex numbers have the form

realPart + *imaginaryPart* * *i*

where *i* is

$$\sqrt{-1}$$

Write a program to test your class. Use floating-point variables to represent the private data of the class. Provide a constructor that enables an object of this class to be initialized when it's declared. Provide a no-argument constructor with default values in case no initializers are provided. Provide public methods that perform the following operations:

    a) Add two Complex numbers: The real parts are added together and the imaginary parts are added together.

    b) Subtract two Complex numbers: The real part of the right operand is subtracted from the real part of the left operand, and the imaginary part of the right operand is subtracted from the imaginary part of the left operand.

    c) Print Complex numbers in the form (a, b), where a is the real part and b is the imaginary part.

8.13 *(Date and Time Class)* Create class DateAndTime that combines the modified Time2 class of Exercise 8.7 and the modified Date class of Exercise 8.8. Modify method incrementHour to call method nextDay if the time is incremented into the next day. Modify methods toString and toUniversalString to output the date in addition to the time. Write a program to test the new class DateAndTime. Specifically, test incrementing the time to the next day.

8.14 *(Set of Integers)* Create class IntegerSet. Each IntegerSet object can hold integers in the range 0–100. The set is represented by an array of booleans. Array element a[i] is true if integer *i* is in the set. Array element a[j] is false if integer *j* is not in the set. The no-argument constructor initializes the array to the "empty set" (i.e., a all false values).

Provide the following methods: Method union creates a set that is the set-theoretic union of two existing sets (i.e., an element of the new set's array is set to true if that element is true in either or both of the existing sets—otherwise, the new set's element is set to false). Method intersection creates a set which is the set-theoretic intersection of two existing sets (i.e., an element of the new set's array is set to false if that element is false in either or both of the existing sets—otherwise, the new set's element is set to true). Method insertElement inserts a new integer *k* into a set (by setting a[k] to true). Method deleteElement deletes integer *m* (by setting a[m] to false). Method toString returns a String containing a set as a list of numbers separated by spaces. Include only those elements that are present in the set. Use --- to represent an empty set. Method isEqualTo determines whether two sets are equal. Write a program to test class IntegerSet. Instantiate several IntegerSet objects. Test that all your methods work properly.

8.15 *(Date Class)* Create class Date with the following capabilities:

    a) Output the date in multiple formats, such as

```
MM/DD/YYYY
June 14, 1992
DDD YYYY
```

    b) Use overloaded constructors to create Date objects initialized with dates of the formats in part (a). In the first case the constructor should receive three integer values. In the second case it should receive a String and two integer values. In the third case it should receive two integer values, the first of which represents the day number in the year. [*Hint:* To convert the String representation of the month to a numeric value, compare Strings using the equals method. For example, if s1 and s2 are Strings, the method call s1.equals(s2) returns true if the Strings are identical and otherwise returns false.]

8.16 *(Rational Numbers)* Create a class called Rational for performing arithmetic with fractions. Write a program to test your class. Use integer variables to represent the private instance variables of the class—the numerator and the denominator. Provide a constructor that enables an object of this class to be initialized when it's declared. The constructor should store the fraction in reduced form. The fraction

> 2/4

is equivalent to 1/2 and would be stored in the object as 1 in the numerator and 2 in the denominator. Provide a no-argument constructor with default values in case no initializers are provided. Provide public methods that perform each of the following operations:

a) Add two Rational numbers: The result of the addition should be stored in reduced form.

b) Subtract two Rational numbers: The result of the subtraction should be stored in reduced form.

c) Multiply two Rational numbers: The result of the multiplication should be stored in reduced form.

d) Divide two Rational numbers: The result of the division should be stored in reduced form.

e) Return a String representation of a Rational number in the form a/b, where a is the numerator and b is the denominator.

f) Return a String representation of a Rational number in floating-point format. (Consider providing formatting capabilities that enable the user of the class to specify the number of digits of precision to the right of the decimal point.)

8.17 *(Huge Integer Class)* Create a class HugeInteger which uses a 40-element array of digits to store integers as large as 40 digits each. Provide methods parse, toString, add and subtract. Method parse should receive a String, extract each digit using method charAt and place the integer equivalent of each digit into the integer array. For comparing HugeInteger objects, provide the following methods: isEqualTo, isNotEqualTo, isGreaterThan, isLessThan, isGreaterThanOrEqualTo and isLessThanOrEqualTo. Each of these is a predicate method that returns true if the relationship holds between the two HugeInteger objects and returns false if the relationship does not hold. Provide a predicate method isZero. If you feel ambitious, also provide methods multiply, divide and remainder. [*Note:* Primitive boolean values can be output as the word "true" or the word "false" with format specifier %b.]

8.18 *(Tic-Tac-Toe)* Create a class TicTacToe that will enable you to write a program to play Tic-Tac-Toe. The class contains a private 3-by-3 two-dimensional array. Use an enumeration to represent the value in each cell of the array. The enumeration's constants should be named X, O and EMPTY (for a position that does not contain an X or an O). The constructor should initialize the board elements to EMPTY. Allow two human players. Wherever the first player moves, place an X in the specified square, and place an O wherever the second player moves. Each move must be to an empty square. After each move, determine whether the game has been won and whether it's a draw. If you feel ambitious, modify your program so that the computer makes the moves for one of the players. Also, allow the player to specify whether he or she wants to go first or second. If you feel exceptionally ambitious, develop a program that will play three-dimensional Tic-Tac-Toe on a 4-by-4-by-4 board [*Note:* This is an extremely challenging project!].

Making a Difference

8.19 *(Air Traffic Control)* Every day, according to the National Air Traffic Controllers Association (www.natca.org/mediacenter/bythenumbers.msp), there are more than 87,000 flights in the United States, including commercial flights, cargo flights, and so on, and the long-term trend is that air traffic activity will increase along with the population. As air traffic grows, so do the challenges to air traffic controllers, who monitor the flights and provide instructions to the pilots to ensure safety in the skies.

In this exercise, you'll create a Flight class that could be used in a simple air-traffic-control simulator. The application's main method will act as air traffic control. Visit sites such as

> www.howstuffworks.com/air-traffic-control.htm

to research how the air-traffic-control system works. Then identify some key attributes of a Flight in an air-traffic-control system. Think about the different states a plane could be in from the time it's parked at an airport gate until it arrives at its destination—parked, taxiing, waiting to take off, taking off, climbing, and so on. Use a FlightStatus enumeration to represent these states. The attributes might include the plane's make and model, current air speed, current altitude, direction, carrier, departure time, estimated arrival time, origin and destination. The origin and destination should be specified using standard three-letter airport codes, such as BOS for Boston and LAX for Los Angeles (these codes are available at world-airport-codes.com). Provide *set* and *get* methods to manipulate these and any other attributes you identify. Next, identify the class's behaviors and implement them as methods of the class. Include behaviors such as changeAltitude, reduceSpeed and beginLandingApproach. The Flight constructor should initialize a Flight's attributes. You should also provide a toString method that returns a String representation of a Flight's current status (e.g., parked at the gate, taxiing, taking off, changing altitude). This String should include all of the object's instance-variable values.

When the application executes, main will display the message, "Air Traffic Control Simulator", then will create and interact with three Flight objects representing planes that are currently flying or preparing to fly. For simplicity, the Flight's confirmation of each action will be a message displayed on the screen when the appropriate method is called on the object. For example, if you call a flight's changeAltitude method, the method should:

a) Display a message containing the airline, flight number, "changing altitude", the current altitude and the new altitude.

b) Change the state of the status instance variable to CHANGING_ALTITUDE.

c) Change the value of the newAltitude instance variable.

In main, create and initialize three Flight objects that are in different states—for example, one could be at the gate, one could be preparing for takeoff and one could be preparing for landing. The main method should send messages to (invoke methods on) the Flight objects. As a Flight object receives each message, it should display a confirmation message from the method being called—such as "[Airline name] [Flight number] changing altitude from 20000 to 25000 feet." The method should also update the appropriate state information in the Flight object. For example, if Air Traffic Control sends a message like "[Airline] [flight number] descend to 12000 feet," the program should execute a method call like flight1.changeAltitude(12000), which would display a confirmation message and would set instance variable newAltitude to 12000. [*Note:* Assume the Flight's currentAltitude instance variable is being set automatically by the plane's altimeter.]

Object-Oriented Programming: Inheritance

9

Say not you know another entirely, till you have divided an inheritance with him.
—Johann Kasper Lavater

This method is to define as the number of a class the class of all classes similar to the given class.
—Bertrand Russell

Good as it is to inherit a library, it is better to collect one.
—Augustine Birrell

Save base authority from others' books.
—William Shakespeare

Objectives

In this chapter you'll learn:

- How inheritance promotes software reusability.
- The notions of superclasses and subclasses.
- To use keyword **extends** to create a class that inherits attributes and behaviors from another class.
- To use access modifier **protected** to give subclass methods access to superclass members.
- To access superclass members with **super**.
- How constructors are used in inheritance hierarchies.
- The methods of class **Object**, the direct or indirect superclass of all Java classes.

9.1 Introduction

This chapter continues our discussion of object-oriented programming (OOP) by introducing one of its primary capabilities—inheritance, which is a form of software reuse in which a new class is created by absorbing an existing class's members and embellishing them with new or modified capabilities. With inheritance, you can save time during program development by basing new classes on existing proven and debugged high-quality software. This also increases the likelihood that a system will be implemented and maintained effectively.

When creating a class, rather than declaring completely new members, you can designate that the new class should inherit the members of an existing class. The existing class is called the superclass, and the new class is the subclass. (The C++ programming language refers to the superclass as the base class and the subclass as the derived class.) Each subclass can become a superclass for future subclasses.

A subclass can add its own fields and methods. Therefore, a subclass is more specific than its superclass and represents a more specialized group of objects. The subclass exhibits the behaviors of its superclass and can add behaviors that are specific to the subclass. This is why inheritance is sometimes referred to as specialization.

The direct superclass is the superclass from which the subclass explicitly inherits. An indirect superclass is any class above the direct superclass in the class hierarchy, which defines the inheritance relationships between classes. In Java, the class hierarchy begins with class Object (in package java.lang), which every class in Java directly or indirectly extends (or "inherits from"). Section 9.7 lists the methods of class Object that are inherited by all other Java classes. Java supports only single inheritance, in which each class is derived from exactly one direct superclass. Unlike C++, Java does not support multiple inheritance (which occurs when a class is derived from more than one direct superclass). Chapter 10, Object-Oriented Programming: Polymorphism, explains how to use Java interfaces to realize many of the benefits of multiple inheritance while avoiding the associated problems.

We distinguish between the *is-a* **relationship** and the *has-a* **relationship**. *Is-a* represents inheritance. In an *is-a* relationship, an object of a subclass can also be treated as an object of its superclass. For example, a car *is a* vehicle. By contrast, *has-a* represents composition (see Chapter 8). In a *has-a* relationship, an object contains as members references to other objects. For example, a car *has a* steering wheel (and a car object has a reference to a steering wheel object).

New classes can inherit from classes in **class libraries**. Organizations develop their own class libraries and can take advantage of others available worldwide. Some day, most new software likely will be constructed from **standardized reusable components**, just as automobiles and most computer hardware are constructed today. This will facilitate the development of more powerful, abundant and economical software.

9.2 Superclasses and Subclasses

Often, an object of one class *is an* object of another class as well. For example, in geometry, a rectangle *is a* quadrilateral—a four-sided shape—as are squares, parallelograms and trapezoids. Thus, in Java, class `Rectangle` can be said to inherit from class `Quadrilateral`. In this context, class `Quadrilateral` is a superclass and class `Rectangle` is a subclass. A rectangle *is a* specific type of quadrilateral, but it's incorrect to claim that every quadrilateral *is a* rectangle—the quadrilateral could be a parallelogram or some other shape. Figure 9.1 lists several simple examples of superclasses and subclasses—note that superclasses tend to be "more general" and subclasses "more specific."

Because every subclass object *is an* object of its superclass, and one superclass can have many subclasses, the set of objects represented by a superclass is typically larger than the set of objects represented by any of its subclasses. For example, the superclass `Vehicle` represents all vehicles, including cars, trucks, boats, bicycles and so on. By contrast, subclass `Car` represents a smaller, more specific subset of vehicles.

Superclass	Subclasses
Student	GraduateStudent, UndergraduateStudent
Shape	Circle, Triangle, Rectangle, Sphere, Cube
Loan	CarLoan, HomeImprovementLoan, MortgageLoan
Employee	Faculty, Staff
BankAccount	CheckingAccount, SavingsAccount

Fig. 9.1 | Inheritance examples.

Inheritance relationships form treelike hierarchical structures. A superclass exists in a hierarchical relationship with its subclasses. Let's develop a sample class hierarchy (Fig. 9.2), also called an **inheritance hierarchy**. A university community has thousands of members, including employees, students and alumni. Employees are either faculty or staff members. Faculty members are either administrators (e.g., deans and department chairpersons) or teachers. Note that the hierarchy could contain many other classes. For example, students can be graduate or undergraduate students. Undergraduate students can be freshmen, sophomores, juniors or seniors.

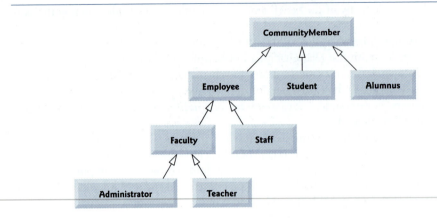

Fig. 9.2 | Inheritance hierarchy for university CommunityMembers.

Each arrow in the hierarchy represents an *is-a* relationship. As we follow the arrows upward in this class hierarchy, we can state, for instance, that "an Employee *is a* CommunityMember" and "a Teacher *is a* Faculty member." CommunityMember is the direct superclass of Employee, Student and Alumnus and is an indirect superclass of all the other classes in the diagram. Starting from the bottom, you can follow the arrows and apply the *is-a* relationship up to the topmost superclass. For example, an Administrator *is a* Faculty member, *is an* Employee, *is a* CommunityMember and, of course, *is an* Object.

Now consider the Shape inheritance hierarchy in Fig. 9.3. This hierarchy begins with superclass Shape, which is extended by subclasses TwoDimensionalShape and ThreeDimensionalShape—Shapes are either TwoDimensionalShapes or ThreeDimensionalShapes. The third level of this hierarchy contains specific types of TwoDimensionalShapes and ThreeDimensionalShapes. As in Fig. 9.2, we can follow the arrows from the bottom of the diagram to the topmost superclass in this class hierarchy to identify several *is-a* relationships. For instance, a Triangle *is a* TwoDimensionalShape and *is a* Shape, while a Sphere *is a* ThreeDimensionalShape and *is a* Shape. Note that this hierarchy could contain many other classes. For example, ellipses and trapezoids are TwoDimensionalShapes.

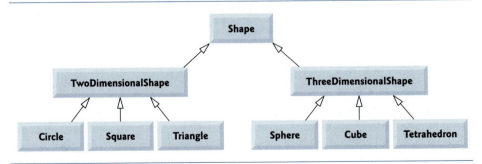

Fig. 9.3 | Inheritance hierarchy for Shapes.

Not every class relationship is an inheritance relationship. In Chapter 8, we discussed the *has-a* relationship, in which classes have members that are references to objects of other classes. Such relationships create classes by composition of existing classes. For example, given the classes `Employee`, `BirthDate` and `TelephoneNumber`, it's improper to say that an `Employee` *is a* `BirthDate` or that an `Employee` *is a* `TelephoneNumber`. However, an `Employee` *has a* `BirthDate`, and an `Employee` *has a* `TelephoneNumber`.

It's possible to treat superclass objects and subclass objects similarly—their commonalities are expressed in the members of the superclass. Objects of all classes that extend a common superclass can be treated as objects of that superclass (i.e., such objects have an *is-a* relationship with the superclass). Later in this chapter and in Chapter 10, Object-Oriented Programming: Polymorphism, we consider many examples that take advantage of the *is-a* relationship.

One problem with inheritance is that a subclass can inherit methods that it does not need or should not have. Even when a superclass method is appropriate for a subclass, that subclass often needs a customized version of the method. In such cases, the subclass can override (redefine) the superclass method with an appropriate implementation, as we'll see often in the chapter's code examples.

9.3 protected Members

Chapter 8 discussed access modifiers `public` and `private`. A class's `public` members are accessible wherever the program has a reference to an object of that class or one of its subclasses. A class's `private` members are accessible only within the class itself. In this section, we introduce access modifier **protected**. Using `protected` access offers an intermediate level of access between `public` and `private`. A superclass's `protected` members can be accessed by members of that superclass, by members of its subclasses and by members of other classes in the same package—`protected` members also have package access.

All `public` and `protected` superclass members retain their original access modifier when they become members of the subclass—`public` members of the superclass become `public` members of the subclass, and `protected` members of the superclass become `protected` members of the subclass. A superclass's `private` members are not accessible outside the class itself. Rather, they're hidden in its subclasses and can be accessed only through the `public` or `protected` methods inherited from the superclass.

Subclass methods can refer to `public` and `protected` members inherited from the superclass simply by using the member names. When a subclass method overrides an inherited superclass method, the superclass method can be accessed from the subclass by preceding the superclass method name with keyword **super** and a dot (.) separator. We discuss accessing overridden members of the superclass in Section 9.4.

Software Engineering Observation 9.1

Methods of a subclass cannot directly access `private` members of their superclass. A subclass can change the state of `private` superclass instance variables only through non-`private` methods provided in the superclass and inherited by the subclass.

Software Engineering Observation 9.2

Declaring `private` instance variables helps you test, debug and correctly modify systems. If a subclass could access its superclass's `private` instance variables, classes that inherit from that subclass could access the instance variables as well. This would propagate access to what should be `private` instance variables, and the benefits of information hiding would be lost.

9.4 Relationship between Superclasses and Subclasses

We now use an inheritance hierarchy containing types of employees in a company's payroll application to discuss the relationship between a superclass and its subclass. In this company, commission employees (who will be represented as objects of a superclass) are paid a percentage of their sales, while base-salaried commission employees (who will be represented as objects of a subclass) receive a base salary *plus* a percentage of their sales.

We divide our discussion of the relationship between these classes into five examples. The first declares class CommissionEmployee, which directly inherits from class Object and declares as private instance variables a first name, last name, social security number, commission rate and gross (i.e., total) sales amount.

The second example declares class BasePlusCommissionEmployee, which also directly inherits from class Object and declares as private instance variables a first name, last name, social security number, commission rate, gross sales amount and base salary. We create this class by writing every line of code the class requires—we'll soon see that it's much more efficient to create it by inheriting from class CommissionEmployee.

The third example declares a new BasePlusCommissionEmployee class that extends class CommissionEmployee (i.e., a BasePlusCommissionEmployee *is a* CommissionEmployee who also has a base salary). This software reuse lets us *write less code* when developing the new subclass. In this example, class BasePlusCommissionEmployee attempts to access class CommissionEmployee's private members—this results in compilation errors, because the subclass cannot access the superclass's private instance variables.

The fourth example shows that if CommissionEmployee's instance variables are declared as protected, the BasePlusCommissionEmployee subclass can access that data directly. Both BasePlusCommissionEmployee classes contain identical functionality, but we show how the inherited version is easier to create and manage.

After we discuss the convenience of using protected instance variables, we create the fifth example, which sets the CommissionEmployee instance variables back to private to enforce good software engineering. Then we show how the BasePlusCommissionEmployee subclass can use CommissionEmployee's public methods to manipulate (in a controlled manner) the private instance variables inherited from CommissionEmployee.

9.4.1 Creating and Using a CommissionEmployee Class

We begin by declaring class CommissionEmployee (Fig. 9.4). Line 4 begins the class declaration and indicates that class CommissionEmployee **extends** (i.e., inherits from) class **Object** (from package java.lang). This causes class CommissionEmployee to inherit the class Object's methods—class Object does not have any fields. If you don't explicitly specify which class a new class extends, the class extends Object implicitly. For this reason, you typically will not include "extends Object" in your code—we do so in this example only for demonstration purposes.

```
1   // Fig. 9.4: CommissionEmployee.java
2   // CommissionEmployee class represents an employee paid a
3   // percentage of gross sales.
```

Fig. 9.4 | CommissionEmployee class represents an employee paid a percentage of gross sales. (Part 1 of 3.)

```
 4   public class CommissionEmployee extends Object
 5   {
 6      private String firstName;
 7      private String lastName;
 8      private String socialSecurityNumber;
 9      private double grossSales; // gross weekly sales
10      private double commissionRate; // commission percentage
11
12      // five-argument constructor
13      public CommissionEmployee( String first, String last, String ssn,
14         double sales, double rate )
15      {
16         // implicit call to Object constructor occurs here
17         firstName = first;
18         lastName = last;
19         socialSecurityNumber = ssn;
20         setGrossSales( sales ); // validate and store gross sales
21         setCommissionRate( rate ); // validate and store commission rate
22      } // end five-argument CommissionEmployee constructor
23
24      // set first name
25      public void setFirstName( String first )
26      {
27         firstName = first; // should validate
28      } // end method setFirstName
29
30      // return first name
31      public String getFirstName()
32      {
33         return firstName;
34      } // end method getFirstName
35
36      // set last name
37      public void setLastName( String last )
38      {
39         lastName = last; // should validate
40      } // end method setLastName
41
42      // return last name
43      public String getLastName()
44      {
45         return lastName;
46      } // end method getLastName
47
48      // set social security number
49      public void setSocialSecurityNumber( String ssn )
50      {
51         socialSecurityNumber = ssn; // should validate
52      } // end method setSocialSecurityNumber
53
54      // return social security number
55      public String getSocialSecurityNumber()
56      {
```

Fig. 9.4 | CommissionEmployee class represents an employee paid a percentage of gross sales. (Part 2 of 3.)

```
57          return socialSecurityNumber;
58      } // end method getSocialSecurityNumber
59
60      // set gross sales amount
61      public void setGrossSales( double sales )
62      {
63          grossSales = ( sales < 0.0 ) ? 0.0 : sales;
64      } // end method setGrossSales
65
66      // return gross sales amount
67      public double getGrossSales()
68      {
69          return grossSales;
70      } // end method getGrossSales
71
72      // set commission rate
73      public void setCommissionRate( double rate )
74      {
75          commissionRate = ( rate > 0.0 && rate < 1.0 ) ? rate : 0.0;
76      } // end method setCommissionRate
77
78      // return commission rate
79      public double getCommissionRate()
80      {
81          return commissionRate;
82      } // end method getCommissionRate
83
84      // calculate earnings
85      public double earnings()
86      {
87          return commissionRate * grossSales;
88      } // end method earnings
89
90      // return String representation of CommissionEmployee object
91      @Override // indicates that this method overrides a superclass method
92      public String toString()
93      {
94          return String.format( "%s: %s %s\n%s: %s\n%s: %.2f\n%s: %.2f",
95              "commission employee", firstName, lastName,
96              "social security number", socialSecurityNumber,
97              "gross sales", grossSales,
98              "commission rate", commissionRate );
99      } // end method toString
100 } // end class CommissionEmployee
```

Fig. 9.4 | CommissionEmployee class represents an employee paid a percentage of gross sales. (Part 3 of 3.)

Overview of Class CommissionEmployee's Methods and Instance Variables

Class CommissionEmployee's public services include a constructor (lines 13–22) and methods earnings (lines 85–88) and toString (lines 91–99). Lines 25–82 declare public *get* and *set* methods for the class's instance variables (declared in lines 6–10) firstName, lastName, socialSecurityNumber, grossSales and commissionRate. The class declares its instance variables as private, so objects of other classes cannot directly access these variables. Declaring instance variables as `private` and providing *get* and *set* methods to manipulate and validate them helps enforce good software engineering. Methods `set-GrossSales` and `setCommissionRate`, for example, validate their arguments before assigning the values to instance variables `grossSales` and `commissionRate`. In a real-world, business-critical application, we'd also perform validation in the class's other *set* methods.

Class *CommissionEmployee's Constructor*

Constructors are not inherited, so class `CommissionEmployee` does not inherit class `Object`'s constructor. However, a superclass's constructors are still available to subclasses. In fact, the first task of any subclass constructor is to call its direct superclass's constructor, either explicitly or implicitly (if no constructor call is specified), to ensure that the instance variables inherited from the superclass are initialized properly. In this example, class `CommissionEmployee`'s constructor calls class `Object`'s constructor implicitly. The syntax for calling a superclass constructor explicitly is discussed in Section 9.4.3. If the code does not include an explicit call to the superclass constructor, Java implicitly calls the superclass's default or no-argument constructor. The comment in line 16 of Fig. 9.4 indicates where the implicit call to the superclass `Object`'s default constructor is made (you do not write the code for this call). `Object`'s default (empty) constructor does nothing. Note that even if a class does not have constructors, the default constructor that the compiler implicitly declares for the class will call the superclass's default or no-argument constructor.

After the implicit call to `Object`'s constructor, lines 17–21 of `CommissionEmployee`'s constructor assign values to the class's instance variables. Note that we do not validate the values of arguments `first`, `last` and `ssn` before assigning them to the corresponding instance variables. We could validate the first and last names—perhaps to ensure that they're of a reasonable length. Similarly, a social security number could be validated to ensure that it contains nine digits, with or without dashes (e.g., 123-45-6789 or 123456789).

Class *CommissionEmployee's* `earnings` *Method*

Method `earnings` (lines 85–88) calculates a `CommissionEmployee`'s earnings. Line 87 multiplies the `commissionRate` by the `grossSales` and returns the result.

Class *CommissionEmployee's* `toString` *Method and the* `@Override` *Annotation*

Method `toString` (lines 91–99) is special—it's one of the methods that every class inherits directly or indirectly from class `Object` (summarized in Section 9.7). Method `toString` returns a `String` representing an object. It's called implicitly whenever an object must be converted to a `String` representation, such as when an object is output by `printf` or `String` method `format` using the `%s` format specifier. Class `Object`'s `toString` method returns a `String` that includes the name of the object's class. It's primarily a placeholder that can be overridden by a subclass to specify an appropriate `String` representation of the data in a subclass object. Method `toString` of class `CommissionEmployee` overrides (redefines) class `Object`'s `toString` method. When invoked, `CommissionEmployee`'s `toString` method uses `String` method `format` to return a `String` containing information about the `CommissionEmployee`. To override a superclass method, a subclass must declare a method with the same signature (method name, number of parameters, parameter types and order of parameter types) as the superclass method—`Object`'s `toString` method takes no parameters, so `CommissionEmployee` declares `toString` with no parameters.

Line 91 uses the **@Override annotation** to indicate that method `toString` should override a superclass method. Annotations have several purposes. For example, when you attempt to override a superclass method, common errors include naming the subclass method incorrectly, or using the wrong number or types of parameters in the parameter list. Each of these problems creates an unintentional overload of the superclass method. If you then attempt to call the method on a subclass object, the superclass's version is invoked and the subclass version is ignored—potentially leading to subtle logic errors. When the compiler encounters a method declared with @Override, it compares the method's signature with the superclass's method signatures. If there is not an exact match, the compiler issues an error message, such as "method does not override or implement a method from a supertype." This indicates that you've accidentally overloaded a superclass method. You can then fix your method's signature so that it matches one in the superclass.

As you'll see when we discuss web applications and web services in Chapters 29–31, annotations can also add complex support code to your classes to simplify the development process and can be used by servers to configure certain aspects of web applications.

Common Programming Error 9.1

Using an incorrect method signature when attempting to override a superclass method causes an unintentional method overload that can lead to subtle logic errors.

Error-Prevention Tip 9.1

Declare overridden methods with the @Override annotation to ensure at compilation time that you defined their signatures correctly. It's always better to find errors at compile time rather than at runtime.

Common Programming Error 9.2

It's a syntax error to override a method with a more restricted access modifier—a public method of the superclass cannot become a protected or private method in the subclass; a protected method of the superclass cannot become a private method in the subclass. Doing so would break the is-a relationship in which it's required that all subclass objects be able to respond to method calls that are made to public methods declared in the superclass. If a public method, for example, could be overridden as a protected or private method, the subclass objects would not be able to respond to the same method calls as superclass objects. Once a method is declared public in a superclass, the method remains public for all that class's direct and indirect subclasses.

Class *CommissionEmployeeTest*

Figure 9.5 tests class CommissionEmployee. Lines 9–10 instantiate a CommissionEmployee object and invoke CommissionEmployee's constructor (lines 13–22 of Fig. 9.4) to initialize it with "Sue" as the first name, "Jones" as the last name, "222-22-2222" as the social security number, 10000 as the gross sales amount and .06 as the commission rate. Lines 15–24 use CommissionEmployee's *get* methods to retrieve the object's instance-variable values for output. Lines 26–27 invoke the object's methods setGrossSales and setCommissionRate to change the values of instance variables grossSales and commissionRate. Lines 29–30 output the String representation of the updated CommissionEmployee. Note that when an object is output using the %s format specifier, the object's toString method is invoked implicitly to obtain the object's String representation. [*Note:* In this chapter, we do not use the earnings methods of our classes; however, these methods are used extensively in Chapter 10.]

```
 1   // Fig. 9.5: CommissionEmployeeTest.java
 2   // CommissionEmployee class test program.
 3
 4   public class CommissionEmployeeTest
 5   {
 6      public static void main( String[] args )
 7      {
 8         // instantiate CommissionEmployee object
 9         CommissionEmployee employee = new CommissionEmployee(
10            "Sue", "Jones", "222-22-2222", 10000, .06 );
11
12         // get commission employee data
13         System.out.println(
14            "Employee information obtained by get methods: \n" );
15         System.out.printf( "%s %s\n", "First name is",
16            employee.getFirstName() );
17         System.out.printf( "%s %s\n", "Last name is",
18            employee.getLastName() );
19         System.out.printf( "%s %s\n", "Social security number is",
20            employee.getSocialSecurityNumber() );
21         System.out.printf( "%s %.2f\n", "Gross sales is",
22            employee.getGrossSales() );
23         System.out.printf( "%s %.2f\n", "Commission rate is",
24            employee.getCommissionRate() );
25
26         employee.setGrossSales( 500 ); // set gross sales
27         employee.setCommissionRate( .1 ); // set commission rate
28
29         System.out.printf( "\n%s:\n\n%s\n",
30            "Updated employee information obtained by toString", employee );
31      } // end main
32   } // end class CommissionEmployeeTest
```

```
Employee information obtained by get methods:

First name is Sue
Last name is Jones
Social security number is 222-22-2222
Gross sales is 10000.00
Commission rate is 0.06

Updated employee information obtained by toString:

commission employee: Sue Jones
social security number: 222-22-2222
gross sales: 500.00
commission rate: 0.10
```

Fig. 9.5 | CommissionEmployee class test program.

9.4.2 Creating and Using a BasePlusCommissionEmployee Class

We now discuss the second part of our introduction to inheritance by declaring and testing (a completely new and independent) class BasePlusCommissionEmployee (Fig. 9.6), which contains a first name, last name, social security number, gross sales amount, commission rate *and* base salary. Class BasePlusCommissionEmployee's public services include a BasePlusCommissionEmployee constructor (lines 15–25) and methods earnings (lines 100–103) and toString (lines 106–115). Lines 28–97 declare public *get* and *set* methods for the class's private instance variables (declared in lines 7–12) firstName, lastName, socialSecurityNumber, grossSales, commissionRate *and* baseSalary. These variables and methods encapsulate all the necessary features of a base-salaried commission employee. Note the similarity between this class and class CommissionEmployee (Fig. 9.4)—in this example, we'll not yet exploit that similarity.

```java
1   // Fig. 9.6: BasePlusCommissionEmployee.java
2   // BasePlusCommissionEmployee class represents an employee that receives
3   // a base salary in addition to commission.
4
5   public class BasePlusCommissionEmployee
6   {
7      private String firstName;
8      private String lastName;
9      private String socialSecurityNumber;
10     private double grossSales; // gross weekly sales
11     private double commissionRate; // commission percentage
12     private double baseSalary; // base salary per week
13
14     // six-argument constructor
15     public BasePlusCommissionEmployee( String first, String last,
16        String ssn, double sales, double rate, double salary )
17     {
18        // implicit call to Object constructor occurs here
19        firstName = first;
20        lastName = last;
21        socialSecurityNumber = ssn;
22        setGrossSales( sales ); // validate and store gross sales
23        setCommissionRate( rate ); // validate and store commission rate
24        setBaseSalary( salary ); // validate and store base salary
25     } // end six-argument BasePlusCommissionEmployee constructor
26
27     // set first name
28     public void setFirstName( String first )
29     {
30        firstName = first; // should validate
31     } // end method setFirstName
32
33     // return first name
34     public String getFirstName()
35     {
36        return firstName;
37     } // end method getFirstName
38
39     // set last name
40     public void setLastName( String last )
41     {
42        lastName = last; // should validate
43     } // end method setLastName
44
```

Fig. 9.6 | BasePlusCommissionEmployee class represents an employee who receives a base salary in addition to a commission. (Part 1 of 3.)

```
45      // return last name
46      public String getLastName()
47      {
48         return lastName;
49      } // end method getLastName
50
51      // set social security number
52      public void setSocialSecurityNumber( String ssn )
53      {
54         socialSecurityNumber = ssn; // should validate
55      } // end method setSocialSecurityNumber
56
57      // return social security number
58      public String getSocialSecurityNumber()
59      {
60         return socialSecurityNumber;
61      } // end method getSocialSecurityNumber
62
63      // set gross sales amount
64      public void setGrossSales( double sales )
65      {
66         grossSales = ( sales < 0.0 ) ? 0.0 : sales;
67      } // end method setGrossSales
68
69      // return gross sales amount
70      public double getGrossSales()
71      {
72         return grossSales;
73      } // end method getGrossSales
74
75      // set commission rate
76      public void setCommissionRate( double rate )
77      {
78         commissionRate = ( rate > 0.0 && rate < 1.0 ) ? rate : 0.0;
79      } // end method setCommissionRate
80
81      // return commission rate
82      public double getCommissionRate()
83      {
84         return commissionRate;
85      } // end method getCommissionRate
86
87      // set base salary
88      public void setBaseSalary( double salary )
89      {
90         baseSalary = ( salary < 0.0 ) ? 0.0 : salary;
91      } // end method setBaseSalary
92
93      // return base salary
94      public double getBaseSalary()
95      {
96         return baseSalary;
97      } // end method getBaseSalary
```

Fig. 9.6 | BasePlusCommissionEmployee class represents an employee who receives a base salary in addition to a commission. (Part 2 of 3.)

```
 98
 99     // calculate earnings
100     public double earnings()
101     {
102        return baseSalary + ( commissionRate * grossSales );
103     } // end method earnings
104
105     // return String representation of BasePlusCommissionEmployee
106     @Override // indicates that this method overrides a superclass method
107     public String toString()
108     {
109        return String.format(
110           "%s: %s %s\n%s: %s\n%s: %.2f\n%s: %.2f\n%s: %.2f",
111           "base-salaried commission employee", firstName, lastName,
112           "social security number", socialSecurityNumber,
113           "gross sales", grossSales, "commission rate", commissionRate,
114           "base salary", baseSalary );
115     } // end method toString
116  } // end class BasePlusCommissionEmployee
```

Fig. 9.6 | BasePlusCommissionEmployee class represents an employee who receives a base salary in addition to a commission. (Part 3 of 3.)

Note that class BasePlusCommissionEmployee does not specify "extends Object" in line 5, so the class implicitly extends Object. Also, like class CommissionEmployee's constructor (lines 13–22 of Fig. 9.4), class BasePlusCommissionEmployee's constructor invokes class Object's default constructor implicitly, as noted in the comment in line 18.

Class BasePlusCommissionEmployee's earnings method (lines 100–103) returns the result of adding the BasePlusCommissionEmployee's base salary to the product of the commission rate and the employee's gross sales.

Class BasePlusCommissionEmployee overrides Object method toString to return a String containing the BasePlusCommissionEmployee's information. Once again, we use format specifier %.2f to format the gross sales, commission rate and base salary with two digits of precision to the right of the decimal point (line 110).

*Testing Class **BasePlusCommissionEmployee***

Figure 9.7 tests class BasePlusCommissionEmployee. Lines 9–11 create a BasePlusCommissionEmployee object and pass "Bob", "Lewis", "333-33-3333", 5000, .04 and 300 to the constructor as the first name, last name, social security number, gross sales, commission rate and base salary, respectively. Lines 16–27 use BasePlusCommissionEmployee's *get* methods to retrieve the values of the object's instance variables for output. Line 29 invokes the object's setBaseSalary method to change the base salary. Method setBaseSalary (Fig. 9.6, lines 88–91) ensures that instance variable baseSalary is not assigned a negative value, because an employee's base salary cannot be negative. Lines 31–33 of Fig. 9.7 invoke method toString explicitly to get the object's String representation.

```
 1   // Fig. 9.7: BasePlusCommissionEmployeeTest.java
 2   // BasePlusCommissionEmployee test program.
 3
```

Fig. 9.7 | BasePlusCommissionEmployee test program. (Part 1 of 2.)

```
4   public class BasePlusCommissionEmployeeTest
5   {
6      public static void main( String[] args )
7      {
8         // instantiate BasePlusCommissionEmployee object
9         BasePlusCommissionEmployee employee =
10           new BasePlusCommissionEmployee(
11           "Bob", "Lewis", "333-33-3333", 5000, .04, 300 );
12
13        // get base-salaried commission employee data
14        System.out.println(
15           "Employee information obtained by get methods: \n" );
16        System.out.printf( "%s %s\n", "First name is",
17           employee.getFirstName() );
18        System.out.printf( "%s %s\n", "Last name is",
19           employee.getLastName() );
20        System.out.printf( "%s %s\n", "Social security number is",
21           employee.getSocialSecurityNumber() );
22        System.out.printf( "%s %.2f\n", "Gross sales is",
23           employee.getGrossSales() );
24        System.out.printf( "%s %.2f\n", "Commission rate is",
25           employee.getCommissionRate() );
26        System.out.printf( "%s %.2f\n", "Base salary is",
27           employee.getBaseSalary() );
28
29        employee.setBaseSalary( 1000 ); // set base salary
30
31        System.out.printf( "\n%s:\n\n%s\n",
32           "Updated employee information obtained by toString",
33           employee.toString() );
34     } // end main
35  } // end class BasePlusCommissionEmployeeTest
```

```
Employee information obtained by get methods:

First name is Bob
Last name is Lewis
Social security number is 333-33-3333
Gross sales is 5000.00
Commission rate is 0.04
Base salary is 300.00

Updated employee information obtained by toString:

base-salaried commission employee: Bob Lewis
social security number: 333-33-3333
gross sales: 5000.00
commission rate: 0.04
base salary: 1000.00
```

Fig. 9.7 | BasePlusCommissionEmployee test program. (Part 2 of 2.)

Notes on Class *BasePlusCommissionEmployee*

Much of class BasePlusCommissionEmployee's code (Fig. 9.6) is similar, or identical, to that of class CommissionEmployee (Fig. 9.4). For example, private instance variables firstName and lastName and methods setFirstName, getFirstName, setLastName and getLastName are identical to those of class CommissionEmployee. The classes also both contain private instance variables socialSecurityNumber, commissionRate and gross-Sales, and corresponding *get* and *set* methods. In addition, the BasePlusCommissionEmployee constructor is almost identical to that of class CommissionEmployee, except that BasePlusCommissionEmployee's constructor also sets the baseSalary. The other additions to class BasePlusCommissionEmployee are private instance variable baseSalary and methods setBaseSalary and getBaseSalary. Class BasePlusCommissionEmployee's toString method is nearly identical to that of class CommissionEmployee except that BasePlusCommissionEmployee's toString also outputs instance variable baseSalary with two digits of precision to the right of the decimal point.

We literally *copied* code from class CommissionEmployee and *pasted* it into class BasePlusCommissionEmployee, then modified class BasePlusCommissionEmployee to include a base salary and methods that manipulate the base salary. This "copy-and-paste" approach is often error prone and time consuming. Worse yet, it spreads copies of the same code throughout a system, creating a code-maintenance nightmare. Is there a way to "absorb" the instance variables and methods of one class in a way that makes them part of other classes without duplicating code? Next we answer this question, using a more elegant approach to building classes that emphasizes the benefits of inheritance.

Software Engineering Observation 9.3

With inheritance, the common instance variables and methods of all the classes in the hierarchy are declared in a superclass. When changes are made for these common features in the superclass—subclasses then inherit the changes. Without inheritance, changes would need to be made to all the source-code files that contain a copy of the code in question.

9.4.3 Creating a CommissionEmployee– BasePlusCommissionEmployee Inheritance Hierarchy

Now we declare a new BasePlusCommissionEmployee class (Fig. 9.8), which extends class CommissionEmployee (Fig. 9.4). A BasePlusCommissionEmployee object *is a* CommissionEmployee, because inheritance passes on class CommissionEmployee's capabilities. Class BasePlusCommissionEmployee also has instance variable baseSalary (Fig. 9.8, line 6). Keyword extends (line 4) indicates inheritance. Subclass BasePlusCommissionEmployee inherits CommissionEmployee's instance variables and methods—recall that only the superclass's public and protected members are directly accessible in the subclass. The CommissionEmployee constructor is not inherited. So, the public BasePlusCommissionEmployee services include its constructor (lines 9–16), public methods inherited from CommissionEmployee, method setBaseSalary (lines 19–22), method getBaseSalary (lines 25–28), method earnings (lines 31–36) and method toString (lines 39–49). Methods earnings and toString override the corresponding methods in class CommissionEmployee because the superclass versions of these methods do not properly calculate a BasePlusCommissionEmployee's earnings or return an appropriate String representation.

```
1   // Fig. 9.8: BasePlusCommissionEmployee.java
2   // private superclass members cannot be accessed in a subclass.
3
```

Fig. 9.8 | private superclass members cannot be accessed in a subclass. (Part 1 of 3.)

```
4   public class BasePlusCommissionEmployee extends CommissionEmployee
5   {
6      private double baseSalary; // base salary per week
7
8      // six-argument constructor
9      public BasePlusCommissionEmployee( String first, String last,
10        String ssn, double sales, double rate, double salary )
11     {
12        // explicit call to superclass CommissionEmployee constructor
13        super( first, last, ssn, sales, rate );
14
15        setBaseSalary( salary ); // validate and store base salary
16     } // end six-argument BasePlusCommissionEmployee constructor
17
18     // set base salary
19     public void setBaseSalary( double salary )
20     {
21        baseSalary = ( salary < 0.0 ) ? 0.0 : salary;
22     } // end method setBaseSalary
23
24     // return base salary
25     public double getBaseSalary()
26     {
27        return baseSalary;
28     } // end method getBaseSalary
29
30     // calculate earnings
31     @Override // indicates that this method overrides a superclass method
32     public double earnings()
33     {
34        // not allowed: commissionRate and grossSales private in superclass
35        return baseSalary + ( commissionRate * grossSales );
36     } // end method earnings
37
38     // return String representation of BasePlusCommissionEmployee
39     @Override // indicates that this method overrides a superclass method
40     public String toString()
41     {
42        // not allowed: attempts to access private superclass members
43        return String.format(
44           "%s: %s %s\n%s: %s\n%s: %.2f\n%s: %.2f\n%s: %.2f",
45           "base-salaried commission employee", firstName, lastName,
46           "social security number", socialSecurityNumber,
47           "gross sales", grossSales, "commission rate", commissionRate,
48           "base salary", baseSalary );
49     } // end method toString
50  } // end class BasePlusCommissionEmployee
```

```
BasePlusCommissionEmployee.java:35: commissionRate has private access in
CommissionEmployee
      return baseSalary + ( commissionRate * grossSales );
                            ^
```
(continued...)

Fig. 9.8 | private superclass members cannot be accessed in a subclass. (Part 2 of 3.)

```
BasePlusCommissionEmployee.java:35: grossSales has private access in
CommissionEmployee
      return baseSalary + ( commissionRate * grossSales );
                                             ^
BasePlusCommissionEmployee.java:45: firstName has private access in
CommissionEmployee
        "base-salaried commission employee", firstName, lastName,
                                              ^
BasePlusCommissionEmployee.java:45: lastName has private access in
CommissionEmployee
        "base-salaried commission employee", firstName, lastName,
                                                         ^
BasePlusCommissionEmployee.java:46: socialSecurityNumber has private access in
CommissionEmployee
        "social security number", socialSecurityNumber,
                                  ^
BasePlusCommissionEmployee.java:47: grossSales has private access in
CommissionEmployee
        "gross sales", grossSales, "commission rate", commissionRate,
                       ^
BasePlusCommissionEmployee.java:47: commissionRate has private access in
CommissionEmployee
        "gross sales", grossSales, "commission rate", commissionRate,
                                                      ^
7 errors
```

Fig. 9.8 | private superclass members cannot be accessed in a subclass. (Part 3 of 3.)

Each subclass constructor must implicitly or explicitly call its superclass constructor to initialize the instance variables inherited from the superclass. Line 13 in BasePlusCommissionEmployee's six-argument constructor (lines 9–16) explicitly calls class CommissionEmployee's five-argument constructor (declared at lines 13–22 of Fig. 9.4) to initialize the superclass portion of a BasePlusCommissionEmployee object (i.e., variables firstName, lastName, socialSecurityNumber, grossSales and commissionRate). We do this by using the superclass constructor call syntax—keyword super, followed by a set of parentheses containing the superclass constructor arguments. The arguments first, last, ssn, sales and rate are used to initialize superclass members firstName, lastName, socialSecurityNumber, grossSales and commissionRate, respectively. If BasePlusCommissionEmployee's constructor did not invoke the superclass's constructor explicitly, Java would attempt to invoke the superclass's no-argument or default constructor. Class CommissionEmployee does not have such a constructor, so the compiler would issue an error. The explicit superclass constructor call in line 13 of Fig. 9.8 must be the first statement in the subclass constructor's body. When a superclass contains a no-argument constructor, you can use super() to call that constructor explicitly, but this is rarely done.

Common Programming Error 9.3

A compilation error occurs if a subclass constructor calls a superclass constructor with arguments that do not match the number and types of parameters in one of the superclass's constructors.

The compiler generates errors for line 35 of Fig. 9.8 because superclass CommissionEmployee's instance variables commissionRate and grossSales are private—subclass BasePlusCommissionEmployee's methods are not allowed to access superclass CommissionEmployee's private instance variables. Note that we used red text in Fig. 9.8 to indicate erroneous code. The compiler issues additional errors at lines 45–47 of BasePlusCommissionEmployee's toString method for the same reason. The errors in BasePlusCommissionEmployee could have been prevented by using the *get* methods inherited from class CommissionEmployee. For example, line 35 could have used getCommissionRate and getGrossSales to access CommissionEmployee's private instance variables commissionRate and grossSales, respectively. Lines 45–47 also could have used appropriate *get* methods to retrieve the values of the superclass's instance variables.

9.4.4 CommissionEmployee–BasePlusCommissionEmployee Inheritance Hierarchy Using protected Instance Variables

To enable class BasePlusCommissionEmployee to directly access superclass instance variables firstName, lastName, socialSecurityNumber, grossSales and commissionRate, we can declare those members as protected in the superclass. As we discussed in Section 9.3, a superclass's protected members *are* accessible by all subclasses of that superclass. In the new CommissionEmployee class, we modified only lines 6–10 to declare the instance variables with the protected access modifier as follows:

```
protected String firstName;
protected String lastName;
protected String socialSecurityNumber;
protected double grossSales; // gross weekly sales
protected double commissionRate; // commission percentage
```

The rest of the class declaration (which is not shown here) is identical to that of Fig. 9.4.

We could have declared CommissionEmployee's instance variables public to enable subclass BasePlusCommissionEmployee to access them. However, declaring public instance variables is poor software engineering because it allows unrestricted access to the instance variables, greatly increasing the chance of errors. With protected instance variables, the subclass gets access to the instance variables, but classes that are not subclasses and classes that are not in the same package cannot access these variables directly—recall that protected class members are also visible to other classes in the same package.

Class *BasePlusCommissionEmployee*

Class BasePlusCommissionEmployee (Fig. 9.9) extends the new version of class CommissionEmployee with protected instance variables. BasePlusCommissionEmployee objects inherit CommissionEmployee's protected instance variables firstName, lastName, socialSecurityNumber, grossSales and commissionRate—all these variables are now protected members of BasePlusCommissionEmployee. As a result, the compiler does not generate errors when compiling line 33 of method earnings and lines 42–44 of method toString. If another class extends this version of class BasePlusCommissionEmployee, the new subclass also can access the protected members.

```
1   // Fig. 9.9: BasePlusCommissionEmployee.java
2   // BasePlusCommissionEmployee inherits protected instance
3   // variables from CommissionEmployee.
```

Fig. 9.9 | BasePlusCommissionEmployee inherits protected instance variables from CommissionEmployee. (Part 1 of 2.)

```
4
5   public class BasePlusCommissionEmployee extends CommissionEmployee
6   {
7      private double baseSalary; // base salary per week
8
9      // six-argument constructor
10     public BasePlusCommissionEmployee( String first, String last,
11        String ssn, double sales, double rate, double salary )
12     {
13        super( first, last, ssn, sales, rate );
14        setBaseSalary( salary ); // validate and store base salary
15     } // end six-argument BasePlusCommissionEmployee constructor
16
17     // set base salary
18     public void setBaseSalary( double salary )
19     {
20        baseSalary = ( salary < 0.0 ) ? 0.0 : salary;
21     } // end method setBaseSalary
22
23     // return base salary
24     public double getBaseSalary()
25     {
26        return baseSalary;
27     } // end method getBaseSalary
28
29     // calculate earnings
30     @Override // indicates that this method overrides a superclass method
31     public double earnings()
32     {
33        return baseSalary + ( commissionRate * grossSales );
34     } // end method earnings
35
36     // return String representation of BasePlusCommissionEmployee
37     @Override // indicates that this method overrides a superclass method
38     public String toString()
39     {
40        return String.format(
41           "%s: %s %s\n%s: %s\n%s: %.2f\n%s: %.2f\n%s: %.2f",
42           "base-salaried commission employee", firstName, lastName,
43           "social security number", socialSecurityNumber,
44           "gross sales", grossSales, "commission rate", commissionRate,
45           "base salary", baseSalary );
46     } // end method toString
47  } // end class BasePlusCommissionEmployee
```

Fig. 9.9 | BasePlusCommissionEmployee inherits protected instance variables from CommissionEmployee. (Part 2 of 2.)

When you create a BasePlusCommissionEmployee object, it contains all instance variables declared in the class hierarchy to that point—i.e., those from classes Object, CommissionEmployee and BasePlusCommissionEmployee. Class BasePlusCommissionEmployee does not inherit class CommissionEmployee's constructor. However, class BasePlusCommissionEmployee's six-argument constructor (lines 10–15) calls class CommissionEmployee's five-argument constructor explicitly to initialize the instance variables that

BasePlusCommissionEmployee inherited from class CommissionEmployee. Similarly, class CommissionEmployee's constructor calls class Object's constructor. BasePlusCommissionEmployee's constructor must do this explicitly because CommissionEmployee does not provide a no-argument constructor that could be invoked implicitly.

Testing Class *BasePlusCommissionEmployee*
The BasePlusCommissionEmployeeTest class for this example is identical to that of Fig. 9.7 and produces the same output, so we do not show it here. Although the version of class BasePlusCommissionEmployee in Fig. 9.6 does not use inheritance and the version in Fig. 9.9 does, *both classes provide the same functionality*. The source code in Fig. 9.9 (47 lines) is considerably shorter than that in Fig. 9.6 (116 lines), because most of Base-PlusCommissionEmployee's functionality is now inherited from CommissionEmployee—there is now only one copy of the CommissionEmployee functionality. This makes the code easier to maintain, modify and debug, because the code related to a commission employee exists only in class CommissionEmployee.

Notes on Using *protected* Instance Variables
In this example, we declared superclass instance variables as protected so that subclasses could access them. Inheriting protected instance variables slightly increases performance, because we can directly access the variables in the subclass without incurring the overhead of a *set* or *get* method call. In most cases, however, it's better to use private instance variables to encourage proper software engineering, and leave code optimization issues to the compiler. Your code will be easier to maintain, modify and debug.

Using protected instance variables creates several potential problems. First, the subclass object can set an inherited variable's value directly without using a *set* method. Therefore, a subclass object can assign an invalid value to the variable, possibly leaving the object in an inconsistent state. For example, if we were to declare CommissionEmployee's instance variable grossSales as protected, a subclass object (e.g., BasePlusCommissionEmployee) could then assign a negative value to grossSales. Another problem with using protected instance variables is that subclass methods are more likely to be written so that they depend on the superclass's data implementation. In practice, subclasses should depend only on the superclass services (i.e., non-private methods) and not on the superclass data implementation. With protected instance variables in the superclass, we may need to modify all the subclasses of the superclass if the superclass implementation changes. For example, if for some reason we were to change the names of instance variables firstName and lastName to first and last, then we would have to do so for all occurrences in which a subclass directly references superclass instance variables firstName and lastName. In such a case, the software is said to be fragile or brittle, because a small change in the superclass can "break" subclass implementation. You should be able to change the superclass implementation while still providing the same services to the subclasses. Of course, if the superclass services change, we must reimplement our subclasses. A third problem is that a class's protected members are visible to all classes in the same package as the class containing the protected members—this is not always desirable.

Software Engineering Observation 9.4
Use the protected *access modifier when a superclass should provide a method only to its subclasses and other classes in the same package, but not to other clients.*

Software Engineering Observation 9.5

Declaring superclass instance variables private *(as opposed to* protected*) enables the superclass implementation of these instance variables to change without affecting subclass implementations.*

Error-Prevention Tip 9.2

When possible, do not include protected *instance variables in a superclass. Instead, include non-private methods that access* private *instance variables. This will help ensure that objects of the class maintain consistent states.*

9.4.5 CommissionEmployee–BasePlusCommissionEmployee Inheritance Hierarchy Using private Instance Variables

Let's reexamine our hierarchy once more, this time using good software engineering practices. Class CommissionEmployee (Fig. 9.10) declares instance variables firstName, lastName, socialSecurityNumber, grossSales and commissionRate as private (lines 6–10) and provides public methods setFirstName, getFirstName, setLastName, getLastName, setSocialSecurityNumber, getSocialSecurityNumber, setGrossSales, getGrossSales, setCommissionRate, getCommissionRate, earnings and toString for manipulating these values. Note that methods earnings (lines 85–88) and toString (lines 91–99) use the class's *get* methods to obtain the values of its instance variables. If we decide to change the instance-variable names, the earnings and toString declarations will not require modification—only the bodies of the *get* and *set* methods that directly manipulate the instance variables will need to change. Note that these changes occur solely within the superclass—no changes to the subclass are needed. Localizing the effects of changes like this is a good software engineering practice. Subclass BasePlusCommissionEmployee (Fig. 9.11) inherits CommissionEmployee's non-private methods and can access the private superclass members via those methods.

```
 1  // Fig. 9.10: CommissionEmployee.java
 2  // CommissionEmployee class uses methods to manipulate its
 3  // private instance variables.
 4  public class CommissionEmployee
 5  {
 6     private String firstName;
 7     private String lastName;
 8     private String socialSecurityNumber;
 9     private double grossSales; // gross weekly sales
10     private double commissionRate; // commission percentage
11
12     // five-argument constructor
13     public CommissionEmployee( String first, String last, String ssn,
14        double sales, double rate )
15     {
16        // implicit call to Object constructor occurs here
17        firstName = first;
18        lastName = last;
19        socialSecurityNumber = ssn;
```

Fig. 9.10 | CommissionEmployee class uses methods to manipulate its private instance variables. (Part 1 of 3.)

```
20        setGrossSales( sales ); // validate and store gross sales
21        setCommissionRate( rate ); // validate and store commission rate
22    } // end five-argument CommissionEmployee constructor
23
24    // set first name
25    public void setFirstName( String first )
26    {
27        firstName = first; // should validate
28    } // end method setFirstName
29
30    // return first name
31    public String getFirstName()
32    {
33        return firstName;
34    } // end method getFirstName
35
36    // set last name
37    public void setLastName( String last )
38    {
39        lastName = last; // should validate
40    } // end method setLastName
41
42    // return last name
43    public String getLastName()
44    {
45        return lastName;
46    } // end method getLastName
47
48    // set social security number
49    public void setSocialSecurityNumber( String ssn )
50    {
51        socialSecurityNumber = ssn; // should validate
52    } // end method setSocialSecurityNumber
53
54    // return social security number
55    public String getSocialSecurityNumber()
56    {
57        return socialSecurityNumber;
58    } // end method getSocialSecurityNumber
59
60    // set gross sales amount
61    public void setGrossSales( double sales )
62    {
63        grossSales = ( sales < 0.0 ) ? 0.0 : sales;
64    } // end method setGrossSales
65
66    // return gross sales amount
67    public double getGrossSales()
68    {
69        return grossSales;
70    } // end method getGrossSales
71
```

Fig. 9.10 | CommissionEmployee class uses methods to manipulate its private instance variables. (Part 2 of 3.)

```
72      // set commission rate
73      public void setCommissionRate( double rate )
74      {
75         commissionRate = ( rate > 0.0 && rate < 1.0 ) ? rate : 0.0;
76      } // end method setCommissionRate
77
78      // return commission rate
79      public double getCommissionRate()
80      {
81         return commissionRate;
82      } // end method getCommissionRate
83
84      // calculate earnings
85      public double earnings()
86      {
87         return getCommissionRate() * getGrossSales();
88      } // end method earnings
89
90      // return String representation of CommissionEmployee object
91      @Override // indicates that this method overrides a superclass method
92      public String toString()
93      {
94         return String.format( "%s: %s %s\n%s: %s\n%s: %.2f\n%s: %.2f",
95            "commission employee", getFirstName(), getLastName(),
96            "social security number", getSocialSecurityNumber(),
97            "gross sales", getGrossSales(),
98            "commission rate", getCommissionRate() );
99      } // end method toString
100  } // end class CommissionEmployee
```

Fig. 9.10 | CommissionEmployee class uses methods to manipulate its private instance variables. (Part 3 of 3.)

Class BasePlusCommissionEmployee (Fig. 9.11) has several changes that distinguish it from Fig. 9.9. Methods earnings (Fig. 9.11, lines 31–35) and toString (lines 38–43) each invoke method getBaseSalary to obtain the base salary value, rather than accessing baseSalary directly. If we decide to rename instance variable baseSalary, only the bodies of method setBaseSalary and getBaseSalary will need to change.

```
1    // Fig. 9.11: BasePlusCommissionEmployee.java
2    // BasePlusCommissionEmployee class inherits from CommissionEmployee
3    // and accesses the superclass's private data via inherited
4    // public methods.
5
6    public class BasePlusCommissionEmployee extends CommissionEmployee
7    {
8       private double baseSalary; // base salary per week
9
```

Fig. 9.11 | BasePlusCommissionEmployee class inherits from CommissionEmployee and accesses the superclass's private data via inherited public methods. (Part 1 of 2.)

```
10      // six-argument constructor
11      public BasePlusCommissionEmployee( String first, String last,
12         String ssn, double sales, double rate, double salary )
13      {
14         super( first, last, ssn, sales, rate );
15         setBaseSalary( salary ); // validate and store base salary
16      } // end six-argument BasePlusCommissionEmployee constructor
17
18      // set base salary
19      public void setBaseSalary( double salary )
20      {
21         baseSalary = ( salary < 0.0 ) ? 0.0 : salary;
22      } // end method setBaseSalary
23
24      // return base salary
25      public double getBaseSalary()
26      {
27         return baseSalary;
28      } // end method getBaseSalary
29
30      // calculate earnings
31      @Override // indicates that this method overrides a superclass method
32      public double earnings()
33      {
34         return getBaseSalary() + super.earnings();
35      } // end method earnings
36
37      // return String representation of BasePlusCommissionEmployee
38      @Override // indicates that this method overrides a superclass method
39      public String toString()
40      {
41         return String.format( "%s %s\n%s: %.2f", "base-salaried",
42            super.toString(), "base salary", getBaseSalary() );
43      } // end method toString
44   } // end class BasePlusCommissionEmployee
```

Fig. 9.11 | BasePlusCommissionEmployee class inherits from CommissionEmployee and accesses the superclass's private data via inherited public methods. (Part 2 of 2.)

Class *BasePlusCommissionEmployee's earnings Method*

Method earnings (Fig. 9.11, lines 31–35) overrides class CommissionEmployee's earnings method (Fig. 9.10, lines 85–88) to calculate a base-salaried commission employee's earnings. The new version obtains the portion of the earnings based on commission alone by calling CommissionEmployee's earnings method with super.earnings() (Fig. 9.11, line 34). BasePlusCommissionEmployee's earnings method then adds the base salary to this value to calculate the total earnings. Note the syntax used to invoke an overridden superclass method from a subclass—place the keyword super and a dot (.) separator before the superclass method name. This method invocation is a good software engineering practice—if a method performs all or some of the actions needed by another method, call that method rather than duplicate its code. By having BasePlusCommissionEmployee's earnings method invoke CommissionEmployee's earnings method to calculate part of a BasePlusCommissionEmployee object's earnings, we avoid duplicating the code and reduce code-maintenance problems. If we did not use "super." then BasePlusCommissionEmployee's `earnings` method would call itself rather than the superclass version. This would result in a phenomenon we study in Chapter 18 called infinite recursion, which would eventually cause the method call stack to overflow—a fatal runtime error.

Common Programming Error 9.4

When a superclass method is overridden in a subclass, the subclass version often calls the superclass version to do a portion of the work. Failure to prefix the superclass method name with the keyword `super` and a dot (`.`) separator when calling the superclass's method causes the subclass method to call itself, potentially creating an error called infinite recursion. Recursion, used correctly, is a powerful capability discussed in Chapter 18, Recursion.

Class *BasePlusCommissionEmployee*'s *toString Method*

Similarly, `BasePlusCommissionEmployee`'s `toString` method (Fig. 9.11, lines 38–43) overrides class `CommissionEmployee`'s `toString` method (Fig. 9.10, lines 91–99) to return a `String` representation that is appropriate for a base-salaried commission employee. The new version creates part of a `BasePlusCommissionEmployee` object's `String` representation (i.e., the `String` `"commission employee"` and the values of class `CommissionEmployee`'s `private` instance variables) by calling `CommissionEmployee`'s `toString` method with the expression `super.toString()` (Fig. 9.11, line 42). `BasePlusCommissionEmployee`'s `toString` method then outputs the remainder of a `BasePlusCommissionEmployee` object's `String` representation (i.e., the value of class `BasePlusCommissionEmployee`'s base salary).

Testing Class *BasePlusCommissionEmployee*

Class `BasePlusCommissionEmployeeTest` performs the same manipulations on a `BasePlusCommissionEmployee` object as in Fig. 9.7 and produces the same output, so we do not show it here. Although each `BasePlusCommissionEmployee` class you've seen behaves identically, the version in Fig. 9.11 is the best engineered. By using inheritance and by calling methods that hide the data and ensure consistency, we've efficiently and effectively constructed a well-engineered class.

Summary of the Inheritance Examples in Sections 9.4.1—9.4.5

You've now seen a set of examples that were designed to teach good software engineering with inheritance. You used the keyword `extends` to create a subclass using inheritance, used `protected` superclass members to enable a subclass to access inherited superclass instance variables, and overrode superclass methods to provide versions that are more appropriate for subclass objects. In addition, you applied software engineering techniques from Chapter 8 and this chapter to create classes that are easy to maintain, modify and debug.

9.5 Constructors in Subclasses

As we explained in the preceding section, instantiating a subclass object begins a chain of constructor calls in which the subclass constructor, before performing its own tasks, invokes its direct superclass's constructor either explicitly via the `super` reference or implicitly calling the superclass's default constructor or no-argument constructor. Similarly, if the superclass is derived from another class—as is, of course, every class except `Object`—the superclass constructor invokes the constructor of the next class up the hierarchy, and so on. The last constructor called in the chain is *always* the constructor for class `Object`. The original subclass constructor's body finishes executing last. Each superclass's constructor manipulates the superclass instance variables that the subclass object inherits. For example, consider again the CommissionEmployee–BasePlusCommissionEmployee hierarchy from Fig. 9.10 and Fig. 9.11. When a program creates a BasePlusCommissionEmployee object, its constructor is called. That constructor calls CommissionEmployee's constructor, which in turn calls Object's constructor. Class Object's constructor has an empty body, so it immediately returns control to CommissionEmployee's constructor, which then initializes the CommissionEmployee private instance variables that are part of the Base-PlusCommissionEmployee object. When CommissionEmployee's constructor completes execution, it returns control to BasePlusCommissionEmployee's constructor, which initializes the BasePlusCommissionEmployee object's baseSalary.

Software Engineering Observation 9.6

When a program creates a subclass object, the subclass constructor immediately calls the superclass constructor (explicitly, via super, or implicitly). The superclass constructor's body executes to initialize the superclass's instance variables that are part of the subclass object, then the subclass constructor's body executes to initialize the subclass-only instance variables. Java ensures that even if a constructor does not assign a value to an instance variable, the variable is still initialized to its default value (e.g., 0 for primitive numeric types, false for booleans, null for references).

9.6 Software Engineering with Inheritance

When you extend a class, the new class inherits the superclass's members—though the private superclass members are hidden in the new class. You can customize the new class to meet your needs by including additional members and by overriding superclass members. Doing this does not require the subclass programmer to change (or even have access to) the superclass's source code. Java simply requires access to the superclass's .class file so it can compile and execute any program that uses or extends the superclass. This powerful capability is attractive to independent software vendors (ISVs), who can develop proprietary classes for sale or license and make them available to users in bytecode format. Users then can derive new classes from these library classes rapidly and without accessing the ISVs' proprietary source code.

Software Engineering Observation 9.7

Although inheriting from a class does not require access to the class's source code, developers often insist on seeing the source code to understand how the class is implemented. Developers in industry want to ensure that they're extending a solid class—for example, a class that performs well and is implemented robustly and securely.

It's sometimes difficult to appreciate the scope of the problems faced by designers who work on large-scale software projects. People experienced with such projects say that effective software reuse improves the software-development process. Object-oriented programming facilitates software reuse, often significantly shortening development time.

The availability of substantial and useful class libraries delivers the maximum benefits of software reuse through inheritance. The standard Java class libraries that are shipped with Java tend to be rather general purpose, encouraging broad software reuse. Many other class libraries exist.

Reading subclass declarations can be confusing, because inherited members are not declared explicitly in the subclasses but are nevertheless present in them. A similar problem exists in documenting subclass members.

Software Engineering Observation 9.8

At the design stage in an object-oriented system, you'll often find that certain classes are closely related. You should "factor out" common instance variables and methods and place them in a superclass. Then use inheritance to develop subclasses, specializing them with capabilities beyond those inherited from the superclass.

Software Engineering Observation 9.9

Declaring a subclass does not affect its superclass's source code. Inheritance preserves the integrity of the superclass.

Software Engineering Observation 9.10

Just as designers of non-object-oriented systems should avoid method proliferation, designers of object-oriented systems should avoid class proliferation. Such proliferation creates management problems and can hinder software reusability, because in a huge class library it becomes difficult to locate the most appropriate classes. The alternative is to create fewer classes that provide more substantial functionality, but such classes might prove cumbersome.

Performance Tip 9.1

If subclasses are larger than they need to be (i.e., contain too much functionality), memory and processing resources might be wasted. Extend the superclass that contains the functionality closest to what you need.

9.7 Object Class

As we discussed earlier in this chapter, all classes in Java inherit directly or indirectly from the Object class (package java.lang), so its 11 methods are inherited by all other classes. Figure 9.12 summarizes Object's methods.

Method	Description
clone	This protected method, which takes no arguments and returns an Object reference, makes a copy of the object on which it's called. The default implementation performs a so-called shallow copy—instance-variable values in one object are copied into another object of the same type. For reference types, only the references are copied. A typical overridden clone method's implementation would perform a deep copy that creates a new object for each reference-type instance variable. Implementing clone correctly is difficult. For this reason, its use is discouraged. Many industry experts suggest that object serialization should be used instead. We discuss object serialization in Chapter 17, Files, Streams and Object Serialization.
equals	This method compares two objects for equality and returns true if they're equal and false otherwise. The method takes any Object as an argument. When objects of a particular class must be compared for equality, the class should override method equals to compare the *contents* of the two objects.

Fig. 9.12 | Object methods. (Part 1 of 2.)

Method	Description
equals *(cont.)*	For the requirements of implementing this method, refer to the method's documentation at java.sun.com/javase/6/docs/api/java/lang/ Object.html# equals(java.lang.Object). The default equals implementation uses operator == to determine whether two references *refer to the same object* in memory. Section 6.15.3 demonstrated class String's equals method and differentiated between comparing String objects with == and with equals.
finalize	This protected method (introduced in Section 8.10) is called by the garbage collector to perform termination housekeeping on an object just before the garbage collector reclaims the object's memory. Recall that it's unclear whether, or when, method finalize will be called. For this reason, most programmers should avoid method finalize.
getClass	Every object in Java knows its own type at execution time. Method getClass (used in Sections 10.5, 14.5 and 24.3) returns an object of class Class (package java.lang) that contains information about the object's type, such as its class name (returned by Class method getName). For more about class Class visit java.sun.com/javase/6/docs/api/java/lang/Class.html.
hashCode	Hashcodes are int values that are useful for high-speed storage and retrieval of information stored in a data structure that is known as a hashtable (discussed in Section 20.11). This method is also called as part of class Object's default toString method implementation.
wait, notify, notifyAll	Methods notify, notifyAll and the three overloaded versions of wait are related to multithreading, which is discussed in Chapter 26.
toString	This method (introduced in Section 9.4.1) returns a String representation of an object. The default implementation of this method returns the package name and class name of the object's class followed by a hexadecimal representation of the value returned by the object's hashCode method.

Fig. 9.12 | Object methods. (Part 2 of 2.)

We discuss several Object methods throughout this book (as indicated in Fig. 9.12). You can learn more about Object's methods in Object's online API documentation and in *The Java Tutorial* at the following sites:

```
java.sun.com/javase/6/docs/api/java/lang/Object.html
java.sun.com/docs/books/tutorial/java/IandI/objectclass.html
```

Recall from Chapter 6 that arrays are objects. As a result, like all other objects, arrays inherit the members of class Object. Note that every array has an overridden clone method that copies the array. However, if the array stores references to objects, the objects are not copied—a shallow copy is performed. For more information about the relationship between arrays and class Object, see *Java Language Specification,* Chapter 10, at

```
java.sun.com/docs/books/jls/third_edition/html/arrays.html
```

9.8 (Optional) GUI and Graphics Case Study: Displaying Text and Images Using Labels

Programs often use labels when they need to display information or instructions to the user in a graphical user interface. Labels are a convenient way of identifying GUI components on the screen and keeping the user informed about the current state of the program. In Java, an object of class JLabel (from package javax.swing) can display text, an image or both. The example in Fig. 9.13 demonstrates several JLabel features, including a plain text label, an image label and a label with both text and an image.

```java
1   // Fig 9.13: LabelDemo.java
2   // Demonstrates the use of labels.
3   import java.awt.BorderLayout;
4   import javax.swing.ImageIcon;
5   import javax.swing.JLabel;
6   import javax.swing.JFrame;
7
8   public class LabelDemo
9   {
10     public static void main( String[] args )
11     {
12        // Create a label with plain text
13        JLabel northLabel = new JLabel( "North" );
14
15        // create an icon from an image so we can put it on a JLabel
16        ImageIcon labelIcon = new ImageIcon( "GUItip.gif" );
17
18        // create a label with an Icon instead of text
19        JLabel centerLabel = new JLabel( labelIcon );
20
21        // create another label with an Icon
22        JLabel southLabel = new JLabel( labelIcon );
23
24        // set the label to display text (as well as an icon)
25        southLabel.setText( "South" );
26
27        // create a frame to hold the labels
28        JFrame application = new JFrame();
29
30        application.setDefaultCloseOperation( JFrame.EXIT_ON_CLOSE );
31
32        // add the labels to the frame; the second argument specifies
33        // where on the frame to add the label
34        application.add( northLabel, BorderLayout.NORTH );
35        application.add( centerLabel, BorderLayout.CENTER );
36        application.add( southLabel, BorderLayout.SOUTH );
37
38        application.setSize( 300, 300 ); // set the size of the frame
39        application.setVisible( true ); // show the frame
40     } // end main
41  } // end class LabelDemo
```

Fig. 9.13 | JLabel with text and with images. (Part 1 of 2.)

Fig. 9.13 | JLabel with text and with images. (Part 2 of 2.)

Lines 3–6 import the classes we need to display JLabels. BorderLayout from package java.awt contains constants that specify where we can place GUI components in the JFrame. Class **ImageIcon** represents an image that can be displayed on a JLabel, and class JFrame represents the window that will contain all the labels.

Line 13 creates a JLabel that displays its constructor argument—the string "North". Line 16 declares local variable labelIcon and assigns it a new ImageIcon. The constructor for ImageIcon receives a String that specifies the path to the image. Since we specify only a file name, Java assumes that it's in the same directory as class LabelDemo. ImageIcon can load images in GIF, JPEG and PNG image formats. Line 19 declares and initializes local variable centerLabel with a JLabel that displays the labelIcon. Line 22 declares and initializes local variable southLabel with a JLabel similar to the one in line 19. However, line 25 calls method **setText** to change the text the label displays. Method setText can be called on any JLabel to change its text. This JLabel displays both the icon and the text.

Line 28 creates the JFrame that displays the JLabels, and line 30 indicates that the program should terminate when the JFrame is closed. We attach the labels to the JFrame in lines 34–36 by calling an overloaded version of method add that takes two parameters. The first parameter is the component we want to attach, and the second is the region in which it should be placed. Each JFrame has an associated *layout* that helps the JFrame position the GUI components that are attached to it. The default layout for a JFrame is known as a **BorderLayout** and has five regions—NORTH (top), SOUTH (bottom), EAST (right side), WEST (left side) and CENTER. Each of these is declared as a constant in class BorderLayout. When calling method add with one argument, the JFrame places the component in the CENTER automatically. If a position already contains a component, then the new component takes its place. Lines 38 and 39 set the size of the JFrame and make it visible on screen.

GUI and Graphics Case Study Exercise

9.1   Modify GUI and Graphics Case Study Exercise 8.1 to include a JLabel as a status bar that displays counts representing the number of each shape displayed. Class DrawPanel should declare a method that returns a String containing the status text. In main, first create the DrawPanel, then create the JLabel with the status text as an argument to the JLabel's constructor. Attach the JLabel to the SOUTH region of the JFrame, as shown in Fig. 9.14.

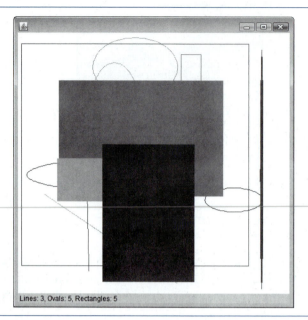

Fig. 9.14 | JLabel displaying shape statistics.

9.9 Wrap-Up

This chapter introduced inheritance—the ability to create classes by absorbing an existing class's members and embellishing them with new capabilities. You learned the notions of superclasses and subclasses and used keyword extends to create a subclass that inherits members from a superclass. We showed how to use the @Override annotation to prevent unintended overloading by indicating that a method overrides a superclass method. We introduced the access modifier protected; subclass methods can directly access protected superclass members. You learned how to use super to access overridden superclass members. You also saw how constructors are used in inheritance hierarchies. Finally, you learned about class Object's methods, the direct or indirect superclass of all java classes.

In Chapter 10, Object-Oriented Programming: Polymorphism, we build on our discussion of inheritance by introducing polymorphism—an object-oriented concept that enables us to write programs that conveniently handle, in a more general manner, objects of a wide variety of classes related by inheritance. After studying Chapter 10, you'll be familiar with classes, objects, encapsulation, inheritance and polymorphism—the key technologies of object-oriented programming.

Summary

Section 9.1 Introduction
- Inheritance reduces program-development time.
- The direct superclass of a subclass (specified by the keyword extends in the first line of a class declaration) is the superclass from which the subclass inherits. An indirect superclass of a subclass is two or more levels up the class hierarchy from that subclass.

- In single inheritance, a class is derived from one direct superclass. In multiple inheritance, a class is derived from more than one direct superclass. Java does not support multiple inheritance.
- A subclass is more specific than its superclass and represents a smaller group of objects.
- Every object of a subclass is also an object of that class's superclass. However, a superclass object is not an object of its class's subclasses.
- An *is-a* relationship represents inheritance. In an *is-a* relationship, an object of a subclass also can be treated as an object of its superclass.
- A *has-a* relationship represents composition. In a *has-a* relationship, a class object contains references to objects of other classes.

Section 9.2 Superclasses and Subclasses
- Single-inheritance relationships form treelike hierarchical structures—a superclass exists in a hierarchical relationship with its subclasses.

Section 9.3 protected Members
- A superclass's `public` members are accessible wherever the program has a reference to an object of that superclass or one of its subclasses.
- A superclass's `private` members can be accessed directly only within the superclass's declaration.
- A superclass's `protected` members have an intermediate level of protection between `public` and `private` access. They can be accessed by members of the superclass, by members of its subclasses and by members of other classes in the same package.
- A superclass's `private` members are hidden in its subclasses and can be accessed only through the `public` or `protected` methods inherited from the superclass.
- When a subclass method overrides a superclass method, the superclass method can be accessed from the subclass if the superclass method name is preceded by `super` and a dot (.) separator.

Section 9.4 Relationship between Superclasses and Subclasses
- A subclass cannot access the `private` members of its superclass—allowing this would violate the encapsulation of the superclass. A subclass can, however, access the non-`private` members of its superclass.
- A subclass can invoke a constructor of its superclass by using the keyword `super`, followed by a set of parentheses containing the superclass constructor arguments. This must appear as the first statement in the subclass constructor's body.
- A superclass method can be overridden in a subclass to declare an appropriate implementation for the subclass.
- The annotation `@Override` indicates that a method should override a superclass method. When the compiler encounters a method declared with `@Override`, it compares the method's signature with the superclass's method signatures. If there is not an exact match, the compiler issues an error message, such as "method does not override or implement a method from a supertype."
- Method `toString` takes no arguments and returns a `String`. The `Object` class's `toString` method is normally overridden by a subclass.
- When an object is output using the `%s` format specifier, the object's `toString` method is called implicitly to obtain its `String` representation.

Section 9.5 Constructors in Subclasses
- The first task of any subclass constructor is to call its direct superclass's constructor, either explicitly or implicitly, to ensure that the instance variables inherited from the superclass are initialized.

Section 9.6 Software Engineering with Inheritance
- Declaring instance variables private, while providing non-private methods to manipulate and perform validation, helps enforce good software engineering.

Section 9.7 Object Class
- See the table of class Object's methods in Fig. 9.12.

Terminology

base class 374	Object class 378
brittle software 393	override a superclass method 377
class hierarchy 374	@Override annotation 381
deep copy 400	protected access modifier 377
derived class 374	reusable software components 375
direct superclass 374	shallow copy 400
extend a class 374	single inheritance 374
extends keyword 378	specialization 374
fragile software 393	standardized reusable component 375
has-a relationship 375	subclass 374
indirect superclass 374	super keyword 377
inheritance 374	superclass 374
inheritance hierarchy 375	superclass constructor call syntax 390
is-a relationship 375	

Self-Review Exercises

9.1 Fill in the blanks in each of the following statements:

a) _____ is a form of software reusability in which new classes acquire the members of existing classes and embellish those classes with new capabilities.

b) A superclass's _____ members can be accessed in the superclass declaration *and* in subclass declarations.

c) In a(n) _____ relationship, an object of a subclass can also be treated as an object of its superclass.

d) In a(n) _____ relationship, a class object has references to objects of other classes as members.

e) In single inheritance, a class exists in a(n) _____ relationship with its subclasses.

f) A superclass's _____ members are accessible anywhere that the program has a reference to an object of that superclass or to an object of one of its subclasses.

g) When an object of a subclass is instantiated, a superclass _____ is called implicitly or explicitly.

h) Subclass constructors can call superclass constructors via the _____ keyword.

9.2 State whether each of the following is *true* or *false*. If a statement is *false*, explain why.

a) Superclass constructors are not inherited by subclasses.

b) A *has-a* relationship is implemented via inheritance.

c) A Car class has an *is-a* relationship with the SteeringWheel and Brakes classes.

d) When a subclass redefines a superclass method by using the same signature, the subclass is said to overload that superclass method.

Answers to Self-Review Exercises

9.1 a) Inheritance. b) public and protected. c) *is-a* or inheritance. d) *has-a* or composition. e) hierarchical. f) public. g) constructor. h) super.

9.2   a) True. b) False. A *has-a* relationship is implemented via composition. An *is-a* relationship is implemented via inheritance. c) False. This is an example of a *has-a* relationship. Class Car has an *is-a* relationship with class Vehicle. d) False. This is known as overriding, not overloading—an overloaded method has the same name, but a different signature.

Exercises

9.3   Many programs written with inheritance could be written with composition instead, and vice versa. Rewrite class BasePlusCommissionEmployee (Fig. 9.11) of the CommissionEmployee–BasePlusCommissionEmployee hierarchy to use composition rather than inheritance.

9.4   Discuss the ways in which inheritance promotes software reuse, saves time during program development and helps prevent errors.

9.5   Draw an inheritance hierarchy for students at a university similar to the hierarchy shown in Fig. 9.2. Use Student as the superclass of the hierarchy, then extend Student with classes UndergraduateStudent and GraduateStudent. Continue to extend the hierarchy as deep (i.e., as many levels) as possible. For example, Freshman, Sophomore, Junior and Senior might extend UndergraduateStudent, and DoctoralStudent and MastersStudent might be subclasses of GraduateStudent. After drawing the hierarchy, discuss the relationships that exist between the classes. [*Note:* You do not need to write any code for this exercise.]

9.6   The world of shapes is much richer than the shapes included in the inheritance hierarchy of Fig. 9.3. Write down all the shapes you can think of—both two-dimensional and three-dimensional—and form them into a more complete Shape hierarchy with as many levels as possible. Your hierarchy should have class Shape at the top. Classes TwoDimensionalShape and ThreeDimensionalShape should extend Shape. Add additional subclasses, such as Quadrilateral and Sphere, at their correct locations in the hierarchy as necessary.

9.7   Some programmers prefer not to use protected access, because they believe it breaks the encapsulation of the superclass. Discuss the relative merits of using protected access vs. using private access in superclasses.

9.8   Write an inheritance hierarchy for classes Quadrilateral, Trapezoid, Parallelogram, Rectangle and Square. Use Quadrilateral as the superclass of the hierarchy. Create and use a Point class to represent the points in each shape. Make the hierarchy as deep (i.e., as many levels) as possible. Specify the instance variables and methods for each class. The private instance variables of Quadrilateral should be the *x-y* coordinate pairs for the four endpoints of the Quadrilateral. Write a program that instantiates objects of your classes and outputs each object's area (except Quadrilateral).

10

Object-Oriented Programming: Polymorphism

One Ring to rule them all, One Ring to find them,
One Ring to bring them all and in the darkness bind them.
—John Ronald Reuel Tolkien

General propositions do not decide concrete cases.
—Oliver Wendell Holmes

A philosopher of imposing stature doesn't think in a vacuum. Even his most abstract ideas are, to some extent, conditioned by what is or is not known in the time when he lives.
—Alfred North Whitehead

Why art thou cast down, O my soul?
—Psalms 42:5

Objectives

In this chapter you'll learn:

- The concept of polymorphism.
- To use overridden methods to effect polymorphism.
- To distinguish between abstract and concrete classes.
- To declare abstract methods to create abstract classes.
- How polymorphism makes systems extensible and maintainable.
- To determine an object's type at execution time.
- To declare and implement interfaces.

10.1 Introduction

We continue our study of object-oriented programming by explaining and demonstrating polymorphism with inheritance hierarchies. Polymorphism enables you to "program in the general" rather than "program in the specific." In particular, polymorphism enables you to write programs that process objects that share the same superclass (either directly or indirectly) as if they're all objects of the superclass; this can simplify programming.

Consider the following example of polymorphism. Suppose we create a program that simulates the movement of several types of animals for a biological study. Classes Fish, Frog and Bird represent the three types of animals under investigation. Imagine that each class extends superclass Animal, which contains a method move and maintains an animal's current location as *x-y* coordinates. Each subclass implements method move. Our program maintains an Animal array containing references to objects of the various Animal subclasses. To simulate the animals' movements, the program sends each object the same message once per second—namely, move. However, each specific type of Animal responds to a move message in a unique way—a Fish might swim three feet, a Frog might jump five feet and a Bird might fly ten feet. The program issues the *same* message (i.e., move) to each animal object, but each object knows how to modify its *x-y* coordinates appropriately for its *specific* type of movement. Relying on each object to know how to "do the right thing" (i.e., do what is appropriate for that type of object) in response to the same method call is the key concept of polymorphism. The same message (in this case, move) sent to a variety of objects has "many forms" of results—hence the term polymorphism.

Implementing for Extensibility

With polymorphism, we can design and implement systems that are easily extensible—new classes can be added with little or no modification to the general portions of the program, as long as the new classes are part of the inheritance hierarchy that the program processes generically. The only parts of a program that must be altered to accommodate new classes are those that require direct knowledge of the new classes that we add to the hierarchy. For example, if we extend class Animal to create class Tortoise (which might respond to a move message by crawling one inch), we need to write only the Tortoise class and the part of the simulation that instantiates a Tortoise object. The portions of the simulation that process each Animal generically can remain the same.

Chapter Overview

This chapter has several parts. First, we discuss common examples of polymorphism. We then provide a small example demonstrating polymorphic behavior. We use superclass references to manipulate both superclass objects and subclass objects polymorphically.

We then present a case study that revisits the employee hierarchy of Section 9.4.5. We develop a simple payroll application that polymorphically calculates the weekly pay of several different types of employees using each employee's earnings method. Though the earnings of each type of employee are calculated in a specific way, polymorphism allows us to process the employees "in the general." In the case study, we enlarge the hierarchy to include two new classes—SalariedEmployee (for people paid a fixed weekly salary) and HourlyEmployee (for people paid an hourly salary and "time-and-a-half" for overtime). We declare a common set of functionality for all the classes in the updated hierarchy in an "abstract" class, Employee, from which "concrete"classes SalariedEmployee, HourlyEmployee and CommissionEmployee inherit directly and "concrete" class BasePlusCommissionEmployee inherits indirectly. As you'll soon see, when we invoke each employee's earnings method off a superclass Employee reference, the correct earnings subclass calculation is performed, due to Java's polymorphic capabilities.

Programming in the Specific

Occasionally, when performing polymorphic processing, we need to program "in the specific." Our Employee case study demonstrates that a program can determine the type of an object at *execution* time and act on that object accordingly. In the case study, we've decided that BasePlusCommissionEmployees should receive 10% raises on their base salaries. So, we use these capabilities to determine whether a particular employee object *is a* BasePlusCommissionEmployee. If so, we increase that employee's base salary by 10%.

Interfaces

The chapter continues with an introduction to Java interfaces. An interface describes a set of methods that can be called on an object, but does not provide concrete implementations for all the methods. You can declare classes that **implement** (i.e., provide concrete implementations for the methods of) one or more interfaces. Each interface method must be declared in all the classes that explicitly implement the interface. Once a class implements an interface, all objects of that class have an *is-a* relationship with the interface type, and all objects of the class are guaranteed to provide the functionality described by the interface. This is true of all subclasses of that class as well.

Interfaces are particularly useful for assigning common functionality to possibly unrelated classes. This allows objects of unrelated classes to be processed polymorphically—objects of classes that implement the same interface can respond to all of the interface method calls. To demonstrate creating and using interfaces, we modify our payroll application to create a general accounts payable application that can calculate payments due for company employees and invoice amounts to be billed for purchased goods. As you'll see, interfaces enable polymorphic capabilities similar to those possible with inheritance.

10.2 Polymorphism Examples

We now consider several additional examples of polymorphism.

Quadrilaterals

If class `Rectangle` is derived from class `Quadrilateral`, then a `Rectangle` object is a more specific version of a `Quadrilateral`. Any operation (e.g., calculating the perimeter or the area) that can be performed on a `Quadrilateral` can also be performed on a `Rectangle`. These operations can also be performed on other `Quadrilateral`s, such as `Square`s, `Parallelogram`s and `Trapezoid`s. The polymorphism occurs when a program invokes a method through a superclass `Quadrilateral` variable—at execution time, the correct subclass version of the method is called, based on the type of the reference stored in the superclass variable. You'll see a simple code example that illustrates this process in Section 10.3.

Space Objects in a Video Game

Suppose we design a video game that manipulates objects of classes `Martian`, `Venusian`, `Plutonian`, `SpaceShip` and `LaserBeam`. Imagine that each class inherits from the superclass `SpaceObject`, which contains method `draw`. Each subclass implements this method. A screen manager maintains a collection (e.g., a `SpaceObject` array) of references to objects of the various classes. To refresh the screen, the screen manager periodically sends each object the same message—namely, `draw`. However, each object responds in a unique way. For example, a `Martian` object might draw itself in red with green eyes and the appropriate number of antennae. A `SpaceShip` object might draw itself as a bright silver flying saucer. A `LaserBeam` object might draw itself as a bright red beam across the screen. Again, the *same* message (in this case, `draw`) sent to a variety of objects has "many forms" of results.

A screen manager might use polymorphism to facilitate adding new classes to a system with minimal modifications to the system's code. Suppose that we want to add `Mercurian` objects to our video game. To do so, we'd build a class `Mercurian` that extends `SpaceObject` and provides its own `draw` method implementation. When `Mercurian` objects appear in the `SpaceObject` collection, the screen manager code invokes method `draw`, exactly as it does for every other object in the collection, regardless of its type. So the new `Mercurian` objects simply "plug right in" without any modification of the screen manager code by the programmer. Thus, without modifying the system (other than to build new classes and modify the code that creates new objects), you can use polymorphism to conveniently include additional types that were not envisioned when the system was created.

Software Engineering Observation 10.1

Polymorphism enables you to deal in generalities and let the execution-time environment handle the specifics. You can command objects to behave in manners appropriate to those objects, without knowing their types (as long as the objects belong to the same inheritance hierarchy).

Software Engineering Observation 10.2

Polymorphism promotes extensibility: Software that invokes polymorphic behavior is independent of the object types to which messages are sent. New object types that can respond to existing method calls can be incorporated into a system without modifying the base system. Only client code that instantiates new objects must be modified to accommodate new types.

10.3 Demonstrating Polymorphic Behavior

Section 9.4 created a class hierarchy, in which class `BasePlusCommissionEmployee` inherited from `CommissionEmployee`. The examples in that section manipulated `CommissionEmployee` and `BasePlusCommissionEmployee` objects by using references to them to invoke their methods—we aimed superclass variables at superclass objects and subclass variables at subclass objects. These assignments are natural and straightforward—superclass variables are intended to refer to superclass objects, and subclass variables are intended to refer to subclass objects. However, as you'll soon see, other assignments are possible.

In the next example, we aim a superclass reference at a subclass object. We then show how invoking a method on a subclass object via a superclass reference invokes the subclass functionality—the type of the *referenced object*, not the type of the *variable*, determines which method is called. This example demonstrates that an object of a subclass can be treated as an object of its superclass, enabling various interesting manipulations. A program can create an array of superclass variables that refer to objects of many subclass types. This is allowed because each subclass object *is an* object of its superclass. For instance, we can assign the reference of a `BasePlusCommissionEmployee` object to a superclass `CommissionEmployee` variable, because a `BasePlusCommissionEmployee` *is a* `CommissionEmployee`—we can treat a `BasePlusCommissionEmployee` as a `CommissionEmployee`.

As you'll learn later in the chapter, you cannot treat a superclass object as a subclass object, because a superclass object is *not* an object of any of its subclasses. For example, we cannot assign the reference of a `CommissionEmployee` object to a subclass `BasePlusCommissionEmployee` variable, because a `CommissionEmployee` is not a `BasePlusCommissionEmployee`—a `CommissionEmployee` does not have a `baseSalary` instance variable and does not have methods `setBaseSalary` and `getBaseSalary`. The *is-a* relationship applies only *up the hierarchy* from a subclass to its direct (and indirect) superclasses, and not vice versa (i.e., not down the hierarchy from a superclass to its subclasses).

The Java compiler *does* allow the assignment of a superclass reference to a subclass variable if we explicitly cast the superclass reference to the subclass type—a technique we discuss in Section 10.5. Why would we ever want to perform such an assignment? A superclass reference can be used to invoke only the methods declared in the superclass—attempting to invoke subclass-only methods through a superclass reference results in compilation errors. If a program needs to perform a subclass-specific operation on a subclass object referenced by a superclass variable, the program must first cast the superclass reference to a subclass reference through a technique known as **downcasting**. This enables the program to invoke subclass methods that are not in the superclass. We show a downcasting example in Section 10.5.

The example in Fig. 10.1 demonstrates three ways to use superclass and subclass variables to store references to superclass and subclass objects. The first two are straightforward—as in Section 9.4, we assign a superclass reference to a superclass variable, and we assign a subclass reference to a subclass variable. Then we demonstrate the relationship between subclasses and superclasses (i.e., the *is-a* relationship) by assigning a subclass reference to a superclass variable. [*Note:* This program uses classes `CommissionEmployee` and `BasePlusCommissionEmployee` from Fig. 9.10 and Fig. 9.11, respectively.]

In Fig. 10.1, lines 10–11 create a `CommissionEmployee` object and assign its reference to a `CommissionEmployee` variable. Lines 14–16 create a `BasePlusCommissionEmployee` object and assign its reference to a `BasePlusCommissionEmployee` variable. These assignments are natural—for example, a `CommissionEmployee` variable's primary purpose is to hold a reference to a `CommissionEmployee` object. Lines 19–21 use `commissionEmployee` to invoke `toString` explicitly. Because `commissionEmployee` refers to a `CommissionEmployee` object, superclass `CommissionEmployee`'s version of `toString` is called. Similarly, lines 24–27 use `basePlusCommissionEmployee` to invoke `toString` explicitly on the `BasePlusCommissionEmployee` object. This invokes subclass `BasePlusCommissionEmployee`'s version of `toString`.

```
 1   // Fig. 10.1: PolymorphismTest.java
 2   // Assigning superclass and subclass references to superclass and
 3   // subclass variables.
 4
 5   public class PolymorphismTest
 6   {
 7      public static void main( String[] args )
 8      {
 9         // assign superclass reference to superclass variable
10         CommissionEmployee commissionEmployee = new CommissionEmployee(
11            "Sue", "Jones", "222-22-2222", 10000, .06 );
12
13         // assign subclass reference to subclass variable
14         BasePlusCommissionEmployee basePlusCommissionEmployee =
15            new BasePlusCommissionEmployee(
16            "Bob", "Lewis", "333-33-3333", 5000, .04, 300 );
17
18         // invoke toString on superclass object using superclass variable
19         System.out.printf( "%s %s:\n\n%s\n\n",
20            "Call CommissionEmployee's toString with superclass reference ",
21            "to superclass object", commissionEmployee.toString() );
22
23         // invoke toString on subclass object using subclass variable
24         System.out.printf( "%s %s:\n\n%s\n\n",
25            "Call BasePlusCommissionEmployee's toString with subclass",
26            "reference to subclass object",
27            basePlusCommissionEmployee.toString() );
28
29         // invoke toString on subclass object using superclass variable
30         CommissionEmployee commissionEmployee2 =
31            basePlusCommissionEmployee;
32         System.out.printf( "%s %s:\n\n%s\n",
33            "Call BasePlusCommissionEmployee's toString with superclass",
34            "reference to subclass object", commissionEmployee2.toString() );
35      } // end main
36   } // end class PolymorphismTest
```

```
Call CommissionEmployee's toString with superclass reference to superclass ob-
ject:

commission employee: Sue Jones
social security number: 222-22-2222
gross sales: 10000.00
commission rate: 0.06
```

Fig. 10.1 | Assigning superclass and subclass references to superclass and subclass variables. (Part 1 of 2.)

```
Call BasePlusCommissionEmployee's toString with subclass reference to
subclass object:

base-salaried commission employee: Bob Lewis
social security number: 333-33-3333
gross sales: 5000.00
commission rate: 0.04
base salary: 300.00

Call BasePlusCommissionEmployee's toString with superclass reference to
subclass object:

base-salaried commission employee: Bob Lewis
social security number: 333-33-3333
gross sales: 5000.00
commission rate: 0.04
base salary: 300.00
```

Fig. 10.1 | Assigning superclass and subclass references to superclass and subclass variables.
(Part 2 of 2.)

Lines 30–31 then assign the reference of subclass object basePlusCommissionEmployee to a superclass CommissionEmployee variable, which lines 32–34 use to invoke method toString. *When a superclass variable contains a reference to a subclass object, and that reference is used to call a method, the subclass version of the method is called.* Hence, commissionEmployee2.toString() in line 34 actually calls class BasePlusCommissionEmployee's toString method. The Java compiler allows this "crossover" because an object of a subclass *is an* object of its superclass (but not vice versa). When the compiler encounters a method call made through a variable, the compiler determines if the method can be called by checking the variable's class type. If that class contains the proper method declaration (or inherits one), the call is compiled. At execution time, the type of the object to which the variable refers determines the actual method to use. This process, called dynamic binding, is discussed in detail in Section 10.5.

10.4 Abstract Classes and Methods

When we think of a class, we assume that programs will create objects of that type. Sometimes it's useful to declare classes—called **abstract classes**—for which you never intend to create objects. Because they're used only as superclasses in inheritance hierarchies, we refer to them as **abstract superclasses**. These classes cannot be used to instantiate objects, because, as we'll soon see, abstract classes are incomplete. Subclasses must declare the "missing pieces" to become "concrete" classes, from which you can instantiate objects. Otherwise, these subclasses, too, will be abstract. We demonstrate abstract classes in Section 10.5.

Purpose of Abstract Classes
An abstract class's purpose is to provide an appropriate superclass from which other classes can inherit and thus share a common design. In the Shape hierarchy of Fig. 9.3, for example, subclasses inherit the notion of what it means to be a Shape—perhaps common attributes such as location, color and borderThickness, and behaviors such as draw, move, resize and changeColor. Classes that can be used to instantiate objects are called **concrete classes**. Such classes provide implementations of every method they declare (some of the implementations can be inherited). For example, we could derive concrete classes Circle,

Square and Triangle from abstract superclass TwoDimensionalShape. Similarly, we could derive concrete classes Sphere, Cube and Tetrahedron from abstract superclass ThreeDimensionalShape. Abstract superclasses are too general to create real objects—they specify only what is common among subclasses. We need to be more specific before we can create objects. For example, if you send the draw message to abstract class TwoDimensionalShape, it knows that two-dimensional shapes should be drawable, but it does not know what specific shape to draw, so it cannot implement a real draw method. Concrete classes provide the specifics that make it reasonable to instantiate objects.

Not all hierarchies contain abstract classes. However, programmers often write client code that uses only abstract superclass types to reduce client code's dependencies on a range of subclass types. For example, you can write a method with a parameter of an abstract superclass type. When called, such a method can receive an object of any concrete class that directly or indirectly extends the superclass specified as the parameter's type.

Abstract classes sometimes constitute several levels of a hierarchy. For example, the Shape hierarchy of Fig. 9.3 begins with abstract class Shape. On the next level of the hierarchy are abstract classes TwoDimensionalShape and ThreeDimensionalShape. The next level of the hierarchy declares concrete classes for TwoDimensionalShapes (Circle, Square and Triangle) and for ThreeDimensionalShapes (Sphere, Cube and Tetrahedron).

Declaring an Abstract Class and Abstract Methods
You make a class abstract by declaring it with keyword **abstract**. An abstract class normally contains one or more **abstract methods**. An abstract method is one with keyword abstract in its declaration, as in

```
public abstract void draw(); // abstract method
```

Abstract methods do not provide implementations. A class that contains any abstract methods must be explicitly declared as an abstract class even if that class contains some concrete (nonabstract) methods. Each concrete subclass of an abstract superclass also must provide concrete implementations of each of the superclass's abstract methods. Constructors and static methods cannot be declared abstract. Constructors are not inherited, so an abstract constructor could never be implemented. Though non-private static methods are inherited, they cannot be overridden. Since abstract methods are meant to be overridden so that they can process objects based on their types, it would not make sense to declare a static method as abstract.

Software Engineering Observation 10.3
An abstract class declares common attributes and behaviors (both abstract and concrete) of the various classes in a class hierarchy. An abstract class typically contains one or more abstract methods that subclasses must override if they're to be concrete. The instance variables and concrete methods of an abstract class are subject to the normal rules of inheritance.

Common Programming Error 10.1
Attempting to instantiate an object of an abstract class is a compilation error.

Common Programming Error 10.2
Failure to implement a superclass's abstract methods in a subclass is a compilation error unless the subclass is also declared abstract.

Using Abstract Classes to Declare Variables

Although we cannot instantiate objects of abstract superclasses, you'll soon see that we *can* use abstract superclasses to declare variables that can hold references to objects of any concrete class derived from those abstract superclasses. Programs typically use such variables to manipulate subclass objects polymorphically. You also can use abstract superclass names to invoke static methods declared in those abstract superclasses.

Consider another application of polymorphism. A drawing program needs to display many shapes, including types of new shapes that you will add to the system after writing the drawing program. The drawing program might need to display shapes, such as Circles, Triangles, Rectangles or others, that derive from abstract class Shape. The drawing program uses Shape variables to manage the objects that are displayed. To draw any object in this inheritance hierarchy, the drawing program uses a superclass Shape variable containing a reference to the subclass object to invoke the object's draw method. This method is declared abstract in superclass Shape, so each concrete subclass *must* implement method draw in a manner specific to that shape—each object in the Shape inheritance hierarchy *knows how to draw itself*. The drawing program does not have to worry about the type of each object or whether the program has ever encountered objects of that type.

Layered Software Systems

Polymorphism is particularly effective for implementing so-called layered software systems. In operating systems, for example, each type of physical device could operate quite differently from the others. Even so, commands to read or write data from and to devices may have a certain uniformity. For each device, the operating system uses a piece of software called a device driver to control all communication between the system and the device. The write message sent to a device-driver object needs to be interpreted specifically in the context of that driver and how it manipulates devices of a specific type. However, the write call itself really is no different from the write to any other device in the system—place some number of bytes from memory onto that device. An object-oriented operating system might use an abstract superclass to provide an "interface" appropriate for all device drivers. Then, through inheritance from that abstract superclass, subclasses are formed that all behave similarly. The device-driver methods are declared as abstract methods in the abstract superclass. The implementations of these abstract methods are provided in the subclasses that correspond to the specific types of device drivers. New devices are always being developed, often long after the operating system has been released. When you buy a new device, it comes with a device driver provided by the device vendor. The device is immediately operational after you connect it to your computer and install the driver. This is another elegant example of how polymorphism makes systems extensible.

10.5 Case Study: Payroll System Using Polymorphism

This section reexamines the CommissionEmployee-BasePlusCommissionEmployee hierarchy that we explored throughout Section 9.4. Now we use an abstract method and polymorphism to perform payroll calculations based on the type of inheritance hierarchy headed by an employee. We create an enhanced employee inheritance hierarchy to meet the following requirements:

A company pays its employees on a weekly basis. The employees are of four types: Salaried employees are paid a fixed weekly salary regardless of the number of hours worked, hourly employees are paid by the hour and receive overtime pay (i.e., 1.5 times their hourly salary rate) for all hours worked in excess of 40 hours, commission employees are paid a percentage of their sales and base-salaried commission employees receive a base salary plus a percentage of their sales. For the current pay period, the company has decided to reward salaried-commission employees by adding 10% to their base salaries. The company wants to write a Java application that performs its payroll calculations polymorphically.

We use abstract class Employee to represent the general concept of an employee. The classes that extend Employee are SalariedEmployee, CommissionEmployee and HourlyEmployee. Class BasePlusCommissionEmployee—which extends CommissionEmployee—represents the last employee type. The UML class diagram in Fig. 10.2 shows the inheritance hierarchy for our polymorphic employee-payroll application. Note that abstract class name Employee is italicized—a convention of the UML.

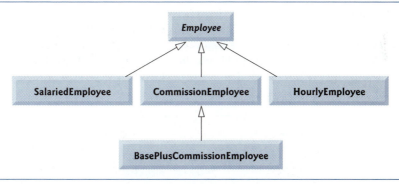

Fig. 10.2 | Employee hierarchy UML class diagram.

Abstract superclass Employee declares the "interface" to the hierarchy—that is, the set of methods that a program can invoke on all Employee objects. We use the term "interface" here in a general sense to refer to the various ways programs can communicate with objects of any Employee subclass. Be careful not to confuse the general notion of an "interface" with the formal notion of a Java interface, the subject of Section 10.7. Each employee, regardless of the way his or her earnings are calculated, has a first name, a last name and a social security number, so private instance variables firstName, lastName and socialSecurityNumber appear in abstract superclass Employee.

The following sections implement the Employee class hierarchy of Fig. 10.2. The first section implements abstract superclass Employee. The next four sections each implement one of the concrete classes. The last section implements a test program that builds objects of all these classes and processes those objects polymorphically.

10.5.1 Abstract Superclass Employee

Class Employee (Fig. 10.4) provides methods earnings and toString, in addition to the *get* and *set* methods that manipulate Employee's instance variables. An earnings method certainly applies generically to all employees. But each earnings calculation depends on the employee's class. So we declare earnings as abstract in superclass Employee because a default implementation does not make sense for that method—there is not enough information to determine what amount earnings should return. Each subclass overrides earnings with an appropriate implementation. To calculate an employee's earnings, the program assigns to a superclass `Employee` variable a reference to the employee's object, then invokes the `earnings` method on that variable. We maintain an array of `Employee` variables, each holding a reference to an `Employee` object. (Of course, there cannot be `Employee` objects, because `Employee` is an abstract class. Because of inheritance, however, all objects of all subclasses of `Employee` may nevertheless be thought of as `Employee` objects.) The program will iterate through the array and call method `earnings` for each `Employee` object. Java processes these method calls polymorphically. Including `earnings` as an `abstract` method in `Employee` enables the calls to `earnings` through `Employee` variables to compile and forces every direct concrete subclass of `Employee` to override `earnings`.

Method `toString` in class `Employee` returns a `String` containing the first name, last name and social security number of the employee. As we'll see, each subclass of `Employee` overrides method `toString` to create a `String` representation of an object of that class that contains the employee's type (e.g., `"salaried employee:"`) followed by the rest of the employee's information.

The diagram in Fig. 10.3 shows each of the five classes in the hierarchy down the left side and methods `earnings` and `toString` across the top. For each class, the diagram shows the desired results of each method. We do not list superclass `Employee`'s *get* and *set* methods because they're not overridden in any of the subclasses—each of these methods is inherited and used "as is" by each subclass.

	earnings	toString
Employee	abstract	*firstName lastName* `social security number:` *SSN*
Salaried-Employee	weeklySalary	`salaried employee:` *firstName lastName* `social security number:` *SSN* `weekly salary:` *weeklysalary*

Hourly-Employee	`if (hours <= 40)`
	    `wage * hours`
	`else if (hours > 40)`
	`{`
	    `40 * wage +`
	    `( hours - 40 ) *`
	    `wage * 1.5`
	`}`
		`hourly employee:` *firstName lastName*
		`social security number:` *SSN*
		`hourly wage:` *wage*`; hours worked:` *hours*

Commission-Employee	commissionRate * grossSales	`commission employee:` *firstName lastName* `social security number:` *SSN* `gross sales:` *grossSales*`;` `commission rate:` *commissionRate*

BasePlus-Commission-Employee	(commissionRate *
	grossSales) +
	baseSalary
		`base salaried commission employee:`
		    firstName lastName
		`social security number:` *SSN*
		`gross sales:` *grossSales*`;`
		`commission rate:` *commissionRate*`;`
		`base salary:` *baseSalary*

Fig. 10.3 | Polymorphic interface for the `Employee` hierarchy classes.

Let's consider class `Employee`'s declaration (Fig. 10.4). The class includes a constructor that takes the first name, last name and social security number as arguments (lines 11–16); *get* methods that return the first name, last name and social security number (lines 25–28, 37–40 and 49–52, respectively); *set* methods that set the first name, last name and social security number (lines 19–22, 31–34 and 43–46, respectively); method `toString` (lines 55–60), which returns the `String` representation of an `Employee`; and abstract method `earnings` (line 63), which will be implemented by each of the concrete subclasses. Note that the `Employee` constructor does not validate the social security number in this example. Normally, such validation should be provided.

```java
1   // Fig. 10.4: Employee.java
2   // Employee abstract superclass.
3
4   public abstract class Employee
5   {
6      private String firstName;
7      private String lastName;
8      private String socialSecurityNumber;
9
10     // three-argument constructor
11     public Employee( String first, String last, String ssn )
12     {
13        firstName = first;
14        lastName = last;
15        socialSecurityNumber = ssn;
16     } // end three-argument Employee constructor
17
18     // set first name
19     public void setFirstName( String first )
20     {
21        firstName = first; // should validate
22     } // end method setFirstName
23
24     // return first name
25     public String getFirstName()
26     {
27        return firstName;
28     } // end method getFirstName
29
30     // set last name
31     public void setLastName( String last )
32     {
33        lastName = last; // should validate
34     } // end method setLastName
35
36     // return last name
37     public String getLastName()
38     {
39        return lastName;
40     } // end method getLastName
41
```

Fig. 10.4 | Employee abstract superclass. (Part 1 of 2.)

```
42        // set social security number
43        public void setSocialSecurityNumber( String ssn )
44        {
45           socialSecurityNumber = ssn; // should validate
46        } // end method setSocialSecurityNumber
47
48        // return social security number
49        public String getSocialSecurityNumber()
50        {
51           return socialSecurityNumber;
52        } // end method getSocialSecurityNumber
53
54        // return String representation of Employee object
55        @Override
56        public String toString()
57        {
58           return String.format( "%s %s\nsocial security number: %s",
59              getFirstName(), getLastName(), getSocialSecurityNumber() );
60        } // end method toString
61
62        // abstract method overridden by concrete subclasses
63        public abstract double earnings(); // no implementation here
64     } // end abstract class Employee
```

Fig. 10.4 | `Employee` abstract superclass. (Part 2 of 2.)

Why did we decide to declare `earnings` as an `abstract` method? It simply does not make sense to provide an implementation of this method in class `Employee`. We cannot calculate the earnings for a general `Employee`—we first must know the specific type of `Employee` to determine the appropriate earnings calculation. By declaring this method abstract, we indicate that each concrete subclass *must* provide an appropriate `earnings` implementation and that a program will be able to use superclass `Employee` variables to invoke method `earnings` polymorphically for any type of `Employee`.

10.5.2 Concrete Subclass SalariedEmployee

Class `SalariedEmployee` (Fig. 10.5) extends class `Employee` (line 4) and overrides abstract method `earnings` (lines 29–33), which makes `SalariedEmployee` a concrete class. The class includes a constructor (lines 9–14) that takes a first name, a last name, a social security number and a weekly salary as arguments; a *set* method to assign a new nonnegative value to instance variable `weeklySalary` (lines 17–20); a *get* method to return `weeklySalary`'s value (lines 23–26); a method `earnings` (lines 29–33) to calculate a `SalariedEmployee`'s earnings; and a method `toString` (lines 36–41), which returns a `String` including the employee's type, namely, `"salaried employee: "` followed by employee-specific information produced by superclass `Employee`'s `toString` method and `SalariedEmployee`'s `getWeeklySalary` method. Class `SalariedEmployee`'s constructor passes the first name, last name and social security number to the `Employee` constructor (line 12) to initialize the `private` instance variables not inherited from the superclass. Method `earnings` overrides `Employee`'s abstract method `earnings` to provide a concrete implementation that returns the `SalariedEmployee`'s weekly salary. If we do not implement `earnings`, class `SalariedEmployee` must be declared abstract—otherwise, class `Sala-`

riedEmployee will not compile. Of course, we want `SalariedEmployee` here to be a concrete class in this example.

```java
1   // Fig. 10.5: SalariedEmployee.java
2   // SalariedEmployee concrete class extends abstract class Employee.
3
4   public class SalariedEmployee extends Employee
5   {
6      private double weeklySalary;
7
8      // four-argument constructor
9      public SalariedEmployee( String first, String last, String ssn,
10        double salary )
11     {
12        super( first, last, ssn ); // pass to Employee constructor
13        setWeeklySalary( salary ); // validate and store salary
14     } // end four-argument SalariedEmployee constructor
15
16     // set salary
17     public void setWeeklySalary( double salary )
18     {
19        weeklySalary = salary < 0.0 ? 0.0 : salary;
20     } // end method setWeeklySalary
21
22     // return salary
23     public double getWeeklySalary()
24     {
25        return weeklySalary;
26     } // end method getWeeklySalary
27
28     // calculate earnings; override abstract method earnings in Employee
29     @Override
30     public double earnings()
31     {
32        return getWeeklySalary();
33     } // end method earnings
34
35     // return String representation of SalariedEmployee object
36     @Override
37     public String toString()
38     {
39        return String.format( "salaried employee: %s\n%s: $%,.2f",
40           super.toString(), "weekly salary", getWeeklySalary() );
41     } // end method toString
42   } // end class SalariedEmployee
```

Fig. 10.5 | `SalariedEmployee` concrete class extends abstract class `Employee`.

Method `toString` (lines 36–41) of class `SalariedEmployee` overrides `Employee` method `toString`. If class `SalariedEmployee` did not override `toString`, `SalariedEmployee` would have inherited the `Employee` version of `toString`. In that case, `SalariedEmployee`'s `toString` method would simply return the employee's full name and social security number, which does not adequately represent a `SalariedEmployee`. To produce a complete String representation of a SalariedEmployee, the subclass's toString method returns "salaried employee: " followed by the superclass Employee-specific information (i.e., first name, last name and social security number) obtained by invoking the superclass's toString method (line 40)—this is a nice example of code reuse. The String representation of a SalariedEmployee also contains the employee's weekly salary obtained by invoking the class's getWeeklySalary method.

10.5.3 Concrete Subclass HourlyEmployee

Class HourlyEmployee (Fig. 10.6) also extends Employee (line 4). The class includes a constructor (lines 10–16) that takes as arguments a first name, a last name, a social security number, an hourly wage and the number of hours worked. Lines 19–22 and 31–35 declare set methods that assign new values to instance variables wage and hours, respectively. Method setWage (lines 19–22) ensures that wage is nonnegative, and method setHours (lines 31–35) ensures that hours is between 0 and 168 (the total number of hours in a week) inclusive. Class HourlyEmployee also includes get methods (lines 25–28 and 38–41) to return the values of wage and hours, respectively; a method earnings (lines 44–51) to calculate an HourlyEmployee's earnings; and a method toString (lines 54–60), which returns a String containing the employee's type ("hourly employee: ") and the employee-specific information. Note that the HourlyEmployee constructor, like the SalariedEmployee constructor, passes the first name, last name and social security number to the superclass Employee constructor (line 13) to initialize the private instance variables. In addition, method toString calls superclass method toString (line 58) to obtain the Employee-specific information (i.e., first name, last name and social security number)—this is another nice example of code reuse.

```java
1   // Fig. 10.6: HourlyEmployee.java
2   // HourlyEmployee class extends Employee.
3
4   public class HourlyEmployee extends Employee
5   {
6      private double wage; // wage per hour
7      private double hours; // hours worked for week
8
9      // five-argument constructor
10     public HourlyEmployee( String first, String last, String ssn,
11        double hourlyWage, double hoursWorked )
12     {
13        super( first, last, ssn );
14        setWage( hourlyWage ); // validate hourly wage
15        setHours( hoursWorked ); // validate hours worked
16     } // end five-argument HourlyEmployee constructor
17
18     // set wage
19     public void setWage( double hourlyWage )
20     {
21        wage = ( hourlyWage < 0.0 ) ? 0.0 : hourlyWage;
22     } // end method setWage
23
```

Fig. 10.6 | HourlyEmployee class derived from Employee. (Part 1 of 2.)

```
24          // return wage
25          public double getWage()
26          {
27             return wage;
28          } // end method getWage
29
30          // set hours worked
31          public void setHours( double hoursWorked )
32          {
33             hours = ( ( hoursWorked >= 0.0 ) && ( hoursWorked <= 168.0 ) ) ?
34                hoursWorked : 0.0;
35          } // end method setHours
36
37          // return hours worked
38          public double getHours()
39          {
40             return hours;
41          } // end method getHours
42
43          // calculate earnings; override abstract method earnings in Employee
44          @Override
45          public double earnings()
46          {
47             if ( getHours() <= 40 ) // no overtime
48                return getWage() * getHours();
49             else
50                return 40 * getWage() + ( gethours() - 40 ) * getWage() * 1.5;
51          } // end method earnings
52
53          // return String representation of HourlyEmployee object
54          @Override
55          public String toString()
56          {
57             return String.format( "hourly employee: %s\n%s: $%,.2f; %s: %,.2f",
58                super.toString(), "hourly wage", getWage(),
59                "hours worked", getHours() );
60          } // end method toString
61       } // end class HourlyEmployee
```

Fig. 10.6 | HourlyEmployee class derived from Employee. (Part 2 of 2.)

10.5.4 Concrete Subclass CommissionEmployee

Class CommissionEmployee (Fig. 10.7) extends class Employee (line 4). The class includes a constructor (lines 10–16) that takes a first name, a last name, a social security number, a sales amount and a commission rate; *set* methods (lines 19–22 and 31–34) to assign new values to instance variables commissionRate and grossSales, respectively; *get* methods (lines 25–28 and 37–40) that retrieve the values of these instance variables; method earnings (lines 43–47) to calculate a CommissionEmployee's earnings; and method toString (lines 50–57), which returns the employee's type, namely, "commission employee: " and employee-specific information. The constructor also passes the first name, last name and social security number to Employee's constructor (line 13) to initialize Employee's private instance variables. Method toString calls superclass method toString (line 54) to obtain the Employee-specific information (i.e., first name, last name and social security number).

```
 1   // Fig. 10.7: CommissionEmployee.java
 2   // CommissionEmployee class extends Employee.
 3
 4   public class CommissionEmployee extends Employee
 5   {
 6      private double grossSales; // gross weekly sales
 7      private double commissionRate; // commission percentage
 8
 9      // five-argument constructor
10      public CommissionEmployee( String first, String last, String ssn,
11         double sales, double rate )
12      {
13         super( first, last, ssn );
14         setGrossSales( sales );
15         setCommissionRate( rate );
16      } // end five-argument CommissionEmployee constructor
17
18      // set commission rate
19      public void setCommissionRate( double rate )
20      {
21         commissionRate = ( rate > 0.0 && rate < 1.0 ) ? rate : 0.0;
22      } // end method setCommissionRate
23
24      // return commission rate
25      public double getCommissionRate()
26      {
27         return commissionRate;
28      } // end method getCommissionRate
29
30      // set gross sales amount
31      public void setGrossSales( double sales )
32      {
33         grossSales = ( sales < 0.0 ) ? 0.0 : sales;
34      } // end method setGrossSales
35
36      // return gross sales amount
37      public double getGrossSales()
38      {
39         return grossSales;
40      } // end method getGrossSales
41
42      // calculate earnings; override abstract method earnings in Employee
43      @Override
44      public double earnings()
45      {
46         return getCommissionRate() * getGrossSales();
47      } // end method earnings
48
49      // return String representation of CommissionEmployee object
50      @Override
51      public String toString()
52      {
53         return String.format( "%s: %s\n%s: $%,.2f; %s: %.2f",
54            "commission employee", super.toString(),
```

Fig. 10.7 | CommissionEmployee class derived from Employee. (Part 1 of 2.)

```
55              "gross sales", getGrossSales(),
56              "commission rate", getCommissionRate() );
57      } // end method toString
58  } // end class CommissionEmployee
```

Fig. 10.7 | CommissionEmployee class derived from Employee. (Part 2 of 2.)

10.5.5 Indirect Concrete Subclass BasePlusCommissionEmployee

Class BasePlusCommissionEmployee (Fig. 10.8) extends class CommissionEmployee (line 4) and therefore is an indirect subclass of class Employee. Class BasePlusCommission-Employee has a constructor (lines 9–14) that takes as arguments a first name, a last name, a social security number, a sales amount, a commission rate and a base salary. It then passes the first name, last name, social security number, sales amount and commission rate to the CommissionEmployee constructor (line 12) to initialize the inherited members. Base-PlusCommissionEmployee also contains a *set* method (lines 17–20) to assign a new value to instance variable baseSalary and a *get* method (lines 23–26) to return baseSalary's value. Method earnings (lines 29–33) calculates a BasePlusCommissionEmployee's earnings. Note that line 32 in method earnings calls superclass CommissionEmployee's earnings method to calculate the commission-based portion of the employee's earnings. This is a nice example of code reuse. BasePlusCommissionEmployee's toString method (lines 36–42) creates a String representation of a BasePlusCommissionEmployee that contains "base-salaried", followed by the String obtained by invoking superclass Commission-Employee's toString method (another example of code reuse), then the base salary. The result is a String beginning with "base-salaried commission employee" followed by the rest of the BasePlusCommissionEmployee's information. Recall that CommissionEmploy-ee's toString obtains the employee's first name, last name and social security number by invoking the toString method of its superclass (i.e., Employee)—yet another example of code reuse. Note that BasePlusCommissionEmployee's toString initiates a chain of method calls that span all three levels of the Employee hierarchy.

```
1   // Fig. 10.8: BasePlusCommissionEmployee.java
2   // BasePlusCommissionEmployee class extends CommissionEmployee.
3
4   public class BasePlusCommissionEmployee extends CommissionEmployee
5   {
6      private double baseSalary; // base salary per week
7
8      // six-argument constructor
9      public BasePlusCommissionEmployee( String first, String last,
10        String ssn, double sales, double rate, double salary )
11     {
12        super( first, last, ssn, sales, rate );
13        setBaseSalary( salary ); // validate and store base salary
14     } // end six-argument BasePlusCommissionEmployee constructor
15
16     // set base salary
17     public void setBaseSalary( double salary )
18     {
```

Fig. 10.8 | BasePlusCommissionEmployee class extends CommissionEmployee. (Part 1 of 2.)

```
19              baseSalary = ( salary < 0.0 ) ? 0.0 : salary; // non-negative
20          } // end method setBaseSalary
21
22          // return base salary
23          public double getBaseSalary()
24          {
25              return baseSalary;
26          } // end method getBaseSalary
27
28          // calculate earnings; override method earnings in CommissionEmployee
29          @Override
30          public double earnings()
31          {
32              return getBaseSalary() + super.earnings();
33          } // end method earnings
34
35          // return String representation of BasePlusCommissionEmployee object
36          @Override
37          public String toString()
38          {
39              return String.format( "%s %s; %s: $%,.2f",
40                  "base-salaried", super.toString(),
41                  "base salary", getBaseSalary() );
42          } // end method toString
43      } // end class BasePlusCommissionEmployee
```

Fig. 10.8 | BasePlusCommissionEmployee class extends CommissionEmployee. (Part 2 of 2.)

10.5.6 Polymorphic Processing, Operator instanceof and Downcasting

To test our Employee hierarchy, the application in Fig. 10.9 creates an object of each of the four concrete classes SalariedEmployee, HourlyEmployee, CommissionEmployee and BasePlusCommissionEmployee. The program manipulates these objects nonpolymorphically, via variables of each object's own type, then polymorphically, using an array of Employee variables. While processing the objects polymorphically, the program increases the base salary of each BasePlusCommissionEmployee by 10%—this requires *determining the object's type at execution time*. Finally, the program polymorphically determines and outputs the type of each object in the Employee array. Lines 9–18 create objects of each of the four concrete Employee subclasses. Lines 22–30 output the String representation and earnings of each of these objects nonpolymorphically. Note that each object's toString method is called implicitly by printf when the object is output as a String with the %s format specifier.

```
1   // Fig. 10.9: PayrollSystemTest.java
2   // Employee hierarchy test program.
3
4   public class PayrollSystemTest
5   {
6       public static void main( String[] args )
7       {
```

Fig. 10.9 | Employee hierarchy test program. (Part 1 of 4.)

```
 8        // create subclass objects
 9        SalariedEmployee salariedEmployee =
10           new SalariedEmployee( "John", "Smith", "111-11-1111", 800.00 );
11        HourlyEmployee hourlyEmployee =
12           new HourlyEmployee( "Karen", "Price", "222-22-2222", 16.75, 40 );
13        CommissionEmployee commissionEmployee =
14           new CommissionEmployee(
15           "Sue", "Jones", "333-33-3333", 10000, .06 );
16        BasePlusCommissionEmployee basePlusCommissionEmployee =
17           new BasePlusCommissionEmployee(
18           "Bob", "Lewis", "444-44-4444", 5000, .04, 300 );
19
20        System.out.println( "Employees processed individually:\n" );
21
22        System.out.printf( "%s\n%s: $%,.2f\n\n",
23           salariedEmployee, "earned", salariedEmployee.earnings() );
24        System.out.printf( "%s\n%s: $%,.2f\n\n",
25           hourlyEmployee, "earned", hourlyEmployee.earnings() );
26        System.out.printf( "%s\n%s: $%,.2f\n\n",
27           commissionEmployee, "earned", commissionEmployee.earnings() );
28        System.out.printf( "%s\n%s: $%,.2f\n\n",
29           basePlusCommissionEmployee,
30           "earned", basePlusCommissionEmployee.earnings() );
31
32        // create four-element Employee array
33        Employee[] employees = new Employee[ 4 ];
34
35        // initialize array with Employees
36        employees[ 0 ] = salariedEmployee;
37        employees[ 1 ] = hourlyEmployee;
38        employees[ 2 ] = commissionEmployee;
39        employees[ 3 ] = basePlusCommissionEmployee;
40
41        System.out.println( "Employees processed polymorphically:\n" );
42
43        // generically process each element in array employees
44        for ( Employee currentEmployee : employees )
45        {
46           System.out.println( currentEmployee ); // invokes toString
47
48           // determine whether element is a BasePlusCommissionEmployee
49           if ( currentEmployee instanceof BasePlusCommissionEmployee )
50           {
51              // downcast Employee reference to
52              // BasePlusCommissionEmployee reference
53              BasePlusCommissionEmployee employee =
54                 ( BasePlusCommissionEmployee ) currentEmployee;
55
56              employee.setBaseSalary( 1.10 * employee.getBaseSalary() );
57
58              System.out.printf(
59                 "new base salary with 10%% increase is: $%,.2f\n",
60                 employee.getBaseSalary() );
61           } // end if
```

Fig. 10.9 | Employee hierarchy test program. (Part 2 of 4.)

```
62
63              System.out.printf(
64                  "earned $%,.2f\n\n", currentEmployee.earnings() );
65          } // end for
66
67          // get type name of each object in employees array
68          for ( int j = 0; j < employees.length; j++ )
69              System.out.printf( "Employee %d is a %s\n", j,
70                  employees[ j ].getClass().getName() );
71      } // end main
72  } // end class PayrollSystemTest
```

```
Employees processed individually:

salaried employee: John Smith
social security number: 111-11-1111
weekly salary: $800.00
earned: $800.00

hourly employee: Karen Price
social security number: 222-22-2222
hourly wage: $16.75; hours worked: 40.00
earned: $670.00

commission employee: Sue Jones
social security number: 333-33-3333
gross sales: $10,000.00; commission rate: 0.06
earned: $600.00

base-salaried commission employee: Bob Lewis
social security number: 444-44-4444
gross sales: $5,000.00; commission rate: 0.04; base salary: $300.00
earned: $500.00

Employees processed polymorphically:

salaried employee: John Smith
social security number: 111-11-1111
weekly salary: $800.00
earned $800.00

hourly employee: Karen Price
social security number: 222-22-2222
hourly wage: $16.75; hours worked: 40.00
earned $670.00

commission employee: Sue Jones
social security number: 333-33-3333
gross sales: $10,000.00; commission rate: 0.06
earned $600.00

base-salaried commission employee: Bob Lewis
social security number: 444-44-4444
gross sales: $5,000.00; commission rate: 0.04; base salary: $300.00
new base salary with 10% increase is: $330.00
earned $530.00
```

Fig. 10.9 | Employee hierarchy test program. (Part 3 of 4.)

```
Employee 0 is a SalariedEmployee
Employee 1 is a HourlyEmployee
Employee 2 is a CommissionEmployee
Employee 3 is a BasePlusCommissionEmployee
```

Fig. 10.9 | Employee hierarchy test program. (Part 4 of 4.)

Creating the Array of *Employees*

Line 33 declares employees and assigns it an array of four Employee variables. Line 36 assigns the reference to a SalariedEmployee object to employees[0]. Line 37 assigns the reference to an HourlyEmployee object to employees[1]. Line 38 assigns the reference to a CommissionEmployee object to employees[2]. Line 39 assigns the reference to a BasePlusCommissionEmployee object to employee[3]. These assignments are allowed, because a SalariedEmployee *is an* Employee, an HourlyEmployee *is an* Employee, a CommissionEmployee *is an* Employee and a BasePlusCommissionEmployee *is an* Employee. Therefore, we can assign the references of SalariedEmployee, HourlyEmployee, CommissionEmployee and BasePlusCommissionEmployee objects to superclass Employee variables, *even though Employee is an abstract class.*

Polymorphically Processing *Employees*

Lines 44–65 iterate through array employees and invoke methods toString and earnings with Employee variable currentEmployee, which is assigned the reference to a different Employee in the array on each iteration. The output illustrates that the appropriate methods for each class are indeed invoked. All calls to method toString and earnings are resolved at execution time, based on the type of the object to which currentEmployee refers. This process is known as **dynamic binding** or **late binding**. For example, line 46 implicitly invokes method toString of the object to which currentEmployee refers. As a result of dynamic binding, Java decides which class's toString method to call *at execution time rather than at compile time.* Note that only the methods of class Employee can be called via an Employee variable (and Employee, of course, includes the methods of class Object). A superclass reference can be used to invoke only methods of the superclass—the subclass method implementations are invoked polymorphically.

Performing Type-Specific Operations on *BasePlusCommissionEmployees*

We perform special processing on BasePlusCommissionEmployee objects—as we encounter these objects, we increase their base salary by 10%. When processing objects polymorphically, we typically do not need to worry about the "specifics," but to adjust the base salary, we do have to determine the specific type of Employee object at execution time. Line 49 uses the **instanceof** operator to determine whether a particular Employee object's type is BasePlusCommissionEmployee. The condition in line 49 is true if the object referenced by currentEmployee *is a* BasePlusCommissionEmployee. This would also be true for any object of a BasePlusCommissionEmployee subclass because of the *is-a* relationship a subclass has with its superclass. Lines 53–54 downcast currentEmployee from type Employee to type BasePlusCommissionEmployee—this cast is allowed only if the object has an *is-a* relationship with BasePlusCommissionEmployee. The condition at line 49 ensures that this is the case. This cast is required if we are to invoke subclass BasePlusCommissionEmployee methods getBaseSalary and setBaseSalary on the current Employee object—

as you'll see momentarily, attempting to invoke a subclass-only method directly on a superclass reference is a compilation error.

Common Programming Error 10.3
Assigning a superclass variable to a subclass variable (without an explicit cast) is a compilation error.

Software Engineering Observation 10.4
If at execution time the reference of a subclass object has been assigned to a variable of one of its direct or indirect superclasses, it's acceptable to downcast the reference stored in that superclass variable back to a reference of the subclass type. Before performing such a cast, use the instanceof *operator to ensure that the object is indeed an object of an appropriate subclass type.*

Common Programming Error 10.4
When downcasting an object, a ClassCastException *occurs if at execution time the object does not have an* is-a *relationship with the type specified in the cast operator. A reference can be cast only to its own type or to the type of one of its superclasses.*

If the instanceof expression in line 49 is true, lines 53–60 perform the special processing required for the BasePlusCommissionEmployee object. Using BasePlusCommissionEmployee variable employee, line 56 invokes subclass-only methods getBaseSalary and setBaseSalary to retrieve and update the employee's base salary with the 10% raise.

Calling **earnings** *Polymorphically*
Lines 63–64 invoke method earnings on currentEmployee, which polymorphically calls the appropriate subclass object's earnings method. Obtaining the earnings of the SalariedEmployee, HourlyEmployee and CommissionEmployee polymorphically in lines 63–64 produces the same results as obtaining these employees' earnings individually in lines 22–27. The earnings amount obtained for the BasePlusCommissionEmployee in lines 63–64 is higher than that obtained in lines 28–30, due to the 10% increase in its base salary.

Polymorphically Processing **Employee***s*
Lines 68–70 display each employee's type as a String. Every object in Java knows its own class and can access this information through the **getClass** method, which all classes inherit from class Object. The getClass method returns an object of type **Class** (from package java.lang), which contains information about the object's type, including its class name. Line 70 invokes getClass on the current object to get its runtime class. The result of the getClass call is used to invoke **getName** to get the object's class name. To learn more about class Class, see its online documentation at java.sun.com/javase/6/docs/api/java/lang/Class.html.

Avoiding Compilation Errors with Downcasting
In the previous example, we avoided several compilation errors by downcasting an Employee variable to a BasePlusCommissionEmployee variable in lines 53–54. If you remove the cast operator (BasePlusCommissionEmployee) from line 54 and attempt to assign Employee variable currentEmployee directly to BasePlusCommissionEmployee variable employee, you'll receive an "incompatible types" compilation error. This error indicates that the attempt to assign the reference of superclass object currentEmployee to subclass variable employee is not allowed. The compiler prevents this assignment because a Com-

missionEmployee is not a `BasePlusCommissionEmployee`—the *is-a* relationship applies only between the subclass and its superclasses, not vice versa.

Similarly, if lines 56 and 60 used superclass variable `currentEmployee` to invoke subclass-only methods `getBaseSalary` and `setBaseSalary`, we'd receive "cannot find symbol" compilation errors on these lines. Attempting to invoke subclass-only methods via a superclass variable is not allowed—even though lines 56 and 60 execute only if `instanceof` in line 49 returns `true` to indicate that `currentEmployee` holds a reference to a `BasePlusCommissionEmployee` object. Using a superclass `Employee` variable, we can invoke only methods found in class `Employee`—`earnings`, `toString` and `Employee`'s *get* and *set* methods.

Software Engineering Observation 10.5
Although the actual method that is called depends on the runtime type of the object to which a variable refers, a variable can be used to invoke only those methods that are members of that variable's type, which the compiler verifies.

10.5.7 Summary of the Allowed Assignments Between Superclass and Subclass Variables

Now that you've seen a complete application that processes diverse subclass objects polymorphically, we summarize what you can and cannot do with superclass and subclass objects and variables. Although a subclass object also *is a* superclass object, the two objects are nevertheless different. As discussed previously, subclass objects can be treated as if they were superclass objects. But because the subclass can have additional subclass-only members, assigning a superclass reference to a subclass variable is not allowed without an explicit cast—such an assignment would leave the subclass members undefined for the superclass object.

We've discussed four ways to assign superclass and subclass references to variables of superclass and subclass types:

1. Assigning a superclass reference to a superclass variable is straightforward.

2. Assigning a subclass reference to a subclass variable is straightforward.

3. Assigning a subclass reference to a superclass variable is safe, because the subclass object *is an* object of its superclass. However, the superclass variable can be used to refer only to superclass members. If this code refers to subclass-only members through the superclass variable, the compiler reports errors.

4. Attempting to assign a superclass reference to a subclass variable is a compilation error. To avoid this error, the superclass reference must be cast to a subclass type explicitly. At *execution time*, if the object to which the reference refers is not a subclass object, an exception will occur. (For more on exception handling, see Chapter 11.) You should use the `instanceof` operator to ensure that such a cast is performed only if the object is a subclass object.

10.6 **final** Methods and Classes

We saw in Sections 5.3 and 5.10 that variables can be declared **final** to indicate that they cannot be modified after they're initialized—such variables represent constant values. It's also possible to declare methods, method parameters and classes with the **final** modifier.

Final Methods Cannot Be Overridden

A **final method** in a superclass cannot be overridden in a subclass. Methods that are declared `private` are implicitly `final`, because it's not possible to override them in a subclass. Methods that are declared `static` are also implicitly `final`. A `final` method's declaration can never change, so all subclasses use the same method implementation, and calls to `final` methods are resolved at compile time—this is known as **static binding**.

Final Classes Cannot Be Superclasses

A **final class** that is declared `final` cannot be a superclass (i.e., a class cannot extend a `final` class). All methods in a `final` class are implicitly `final`. Class `String` is an example of a `final` class. If you were allowed to create a subclass of `String`, objects of that subclass could be used wherever `String`s are expected. Since class `String` cannot be extended, programs that use `String`s can rely on the functionality of `String` objects as specified in the Java API. Making the class `final` also prevents programmers from creating subclasses that might bypass security restrictions. For more insights on the use of keyword `final`, visit

> `java.sun.com/docs/books/tutorial/java/IandI/final.html`

and

> `www.ibm.com/developerworks/java/library/j-jtp1029.html`

Common Programming Error 10.5

Attempting to declare a subclass of a `final` class is a compilation error.

Software Engineering Observation 10.6

In the Java API, the vast majority of classes are not declared `final`. This enables inheritance and polymorphism. However, in some cases, it's important to declare classes `final`—typically for security reasons.

10.7 Case Study: Creating and Using Interfaces

Our next example (Figs. 10.11–10.15) reexamines the payroll system of Section 10.5. Suppose that the company involved wishes to perform several accounting operations in a single accounts payable application—in addition to calculating the earnings that must be paid to each employee, the company must also calculate the payment due on each of several invoices (i.e., bills for goods purchased). Though applied to unrelated things (i.e., employees and invoices), both operations have to do with obtaining some kind of payment amount. For an employee, the payment refers to the employee's earnings. For an invoice, the payment refers to the total cost of the goods listed on the invoice. Can we calculate such different things as the payments due for employees and invoices in a single application polymorphically? Does Java offer a capability requiring that unrelated classes implement a set of common methods (e.g., a method that calculates a payment amount)? Java **interfaces** offer exactly this capability.

Standardizing Interactions

Interfaces define and standardize the ways in which things such as people and systems can interact with one another. For example, the controls on a radio serve as an interface between radio users and a radio's internal components. The controls allow users to perform only a limited set of operations (e.g., change the station, adjust the volume, choose between AM and FM), and different radios may implement the controls in different ways (e.g., using push buttons, dials, voice commands). The interface specifies *what* operations a radio must permit users to perform but does not specify *how* the operations are performed.

Software Objects Communicate Via Interfaces

Software objects also communicate via interfaces. A Java interface describes a set of methods that can be called on an object to tell it, for example, to perform some task or return some piece of information. The next example introduces an interface named `Payable` to describe the functionality of any object that must be capable of being paid and thus must offer a method to determine the proper payment amount due. An interface declaration begins with the keyword `interface` and contains only constants and `abstract` methods. Unlike classes, all interface members must be `public`, and *interfaces may not specify any implementation details*, such as concrete method declarations and instance variables. All methods declared in an interface are implicitly `public abstract` methods, and all fields are implicitly `public`, `static` and `final`. [*Note:* As of Java SE 5, it became a better programming practice to declare sets of constants as enumerations with keyword `enum`. See Section 5.10 for an introduction to `enum` and Section 8.9 for additional `enum` details.]

Good Programming Practice 10.1

According to Chapter 9 of the Java Language Specification, *it's proper style to declare an interface's methods without keywords* `public` *and* `abstract`, *because they're redundant in interface method declarations. Similarly, constants should be declared without keywords* `public`, `static` *and* `final`, *because they, too, are redundant.*

Using an Interface

To use an interface, a concrete class must specify that it `implements` the interface and must declare each method in the interface with the signature specified in the interface declaration. To specify that a class implements an interface add the `implements` keyword and the name of the interface to the end of your class declaration's first line. A class that does not implement all the methods of the interface is an abstract class and must be declared `abstract`. Implementing an interface is like signing a contract with the compiler that states, "I will declare all the methods specified by the interface or I will declare my class abstract."

Common Programming Error 10.6

Failing to implement any method of an interface in a concrete class that `implements` *the interface results in a compilation error indicating that the class must be declared abstract.*

Relating Disparate Types

An interface is often used when disparate (i.e., unrelated) classes need to share common methods and constants. This allows objects of unrelated classes to be processed polymorphically—objects of classes that implement the same interface can respond to the same method calls. You can create an interface that describes the desired functionality, then implement this interface in any classes that require that functionality. For example, in the accounts payable application developed in this section, we implement interface `Payable` in any class that must be able to calculate a payment amount (e.g., `Employee`, `Invoice`).

Interfaces vs. Abstract Classes

An interface is often used in place of an abstract class when there is no default implementation to inherit—that is, no fields and no default method implementations. Like public abstract classes, interfaces are typically public types. Like a public class, a public interface must be declared in a file with the same name as the interface and the .java file-name extension.

Tagging Interfaces

We'll see in Chapter 17, Files, Streams and Object Serialization, the notion of "tagging interfaces"—empty interfaces that have *no* methods or constant values. They're used to add *is-a* relationships to classes. For example, in Chapter 17 we'll discuss a Java mechanism called object serialization, which can convert objects to byte representations and can convert those byte representations back to objects. To enable this mechanism to work with your objects, you simply have to mark them as Serializable by adding implements Serializable to the end of your class declaration's first line. Then, all the objects of your class have the *is-a* relationship with Serializable.

10.7.1 Developing a Payable Hierarchy

To build an application that can determine payments for employees and invoices alike, we first create interface Payable, which contains method getPaymentAmount that returns a double amount that must be paid for an object of any class that implements the interface. Method getPaymentAmount is a general-purpose version of method earnings of the Employee hierarchy—method earnings calculates a payment amount specifically for an Employee, while getPaymentAmount can be applied to a broad range of unrelated objects. After declaring interface Payable, we introduce class Invoice, which implements interface Payable. We then modify class Employee such that it also implements interface Payable. Finally, we update Employee subclass SalariedEmployee to "fit" into the Payable hierarchy by renaming SalariedEmployee method earnings as getPaymentAmount.

Good Programming Practice 10.2

When declaring a method in an interface, choose a method name that describes the method's purpose in a general manner, because the method may be implemented by many unrelated classes.

Classes Invoice and Employee both represent things for which the company must be able to calculate a payment amount. Both classes implement the Payable interface, so a program can invoke method getPaymentAmount on Invoice objects and Employee objects alike. As we'll soon see, this enables the polymorphic processing of Invoices and Employees required for the company's accounts payable application.

The UML class diagram in Fig. 10.10 shows the hierarchy used in our accounts payable application. The hierarchy begins with interface Payable. The UML distinguishes an interface from other classes by placing the word "interface" in guillemets (« and ») above the interface name. The UML expresses the relationship between a class and an interface through a relationship known as realization. A class is said to "realize," or implement, the methods of an interface. A class diagram models a realization as a dashed arrow with a hollow arrowhead pointing from the implementing class to the interface. The diagram in Fig. 10.10 indicates that classes Invoice and Employee each realize (i.e., implement) interface Payable. Note that, as in the class diagram of Fig. 10.2, class Employee appears in italics, indicating that it's an abstract class. Concrete class SalariedEmployee extends Employee and *inherits its superclass's realization relationship* with interface Payable.

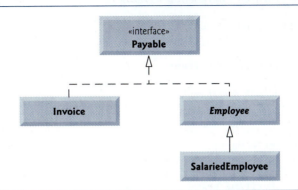

Fig. 10.10 | Payable interface hierarchy UML class diagram.

10.7.2 Interface Payable

The declaration of interface Payable begins in Fig. 10.11 at line 4. Interface Payable contains public abstract method getPaymentAmount (line 6). Note that the method is not explicitly declared public or abstract. Interface methods are always public and abstract, so they do not need to be declared as such. Interface Payable has only one method—interfaces can have any number of methods. In addition, method getPaymentAmount has no parameters, but interface methods *can* have parameters. Note that interfaces may also contain fields that are implicitly final and static.

```
1   // Fig. 10.11: Payable.java
2   // Payable interface declaration.
3
4   public interface Payable
5   {
6      double getPaymentAmount(); // calculate payment; no implementation
7   } // end interface Payable
```

Fig. 10.11 | Payable interface declaration.

10.7.3 Class Invoice

We now create class Invoice (Fig. 10.12) to represent a simple invoice that contains billing information for only one kind of part. The class declares private instance variables partNumber, partDescription, quantity and pricePerItem (in lines 6–9) that indicate the part number, a description of the part, the quantity of the part ordered and the price per item. Class Invoice also contains a constructor (lines 12–19), *get* and *set* methods (lines 22–67) that manipulate the class's instance variables and a toString method (lines 70–76) that returns a String representation of an Invoice object. Note that methods setQuantity (lines 46–49) and setPricePerItem (lines 58–61) ensure that quantity and pricePerItem obtain only nonnegative values.

```java
 1   // Fig. 10.12: Invoice.java
 2   // Invoice class implements Payable.
 3
 4   public class Invoice implements Payable
 5   {
 6      private String partNumber;
 7      private String partDescription;
 8      private int quantity;
 9      private double pricePerItem;
10
11      // four-argument constructor
12      public Invoice( String part, String description, int count,
13         double price )
14      {
15         partNumber = part;
16         partDescription = description;
17         setQuantity( count ); // validate and store quantity
18         setPricePerItem( price ); // validate and store price per item
19      } // end four-argument Invoice constructor
20
21      // set part number
22      public void setPartNumber( String part )
23      {
24         partNumber = part; // should validate
25      } // end method setPartNumber
26
27      // get part number
28      public String getPartNumber()
29      {
30         return partNumber;
31      } // end method getPartNumber
32
33      // set description
34      public void setPartDescription( String description )
35      {
36         partDescription = description; // should validate
37      } // end method setPartDescription
38
39      // get description
40      public String getPartDescription()
41      {
42         return partDescription;
43      } // end method getPartDescription
44
45      // set quantity
46      public void setQuantity( int count )
47      {
48         quantity = ( count < 0 ) ? 0 : count; // quantity cannot be negative
49      } // end method setQuantity
50
51      // get quantity
52      public int getQuantity()
53      {
```

Fig. 10.12 | Invoice class that implements Payable. (Part 1 of 2.)

```
54          return quantity;
55      } // end method getQuantity
56
57      // set price per item
58      public void setPricePerItem( double price )
59      {
60          pricePerItem = ( price < 0.0 ) ? 0.0 : price; // validate price
61      } // end method setPricePerItem
62
63      // get price per item
64      public double getPricePerItem()
65      {
66          return pricePerItem;
67      } // end method getPricePerItem
68
69      // return String representation of Invoice object
70      @Override
71      public String toString()
72      {
73          return String.format( "%s: \n%s: %s (%s) \n%s: %d \n%s: $%,.2f",
74              "invoice", "part number", getPartNumber(), getPartDescription(),
75              "quantity", getQuantity(), "price per item", getPricePerItem() );
76      } // end method toString
77
78      // method required to carry out contract with interface Payable
79      @Override
80      public double getPaymentAmount()
81      {
82          return getQuantity() * getPricePerItem(); // calculate total cost
83      } // end method getPaymentAmount
84  } // end class Invoice
```

Fig. 10.12 | Invoice class that implements Payable. (Part 2 of 2.)

Line 4 indicates that class Invoice implements interface Payable. Like all classes, class Invoice also implicitly extends Object. Java does not allow subclasses to inherit from more than one superclass, but it allows a class to inherit from one superclass and implement as many interfaces as it needs. To implement more than one interface, use a comma-separated list of interface names after keyword implements in the class declaration, as in:

> public class *ClassName* extends *SuperclassName* implements *FirstInterface*, *SecondInterface*, ...

Software Engineering Observation 10.7

All objects of a class that implement multiple interfaces have the is-a *relationship with each implemented interface type.*

Class Invoice implements the one method in interface Payable—method getPaymentAmount is declared in lines 79–83. The method calculates the total payment required to pay the invoice. The method multiplies the values of quantity and pricePerItem (obtained through the appropriate *get* methods) and returns the result (line 82). This method satisfies the implementation requirement for this method in interface Payable—we've fulfilled the interface contract with the compiler.

10.7.4 Modifying Class `Employee` to Implement Interface `Payable`

We now modify class `Employee` such that it implements interface `Payable`. Figure 10.13 contains the modified class, which is identical to that of Fig. 10.4 with two exceptions. First, line 4 of Fig. 10.13 indicates that class `Employee` now `implements` interface `Payable`. So we must rename `earnings` to `getPaymentAmount` throughout the `Employee` hierarchy. As with method `earnings` in the version of class `Employee` in Fig. 10.4, however, it does not make sense to implement method `getPaymentAmount` in class `Employee` because we cannot calculate the earnings payment owed to a general `Employee`—we must first know the specific type of `Employee`. In Fig. 10.4, we declared method `earnings` as abstract for this reason, so class `Employee` had to be declared `abstract`. This forced each `Employee` concrete subclass to override `earnings` with an implementation.

In Fig. 10.13, we handle this situation differently. Recall that when a class implements an interface, it makes a contract with the compiler stating either that the class will implement each of the methods in the interface or that the class will be declared `abstract`. If the latter option is chosen, we do not need to declare the interface methods as `abstract` in the abstract class—they're already implicitly declared as such in the interface. Any concrete subclass of the abstract class must implement the interface methods to fulfill the superclass's contract with the compiler. If the subclass does not do so, it too must be declared `abstract`. As indicated by the comments in lines 62–63, class `Employee` of Fig. 10.13 does not implement method `getPaymentAmount`, so the class is declared `abstract`. Each direct `Employee` subclass inherits the superclass's contract to implement method `getPaymentAmount` and thus must implement this method to become a concrete class for which objects can be instantiated. A class that extends one of `Employee`'s concrete subclasses will inherit an implementation of `getPaymentAmount` and thus will also be a concrete class.

```
1   // Fig. 10.13: Employee.java
2   // Employee abstract superclass implements Payable.
3
4   public abstract class Employee implements Payable
5   {
6      private String firstName;
7      private String lastName;
8      private String socialSecurityNumber;
9
10     // three-argument constructor
11     public Employee( String first, String last, String ssn )
12     {
13        firstName = first;
14        lastName = last;
15        socialSecurityNumber = ssn;
16     } // end three-argument Employee constructor
17
18     // set first name
19     public void setFirstName( String first )
20     {
21        firstName = first; // should validate
22     } // end method setFirstName
```

Fig. 10.13 | `Employee` class that implements `Payable`. (Part 1 of 2.)

```
23
24        // return first name
25        public String getFirstName()
26        {
27           return firstName;
28        } // end method getFirstName
29
30        // set last name
31        public void setLastName( String last )
32        {
33           lastName = last; // should validate
34        } // end method setLastName
35
36        // return last name
37        public String getLastName()
38        {
39           return lastName;
40        } // end method getLastName
41
42        // set social security number
43        public void setSocialSecurityNumber( String ssn )
44        {
45           socialSecurityNumber = ssn; // should validate
46        } // end method setSocialSecurityNumber
47
48        // return social security number
49        public String getSocialSecurityNumber()
50        {
51           return socialSecurityNumber;
52        } // end method getSocialSecurityNumber
53
54        // return String representation of Employee object
55        @Override
56        public String toString()
57        {
58           return String.format( "%s %s\nsocial security number: %s",
59              getFirstName(), getLastName(), getSocialSecurityNumber() );
60        } // end method toString
61
62        // Note: We do not implement Payable method getPaymentAmount here so
63        // this class must be declared abstract to avoid a compilation error.
64     } // end abstract class Employee
```

Fig. 10.13 | Employee class that implements Payable. (Part 2 of 2.)

10.7.5 Modifying Class SalariedEmployee for Use in the Payable Hierarchy

Figure 10.14 contains a modified SalariedEmployee class that extends Employee and fulfills superclass Employee's contract to implement Payable method getPaymentAmount. This version of SalariedEmployee is identical to that of Fig. 10.5, but it replaces method earnings with method getPaymentAmount (lines 30–34). Recall that the Payable version of the method has a more general name to be applicable to possibly disparate classes. The remaining Employee subclasses (e.g., HourlyEmployee, CommissionEmployee and BasePlusCommissionEmployee) also must be modified to contain method getPaymentAmount in place of earnings to reflect the fact that Employee now implements Payable. We leave these modifications as an exercise (Exercise 10.11) and use only SalariedEmployee in our test program here. Exercise 10.12 asks you to implement interface Payable in the entire Employee class hierarchy of Figs. 10.4–10.9 without modifying the Employee subclasses.

```java
1   // Fig. 10.14: SalariedEmployee.java
2   // SalariedEmployee class extends Employee, which implements Payable.
3
4   public class SalariedEmployee extends Employee
5   {
6      private double weeklySalary;
7
8      // four-argument constructor
9      public SalariedEmployee( String first, String last, String ssn,
10        double salary )
11     {
12        super( first, last, ssn ); // pass to Employee constructor
13        setWeeklySalary( salary ); // validate and store salary
14     } // end four-argument SalariedEmployee constructor
15
16     // set salary
17     public void setWeeklySalary( double salary )
18     {
19        weeklySalary = salary < 0.0 ? 0.0 : salary;
20     } // end method setWeeklySalary
21
22     // return salary
23     public double getWeeklySalary()
24     {
25        return weeklySalary;
26     } // end method getWeeklySalary
27
28     // calculate earnings; implement interface Payable method that was
29     // abstract in superclass Employee
30     @Override
31     public double getPaymentAmount()
32     {
33        return getWeeklySalary();
34     } // end method getPaymentAmount
35
36     // return String representation of SalariedEmployee object
37     @Override
38     public String toString()
39     {
40        return String.format( "salaried employee: %s\n%s: $%,.2f",
41           super.toString(), "weekly salary", getWeeklySalary() );
42     } // end method toString
43  } // end class SalariedEmployee
```

Fig. 10.14 | SalariedEmployee class that implements interface Payable method getPaymentAmount.

When a class implements an interface, the same *is-a* relationship provided by inheritance applies. Class Employee implements Payable, so we can say that an Employee *is a*

Payable. In fact, objects of any classes that extend Employee are also Payable objects. SalariedEmployee objects, for instance, are Payable objects. Objects of any subclasses of the class that implements the interface can also be thought of as objects of the interface type. Thus, just as we can assign the reference of a SalariedEmployee object to a superclass Employee variable, we can assign the reference of a SalariedEmployee object to an interface Payable variable. Invoice implements Payable, so an Invoice object also *is a* Payable object, and we can assign the reference of an Invoice object to a Payable variable.

Software Engineering Observation 10.8
When a method parameter is declared with a superclass or interface type, the method processes the object received as an argument polymorphically.

Software Engineering Observation 10.9
Using a superclass reference, we can polymorphically invoke any method declared in the superclass and its superclasses (e.g., class Object). Using an interface reference, we can polymorphically invoke any method declared in the interface, its superinterfaces (one interface can extend another) and in class Object—a variable of an interface type must refer to an object to call methods, and all objects have the methods of class Object.

10.7.6 Using Interface Payable to Process Invoices and Employees Polymorphically

PayableInterfaceTest (Fig. 10.15) illustrates that interface Payable can be used to process a set of Invoices and Employees polymorphically in a single application. Line 9 declares payableObjects and assigns it an array of four Payable variables. Lines 12–13 assign the references of Invoice objects to the first two elements of payableObjects. Lines 14–17 then assign the references of SalariedEmployee objects to the remaining two elements of payableObjects. These assignments are allowed because an Invoice *is a* Payable, a SalariedEmployee *is an* Employee and an Employee *is a* Payable. Lines 23–29 use the enhanced for statement to polymorphically process each Payable object in payableObjects, printing the object as a String, along with the payment amount due. Note that line 27 invokes method toString via a Payable interface reference, even though toString is not declared in interface Payable—all references (including those of interface types) refer to objects that extend Object and therefore have a toString method. (Note that toString also can be invoked implicitly here.) Line 28 invokes Payable method getPaymentAmount to obtain the payment amount for each object in payableObjects, regardless of the actual type of the object. The output reveals that the method calls in lines 27–28 invoke the appropriate class's implementation of methods toString and getPaymentAmount. For instance, when currentPayable refers to an Invoice during the first iteration of the for loop, class Invoice's toString and getPaymentAmount execute.

```
1   // Fig. 10.15: PayableInterfaceTest.java
2   // Tests interface Payable.
3
```

Fig. 10.15 | Payable interface test program processing Invoices and Employees polymorphically. (Part 1 of 2.)

```
4   public class PayableInterfaceTest
5   {
6      public static void main( String[] args )
7      {
8         // create four-element Payable array
9         Payable[] payableObjects = new Payable[ 4 ];
10
11        // populate array with objects that implement Payable
12        payableObjects[ 0 ] = new Invoice( "01234", "seat", 2, 375.00 );
13        payableObjects[ 1 ] = new Invoice( "56789", "tire", 4, 79.95 );
14        payableObjects[ 2 ] =
15           new SalariedEmployee( "John", "Smith", "111-11-1111", 800.00 );
16        payableObjects[ 3 ] =
17           new SalariedEmployee( "Lisa", "Barnes", "888-88-8888", 1200.00 );
18
19        System.out.println(
20           "Invoices and Employees processed polymorphically:\n" );
21
22        // generically process each element in array payableObjects
23        for ( Payable currentPayable : payableObjects )
24        {
25           // output currentPayable and its appropriate payment amount
26           System.out.printf( "%s \n%s: $%,.2f\n\n",
27              currentPayable.toString(),
28              "payment due", currentPayable.getPaymentAmount() );
29        } // end for
30     } // end main
31  } // end class PayableInterfaceTest
```

```
Invoices and Employees processed polymorphically:

invoice:
part number: 01234 (seat)
quantity: 2
price per item: $375.00
payment due: $750.00

invoice:
part number: 56789 (tire)
quantity: 4
price per item: $79.95
payment due: $319.80

salaried employee: John Smith
social security number: 111-11-1111
weekly salary: $800.00
payment due: $800.00

salaried employee: Lisa Barnes
social security number: 888-88-8888
weekly salary: $1,200.00
payment due: $1,200.00
```

Fig. 10.15 | Payable interface test program processing Invoices and Employees polymorphically. (Part 2 of 2.)

10.7.7 Common Interfaces of the Java API

In this section, we overview several common interfaces found in the Java API. The power and flexibility of interfaces is used frequently throughout the Java API. These interfaces are implemented and used in the same manner as the interfaces you create (e.g., interface Payable in Section 10.7.2). The Java API's interfaces enable you to use your own classes within the frameworks provided by Java, such as comparing objects of your own types and creating tasks that can execute concurrently with other tasks in the same program. Figure 10.16 presents a brief overview of a few of the more popular interfaces of the Java API that we use in *Java How to Program*.

Interface	Description
Comparable	Java contains several comparison operators (e.g., <, <=, >, >=, ==, !=) that allow you to compare primitive values. However, these operators cannot be used to compare objects. Interface Comparable is used to allow objects of a class that implements the interface to be compared to one another. Interface Comparable is commonly used for ordering objects in a collection such as an array. We use Comparable in Chapter 20, Generic Collections, and Chapter 21, Generic Classes and Methods.
Serializable	An interface used to identify classes whose objects can be written to (i.e., serialized) or read from (i.e., deserialized) some type of storage (e.g., file on disk, database field) or transmitted across a network. We use Serializable in Chapter 17, Files, Streams and Object Serialization, and Chapter 27, Networking.
Runnable	Implemented by any class for which objects of that class should be able to execute in parallel using a technique called multithreading (discussed in Chapter 26, Multithreading). The interface contains one method, run, which describes the behavior of an object when executed.
GUI event-listener interfaces	You work with graphical user interfaces (GUIs) every day. In your web browser, you might type the address of a website to visit, or you might click a button to return to a previous site. The browser responds to your interaction and performs the desired task. Your interaction is known as an event, and the code that the browser uses to respond to an event is known as an event handler. In Chapter 14, GUI Components: Part 1, and Chapter 25, GUI Components: Part 2, you'll learn how to build GUIs and event handlers that respond to user interactions. Event handlers are declared in classes that implement an appropriate event-listener interface. Each event-listener interface specifies one or more methods that must be implemented to respond to user interactions.
SwingConstants	Contains a set of constants used in GUI programming to position GUI elements on the screen. We explore GUI programming in Chapters 14 and 25.

Fig. 10.16 | Common interfaces of the Java API.

10.8 (Optional) GUI and Graphics Case Study: Drawing with Polymorphism

You may have noticed in the drawing program created in GUI and Graphics Case Study Exercise 8.1 (and modified in GUI and Graphics Case Study Exercise 9.1) that shape classes have many similarities. Using inheritance, we can "factor out" the common features from all three classes and place them in a single shape superclass. Then, using variables of the superclass type, we can manipulate objects of all three shape types polymorphically. Removing the redundancy in the code will result in a smaller, more flexible program that is easier to maintain.

GUI and Graphics Case Study Exercises

10.1 Modify the MyLine, MyOval and MyRectangle classes of GUI and Graphics Case Study Exercise 8.1 and Exercise 9.1 to create the class hierarchy in Fig. 10.17. Classes of the MyShape hierarchy should be "smart" shape classes that know how to draw themselves (if provided with a Graphics object that tells them where to draw). Once the program creates an object from this hierarchy, it can manipulate it polymorphically for the rest of its lifetime as a MyShape.

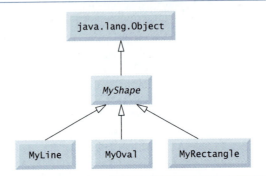

Fig. 10.17 | MyShape hierarchy.

In your solution, class MyShape in Fig. 10.17 *must* be abstract. Since MyShape represents any shape in general, you cannot implement a draw method without knowing exactly what shape it is. The data representing the coordinates and color of the shapes in the hierarchy should be declared as private members of class MyShape. In addition to the common data, class MyShape should declare the following methods:

    a) A no-argument constructor that sets all the coordinates of the shape to 0 and the color to Color.BLACK.

    b) A constructor that initializes the coordinates and color to the values of the arguments supplied.

    c) *Set* methods for the individual coordinates and color that allow the programmer to set any piece of data independently for a shape in the hierarchy.

    d) *Get* methods for the individual coordinates and color that allow the programmer to retrieve any piece of data independently for a shape in the hierarchy.

    e) The abstract method

```
public abstract void draw( Graphics g );
```

       which will be called from the program's paintComponent method to draw a shape on the screen.

To ensure proper encapsulation, all data in class MyShape must be private. This requires declaring proper *set* and *get* methods to manipulate the data. Class MyLine should provide a no-argument constructor and a constructor with arguments for the coordinates and color. Classes MyOval and MyRectangle should provide a no-argument constructor and a constructor with arguments for the coordinates, color and determining whether the shape is filled. The no-argument constructor should, in addition to setting the default values, set the shape to be an unfilled shape.

You can draw lines, rectangles and ovals if you know two points in space. Lines require *x1*, *y1*, *x2* and *y2* coordinates. The drawLine method of the Graphics class will connect the two points supplied with a line. If you have the same four coordinate values (*x1*, *y1*, *x2* and *y2*) for ovals and rectangles, you can calculate the four arguments needed to draw them. Each requires an upper-left *x*-coordinate value (the smaller of the two *x*-coordinate values), an upper-left *y*-coordinate value (the smaller of the two *y*-coordinate values), a *width* (the absolute value of the difference between the two *x*-coordinate values) and a *height* (the absolute value of the difference between the two *y*-coordinate values). Rectangles and ovals should also have a filled flag that determines whether to draw the shape as a filled shape.

There should be no MyLine, MyOval or MyRectangle variables in the program—only MyShape variables that contain references to MyLine, MyOval and MyRectangle objects. The program should generate random shapes and store them in an array of type MyShape. Method paintComponent should walk through the MyShape array and draw every shape (i.e., polymorphically calling every shape's draw method).

Allow the user to specify (via an input dialog) the number of shapes to generate. The program will then generate and display the shapes along with a status bar that informs the user how many of each shape were created.

10.2 *(Drawing Application Modification)* In Exercise 10.1, you created a MyShape hierarchy in which classes MyLine, MyOval and MyRectangle extend MyShape directly. If your hierarchy was properly designed, you should be able to see the similarities between the MyOval and MyRectangle classes. Redesign and reimplement the code for the MyOval and MyRectangle classes to "factor out" the common features into the abstract class MyBoundedShape to produce the hierarchy in Fig. 10.18.

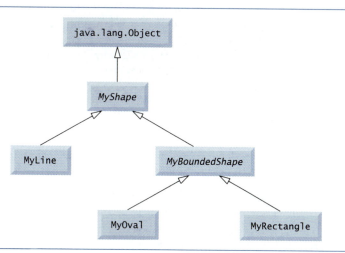

Fig. 10.18 | MyShape hierarchy with MyBoundedShape.

Class MyBoundedShape should declare two constructors that mimic those of class MyShape, only with an added parameter to set whether the shape is filled. Class MyBoundedShape should also declare *get* and *set* methods for manipulating the filled flag and methods that calculate the upper-left *x*-coordinate, upper-left *y*-coordinate, width and height. Remember, the values needed to draw an oval or a rectangle can be calculated from two *(x, y)* coordinates. If designed properly, the new MyOval and MyRectangle classes should each have two constructors and a draw method.

10.9 Wrap-Up

This chapter introduced polymorphism—the ability to process objects that share the same superclass in a class hierarchy as if they're all objects of the superclass. The chapter discussed how polymorphism makes systems extensible and maintainable, then demonstrated how to use overridden methods to effect polymorphic behavior. We introduced abstract classes, which allow you to provide an appropriate superclass from which other classes can inherit. You learned that an abstract class can declare abstract methods that each subclass must implement to become a concrete class and that a program can use variables of an abstract class to invoke the subclasses' implementations of abstract methods polymorphically. You also learned how to determine an object's type at execution time. We discussed the concepts of final methods and classes. Finally, the chapter discussed declaring and implementing an interface as another way to achieve polymorphic behavior.

You should now be familiar with classes, objects, encapsulation, inheritance, interfaces and polymorphism—the most essential aspects of object-oriented programming.

In the next chapter, you'll learn about exceptions, useful for handling errors during a program's execution. Exception handling provides for more robust programs.

Summary

Section 10.1 Introduction
- Polymorphism enables us to write programs that process objects that share the same superclass in a class hierarchy as if they're all objects of the superclass; this can simplify programming.
- With polymorphism, we can design and implement systems that are easily extensible—new classes can be added with little or no modification to the general portions of the program, as long as the new classes are part of the same inheritance hierarchy. The only parts of a program that must be altered to accommodate new classes are those that require direct knowledge of the new classes that you add to the hierarchy.

Section 10.3 Demonstrating Polymorphic Behavior
- When the compiler encounters a method call made through a variable, the compiler determines if the method can be called by checking the variable's class type. If that class contains the proper method declaration (or inherits one), the call is compiled. At execution time, the type of the object to which the variable refers determines the actual method to use.

Section 10.4 Abstract Classes and Methods
- Abstract classes cannot be used to instantiate objects, because they're incomplete.
- The primary purpose of an abstract class is to provide an appropriate superclass from which other classes can inherit and thus share a common design.
- Classes that can be used to instantiate objects are called concrete classes. Such classes provide implementations of every method they declare (some of the implementations can be inherited).
- Not all inheritance hierarchies contain abstract classes. However, programmers often write client code that uses only abstract superclass types to reduce client code's dependencies on a range of specific subclass types.

- Abstract classes sometimes constitute several levels of a hierarchy.

- You make a class abstract by declaring it with keyword abstract. An abstract class normally contains one or more abstract methods.

- Abstract methods do not provide implementations.

- A class that contains any abstract methods must be declared as an abstract class even if it contains some concrete methods. Each concrete subclass of an abstract superclass must provide concrete implementations of each of the superclass's abstract methods.

- Constructors and static methods cannot be declared abstract.

- You *can* use abstract superclasses to declare variables that can hold references to objects of any concrete class derived from those abstract superclasses. Programs typically use such variables to manipulate subclass objects polymorphically.

- Polymorphism is particularly effective for implementing layered software systems.

Section 10.5 Case Study: Payroll System Using Polymorphism

- Including an abstract method in a superclass forces every direct subclass of the superclass to override the abstract method in order to become a concrete class. This enables the hierarchy designer to demand that each concrete subclass provide an appropriate method implementation.

- Most method calls are resolved at execution time, based on the type of the object being manipulated. This process is known as dynamic binding or late binding.

- A superclass variable can be used to invoke only methods declared in the superclass (and the superclass can invoke overridden versions of these in the subclass).

- The instanceof operator can be used to determine whether a particular object's type has the *is-a* relationship with a specific type.

- Every object in Java knows its own class and can access it through method getClass, which all classes inherit from class Object. Method getClass returns an object of type Class (package java.lang), which contains information about the object's type, including its class name.

- The *is-a* relationship applies only between the subclass and its superclasses, not vice versa.

Section 10.6 final Methods and Classes

- A method that is declared final in a superclass cannot be overridden in a subclass.

- Methods declared private are implicitly final, because you can't override them in a subclass.

- Methods that are declared static are implicitly final.

- A final method's declaration can never change, so all subclasses use the same method implementation, and calls to final methods are resolved at compile time—this is known as static binding.

- Since the compiler knows that final methods cannot be overridden, it can optimize programs by removing calls to final methods and replacing them with the expanded code of their declarations at each method-call location—a technique known as inlining the code.

- A class that is declared final cannot be a superclass.

- All methods in a final class are implicitly final.

Section 10.7 Case Study: Creating and Using Interfaces

- An interface specifies *what* operations are allowed but not *how* the operations are performed.

- A Java interface describes a set of methods that can be called on an object.

- An interface declaration begins with the keyword interface.

- All interface members must be public, and interfaces may not specify any implementation details, such as concrete method declarations and instance variables.

- All methods declared in an interface are implicitly `public abstract` methods and all fields are implicitly `public`, `static` and `final`.

- To use an interface, a concrete class must specify that it `implements` the interface and must declare each interface method with the signature specified in the interface declaration. A class that does not implement all the interface's methods must be declared `abstract`.

- Implementing an interface is like signing a contract with the compiler that states, "I will declare all the methods specified by the interface or I will declare my class `abstract`."

- An interface is typically used when disparate (i.e., unrelated) classes need to share common methods and constants. This allows objects of unrelated classes to be processed polymorphically—objects of classes that implement the same interface can respond to the same method calls.

- You can create an interface that describes the desired functionality, then implement the interface in any classes that require that functionality.

- An interface is often used in place of an `abstract` class when there is no default implementation to inherit—that is, no instance variables and no default method implementations.

- Like `public abstract` classes, interfaces are typically `public` types, so they're normally declared in files by themselves with the same name as the interface and the `.java` file-name extension.

- Java does not allow subclasses to inherit from more than one superclass, but it does allow a class to inherit from a superclass and implement more than one interface.

- All objects of a class that implement multiple interfaces have the *is-a* relationship with each implemented interface type.

- An interface can declare constants. The constants are implicitly `public`, `static` and `final`.

Terminology

abstract class 414
abstract keyword 415
abstract method 415
abstract superclass 414
Class class 430
concrete class 414
downcasting 412
dynamic binding 429
final class 432
final method 432
getClass method of class Object 430

getName method of class Class 430
implement an interface 410
implements keyword 433
instanceof operator 429
interface 432
interface declaration 433
interface keyword 433
late binding 429
polymorphism 409
realization in the UML 434
static binding 432

Self-Review Exercises

10.1 Fill in the blanks in each of the following statements:
a) If a class contains at least one abstract method, it's a(n) _____ class.
b) Classes from which objects can be instantiated are called _____ classes.
c) _____ involves using a superclass variable to invoke methods on superclass and subclass objects, enabling you to "program in the general."
d) Methods that are not interface methods and that do not provide implementations must be declared using keyword _____.
e) Casting a reference stored in a superclass variable to a subclass type is called _____.

10.2 State whether each of the statements that follows is *true* or *false*. If *false*, explain why.
a) All methods in an `abstract` class must be declared as `abstract` methods.
b) Invoking a subclass-only method through a subclass variable is not allowed.
c) If a superclass declares an `abstract` method, a subclass must implement that method.

d) An object of a class that implements an interface may be thought of as an object of that interface type.

Answers to Self-Review Exercises

10.1 a) abstract. b) concrete. c) Polymorphism. d) abstract. e) downcasting.

10.2 a) False. An abstract class can include methods with implementations and abstract methods. b) False. Trying to invoke a subclass-only method with a superclass variable is no allowed. c) False. Only a concrete subclass must implement the method. d) True.

Exercises

10.3 How does polymorphism enable you to program "in the general" rather than "in the specific"? Discuss the key advantages of programming "in the general."

10.4 What are abstract methods? Describe the circumstances in which an abstract method would be appropriate.

10.5 How does polymorphism promote extensibility?

10.6 Discuss four ways in which you can assign superclass and subclass references to variables of superclass and subclass types.

10.7 Compare and contrast abstract classes and interfaces. Why would you use an abstract class? Why would you use an interface?

10.8 *(Payroll System Modification)* Modify the payroll system of Figs. 10.4–10.9 to include private instance variable birthDate in class Employee. Use class Date of Fig. 8.7 to represent an employee's birthday. Add *get* methods to class Date. Assume that payroll is processed once per month. Create an array of Employee variables to store references to the various employee objects. In a loop, calculate the payroll for each Employee (polymorphically), and add a $100.00 bonus to the person's payroll amount if the current month is the one in which the Employee's birthday occurs.

10.9 *(Shape Hierarchy)* Implement the Shape hierarchy shown in Fig. 9.3. Each TwoDimensionalShape should contain method getArea to calculate the area of the two-dimensional shape. Each ThreeDimensionalShape should have methods getArea and getVolume to calculate the surface area and volume, respectively, of the three-dimensional shape. Create a program that uses an array of Shape references to objects of each concrete class in the hierarchy. The program should print a text description of the object to which each array element refers. Also, in the loop that processes all the shapes in the array, determine whether each shape is a TwoDimensionalShape or a ThreeDimensionalShape. If it's a TwoDimensionalShape, display its area. If it's a ThreeDimensionalShape, display its area and volume.

10.10 *(Payroll System Modification)* Modify the payroll system of Figs. 10.4–10.9 to include an additional Employee subclass PieceWorker that represents an employee whose pay is based on the number of pieces of merchandise produced. Class PieceWorker should contain private instance variables wage (to store the employee's wage per piece) and pieces (to store the number of pieces produced). Provide a concrete implementation of method earnings in class PieceWorker that calculates the employee's earnings by multiplying the number of pieces produced by the wage per piece. Create an array of Employee variables to store references to objects of each concrete class in the new Employee hierarchy. For each Employee, display its String representation and earnings.

10.11 *(Accounts Payable System Modification)* In this exercise, we modify the accounts payable application of Figs. 10.11–10.15 to include the complete functionality of the payroll application of Figs. 10.4–10.9. The application should still process two Invoice objects, but now should process one object of each of the four Employee subclasses. If the object currently being processed is a BasePlusCommissionEmployee, the application should increase the BasePlusCommissionEmployee's base salary by 10%. Finally, the application should output the payment amount for each object. Complete the following steps to create the new application:

    a) Modify classes HourlyEmployee (Fig. 10.6) and CommissionEmployee (Fig. 10.7) to place them in the Payable hierarchy as subclasses of the version of Employee (Fig. 10.13) that implements Payable. [*Hint:* Change the name of method earnings to getPaymentAmount in each subclass so that the class satisfies its inherited contract with interface Payable.]

    b) Modify class BasePlusCommissionEmployee (Fig. 10.8) such that it extends the version of class CommissionEmployee created in part (a).

    c) Modify PayableInterfaceTest (Fig. 10.15) to polymorphically process two Invoices, one SalariedEmployee, one HourlyEmployee, one CommissionEmployee and one BasePlusCommissionEmployee. First output a String representation of each Payable object. Next, if an object is a BasePlusCommissionEmployee, increase its base salary by 10%. Finally, output the payment amount for each Payable object.

10.12 (*Accounts Payable System Modification*) It's possible to include the functionality of the payroll application (Figs. 10.4–10.9) in the accounts payable application without modifying Employee subclasses SalariedEmployee, HourlyEmployee, CommissionEmployee or BasePlusCommissionEmplyee. To do so, you can modify class Employee (Fig. 10.4) to implement interface Payable and declare method getPaymentAmount to invoke method earnings. Method getPaymentAmount would then be inherited by the subclasses in the Employee hierarchy. When getPaymentAmount is called for a particular subclass object, it polymorphically invokes the appropriate earnings method for that subclass. Reimplement Exercise 10.11 using the original Employee hierarchy from the payroll application of Figs. 10.4–10.9. Modify class Employee as described in this exercise, and *do not* modify any of class Employee's subclasses.

Making a Difference

10.13 (*CarbonFootprint Interface: Polymorphism*) Using interfaces, as you learned in this chapter, you can specify similar behaviors for possibly disparate classes. Governments and companies worldwide are becoming increasingly concerned with carbon footprints (annual releases of carbon dioxide into the atmosphere) from buildings burning various types of fuels for heat, vehicles burning fuels for power, and the like. Many scientists blame these greenhouse gases for the phenomenon called global warming. Create three small classes unrelated by inheritance—classes Building, Car and Bicycle. Give each class some unique appropriate attributes and behaviors that it does not have in common with other classes. Write an interface CarbonFootprint with a getCarbonFootprint method. Have each of your classes implement that interface, so that its getCarbonFootprint method calculates an appropriate carbon footprint for that class (check out a few websites that explain how to calculate carbon footprints). Write an application that creates objects of each of the three classes, places references to those objects in ArrayList<CarbonFootprint>, then iterates through the ArrayList, polymorphically invoking each object's getCarbonFootprint method. For each object, print some identifying information and the object's carbon footprint.

Exception Handling

11

It is common sense to take a method and try it. If it fails, admit it frankly and try another. But above all, try something.
—Franklin Delano Roosevelt

If they're running and they don't look where they're going I have to come out from somewhere and catch them.
—Jerome David Salinger

Objectives

In this chapter you'll learn:

- What exceptions are.
- How exception and error handling works.
- To use **try**, **throw** and **catch** to detect, indicate and handle exceptions, respectively.
- To use the **finally** block to release resources.
- How stack unwinding enables exceptions not caught in one scope to be caught in another.
- How stack traces help in debugging.
- How exceptions are arranged in an exception-class hierarchy.
- To declare new exception classes.
- To create chained exceptions that maintain complete stack-trace information.

11.1 Introduction

In this chapter, we introduce **exception handling**. An **exception** is an indication of a problem that occurs during a program's execution. The name "exception" implies that the problem occurs infrequently. With exception handling, a program can continue executing (rather than terminating) after dealing with a problem. This helps ensure the kind of robust applications that contribute to what is called mission-critical or business-critical computing. A more severe problem could prevent a program from continuing normal execution, instead requiring it to notify the user of the problem before terminating in a controlled manner. Java enables you to deal with exception handling easily from the inception of a project. The features presented in this chapter help you write **robust** and **fault-tolerant programs** (i.e., programs that can deal with problems as they arise and continue executing). Java exception handling is based in part on Andrew Koenig's and Bjarne Stroustrup's paper, "Exception Handling for C++ (revised)."[1]

 Error-Prevention Tip 11.1
Exception handling helps improve a program's fault tolerance.

In earlier chapters you've been briefly introduced to exceptions. In Chapter 6 you learned that an `ArrayIndexOutOfBoundsException` occurs when an attempt is made to access an element past either end of an array. Such a problem may occur, for example, if there is an "off-by-one" error in a `for` statement that manipulates an array. In Chapter 10 we introduced the `ClassCastException`, which occurs when an attempt is made to cast an object that does not have an *is-a* relationship with the type specified in the cast operator. A `NullPointerException` can occur when a `null` reference is used where an object is expected—for example, when an attempt is made to use a reference-type instance variable before it is initialized. Throughout this text you've also used class `Scanner`—which, as you'll see in this chapter, also may cause exceptions.

We begin with an overview of exception-handling concepts, then demonstrate basic exception-handling techniques. We show these techniques in action by handling an excep-

---

1. A. Koenig, and B. Stroustrup. "Exception Handling for C++ (revised)," *Proceedings of the Usenix C++ Conference*, pp. 149–176, San Francisco, April 1990.

tion that occurs when a method attempts to divide an integer by zero. Next, we introduce several classes at the top of Java's exception-handling class hierarchy. As you'll see, only classes that extend `Throwable` (package `java.lang`) directly or indirectly can be used with exception handling. We then show how to use chained exceptions. When you invoke a method that indicates an exception, you can throw another exception and chain the original one to the new one—this enables you to add application-specific information to the orginal exception. Next, we introduce preconditions and postconditions, which must be true when your methods are called and when they return, respectively. Finally, we present assertions, which you can use at development time to help debug your code.

[*Note:* If you execute the examples in this chapter from an IDE, such as Eclipse or Net-Beans, the outputs of your programs might differ from those shown here.]

11.2 Error-Handling Overview

Programs frequently test conditions to determine how program execution should proceed. Consider the following pseudocode:

> *Perform a task*
>
> *If the preceding task did not execute correctly*
> *Perform error processing*
>
> *Perform next task*
>
> *If the preceding task did not execute correctly*
> *Perform error processing*
>
> ...

This pseudocode begins by performing a task; then tests whether it executed correctly. If not, we perform error processing. Otherwise, we continue with the next task. Although this form of error handling works, intermixing program and error-handling logic can make programs difficult to read, modify, maintain and debug—especially in large applications.

Performance Tip 11.1

If the potential problems occur infrequently, intermixing program and error-handling logic can degrade program performance, because the program must perform potentially frequent tests to determine whether the task executed correctly and the next task can be performed.

Exception handling enables you to remove error-handling code from the "main line" of program execution, improving program clarity and enhancing modifiability. You can decide to handle any exceptions you choose—all exceptions, all exceptions of a certain type or all exceptions of a group of related types (i.e., exception types that are related through a superclass in an inheritance hierarchy). Such flexibility reduces the likelihood that errors will be overlooked, thus making programs more robust.

11.3 Example: Divide by Zero without Exception Handling

First we demonstrate what happens when errors arise in an application that does not use exception handling. Figure 11.1 prompts the user for two integers and passes them to method `quotient`, which calculates the integer quotient and returns an `int` result. In this example, you'll see that exceptions are **thrown** (i.e., the exception occurs) when a method detects a problem and is unable to handle it. Note that `quotient` is declared `static`, so `main` can call it directly without creating a `DivideByZeroNoExceptionHandling` object.

The first of the three sample executions in Fig. 11.1 shows a successful division. In the second sample execution, the user enters the value 0 as the denominator. Notice that several lines of information are displayed in response to this invalid input. This information is known as a **stack trace**, which includes the name of the exception (`java.lang.ArithmeticException`) in a descriptive message that indicates the problem that occurred and the method-call stack (i.e., the call chain) at the time it occurred. The stack trace includes the path of execution that led to the exception method by method. This information helps you debug the program. The first line specifies that an `ArithmeticException` has occurred. The text after the name of the exception ("/ by zero") indicates that this exception occurred as a result of an attempt to divide by zero. Java does not allow division by zero in integer arithmetic. When division by zero in integer arithmetic occurs, Java throws an **ArithmeticException**. ArithmeticExceptions can arise from a number of different problems in arithmetic, so the extra data ("/ by zero") provides more specific information. [*Note:* Java *does* allow division by zero with floating-point values. Such a calculation results in the value positive or negative infinity, which is represented in Java as a floating-point value (but displays as the string `Infinity` or `-Infinity`). If 0.0 is divided by 0.0, the result is NaN (not a number), which is also represented in Java as a floating-point value (but displays as NaN).]

```
1   // Fig. 11.1: DivideByZeroNoExceptionHandling.java
2   // Integer division without exception handling.
3   import java.util.Scanner;
4
5   public class DivideByZeroNoExceptionHandling
6   {
7      // demonstrates throwing an exception when a divide-by-zero occurs
8      public static int quotient( int numerator, int denominator )
9      {
10        return numerator / denominator; // possible division by zero
11     } // end method quotient
12
13     public static void main( String[] args )
14     {
15        Scanner scanner = new Scanner( System.in ); // scanner for input
16
17        System.out.print( "Please enter an integer numerator: " );
18        int numerator = scanner.nextInt();
19        System.out.print( "Please enter an integer denominator: " );
20        int denominator = scanner.nextInt();
21
22        int result = quotient( numerator, denominator );
23        System.out.printf(
24           "\nResult: %d / %d = %d\n", numerator, denominator, result );
25     } // end main
26  } // end class DivideByZeroNoExceptionHandling
```

Fig. 11.1 | Integer division without exception handling. (Part 1 of 2.)

```
Please enter an integer numerator: 100
Please enter an integer denominator: 7

Result: 100 / 7 = 14
```

```
Please enter an integer numerator: 100
Please enter an integer denominator: 0
Exception in thread "main" java.lang.ArithmeticException: / by zero
        at DivideByZeroNoExceptionHandling.quotient(
            DivideByZeroNoExceptionHandling.java:10)
        at DivideByZeroNoExceptionHandling.main(
            DivideByZeroNoExceptionHandling.java:22)
```

```
Please enter an integer numerator: 100
Please enter an integer denominator: hello
Exception in thread "main" java.util.InputMismatchException
        at java.util.Scanner.throwFor(Unknown Source)
        at java.util.Scanner.next(Unknown Source)
        at java.util.Scanner.nextInt(Unknown Source)
        at java.util.Scanner.nextInt(Unknown Source)
        at DivideByZeroNoExceptionHandling.main(
            DivideByZeroNoExceptionHandling.java:20)
```

Fig. 11.1 | Integer division without exception handling. (Part 2 of 2.)

Starting from the last line of the stack trace, we see that the exception was detected in line 22 of method main. Each line of the stack trace contains the class name and method (DivideByZeroNoExceptionHandling.main) followed by the file name and line number (DivideByZeroNoExceptionHandling.java:22). Moving up the stack trace, we see that the exception occurs in line 10, in method quotient. The top row of the call chain indicates the throw point—the initial point at which the exception occurs. The throw point of this exception is in line 10 of method quotient.

In the third execution, the user enters the string "hello" as the denominator. Notice again that a stack trace is displayed. This informs us that an InputMismatchException has occurred (package java.util). Our prior examples that read numeric values from the user assumed that the user would input a proper integer value. However, users sometimes make mistakes and input noninteger values. An **InputMismatchException** occurs when Scanner method nextInt receives a string that does not represent a valid integer. Starting from the end of the stack trace, we see that the exception was detected in line 20 of method main. Moving up the stack trace, we see that the exception occurred in method nextInt. Notice that in place of the file name and line number, we are provided with the text Unknown Source. This means that the so-called debugging symbols that provide the filename and line number information for that method's class were not available to the JVM—this is typically the case for the classes of the Java API. Many IDEs have access to the Java API source code and will display file names in stack traces.

Notice that in the sample executions of Fig. 11.1 when exceptions occur and stack traces are displayed, the program also exits. This does not always occur in Java—sometimes a program may continue even though an exception has occurred and a stack trace has been printed. In such cases, the application may produce unexpected results. The next section demonstrates how to handle these exceptions.

In Fig. 11.1 both types of exceptions were detected in method main. In the next example, we'll see how to handle these exceptions to enable the program to run to normal completion.

11.4 Example: Handling ArithmeticExceptions and InputMismatchExceptions

The application in Fig. 11.2, which is based on Fig. 11.1, uses exception handling to process any ArithmeticExceptions and InputMistmatchExceptions that arise. The application still prompts the user for two integers and passes them to method quotient, which calculates the quotient and returns an int result. This version of the application uses exception handling so that if the user makes a mistake, the program catches and handles (i.e., deals with) the exception—in this case, allowing the user to try to enter the input again. Note that quotient is declared static, so main can call it directly without instantiating a DivideByZeroWithExceptionHandling object.

```java
1  // Fig. 11.2: DivideByZeroWithExceptionHandling.java
2  // Handling ArithmeticExceptions and InputMismatchExceptions.
3  import java.util.InputMismatchException;
4  import java.util.Scanner;
5
6  public class DivideByZeroWithExceptionHandling
7  {
8     // demonstrates throwing an exception when a divide-by-zero occurs
9     public static int quotient( int numerator, int denominator )
10       throws ArithmeticException
11    {
12       return numerator / denominator; // possible division by zero
13    } // end method quotient
14
15    public static void main( String[] args )
16    {
17       Scanner scanner = new Scanner( System.in ); // scanner for input
18       boolean continueLoop = true; // determines if more input is needed
19
20       do
21       {
22          try // read two numbers and calculate quotient
23          {
24             System.out.print( "Please enter an integer numerator: " );
25             int numerator = scanner.nextInt();
26             System.out.print( "Please enter an integer denominator: " );
27             int denominator = scanner.nextInt();
28
29             int result = quotient( numerator, denominator );
30             System.out.printf( "\nResult: %d / %d = %d\n", numerator,
31                denominator, result );
32             continueLoop = false; // input successful; end looping
33          } // end try
34          catch ( InputMismatchException inputMismatchException )
35          {
```

Fig. 11.2 | Handling ArithmeticExceptions and InputMismatchExceptions. (Part 1 of 2.)

```
36          System.err.printf( "\nException: %s\n",
37            inputMismatchException );
38          scanner.nextLine(); // discard input so user can try again
39          System.out.println(
40            "You must enter integers. Please try again.\n" );
41        } // end catch
42        catch ( ArithmeticException arithmeticException )
43        {
44          System.err.printf( "\nException: %s\n", arithmeticException );
45          System.out.println(
46            "Zero is an invalid denominator. Please try again.\n" );
47        } // end catch
48      } while ( continueLoop ); // end do...while
49    } // end main
50  } // end class DivideByZeroWithExceptionHandling
```

```
Please enter an integer numerator: 100
Please enter an integer denominator: 7

Result: 100 / 7 = 14
```

```
Please enter an integer numerator: 100
Please enter an integer denominator: 0

Exception: java.lang.ArithmeticException: / by zero
Zero is an invalid denominator. Please try again.

Please enter an integer numerator: 100
Please enter an integer denominator: 7

Result: 100 / 7 = 14
```

```
Please enter an integer numerator: 100
Please enter an integer denominator: hello

Exception: java.util.InputMismatchException
You must enter integers. Please try again.

Please enter an integer numerator: 100
Please enter an integer denominator: 7

Result: 100 / 7 = 14
```

Fig. 11.2 | Handling ArithmeticExceptions and InputMismatchExceptions. (Part 2 of 2.)

The first sample execution in Fig. 11.2 is a successful one that does not encounter any problems. In the second execution the user enters a zero denominator, and an ArithmeticException exception occurs. In the third execution the user enters the string "hello" as the denominator, and an InputMismatchException occurs. For each exception, the user is informed of the mistake and asked to try again, then is prompted for two new integers. In each sample execution, the program runs successfully to completion.

Class `InputMismatchException` is imported in line 3. Class `ArithmeticException` does not need to be imported because it's in package `java.lang`. Line 18 creates the `boolean` variable `continueLoop`, which is `true` if the user has not yet entered valid input. Lines 20–48 repeatedly ask users for input until a valid input is received.

Enclosing Code in a *try* Block

Lines 22–33 contain a **try block**, which encloses the code that might `throw` an exception and the code that should not execute if an exception occurs (i.e., if an exception occurs, the remaining code in the `try` block will be skipped). A `try` block consists of the keyword `try` followed by a block of code enclosed in curly braces. [*Note:* The term "try block" sometimes refers only to the block of code that follows the `try` keyword (not including the `try` keyword itself). For simplicity, we use the term "try block" to refer to the block of code that follows the `try` keyword, as well as the `try` keyword.] The statements that read the integers from the keyboard (lines 25 and 27) each use method `nextInt` to read an `int` value. Method `nextInt` throws an `InputMismatchException` if the value read in is not an integer.

The division that can cause an `ArithmeticException` is not performed in the `try` block. Rather, the call to method `quotient` (line 29) invokes the code that attempts the division (line 12); the JVM throws an `ArithmeticException` object when the denominator is zero.

Software Engineering Observation 11.1

Exceptions may surface through explicitly mentioned code in a try block, through calls to other methods, through deeply nested method calls initiated by code in a try block or from the Java Virtual Machine as it executes Java bytecodes.

Catching Exceptions

The `try` block in this example is followed by two `catch` blocks—one that handles an `InputMismatchException` (lines 34–41) and one that handles an `ArithmeticException` (lines 42–47). A **catch block** (also called a **catch clause** or **exception handler**) catches (i.e., receives) and handles an exception. A `catch` block begins with the keyword `catch` and is followed by a parameter in parentheses (called the exception parameter, discussed shortly) and a block of code enclosed in curly braces. [*Note:* The term "catch clause" is sometimes used to refer to the keyword `catch` followed by a block of code, whereas the term "catch block" refers to only the block of code following the `catch` keyword, but not including it. For simplicity, we use the term "catch block" to refer to the block of code following the `catch` keyword, as well as the keyword itself.]

At least one `catch` block or a **finally block** (discussed in Section 11.7) must immediately follow the `try` block. Each `catch` block specifies in parentheses an **exception parameter** that identifies the exception type the handler can process. When an exception occurs in a `try` block, the `catch` block that executes is the first one whose type matches the type of the exception that occurred (i.e., the type in the `catch` block matches the thrown exception type exactly or is a superclass of it). The exception parameter's name enables the `catch` block to interact with a caught exception object—e.g., to implicitly invoke the caught exception's `toString` method (as in lines 37 and 44), which displays basic information about the exception. Notice that we use the **System.err (standard error stream) object** to output error messages. By default, `System.err`'s print methods, like those of `System.out`, display data to the command prompt.

Line 38 of the first `catch` block calls `Scanner` method `nextLine`. Because an `Input-MismatchException` occurred, the call to method `nextInt` never successfully read in the user's data—so we read that input with a call to method `nextLine`. We do not do anything with the input at this point, because we know that it's invalid. Each `catch` block displays an error message and asks the user to try again. After either `catch` block terminates, the user is prompted for input. We'll soon take a deeper look at how this flow of control works in exception handling.

Common Programming Error 11.1
It's a syntax error to place code between a `try` block and its corresponding `catch` blocks.

Common Programming Error 11.2
Each `catch` block can have only a single parameter—specifying a comma-separated list of exception parameters is a syntax error.

An **uncaught exception** is an one for which there are no matching `catch` blocks. You saw uncaught exceptions in the second and third outputs of Fig. 11.1. Recall that when exceptions occurred in that example, the application terminated early (after displaying the exception's stack trace). This does not always occur as a result of uncaught exceptions. As you'll learn in Chapter 26, Multithreading, Java uses a multithreaded model of program execution. Each **thread** is a parallel activity. One program can have many threads. If a program has only one thread, an uncaught exception will cause the program to terminate. If a program has multiple threads, an uncaught exception will terminate only the thread where the exception occurred. In such programs, however, certain threads may rely on others, and if one thread terminates due to an uncaught exception, there may be adverse effects to the rest of the program.

Termination Model of Exception Handling

If an exception occurs in a `try` block (such as an `InputMismatchException` being thrown as a result of the code at line 25 of Fig. 11.2), the `try` block terminates immediately and program control transfers to the first of the following `catch` blocks in which the exception parameter's type matches the thrown exception's type. In Fig. 11.2, the first `catch` block catches `InputMismatchExceptions` (which occur if invalid input is entered) and the second `catch` block catches `ArithmeticExceptions` (which occur if an attempt is made to divide by zero). After the exception is handled, program control does not return to the throw point, because the `try` block has expired (and its local variables have been lost). Rather, control resumes after the last `catch` block. This is known as the **termination model of exception handling**. Some languages use the **resumption model of exception handling**, in which, after an exception is handled, control resumes just after the throw point.

Notice that we name our exception parameters (`inputMismatchException` and `arithmeticException`) based on their type. Java programmers often simply use the letter e as the name of their exception parameters.

Good Programming Practice 11.1
Using an exception-parameter name that reflects the parameter's type promotes clarity by reminding you of the type of exception being handled.

After executing a catch block, this program's flow of control proceeds to the first statement after the last catch block (line 48 in this case). The condition in the do...while statement is true (variable continueLoop contains its initial value of true), so control returns to the beginning of the loop and the user is once again prompted for input. This control statement will loop until valid input is entered. At that point, program control reaches line 32, which assigns false to variable continueLoop. The try block then terminates. If no exceptions are thrown in the try block, the catch blocks are skipped and control continues with the first statement after the catch blocks (we'll learn about another possibility when we discuss the finally block in Section 11.7). Now the condition for the do...while loop is false, and method main ends.

The try block and its corresponding catch and/or finally blocks form a **try statement**. Do not confuse the terms "try block" and "try statement"—the latter includes the try block as well as the following catch blocks and/or finally block.

As with any other block of code, when a try block terminates, local variables declared in the block go out of scope and are no longer accessible; thus, the local variables of a try block are not accessible in the corresponding catch blocks. When a catch block terminates, local variables declared within the catch block (including the exception parameter of that catch block) also go out of scope and are destroyed. Any remaining catch blocks in the try statement are ignored, and execution resumes at the first line of code after the try...catch sequence—this will be a finally block, if one is present.

Using the **throws** Clause

Now let's examine method quotient (Fig. 11.2, lines 9–13). The portion of the method declaration located at line 10 is known as a **throws clause**. A throws clause specifies the exceptions the method throws. This clause appears after the method's parameter list and before the method's body. It contains a comma-separated list of the exceptions that the method will throw if various problems occur. Such exceptions may be thrown by statements in the method's body or by methods called from the body. A method can throw exceptions of the classes listed in its throws clause or of their subclasses. We've added the throws clause to this application to indicate to the rest of the program that this method may throw an ArithmeticException. Clients of method quotient are thus informed that the method may throw an ArithmeticException. You'll learn more about the throws clause in Section 11.6.

 Error-Prevention Tip 11.2
Read the online API documentation for a method before using that method in a program. The documentation specifies the exceptions thrown by the method (if any) and indicates reasons why such exceptions may occur. Next, read the online API documentation for the specified exception classes. The documentation for an exception class typically contains potential reasons that such exceptions occur. Finally, provide for handling those exceptions in your program.

When line 12 executes, if the denominator is zero, the JVM throws an ArithmeticException object. This object will be caught by the catch block at lines 42–47, which displays basic information about the exception by implicitly invoking the exception's toString method, then asks the user to try again.

If the denominator is not zero, method quotient performs the division and returns the result to the point of invocation of method quotient in the try block (line 29). Lines

30–31 display the result of the calculation and line 32 sets `continueLoop` to `false`. In this case, the `try` block completes successfully, so the program skips the `catch` blocks and fails the condition at line 48, and method `main` completes execution normally.

Note that when `quotient` throws an `ArithmeticException`, `quotient` terminates and does not return a value, and `quotient`'s local variables go out of scope (and are destroyed). If `quotient` contained local variables that were references to objects and there were no other references to those objects, the objects would be marked for garbage collection. Also, when an exception occurs, the `try` block from which `quotient` was called terminates before lines 30–32 can execute. Here, too, if local variables were created in the `try` block prior to the exception's being thrown, these variables would go out of scope.

If an `InputMismatchException` is generated by lines 25 or 27, the `try` block terminates and execution continues with the `catch` block at lines 34–41. In this case, method `quotient` is not called. Then method `main` continues after the last `catch` block (line 48).

11.5 When to Use Exception Handling

Exception handling is designed to process **synchronous errors**, which occur when a statement executes. Common examples we'll see throughout the book are out-of-range array indices, arithmetic overflow (i.e., a value outside the representable range of values), division by zero, invalid method parameters, thread interruption (as we'll see in Chapter 26) and unsuccessful memory allocation (due to lack of memory). Exception handling is not designed to process problems associated with **asynchronous events** (e.g., disk I/O completions, network message arrivals, mouse clicks and keystrokes), which occur in parallel with, and independent of, the program's flow of control.

Software Engineering Observation 11.2

Incorporate your exception-handling strategy into your system from the inception of the design process. Including exception handling after a system has been implemented can be difficult.

Software Engineering Observation 11.3

Exception handling provides a single, uniform technique for processing problems. This helps programmers working on large projects understand each other's error-processing code.

Software Engineering Observation 11.4

Exception handling simplifies combining software components and enables them to work together effectively by enabling predefined components to communicate problems to application-specific components, which can then process the problems in an application-specific manner.

11.6 Java Exception Hierarchy

All Java exception classes inherit directly or indirectly from class **Exception**, forming an inheritance hierarchy. You can extend this hierarchy with your own exception classes.

Figure 11.3 shows a small portion of the inheritance hierarchy for class **Throwable** (a subclass of `Object`), which is the superclass of class `Exception`. Only `Throwable` objects can be used with the exception-handling mechanism. Class `Throwable` has two subclasses: `Exception` and `Error`. Class `Exception` and its subclasses—for instance, `RuntimeException` (package `java.lang`) and `IOException` (package `java.io`)—represent exceptional situations that can occur in a Java program and that can be caught by the application. Class **Error** and its subclasses represent abnormal situations that happen in the JVM. Errors happen infrequently and should not be caught by applications—it's usually not possible for applications to recover from Errors.

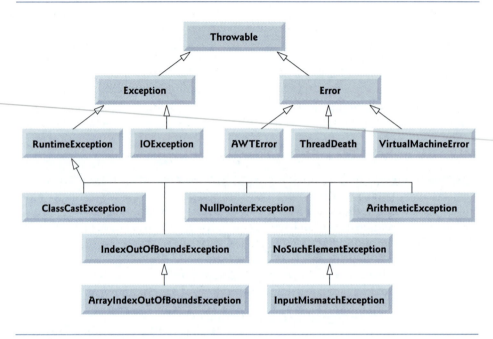

Fig. 11.3 | Portion of class `Throwable`'s inheritance hierarchy.

The Java exception hierarchy contains hundreds of classes. Information about Java's exception classes can be found throughout the Java API. You can view Throwable's documentation at `java.sun.com/javase/6/docs/api/java/lang/Throwable.html`. From there, you can look at this class's subclasses to get more information about Java's Exceptions and Errors.

Checked vs. Unchecked Exceptions

Java distinguishes between **checked exceptions** and **unchecked exceptions**. This distinction is important, because the Java compiler enforces a **catch-or-declare requirement** for checked exceptions. An exception's type determines whether it is checked or unchecked. All exception types that are direct or indirect subclasses of class **RuntimeException** (package java.lang) are unchecked exceptions. These are typically caused by defects in your program's code. Examples of unchecked exceptions include ArrayIndexOutOfBoundsExceptions (discussed in Chapter 6) and ArithmeticExceptions (shown in Fig. 11.3). All classes that inherit from class Exception but not class RuntimeException are considered to be checked exceptions. Such exceptions are typically caused by conditions that are not in the control of the program—for example, in file processing, the program can't open a file because the file does not exist. Classes that inherit from class Error are considered to be unchecked.

The compiler *checks* each method call and method declaration to determine whether the method throws checked exceptions. If so, the compiler verifies that the checked exception is caught or is declared in a `throws` clause. We show how to catch and declare checked exceptions in the next several examples. Recall from Section 11.4 that the `throws` clause specifies the exceptions a method throws. Such exceptions are not caught in the method's body. To satisfy the *catch* part of the catch-or-declare requirement, the code that generates the exception must be wrapped in a `try` block and must provide a `catch` handler for the checked-exception type (or one of its superclass types). To satisfy the *declare* part of the catch-or-declare requirement, the method containing the code that generates the exception must provide a `throws` clause containing the checked-exception type after its parameter list and before its method body. If the catch-or-declare requirement is not satisfied, the compiler will issue an error message indicating that the exception must be caught or declared. This forces you to think about the problems that may occur when a method that throws checked exceptions is called.

Software Engineering Observation 11.5

You must deal with checked exceptions. This results in more robust code than would be created if you were able to simply ignore the exceptions.

Common Programming Error 11.3

A compilation error occurs if a method explicitly attempts to throw a checked exception (or calls another method that throws a checked exception) and that exception is not listed in that method's `throws` clause.

Common Programming Error 11.4

If a subclass method overrides a superclass method, it's an error for the subclass method to list more exceptions in its `throws` clause than the overridden superclass method does. However, a subclass's `throws` clause can contain a subset of a superclass's `throws` list.

Software Engineering Observation 11.6

If your method calls other methods that explicitly throw checked exceptions, those exceptions must be caught or declared in your method. If an exception can be handled meaningfully in a method, the method should catch the exception rather than declare it.

Unlike checked exceptions, the Java compiler does not check the code to determine whether an unchecked exception is caught or declared. Unchecked exceptions typically can be prevented by proper coding. For example, the unchecked `ArithmeticException` thrown by method `quotient` (lines 9–13) in Fig. 11.2 can be avoided if the method ensures that the denominator is not zero before attempting to perform the division. Unchecked exceptions are not required to be listed in a method's `throws` clause—even if they are, it's not required that such exceptions be caught by an application.

Software Engineering Observation 11.7

Although the compiler does not enforce the catch-or-declare requirement for unchecked exceptions, provide appropriate exception-handling code when it's known that such exceptions might occur. For example, a program should process the `NumberFormatException` from `Integer` method `parseInt`, even though `NumberFormatException` (an indirect subclass of `RuntimeException`) is an unchecked exception type. This makes your programs more robust.

Catching Subclass Exceptions

If a catch handler is written to catch superclass-type exception objects, it can also catch all objects of that class's subclasses. This enables catch to handle related errors with a concise notation and allows for polymorphic processing of related exceptions. You can certainly catch each subclass type individually if those exceptions require different processing. Catching related exceptions in one catch block makes sense only if the handling behavior is the same for all subclasses.

Only the First Matching catch Executes

If there are multiple catch blocks that match a particular exception type, only the first matching catch block executes when an exception of that type occurs. It's a compilation error to catch the *exact same type* in two different catch blocks associated with a particular try block. However, there may be several catch blocks that match an exception—i.e., several catch blocks whose types are the same as the exception type or a superclass of that type. For instance, we could follow a catch block for type ArithmeticException with a catch block for type Exception—both would match ArithmeticExceptions, but only the first matching catch block would execute.

Error-Prevention Tip 11.3

Catching subclass types individually is subject to error if you forget to test for one or more of the subclass types explicitly; catching the superclass guarantees that objects of all subclasses will be caught. Positioning a catch block for the superclass type after all other subclass catch blocks for subclasses of that superclass ensures that all subclass exceptions are eventually caught.

Common Programming Error 11.5

Placing a catch block for a superclass exception type before other catch blocks that catch subclass exception types would prevent those catch blocks from executing, so a compilation error occurs.

11.7 finally Block

Programs that obtain certain types of resources must return them to the system explicitly to avoid so-called resource leaks. In programming languages such as C and C++, the most common kind of resource leak is a memory leak. Java performs automatic garbage collection of memory no longer used by programs, thus avoiding most memory leaks. However, other types of resource leaks can occur. For example, files, database connections and network connections that are not closed properly after they're no longer needed might not be available for use in other programs.

Error-Prevention Tip 11.4

A subtle issue is that Java does not entirely eliminate memory leaks. Java will not garbage-collect an object until there are no remaining references to it. Thus, if programmers erroneously keep references to unwanted objects, memory leaks can occur. To help avoid this problem, set reference-type variables to null, when they're no longer needed.

The finally block (which consists of the finally keyword, followed by code enclosed in curly braces), sometimes referred to as the **finally clause**, is optional. If it's present, it's placed after the last catch block, as in Fig. 11.4.

```
try
{
    statements
    resource-acquisition statements
} // end try
catch ( AKindOfException exception1 )
{
    exception-handling statements
} // end catch
...
catch ( AnotherKindOfException exception2 )
{
    exception-handling statements
} // end catch
finally
{
    statements
    resource-release statements
} // end finally
```

Fig. 11.4 | A try statement with a finally block.

Java guarantees that the finally block will execute whether or not an exception is thrown in the corresponding try block. Java also guarantees that the finally block will execute if a try block exits by using a return, break or continue statement or simply by reaching its closing right brace. The finally block will *not* execute if the application exits early from a try block by calling method **System.exit**. This method, which we demonstrate in Chapter 17, immediately terminates an application.

Because a finally block almost always executes, it typically contains resource-release code. Suppose a resource is allocated in a try block. If no exception occurs, the catch blocks are skipped and control proceeds to the finally block, which frees the resource. Control then proceeds to the first statement after the finally block. If an exception occurs in the try block, the try block terminates. If the program catches the exception in one of the corresponding catch blocks, it processes the exception, then the finally block releases the resource and control proceeds to the first statement after the finally block. If the program doesn't catch the exception, the finally block still releases the resource and an attempt is made to catch the exception in a calling method.

Error-Prevention Tip 11.5
The finally block is an ideal place to release resources acquired in a try block (such as opened files), which helps eliminate resource leaks.

Performance Tip 11.2
Always release a resource explicitly and at the earliest possible moment at which it's no longer needed. This makes resources available for reuse, thus improving resource utilization.

If an exception that occurs in a try block cannot be caught by one of that try block's catch handlers, the program skips the rest of the try block and control proceeds to the finally block. Then the program passes the exception to the next outer try block—normally in the calling method—where an associated catch block might catch it. This process can occur through many levels of try blocks. Also, the exception could go uncaught.

If a `catch` block throws an exception, the `finally` block still executes. Then the exception is passed to the next outer `try` block—again, normally in the calling method.

Figure 11.5 demonstrates that the `finally` block executes even if an exception is not thrown in the corresponding `try` block. The program contains `static` methods `main` (lines 6–18), `throwException` (lines 21–44) and `doesNotThrowException` (lines 47–64). Methods `throwException` and `doesNotThrowException` are declared `static`, so `main` can call them directly without instantiating a `UsingExceptions` object.

```java
1   // Fig. 11.5: UsingExceptions.java
2   // try...catch...finally exception handling mechanism.
3
4   public class UsingExceptions
5   {
6      public static void main( String[] args )
7      {
8         try
9         {
10           throwException(); // call method throwException
11        } // end try
12        catch ( Exception exception ) // exception thrown by throwException
13        {
14           System.err.println( "Exception handled in main" );
15        } // end catch
16
17        doesNotThrowException();
18     } // end main
19
20     // demonstrate try...catch...finally
21     public static void throwException() throws Exception
22     {
23        try // throw an exception and immediately catch it
24        {
25           System.out.println( "Method throwException" );
26           throw new Exception(); // generate exception
27        } // end try
28        catch ( Exception exception ) // catch exception thrown in try
29        {
30           System.err.println(
31              "Exception handled in method throwException" );
32           throw exception; // rethrow for further processing
33
34           // code here would not be reached; would cause compilation errors
35
36        } // end catch
37        finally // executes regardless of what occurs in try...catch
38        {
39           System.err.println( "Finally executed in throwException" );
40        } // end finally
41
42        // code here would not be reached; would cause compilation errors
43
44     } // end method throwException
```

Fig. 11.5 | try...catch...finally exception-handling mechanism. (Part 1 of 2.)

```
45
46         // demonstrate finally when no exception occurs
47         public static void doesNotThrowException()
48         {
49            try // try block does not throw an exception
50            {
51               System.out.println( "Method doesNotThrowException" );
52            } // end try
53            catch ( Exception exception ) // does not execute
54            {
55               System.err.println( exception );
56            } // end catch
57            finally // executes regardless of what occurs in try...catch
58            {
59               System.err.println(
60                  "Finally executed in doesNotThrowException" );
61            } // end finally
62
63            System.out.println( "End of method doesNotThrowException" );
64         } // end method doesNotThrowException
65      } // end class UsingExceptions
```

```
Method throwException
Exception handled in method throwException
Finally executed in throwException
Exception handled in main
Method doesNotThrowException
Finally executed in doesNotThrowException
End of method doesNotThrowException
```

Fig. 11.5 | try...catch...finally exception-handling mechanism. (Part 2 of 2.)

Both System.out and System.err are **streams**—a sequence of bytes. While System.out (known as the **standard output stream**) is used to display a program's output, System.err (known as the **standard error stream**) is used to display a program's errors. Output from these streams can be redirected (i.e., sent to somewhere other than the command prompt, such as to a file). Using two different streams enables you to easily separate error messages from other output. For instance, data output from System.err could be sent to a log file, while data output from System.out can be displayed on the screen. For simplicity, this chapter will not redirect output from System.err, but will display such messages to the command prompt. You'll learn more about streams in Chapter 17, Files, Streams and Object Serialization.

*Throwing Exceptions Using the **throw** Statement*
Method main (Fig. 11.5) begins executing, enters its try block and immediately calls method throwException (line 10). Method throwException throws an Exception. The statement at line 26 is known as a **throw statement**—it's executed to indicate that an exception has occurred. So far, you've only caught exceptions thrown by called methods. You can throw exceptions by using the throw statement. Just as with exceptions thrown by the Java API's methods, this indicates to client applications that an error has occurred. A throw statement specifies an object to be thrown. The operand of a throw can be of any class derived from class Throwable.

Software Engineering Observation 11.8

When toString *is invoked on any* Throwable *object, its resulting* string *includes the descriptive* string *that was supplied to the constructor, or simply the class name if no* string *was supplied.*

Software Engineering Observation 11.9

An object can be thrown without containing information about the problem that occurred. In this case, simply knowing that an exception of a particular type occurred may provide sufficient information for the handler to process the problem correctly.

Software Engineering Observation 11.10

Exceptions can be thrown from constructors. When an error is detected in a constructor, an exception should be thrown to avoid creating an improperly formed object.

Rethrowing Exceptions

Line 32 of Fig. 11.5 rethrows the exception. Exceptions are rethrown when a catch block, upon receiving an exception, decides either that it cannot process that exception or that it can only partially process it. Rethrowing an exception defers the exception handling (or perhaps a portion of it) to another catch block associated with an outer try statement. An exception is rethrown by using the throw keyword, followed by a reference to the exception object that was just caught. Note that exceptions cannot be rethrown from a finally block, as the exception parameter (a local variable) from the catch block no longer exists.

When a rethrow occurs, the next enclosing try block detects the rethrown exception, and that try block's catch blocks attempt to handle it. In this case, the next enclosing try block is found at lines 8–11 in method main. Before the rethrown exception is handled, however, the finally block (lines 37–40) executes. Then method main detects the rethrown exception in the try block and handles it in the catch block (lines 12–15).

Next, main calls method doesNotThrowException (line 17). No exception is thrown in doesNotThrowException's try block (lines 49–52), so the program skips the catch block (lines 53–56), but the finally block (lines 57–61) nevertheless executes. Control proceeds to the statement after the finally block (line 63). Then control returns to main and the program terminates.

Common Programming Error 11.6

If an exception has not been caught when control enters a finally block and the finally block throws an exception that is not caught in the finally block, the first exception will be lost and the exception from the finally block will be returned to the calling method.

Error-Prevention Tip 11.6

Avoid placing code that can throw an exception in a finally block. If such code is required, enclose the code in a try...catch within the finally block.

Common Programming Error 11.7

Assuming that an exception thrown from a catch block will be processed by that catch block or any other catch block associated with the same try statement can lead to logic errors.

Good Programming Practice 11.2

Java's exception-handling mechanism is intended to remove error-processing code from the main line of a program's code to improve program clarity. Do not place try...catch... finally *around every statement that may throw an exception. This makes programs difficult to read. Rather, place one try block around a significant portion of your code, follow that* try *block with* catch *blocks that handle each possible exception and follow the* catch *blocks with a single* finally *block (if one is required).*

11.8 Stack Unwinding

When an exception is thrown but not caught in a particular scope, the method-call stack is "unwound," and an attempt is made to catch the exception in the next outer try block. This process is called **stack unwinding**. Unwinding the method-call stack means that the method in which the exception was not caught terminates, all local variables in that method go out of scope and control returns to the statement that originally invoked that method. If a try block encloses that statement, an attempt is made to catch the exception. If a try block does not enclose that statement or if the exception is not caught, stack unwinding occurs again. Figure 11.6 demonstrates stack unwinding.

```java
1   // Fig. 11.6: UsingExceptions.java
2   // Stack unwinding.
3
4   public class UsingExceptions
5   {
6      public static void main( String[] args )
7      {
8         try // call throwException to demonstrate stack unwinding
9         {
10            throwException();
11         } // end try
12         catch ( Exception exception ) // exception thrown in throwException
13         {
14            System.err.println( "Exception handled in main" );
15         } // end catch
16      } // end main
17
18      // throwException throws exception that is not caught in this method
19      public static void throwException() throws Exception
20      {
21         try // throw an exception and catch it in main
22         {
23            System.out.println( "Method throwException" );
24            throw new Exception(); // generate exception
25         } // end try
26         catch ( RuntimeException runtimeException ) // catch incorrect type
27         {
28            System.err.println(
29               "Exception handled in method throwException" );
30         } // end catch
```

Fig. 11.6 | Stack unwinding. (Part 1 of 2.)

```
31         finally // finally block always executes
32         {
33            System.err.println( "Finally is always executed" );
34         } // end finally
35      } // end method throwException
36   } // end class UsingExceptions
```

```
Method throwException
Finally is always executed
Exception handled in main
```

Fig. 11.6 | Stack unwinding. (Part 2 of 2.)

When method main executes, line 10 in the try block calls method throwException (lines 19–35). In the try block of method throwException (lines 21–25), line 24 throws an Exception. This terminates the try block immediately, and control skips the catch block at line 26, because the type being caught (RuntimeException) is not an exact match with the thrown type (Exception) and is not a superclass of it. Method throwException terminates (but not until its finally block executes) and returns control to line 10—the point from which it was called in the program. Line 10 is in an enclosing try block. The exception has not yet been handled, so the try block terminates and an attempt is made to catch the exception at line 12. The type being caught (Exception) *does* match the thrown type. Consequently, the catch block processes the exception, and the program terminates at the end of main. If there were no matching catch blocks, and the exception is not declared in each method that throws it, a compilation error would occur. Remember that this is not always the case—for unchecked exceptions, the application will compile, but will run with unexpected results.

11.9 printStackTrace, getStackTrace and getMessage

Recall from Section 11.6 that exceptions derive from class Throwable. Class Throwable offers a **printStackTrace** method that outputs to the standard error stream the stack trace (discussed in Section 11.3). Often, this is helpful in testing and debugging. Class Throwable also provides a **getStackTrace** method that retrieves the stack-trace information that might be printed by printStackTrace. Class Throwable's **getMessage** method returns the descriptive string stored in an exception. The example in this section demonstrates these three methods.

Error-Prevention Tip 11.7

An exception that is not caught in an application causes Java's default exception handler to run. This displays the name of the exception, a descriptive message that indicates the problem that occurred and a complete execution stack trace. In an application with a single thread of execution, the application terminates. In an application with multiple threads, the thread that caused the exception terminates.

Error-Prevention Tip 11.8

Throwable method toString (inherited by all Throwable subclasses) returns a string containing the name of the exception's class and a descriptive message.

Figure 11.7 demonstrates getMessage, printStackTrace and getStackTrace. If we wanted to output the stack-trace information to streams other than the standard error stream, we could use the information returned from getStackTrace and output it to another stream or use one of the overloaded versions of method printStackTrace. Sending data to other streams is discussed in Chapter 17, Files, Streams and Object Serialization.

```java
1   // Fig. 11.7: UsingExceptions.java
2   // Throwable methods getMessage, getStackTrace and printStackTrace.
3
4   public class UsingExceptions
5   {
6      public static void main( String[] args )
7      {
8         try
9         {
10           method1(); // call method1
11        } // end try
12        catch ( Exception exception ) // catch exception thrown in method1
13        {
14           System.err.printf( "%s\n\n", exception.getMessage() );
15           exception.printStackTrace(); // print exception stack trace
16
17           // obtain the stack-trace information
18           StackTraceElement[] traceElements = exception.getStackTrace();
19
20           System.out.println( "\nStack trace from getStackTrace:" );
21           System.out.println( "Class\t\tFile\t\t\tLine\tMethod" );
22
23           // loop through traceElements to get exception description
24           for ( StackTraceElement element : traceElements )
25           {
26              System.out.printf( "%s\t", element.getClassName() );
27              System.out.printf( "%s\t", element.getFileName() );
28              System.out.printf( "%s\t", element.getLineNumber() );
29              System.out.printf( "%s\n", element.getMethodName() );
30           } // end for
31        } // end catch
32     } // end main
33
34     // call method2; throw exceptions back to main
35     public static void method1() throws Exception
36     {
37        method2();
38     } // end method method1
39
40     // call method3; throw exceptions back to method1
41     public static void method2() throws Exception
42     {
43        method3();
44     } // end method method2
```

Fig. 11.7 | Throwable methods getMessage, getStackTrace and printStackTrace. (Part 1 of 2.)

```
45
46        // throw Exception back to method2
47        public static void method3() throws Exception
48        {
49            throw new Exception( "Exception thrown in method3" );
50        } // end method method3
51    } // end class UsingExceptions
```

```
Exception thrown in method3

java.lang.Exception: Exception thrown in method3
        at UsingExceptions.method3(UsingExceptions.java:49)
        at UsingExceptions.method2(UsingExceptions.java:43)
        at UsingExceptions.method1(UsingExceptions.java:37)
        at UsingExceptions.main(UsingExceptions.java:10)

Stack trace from getStackTrace:
Class           File                   Line    Method
UsingExceptions UsingExceptions.java   49      method3
UsingExceptions UsingExceptions.java   43      method2
UsingExceptions UsingExceptions.java   37      method1
UsingExceptions UsingExceptions.java   10      main
```

Fig. 11.7 | Throwable methods getMessage, getStackTrace and printStackTrace. (Part 2 of 2.)

In main, the try block (lines 8–11) calls method1 (declared at lines 35–38), which in turn calls method2 (declared at lines 41–44), which in turn calls method3 (declared at lines 47–50). Line 49 of method3 throws an Exception object—this is the throw point. Because the throw statement at line 49 is not enclosed in a try block, stack unwinding occurs—method3 terminates at line 49, then returns control to the statement in method2 that invoked method3 (i.e., line 43). Because no try block encloses line 43, stack unwinding occurs again—method2 terminates at line 43 and returns control to the statement in method1 that invoked method2 (i.e., line 37). Because no try block encloses line 37, stack unwinding occurs one more time—method1 terminates at line 37 and returns control to the statement in main that invoked method1 (i.e., line 10). The try block at lines 8–11 encloses this statement. The exception has not been handled, so the try block terminates and the first matching catch block (lines 12–31) catches and processes the exception.

Line 14 invokes the exception's getMessage method to get the exception description. Line 15 invokes the exception's printStackTrace method to output the stack trace that indicates where the exception occurred. Line 18 invokes the exception's getStackTrace method to obtain the stack-trace information as an array of **StackTraceElement** objects. Lines 24–30 get each StackTraceElement in the array and invoke its methods **getClassName**, **getFileName**, **getLineNumber** and **getMethodName** to get the class name, file name, line number and method name, respectively, for that StackTraceElement. Each StackTraceElement represents one method call on the method-call stack.

The output in Fig. 11.7 shows that the stack-trace information printed by printStackTrace follows the pattern: *className.methodName(fileName:lineNumber)*, where *className*, *methodName* and *fileName* indicate the names of the class, method and file in which the exception occurred, respectively, and the *lineNumber* indicates where in the file the exception occurred. You saw this in the output for Fig. 11.1. Method getStackTrace enables custom processing of the exception information. Compare the output of print-StackTrace with the output created from the StackTraceElements to see that both contain the same stack-trace information.

Software Engineering Observation 11.11

Never ignore an exception you catch. At least use printStackTrace to output an error message. This will inform users that a problem exists, so that they can take appropriate actions.

11.10 Chained Exceptions

Sometimes a method responds to an exception by throwing a different exception type that is specific to the current application. If a catch block throws a new exception, the original exception's information and stack trace are lost. Earlier Java versions provided no mechanism to wrap the original exception information with the new exception's information to provide a complete stack trace showing where the original problem occurred. This made debugging such problems particularly difficult. **Chained exceptions** enable an exception object to maintain the complete stack-trace information from the original exception. Figure 11.8 demonstrates chained exceptions.

```java
1   // Fig. 11.8: UsingChainedExceptions.java
2   // Chained exceptions.
3
4   public class UsingChainedExceptions
5   {
6      public static void main( String[] args )
7      {
8         try
9         {
10            method1(); // call method1
11         } // end try
12         catch ( Exception exception ) // exceptions thrown from method1
13         {
14            exception.printStackTrace();
15         } // end catch
16      } // end main
17
18      // call method2; throw exceptions back to main
19      public static void method1() throws Exception
20      {
21         try
22         {
23            method2(); // call method2
24         } // end try
25         catch ( Exception exception ) // exception thrown from method2
26         {
27            throw new Exception( "Exception thrown in method1", exception );
28         } // end catch
29      } // end method method1
30
```

Fig. 11.8 | Chained exceptions. (Part 1 of 2.)

```
31      // call method3; throw exceptions back to method1
32      public static void method2() throws Exception
33      {
34         try
35         {
36            method3(); // call method3
37         } // end try
38         catch ( Exception exception ) // exception thrown from method3
39         {
40            throw new Exception( "Exception thrown in method2", exception );
41         } // end catch
42      } // end method method2
43
44      // throw Exception back to method2
45      public static void method3() throws Exception
46      {
47         throw new Exception( "Exception thrown in method3" );
48      } // end method method3
49   } // end class UsingChainedExceptions
```

```
java.lang.Exception: Exception thrown in method1
        at UsingChainedExceptions.method1(UsingChainedExceptions.java:27)
        at UsingChainedExceptions.main(UsingChainedExceptions.java:10)
Caused by: java.lang.Exception: Exception thrown in method2
        at UsingChainedExceptions.method2(UsingChainedExceptions.java:40)
        at UsingChainedExceptions.method1(UsingChainedExceptions.java:23)
        ... 1 more
Caused by: java.lang.Exception: Exception thrown in method3
        at UsingChainedExceptions.method3(UsingChainedExceptions.java:47)
        at UsingChainedExceptions.method2(UsingChainedExceptions.java:36)
        ... 2 more
```

Fig. 11.8 | Chained exceptions. (Part 2 of 2.)

The program consists of four methods—main (lines 6–16), method1 (lines 19–29), method2 (lines 32–42) and method3 (lines 45–48). Line 10 in method main's try block calls method1. Line 23 in method1's try block calls method2. Line 36 in method2's try block calls method3. In method3, line 47 throws a new Exception. Because this statement is not in a try block, method3 terminates, and the exception is returned to the calling method (method2) at line 36. This statement *is* in a try block; therefore, the try block terminates and the exception is caught at lines 38–41. Line 40 in the catch block throws a new exception. In this case, the Exception constructor with two arguments is called. The second argument represents the exception that was the original cause of the problem. In this program, that exception occurred at line 47. Because an exception is thrown from the catch block, method2 terminates and returns the new exception to the calling method (method1) at line 23. Once again, this statement is in a try block, so the try block terminates and the exception is caught at lines 25–28. Line 27 in the catch block throws a new exception and uses the exception that was caught as the second argument to the Exception constructor. Because an exception is thrown from the catch block, method1 terminates and returns the new exception to the calling method (main) at line 10. The try block in main terminates, and the exception is caught at lines 12–15. Line 14 prints a stack trace.

Notice in the program output that the first three lines show the most recent exception that was thrown (i.e., the one from method1 at line 27). The next four lines indicate the exception that was thrown from method2 at line 40. Finally, the last four lines represent the exception that was thrown from method3 at line 47. Also notice that, as you read the output in reverse, it shows how many more chained exceptions remain.

11.11 Declaring New Exception Types

Most Java programmers use existing classes from the Java API, third-party vendors and freely available class libraries (usually downloadable from the Internet) to build Java applications. The methods of those classes typically are declared to throw appropriate exceptions when problems occur. You write code that processes these existing exceptions to make programs more robust.

If you build classes that other programmers will use, you might find it useful to declare your own exception classes that are specific to the problems that can occur when another programmer uses your reusable classes.

Software Engineering Observation 11.12

If possible, indicate exceptions from your methods by using existing exception classes, rather than creating new ones. The Java API contains many exception classes that might be suitable for the type of problems your methods need to indicate.

A new exception class must extend an existing exception class to ensure that the class can be used with the exception-handling mechanism. Like any other class, an exception class can contain fields and methods. However, a typical new exception class contains only four constructors: one that takes no arguments and passes a default error message String to the superclass constructor; one that receives a customized error message as a String and passes it to the superclass constructor; one that receives a customized error message as a String and a Throwable (for chaining exceptions) and passes both to the superclass constructor; and one that receives a Throwable (for chaining exceptions) and passes it to the superclass constructor.

Good Programming Practice 11.3

Associating each type of serious execution-time malfunction with an appropriately named Exception *class improves program clarity.*

Software Engineering Observation 11.13

When defining your own exception type, study the existing exception classes in the Java API and try to extend a related exception class. For example, if you are creating a new class to represent when a method attempts a division by zero, you might extend class ArithmeticException *because division by zero occurs during arithmetic. If the existing classes are not appropriate superclasses for your new exception class, decide whether your new class should be a checked or an unchecked exception class. The new exception class should be a checked exception (i.e., extend* Exception *but not* RuntimeException*) if clients should be required to handle the exception. The client application should be able to reasonably recover from such an exception. The new exception class should extend* RuntimeException *if the client code should be able to ignore the exception (i.e., the exception is an unchecked one).*

In Chapter 22, Custom Generic Data Structures, we provide an example of a custom exception class. We declare a reusable class called `List` that is capable of storing a list of references to objects. Some operations typically performed on a `List` are not allowed if the `List` is empty, such as removing an item from the front or back of the list. For this reason, some `List` methods throw exceptions of exception class `EmptyListException`.

Good Programming Practice 11.4
By convention, all exception-class names should end with the word `Exception`.

11.12 Preconditions and Postconditions

Programmers spend significant amounts of time maintaining and debugging code. To facilitate these tasks and to improve the overall design, they can specify the expected states before and after a method's execution. These states are called preconditions and postconditions, respectively.

A **precondition** must be true when a method is invoked. Preconditions describe constraints on method parameters and any other expectations the method has about the current state of a program just before it begins executing. If the preconditions are not met, then the method's behavior is undefined—it may throw an exception, proceed with an illegal value or attempt to recover from the error. You should never expect consistent behavior if the preconditions are not satisfied.

A **postcondition** is true after the method successfully returns. Postconditions describe constraints on the return value and any other side effects the method may have. When calling a method, you may assume that a method fulfills all of its postconditions. If you are writing your own method, you should document all postconditions so that others know what to expect when they call your method, and you should make certain that your method honors all its postconditions if its preconditions are indeed met.

When their preconditions or postconditions are not met, methods typically throw exceptions. As an example, examine `String` method `charAt`, which has one `int` parameter—an index in the `String`. For a precondition, method `charAt` assumes that `index` is greater than or equal to zero and less than the length of the `String`. If the precondition is met, the postcondition states that the method will return the character at the position in the `String` specified by the parameter `index`. Otherwise, the method throws an `IndexOutOfBoundsException`. We trust that method `charAt` satisfies its postcondition, provided that we meet the precondition. We need not be concerned with the details of how the method actually retrieves the character at the index.

Some programmers state the preconditions and postconditions informally as part of the general method specification, while others prefer a more formal approach by explicitly defining them. When designing your own methods, you should state the preconditions and postconditions in a comment before the method declaration in whichever manner you prefer. Stating the preconditions and postconditions before writing a method will also help guide you as you implement the method.

11.13 Assertions

When implementing and debugging a class, it's sometimes useful to state conditions that should be true at a particular point in a method. These conditions, called **assertions**, help ensure a program's validity by catching potential bugs and identifying possible logic errors during development. Preconditions and postconditions are two types of assertions. Preconditions are assertions about its state when a method is invoked, and postconditions are assertions about a program's state after a method finishes.

While assertions can be stated as comments to guide you during program development, Java includes two versions of the **assert** statement for validating assertions programmatically. The **assert** statement evaluates a **boolean** expression and, if **false**, throws an **AssertionError** (a subclass of Error). The first form of the **assert** statement is

> **assert** *expression*;

which throws an **AssertionError** if *expression* is **false**. The second form is

> **assert** *expression1* : *expression2*;

which evaluates *expression1* and throws an **AssertionError** with *expression2* as the error message if *expression1* is **false**.

You can use assertions to programmatically implement preconditions and postconditions or to verify any other intermediate states that help you ensure your code is working correctly. Figure 11.9 demonstrates the **assert** statement. Line 11 prompts the user to enter a number between 0 and 10, then line 12 reads the number. Line 15 determines whether the user entered a number within the valid range. If the number is out of range, the **assert** statement reports an error; otherwise, the program proceeds normally.

```java
1   // Fig. 11.9: AssertTest.java
2   // Checking with assert that a value is within range
3   import java.util.Scanner;
4
5   public class AssertTest
6   {
7      public static void main( String[] args )
8      {
9         Scanner input = new Scanner( System.in );
10
11         System.out.print( "Enter a number between 0 and 10: " );
12         int number = input.nextInt();
13
14         // assert that the value is >= 0 and <= 10
15         assert ( number >= 0 && number <= 10 ) : "bad number: " + number;
16
17         System.out.printf( "You entered %d\n", number );
18      } // end main
19   } // end class AssertTest
```

```
Enter a number between 0 and 10: 5
You entered 5
```

```
Enter a number between 0 and 10: 50
Exception in thread "main" java.lang.AssertionError: bad number: 50
        at AssertTest.main(AssertTest.java:15)
```

Fig. 11.9 | Checking with assert that a value is within range.

You use assertions primarily for debugging and identifying logic errors in an application. You must explicitly enable assertions when executing a program, because they reduce performance and are unnecessary for the program's user. To do so, use the `java` command's `-ea` command-line option, as in

```
java -ea AssertTest
```

Users should not encounter any `AssertionError`s through normal execution of a properly written program. Such errors should only indicate bugs in the implementation. As a result, you should never catch an `AssertionError`. Rather, you should allow the program to terminate when the error occurs, so you can see the error message, then locate and fix the source of the problem. Since application users can choose not to enable assertions at runtime, you should not use `assert` to indicate runtime problems in production code. Rather, you should use the exception mechanism for this purpose.

11.14 Wrap-Up

In this chapter, you learned how to use exception handling to deal with errors. You learned that exception handling enables you to remove error-handling code from the "main line" of the program's execution. We showed how to use `try` blocks to enclose code that may throw an exception, and how to use `catch` blocks to deal with exceptions that may arise. You learned about the termination model of exception handling, which dictates that after an exception is handled, program control does not return to the throw point. We discussed checked vs. unchecked exceptions, and how to specify with the `throws` clause the exceptions that a method might throw. You learned how to use the `finally` block to release resources whether or not an exception occurs. You also learned how to throw and rethrow exceptions. We showed how to obtain information about an exception using methods `printStackTrace`, `getStackTrace` and `getMessage`. Next, we presented chained exceptions, which allow you to wrap original exception information with new exception information. Then, we showed how to create your own exception classes. We introduced preconditions and postconditions to help programmers using your methods understand conditions that must be true when the method is called and when it returns. When preconditions and postconditions are not met, methods typically throw exceptions. Finally, we discussed the `assert` statement and how it can be used to help you debug your programs. In particular, `assert` can be used to ensure that preconditions and postconditions are met. In the next chapter, we begin our two-chapter, optional case study on object-oriented design with the UML.

Summary

Section 11.1 Introduction
- An exception is an indication of a problem that occurs during a program's execution.
- Exception handling enables programmers to create applications that can resolve exceptions.

Section 11.2 Error-Handling Overview
- Exception handling enables you to remove error-handling code from the "main line" of the program's execution, improving program clarity and enhancing modifiability.

Section 11.3 Example: Divide by Zero without Exception Handling

- Exceptions are thrown when a method detects a problem and is unable to handle it.

- An exception's stack trace includes the name of the exception in a message that indicates the problem that occurred and the complete method-call stack at the time the exception occurred.

- The point in the program at which an exception occurs is called the throw point.

Section 11.4 Example: Handling `ArithmeticExceptions` and `InputMismatchExceptions`

- A `try` block encloses code that might `throw` an exception and code that should not execute if that exception occurs.

- Exceptions may surface through explicitly mentioned code in a `try` block, through calls to other methods or even through deeply nested method calls initiated by code in the `try` block.

- A `catch` block begins with the keyword `catch` and an exception parameter followed by a block of code that handles the exception. This code executes when the `try` block detects the exception.

- An uncaught exception is an exception that occurs for which there are no matching `catch` blocks.

- An uncaught exception will cause a program to terminate early if that program contains only one thread. Otherwise, only the thread where the exception occurred will terminate. The rest of the program will run but possibly with adverse results.

- At least one `catch` block or a `finally` block must immediately follow the `try` block.

- A `catch` block specifies in parentheses an exception parameter identifying the exception type to handle. The parameter's name enables the `catch` block to interact with a caught exception object.

- If an exception occurs in a `try` block, the `try` block terminates immediately and program control transfers to the first `catch` block with a parameter type that matches the thrown exception's type.

- After an exception is handled, program control does not return to the throw point, because the `try` block has expired. This is known as the termination model of exception handling.

- If there are multiple matching `catch` blocks when an exception occurs, only the first is executed.

- A `throws` clause specifies a comma-separated list of exceptions that the method might throw, and appears after the method's parameter list and before the method body.

Section 11.5 When to Use Exception Handling

- Exception handling processes synchronous errors, which occur when a statement executes.

- Exception handling is not designed to process problems associated with asynchronous events, which occur in parallel with, and independent of, the program's flow of control.

Section 11.6 Java Exception Hierarchy

- All Java exception classes inherit directly or indirectly from class `Exception`.

- Programmers can extend the Java exception hierarchy with their own exception classes.

- Class `Throwable` is the superclass of class `Exception` and is therefore also the superclass of all exceptions. Only `Throwable` objects can be used with the exception-handling mechanism.

- Class `Throwable` has two subclasses: `Exception` and `Error`.

- Class `Exception` and its subclasses represent problems that could occur in a Java program and be caught by the application.

- Class `Error` and its subclasses represent problems that could happen in the Java runtime system. `Errors` happen infrequently and typically should not be caught by an application.

- Java distinguishes between two categories of exceptions: checked and unchecked.

- The Java compiler does not check to determine if an unchecked exception is caught or declared. Unchecked exceptions typically can be prevented by proper coding.

- Subclasses of `RuntimeException` represent unchecked exceptions. All exception types that inherit from class `Exception` but not from `RuntimeException` are checked.

- If a `catch` block is written to catch exception objects of a superclass type, it can also catch all objects of that class's subclasses. This allows for polymorphic processing of related exceptions.

Section 11.7 `finally` block

- Programs that obtain certain types of resources must return them to the system explicitly to avoid so-called resource leaks. Resource-release code typically is placed in a `finally` block.

- The `finally` block is optional. If it's present, it's placed after the last `catch` block.

- Java guarantees that the `finally` block will execute whether or not an exception is thrown in the corresponding `try` block or any of its corresponding `catch` blocks.

- If an exception cannot be caught by one of that `try` block's associated `catch` handlers, control proceeds to the `finally` block. Then the exception is passed to the next outer `try` block.

- If a `catch` block throws an exception, the `finally` block still executes. Then the exception is passed to the next outer `try` block.

- A `throw` statement can throw any `Throwable` object.

Section 11.8 Stack Unwinding

- Exceptions are rethrown when a `catch` block, upon receiving an exception, decides either that it cannot process that exception or that it can only partially process it. Rethrowing an exception defers the exception handling (or perhaps a portion of it) to another `catch` block.

- When a rethrow occurs, the next enclosing `try` block detects the rethrown exception, and that `try` block's `catch` blocks attempt to handle it.

- When an exception is thrown but not caught in a particular scope, the method-call stack is unwound, and an attempt is made to `catch` the exception in the next outer `try` statement.

Section 11.9 `printStackTrace`, `getStackTrace` and `getMessage`

- Class `Throwable` offers a `printStackTrace` method that prints the method-call stack. Often, this is helpful in testing and debugging.

- Class `Throwable` also provides a `getStackTrace` method that obtains the same stack-trace information that is printed by `printStackTrace`.

- Class `Throwable`'s `getMessage` method returns the descriptive string stored in an exception.

- Method `getStackTrace` obtains the stack-trace information as an array of `StackTraceElement` objects. Each `StackTraceElement` represents one method call on the method-call stack.

- `StackTraceElement` methods `getClassName`, `getFileName`, `getLineNumber` and `getMethodName` get the class name, file name, line number and method name, respectively.

Section 11.10 Chained Exceptions

- Chained exceptions enable an exception object to maintain the complete stack-trace information, including information about previous exceptions that caused the current exception.

Section 11.11 Declaring New Exception Types

- A new exception class must extend an existing exception class to ensure that the class can be used with the exception-handling mechanism.

Section 11.12 Preconditions and Postconditions

- A method's precondition is a condition that must be true when the method is invoked.

- A method's postcondition is a condition that is true after the method successfully returns.

- When designing your own methods, you should state the preconditions and postconditions in a comment before the method declaration.

Section 11.13 Assertions
- Assertions help ensure a program's validity by catching potential bugs and identifying possible logic errors.
- Java includes two versions of an `assert` statement for validating assertions programatically.
- To enable assertions at runtime, use the -ea switch when running the `java` command.

Terminology

ArithmeticException class 454
assert statement 477
assertion 476
AssertionError class 477
asynchronous event 461
catch block 458
catch clause 458
catch keyword 458
catch-or-declare requirement 462
chained exceptions 473
checked exception 462
Error class 462
exception 452
Exception class 461
exception handler 458
exception handling 452
exception parameter 458
exit method of class System 465
fault-tolerant program 452
finally block 458
finally clause 464
finally keyword 458
getClassName method of class
    StackTraceElement 472
getFileName method of class
    StackTraceElement 472
getLineNumber method of class
    StackTraceElement 472
getMessage method of class Throwable 470
getMethodName method of class
    StackTraceElement 472
getStackTrace method of class Throwable 470

InputMismatchException class 455
postcondition 476
precondition 476
printStackTrace method of class Throwable
    470
resource leak 464
resumption model of exception handling 459
rethrow an exception 468
rintStackTrace 470
robust application 452
RuntimeException class 462
stack trace 454
stack unwinding 469
StackTraceElement class 472
standard error stream 467
standard output stream 467
stream 467
synchronous error 461
termination model of exception handling 459
thread 459
throw an exception 454
throw keyword 468
throw point 455
throw statement 467
Throwable class 461
throws clause 460
throws keyword 460
try block 458
try keyword 458
try statement 460
uncaught exception 459
unchecked exception 462

Self-Review Exercises

11.1 List five common examples of exceptions.

11.2 Give several reasons why exception-handling techniques should not be used for conventional program control.

11.3 Why are exceptions particularly appropriate for dealing with errors produced by methods of classes in the Java API?

11.4   What is a "resource leak"?

11.5   If no exceptions are thrown in a try block, where does control proceed to when the try block completes execution?

11.6   Give a key advantage of using catch(Exception *exceptionName*).

11.7   Should a conventional application catch Error objects? Explain.

11.8   What happens if no catch handler matches the type of a thrown object?

11.9   What happens if several catch blocks match the type of the thrown object?

11.10   Why would a programmer specify a superclass type as the type in a catch block?

11.11   What is the key reason for using finally blocks?

11.12   What happens when a catch block throws an Exception?

11.13   What does the statement throw *exceptionReference* do in a catch block?

11.14   What happens to a local reference in a try block when that block throws an Exception?

Answers to Self-Review Exercises

11.1   Memory exhaustion, array index out of bounds, arithmetic overflow, division by zero, invalid method parameters.

11.2   (a) Exception handling is designed to handle infrequently occurring situations that often result in program termination, not situations that arise all the time. (b) Flow of control with conventional control structures is generally clearer and more efficient than with exceptions. (c) The additional exceptions can get in the way of genuine error-type exceptions. It becomes more difficult for you to keep track of the larger number of exception cases.

11.3   It's unlikely that methods of classes in the Java API could perform error processing that would meet the unique needs of all users.

11.4   A "resource leak" occurs when an executing program does not properly release a resource when it's no longer needed.

11.5   The catch blocks for that try statement are skipped, and the program resumes execution after the last catch block. If there is a finally block, it's executed first; then the program resumes execution after the finally block.

11.6   The form catch(Exception *exceptionName*) catches any type of exception thrown in a try block. An advantage is that no thrown Exception can slip by without being caught. You can then decide to handle the exception or possibly rethrow it.

11.7   Errors are usually serious problems with the underlying Java system; most programs will not want to catch Errors because they will not be able to recover from them.

11.8   This causes the search for a match to continue in the next enclosing try statement. If there is a finally block, it will be executed before the exception goes to the next enclosing try statement. If there are no enclosing try statements for which there are matching catch blocks and the exceptions are declared (or unchecked), a stack trace is printed and the current thread terminates early. If the exceptions are checked, but not caught or declared, compilation errors occur.

11.9   The first matching catch block after the try block is executed.

11.10   This enables a program to catch related types of exceptions and process them in a uniform manner. However, it's often useful to process the subclass types individually for more precise exception handling.

11.11   The finally block is the preferred means for releasing resources to prevent resource leaks.

11.12 First, control passes to the `finally` block if there is one. Then the exception will be processed by a `catch` block (if one exists) associated with an enclosing `try` block (if one exists).

11.13 It rethrows the exception for processing by an exception handler of an enclosing `try` statement, after the `finally` block of the current `try` statement executes.

11.14 The reference goes out of scope. If the referenced object becomes unreachable, the object can be garbage collected.

Exercises

11.15 List the various exceptional conditions that have occurred in programs throughout this text so far. List as many additional exceptional conditions as you can. For each of these, describe briefly how a program typically would handle the exception by using the exception-handling techniques discussed in this chapter. Typical exceptions include division by zero and array index out of bounds.

11.16 Until this chapter, we've found dealing with errors detected by constructors to be a bit awkward. Explain why exception handling is an effective means for dealing with constructor failure.

11.17 *(Catching Exceptions with Superclasses)* Use inheritance to create an exception superclass (called `ExceptionA`) and exception subclasses `ExceptionB` and `ExceptionC`, where `ExceptionB` inherits from `ExceptionA` and `ExceptionC` inherits from `ExceptionB`. Write a program to demonstrate that the `catch` block for type `ExceptionA` catches exceptions of types `ExceptionB` and `ExceptionC`.

11.18 *(Catching Exceptions Using Class `Exception`)* Write a program that demonstrates how various exceptions are caught with

        `catch ( Exception exception )`

This time, define classes `ExceptionA` (which inherits from class `Exception`) and `ExceptionB` (which inherits from class `ExceptionA`). In your program, create `try` blocks that throw exceptions of types `ExceptionA`, `ExceptionB`, `NullPointerException` and `IOException`. All exceptions should be caught with `catch` blocks specifying type `Exception`.

11.19 *(Order of `catch` Blocks)* Write a program that shows that the order of `catch` blocks is important. If you try to catch a superclass exception type before a subclass type, the compiler should generate errors.

11.20 *(Constructor Failure)* Write a program that shows a constructor passing information about constructor failure to an exception handler. Define class `SomeClass`, which throws an `Exception` in the constructor. Your program should try to create an object of type `SomeClass` and catch the exception that is thrown from the constructor.

11.21 *(Rethrowing Exceptions)* Write a program that illustrates rethrowing an exception. Define methods `someMethod` and `someMethod2`. Method `someMethod2` should initially throw an exception. Method `someMethod` should call `someMethod2`, catch the exception and rethrow it. Call `someMethod` from method `main`, and catch the rethrown exception. Print the stack trace of this exception.

11.22 *(Catching Exceptions Using Outer Scopes)* Write a program showing that a method with its own `try` block does not have to catch every possible error generated within the `try`. Some exceptions can slip through to, and be handled in, other scopes.

12

ATM Case Study, Part 1: Object-Oriented Design with the UML

Action speaks louder than words but not nearly as often.
—Mark Twain

Always design a thing by considering it in its next larger context.
—Eliel Saarinen

Oh, life is a glorious cycle of song.
—Dorothy Parker

The Wright brothers' design ... allowed them to survive long enough to learn how to fly.
—Michael Potts

Objectives

In this chapter you'll learn:

- A simple object-oriented design methodology.

- What a requirements document is.

- To identify classes and class attributes from a requirements document.

- To identify objects' states, activities and operations from a requirements document.

- To determine the collaborations among objects in a system.

- To work with various UML diagrams to graphically model an object-oriented system.

12.1 Case Study Introduction

Now we begin the optional portion of our object-oriented design and implementation case study. In this chapter and Chapter 13, you'll design and implement an object-oriented automated teller machine (ATM) software system. The case study provides you with a concise, carefully paced, complete design and implementation experience. In Sections 12.2 12.7 and 13.2–13.3, you'll perform the steps of an object-oriented design (OOD) process using the UML while relating these steps to the object-oriented concepts discussed in Chapters 2–10. In this chapter, you'll work with six popular types of UML diagrams to graphically represent the design. In Chapter 13, you'll tune the design with inheritance, then fully implement the ATM in a 673-line Java application (Section 13.4).

This is not an exercise; rather, it's an end-to-end learning experience that concludes with a detailed walkthrough of the complete Java code that implements our design. It will acquaint you with the kinds of substantial problems encountered in industry.

These chapters can be studied as a continuous unit after you've completed the introduction to object-oriented programming in Chapters 8–11. Or, you can pace the sections one at a time after Chapters 2–8 and 10. Each section of the case study begins with a note telling you the chapter after which it can be covered.

12.2 Examining the Requirements Document

[*Note:* **This section can be taught after Chapter 2.**]
We begin our design process by presenting a **requirements document** that specifies the purpose of the ATM system and *what* it must do. Throughout the case study, we refer often to this requirements document.

Requirements Document
A local bank intends to install a new automated teller machine (ATM) to allow users (i.e., bank customers) to perform basic financial transactions (Fig. 12.1). Each user can have only one account at the bank. ATM users should be able to view their account balance, withdraw cash (i.e., take money out of an account) and deposit funds (i.e., place money into an account). The user interface of the automated teller machine contains:

- a screen that displays messages to the user
- a keypad that receives numeric input from the user
- a cash dispenser that dispenses cash to the user and
- a deposit slot that receives deposit envelopes from the user.

The cash dispenser begins each day loaded with 500 $20 bills. [*Note:* Owing to the limited scope of this case study, certain elements of the ATM described here do not accurately mimic those of a real ATM. For example, a real ATM typically contains a device that reads a user's account number from an ATM card, whereas this ATM asks the user to type the account number on the keypad. A real ATM also usually prints a receipt at the end of a session, but all output from this ATM appears on the screen.]

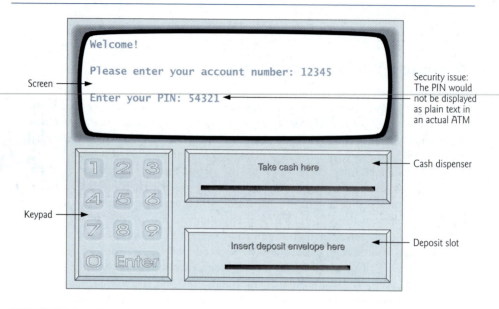

Fig. 12.1 | Automated teller machine user interface.

The bank wants you to develop software to perform the financial transactions initiated by bank customers through the ATM. The bank will integrate the software with the ATM's hardware at a later time. The software should encapsulate the functionality of the hardware devices (e.g., cash dispenser, deposit slot) within software components, but it need not concern itself with how these devices perform their duties. The ATM hardware has not been developed yet, so instead of writing your software to run on the ATM, you should develop a first version to run on a personal computer. This version should use the computer's monitor to simulate the ATM's screen, and the computer's keyboard to simulate the ATM's keypad.

An ATM session consists of authenticating a user (i.e., proving the user's identity) based on an account number and personal identification number (PIN), followed by creating and executing financial transactions. To authenticate a user and perform transactions, the ATM must interact with the bank's account information database (i.e., an organized collection of data stored on a computer; we study database access in Chapter 28). For each bank account, the database stores an account number, a PIN and a balance indicating the amount of money in the account. [*Note:* We assume that the bank plans to build only one ATM, so we need not worry about multiple ATMs accessing this database at the same time. Furthermore, we assume that the bank does not make any changes to the information in the database while a user is accessing the ATM. Also, any business system like an ATM faces reasonably complicated security issues that are beyond the scope of a first or second programming course. We make the simplifying assumption, however, that the bank trusts the ATM to access and manipulate the information in the database without significant security measures.]

Upon first approaching the ATM (assuming no one is currently using it), the user should experience the following sequence of events (shown in Fig. 12.1):

1. The screen displays Welcome! and prompts the user to enter an account number.

2. The user enters a five-digit account number using the keypad.

3. The screen prompts the user to enter the PIN (personal identification number) associated with the specified account number.

4. The user enters a five-digit PIN using the keypad.[1]

5. If the user enters a valid account number and the correct PIN for that account, the screen displays the main menu (Fig. 12.2). If the user enters an invalid account number or an incorrect PIN, the screen displays an appropriate message, then the ATM returns to *Step 1* to restart the authentication process.

Fig. 12.2 | ATM main menu.

After the ATM authenticates the user, the main menu (Fig. 12.2) should contain a numbered option for each of the three types of transactions: balance inquiry (option 1),

---

1. In this simple, command-line, text-based ATM, as you type the PIN, it appears on the screen. This is an obvious security breach—you would not want someone looking over your shoulder at an ATM and seeing your PIN displayed on the screen. In Chapter 14, we introduce the JPasswordField GUI component, which displays asterisks as the user types—making it more appropriate for entering PIN numbers and passwords. Exercise 14.18 asks you to build a GUI-based version of the ATM and to use a JPasswordField to obtain the user's PIN.

withdrawal (option 2) and deposit (option 3). It also should contain an option to allow the user to exit the system (option 4). The user then chooses either to perform a transaction (by entering 1, 2 or 3) or to exit the system (by entering 4).

If the user enters 1 to make a balance inquiry, the screen displays the user's account balance. To do so, the ATM must retrieve the balance from the bank's database.

The following steps describe what occurs when the user enters 2 to make a withdrawal:

1. The screen displays a menu (shown in Fig. 12.3) containing standard withdrawal amounts: $20 (option 1), $40 (option 2), $60 (option 3), $100 (option 4) and $200 (option 5). The menu also contains an option to allow the user to cancel the transaction (option 6).

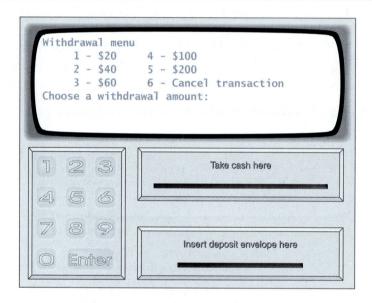

Fig. 12.3 | ATM withdrawal menu.

2. The user enters a menu selection using the keypad.

3. If the withdrawal amount chosen is greater than the user's account balance, the screen displays a message stating this and telling the user to choose a smaller amount. The ATM then returns to *Step 1*. If the withdrawal amount chosen is less than or equal to the user's account balance (i.e., an acceptable amount), the ATM proceeds to *Step 4*. If the user chooses to cancel the transaction (option 6), the ATM displays the main menu and waits for user input.

4. If the cash dispenser contains enough cash, the ATM proceeds to *Step 5*. Otherwise, the screen displays a message indicating the problem and telling the user to choose a smaller withdrawal amount. The ATM then returns to *Step 1*.

5. The ATM debits the withdrawal amount from the user's account in the bank's database (i.e., subtracts the withdrawal amount from the user's account balance).

6. The cash dispenser dispenses the desired amount of money to the user.

7. The screen displays a message reminding the user to take the money.

The following steps describe the actions that occur when the user enters 3 (when viewing the main menu of Fig. 12.2) to make a deposit:

1. The screen prompts the user to enter a deposit amount or type 0 (zero) to cancel.

2. The user enters a deposit amount or 0 using the keypad. [*Note:* The keypad does not contain a decimal point or a dollar sign, so the user cannot type a real dollar amount (e.g., $27.25). Instead, the user must enter a deposit amount as a number of cents (e.g., 2725). The ATM then divides this number by 100 to obtain a number representing a dollar amount (e.g., $2725 \div 100 = 27.25$).]

3. If the user specifies a deposit amount, the ATM proceeds to *Step 4*. If the user chooses to cancel the transaction (by entering 0), the ATM displays the main menu and waits for user input.

4. The screen displays a message telling the user to insert a deposit envelope.

5. If the deposit slot receives a deposit envelope within two minutes, the ATM credits the deposit amount to the user's account in the bank's database (i.e., adds the deposit amount to the user's account balance). [*Note:* This money is not immediately available for withdrawal. The bank first must physically verify the amount of cash in the deposit envelope, and any checks in the envelope must clear (i.e., money must be transferred from the check writer's account to the check recipient's account). When either of these events occurs, the bank appropriately updates the user's balance stored in its database. This occurs independently of the ATM system.] If the deposit slot does not receive a deposit envelope within this time period, the screen displays a message that the system has canceled the transaction due to inactivity. The ATM then displays the main menu and waits for user input.

After the system successfully executes a transaction, it should return to the main menu so that the user can perform additional transactions. If the user exits the system, the screen should display a thank you message, then display the welcome message for the next user.

Analyzing the ATM System
The preceding statement is a simplified example of a requirements document. Typically, such a document is the result of a detailed process of **requirements gathering**, which might include interviews with possible users of the system and specialists in fields related to the system. For example, a systems analyst who is hired to prepare a requirements document for banking software (e.g., the ATM system described here) might interview banking experts to gain a better understanding of what the software must do. The analyst would use the information gained to compile a list of **system requirements** to guide systems designers as they design the system.

The process of requirements gathering is a key task of the first stage of the software life cycle. The **software life cycle** specifies the stages through which software goes from the time it's first conceived to the time it's retired from use. These stages typically include: analysis, design, implementation, testing and debugging, deployment, maintenance and retirement. Several software life-cycle models exist, each with its own preferences and specifications for when and how often software engineers should perform each of these stages.

Waterfall models perform each stage once in succession, whereas **iterative models** may repeat one or more stages several times throughout a product's life cycle.

The analysis stage focuses on defining the problem to be solved. When designing any system, one must *solve the problem right*, but of equal importance, one must *solve the right problem*. Systems analysts collect the requirements that indicate the specific problem to solve. Our requirements document describes the requirements of our ATM system in sufficient detail that you need not go through an extensive analysis stage—it's been done for you.

To capture what a proposed system should do, developers often employ a technique known as **use case modeling**. This process identifies the **use cases** of the system, each representing a different capability that the system provides to its clients. For example, ATMs typically have several use cases, such as "View Account Balance," "Withdraw Cash," "Deposit Funds," "Transfer Funds Between Accounts" and "Buy Postage Stamps." The simplified ATM system we build in this case study allows only the first three.

Each use case describes a typical scenario for which the user uses the system. You've already read descriptions of the ATM system's use cases in the requirements document; the lists of steps required to perform each transaction type (i.e., balance inquiry, withdrawal and deposit) actually described the three use cases of our ATM—"View Account Balance," "Withdraw Cash" and "Deposit Funds," respectively.

Use Case Diagrams

We now introduce the first of several UML diagrams in the case study. We create a **use case diagram** to model the interactions between a system's clients (in this case study, bank customers) and its use cases. The goal is to show the kinds of interactions users have with a system without providing the details—these are provided in other UML diagrams (which we present throughout this case study). Use case diagrams are often accompanied by informal text that gives more detail—like the text that appears in the requirements document. Use case diagrams are produced during the analysis stage of the software life cycle. In larger systems, use case diagrams are indispensable tools that help system designers remain focused on satisfying the users' needs.

Figure 12.4 shows the use case diagram for our ATM system. The stick figure represents an **actor**, which defines the roles that an external entity—such as a person or another system—plays when interacting with the system. For our automated teller machine, the actor is a User who can view an account balance, withdraw cash and deposit funds from the ATM. The User is not an actual person, but instead comprises the roles that a real person—when playing the part of a User—can play while interacting with the ATM. Note that a use case diagram can include multiple actors. For example, the use case diagram for a real bank's ATM system might also include an actor named Administrator who refills the cash dispenser each day.

Our requirements document supplies the actors—"ATM users should be able to view their account balance, withdraw cash and deposit funds." Therefore, the actor in each of the three use cases is the user who interacts with the ATM. An external entity—a real person—plays the part of the user to perform financial transactions. Figure 12.4 shows one actor, whose name, User, appears below the actor in the diagram. The UML models each use case as an oval connected to an actor with a solid line.

Software engineers (more precisely, systems designers) must analyze the requirements document or a set of use cases and design the system before programmers implement it in

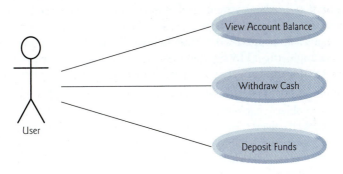

Fig. 12.4 | Use case diagram for the ATM system from the User's perspective.

a particular programming language. During the analysis stage, systems designers focus on understanding the requirements document to produce a high-level specification that describes *what* the system is supposed to do. The output of the design stage—a **design specification**—should specify clearly *how* the system should be constructed to satisfy these requirements. In the next several sections, we perform the steps of a simple object-oriented design (OOD) process on the ATM system to produce a design specification containing a collection of UML diagrams and supporting text.

The UML is designed for use with any OOD process. Many such processes exist, the best known of which is the Rational Unified Process™ (RUP) developed by Rational Software Corporation, now part of IBM. RUP is a rich process intended for designing "industrial strength" applications. For this case study, we present our own simplified design process, designed for students in first and second programming courses.

Designing the ATM System

We now begin the design stage of our ATM system. A **system** is a set of components that interact to solve a problem. For example, to perform the ATM system's designated tasks, our ATM system has a user interface (Fig. 12.1), and contains software that executes financial transactions and interacts with a database of bank account information. **System structure** describes the system's objects and their interrelationships. **System behavior** describes how the system changes as its objects interact with one another.

Every system has both structure and behavior—designers must specify both. There are several types of system structures and behaviors. For example, the interactions among objects in the system differ from those between the user and the system, yet both constitute a portion of the system behavior.

The UML 2 standard specifies 13 diagram types for documenting the system models. Each models a distinct characteristic of a system's structure or behavior—six diagrams relate to system structure, the remaining seven to system behavior. We list here only the six diagram types used in our case study—one models system structure; the other five model system behavior. We provide an overview of the remaining seven UML diagram types in Appendix P, UML 2: Additional Diagram Types.

1. **Use case diagrams**, such as the one in Fig. 12.4, model the interactions between a system and its external entities (actors) in terms of use cases (system capabilities, such as "View Account Balance," "Withdraw Cash" and "Deposit Funds").

2. **Class diagrams**, which you'll study in Section 12.3, model the classes, or "building blocks," used in a system. Each noun or "thing" described in the requirements document is a candidate to be a class in the system (e.g., Account, Keypad). Class diagrams help us specify the structural relationships between parts of the system. For example, the ATM system class diagram will specify that the ATM is physically composed of a screen, a keypad, a cash dispenser and a deposit slot.

3. **State machine diagrams**, which you'll study in Section 12.5, model the ways in which an object changes state. An object's **state** is indicated by the values of all its attributes at a given time. When an object changes state, it may behave differently in the system. For example, after validating a user's PIN, the ATM transitions from the "user not authenticated" state to the "user authenticated" state, at which point it allows the user to perform financial transactions (e.g., view account balance, withdraw cash, deposit funds).

4. **Activity diagrams**, which you'll also study in Section 12.5, model an object's **activity**—is workflow (sequence of events) during program execution. An activity diagram models the actions the object performs and specifies the order in which it performs them. For example, an activity diagram shows that the ATM must obtain the balance of the user's account (from the bank's account information database) *before* the screen can display the balance to the user.

5. **Communication diagrams** (called **collaboration diagrams** in earlier versions of the UML) model the interactions among objects in a system, with an emphasis on *what* interactions occur. You'll learn in Section 12.7 that these diagrams show which objects must interact to perform an ATM transaction. For example, the ATM must communicate with the bank's account information database to retrieve an account balance.

6. **Sequence diagrams** also model the interactions among the objects in a system, but unlike communication diagrams, they emphasize *when* interactions occur. You'll learn in Section 12.7 that these diagrams help show the order in which interactions occur in executing a financial transaction. For example, the screen prompts the user to enter a withdrawal amount before cash is dispensed.

In Section 12.3, we continue designing our ATM system by identifying the classes from the requirements document. We accomplish this by extracting key nouns and noun phrases from the requirements document. Using these classes, we develop our first draft of the class diagram that models the structure of our ATM system.

Web Resources

We've created an extensive UML Resource Center that contains many links to additional information, including introductions, tutorials, blogs, books, certification, conferences, developer tools, documentation, e-books, FAQs, forums, groups, UML in Java, podcasts, security, tools, downloads, training courses, videos and more. We encourage you to browse our UML Resource Center at www.deitel.com/UML/ to learn more.

Self-Review Exercises for Section 12.2

12.1 Suppose we enabled a user of our ATM system to transfer money between two bank accounts. Modify the use case diagram of Fig. 12.4 to reflect this change.

12.2 _____ model the interactions among objects in a system with an emphasis on *when* these interactions occur.
- a) Class diagrams
- b) Sequence diagrams
- c) Communication diagrams
- d) Activity diagrams

12.3 Which of the following choices lists stages of a typical software life cycle in sequential order?
- a) design, analysis, implementation, testing
- b) design, analysis, testing, implementation
- c) analysis, design, testing, implementation
- d) analysis, design, implementation, testing

12.3 Identifying the Classes in a Requirements Document

[*Note:* **This section can be taught after Chapter 7.**]
Now we begin designing the ATM system. In this section, we identify the classes that are needed to build the system by analyzing the *nouns* and *noun phrases* that appear in the requirements document. We introduce UML class diagrams to model these classes. This is an important first step in defining the system's structure.

Identifying the Classes in a System

We begin our OOD process by identifying the classes required to build the ATM system. We'll eventually describe these classes using UML class diagrams and implement these classes in Java. First, we review the requirements document of Section 12.2 and identify key nouns and noun phrases to help us identify classes that comprise the ATM system. We may decide that some of these nouns and noun phrases are actually attributes of other classes in the system. We may also conclude that some of the nouns do not correspond to parts of the system and thus should not be modeled at all. Additional classes may become apparent to us as we proceed through the design process.

Figure 12.5 lists the nouns and noun phrases found in the requirements document of Section 12.2. We list them from left to right in the order in which we first encounter them. We list only the singular form of each.

Nouns and noun phrases in the ATM requirements document			
bank	money / funds	account number	ATM
screen	PIN	user	keypad
bank database	customer	cash dispenser	balance inquiry
transaction	$20 bill / cash	withdrawal	account
deposit slot	deposit	balance	deposit envelope

Fig. 12.5 | Nouns and noun phrases in the ATM requirements document.

We create classes only for the nouns and noun phrases that have significance in the ATM system. We don't model "bank" as a class, because the bank is not a part of the ATM system—the bank simply wants us to build the ATM. "Customer" and "user" also represent outside entities—they're important because they *interact* with our ATM system, but we do not need to model them as classes in the ATM software. Recall that we modeled an ATM user (i.e., a bank customer) as the actor in the use case diagram of Fig. 12.4.

We do not model "$20 bill" or "deposit envelope" as classes. These are physical objects in the real world, but they're not part of what is being automated. We can adequately represent the presence of bills in the system using an attribute of the class that models the cash dispenser. (We assign attributes to the ATM system's classes in Section 12.4.) For example, the cash dispenser maintains a count of the number of bills it contains. The requirements document does not say anything about what the system should do with deposit envelopes after it receives them. We can assume that simply acknowledging the receipt of an envelope—an operation performed by the class that models the deposit slot—is sufficient to represent the presence of an envelope in the system. (We assign operations to the ATM system's classes in Section 12.6.)

In our simplified ATM system, representing various amounts of "money," including an account's "balance," as attributes of classes seems most appropriate. Likewise, the nouns "account number" and "PIN" represent significant pieces of information in the ATM system. They're important attributes of a bank account. They do not, however, exhibit behaviors. Thus, we can most appropriately model them as attributes of an account class.

Though the requirements document frequently describes a "transaction" in a general sense, we do not model the broad notion of a financial transaction at this time. Instead, we model the three types of transactions (i.e., "balance inquiry," "withdrawal" and "deposit") as individual classes. These classes possess specific attributes needed for executing the transactions they represent. For example, a withdrawal needs to know the amount of the withdrawal. A balance inquiry, however, does not require any additional data other than the account number. Furthermore, the three transaction classes exhibit unique behaviors. A withdrawal includes dispensing cash to the user, whereas a deposit involves receiving deposit envelopes from the user. [*Note:* In Section 13.3, we "factor out" common features of all transactions into a general "transaction" class using the object-oriented concept of inheritance.]

We determine the classes for our system based on the remaining nouns and noun phrases from Fig. 12.5. Each of these refers to one or more of the following:

- ATM
- screen
- keypad
- cash dispenser
- deposit slot
- account
- bank database
- balance inquiry
- withdrawal
- deposit

The elements of this list are likely to be classes that we'll need to implement our system.

We can now model the classes in our system based on the list we've created. We capitalize class names in the design process—a UML convention—as we'll do when we write the actual Java code that implements our design. If the name of a class contains more than one word, we run the words together and capitalize each word (e.g., `MultipleWordName`). Using this convention, we create classes `ATM`, `Screen`, `Keypad`, `CashDispenser`, `Deposit-Slot`, `Account`, `BankDatabase`, `BalanceInquiry`, `Withdrawal` and `Deposit`. We construct our system using these classes as building blocks. Before we begin building the system, however, we must gain a better understanding of how the classes relate to one another.

Modeling Classes

The UML enables us to model, via **class diagrams**, the classes in the ATM system and their interrelationships. Figure 12.6 represents class `ATM`. Each class is modeled as a rectangle with three compartments. The top one contains the name of the class centered horizontally in boldface. The middle compartment contains the class's attributes. (We discuss attributes in Sections 12.4–12.5.) The bottom compartment contains the class's operations (discussed in Section 12.6). In Fig. 12.6, the middle and bottom compartments are empty because we've not yet determined this class's attributes and operations.

Fig. 12.6 | Representing a class in the UML using a class diagram.

Class diagrams also show the relationships between the classes of the system. Figure 12.7 shows how our classes `ATM` and `Withdrawal` relate to one another. For the moment, for simplicity, we choose to model only this subset of classes. We present a more complete class diagram later in this section. Notice that the rectangles representing classes in this diagram are not subdivided into compartments. The UML allows the suppression of class attributes and operations in this manner to create more readable diagrams, when appropriate. Such a diagram is said to be an **elided diagram**—one in which some information, such as the contents of the second and third compartments, is not modeled. We'll place information in these compartments in Sections 12.4–12.6.

Fig. 12.7 | Class diagram showing an association among classes.

In Fig. 12.7, the solid line that connects the two classes represents an **association**—a relationship between classes. The numbers near each end of the line are **multiplicity** values, which indicate how many objects of each class participate in the association. In this case, following the line from left to right reveals that, at any given moment, one `ATM` object participates in an association with either zero or one `Withdrawal` objects—zero if the current user is not currently performing a transaction or has requested a different type of transaction, and one if the user has requested a withdrawal. The UML can model many types of multiplicity. Figure 12.8 lists and explains the multiplicity types.

Symbol	Meaning
0	None
1	One
m	An integer value
0..1	Zero or one
m, n	m or n
$m..n$	At least m, but not more than n
*	Any nonnegative integer (zero or more)
0..*	Zero or more (identical to *)
1..*	One or more

Fig. 12.8 | Multiplicity types.

An association can be named. For example, the word Executes above the line connecting classes ATM and Withdrawal in Fig. 12.7 indicates the name of that association. This part of the diagram reads "one object of class ATM executes zero or one objects of class Withdrawal." Note that association names are *directional*, as indicated by the filled arrowhead—so it would be improper, for example, to read the preceding association from right to left as "zero or one objects of class Withdrawal execute one object of class ATM."

The word currentTransaction at the Withdrawal end of the association line in Fig. 12.7 is a **role name**, identifying the role the Withdrawal object plays in its relationship with the ATM. A role name adds meaning to an association between classes by identifying the role a class plays in the context of an association. A class can play several roles in the same system. For example, in a school personnel system, a person may play the role of "professor" when relating to students. The same person may take on the role of "colleague" when participating in an association with another professor, and "coach" when coaching student athletes. In Fig. 12.7, the role name currentTransaction indicates that the Withdrawal object participating in the Executes association with an object of class ATM represents the transaction currently being processed by the ATM. In other contexts, a Withdrawal object may take on other roles (e.g., the "previous transaction"). Notice that we do not specify a role name for the ATM end of the Executes association. Role names in class diagrams are often omitted when the meaning of an association is clear without them.

In addition to indicating simple relationships, associations can specify more complex relationships, such as objects of one class being "composed of" objects of other classes. Consider a real-world automated teller machine. What "pieces" does a manufacturer put together to build a working ATM? Our requirements document tells us that the ATM is composed of a screen, a keypad, a cash dispenser and a deposit slot.

In Fig. 12.9, the **solid diamonds** attached to the ATM class's association lines indicate that ATM has a **composition** relationship with classes Screen, Keypad, CashDispenser and DepositSlot. Composition implies a whole/part relationship. The class that has the composition symbol (the solid diamond) on its end of the association line is the whole (in this case, ATM), and the classes on the other end of the association lines are the parts—in this case, Screen, Keypad, CashDispenser and DepositSlot. The compositions in Fig. 12.9 indicate that an object of class ATM is formed from one object of class Screen, one object of class CashDispenser, one object of class Keypad and one object of class DepositSlot.

The ATM *has a* screen, a keypad, a cash dispenser and a deposit slot. (As we saw in Chapter 9, the *is-a* relationship defines inheritance. We'll see in Section 13.3 that there's a nice opportunity to use inheritance in the ATM system design.)

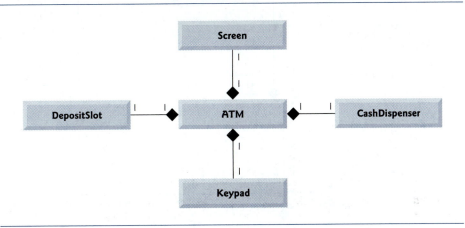

Fig. 12.9 | Class diagram showing composition relationships.

According to the UML specification (`www.omg.org/technology/documents/formal/uml.htm`), composition relationships have the following properties:

1. Only one class in the relationship can represent the whole (i.e., the diamond can be placed on only one end of the association line). For example, either the screen is part of the ATM or the ATM is part of the screen, but the screen and the ATM cannot both represent the whole in the relationship.

2. The parts in the composition relationship exist only as long as the whole does, and the whole is responsible for the creation and destruction of its parts. For example, the act of constructing an ATM includes manufacturing its parts. Also, if the ATM is destroyed, its screen, keypad, cash dispenser and deposit slot are also destroyed.

3. A part may belong to only one whole at a time, although it may be removed and attached to another whole, which then assumes responsibility for the part.

The solid diamonds in our class diagrams indicate composition relationships that fulfill these properties. If a *has-a* relationship does not satisfy one or more of these criteria, the UML specifies that **hollow diamonds** be attached to the ends of association lines to indicate **aggregation**—a weaker form of composition. For example, a personal computer and a computer monitor participate in an aggregation relationship—the computer *has a* monitor, but the two parts can exist independently, and the same monitor can be attached to multiple computers at once, thus violating composition's second and third properties.

Figure 12.10 shows a class diagram for the ATM system. This diagram models most of the classes that we identified earlier in this section, as well as the associations between them that we can infer from the requirements document. [*Note:* Classes `BalanceInquiry` and `Deposit` participate in associations similar to those of class `Withdrawal`, so we've chosen to omit them from this diagram to keep it simple. In Section 13.3, we expand our class diagram to include all the classes in the ATM system.]

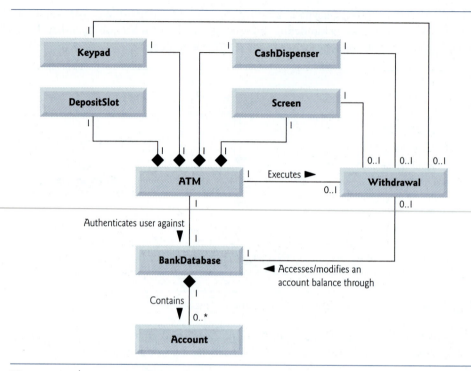

Fig. 12.10 | Class diagram for the ATM system model.

Figure 12.10 presents a graphical model of ATM system's structure. It includes classes BankDatabase and Account, and several associations that were not present in either Fig. 12.7 or Fig. 12.9. It shows that class ATM has a **one-to-one relationship** with class BankDatabase—one ATM object authenticates users against one BankDatabase object. In Fig. 12.10, we also model the fact that the bank's database contains information about many accounts—one BankDatabase object participates in a composition relationship with zero or more Account objects. The multiplicity value 0..* at the Account end of the association between class BankDatabase and class Account indicates that zero or more objects of class Account take part in the association. Class BankDatabase has a **one-to-many relationship** with class Account—the BankDatabase contains many Accounts. Similarly, class Account has a **many-to-one relationship** with class BankDatabase—there can be many Accounts stored in the BankDatabase. [*Note:* Recall from Fig. 12.8 that the multiplicity value * is identical to 0..*. We include 0..* in our class diagrams for clarity.]

Figure 12.10 also indicates that at any given time 0 or 1 Withdrawal objects can exist. If the user is performing a withdrawal, "one object of class Withdrawal accesses/modifies an account balance through one object of class BankDatabase." We could have created an association directly between class Withdrawal and class Account. The requirements document, however, states that the "ATM must interact with the bank's account information database" to perform transactions. A bank account contains sensitive information, and systems engineers must always consider the security of personal data when designing a system. Thus, only the BankDatabase can access and manipulate an account directly. All other parts of the system must interact with the database to retrieve or update account information (e.g., an account balance).

The class diagram in Fig. 12.10 also models associations between class `Withdrawal` and classes `Screen`, `CashDispenser` and `Keypad`. A withdrawal transaction includes prompting the user to choose a withdrawal amount, and receiving numeric input. These actions require the use of the screen and the keypad, respectively. Furthermore, dispensing cash to the user requires access to the cash dispenser.

Classes `BalanceInquiry` and `Deposit`, though not shown in Fig. 12.10, take part in several associations with the other classes of the ATM system. Like class `Withdrawal`, each of these classes associates with classes `ATM` and `BankDatabase`. An object of class `Balance-Inquiry` also associates with an object of class `Screen` to display the balance of an account to the user. Class `Deposit` associates with classes `Screen`, `Keypad` and `DepositSlot`. Like withdrawals, deposit transactions require use of the screen and the keypad to display prompts and receive input, respectively. To receive deposit envelopes, an object of class `Deposit` accesses the deposit slot.

We've now identified the initial classes in our ATM system—we may discover others as we proceed with the design and implementation. In Section 12.4 we determine the attributes for each of these classes, and in Section 12.5 we use these attributes to examine how the system changes over time.

Self-Review Exercises for Section 12.3

12.4 Suppose we have a class `Car` that represents a car. Think of some of the different pieces that a manufacturer would put together to produce a whole car. Create a class diagram (similar to Fig. 12.9) that models some of the composition relationships of class `Car`.

12.5 Suppose we have a class `File` that represents an electronic document in a standalone, non-networked computer represented by class `Computer`. What sort of association exists between class `Computer` and class `File`?
    a) Class `Computer` has a one-to-one relationship with class `File`.
    b) Class `Computer` has a many-to-one relationship with class `File`.
    c) Class `Computer` has a one-to-many relationship with class `File`.
    d) Class `Computer` has a many-to-many relationship with class `File`.

12.6 State whether the following statement is *true* or *false*, and if *false*, explain why: A UML diagram in which a class's second and third compartments are not modeled is said to be an elided diagram.

12.7 Modify the class diagram of Fig. 12.10 to include class `Deposit` instead of class `Withdrawal`.

12.4 Identifying Class Attributes

[*Note:* **This section can be taught after Chapter 3.**]
In Section 12.3, we began the first stage of an object-oriented design (OOD) for our ATM system—analyzing the requirements document and identifying the classes needed to implement the system. We listed the nouns and noun phrases in the requirements document and identified a class for each one that plays a significant role in the ATM system. We then modeled the classes and their relationships in a UML class diagram (Fig. 12.10).

Classes have attributes (data) and operations (behaviors). Class attributes are implemented in Java programs as fields, and class operations are implemented as methods. In this section, we determine many of the attributes needed in the ATM system. In Section 12.5 we examine how these attributes represent an object's state. In Section 12.6 we determine class operations.

Identifying Attributes

Consider the attributes of some real-world objects: A person's attributes include height, weight and whether the person is left-handed, right-handed or ambidextrous. A radio's attributes include its station, volume and AM or FM settings. A car's attributes include its speedometer and odometer readings, the amount of gas in its tank and what gear it's in. A personal computer's attributes include its manufacturer (e.g., Dell, Sun, Apple or IBM), type of screen (e.g., LCD or CRT), main memory size and hard disk size.

We can identify many attributes of the classes in our system by looking for descriptive words and phrases in the requirements document. For each such word and phrase we find that plays a significant role in the ATM system, we create an attribute and assign it to one or more of the classes identified in Section 12.3. We also create attributes to represent any additional data that a class may need, as such needs become clear throughout the design process.

Figure 12.11 lists the words or phrases from the requirements document that describe each class. We formed this list by reading the requirements document and identifying any words or phrases that refer to characteristics of the classes in the system. For example, the requirements document describes the steps taken to obtain a "withdrawal amount," so we list "amount" next to class `Withdrawal`.

Class	Descriptive words and phrases
`ATM`	user is authenticated
`BalanceInquiry`	account number
`Withdrawal`	account number
	amount
`Deposit`	account number
	amount
`BankDatabase`	*[no descriptive words or phrases]*
`Account`	account number
	PIN
	balance
`Screen`	*[no descriptive words or phrases]*
`Keypad`	*[no descriptive words or phrases]*
`CashDispenser`	begins each day loaded with 500 $20 bills
`DepositSlot`	*[no descriptive words or phrases]*

Fig. 12.11 | Descriptive words and phrases from the ATM requirements document.

Figure 12.11 leads us to create one attribute of class `ATM`. Class `ATM` maintains information about the state of the ATM. The phrase "user is authenticated" describes a state of the ATM (we introduce states in Section 12.5), so we include `userAuthenticated` as a **Boolean attribute** (i.e., an attribute that has a value of either `true` or `false`) in class `ATM`. Note that the `Boolean` attribute type in the UML is equivalent to the `boolean` type in Java. This attribute indicates whether the ATM has successfully authenticated the current user—userAuthenticated must be true for the system to allow the user to perform transactions and access account information. This attribute helps ensure the security of the data in the system.

Classes BalanceInquiry, Withdrawal and Deposit share one attribute. Each transaction involves an "account number" that corresponds to the account of the user making the transaction. We assign an integer attribute accountNumber to each transaction class to identify the account to which an object of the class applies.

Descriptive words and phrases in the requirements document also suggest some differences in the attributes required by each transaction class. The requirements document indicates that to withdraw cash or deposit funds, users must input a specific "amount" of money to be withdrawn or deposited, respectively. Thus, we assign to classes Withdrawal and Deposit an attribute amount to store the value supplied by the user. The amounts of money related to a withdrawal and a deposit are defining characteristics of these transactions that the system requires for these transactions to take place. Class BalanceInquiry, however, needs no additional data to perform its task—it requires only an account number to indicate the account whose balance should be retrieved.

Class Account has several attributes. The requirements document states that each bank account has an "account number" and "PIN," which the system uses for identifying accounts and authenticating users. We assign to class Account two integer attributes: accountNumber and pin. The requirements document also specifies that an account maintains a "balance" of the amount of money in the account and that money the user deposits does not become available for a withdrawal until the bank verifies the amount of cash in the deposit envelope, and any checks in the envelope clear. An account must still record the amount of money that a user deposits, however. Therefore, we decide that an account should represent a balance using two attributes: availableBalance and totalBalance. Attribute availableBalance tracks the amount of money that a user can withdraw from the account. Attribute totalBalance refers to the total amount of money that the user has "on deposit" (i.e., the amount of money available, plus the amount waiting to be verified or cleared). For example, suppose an ATM user deposits $50.00 into an empty account. The totalBalance attribute would increase to $50.00 to record the deposit, but the availableBalance would remain at $0.

[*Note:* We assume that the bank updates the availableBalance attribute of an Account some length of time after the ATM transaction occurs, in response to confirming that $50 worth of cash or checks was found in the deposit envelope. We assume that this update occurs through a transaction that a bank employee performs using some piece of bank software other than the ATM. Thus, we do not discuss this transaction in our case study.]

Class CashDispenser has one attribute. The requirements document states that the cash dispenser "begins each day loaded with 500 $20 bills." The cash dispenser must keep track of the number of bills it contains to determine whether enough cash is on hand to satisfy withdrawal requests. We assign to class CashDispenser an integer attribute count, which is initially set to 500.

For real problems in industry, there is no guarantee that requirements documents will be precise enough for the object-oriented systems designer to determine all the attributes or even all the classes. The need for additional classes, attributes and behaviors may become clear as the design process proceeds. As we progress through this case study, we will continue to add, modify and delete information about the classes in our system.

Modeling Attributes

The class diagram in Fig. 12.12 lists some of the attributes for the classes in our system—the descriptive words and phrases in Fig. 12.11 lead us to identify these attributes. For simplicity, Fig. 12.12 does not show the associations among classes—we showed these in Fig. 12.10. This is a common practice of systems designers when designs are being developed. Recall from Section 12.3 that in the UML, a class's attributes are placed in the middle compartment of the class's rectangle. We list each attribute's name and type separated by a colon (:), followed in some cases by an equal sign (=) and an initial value.

Consider the `userAuthenticated` attribute of class ATM:

> `userAuthenticated : Boolean = false`

This attribute declaration contains three pieces of information about the attribute. The **attribute name** is `userAuthenticated`. The **attribute type** is `Boolean`. In Java, an attribute can be represented by a primitive type, such as `boolean`, `int` or `double`, or a reference type like a class. We've chosen to model only primitive-type attributes in Fig. 12.12—we discuss the reasoning behind this decision shortly. [*Note:* The attribute types in Fig. 12.12 are in UML notation. We'll associate the types `Boolean`, `Integer` and `Double` in the UML diagram with the primitive types `boolean`, `int` and `double` in Java, respectively.]

We can also indicate an initial value for an attribute. The `userAuthenticated` attribute in class ATM has an initial value of `false`. This indicates that the system initially does

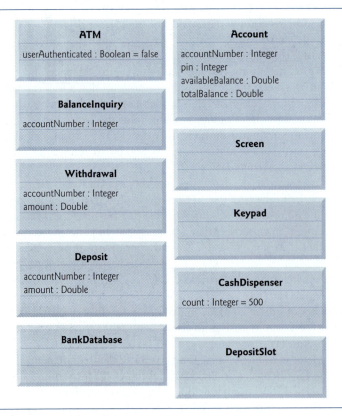

Fig. 12.12 | Classes with attributes.

not consider the user to be authenticated. If an attribute has no initial value specified, only its name and type (separated by a colon) are shown. For example, the `accountNumber` attribute of class `BalanceInquiry` is an integer. Here we show no initial value, because the value of this attribute is a number that we do not yet know. This number will be determined at execution time based on the account number entered by the current ATM user.

Figure 12.12 does not include attributes for classes `Screen`, `Keypad` and `DepositSlot`. These are important components of our system, for which our design process has not yet revealed any attributes. We may discover some, however, in the remaining phases of design or when we implement these classes in Java. This is perfectly normal.

Software Engineering Observation 12.1

At early stages in the design process, classes often lack attributes (and operations). Such classes should not be eliminated, however, because attributes (and operations) may become evident in the later phases of design and implementation.

Note that Fig. 12.12 also does not include attributes for class `BankDatabase`. Recall that attributes in Java can be represented by either primitive types or reference types. We've chosen to include only primitive-type attributes in the class diagram in Fig. 12.12 (and in similar class diagrams throughout the case study). A reference-type attribute is modeled more clearly as an association between the class holding the reference and the class of the object to which the reference points. For example, the class diagram in Fig. 12.10 indicates that class `BankDatabase` participates in a composition relationship with zero or more `Account` objects. From this composition, we can determine that when we implement the ATM system in Java, we'll be required to create an attribute of class `BankDatabase` to hold references to zero or more `Account` objects. Similarly, we can determine reference-type attributes of class `ATM` that correspond to its composition relationships with classes `Screen`, `Keypad`, `CashDispenser` and `DepositSlot`. These composition-based attributes would be redundant if modeled in Fig. 12.12, because the compositions modeled in Fig. 12.10 already convey the fact that the database contains information about zero or more accounts and that an ATM is composed of a screen, keypad, cash dispenser and deposit slot. Software developers typically model these whole/part relationships as compositions rather than as attributes required to implement the relationships.

The class diagram in Fig. 12.12 provides a solid basis for the structure of our model, but the diagram is not complete. In Section 12.5 we identify the states and activities of the objects in the model, and in Section 12.6 we identify the operations that the objects perform. As we present more of the UML and object-oriented design, we'll continue to strengthen the structure of our model.

Self-Review Exercises for Section 12.4

12.8   We typically identify the attributes of the classes in our system by analyzing the _____ in the requirements document.
    a) nouns and noun phrases
    b) descriptive words and phrases
    c) verbs and verb phrases
    d) All of the above.

12.9   Which of the following is not an attribute of an airplane?
    a) length
    b) wingspan

    c) fly

    d) number of seats

12.10 Describe the meaning of the following attribute declaration of class `CashDispenser` in the class diagram in Fig. 12.12:

```
count : Integer = 500
```

12.5 Identifying Objects' States and Activities

[*Note:* **This section can be taught after Chapter 4.**]

In Section 12.4, we identified many of the class attributes needed to implement the ATM system and added them to the class diagram in Fig. 12.12. We now show how these attributes represent an object's state. We identify some key states that our objects may occupy and discuss how objects change state in response to various events occurring in the system. We also discuss the workflow, or **activities**, that objects perform in the ATM system, and we present the activities of `BalanceInquiry` and `Withdrawal` transaction objects.

State Machine Diagrams

Each object in a system goes through a series of states. An object's state is indicated by the values of its attributes at a given time. **State machine diagrams** (commonly called **state diagrams**) model several states of an object and show under what circumstances the object changes state. Unlike the class diagrams presented in earlier case study sections, which focused primarily on the system's structure, state diagrams model some of the system's behavior.

    Figure 12.13 is a simple state diagram that models some of the states of an object of class `ATM`. The UML represents each state in a state diagram as a **rounded rectangle** with the name of the state placed inside it. A **solid circle** with an attached stick ($\rightarrow$) arrowhead designates the **initial state**. Recall that we modeled this state information as the `Boolean` attribute `userAuthenticated` in the class diagram of Fig. 12.12. This attribute is initialized to `false`, or the "User not authenticated" state, according to the state diagram.

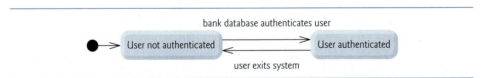

Fig. 12.13 | State diagram for the ATM object.

    The arrows with stick ($\rightarrow$) arrowhead indicate **transitions** between states. An object can transition from one state to another in response to various events that occur in the system. The name or description of the event that causes a transition is written near the line that corresponds to the transition. For example, the ATM object changes from the "User not authenticated" to the "User authenticated" state after the database authenticates the user. Recall from the requirements document that the database authenticates a user by comparing the account number and PIN entered by the user with those of an account in the database. If the user has entered a valid account number and the correct PIN, the ATM object transitions to the "User authenticated" state and changes its `userAuthenticated` attribute to a value of `true`. When the user exits the system by choosing the "exit" option from the main menu, the ATM object returns to the "User not authenticated" state.

Software Engineering Observation 12.2

Software designers do not generally create state diagrams showing every possible state and state transition for all attributes—there are simply too many of them. State diagrams typically show only key states and state transitions.

Activity Diagrams

Like a state diagram, an activity diagram models aspects of system behavior. Unlike a state diagram, an activity diagram models an object's **workflow** (sequence of events) during program execution. An activity diagram models the **actions** the object will perform and in what order. The activity diagram in Fig. 12.14 models the actions involved in executing a balance-inquiry transaction. We assume that a `BalanceInquiry` object has already been initialized and assigned a valid account number (that of the current user), so the object knows which balance to retrieve. The diagram includes the actions that occur after the user selects a balance inquiry from the main menu and before the ATM returns the user to the main menu—a `BalanceInquiry` object does not perform or initiate these actions, so we do not model them here. The diagram begins with retrieving the balance of the account from the database. Next, the `BalanceInquiry` displays the balance on the screen. This action completes the execution of the transaction. Recall that we've chosen to represent an account balance as both the `availableBalance` and `totalBalance` attributes of class `Account`, so the actions modeled in Fig. 12.14 refer to the retrieval and display of *both* balance attributes.

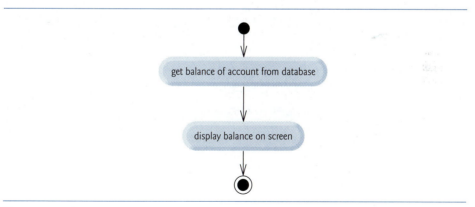

Fig. 12.14 | Activity diagram for a `BalanceInquiry` object.

The UML represents an action in an activity diagram as an action state modeled by a rectangle with its left and right sides replaced by arcs curving outward. Each action state contains an action expression—for example, "get balance of account from database"—that specifies an action to be performed. An arrow with a stick ($\twoheadrightarrow$) arrowhead connects two action states, indicating the order in which the actions represented by the action states occur. The solid circle (at the top of Fig. 12.14) represents the activity's initial state—the beginning of the workflow before the object performs the modeled actions. In this case, the transaction first executes the "get balance of account from database" action expression. The transaction then displays both balances on the screen. The solid circle enclosed in an open circle (at the bottom of Fig. 12.14) represents the final state—the end of the workflow after the object performs the modeled actions. We used UML activity diagrams to illustrate the flow of control for the control statements presented in Chapters 3–4.

Figure 12.15 shows an activity diagram for a withdrawal transaction. We assume that a Withdrawal object has been assigned a valid account number. We do not model the user

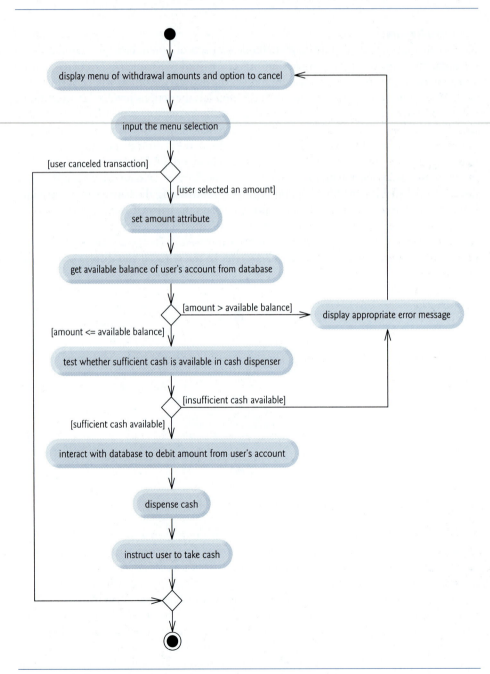

Fig. 12.15 | Activity diagram for a withdrawal transaction.

selecting a withdrawal from the main menu or the ATM returning the user to the main menu because these are not actions performed by a `Withdrawal` object. The transaction first displays a menu of standard withdrawal amounts (shown in Fig. 12.3) and an option to cancel the transaction. The transaction then receives a menu selection from the user. The activity flow now arrives at a decision (a fork indicated by the small diamond symbol). [*Note:* A decision was known as a branch in earlier versions of the UML.] This point determines the next action based on the associated guard condition (in square brackets next to the transition), which states that the transition occurs if this guard condition is met. If the user cancels the transaction by choosing the "cancel" option from the menu, the activity flow immediately skips to the final state. Note the merge (indicated by the small diamond symbol) where the cancellation flow of activity joins the main flow of activity before reaching the activity's final state. If the user selects a withdrawal amount from the menu, `Withdrawal` sets `amount` (an attribute originally modeled in Fig. 12.12) to the value chosen by the user.

After setting the withdrawal amount, the transaction retrieves the available balance of the user's account (i.e., the `availableBalance` attribute of the user's `Account` object) from the database. The activity flow then arrives at another decision. If the requested withdrawal amount exceeds the user's available balance, the system displays an appropriate error message informing the user of the problem, then returns to the beginning of the activity diagram and prompts the user to input a new amount. If the requested withdrawal amount is less than or equal to the user's available balance, the transaction proceeds. The transaction next tests whether the cash dispenser has enough cash remaining to satisfy the withdrawal request. If it does not, the transaction displays an appropriate error message, then returns to the beginning of the activity diagram and prompts the user to choose a new amount. If sufficient cash is available, the transaction interacts with the database to debit the withdrawal amount from the user's account (i.e., subtract the amount from both the `availableBalance` and `totalBalance` attributes of the user's `Account` object). The transaction then dispenses the desired amount of cash and instructs the user to take it. Finally, the main flow of activity merges with the cancellation flow of activity before reaching the final state.

We've taken the first steps in modeling the ATM software system's behavior and have shown how an object's attributes participate in performing the object's activities. In Section 12.6, we investigate the behaviors for all classes to give a more accurate interpretation of the system behavior by filling in the third compartments of the classes in our class diagram.

Self-Review Exercises for Section 12.5

12.11 State whether the following statement is *true* or *false*, and if *false*, explain why: State diagrams model structural aspects of a system.

12.12 An activity diagram models the _____ that an object performs and the order in which it performs them.
   a) actions
   b) attributes
   c) states
   d) state transitions

12.13 Based on the requirements document, create an activity diagram for a deposit transaction.

12.6 Identifying Class Operations

[*Note:* **This section can be taught after Chapter 5.**]

In this section, we determine some of the class operations (or behaviors) needed to implement the ATM system. An operation is a service that objects of a class provide to clients (users) of the class. Consider the operations of some real-world objects. A radio's operations include setting its station and volume (typically invoked by a person's adjusting the radio's controls). A car's operations include accelerating (invoked by the driver's pressing the accelerator pedal), decelerating (invoked by the driver's pressing the brake pedal or releasing the gas pedal), turning and shifting gears. Software objects can offer operations as well—for example, a software graphics object might offer operations for drawing a circle, drawing a line, drawing a square and the like. A spreadsheet software object might offer operations like printing the spreadsheet, totaling the elements in a row or column and graphing information in the spreadsheet as a bar chart or pie chart.

We can derive many of the class operations by examining the key verbs and verb phrases in the requirements document. We then relate these verbs and verb phrases to classes in our system (Fig. 12.16). The verb phrases in Fig. 12.16 help us determine the operations of each class.

Class	Verbs and verb phrases
ATM	executes financial transactions
BalanceInquiry	*[none in the requirements document]*
Withdrawal	*[none in the requirements document]*
Deposit	*[none in the requirements document]*
BankDatabase	authenticates a user, retrieves an account balance, credits a deposit amount to an account, debits a withdrawal amount from an account
Account	retrieves an account balance, credits a deposit amount to an account, debits a withdrawal amount from an account
Screen	displays a message to the user
Keypad	receives numeric input from the user
CashDispenser	dispenses cash, indicates whether it contains enough cash to satisfy a withdrawal request
DepositSlot	receives a deposit envelope

Fig. 12.16 | Verbs and verb phrases for each class in the ATM system.

Modeling Operations

To identify operations, we examine the verb phrases listed for each class in Fig. 12.16. The "executes financial transactions" phrase associated with class ATM implies that class ATM instructs transactions to execute. Therefore, classes BalanceInquiry, Withdrawal and Deposit each need an operation to provide this service to the ATM. We place this operation (which we've named execute) in the third compartment of the three transaction classes in the updated class diagram of Fig. 12.17. During an ATM session, the ATM object will invoke these transaction operations as necessary.

Fig. 12.17 | Classes in the ATM system with attributes and operations.

The UML represents operations (which are implemented as methods in Java) by listing the operation name, followed by a comma-separated list of parameters in parentheses, a colon and the return type:

operationName(*parameter1*, *parameter2*, ..., *parameterN*) : *return type*

Each parameter in the comma-separated parameter list consists of a parameter name, followed by a colon and the parameter type:

parameterName : *parameterType*

For the moment, we do not list the parameters of our operations—we'll identify and model some of them shortly. For some of the operations, we do not yet know the return types, so we also omit them from the diagram. These omissions are perfectly normal at this point. As our design and implementation proceed, we'll add the remaining return types.

Authenticating a User

Figure 12.16 lists the phrase "authenticates a user" next to class BankDatabase—the database is the object that contains the account information necessary to determine whether the account number and PIN entered by a user match those of an account held at the bank. Therefore, class BankDatabase needs an operation that provides an authentication service to the ATM. We place the operation authenticateUser in the third compartment of class BankDatabase (Fig. 12.17). However, an object of class Account, not class Bank-Database, stores the account number and PIN that must be accessed to authenticate a user, so class Account must provide a service to validate a PIN obtained through user input against a PIN stored in an Account object. Therefore, we add a validatePIN operation to class Account. Note that we specify a return type of Boolean for the authenticateUser and validatePIN operations. Each operation returns a value indicating either that the operation was successful in performing its task (i.e., a return value of true) or that it was not (i.e., a return value of false).

Other BankDatabase and Account Operations

Figure 12.16 lists several additional verb phrases for class BankDatabase: "retrieves an account balance," "credits a deposit amount to an account" and "debits a withdrawal amount from an account." Like "authenticates a user," these remaining phrases refer to services that the database must provide to the ATM, because the database holds all the account data used to authenticate a user and perform ATM transactions. However, objects of class Account actually perform the operations to which these phrases refer. Thus, we assign an operation to both class BankDatabase and class Account to correspond to each of these phrases. Recall from Section 12.3 that, because a bank account contains sensitive information, we do not allow the ATM to access accounts directly. The database acts as an intermediary between the ATM and the account data, thus preventing unauthorized access. As we'll see in Section 12.7, class ATM invokes the operations of class BankDatabase, each of which in turn invokes the operation with the same name in class Account.

Getting the Balances

The phrase "retrieves an account balance" suggests that classes BankDatabase and Account each need a getBalance operation. However, recall that we created two attributes in class Account to represent a balance—availableBalance and totalBalance. A balance inquiry requires access to both balance attributes so that it can display them to the user, but a withdrawal needs to check only the value of availableBalance. To allow objects in the system to obtain each balance attribute individually, we add operations getAvailable-Balance and getTotalBalance to the third compartment of classes BankDatabase and Account (Fig. 12.17). We specify a return type of Double for these operations because the balance attributes they retrieve are of type Double.

Crediting and Debiting an Account

The phrases "credits a deposit amount to an account" and "debits a withdrawal amount from an account" indicate that classes BankDatabase and Account must perform operations to update an account during a deposit and withdrawal, respectively. We therefore assign credit and debit operations to classes BankDatabase and Account. You may recall that crediting an account (as in a deposit) adds an amount only to the totalBalance attribute. Debiting an account (as in a withdrawal), on the other hand, subtracts the amount from both balance attributes. We hide these implementation details inside class Account. This is a good example of encapsulation and information hiding.

Deposit Confirmations Performed by Another Banking System

If this were a real ATM system, classes `BankDatabase` and `Account` would also provide a set of operations to allow another banking system to update a user's account balance after either confirming or rejecting all or part of a deposit. Operation `confirmDepositAmount`, for example, would add an amount to the `availableBalance` attribute, thus making deposited funds available for withdrawal. Operation `rejectDepositAmount` would subtract an amount from the `totalBalance` attribute to indicate that a specified amount, which had recently been deposited through the ATM and added to the `totalBalance`, was not found in the deposit envelope. The bank would invoke this operation after determining either that the user failed to include the correct amount of cash or that any checks did not clear (i.e., they "bounced"). While adding these operations would make our system more complete, we do not include them in our class diagrams or our implementation because they're beyond the scope of the case study.

Displaying Messages

Class `Screen` "displays a message to the user" at various times in an ATM session. All visual output occurs through the screen of the ATM. The requirements document describes many types of messages (e.g., a welcome message, an error message, a thank you message) that the screen displays to the user. The requirements document also indicates that the screen displays prompts and menus to the user. However, a prompt is really just a message describing what the user should input next, and a menu is essentially a type of prompt consisting of a series of messages (i.e., menu options) displayed consecutively. Therefore, rather than assign class `Screen` an individual operation to display each type of message, prompt and menu, we simply create one operation that can display any message specified by a parameter. We place this operation (`displayMessage`) in the third compartment of class `Screen` in our class diagram (Fig. 12.17). Note that we do not worry about the parameter of this operation at this time—we model it later in this section.

Keyboard Input

From the phrase "receives numeric input from the user" listed by class `Keypad` in Fig. 12.16, we conclude that class `Keypad` should perform a `getInput` operation. Because the ATM's keypad, unlike a computer keyboard, contains only the numbers 0–9, we specify that this operation returns an integer value. Recall from the requirements document that in different situations the user may be required to enter a different type of number (e.g., an account number, a PIN, the number of a menu option, a deposit amount as a number of cents). Class `Keypad` simply obtains a numeric value for a client of the class— it does not determine whether the value meets any specific criteria. Any class that uses this operation must verify that the user entered an appropriate number in a given situation, then respond accordingly (i.e., display an error message via class `Screen`). [*Note:* When we implement the system, we simulate the ATM's keypad with a computer keyboard, and for simplicity we assume that the user does not enter nonnumeric input using keys on the computer keyboard that do not appear on the ATM's keypad.]

Dispensing Cash

Figure 12.16 lists "dispenses cash" for class `CashDispenser`. Therefore, we create operation `dispenseCash` and list it under class `CashDispenser` in Fig. 12.17. Class `CashDispenser` also "indicates whether it contains enough cash to satisfy a withdrawal request."

Thus, we include `isSufficientCashAvailable`, an operation that returns a value of UML type `Boolean`, in class `CashDispenser`.

Figure 12.16 also lists "receives a deposit envelope" for class `DepositSlot`. The deposit slot must indicate whether it received an envelope, so we place an operation `isEnvelopeReceived`, which returns a `Boolean` value, in the third compartment of class `DepositSlot`. [*Note:* A real hardware deposit slot would most likely send the ATM a signal to indicate that an envelope was received. We simulate this behavior, however, with an operation in class `DepositSlot` that class ATM can invoke to find out whether the deposit slot received an envelope.]

Class **ATM**

We do not list any operations for class ATM at this time. We are not yet aware of any services that class ATM provides to other classes in the system. When we implement the system with Java code, however, operations of this class, and additional operations of the other classes in the system, may emerge.

Identifying and Modeling Operation Parameters for Class **BankDatabase**

So far, we've not been concerned with the parameters of our operations—we've attempted to gain only a basic understanding of the operations of each class. Let's now take a closer look at some operation parameters. We identify an operation's parameters by examining what data the operation requires to perform its assigned task.

Consider `BankDatabase`'s `authenticateUser` operation. To authenticate a user, this operation must know the account number and PIN supplied by the user. So we specify that `authenticateUser` takes integer parameters `userAccountNumber` and `userPIN`, which the operation must compare to an `Account` object's account number and PIN in the database. We prefix these parameter names with "user" to avoid confusion between the operation's parameter names and class `Account`'s attribute names. We list these parameters in the class diagram in Fig. 12.18 that models only class `BankDatabase`. [*Note:* It's perfectly normal to model only one class. In this case, we're examining the parameters of this one class, so we omit the other classes. In class diagrams later in the case study, in which parameters are no longer the focus of our attention, we omit these parameters to save space. Remember, however, that the operations listed in these diagrams still have parameters.]

BankDatabase
authenticateUser(userAccountNumber : Integer, userPIN : Integer) : Boolean getAvailableBalance(userAccountNumber : Integer) : Double getTotalBalance(userAccountNumber : Integer) : Double credit(userAccountNumber : Integer, amount : Double) debit(userAccountNumber : Integer, amount : Double)

Fig. 12.18 | Class `BankDatabase` with operation parameters.

Recall that the UML models each parameter in an operation's comma-separated parameter list by listing the parameter name, followed by a colon and the parameter type (in UML notation). Figure 12.18 thus specifies that operation `authenticateUser` takes two parameters—userAccountNumber and userPIN, both of type Integer. When we implement the system in Java, we'll represent these parameters with int values.

Class BankDatabase operations getAvailableBalance, getTotalBalance, credit and debit also each require a userAccountNumber parameter to identify the account to which the database must apply the operations, so we include these parameters in the class diagram of Fig. 12.18. In addition, operations credit and debit each require a Double parameter amount to specify the amount of money to be credited or debited, respectively.

Identifying and Modeling Operation Parameters for Class *Account*

Figure 12.19 models class Account's operation parameters. Operation validatePIN requires only a userPIN parameter, which contains the user-specified PIN to be compared with the account's PIN. Like their BankDatabase counterparts, operations credit and debit in class Account each require a Double parameter amount that indicates the amount of money involved in the operation. Operations getAvailableBalance and getTotal-Balance in class Account require no additional data to perform their tasks. Note that class Account's operations do not require an account-number parameter to distinguish between Accounts, because these operations can be invoked only on a specific Account object.

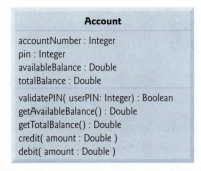

Fig. 12.19 | Class Account with operation parameters.

Identifying and Modeling Operation Parameters for Class *Screen*

Figure 12.20 models class Screen with a parameter specified for operation display-Message. This operation requires only a String parameter message that indicates the text to be displayed. Recall that the parameter types listed in our class diagrams are in UML notation, so the String type listed in Fig. 12.20 refers to the UML type. When we implement the system in Java, we'll use the Java class String to represent this parameter.

Fig. 12.20 | Class Screen with operation parameters.

Identifying and Modeling Operation Parameters for Class *CashDispenser*

Figure 12.21 specifies that operation dispenseCash of class CashDispenser takes a Double parameter amount to indicate the amount of cash (in dollars) to be dispensed. Operation isSufficientCashAvailable also takes a Double parameter amount to indicate the amount of cash in question.

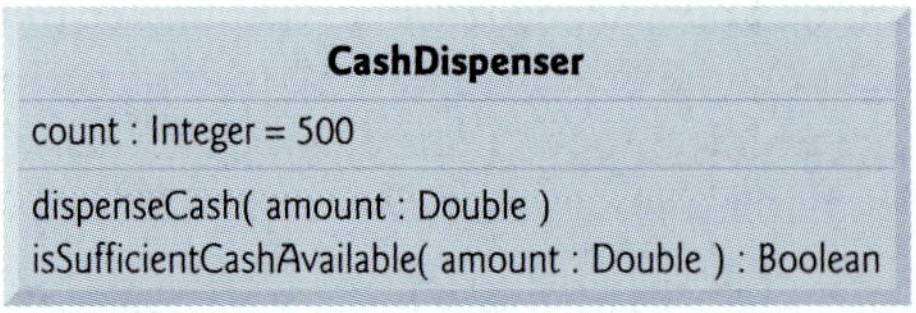

CashDispenser
count : Integer = 500
dispenseCash(amount : Double) isSufficientCashAvailable(amount : Double) : Boolean

Fig. 12.21 | Class CashDispenser with operation parameters.

Identifying and Modeling Operation Parameters for Other Classes

Note that we do not discuss parameters for operation execute of classes BalanceInquiry, Withdrawal and Deposit, operation getInput of class Keypad and operation isEnvelopeReceived of class DepositSlot. At this point in our design process, we cannot determine whether these operations require additional data, so we leave their parameter lists empty. Later, we may decide to add parameters.

In this section, we've determined many of the operations performed by the classes in the ATM system. We've identified the parameters and return types of some of the operations. As we continue our design process, the number of operations belonging to each class may vary—we might find that new operations are needed or that some current operations are unnecessary. We also might determine that some of our class operations need additional parameters and different return types, or that some parameters are unnecessary or require different types.

Self-Review Exercises for Section 12.6

12.14 Which of the following is not a behavior?
a) reading data from a file
b) printing output
c) text output
d) obtaining input from the user

12.15 If you were to add to the ATM system an operation that returns the amount attribute of class Withdrawal, how and where would you specify this operation in the class diagram of Fig. 12.17?

12.16 Describe the meaning of the following operation listing that might appear in a class diagram for an object-oriented design of a calculator:

```
add( x : Integer, y : Integer ) : Integer
```

12.7 Indicating Collaboration Among Objects

[*Note:* This section can be taught after Chapter 6.]

In this section, we concentrate on the collaborations (interactions) among objects. When two objects communicate with each other to accomplish a task, they're said to collaborate—objects do this by invoking one another's operations. A collaboration consists of an object of one class sending a message to an object of another class. Messages are sent in Java via method calls.

In Section 12.6, we determined many of the operations of the classes in our system. In this section, we concentrate on the messages that invoke these operations. To identify the collaborations in the system, we return to the requirements document in Section 12.2. Recall that this document specifies the range of activities that occur during an ATM session (e.g., authenticating a user, performing transactions). The steps used to describe how the system must perform each of these tasks are our first indication of the collaborations in our system. As we proceed through this section and Chapter 13, we may discover additional collaborations.

Identifying the Collaborations in a System

We identify the collaborations in the system by carefully reading the sections of the requirements document that specify what the ATM should do to authenticate a user and to perform each transaction type. For each action or step described, we decide which objects in our system must interact to achieve the desired result. We identify one object as the sending object and another as the receiving object. We then select one of the receiving object's operations (identified in Section 12.6) that must be invoked by the sending object to produce the proper behavior. For example, the ATM displays a welcome message when idle. We know that an object of class Screen displays a message to the user via its displayMessage operation. Thus, we decide that the system can display a welcome message by employing a collaboration between the ATM and the Screen in which the ATM sends a displayMessage message to the Screen by invoking the displayMessage operation of class Screen. [*Note:* To avoid repeating the phrase "an object of class...," we refer to an object by using its class name preceded by an article (e.g., "a," "an" or "the")—for example, "the ATM" refers to an object of class ATM.]

Figure 12.22 lists the collaborations that can be derived from the requirements document. For each sending object, we list the collaborations in the order in which they first occur during an ATM session (i.e., the order in which they're discussed in the requirements document). We list each collaboration involving a unique sender, message and recipient only once, even though the collaborations may occur at several different times throughout an ATM session. For example, the first row in Fig. 12.22 indicates that the ATM collaborates with the Screen whenever the ATM needs to display a message to the user.

Let's consider the collaborations in Fig. 12.22. Before allowing a user to perform any transactions, the ATM must prompt the user to enter an account number, then to enter a PIN. It accomplishes these tasks by sending a displayMessage message to the Screen. Both actions refer to the same collaboration between the ATM and the Screen, which is already listed in Fig. 12.22. The ATM obtains input in response to a prompt by sending a getInput message to the Keypad. Next, the ATM must determine whether the user-specified account number and PIN match those of an account in the database. It does so by sending an authenticateUser message to the BankDatabase. Recall that the BankDatabase cannot authenticate a user directly—only the user's Account (i.e., the Account that contains the account number specified by the user) can access the user's PIN on record to authenticate the user. Figure 12.22 therefore lists a collaboration in which the BankDatabase sends a validatePIN message to an Account.

After the user is authenticated, the ATM displays the main menu by sending a series of displayMessage messages to the Screen and obtains input containing a menu selection by sending a getInput message to the Keypad. We've already accounted for these collaborations, so we do not add anything to Fig. 12.22. After the user chooses a type of transaction to perform, the ATM executes the transaction by sending an execute message to an object of the appropriate transaction class (i.e., a BalanceInquiry, a Withdrawal or a

An object of class...	sends the message...	to an object of class...
ATM	displayMessage	Screen
	getInput	Keypad
	authenticateUser	BankDatabase
	execute	BalanceInquiry
	execute	Withdrawal
	execute	Deposit
BalanceInquiry	getAvailableBalance	BankDatabase
	getTotalBalance	BankDatabase
	displayMessage	Screen
Withdrawal	displayMessage	Screen
	getInput	Keypad
	getAvailableBalance	BankDatabase
	isSufficientCashAvailable	CashDispenser
	debit	BankDatabase
	dispenseCash	CashDispenser
Deposit	displayMessage	Screen
	getInput	Keypad
	isEnvelopeReceived	DepositSlot
	credit	BankDatabase
BankDatabase	validatePIN	Account
	getAvailableBalance	Account
	getTotalBalance	Account
	debit	Account
	credit	Account

Fig. 12.22 | Collaborations in the ATM system.

Deposit). For example, if the user chooses to perform a balance inquiry, the ATM sends an execute message to a BalanceInquiry.

Further examination of the requirements document reveals the collaborations involved in executing each transaction type. A BalanceInquiry retrieves the amount of money available in the user's account by sending a getAvailableBalance message to the BankDatabase, which responds by sending a getAvailableBalance message to the user's Account. Similarly, the BalanceInquiry retrieves the amount of money on deposit by sending a getTotalBalance message to the BankDatabase, which sends the same message to the user's Account. To display both parts of the user's account balance at the same time, the BalanceInquiry sends a displayMessage message to the Screen.

A Withdrawal responds to an execute message by sending displayMessage messages to the Screen to display a menu of standard withdrawal amounts (i.e., $20, $40, $60, $100, $200). The Withdrawal sends a getInput message to the Keypad to obtain the user's selection. Next, the Withdrawal determines whether the requested amount is less than or equal to the user's account balance. The Withdrawal can obtain the amount of money available by sending a getAvailableBalance message to the BankDatabase. The Withdrawal then tests whether the cash dispenser contains enough cash by sending an isSufficientCashAvailable message to the CashDispenser. A Withdrawal sends a debit message to the BankDatabase to decrease the user's account balance. The BankDatabase in turn sends the same message to the appropriate Account, which decreases both the totalBalance and the availableBalance. To dispense the requested amount of cash, the Withdrawal sends a dispenseCash message to the CashDispenser. Finally, the Withdrawal sends a displayMessage message to the Screen, instructing the user to take the cash.

A `Deposit` responds to an `execute` message first by sending a `displayMessage` message to the `Screen` to prompt the user for a deposit amount. The `Deposit` sends a `getInput` message to the `Keypad` to obtain the user's input. The `Deposit` then sends a `displayMessage` message to the `Screen` to tell the user to insert a deposit envelope. To determine whether the deposit slot received an incoming deposit envelope, the `Deposit` sends an `isEnvelopeReceived` message to the `DepositSlot`. The `Deposit` updates the user's account by sending a `credit` message to the `BankDatabase`, which subsequently sends a `credit` message to the user's `Account`. Recall that crediting funds to an `Account` increases the `totalBalance` but not the `availableBalance`.

Interaction Diagrams

Now that we've identified possible collaborations between our ATM system's objects, let's graphically model these interactions using the UML. The UML provides several types of **interaction diagrams** that model the behavior of a system by modeling how objects interact. The **communication diagram** emphasizes *which objects* participate in collaborations. [*Note:* Communication diagrams were called **collaboration diagrams** in earlier versions of the UML.] Like the communication diagram, the **sequence diagram** shows collaborations among objects, but it emphasizes *when* messages are sent between objects *over time*.

Communication Diagrams

Figure 12.23 shows a communication diagram that models the ATM executing a `BalanceInquiry`. Objects are modeled in the UML as rectangles containing names in the form `objectName : ClassName`. In this example, which involves only one object of each type, we disregard the object name and list only a colon followed by the class name. [*Note:* Specifying each object's name in a communication diagram is recommended when modeling multiple objects of the same type.] Communicating objects are connected with solid lines, and messages are passed between objects along these lines in the direction shown by arrows. The name of the message, which appears next to the arrow, is the name of an operation (i.e., a method in Java) belonging to the receiving object—think of the name as a "service" that the receiving object provides to sending objects (its clients).

Fig. 12.23 | Communication diagram of the ATM executing a balance inquiry.

The solid filled arrow represents a message—or **synchronous call**—in the UML and a method call in Java. This arrow indicates that the flow of control is from the sending object (the ATM) to the receiving object (a `BalanceInquiry`). Since this is a synchronous call, the sending object may not send another message, or do anything at all, until the receiving object processes the message and returns control to the sending object. The sender just waits. In Fig. 12.23, the ATM calls `BalanceInquiry` method `execute` and may not send another message until `execute` has finished and returns control to the ATM. [*Note:* If this were an **asynchronous call**, represented by a stick (➤) arrowhead, the sending object would not have to wait for the receiving object to return control—it would continue sending additional messages immediately following the asynchronous call. Asynchronous calls are implemented in Java using a technique called multithreading, which is discussed in Chapter 26, Multithreading.]

Sequence of Messages in a Communication Diagram

Figure 12.24 shows a communication diagram that models the interactions among system objects when an object of class BalanceInquiry executes. We assume that the object's accountNumber attribute contains the account number of the current user. The collaborations in Fig. 12.24 begin after the ATM sends an execute message to a BalanceInquiry (i.e., the interaction modeled in Fig. 12.23). The number to the left of a message name indicates the order in which the message is passed. The **sequence of messages** in a communication diagram progresses in numerical order from least to greatest. In this diagram, the numbering starts with message 1 and ends with message 3. The BalanceInquiry first sends a getAvailableBalance message to the BankDatabase (message 1), then sends a getTotalBalance message to the BankDatabase (message 2). Within the parentheses following a message name, we can specify a comma-separated list of the names of the parameters sent with the message (i.e., arguments in a Java method call)—the BalanceInquiry passes attribute accountNumber with its messages to the BankDatabase to indicate which Account's balance information to retrieve. Recall from Fig. 12.18 that operations getAvailableBalance and getTotalBalance of class BankDatabase each require a parameter to identify an account. The BalanceInquiry next displays the availableBalance and the totalBalance to the user by passing a displayMessage message to the Screen (message 3) that includes a parameter indicating the message to be displayed.

Note that Fig. 12.24 models two additional messages passing from the BankDatabase to an Account (message 1.1 and message 2.1). To provide the ATM with the two balances of the user's Account (as requested by messages 1 and 2), the BankDatabase must pass a

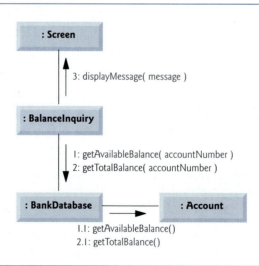

Fig. 12.24 | Communication diagram for executing a balance inquiry.

getAvailableBalance and a getTotalBalance message to the user's Account. Such messages passed within the handling of another message are called **nested messages**. The UML recommends using a decimal numbering scheme to indicate nested messages. For example, message 1.1 is the first message nested in message 1—the BankDatabase passes a getAvailableBalance message during BankDatabase's processing of a message by the same name. [*Note:* If the BankDatabase needed to pass a second nested message while processing message 1, the second message would be numbered 1.2.] A message may be passed only when all the nested messages from the previous message have been passed. For example, the BalanceInquiry passes message 3 only after messages 2 and 2.1 have been passed, in that order.

The nested numbering scheme used in communication diagrams helps clarify precisely when and in what context each message is passed. For example, if we numbered the messages in Fig. 12.24 using a flat numbering scheme (i.e., 1, 2, 3, 4, 5), someone looking at the diagram might not be able to determine that BankDatabase passes the getAvailableBalance message (message 1.1) to an Account *during* the BankDatabase's processing of message 1, as opposed to *after* completing the processing of message 1. The nested decimal numbers make it clear that the second getAvailableBalance message (message 1.1) is passed to an Account within the handling of the first getAvailableBalance message (message 1) by the BankDatabase.

Sequence Diagrams

Communication diagrams emphasize the participants in collaborations, but model their timing a bit awkwardly. A sequence diagram helps model the timing of collaborations more clearly. Figure 12.25 shows a sequence diagram modeling the sequence of interactions that occur when a Withdrawal executes. The dotted line extending down from an object's rectangle is that object's lifeline, which represents the progression of time. Actions occur along an object's lifeline in chronological order from top to bottom—an action near the top happens before one near the bottom.

Message passing in sequence diagrams is similar to message passing in communication diagrams. A solid arrow with a filled arrowhead extending from the sending object to the receiving object represents a message between two objects. The arrowhead points to an activation on the receiving object's lifeline. An activation, shown as a thin vertical rectangle, indicates that an object is executing. When an object returns control, a return message, represented as a dashed line with a stick ($\rightarrow$) arrowhead, extends from the activation of the object returning control to the activation of the object that initially sent the message. To eliminate clutter, we omit the return-message arrows—the UML allows this practice to make diagrams more readable. Like communication diagrams, sequence diagrams can indicate message parameters between the parentheses following a message name.

The sequence of messages in Fig. 12.25 begins when a Withdrawal prompts the user to choose a withdrawal amount by sending a displayMessage message to the Screen. The Withdrawal then sends a getInput message to the Keypad, which obtains input from the user. We've already modeled the control logic involved in a Withdrawal in the activity diagram of Fig. 12.15, so we do not show this logic in the sequence diagram of Fig. 12.25. Instead, we model the best-case scenario in which the balance of the user's account is greater than or equal to the chosen withdrawal amount, and the cash dispenser contains a sufficient amount of cash to satisfy the request. You can model control logic in a sequence diagram with UML frames (which are not covered in this case study). For a quick overview of UML frames, visit www.agilemodeling.com/style/frame.htm.

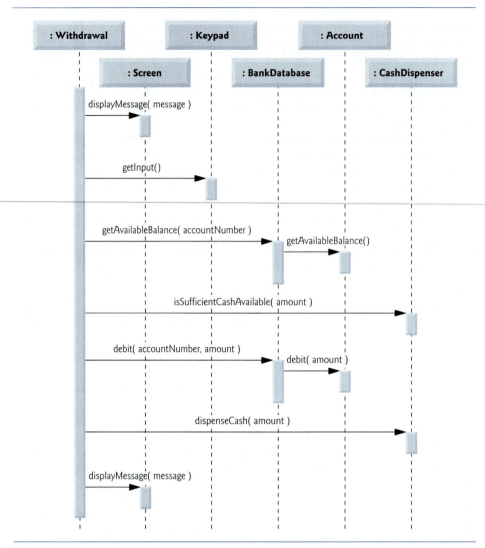

Fig. 12.25 | Sequence diagram that models a Withdrawal executing.

After obtaining a withdrawal amount, the Withdrawal sends a getAvailableBalance message to the BankDatabase, which in turn sends a getAvailableBalance message to the user's Account. Assuming that the user's account has enough money available to permit the transaction, the Withdrawal next sends an isSufficientCashAvailable message to the CashDispenser. Assuming that there is enough cash available, the Withdrawal decreases the balance of the user's account (i.e., both the totalBalance and the availableBalance) by sending a debit message to the BankDatabase. The BankDatabase responds by sending a debit message to the user's Account. Finally, the Withdrawal sends a dispenseCash message to the CashDispenser and a displayMessage message to the Screen, telling the user to remove the cash from the machine.

We've identified the collaborations among objects in the ATM system and modeled some of these collaborations using UML interaction diagrams—both communication diagrams and sequence diagrams. In Section 13.2, we enhance the structure of our model to complete a preliminary object-oriented design, then we begin implementing the ATM system in Java.

Self-Review Exercises for Section 12.7

12.17 A(n) _____ consists of an object of one class sending a message to an object of another class.

- a) association
- b) aggregation
- c) collaboration
- d) composition

12.18 Which form of interaction diagram emphasizes *what* collaborations occur? Which form emphasizes *when* collaborations occur?

12.19 Create a sequence diagram that models the interactions among objects in the ATM system that occur when a Deposit executes successfully, and explain the sequence of messages modeled by the diagram.

12.8 Wrap-Up

In this chapter, you learned how to work from a detailed requirements document to develop an object-oriented design. You worked with six popular types of UML diagrams to graphically model an object-oriented automated teller machine software system. In Chapter 13, we tune the design using inheritance, then completely implement the design in a 673-line Java application.

Answers to Self-Review Exercises

12.1 Figure 12.26 contains a use case diagram for a modified version of our ATM system that also allows users to transfer money between accounts.

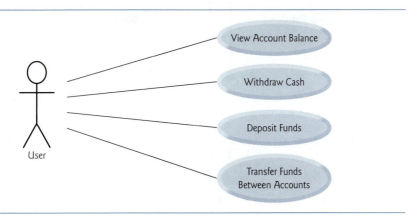

Fig. 12.26 | Use case diagram for a modified version of our ATM system that also allows users to transfer money between accounts.

12.2 b.

12.3 d.

12.4 [*Note:* Student answers may vary.] Figure 12.27 presents a class diagram that shows some of the composition relationships of a class Car.

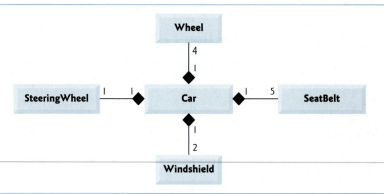

Fig. 12.27 | Class diagram showing composition relationships of a class Car.

12.5 c. [*Note:* In a computer network, this relationship could be many-to-many.]

12.6 True.

12.7 Figure 12.28 presents a class diagram for the ATM including class Deposit instead of class Withdrawal (as in Fig. 12.10). Note that Deposit does not access CashDispenser, but does access DepositSlot.

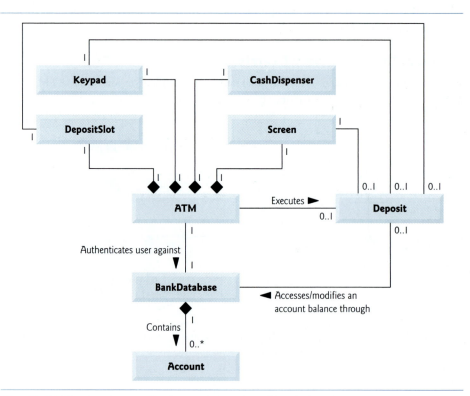

Fig. 12.28 | Class diagram for the ATM system model including class Deposit.

12.8 b.

12.9 c. Fly is an operation or behavior of an airplane, not an attribute.

12.10 This indicates that count is an Integer with an initial value of 500. This attribute keeps track of the number of bills available in the CashDispenser at any given time.

12.11 False. State diagrams model some of the behavior of a system.

12.12 a.

12.13 Figure 12.29 models the actions that occur after the user chooses the deposit option from the main menu and before the ATM returns the user to the main menu. Recall that part of receiving a deposit amount from the user involves converting an integer number of cents to a dollar amount. Also recall that crediting a deposit amount to an account increases only the totalBalance attribute of the user's Account object. The bank updates the availableBalance attribute of the user's Account object only after confirming the amount of cash in the deposit envelope and after the enclosed checks clear—this occurs independently of the ATM system.

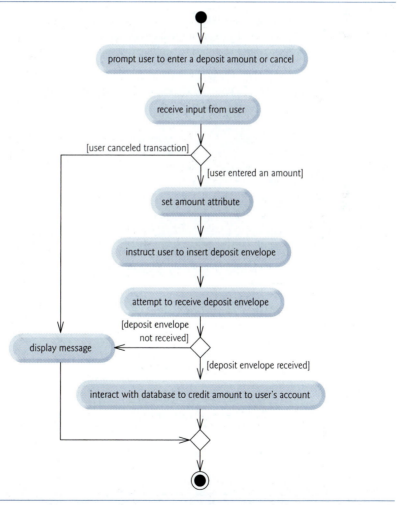

Fig. 12.29 | Activity diagram for a deposit transaction.

12.14 c.

12.15 To specify an operation that retrieves the amount attribute of class Withdrawal, the following operation listing would be placed in the operation (i.e., third) compartment of class Withdrawal:

    getAmount( ) : Double

12.16 This operation listing indicates an operation named add that takes integers x and y as parameters and returns an integer value.

12.17 c.

12.18 Communication diagrams emphasize *what* collaborations occur. Sequence diagrams emphasize *when* collaborations occur.

12.19 Figure 12.30 presents a sequence diagram that models the interactions between objects in the ATM system that occur when a Deposit executes successfully. A Deposit first sends a displayMessage message to the Screen to ask the user to enter a deposit amount. Next the Deposit sends a getInput message to the Keypad to receive input from the user. The Deposit then instructs the user to enter a deposit envelope by sending a displayMessage message to the Screen. The Deposit next sends an isEnvelopeReceived message to the DepositSlot to confirm that the deposit envelope has been received by the ATM. Finally, the Deposit increases the totalBalance attribute (but not the availableBalance attribute) of the user's Account by sending a credit message to the BankDatabase. The BankDatabase responds by sending the same message to the user's Account.

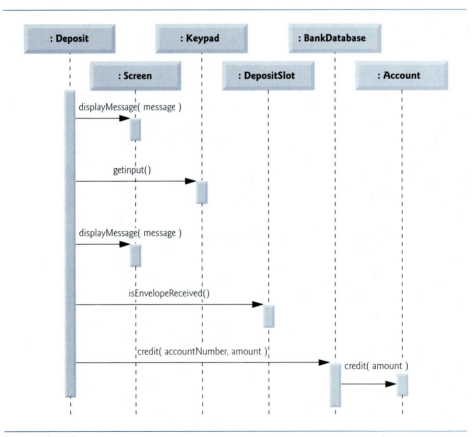

Fig. 12.30 | Sequence diagram that models a Deposit executing.

ATM Case Study Part 2: Implementing an Object-Oriented Design

13

You can't work in the abstract.
—I. M. Pei

To generalize means to think.
—Georg Wilhelm Friedrich Hegel

We are all gifted. That is our inheritance.
—Ethel Waters

Let me walk through the fields of paper touching with my wand dry stems and stunted butterflies...
—Denise Levertov

Objectives

In this chapter you'll:

- Incorporate inheritance into the design of the ATM.

- Incorporate polymorphism into the design of the ATM.

- Fully implement in Java the UML-based object-oriented design of the ATM software.

- Study a detailed code walkthrough of the ATM software system that explains the implementation issues.

13.1 Introduction

In Chapter 12, we developed an object-oriented design for our ATM system. We now begin implementing our object-oriented design in Java. In Section 13.2, we show how to convert class diagrams to Java code. In Section 13.3, we tune the design with inheritance and polymorphism. Then we present a full Java code implementation of the ATM software in Section 13.4. The code is carefully commented and the discussions of the implementation are thorough and precise. Studying this application provides the opportunity for you to see a more substantial application of the kind you are likely to encounter in industry.

13.2 Starting to Program the Classes of the ATM System

[*Note:* This section can be taught after Chapter 8.]

Visibility
We now apply access modifiers to the members of our classes. We've introduced access modifiers public and private. Access modifiers determine the visibility or accessibility of an object's attributes and methods to other objects. Before we can begin implementing our design, we must consider which attributes and methods of our classes should be public and which should be private.

We've observed that attributes normally should be private and that methods invoked by clients of a given class should be public. Methods that are called as "utility methods" only by other methods of the class normally should be private. The UML employs visibility markers for modeling the visibility of attributes and operations. Public visibility is indicated by placing a plus sign (+) before an operation or an attribute, whereas a minus sign (–) indicates private visibility. Figure 13.1 shows our updated class diagram with visibility markers included. [*Note:* We do not include any operation parameters in Fig. 13.1—this is perfectly normal. Adding visibility markers does not affect the parameters already modeled in the class diagrams of Figs. 12.17–12.21.]

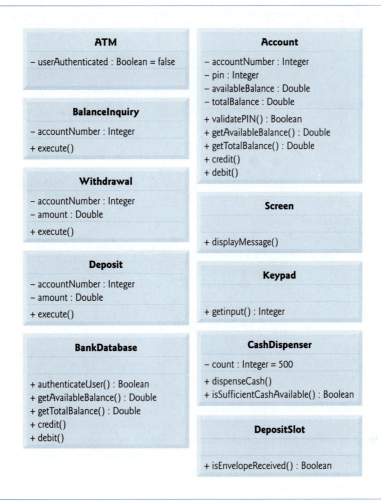

Fig. 13.1 | Class diagram with visibility markers.

Navigability

Before we begin implementing our design in Java, we introduce an additional UML notation. The class diagram in Fig. 13.2 further refines the relationships among classes in the ATM system by adding navigability arrows to the association lines. Navigability arrows (represented as arrows with stick (⟶) arrowhead in the class diagram) indicate in the direction which an association can be traversed. When implementing a system designed using the UML, programmers use navigability arrows to determine which objects need references to other objects. For example, the navigability arrow pointing from class ATM to class BankDatabase indicates that we can navigate from the former to the latter, thereby enabling the ATM to invoke the BankDatabase's operations. However, since Fig. 13.2 does not contain a navigability arrow pointing from class BankDatabase to class ATM, the Bank-Database cannot access the ATM's operations. Note that associations in a class diagram that have navigability arrows at both ends or have none at all indicate bidirectional navigability—navigation can proceed in either direction across the association.

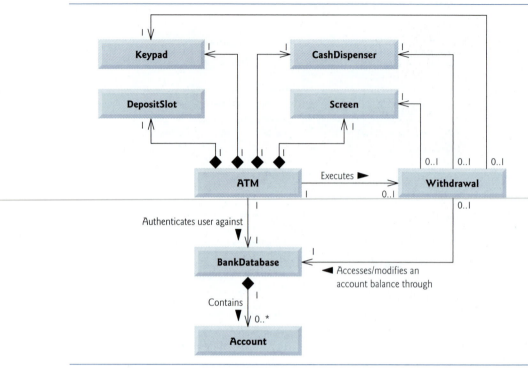

Fig. 13.2 | Class diagram with navigability arrows.

Like the class diagram of Fig. 12.10, that of Fig. 13.2 omits classes `BalanceInquiry` and `Deposit` for simplicity. The navigability of the associations in which these classes participate closely parallels that of class `Withdrawal`. Recall from Section 12.3 that `Balance-Inquiry` has an association with class `Screen`. We can navigate from class `BalanceInquiry` to class `Screen` along this association, but we cannot navigate from class `Screen` to class `BalanceInquiry`. Thus, if we were to model class `BalanceInquiry` in Fig. 13.2, we would place a navigability arrow at class `Screen`'s end of this association. Also recall that class `Deposit` associates with classes `Screen`, `Keypad` and `DepositSlot`. We can navigate from class `Deposit` to each of these classes, but not vice versa. We therefore would place navigability arrows at the `Screen`, `Keypad` and `DepositSlot` ends of these associations. [*Note:* We model these additional classes and associations in our final class diagram in Section 13.3, after we've simplified the structure of our system by incorporating the object-oriented concept of inheritance.]

Implementing the ATM System from Its UML Design

We are now ready to begin implementing the ATM system. We first convert the classes in the diagrams of Fig. 13.1 and Fig. 13.2 into Java code. The code will represent the "skeleton" of the system. In Section 13.3, we modify the code to incorporate inheritance. In Section 13.4, we present the complete working Java code for our model.

As an example, we develop the code from our design of class `Withdrawal` in Fig. 13.1. We use this figure to determine the attributes and operations of the class. We use the UML model in Fig. 13.2 to determine the associations among classes. We follow the following four guidelines for each class:

1. Use the name located in the first compartment to declare the class as a `public` class with an empty no-argument constructor. We include this constructor simply as a placeholder to remind us that most classes will indeed need custom constructors. In Section 13.4, when we complete a working version of this class, we'll add any necessary arguments and code the body of the constructor as needed. For example, class `Withdrawal` yields the code in Fig. 13.3. [*Note:* If we find that the class's instance variables require only default initialization, then we'll remove the empty no-argument constructor because it's unnecessary.]

```
1   // Class Withdrawal represents an ATM withdrawal transaction
2   public class Withdrawal
3   {
4      // no-argument constructor
5      public Withdrawal()
6      {
7      } // end no-argument Withdrawal constructor
8   } // end class Withdrawal
```

Fig. 13.3 | Java code for class `Withdrawal` based on Figs. 13.1–13.2.

2. Use the attributes located in the second compartment to declare the instance variables. For example, the `private` attributes `accountNumber` and `amount` of class `Withdrawal` yield the code in Fig. 13.4. [*Note:* The constructor of the complete working version of this class will assign values to these attributes.]

```
1   // Class Withdrawal represents an ATM withdrawal transaction
2   public class Withdrawal
3   {
4      // attributes
5      private int accountNumber; // account to withdraw funds from
6      private double amount; // amount to withdraw
7
8      // no-argument constructor
9      public Withdrawal()
10     {
11     } // end no-argument Withdrawal constructor
12  } // end class Withdrawal
```

Fig. 13.4 | Java code for class `Withdrawal` based on Figs. 13.1–13.2.

3. Use the associations described in the class diagram to declare the references to other objects. For example, according to Fig. 13.2, `Withdrawal` can access one object of class `Screen`, one object of class `Keypad`, one object of class `CashDispenser` and one object of class `BankDatabase`. This yields the code in Fig. 13.5. [*Note:* The constructor of the complete working version of this class will initialize these instance variables with references to actual objects.]

4. Use the operations located in the third compartment of Fig. 13.1 to declare the shells of the methods. If we have not yet specified a return type for an operation,

we declare the method with return type void. Refer to the class diagrams of Figs. 12.17–12.21 to declare any necessary parameters. For example, adding the public operation execute in class Withdrawal, which has an empty parameter list, yields the code in Fig. 13.6. [*Note:* We code the bodies of methods when we implement the complete system in Section 13.4.]

This concludes our discussion of the basics of generating classes from UML diagrams.

```java
1   // Class Withdrawal represents an ATM withdrawal transaction
2   public class Withdrawal
3   {
4      // attributes
5      private int accountNumber; // account to withdraw funds from
6      private double amount; // amount to withdraw
7
8      // references to associated objects
9      private Screen screen; // ATM's screen
10     private Keypad keypad; // ATM's keypad
11     private CashDispenser cashDispenser; // ATM's cash dispenser
12     private BankDatabase bankDatabase; // account info database
13
14     // no-argument constructor
15     public Withdrawal()
16     {
17     } // end no-argument Withdrawal constructor
18  } // end class Withdrawal
```

Fig. 13.5 | Java code for class Withdrawal based on Figs. 13.1–13.2.

```java
1   // Class Withdrawal represents an ATM withdrawal transaction
2   public class Withdrawal
3   {
4      // attributes
5      private int accountNumber; // account to withdraw funds from
6      private double amount; // amount to withdraw
7
8      // references to associated objects
9      private Screen screen; // ATM's screen
10     private Keypad keypad; // ATM's keypad
11     private CashDispenser cashDispenser; // ATM's cash dispenser
12     private BankDatabase bankDatabase; // account info database
13
14     // no-argument constructor
15     public Withdrawal()
16     {
17     } // end no-argument Withdrawal constructor
18
19     // operations
20     public void execute()
21     {
22     } // end method execute
23  } // end class Withdrawal
```

Fig. 13.6 | Java code for class Withdrawal based on Figs. 13.1–13.2.

Self-Review Exercises for Section 13.2

13.1   State whether the following statement is *true* or *false*, and if *false*, explain why: If an attribute of a class is marked with a minus sign (-) in a class diagram, the attribute is not directly accessible outside the class.

13.2   In Fig. 13.2, the association between the ATM and the Screen indicates that:
a) we can navigate from the Screen to the ATM
b) we can navigate from the ATM to the Screen
c) Both (a) and (b); the association is bidirectional
d) None of the above

13.3   Write Java code to begin implementing the design for class Keypad.

13.3 Incorporating Inheritance and Polymorphism into the ATM System

[*Note:* **This section can be taught after Chapter 10.**]
We now revisit our ATM system design to see how it might benefit from inheritance. To apply inheritance, we first look for commonality among classes in the system. We create an inheritance hierarchy to model similar (yet not identical) classes in a more elegant and efficient manner. We then modify our class diagram to incorporate the new inheritance relationships. Finally, we demonstrate how our updated design is translated into Java code.

In Section 12.3, we encountered the problem of representing a financial transaction in the system. Rather than create one class to represent all transaction types, we decided to create three individual transaction classes—BalanceInquiry, Withdrawal and Deposit— to represent the transactions that the ATM system can perform. Figure 13.7 shows the attributes and operations of classes BalanceInquiry, Withdrawal and Deposit. Note that these classes have one attribute (accountNumber) and one operation (execute) in common. Each class requires attribute accountNumber to specify the account to which the transaction applies. Each class contains operation execute, which the ATM invokes to perform the transaction. Clearly, BalanceInquiry, Withdrawal and Deposit represent *types of* transactions. Figure 13.7 reveals commonality among the transaction classes, so using inheritance to factor out the common features seems appropriate for designing classes BalanceInquiry, Withdrawal and Deposit. We place the common functionality in a superclass, Transaction, that classes BalanceInquiry, Withdrawal and Deposit extend.

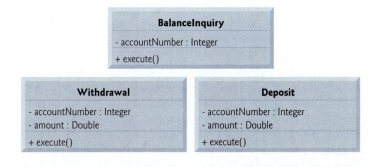

Fig. 13.7 | Attributes and operations of BalanceInquiry, Withdrawal and Deposit.

Generalization

The UML specifies a relationship called a **generalization** to model inheritance. Figure 13.8 is the class diagram that models the generalization of superclass Transaction and subclasses BalanceInquiry, Withdrawal and Deposit. The arrows with triangular hollow arrowheads indicate that classes BalanceInquiry, Withdrawal and Deposit extend class Transaction. Class Transaction is said to be a generalization of classes BalanceInquiry, Withdrawal and Deposit. Class BalanceInquiry, Withdrawal and Deposit are said to be **specializations** of class Transaction.

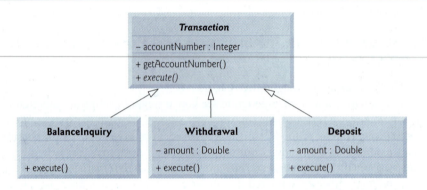

Fig. 13.8 | Class diagram modeling generalization of superclass Transaction and subclasses BalanceInquiry, Withdrawal and Deposit. Note that abstract class names (e.g., Transaction) and method names (e.g., execute in class Transaction) appear in italics.

Classes BalanceInquiry, Withdrawal and Deposit share integer attribute account-Number, so we factor out this common attribute and place it in superclass Transaction. We no longer list accountNumber in the second compartment of each subclass, because the three subclasses inherit this attribute from Transaction. Recall, however, that subclasses cannot directly access private attributes of a superclass. We therefore include public method getAccountNumber in class Transaction. Each subclass will inherit this method, enabling the subclass to access its accountNumber as needed to execute a transaction.

According to Fig. 13.7, classes BalanceInquiry, Withdrawal and Deposit also share operation execute, so we placed public method execute in superclass Transaction. However, it does not make sense to implement execute in class Transaction, because the functionality that this method provides depends on the type of the actual transaction. We therefore declare method execute as abstract in superclass Transaction. Any class that contains at least one abstract method must also be declared abstract. This forces any subclass of Transaction that must be a concrete class (i.e., BalanceInquiry, Withdrawal and Deposit) to implement method execute. The UML requires that we place abstract class names (and abstract methods) in italics, so Transaction and its method execute appear in italics in Fig. 13.8. Note that method execute is not italicized in subclasses BalanceInquiry, Withdrawal and Deposit. Each subclass overrides superclass Transaction's execute method with a concrete implementation that performs the steps appropriate for completing that type of transaction. Note that Fig. 13.8 includes operation execute in the third compartment of classes BalanceInquiry, Withdrawal and Deposit, because each class has a different concrete implementation of the overridden method.

*Processing **Transactions** Polymorphically*

Polymorphism provides the ATM with an elegant way to execute all transactions "in the general." For example, suppose a user chooses to perform a balance inquiry. The ATM sets a Transaction reference to a new BalanceInquiry object. When the ATM uses its Transaction reference to invoke method execute, BalanceInquiry's version of execute is called.

This polymorphic approach also makes the system easily extensible. Should we wish to create a new transaction type (e.g., funds transfer or bill payment), we would just create an additional Transaction subclass that overrides the execute method with a version of the method appropriate for executing the new transaction type. We would need to make only minimal changes to the system code to allow users to choose the new transaction type from the main menu and for the ATM to instantiate and execute objects of the new subclass. The ATM could execute transactions of the new type using the current code, because it executes all transactions polymorphically using a general Transaction reference.

Recall that an abstract class like Transaction is one for which the programmer never intends to instantiate objects. An abstract class simply declares common attributes and behaviors of its subclasses in an inheritance hierarchy. Class Transaction defines the concept of what it means to be a transaction that has an account number and executes. You may wonder why we bother to include abstract method execute in class Transaction if it lacks a concrete implementation. Conceptually, we include it because it corresponds to the defining behavior of all transactions—executing. Technically, we must include method execute in superclass Transaction so that the ATM (or any other class) can polymorphically invoke each subclass's overridden version of this method through a Transaction reference. Also, from a software engineering perspective, including an abstract method in a superclass forces the implementor of the subclasses to override that method with concrete implementations in the subclasses, or else the subclasses, too, will be abstract, preventing objects of those subclasses from being instantiated.

*Additional Attribute of Classes **Withdrawal** and **Deposit***

Subclasses BalanceInquiry, Withdrawal and Deposit inherit attribute accountNumber from superclass Transaction, but classes Withdrawal and Deposit contain the additional attribute amount that distinguishes them from class BalanceInquiry. Classes Withdrawal and Deposit require this additional attribute to store the amount of money that the user wishes to withdraw or deposit. Class BalanceInquiry has no need for such an attribute and requires only an account number to execute. Even though two of the three Transaction subclasses share this attribute, we do not place it in superclass Transaction—we place only features common to all the subclasses in the superclass, otherwise subclasses could inherit attributes (and methods) that they do not need and should not have.

*Class Diagram with **Transaction** Hierarchy Incorporated*

Figure 13.9 presents an updated class diagram of our model that incorporates inheritance and introduces class Transaction. We model an association between class ATM and class Transaction to show that the ATM, at any given moment, either is executing a transaction or is not (i.e., zero or one objects of type Transaction exist in the system at a time). Because a Withdrawal is a type of Transaction, we no longer draw an association line directly between class ATM and class Withdrawal. Subclass Withdrawal inherits superclass Transaction's association with class ATM. Subclasses BalanceInquiry and Deposit inherit this association, too, so the previously omitted associations between ATM and classes BalanceInquiry and Deposit no longer exist either.

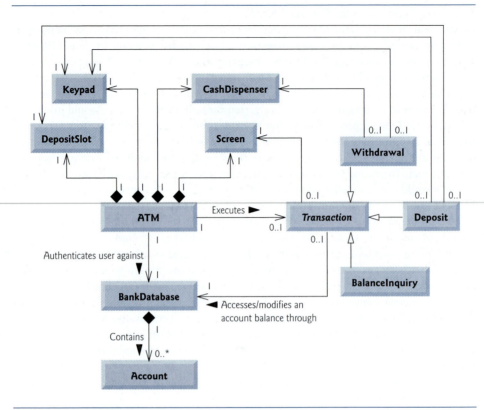

Fig. 13.9 | Class diagram of the ATM system (incorporating inheritance). Note that the abstract class name `Transaction` appears in italics.

We also add an association between class `Transaction` and the `BankDatabase` (Fig. 13.9). All `Transaction`s require a reference to the `BankDatabase` so they can access and modify account information. Because each `Transaction` subclass inherits this reference, we no longer model the association between class `Withdrawal` and the `BankDatabase`. Similarly, the previously omitted associations between the `BankDatabase` and classes `BalanceInquiry` and `Deposit` no longer exist.

We show an association between class `Transaction` and the `Screen`. All `Transaction`s display output to the user via the `Screen`. Thus, we no longer include the association previously modeled between `Withdrawal` and the `Screen`, although `Withdrawal` still participates in associations with the `CashDispenser` and the `Keypad`. Our class diagram incorporating inheritance also models `Deposit` and `BalanceInquiry`. We show associations between `Deposit` and both the `DepositSlot` and the `Keypad`. Note that class `BalanceInquiry` takes part in no associations other than those inherited from class `Transaction`—a `BalanceInquiry` needs to interact only with the `BankDatabase` and with the `Screen`.

Figure 13.1 showed attributes and operations with visibility markers. Now in Fig. 13.10 we present a modified class diagram that incorporates inheritance. This abbreviated diagram does not show inheritance relationships, but instead shows the attributes and methods after we've employed inheritance in our system. To save space, as we did in

Fig. 12.12, we do not include those attributes shown by associations in Fig. 13.9—we do, however, include them in the Java implementation in Section 13.4. We also omit all operation parameters, as we did in Fig. 13.1—incorporating inheritance does not affect the parameters already modeled in Figs. 12.17–12.21.

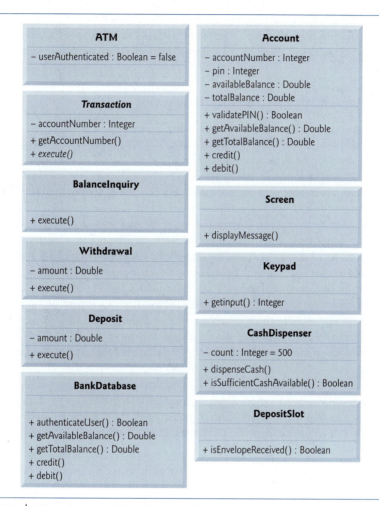

Fig. 13.10 | Class diagram with attributes and operations (incorporating inheritance). Note that the abstract class name `Transaction` and the abstract method name `execute` in class `Transaction` appear in italics.

Software Engineering Observation 13.1

A complete class diagram shows all the associations among classes and all the attributes and operations for each class. When the number of class attributes, methods and associations is substantial (as in Figs. 13.9 and 13.10), a good practice that promotes readability is to divide this information between two class diagrams—one focusing on associations and the other on attributes and methods.

13.3.1 Implementing the ATM System Design (Incorporating Inheritance)

In Section 13.2, we began implementing the ATM system design in Java code. We now modify our implementation to incorporate inheritance, using class Withdrawal as an example.

1. If a class A is a generalization of class B, then class B extends class A in the class declaration. For example, abstract superclass Transaction is a generalization of class Withdrawal. Figure 13.11 shows the declaration of class Withdrawal.

```
 1  // Class Withdrawal represents an ATM withdrawal transaction
 2  public class Withdrawal extends Transaction
 3  {
 4  } // end class Withdrawal
```

Fig. 13.11 | Java code for shell of class Withdrawal.

2. If class A is an abstract class and class B is a subclass of class A, then class B must implement the abstract methods of class A if class B is to be a concrete class. For example, class Transaction contains abstract method execute, so class Withdrawal must implement this method if we want to instantiate a Withdrawal object. Figure 13.12 is the Java code for class Withdrawal from Fig. 13.9 and Fig. 13.10. Class Withdrawal inherits field accountNumber from superclass Transaction, so Withdrawal does not need to declare this field. Class Withdrawal also inherits references to the Screen and the BankDatabase from its superclass Transaction, so we do not include these references in our code. Figure 13.10 specifies attribute amount and operation execute for class Withdrawal. Line 6 of Fig. 13.12 declares a field for attribute amount. Lines 16–19 declare the shell of a method for operation execute. Recall that subclass Withdrawal must provide a concrete implementation of the abstract method execute in superclass Transaction. The keypad and cashDispenser references (lines 7–8) are fields derived from Withdrawal's associations in Fig. 13.9. [*Note:* The constructor in the complete working version of this class will initialize these references to actual objects.]

```
 1  // Withdrawal.java
 2  // Generated using the class diagrams in Fig. 13.9 and Fig. 13.10
 3  public class Withdrawal extends Transaction
 4  {
 5     // attributes
 6     private double amount; // amount to withdraw
 7     private Keypad keypad; // reference to keypad
 8     private CashDispenser cashDispenser; // reference to cash dispenser
 9
10     // no-argument constructor
11     public Withdrawal()
12     {
13     } // end no-argument Withdrawal constructor
14
```

Fig. 13.12 | Java code for class Withdrawal based on Figs. 13.9 and 13.10. (Part 1 of 2.)

```
15      // method overriding execute
16      @Override
17      public void execute()
18      {
19      } // end method execute
20  } // end class Withdrawal
```

Fig. 13.12 | Java code for class Withdrawal based on Figs. 13.9 and 13.10. (Part 2 of 2.)

Software Engineering Observation 13.2

Several UML modeling tools can convert UML-based designs into Java code, speeding the implementation process considerably. For more information on these tools, visit our UML Resource Center at www.deitel.com/UML/.

Congratulations on completing the case study's design portion! We implement the ATM system in Java code in Section 13.4. We recommend that you carefully read the code and its description. The code is abundantly commented and precisely follows the design with which you're now familiar. The accompanying description is carefully written to guide your understanding of the implementation based on the UML design. Mastering this code is a wonderful culminating accomplishment after studying Sections 12.2–12.7 and 13.2–13.3.

Self-Review Exercises for Section 13.3

13.4   The UML uses an arrow with a _____ to indicate a generalization relationship.
a) solid filled arrowhead
b) triangular hollow arrowhead
c) diamond-shaped hollow arrowhead
d) stick arrowhead

13.5   State whether the following statement is *true* or *false*, and if *false*, explain why: The UML requires that we underline abstract class names and method names.

13.6   Write Java code to begin implementing the design for class Transaction specified in Figs. 13.9 and 13.10. Be sure to include private reference-type attributes based on class Transaction's associations. Also be sure to include public *get* methods that provide access to any of these private attributes that the subclasses require to perform their tasks.

13.4 ATM Case Study Implementation

This section contains the complete working 673-line implementation of the ATM system. We consider the classes in the order in which we identified them in Section 12.3—ATM, Screen, Keypad, CashDispenser, DepositSlot, Account, BankDatabase, Transaction, BalanceInquiry, Withdrawal and Deposit.

We apply the guidelines discussed in Sections 13.2—13.3 to code these classes based on how we modeled them in the UML class diagrams of Figs. 13.9 and 13.10. To develop the bodies of class methods, we refer to the activity diagrams in Section 12.5 and the communication and sequence diagrams presented in Section 12.7. Note that our ATM design does not specify all the program logic and may not specify all the attributes and operations required to complete the ATM implementation. This is a normal part of the object-oriented design process. As we implement the system, we complete the program logic and add attributes and behaviors as necessary to construct the ATM system specified by the requirements document in Section 12.2.

We conclude the discussion by presenting a Java application (ATMCaseStudy) that starts the ATM and puts the other classes in the system in use. Recall that we are developing a first version of the ATM system that runs on a personal computer and uses the computer's keyboard and monitor to approximate the ATM's keypad and screen. We also only simulate the actions of the ATM's cash dispenser and deposit slot. We attempt to implement the system, however, so that real hardware versions of these devices could be integrated without significant changes in the code.

13.4.1 Class ATM

Class ATM (Fig. 13.13) represents the ATM as a whole. Lines 6–12 implement the class's attributes. We determine all but one of these attributes from the UML class diagrams of Figs. 13.9 and 13.10. Note that we implement the UML Boolean attribute user-Authenticated in Fig. 13.10 as a boolean in Java (line 6). Line 7 declares an attribute not found in our UML design—an int attribute currentAccountNumber that keeps track of the account number of the current authenticated user. We'll soon see how the class uses this attribute. Lines 8–12 declare reference-type attributes corresponding to the ATM class's associations modeled in the class diagram of Fig. 13.9. These attributes allow the ATM to access its parts (i.e., its Screen, Keypad, CashDispenser and DepositSlot) and interact with the bank's account-information database (i.e., a BankDatabase object).

```java
1   // ATM.java
2   // Represents an automated teller machine
3
4   public class ATM
5   {
6      private boolean userAuthenticated; // whether user is authenticated
7      private int currentAccountNumber; // current user's account number
8      private Screen screen; // ATM's screen
9      private Keypad keypad; // ATM's keypad
10     private CashDispenser cashDispenser; // ATM's cash dispenser
11     private DepositSlot depositSlot; // ATM's deposit slot
12     private BankDatabase bankDatabase; // account information database
13
14     // constants corresponding to main menu options
15     private static final int BALANCE_INQUIRY = 1;
16     private static final int WITHDRAWAL = 2;
17     private static final int DEPOSIT = 3;
18     private static final int EXIT = 4;
19
20     // no-argument ATM constructor initializes instance variables
21     public ATM()
22     {
23        userAuthenticated = false; // user is not authenticated to start
24        currentAccountNumber = 0; // no current account number to start
25        screen = new Screen(); // create screen
26        keypad = new Keypad(); // create keypad
27        cashDispenser = new CashDispenser(); // create cash dispenser
```

Fig. 13.13 | Class ATM represents the ATM. (Part 1 of 4.)

```
28          depositSlot = new DepositSlot(); // create deposit slot
29          bankDatabase = new BankDatabase(); // create acct info database
30      } // end no-argument ATM constructor
31
32      // start ATM
33      public void run()
34      {
35          // welcome and authenticate user; perform transactions
36          while ( true )
37          {
38              // loop while user is not yet authenticated
39              while ( !userAuthenticated )
40              {
41                  screen.displayMessageLine( "\nWelcome!" );
42                  authenticateUser(); // authenticate user
43              } // end while
44
45              performTransactions(); // user is now authenticated
46              userAuthenticated = false; // reset before next ATM session
47              currentAccountNumber = 0; // reset before next ATM session
48              screen.displayMessageLine( "\nThank you! Goodbye!" );
49          } // end while
50      } // end method run
51
52      // attempts to authenticate user against database
53      private void authenticateUser()
54      {
55          screen.displayMessage( "\nPlease enter your account number: " );
56          int accountNumber = keypad.getInput(); // input account number
57          screen.displayMessage( "\nEnter your PIN: " ); // prompt for PIN
58          int pin = keypad.getInput(); // input PIN
59
60          // set userAuthenticated to boolean value returned by database
61          userAuthenticated =
62              bankDatabase.authenticateUser( accountNumber, pin );
63
64          // check whether authentication succeeded
65          if ( userAuthenticated )
66          {
67              currentAccountNumber = accountNumber; // save user's account #
68          } // end if
69          else
70              screen.displayMessageLine(
71                  "Invalid account number or PIN. Please try again." );
72      } // end method authenticateUser
73
74      // display the main menu and perform transactions
75      private void performTransactions()
76      {
77          // local variable to store transaction currently being processed
78          Transaction currentTransaction = null;
79
80          boolean userExited = false; // user has not chosen to exit
```

Fig. 13.13 | Class ATM represents the ATM. (Part 2 of 4.)

```
81
82          // loop while user has not chosen option to exit system
83          while ( !userExited )
84          {
85             // show main menu and get user selection
86             int mainMenuSelection = displayMainMenu();
87
88             // decide how to proceed based on user's menu selection
89             switch ( mainMenuSelection )
90             {
91                // user chose to perform one of three transaction types
92                case BALANCE_INQUIRY:
93                case WITHDRAWAL:
94                case DEPOSIT:
95
96                   // initialize as new object of chosen type
97                   currentTransaction =
98                      createTransaction( mainMenuSelection );
99
100                  currentTransaction.execute(); // execute transaction
101                  break;
102               case EXIT: // user chose to terminate session
103                  screen.displayMessageLine( "\nExiting the system..." );
104                  userExited = true; // this ATM session should end
105                  break;
106               default: // user did not enter an integer from 1-4
107                  screen.displayMessageLine(
108                     "\nYou did not enter a valid selection. Try again." );
109                  break;
110            } // end switch
111         } // end while
112      } // end method performTransactions
113
114      // display the main menu and return an input selection
115      private int displayMainMenu()
116      {
117         screen.displayMessageLine( "\nMain menu:" );
118         screen.displayMessageLine( "1 - View my balance" );
119         screen.displayMessageLine( "2 - Withdraw cash" );
120         screen.displayMessageLine( "3 - Deposit funds" );
121         screen.displayMessageLine( "4 - Exit\n" );
122         screen.displayMessage( "Enter a choice: " );
123         return keypad.getInput(); // return user's selection
124      } // end method displayMainMenu
125
126      // return object of specified Transaction subclass
127      private Transaction createTransaction( int type )
128      {
129         Transaction temp = null; // temporary Transaction variable
130
131         // determine which type of Transaction to create
132         switch ( type )
133         {
```

Fig. 13.13 | Class ATM represents the ATM. (Part 3 of 4.)

```
134              case BALANCE_INQUIRY: // create new BalanceInquiry transaction
135                 temp = new BalanceInquiry(
136                    currentAccountNumber, screen, bankDatabase );
137                 break;
138              case WITHDRAWAL: // create new Withdrawal transaction
139                 temp = new Withdrawal( currentAccountNumber, screen,
140                    bankDatabase, keypad, cashDispenser );
141                 break;
142              case DEPOSIT: // create new Deposit transaction
143                 temp = new Deposit( currentAccountNumber, screen,
144                    bankDatabase, keypad, depositSlot );
145                 break;
146           } // end switch
147
148           return temp; // return the newly created object
149        } // end method createTransaction
150  } // end class ATM
```

Fig. 13.13 | Class ATM represents the ATM. (Part 4 of 4.)

Lines 15–18 declare integer constants that correspond to the four options in the ATM's main menu (i.e., balance inquiry, withdrawal, deposit and exit). Lines 21–30 declare the constructor, which initializes the class's attributes. When an ATM object is first created, no user is authenticated, so line 23 initializes userAuthenticated to false. Likewise, line 24 initializes currentAccountNumber to 0 because there is no current user yet. Lines 25–28 instantiate new objects to represent the ATM's parts. Recall that class ATM has composition relationships with classes Screen, Keypad, CashDispenser and DepositSlot, so class ATM is responsible for their creation. Line 29 creates a new BankDatabase. [*Note: If this were a real ATM system, the ATM class would receive a reference to an existing database object created by the bank. However, in this implementation we are only simulating the bank's database, so class ATM creates the BankDatabase object with which it interacts.*]

ATM *Method* run

The class diagram of Fig. 13.10 does not list any operations for class ATM. We now implement one operation (i.e., public method) in class ATM that allows an external client of the class (i.e., class ATMCaseStudy) to tell the ATM to run. ATM method run (lines 33–50) uses an infinite loop (lines 36–49) to repeatedly welcome a user, attempt to authenticate the user and, if authentication succeeds, allow the user to perform transactions. After an authenticated user performs the desired transactions and chooses to exit, the ATM resets itself, displays a goodbye message to the user and restarts the process. We use an infinite loop here to simulate the fact that an ATM appears to run continuously until the bank turns it off (an action beyond the user's control). An ATM user has the option to exit the system but not the ability to turn off the ATM completely.

Authenticating a User

In method run's infinite loop, lines 39–43 cause the ATM to repeatedly welcome and attempt to authenticate the user as long as the user has not been authenticated (i.e., !userAuthenticated is true). Line 41 invokes method displayMessageLine of the ATM's screen to display a welcome message. Like Screen method displayMessage designed in the case study, method displayMessageLine (declared in lines 13–16 of Fig. 13.14) displays a message to the user, but this method also outputs a newline after the message. We've added this method during implementation to give class Screen's clients more control over the placement of displayed messages. Line 42 invokes class ATM's private utility method authenticateUser (declared in lines 53–72) to attempt to authenticate the user.

We refer to the requirements document to determine the steps necessary to authenticate the user before allowing transactions to occur. Line 55 of method authenticateUser invokes method displayMessage of the screen to prompt the user to enter an account number. Line 56 invokes method getInput of the keypad to obtain the user's input, then stores the integer value entered by the user in a local variable accountNumber. Method authenticateUser next prompts the user to enter a PIN (line 57), and stores the PIN input by the user in a local variable pin (line 58). Next, lines 61–62 attempt to authenticate the user by passing the accountNumber and pin entered by the user to the bankDatabase's authenticateUser method. Class ATM sets its userAuthenticated attribute to the boolean value returned by this method—userAuthenticated becomes true if authentication succeeds (i.e., accountNumber and pin match those of an existing Account in bankDatabase) and remains false otherwise. If userAuthenticated is true, line 67 saves the account number entered by the user (i.e., accountNumber) in the ATM attribute currentAccountNumber. The other ATM methods use this variable whenever an ATM session requires access to the user's account number. If userAuthenticated is false, lines 70–71 use the screen's displayMessageLine method to indicate that an invalid account number and/or PIN was entered and the user must try again. Note that we set currentAccountNumber only after authenticating the user's account number and the associated PIN—if the database could not authenticate the user, currentAccountNumber remains 0.

After method run attempts to authenticate the user (line 42), if userAuthenticated is still false, the while loop in lines 39–43 executes again. If userAuthenticated is now true, the loop terminates and control continues with line 45, which calls class ATM's utility method performTransactions.

Performing Transactions
Method performTransactions (lines 75–112) carries out an ATM session for an authenticated user. Line 78 declares a local Transaction variable to which we will assign a BalanceInquiry, Withdrawal or Deposit object representing the ATM transaction currently being processed. Note that we use a Transaction variable here to allow us to take advantage of polymorphism. Also note that we name this variable after the role name included in the class diagram of Fig. 12.7—currentTransaction. Line 80 declares another local variable—a boolean called userExited that keeps track of whether the user has chosen to exit. This variable controls a while loop (lines 83–111) that allows the user to execute an unlimited number of transactions before choosing to exit. Within this loop, line 86 displays the main menu and obtains the user's menu selection by calling an ATM utility method displayMainMenu (declared in lines 115–124). This method displays the main menu by invoking methods of the ATM's screen and returns a menu selection obtained from the user through the ATM's keypad. Line 86 stores the user's selection returned by displayMainMenu in local variable mainMenuSelection.

After obtaining a main menu selection, method performTransactions uses a switch statement (lines 89–110) to respond to the selection appropriately. If mainMenuSelection is equal to any of the three integer constants representing transaction types (i.e., if the user chose to perform a transaction), lines 97–98 call utility method createTransaction (declared in lines 127–149) to return a newly instantiated object of the type that corresponds to the selected transaction. Variable currentTransaction is assigned the reference returned by createTransaction, then line 100 invokes method execute of this transaction to execute it. We'll discuss Transaction method execute and the three Transaction subclasses shortly. We assign the Transaction variable currentTransaction an object of one of the three Transaction subclasses so that we can execute transactions polymorphically. For example, if the user chooses to perform a balance inquiry, mainMenuSelection equals BALANCE_INQUIRY, leading createTransaction to return a BalanceInquiry object. Thus, currentTransaction refers to a BalanceInquiry, and invoking currentTransaction.execute() results in BalanceInquiry's version of execute being called.

Creating a Transaction

Method createTransaction (lines 127–149) uses a switch statement (lines 132–146) to instantiate a new Transaction subclass object of the type indicated by the parameter type. Recall that method performTransactions passes mainMenuSelection to this method only when mainMenuSelection contains a value corresponding to one of the three transaction types. Therefore type is BALANCE_INQUIRY, WITHDRAWAL or DEPOSIT. Each case in the switch statement instantiates a new object by calling the appropriate Transaction subclass constructor. Each constructor has a unique parameter list, based on the specific data required to initialize the subclass object. A BalanceInquiry requires only the account number of the current user and references to the ATM's screen and the bankDatabase. In addition to these parameters, a Withdrawal requires references to the ATM's keypad and cashDispenser, and a Deposit requires references to the ATM's keypad and depositSlot. We discuss the transaction classes in more detail in Sections 13.4.8—13.4.11.

Exiting the Main Menu and Processing Invalid Selections

After executing a transaction (line 100 in performTransactions), userExited remains false and lines 83–111 repeat, returning the user to the main menu. However, if a user does not perform a transaction and instead selects the main menu option to exit, line 104 sets userExited to true, causing the condition of the while loop (!userExited) to become false. This while is the final statement of method performTransactions, so control returns to the calling method run. If the user enters an invalid main menu selection (i.e., not an integer from 1–4), lines 107–108 display an appropriate error message, userExited remains false and the user returns to the main menu to try again.

Awaiting the Next ATM User

When performTransactions returns control to method run, the user has chosen to exit the system, so lines 46–47 reset the ATM's attributes userAuthenticated and currentAccountNumber to prepare for the next ATM user. Line 48 displays a goodbye message before the ATM starts over and welcomes the next user.

13.4.2 Class Screen

Class Screen (Fig. 13.14) represents the screen of the ATM and encapsulates all aspects of displaying output to the user. Class Screen approximates a real ATM's screen with a computer monitor and outputs text messages using standard console output methods System.out.print, System.out.println and System.out.printf. In this case study, we designed class Screen to have one operation—displayMessage. For greater flexibility in displaying messages to the Screen, we now declare three Screen methods—displayMessage, displayMessageLine and displayDollarAmount.

```
 1   // Screen.java
 2   // Represents the screen of the ATM
 3
 4   public class Screen
 5   {
 6      // display a message without a carriage return
 7      public void displayMessage( String message )
 8      {
 9         System.out.print( message );
10      } // end method displayMessage
11
12      // display a message with a carriage return
13      public void displayMessageLine( String message )
14      {
15         System.out.println( message );
16      } // end method displayMessageLine
17
18      // displays a dollar amount
19      public void displayDollarAmount( double amount )
20      {
21         System.out.printf( "$%,.2f", amount );
22      } // end method displayDollarAmount
23   } // end class Screen
```

Fig. 13.14 | Class Screen represents the screen of the ATM.

Method displayMessage (lines 7–10) takes a String argument and prints it to the console. The cursor stays on the same line, making this method appropriate for displaying prompts to the user. Method displayMessageLine (lines 13–16) does the same using System.out.println, which outputs a newline to move the cursor to the next line. Finally, method displayDollarAmount (lines 19–22) outputs a properly formatted dollar amount (e.g., $1,234.56). Line 21 uses System.out.printf to output a double value formatted with commas to increase readability and two decimal places.

13.4.3 Class Keypad

Class Keypad (Fig. 13.15) represents the keypad of the ATM and is responsible for receiving all user input. Recall that we are simulating this hardware, so we use the computer's keyboard to approximate the keypad. We use class Scanner to obtain console input from the user. A computer keyboard contains many keys not found on the ATM's keypad. However, we assume that the user presses only the keys on the computer keyboard that also appear on the keypad—the keys numbered 0–9 and the *Enter* key.

```
 1   // Keypad.java
 2   // Represents the keypad of the ATM
 3   import java.util.Scanner; // program uses Scanner to obtain user input
 4
 5   public class Keypad
 6   {
 7      private Scanner input; // reads data from the command line
```

Fig. 13.15 | Class Keypad represents the ATM's keypad. (Part 1 of 2.)

```
 8
 9      // no-argument constructor initializes the Scanner
10      public Keypad()
11      {
12         input = new Scanner( System.in );
13      } // end no-argument Keypad constructor
14
15      // return an integer value entered by user
16      public int getInput()
17      {
18         return input.nextInt(); // we assume that user enters an integer
19      } // end method getInput
20   } // end class Keypad
```

Fig. 13.15 | Class Keypad represents the ATM's keypad. (Part 2 of 2.)

Line 3 of class Keypad imports class Scanner for use in class Keypad. Line 7 declares Scanner variable input as an instance variable. Line 12 in the constructor creates a new Scanner object that reads input from the standard input stream (System.in) and assigns the object's reference to variable input. Method getInput (declared in lines 16–19) invokes Scanner method nextInt (line 18) to return the next integer input by the user. [*Note:* Method nextInt can throw an InputMismatchException if the user enters non-integer input. Because the real ATM's keypad permits only integer input, we assume that no exception will occur and do not attempt to fix this problem. See Chapter 11, Exception Handling, for information on catching exceptions.] Recall that nextInt obtains all the input used by the ATM. Keypad's getInput method simply returns the integer input by the user. If a client of class Keypad requires input that satisfies some criteria (i.e., a number corresponding to a valid menu option), the client must perform the error checking.

13.4.4 Class CashDispenser

Class CashDispenser (Fig. 13.16) represents the cash dispenser of the ATM. Line 7 declares constant INITIAL_COUNT, which indicates the initial count of bills in the cash dispenser when the ATM starts (i.e., 500). Line 8 implements attribute count (modeled in Fig. 13.10), which keeps track of the number of bills remaining in the CashDispenser at any time. The constructor (lines 11–14) sets count to the initial count. CashDispenser has two public methods—dispenseCash (lines 17–21) and isSufficientCashAvailable (lines 24–32). The class trusts that a client (i.e., Withdrawal) calls dispenseCash only after establishing that sufficient cash is available by calling isSufficientCashAvailable. Thus, dispenseCash simply simulates dispensing the requested amount without checking whether sufficient cash is available.

```
1   // CashDispenser.java
2   // Represents the cash dispenser of the ATM
3
4   public class CashDispenser
5   {
```

Fig. 13.16 | Class CashDispenser represents the ATM's cash dispenser. (Part 1 of 2.)

```
6     // the default initial number of bills in the cash dispenser
7     private final static int INITIAL_COUNT = 500;
8     private int count; // number of $20 bills remaining
9
10    // no-argument CashDispenser constructor initializes count to default
11    public CashDispenser()
12    {
13       count = INITIAL_COUNT; // set count attribute to default
14    } // end CashDispenser constructor
15
16    // simulates dispensing of specified amount of cash
17    public void dispenseCash( int amount )
18    {
19       int billsRequired = amount / 20; // number of $20 bills required
20       count -= billsRequired; // update the count of bills
21    } // end method dispenseCash
22
23    // indicates whether cash dispenser can dispense desired amount
24    public boolean isSufficientCashAvailable( int amount )
25    {
26       int billsRequired = amount / 20; // number of $20 bills required
27
28       if ( count >= billsRequired  )
29          return true; // enough bills available
30       else
31          return false; // not enough bills available
32    } // end method isSufficientCashAvailable
33 } // end class CashDispenser
```

Fig. 13.16 | Class `CashDispenser` represents the ATM's cash dispenser. (Part 2 of 2.)

Method `isSufficientCashAvailable` (lines 24–32) has a parameter amount that specifies the amount of cash in question. Line 26 calculates the number of $20 bills required to dispense the specified amount. The ATM allows the user to choose only withdrawal amounts that are multiples of $20, so we divide amount by 20 to obtain the number of billsRequired. Lines 28–31 return true if the CashDispenser's count is greater than or equal to billsRequired (i.e., enough bills are available) and false otherwise (i.e., not enough bills). For example, if a user wishes to withdraw $80 (i.e., billsRequired is 4), but only three bills remain (i.e., count is 3), the method returns false.

Method dispenseCash (lines 17–21) simulates cash dispensing. If our system were hooked up to a real hardware cash dispenser, this method would interact with the device to physically dispense cash. Our version of the method simply decreases the count of bills remaining by the number required to dispense the specified amount (line 20). Note that it's the responsibility of the client of the class (i.e., Withdrawal) to inform the user that cash has been dispensed—CashDispenser cannot interact directly with Screen.

13.4.5 Class DepositSlot

Class DepositSlot (Fig. 13.17) represents the ATM's deposit slot. Like class CashDispenser, class DepositSlot merely simulates the functionality of a real hardware deposit slot. DepositSlot has no attributes and only one method—isEnvelopeReceived (lines 8–11)—which indicates whether a deposit envelope was received.

```
 I   // DepositSlot.java
 2   // Represents the deposit slot of the ATM
 3
 4   public class DepositSlot
 5   {
 6      // indicates whether envelope was received (always returns true,
 7      // because this is only a software simulation of a real deposit slot)
 8      public boolean isEnvelopeReceived()
 9      {
10         return true; // deposit envelope was received
11      } // end method isEnvelopeReceived
12   } // end class DepositSlot
```

Fig. 13.17 | Class `DepositSlot` represents the ATM's deposit slot.

Recall from the requirements document that the ATM allows the user up to two minutes to insert an envelope. The current version of method `isEnvelopeReceived` simply returns `true` immediately (line 10), because this is only a software simulation, and we assume that the user has inserted an envelope within the required time frame. If an actual hardware deposit slot were connected to our system, method `isEnvelopeReceived` might be implemented to wait for a maximum of two minutes to receive a signal from the hardware deposit slot indicating that the user has indeed inserted a deposit envelope. If `isEnvelopeReceived` were to receive such a signal within two minutes, the method would return `true`. If two minutes elapsed and the method still had not received a signal, then the method would return `false`.

13.4.6 Class Account

Class `Account` (Fig. 13.18) represents a bank account. Each `Account` has four attributes (modeled in Fig. 13.10)—accountNumber, pin, availableBalance and totalBalance. Lines 6–9 implement these attributes as `private` fields. Variable `availableBalance` represents the amount of funds available for withdrawal. Variable `totalBalance` represents the amount of funds available, plus the amount of deposited funds still pending confirmation or clearance.

```
 I   // Account.java
 2   // Represents a bank account
 3
 4   public class Account
 5   {
 6      private int accountNumber; // account number
 7      private int pin; // PIN for authentication
 8      private double availableBalance; // funds available for withdrawal
 9      private double totalBalance; // funds available + pending deposits
10
11      // Account constructor initializes attributes
12      public Account( int theAccountNumber, int thePIN,
13         double theAvailableBalance, double theTotalBalance )
14      {
15         accountNumber = theAccountNumber;
```

Fig. 13.18 | Class `Account` represents a bank account. (Part I of 2.)

```
16            pin = thePIN;
17            availableBalance = theAvailableBalance;
18            totalBalance = theTotalBalance;
19        } // end Account constructor
20
21        // determines whether a user-specified PIN matches PIN in Account
22        public boolean validatePIN( int userPIN )
23        {
24            if ( userPIN == pin )
25                return true;
26            else
27                return false;
28        } // end method validatePIN
29
30        // returns available balance
31        public double getAvailableBalance()
32        {
33            return availableBalance;
34        } // end getAvailableBalance
35
36        // returns the total balance
37        public double getTotalBalance()
38        {
39            return totalBalance;
40        } // end method getTotalBalance
41
42        // credits an amount to the account
43        public void credit( double amount )
44        {
45            totalBalance += amount; // add to total balance
46        } // end method credit
47
48        // debits an amount from the account
49        public void debit( double amount )
50        {
51            availableBalance -= amount; // subtract from available balance
52            totalBalance -= amount; // subtract from total balance
53        } // end method debit
54
55        // returns account number
56        public int getAccountNumber()
57        {
58            return accountNumber;
59        } // end method getAccountNumber
60    } // end class Account
```

Fig. 13.18 | Class Account represents a bank account. (Part 2 of 2.)

The Account class has a constructor (lines 12–19) that takes an account number, the PIN established for the account, the account's initial available balance and the account's initial total balance as arguments. Lines 15–18 assign these values to the class's attributes (i.e., fields).

Method validatePIN (lines 22–28) determines whether a user-specified PIN (i.e., parameter userPIN) matches the PIN associated with the account (i.e., attribute pin).

Recall that we modeled this method's parameter userPIN in Fig. 12.19. If the two PINs match, the method returns true (line 25); otherwise, it returns false (line 27).

Methods getAvailableBalance (lines 31–34) and getTotalBalance (lines 37–40) are *get* methods that return the values of double attributes availableBalance and total-Balance, respectively.

Method credit (lines 43–46) adds an amount of money (i.e., parameter amount) to an Account as part of a deposit transaction. Note that this method adds the amount only to attribute totalBalance (line 45). The money credited to an account during a deposit does not become available immediately, so we modify only the total balance. We assume that the bank updates the available balance appropriately at a later time. Our implementation of class Account includes only methods required for carrying out ATM transactions. Therefore, we omit the methods that some other bank system would invoke to add to attribute availableBalance (to confirm a deposit) or subtract from attribute totalBalance (to reject a deposit).

Method debit (lines 49–53) subtracts an amount of money (i.e., parameter amount) from an Account as part of a withdrawal transaction. This method subtracts the amount from both attribute availableBalance (line 51) and attribute totalBalance (line 52), because a withdrawal affects both measures of an account balance.

Method getAccountNumber (lines 56–59) provides access to an Account's account-Number. We include this method in our implementation so that a client of the class (i.e., BankDatabase) can identify a particular Account. For example, BankDatabase contains many Account objects, and it can invoke this method on each of its Account objects to locate the one with a specific account number.

13.4.7 Class BankDatabase

Class BankDatabase (Fig. 13.19) models the bank's database with which the ATM interacts to access and modify a user's account information. [*Note:* We study database access in Chapter 28. For now we model the database as an array. An exercise in Chapter 28 asks you to reimplement this portion of the ATM using an actual database.]

```
1   // BankDatabase.java
2   // Represents the bank account information database
3
4   public class BankDatabase
5   {
6      private Account[] accounts; // array of Accounts
7
8      // no-argument BankDatabase constructor initializes accounts
9      public BankDatabase()
10     {
11        accounts = new Account[ 2 ]; // just 2 accounts for testing
12        accounts[ 0 ] = new Account( 12345, 54321, 1000.0, 1200.0 );
13        accounts[ 1 ] = new Account( 98765, 56789, 200.0, 200.0 );
14     } // end no-argument BankDatabase constructor
15
```

Fig. 13.19 | Class BankDatabase represents the bank's account information database. (Part 1 of 2.)

```
16      // retrieve Account object containing specified account number
17      private Account getAccount( int accountNumber )
18      {
19         // loop through accounts searching for matching account number
20         for ( Account currentAccount : accounts )
21         {
22            // return current account if match found
23            if ( currentAccount.getAccountNumber() == accountNumber )
24               return currentAccount;
25         } // end for
26
27         return null; // if no matching account was found, return null
28      } // end method getAccount
29
30      // determine whether user-specified account number and PIN match
31      // those of an account in the database
32      public boolean authenticateUser( int userAccountNumber, int userPIN )
33      {
34         // attempt to retrieve the account with the account number
35         Account userAccount = getAccount( userAccountNumber );
36
37         // if account exists, return result of Account method validatePIN
38         if ( userAccount != null )
39            return userAccount.validatePIN( userPIN );
40         else
41            return false; // account number not found, so return false
42      } // end method authenticateUser
43
44      // return available balance of Account with specified account number
45      public double getAvailableBalance( int userAccountNumber )
46      {
47         return getAccount( userAccountNumber ).getAvailableBalance();
48      } // end method getAvailableBalance
49
50      // return total balance of Account with specified account number
51      public double getTotalBalance( int userAccountNumber )
52      {
53         return getAccount( userAccountNumber ).getTotalBalance();
54      } // end method getTotalBalance
55
56      // credit an amount to Account with specified account number
57      public void credit( int userAccountNumber, double amount )
58      {
59         getAccount( userAccountNumber ).credit( amount );
60      } // end method credit
61
62      // debit an amount from Account with specified account number
63      public void debit( int userAccountNumber, double amount )
64      {
65         getAccount( userAccountNumber ).debit( amount );
66      } // end method debit
67   } // end class BankDatabase
```

Fig. 13.19 | Class BankDatabase represents the bank's account information database. (Part 2 of 2.)

We determine one reference-type attribute for class BankDatabase based on its composition relationship with class Account. Recall from Fig. 13.9 that a BankDatabase is composed of zero or more objects of class Account. Line 6 implements attribute accounts—an array of Account objects—to implement this composition relationship. Class BankDatabase has a no-argument constructor (lines 9–14) that initializes accounts to contain a set of new Account objects. For the sake of testing the system, we declare accounts to hold just two array elements (line 11), which we instantiate as new Account objects with test data (lines 12–13). Note that the Account constructor has four parameters—the account number, the PIN assigned to the account, the initial available balance and the initial total balance. Recall that class BankDatabase serves as an intermediary between class ATM and the actual Account objects that contain a user's account information. Thus, the methods of class BankDatabase do nothing more than invoke the corresponding methods of the Account object belonging to the current ATM user.

We include private utility method getAccount (lines 17–28) to allow the BankDatabase to obtain a reference to a particular Account within array accounts. To locate the user's Account, the BankDatabase compares the value returned by method getAccountNumber for each element of accounts to a specified account number until it finds a match. Lines 20–25 traverse the accounts array. If the account number of currentAccount equals the value of parameter accountNumber, the method immediately returns the currentAccount. If no account has the given account number, then line 27 returns null.

Method authenticateUser (lines 32–42) proves or disproves the identity of an ATM user. This method takes a user-specified account number and PIN as arguments and indicates whether they match the account number and PIN of an Account in the database. Line 35 calls method getAccount, which returns either an Account with userAccountNumber as its account number or null to indicate that userAccountNumber is invalid. If getAccount returns an Account object, line 39 returns the boolean value returned by that object's validatePIN method. BankDatabase's authenticateUser method does not perform the PIN comparison itself—rather, it forwards userPIN to the Account object's validatePIN method to do so. The value returned by Account method validatePIN indicates whether the user-specified PIN matches the PIN of the user's Account, so method authenticateUser simply returns this value to the class's client (i.e., ATM).

BankDatabase trusts the ATM to invoke method authenticateUser and receive a return value of true before allowing the user to perform transactions. BankDatabase also trusts that each Transaction object created by the ATM contains the valid account number of the current authenticated user and that this is the account number passed to the remaining BankDatabase methods as argument userAccountNumber. Methods getAvailableBalance (lines 45–48), getTotalBalance (lines 51–54), credit (lines 57–60) and debit (lines 63–66) therefore simply retrieve the user's Account object with utility method getAccount, then invoke the appropriate Account method on that object. We know that the calls to getAccount from these methods will never return null, because userAccountNumber must refer to an existing Account. Methods getAvailableBalance and getTotalBalance return the values returned by the corresponding Account methods. Also note that credit and debit simply redirect parameter amount to the Account methods they invoke.

13.4.8 Class Transaction

Class Transaction (Fig. 13.20) is an abstract superclass that represents the notion of an ATM transaction. It contains the common features of subclasses BalanceInquiry, Withdrawal and Deposit. This class expands upon the "skeleton" code first developed in Section 13.3. Line 4 declares this class to be abstract. Lines 6–8 declare the class's private attributes. Recall from the class diagram of Fig. 13.10 that class Transaction contains an attribute accountNumber (line 6) that indicates the account involved in the Transaction. We derive attributes screen (line 7) and bankDatabase (line 8) from class Transaction's associations modeled in Fig. 13.9—all transactions require access to the ATM's screen and the bank's database.

```java
 1   // Transaction.java
 2   // Abstract superclass Transaction represents an ATM transaction
 3
 4   public abstract class Transaction
 5   {
 6      private int accountNumber; // indicates account involved
 7      private Screen screen; // ATM's screen
 8      private BankDatabase bankDatabase; // account info database
 9
10      // Transaction constructor invoked by subclasses using super()
11      public Transaction( int userAccountNumber, Screen atmScreen,
12         BankDatabase atmBankDatabase )
13      {
14         accountNumber = userAccountNumber;
15         screen = atmScreen;
16         bankDatabase = atmBankDatabase;
17      } // end Transaction constructor
18
19      // return account number
20      public int getAccountNumber()
21      {
22         return accountNumber;
23      } // end method getAccountNumber
24
25      // return reference to screen
26      public Screen getScreen()
27      {
28         return screen;
29      } // end method getScreen
30
31      // return reference to bank database
32      public BankDatabase getBankDatabase()
33      {
34         return bankDatabase;
35      } // end method getBankDatabase
36
37      // perform the transaction (overridden by each subclass)
38      abstract public void execute();
39   } // end class Transaction
```

Fig. 13.20 | Abstract superclass Transaction represents an ATM transaction.

Class Transaction has a constructor (lines 11–17) that takes as arguments the current user's account number and references to the ATM's screen and the bank's database. Because Transaction is an abstract class, this constructor will be called only by the constructors of the Transaction subclasses.

The class has three `public` *get* methods—getAccountNumber (lines 20–23), get-Screen (lines 26–29) and getBankDatabase (lines 32–35). These are inherited by Transaction subclasses and used to gain access to class Transaction's private attributes.

Class Transaction also declares abstract method execute (line 38). It does not make sense to provide this method's implementation, because a generic transaction cannot be executed. So, we declare this method abstract and force each Transaction subclass to provide a concrete implementation that executes that particular type of transaction.

13.4.9 Class BalanceInquiry

Class BalanceInquiry (Fig. 13.21) extends Transaction and represents a balance-inquiry ATM transaction. BalanceInquiry does not have any attributes of its own, but it inherits Transaction attributes accountNumber, screen and bankDatabase, which are accessible through Transaction's public *get* methods. The BalanceInquiry constructor takes arguments corresponding to these attributes and simply forwards them to Transaction's constructor using super (line 10).

Class BalanceInquiry overrides Transaction's abstract method execute to provide a concrete implementation (lines 14–36) that performs the steps involved in a balance inquiry. Lines 18–19 get references to the bank database and the ATM's screen by invoking methods inherited from superclass Transaction. Lines 22–23 retrieve the available balance of the account involved by invoking method getAvailableBalance of bankDatabase. Note that line 23 uses inherited method getAccountNumber to get the account number of the current user, which it then passes to getAvailableBalance. Lines 26–27 retrieve the total balance of the current user's account. Lines 30–35 display the balance information on the ATM's screen. Recall that displayDollarAmount takes a double argument and outputs it to the screen formatted as a dollar amount. For example, if a user's availableBalance is 1000.5, line 32 outputs $1,000.50. Note that line 35 inserts a blank line of output to separate the balance information from subsequent output (i.e., the main menu repeated by class ATM after executing the BalanceInquiry).

```
1   // BalanceInquiry.java
2   // Represents a balance inquiry ATM transaction
3
4   public class BalanceInquiry extends Transaction
5   {
6      // BalanceInquiry constructor
7      public BalanceInquiry( int userAccountNumber, Screen atmScreen,
8         BankDatabase atmBankDatabase )
9      {
10        super( userAccountNumber, atmScreen, atmBankDatabase );
11     } // end BalanceInquiry constructor
12
13     // performs the transaction
14     @Override
15     public void execute()
16     {
17        // get references to bank database and screen
18        BankDatabase bankDatabase = getBankDatabase();
19        Screen screen = getScreen();
```

Fig. 13.21 | Class BalanceInquiry represents a balance-inquiry ATM transaction. (Part 1 of 2.)

```
20
21        // get the available balance for the account involved
22        double availableBalance =
23           bankDatabase.getAvailableBalance( getAccountNumber() );
24
25        // get the total balance for the account involved
26        double totalBalance =
27           bankDatabase.getTotalBalance( getAccountNumber() );
28
29        // display the balance information on the screen
30        screen.displayMessageLine( "\nBalance Information:" );
31        screen.displayMessage( " - Available balance: " );
32        screen.displayDollarAmount( availableBalance );
33        screen.displayMessage( "\n - Total balance:      " );
34        screen.displayDollarAmount( totalBalance );
35        screen.displayMessageLine( "" );
36     } // end method execute
37  } // end class BalanceInquiry
```

Fig. 13.21 | Class `BalanceInquiry` represents a balance-inquiry ATM transaction. (Part 2 of 2.)

13.4.10 Class `Withdrawal`

Class `Withdrawal` (Fig. 13.22) extends `Transaction` and represents a withdrawal ATM transaction. This class expands upon the "skeleton" code for this class developed in Fig. 13.12. Recall from the class diagram of Fig. 13.10 that class `Withdrawal` has one attribute, amount, which line 6 implements as an `int` field. Figure 13.9 models associations between class `Withdrawal` and classes `Keypad` and `CashDispenser`, for which lines 7–8 implement reference-type attributes keypad and cashDispenser, respectively. Line 11 declares a constant corresponding to the cancel menu option. We'll soon discuss how the class uses this constant.

```
1   // Withdrawal.java
2   // Represents a withdrawal ATM transaction
3
4   public class Withdrawal extends Transaction
5   {
6      private int amount; // amount to withdraw
7      private Keypad keypad; // reference to keypad
8      private CashDispenser cashDispenser; // reference to cash dispenser
9
10     // constant corresponding to menu option to cancel
11     private final static int CANCELED = 6;
12
13     // Withdrawal constructor
14     public Withdrawal( int userAccountNumber, Screen atmScreen,
15        BankDatabase atmBankDatabase, Keypad atmKeypad,
16        CashDispenser atmCashDispenser )
17     {
18        // initialize superclass variables
19        super( userAccountNumber, atmScreen, atmBankDatabase );
```

Fig. 13.22 | Class `Withdrawal` represents a withdrawal ATM transaction. (Part 1 of 4.)

```
20
21          // initialize references to keypad and cash dispenser
22          keypad = atmKeypad;
23          cashDispenser = atmCashDispenser;
24       } // end Withdrawal constructor
25
26       // perform transaction
27       @Override
28       public void execute()
29       {
30          boolean cashDispensed = false; // cash was not dispensed yet
31          double availableBalance; // amount available for withdrawal
32
33          // get references to bank database and screen
34          BankDatabase bankDatabase = getBankDatabase();
35          Screen screen = getScreen();
36
37          // loop until cash is dispensed or the user cancels
38          do
39          {
40             // obtain a chosen withdrawal amount from the user
41             amount = displayMenuOfAmounts();
42
43             // check whether user chose a withdrawal amount or canceled
44             if ( amount != CANCELED )
45             {
46                // get available balance of account involved
47                availableBalance =
48                   bankDatabase.getAvailableBalance( getAccountNumber() );
49
50                // check whether the user has enough money in the account
51                if ( amount <= availableBalance )
52                {
53                   // check whether the cash dispenser has enough money
54                   if ( cashDispenser.isSufficientCashAvailable( amount ) )
55                   {
56                      // update the account involved to reflect the withdrawal
57                      bankDatabase.debit( getAccountNumber(), amount );
58
59                      cashDispenser.dispenseCash( amount ); // dispense cash
60                      cashDispensed = true; // cash was dispensed
61
62                      // instruct user to take cash
63                      screen.displayMessageLine( "\nYour cash has been" +
64                         " dispensed. Please take your cash now." );
65                   } // end if
66                   else // cash dispenser does not have enough cash
67                      screen.displayMessageLine(
68                         "\nInsufficient cash available in the ATM." +
69                         "\n\nPlease choose a smaller amount." );
70                } // end if
71                else // not enough money available in user's account
72                {
```

Fig. 13.22 | Class Withdrawal represents a withdrawal ATM transaction. (Part 2 of 4.)

```
73                  screen.displayMessageLine(
74                     "\nInsufficient funds in your account." +
75                     "\n\nPlease choose a smaller amount." );
76               } // end else
77            } // end if
78            else // user chose cancel menu option
79            {
80               screen.displayMessageLine( "\nCanceling transaction..." );
81               return; // return to main menu because user canceled
82            } // end else
83         } while ( !cashDispensed );
84
85      } // end method execute
86
87      // display a menu of withdrawal amounts and the option to cancel;
88      // return the chosen amount or 0 if the user chooses to cancel
89      private int displayMenuOfAmounts()
90      {
91         int userChoice = 0; // local variable to store return value
92
93         Screen screen = getScreen(); // get screen reference
94
95         // array of amounts to correspond to menu numbers
96         int[] amounts = { 0, 20, 40, 60, 100, 200 };
97
98         // loop while no valid choice has been made
99         while ( userChoice == 0 )
100        {
101           // display the menu
102           screen.displayMessageLine( "\nWithdrawal Menu:" );
103           screen.displayMessageLine( "1 - $20" );
104           screen.displayMessageLine( "2 - $40" );
105           screen.displayMessageLine( "3 - $60" );
106           screen.displayMessageLine( "4 - $100" );
107           screen.displayMessageLine( "5 - $200" );
108           screen.displayMessageLine( "6 - Cancel transaction" );
109           screen.displayMessage( "\nChoose a withdrawal amount: " );
110
111           int input = keypad.getInput(); // get user input through keypad
112
113           // determine how to proceed based on the input value
114           switch ( input )
115           {
116              case 1: // if the user chose a withdrawal amount
117              case 2: // (i.e., chose option 1, 2, 3, 4 or 5), return the
118              case 3: // corresponding amount from amounts array
119              case 4:
120              case 5:
121                 userChoice = amounts[ input ]; // save user's choice
122                 break;
123              case CANCELED: // the user chose to cancel
124                 userChoice = CANCELED; // save user's choice
125                 break;
```

Fig. 13.22 | Class `Withdrawal` represents a withdrawal ATM transaction. (Part 3 of 4.)

```
126                    default: // the user did not enter a value from 1-6
127                        screen.displayMessageLine(
128                            "\nInvalid selection. Try again." );
129                } // end switch
130            } // end while
131
132            return userChoice; // return withdrawal amount or CANCELED
133        } // end method displayMenuOfAmounts
134    } // end class Withdrawal
```

Fig. 13.22 | Class Withdrawal represents a withdrawal ATM transaction. (Part 4 of 4.)

Class Withdrawal's constructor (lines 14–24) has five parameters. It uses super to pass parameters userAccountNumber, atmScreen and atmBankDatabase to superclass Transaction's constructor to set the attributes that Withdrawal inherits from Transaction. The constructor also takes references atmKeypad and atmCashDispenser as parameters and assigns them to reference-type attributes keypad and cashDispenser.

Class Withdrawal overrides Transaction method execute with a concrete implementation (lines 27–85) that performs the steps of a withdrawal. Line 30 declares and initializes a local boolean variable cashDispensed, which indicates whether cash has been dispensed (i.e., whether the transaction has completed successfully) and is initially false. Line 31 declares local double variable availableBalance, which will store the user's available balance during a withdrawal transaction. Lines 34–35 get references to the bank database and the ATM's screen by invoking methods inherited from superclass Transaction.

Lines 38–83 contain a do...while statement that executes its body until cash is dispensed (i.e., until cashDispensed becomes true) or until the user chooses to cancel (in which case, the loop terminates). We use this loop to continuously return the user to the start of the transaction if an error occurs (i.e., the requested withdrawal amount is greater than the user's available balance or greater than the amount of cash in the cash dispenser). Line 41 displays a menu of withdrawal amounts and obtains a user selection by calling private utility method displayMenuOfAmounts (declared in lines 89–133). This method displays the menu of amounts and returns either an int withdrawal amount or an int constant CANCELED to indicate that the user has chosen to cancel the transaction.

Method displayMenuOfAmounts (lines 89–133) first declares local variable userChoice (initially 0) to store the value that the method will return (line 91). Line 93 gets a reference to the screen by calling method getScreen inherited from superclass Transaction. Line 96 declares an integer array of withdrawal amounts that correspond to the amounts displayed in the withdrawal menu. We ignore the first element in the array (index 0) because the menu has no option 0. The while statement at lines 99–130 repeats until userChoice takes on a value other than 0. We'll see shortly that this occurs when the user makes a valid selection from the menu. Lines 102–109 display the withdrawal menu on the screen and prompt the user to enter a choice. Line 111 obtains integer input through the keypad. The switch statement at lines 114–129 determines how to proceed based on the user's input. If the user selects a number between 1 and 5, line 121 sets userChoice to the value of the element in amounts at index input. For example, if the user enters 3 to withdraw $60, line 121 sets userChoice to the value of amounts[3] (i.e., 60). Line 122 terminates the switch. Variable userChoice no longer equals 0, so the while at lines 99–130 terminates and line 132 returns userChoice. If the user selects the cancel menu option, lines 124–125 execute, setting userChoice to CANCELED and causing the method to return this value. If the user does not enter a valid menu selection, lines 127–128 display an error message and the user is returned to the withdrawal menu.

Line 44 in method execute determines whether the user has selected a withdrawal amount or chosen to cancel. If the user cancels, lines 80–81 execute and display an appropriate message to the user before returning control to the calling method (i.e., ATM method performTransactions). If the user has chosen a withdrawal amount, lines 47–48 retrieve the available balance of the current user's Account and store it in variable availableBalance. Next, the if statement at line 51 determines whether the selected amount is less than or equal to the user's available balance. If it's not, lines 73–75 display an appropriate error message. Control then continues to the end of the do…while, and the loop repeats because cashDispensed is still false. If the user's balance is high enough, the if statement at line 54 determines whether the cash dispenser has enough money to satisfy the withdrawal request by invoking the cashDispenser's isSufficientCashAvailable method. If this method returns false, lines 67–69 display an appropriate error message and the do…while repeats. If sufficient cash is available, then the requirements for the withdrawal are satisfied, and line 57 debits amount from the user's account in the database. Lines 59–60 then instruct the cash dispenser to dispense the cash to the user and set cashDispensed to true. Finally, lines 63–64 display a message to the user that cash has been dispensed. Because cashDispensed is now true, control continues after the do…while. No additional statements appear below the loop, so the method returns control to class ATM.

13.4.11 Class Deposit

Class Deposit (Fig. 13.23) extends Transaction and represents a deposit transaction. Recall from Fig. 13.10 that class Deposit has one attribute amount, which line 6 implements as an int field. Lines 7–8 create reference-type attributes keypad and depositSlot that implement the associations between class Deposit and classes Keypad and DepositSlot modeled in Fig. 13.9. Line 9 declares a constant CANCELED that corresponds to the value a user enters to cancel. We'll soon discuss how the class uses this constant.

```
1   // Deposit.java
2   // Represents a deposit ATM transaction
3
4   public class Deposit extends Transaction
5   {
6      private double amount; // amount to deposit
7      private Keypad keypad; // reference to keypad
8      private DepositSlot depositSlot; // reference to deposit slot
9      private final static int CANCELED = 0; // constant for cancel option
10
11     // Deposit constructor
12     public Deposit( int userAccountNumber, Screen atmScreen,
13        BankDatabase atmBankDatabase, Keypad atmKeypad,
14        DepositSlot atmDepositSlot )
15     {
16        // initialize superclass variables
17        super( userAccountNumber, atmScreen, atmBankDatabase );
18
```

Fig. 13.23 | Class Deposit represents a deposit ATM transaction. (Part 1 of 3.)

```
19          // initialize references to keypad and deposit slot
20          keypad = atmKeypad;
21          depositSlot = atmDepositSlot;
22      } // end Deposit constructor
23
24      // perform transaction
25      @Override
26      public void execute()
27      {
28          BankDatabase bankDatabase = getBankDatabase(); // get reference
29          Screen screen = getScreen(); // get reference
30
31          amount = promptForDepositAmount(); // get deposit amount from user
32
33          // check whether user entered a deposit amount or canceled
34          if ( amount != CANCELED )
35          {
36              // request deposit envelope containing specified amount
37              screen.displayMessage(
38                  "\nPlease insert a deposit envelope containing " );
39              screen.displayDollarAmount( amount );
40              screen.displayMessageLine( "." );
41
42              // receive deposit envelope
43              boolean envelopeReceived = depositSlot.isEnvelopeReceived();
44
45              // check whether deposit envelope was received
46              if ( envelopeReceived )
47              {
48                  screen.displayMessageLine( "\nYour envelope has been " +
49                      "received.\nNOTE: The money just deposited will not " +
50                      "be available until we verify the amount of any " +
51                      "enclosed cash and your checks clear." );
52
53                  // credit account to reflect the deposit
54                  bankDatabase.credit( getAccountNumber(), amount );
55              } // end if
56              else // deposit envelope not received
57              {
58                  screen.displayMessageLine( "\nYou did not insert an " +
59                      "envelope, so the ATM has canceled your transaction." );
60              } // end else
61          } // end if
62          else // user canceled instead of entering amount
63          {
64              screen.displayMessageLine( "\nCanceling transaction..." );
65          } // end else
66      } // end method execute
67
68      // prompt user to enter a deposit amount in cents
69      private double promptForDepositAmount()
70      {
71          Screen screen = getScreen(); // get reference to screen
72
```

Fig. 13.23 | Class Deposit represents a deposit ATM transaction. (Part 2 of 3.)

```
73              // display the prompt
74              screen.displayMessage( "\nPlease enter a deposit amount in " +
75                 "CENTS (or 0 to cancel): " );
76              int input = keypad.getInput(); // receive input of deposit amount
77
78              // check whether the user canceled or entered a valid amount
79              if ( input == CANCELED )
80                 return CANCELED;
81              else
82              {
83                 return ( double ) input / 100; // return dollar amount
84              } // end else
85           } // end method promptForDepositAmount
86        } // end class Deposit
```

Fig. 13.23 | Class `Deposit` represents a deposit ATM transaction. (Part 3 of 3.)

Like `Withdrawal`, class `Deposit` contains a constructor (lines 12–22) that passes three parameters to superclass `Transaction`'s constructor. The constructor also has parameters atmKeypad and atmDepositSlot, which it assigns to corresponding attributes (lines 20–21).

Method `execute` (lines 25–66) overrides the abstract version in superclass `Transaction` with a concrete implementation that performs the steps required in a deposit transaction. Lines 28–29 get references to the database and the screen. Line 31 prompts the user to enter a deposit amount by invoking `private` utility method promptForDepositAmount (declared in lines 69–85) and sets attribute amount to the value returned. Method promptForDepositAmount asks the user to enter a deposit amount as an integer number of cents (because the ATM's keypad does not contain a decimal point; this is consistent with many real ATMs) and returns the `double` value representing the dollar amount to be deposited.

Line 71 in method promptForDepositAmount gets a reference to the ATM's screen. Lines 74–75 display a message on the screen asking the user to input a deposit amount as a number of cents or "0" to cancel the transaction. Line 76 receives the user's input from the keypad. The `if` statement at lines 79–84 determines whether the user has entered a real deposit amount or chosen to cancel. If the latter, line 80 returns the constant CANCELED. Otherwise, line 83 returns the deposit amount after converting from the number of cents to a dollar amount by casting input to a `double`, then dividing by 100. For example, if the user enters 125 as the number of cents, line 83 returns 125.0 divided by 100, or 1.25—125 cents is $1.25.

Lines 34–65 in method `execute` determine whether the user has chosen to cancel the transaction instead of entering a deposit amount. If the user cancels, line 64 displays an appropriate message, and the method returns. If the user enters a deposit amount, lines 37–40 instruct the user to insert a deposit envelope with the correct amount. Recall that `Screen` method displayDollarAmount outputs a `double` formatted as a dollar amount.

Line 43 sets a local `boolean` variable to the value returned by depositSlot's isEnvelopeReceived method, indicating whether a deposit envelope has been received. Recall that we coded method isEnvelopeReceived (lines 8–11 of Fig. 13.17) to always return `true`, because we are simulating the functionality of the deposit slot and assume that the user always inserts an envelope. However, we code method execute of class `Deposit` to test for the possibility that the user does not insert an envelope—good software engineering demands that programs account for all possible return values. Thus, class `Deposit` is prepared for future versions of isEnvelopeReceived that could return false. Lines 48–54 execute if the deposit slot receives an envelope. Lines 48–51 display an appropriate message to the user. Line 54 then credits the deposit amount to the user's account in the database. Lines 58–59 will execute if the deposit slot does not receive a deposit envelope. In this case, we display a message to the user stating that the ATM has canceled the transaction. The method then returns without modifying the user's account.

13.4.12 Class ATMCaseStudy

Class ATMCaseStudy (Fig. 13.24) is a simple class that allows us to start, or "turn on," the ATM and test the implementation of our ATM system model. Class ATMCaseStudy's main method (lines 7–11) does nothing more than instantiate a new ATM object named theATM (line 9) and invoke its run method (line 10) to start the ATM.

```java
1   // ATMCaseStudy.java
2   // Driver program for the ATM case study
3
4   public class ATMCaseStudy
5   {
6      // main method creates and runs the ATM
7      public static void main( String[] args )
8      {
9         ATM theATM = new ATM();
10        theATM.run();
11     } // end main
12  } // end class ATMCaseStudy
```

Fig. 13.24 | ATMCaseStudy.java starts the ATM.

13.5 Wrap-Up

In this chapter, you used inheritance to tune the design of the ATM software system, and you fully implemented the ATM in Java. Congratulations on completing the entire ATM case study! We hope you found this experience to be valuable and that it reinforced many of the object-oriented programming concepts that you've learned. In the next chapter, we take a deeper look at graphical user interfaces (GUIs).

Answers to Self-Review Exercises

13.1   True. The minus sign (–) indicates private visibility.

13.2   b.

13.3   The design for class Keypad yields the code in Fig. 13.25. Recall that class Keypad has no attributes for the moment, but attributes may become apparent as we continue the implementation. Also note that if we were designing a real ATM, method getInput would need to interact with the ATM's keypad hardware. We'll actually do input from the keyboard of a personal computer when we write the complete Java code in Section 13.4.

13.4   b.

13.5   False. The UML requires that we italicize abstract class names and method names.

13.6   The design for class Transaction yields the code in Fig. 13.26. The bodies of the class constructor and methods are completed in Section 13.4. When fully implemented, methods getScreen and getBankDatabase will return superclass Transaction's private reference attributes screen and bankDatabase, respectively. These methods allow the Transaction subclasses to access the ATM's screen and interact with the bank's database.

```
1  // Class Keypad represents an ATM's keypad
2  public class Keypad
3  {
4      // no attributes have been specified yet
5
6      // no-argument constructor
7      public Keypad()
8      {
9      } // end no-argument Keypad constructor
10
11     // operations
12     public int getInput()
13     {
14     } // end method getInput
15 } // end class Keypad
```

Fig. 13.25 | Java code for class Keypad based on Figs. 13.1–13.2.

```
1  // Abstract class Transaction represents an ATM transaction
2  public abstract class Transaction
3  {
4      // attributes
5      private int accountNumber; // indicates account involved
6      private Screen screen; // ATM's screen
7      private BankDatabase bankDatabase; // account info database
8
9      // no-argument constructor invoked by subclasses using super()
10     public Transaction()
11     {
12     } // end no-argument Transaction constructor
13
14     // return account number
15     public int getAccountNumber()
16     {
17     } // end method getAccountNumber
18
19     // return reference to screen
20     public Screen getScreen()
21     {
22     } // end method getScreen
23
24     // return reference to bank database
25     public BankDatabase getBankDatabase()
26     {
27     } // end method getBankDatabase
28
29     // abstract method overridden by subclasses
30     public abstract void execute();
31 } // end class Transaction
```

Fig. 13.26 | Java code for class Transaction based on Figs. 13.9 and 13.10.

GUI Components: Part 1

Objectives

In this chapter you'll learn:

- The design principles of graphical user interfaces (GUIs).

- How to use Java's new, elegant, cross-platform Nimbus look-and-feel.

- To build GUIs and handle events generated by user interactions with GUIs.

- To understand the packages containing GUI components, event-handling classes and interfaces.

- To create and manipulate buttons, labels, lists, text fields and panels.

- To handle mouse events and keyboard events.

- To use layout managers to arrange GUI components

14.1 Introduction

A **graphical user interface (GUI)** presents a user-friendly mechanism for interacting with an application. A GUI (pronounced "GOO-ee") gives an application a distinctive "look" and "feel." Providing different applications with consistent, intuitive user-interface components gives users a sense of familiarity with a new application, so that they can learn it more quickly and use it more productively.

Look-and-Feel Observation 14.1

Consistent user interfaces enable a user to learn new applications faster.

GUIs are built from **GUI components**. These are sometimes called **controls** or **widgets**—short for **window gadgets**. A GUI component is an object with which the user interacts via the mouse, the keyboard or another form of input, such as voice recognition. In this chapter and Chapter 25, GUI Components: Part 2, you'll learn about many of Java's GUI components. We also cover other GUI components as they're needed throughout the rest of the book.

Many IDEs provide GUI design tools in which you can specify a component's exact size and location in a visual manner by using the mouse. The IDE generates the GUI code for you. Though this greatly simplifies creating GUIs, each IDE has different capabilities and generates different code. For this reason, we wrote the GUI code by hand.

As an example of a GUI, consider Fig. 14.1, which shows the SwingSet3 application that is available at `download.java.net/javadesktop/swingset3/SwingSet3.jnlp`. This application is a nice way for you to browse through the various GUI components provided by Java's Swing GUI APIs. Simply click a component name (e.g., `JFrame`, `JTabbedPane`, etc.) in the **GUI Components** area at the left of the window to see a demonstration of the GUI component in the right side of the window. The source code for each demo is shown in the text area at the bottom of the window. We've labeled a few of the GUI components in the application. At the top of the window is a **title bar** that contains the window's title. Below that is a **menu bar** containing **menus** (**File** and **View**). In the top-right region of the window is a set of **buttons**—typically, users press buttons to perform tasks. In the **GUI Components** area of the window is a **combo box**; the user can click the down arrow at the right side of the box to select from a list of items. The menus, buttons and combo box are part of the application's GUI. They enable you to interact with the application.

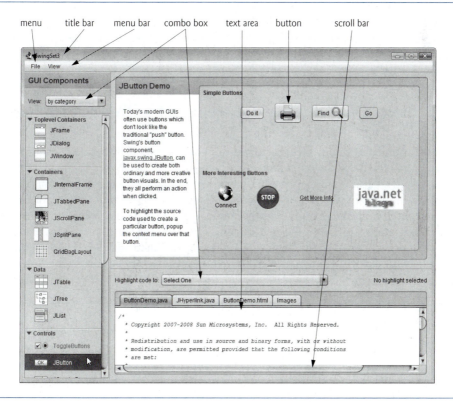

Fig. 14.1 | SwingSet3 application demonstrates many of Java's Swing GUI components.

14.2 Java's New Nimbus Look-and-Feel

As of Java SE 6 update 10, Java comes bundled with a new, elegant, cross-platform look-and-feel known as **Nimbus**. For GUI screen captures like Fig. 14.1, we've configured our systems to use Nimbus as the default look-and-feel. There are three ways that you can use Nimbus:

1. Set it as the default for all Java applications that run on your computer.

2. Set it as the look-and-feel at the time that you launch an application by passing a command-line argument to the java command.

3. Set it as the look-and-feel programatically in your application (see Section 25.6).

To set Nimbus as the default for all Java applications, you must create a text file named swing.properties in the lib folder of both your JDK installation folder and your JRE installation folder. Place the following line of code in the file:

```
swing.defaultlaf=com.sun.java.swing.plaf.nimbus.NimbusLookAndFeel
```

For more information on locating these installation folders visit java.sun.com/javase/ 6/webnotes/install/index.html. [*Note:* In addition to the standalone JRE, there is a JRE nested in your JDK's installation folder. If you are using an IDE that depends on the JDK (e.g., NetBeans), you may also need to place the swing.properties file in the nested jre folder's lib folder.]

If you prefer to select Nimbus on an application-by-application basis, place the following command-line argument after the java command and before the application's name when you run the application:

```
-Dswing.defaultlaf=com.sun.java.swing.plaf.nimbus.NimbusLookAndFeel
```

14.3 Simple GUI-Based Input/Output with JOptionPane

The applications in Chapters 2–10 display text in the command window and obtain input from the command window. Most applications you use on a daily basis use windows or **dialog boxes** (also called **dialogs**) to interact with the user. For example, an e-mail program allows you to type and read messages in a window the program provides. Typically, dialog boxes are windows in which programs display important messages to the user or obtain information from the user. Java's **JOptionPane** class (package javax.swing) provides prebuilt dialog boxes for both input and output. These dialogs are displayed by invoking static JOptionPane methods. Figure 14.2 presents a simple addition application that uses two **input dialogs** to obtain integers from the user and a **message dialog** to display the sum of the integers the user enters.

```java
1  // Fig. 14.2: Addition.java
2  // Addition program that uses JOptionPane for input and output.
3  import javax.swing.JOptionPane; // program uses JOptionPane
4
5  public class Addition
6  {
7     public static void main( String[] args )
8     {
9        // obtain user input from JOptionPane input dialogs
10       String firstNumber =
11          JOptionPane.showInputDialog( "Enter first integer" );
12       String secondNumber =
13          JOptionPane.showInputDialog( "Enter second integer" );
14
```

Fig. 14.2 | Addition program that uses JOptionPane for input and output. (Part 1 of 2.)

```
15      // convert String inputs to int values for use in a calculation
16      int number1 = Integer.parseInt( firstNumber );
17      int number2 = Integer.parseInt( secondNumber );
18
19      int sum = number1 + number2; // add numbers
20
21      // display result in a JOptionPane message dialog
22      JOptionPane.showMessageDialog( null, "The sum is " + sum,
23         "Sum of Two Integers", JOptionPane.PLAIN_MESSAGE );
24   } // end method main
25 } // end class Addition
```

(a) Input dialog displayed by lines 10–11

Prompt to the user

When the user clicks **OK**, `showInputDialog` returns to the program the **100** typed by the user as a `String`. The program must convert the `String` to an `int`

Text field in which the user types a value

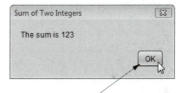

(b) Input dialog displayed by lines 12–13

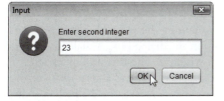

(c) Message dialog displayed by lines 22–23

When the user clicks **OK**, the message dialog is dismissed (removed from the screen).

Fig. 14.2 | Addition program that uses `JOptionPane` for input and output. (Part 2 of 2.)

Input Dialogs

Line 3 imports class `JOptionPane`. Lines 10–11 declare the local `String` variable first-Number and assign it the result of the call to `JOptionPane` static method **showInputDialog**. This method displays an input dialog (see the first screen capture in Fig. 14.2), using the method's `String` argument ("Enter first integer") as a prompt.

Look-and-Feel Observation 14.2

The prompt in an input dialog typically uses sentence-style capitalization—a style that capitalizes only the first letter of the first word in the text unless the word is a proper noun (for example, Jones).

The user types characters in the text field, then clicks **OK** or presses the *Enter* key to submit the `String` to the program. Clicking **OK** also **dismisses (hides) the dialog**. [*Note:* If you type in the text field and nothing appears, activate the text field by clicking it with the mouse.] Unlike `Scanner`, which can be used to input values of several types from the user at the keyboard, an input dialog can input only `Strings`. This is typical of most GUI components. The user can type any characters in the input dialog's text field. Our program assumes that the user enters a valid integer. If the user clicks **Cancel**, showInputDialog returns null. If the user either types a noninteger value or clicks the **Cancel** button in the input dialog, an exception will occur and the program will not operate correctly. Chapter 11, Exception Handling, discussed how to handle such errors. Lines 12–13 display another input dialog that prompts the user to enter the second integer. Note that each JOptionPane dialog that you display is a so called **modal dialog**—while the dialog is on the screen, the user cannot interact with the rest of the application.

Look-and-Feel Observation 14.3

Do not overuse modal dialogs as they can reduce the usability of your applications. Use a modal dialog only when it's necessary to prevent users from interacting with the rest of an application until they dismiss the dialog.

Converting *Strings* to *int* Values

To perform the calculation, we convert the Strings that the user entered to int values. Recall that the Integer class's static method parseInt converts its String argument to an int value. Lines 16–17 assign the converted values to local variables number1 and number2. Then, line 19 sums these values and assigns the result to local variable sum.

Message Dialogs

Lines 22–23 use JOptionPane static method **showMessageDialog** to display a message dialog (the last screen capture of Fig. 14.2) containing the sum. The first argument helps the Java application determine where to position the dialog box. A dialog is typically displayed from a GUI application with its own window. The first argument refers to that window (known as the parent window) and causes the dialog to appear centered over parent (as we'll do in Section 14.9). If the first argument is null, the dialog box is displayed at the center of your screen. The second argument is the message to display—in this case, the result of concatenating the String "The sum is " and the value of sum. The third argument—"Sum of Two Integers"—is the String that should appear in the title bar at the top of the dialog. The fourth argument—JOptionPane.PLAIN_MESSAGE—is the type of message dialog to display. A PLAIN_MESSAGE dialog does not display an icon to the left of the message. Class JOptionPane provides several overloaded versions of methods showInputDialog and showMessageDialog, as well as methods that display other dialog types. For complete information on class JOptionPane, visit java.sun.com/javase/6/docs/api/javax/swing/JOptionPane.html.

Look-and-Feel Observation 14.4

*The title bar of a window typically uses **book-title capitalization**—a style that capitalizes the first letter of each significant word in the text and does not end with any punctuation (for example, Capitalization in a Book Title).*

JOptionPane *Message Dialog Constants*

The constants that represent the message dialog types are shown in Fig. 14.3. All message dialog types except PLAIN_MESSAGE display an icon to the left of the message. These icons provide a visual indication of the message's importance to the user. Note that a QUESTION_MESSAGE icon is the default icon for an input dialog box (see Fig. 14.2).

Message dialog type	Icon	Description
ERROR_MESSAGE		Indicates an error to the user.
INFORMATION_MESSAGE		Indicates an informational message to the user.
WARNING_MESSAGE		Warns the user of a potential problem.
QUESTION_MESSAGE		Poses a question to the user. This dialog normally requires a response, such as clicking a **Yes** or a **No** button.
PLAIN_MESSAGE	no icon	A dialog that contains a message, but no icon.

Fig. 14.3 | JOptionPane static constants for message dialogs.

14.4 Overview of Swing Components

Though it's possible to perform input and output using the JOptionPane dialogs presented in Section 14.3, most GUI applications require more elaborate, customized user interfaces. The remainder of this chapter discusses many GUI components that enable application developers to create robust GUIs. Figure 14.4 lists several **Swing GUI components** from package `javax.swing` that are used to build Java GUIs. Most Swing components are pure Java components—they're written, manipulated and displayed completely in Java. They're part of the **Java Foundation Classes (JFC)**—Java's libraries for cross-platform GUI development. Visit java.sun.com/javase/technologies/desktop/ for more information on JFC and Java desktop technologies.

Component	Description
JLabel	Displays uneditable text or icons.
JTextField	Enables user to enter data from the keyboard. Can also be used to display editable or uneditable text.
JButton	Triggers an event when clicked with the mouse.
JCheckBox	Specifies an option that can be selected or not selected.
JComboBox	Provides a drop-down list of items from which the user can make a selection by clicking an item or possibly by typing into the box.
JList	Provides a list of items from which the user can make a selection by clicking on any item in the list. Multiple elements can be selected.
JPanel	Provides an area in which components can be placed and organized. Can also be used as a drawing area for graphics.

Fig. 14.4 | Some basic GUI components.

Swing vs. AWT
There are actually two sets of GUI components in Java. Before Swing was introduced in Java SE 1.2, Java GUIs were built with components from the **Abstract Window Toolkit**

(AWT) in package `java.awt`. When a Java application with an AWT GUI executes on different Java platforms, the application's GUI components display differently on each platform. Consider an application that displays an object of type `Button` (package `java.awt`). On a computer running the Microsoft Windows operating system, the `Button` will have the same appearance as the buttons in other Windows applications. Similarly, on a computer running the Apple Mac OS X operating system, the `Button` will have the same look-and-feel as the buttons in other Macintosh applications. Sometimes, the manner in which a user can interact with a particular AWT component differs between platforms.

Together, the appearance and the way in which the user interacts with the application are known as that application's **look-and-feel**. Swing GUI components allow you to specify a uniform look-and-feel for your application across all platforms or to use each platform's custom look-and-feel. An application can even change the look-and-feel during execution to enable users to choose their own preferred look-and-feel.

Portability Tip 14.1

Swing components are implemented in Java, so they're more portable and flexible than the original Java GUI components from package `java.awt`, which were based on the GUI components of the underlying platform. For this reason, Swing GUI components are generally preferred.

Lightweight vs. Heavyweight GUI Components

Most Swing components are not tied to actual GUI components of the underlying platform. Such GUI components are known as **lightweight components**. AWT components (many of which parallel the Swing components) are tied to the local platform and are called **heavyweight components**, because they rely on the local platform's **windowing system** to determine their functionality and their look-and-feel.

Several Swing components are heavyweight components. Like AWT components, heavyweight Swing GUI components require direct interaction with the local windowing system, which may restrict their appearance and functionality, making them less flexible than lightweight components.

Portability Tip 14.2

The look-and-feel of a GUI defined with heavyweight GUI components from package `java.awt` may vary across platforms. Because heavyweight components are tied to the local-platform GUI, the look-and-feel varies from platform to platform.

Superclasses of Swing's Lightweight GUI Components

The UML class diagram of Fig. 14.5 shows an inheritance hierarchy of classes from which lightweight Swing components inherit their common attributes and behaviors.

Software Engineering Observation 14.1

Study the attributes and behaviors of the classes in the class hierarchy of Fig. 14.5. These classes declare the features that are common to most Swing components.

Class **Component** (package `java.awt`) is a subclass of `Object` that declares many of the attributes and behaviors common to the GUI components in packages `java.awt` and `javax.swing`. Most GUI components extend class `Component` directly or indirectly. Visit `java.sun.com/javase/6/docs/api/java/awt/Component.html` for a complete list of these common features.

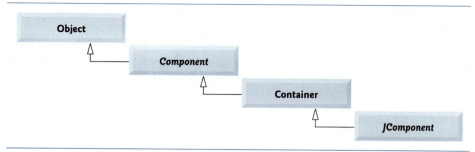

Fig. 14.5 | Common superclasses of many of the Swing components.

Class **Container** (package java.awt) is a subclass of Component. As you'll soon see, Components are attached to Containers (such as windows) so that they can be organized and displayed on the screen. Any object that *is a* Container can be used to organize other Components in a GUI. Because a Container *is a* Component, you can place Containers in other Containers to help organize a GUI. Visit java.sun.com/javase/6/docs/api/java/awt/Container.html for a complete list of the Container features that are common to Swing lightweight components.

Class **JComponent** (package javax.swing) is a subclass of Container. JComponent is the superclass of all lightweight Swing components and declares their common attributes and behaviors. Because JComponent is a subclass of Container, all lightweight Swing components are also Containers. Some common lightweight component features supported by JComponent include:

1. A **pluggable look-and-feel** that can be used to customize the appearance of components (e.g., for use on particular platforms). You'll see an example of this in Section 25.6.

2. Shortcut keys (called **mnemonics**) for direct access to GUI components through the keyboard. You'll see an example of this in Section 25.4.

3. Common event-handling capabilities for cases where several GUI components initiate the same actions in an application.

4. Brief descriptions of a GUI component's purpose (called **tool tips**) that are displayed when the mouse cursor is positioned over the component for a short time. You'll see an example of this in the next section.

5. Support for accessibility, such as braille screen readers for the visually impaired.

6. Support for user-interface **localization**—that is, customizing the user interface to display in different languages and use local cultural conventions.

Visit java.sun.com/javase/6/docs/api/javax/swing/JComponent.html for more details on the common lightweight component features.

14.5 Displaying Text and Images in a Window

Our next example introduces a framework for building GUI applications. This framework uses several concepts that you'll see in many of our GUI applications. This is our first example in which the application appears in its own window. Most windows you'll create that can contain Swing GUI components are instances of class JFrame or a subclass of

JFrame. JFrame is an indirect subclass of class java.awt.Window that provides the basic attributes and behaviors of a window—a title bar at the top, and buttons to minimize, maximize and close the window. Since an application's GUI is typically specific to the application, most of our examples will consist of two classes—a subclass of JFrame that helps us demonstrate new GUI concepts and an application class in which main creates and displays the application's primary window.

Labeling GUI Components

A typical GUI consists of many components. In a large GUI, it can be difficult to identify the purpose of every component. So GUI designers often provide text stating each component's purpose. Such text is known as a label and is created with class **JLabel**—a subclass of JComponent. A JLabel displays read-only text, an image, or both text and an image. Applications rarely change a label's contents after creating it.

 Look-and-Feel Observation 14.5

Text in a JLabel normally uses sentence-style capitalization.

The application of Figs. 14.6–14.7 demonstrates several JLabel features and presents the framework we use in most of our GUI examples. We did not highlight the code in this example, since most of it is new. [*Note:* There are many more features for each GUI component than we can cover in our examples. To learn the complete details of each GUI component, visit its page in the online documentation. For class JLabel, visit java.sun.com/javase/6/docs/api/javax/swing/JLabel.html.]

```java
1   // Fig. 14.6: LabelFrame.java
2   // Demonstrating the JLabel class.
3   import java.awt.FlowLayout; // specifies how components are arranged
4   import javax.swing.JFrame; // provides basic window features
5   import javax.swing.JLabel; // displays text and images
6   import javax.swing.SwingConstants; // common constants used with Swing
7   import javax.swing.Icon; // interface used to manipulate images
8   import javax.swing.ImageIcon; // loads images
9
10  public class LabelFrame extends JFrame
11  {
12     private JLabel label1; // JLabel with just text
13     private JLabel label2; // JLabel constructed with text and icon
14     private JLabel label3; // JLabel with added text and icon
15
16     // LabelFrame constructor adds JLabels to JFrame
17     public LabelFrame()
18     {
19        super( "Testing JLabel" );
20        setLayout( new FlowLayout() ); // set frame layout
21
22        // JLabel constructor with a string argument
23        label1 = new JLabel( "Label with text" );
24        label1.setToolTipText( "This is label1" );
25        add( label1 ); // add label1 to JFrame
```

Fig. 14.6 | JLabels with text and icons. (Part 1 of 2.)

```
26
27          // JLabel constructor with string, Icon and alignment arguments
28          Icon bug = new ImageIcon( getClass().getResource( "bug1.png" ) );
29          label2 = new JLabel( "Label with text and icon", bug,
30             SwingConstants.LEFT );
31          label2.setToolTipText( "This is label2" );
32          add( label2 ); // add label2 to JFrame
33
34          label3 = new JLabel(); // JLabel constructor no arguments
35          label3.setText( "Label with icon and text at bottom" );
36          label3.setIcon( bug ); // add icon to JLabel
37          label3.setHorizontalTextPosition( SwingConstants.CENTER );
38          label3.setVerticalTextPosition( SwingConstants.BOTTOM );
39          label3.setToolTipText( "This is label3" );
40          add( label3 ); // add label3 to JFrame
41       } // end LabelFrame constructor
42    } // end class LabelFrame
```

Fig. 14.6 | JLabels with text and icons. (Part 2 of 2.)

```
1    // Fig. 14.7: LabelTest.java
2    // Testing LabelFrame.
3    import javax.swing.JFrame;
4
5    public class LabelTest
6    {
7       public static void main( String[] args )
8       {
9          LabelFrame labelFrame = new LabelFrame(); // create LabelFrame
10          labelFrame.setDefaultCloseOperation( JFrame.EXIT_ON_CLOSE );
11          labelFrame.setSize( 260, 180 ); // set frame size
12          labelFrame.setVisible( true ); // display frame
13       } // end main
14    } // end class LabelTest
```

Fig. 14.7 | Test class for LabelFrame.

Class LabelFrame (Fig. 14.6) is a subclass of JFrame. We'll use an instance of class LabelFrame to display a window containing three JLabels. Lines 3–8 import the classes used in class LabelFrame. The class extends JFrame to inherit the features of a window. Lines 12–14 declare the three JLabel instance variables, each of which is instantiated in the LabelFrame constructor (lines 17–41). Typically, the JFrame subclass's constructor builds the GUI that is displayed in the window when the application executes. Line 19 invokes superclass JFrame's constructor with the argument "Testing JLabel". JFrame's constructor uses this String as the text in the window's title bar.

Specifying the Layout

When building a GUI, you must attach each GUI component to a container, such as a window created with a JFrame. Also, you typically must decide where to position each GUI component. This is known as specifying the layout of the GUI components. As you'll learn at the end of this chapter and in Chapter 25, Java provides several layout managers that can help you position components.

Many integrated development environments provide GUI design tools in which you can specify the exact size and location of a component in a visual manner by using the mouse; then the IDE will generate the GUI code for you. Though such IDEs can greatly simplify GUI creation, they're each different in capability.

To ensure that this book's examples can be used with any IDE, we did not use an IDE to create the GUI code. For this reason, we use Java's layout managers in our GUI examples. One such layout manager is FlowLayout, in which GUI components are placed on a container from left to right in the order in which the program attaches them to the container. When there is no more room to fit components left to right, components continue to display left to right on the next line. If the container is resized, a FlowLayout reflows (i.e., rearranges) the components to accommodate the new width of the container, possibly with fewer or more rows of GUI components. Every container has a default layout, which we are changing for LabelFrame to a FlowLayout (line 20). Method **setLayout** is inherited into class LabelFrame indirectly from class Container. The argument to the method must be an object of a class that implements the LayoutManager interface (e.g., FlowLayout). Line 20 creates a new FlowLayout object and passes its reference as the argument to setLayout.

Creating and Attaching **label1**

Now that we've specified the window's layout, we can begin creating and attaching GUI components to the window. Line 23 creates a JLabel object and passes "Label with text" to the constructor. The JLabel displays this text on the screen as part of the application's GUI. Line 24 uses method **setToolTipText** (inherited by JLabel from JComponent) to specify the tool tip that is displayed when the user positions the mouse cursor over the JLabel in the GUI. You can see a sample tool tip in the second screen capture of Fig. 14.7. When you execute this application, try positioning the mouse over each JLabel to see its tool tip. Line 25 attaches label1 to the LabelFrame by passing label1 to the **add** method, which is inherited indirectly from class Container.

Common Programming Error 14.1

If you do not explicitly add a GUI component to a container, the GUI component will not be displayed when the container appears on the screen.

Look-and-Feel Observation 14.6

Use tool tips to add descriptive text to your GUI components. This text helps the user determine the GUI component's purpose in the user interface.

Creating and Attaching **label2**

Icons are a popular way to enhance the look-and-feel of an application and are also commonly used to indicate functionality. For examples, most of today's VCRs and DVD players use the same icon to play a tape or DVD. Several Swing components can display images. An icon is normally specified with an `Icon` argument to a constructor or to the component's `setIcon` method. An Icon is an object of any class that implements interface Icon (package `javax.swing`). One such class is `ImageIcon` (package `javax.swing`), which supports several image formats, including **Graphics Interchange Format (GIF)**, **Portable Network Graphics (PNG)** and **Joint Photographic Experts Group (JPEG)**. File names for each of these types end with `.gif`, `.png` or `.jpg` (or `.jpeg`), respectively. We discuss images in more detail in Chapter 24, Multimedia: Applets and Applications.

Line 28 declares an `ImageIcon`. The file `bug1.png` contains the image to load and store in the `ImageIcon` object. This image is included in the directory for this example. The ImageIcon object is assigned to Icon reference bug. Remember, class ImageIcon implements interface Icon; an ImageIcon *is an* Icon.

In line 28, the expression `getClass().getResource("bug1.png")` invokes method **getClass** (inherited indirectly from class Object) to retrieve a reference to the Class object that represents the LabelFrame class declaration. That reference is then used to invoke Class method **getResource**, which returns the location of the image as a URL. The ImageIcon constructor uses the URL to locate the image, then loads it into memory. As we discussed in Chapter 1, the JVM loads class declarations into memory, using a class loader. The class loader knows where each class it loads is located on disk. Method get-Resource uses the Class object's class loader to determine the location of a resource, such as an image file. In this example, the image file is stored in the same location as the Label-Frame.class file. The techniques described here enable an application to load image files from locations that are relative to LabelFrame's `.class` file on disk.

A JLabel can display an Icon. Lines 29–30 use another JLabel constructor to create a JLabel that displays the text "Label with text and icon" and the Icon bug created in line 28. The last constructor argument indicates that the label's contents are left justified, or left aligned (i.e., the icon and text are at the left side of the label's area on the screen). Interface **SwingConstants** (package `javax.swing`) declares a set of common integer constants (such as SwingConstants.LEFT) that are used with many Swing components. By default, the text appears to the right of the image when a label contains both text and an image. Note that the horizontal and vertical alignments of a JLabel can be set with methods **setHorizontalAlignment** and **setVerticalAlignment**, respectively. Line 31 specifies the tool-tip text for label2, and line 32 adds label2 to the JFrame.

Creating and Attaching *label3*

Class JLabel provides methods to change a label's appearance after it has been instantiated. Line 34 creates a JLabel and invokes its no-argument constructor. Such a label initially has no text or Icon. Line 35 uses JLabel method **setText** to set the text displayed on the label. The corresponding method **getText** retrieves the current text displayed on a label. Line 36 uses JLabel method **setIcon** to specify the Icon to display on the label. The corresponding method **getIcon** retrieves the current Icon displayed on a label. Lines 37–38 use JLabel methods **setHorizontalTextPosition** and **setVerticalTextPosition** to specify the text position in the label. In this case, the text will be centered horizontally and will appear at the bottom of the label. Thus, the Icon will appear above the text. The horizontal-position constants in SwingConstants are LEFT, CENTER and RIGHT (Fig. 14.8). The vertical-position constants in SwingConstants are TOP, CENTER and BOTTOM (Fig. 14.8). Line 39 sets the tool-tip text for label3. Line 40 adds label3 to the JFrame.

Constant	Description
Horizontal-position constants	
SwingConstants.LEFT	Place text on the left.
SwingConstants.CENTER	Place text in the center.
SwingConstants.RIGHT	Place text on the right.
Vertical-position constants	
SwingConstants.TOP	Place text at the top.
SwingConstants.CENTER	Place text in the center.
SwingConstants.BOTTOM	Place text at the bottom.

Fig. 14.8 | Positioning constants.

Creating and Displaying a *LabelFrame* Window

Class LabelTest (Fig. 14.7) creates an object of class LabelFrame (line 9), then specifies the default close operation for the window. By default, closing a window simply hides the window. However, when the user closes the LabelFrame window, we would like the application to terminate. Line 10 invokes LabelFrame's **setDefaultCloseOperation** method (inherited from class JFrame) with constant **JFrame.EXIT_ON_CLOSE** as the argument to indicate that the program should terminate when the window is closed by the user. This line is important. Without it the application will not terminate when the user closes the window. Next, line 11 invokes LabelFrame's **setSize** method to specify the width and height of the window in pixels. Finally, line 12 invokes LabelFrame's **setVisible** method with the argument true to display the window on the screen. Try resizing the window to see how the FlowLayout changes the JLabel positions as the window width changes.

14.6 Text Fields and an Introduction to Event Handling with Nested Classes

Normally, a user interacts with an application's GUI to indicate the tasks that the application should perform. For example, when you write an e-mail in an e-mail application, clicking the **Send** button tells the application to send the e-mail to the specified e-mail addresses. GUIs are event driven. When the user interacts with a GUI component, the interaction—known as an event—drives the program to perform a task. Some common user interactions that cause an application to perform a task include clicking a button, typing in a text field, selecting an item from a menu, closing a window and moving the mouse. The code that performs a task in response to an event is called an event handler, and the overall process of responding to events is known as event handling.

Let's consider two other GUI components that can generate events—**JTextFields** and **JPasswordFields** (package javax.swing). Class JTextField extends class **JTextComponent** (package javax.swing.text), which provides many features common to Swing's text-based components. Class JPasswordField extends JTextField and adds methods that are specific to processing passwords. Each of these components is a single-line area in which the user can enter text via the keyboard. Applications can also display text in a JTextField (see the output of Fig. 14.10). A JPasswordField shows that characters are being typed as the user enters them, but hides the actual characters with an **echo character**, assuming that they represent a password that should remain known only to the user.

When the user types data into a JTextField or a JPasswordField, then presses *Enter*, an event occurs. Our next example demonstrates how a program can perform a task in response to that event. The techniques shown here are applicable to all GUI components that generate events.

The application of Figs. 14.9–14.10 uses classes JTextField and JPasswordField to create and manipulate four text fields. When the user types in one of the text fields, then presses *Enter*, the application displays a message dialog box containing the text the user typed. You can type only in the text field that is "in **focus**." A component receives the focus when the user clicks the component. This is important, because the text field with the focus is the one that generates an event when the user presses *Enter*. In this example, when the user presses *Enter* in the JPasswordField, the password is revealed. We begin by discussing the setup of the GUI, then discuss the event-handling code.

```
1   // Fig. 14.9: TextFieldFrame.java
2   // Demonstrating the JTextField class.
3   import java.awt.FlowLayout;
4   import java.awt.event.ActionListener;
5   import java.awt.event.ActionEvent;
6   import javax.swing.JFrame;
7   import javax.swing.JTextField;
8   import javax.swing.JPasswordField;
9   import javax.swing.JOptionPane;
10
11  public class TextFieldFrame extends JFrame
12  {
13     private JTextField textField1; // text field with set size
14     private JTextField textField2; // text field constructed with text
15     private JTextField textField3; // text field with text and size
16     private JPasswordField passwordField; // password field with text
17
18     // TextFieldFrame constructor adds JTextFields to JFrame
19     public TextFieldFrame()
20     {
21        super( "Testing JTextField and JPasswordField" );
22        setLayout( new FlowLayout() ); // set frame layout
23
24        // construct textfield with 10 columns
25        textField1 = new JTextField( 10 );
26        add( textField1 ); // add textField1 to JFrame
27
28        // construct textfield with default text
29        textField2 = new JTextField( "Enter text here" );
30        add( textField2 ); // add textField2 to JFrame
31
32        // construct textfield with default text and 21 columns
33        textField3 = new JTextField( "Uneditable text field", 21 );
34        textField3.setEditable( false ); // disable editing
35        add( textField3 ); // add textField3 to JFrame
36
```

Fig. 14.9 | JTextFields and JPasswordFields. (Part 1 of 2.)

```
37        // construct passwordfield with default text
38        passwordField = new JPasswordField( "Hidden text" );
39        add( passwordField ); // add passwordField to JFrame
40
41        // register event handlers
42        TextFieldHandler handler = new TextFieldHandler();
43        textField1.addActionListener( handler );
44        textField2.addActionListener( handler );
45        textField3.addActionListener( handler );
46        passwordField.addActionListener( handler );
47     } // end TextFieldFrame constructor
48
49     // private inner class for event handling
50     private class TextFieldHandler implements ActionListener
51     {
52        // process text field events
53        public void actionPerformed( ActionEvent event )
54        {
55           String string = ""; // declare string to display
56
57           // user pressed Enter in JTextField textField1
58           if ( event.getSource() == textField1 )
59              string = String.format( "textField1: %s",
60                 event.getActionCommand() );
61
62           // user pressed Enter in JTextField textField2
63           else if ( event.getSource() == textField2 )
64              string = String.format( "textField2: %s",
65                 event.getActionCommand() );
66
67           // user pressed Enter in JTextField textField3
68           else if ( event.getSource() == textField3 )
69              string = String.format( "textField3: %s",
70                 event.getActionCommand() );
71
72           // user pressed Enter in JTextField passwordField
73           else if ( event.getSource() == passwordField )
74              string = String.format( "passwordField: %s",
75                 event.getActionCommand() );
76
77           // display JTextField content
78           JOptionPane.showMessageDialog( null, string );
79        } // end method actionPerformed
80     } // end private inner class TextFieldHandler
81  } // end class TextFieldFrame
```

Fig. 14.9 | JTextFields and JPasswordFields. (Part 2 of 2.)

```
1  // Fig. 14.10: TextFieldTest.java
2  // Testing TextFieldFrame.
3  import javax.swing.JFrame;
4
```

Fig. 14.10 | Test class for TextFieldFrame. (Part 1 of 2.)

```
5   public class TextFieldTest
6   {
7      public static void main( String[] args )
8      {
9         TextFieldFrame textFieldFrame = new TextFieldFrame();
10        textFieldFrame.setDefaultCloseOperation( JFrame.EXIT_ON_CLOSE );
11        textFieldFrame.setSize( 350, 100 ); // set frame size
12        textFieldFrame.setVisible( true ); // display frame
13     } // end main
14  } // end class TextFieldTest
```

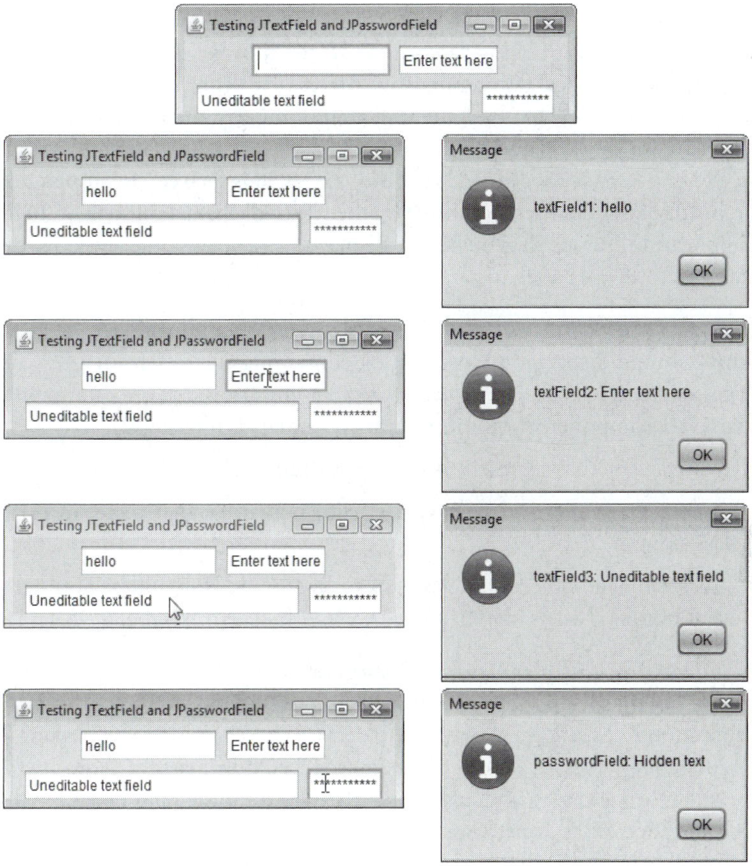

Fig. 14.10 | Test class for `TextFieldFrame`. (Part 2 of 2.)

Lines 3–9 import the classes and interfaces we use in this example. Class `TextField-Frame` extends `JFrame` and declares three `JTextField` variables and a `JPasswordField` variable (lines 13–16). Each of the corresponding text fields is instantiated and attached to the `TextFieldFrame` in the constructor (lines 19–47).

Creating the GUI
Line 22 sets the `TextFieldFrame`'s layout to `FlowLayout`. Line 25 creates `textField1` with 10 columns of text. A text column's width in pixels is determined by the average width of

a character in the text field's current font. When text is displayed in a text field and the text is wider than the field itself, a portion of the text at the right side is not visible. If you are typing in a text field and the cursor reaches the right edge, the text at the left edge is pushed off the left side of the field and is no longer visible. Users can use the left and right arrow keys to move through the complete text, even though the entire text is not visible at one time. Line 26 adds textField1 to the JFrame.

Line 29 creates textField2 with the initial text "Enter text here" to display in the text field. The width of the field is determined by the width of the default text specified in the constructor. Line 30 adds textField2 to the JFrame.

Line 33 creates textField3 and calls the JTextField constructor with two arguments—the default text "Uneditable text field" to display and the number of columns (21). The width of the text field is determined by the number of columns specified. Line 34 uses method **setEditable** (inherited by JTextField from class JTextComponent) to make the text field uneditable—i.e., the user cannot modify the text in the field. Line 35 adds textField3 to the JFrame.

Line 38 creates passwordField with the text "Hidden text" to display in the text field. The width of the field is determined by the width of the default text. When you execute the application, notice that the text is displayed as a string of asterisks. Line 39 adds passwordField to the JFrame.

Steps Required to Set Up Event Handling for a GUI Component

This example should display a message dialog containing the text from a text field when the user presses *Enter* in that text field. Before an application can respond to an event for a particular GUI component, you must perform several coding steps:

1. Create a class that represents the event handler.

2. Implement an appropriate interface, known as an **event-listener interface**, in the class from *Step 1*.

3. Indicate that an object of the class from *Steps 1* and *2* should be notified when the event occurs. This is known as **registering the event handler**.

Using a Nested Class to Implement an Event Handler

All the classes discussed so far were so-called **top-level classes**—that is, they were not declared inside another class. Java allows you to declare classes inside other classes—these are called **nested classes**. Nested classes can be static or non-static. Non-static nested classes are called **inner classes** and are frequently used to implement event handlers.

Before an object of an inner class can be created, there must first be an object of the top-level class that contains the inner class. This is required because an inner-class object implicitly has a reference to an object of its top-level class. There is also a special relationship between these objects—the inner-class object is allowed to directly access all the variables and methods of the outer class. A nested class that is static does not require an object of its top-level class and does not implicitly have a reference to an object of the top-level class. As you'll see in Chapter 15, Graphics and Java 2D™, the Java 2D graphics API uses static nested classes extensively.

Software Engineering Observation 14.2

An inner class is allowed to directly access all of its top-level class's variables and methods.

The event handling in this example is performed by an object of the private inner class TextFieldHandler (lines 50–80). This class is private because it will be used only to create event handlers for the text fields in top-level class TextFieldFrame. As with other class members, inner classes can be declared public, protected or private. Since event handlers tend to be specific to the application in which they're defined, they're often implemented as private inner classes or, as you'll learn in Section 14.11, as anonymous inner classes.

GUI components can generate many events in response to user interactions. Each event is represented by a class and can be processed only by the appropriate type of event handler. Normally, a component's supported events are described in the Java API documentation for that component's class and its superclasses. When the user presses *Enter* in a JTextField or JPasswordField, an **ActionEvent** (package java.awt.event) occurs. Such an event is processed by an object that implements the interface **ActionListener** (package java.awt.event). The information discussed here is available in the Java API documentation for classes JTextField and ActionEvent. Since JPasswordField is a subclass of JTextField, JPasswordField supports the same events.

To prepare to handle the events in this example, inner class TextFieldHandler implements interface ActionListener and declares the only method in that interface—actionPerformed (lines 53–79). This method specifies the tasks to perform when an ActionEvent occurs. So, inner class TextFieldHandler satisfies *Steps 1* and *2* listed earlier in this section. We'll discuss the details of method actionPerformed shortly.

Registering the Event Handler for Each Text Field

In the TextFieldFrame constructor, line 42 creates a TextFieldHandler object and assigns it to variable handler. This object's actionPerformed method will be called automatically when the user presses *Enter* in any of the GUI's text fields. However, before this can occur, the program must register this object as the event handler for each text field. Lines 43–46 are the event-registration statements that specify handler as the event handler for the three JTextFields and the JPasswordField. The application calls JTextField method **addActionListener** to register the event handler for each component. This method receives as its argument an ActionListener object, which can be an object of any class that implements ActionListener. The object handler *is an* ActionListener, because class TextFieldHandler implements ActionListener. After lines 43–46 execute, the object handler **listens for events**. Now, when the user presses *Enter* in any of these four text fields, method actionPerformed (line 53–79) in class TextFieldHandler is called to handle the event. If an event handler is not registered for a particular text field, the event that occurs when the user presses *Enter* in that text field is **consumed**—i.e., it's simply ignored by the application.

Software Engineering Observation 14.3
The event listener for an event must implement the appropriate event-listener interface.

Common Programming Error 14.2
Forgetting to register an event-handler object for a particular GUI component's event type causes events of that type to be ignored.

Details of Class **TextFieldHandler's** `actionPerformed` *Method*
In this example, we are using one event-handling object's `actionPerformed` method (lines
53–79) to handle the events generated by four text fields. Since we'd like to output the
name of each text field's instance variable for demonstration purposes, we must determine
which text field generated the event each time `actionPerformed` is called. The GUI component with which the user interacts is the **event source**. In this example, the event source
is one of the text fields or the password field. When the user presses *Enter* while one of
these GUI components has the focus, the system creates a unique `ActionEvent` object that
contains information about the event that just occurred, such as the event source and the
text in the text field. The system then passes this `ActionEvent` object in a method call to
the event listener's `actionPerformed` method. In this example, we display some of that information in a message dialog. Line 55 declares the `String` that will be displayed. The variable is initialized with the **empty string**—a `String` containing no characters. The compiler
requires this in case none of the branches of the nested `if` in lines 58–75 executes.

   `ActionEvent` method `getSource` (which is inherited into `ActionEvent` from class
`EventObject` and called in lines 58, 63, 68 and 73) returns a reference to the event source.
The condition in line 58 asks, "Is the event source `textField1`?" This condition compares
the references on either side of the `==` operator to determine if they refer to the same object.
If they both refer to `textField1`, the program knows that the user pressed *Enter* in
`textField1`. In this case, lines 59–60 create a `String` containing the message that line 78
displays in a message dialog. Line 60 uses `ActionEvent` method **getActionCommand** to
obtain the text the user typed in the text field that generated the event.

   In this example, we display the text of the password in the `JPasswordField` when the
user presses *Enter* in that field. Sometimes it's necessary to programatically process the
characters in a password. Class `JPasswordField` method **getPassword** returns the password's characters as an array of type `char`.

Class **TextFieldTest**
Class `TextFieldTest` (Fig. 14.10) contains the `main` method that executes this application
and displays an object of class `TextFieldFrame`. When you execute the application, note
that even the uneditable `JTextField` (`textField3`) can generate an `ActionEvent`. To test
this, click the text field to give it the focus, then press *Enter*. Also note that the actual text
of the password is displayed when you press *Enter* in the `JPasswordField`. Of course, you
would normally not display the password!

   This application used a single object of class `TextFieldHandler` as the event listener
for four text fields. Starting in Section 14.10, you'll see that it's possible to declare several
event-listener objects of the same type and register each object for a separate GUI component's event. This technique enables us to eliminate the `if...else` logic used in this
example's event handler by providing separate event handlers for each component's events.

14.7 Common GUI Event Types and Listener Interfaces

In Section 14.6, you learned that information about the event that occurs when the user
presses *Enter* in a text field is stored in an `ActionEvent` object. Many different types of
events can occur when the user interacts with a GUI. The event information is stored in
an object of a class that extends `AWTEvent` (from package `java.awt`). Figure 14.11 illustrates a hierarchy containing many event classes from the package **java.awt.event**. Some
of these are discussed in this chapter and Chapter 25. These event types are used with both

AWT and Swing components. Additional event types that are specific to Swing GUI components are declared in package `javax.swing.event`.

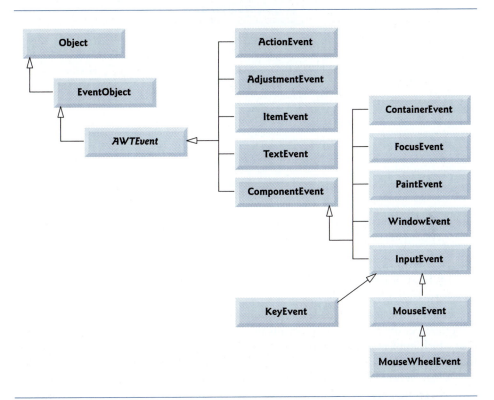

Fig. 14.11 | Some event classes of package `java.awt.event`.

Let's summarize the three parts to the event-handling mechanism that you saw in Section 14.6—the event source, the event object and the event listener. The event source is the GUI component with which the user interacts. The event object encapsulates information about the event that occurred, such as a reference to the event source and any event-specific information that may be required by the event listener for it to handle the event. The event listener is an object that is notified by the event source when an event occurs; in effect, it "listens" for an event, and one of its methods executes in response to the event. A method of the event listener receives an event object when the event listener is notified of the event. The event listener then uses the event object to respond to the event. This event-handling model is known as the delegation event model—an event's processing is delegated to an object (the event listener) in the application.

For each event-object type, there is typically a corresponding event-listener interface. An event listener for a GUI event is an object of a class that implements one or more of the event-listener interfaces from packages `java.awt.event` and `javax.swing.event`. Many of the event-listener types are common to both Swing and AWT components. Such types are declared in package `java.awt.event`, and some of them are shown in Fig. 14.12. Additional event-listener types that are specific to Swing components are declared in package `javax.swing.event`.

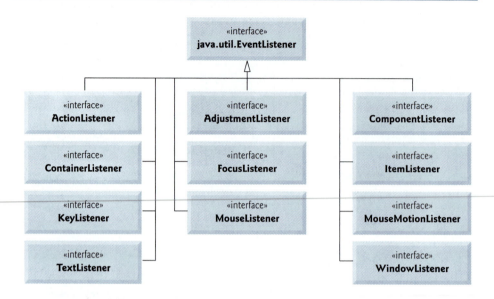

Fig. 14.12 | Some common event-listener interfaces of package `java.awt.event`.

Each event-listener interface specifies one or more event-handling methods that must be declared in the class that implements the interface. Recall from Section 10.7 that any class which implements an interface must declare all the `abstract` methods of that interface; otherwise, the class is an `abstract` class and cannot be used to create objects.

When an event occurs, the GUI component with which the user interacted notifies its registered listeners by calling each listener's appropriate event-handling method. For example, when the user presses the *Enter* key in a `JTextField`, the registered listener's `actionPerformed` method is called. How did the event handler get registered? How does the GUI component know to call `actionPerformed` rather than another event-handling method? We answer these questions and diagram the interaction in the next section.

14.8 How Event Handling Works

Let's illustrate how the event-handling mechanism works, using `textField1` from the example of Fig. 14.9. We have two remaining open questions from Section 14.7:

1. How did the event handler get registered?
2. How does the GUI component know to call `actionPerformed` rather than some other event-handling method?

The first question is answered by the event registration performed in lines 43–46 of Fig. 14.9. Figure 14.13 diagrams `JTextField` variable `textField1`, `TextFieldHandler` variable `handler` and the objects to which they refer.

Registering Events
Every `JComponent` has an instance variable called `listenerList` that refers to an object of class **EventListenerList** (package `javax.swing.event`). Each object of a `JComponent`

subclass maintains references to its registered listeners in the `listenerList`. For simplicity, we've diagramed `listenerList` as an array below the `JTextField` object in Fig. 14.13.

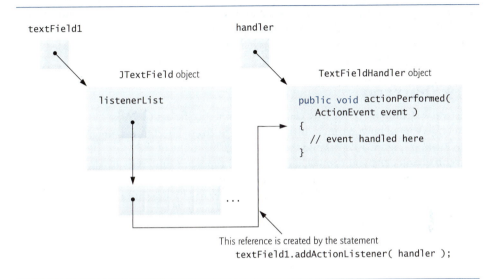

Fig. 14.13 | Event registration for `JTextField` `textField1`.

When line 43 of Fig. 14.9

```
textField1.addActionListener( handler );
```

executes, a new entry containing a reference to the `TextFieldHandler` object is placed in `textField1`'s `listenerList`. Although not shown in the diagram, this new entry also includes the listener's type (in this case, `ActionListener`). Using this mechanism, each lightweight Swing GUI component maintains its own list of listeners that were registered to handle the component's events.

Event-Handler Invocation

The event-listener type is important in answering the second question: How does the GUI component know to call `actionPerformed` rather than another method? Every GUI component supports several event types, including **mouse events, key events** and others. When an event occurs, the event is **dispatched** only to the event listeners of the appropriate type. Dispatching is simply the process by which the GUI component calls an event-handling method on each of its listeners that are registered for the event type that occurred.

Each event type has one or more corresponding event-listener interfaces. For example, `ActionEvents` are handled by `ActionListeners`, **MouseEvents** are handled by **MouseListeners** and **MouseMotionListeners**, and `KeyEvents` are handled by **KeyListeners**. When an event occurs, the GUI component receives (from the JVM) a unique **event ID** specifying the event type. The GUI component uses the event ID to decide the listener type to which the event should be dispatched and to decide which method to call on each listener object. For an `ActionEvent`, the event is dispatched to every registered `ActionListener`'s `actionPerformed` method (the only method in interface `ActionListener`). For a Mouse-Event, the event is dispatched to every registered `MouseListener` or `MouseMotionLis-`

tener, depending on the mouse event that occurs. The `MouseEvent`'s event ID determines which of the several mouse event-handling methods are called. All these decisions are handled for you by the GUI components. All you need to do is register an event handler for the particular event type that your application requires, and the GUI component will ensure that the event handler's appropriate method gets called when the event occurs. [*Note:* We discuss other event types and event-listener interfaces as they're needed with each new component we introduce.]

14.9 JButton

A button is a component the user clicks to trigger a specific action. A Java application can use several types of buttons, including command buttons, checkboxes, toggle buttons and radio buttons. Figure 14.14 shows the inheritance hierarchy of the Swing buttons we cover in this chapter. As you can see, all the button types are subclasses of **AbstractButton** (package `javax.swing`), which declares the common features of Swing buttons. In this section, we concentrate on buttons that are typically used to initiate a command.

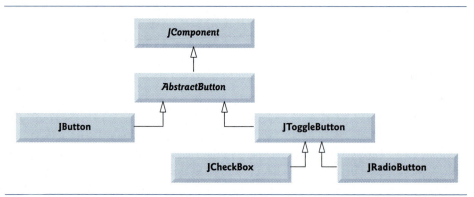

Fig. 14.14 | Swing button hierarchy.

Look-and-Feel Observation 14.7
Buttons typically use book-title capitalization.

A command button (see Fig. 14.16's output) generates an `ActionEvent` when the user clicks it. Command buttons are created with class **JButton**. The text on the face of a JButton is called a button label. A GUI can have many JButtons, but each button label typically should be unique in the portion of the GUI that is currently displayed.

Look-and-Feel Observation 14.8
Having more than one JButton with the same label makes the JButtons ambiguous to the user. Provide a unique label for each button.

The application of Figs. 14.15 and 14.16 creates two JButtons and demonstrates that JButtons support the display of `Icon`s. Event handling for the buttons is performed by a single instance of inner class `ButtonHandler` (lines 39–47).

```
 1    // Fig. 14.15: ButtonFrame.java
 2    // Creating JButtons.
 3    import java.awt.FlowLayout;
 4    import java.awt.event.ActionListener;
 5    import java.awt.event.ActionEvent;
 6    import javax.swing.JFrame;
 7    import javax.swing.JButton;
 8    import javax.swing.Icon;
 9    import javax.swing.ImageIcon;
10    import javax.swing.JOptionPane;
11
12    public class ButtonFrame extends JFrame
13    {
14       private JButton plainJButton; // button with just text
15       private JButton fancyJButton; // button with icons
16
17       // ButtonFrame adds JButtons to JFrame
18       public ButtonFrame()
19       {
20          super( "Testing Buttons" );
21          setLayout( new FlowLayout() ); // set frame layout
22
23          plainJButton = new JButton( "Plain Button" ); // button with text
24          add( plainJButton ); // add plainJButton to JFrame
25
26          Icon bug1 = new ImageIcon( getClass().getResource( "bug1.gif" ) );
27          Icon bug2 = new ImageIcon( getClass().getResource( "bug2.gif" ) );
28          fancyJButton = new JButton( "Fancy Button", bug1 ); // set image
29          fancyJButton.setRolloverIcon( bug2 ); // set rollover image
30          add( fancyJButton ); // add fancyJButton to JFrame
31
32          // create new ButtonHandler for button event handling
33          ButtonHandler handler = new ButtonHandler();
34          fancyJButton.addActionListener( handler );
35          plainJButton.addActionListener( handler );
36       } // end ButtonFrame constructor
37
38       // inner class for button event handling
39       private class ButtonHandler implements ActionListener
40       {
41          // handle button event
42          public void actionPerformed( ActionEvent event )
43          {
44             JOptionPane.showMessageDialog( ButtonFrame.this, String.format(
45                "You pressed: %s", event.getActionCommand() ) );
46          } // end method actionPerformed
47       } // end private inner class ButtonHandler
48    } // end class ButtonFrame
```

Fig. 14.15 | Command buttons and action events.

Lines 14–15 declare JButton variables plainJButton and fancyJButton. The corresponding objects are instantiated in the constructor. Line 23 creates plainJButton with the button label "Plain Button". Line 24 adds the JButton to the JFrame.

```
 1   // Fig. 14.16: ButtonTest.java
 2   // Testing ButtonFrame.
 3   import javax.swing.JFrame;
 4
 5   public class ButtonTest
 6   {
 7      public static void main( String[] args )
 8      {
 9         ButtonFrame buttonFrame = new ButtonFrame(); // create ButtonFrame
10         buttonFrame.setDefaultCloseOperation( JFrame.EXIT_ON_CLOSE );
11         buttonFrame.setSize( 275, 110 ); // set frame size
12         buttonFrame.setVisible( true ); // display frame
13      } // end main
14   } // end class ButtonTest
```

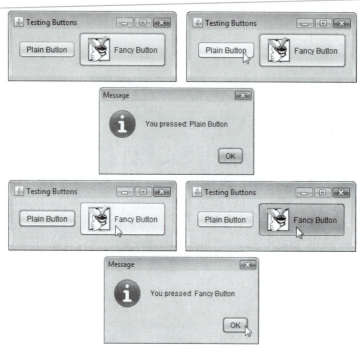

Fig. 14.16 | Test class for `ButtonFrame`.

A `JButton` can display an `Icon`. To provide the user with an extra level of visual inter-action with the GUI, a `JButton` can also have a **rollover Icon**—an `Icon` that is displayed when the user positions the mouse over the `JButton`. The icon on the `JButton` changes as the mouse moves in and out of the `JButton`'s area on the screen. Lines 26–27 (Fig. 14.15) create two `ImageIcon` objects that represent the default `Icon` and rollover `Icon` for the `JButton` created at line 28. Both statements assume that the image files are stored in the same directory as the application. Images are commonly placed in the same directory as the application or a subdirectory like `images`). These image files have been provided for you with the example.

Line 28 creates `fancyButton` with the text `"Fancy Button"` and the icon `bug1`. By default, the text is displayed to the right of the icon. Line 29 uses **setRolloverIcon** (inherited from class `AbstractButton`) to specify the image displayed on the `JButton` when the user positions the mouse over it. Line 30 adds the `JButton` to the `JFrame`.

> ### Look-and-Feel Observation 14.9
> *Because class `AbstractButton` supports displaying text and images on a button, all sub-classes of `AbstractButton` also support displaying text and images.*

> ### Look-and-Feel Observation 14.10
> *Using rollover icons for `JButtons` provides users with visual feedback indicating that when they click the mouse while the cursor is positioned over the `JButton`, an action will occur.*

`JButtons`, like `JTextFields`, generate `ActionEvents` that can be processed by any `ActionListener` object. Lines 33–35 create an object of `private` inner class `ButtonHandler` and use `addActionListener` to register it as the event handler for each `JButton`. Class `ButtonHandler` (lines 39–47) declares `actionPerformed` to display a message dialog box containing the label for the button the user pressed. For a `JButton` event, `ActionEvent` method `getActionCommand` returns the label on the `JButton`.

Accessing the `this` Reference in an Object of a Top-Level Class From an Inner Class
When you execute this application and click one of its buttons, notice that the message dialog that appears is centered over the application's window. This occurs because the call to `JOptionPane` method `showMessageDialog` (lines 44–45 of Fig. 14.15) uses `ButtonFrame.this` rather than `null` as the first argument. When this argument is not `null`, it represents the so-called parent GUI component of the message dialog (in this case the application window is the parent component) and enables the dialog to be centered over that component when the dialog is displayed. `ButtonFrame.this` represents the `this` reference of the object of top-level class `ButtonFrame`.

> ### Software Engineering Observation 14.4
> *When used in an inner class, keyword `this` refers to the current inner-class object being manipulated. An inner-class method can use its outer-class object's `this` by preceding `this` with the outer-class name and a dot, as in `ButtonFrame.this`.*

14.10 Buttons That Maintain State

The Swing GUI components contain three types of **state buttons**—**`JToggleButton`**, **`JCheckBox`** and **`JRadioButton`**—that have on/off or true/false values. Classes `JCheckBox` and `JRadioButton` are subclasses of `JToggleButton` (Fig. 14.14). A `JRadioButton` is different from a `JCheckBox` in that normally several `JRadioButtons` are grouped together and are mutually exclusive—only one in the group can be selected at any time, just like the buttons on a car radio. We first discuss class `JCheckBox`.

14.10.1 JCheckBox

The application of Figs. 14.17–14.18 uses two `JCheckBoxes` to select the desired font style of the text displayed in a `JTextField`. When selected, one applies a bold style and the other an italic style. If both are selected, the style is bold and italic. When the application initially executes, neither `JCheckBox` is checked (i.e., they're both `false`), so the font is plain. Class `CheckBoxTest` (Fig. 14.18) contains the `main` method that executes this application.

```
 1    // Fig. 14.17: CheckBoxFrame.java
 2    // Creating JCheckBox buttons.
 3    import java.awt.FlowLayout;
 4    import java.awt.Font;
 5    import java.awt.event.ItemListener;
 6    import java.awt.event.ItemEvent;
 7    import javax.swing.JFrame;
 8    import javax.swing.JTextField;
 9    import javax.swing.JCheckBox;
10
11    public class CheckBoxFrame extends JFrame
12    {
13       private JTextField textField; // displays text in changing fonts
14       private JCheckBox boldJCheckBox; // to select/deselect bold
15       private JCheckBox italicJCheckBox; // to select/deselect italic
16
17       // CheckBoxFrame constructor adds JCheckBoxes to JFrame
18       public CheckBoxFrame()
19       {
20          super( "JCheckBox Test" );
21          setLayout( new FlowLayout() ); // set frame layout
22
23          // set up JTextField and set its font
24          textField = new JTextField( "Watch the font style change", 20 );
25          textField.setFont( new Font( "Serif", Font.PLAIN, 14 ) );
26          add( textField ); // add textField to JFrame
27
28          boldJCheckBox = new JCheckBox( "Bold" ); // create bold checkbox
29          italicJCheckBox = new JCheckBox( "Italic" ); // create italic
30          add( boldJCheckBox ); // add bold checkbox to JFrame
31          add( italicJCheckBox ); // add italic checkbox to JFrame
32
33          // register listeners for JCheckBoxes
34          CheckBoxHandler handler = new CheckBoxHandler();
35          boldJCheckBox.addItemListener( handler );
36          italicJCheckBox.addItemListener( handler );
37       } // end CheckBoxFrame constructor
38
39       // private inner class for ItemListener event handling
40       private class CheckBoxHandler implements ItemListener
41       {
42          // respond to checkbox events
43          public void itemStateChanged( ItemEvent event )
44          {
45             Font font = null; // stores the new Font
46
47             // determine which CheckBoxes are checked and create Font
48             if ( boldJCheckBox.isSelected() && italicJCheckBox.isSelected() )
49                font = new Font( "Serif", Font.BOLD + Font.ITALIC, 14 );
50             else if ( boldJCheckBox.isSelected() )
51                font = new Font( "Serif", Font.BOLD, 14 );
52             else if ( italicJCheckBox.isSelected() )
53                font = new Font( "Serif", Font.ITALIC, 14 );
```

Fig. 14.17 | JCheckBox buttons and item events. (Part 1 of 2.)

```
54              else
55                 font = new Font( "Serif", Font.PLAIN, 14 );
56
57              textField.setFont( font ); // set textField's font
58          } // end method itemStateChanged
59       } // end private inner class CheckBoxHandler
60    } // end class CheckBoxFrame
```

Fig. 14.17 | JCheckBox buttons and item events. (Part 2 of 2.)

```
1    // Fig. 14.18: CheckBoxTest.java
2    // Testing CheckBoxFrame.
3    import javax.swing.JFrame;
4
5    public class CheckBoxTest
6    {
7       public static void main( String[] args )
8       {
9          CheckBoxFrame checkBoxFrame = new CheckBoxFrame();
10         checkBoxFrame.setDefaultCloseOperation( JFrame.EXIT_ON_CLOSE );
11         checkBoxFrame.setSize( 275, 100 ); // set frame size
12         checkBoxFrame.setVisible( true ); // display frame
13      } // end main
14   } // end class CheckBoxTest
```

Fig. 14.18 | Test class for CheckBoxFrame.

After the JTextField is created and initialized (Fig. 14.17, line 24), line 25 uses method **setFont** (inherited by JTextField indirectly from class Component) to set the font of the JTextField to a new object of class **Font** (package java.awt). The new Font is initialized with "Serif" (a generic font name that represents a font such as Times and is supported on all Java platforms), Font.PLAIN style and 14-point size. Next, lines 28–29 create two JCheckBox objects. The String passed to the JCheckBox constructor is the checkbox label that appears to the right of the JCheckBox by default.

When the user clicks a JCheckBox, an **ItemEvent** occurs. This event can be handled by an **ItemListener** object, which must implement method **itemStateChanged**. In this example, the event handling is performed by an instance of private inner class CheckBoxHandler (lines 40–59). Lines 34–36 create an instance of class CheckBoxHandler and register it with method **addItemListener** as the listener for both the JCheckBox objects.

CheckBoxHandler method itemStateChanged (lines 43–58) is called when the user clicks the boldJCheckBox or the italicJCheckBox. In this example, we don't need to know which of the two JCheckBoxes was clicked, just whether or not each one is checked.

Line 48 uses JCheckBox method **isSelected** to determine if both JCheckBoxes are selected. If so, line 49 creates a bold italic font by adding the Font constants Font.BOLD and Font.ITALIC for the font-style argument of the Font constructor. Line 50 determines whether the boldJCheckBox is selected, and if so line 51 creates a bold font. Line 52 determines whether the italicJCheckBox is selected, and if so line 53 creates an italic font. If none of the preceding conditions are true, line 55 creates a plain font using the Font constant Font.PLAIN. Finally, line 57 sets textField's new font, which changes the font in the JTextField on the screen.

Relationship Between an Inner Class and Its Top-Level Class

You may have noticed that class CheckBoxHandler used variables boldJCheckBox (Fig. 14.17, lines 48 and 50), italicJCheckBox (lines 48 and 52) and textField (line 57) even though these variables are not declared in the inner class. Recall that an inner class has a special relationship with its top-level class—it is allowed to access all the variables and methods of the top-level class. CheckBoxHandler method itemStateChanged (line 43–58) uses this relationship to determine which JCheckBoxes are checked and to set the font on the JTextField. Notice that none of the code in inner class CheckBoxHandler requires an explicit reference to the top-level class object.

14.10.2 JRadioButton

Radio buttons (declared with class JRadioButton) are similar to checkboxes in that they have two states—selected and not selected (also called deselected). However, radio buttons normally appear as a **group** in which only one button can be selected at a time (see the output of Fig. 14.20). Selecting a different radio button forces all others to be deselected. Radio buttons are used to represent **mutually exclusive options** (i.e., multiple options in the group cannot be selected at the same time). The logical relationship between radio buttons is maintained by a **ButtonGroup** object (package javax.swing), which itself is not a GUI component. A ButtonGroup object organizes a group of buttons and is not itself displayed in a user interface. Rather, the individual JRadioButton objects from the group are displayed in the GUI.

Common Programming Error 14.3

Adding a ButtonGroup object (or an object of any other class that does not derive from Component) to a container results in a compilation error.

The application of Figs. 14.19–14.20 is similar to that of Figs. 14.17–14.18. The user can alter the font style of a JTextField's text. The application uses radio buttons that permit only a single font style in the group to be selected at a time. Class RadioButtonTest (Fig. 14.20) contains the main method that executes this application.

```
1   // Fig. 14.19: RadioButtonFrame.java
2   // Creating radio buttons using ButtonGroup and JRadioButton.
3   import java.awt.FlowLayout;
4   import java.awt.Font;
5   import java.awt.event.ItemListener;
6   import java.awt.event.ItemEvent;
7   import javax.swing.JFrame;
```

Fig. 14.19 | JRadioButtons and ButtonGroups. (Part 1 of 3.)

```
 8   import javax.swing.JTextField;
 9   import javax.swing.JRadioButton;
10   import javax.swing.ButtonGroup;
11
12   public class RadioButtonFrame extends JFrame
13   {
14      private JTextField textField; // used to display font changes
15      private Font plainFont; // font for plain text
16      private Font boldFont; // font for bold text
17      private Font italicFont; // font for italic text
18      private Font boldItalicFont; // font for bold and italic text
19      private JRadioButton plainJRadioButton; // selects plain text
20      private JRadioButton boldJRadioButton; // selects bold text
21      private JRadioButton italicJRadioButton; // selects italic text
22      private JRadioButton boldItalicJRadioButton; // bold and italic
23      private ButtonGroup radioGroup; // buttongroup to hold radio buttons
24
25      // RadioButtonFrame constructor adds JRadioButtons to JFrame
26      public RadioButtonFrame()
27      {
28         super( "RadioButton Test" );
29         setLayout( new FlowLayout() ); // set frame layout
30
31         textField = new JTextField( "Watch the font style change", 25 );
32         add( textField ); // add textField to JFrame
33
34         // create radio buttons
35         plainJRadioButton = new JRadioButton( "Plain", true );
36         boldJRadioButton = new JRadioButton( "Bold", false );
37         italicJRadioButton = new JRadioButton( "Italic", false );
38         boldItalicJRadioButton = new JRadioButton( "Bold/Italic", false );
39         add( plainJRadioButton ); // add plain button to JFrame
40         add( boldJRadioButton ); // add bold button to JFrame
41         add( italicJRadioButton ); // add italic button to JFrame
42         add( boldItalicJRadioButton ); // add bold and italic button
43
44         // create logical relationship between JRadioButtons
45         radioGroup = new ButtonGroup(); // create ButtonGroup
46         radioGroup.add( plainJRadioButton ); // add plain to group
47         radioGroup.add( boldJRadioButton ); // add bold to group
48         radioGroup.add( italicJRadioButton ); // add italic to group
49         radioGroup.add( boldItalicJRadioButton ); // add bold and italic
50
51         // create font objects
52         plainFont = new Font( "Serif", Font.PLAIN, 14 );
53         boldFont = new Font( "Serif", Font.BOLD, 14 );
54         italicFont = new Font( "Serif", Font.ITALIC, 14 );
55         boldItalicFont = new Font( "Serif", Font.BOLD + Font.ITALIC, 14 );
56         textField.setFont( plainFont ); // set initial font to plain
57
58         // register events for JRadioButtons
59         plainJRadioButton.addItemListener(
60            new RadioButtonHandler( plainFont ) );
```

Fig. 14.19 | JRadioButtons and ButtonGroups. (Part 2 of 3.)

```
61          boldJRadioButton.addItemListener(
62             new RadioButtonHandler( boldFont ) );
63          italicJRadioButton.addItemListener(
64             new RadioButtonHandler( italicFont ) );
65          boldItalicJRadioButton.addItemListener(
66             new RadioButtonHandler( boldItalicFont ) );
67       } // end RadioButtonFrame constructor
68
69       // private inner class to handle radio button events
70       private class RadioButtonHandler implements ItemListener
71       {
72          private Font font; // font associated with this listener
73
74          public RadioButtonHandler( Font f )
75          {
76             font = f; // set the font of this listener
77          } // end constructor RadioButtonHandler
78
79          // handle radio button events
80          public void itemStateChanged( ItemEvent event )
81          {
82             textField.setFont( font ); // set font of textField
83          } // end method itemStateChanged
84       } // end private inner class RadioButtonHandler
85    } // end class RadioButtonFrame
```

Fig. 14.19 | JRadioButtons and ButtonGroups. (Part 3 of 3.)

```
1    // Fig. 14.20: RadioButtonTest.java
2    // Testing RadioButtonFrame.
3    import javax.swing.JFrame;
4
5    public class RadioButtonTest
6    {
7       public static void main( String[] args )
8       {
9          RadioButtonFrame radioButtonFrame = new RadioButtonFrame();
10         radioButtonFrame.setDefaultCloseOperation( JFrame.EXIT_ON_CLOSE );
11         radioButtonFrame.setSize( 300, 100 ); // set frame size
12         radioButtonFrame.setVisible( true ); // display frame
13      } // end main
14   } // end class RadioButtonTest
```

Fig. 14.20 | Test class for RadioButtonFrame.

Lines 35–42 in the constructor (Fig. 14.19) create four JRadioButton objects and add them to the JFrame. Each JRadioButton is created with a constructor call like that in line 35. This constructor specifies the label that appears to the right of the JRadioButton by default and the initial state of the JRadioButton. A true second argument indicates that the JRadioButton should appear selected when it's displayed.

Line 45 instantiates ButtonGroup object radioGroup. This object is the "glue" that forms the logical relationship between the four JRadioButton objects and allows only one of the four to be selected at a time. It's possible that no JRadioButtons in a ButtonGroup are selected, but this can occur only if no preselected JRadioButtons are added to the ButtonGroup and the user has not selected a JRadioButton yet. Lines 46–49 use ButtonGroup method **add** to associate each of the JRadioButtons with radioGroup. If more than one selected JRadioButton object is added to the group, the selected one that was added first will be selected when the GUI is displayed.

JRadioButtons, like JCheckBoxes, generate ItemEvents when they're clicked. Lines 59–66 create four instances of inner class RadioButtonHandler (declared at lines 70–84). In this example, each event-listener object is registered to handle the ItemEvent generated when the user clicks a particular JRadioButton. Notice that each RadioButtonHandler object is initialized with a particular Font object (created in lines 52–55).

Class RadioButtonHandler (line 70–84) implements interface ItemListener so it can handle ItemEvents generated by the JRadioButtons. The constructor stores the Font object it receives as an argument in the event-listener object's instance variable font (declared at line 72). When the user clicks a JRadioButton, radioGroup turns off the previously selected JRadioButton and method itemStateChanged (line 80–83) sets the font in the JTextField to the Font stored in the JRadioButton's corresponding event-listener object. Notice that line 82 of inner class RadioButtonHandler uses the top-level class's textField instance variable to set the font.

14.11 JComboBox and Using an Anonymous Inner Class for Event Handling

A combo box (sometimes called a **drop-down list**) enables the user to select one item from a list (Fig. 14.22). Combo boxes are implemented with class **JComboBox**, which extends class JComponent. JComboBoxes generate ItemEvents like JCheckBoxes and JRadioButtons. This example also demonstrates a special form of inner class that is used frequently in event handling. The application (Figs. 14.21–14.22) uses a JComboBox to provide a list of four image-file names from which the user can select one image to display. When the user selects a name, the application displays the corresponding image as an Icon on a JLabel. Class ComboBoxTest (Fig. 14.22) contains the main method that executes this application. The screen captures for this application show the JComboBox list after the selection was made to illustrate which image-file name was selected.

```
1   // Fig. 14.21: ComboBoxFrame.java
2   // JComboBox that displays a list of image names.
3   import java.awt.FlowLayout;
4   import java.awt.event.ItemListener;
5   import java.awt.event.ItemEvent;
```

Fig. 14.21 | JComboBox that displays a list of image names. (Part 1 of 2.)

```
 6   import javax.swing.JFrame;
 7   import javax.swing.JLabel;
 8   import javax.swing.JComboBox;
 9   import javax.swing.Icon;
10   import javax.swing.ImageIcon;
11
12   public class ComboBoxFrame extends JFrame
13   {
14      private JComboBox imagesJComboBox; // combobox to hold names of icons
15      private JLabel label; // label to display selected icon
16
17      private static final String[] names =
18         { "bug1.gif", "bug2.gif",  "travelbug.gif", "buganim.gif" };
19      private Icon[] icons = {
20         new ImageIcon( getClass().getResource( names[ 0 ] ) ),
21         new ImageIcon( getClass().getResource( names[ 1 ] ) ),
22         new ImageIcon( getClass().getResource( names[ 2 ] ) ),
23         new ImageIcon( getClass().getResource( names[ 3 ] ) ) };
24
25      // ComboBoxFrame constructor adds JComboBox to JFrame
26      public ComboBoxFrame()
27      {
28         super( "Testing JComboBox" );
29         setLayout( new FlowLayout() ); // set frame layout
30
31         imagesJComboBox = new JComboBox( names ); // set up JComboBox
32         imagesJComboBox.setMaximumRowCount( 3 ); // display three rows
33
34         imagesJComboBox.addItemListener(
35            new ItemListener() // anonymous inner class
36            {
37               // handle JComboBox event
38               public void itemStateChanged( ItemEvent event )
39               {
40                  // determine whether item selected
41                  if ( event.getStateChange() == ItemEvent.SELECTED )
42                     label.setIcon( icons[
43                        imagesJComboBox.getSelectedIndex() ] );
44               } // end method itemStateChanged
45            } // end anonymous inner class
46         ); // end call to addItemListener
47
48         add( imagesJComboBox ); // add combobox to JFrame
49         label = new JLabel( icons[ 0 ] ); // display first icon
50         add( label ); // add label to JFrame
51      } // end ComboBoxFrame constructor
52   } // end class ComboBoxFrame
```

Fig. 14.21 | JComboBox that displays a list of image names. (Part 2 of 2.)

```
1   // Fig. 14.22: ComboBoxTest.java
2   // Testing ComboBoxFrame.
3   import javax.swing.JFrame;
```

Fig. 14.22 | Testing ComboBoxFrame. (Part 1 of 2.)

```
 4
 5   public class ComboBoxTest
 6   {
 7      public static void main( String[] args )
 8      {
 9         ComboBoxFrame comboBoxFrame = new ComboBoxFrame();
10         comboBoxFrame.setDefaultCloseOperation( JFrame.EXIT_ON_CLOSE );
11         comboBoxFrame.setSize( 350, 150 ); // set frame size
12         comboBoxFrame.setVisible( true ); // display frame
13      } // end main
14   } // end class ComboBoxTest
```

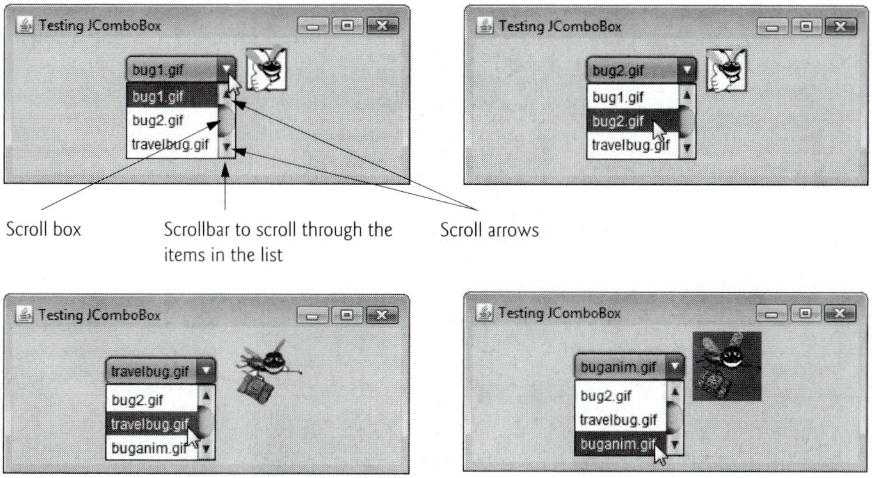

Scroll box   Scrollbar to scroll through the   Scroll arrows
                    items in the list

Fig. 14.22 | Testing ComboBoxFrame. (Part 2 of 2.)

Lines 19–23 (Fig. 14.21) declare and initialize array icons with four new ImageIcon objects. String array names (lines 17–18) contains the names of the four image files that are stored in the same directory as the application.

At line 31, the constructor initializes a JComboBox object with the Strings in array names as the elements in the list. Each item in the list has an **index**. The first item is added at index 0, the next at index 1 and so forth. The first item added to a JComboBox appears as the currently selected item when the JComboBox is displayed. Other items are selected by clicking the JComboBox, then selecting an item from the list that appears.

Line 32 uses JComboBox method **setMaximumRowCount** to set the maximum number of elements that are displayed when the user clicks the JComboBox. If there are additional items, the JComboBox provides a **scrollbar** (see the first screen capture) that allows the user to scroll through all the elements in the list. The user can click the **scroll arrows** at the top and bottom of the scrollbar to move up and down through the list one element at a time, or else drag the **scroll box** in the middle of the scrollbar up and down. To drag the scroll box, position the mouse cursor on it, hold the mouse button down and move the mouse. [*Note:* In this example, the drop-down list is too short to drag the scroll box, so you can click the up and down arrows or use your mouse's wheel to scroll through the four items in the list.

Line 48 attaches the JComboBox to the ComboBoxFrame's FlowLayout (set in line 29). Line 49 creates the JLabel that displays ImageIcons and initializes it with the first Image-Icon in array icons. Line 50 attaches the JLabel to the ComboBoxFrame's FlowLayout.

Using an Anonymous Inner Class for Event Handling
Lines 34–46 are one statement that declares the event listener's class, creates an object of that class and registers it as the listener for imagesJComboBox's ItemEvents. This event-listener object is an instance of an anonymous inner class—an inner class that is declared without a name and typically appears inside a method declaration. As with other inner classes, an anonymous inner class can access its top-level class's members. However, an anonymous inner class has limited access to the local variables of the method in which it's declared. Since an anonymous inner class has no name, one object of the anonymous inner class must be created at the point where the class is declared (starting at line 35).

Lines 34–46 are a call to imagesJComboBox's addItemListener method. The argument to this method must be an object that *is an* ItemListener (i.e., any object of a class that implements ItemListener). Lines 35–45 are a class-instance creation expression that declares an anonymous inner class and creates one object of that class. A reference to that object is then passed as the argument to addItemListener. The syntax ItemListener() after new begins the declaration of an anonymous inner class that implements interface ItemListener. This is similar to beginning a class declaration with

```
public class MyHandler implements ItemListener
```

The parentheses after ItemListener indicate a call to the default constructor of the anonymous inner class.

The opening left brace at 36 and the closing right brace at line 45 delimit the body of the anonymous inner class. Lines 38–44 declare the ItemListener's itemStateChanged method. When the user makes a selection from imagesJComboBox, this method sets label's Icon. The Icon is selected from array icons by determining the index of the selected item in the JComboBox with method getSelectedIndex in line 43. Note that for each item selected from a JComboBox, another item is first deselected—so two ItemEvents occur when an item is selected. We wish to display only the icon for the item the user just selected. For this reason, line 41 determines whether ItemEvent method getStateChange returns ItemEvent.SELECTED. If so, lines 42–43 set label's icon.

The syntax shown in lines 35–45 for creating an event handler with an anonymous inner class is similar to the code that would be generated by a Java integrated development environment (IDE). Typically, an IDE enables you to design a GUI visually, then it generates code that implements the GUI. You simply insert statements in the event-handling methods that declare how to handle each event.

14.12 JList

A list displays a series of items from which the user may select one or more items (see the output of Fig. 14.24). Lists are created with class JList, which directly extends class JComponent. Class JList supports **single-selection lists** (which allow only one item to be selected at a time) and **multiple-selection lists** (which allow any number of items to be selected). In this section, we discuss single-selection lists.

The application of Figs. 14.23–14.24 creates a JList containing 13 color names. When a color name is clicked in the JList, a **ListSelectionEvent** occurs and the application changes the background color of the application window to the selected color. Class ListTest (Fig. 14.24) contains the main method that executes this application.

```java
1   // Fig. 14.23: ListFrame.java
2   // JList that displays a list of colors.
3   import java.awt.FlowLayout;
4   import java.awt.Color;
5   import javax.swing.JFrame;
6   import javax.swing.JList;
7   import javax.swing.JScrollPane;
8   import javax.swing.event.ListSelectionListener;
9   import javax.swing.event.ListSelectionEvent;
10  import javax.swing.ListSelectionModel;
11
12  public class ListFrame extends JFrame
13  {
14     private JList colorJList; // list to display colors
15     private static final String[] colorNames = { "Black", "Blue", "Cyan",
16        "Dark Gray", "Gray", "Green", "Light Gray", "Magenta",
17        "Orange", "Pink", "Red", "White", "Yellow" };
18     private static final Color[] colors = { Color.BLACK, Color.BLUE,
19        Color.CYAN, Color.DARK_GRAY, Color.GRAY, Color.GREEN,
20        Color.LIGHT_GRAY, Color.MAGENTA, Color.ORANGE, Color.PINK,
21        Color.RED, Color.WHITE, Color.YELLOW };
22
23     // ListFrame constructor add JScrollPane containing JList to JFrame
24     public ListFrame()
25     {
26        super( "List Test" );
27        setLayout( new FlowLayout() ); // set frame layout
28
29        colorJList = new JList( colorNames ); // create with colorNames
30        colorJList.setVisibleRowCount( 5 ); // display five rows at once
31
32        // do not allow multiple selections
33        colorJList.setSelectionMode( ListSelectionModel.SINGLE_SELECTION );
```

Fig. 14.23 | JList that displays a list of colors. (Part 1 of 2.)

```
34
35          // add a JScrollPane containing JList to frame
36          add( new JScrollPane( colorJList ) );
37
38          colorJList.addListSelectionListener(
39             new ListSelectionListener() // anonymous inner class
40             {
41                // handle list selection events
42                public void valueChanged( ListSelectionEvent event )
43                {
44                   getContentPane().setBackground(
45                      colors[ colorJList.getSelectedIndex() ] );
46                } // end method valueChanged
47             } // end anonymous inner class
48          ); // end call to addListSelectionListener
49       } // end ListFrame constructor
50    } // end class ListFrame
```

Fig. 14.23 | JList that displays a list of colors. (Part 2 of 2.)

```
1   // Fig. 14.24: ListTest.java
2   // Selecting colors from a JList.
3   import javax.swing.JFrame;
4
5   public class ListTest
6   {
7      public static void main( String[] args )
8      {
9         ListFrame listFrame = new ListFrame(); // create ListFrame
10        listFrame.setDefaultCloseOperation( JFrame.EXIT_ON_CLOSE );
11        listFrame.setSize( 350, 150 ); // set frame size
12        listFrame.setVisible( true ); // display frame
13     } // end main
14  } // end class ListTest
```

Fig. 14.24 | Test class for ListFrame.

Line 29 (Fig. 14.23) creates JList object colorJList. The argument to the JList constructor is the array of Objects (in this case Strings) to display in the list. Line 30 uses JList method **setVisibleRowCount** to determine the number of items visible in the list.

Line 33 uses JList method **setSelectionMode** to specify the list's **selection mode**. Class **ListSelectionModel** (of package javax.swing) declares three constants that specify a JList's selection mode—**SINGLE_SELECTION** (which allows only one item to be selected at a time), **SINGLE_INTERVAL_SELECTION** (for a multiple-selection list that allows selection of several contiguous items) and **MULTIPLE_INTERVAL_SELECTION** (for a multiple-selection list that does not restrict the items that can be selected).

Unlike a JComboBox, a JList *does not* provide a scrollbar if there are more items in the list than the number of visible rows. In this case, a **JScrollPane** object is used to provide the scrolling capability. Line 36 adds a new instance of class JScrollPane to the JFrame. The JScrollPane constructor receives as its argument the JComponent that needs scrolling functionality (in this case, colorJList). Notice in the screen captures that a scrollbar created by the JScrollPane appears at the right side of the JList. By default, the scrollbar appears only when the number of items in the JList exceeds the number of visible items.

Lines 38–48 use JList method **addListSelectionListener** to register an object that implements **ListSelectionListener** (package javax.swing.event) as the listener for the JList's selection events. Once again, we use an instance of an anonymous inner class (lines 39–47) as the listener. In this example, when the user makes a selection from colorJList, method **valueChanged** (line 42–46) should change the background color of the List-Frame to the selected color. This is accomplished in lines 44–45. Note the use of JFrame method **getContentPane** in line 44. Each JFrame actually consists of three layers—the background, the content pane and the glass pane. The content pane appears in front of the background and is where the GUI components in the JFrame are displayed. The glass pane is used to display tool tips and other items that should appear in front of the GUI components on the screen. The content pane completely hides the background of the JFrame; thus, to change the background color behind the GUI components, you must change the content pane's background color. Method getContentPane returns a reference to the JFrame's content pane (an object of class Container). In line 44, we then use that reference to call method **setBackground**, which sets the content pane's background color to an element in the colors array. The color is selected from the array by using the selected item's index. JList method **getSelectedIndex** returns the selected item's index. As with arrays and JComboBoxes, JList indexing is zero based.

14.13 Multiple-Selection Lists

A **multiple-selection list** enables the user to select many items from a JList (see the output of Fig. 14.26). A SINGLE_INTERVAL_SELECTION list allows selecting a contiguous range of items. To do so, click the first item, then press and hold the *Shift* key while clicking the last item in the range. A MULTIPLE_INTERVAL_SELECTION list (the default) allows continuous range selection as described for a SINGLE_INTERVAL_SELECTION list. Such a list also allows miscellaneous items to be selected by pressing and holding the *Ctrl* key (sometimes called the *Control* key) while clicking each item to select. To deselect an item, press and hold the *Ctrl* key while clicking the item a second time.

The application of Figs. 14.25–14.26 uses multiple-selection lists to copy items from one JList to another. One list is a MULTIPLE_INTERVAL_SELECTION list and the other is a SINGLE_INTERVAL_SELECTION list. When you execute the application, try using the selection techniques described previously to select items in both lists.

```
1   // Fig. 14.25: MultipleSelectionFrame.java
2   // Copying items from one List to another.
3   import java.awt.FlowLayout;
```

Fig. 14.25 | JList that allows multiple selections. (Part 1 of 2.)

```java
 4  import java.awt.event.ActionListener;
 5  import java.awt.event.ActionEvent;
 6  import javax.swing.JFrame;
 7  import javax.swing.JList;
 8  import javax.swing.JButton;
 9  import javax.swing.JScrollPane;
10  import javax.swing.ListSelectionModel;
11
12  public class MultipleSelectionFrame extends JFrame
13  {
14     private JList colorJList; // list to hold color names
15     private JList copyJList; // list to copy color names into
16     private JButton copyJButton; // button to copy selected names
17     private static final String[] colorNames = { "Black", "Blue", "Cyan",
18        "Dark Gray", "Gray", "Green", "Light Gray", "Magenta", "Orange",
19        "Pink", "Red", "White", "Yellow" };
20
21     // MultipleSelectionFrame constructor
22     public MultipleSelectionFrame()
23     {
24        super( "Multiple Selection Lists" );
25        setLayout( new FlowLayout() ); // set frame layout
26
27        colorJList = new JList( colorNames ); // holds names of all colors
28        colorJList.setVisibleRowCount( 5 ); // show five rows
29        colorJList.setSelectionMode(
30           ListSelectionModel.MULTIPLE_INTERVAL_SELECTION );
31        add( new JScrollPane( colorJList ) ); // add list with scrollpane
32
33        copyJButton = new JButton( "Copy >>>" ); // create copy button
34        copyJButton.addActionListener(
35
36           new ActionListener() // anonymous inner class
37           {
38              // handle button event
39              public void actionPerformed( ActionEvent event )
40              {
41                 // place selected values in copyJList
42                 copyJList.setListData( colorJList.getSelectedValues() );
43              } // end method actionPerformed
44           } // end anonymous inner class
45        ); // end call to addActionListener
46
47        add( copyJButton ); // add copy button to JFrame
48
49        copyJList = new JList(); // create list to hold copied color names
50        copyJList.setVisibleRowCount( 5 ); // show 5 rows
51        copyJList.setFixedCellWidth( 100 ); // set width
52        copyJList.setFixedCellHeight( 15 ); // set height
53        copyJList.setSelectionMode(
54           ListSelectionModel.SINGLE_INTERVAL_SELECTION );
55        add( new JScrollPane( copyJList ) ); // add list with scrollpane
56     } // end MultipleSelectionFrame constructor
57  } // end class MultipleSelectionFrame
```

Fig. 14.25 | JList that allows multiple selections. (Part 2 of 2.)

```
1   // Fig. 14.26: MultipleSelectionTest.java
2   // Testing MultipleSelectionFrame.
3   import javax.swing.JFrame;
4
5   public class MultipleSelectionTest
6   {
7      public static void main( String[] args )
8      {
9         MultipleSelectionFrame multipleSelectionFrame =
10            new MultipleSelectionFrame();
11         multipleSelectionFrame.setDefaultCloseOperation(
12            JFrame.EXIT_ON_CLOSE );
13         multipleSelectionFrame.setSize( 350, 150 ); // set frame size
14         multipleSelectionFrame.setVisible( true ); // display frame
15      } // end main
16   } // end class MultipleSelectionTest
```

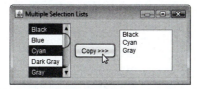

Fig. 14.26 | Test class for `MultipleSelectionFrame`.

Line 27 of Fig. 14.25 creates `JList` `colorJList` and initializes it with the `String`s in the array `colorNames`. Line 28 sets the number of visible rows in `colorJList` to 5. Lines 29–30 specify that `colorJList` is a `MULTIPLE_INTERVAL_SELECTION` list. Line 31 adds a new `JScrollPane` containing `colorJList` to the `JFrame`. Lines 49–55 perform similar tasks for `copyJList`, which is declared as a `SINGLE_INTERVAL_SELECTION` list. If a `JList` does not contain items it will not diplay in a `FlowLayout`. For this reason, line 51–52 use `JList` methods **`setFixedCellWidth`** and **`setFixedCellHeight`** to set `copyJList`'s width to 100 pixels and the height of each item in the `JList` to 15 pixels, respectively.

There are no events to indicate that a user has made multiple selections in a multiple-selection list. Normally, an event generated by another GUI component (known as an **external event**) specifies when the multiple selections in a `JList` should be processed. In this example, the user clicks the `JButton` called `copyJButton` to trigger the event that copies the selected items in `colorJList` to `copyJList`.

Lines 34–45 declare, create and register an `ActionListener` for the `copyJButton`. When the user clicks `copyJButton`, method `actionPerformed` (lines 39–43) uses `JList` method **`setListData`** to set the items displayed in `copyJList`. Line 42 calls `colorJList`'s method **`getSelectedValues`**, which returns an array of `Object`s representing the selected items in `colorJList`. In this example, the returned array is passed as the argument to `copyJList`'s `setListData` method.

You might be wondering why `copyJList` can be used in line 42 even though the application does not create the object to which it refers until line 49. Remember that method `actionPerformed` (lines 39–43) does not execute until the user presses the `copyJButton`, which cannot occur until after the constructor completes execution and the application displays the GUI. At that point in the application's execution, `copyJList` is already initialized with a new `JList` object.

14.14 Mouse Event Handling

This section presents the **MouseListener** and **MouseMotionListener** event-listener interfaces for handling mouse events. Mouse events can be trapped for any GUI component that derives from java.awt.Component. The methods of interfaces MouseListener and MouseMotionListener are summarized in Figure 14.27. Package javax.swing.event contains interface **MouseInputListener**, which extends interfaces MouseListener and MouseMotionListener to create a single interface containing all the MouseListener and MouseMotionListener methods. The MouseListener and MouseMotionListener methods are called when the mouse interacts with a Component if appropriate event-listener objects are registered for that Component.

MouseListener and MouseMotionListener interface methods

Methods of interface MouseListener

`public void mousePressed( MouseEvent event )`

> Called when a mouse button is pressed while the mouse cursor is on a component.

`public void mouseClicked( MouseEvent event )`

> Called when a mouse button is pressed and released while the mouse cursor remains stationary on a component. This event is always preceded by a call to mousePressed.

`public void mouseReleased( MouseEvent event )`

> Called when a mouse button is released after being pressed. This event is always preceded by a call to mousePressed and one or more calls to mouseDragged.

`public void mouseEntered( MouseEvent event )`

> Called when the mouse cursor enters the bounds of a component.

`public void mouseExited( MouseEvent event )`

> Called when the mouse cursor leaves the bounds of a component.

Methods of interface MouseMotionListener

`public void mouseDragged( MouseEvent event )`

> Called when the mouse button is pressed while the mouse cursor is on a component and the mouse is moved while the mouse button remains pressed. This event is always preceded by a call to mousePressed. All drag events are sent to the component on which the user began to drag the mouse.

`public void mouseMoved( MouseEvent event )`

> Called when the mouse is moved (with no mouse buttons pressed) when the mouse cursor is on a component. All move events are sent to the component over which the mouse is currently positioned.

Fig. 14.27 | MouseListener and MouseMotionListener interface methods.

Each of the mouse event-handling methods receives as an argument a **MouseEvent** object that contains information about the mouse event that occurred, including the *x*- and *y*-coordinates of the location where the event occurred. These coordinates are measured from the upper-left corner of the GUI component on which the event occurred. The *x*-coordinates start at 0 and increase from left to right. The *y*-coordinates start at 0 and increase from top to bottom. The methods and constants of class **InputEvent** (Mouse-Event's superclass) enable you to determine which mouse button the user clicked.

Software Engineering Observation 14.7

Method calls to mouseDragged are sent to the MouseMotionListener for the Component on which a mouse drag operation started. Similarly, the mouseReleased method call at the end of a drag operation is sent to the MouseListener for the Component on which the drag operation started.

Java also provides interface **MouseWheelListener** to enable applications to respond to the rotation of a mouse wheel. This interface declares method **mouseWheelMoved**, which receives a **MouseWheelEvent** as its argument. Class MouseWheelEvent (a subclass of Mouse-Event) contains methods that enable the event handler to obtain information about the amount of wheel rotation.

Tracking Mouse Events on a *JPanel*

The MouseTracker application (Figs. 14.28–14.29) demonstrates the MouseListener and MouseMotionListener interface methods. The event-handler class (lines 36–90) implements both interfaces. Note that you must declare all seven methods from these two interfaces when your class implements them both. Each mouse event in this example displays a String in the JLabel called statusBar that is attached to the bottom of the window.

```java
1   // Fig. 14.28: MouseTrackerFrame.java
2   // Demonstrating mouse events.
3   import java.awt.Color;
4   import java.awt.BorderLayout;
5   import java.awt.event.MouseListener;
6   import java.awt.event.MouseMotionListener;
7   import java.awt.event.MouseEvent;
8   import javax.swing.JFrame;
9   import javax.swing.JLabel;
10  import javax.swing.JPanel;
11
12  public class MouseTrackerFrame extends JFrame
13  {
14     private JPanel mousePanel; // panel in which mouse events will occur
15     private JLabel statusBar; // label that displays event information
16
17     // MouseTrackerFrame constructor sets up GUI and
18     // registers mouse event handlers
19     public MouseTrackerFrame()
20     {
21        super( "Demonstrating Mouse Events" );
22
23        mousePanel = new JPanel(); // create panel
24        mousePanel.setBackground( Color.WHITE ); // set background color
25        add( mousePanel, BorderLayout.CENTER ); // add panel to JFrame
26
27        statusBar = new JLabel( "Mouse outside JPanel" );
28        add( statusBar, BorderLayout.SOUTH ); // add label to JFrame
```

Fig. 14.28 | Mouse event handling. (Part 1 of 3.)

```
29
30          // create and register listener for mouse and mouse motion events
31          MouseHandler handler = new MouseHandler();
32          mousePanel.addMouseListener( handler );
33          mousePanel.addMouseMotionListener( handler );
34       } // end MouseTrackerFrame constructor
35
36       private class MouseHandler implements MouseListener,
37          MouseMotionListener
38       {
39          // MouseListener event handlers
40          // handle event when mouse released immediately after press
41          public void mouseClicked( MouseEvent event )
42          {
43             statusBar.setText( String.format( "Clicked at [%d, %d]",
44                event.getX(), event.getY() ) );
45          } // end method mouseClicked
46
47          // handle event when mouse pressed
48          public void mousePressed( MouseEvent event )
49          {
50             statusBar.setText( String.format( "Pressed at [%d, %d]",
51                event.getX(), event.getY() ) );
52          } // end method mousePressed
53
54          // handle event when mouse released
55          public void mouseReleased( MouseEvent event )
56          {
57             statusBar.setText( String.format( "Released at [%d, %d]",
58                event.getX(), event.getY() ) );
59          } // end method mouseReleased
60
61          // handle event when mouse enters area
62          public void mouseEntered( MouseEvent event )
63          {
64             statusBar.setText( String.format( "Mouse entered at [%d, %d]",
65                event.getX(), event.getY() ) );
66             mousePanel.setBackground( Color.GREEN );
67          } // end method mouseEntered
68
69          // handle event when mouse exits area
70          public void mouseExited( MouseEvent event )
71          {
72             statusBar.setText( "Mouse outside JPanel" );
73             mousePanel.setBackground( Color.WHITE );
74          } // end method mouseExited
75
76          // MouseMotionListener event handlers
77          // handle event when user drags mouse with button pressed
78          public void mouseDragged( MouseEvent event )
79          {
80             statusBar.setText( String.format( "Dragged at [%d, %d]",
81                event.getX(), event.getY() ) );
82          } // end method mouseDragged
```

Fig. 14.28 | Mouse event handling. (Part 2 of 3.)

```
83
84          // handle event when user moves mouse
85          public void mouseMoved( MouseEvent event )
86          {
87             statusBar.setText( String.format( "Moved at [%d, %d]",
88                event.getX(), event.getY() ) );
89          } // end method mouseMoved
90       } // end inner class MouseHandler
91    } // end class MouseTrackerFrame
```

Fig. 14.28 | Mouse event handling. (Part 3 of 3.)

```
1    // Fig. 14.29: MouseTrackerFrame.java
2    // Testing MouseTrackerFrame.
3    import javax.swing.JFrame;
4
5    public class MouseTracker
6    {
7       public static void main( String[] args )
8       {
9          MouseTrackerFrame mouseTrackerFrame = new MouseTrackerFrame();
10         mouseTrackerFrame.setDefaultCloseOperation( JFrame.EXIT_ON_CLOSE );
11         mouseTrackerFrame.setSize( 300, 100 ); // set frame size
12         mouseTrackerFrame.setVisible( true ); // display frame
13      } // end main
14   } // end class MouseTracker
```

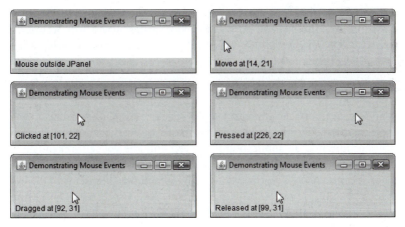

Fig. 14.29 | Test class for MouseTrackerFrame.

Line 23 in Fig. 14.28 creates JPanel mousePanel. This JPanel's mouse events will be tracked by the application. Line 24 sets mousePanel's background color to white. When the user moves the mouse into the mousePanel, the application will change mousePanel's background color to green. When the user moves the mouse out of the mousePanel, the application will change the background color back to white. Line 25 attaches mousePanel to the JFrame. As you learned in Section 14.5, you typically must specify the layout of the GUI components in a JFrame. In that section, we introduced the layout manager Flow-

Layout. Here we use the default layout of a JFrame's content pane—**BorderLayout**. This layout manager arranges components into five regions: **NORTH, SOUTH, EAST, WEST** and **CENTER**. NORTH corresponds to the top of the container. This example uses the CENTER and SOUTH regions. Line 25 uses a two-argument version of method add to place mousePanel in the CENTER region. The BorderLayout automatically sizes the component in the CENTER to use all the space in the JFrame that is not occupied by components in the other regions. Section 14.18.2 discusses BorderLayout in more detail.

Lines 27–28 in the constructor declare JLabel statusBar and attach it to the JFrame's SOUTH region. This JLabel occupies the width of the JFrame. The region's height is determined by the JLabel.

Line 31 creates an instance of inner class MouseHandler (lines 36–90) called handler that responds to mouse events. Lines 32–33 register handler as the listener for mousePanel's mouse events. Methods **addMouseListener** and **addMouseMotionListener** are inherited indirectly from class Component and can be used to register MouseListeners and MouseMotionListeners, respectively. A MouseHandler object *is a* MouseListener and *is a* MouseMotionListener because the class implements both interfaces. Note that we chose to implement both interfaces here to demonstrate a class that implements more than one interface, but we could have implemented interface MouseInputListener instead.]

When the mouse enters and exits mousePanel's area, methods mouseEntered (lines 62–67) and mouseExited (lines 70–74) are called, respectively. Method mouseEntered displays a message in the statusBar indicating that the mouse entered the JPanel and changes the background color to green. Method mouseExited displays a message in the statusBar indicating that the mouse is outside the JPanel (see the first sample output window) and changes the background color to white.

When any of the other five events occurs, it displays a message in the statusBar that includes a string containing the event and the coordinates at which it occurred. Mouse-Event methods **getX** and **getY** return the *x*- and *y*-coordinates, respectively, of the mouse at the time the event occurred.

14.15 Adapter Classes

Many event-listener interfaces, such as MouseListener and MouseMotionListener, contain multiple methods. It's not always desirable to declare every method in an event-listener interface. For instance, an application may need only the mouseClicked handler from MouseListener or the mouseDragged handler from MouseMotionListener. Interface WindowListener specifies seven window event-handling methods. For many of the listener interfaces that have multiple methods, packages java.awt.event and javax.swing.event provide event-listener adapter classes. An **adapter class** implements an interface and provides a default implementation (with an empty method body) of each method in the interface. Figure 14.30 shows several java.awt.event adapter classes and the interfaces they implement. You can extend an adapter class to inherit the default implementation of every method and subsequently override only the method(s) you need for event handling.

Software Engineering Observation 14.8

When a class implements an interface, the class has an is-a relationship with that interface. All direct and indirect subclasses of that class inherit this interface. Thus, an object of a class that extends an event-adapter class is an object of the corresponding event-listener type (e.g., an object of a subclass of MouseAdapter is a MouseListener).

Event-adapter class in `java.awt.event`	Implements interface
ComponentAdapter	ComponentListener
ContainerAdapter	ContainerListener
FocusAdapter	FocusListener
KeyAdapter	KeyListener
MouseAdapter	MouseListener
MouseMotionAdapter	MouseMotionListener
WindowAdapter	WindowListener

Fig. 14.30 | Event-adapter classes and the interfaces they implement in package `java.awt.event`.

Extending *MouseAdapter*

The application of Figs. 14.31–14.32 demonstrates how to determine the number of mouse clicks (i.e., the click count) and how to distinguish between the different mouse buttons. The event listener in this application is an object of inner class `MouseClickHandler` (lines 25–45) that extends `MouseAdapter`, so we can declare just the `mouseClicked` method we need in this example.

```
1   // Fig. 14.31: MouseDetailsFrame.java
2   // Demonstrating mouse clicks and distinguishing between mouse buttons.
3   import java.awt.BorderLayout;
4   import java.awt.event.MouseAdapter;
5   import java.awt.event.MouseEvent;
6   import javax.swing.JFrame;
7   import javax.swing.JLabel;
8
9   public class MouseDetailsFrame extends JFrame
10  {
11     private String details; // String that is displayed in the statusBar
12     private JLabel statusBar; // JLabel that appears at bottom of window
13
14     // constructor sets title bar String and register mouse listener
15     public MouseDetailsFrame()
16     {
17        super( "Mouse clicks and buttons" );
18
19        statusBar = new JLabel( "Click the mouse" );
20        add( statusBar, BorderLayout.SOUTH );
21        addMouseListener( new MouseClickHandler() ); // add handler
22     } // end MouseDetailsFrame constructor
23
24     // inner class to handle mouse events
25     private class MouseClickHandler extends MouseAdapter
26     {
27        // handle mouse-click event and determine which button was pressed
28        public void mouseClicked( MouseEvent event )
29        {
30           int xPos = event.getX(); // get x-position of mouse
```

Fig. 14.31 | Left, center and right mouse-button clicks. (Part 1 of 2.)

```
31              int yPos = event.getY(); // get y-position of mouse
32
33          details = String.format( "Clicked %d time(s)",
34              event.getClickCount() );
35
36          if ( event.isMetaDown() ) // right mouse button
37              details += " with right mouse button";
38          else if ( event.isAltDown() ) // middle mouse button
39              details += " with center mouse button";
40          else // left mouse button
41              details += " with left mouse button";
42
43          statusBar.setText( details ); // display message in statusBar
44       } // end method mouseClicked
45    } // end private inner class MouseClickHandler
46 } // end class MouseDetailsFrame
```

Fig. 14.31 | Left, center and right mouse-button clicks. (Part 2 of 2.)

```
1  // Fig. 14.32: MouseDetails.java
2  // Testing MouseDetailsFrame.
3  import javax.swing.JFrame;
4
5  public class MouseDetails
6  {
7     public static void main( String[] args )
8     {
9        MouseDetailsFrame mouseDetailsFrame = new MouseDetailsFrame();
10       mouseDetailsFrame.setDefaultCloseOperation( JFrame.EXIT_ON_CLOSE );
11       mouseDetailsFrame.setSize( 400, 150 ); // set frame size
12       mouseDetailsFrame.setVisible( true ); // display frame
13    } // end main
14 } // end class MouseDetails
```

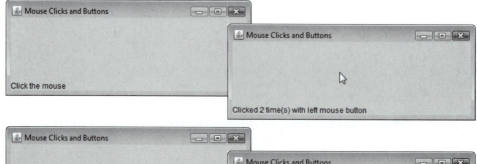

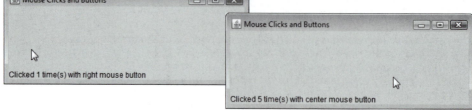

Fig. 14.32 | Test class for MouseDetailsFrame.

Common Programming Error 14.4

If you extend an adapter class and misspell the name of the method you are overriding, your method simply becomes another method in the class. This is a logic error that is difficult to detect, since the program will call the empty version of the method inherited from the adapter class.

A user of a Java application may be on a system with a one-, two- or three-button mouse. Java provides a mechanism to distinguish among mouse buttons. Class Mouse-Event inherits several methods from class InputEvent that can distinguish among mouse buttons on a multibutton mouse or can mimic a multibutton mouse with a combined keystroke and mouse-button click. Figure 14.33 shows the InputEvent methods used to distinguish among mouse-button clicks. Java assumes that every mouse contains a left mouse button. Thus, it's simple to test for a left-mouse-button click. However, users with a one- or two-button mouse must use a combination of keystrokes and mouse-button clicks at the same time to simulate the missing buttons on the mouse. In the case of a one- or two-button mouse, a Java application assumes that the center mouse button is clicked if the user holds down the *Alt* key and clicks the left mouse button on a two-button mouse or the only mouse button on a one-button mouse. In the case of a one-button mouse, a Java application assumes that the right mouse button is clicked if the user holds down the *Meta* key (sometimes called the *Command* key or the "Apple" key on a Mac) and clicks the mouse button.

InputEvent method	Description
isMetaDown()	Returns true when the user clicks the right mouse button on a mouse with two or three buttons. To simulate a right-mouse-button click on a one-button mouse, the user can hold down the *Meta* key on the keyboard and click the mouse button.
isAltDown()	Returns true when the user clicks the middle mouse button on a mouse with three buttons. To simulate a middle-mouse-button click on a one- or two-button mouse, the user can press the *Alt* key and click the only or left mouse button, respectively.

Fig. 14.33 | InputEvent methods that help distinguish among left-, center- and right-mouse-button clicks.

Line 21 of Fig. 14.31 registers a MouseListener for the MouseDetailsFrame. The event listener is an object of class MouseClickHandler, which extends MouseAdapter. This enables us to declare only method mouseClicked (lines 28–44). This method first captures the coordinates where the event occurred and stores them in local variables xPos and yPos (lines 30–31). Lines 33–34 create a String called details containing the number of consecutive mouse clicks, which is returned by MouseEvent method **getClickCount** at line 34. Lines 36–41 use methods **isMetaDown** and **isAltDown** to determine which mouse button the user clicked and append an appropriate String to details in each case. The resulting String is displayed in the statusBar. Class MouseDetails (Fig. 14.32) contains the main method that executes the application. Try clicking with each of your mouse's buttons repeatedly to see the click count increment.

14.16 JPanel Subclass for Drawing with the Mouse

Section 14.14 showed how to track mouse events in a JPanel. In this section, we use a JPanel as a dedicated drawing area in which the user can draw by dragging the mouse. In addition, this section demonstrates an event listener that extends an adapter class.

Method paintComponent

Lightweight Swing components that extend class JComponent (such as JPanel) contain method **paintComponent**, which is called when a lightweight Swing component is displayed. By overriding this method, you can specify how to draw shapes using Java's graphics capabilities. When customizing a JPanel for use as a dedicated drawing area, the subclass should override method paintComponent and call the superclass version of paintComponent as the first statement in the body of the overridden method to ensure that the component displays correctly. The reason is that subclasses of JComponent support **transparency**. To display a component correctly, the program must determine whether the component is transparent. The code that determines this is in superclass JComponent's paintComponent implementation. When a component is transparent, paintComponent will not clear its background when the program displays the component. When a component is **opaque**, paintComponent clears the component's background before the component is displayed. If the superclass version of paintComponent is not called, an opaque GUI component typically will not display correctly on the user interface. Also, if the superclass version is called after performing the customized drawing statements, the results typically will be erased. The transparency of a Swing lightweight component can be set with method **setOpaque** (a false argument indicates that the component is transparent).

Look-and-Feel Observation 14.12

Most Swing GUI components can be transparent or opaque. If a Swing GUI component is opaque, its background will be cleared when its paintComponent method is called. Only opaque components can display a customized background color. JPanel objects are opaque by default.

Error-Prevention Tip 14.1

In a JComponent subclass's paintComponent method, the first statement should always call to the superclass's paintComponent method to ensure that an object of the subclass displays correctly.

Common Programming Error 14.5

If an overridden paintComponent method does not call the superclass's version, the subclass component may not display properly. If an overridden paintComponent method calls the superclass's version after other drawing is performed, the drawing will be erased.

Defining the Custom Drawing Area

The Painter application of Figs. 14.34–14.35 demonstrates a customized subclass of JPanel that is used to create a dedicated drawing area. The application uses the mouse-Dragged event handler to create a simple drawing application. The user can draw pictures by dragging the mouse on the JPanel. This example does not use method mouseMoved, so our event-listener class (the anonymous inner class at lines 22–34) extends Mouse-

MotionAdapter. Since this class already declares both mouseMoved and mouseDragged, we can simply override mouseDragged to provide the event handling this application requires.

```java
1   // Fig. 14.34: PaintPanel.java
2   // Using class MouseMotionAdapter.
3   import java.awt.Point;
4   import java.awt.Graphics;
5   import java.awt.event.MouseEvent;
6   import java.awt.event.MouseMotionAdapter;
7   import javax.swing.JPanel;
8
9   public class PaintPanel extends JPanel
10  {
11     private int pointCount = 0; // count number of points
12
13     // array of 10000 java.awt.Point references
14     private Point[] points = new Point[ 10000 ];
15
16     // set up GUI and register mouse event handler
17     public PaintPanel()
18     {
19        // handle frame mouse motion event
20        addMouseMotionListener(
21
22           new MouseMotionAdapter() // anonymous inner class
23           {
24              // store drag coordinates and repaint
25              public void mouseDragged( MouseEvent event )
26              {
27                 if ( pointCount < points.length )
28                 {
29                    points[ pointCount ] = event.getPoint(); // find point
30                    pointCount++; // increment number of points in array
31                    repaint(); // repaint JFrame
32                 } // end if
33              } // end method mouseDragged
34           } // end anonymous inner class
35        ); // end call to addMouseMotionListener
36     } // end PaintPanel constructor
37
38     // draw ovals in a 4-by-4 bounding box at specified locations on window
39     public void paintComponent( Graphics g )
40     {
41        super.paintComponent( g ); // clears drawing area
42
43        // draw all points in array
44        for ( int i = 0; i < pointCount; i++ )
45           g.fillOval( points[ i ].x, points[ i ].y, 4, 4 );
46     } // end method paintComponent
47  } // end class PaintPanel
```

Fig. 14.34 | Adapter class used to implement event handlers.

Class PaintPanel (Fig. 14.34) extends JPanel to create the dedicated drawing area. Lines 3–7 import the classes used in class PaintPanel. Class **Point** (package java.awt) represents an *x-y* coordinate. We use objects of this class to store the coordinates of each mouse drag event. Class **Graphics** is used to draw.

In this example, we use an array of 10,000 Points (line 14) to store the location at which each mouse drag event occurs. As you'll see, method paintComponent uses these Points to draw. Instance variable pointCount (line 11) maintains the total number of Points captured from mouse drag events so far.

Lines 20–35 register a MouseMotionListener to listen for the PaintPanel's mouse motion events. Lines 22–34 create an object of an anonymous inner class that extends the adapter class MouseMotionAdapter. Recall that MouseMotionAdapter implements Mouse-MotionListener, so the anonymous inner class object is a MouseMotionListener. The anonymous inner class inherits default mouseMoved and mouseDragged implementations, so it already implements all the interface's methods. However, the default methods do nothing when they're called. So, we override method mouseDragged at lines 25–33 to capture the coordinates of a mouse drag event and store them as a Point object. Line 27 ensures that we store the event's coordinates only if there are still empty elements in the array. If so, line 29 invokes the MouseEvent's **getPoint** method to obtain the Point where the event occurred and stores it in the array at index pointCount. Line 30 increments the pointCount, and line 31 calls method **repaint** (inherited indirectly from class Component) to indicate that the PaintPanel should be refreshed on the screen as soon as possible with a call to the PaintPanel's paintComponent method.

Method paintComponent (lines 39–46), which receives a Graphics parameter, is called automatically any time the PaintPanel needs to be displayed on the screen (such as when the GUI is first displayed) or refreshed on the screen (such as when method repaint is called or when the GUI component was hidden by another window on the screen and subsequently becomes visible again).

Look-and-Feel Observation 14.13

Calling repaint *for a Swing GUI component indicates that the component should be refreshed on the screen as soon as possible. The background of the GUI component is cleared only if the component is opaque. JComponent method* setOpaque *can be passed a* boolean *argument indicating whether the component is opaque (*true*) or transparent (*false*).*

Line 41 invokes the superclass version of paintComponent to clear the PaintPanel's background (JPanels are opaque by default). Lines 44–45 draw an oval at the location specified by each Point in the array (up to the pointCount). Graphics method **fillOval** draws a solid oval. The method's four parameters represent a rectangular area (called the bounding box) in which the oval is displayed. The first two parameters are the upper-left *x*-coordinate and the upper-left *y*-coordinate of the rectangular area. The last two coordinates represent the rectangular area's width and height. Method fillOval draws the oval so it touches the middle of each side of the rectangular area. In line 45, the first two arguments are specified by using class Point's two public instance variables—x and y. The loop terminates when pointCount points have been displayed. You'll learn more Graphics features in Chapter 15.

Look-and-Feel Observation 14.14

Drawing on any GUI component is performed with coordinates that are measured from the upper-left corner (0, 0) of that GUI component, not the upper-left corner of the screen.

*Using the Custom **JPanel** in an Application*

Class Painter (Fig. 14.35) contains the main method that executes this application. Line
14 creates a PaintPanel object on which the user can drag the mouse to draw. Line 15
attaches the PaintPanel to the JFrame.

```
1   // Fig. 14.35: Painter.java
2   // Testing PaintPanel.
3   import java.awt.BorderLayout;
4   import javax.swing.JFrame;
5   import javax.swing.JLabel;
6
7   public class Painter
8   {
9      public static void main( String[] args )
10     {
11        // create JFrame
12        JFrame application = new JFrame( "A simple paint program" );
13
14        PaintPanel paintPanel = new PaintPanel(); // create paint panel
15        application.add( paintPanel, BorderLayout.CENTER ); // in center
16
17        // create a label and place it in SOUTH of BorderLayout
18        application.add( new JLabel( "Drag the mouse to draw" ),
19           BorderLayout.SOUTH );
20
21        application.setDefaultCloseOperation( JFrame.EXIT_ON_CLOSE );
22        application.setSize( 400, 200 ); // set frame size
23        application.setVisible( true ); // display frame
24     } // end main
25  } // end class Painter
```

Fig. 14.35 | Test class for PaintFrame.

14.17 Key Event Handling

This section presents the KeyListener interface for handling **key events**. Key events are
generated when keys on the keyboard are pressed and released. A class that implements
KeyListener must provide declarations for methods **keyPressed**, **keyReleased** and **key-
Typed**, each of which receives a KeyEvent as its argument. Class KeyEvent is a subclass of
InputEvent. Method keyPressed is called in response to pressing any key. Method key-
Typed is called in response to pressing any key that is not an **action key**. (The action keys
are any arrow key, *Home, End, Page Up, Page Down*, any function key, etc.) Method key-
Released is called when the key is released after any keyPressed or keyTyped event.

The application of Figs. 14.36–14.37 demonstrates the KeyListener methods. Class KeyDemoFrame implements the KeyListener interface, so all three methods are declared in the application.

```java
1   // Fig. 14.36: KeyDemoFrame.java
2   // Demonstrating keystroke events.
3   import java.awt.Color;
4   import java.awt.event.KeyListener;
5   import java.awt.event.KeyEvent;
6   import javax.swing.JFrame;
7   import javax.swing.JTextArea;
8
9   public class KeyDemoFrame extends JFrame implements KeyListener
10  {
11     private String line1 = ""; // first line of textarea
12     private String line2 = ""; // second line of textarea
13     private String line3 = ""; // third line of textarea
14     private JTextArea textArea; // textarea to display output
15
16     // KeyDemoFrame constructor
17     public KeyDemoFrame()
18     {
19        super( "Demonstrating Keystroke Events" );
20
21        textArea = new JTextArea( 10, 15 ); // set up JTextArea
22        textArea.setText( "Press any key on the keyboard..." );
23        textArea.setEnabled( false ); // disable textarea
24        textArea.setDisabledTextColor( Color.BLACK ); // set text color
25        add( textArea ); // add textarea to JFrame
26
27        addKeyListener( this ); // allow frame to process key events
28     } // end KeyDemoFrame constructor
29
30     // handle press of any key
31     public void keyPressed( KeyEvent event )
32     {
33        line1 = String.format( "Key pressed: %s",
34           KeyEvent.getKeyText( event.getKeyCode() ) ); // show pressed key
35        setLines2and3( event ); // set output lines two and three
36     } // end method keyPressed
37
38     // handle release of any key
39     public void keyReleased( KeyEvent event )
40     {
41        line1 = String.format( "Key released: %s",
42           KeyEvent.getKeyText( event.getKeyCode() ) ); // show released key
43        setLines2and3( event ); // set output lines two and three
44     } // end method keyReleased
45
46     // handle press of an action key
47     public void keyTyped( KeyEvent event )
48     {
49        line1 = String.format( "Key typed: %s", event.getKeyChar() );
```

Fig. 14.36 | Key event handling. (Part 1 of 2.)

```
50          setLines2and3( event ); // set output lines two and three
51    } // end method keyTyped
52
53    // set second and third lines of output
54    private void setLines2and3( KeyEvent event )
55    {
56       line2 = String.format( "This key is %san action key",
57          ( event.isActionKey() ? "" : "not " ) );
58
59       String temp = KeyEvent.getKeyModifiersText( event.getModifiers() );
60
61       line3 = String.format( "Modifier keys pressed: %s",
62          ( temp.equals( "" ) ? "none" : temp ) ); // output modifiers
63
64       textArea.setText( String.format( "%s\n%s\n%s\n",
65          line1, line2, line3 ) ); // output three lines of text
66    } // end method setLines2and3
67 } // end class KeyDemoFrame
```

Fig. 14.36 | Key event handling. (Part 2 of 2.)

```
1  // Fig. 14.37: KeyDemo.java
2  // Testing KeyDemoFrame.
3  import javax.swing.JFrame;
4
5  public class KeyDemo
6  {
7     public static void main( String[] args )
8     {
9        KeyDemoFrame keyDemoFrame = new KeyDemoFrame();
10       keyDemoFrame.setDefaultCloseOperation( JFrame.EXIT_ON_CLOSE );
11       keyDemoFrame.setSize( 350, 100 ); // set frame size
12       keyDemoFrame.setVisible( true ); // display frame
13    } // end main
14 } // end class KeyDemo
```

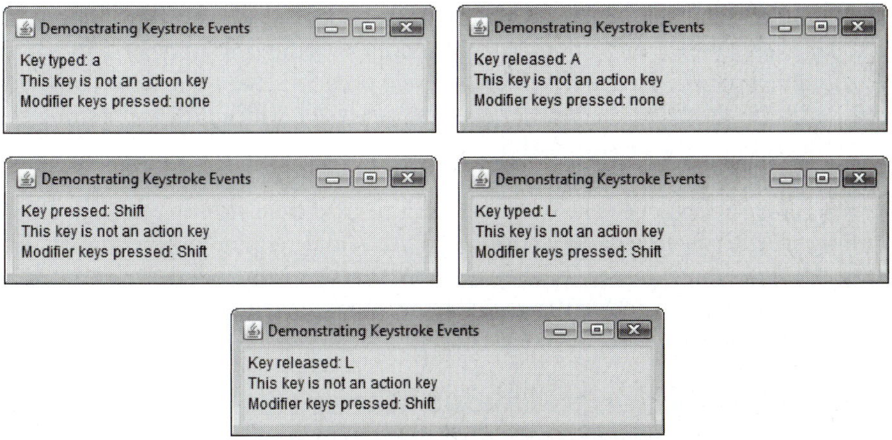

Fig. 14.37 | Test class for KeyDemoFrame. (Part 1 of 2.)

Fig. 14.37 | Test class for `KeyDemoFrame`. (Part 2 of 2.)

The constructor (Fig. 14.36, lines 17–28) registers the application to handle its own key events by using method **addKeyListener** at line 27. Method addKeyListener is declared in class Component, so every subclass of Component can notify KeyListener objects of key events for that Component.

At line 25, the constructor adds JTextArea textArea (where the application's output is displayed) to the JFrame. A JTextArea is a multiline area in which you can display text. (We discuss JTextAreas in more detail in Section 14.20.) Notice in the screen captures that textArea occupies the entire window. This is due to the JFrame's default Border-Layout (discussed in Section 14.18.2 and demonstrated in Fig. 14.41). When a single Component is added to a BorderLayout, the Component occupies the entire Container. Line 23 disables the JTextArea so the user cannot type in it. This causes the text in the JTextArea to become gray. Line 24 uses method **setDisabledTextColor** to change the text color in the JTextArea to black for readability.

Methods keyPressed (lines 31–36) and keyReleased (lines 39–44) use KeyEvent method **getKeyCode** to get the virtual key code of the pressed key. Class KeyEvent contains virtual key-code constants that represents every key on the keyboard. These constants can be compared with getKeyCode's return value to test for individual keys on the keyboard. The value returned by getKeyCode is passed to static KeyEvent method **getKeyText**, which returns a string containing the name of the key that was pressed. For a complete list of virtual key constants, see the on-line documentation for class KeyEvent (package java.awt.event). Method keyTyped (lines 47–51) uses KeyEvent method **getKeyChar** (which returns a char) to get the Unicode value of the character typed.

All three event-handling methods finish by calling method setLines2and3 (lines 54–66) and passing it the KeyEvent object. This method uses KeyEvent method **isActionKey** (line 57) to determine whether the key in the event was an action key. Also, InputEvent method **getModifiers** is called (line 59) to determine whether any modifier keys (such as *Shift*, *Alt* and *Ctrl*) were pressed when the key event occurred. The result of this method is passed to static KeyEvent method **getKeyModifiersText**, which produces a string containing the names of the pressed modifier keys.

[*Note:* If you need to test for a specific key on the keyboard, class KeyEvent provides a key constant for each one. These constants can be used from the key event handlers to determine whether a particular key was pressed. Also, to determine whether the *Alt*, *Ctrl*, *Meta* and *Shift* keys are pressed individually, InputEvent methods **isAltDown**, **isControlDown**, **isMetaDown** and **isShiftDown** each return a boolean indicating whether the particular key was pressed during the key event.]

14.18 Introduction to Layout Managers

Layout managers arrange GUI components in a container for presentation purposes. You can use the layout managers for basic layout capabilities instead of determining every GUI component's exact position and size. This functionality enables you to concentrate on the basic look-and-feel and lets the layout managers process most of the layout details. All layout managers implement the interface **LayoutManager** (in package java.awt). Class Container's setLayout method takes an object that implements the LayoutManager interface as an argument. There are basically three ways for you to arrange components in a GUI:

1. Absolute positioning: This provides the greatest level of control over a GUI's appearance. By setting a Container's layout to null, you can specify the absolute position of each GUI component with respect to the upper-left corner of the Container by using Component methods setSize and setLocation or setBounds. If you do this, you also must specify each GUI component's size. Programming a GUI with absolute positioning can be tedious, unless you have an integrated development environment (IDE) that can generate the code for you.

2. Layout managers: Using layout managers to position elements can be simpler and faster than creating a GUI with absolute positioning, but you lose some control over the size and the precise positioning of GUI components.

3. Visual programming in an IDE: IDEs provide tools that make it easy to create GUIs. Each IDE typically provides a **GUI design tool** that allows you to drag and drop GUI components from a tool box onto a design area. You can then position, size and align GUI components as you like. The IDE generates the Java code that creates the GUI. In addition, you can typically add event-handling code for a particular component by double-clicking the component. Some design tools also allow you to use the layout managers described in this chapter and in Chapter 25.

Look-and-Feel Observation 14.15

Most Java IDEs provide GUI design tools for visually designing a GUI; the tools then write Java code that creates the GUI. Such tools often provide greater control over the size, position and alignment of GUI components than do the built-in layout managers.

Look-and-Feel Observation 14.16

It's possible to set a Container's layout to null, which indicates that no layout manager should be used. In a Container without a layout manager, you must position and size the components in the given container and take care that, on resize events, all components are repositioned as necessary. A component's resize events can be processed by a Component-Listener.

Figure 14.38 summarizes the layout managers presented in this chapter. Others are discussed in Chapter 25 and the powerful GroupLayout layout manager is discussed in Appendix I.

Layout manager	Description
FlowLayout	Default for javax.swing.JPanel. Places components sequentially (left to right) in the order they were added. It's also possible to specify the order of the components by using the Container method add, which takes a Component and an integer index position as arguments.

Fig. 14.38 | Layout managers. (Part 1 of 2.)

Layout manager	Description
BorderLayout	Default for JFrames (and other windows). Arranges the components into five areas: NORTH, SOUTH, EAST, WEST and CENTER.
GridLayout	Arranges the components into rows and columns.

Fig. 14.38 │ Layout managers. (Part 2 of 2.)

14.18.1 FlowLayout

FlowLayout is the simplest layout manager. GUI components are placed on a container from left to right in the order in which they're added to the container. When the edge of the container is reached, components continue to display on the next line. Class FlowLayout allows GUI components to be left aligned, centered (the default) and right aligned.

The application of Figs. 14.39–14.40 creates three JButton objects and adds them to the application, using a FlowLayout layout manager. The components are center aligned by default. When the user clicks **Left**, the alignment for the layout manager is changed to a left-aligned FlowLayout. When the user clicks **Right**, the alignment for the layout manager is changed to a right-aligned FlowLayout. When the user clicks **Center**, the alignment for the layout manager is changed to a center-aligned FlowLayout. Each button has its own event handler that is declared with an anonymous inner class that implements ActionListener. The sample output windows show each of the FlowLayout alignments. Also, the last sample output window shows the centered alignment after the window has been resized to a smaller width. Notice that the button **Right** flows onto a new line.

As seen previously, a container's layout is set with method setLayout of class Container. Line 25 sets the layout manager to the FlowLayout declared at line 23. Normally, the layout is set before any GUI components are added to a container.

Look-and-Feel Observation 14.17

Each individual container can have only one layout manager, but multiple containers in the same application can each use different layout managers.

```
1   // Fig. 14.39: FlowLayoutFrame.java
2   // Demonstrating FlowLayout alignments.
3   import java.awt.FlowLayout;
4   import java.awt.Container;
5   import java.awt.event.ActionListener;
6   import java.awt.event.ActionEvent;
7   import javax.swing.JFrame;
8   import javax.swing.JButton;
9
10  public class FlowLayoutFrame extends JFrame
11  {
12      private JButton leftJButton; // button to set alignment left
13      private JButton centerJButton; // button to set alignment center
14      private JButton rightJButton; // button to set alignment right
15      private FlowLayout layout; // layout object
16      private Container container; // container to set layout
```

Fig. 14.39 │ FlowLayout allows components to flow over multiple lines. (Part 1 of 3.)

```
17
18       // set up GUI and register button listeners
19       public FlowLayoutFrame()
20       {
21          super( "FlowLayout Demo" );
22
23          layout = new FlowLayout(); // create FlowLayout
24          container = getContentPane(); // get container to layout
25          setLayout( layout ); // set frame layout
26
27          // set up leftJButton and register listener
28          leftJButton = new JButton( "Left" ); // create Left button
29          add( leftJButton ); // add Left button to frame
30          leftJButton.addActionListener(
31
32             new ActionListener() // anonymous inner class
33             {
34                // process leftJButton event
35                public void actionPerformed( ActionEvent event )
36                {
37                   layout.setAlignment( FlowLayout.LEFT );
38
39                   // realign attached components
40                   layout.layoutContainer( container );
41                } // end method actionPerformed
42             } // end anonymous inner class
43          ); // end call to addActionListener
44
45          // set up centerJButton and register listener
46          centerJButton = new JButton( "Center" ); // create Center button
47          add( centerJButton ); // add Center button to frame
48          centerJButton.addActionListener(
49
50             new ActionListener() // anonymous inner class
51             {
52                // process centerJButton event
53                public void actionPerformed( ActionEvent event )
54                {
55                   layout.setAlignment( FlowLayout.CENTER );
56
57                   // realign attached components
58                   layout.layoutContainer( container );
59                } // end method actionPerformed
60             } // end anonymous inner class
61          ); // end call to addActionListener
62
63          // set up rightJButton and register listener
64          rightJButton = new JButton( "Right" ); // create Right button
65          add( rightJButton ); // add Right button to frame
66          rightJButton.addActionListener(
67
68             new ActionListener() // anonymous inner class
69             {
```

Fig. 14.39 | FlowLayout allows components to flow over multiple lines. (Part 2 of 3.)

```
70                    // process rightJButton event
71                    public void actionPerformed( ActionEvent event )
72                    {
73                       layout.setAlignment( FlowLayout.RIGHT );
74
75                       // realign attached components
76                       layout.layoutContainer( container );
77                    } // end method actionPerformed
78                 } // end anonymous inner class
79              ); // end call to addActionListener
80        } // end FlowLayoutFrame constructor
81  } // end class FlowLayoutFrame
```

Fig. 14.39 | FlowLayout allows components to flow over multiple lines. (Part 3 of 3.)

```
1   // Fig. 14.40: FlowLayoutDemo.java
2   // Testing FlowLayoutFrame.
3   import javax.swing.JFrame;
4
5   public class FlowLayoutDemo
6   {
7      public static void main( String[] args )
8      {
9         FlowLayoutFrame flowLayoutFrame = new FlowLayoutFrame();
10        flowLayoutFrame.setDefaultCloseOperation( JFrame.EXIT_ON_CLOSE );
11        flowLayoutFrame.setSize( 300, 75 ); // set frame size
12        flowLayoutFrame.setVisible( true ); // display frame
13     } // end main
14  } // end class FlowLayoutDemo
```

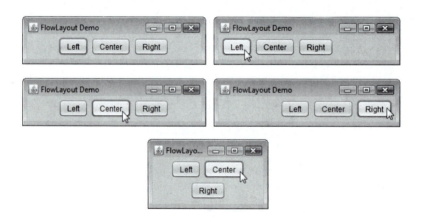

Fig. 14.40 | Test class for FlowLayoutFrame.

Note that each button's event handler is specified with a separate anonymous inner-class object (Fig. 14.39, lines 30–43, 48–61 and 66–79, respectively) and method action-Performed in each case executes two statements. For example, line 37 in the event handler for leftJButton uses FlowLayout method **setAlignment** to change the alignment for the

FlowLayout to a left-aligned (**FlowLayout.LEFT**) FlowLayout. Line 40 uses LayoutManager interface method **layoutContainer** (which is inherited by all layout managers) to specify that the JFrame should be rearranged based on the adjusted layout. According to which button was clicked, the actionPerformed method for each button sets the FlowLayout's alignment to FlowLayout.LEFT (line 37), **FlowLayout.CENTER** (line 55) or **FlowLayout.RIGHT** (line 73).

14.18.2 BorderLayout

The BorderLayout layout manager (the default layout manager for a JFrame) arranges components into five regions: NORTH, SOUTH, EAST, WEST and CENTER. NORTH corresponds to the top of the container. Class BorderLayout extends Object and implements interface **LayoutManager2** (a subinterface of LayoutManager that adds several methods for enhanced layout processing).

A BorderLayout limits a Container to containing at most five components—one in each region. The component placed in each region can be a container to which other components are attached. The components placed in the NORTH and SOUTH regions extend horizontally to the sides of the container and are as tall as the components placed in those regions. The EAST and WEST regions expand vertically between the NORTH and SOUTH regions and are as wide as the components placed in those regions. The component placed in the CENTER region expands to fill all remaining space in the layout (which is the reason the JTextArea in Fig. 14.37 occupies the entire window). If all five regions are occupied, the entire container's space is covered by GUI components. If the NORTH or SOUTH region is not occupied, the GUI components in the EAST, CENTER and WEST regions expand vertically to fill the remaining space. If the EAST or WEST region is not occupied, the GUI component in the CENTER region expands horizontally to fill the remaining space. If the CENTER region is not occupied, the area is left empty—the other GUI components do not expand to fill the remaining space. The application of Figs. 14.41–14.42 demonstrates the BorderLayout layout manager by using five JButtons.

```
1   // Fig. 14.41: BorderLayoutFrame.java
2   // Demonstrating BorderLayout.
3   import java.awt.BorderLayout;
4   import java.awt.event.ActionListener;
5   import java.awt.event.ActionEvent;
6   import javax.swing.JFrame;
7   import javax.swing.JButton;
8
9   public class BorderLayoutFrame extends JFrame implements ActionListener
10  {
11     private JButton[] buttons; // array of buttons to hide portions
12     private static final String[] names = { "Hide North", "Hide South",
13        "Hide East", "Hide West", "Hide Center" };
14     private BorderLayout layout; // borderlayout object
15
16     // set up GUI and event handling
17     public BorderLayoutFrame()
18     {
```

Fig. 14.41 | BorderLayout containing five buttons. (Part 1 of 2.)

```
19              super( "BorderLayout Demo" );
20
21              layout = new BorderLayout( 5, 5 ); // 5 pixel gaps
22              setLayout( layout ); // set frame layout
23              buttons = new JButton[ names.length ]; // set size of array
24
25              // create JButtons and register listeners for them
26              for ( int count = 0; count < names.length; count++ )
27              {
28                 buttons[ count ] = new JButton( names[ count ] );
29                 buttons[ count ].addActionListener( this );
30              } // end for
31
32              add( buttons[ 0 ], BorderLayout.NORTH ); // add button to north
33              add( buttons[ 1 ], BorderLayout.SOUTH ); // add button to south
34              add( buttons[ 2 ], BorderLayout.EAST ); // add button to east
35              add( buttons[ 3 ], BorderLayout.WEST ); // add button to west
36              add( buttons[ 4 ], BorderLayout.CENTER ); // add button to center
37           } // end BorderLayoutFrame constructor
38
39           // handle button events
40           public void actionPerformed( ActionEvent event )
41           {
42              // check event source and lay out content pane correspondingly
43              for ( JButton button : buttons )
44              {
45                 if ( event.getSource() == button )
46                    button.setVisible( false ); // hide button clicked
47                 else
48                    button.setVisible( true ); // show other buttons
49              } // end for
50
51              layout.layoutContainer( getContentPane() ); // lay out content pane
52           } // end method actionPerformed
53        } // end class BorderLayoutFrame
```

Fig. 14.41 | BorderLayout containing five buttons. (Part 2 of 2.)

```
1   // Fig. 14.42: BorderLayoutDemo.java
2   // Testing BorderLayoutFrame.
3   import javax.swing.JFrame;
4
5   public class BorderLayoutDemo
6   {
7      public static void main( String[] args )
8      {
9         BorderLayoutFrame borderLayoutFrame = new BorderLayoutFrame();
10        borderLayoutFrame.setDefaultCloseOperation( JFrame.EXIT_ON_CLOSE );
11        borderLayoutFrame.setSize( 300, 200 ); // set frame size
12        borderLayoutFrame.setVisible( true ); // display frame
13     } // end main
14  } // end class BorderLayoutDemo
```

Fig. 14.42 | Test class for BorderLayoutFrame. (Part 1 of 2.)

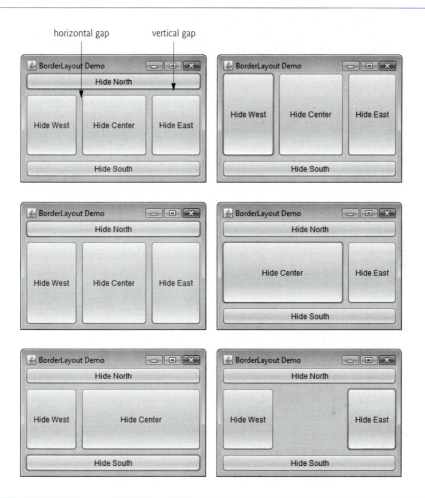

Fig. 14.42 | Test class for BorderLayoutFrame. (Part 2 of 2.)

Line 21 of Fig. 14.41 creates a BorderLayout. The constructor arguments specify the number of pixels between components that are arranged horizontally (**horizontal gap space**) and between components that are arranged vertically (**vertical gap space**), respectively. The default is one pixel of gap space horizontally and vertically. Line 22 uses method setLayout to set the content pane's layout to layout.

We add Components to a BorderLayout with another version of Container method add that takes two arguments—the Component to add and the region in which the Component should appear. For example, line 32 specifies that buttons[0] should appear in the NORTH region. The components can be added in any order, but only one component should be added to each region.

Look-and-Feel Observation 14.18

If no region is specified when adding a Component to a BorderLayout, the layout manager assumes that the Component should be added to region BorderLayout.CENTER.

Common Programming Error 14.6

When more than one component is added to a region in a BorderLayout, only the last component added to that region will be displayed. There is no error that indicates this problem.

Note that class `BorderLayoutFrame` implements `ActionListener` directly in this example, so the `BorderLayoutFrame` will handle the events of the `JButton`s. For this reason, line 29 passes the `this` reference to the `addActionListener` method of each `JButton`. When the user clicks a particular `JButton` in the layout, method action-Performed (lines 40–52) executes. The enhanced for statement at lines 43–49 uses an `if...else` to hide the particular `JButton` that generated the event. Method **setVisible** (inherited into `JButton` from class `Component`) is called with a `false` argument (line 46) to hide the `JButton`. If the current `JButton` in the array is not the one that generated the event, method `setVisible` is called with a `true` argument (line 48) to ensure that the `JButton` is displayed on the screen. Line 51 uses `LayoutManager` method `layoutContainer` to recalculate the layout of the content pane. Notice in the screen captures of Fig. 14.42 that certain regions in the `BorderLayout` change shape as `JButton`s are hidden and displayed in other regions. Try resizing the application window to see how the various regions resize based on the window's width and height. For more complex layouts, group components in `JPanel`s, each with a separate layout manager. Place the `JPanel`s on the `JFrame` using either the default `BorderLayout` or some other layout.

14.18.3 GridLayout

The **GridLayout** layout manager divides the container into a grid so that components can be placed in rows and columns. Class `GridLayout` inherits directly from class `Object` and implements interface `LayoutManager`. Every `Component` in a `GridLayout` has the same width and height. Components are added to a `GridLayout` starting at the top-left cell of the grid and proceeding left to right until the row is full. Then the process continues left to right on the next row of the grid, and so on. The application of Figs. 14.43–14.44 demonstrates the `GridLayout` layout manager by using six `JButton`s.

```
1   // Fig. 14.43: GridLayoutFrame.java
2   // Demonstrating GridLayout.
3   import java.awt.GridLayout;
4   import java.awt.Container;
5   import java.awt.event.ActionListener;
6   import java.awt.event.ActionEvent;
7   import javax.swing.JFrame;
8   import javax.swing.JButton;
9
10  public class GridLayoutFrame extends JFrame implements ActionListener
11  {
12     private JButton[] buttons; // array of buttons
13     private static final String[] names =
14        { "one", "two", "three", "four", "five", "six" };
15     private boolean toggle = true; // toggle between two layouts
```

Fig. 14.43 | GridLayout containing six buttons. (Part 1 of 2.)

```
16      private Container container; // frame container
17      private GridLayout gridLayout1; // first gridlayout
18      private GridLayout gridLayout2; // second gridlayout
19
20      // no-argument constructor
21      public GridLayoutFrame()
22      {
23          super( "GridLayout Demo" );
24          gridLayout1 = new GridLayout( 2, 3, 5, 5 ); // 2 by 3; gaps of 5
25          gridLayout2 = new GridLayout( 3, 2 ); // 3 by 2; no gaps
26          container = getContentPane(); // get content pane
27          setLayout( gridLayout1 ); // set JFrame layout
28          buttons = new JButton[ names.length ]; // create array of JButtons
29
30          for ( int count = 0; count < names.length; count++ )
31          {
32              buttons[ count ] = new JButton( names[ count ] );
33              buttons[ count ].addActionListener( this ); // register listener
34              add( buttons[ count ] ); // add button to JFrame
35          } // end for
36      } // end GridLayoutFrame constructor
37
38      // handle button events by toggling between layouts
39      public void actionPerformed( ActionEvent event )
40      {
41          if ( toggle )
42              container.setLayout( gridLayout2 ); // set layout to second
43          else
44              container.setLayout( gridLayout1 ); // set layout to first
45
46          toggle = !toggle; // set toggle to opposite value
47          container.validate(); // re-lay out container
48      } // end method actionPerformed
49  } // end class GridLayoutFrame
```

Fig. 14.43 | GridLayout containing six buttons. (Part 2 of 2.)

Lines 24–25 create two GridLayout objects. The GridLayout constructor used at line 24 specifies a GridLayout with 2 rows, 3 columns, 5 pixels of horizontal-gap space between Components in the grid and 5 pixels of vertical-gap space between Components in the grid. The GridLayout constructor used at line 25 specifies a GridLayout with 3 rows and 2 columns that uses the default gap space (1 pixel).

The JButton objects in this example initially are arranged using gridLayout1 (set for the content pane at line 27 with method setLayout). The first component is added to the first column of the first row. The next component is added to the second column of the first row, and so on. When a JButton is pressed, method actionPerformed (lines 39–48) is called. Every call to actionPerformed toggles the layout between gridLayout2 and gridLayout1, using boolean variable toggle to determine the next layout to set.

Line 47 shows another way to reformat a container for which the layout has changed. Container method **validate** recomputes the container's layout based on the current layout manager for the Container and the current set of displayed GUI components.

```
 1   // Fig. 14.44: GridLayoutDemo.java
 2   // Testing GridLayoutFrame.
 3   import javax.swing.JFrame;
 4
 5   public class GridLayoutDemo
 6   {
 7      public static void main( String[] args )
 8      {
 9         GridLayoutFrame gridLayoutFrame = new GridLayoutFrame();
10         gridLayoutFrame.setDefaultCloseOperation( JFrame.EXIT_ON_CLOSE );
11         gridLayoutFrame.setSize( 300, 200 ); // set frame size
12         gridLayoutFrame.setVisible( true ); // display frame
13      } // end main
14   } // end class GridLayoutDemo
```

Fig. 14.44 | Test class for `GridLayoutFrame`.

14.19 Using Panels to Manage More Complex Layouts

Complex GUIs (like Fig. 14.1) require that each component be placed in an exact location. They often consist of multiple panels, with each panel's components arranged in a specific layout. Class `JPanel` extends `JComponent` and `JComponent` extends class `Container`, so every `JPanel` is a `Container`. Thus, every `JPanel` may have components, including other panels, attached to it with `Container` method `add`. The application of Figs. 14.45–14.46 demonstrates how a `JPanel` can be used to create a more complex layout in which several `JButtons` are placed in the `SOUTH` region of a `BorderLayout`.

After `JPanel` `buttonJPanel` is declared (line 11) and created (line 19), line 20 sets `buttonJPanel`'s layout to a `GridLayout` of one row and five columns (there are five `JButtons` in array `buttons`). Lines 23–27 add the `JButtons` in the array to the `JPanel`. Line 26 adds the buttons directly to the `JPanel`—class `JPanel` does not have a content pane, unlike a `JFrame`. Line 29 uses the `JFrame`'s default `BorderLayout` to add `buttonJPanel` to the `SOUTH` region. Note that the `SOUTH` region is as tall as the buttons on `buttonJPanel`. A `JPanel` is sized to the components it contains. As more components are added, the `JPanel` grows (according to the restrictions of its layout manager) to accommodate the components. Resize the window to see how the layout manager affects the size of the `JButtons`.

```
 1   // Fig. 14.45: PanelFrame.java
 2   // Using a JPanel to help lay out components.
 3   import java.awt.GridLayout;
 4   import java.awt.BorderLayout;
```

Fig. 14.45 | `JPanel` with five `JButtons` in a `GridLayout` attached to the `SOUTH` region of a `BorderLayout`. (Part 1 of 2.)

```
 5    import javax.swing.JFrame;
 6    import javax.swing.JPanel;
 7    import javax.swing.JButton;
 8
 9    public class PanelFrame extends JFrame
10    {
11       private JPanel buttonJPanel; // panel to hold buttons
12       private JButton[] buttons; // array of buttons
13
14       // no-argument constructor
15       public PanelFrame()
16       {
17          super( "Panel Demo" );
18          buttons = new JButton[ 5 ]; // create buttons array
19          buttonJPanel = new JPanel(); // set up panel
20          buttonJPanel.setLayout( new GridLayout( 1, buttons.length ) );
21
22          // create and add buttons
23          for ( int count = 0; count < buttons.length; count++ )
24          {
25             buttons[ count ] = new JButton( "Button " + ( count + 1 ) );
26             buttonJPanel.add( buttons[ count ] ); // add button to panel
27          } // end for
28
29          add( buttonJPanel, BorderLayout.SOUTH ); // add panel to JFrame
30       } // end PanelFrame constructor
31    } // end class PanelFrame
```

Fig. 14.45 | JPanel with five JButtons in a GridLayout attached to the SOUTH region of a BorderLayout. (Part 2 of 2.)

```
 1    // Fig. 14.46: PanelDemo.java
 2    // Testing PanelFrame.
 3    import javax.swing.JFrame;
 4
 5    public class PanelDemo extends JFrame
 6    {
 7       public static void main( String[] args )
 8       {
 9          PanelFrame panelFrame = new PanelFrame();
10          panelFrame.setDefaultCloseOperation( JFrame.EXIT_ON_CLOSE );
11          panelFrame.setSize( 450, 200 ); // set frame size
12          panelFrame.setVisible( true ); // display frame
13       } // end main
14    } // end class PanelDemo
```

Fig. 14.46 | Test class for PanelFrame.

14.20 JTextArea

A **JTextArea** provides an area for manipulating multiple lines of text. Like class JText-Field, JTextArea is a subclass of JTextComponent, which declares common methods for JTextFields, JTextAreas and several other text-based GUI components.

The application in Figs. 14.47–14.48 demonstrates JTextAreas. One JTextArea displays text that the user can select. The other is uneditable and is used to display the text the user selected in the first JTextArea. Unlike JTextFields, JTextAreas do not have action events—when you press *Enter* while typing in a JTextArea, the cursor simply moves to the next line. As with multiple-selection JLists (Section 14.13), an external event from another GUI component indicates when to process the text in a JTextArea. For example, when typing an e-mail message, you normally click a **Send** button to send the text of the message to the recipient. Similarly, when editing a document in a word processor, you normally save the file by selecting a **Save** or **Save As...** menu item. In this program, the button **Copy >>>** generates the external event that copies the selected text in the left JTextArea and displays it in the right JTextArea.

```java
1   // Fig. 14.47: TextAreaFrame.java
2   // Copying selected text from one textarea to another.
3   import java.awt.event.ActionListener;
4   import java.awt.event.ActionEvent;
5   import javax.swing.Box;
6   import javax.swing.JFrame;
7   import javax.swing.JTextArea;
8   import javax.swing.JButton;
9   import javax.swing.JScrollPane;
10
11  public class TextAreaFrame extends JFrame
12  {
13     private JTextArea textArea1; // displays demo string
14     private JTextArea textArea2; // highlighted text is copied here
15     private JButton copyJButton; // initiates copying of text
16
17     // no-argument constructor
18     public TextAreaFrame()
19     {
20        super( "TextArea Demo" );
21        Box box = Box.createHorizontalBox(); // create box
22        String demo = "This is a demo string to\n" +
23           "illustrate copying text\nfrom one textarea to \n" +
24           "another textarea using an\nexternal event\n";
25
26        textArea1 = new JTextArea( demo, 10, 15 ); // create textarea1
27        box.add( new JScrollPane( textArea1 ) ); // add scrollpane
28
29        copyJButton = new JButton( "Copy >>>" ); // create copy button
30        box.add( copyJButton ); // add copy button to box
31        copyJButton.addActionListener(
32
33           new ActionListener() // anonymous inner class
34           {
```

Fig. 14.47 | Copying selected text from one JTextArea to another. (Part 1 of 2.)

```
35                    // set text in textArea2 to selected text from textArea1
36                    public void actionPerformed( ActionEvent event )
37                    {
38                       textArea2.setText( textArea1.getSelectedText() );
39                    } // end method actionPerformed
40                 } // end anonymous inner class
41              ); // end call to addActionListener
42
43              textArea2 = new JTextArea( 10, 15 ); // create second textarea
44              textArea2.setEditable( false ); // disable editing
45              box.add( new JScrollPane( textArea2 ) ); // add scrollpane
46
47              add( box ); // add box to frame
48           } // end TextAreaFrame constructor
49        } // end class TextAreaFrame
```

Fig. 14.47 | Copying selected text from one `JTextArea` to another. (Part 2 of 2.)

```
1    // Fig. 14.48: TextAreaDemo.java
2    // Copying selected text from one textarea to another.
3    import javax.swing.JFrame;
4
5    public class TextAreaDemo
6    {
7       public static void main( String[] args )
8       {
9          TextAreaFrame textAreaFrame = new TextAreaFrame();
10         textAreaFrame.setDefaultCloseOperation( JFrame.EXIT_ON_CLOSE );
11         textAreaFrame.setSize( 425, 200 ); // set frame size
12         textAreaFrame.setVisible( true ); // display frame
13      } // end main
14   } // end class TextAreaDemo
```

 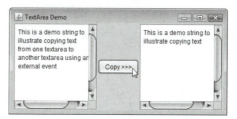

Fig. 14.48 | Test class for `TextAreaFrame`.

In the constructor (lines 18–48), line 21 creates a **Box** container (package `javax.swing`) to organize the GUI components. Box is a subclass of `Container` that uses a **BoxLayout** layout manager (discussed in detail in Section 25.9) to arrange the GUI components either horizontally or vertically. Box's `static` method **createHorizontalBox** creates a Box that arranges components from left to right in the order that they're attached.

Lines 26 and 43 create JTextAreas textArea1 and textArea2. Line 26 uses JText-Area's three-argument constructor, which takes a String representing the initial text and two ints specifying that the JTextArea has 10 rows and 15 columns. Line 43 uses JText-Area's two-argument constructor, specifying that the JTextArea has 10 rows and 15 columns. Line 26 specifies that demo should be displayed as the default JTextArea content. A JTextArea does not provide scrollbars if it cannot display its complete contents. So, line 27 creates a JScrollPane object, initializes it with textArea1 and attaches it to container box. By default, horizontal and vertical scrollbars appear as necessary in a JScrollPane.

Lines 29–41 create JButton object copyJButton with the label "Copy >>>", add copyJButton to container box and register the event handler for copyJButton's ActionEvent. This button provides the external event that determines when the program should copy the selected text in textArea1 to textArea2. When the user clicks copyJButton, line 38 in actionPerformed indicates that method getSelectedText (inherited into JTextArea from JTextComponent) should return the selected text from textArea1. The user selects text by dragging the mouse over the desired text to highlight it. Method setText changes the text in textArea2 to the string returned by getSelectedText.

Lines 43–45 create textArea2, set its editable property to false and add it to container box. Line 47 adds box to the JFrame. Recall from Section 14.18 that the default layout of a JFrame is a BorderLayout and that the add method by default attaches its argument to the CENTER of the BorderLayout.

When text reaches the right edge of a JTextArea the text can wrap to the next line. This is referred to as **line wrapping**. By default, JTextArea does not wrap lines.

 Look-and-Feel Observation 14.19

To provide line wrapping functionality for a JTextArea, invoke JTextArea method set-LineWrap with a true argument.

JScrollPane *Scrollbar Policies*

This example uses a JScrollPane to provide scrolling for a JTextArea. By default, JScrollPane displays scrollbars only if they're required. You can set the horizontal and vertical **scrollbar policies** of a JScrollPane when it's constructed. If a program has a reference to a JScrollPane, the program can use JScrollPane methods **setHorizontal-ScrollBarPolicy** and **setVerticalScrollBarPolicy** to change the scrollbar policies at any time. Class JScrollPane declares the constants

```
JScrollPane.VERTICAL_SCROLLBAR_ALWAYS
JScrollPane.HORIZONTAL_SCROLLBAR_ALWAYS
```

to indicate that a scrollbar should always appear, constants

```
JScrollPane.VERTICAL_SCROLLBAR_AS_NEEDED
JScrollPane.HORIZONTAL_SCROLLBAR_AS_NEEDED
```

to indicate that a scrollbar should appear only if necessary (the defaults) and constants

```
JScrollPane.VERTICAL_SCROLLBAR_NEVER
JScrollPane.HORIZONTAL_SCROLLBAR_NEVER
```

to indicate that a scrollbar should never appear. If the horizontal scrollbar policy is set to JScrollPane.HORIZONTAL_SCROLLBAR_NEVER, a JTextArea attached to the JScrollPane will automatically wrap lines.

14.21 Wrap-Up

In this chapter, you learned many GUI components and how to implement event handling. You also learned about nested classes, inner classes and anonymous inner classes.

You saw the special relationship between an inner-class object and an object of its top-level class. You learned how to use JOptionPane dialogs to obtain text input from the user and how to display messages to the user. You also learned how to create applications that execute in their own windows. We discussed class JFrame and components that enable a user to interact with an application. We also showed you how to display text and images to the user. You learned how to customize JPanels to create custom drawing areas, which you'll use extensively in the next chapter. You saw how to organize components on a window using layout managers and how to creating more complex GUIs by using JPanels to organize components. Finally, you learned about the JTextArea component in which a user can enter text and an application can display text. In Chapter 25, you'll learn about more advanced GUI components, such as sliders, menus and more complex layout managers. In the next chapter, you'll learn how to add graphics to your GUI application. Graphics allow you to draw shapes and text with colors and styles.

Summary

Section 14.1 Introduction
- A graphical user interface (GUI) presents a user-friendly mechanism for interacting with an application. A GUI gives an application a distinctive "look" and "feel."
- Providing different applications with consistent, intuitive user-interface components gives users a sense of familarity with a new application, so that they can learn it more quickly.
- GUIs are built from GUI components—sometimes called controls or widgets.

Section 14.2 Java's New Nimbus Look-and-Feel
- As of Java SE 6 update 10, Java comes bundled with a new, elegant, cross-platform look-and-feel known as Nimbus.
- To set Nimbus as the default for all Java applications, you must create a swing.properties text file in the lib folder of both your JDK installation folder and your JRE installation folder. Place the following line of code in the file:

      swing.defaultlaf=com.sun.java.swing.plaf.nimbus.NimbusLookAndFeel

- To select Nimbus on an application-by-application basis, place the following command-line argument after the java command and before the application's name when you run the application:

      -Dswing.defaultlaf=com.sun.java.swing.plaf.nimbus.NimbusLookAndFeel

Section 14.3 Simple GUI-Based Input/Output with JOptionPane
- Most applications use windows or dialog boxes (also called dialogs) to interact with the user.
- Class JOptionPane (package javax.swing) provides prebuilt dialog boxes for both input and output. JOptionPane static method showInputDialog displays an input dialog.
- A prompt typically uses sentence-style capitalization—capitalizing only the first letter of the first word in the text unless the word is a proper noun.
- An input dialog can input only input Strings. This is typical of most GUI components.
- JOptionPane static method showMessageDialog displays a message dialog.

Section 14.4 Overview of Swing Components
- Most Swing GUI components are located in package javax.swing.

- Together, the appearance and the way in which the user interacts with the application are known as that application's look-and-feel. Swing GUI components allow you to specify a uniform look-and-feel for your application across all platforms or to use each platform's custom look-and-feel.

- Lightweight Swing components are not tied to actual GUI components supported by the underlying platform on which an application executes.

- Several Swing components are heavyweight components that require direct interaction with the local windowing system, which may restrict their appearance and functionality.

- Class `Component` (package `java.awt`) declares many of the attributes and behaviors common to the GUI components in packages `java.awt` and `javax.swing`.

- Class `Container` (package `java.awt`) is a subclass of `Component`. `Components` are attached to `Containers` so the `Components` can be organized and displayed on the screen.

- Class `JComponent` (package `javax.swing`) is a subclass of `Container`. `JComponent` is the superclass of all lightweight Swing components and declares their common attributes and behaviors.

- Some common `JComponent` features include a pluggable look-and-feel, shortcut keys called mnemonics, tool tips, support for assistive technologies and support for user-interface localization.

Section 14.5 Displaying Text and Images in a Window

- Class `JFrame` provides the basic attributes and behaviors of a window.

- A `JLabel` displays read-only text, an image, or both text and an image. Text in a `JLabel` normally uses sentence-style capitalization.

- Each GUI component must be attached to a container, such as a window created with a `JFrame`.

- Many IDEs provide GUI design tools in which you can specify the exact size and location of a component by using the mouse; then the IDE will generate the GUI code for you.

- `JComponent` method `setToolTipText` specifies the tool tip that is displayed when the user positions the mouse cursor over a lightweight component.

- `Container` method `add` attaches a GUI component to a `Container`.

- Class `ImageIcon` supports several image formats, including GIF, PNG and JPEG.

- Method `getClass` (of class `Object`) retrieves a reference to the `Class` object that represents the the class declaration for the object on which the method is called.

- `Class` method `getResource` returns the location of its argument as a URL. Method `getResource` uses the `Class` object's class loader to determine the location of the resource.

- Interface `SwingConstants` (package `javax.swing`) declares common integer constants that are used with many Swing components.

- The horizontal and vertical alignments of a `JLabel` can be set with methods `setHorizontalAlignment` and `setVerticalAlignment`, respectively.

- `JLabel` method `setText` sets the text displayed on a label. The corresponding method `getText` retrieves the current text displayed on a label.

- `JLabel` method `setIcon` specifies the `Icon` to display on a label. The corresponding method `getIcon` retrieves the current `Icon` displayed on a label.

- `JLabel` methods `setHorizontalTextPosition` and `setVerticalTextPosition` specify the text position in the label.

- `JFrame` method `setDefaultCloseOperation` with constant `JFrame.EXIT_ON_CLOSE` as the argument indicates that the program should terminate when the window is closed by the user.

- `Component` method `setSize` specifies the width and height of a component.

- `Component` method `setVisible` with the argument `true` displays a `JFrame` on the screen.

Section 14.6 Text Fields and an Introduction to Event Handling with Nested Classes

- GUIs are event driven—when the user interacts with a GUI component, events drive the program to perform tasks.

- The code that performs a task in response to an event is called an event handler and the overall process of responding to events is known as event handling.

- Class JTextField extends class JTextComponent (package javax.swing.text), which provides common text-based component features. Class JPasswordField extends JTextField and adds several methods that are specific to processing passwords.

- A JPasswordField shows that characters are being typed as the user enters them, but hides the actual characters with echo characters.

- A component receives the focus when the user clicks the component.

- JTextComponent method setEditable can be used to make a text field uneditable.

- To respond to an event for a particular GUI component, you must: 1) Create a class that represents the event handler. 2) Implement an appropriate event-listener interface in the class from *Step 1*. 3) Indicate that an object of the class from *Steps 1* and *2* should be notified when the event occurs. This is known as registering the event handler.

- Nested classes can be static or non-static. Non-static nested classes are called inner classes and are frequently used for event handling.

- An object of a non-static inner class must be created by an object of the top-level class that contains the inner class.

- An inner-class object can directly access the instance variables and methods of its top-level class.

- A nested class that is static does not require an object of its top-level class and does not implicitly have a reference to an object of the top-level class.

- Pressing *Enter* in a JTextField or JPasswordField generates an ActionEvent (from package java.awt.event) that can be handled by an ActionListener (package java.awt.event).

- JTextField method addActionListener registers the event handler for that ActionEvent of a text field. This method receives as its argument an ActionListener object.

- The GUI component with which the user interacts is the event source.

- An ActionEvent object contains information about the event that just occurred, such as the event source and the text in the text field.

- ActionEvent method getSource returns a reference to the event source. ActionEvent method getActionCommand returns the text the user typed in a text field or the label on a JButton.

- JPasswordField method getPassword returns the password the user typed.

Section 14.7 Common GUI Event Types and Listener Interfaces

- Each event-object type typically has a corresponding event-listener interface that specifies one or more event-handling methods which must be declared in the class that implements the interface.

Section 14.8 How Event Handling Works

- When an event occurs, the GUI component with which the user interacted notifies its registered listeners by calling each listener's appropriate event-handling method.

- Every JComponent has an EventListenerList (package javax.swing.event) in which references to registered listeners are stored.

- Every GUI component supports several event types. When an event occurs, the event is dispatched only to the event listeners of the appropriate type. The GUI component receives a unique event ID specifying the event type, which it uses to decide the listener type to which the event should be dispatched and which method to call on each listener object.

Section 14.9 JButton

- A button is a component the user clicks to trigger an action. All the button types are subclasses of AbstractButton (package javax.swing). Button labels typically use book-title capitalization.

- Command buttons are created with class JButton.

- A JButton can display an Icon. A JButton can also have a rollover Icon—an Icon that is displayed when the user positions the mouse over the button.

- Method setRolloverIcon (of class AbstractButton) specifies the image displayed on a button when the user positions the mouse over it.

Section 14.10 Buttons That Maintain State

- There are three Swing state button types—JToggleButton, JCheckBox and JRadioButton.

- Classes JCheckBox and JRadioButton are subclasses of JToggleButton.

- Component method setFont sets the component's font to a new Font object (package java.awt).

- Clicking a JCheckBox causes an ItemEvent that can be handled by an ItemListener object (which must implement method itemStateChanged). Method addItemListener registers the listener for the ItemEvent of a JCheckBox or JRadioButton object.

- JCheckBox method isSelected determines whether a JCheckBox is selected.

- JRadioButtons are similar to JCheckBoxes in that they have two states—selected and not selected. However, radio buttons normally appear as a group in which only one button can be selected at a time. Selecting a different radio button forces all others to be deselected.

- JRadioButtons are used to represent mutually exclusive options.

- The logical relationship between JRadioButtons is maintained by a ButtonGroup object.

- ButtonGroup method add associates each JRadioButton with a ButtonGroup. If more than one selected JRadioButton object is added to a group, the selected one that was added first will be selected when the GUI is displayed.

- JRadioButtons generate ItemEvents when they're clicked.

Section 14.11 JComboBox and Using an Anonymous Inner Class for Event Handling

- A JComboBox provides a list of items from which the user can make a single selection. JComboBoxes generate ItemEvents.

- Each item in a JComboBox has an index. The first item added to a JComboBox appears as the currently selected item when the JComboBox is displayed. Other items are selected by clicking the JComboBox, which expands into a list from which the user can make a selection.

- JComboBox method setMaximumRowCount sets the maximum number of elements that are displayed when the user clicks the JComboBox. If there are more items, the JComboBox provides a scrollbar that allows the user to scroll through all the elements in the list.

- An anonymous inner class is a special form of inner class that is declared without a name and typically appears inside a method declaration. Since an anonymous inner class has no name, one object of the anonymous inner class must be created at the point where the class is declared.

- JComboBox method getSelectedIndex returns the index of the selected item.

Section 14.12 JList

- A JList displays a series of items from which the user may select one or more items. Class JList supports single-selection lists and multiple-selection lists.

- When the user clicks an item in a JList, a ListSelectionEvent occurs. JList method addListSelectionListener registers a ListSelectionListener for a JList's selection events. A ListSelectionListener (package javax.swing.event) must implement method valueChanged.

- JList method `setVisibleRowCount` specifies the number of items that are visible in the list.

- JList method `setSelectionMode` specifies a list's selection mode.

- A `JList` does not provide a scrollbar if there are more items in the list than the number of visible rows. In this case, a `JScrollPane` object can be used to provide the scrolling capability.

- `JFrame` method `getContentPane` returns a reference to the `JFrame`'s content pane where GUI components are displayed.

- JList method `getSelectedIndex` returns the selected item's index.

Section 14.13 Multiple-Selection Lists

- A multiple-selection list enables the user to select many items from a `JList`.

- JList method `setFixedCellWidth` sets a `JList`'s width. Method `setFixedCellHeight` sets the height of each item in a `JList`.

- There are no events to indicate that a user has made multiple selections in a multiple-selection list. Normally, an external event generated by another GUI component (such as a `JButton`) specifies when the multiple selections in a `JList` should be processed.

- JList method `setListData` sets the items displayed in a `JList`. `JList` method `getSelectedValues` returns an array of `Objects` representing the selected items in a `JList`.

Section 14.14 Mouse Event Handling

- The `MouseListener` and `MouseMotionListener` event-listener interfaces are used to handle mouse events. Mouse events can be trapped for any GUI component that extends `Component`.

- Interface `MouseInputListener` (package `javax.swing.event`) extends interfaces `MouseListener` and `MouseMotionListener` to create a single interface containing all their methods.

- Each mouse event-handling method receives a `MouseEvent` object that contains information about the event, including the x- and y-coordinates where the event occurred. Coordinates are measured from the upper-left corner of the GUI component on which the event occurred.

- The methods and constants of class `InputEvent` (`MouseEvent`'s superclass) enable an application to determine which mouse button the user clicked.

- Interface `MouseWheelListener` enables applications to respond to the rotation of a mouse wheel.

Section 14.15 Adapter Classes

- Many event-listener interfaces contain multiple methods. For many of these interfaces, packages `java.awt.event` and `javax.swing.event` provide event-listener adapter classes. An adapter class implements an interface and provides default implementations of its methods. Extend an adapter class to inherit the default method implementations then override the method(s) you need.

- `MouseEvent` method `getClickCount` returns the number of consecutive mouse-button clicks. Methods `isMetaDown` and `isAltDown` determine which mouse button the user clicked.

Section 14.16 **JPanel** Subclass for Drawing with the Mouse

- Lightweight Swing components that extend class `JComponent` contain method `paintComponent`, which is called when a lightweight Swing component is displayed. By overriding this method, you can specify how to draw shapes using Java's graphics capabilities.

- When customizing a `JPanel` for drawing, the subclass should override method `paintComponent` and call the superclass version as the first statement in the body of the overridden method.

- Subclasses of `JComponent` support transparency. When a component is opaque, `paintComponent` clears the component's background before the component is displayed.

- The transparency of a Swing lightweight component can be set with method `setOpaque` (a `false` argument indicates that the component is transparent).

- Class Point (package java.awt) represents an *x-y* coordinate.

- Class Graphics is used to draw.

- MouseEvent method getPoint obtains the Point where a mouse event occurred.

- Method repaint (inherited indirectly from class Component) indicates that a component should be refreshed on the screen as soon as possible.

- Method paintComponent receives a Graphics parameter and is called automatically any time a lightweight component needs to be displayed on the screen.

- Graphics method fillOval draws a solid oval. The first two arguments are the upper-left *x*-coordinate and the upper-left *y*-coordinate of the bounding box. The last two arguments represent the bounding box's width and height.

Section 14.17 Key Event Handling

- Interface KeyListener is used to handle key events that are generated when keys on the keyboard are pressed and released. Method addKeyListener of class Component registers a KeyListener.

- KeyEvent method getKeyCode gets the virtual key code of the key that was pressed. Class KeyEvent maintains a set of virtual key-code constants that represent every key on the keyboard.

- KeyEvent method getKeyText returns a string containing the name of the key that was pressed.

- KeyEvent method getKeyChar gets the Unicode value of the character typed.

- KeyEvent method isActionKey determines whether the key in an event was an action key.

- InputEvent method getModifiers determines whether any modifier keys (such as *Shift*, *Alt* and *Ctrl*) were pressed when the key event occurred.

- KeyEvent method getKeyModifiersText produces a string containing the names of the pressed modifier keys.

Section 14.18 Introduction to Layout Managers

- Layout managers arrange GUI components in a container for presentation purposes.

- All layout managers implement the interface LayoutManager (package java.awt).

- Container method setLayout specifies the layout of a container.

- FlowLayout places components left to right in the order in which they're added to the container. When the edge of the container is reached, components continue to display on the next line. FlowLayout allows GUI components to be left aligned, centered (the default) and right aligned.

- FlowLayout method setAlignment changes the alignment for a FlowLayout.

- BorderLayout (the default for a JFrame) arranges components into five regions: NORTH, SOUTH, EAST, WEST and CENTER. NORTH corresponds to the top of the container.

- A BorderLayout limits a Container to containing at most five components—one in each region.

- GridLayout divides a container into a grid of rows and columns.

- Container method validate recomputes a container's layout based on the current layout manager for the Container and the current set of displayed GUI components.

Section 14.19 Using Panels to Manage More Complex Layouts

- Complex GUIs often consist of multiple panels, with each panel's components arranged in a specific layout. Every JPanel may have components, including other panels, attached to it with Container method add.

Section 14.20 JTextArea

- A JTextArea provides an area for manipulating multiple lines of text. JTextArea is a subclass of JTextComponent.

- Class Box is a subclass of Container that uses a BoxLayout layout manager to arrange the GUI components either horizontally or vertically.
- Box static method createHorizontalBox creates a Box that arranges components from left to right in the order that they're attached.
- Method getSelectedText returns the selected text from a JTextArea.
- You can set the horizontal and vertical scrollbar policies of a JScrollPane when it's constructed. JScrollPane methods setHorizontalScrollBarPolicy, and setVerticalScrollBarPolicy can be used to change the scrollbar policies at any time.

Terminology

Self-Review Exercises

14.1   Fill in the blanks in each of the following statements:

a) Method _____ is called when the mouse is moved with no buttons pressed and an event listener is registered to handle the event.

b) Text that cannot be modified by the user is called _____ text.

c) A(n) _____ arranges GUI components in a Container.

d) The add method for attaching GUI components is a method of class _____.

e) GUI is an acronym for _____.

f) Method _____ is used to specify the layout manager for a container.

g) A mouseDragged method call is preceded by a(n) _____ method call and followed by a(n) _____ method call.

h) Class _____ contains methods that display message dialogs and input dialogs.

i) An input dialog capable of receiving input from the user is displayed with method _____ of class _____.

j) A dialog capable of displaying a message to the user is displayed with method _____ of class _____.

k) Both `JTextFields` and `JTextAreas` directly extend class _____.

14.2 Determine whether each statement is *true* or *false*. If *false*, explain why.

a) `BorderLayout` is the default layout manager for a `JFrame`'s content pane.

b) When the mouse cursor is moved into the bounds of a GUI component, method `mouseOver` is called.

c) A `JPanel` cannot be added to another `JPanel`.

d) In a `BorderLayout`, two buttons added to the `NORTH` region will be placed side by side.

e) A maximum of five components can be added to a `BorderLayout`.

f) Inner classes are not allowed to access the members of the enclosing class.

g) A `JTextArea`'s text is always read-only.

h) Class `JTextArea` is a direct subclass of class `Component`.

14.3 Find the error(s) in each of the following statements, and explain how to correct it (them):

a) `buttonName = JButton( "Caption" );`

b) `JLabel aLabel, JLabel;    // create references`

c) `txtField = new JTextField( 50, "Default Text" );`

d)
```
setLayout( new BorderLayout() );
button1 = new JButton( "North Star" );
button2 = new JButton( "South Pole" );
add( button1 );
add( button2 );
```

Answers to Self-Review Exercises

14.1 a) mouseMoved. b) uneditable (read-only). c) layout manager. d) `Container`. e) graphical user interface. f) setLayout. g) mousePressed, mouseReleased. h) JOptionPane. i) showInputDialog, JOptionPane. j) showMessageDialog, JOptionPane. k) JTextComponent.

14.2
a) True.

b) False. Method `mouseEntered` is called.

c) False. A `JPanel` can be added to another `JPanel`, because `JPanel` is an indirect subclass of `Component`. So, a `JPanel` is a `Component`. Any `Component` can be added to a `Container`.

d) False. Only the last button added will be displayed. Remember that only one component should be added to each region in a `BorderLayout`.

e) True. [*Note:* Panels containing multiple components can be added to each region.]

f) False. Inner classes have access to all members of the enclosing class declaration.

g) False. `JTextAreas` are editable by default.

h) False. `JTextArea` derives from class `JTextComponent`.

14.3
a) `new` is needed to create an object.

b) `JLabel` is a class name and cannot be used as a variable name.

c) The arguments passed to the constructor are reversed. The `String` must be passed first.

d) `BorderLayout` has been set, and components are being added without specifying the region, so both are added to the center region. Proper `add` statements might be
```
add( button1, BorderLayout.NORTH );
add( button2, BorderLayout.SOUTH );
```

Exercises

14.4 Fill in the blanks in each of the following statements:

a) The `JTextField` class directly extends class _____.

b) `Container` method _____ attaches a GUI component to a container.

   c) Method _____ is called when a mouse button is released (without moving the mouse).

   d) The _____ class is used to create a group of JRadioButtons.

14.5 Determine whether each statement is *true* or *false*. If *false*, explain why.

   a) Only one layout manager can be used per Container.

   b) GUI components can be added to a Container in any order in a BorderLayout.

   c) JRadioButtons provide a series of mutually exclusive options (i.e., only one can be true at a time).

   d) Graphics method setFont is used to set the font for text fields.

   e) A JList displays a scrollbar if there are more items in the list than can be displayed.

   f) A Mouse object has a method called mouseDragged.

14.6 Determine whether each statement is *true* or *false*. If *false*, explain why.

   a) A JPanel is a JComponent.

   b) A JPanel is a Component.

   c) A JLabel is a Container.

   d) A JList is a JPanel.

   e) An AbstractButton is a JButton.

   f) A JTextField is an Object.

   g) ButtonGroup is a subclass of JComponent.

14.7 Find any errors in each of the following lines of code, and explain how to correct them.

   a) `import javax.swing.JFrame`

   b) `panelObject.GridLayout( 8, 8 ); // set GridLayout`

   c) `container.setLayout( new FlowLayout( FlowLayout.DEFAULT ) );`

   d) `container.add( eastButton, EAST );  // BorderLayout`

14.8 Create the following GUI. You do not have to provide any functionality.

14.9 Create the following GUI. You do not have to provide any functionality.

14.10 Create the following GUI. You do not have to provide any functionality.

14.11 Create the following GUI. You do not have to provide any functionality.

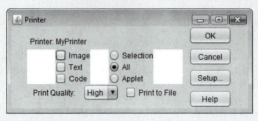

14.12 *(Temperature Conversion)* Write a temperature-conversion application that converts from Fahrenheit to Celsius. The Fahrenheit temperature should be entered from the keyboard (via a JTextField). A JLabel should be used to display the converted temperature. Use the following formula for the conversion:

$$Celsius = \frac{5}{9} \times (\ Fahrenheit - 32\ )$$

14.13 *(Temperature Conversion Modification)* Enhance the temperature-conversion application of Exercise 14.12 by adding the Kelvin temperature scale. The application should also allow the user to make conversions between any two scales. Use the following formula for the conversion between Kelvin and Celsius (in addition to the formula in Exercise 14.12):

$$Kelvin = Celsius + 273.15$$

14.14 *(Guess the Number Game)* Write an application that plays "guess the number" as follows: Your application chooses the number to be guessed by selecting an integer at random in the range 1–1000. The application then displays the following in a label:

```
I have a number between 1 and 1000. Can you guess my number?
Please enter your first guess.
```

A JTextField should be used to input the guess. As each guess is input, the background color should change to either red or blue. Red indicates that the user is getting "warmer," and blue, "colder." A JLabel should display either "Too High" or "Too Low" to help the user zero in. When the user gets the correct answer, "Correct!" should be displayed, and the JTextField used for input should be changed to be uneditable. A JButton should be provided to allow the user to play the game again. When the JButton is clicked, a new random number should be generated and the input JTextField changed to be editable.

14.15 *(Displaying Events)* It's often useful to display the events that occur during the execution of an application. This can help you understand when the events occur and how they're generated. Write an application that enables the user to generate and process every event discussed in this chapter. The application should provide methods from the ActionListener, ItemListener, ListSelectionListener, MouseListener, MouseMotionListener and KeyListener interfaces to display messages when the events occur. Use method toString to convert the event objects received in each event handler into Strings that can be displayed. Method toString creates a String containing all the information in the event object.

14.16 *(GUI-Based Craps Game)* Modify the application of Section 5.10 to provide a GUI that enables the user to click a JButton to roll the dice. The application should also display four JLabels and four JTextFields, with one JLabel for each JTextField. The JTextFields should be used to display the values of each die and the sum of the dice after each roll. The point should be displayed in the fourth JTextField when the user does not win or lose on the first roll and should continue to be displayed until the game is lost.

(Optional) GUI and Graphics Case Study Exercise: Expanding the Interface

14.17   *(Interactive Drawing Application)* In this exercise, you'll implement a GUI application that uses the MyShape hierarchy from the GUI case study Exercise 10.2 to create an interactive drawing application. You'll create two classes for the GUI and provide a test class that launches the application. The classes of the MyShape hierarchy require no additional changes.

The first class to create is a subclass of JPanel called DrawPanel, which represents the area on which the user draws the shapes. Class DrawPanel should have the following instance variables:

- a) An array shapes of type MyShape that will store all the shapes the user draws.
- b) An integer shapeCount that counts the number of shapes in the array.
- c) An integer shapeType that determines the type of shape to draw.
- d) A MyShape currentShape that represents the current shape the user is drawing.
- e) A Color currentColor that represents the current drawing color.
- f) A boolean filledShape that determines whether to draw a filled shape.
- g) A JLabel statusLabel that represents the status bar. The status bar will display the co-ordinates of the current mouse position.

Class DrawPanel should also declare the following methods:

- a) Overridden method paintComponent that draws the shapes in the array. Use instance variable shapeCount to determine how many shapes to draw. Method paintComponent should also call currentShape's draw method, provided that currentShape is not null.
- b) Set methods for the shapeType, currentColor and filledShape.
- c) Method clearLastShape should clear the last shape drawn by decrementing instance variable shapeCount. Ensure that shapeCount is never less than zero.
- d) Method clearDrawing should remove all the shapes in the current drawing by setting shapeCount to zero.

Methods clearLastShape and clearDrawing should call method repaint (inherited from JPanel) to refresh the drawing on the DrawPanel by indicating that the system should call method paint-Component.

Class DrawPanel should also provide event handling to enable the user to draw with the mouse. Create a single inner class that both extends MouseAdapter and implements MouseMotion-Listener to handle all mouse events in one class.

In the inner class, override method mousePressed so that it assigns currentShape a new shape of the type specified by shapeType and initializes both points to the mouse position. Next, override method mouseReleased to finish drawing the current shape and place it in the array. Set the second point of currentShape to the current mouse position and add currentShape to the array. Instance variable shapeCount determines the insertion index. Set currentShape to null and call method repaint to update the drawing with the new shape.

Override method mouseMoved to set the text of the statusLabel so that it displays the mouse coordinates—this will update the label with the coordinates every time the user moves (but does not drag) the mouse within the DrawPanel. Next, override method mouseDragged so that it sets the second point of the currentShape to the current mouse position and calls method repaint. This will allow the user to see the shape while dragging the mouse. Also, update the JLabel in mouse-Dragged with the current position of the mouse.

Create a constructor for DrawPanel that has a single JLabel parameter. In the constructor, initialize statusLabel with the value passed to the parameter. Also initialize array shapes with 100 entries, shapeCount to 0, shapeType to the value that represents a line, currentShape to null and currentColor to Color.BLACK. The constructor should then set the background color of the Draw-Panel to Color.WHITE and register the MouseListener and MouseMotionListener so the JPanel properly handles mouse events.

Next, create a JFrame subclass called DrawFrame that provides a GUI that enables the user to control various aspects of drawing. For the layout of the DrawFrame, we recommend a BorderLay-out, with the components in the NORTH region, the main drawing panel in the CENTER region, and a status bar in the SOUTH region, as in Fig. 14.49. In the top panel, create the components listed below. Each component's event handler should call the appropriate method in class DrawPanel.

    a) A button to undo the last shape drawn.

    b) A button to clear all shapes from the drawing.

    c) A combo box for selecting the color from the 13 predefined colors.

    d) A combo box for selecting the shape to draw.

    e) A checkbox that specifies whether a shape should be filled or unfilled.

Declare and create the interface components in DrawFrame's constructor. You'll need to create the status bar JLabel before you create the DrawPanel, so you can pass the JLabel as an argument to DrawPanel's constructor. Finally, create a test class that initializes and displays the DrawFrame to execute the application.

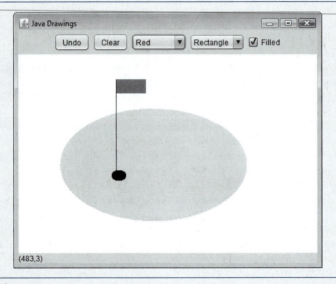

Fig. 14.49 | Interface for drawing shapes.

14.18 *(GUI-Based Version of the ATM Case Study)* Reimplement the ATM Case Study of Chapters 12–13 as a GUI-based application. Use GUI components to approximate the ATM user interface shown in Fig. 12.1. For the cash dispenser and the deposit slot use JButtons labeled **Remove Cash** and **Insert Envelope**. This will enable the application to receive events indicating when the user takes the cash and inserts a deposit envelope, respectively.

Making a Difference

14.19 *(Ecofont)* Ecofont (www.ecofont.eu/ecofont_en.html)—developed by SPRANQ (a Netherlands-based company)—is a free, open-source computer font designed to reduce by as much as 20% the amount of ink used for printing, thus reducing also the number of ink cartridges used and the environmental impact of the manufacturing and shipping processes (using less energy, less fuel for shipping, and so on). The font, based on sans-serif Verdana, has small circular "holes" in the letters that are not visible in smaller sizes—such as the 9- or 10-point type frequently used. Download Ecofont, then install the font file Spranq_eco_sans_regular.ttf using the instructions from the Ecofont website. Next, develop a GUI-based program that allows you to type in a text string to be displayed in the Ecofont. Create **Increase Font Size** and **Decrease Font Size** buttons that allow you to scale up or down by one point at a time. Start with a default font size of 9 points. As you scale up, you'll be able to see the holes in the letters more clearly. As you scale down, the holes will be less apparent. What is the smallest font size at which you begin to notice the holes?

14.20 *(Typing Tutor: Tuning a Crucial Skill in the Computer Age)* Typing quickly and correctly is an essential skill for working effectively with computers and the Internet. In this exercise, you'll build a GUI application that can help users learn to "touch type" (i.e., type correctly without looking at the keyboard). The application should display a *virtual keyboard* (Fig. 14.50) and should allow the user to watch what he or she is typing on the screen without looking at the *actual keyboard*. Use JButtons to represent the keys. As the user presses each key, the application highlights the corresponding JButton on the GUI and adds the character to a JTextArea that shows what the user has typed so far. [*Hint:* To highlight a JButton, use its setBackground method to change its background color. When the key is released, reset its original background color. You can obtain the JButton's original background color with the getBackground method before you change its color.]

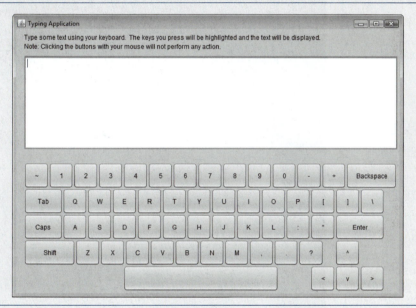

Fig. 14.50 | Typing tutor.

You can test your program by typing a pangram—a phrase that contains every letter of the alphabet at least once—such as "The quick brown fox jumped over a lazy dog." You can find other pangrams on the web.

To make the program more interesting you could monitor the user's accuracy. You could have the user type specific phrases that you've prestored in your program and that you display on the screen above the virtual keyboard. You could keep track of how many keystrokes the user types correctly and how many are typed incorrectly. You could also keep track of which keys the user is having difficulty with and display a report showing those keys.

15

Graphics and Java 2D™

One picture is worth ten thousand words.
—Chinese proverb

Treat nature in terms of the cylinder, the sphere, the cone, all in perspective.
—Paul Cézanne

Colors, like features, follow the changes of the emotions.
—Pablo Picasso

Objectives

In this chapter you'll learn:

- To understand graphics contexts and graphics objects.

- To manipulate colors and fonts.

- To use methods of class `Graphics` to draw lines, rectangles, rectangles with rounded corners, three-dimensional rectangles, ovals, arcs and polygons.

- To use methods of class `Graphics2D` from the `Java 2D` API to draw lines, rectangles, rectangles with rounded corners, ellipses, arcs and general paths.

- To specify `Paint` and `Stroke` characteristics of shapes displayed with `Graphics2D`.

15.1 Introduction

In this chapter, we overview several of Java's capabilities for drawing two-dimensional shapes, controlling colors and controlling fonts. One of Java's initial appeals was its support for graphics that enabled programmers to visually enhance their applications. Java now contains many more sophisticated drawing capabilities as part of the Java 2D™ API. This chapter begins with an introduction to many of Java's original drawing capabilities. Next we present several of the more powerful Java 2D capabilities, such as controlling the style of lines used to draw shapes and the way shapes are filled with color and patterns.

Figure 15.1 shows a portion of the Java class hierarchy that includes several of the basic graphics classes and Java 2D API classes and interfaces covered in this chapter. Class `Color` contains methods and constants for manipulating colors. Class `JComponent` contains method `paintComponent`, which is used to draw graphics on a component. Class `Font` contains methods and constants for manipulating fonts. Class `FontMetrics` contains methods for obtaining font information. Class `Graphics` contains methods for drawing strings, lines, rectangles and other shapes. Class `Graphics2D`, which extends class `Graphics`, is used for drawing with the Java 2D API. Class `Polygon` contains methods for creating polygons. The bottom half of the figure lists several classes and interfaces from the Java 2D API. Class `BasicStroke` helps specify the drawing characteristics of lines. Classes `GradientPaint` and `TexturePaint` help specify the characteristics for filling shapes with colors or patterns. Classes `GeneralPath`, `Line2D`, `Arc2D`, `Ellipse2D`, `Rectangle2D` and `RoundRectangle2D` represent several Java 2D shapes. [*Note:* We begin by discussing Java's original graphics capabilities, then move on to the Java 2D API. The classes that were part of Java's original graphics capabilities are now considered to be part of the Java 2D API.]

To begin drawing in Java, we must first understand Java's **coordinate system** (Fig. 15.2), which is a scheme for identifying every point on the screen. By default, the upper-left corner of a GUI component (e.g., a window) has the coordinates (0, 0). A coordinate pair is composed of an *x-coordinate* (the **horizontal coordinate**) and a *y-coordinate* (the **vertical coordinate**). The *x*-coordinate is the horizontal distance moving right from the left of the screen. The *y*-coordinate is the vertical distance moving down from the top of the screen. The *x*-axis describes every horizontal coordinate, and the *y*-axis every vertical coordinate. The coordinates are used to indicate where graphics should be displayed on a screen. Coordinate units are measured in **pixels** (which stands for "picture element"). A pixel is a display monitor's smallest unit of resolution.

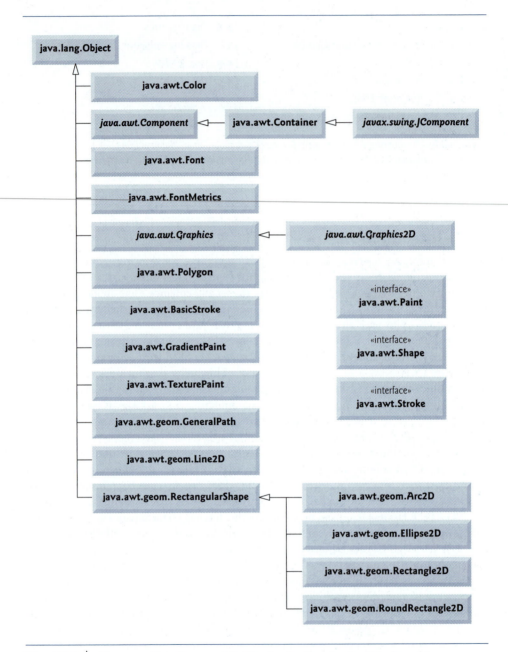

Fig. 15.1 | Classes and interfaces used in this chapter from Java's original graphics capabilities and from the Java 2D API.

Portability Tip 15.1
Different display monitors have different resolutions (i.e., the density of the pixels varies). This can cause graphics to appear in different sizes on different monitors or on the same monitor with different settings.

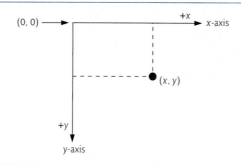

Fig. 15.2 | Java coordinate system. Units are measured in pixels.

15.2 Graphics Contexts and Graphics Objects

A **graphics context** enables drawing on the screen. A Graphics object manages a graphics context and draws pixels on the screen that represent text and other graphical objects (e.g., lines, ellipses, rectangles and other polygons). Graphics objects contain methods for drawing, font manipulation, color manipulation and the like.

Class Graphics is an abstract class (i.e., Graphics objects cannot be instantiated). This contributes to Java's portability. Because drawing is performed differently on every platform that supports Java, there cannot be only one implementation of the drawing capabilities across all systems. For example, the graphics capabilities that enable a PC running Microsoft Windows to draw a rectangle are different from those that enable a Linux workstation to draw a rectangle—and they're both different from the graphics capabilities that enable a Macintosh to draw a rectangle. When Java is implemented on each platform, a subclass of Graphics is created that implements the drawing capabilities. This implementation is hidden by class Graphics, which supplies the interface that enables us to use graphics in a platform-independent manner.

Recall from Chapter 14 that class Component is the superclass for many of the classes in package java.awt. Class JComponent (package javax.swing), which inherits indirectly from class Component, contains a paintComponent method that can be used to draw graphics. Method paintComponent takes a Graphics object as an argument. This object is passed to the paintComponent method by the system when a lightweight Swing component needs to be repainted. The header for the paintComponent method is

```
public void paintComponent( Graphics g )
```

Parameter g receives a reference to an instance of the system-specific subclass that Graphics extends. The preceding method header should look familiar to you—it's the same one we used in some of the applications in Chapter 14. Actually, class JComponent is a superclass of JPanel. Many capabilities of class JPanel are inherited from class JComponent.

You seldom call method paintComponent directly, because drawing graphics is an event-driven process. As we mentioned in Chapter 11, Java uses a multithreaded model of program execution. Each thread is a parallel activity. Each program can have many threads. When you create a GUI-based application, one of those threads is known as the **event-dispatch thread (EDT)** and it is used to process all GUI events. All drawing and manipulation of GUI components should be performed in that thread. When a GUI application executes, the application container calls method paintComponent (in the event-dispatch thread) for each lightweight component as the GUI is displayed. For paintComponent to be called again, an event must occur (such as covering and uncovering the component with another window).

If you need paintComponent to execute (i.e., if you want to update the graphics drawn on a Swing component), you can call method **repaint**, which is inherited by all JComponents indirectly from class Component (package java.awt). Method repaint is frequently called to request a call to method paintComponent. The header for repaint is

```
public void repaint()
```

15.3 Color Control

Class Color declares methods and constants for manipulating colors in a Java program. The predeclared color constants are summarized in Fig. 15.3, and several color methods and constructors are summarized in Fig. 15.4. Note that two of the methods in Fig. 15.4 are Graphics methods that are specific to colors.

Color constant	RGB value
public final static Color RED	255, 0, 0
public final static Color GREEN	0, 255, 0
public final static Color BLUE	0, 0, 255
public final static Color ORANGE	255, 200, 0
public final static Color PINK	255, 175, 175
public final static Color CYAN	0, 255, 255
public final static Color MAGENTA	255, 0, 255
public final static Color YELLOW	255, 255, 0
public final static Color BLACK	0, 0, 0
public final static Color WHITE	255, 255, 255
public final static Color GRAY	128, 128, 128
public final static Color LIGHT_GRAY	192, 192, 192
public final static Color DARK_GRAY	64, 64, 64

Fig. 15.3 | Color constants and their RGB values.

Method	Description
Color constructors and methods	
public Color(int r, int g, int b)	Creates a color based on red, green and blue components expressed as integers from 0 to 255.
public Color(float r, float g, float b)	Creates a color based on red, green and blue components expressed as floating-point values from 0.0 to 1.0.

Fig. 15.4 | Color methods and color-related Graphics methods. (Part 1 of 2.)

Method	Description
`public int getRed()`	
	Returns a value between 0 and 255 representing the red content.
`public int getGreen()`	
	Returns a value between 0 and 255 representing the green content.
`public int getBlue()`	
	Returns a value between 0 and 255 representing the blue content.
Graphics methods for manipulating `Color`*s*	
`public Color getColor()`	
	Returns `Color` object representing current color for the graphics context.
`public void setColor( Color c )`	
	Sets the current color for drawing with the graphics context.

Fig. 15.4 | Color methods and color-related `Graphics` methods. (Part 2 of 2.)

Every color is created from a red, a green and a blue component. Together these components are called **RGB values**. All three RGB components can be integers in the range from 0 to 255, or they can be floating-point values in the range 0.0 to 1.0. The first RGB component specifies the amount of red, the second the amount of green and the third the amount of blue. The larger the RGB value, the greater the amount of that particular color. Java enables you to choose from $256 \times 256 \times 256$ (approximately 16.7 million) colors. Not all computers are capable of displaying all these colors. The computer will display the closest color it can.

Two of class `Color`'s constructors are shown in Fig. 15.4—one that takes three `int` arguments and one that takes three `float` arguments, with each argument specifying the amount of red, green and blue. The `int` values must be in the range 0–255 and the `float` values must be in the range 0.0–1.0. The new `Color` object will have the specified amounts of red, green and blue. `Color` methods **getRed**, **getGreen** and **getBlue** return integer values from 0 to 255 representing the amounts of red, green and blue, respectively. `Graphics` method **getColor** returns a `Color` object representing the current drawing color. `Graphics` method **setColor** sets the current drawing color.

Drawing in Different Colors
Figures 15.5–15.6 demonstrate several methods from Fig. 15.4 by drawing filled rectangles and `String`s in several different colors. When the application begins execution, class `ColorJPanel`'s `paintComponent` method (lines 10–37 of Fig. 15.5) is called to paint the window. Line 17 uses `Graphics` method `setColor` to set the drawing color. Method `setColor` receives a `Color` object. The expression `new Color( 255, 0, 0 )` creates a new `Color` object that represents red (red value 255, and 0 for the green and blue values). Line 18 uses `Graphics` method **fillRect** to draw a filled rectangle in the current color. Method `fillRect` draws a rectangle based on its four arguments. The first two integer values represent the upper-left *x*-coordinate and upper-left *y*-coordinate, where the `Graphics` object begins drawing the rectangle. The third and fourth arguments are nonnegative integers that represent the width and the height of the rectangle in pixels, respectively. A rectangle drawn using method `fillRect` is filled by the current color of the `Graphics` object.

```
1    // Fig. 15.5: ColorJPanel.java
2    // Demonstrating Colors.
3    import java.awt.Graphics;
4    import java.awt.Color;
5    import javax.swing.JPanel;
6
7    public class ColorJPanel extends JPanel
8    {
9       // draw rectangles and Strings in different colors
10      public void paintComponent( Graphics g )
11      {
12         super.paintComponent( g ); // call superclass's paintComponent
13
14         this.setBackground( Color.WHITE );
15
16         // set new drawing color using integers
17         g.setColor( new Color( 255, 0, 0 ) );
18         g.fillRect( 15, 25, 100, 20 );
19         g.drawString( "Current RGB: " + g.getColor(), 130, 40 );
20
21         // set new drawing color using floats
22         g.setColor( new Color( 0.50f, 0.75f, 0.0f ) );
23         g.fillRect( 15, 50, 100, 20 );
24         g.drawString( "Current RGB: " + g.getColor(), 130, 65 );
25
26         // set new drawing color using static Color objects
27         g.setColor( Color.BLUE );
28         g.fillRect( 15, 75, 100, 20 );
29         g.drawString( "Current RGB: " + g.getColor(), 130, 90 );
30
31         // display individual RGB values
32         Color color = Color.MAGENTA;
33         g.setColor( color );
34         g.fillRect( 15, 100, 100, 20 );
35         g.drawString( "RGB values: " + color.getRed() + ", " +
36            color.getGreen() + ", " + color.getBlue(), 130, 115 );
37      } // end method paintComponent
38   } // end class ColorJPanel
```

Fig. 15.5 | Color changed for drawing.

```
1    // Fig. 15.6: ShowColors.java
2    // Demonstrating Colors.
3    import javax.swing.JFrame;
4
5    public class ShowColors
6    {
7       // execute application
8       public static void main( String[] args )
9       {
10         // create frame for ColorJPanel
11         JFrame frame = new JFrame( "Using colors" );
12         frame.setDefaultCloseOperation( JFrame.EXIT_ON_CLOSE );
```

Fig. 15.6 | Creating JFrame to display colors on JPanel. (Part 1 of 2.)

```
13
14              ColorJPanel colorJPanel = new ColorJPanel(); // create ColorJPanel
15              frame.add( colorJPanel ); // add colorJPanel to frame
16              frame.setSize( 400, 180 ); // set frame size
17              frame.setVisible( true ); // display frame
18         } // end main
19    } // end class ShowColors
```

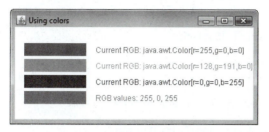

Fig. 15.6 | Creating JFrame to display colors on JPanel. (Part 2 of 2.)

Line 19 (Fig. 15.5) uses Graphics method **drawString** to draw a String in the current color. The expression g.getColor() retrieves the current color from the Graphics object. We then concatenate the Color with string "Current RGB: ", resulting in an implicit call to class Color's toString method. The String representation of a Color contains the class name and package (java.awt.Color) and the red, green and blue values.

Look-and-Feel Observation 15.1

Everyone perceives colors differently. Choose your colors carefully to ensure that your application is readable, both for people who can perceive color and for those who are color blind. Try to avoid using many different colors in close proximity.

Lines 22–24 and 27–29 perform the same tasks again. Line 22 uses the Color constructor with three float arguments to create a dark green color (0.50f for red, 0.75f for green and 0.0f for blue). Note the syntax of the values. The letter f appended to a floating-point literal indicates that the literal should be treated as type float. Recall that by default, floating-point literals are treated as type double.

Line 27 sets the current drawing color to one of the predeclared Color constants (Color.BLUE). The Color constants are static, so they're created when class Color is loaded into memory at execution time.

The statement in lines 35–36 makes calls to Color methods getRed, getGreen and getBlue on the predeclared Color.MAGENTA constant. Method main of class ShowColors (lines 8–18 of Fig. 15.6) creates the JFrame that will contain a ColorJPanel object where the colors will be displayed.

Software Engineering Observation 15.1

To change the color, you must create a new Color object (or use one of the predeclared Color constants). Like String objects, Color objects are immutable (not modifiable).

Package javax.swing provides the **JColorChooser** GUI component that enables application users to select colors. The application of Figs. 15.7–15.8 demonstrates a JColorChooser dialog. When you click the **Change Color** button, a JColorChooser dialog appears. When you select a color and press the dialog's **OK** button, the background color of the application window changes.

```java
 1   // Fig. 15.7: ShowColors2JFrame.java
 2   // Choosing colors with JColorChooser.
 3   import java.awt.BorderLayout;
 4   import java.awt.Color;
 5   import java.awt.event.ActionEvent;
 6   import java.awt.event.ActionListener;
 7   import javax.swing.JButton;
 8   import javax.swing.JFrame;
 9   import javax.swing.JColorChooser;
10   import javax.swing.JPanel;
11
12   public class ShowColors2JFrame extends JFrame
13   {
14      private JButton changeColorJButton;
15      private Color color = Color.LIGHT_GRAY;
16      private JPanel colorJPanel;
17
18      // set up GUI
19      public ShowColors2JFrame()
20      {
21         super( "Using JColorChooser" );
22
23         // create JPanel for display color
24         colorJPanel = new JPanel();
25         colorJPanel.setBackground( color );
26
27         // set up changeColorJButton and register its event handler
28         changeColorJButton = new JButton( "Change Color" );
29         changeColorJButton.addActionListener(
30
31            new ActionListener() // anonymous inner class
32            {
33               // display JColorChooser when user clicks button
34               public void actionPerformed( ActionEvent event )
35               {
36                  color = JColorChooser.showDialog(
37                     ShowColors2JFrame.this, "Choose a color", color );
38
39                  // set default color, if no color is returned
40                  if ( color == null )
41                     color = Color.LIGHT_GRAY;
42
43                  // change content pane's background color
44                  colorJPanel.setBackground( color );
45               } // end method actionPerformed
46            } // end anonymous inner class
47         ); // end call to addActionListener
48
49         add( colorJPanel, BorderLayout.CENTER ); // add colorJPanel
50         add( changeColorJButton, BorderLayout.SOUTH ); // add button
```

Fig. 15.7 | JColorChooser dialog. (Part 1 of 2.)

```
51
52          setSize( 400, 130 ); // set frame size
53          setVisible( true ); // display frame
54      } // end ShowColor2JFrame constructor
55  } // end class ShowColors2JFrame
```

Fig. 15.7 | JColorChooser dialog. (Part 2 of 2.)

```
 1  // Fig. 15.8: ShowColors2.java
 2  // Choosing colors with JColorChooser.
 3  import javax.swing.JFrame;
 4
 5  public class ShowColors2
 6  {
 7      // execute application
 8      public static void main( String[] args )
 9      {
10          ShowColors2JFrame application = new ShowColors2JFrame();
11          application.setDefaultCloseOperation( JFrame.EXIT_ON_CLOSE );
12      } // end main
13  } // end class ShowColors2
```

(a) Initial application window.

(b) JColorChooser window.

Select a color from one of the color swatches.

(c) Application window after changing JPanel's background color.

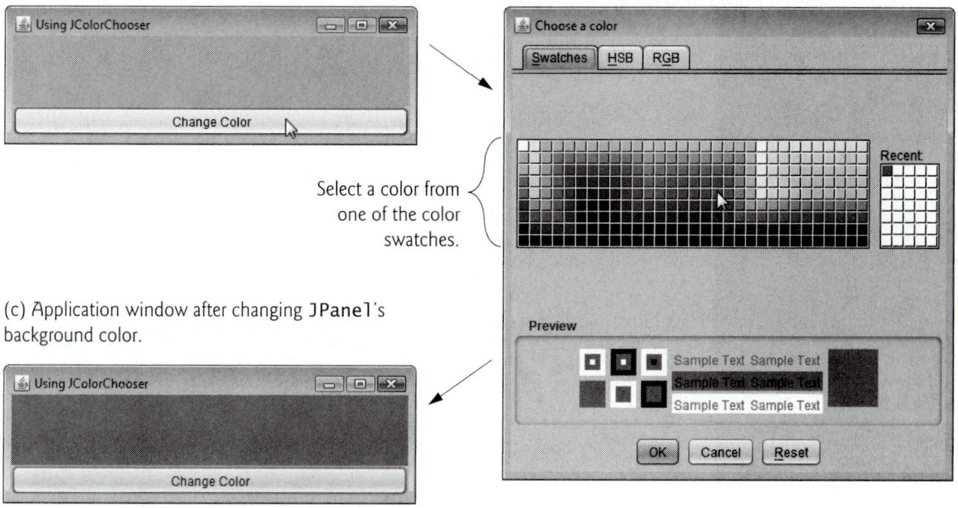

Fig. 15.8 | Choosing colors with JColorChooser.

Class JColorChooser provides static method **showDialog**, which creates a JColor-Chooser object, attaches it to a dialog box and displays the dialog. Lines 36–37 of Fig. 15.7 invoke this method to display the color chooser dialog. Method showDialog returns the selected Color object, or null if the user presses **Cancel** or closes the dialog without pressing **OK**. The method takes three arguments—a reference to its parent Component, a String to display in the title bar of the dialog and the initial selected Color for the dialog. The parent component is a reference to the window from which the dialog is displayed (in this case the JFrame, with the reference name frame). The dialog will be centered on the parent. If the parent is `null`, the dialog is centered on the screen. While the color chooser dialog is on the screen, the user cannot interact with the parent component until the dialog is dismissed. This type of dialog is called a modal dialog.

After the user selects a color, lines 40–41 determine whether `color` is `null`, and, if so, set `color` to `Color.LIGHT_GRAY`. Line 44 invokes method `setBackground` to change the background color of the `JPanel`. Method `setBackground` is one of the many `Component` methods that can be used on most GUI components. Note that the user can continue to use the **Change Color** button to change the background color of the application. Figure 15.8 contains method `main`, which executes the program.

Figure 15.8(b) shows the default `JColorChooser` dialog that allows the user to select a color from a variety of **color swatches**. Note that there are actually three tabs across the top of the dialog—**Swatches**, **HSB** and **RGB**. These represent three different ways to select a color. The **HSB** tab allows you to select a color based on **hue, saturation** and **brightness**—values that are used to define the amount of light in a color. We do not discuss HSB values. For more information on them, visit `whatis.techtarget.com/definition/0,,sid9_gci212262,00.html`. The **RGB** tab allows you to select a color by using sliders to select the red, green and blue components. The **HSB** and **RGB** tabs are shown in Fig. 15.9.

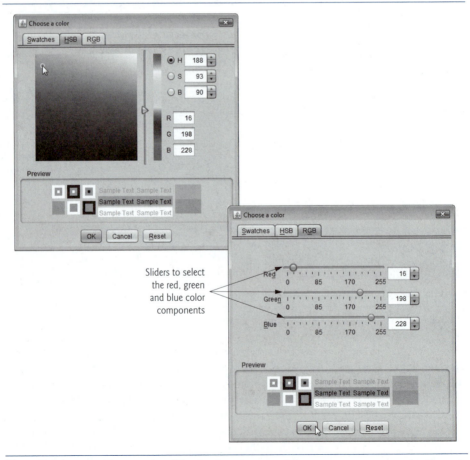

Sliders to select the red, green and blue color components

Fig. 15.9 | HSB and RGB tabs of the `JColorChooser` dialog.

15.4 Manipulating Fonts

This section introduces methods and constants for manipulating fonts. Most font methods and font constants are part of class Font. Some methods of class Font and class Graphics are summarized in Fig. 15.10.

Method or constant	Description
Font constants, constructors and methods	
`public final static int PLAIN`	A constant representing a plain font style.
`public final static int BOLD`	A constant representing a bold font style.
`public final static int ITALIC`	A constant representing an italic font style.
`public Font( String name, int style, int size )`	Creates a Font object with the specified font name, style and size.
`public int getStyle()`	Returns an int indicating the current font style.
`public int getSize()`	Returns an int indicating the current font size.
`public String getName()`	Returns the current font name as a string.
`public String getFamily()`	Returns the font's family name as a string.
`public boolean isPlain()`	Returns true if the font is plain, else false.
`public boolean isBold()`	Returns true if the font is bold, else false.
`public boolean isItalic()`	Returns true if the font is italic, else false.
Graphics methods for manipulating Fonts	
`public Font getFont()`	Returns a Font object reference representing the current font.
`public void setFont( Font f )`	Sets the current font to the font, style and size specified by the Font object reference f.

Fig. 15.10 | Font-related methods and constants.

Class Font's constructor takes three arguments—the **font name**, **font style** and **font size**. The font name is any font currently supported by the system on which the program is running, such as standard Java fonts Monospaced, SansSerif and Serif. The font style is **Font.PLAIN**, **Font.ITALIC** or **Font.BOLD** (each is a static field of class Font). Font styles can be used in combination (e.g., Font.ITALIC + Font.BOLD). The font size is measured in points. A **point** is 1/72 of an inch. Graphics method **setFont** sets the current drawing font—the font in which text will be displayed—to its Font argument.

Portability Tip 15.2

The number of fonts varies across systems. Java provides five font names—Serif, Monospaced, SansSerif, Dialog and DialogInput—that can be used on all Java platforms. The Java runtime environment (JRE) on each platform maps these logical font names to actual fonts installed on the platform. The actual fonts used may vary by platform.

The application of Figs. 15.11–15.12 displays text in four different fonts, with each font in a different size. Figure 15.11 uses the Font constructor to initialize Font objects (in lines 16, 20, 24 and 29) that are each passed to Graphics method setFont to change the drawing font. Each call to the Font constructor passes a font name (Serif, Monospaced or SansSerif) as a string, a font style (Font.PLAIN, Font.ITALIC or Font.BOLD) and a font size. Once Graphics method setFont is invoked, all text displayed following the call will appear in the new font until the font is changed. Each font's information is displayed in lines 17, 21, 25 and 30–31 using method drawString. Note that the coordinate passed to drawString corresponds to the lower-left corner of the baseline of the font. Line 28 changes the drawing color to red, so the next string displayed appears in red. Lines 30–31 display information about the final Font object. Method **getFont** of class Graphics returns a Font object representing the current font. Method **getName** returns the current font name as a string. Method **getSize** returns the font size in points.

Figure 15.12 contains method main, which creates a JFrame. We add a FontJPanel object to this JFrame (line 15), which displays the graphics created in Fig. 15.11.

Software Engineering Observation 15.2

To change the font, you must create a new Font object. Font objects are immutable—class Font has no set methods to change the characteristics of the current font.

```
1   // Fig. 15.11: FontJPanel.java
2   // Display strings in different fonts and colors.
3   import java.awt.Font;
4   import java.awt.Color;
5   import java.awt.Graphics;
6   import javax.swing.JPanel;
7
8   public class FontJPanel extends JPanel
9   {
10     // display Strings in different fonts and colors
11     public void paintComponent( Graphics g )
12     {
13        super.paintComponent( g ); // call superclass's paintComponent
14
15        // set font to Serif (Times), bold, 12pt and draw a string
16        g.setFont( new Font( "Serif", Font.BOLD, 12 ) );
17        g.drawString( "Serif 12 point bold.", 20, 30 );
18
19        // set font to Monospaced (Courier), italic, 24pt and draw a string
20        g.setFont( new Font( "Monospaced", Font.ITALIC, 24 ) );
21        g.drawString( "Monospaced 24 point italic.", 20, 50 );
22
23        // set font to SansSerif (Helvetica), plain, 14pt and draw a string
24        g.setFont( new Font( "SansSerif", Font.PLAIN, 14 ) );
25        g.drawString( "SansSerif 14 point plain.", 20, 70 );
26
27        // set font to Serif (Times), bold/italic, 18pt and draw a string
28        g.setColor( Color.RED );
29        g.setFont( new Font( "Serif", Font.BOLD + Font.ITALIC, 18 ) );
30        g.drawString( g.getFont().getName() + " " + g.getFont().getSize() +
31           " point bold italic.", 20, 90 );
32     } // end method paintComponent
33  } // end class FontJPanel
```

Fig. 15.11 | Graphics method setFont changes the drawing font.

```
 1   // Fig. 15.12: Fonts.java
 2   // Using fonts.
 3   import javax.swing.JFrame;
 4
 5   public class Fonts
 6   {
 7      // execute application
 8      public static void main( String[] args )
 9      {
10         // create frame for FontJPanel
11         JFrame frame = new JFrame( "Using fonts" );
12         frame.setDefaultCloseOperation( JFrame.EXIT_ON_CLOSE );
13
14         FontJPanel fontJPanel = new FontJPanel(); // create FontJPanel
15         frame.add( fontJPanel ); // add fontJPanel to frame
16         frame.setSize( 420, 150 ); // set frame size
17         frame.setVisible( true ); // display frame
18      } // end main
19   } // end class Fonts
```

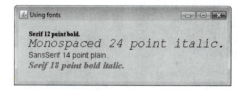

Fig. 15.12 | Creating a JFrame to display fonts.

Font Metrics

Sometimes it's necessary to get information about the current drawing font, such as its name, style and size. Several Font methods used to get font information are summarized in Fig. 15.10. Method **getStyle** returns an integer value representing the current style. The integer value returned is either Font.PLAIN, Font.ITALIC, Font.BOLD or the combination of Font.ITALIC and Font.BOLD. Method **getFamily** returns the name of the font family to which the current font belongs. The name of the font family is platform specific. Font methods are also available to test the style of the current font, and these too are summarized in Fig. 15.10. Methods **isPlain**, **isBold** and **isItalic** return true if the current font style is plain, bold or italic, respectively.

Figure 15.13 illustrates some of the common **font metrics**, which provide precise information about a font, such as **height**, **descent** (the amount a character dips below the

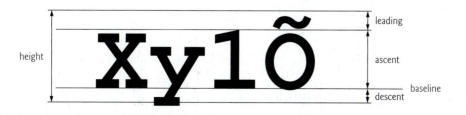

Fig. 15.13 | Font metrics.

baseline), ascent (the amount a character rises above the baseline) and leading (the difference between the descent of one line of text and the ascent of the line of text below it—that is, the interline spacing).

Class `FontMetrics` declares several methods for obtaining font metrics. These methods and Graphics method `getFontMetrics` are summarized in Fig. 15.14. The application of Figs. 15.15–15.16 uses the methods of Fig. 15.14 to obtain font metric information for two fonts.

Method	Description
FontMetrics methods	
`public int getAscent()`	Returns the ascent of a font in points.
`public int getDescent()`	Returns the descent of a font in points.
`public int getLeading()`	Returns the leading of a font in points.
`public int getHeight()`	Returns the height of a font in points.
Graphics methods for getting a Font's FontMetrics	
`public FontMetrics getFontMetrics()`	
	Returns the FontMetrics object for the current drawing Font.
`public FontMetrics getFontMetrics( Font f )`	
	Returns the FontMetrics object for the specified Font argument.

Fig. 15.14 | FontMetrics and Graphics methods for obtaining font metrics.

```
1   // Fig. 15.15: MetricsJPanel.java
2   // FontMetrics and Graphics methods useful for obtaining font metrics.
3   import java.awt.Font;
4   import java.awt.FontMetrics;
5   import java.awt.Graphics;
6   import javax.swing.JPanel;
7
8   public class MetricsJPanel extends JPanel
9   {
10      // display font metrics
11      public void paintComponent( Graphics g )
12      {
13         super.paintComponent( g ); // call superclass's paintComponent
14
15         g.setFont( new Font( "SansSerif", Font.BOLD, 12 ) );
16         FontMetrics metrics = g.getFontMetrics();
17         g.drawString( "Current font: " + g.getFont(), 10, 30 );
18         g.drawString( "Ascent: " + metrics.getAscent(), 10, 45 );
19         g.drawString( "Descent: " + metrics.getDescent(), 10, 60 );
20         g.drawString( "Height: " + metrics.getHeight(), 10, 75 );
21         g.drawString( "Leading: " + metrics.getLeading(), 10, 90 );
22
23         Font font = new Font( "Serif", Font.ITALIC, 14 );
24         metrics = g.getFontMetrics( font );
```

Fig. 15.15 | Font metrics. (Part 1 of 2.)

```
25          g.setFont( font );
26          g.drawString( "Current font: " + font, 10, 120 );
27          g.drawString( "Ascent: " + metrics.getAscent(), 10, 135 );
28          g.drawString( "Descent: " + metrics.getDescent(), 10, 150 );
29          g.drawString( "Height: " + metrics.getHeight(), 10, 165 );
30          g.drawString( "Leading: " + metrics.getLeading(), 10, 180 );
31      } // end method paintComponent
32  } // end class MetricsJPanel
```

Fig. 15.15 | Font metrics. (Part 2 of 2.)

```
1   // Fig. 15.16: Metrics.java
2   // Displaying font metrics.
3   import javax.swing.JFrame;
4
5   public class Metrics
6   {
7       // execute application
8       public static void main( String[] args )
9       {
10          // create frame for MetricsJPanel
11          JFrame frame = new JFrame( "Demonstrating FontMetrics" );
12          frame.setDefaultCloseOperation( JFrame.EXIT_ON_CLOSE );
13
14          MetricsJPanel metricsJPanel = new MetricsJPanel();
15          frame.add( metricsJPanel ); // add metricsJPanel to frame
16          frame.setSize( 510, 240 ); // set frame size
17          frame.setVisible( true ); // display frame
18      } // end main
19  } // end class Metrics
```

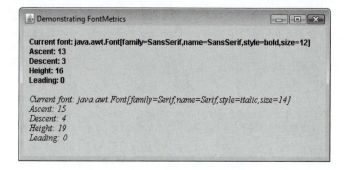

Fig. 15.16 | Creating JFrame to display font metric information.

Line 15 of Fig. 15.15 creates and sets the current drawing font to a SansSerif, bold, 12-point font. Line 16 uses Graphics method getFontMetrics to obtain the FontMetrics object for the current font. Line 17 outputs the String representation of the Font returned by g.getFont(). Lines 18–21 use FontMetric methods to obtain the ascent, descent, height and leading for the font.

Line 23 creates a new Serif, italic, 14-point font. Line 24 uses a second version of Graphics method getFontMetrics, which accepts a Font argument and returns a corresponding `FontMetrics` object. Lines 27–30 obtain the ascent, descent, height and leading for the font. Note that the font metrics are slightly different for the two fonts.

15.5 Drawing Lines, Rectangles and Ovals

This section presents `Graphics` methods for drawing lines, rectangles and ovals. The methods and their parameters are summarized in Fig. 15.17. For each drawing method that requires a `width` and `height` parameter, the `width` and `height` must be nonnegative values. Otherwise, the shape will not display.

Method	Description
`public void drawLine( int x1, int y1, int x2, int y2 )`	
	Draws a line between the point (x1, y1) and the point (x2, y2).
`public void drawRect( int x, int y, int width, int height )`	
	Draws a rectangle of the specified `width` and `height`. The rectangle's top-left corner is located at (x, y). Only the outline of the rectangle is drawn using the `Graphics` object's color—the body of the rectangle is not filled with this color.
`public void fillRect( int x, int y, int width, int height )`	
	Draws a filled rectangle in the current color with the specified `width` and `height`. The rectangle's top-left corner is located at (x, y).
`public void clearRect( int x, int y, int width, int height )`	
	Draws a filled rectangle with the specified `width` and `height` in the current background color. The rectangle's top-left corner is located at (x, y). This method is useful if you want to remove a portion of an image.
`public void drawRoundRect( int x, int y, int width, int height, int arcWidth, int arcHeight )`	
	Draws a rectangle with rounded corners in the current color with the specified `width` and `height`. The `arcWidth` and `arcHeight` determine the rounding of the corners (see Fig. 15.20). Only the outline of the shape is drawn.
`public void fillRoundRect( int x, int y, int width, int height, int arcWidth, int arcHeight )`	
	Draws a filled rectangle in the current color with rounded corners with the specified `width` and `height`. The `arcWidth` and `arcHeight` determine the rounding of the corners (see Fig. 15.20).
`public void draw3DRect( int x, int y, int width, int height, boolean b )`	
	Draws a three-dimensional rectangle in the current color with the specified `width` and `height`. The rectangle's top-left corner is located at (x, y). The rectangle appears raised when b is true and lowered when b is false. Only the outline of the shape is drawn.
`public void fill3DRect( int x, int y, int width, int height, boolean b )`	
	Draws a filled three-dimensional rectangle in the current color with the specified `width` and `height`. The rectangle's top-left corner is located at (x, y). The rectangle appears raised when b is true and lowered when b is false.

Fig. 15.17 | `Graphics` methods that draw lines, rectangles and ovals. (Part 1 of 2.)

Method	Description

`public void drawOval( int x, int y, int width, int height )`

Draws an oval in the current color with the specified width and height. The bounding rectangle's top-left corner is located at (x, y). The oval touches all four sides of the bounding rectangle at the center of each side (see Fig. 15.21). Only the outline of the shape is drawn.

`public void fillOval( int x, int y, int width, int height )`

Draws a filled oval in the current color with the specified width and height. The bounding rectangle's top-left corner is located at (x, y). The oval touches the center of all four sides of the bounding rectangle (see Fig. 15.21).

Fig. 15.17 | Graphics methods that draw lines, rectangles and ovals. (Part 2 of 2.)

The application of Figs. 15.18–15.19 demonstrates drawing a variety of lines, rectangles, three-dimensional rectangles, rounded rectangles and ovals. In Fig. 15.18, line 17 draws a red line, line 20 draws an empty blue rectangle and line 21 draws a filled blue rectangle. Methods **fillRoundRect** (line 24) and **drawRoundRect** (line 25) draw rectangles with rounded corners. Their first two arguments specify the coordinates of the upper-left corner of the bounding rectangle—the area in which the rounded rectangle will be drawn. Note that the upper-left corner coordinates are not the edge of the rounded rectangle, but the coordinates where the edge would be if the rectangle had square corners. The third and fourth arguments specify the width and height of the rectangle. The last two arguments determine the horizontal and vertical diameters of the arc (i.e., the arc width and arc height) used to represent the corners.

```
 1   // Fig. 15.18: LinesRectsOvalsJPanel.java
 2   // Drawing lines, rectangles and ovals.
 3   import java.awt.Color;
 4   import java.awt.Graphics;
 5   import javax.swing.JPanel;
 6
 7   public class LinesRectsOvalsJPanel extends JPanel
 8   {
 9      // display various lines, rectangles and ovals
10      public void paintComponent( Graphics g )
11      {
12         super.paintComponent( g ); // call superclass's paint method
13
14         this.setBackground( Color.WHITE );
15
16         g.setColor( Color.RED );
17         g.drawLine( 5, 30, 380, 30 );
18
19         g.setColor( Color.BLUE );
20         g.drawRect( 5, 40, 90, 55 );
21         g.fillRect( 100, 40, 90, 55 );
22
```

Fig. 15.18 | Drawing lines, rectangles and ovals. (Part 1 of 2.)

```
23          g.setColor( Color.CYAN );
24          g.fillRoundRect( 195, 40, 90, 55, 50, 50 );
25          g.drawRoundRect( 290, 40, 90, 55, 20, 20 );
26
27          g.setColor( Color.GREEN );
28          g.draw3DRect( 5, 100, 90, 55, true );
29          g.fill3DRect( 100, 100, 90, 55, false );
30
31          g.setColor( Color.MAGENTA );
32          g.drawOval( 195, 100, 90, 55 );
33          g.fillOval( 290, 100, 90, 55 );
34       } // end method paintComponent
35    } // end class LinesRectsOvalsJPanel
```

Fig. 15.18 | Drawing lines, rectangles and ovals. (Part 2 of 2.)

```
1    // Fig. 15.19: LinesRectsOvals.java
2    // Drawing lines, rectangles and ovals.
3    import java.awt.Color;
4    import javax.swing.JFrame;
5
6    public class LinesRectsOvals
7    {
8       // execute application
9       public static void main( String[] args )
10      {
11         // create frame for LinesRectsOvalsJPanel
12         JFrame frame =
13            new JFrame( "Drawing lines, rectangles and ovals" );
14         frame.setDefaultCloseOperation( JFrame.EXIT_ON_CLOSE );
15
16         LinesRectsOvalsJPanel linesRectsOvalsJPanel =
17            new LinesRectsOvalsJPanel();
18         linesRectsOvalsJPanel.setBackground( Color.WHITE );
19         frame.add( linesRectsOvalsJPanel ); // add panel to frame
20         frame.setSize( 400, 210 ); // set frame size
21         frame.setVisible( true ); // display frame
22      } // end main
23   } // end class LinesRectsOvals
```

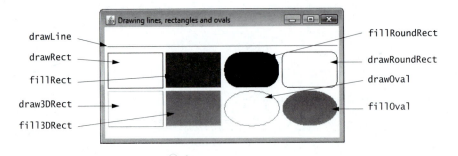

Fig. 15.19 | Creating JFrame to display lines, rectangles and ovals.

Figure 15.20 labels the arc width, arc height, width and height of a rounded rectangle. Using the same value for the arc width and arc height produces a quarter-circle at each corner. When the arc width, arc height, width and height have the same values, the result is a circle. If the values for width and height are the same and the values of arcWidth and arcHeight are 0, the result is a square.

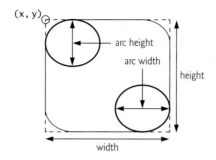

Fig. 15.20 | Arc width and arc height for rounded rectangles.

Methods **draw3DRect** (line 28) and **fill3DRect** (line 29) take the same arguments. The first two specify the top-left corner of the rectangle. The next two arguments specify the width and height of the rectangle, respectively. The last argument determines whether the rectangle is raised (true) or lowered (false). The three-dimensional effect of draw3DRect appears as two edges of the rectangle in the original color and two edges in a slightly darker color. The three-dimensional effect of fill3DRect appears as two edges of the rectangle in the original drawing color and the fill and other two edges in a slightly darker color. Raised rectangles have the original drawing color edges at the top and left of the rectangle. Lowered rectangles have the original drawing color edges at the bottom and right of the rectangle. The three-dimensional effect is difficult to see in some colors.

Methods **drawOval** and **fillOval** (Fig. 15.18, lines 32–33) take the same four arguments. The first two arguments specify the top-left coordinate of the bounding rectangle that contains the oval. The last two arguments specify the width and height of the bounding rectangle, respectively. Figure 15.21 shows an oval bounded by a rectangle. Note that the oval touches the center of all four sides of the bounding rectangle. (The bounding rectangle is not displayed on the screen.)

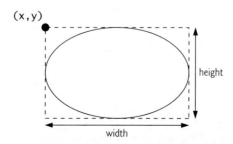

Fig. 15.21 | Oval bounded by a rectangle.

15.6 Drawing Arcs

An arc is drawn as a portion of an oval. Arc angles are measured in degrees. Arcs **sweep** (i.e., move along a curve) from a **starting angle** by the number of degrees specified by their **arc angle**. The starting angle indicates in degrees where the arc begins. The arc angle specifies the total number of degrees through which the arc sweeps. Figure 15.22 illustrates two arcs. The left set of axes shows an arc sweeping from zero degrees to approximately 110 degrees. Arcs that sweep in a counterclockwise direction are measured in **positive degrees**. The set of axes on the right shows an arc sweeping from zero degrees to approximately –110 degrees. Arcs that sweep in a clockwise direction are measured in **negative degrees**. Note the dashed boxes around the arcs in Fig. 15.22. When drawing an arc, we specify a bounding rectangle for an oval. The arc will sweep along part of the oval. Graphics methods **drawArc** and **fillArc** for drawing arcs are summarized in Fig. 15.23.

Fig. 15.22 | Positive and negative arc angles.

Method	Description
public void drawArc(int x, int y, int width, int height, int startAngle, int arcAngle)	
	Draws an arc relative to the bounding rectangle's top-left x- and y-coordinates with the specified width and height. The arc segment is drawn starting at startAngle and sweeps arcAngle degrees.
public void fillArc(int x, int y, int width, int height, int startAngle, int arcAngle)	
	Draws a filled arc (i.e., a sector) relative to the bounding rectangle's top-left x- and y-coordinates with the specified width and height. The arc segment is drawn starting at startAngle and sweeps arcAngle degrees.

Fig. 15.23 | Graphics methods for drawing arcs.

Figures 15.24–12.25 demonstrate the arc methods of Fig. 15.23. The application draws six arcs (three unfilled and three filled). To illustrate the bounding rectangle that helps determine where the arc appears, the first three arcs are displayed inside a red rectangle that has the same x, y, width and height arguments as the arcs.

```
 1   // Fig. 15.24: ArcsJPanel.java
 2   // Drawing arcs.
 3   import java.awt.Color;
 4   import java.awt.Graphics;
 5   import javax.swing.JPanel;
 6
 7   public class ArcsJPanel extends JPanel
 8   {
 9      // draw rectangles and arcs
10      public void paintComponent( Graphics g )
11      {
12         super.paintComponent( g ); // call superclass's paintComponent
13
14         // start at 0 and sweep 360 degrees
15         g.setColor( Color.RED );
16         g.drawRect( 15, 35, 80, 80 );
17         g.setColor( Color.BLACK );
18         g.drawArc( 15, 35, 80, 80, 0, 360 );
19
20         // start at 0 and sweep 110 degrees
21         g.setColor( Color.RED );
22         g.drawRect( 100, 35, 80, 80 );
23         g.setColor( Color.BLACK );
24         g.drawArc( 100, 35, 80, 80, 0, 110 );
25
26         // start at 0 and sweep -270 degrees
27         g.setColor( Color.RED );
28         g.drawRect( 185, 35, 80, 80 );
29         g.setColor( Color.BLACK );
30         g.drawArc( 185, 35, 80, 80, 0, -270 );
31
32         // start at 0 and sweep 360 degrees
33         g.fillArc( 15, 120, 80, 40, 0, 360 );
34
35         // start at 270 and sweep -90 degrees
36         g.fillArc( 100, 120, 80, 40, 270, -90 );
37
38         // start at 0 and sweep -270 degrees
39         g.fillArc( 185, 120, 80, 40, 0, -270 );
40      } // end method paintComponent
41   } // end class ArcsJPanel
```

Fig. 15.24 | Arcs displayed with `drawArc` and `fillArc`.

```
 1   // Fig. 15.25: DrawArcs.java
 2   // Drawing arcs.
 3   import javax.swing.JFrame;
 4
 5   public class DrawArcs
 6   {
 7      // execute application
 8      public static void main( String[] args )
 9      {
```

Fig. 15.25 | Creating JFrame to display arcs. (Part 1 of 2.)

```
10        // create frame for ArcsJPanel
11        JFrame frame = new JFrame( "Drawing Arcs" );
12        frame.setDefaultCloseOperation( JFrame.EXIT_ON_CLOSE );
13
14        ArcsJPanel arcsJPanel = new ArcsJPanel(); // create ArcsJPanel
15        frame.add( arcsJPanel ); // add arcsJPanel to frame
16        frame.setSize( 300, 210 ); // set frame size
17        frame.setVisible( true ); // display frame
18     } // end main
19   } // end class DrawArcs
```

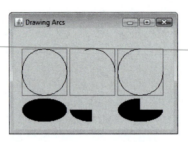

Fig. 15.25 | Creating JFrame to display arcs. (Part 2 of 2.)

15.7 Drawing Polygons and Polylines

Polygons are closed multisided shapes composed of straight-line segments. Polylines are sequences of connected points. Figure 15.26 discusses methods for drawing polygons and polylines. Note that some methods require a **Polygon** object (package java.awt). Class Polygon's constructors are also described in Fig. 15.26. The application of Figs. 15.27–15.28 draws polygons and polylines.

Method	Description
Graphics methods for drawing polygons	
public void drawPolygon(**int**[] xPoints, **int**[] yPoints, **int** points)	
	Draws a polygon. The *x*-coordinate of each point is specified in the xPoints array, and the *y*-coordinate of each point in the yPoints array. The last argument specifies the number of points. This method draws a closed polygon. If the last point is different from the first, the polygon is closed by a line that connects the last point to the first.
public void drawPolyline(**int**[] xPoints, **int**[] yPoints, **int** points)	
	Draws a sequence of connected lines. The *x*-coordinate of each point is specified in the xPoints array, and the *y*-coordinate of each point in the yPoints array. The last argument specifies the number of points. If the last point is different from the first, the polyline is not closed.
public void drawPolygon(Polygon p)	
	Draws the specified polygon.

Fig. 15.26 | Graphics methods for polygons and class Polygon methods. (Part 1 of 2.)

Method	Description
`public void fillPolygon( int[] xPoints, int[] yPoints, int points )`	
	Draws a filled polygon. The *x*-coordinate of each point is specified in the xPoints array, and the *y*-coordinate of each point in the yPoints array. The last argument specifies the number of points. This method draws a closed polygon. If the last point is different from the first, the polygon is closed by a line that connects the last point to the first.
`public void fillPolygon( Polygon p )`	
	Draws the specified filled polygon. The polygon is closed.
Polygon constructors and methods	
`public Polygon()`	
	Constructs a new polygon object. The polygon does not contain any points.
`public Polygon( int[] xValues, int[] yValues, int numberOfPoints )`	
	Constructs a new polygon object. The polygon has numberOfPoints sides, with each point consisting of an *x*-coordinate from xValues and a *y*-coordinate from yValues.
`public void addPoint( int x, int y )`	
	Adds pairs of *x*- and *y*-coordinates to the Polygon.

Fig. 15.26 | Graphics methods for polygons and class Polygon methods. (Part 2 of 2.)

```java
1   // Fig. 15.27: PolygonsJPanel.java
2   // Drawing polygons.
3   import java.awt.Graphics;
4   import java.awt.Polygon;
5   import javax.swing.JPanel;
6
7   public class PolygonsJPanel extends JPanel
8   {
9      // draw polygons and polylines
10     public void paintComponent( Graphics g )
11     {
12        super.paintComponent( g ); // call superclass's paintComponent
13
14        // draw polygon with Polygon object
15        int[] xValues = { 20, 40, 50, 30, 20, 15 };
16        int[] yValues = { 50, 50, 60, 80, 80, 60 };
17        Polygon polygon1 = new Polygon( xValues, yValues, 6 );
18        g.drawPolygon( polygon1 );
19
20        // draw polylines with two arrays
21        int[] xValues2 = { 70, 90, 100, 80, 70, 65, 60 };
22        int[] yValues2 = { 100, 100, 110, 110, 130, 110, 90 };
23        g.drawPolyline( xValues2, yValues2, 7 );
24
25        // fill polygon with two arrays
26        int[] xValues3 = { 120, 140, 150, 190 };
```

Fig. 15.27 | Polygons displayed with drawPolygon and fillPolygon. (Part 1 of 2.)

```
27          int[] yValues3 = { 40, 70, 80, 60 };
28          g.fillPolygon( xValues3, yValues3, 4 );
29
30          // draw filled polygon with Polygon object
31          Polygon polygon2 = new Polygon();
32          polygon2.addPoint( 165, 135 );
33          polygon2.addPoint( 175, 150 );
34          polygon2.addPoint( 270, 200 );
35          polygon2.addPoint( 200, 220 );
36          polygon2.addPoint( 130, 180 );
37          g.fillPolygon( polygon2 );
38       } // end method paintComponent
39    } // end class PolygonsJPanel
```

Fig. 15.27 | Polygons displayed with `drawPolygon` and `fillPolygon`. (Part 2 of 2.)

```
 1    // Fig. 15.28: DrawPolygons.java
 2    // Drawing polygons.
 3    import javax.swing.JFrame;
 4
 5    public class DrawPolygons
 6    {
 7       // execute application
 8       public static void main( String[] args )
 9       {
10          // create frame for PolygonsJPanel
11          JFrame frame = new JFrame( "Drawing Polygons" );
12          frame.setDefaultCloseOperation( JFrame.EXIT_ON_CLOSE );
13
14          PolygonsJPanel polygonsJPanel = new PolygonsJPanel();
15          frame.add( polygonsJPanel ); // add polygonsJPanel to frame
16          frame.setSize( 280, 270 ); // set frame size
17          frame.setVisible( true ); // display frame
18       } // end main
19    } // end class DrawPolygons
```

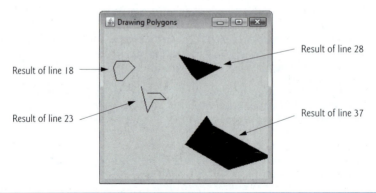

Fig. 15.28 | Creating `JFrame` to display polygons.

Lines 15–16 of Fig. 15.27 create two `int` arrays and use them to specify the points for `Polygon polygon1`. The `Polygon` constructor call in line 17 receives array `xValues`, which contains the *x*-coordinate of each point; array yValues, which contains the *y*-coordinate of each point and 6 (the number of points in the polygon). Line 18 displays polygon1 by passing it as an argument to Graphics method **drawPolygon**.

Lines 21–22 create two int arrays and use them to specify the points for a series of connected lines. Array xValues2 contains the *x*-coordinate of each point and array yValues2 the *y*-coordinate of each point. Line 23 uses Graphics method **drawPolyline** to display the series of connected lines specified with the arguments xValues2, yValues2 and 7 (the number of points).

Lines 26–27 create two int arrays and use them to specify the points of a polygon. Array xValues3 contains the *x*-coordinate of each point and array yValues3 the *y*-coordinate of each point. Line 28 displays a polygon by passing to Graphics method **fillPolygon** the two arrays (xValues3 and yValues3) and the number of points to draw (4).

Common Programming Error 15.1

An ArrayIndexOutOfBoundsException is thrown if the number of points specified in the third argument to method drawPolygon or method fillPolygon is greater than the number of elements in the arrays of coordinates that specify the polygon to display.

Line 31 creates Polygon polygon2 with no points. Lines 32–36 use Polygon method **addPoint** to add pairs of *x*- and *y*-coordinates to the Polygon. Line 37 displays Polygon polygon2 by passing it to Graphics method fillPolygon.

15.8 Java 2D API

The Java 2D API provides advanced two-dimensional graphics capabilities for programmers who require detailed and complex graphical manipulations. The API includes features for processing line art, text and images in packages java.awt, java.awt.image, java.awt.color, java.awt.font, java.awt.geom, java.awt.print and java.awt.image.renderable. The capabilities of the API are far too broad to cover in this textbook. For an overview of the capabilities, see the Java 2D demo (discussed in Chapter 23, Applets and Java Web Start) or visit java.sun.com/javase/6/docs/technotes/guides/2d. In this section, we overview several Java 2D capabilities.

Drawing with the Java 2D API is accomplished with a **Graphics2D** reference (package java.awt). Graphics2D is an abstract subclass of class Graphics, so it has all the graphics capabilities demonstrated earlier in this chapter. In fact, the actual object used to draw in every paintComponent method is an instance of a subclass of Graphics2D that is passed to method paintComponent and accessed via the superclass Graphics. To access Graphics2D capabilities, we must cast the Graphics reference (g) passed to paintComponent into a Graphics2D reference with a statement such as

```
Graphics2D g2d = ( Graphics2D ) g;
```

The next two examples use this technique.

Lines, Rectangles, Round Rectangles, Arcs and Ellipses

This example demonstrates several Java 2D shapes from package java.awt.geom, including **Line2D.Double**, **Rectangle2D.Double**, **RoundRectangle2D.Double**, **Arc2D.Double** and **Ellipse2D.Double**. Note the syntax of each class name. Each class represents a shape with dimensions specified as double values. There is a separate version of each represented with float values (e.g., **Ellipse2D.Float**). In each case, Double is a public static nested class of the class specified to the left of the dot (e.g., `Ellipse2D`). To use the `static` nested class, we simply qualify its name with the outer class name.

In Figs. 15.29–15.30, we draw Java 2D shapes and modify their drawing characteristics, such as changing line thickness, filling shapes with patterns and drawing dashed lines. These are just a few of the many capabilities provided by Java 2D.

```java
1   // Fig. 15.29: ShapesJPanel.java
2   // Demonstrating some Java 2D shapes.
3   import java.awt.Color;
4   import java.awt.Graphics;
5   import java.awt.BasicStroke;
6   import java.awt.GradientPaint;
7   import java.awt.TexturePaint;
8   import java.awt.Rectangle;
9   import java.awt.Graphics2D;
10  import java.awt.geom.Ellipse2D;
11  import java.awt.geom.Rectangle2D;
12  import java.awt.geom.RoundRectangle2D;
13  import java.awt.geom.Arc2D;
14  import java.awt.geom.Line2D;
15  import java.awt.image.BufferedImage;
16  import javax.swing.JPanel;
17
18  public class ShapesJPanel extends JPanel
19  {
20     // draw shapes with Java 2D API
21     public void paintComponent( Graphics g )
22     {
23        super.paintComponent( g ); // call superclass's paintComponent
24
25        Graphics2D g2d = ( Graphics2D ) g; // cast g to Graphics2D
26
27        // draw 2D ellipse filled with a blue-yellow gradient
28        g2d.setPaint( new GradientPaint( 5, 30, Color.BLUE, 35, 100,
29           Color.YELLOW, true ) );
30        g2d.fill( new Ellipse2D.Double( 5, 30, 65, 100 ) );
31
32        // draw 2D rectangle in red
33        g2d.setPaint( Color.RED );
34        g2d.setStroke( new BasicStroke( 10.0f ) );
35        g2d.draw( new Rectangle2D.Double( 80, 30, 65, 100 ) );
36
37        // draw 2D rounded rectangle with a buffered background
38        BufferedImage buffImage = new BufferedImage( 10, 10,
39           BufferedImage.TYPE_INT_RGB );
40
41        // obtain Graphics2D from buffImage and draw on it
42        Graphics2D gg = buffImage.createGraphics();
43        gg.setColor( Color.YELLOW ); // draw in yellow
44        gg.fillRect( 0, 0, 10, 10 ); // draw a filled rectangle
45        gg.setColor( Color.BLACK );  // draw in black
46        gg.drawRect( 1, 1, 6, 6 ); // draw a rectangle
47        gg.setColor( Color.BLUE ); // draw in blue
```

Fig. 15.29 | Java 2D shapes. (Part 1 of 2.)

```
48          gg.fillRect( 1, 1, 3, 3 ); // draw a filled rectangle
49          gg.setColor( Color.RED ); // draw in red
50          gg.fillRect( 4, 4, 3, 3 ); // draw a filled rectangle
51
52          // paint buffImage onto the JFrame
53          g2d.setPaint( new TexturePaint( buffImage,
54             new Rectangle( 10, 10 ) ) );
55          g2d.fill(
56             new RoundRectangle2D.Double( 155, 30, 75, 100, 50, 50 ) );
57
58          // draw 2D pie-shaped arc in white
59          g2d.setPaint( Color.WHITE );
60          g2d.setStroke( new BasicStroke( 6.0f ) );
61          g2d.draw(
62             new Arc2D.Double( 240, 30, 75, 100, 0, 270, Arc2D.PIE ) );
63
64          // draw 2D lines in green and yellow
65          g2d.setPaint( Color.GREEN );
66          g2d.draw( new Line2D.Double( 395, 30, 320, 150 ) );
67
68          // draw 2D line using stroke
69          float[] dashes = { 10 }; // specify dash pattern
70          g2d.setPaint( Color.YELLOW );
71          g2d.setStroke( new BasicStroke( 4, BasicStroke.CAP_ROUND,
72             BasicStroke.JOIN_ROUND, 10, dashes, 0 ) );
73          g2d.draw( new Line2D.Double( 320, 30, 395, 150 ) );
74       } // end method paintComponent
75    } // end class ShapesJPanel
```

Fig. 15.29 | Java 2D shapes. (Part 2 of 2.)

```
 1    // Fig. 15.30: Shapes.java
 2    // Demonstrating some Java 2D shapes.
 3    import javax.swing.JFrame;
 4
 5    public class Shapes
 6    {
 7       // execute application
 8       public static void main( String[] args )
 9       {
10          // create frame for ShapesJPanel
11          JFrame frame = new JFrame( "Drawing 2D shapes" );
12          frame.setDefaultCloseOperation( JFrame.EXIT_ON_CLOSE );
13
14          // create ShapesJPanel
15          ShapesJPanel shapesJPanel = new ShapesJPanel();
16
17          frame.add( shapesJPanel ); // add shapesJPanel to frame
18          frame.setSize( 425, 200 ); // set frame size
19          frame.setVisible( true ); // display frame
20       } // end main
21    } // end class Shapes
```

Fig. 15.30 | Creating JFrame to display shapes. (Part 1 of 2.)

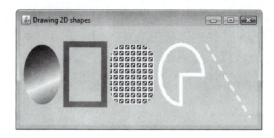

Fig. 15.30 | Creating JFrame to display shapes. (Part 2 of 2.)

Line 25 of Fig. 15.29 casts the Graphics reference received by paintComponent to a Graphics2D reference and assigns it to g2d to allow access to the Java 2D features.

Ovals, Gradient Fills and *Paint* Objects

The first shape we draw is an oval filled with gradually changing colors. Lines 28–29 invoke Graphics2D method **setPaint** to set the **Paint** object that determines the color for the shape to display. A Paint object implements interface java.awt.Paint. It can be something as simple as one of the predeclared Color objects introduced in Section 15.3 (class Color implements Paint), or it can be an instance of the Java 2D API's Gradient-Paint, **SystemColor**, TexturePaint, LinearGradientPaint or RadialGradientPaint classes. In this case, we use a GradientPaint object.

Class GradientPaint helps draw a shape in gradually changing colors—called a **gradient**. The GradientPaint constructor used here requires seven arguments. The first two specify the starting coordinate for the gradient. The third specifies the starting Color for the gradient. The fourth and fifth specify the ending coordinate for the gradient. The sixth specifies the ending Color for the gradient. The last argument specifies whether the gradient is **cyclic** (true) or **acyclic** (false). The two sets of coordinates determine the direction of the gradient. Because the second coordinate (35, 100) is down and to the right of the first coordinate (5, 30), the gradient goes down and to the right at an angle. Because this gradient is cyclic (true), the color starts with blue, gradually becomes yellow, then gradually returns to blue. If the gradient is acyclic, the color transitions from the first color specified (e.g., blue) to the second color (e.g., yellow).

Line 30 uses Graphics2D method **fill** to draw a filled **Shape** object—an object that implements interface Shape (package java.awt). In this case, we display an Ellipse2D.Double object. The Ellipse2D.Double constructor receives four arguments specifying the bounding rectangle for the ellipse to display.

Rectangles, *Strokes*

Next we draw a red rectangle with a thick border. Line 33 invokes setPaint to set the Paint object to Color.RED. Line 34 uses Graphics2D method **setStroke** to set the characteristics of the rectangle's border (or the lines for any other shape). Method setStroke requires as its argument an object that implements interface **Stroke** (package java.awt). In this case, we use an instance of class BasicStroke. Class BasicStroke provides several constructors to specify the width of the line, how the line ends (called the **end caps**), how lines join together (called **line joins**) and the dash attributes of the line (if it's a dashed line). The constructor here specifies that the line should be 10 pixels wide.

Line 35 uses `Graphics2D` method **draw** to draw a `Shape` object—in this case, a `Rectangle2D.Double`. The `Rectangle2D.Double` constructor receives arguments specifying the rectangle's upper-left *x*-coordinate, upper-left *y*-coordinate, width and height.

Rounded Rectangles, *BufferedImages* and *TexturePaint* Objects

Next we draw a rounded rectangle filled with a pattern created in a **BufferedImage** (package `java.awt.image`) object. Lines 38–39 create the `BufferedImage` object. Class `BufferedImage` can be used to produce images in color and grayscale. This particular `BufferedImage` is 10 pixels wide and 10 pixels tall (as specified by the first two arguments of the constructor). The third argument **BufferedImage.TYPE_INT_RGB** indicates that the image is stored in color using the RGB color scheme.

To create the rounded rectangle's fill pattern, we must first draw into the `BufferedImage`. Line 42 creates a `Graphics2D` object (by calling `BufferedImage` method **createGraphics**) that can be used to draw into the `BufferedImage`. Lines 43–50 use methods `setColor`, `fillRect` and `drawRect` (discussed earlier in this chapter) to create the pattern.

Lines 53–54 set the `Paint` object to a new `TexturePaint` (package `java.awt`) object. A `TexturePaint` object uses the image stored in its associated `BufferedImage` (the first constructor argument) as the fill texture for a filled-in shape. The second argument specifies the `Rectangle` area from the `BufferedImage` that will be replicated through the texture. In this case, the `Rectangle` is the same size as the `BufferedImage`. However, a smaller portion of the `BufferedImage` can be used.

Lines 55–56 use `Graphics2D` method `fill` to draw a filled `Shape` object—in this case, a `RoundRectangle2D.Double`. The constructor for class `RoundRectangle2D.Double` receives six arguments specifying the rectangle dimensions and the arc width and arc height used to determine the rounding of the corners.

Arcs

Next we draw a pie-shaped arc with a thick white line. Line 59 sets the `Paint` object to `Color.WHITE`. Line 60 sets the `Stroke` object to a new `BasicStroke` for a line 6 pixels wide. Lines 61–62 use `Graphics2D` method `draw` to draw a `Shape` object—in this case, an `Arc2D.Double`. The `Arc2D.Double` constructor's first four arguments specify the upper-left *x*-coordinate, upper-left *y*-coordinate, width and height of the bounding rectangle for the arc. The fifth argument specifies the start angle. The sixth argument specifies the arc angle. The last argument specifies how the arc is closed. Constant **Arc2D.PIE** indicates that the arc is closed by drawing two lines—one line from the arc's starting point to the center of the bounding rectangle and one line from the center of the bounding rectangle to the ending point. Class `Arc2D` provides two other static constants for specifying how the arc is closed. Constant **Arc2D.CHORD** draws a line from the starting point to the ending point. Constant **Arc2D.OPEN** specifies that the arc should not be closed.

Lines

Finally, we draw two lines using **Line2D** objects—one solid and one dashed. Line 65 sets the `Paint` object to `Color.GREEN`. Line 66 uses `Graphics2D` method `draw` to draw a `Shape` object—in this case, an instance of class `Line2D.Double`. The `Line2D.Double` constructor's arguments specify the starting coordinates and ending coordinates of the line.

Line 69 declares a one-element `float` array containing the value 10. This array describes the dashes in the dashed line. In this case, each dash will be 10 pixels long. To create dashes of different lengths in a pattern, simply provide the length of each dash as an element in the array. Line 70 sets the Paint object to Color.YELLOW. Lines 71–72 set the Stroke object to a new BasicStroke. The line will be 4 pixels wide and will have rounded ends (BasicStroke.CAP_ROUND). If lines join together (as in a rectangle at the corners), their joining will be rounded (BasicStroke.JOIN_ROUND). The dashes argument specifies the dash lengths for the line. The last argument indicates the starting index in the dashes array for the first dash in the pattern. Line 73 then draws a line with the current Stroke.

Creating Your Own Shapes with General Paths

Next we present a general path—a shape constructed from straight lines and complex curves. A general path is represented with an object of class GeneralPath (package java.awt.geom). The application of Figs. 15.31 and 15.32 demonstrates drawing a general path in the shape of a five-pointed star.

```java
1   // Fig. 15.31: Shapes2JPanel.java
2   // Demonstrating a general path.
3   import java.awt.Color;
4   import java.awt.Graphics;
5   import java.awt.Graphics2D;
6   import java.awt.geom.GeneralPath;
7   import java.util.Random;
8   import javax.swing.JPanel;
9
10  public class Shapes2JPanel extends JPanel
11  {
12      // draw general paths
13      public void paintComponent( Graphics g )
14      {
15          super.paintComponent( g ); // call superclass's paintComponent
16          Random random = new Random(); // get random number generator
17
18          int[] xPoints = { 55, 67, 109, 73, 83, 55, 27, 37, 1, 43 };
19          int[] yPoints = { 0, 36, 36, 54, 96, 72, 96, 54, 36, 36 };
20
21          Graphics2D g2d = ( Graphics2D ) g;
22          GeneralPath star = new GeneralPath(); // create GeneralPath object
23
24          // set the initial coordinate of the General Path
25          star.moveTo( xPoints[ 0 ], yPoints[ 0 ] );
26
27          // create the star--this does not draw the star
28          for ( int count = 1; count < xPoints.length; count++ )
29              star.lineTo( xPoints[ count ], yPoints[ count ] );
30
31          star.closePath(); // close the shape
32
33          g2d.translate( 150, 150 ); // translate the origin to (150, 150)
34
35          // rotate around origin and draw stars in random colors
36          for ( int count = 1; count <= 20; count++ )
37          {
38              g2d.rotate( Math.PI / 10.0 ); // rotate coordinate system
```

Fig. 15.31 | Java 2D general paths. (Part 1 of 2.)

```
39
40              // set random drawing color
41              g2d.setColor( new Color( random.nextInt( 256 ),
42                 random.nextInt( 256 ), random.nextInt( 256 ) ) );
43
44              g2d.fill( star ); // draw filled star
45           } // end for
46        } // end method paintComponent
47     } // end class Shapes2JPanel
```

Fig. 15.31 | Java 2D general paths. (Part 2 of 2.)

```
1    // Fig. 15.32: Shapes2.java
2    // Demonstrating a general path.
3    import java.awt.Color;
4    import javax.swing.JFrame;
5
6    public class Shapes2
7    {
8       // execute application
9       public static void main( String[] args )
10      {
11         // create frame for Shapes2JPanel
12         JFrame frame = new JFrame( "Drawing 2D Shapes" );
13         frame.setDefaultCloseOperation( JFrame.EXIT_ON_CLOSE );
14
15         Shapes2JPanel shapes2JPanel = new Shapes2JPanel();
16         frame.add( shapes2JPanel ); // add shapes2JPanel to frame
17         frame.setBackground( Color.WHITE ); // set frame background color
18         frame.setSize( 315, 330 ); // set frame size
19         frame.setVisible( true ); // display frame
20      } // end main
21   } // end class Shapes2
```

Fig. 15.32 | Creating JFrame to display stars.

Lines 18–19 declare two int arrays representing the *x*- and *y*-coordinates of the points in the star. Line 22 creates GeneralPath object star. Line 25 uses GeneralPath method **moveTo** to specify the first point in the star. The for statement in lines 28–29 uses GeneralPath method **lineTo** to draw a line to the next point in the star. Each new call to lineTo draws a line from the previous point to the current point. Line 31 uses General-Path method **closePath** to draw a line from the last point to the point specified in the last call to moveTo. This completes the general path.

Line 33 uses Graphics2D method **translate** to move the drawing origin to location (150, 150). All drawing operations now use location (150, 150) as (0, 0).

The for statement in lines 36–45 draws the star 20 times by rotating it around the new origin point. Line 38 uses Graphics2D method **rotate** to rotate the next displayed shape. The argument specifies the rotation angle in radians (with 360° = 2π radians). Line 44 uses Graphics2D method **fill** to draw a filled version of the star.

15.9 Wrap-Up

In this chapter, you learned how to use Java's graphics capabilities to produce colorful drawings. You learned how to specify the location of an object using Java's coordinate system, and how to draw on a window using the paintComponent method. You were introduced to class Color, and you learned how to use this class to specify different colors using their RGB components. You used the JColorChooser dialog to allow users to select colors in a program. You then learned how to work with fonts when drawing text on a window. You learned how to create a Font object from a font name, style and size, as well as how to access the metrics of a font. From there, you learned how to draw various shapes on a window, such as rectangles (regular, rounded and 3D), ovals and polygons, as well as lines and arcs. You then used the Java 2D API to create more complex shapes and to fill them with gradients or patterns. The chapter concluded with a discussion of general paths, used to construct shapes from straight lines and complex curves. In the next chapter, we discuss class String and its methods. We also introduce regular expressions for pattern matching in strings and demonstrate how to validate user input with regular expressions.

Summary

Section 15.1 Introduction

- Java's coordinate system is a scheme for identifying every point on the screen.
- A coordinate pair has an *x*-coordinate (horizontal) and a *y*-coordinate (vertical).
- Coordinates are used to indicate where graphics should be displayed on a screen.
- Coordinate units are measured in pixels. A pixel is a display monitor's smallest unit of resolution.

Section 15.2 Graphics Contexts and Graphics Objects

- A Java graphics context enables drawing on the screen.
- Class Graphics contains methods for drawing strings, lines, rectangles and other shapes. Methods are also included for font manipulation and color manipulation.
- A Graphics object manages a graphics context and draws pixels on the screen that represent text and other graphical object (e.g., lines, ellipses, rectangles and other polygons).
- Class Graphics is an abstract class. Each Java implementation has a Graphics subclass that provides drawing capabilities. This implementation is hidden from us by class Graphics, which supplies the interface that enables us to use graphics in a platform-independent manner.
- Method paintComponent can be used to draw graphics in any JComponent component.
- Method paintComponent receives a Graphics object that is passed to the method by the system when a lightweight Swing component needs to be repainted.

- You seldom call method paintComponent directly, because drawing graphics is an event-driven process. When an application executes, the application container calls method paintComponent. For paintComponent to be called again, an event must occur.
- When a JComponent is displayed, its paintComponent method is called.
- Calling method repaint on a component updates the graphics drawn on that component.

Section 15.3 Color Control
- Class Color declares methods and constants for manipulating colors in a Java program.
- Every color is created from a red, a green and a blue component. Together these components are called RGB values. The RGB components specify the amount of red, green and blue in a color, respectively. The larger the RGB value, the greater the amount of that particular color.
- Color methods getRed, getGreen and getBlue return int values from 0 to 255 representing the amount of red, green and blue, respectively.
- Graphics method getColor returns a Color object representing the current drawing color.
- Graphics method setColor sets the current drawing color.
- Graphics method fillRect draws a rectangle filled by the current color of the Graphics object.
- Graphics method drawString draws a String in the current color.
- The JColorChooser GUI component enables application users to select colors.
- JColorChooser static method showDialog creates a JColorChooser object, attaches it to a dialog box and displays the dialog. When it is on the screen, the user can interact only with the dialog. This type of dialog is called a modal dialog.

Section 15.4 Manipulating Fonts
- Class Font contains methods and constants for manipulating fonts.
- Class Font's constructor takes three arguments—the font name, font style and font size.
- A Font's font style can be Font.PLAIN, Font.ITALIC or Font.BOLD (each is a static field of class Font). Font styles can be used in combination (e.g., Font.ITALIC + Font.BOLD).
- The font size is measured in points. A point is 1/72 of an inch.
- Graphics method setFont sets the drawing font in which text will be displayed.
- Font method getStyle returns an integer value representing the current Font's style.
- Font method getSize returns the font size in points.
- Font method getName returns the current font name as a string.
- Font method getFamily returns the name of the font family to which the current font belongs. The name of the font family is platform specific.
- Class FontMetrics contains methods for obtaining font information.
- Font metrics include height, descent and leading.

Section 15.5 Drawing Lines, Rectangles and Ovals
- Graphics methods fillRoundRect and drawRoundRect draw rectangles with rounded corners.
- Graphics methods draw3DRect and fill3DRect draw three-dimensional rectangles.
- Graphics methods drawOval and fillOval draw ovals.

Section 15.6 Drawing Arcs
- An arc is drawn as a portion of an oval.
- Arcs sweep from a starting angle by the number of degrees specified by their arc angle.
- Graphics methods drawArc and fillArc are used for drawing arcs.

Section 15.7 Drawing Polygons and Polylines

- Class Polygon contains methods for creating polygons.
- Polygons are closed multisided shapes composed of straight-line segments.
- Polylines are a sequence of connected points.
- Graphics method drawPolyline displays a series of connected lines.
- Graphics methods drawPolygon and fillPolygon are used to draw polygons.
- Polygon method addPoint of class Polygon adds pairs of *x*- and *y*-coordinates to the Polygon.

Section 15.8 Java 2D API

- The Java 2D API provides advanced two-dimensional graphics capabilities.
- Class Graphics2D—a subclass of Graphics—is used for drawing with the Java 2D API.
- The Java 2D API's classes for drawing shapes include Line2D.Double, Rectangle2D.Double, RoundRectangle2D.Double, Arc2D.Double and Ellipse2D.Double.
- Class GradientPaint helps draw a shape in gradually changing colors—called a gradient.
- Graphics2D method fill draws a filled object of any type that implements interface Shape.
- Class BasicStroke helps specify the drawing characteristics of lines.
- Graphics2D method draw is used to draw a Shape object.
- Classes GradientPaint and TexturePaint enable you to fill shapes with colors or patterns.
- A GeneralPath constructed from straight lines and complex curves.
- GeneralPath method moveTo specifies the first point in a general path.
- GeneralPath method lineTo draws a line to the next point in the path. Each new call to lineTo draws a line from the previous point to the current point.
- GeneralPath method closePath draws a line from the last point to the point specified in the last call to moveTo. This completes the general path.
- Graphics2D method translate is used to move the drawing origin to a new location.
- Graphics2D method rotate is used to rotate the next displayed shape.

Terminology

Self-Review Exercises

15.1 Fill in the blanks in each of the following statements:

a) In Java 2D, method _____ of class _____ sets the characteristics of a line used to draw a shape.

b) Class _____ helps specify the fill for a shape such that the fill gradually changes from one color to another.

c) The _____ method of class Graphics draws a line between two points.

d) RGB is short for _____, _____ and _____.

e) Font sizes are measured in units called _____.

    f) Class _____ helps specify the fill for a shape using a pattern drawn in a Buffered-Image.

15.2 State whether each of the following is *true* or *false*. If *false*, explain why.
    a) The first two arguments of Graphics method drawOval specify the center coordinate of the oval.
    b) In the Java coordinate system, *x*-coordinates increase from left to right and *y*-coordinates from top to bottom.
    c) Graphics method fillPolygon draws a filled polygon in the current color.
    d) Graphics method drawArc allows negative angles.
    e) Graphics method getSize returns the size of the current font in centimeters.
    f) Pixel coordinate (0, 0) is located at the exact center of the monitor.

15.3 Find the error(s) in each of the following and explain how to correct them. Assume that g is a Graphics object.
    a) `g.setFont( "SansSerif" );`
    b) `g.erase( x, y, w, h );`   `// clear rectangle at (x, y)`
    c) `Font f = new Font( "Serif", Font.BOLDITALIC, 12 );`
    d) `g.setColor( 255, 255, 0 );` `// change color to yellow`

Answers to Self-Review Exercises

15.1 a) setStroke, Graphics2D. b) GradientPaint. c) drawLine. d) red, green, blue. e) points. f) TexturePaint.

15.2 a) False. The first two arguments specify the upper-left corner of the bounding rectangle.
    b) True.
    c) True.
    d) True.
    e) False. Font sizes are measured in points.
    f) False. The coordinate (0,0) corresponds to the upper-left corner of a GUI component on which drawing occurs.

15.3 a) The setFont method takes a Font object as an argument—not a String.
    b) The Graphics class does not have an erase method. The clearRect method should be used.
    c) Font.BOLDITALIC is not a valid font style. To get a bold italic font, use Font.BOLD + Font.ITALIC.
    d) Method setColor takes a Color object as an argument, not three integers.

Exercises

15.4 Fill in the blanks in each of the following statements:
    a) Class _____ of the Java 2D API is used to draw ovals.
    b) Methods draw and fill of class Graphics2D require an object of type _____ as their argument.
    c) The three constants that specify font style are _____, _____ and _____.
    d) Graphics2D method _____ sets the painting color for Java 2D shapes.

15.5 State whether each of the following is *true* or *false*. If *false*, explain why.
    a) Graphics method drawPolygon automatically connects the endpoints of the polygon.
    b) Graphics method drawLine draws a line between two points.
    c) Graphics method fillArc uses degrees to specify the angle.
    d) In the Java coordinate system, values on the *y*-axis increase from left to right.
    e) Graphics inherits directly from class Object.

    f) `Graphics` is an abstract class.

    g) The `Font` class inherits directly from class `Graphics`.

15.6 *(Concentric Circles Using Method `drawArc`)* Write an application that draws a series of eight concentric circles. The circles should be separated by 10 pixels. Use `Graphics` method `drawArc`.

15.7 *(Concentric Circles Using Class `Ellipse2D.Double`)* Modify your solution to Exercise 15.6 to draw the ovals by using class `Ellipse2D.Double` and method `draw` of class `Graphics2D`.

15.8 *(Random Lines Using Class `Line2D.Double`)* Modify your solution to Exercise 15.7 to draw random lines, in random colors and random line thicknesses. Use class `Line2D.Double` and method `draw` of class `Graphics2D` to draw the lines.

15.9 *(Random Triangles)* Write an application that displays randomly generated triangles in different colors. Each triangle should be filled with a different color. Use class `GeneralPath` and method `fill` of class `Graphics2D` to draw the triangles.

15.10 *(Random Characters)* Write an application that randomly draws characters in different fonts, sizes and colors.

15.11 *(Grid Using Method `drawLine`)* Write an application that draws an 8-by-8 grid. Use `Graphics` method `drawLine`.

15.12 *(Grid Using Class `Line2D.Double`)* Modify your solution to Exercise 15.11 to draw the grid using instances of class `Line2D.Double` and method `draw` of class `Graphics2D`.

15.13 *(Grid Using Method `drawRect`)* Write an application that draws a 10-by-10 grid. Use the `Graphics` method `drawRect`.

15.14 *(Grid Using Class `Rectangle2D.Double`)* Modify your solution to Exercise 15.13 to draw the grid by using class `Rectangle2D.Double` and method `draw` of class `Graphics2D`.

15.15 *(Drawing Tetrahedrons)* Write an application that draws a tetrahedron (a three-dimensional shape with four triangular faces). Use class `GeneralPath` and method `draw` of class `Graphics2D`.

15.16 *(Drawing Cubes)* Write an application that draws a cube. Use class `GeneralPath` and method `draw` of class `Graphics2D`.

15.17 *(Circles Using Class `Ellipse2D.Double`)* Write an application that asks the user to input the radius of a circle as a floating-point number and draws the circle, as well as the values of the circle's diameter, circumference and area. Use the value 3.14159 for π. [*Note:* You may also use the predefined constant `Math.PI` for the value of π. This constant is more precise than the value 3.14159. Class `Math` is declared in the `java.lang` package, so you need not `import` it.] Use the following formulas (r is the radius):

$$diameter = 2r$$
$$circumference = 2\pi r$$
$$area = \pi r^2$$

The user should also be prompted for a set of coordinates in addition to the radius. Then draw the circle, and display its diameter, circumference and area, using an `Ellipse2D.Double` object to represent the circle and method `draw` of class `Graphics2D` to display it.

15.18 *(Screen Saver)* Write an application that simulates a screen saver. The application should randomly draw lines using method `drawLine` of class `Graphics`. After drawing 100 lines, the application should clear itself and start drawing lines again. To allow the program to draw continuously, place a call to `repaint` as the last line in method `paintComponent`. Do you notice any problems with this on your system?

15.19 *(Screen Saver Using Timer)* Package `javax.swing` contains a class called `Timer` that is capable of calling method `actionPerformed` of interface `ActionListener` at a fixed time interval (specified in milliseconds). Modify your solution to Exercise 15.18 to remove the call to `repaint` from method `paintComponent`. Declare your class to implement `ActionListener`. (The `actionPerformed` method should simply call `repaint`.) Declare an instance variable of type `Timer` called `timer` in your class. In the constructor for your class, write the following statements:

```
timer = new Timer( 1000, this );
timer.start();
```

This creates an instance of class `Timer` that will call `this` object's `actionPerformed` method every 1000 milliseconds (i.e., every second).

15.20 *(Screen Saver for a Random Number of Lines)* Modify your solution to Exercise 15.19 to enable the user to enter the number of random lines that should be drawn before the application clears itself and starts drawing lines again. Use a `JTextField` to obtain the value. The user should be able to type a new number into the `JTextField` at any time during the program's execution. Use an inner class to perform event handling for the `JTextField`.

15.21 *(Screen Saver with Shapes)* Modify your solution to Exercise 15.19 such that it uses random-number generation to choose different shapes to display. Use methods of class `Graphics`.

15.22 *(Screen Saver Using the Java 2D API)* Modify your solution to Exercise 15.21 to use classes and drawing capabilities of the Java 2D API. Draw shapes like rectangles and ellipses, with randomly generated gradients. Use class `GradientPaint` to generate the gradient.

15.23 *(Turtle Graphics)* Modify your solution to Exercise 6.21—*Turtle Graphics*—to add a graphical user interface using `JTextFields` and `JButtons`. Draw lines rather than asterisks (*). When the turtle graphics program specifies a move, translate the number of positions into a number of pixels on the screen by multiplying the number of positions by 10 (or any value you choose). Implement the drawing with Java 2D API features.

15.24 *(Knight's Tour)* Produce a graphical version of the Knight's Tour problem (Exercise 6.22, Exercise 6.23 and Exercise 6.26). As each move is made, the appropriate cell of the chessboard should be updated with the proper move number. If the result of the program is a *full tour* or a *closed tour*, the program should display an appropriate message. If you like, use class `Timer` (see Exercise 15.19) to help animate the Knight's Tour.

15.25 *(Tortoise and Hare)* Produce a graphical version of the *Tortoise and Hare* simulation (Exercise 6.28). Simulate the mountain by drawing an arc that extends from the bottom-left corner of the window to the top-right corner. The tortoise and the hare should race up the mountain. Implement the graphical output to actually print the tortoise and the hare on the arc for every move. [*Hint:* Extend the length of the race from 70 to 300 to allow yourself a larger graphics area.]

15.26 *(Drawing Spirals)* Write an application that uses `Graphics` method `drawPolyline` to draw a spiral similar to the one shown in Fig. 15.33.

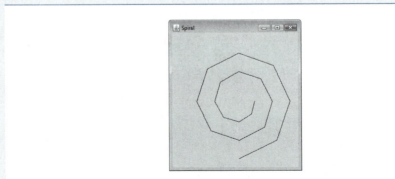

Fig. 15.33 | Spiral drawn using method `drawPolyline`.

15.27 *(Pie Chart)* Write a program that inputs four numbers and graphs them as a pie chart. Use class Arc2D.Double and method fill of class Graphics2D to perform the drawing. Draw each piece of the pie in a separate color.

15.28 *(Selecting Shapes)* Write an application that allows the user to select a shape from a JCombo-Box and draws it 20 times with random locations and dimensions in method paintComponent. The first item in the JComboBox should be the default shape that is displayed the first time paintComponent is called.

15.29 *(Random Colors)* Modify Exercise 15.28 to draw each of the 20 randomly sized shapes in a randomly selected color. Use all 13 predefined Color objects in an array of Colors.

15.30 *(JColorChooser Dialog)* Modify Exercise 15.28 to allow the user to select the color in which shapes should be drawn from a JColorChooser dialog.

(Optional) GUI and Graphics Case Study: Adding Java2D

15.31 Java2D introduces many new capabilities for creating unique and impressive graphics. We'll add a small subset of these features to the drawing application you created in Exercise 14.17. In this version, you'll enable the user to specify gradients for filling shapes and to change stroke characteristics for drawing lines and outlines of shapes. The user will be able to choose which colors compose the gradient and set the width and dash length of the stroke.

First, you must update the MyShape hierarchy to support Java2D functionality. Make the following changes in class MyShape:

    a) Change abstract method draw's parameter type from Graphics to Graphics2D.

    b) Change all variables of type Color to type Paint to enable support for gradients. [*Note:* Recall that class Color implements interface Paint.]

    c) Add an instance variable of type Stroke in class MyShape and a Stroke parameter in the constructor to initialize the new instance variable. The default stroke should be an instance of class BasicStroke.

Classes MyLine, MyBoundedShape, MyOval and MyRectangle should each add a Stroke parameter to their constructors. In the draw methods, each shape should set the Paint and the Stroke before drawing or filling a shape. Since Graphics2D is a subclass of Graphics, we can continue to use Graphics methods drawLine, drawOval, fillOval, and so on. to draw the shapes. When these methods are called, they'll draw the appropriate shape using the specified Paint and Stroke settings.

Next, you'll update the DrawPanel to handle the Java2D features. Change all Color variables to Paint variables. Declare an instance variable currentStroke of type Stroke and provide a *set* method for it. Update the calls to the individual shape constructors to include the Paint and Stroke arguments. In method paintComponent, cast the Graphics reference to type Graphics2D and use the Graphics2D reference in each call to MyShape method draw.

Next, make the new Java2D features accessible from the GUI. Create a JPanel of GUI components for setting the Java2D options. Add these components at the top of the DrawFrame below the panel that currently contains the standard shape controls (see Fig. 15.34). These GUI components should include:

    a) A check box to specify whether to paint using a gradient.

    b) Two JButtons that each show a JColorChooser dialog to allow the user to choose the first and second color in the gradient. (These will replace the JComboBox used for choosing the color in Exercise 14.17.)

    c) A text field for entering the Stroke width.

    d) A text field for entering the Stroke dash length.

    e) A check box for selecting whether to draw a dashed or solid line.

If the user selects to draw with a gradient, set the Paint on the DrawPanel to be a gradient of the two colors chosen by the user. The expression

```
new GradientPaint( 0, 0, color1, 50, 50, color2, true ) )
```

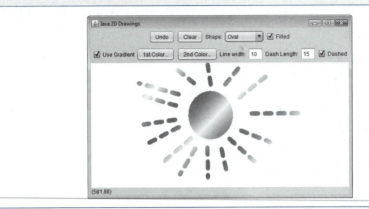

Fig. 15.34 | Drawing with Java2D.

creates a GradientPaint that cycles diagonally from the upper-left to the bottom-right every 50 pixels. Variables color1 and color2 represent the colors chosen by the user. If the user does not select to use a gradient, then simply set the Paint on the DrawPanel to be the first Color chosen by the user.

For strokes, if the user chooses a solid line, then create the Stroke with the expression

```
new BasicStroke( width, BasicStroke.CAP_ROUND, BasicStroke.JOIN_ROUND )
```

where variable width is the width specified by the user in the line-width text field. If the user chooses a dashed line, then create the Stroke with the expression

```
new BasicStroke( width, BasicStroke.CAP_ROUND, BasicStroke.JOIN_ROUND,
    10, dashes, 0 )
```

where width again is the width in the line-width field, and dashes is an array with one element whose value is the length specified in the dash-length field. The Panel and Stroke objects should be passed to the shape object's constructor when the shape is created in DrawPanel.

Making a Difference

15.32 *(Large-Type Displays for People with Low Vision)* The accessibility of computers and the Internet to all people, regardless of disabilities, is becoming more important as these tools play increasing roles in our personal and business lives. According to a recent estimate by the World Health Organization (www.who.int/mediacentre/factsheets/fs282/en/), 124 million people worldwide have low vision. To learn more about low vision, check out the GUI-based low vision simulation at www.webaim.org/simulations/lowvision.php. People with low vision might prefer to choose a font and/or a larger font size when reading electronic documents and web pages. Java has five built-in "logical" fonts that are guaranteed to be available in any Java implementation, including Serif, Sans-serif and Monospaced. Write a GUI application that provides a JTextArea in which the user can type text. Allow the user to select Serif, Sans-serif or Monospaced from a JComboBox. Provide a **Bold** JCheckBox, which, if checked, makes the text bold. Include **Increase Font Size** and **Decrease Font Size** JButtons that allow the user to scale the size of the font up or down, respectively, by one point at a time. Start with a font size of 18 points. For the purposes of this exercise, set the font size on the JComboBox, JButtons and JCheckBox to 20 points so that a person with low vision will be able to read the text on them.

Strings, Characters and Regular Expressions

16

The chief defect of Henry King
Was chewing little bits of string.
—Hilaire Belloc

Vigorous writing is concise. A
sentence should contain no
unnecessary words, a paragraph
no unnecessary sentences.
—William Strunk, Jr.

I have made this letter longer
than usual, because I lack the
time to make it short.
—Blaise Pascal

Objectives

In this chapter you'll learn:

- To create and manipulate mutable character-string objects of class `StringBuilder`.

- To create and manipulate objects of class `Character`.

- To break a `String` object into tokens using `String` method `split`.

- To use regular expressions to validate `String` data entered into an application.

16.1 Introduction

We now continue our introduction to Java's string- and character-processing capabilities. The techniques discussed here (and in Sections 6.14–6.15) are appropriate for validating program input, displaying information to users and other text-based manipulations. They're also appropriate for developing text editors, word processors, page-layout software, computerized typesetting systems and other kinds of text-processing software. This chapter discusses class `StringBuilder` and class `Character` from the `java.lang` package. These classes and class `String` provide the foundation for string and character manipulation in Java. We also discuss regular expressions—a technology that provides applications with powerful capabilities to validate input; the functionality is located in class `String` and classes `Matcher` and `Pattern` from the `java.util.regex` package.

16.2 Class `StringBuilder`

We now discuss the features of class **`StringBuilder`** for creating and manipulating dynamic string information—that is, modifiable strings. Every `StringBuilder` is capable of storing a number of characters specified by its capacity. If the capacity of a `StringBuilder` is exceeded, the capacity expands to accommodate the additional characters.

Performance Tip 16.1

Java can perform certain optimizations involving `String` objects (such as referring to one `String` object from multiple variables) because it knows these objects will not change. Strings (not `StringBuilders`) should be used if the data will not change.

Performance Tip 16.2

In programs that frequently perform string concatenation, or other string modifications, it's often more efficient to implement the modifications with class `StringBuilder`.

Software Engineering Observation 16.1

`StringBuilders` are not thread safe. If multiple threads require access to the same dynamic string information, use class `StringBuffer` in your code. Classes `StringBuilder` and `StringBuffer` provide identical capabilities, but class `StringBuffer` is thread safe. For more details on threading, see Chapter 26.

16.2.1 StringBuilder Constructors

Class `StringBuilder` provides four constructors. We demonstrate three of these in Fig. 16.1. Line 8 uses the no-argument `StringBuilder` constructor to create a `StringBuilder` with no characters in it and an initial capacity of 16 characters (the default for a `StringBuilder`). Line 9 uses the `StringBuilder` constructor that takes an integer argument to create a `StringBuilder` with no characters in it and the initial capacity specified by the integer argument (i.e., 10). Line 10 uses the `StringBuilder` constructor that takes a `String` argument to create a `StringBuilder` containing the characters in the `String` argument. The initial capacity is the number of characters in the `String` argument plus 16.

```java
1   // Fig. 16.1: StringBuilderConstructors.java
2   // StringBuilder constructors.
3
4   public class StringBuilderConstructors
5   {
6      public static void main( String[] args )
7      {
8         StringBuilder buffer1 = new StringBuilder();
9         StringBuilder buffer2 = new StringBuilder( 10 );
10        StringBuilder buffer3 = new StringBuilder( "hello" );
11
12        System.out.printf( "buffer1 = \"%s\"\n", buffer1.toString() );
13        System.out.printf( "buffer2 = \"%s\"\n", buffer2.toString() );
14        System.out.printf( "buffer3 = \"%s\"\n", buffer3.toString() );
15     } // end main
16  } // end class StringBuilderConstructors
```

```
buffer1 = ""
buffer2 = ""
buffer3 = "hello"
```

Fig. 16.1 | `StringBuilder` constructors.

Lines 12–14 use the method `toString` of class `StringBuilder` to output the `StringBuilder`s with the `printf` method. In Section 16.2.4, we discuss how Java uses `StringBuilder` objects to implement the + and += operators for string concatenation.

16.2.2 StringBuilder Methods length, capacity, setLength and ensureCapacity

Class `StringBuilder` provides methods **length** and **capacity** to return the number of characters currently in a `StringBuilder` and the number of characters that can be stored in a `StringBuilder` without allocating more memory, respectively. Method **ensureCapacity** guarantees that a `StringBuilder` has at least the specified capacity. Method `setLength` increases or decreases the length of a `StringBuilder`. Figure 16.2 demonstrates these methods.

The application contains one `StringBuilder` called `buffer`. Line 8 uses the `StringBuilder` constructor that takes a `String` argument to initialize the `StringBuilder` with "Hello, how are you?". Lines 10–11 print the contents, length and capacity of the `StringBuilder`. Note in the output window that the capacity of the `StringBuilder` is

```
 1   // Fig. 16.2: StringBuilderCapLen.java
 2   // StringBuilder length, setLength, capacity and ensureCapacity methods.
 3
 4   public class StringBuilderCapLen
 5   {
 6      public static void main( String[] args )
 7      {
 8         StringBuilder buffer = new StringBuilder( "Hello, how are you?" );
 9
10         System.out.printf( "buffer = %s\nlength = %d\ncapacity = %d\n\n",
11            buffer.toString(), buffer.length(), buffer.capacity() );
12
13         buffer.ensureCapacity( 75 );
14         System.out.printf( "New capacity = %d\n\n", buffer.capacity() );
15
16         buffer.setLength( 10 );
17         System.out.printf( "New length = %d\nbuffer = %s\n",
18            buffer.length(), buffer.toString() );
19      } // end main
20   } // end class StringBuilderCapLen
```

```
buffer = Hello, how are you?
length = 19
capacity = 35

New capacity = 75

New length = 10
buffer = Hello, how
```

Fig. 16.2 | `StringBuilder` length, setLength, capacity and ensureCapacity methods.

initially 35. Recall that the `StringBuilder` constructor that takes a `String` argument initializes the capacity to the length of the string passed as an argument plus 16.

Line 13 uses method `ensureCapacity` to expand the capacity of the `StringBuilder` to a minimum of 75 characters. Actually, if the original capacity is less than the argument, the method ensures a capacity that is the greater of the number specified as an argument and twice the original capacity plus 2. The `StringBuilder`'s current capacity remains unchanged if it's more than the specified capacity.

Performance Tip 16.3

Dynamically increasing the capacity of a `StringBuilder` can take a relatively long time. Executing a large number of these operations can degrade the performance of an application. If a `StringBuilder` is going to increase greatly in size, possibly multiple times, setting its capacity high at the beginning will increase performance.

Line 16 uses method `setLength` to set the length of the `StringBuilder` to 10. If the specified length is less than the current number of characters in the `StringBuilder`, the buffer is truncated to the specified length (i.e., the characters in the `StringBuilder` after the specified length are discarded). If the specified length is greater than the number of characters currently in the `StringBuilder`, null characters (characters with the numeric representation 0) are appended until the total number of characters in the `StringBuilder` is equal to the specified length.

16.2.3 StringBuilder Methods charAt, setCharAt, getChars and reverse

Class StringBuilder provides the **charAt**, **setCharAt**, **getChars** and **reverse** methods to manipulate the characters in a StringBuilder (Fig. 16.3). Method charAt (line 12) takes an integer argument and returns the character in the StringBuilder at that index. Method getChars (line 15) copies characters from a StringBuilder into the character array passed as an argument. This method takes four arguments—the starting index from which characters should be copied in the StringBuilder, the index one past the last character to be copied from the StringBuilder, the character array into which the characters are to be copied and the starting location in the character array where the first character should be placed. Method setCharAt (lines 21 and 22) takes an integer and a character argument and sets the character at the specified position in the StringBuilder to the character argument. Method reverse (line 25) reverses the contents of the String-Builder.

Common Programming Error 16.1

Attempting to access a character that is outside the bounds of a StringBuilder (i.e., with an index less than 0 or greater than or equal to the StringBuilder's length) results in a StringIndexOutOfBoundsException.

```
1   // Fig. 16.3: StringBuilderChars.java
2   // StringBuilder methods charAt, setCharAt, getChars and reverse.
3
4   public class StringBuilderChars
5   {
6      public static void main( String[] args )
7      {
8         StringBuilder buffer = new StringBuilder( "hello there" );
9
10        System.out.printf( "buffer = %s\n", buffer.toString() );
11        System.out.printf( "Character at 0: %s\nCharacter at 4: %s\n\n",
12           buffer.charAt( 0 ), buffer.charAt( 4 ) );
13
14        char[] charArray = new char[ buffer.length() ];
15        buffer.getChars( 0, buffer.length(), charArray, 0 );
16        System.out.print( "The characters are: " );
17
18        for ( char character : charArray )
19           System.out.print( character );
20
21        buffer.setCharAt( 0, 'H' );
22        buffer.setCharAt( 6, 'T' );
23        System.out.printf( "\n\nbuffer = %s", buffer.toString() );
24
25        buffer.reverse();
26        System.out.printf( "\n\nbuffer = %s\n", buffer.toString() );
27     } // end main
28  } // end class StringBuilderChars
```

Fig. 16.3 | StringBuilder methods charAt, setCharAt, getChars and reverse. (Part 1 of 2.)

```
buffer = hello there
Character at 0: h
Character at 4: o

The characters are: hello there

buffer = Hello There

buffer = erehT olleH
```

Fig. 16.3 | StringBuilder methods charAt, setCharAt, getChars and reverse. (Part 2 of 2.)

16.2.4 StringBuilder append Methods

Class StringBuilder provides overloaded **append** methods (Fig. 16.4) to allow values of various types to be appended to the end of a StringBuilder. Versions are provided for each of the primitive types, and for character arrays, Strings, Objects, and more. (Remember that method toString produces a string representation of any Object.) Each method takes its argument, converts it to a string and appends it to the StringBuilder.

```java
1   // Fig. 16.4: StringBuilderAppend.java
2   // StringBuilder append methods.
3
4   public class StringBuilderAppend
5   {
6      public static void main( String[] args )
7      {
8         Object objectRef = "hello";
9         String string = "goodbye";
10        char[] charArray = { 'a', 'b', 'c', 'd', 'e', 'f' };
11        boolean booleanValue = true;
12        char characterValue = 'Z';
13        int integerValue = 7;
14        long longValue = 10000000000L;
15        float floatValue = 2.5f;
16        double doubleValue = 33.333;
17
18        StringBuilder lastBuffer = new StringBuilder( "last buffer" );
19        StringBuilder buffer = new StringBuilder();
20
21        buffer.append( objectRef );
22        buffer.append( "\n" );
23        buffer.append( string );
24        buffer.append( "\n" );
25        buffer.append( charArray );
26        buffer.append( "\n" );
27        buffer.append( charArray, 0, 3 );
28        buffer.append( "\n" );
29        buffer.append( booleanValue );
30        buffer.append( "\n" );
```

Fig. 16.4 | StringBuilder append methods. (Part 1 of 2.)

```
31          buffer.append( characterValue );
32          buffer.append( "\n" );
33          buffer.append( integerValue );
34          buffer.append( "\n" );
35          buffer.append( longValue );
36          buffer.append( "\n" );
37          buffer.append( floatValue );
38          buffer.append( "\n" );
39          buffer.append( doubleValue );
40          buffer.append( "\n" );
41          buffer.append( lastBuffer );
42
43          System.out.printf( "buffer contains %s\n", buffer.toString() );
44       } // end main
45  } // end StringBuilderAppend
```

```
buffer contains hello
goodbye
abcdef
abc
true
Z
7
10000000000
2.5
33.333
last buffer
```

Fig. 16.4 | StringBuilder append methods. (Part 2 of 2.)

Actually, a compiler can use StringBuilder (or StringBuffer) and the append methods to implement the + and += String concatenation operators. For example, assuming the declarations

```
String string1 = "hello";
String string2 = "BC";
int value = 22;
```

the statement

```
String s = string1 + string2 + value;
```

concatenates "hello", "BC" and 22. The concatenation can be performed as follows:

```
String s = new StringBuilder().append( "hello" ).append( "BC" ).
   append( 22 ).toString();
```

First, the preceding statement creates an empty StringBuilder, then appends to it the strings "hello" and "BC" and the integer 22. Next, StringBuilder's toString method converts the StringBuilder to a String object to be assigned to String s. The statement

```
s += "!";
```

can be performed as follows:

```
s = new StringBuilder().append( s ).append( "!" ).toString();
```

First, the preceding statement creates an empty StringBuilder, then it appends to it the current contents of s followed by "!". Next, StringBuilder's method toString converts the StringBuilder to a string representation, and the result is assigned to s.

16.2.5 StringBuilder Insertion and Deletion Methods

Class StringBuilder provides overloaded **insert** methods to insert values of various types at any position in a StringBuilder. Versions are provided for the primitive types and for character arrays, Strings, Objects and CharSequences. Each method takes its second argument, converts it to a String and inserts it at the index specified by the first argument. If the first argument is less than 0 or greater than the StringBuilder's length, a StringIndexOutOfBoundsException occurs. Class StringBuilder also provides methods **delete** and **deleteCharAt** to delete characters at any position in a StringBuilder. Method delete takes two arguments—the starting index and the index one past the end of the characters to delete. All characters beginning at the starting index up to but not including the ending index are deleted. Method deleteCharAt takes one argument—the index of the character to delete. Invalid indices cause both methods to throw a StringIndexOutOfBoundsException. Figure 16.5 demonstrates methods insert, delete and deleteCharAt.

```
1   // Fig. 16.5: StringBuilderInsertDelete.java
2   // StringBuilder methods insert, delete and deleteCharAt.
3
4   public class StringBuilderInsertDelete
5   {
6      public static void main( String[] args )
7      {
8         Object objectRef = "hello";
9         String string = "goodbye";
10        char[] charArray = { 'a', 'b', 'c', 'd', 'e', 'f' };
11        boolean booleanValue = true;
12        char characterValue = 'K';
13        int integerValue = 7;
14        long longValue = 10000000;
15        float floatValue = 2.5f; // f suffix indicates that 2.5 is a float
16        double doubleValue = 33.333;
17
18        StringBuilder buffer = new StringBuilder();
19
20        buffer.insert( 0, objectRef );
21        buffer.insert( 0, "  " ); // each of these contains two spaces
22        buffer.insert( 0, string );
23        buffer.insert( 0, "  " );
24        buffer.insert( 0, charArray );
25        buffer.insert( 0, "  " );
26        buffer.insert( 0, charArray, 3, 3 );
27        buffer.insert( 0, "  " );
28        buffer.insert( 0, booleanValue );
29        buffer.insert( 0, "  " );
30        buffer.insert( 0, characterValue );
31        buffer.insert( 0, "  " );
32        buffer.insert( 0, integerValue );
```

Fig. 16.5 | StringBuilder methods insert, delete and deleteCharAt. (Part 1 of 2.)

```
33        buffer.insert( 0, "   " );
34        buffer.insert( 0, longValue );
35        buffer.insert( 0, "   " );
36        buffer.insert( 0, floatValue );
37        buffer.insert( 0, "   " );
38        buffer.insert( 0, doubleValue );
39
40        System.out.printf(
41           "buffer after inserts:\n%s\n\n", buffer.toString() );
42
43        buffer.deleteCharAt( 10 ); // delete 5 in 2.5
44        buffer.delete( 2, 6 ); // delete .333 in 33.333
45
46        System.out.printf(
47           "buffer after deletes:\n%s\n", buffer.toString() );
48     } // end main
49  } // end class StringBuilderInsertDelete
```

```
buffer after inserts:
33.333  2.5  10000000  7  K  true  def  abcdef  goodbye  hello

buffer after deletes:
33  2.  10000000  7  K  true  def  abcdef  goodbye  hello
```

Fig. 16.5 | StringBuilder methods insert, delete and deleteCharAt. (Part 2 of 2.)

16.3 Class Character

Java provides eight type-wrapper classes—Boolean, Character, Double, Float, Byte, Short, Integer and Long—that enable primitive-type values to be treated as objects. In this section, we present class Character—the type-wrapper class for primitive type char.

Most Character methods are static methods designed for convenience in processing individual char values. These methods take at least a character argument and perform either a test or a manipulation of the character. Class Character also contains a constructor that receives a char argument to initialize a Character object. Most of the methods of class Character are presented in the next three examples. For more information on class Character (and all the type-wrapper classes), see the java.lang package in the Java API documentation.

Figure 16.6 demonstrates static methods that test characters to determine whether they're a specific character type and the static methods that perform case conversions on characters. You can enter any character and apply the methods to the character.

```
1   // Fig. 16.6: StaticCharMethods.java
2   // Character static methods for testing characters and converting case.
3   import java.util.Scanner;
4
5   public class StaticCharMethods
6   {
7      public static void main( String[] args )
8      {
```

Fig. 16.6 | Character static methods for testing characters and converting case. (Part 1 of 3.)

```
 9          Scanner scanner = new Scanner( System.in ); // create scanner
10          System.out.println( "Enter a character and press Enter" );
11          String input = scanner.next();
12          char c = input.charAt( 0 ); // get input character
13
14          // display character info
15          System.out.printf( "is defined: %b\n", Character.isDefined( c ) );
16          System.out.printf( "is digit: %b\n", Character.isDigit( c ) );
17          System.out.printf( "is first character in a Java identifier: %b\n",
18             Character.isJavaIdentifierStart( c ) );
19          System.out.printf( "is part of a Java identifier: %b\n",
20             Character.isJavaIdentifierPart( c ) );
21          System.out.printf( "is letter: %b\n", Character.isLetter( c ) );
22          System.out.printf(
23             "is letter or digit: %b\n", Character.isLetterOrDigit( c ) );
24          System.out.printf(
25             "is lower case: %b\n", Character.isLowerCase( c ) );
26          System.out.printf(
27             "is upper case: %b\n", Character.isUpperCase( c ) );
28          System.out.printf(
29             "to upper case: %s\n", Character.toUpperCase( c ) );
30          System.out.printf(
31             "to lower case: %s\n", Character.toLowerCase( c ) );
32       } // end main
33    } // end class StaticCharMethods
```

```
Enter a character and press Enter
A
is defined: true
is digit: false
is first character in a Java identifier: true
is part of a Java identifier: true
is letter: true
is letter or digit: true
is lower case: false
is upper case: true
to upper case: A
to lower case: a
```

```
Enter a character and press Enter
8
is defined: true
is digit: true
is first character in a Java identifier: false
is part of a Java identifier: true
is letter: false
is letter or digit: true
is lower case: false
is upper case: false
to upper case: 8
to lower case: 8
```

Fig. 16.6 | Character static methods for testing characters and converting case. (Part 2 of 3.)

```
Enter a character and press Enter
$
is defined: true
is digit: false
is first character in a Java identifier: true
is part of a Java identifier: true
is letter: false
is letter or digit: false
is lower case: false
is upper case: false
to upper case: $
to lower case: $
```

Fig. 16.6 | Character static methods for testing characters and converting case. (Part 3 of 3.)

Line 15 uses Character method **isDefined** to determine whether character c is defined in the Unicode character set. If so, the method returns true; otherwise, it returns false. Line 16 uses Character method **isDigit** to determine whether character c is a defined Unicode digit. If so, the method returns true, and otherwise, false.

Line 18 uses Character method **isJavaIdentifierStart** to determine whether c is a character that can be the first character of an identifier in Java—that is, a letter, an underscore (_) or a dollar sign ($). If so, the method returns true, and otherwise, false. Line 20 uses Character method **isJavaIdentifierPart** to determine whether character c is a character that can be used in an identifier in Java—that is, a digit, a letter, an underscore (_) or a dollar sign ($). If so, the method returns true, and otherwise, false.

Line 21 uses Character method **isLetter** to determine whether character c is a letter. If so, the method returns true, and otherwise, false. Line 23 uses Character method **isLetterOrDigit** to determine whether character c is a letter or a digit. If so, the method returns true, and otherwise, false.

Line 25 uses Character method **isLowerCase** to determine whether character c is a lowercase letter. If so, the method returns true, and otherwise, false. Line 27 uses Character method **isUpperCase** to determine whether character c is an uppercase letter. If so, the method returns true, and otherwise, false.

Line 29 uses Character method **toUpperCase** to convert the character c to its uppercase equivalent. The method returns the converted character if the character has an uppercase equivalent, and otherwise, the method returns its original argument. Line 31 uses Character method **toLowerCase** to convert the character c to its lowercase equivalent. The method returns the converted character if the character has a lowercase equivalent, and otherwise, the method returns its original argument.

Character Methods digit and forDigit

Figure 16.7 demonstrates static Character methods **digit** and **forDigit**, which convert characters to digits and digits to characters, respectively, in different number systems. Common number systems include decimal (base 10), octal (base 8), hexadecimal (base 16) and binary (base 2). The base of a number is also known as its **radix**. For more information on conversions between number systems, see Appendix H.

Line 28 uses method forDigit to convert the integer digit into a character in the number system specified by the integer radix (the base of the number). For example, the decimal integer 13 in base 16 (the radix) has the character value 'd'. Lowercase and uppercase letters represent the same value in number systems. Line 35 uses method digit to convert variable character into an integer in the number system specified by the integer radix (the base of the number). For example, the character 'A' is the base 16 (the radix) representation of the base 10 value 10. The radix must be between 2 and 36, inclusive.

```java
1   // Fig. 16.7: StaticCharMethods2.java
2   // Character class static conversion methods.
3   import java.util.Scanner;
4
5   public class StaticCharMethods2
6   {
7      // executes application
8      public static void main( String[] args )
9      {
10         Scanner scanner = new Scanner( System.in );
11
12         // get radix
13         System.out.println( "Please enter a radix:" );
14         int radix = scanner.nextInt();
15
16         // get user choice
17         System.out.printf( "Please choose one:\n1 -- %s\n2 -- %s\n",
18            "Convert digit to character", "Convert character to digit" );
19         int choice = scanner.nextInt();
20
21         // process request
22         switch ( choice )
23         {
24            case 1: // convert digit to character
25               System.out.println( "Enter a digit:" );
26               int digit = scanner.nextInt();
27               System.out.printf( "Convert digit to character: %s\n",
28                  Character.forDigit( digit, radix ) );
29               break;
30
31            case 2: // convert character to digit
32               System.out.println( "Enter a character:" );
33               char character = scanner.next().charAt( 0 );
34               System.out.printf( "Convert character to digit: %s\n",
35                  Character.digit( character, radix ) );
36               break;
37         } // end switch
38      } // end main
39   } // end class StaticCharMethods2
```

```
Please enter a radix:
16
Please choose one:
1 -- Convert digit to character
2 -- Convert character to digit
2
Enter a character:
A
Convert character to digit: 10
```

Fig. 16.7 | Character class static conversion methods. (Part 1 of 2.)

```
Please enter a radix:
16
Please choose one:
1 -- Convert digit to character
2 -- Convert character to digit
1
Enter a digit:
13
Convert digit to character: d
```

Fig. 16.7 | Character class static conversion methods. (Part 2 of 2.)

Figure 16.8 demonstrates the constructor and several non-static methods of class Character—**charValue**, toString and equals. Lines 7–8 instantiate two Character objects by assigning the character constants 'A' and 'a', respectively, to the Character variables. Java automatically converts these char literals into Character objects—a process known as autoboxing that we discuss in more detail in Section 20.4. Line 11 uses Character method charValue to return the char value stored in Character object c1. Line 11 returns a string representation of Character object c2 using method toString. The condition in line 13 uses method equals to determine whether the object c1 has the same contents as the object c2 (i.e., the characters inside each object are equal).

```java
1   // Fig. 16.8: OtherCharMethods.java
2   // Character class non-static methods.
3   public class OtherCharMethods
4   {
5      public static void main( String[] args )
6      {
7         Character c1 = 'A';
8         Character c2 = 'a';
9
10        System.out.printf(
11           "c1 = %s\nc2 = %s\n\n", c1.charValue(), c2.toString() );
12
13        if ( c1.equals( c2 ) )
14           System.out.println( "c1 and c2 are equal\n" );
15        else
16           System.out.println( "c1 and c2 are not equal\n" );
17     } // end main
18  } // end class OtherCharMethods
```

```
c1 = A
c2 = a

c1 and c2 are not equal
```

Fig. 16.8 | Character class non-static methods.

16.4 Tokenizing Strings

When you read a sentence, your mind breaks it into tokens—individual words and punctuation marks that convey meaning to you. Compilers also perform tokenization. They break up statements into individual pieces like keywords, identifiers, operators and other programming-language elements. We now study class String's **split** method, which breaks a String into its component tokens. Tokens are separated from one another by **delimiters**, typically white-space characters such as space, tab, newline and carriage return. Other characters can also be used as delimiters to separate tokens. The application in Fig. 16.9 demonstrates String's split method.

```
1   // Fig. 16.9: TokenTest.java
2   // StringTokenizer object used to tokenize strings.
3   import java.util.Scanner;
4   import java.util.StringTokenizer;
5
6   public class TokenTest
7   {
8      // execute application
9      public static void main( String[] args )
10     {
11        // get sentence
12        Scanner scanner = new Scanner( System.in );
13        System.out.println( "Enter a sentence and press Enter" );
14        String sentence = scanner.nextLine();
15
16        // process user sentence
17        String[] tokens = sentence.split( " " );
18        System.out.printf( "Number of elements: %d\nThe tokens are:\n",
19           tokens.length );
20
21        for ( String token : tokens )
22           System.out.println( token );
23     } // end main
24  } // end class TokenTest
```

```
Enter a sentence and press Enter
This is a sentence with seven tokens
Number of elements: 7
The tokens are:
This
is
a
sentence
with
seven
tokens
```

Fig. 16.9 | StringTokenizer object used to tokenize strings.

When the user presses the *Enter* key, the input sentence is stored in variable sentence. Line 17 invokes String method split with the String argument " ", which returns an array of Strings. The space character in the argument String is the delimiter that method split uses to locate the tokens in the String. As you'll learn in the next section, the argument to method split can be a regular expression for more complex tokenizing. Line 19 displays the length of the array tokens—i.e., the number of tokens in sentence. Lines 21–22 output each token on a separate line.

16.5 Regular Expressions, Class Pattern and Class Matcher

A regular expression is a specially formatted String that describes a search pattern for matching characters in other Strings. They're useful for validating input and ensuring that data is in a particular format. For example, a ZIP code must consist of five digits, and a last name must contain only letters, spaces, apostrophes and hyphens. One application of regular expressions is to facilitate the construction of a compiler. Often, a large and complex regular expression is used to validate the syntax of a program. If the code does not match the regular expression, the compiler knows that there's a syntax error within the code.

Class String provides several methods for performing regular-expression operations, the simplest of which is the matching operation. String method **matches** receives a String that specifies the regular expression and matches the contents of the String object on which it's called to the regular expression. The method returns a boolean indicating whether the match succeeded.

A regular expression consists of literal characters and special symbols. Figure 16.10 specifies some predefined character classes that can be used with regular expressions. A character class is an escape sequence that represents a group of characters. A digit is any numeric character. A word character is any letter (uppercase or lowercase), any digit or the underscore character. A white-space character is a space, a tab, a carriage return, a newline or a form feed. Each character class matches a single character in the String we're attempting to match with the regular expression.

Character	Matches	Character	Matches
\d	any digit	\D	any nondigit
\w	any word character	\W	any nonword character
\s	any white-space character	\S	any nonwhite-space character

Fig. 16.10 | Predefined character classes.

Regular expressions are not limited to these predefined character classes. The expressions employ various operators and other forms of notation to match complex patterns. We examine several of these techniques in the application in Figs. 16.11 and 16.12, which validates user input via regular expressions. [*Note:* This application is not designed to match all possible valid user input.]

```
1    // Fig. 16.11: ValidateInput.java
2    // Validate user information using regular expressions.
3
4    public class ValidateInput
5    {
6       // validate first name
7       public static boolean validateFirstName( String firstName )
8       {
```

Fig. 16.11 | Validating user information using regular expressions. (Part 1 of 2.)

```
 9          return firstName.matches( "[A-Z][a-zA-Z]*" );
10      } // end method validateFirstName
11
12      // validate last name
13      public static boolean validateLastName( String lastName )
14      {
15          return lastName.matches( "[a-zA-z]+([ '-][a-zA-Z]+)*" );
16      } // end method validateLastName
17
18      // validate address
19      public static boolean validateAddress( String address )
20      {
21          return address.matches(
22              "\\d+\\s+([a-zA-Z]+|[a-zA-Z]+\\s[a-zA-Z]+)" );
23      } // end method validateAddress
24
25      // validate city
26      public static boolean validateCity( String city )
27      {
28          return city.matches( "([a-zA-Z]+|[a-zA-Z]+\\s[a-zA-Z]+)" );
29      } // end method validateCity
30
31      // validate state
32      public static boolean validateState( String state )
33      {
34          return state.matches( "([a-zA-Z]+|[a-zA-Z]+\\s[a-zA-Z]+)" ) ;
35      } // end method validateState
36
37      // validate zip
38      public static boolean validateZip( String zip )
39      {
40          return zip.matches( "\\d{5}" );
41      } // end method validateZip
42
43      // validate phone
44      public static boolean validatePhone( String phone )
45      {
46          return phone.matches( "[1-9]\\d{2}-[1-9]\\d{2}-\\d{4}" );
47      } // end method validatePhone
48  } // end class ValidateInput
```

Fig. 16.11 | Validating user information using regular expressions. (Part 2 of 2.)

```
 1  // Fig. 16.12: Validate.java
 2  // Validate user information using regular expressions.
 3  import java.util.Scanner;
 4
 5  public class Validate
 6  {
 7      public static void main( String[] args )
 8      {
 9          // get user input
10          Scanner scanner = new Scanner( System.in );
```

Fig. 16.12 | Inputs and validates data from user using the ValidateInput class. (Part 1 of 3.)

```
11          System.out.println( "Please enter first name:" );
12          String firstName = scanner.nextLine();
13          System.out.println( "Please enter last name:" );
14          String lastName = scanner.nextLine();
15          System.out.println( "Please enter address:" );
16          String address = scanner.nextLine();
17          System.out.println( "Please enter city:" );
18          String city = scanner.nextLine();
19          System.out.println( "Please enter state:" );
20          String state = scanner.nextLine();
21          System.out.println( "Please enter zip:" );
22          String zip = scanner.nextLine();
23          System.out.println( "Please enter phone:" );
24          String phone = scanner.nextLine();
25
26          // validate user input and display error message
27          System.out.println( "\nValidate Result:" );
28
29          if ( !ValidateInput.validateFirstName( firstName ) )
30             System.out.println( "Invalid first name" );
31          else if ( !ValidateInput.validateLastName( lastName ) )
32             System.out.println( "Invalid last name" );
33          else if ( !ValidateInput.validateAddress( address ) )
34             System.out.println( "Invalid address" );
35          else if ( !ValidateInput.validateCity( city ) )
36             System.out.println( "Invalid city" );
37          else if ( !ValidateInput.validateState( state ) )
38             System.out.println( "Invalid state" );
39          else if ( !ValidateInput.validateZip( zip ) )
40             System.out.println( "Invalid zip code" );
41          else if ( !ValidateInput.validatePhone( phone ) )
42             System.out.println( "Invalid phone number" );
43          else
44             System.out.println( "Valid input.  Thank you." );
45       } // end main
46    } // end class Validate
```

```
Please enter first name:
Jane
Please enter last name:
Doe
Please enter address:
123 Some Street
Please enter city:
Some City
Please enter state:
SS
Please enter zip:
123
Please enter phone:
123-456-7890

Validate Result:
Invalid zip code
```

Fig. 16.12 | Inputs and validates data from user using the **ValidateInput** class. (Part 2 of 3.)

```
Please enter first name:
Jane
Please enter last name:
Doe
Please enter address:
123 Some Street
Please enter city:
Some City
Please enter state:
SS
Please enter zip:
12345
Please enter phone:
123-456-7890


Validate Result:
Valid input.  Thank you.
```

Fig. 16.12 | Inputs and validates data from user using the `ValidateInput` class. (Part 3 of 3.)

Figure 16.11 validates user input. Line 9 validates the first name. To match a set of characters that does not have a predefined character class, use square brackets, []. For example, the pattern "[aeiou]" matches a single character that's a vowel. Character ranges are represented by placing a dash (-) between two characters. In the example, "[A-Z]" matches a single uppercase letter. If the first character in the brackets is "^", the expression accepts any character other than those indicated. However, it's important to note that "[^Z]" is not the same as "[A-Y]", which matches uppercase letters A–Y—"[^Z]" matches any character other than capital Z, including lowercase letters and nonletters such as the newline character. Ranges in character classes are determined by the letters' integer values. In this example, "[A-Za-z]" matches all uppercase and lowercase letters. The range "[A-z]" matches all letters and also matches those characters (such as [and \) with an integer value between uppercase Z and lowercase a (for more information on integer values of characters see Appendix B). Like predefined character classes, character classes delimited by square brackets match a single character in the search object.

In line 9, the asterisk after the second character class indicates that any number of letters can be matched. In general, when the regular-expression operator "*" appears in a regular expression, the application attempts to match zero or more occurrences of the subexpression immediately preceding the "*". Operator "+" attempts to match one or more occurrences of the subexpression immediately preceding "+". So both "A*" and "A+" will match "AAA" or "A", but only "A*" will match an empty string.

If method `validateFirstName` returns `true` (line 29 of Fig. 16.12), the application attempts to validate the last name (line 31) by calling `validateLastName` (lines 13–16 of Fig. 16.11). The regular expression to validate the last name matches any number of letters split by spaces, apostrophes or hyphens.

Line 33 of Fig. 16.12 calls method `validateAddress` (lines 19–23 of Fig. 16.11) to validate the address. The first character class matches any digit one or more times (\\d+). Note that two \ characters are used, because \ normally starts an escape sequence in a string. So \\d in a `String` represents the regular expression pattern \d. Then we match one or more white-space characters (\\s+). The character "|" matches the expression to its left or to its right. For example, "Hi (John|Jane)" matches both "Hi John" and "Hi Jane". The parentheses are used to group parts of the regular expression. In this example, the left side of | matches a single word, and the right side matches two words separated by any amount of white space. So the address must contain a number followed by one or two words. Therefore, "10 Broadway" and "10 Main Street" are both valid addresses in this example. The city (lines 26–29 of Fig. 16.11) and state (lines 32–35 of Fig. 16.11) methods also match any word of at least one character or, alternatively, any two words of at least one character if the words are separated by a single space, so both Waltham and West Newton would match.

Quantifiers
The asterisk (*) and plus (+) are formally called **quantifiers**. Figure 16.13 lists all the quantifiers. We've already discussed how the asterisk (*) and plus (+) quantifiers work. All quantifiers affect only the subexpression immediately preceding the quantifier. Quantifier question mark (?) matches zero or one occurrences of the expression that it quantifies. A set of braces containing one number ({n}) matches exactly n occurrences of the expression it quantifies. We demonstrate this quantifier to validate the zip code in Fig. 16.11 at line 40. Including a comma after the number enclosed in braces matches at least n occurrences of the quantified expression. The set of braces containing two numbers ({n,m}), matches between n and m occurrences of the expression that it qualifies. Quantifiers may be applied to patterns enclosed in parentheses to create more complex regular expressions.

Quantifier	Matches
*	Matches zero or more occurrences of the pattern.
+	Matches one or more occurrences of the pattern.
?	Matches zero or one occurrences of the pattern.
{n}	Matches exactly n occurrences.
{$n,$}	Matches at least n occurrences.
{n,m}	Matches between n and m (inclusive) occurrences.

Fig. 16.13 | Quantifiers used in regular expressions.

All of the quantifiers are **greedy**. This means that they'll match as many occurrences as they can as long as the match is still successful. However, if any of these quantifiers is followed by a question mark (?), the quantifier becomes **reluctant** (sometimes called lazy). It then will match as few occurrences as possible as long as the match is still successful.

The zip code regular expression (line 40, Fig. 16.11) matches a digit five times by using the digit character class and a quantifier with the digit 5 between braces. The phone number (line 46, Fig. 16.11) matches three digits (the first one cannot be zero) followed by a dash three more digits (again the first one cannot be zero) a dash and four more digits.

String Method matches checks whether an entire String conforms to a regular expression. For example, we want to accept "Smith" as a last name, but not "9@Smith#". If only a substring matches the regular expression, method matches returns false.

Replacing Substrings and Splitting Strings
Sometimes it's useful to replace parts of a string or to split a string into pieces. For this purpose, class String provides methods **replaceAll**, **replaceFirst** and **split**. These methods are demonstrated in Fig. 16.14.

```
1   // Fig. 16.14: RegexSubstitution.java
2   // String methods replaceFirst, replaceAll and split.
3   import java.util.Arrays;
4
5   public class RegexSubstitution
6   {
7      public static void main( String[] args )
8      {
9         String firstString = "This sentence ends in 5 stars *****";
10        String secondString = "1, 2, 3, 4, 5, 6, 7, 8";
11
12        System.out.printf( "Original String 1: %s\n", firstString );
13
14        // replace '*' with '^'
15        firstString = firstString.replaceAll( "\\*", "^" );
16
17        System.out.printf( "^ substituted for *: %s\n", firstString );
18
19        // replace 'stars' with 'carets'
20        firstString = firstString.replaceAll( "stars", "carets" );
21
22        System.out.printf(
23           "\"carets\" substituted for \"stars\": %s\n", firstString );
24
25        // replace words with 'word'
26        System.out.printf( "Every word replaced by \"word\": %s\n\n",
27           firstString.replaceAll( "\\w+", "word" ) );
28
29        System.out.printf( "Original String 2: %s\n", secondString );
30
31        // replace first three digits with 'digit'
32        for ( int i = 0; i < 3; i++ )
33           secondString = secondString.replaceFirst( "\\d", "digit" );
34
35        System.out.printf(
36           "First 3 digits replaced by \"digit\" : %s\n", secondString );
37
38        System.out.print( "String split at commas: " );
39        String[] results = secondString.split( ",\\s*" ); // split on commas
40        System.out.println( Arrays.toString( results ) );
41     } // end main
42  } // end class RegexSubstitution
```

```
Original String 1: This sentence ends in 5 stars *****
^ substituted for *: This sentence ends in 5 stars ^^^^^
"carets" substituted for "stars": This sentence ends in 5 carets ^^^^^
Every word replaced by "word": word word word word word word ^^^^^

Original String 2: 1, 2, 3, 4, 5, 6, 7, 8
First 3 digits replaced by "digit" : digit, digit, digit, 4, 5, 6, 7, 8
String split at commas: ["digit", "digit", "digit", "4", "5", "6", "7", "8"]
```

Fig. 16.14 | String methods replaceFirst, replaceAll and split.

Method replaceAll replaces text in a String with new text (the second argument) wherever the original String matches a regular expression (the first argument). Line 15 replaces every instance of "*" in firstString with "^". Note that the regular expression ("*") precedes character * with two backslashes. Normally, * is a quantifier indicating that a regular expression should match any number of occurrences of a preceding pattern. However, in line 15, we want to find all occurrences of the literal character *—to do this, we must escape character * with character \. Escaping a special regular-expression character with \ instructs the matching engine to find the actual character. Since the expression is stored in a Java String and \ is a special character in Java Strings, we must include an additional \. So the Java String "*" represents the regular-expression pattern * which matches a single * character in the search string. In line 20, every match for the regular expression "stars" in firstString is replaced with "carets". Line 27 uses replaceAll to replace all words in the string with "word".

Method replaceFirst (line 33) replaces the first occurrence of a pattern match. Java Strings are immutable; therefore, method replaceFirst returns a new String in which the appropriate characters have been replaced. This line takes the original String and replaces it with the String returned by replaceFirst. By iterating three times we replace the first three instances of a digit (\d) in secondString with the text "digit".

Method split divides a String into substrings. The original is broken in any location that matches a specified regular expression. Method split returns an array of Strings containing the substrings between regular-expression matches. In line 39, we use method split to tokenize a String of comma-separated integers. The argument is the regular expression that locates the delimiter. In this case, we use the regular expression ",\\s*" to separate the substrings wherever a comma occurs. By matching any white-space characters, we eliminate extra spaces from the resulting substrings. Note that the commas and white-space characters are not returned as part of the substrings. Again, note that the Java String ",\\s*" represents the regular expression ,\s*. Line 40 uses Arrays method toString to display the contents of array results in square brackets and separated by commas.

Classes *Pattern* and *Matcher*

In addition to the regular-expression capabilities of class String, Java provides other classes in package java.util.regex that help developers manipulate regular expressions. Class **Pattern** represents a regular expression. Class **Matcher** contains both a regular-expression pattern and a CharSequence in which to search for the pattern.

CharSequence (package java.lang) is an interface that allows read access to a sequence of characters. The interface requires that the methods charAt, length, subSequence and toString be declared. Both String and StringBuilder implement interface CharSequence, so an instance of either of these classes can be used with class Matcher.

Common Programming Error 16.2

A regular expression can be tested against an object of any class that implements interface CharSequence, but the regular expression must be a String. Attempting to create a regular expression as a StringBuilder is an error.

If a regular expression will be used only once, static Pattern method **matches** can be used. This method takes a String that specifies the regular expression and a CharSequence on which to perform the match. This method returns a boolean indicating whether the search object (the second argument) matches the regular expression.

If a regular expression will be used more than once (in a loop for example), it's more efficient to use static Pattern method **compile** to create a specific Pattern object for that regular expression. This method receives a String representing the pattern and returns a new Pattern object, which can then be used to call method **matcher**. This method receives a CharSequence to search and returns a Matcher object.

Matcher provides method **matches**, which performs the same task as Pattern method matches, but receives no arguments—the search pattern and search object are encapsulated in the Matcher object. Class Matcher provides other methods, including **find**, **lookingAt**, **replaceFirst** and **replaceAll**.

Figure 16.15 presents a simple example that employs regular expressions. This program matches birthdays against a regular expression. The expression matches only birthdays that do not occur in April and that belong to people whose names begin with "J".

Lines 11–12 create a Pattern by invoking static Pattern method compile. The dot character "." in the regular expression (line 12) matches any single character except a newline character.

```
 1   // Fig. 16.15: RegexMatches.java
 2   // Classes Pattern and Matcher.
 3   import java.util.regex.Matcher;
 4   import java.util.regex.Pattern;
 5
 6   public class RegexMatches
 7   {
 8      public static void main( String[] args )
 9      {
10         // create regular expression
11         Pattern expression =
12            Pattern.compile( "J.*\\d[0-35-9]-\\d\\d-\\d\\d" );
13
14         String string1 = "Jane's Birthday is 05-12-75\n" +
15            "Dave's Birthday is 11-04-68\n" +
16            "John's Birthday is 04-28-73\n" +
17            "Joe's Birthday is 12-17-77";
18
19         // match regular expression to string and print matches
20         Matcher matcher = expression.matcher( string1 );
21
22         while ( matcher.find() )
23            System.out.println( matcher.group() );
24      } // end main
25   } // end class RegexMatches
```

```
Jane's Birthday is 05-12-75
Joe's Birthday is 12-17-77
```

Fig. 16.15 | Classes Pattern and Matcher.

Line 20 creates the Matcher object for the compiled regular expression and the matching sequence (string1). Lines 22–23 use a while loop to iterate through the String. Line 22 uses Matcher method find to attempt to match a piece of the search object to the search pattern. Each call to this method starts at the point where the last call ended, so multiple matches can be found. Matcher method lookingAt performs the same way, except that it always starts from the beginning of the search object and will always find the first match if there is one.

Common Programming Error 16.3

Method matches (from class String, Pattern or Matcher) will return true *only if the entire search object matches the regular expression. Methods* find *and* lookingAt *(from class Matcher) will return* true *if a portion of the search object matches the regular expression.*

Line 23 uses Matcher method **group**, which returns the String from the search object that matches the search pattern. The String that is returned is the one that was last matched by a call to find or lookingAt. The output in Fig. 16.15 shows the two matches that were found in string1.

For more information on regular expressions, visit our Regular Expressions Resource Center at www.deitel.com/regularexpressions/.

16.6 Wrap-Up

In this chapter, you learned about the Character class and some of the methods it declares to handle chars. We discussed the capabilities of the StringBuilder class for creating Strings, and we presented regular expressions, which provide a powerful capability to search and match portions of Strings that fit a particular pattern. In the next chapter, we continue our presentation of file processing, including how entire objects can be stored in files and retrieved for use in programs.

Summary

Section 16.2 Class StringBuilder
- Class StringBuilder provides constructors that enable StringBuilders to be initialized with no characters and an initial capacity of 16 characters, with no characters and an initial capacity specified in the integer argument, or with a copy of the characters of the String argument and an initial capacity that is the number of characters in the String argument plus 16.

- StringBuilder method length returns the number of characters currently stored in a StringBuilder. StringBuilder method capacity returns the number of characters that can be stored in a StringBuilder without allocating more memory.

- StringBuilder method ensureCapacity ensures that a StringBuilder has at least the specified capacity. StringBuilder method setLength increases or decreases the length of a StringBuilder.

- StringBuilder method charAt returns the character at the specified index. StringBuilder method setCharAt sets the character at the specified position. StringBuilder method getChars copies characters in the StringBuilder into the character array passed as an argument.

- StringBuilder's overloaded append methods add primitive-type, character array, String, Object or CharSequence values to the end of a StringBuilder.

- StringBuilder's overloaded insert methods insert primitive-type, character array, String, Object or CharSequence values at any position in a StringBuilder.

Section 16.3 Class Character
- Character method isDefined determines whether a character is in the Unicode character set.
- Character method isDigit determines whether a character is a defined Unicode digit.
- Character method isJavaIdentifierStart determines whether a character can be used as the first character of a Java identifier. Character method isJavaIdentifierPart determines if a character can be used in an identifier.

- Character method isLetter determines if a character is a letter. Character method isLetter-OrDigit determines if a character is a letter or a digit.

- Character method isLowerCase determines whether a character is a lowercase letter. Character method isUpperCase determines whether a character is an uppercase letter.

- Character method toUpperCase converts a character to its uppercase equivalent. Character method toLowerCase converts a character to its lowercase equivalent.

- Character method digit converts its character argument into an integer in the number system specified by its integer argument radix. Character method forDigit converts its integer argument digit into a character in the number system specified by its integer argument radix.

- Character method charValue returns the char stored in a Character object. Character method toString returns a String representation of a Character.

Section 16.4 Tokenizing *Strings*

- Class String's split method tokenizes a String based on the delimiter specified as an argument and returns an array of Strings containing the tokens.

Section 16.5 Regular Expressions, Class *Pattern* and Class *Matcher*

- Regular expressions are sequences of characters and symbols that define a set of strings. They're useful for validating input and ensuring that data is in a particular format.

- String method matches receives a string that specifies the regular expression and matches the contents of the String object on which it's called to the regular expression. The method returns a boolean indicating whether the match succeeded.

- A character class is an escape sequence that represents a group of characters. Each character class matches a single character in the string we are attempting to match with the regular expression.

- A word character (\w) is any letter (uppercase or lowercase), any digit or the underscore character.

- A white-space character (\s) is a space, a tab, a carriage return, a newline or a form feed.

- A digit (\d) is any numeric character.

- To match a set of characters that does not have a predefined character class, use square brackets, []. Ranges can be represented by placing a dash (-) between two characters. If the first character in the brackets is "^", the expression accepts any character other than those indicated.

- When the regular expression operator "*" appears in a regular expression, the program attempts to match zero or more occurrences of the subexpression immediately preceding the "*".

- Operator "+" attempts to match one or more occurrences of the subexpression preceding it.

- The character "|" allows a match of the expression to its left or to its right.

- Parentheses ( ) are used to group parts of the regular expression.

- The asterisk (*) and plus (+) are formally called quantifiers.

- A quantifier affects only the subexpression immediately preceding it.

- Quantifier question mark (?) matches zero or one occurrences of the expression that it quantifies.

- A set of braces containing one number ({n}) matches exactly n occurrences of the expression it quantifies. Including a comma after the number enclosed in braces matches at least n occurrences.

- A set of braces containing two numbers ({n,m}) matches between n and m occurrences of the expression that it qualifies.

- Quantifiers are greedy—they'll match as many occurrences as they can as long as the match is successful. If a quantifier is followed by a question mark (?), the quantifier becomes reluctant, matching as few occurrences as possible as long as the match is successful.

- `String` method `replaceAll` replaces text in a string with new text (the second argument) wherever the original string matches a regular expression (the first argument).

- Escaping a special regular-expression character with a \ instructs the regular-expression matching engine to find the actual character, as opposed to what it represents in a regular expression.

- `String` method `replaceFirst` replaces the first occurrence of a pattern match and returns a new string in which the appropriate characters have been replaced.

- `String` method `split` divides a string into substrings at any location that matches a specified regular expression and returns an array of the substrings.

- Class `Pattern` represents a regular expression.

- Class `Matcher` contains a regular-expression pattern and a `CharSequence` in which to search.

- `CharSequence` is an interface that allows read access to a sequence of characters. Both `String` and `StringBuilder` implement this interface, so they can be used with class `Matcher`.

- If a regular expression will be used only once, static `Pattern` method `matches` takes a string that specifies the regular expression and a `CharSequence` on which to perform the match. This method returns a `boolean` indicating whether the search object matches the regular expression.

- If a regular expression will be used more than once, it's more efficient to use static `Pattern` method `compile` to create a specific `Pattern` object for that regular expression. This method receives a string representing the pattern and returns a new `Pattern` object.

- `Pattern` method `matcher` receives a `CharSequence` to search and returns a `Matcher` object. `Matcher` method `matches` performs the same task as `Pattern` method `matches` but without arguments.

- `Matcher` method `find` attempts to match a piece of the search object to the search pattern. Each call to this method starts at the point where the last call ended, so multiple matches can be found.

- `Matcher` method `lookingAt` performs the same as `find`, except that it always starts from the beginning of the search object and will always find the first match if there is one.

- `Matcher` method `group` returns the string from the search object that matches the search pattern. The string returned is the one that was last matched by a call to `find` or `lookingAt`.

Terminology

Self-Review Exercise

16.1 For each of the following, write a single statement that performs the indicated task:
  a) Compare the string in s1 to the string in s2 for equality of contents.
  b) Append the string s2 to the string s1, using +=.
  c) Determine the length of the string in s1.

Answers to Self-Review Exercise

16.1 a) `s1.equals( s2 )`
  b) `s1 += s2;`
  c) `s1.length()`

Exercises

16.2 *(Random Sentences)* Write an application that uses random-number generation to create sentences. Use four arrays of strings called `article`, `noun`, `verb` and `preposition`. Create a sentence by selecting a word at random from each array in the following order: `article`, `noun`, `verb`, `preposition`, `article` and `noun`. As each word is picked, concatenate it to the previous words in the sentence. The words should be separated by spaces. When the final sentence is output, it should start with a capital letter and end with a period. The application should generate and display 20 sentences.

The article array should contain the articles "the", "a", "one", "some" and "any"; the noun array should contain the nouns "boy", "girl", "dog", "town" and "car"; the verb array should contain the verbs "drove", "jumped", "ran", "walked" and "skipped"; the preposition array should contain the prepositions "to", "from", "over", "under" and "on".

16.3 *(Limericks)* A limerick is a humorous five-line verse in which the first and second lines rhyme with the fifth, and the third line rhymes with the fourth. Using techniques similar to those developed in Exercise 16.2, write a Java application that produces random limericks. Polishing this application to produce good limericks is a challenging problem, but the result will be worth the effort!

16.4 *(Pig Latin)* Write an application that encodes English-language phrases into pig Latin. Pig Latin is a form of coded language. There are many different ways to form pig Latin phrases. For simplicity, use the following algorithm:

To form a pig Latin phrase from an English-language phrase, tokenize the phrase into words with `String` method `split`. To translate each English word into a pig Latin word, place the first letter of the English word at the end of the word and add the letters "ay." Thus, the word "jump" becomes "umpjay," the word "the" becomes "hetay," and the word "computer" becomes "omputer-cay." Blanks between words remain as blanks. Assume the following: The English phrase consists of words separated by blanks, there are no punctuation marks and all words have two or more letters. Method `printLatinWord` should display each word. Each token is passed to method `printLatin-Word` to print the pig Latin word. Enable the user to input the sentence. Keep a running display of all the converted sentences in a text area.

16.5 *(Tokenizing Telephone Numbers)* Write an application that inputs a telephone number as a string in the form (555) 555-5555. The application should `String` method `split` to extract the area code as a token, the first three digits of the phone number as a token and the last four digits of the phone number as a token. The seven digits of the phone number should be concatenated into one string. Both the area code and the phone number should be printed. Remember that you'll have to change delimiter characters during the tokenization process.

16.6 *(Displaying a Sentence with Its Words Reversed)* Write an application that inputs a line of text, tokenizes the line with `String` method `split` and outputs the tokens in reverse order. Use space characters as delimiters.

16.7 *(Tokenizing and Comparing `Strings`)* Write an application that reads a line of text, tokenizes the line using space characters as delimiters and outputs only those words beginning with the letter "b".

16.8 *(Tokenizing and Comparing `Strings`)* Write an application that reads a line of text, tokenizes it using space characters as delimiters and outputs only those words ending with the letters "ED".

16.9 *(Converting `int` Values to Characters)* Write an application that inputs an integer code for a character and displays the corresponding character. Modify this application so that it generates all possible three-digit codes in the range from 000 to 255 and attempts to print the corresponding characters.

16.10 *(Defining Your Own `String` Methods)* Write your own versions of `String` search methods `indexOf` and `lastIndexOf`.

16.11 *(Creating Three-Letter `Strings` from a Five-Letter Word)* Write an application that reads a five-letter word from the user and produces every possible three-letter string that can be derived from the letters of that word. For example, the three-letter words produced from the word "bathe" include "ate," "bat," "bet," "tab," "hat," "the" and "tea."

Special Section: Advanced String-Manipulation Exercises

The preceding exercises are keyed to the text and designed to test your understanding of fundamental string-manipulation concepts. This section includes a collection of intermediate and advanced string-manipulation exercises. You should find these problems challenging, yet entertaining. The problems vary considerably in difficulty. Some require an hour or two of application writing and implementation. Others are useful for lab assignments that might require two or three weeks of study and implementation. Some are challenging term projects.

16.12 *(Text Analysis)* The availability of computers with string-manipulation capabilities has resulted in some rather interesting approaches to analyzing the writings of great authors. Much attention has been focused on whether William Shakespeare ever lived. Some scholars believe there is substantial evidence indicating that Christopher Marlowe actually penned the masterpieces attributed to Shakespeare. Researchers have used computers to find similarities in the writings of these two authors. This exercise examines three methods for analyzing texts with a computer.

    a) Write an application that reads a line of text from the keyboard and prints a table indicating the number of occurrences of each letter of the alphabet in the text. For example, the phrase

```
To be, or not to be: that is the question:
```

       contains one "a," two "b's," no "c's," and so on.

    b) Write an application that reads a line of text and prints a table indicating the number of one-letter words, two-letter words, three-letter words, and so on, appearing in the text. For example, Fig. 16.16 shows the counts for the phrase

```
Whether 'tis nobler in the mind to suffer
```

Word length	Occurrences
1	0
2	2
3	1
4	2 (including 'tis)
5	0
6	2
7	1

Fig. 16.16 | Word-length counts for the string
`"Whether 'tis nobler in the mind to suffer"`.

c) Write an application that reads a line of text and prints a table indicating the number of occurrences of each different word in the text. The application should include the words in the table in the same order in which they appear in the text. For example, the lines

```
To be, or not to be: that is the question:
Whether 'tis nobler in the mind to suffer
```

contain the word "to" three times, the word "be" two times, the word "or" once, etc.

16.13 *(Printing Dates in Various Formats)* Dates are printed in several common formats. Two of the more common formats are

```
04/25/1955 and April 25, 1955
```

Write an application that reads a date in the first format and prints it in the second format.

16.14 *(Check Protection)* Computers are frequently employed in check-writing systems, such as payroll and accounts payable applications. There are many strange stories about weekly paychecks being printed (by mistake) for amounts in excess of $1 million. Incorrect amounts are printed by computerized check-writing systems because of human error or machine failure. Systems designers build controls into their systems to prevent such erroneous checks from being issued.

Another serious problem is the intentional alteration of a check amount by someone who plans to cash a check fraudulently. To prevent a dollar amount from being altered, some computerized check-writing systems employ a technique called check protection. Checks designed for imprinting by computer contain a fixed number of spaces in which the computer may print an amount. Suppose a paycheck contains eight blank spaces in which the computer is supposed to print the amount of a weekly paycheck. If the amount is large, then all eight of the spaces will be filled. For example,

```
1,230.60 (check amount)
--------
12345678 (position numbers)
```

On the other hand, if the amount is less than $1000, then several of the spaces would ordinarily be left blank. For example,

```
   99.87
--------
12345678
```

contains three blank spaces. If a check is printed with blank spaces, it's easier for someone to alter the amount. To prevent alteration, many check-writing systems insert *leading asterisks* to protect the amount as follows:

```
***99.87
--------
12345678
```

Write an application that inputs a dollar amount to be printed on a check, then prints the amount in check-protected format with leading asterisks if necessary. Assume that nine spaces are available for printing the amount.

16.15 *(Writing the Word Equivalent of a Check Amount)* Continuing the discussion in Exercise 16.14, we reiterate the importance of designing check-writing systems to prevent alteration of check amounts. One common security method requires that the amount be written in numbers and spelled out in words as well. Even if someone is able to alter the numerical amount of the check, it's extremely difficult to change the amount in words. Write an application that inputs a numeric check amount that is less than $1000 and writes the word equivalent of the amount. For example, the amount 112.43 should be written as

```
ONE hundred TWELVE and 43/100
```

16.16 *(Morse Code)* Perhaps the most famous of all coding schemes is the Morse code, developed by Samuel Morse in 1832 for use with the telegraph system. The Morse code assigns a series of dots and dashes to each letter of the alphabet, each digit, and a few special characters (e.g., period, comma, colon, semicolon). In sound-oriented systems, the dot represents a short sound and the dash a long sound. Other representations of dots and dashes are used with light-oriented systems and signal-flag systems. Separation between words is indicated by a space or, simply, the absence of a dot or dash. In a sound-oriented system, a space is indicated by a short time during which no sound is transmitted. The international version of the Morse code appears in Fig. 16.17.

Write an application that reads an English-language phrase and encodes it into Morse code. Also write an application that reads a phrase in Morse code and converts it into the English-language equivalent. Use one blank between each Morse-coded letter and three blanks between each Morse-coded word.

Character	Code	Character	Code	Character	Code
A	.-	N	-.	*Digits*	
B	-...	O	---	1	.----
C	-.-.	P	.--.	2	..---
D	-..	Q	--.-	3	...--
E	.	R	.-.	4	....-
F	..-.	S	...	5	.....
G	--.	T	-	6	-....
H	....	U	..-	7	--...
I	..	V	...-	8	---..
J	.---	W	.--	9	----.
K	-.-	X	-..-	0	-----
L	.-..	Y	-.--		
M	--	Z	--..		

Fig. 16.17 | Letters and digits as expressed in international Morse code.

16.17 *(Metric Conversions)* Write an application that will assist the user with metric conversions. Your application should allow the user to specify the names of the units as strings (i.e., centimeters, liters, grams, and so on, for the metric system and inches, quarts, pounds, and so on, for the English system) and should respond to simple questions, such as

```
"How many inches are in 2 meters?"
"How many liters are in 10 quarts?"
```

Your application should recognize invalid conversions. For example, the question

```
"How many feet are in 5 kilograms?"
```

is not meaningful because "feet" is a unit of length, whereas "kilograms" is a unit of mass.

Special Section: Challenging String-Manipulation Projects

16.18 *(Project: A Spelling Checker)* Many popular word-processing software packages have built-in spell checkers. In this project, you are asked to develop your own spell-checker utility. We make suggestions to help get you started. You should then consider adding more capabilities. Use a computerized dictionary (if you have access to one) as a source of words.

Why do we type so many words with incorrect spellings? In some cases, it's because we simply do not know the correct spelling, so we make a best guess. In some cases, it's because we transpose two letters (e.g., "defualt" instead of "default"). Sometimes we double-type a letter accidentally (e.g., "hanndy" instead of "handy"). Sometimes we type a nearby key instead of the one we intended (e.g., "biryhday" instead of "birthday"), and so on.

Design and implement a spell-checker application in Java. Your application should maintain an array wordList of strings. Enable the user to enter these strings. [*Note:* In Chapter 17, we introduce file processing. With this capability, you can obtain the words for the spell checker from a computerized dictionary stored in a file.]

Your application should ask a user to enter a word. The application should then look up that word in the wordList array. If the word is in the array, your application should print "Word is spelled correctly." If the word is not in the array, your application should print "Word is not spelled correctly." Then your application should try to locate other words in wordList that might be the word the user intended to type. For example, you can try all possible single transpositions of adjacent letters to discover that the word "default" is a direct match to a word in wordList. Of course, this implies that your application will check all other single transpositions, such as "edfault," "dfeault," "deafult," "defalut" and "defautl." When you find a new word that matches one in wordList, print it in a message, such as

```
Did you mean "default"?
```

Implement other tests, such as replacing each double letter with a single letter, and any other tests you can develop to improve the value of your spell checker.

16.19 *(Project: A Crossword Puzzle Generator)* Most people have worked a crossword puzzle, but few have ever attempted to generate one. Generating a crossword puzzle is suggested here as a string-manipulation project requiring substantial sophistication and effort.

There are many issues the programmer must resolve to get even the simplest crossword-puzzle-generator application working. For example, how do you represent the grid of a crossword puzzle inside the computer? Should you use a series of strings or two-dimensional arrays?

The programmer needs a source of words (i.e., a computerized dictionary) that can be directly referenced by the application. In what form should these words be stored to facilitate the complex manipulations required by the application?

If you are really ambitious, you'll want to generate the clues portion of the puzzle, in which the brief hints for each across word and each down word are printed. Merely printing a version of the blank puzzle itself is not a simple problem.

Files, Streams and Object Serialization

17

I can only assume that a "Do Not File" document is filed in a "Do Not File" file.
—Senator Frank Church
Senate Intelligence Subcommittee Hearing, 1975

Consciousness ... does not appear to itself chopped up in bits. ... A "river" or a "stream" are the metaphors by which it is most naturally described.
—William James

I read part of it all the way through.
—Samuel Goldwyn

Objectives

In this chapter you'll learn:

- To use class `File` to retrieve information about files and directories.

- The Java input/output stream class hierarchy.

- Sequential-access file processing.

- To use classes `FileInputStream` and `FileOutputStream` to read from and write to files.

- To use classes `ObjectInputStream` and `ObjectOutputStream` to read objects from and write objects to files.

- To use a `JFileChooser` dialog.

17.1 Introduction

In Sections 6.16–6.19, we introduced file-processing concepts. You learned how to create, write to and read from sequential-access text files. Here, we discuss additional file-processing concepts and present sufficient stream-processing capabilities to support the networking features introduced in Chapter 27, Networking.

We discuss several classes in package java.io, then demonstrate retrieving information about files and directories using class File. Next, we devote several sections to the mechanisms for writing data to and reading data from files. First, we create an object-oriented credit-inquiry program using the techniques you learned in Section 6.19. In this program, objects of our own class AccountRecord store the data from each record we read from the file. As you'll see, it is not straightforward to read data from text files back into object form. Fortunately, many object-oriented languages (including Java) provide ways to write objects to and read objects from files (known as object serialization and deserialization). To demonstrate this, we recreate the sequential-access programs that used text files in Section 6.19, this time by storing objects in binary files.

17.2 The java.io Package

Java programs perform file processing by using classes from package **java.io**. This package includes definitions for stream classes, such as **FileInputStream** (for byte-based input from a file), **FileOutputStream** (for byte-based output to a file), **FileReader** (for character-based input from a file) and **FileWriter** (for character-based output to a file), which inherit from classes InputStream, OutputStream, Reader and Writer, respectively (these classes will be discussed later in this chapter). Thus, the methods of the stream classes can also be applied to file streams. You open a file by creating an object of one these stream classes. The object's constructor interacts with the operating system to open the file.

Java contains classes that enable you to perform input and output of objects or variables of primitive data types. The data will still be stored as bytes or characters behind the scenes, allowing you to read or write data in the form of ints, Strings, or other types without having to worry about the details of converting such values to byte format. To perform such input and output, objects of classes **ObjectInputStream** and **ObjectOutputStream** can be used together with the byte-based file stream classes FileInputStream and

FileOutputStream (these classes will be discussed in more detail shortly). The complete hierarchy of classes in package java.io can be viewed in the online documentation at

> java.sun.com/javase/6/docs/api/java/io/package-tree.html

Each class is indented under its superclass. For example, class InputStream is a subclass of Object. To view the details of a class, click its name in the hierarchy.

As you can see in the hierarchy, Java offers many classes for performing input/output operations. We use several of these classes in this chapter to implement file-processing programs that create and manipulate sequential-access files. We also include a detailed example on class **File**, which is useful for obtaining information about files and directories. In Chapter 27, we use stream classes extensively to implement networking applications. Several other classes in the java.io package that we do not use in this chapter are discussed briefly in Section 17.6.

In addition to the java.io classes, you've already seen that character-based input and output can be performed with classes Scanner and Formatter. You've used class Scanner to input data from the keyboard and from a file. You've used class Formatter to output formatted data to a file in a manner similar to method System.out.printf. Appendix G presents the details of formatted output with printf. All these features can be used to format text files as well.

17.3 Class File

This section presents class File, which is particularly useful for retrieving information about files or directories from disk. Objects of class File do not open files or provide any file-processing capabilities. However, File objects are used frequently with objects of other java.io classes to specify files or directories to manipulate.

Creating File Objects

Class File provides four constructors. The one with a String argument specifies the name of a file or directory to associate with the File object. The name can contain path information as well as a file or directory name. A file or directory's path specifies its location on disk. The path includes some or all of the directories leading to the file or directory. An absolute path contains all the directories, starting with the root directory, that lead to a specific file or directory. Every file or directory on a particular disk drive has the same root directory in its path. A relative path normally starts from the directory in which the application began executing and is therefore "relative" to the current directory. The constructor with two String arguments specifies an absolute or relative path as the first argument and the file or directory to associate with the File object as the second argument. The constructor with File and String arguments uses an existing File object that specifies the parent directory of the file or directory specified by the String argument. The fourth constructor uses a URI object to locate the file. A Uniform Resource Identifier (URI) is a more general form of the Uniform Resource Locators (URLs) that are used to locate websites. For example, http://www.deitel.com/ is the URL for the Deitel & Associates website. URIs for locating files vary across operating systems. On Windows platforms, the URI

> file://C:/data.txt

identifies the file data.txt stored in the root directory of the C: drive. On UNIX/Linux platforms, the URI

> file:/home/student/data.txt

identifies the file data.txt stored in the home directory of the user student.

 Error-Prevention Tip 17.1

*Use File method **isFile** to determine whether a File object represents a file (not a directory) before attempting to open the file.*

Figure 17.1 lists some common File methods. The complete list can be viewed at java.sun.com/javase/6/docs/api/java/io/File.html.

Method	Description
boolean canRead()	Returns true if a file is readable by the current application; false otherwise.
boolean canWrite()	Returns true if a file is writable by the current application; false otherwise.
boolean exists()	Returns true if the file or directory represented by the File object exists; false otherwise.
boolean isFile()	Returns true if the name specified as the argument to the File constructor is a file; false otherwise.
boolean isDirectory()	Returns true if the name specified as the argument to the File constructor is a directory; false otherwise.
boolean isAbsolute()	Returns true if the arguments specified to the File constructor indicate an absolute path to a file or directory; false otherwise.
String getAbsolutePath()	Returns a String with the absolute path of the file or directory.
String getName()	Returns a String with the name of the file or directory.
String getPath()	Returns a String with the path of the file or directory.
String getParent()	Returns a String with the parent directory of the file or directory (i.e., the directory in which the file or directory is located).
long length()	Returns the length of the file, in bytes. If the File object represents a directory, an unspecified value is returned.
long lastModified()	Returns a platform-dependent representation of the time at which the file or directory was last modified. The value returned is useful only for comparison with other values returned by this method.
String[] list()	Returns an array of Strings representing a directory's contents. Returns null if the File object does not represent a directory.

Fig. 17.1 | File methods.

Demonstrating Class File

Figure 17.2 prompts the user to enter the name of a file or directory, then uses class File to output information about the file or directory. The program begins by prompting the user for a file or directory (line 12). Line 13 inputs the file name or directory name and passes it to method analyzePath (lines 17–50). The method creates a new File object (line 20) and assigns its reference to name. Line 22 invokes File method exists to determine whether the name input by the user exists (either as a file or as a directory) on the disk. If the name does not exist, control proceeds to lines 46–49 and displays a message to the screen containing the name the user typed, followed by "does not exist." Otherwise, the if statement (lines 22–45) executes. The program outputs the name of the file or directory (line 27), followed by the results of testing the File object with isFile (line 28), isDirectory (line 29) and isAbsolute (line 31). Next, the program displays the values returned by lastModified (line 33), length (line 33), getPath (line 34), getAbsolute-Path (line 35) and getParent (line 35). If the File object represents a directory (line 37), the program obtains a list of the directory's contents as an array of Strings by using File method list (line 39) and displays the list on the screen.

```java
1   // Fig. 17.2: FileDemonstration.java
2   // File class used to obtain file and directory information.
3   import java.io.File;
4   import java.util.Scanner;
5
6   public class FileDemonstration
7   {
8      public static void main( String[] args )
9      {
10        Scanner input = new Scanner( System.in );
11
12        System.out.print( "Enter file or directory name: " );
13        analyzePath( input.nextLine() );
14     } // end main
15
16     // display information about file user specifies
17     public static void analyzePath( String path )
18     {
19        // create File object based on user input
20        File name = new File( path );
21
22        if ( name.exists() ) // if name exists, output information about it
23        {
24           // display file (or directory) information
25           System.out.printf(
26              "%s%s\n%s\n%s\n%s\n%s%s\n%s%s\n%s%s\n%s%s\n%s%s",
27              name.getName(), " exists",
28              ( name.isFile() ? "is a file" : "is not a file" ),
29              ( name.isDirectory() ? "is a directory" :
30                 "is not a directory" ),
31              ( name.isAbsolute() ? "is absolute path" :
32                 "is not absolute path" ), "Last modified: ",
33              name.lastModified(), "Length: ", name.length(),
34              "Path: ", name.getPath(), "Absolute path: ",
35              name.getAbsolutePath(), "Parent: ", name.getParent() );
36
37           if ( name.isDirectory() ) // output directory listing
38           {
39              String[] directory = name.list();
40              System.out.println( "\n\nDirectory contents:\n" );
41
```

Fig. 17.2 | File class used to obtain file and directory information. (Part 1 of 2.)

```
42                 for ( String directoryName : directory )
43                     System.out.println( directoryName );
44             } // end if
45         } // end outer if
46         else // not file or directory, output error message
47         {
48             System.out.printf( "%s %s", path, "does not exist." );
49         } // end else
50     } // end method analyzePath
51 } // end class FileDemonstration
```

```
Enter file or directory name: E:\Program Files\Java\jdk1.6.0_11\demo\jfc
jfc exists
is not a file
is a directory
is absolute path
Last modified: 1228404395024
Length: 4096
Path: E:\Program Files\Java\jdk1.6.0_11\demo\jfc
Absolute path: E:\Program Files\Java\jdk1.6.0_11\demo\jfc
Parent: E:\Program Files\Java\jdk1.6.0_11\demo

Directory contents:

CodePointIM
FileChooserDemo
Font2DTest
Java2D
Laffy
Metalworks
Notepad
SampleTree
Stylepad
SwingApplet
SwingSet2
SwingSet3
```

```
Enter file or directory name: C:\Program Files\Java\jdk1.6.0_11\demo\jfc
\Java2D\README.txt
README.txt exists
is a file
is not a directory
is absolute path
Last modified: 1228404384270
Length: 7518
Path: E:\Program Files\Java\jdk1.6.0_11\demo\jfc\Java2D\README.txt
Absolute path: E:\Program Files\Java\jdk1.6.0_11\demo\jfc\Java2D\README.txt
Parent: E:\Program Files\Java\jdk1.6.0_11\demo\jfc\Java2D
```

Fig. 17.2 | `File` class used to obtain file and directory information. (Part 2 of 2.)

The first output of this program demonstrates a `File` object associated with the `jfc` directory from the JDK. The second output demonstrates a `File` object associated with the `README.txt` file from the Java 2D example that comes with the JDK. In both cases, we specified an absolute path on our computer.

A **separator character** is used to separate directories and files in the path. On a Windows computer, the separator character is a backslash (\). On a UNIX system, it's a forward slash (/). Java processes both characters identically in a path name. For example, if we were to use the path

```
c:\Program Files\Java\jdk1.6.0_11\demo/jfc
```

which employs each separator character, Java would still process the path properly. When building `String`s that represent path information, use `File.separator` to obtain the local computer's proper separator character rather than explicitly using / or \. This constant returns a `String` consisting of one character—the proper separator for the system.

> **Common Programming Error 17.1**
>
> *Using \ as a directory separator rather than \\ in a string literal is a logic error. A single \ indicates that the \ followed by the next character represents an escape sequence. Use \\ to insert a \ in a string literal.*

17.4 Case Study: A Credit-Inquiry Program

Next, we use the sequential-access file processing techniques from Section 6.19 to create an object-oriented credit-inquiry program that retrieves specific data from a text file.

17.4.1 Class AccountRecord

Java imposes no structure on a file—concepts such as records do not exist as part of the Java language. Therefore, you must structure files to meet the requirements of your applications as we did in Section 6.19. The program in Fig. 6.30 created a simple sequential-access file that might be used in an accounts receivable system to keep track of the amounts owed to a company by its credit clients. For each client, the program obtained from the user an account number and the client's name and balance (i.e., the amount the client owes the company for goods and services received). Each client's data constitutes a "record" for that client. This application used the account number as the record key—the file was created and maintained in account-number order. As you recall, we assumed that the user entered the records in account-number order.

Class `AccountRecord` (Fig. 17.3) encapsulates the client record information used by several of the examples in this chapter. We declared class `AccountRecord` in the package `com.deitel.ch17` (line 3), so that it can be imported into several of this chapter's examples for reuse. (Section 8.14 provides information on compiling and using your own packages.) Class `AccountRecord` contains `private` instance variables `account`, `firstName`, `lastName` and `balance` (lines 7–10) and *set* and *get* methods for accessing these fields. Though the *set* methods do not validate the data in this example, they should do so in a industrial-strength system.

```
1   // Fig. 17.3: AccountRecord.java
2   // AccountRecord class maintains information for one account.
3   package com.deitel.ch17; // packaged for reuse
```

Fig. 17.3 | AccountRecord class maintains information for one account. (Part 1 of 3.)

```
4
5   public class AccountRecord
6   {
7      private int account;
8      private String firstName;
9      private String lastName;
10     private double balance;
11
12     // no-argument constructor calls other constructor with default values
13     public AccountRecord()
14     {
15        this( 0, "", "", 0.0 ); // call four-argument constructor
16     } // end no-argument AccountRecord constructor
17
18     // initialize a record
19     public AccountRecord( int acct, String first, String last, double bal )
20     {
21        setAccount( acct );
22        setFirstName( first );
23        setLastName( last );
24        setBalance( bal );
25     } // end four-argument AccountRecord constructor
26
27     // set account number
28     public void setAccount( int acct )
29     {
30        account = acct;
31     } // end method setAccount
32
33     // get account number
34     public int getAccount()
35     {
36        return account;
37     } // end method getAccount
38
39     // set first name
40     public void setFirstName( String first )
41     {
42        firstName = first;
43     } // end method setFirstName
44
45     // get first name
46     public String getFirstName()
47     {
48        return firstName;
49     } // end method getFirstName
50
51     // set last name
52     public void setLastName( String last )
53     {
54        lastName = last;
55     } // end method setLastName
56
```

Fig. 17.3 | AccountRecord class maintains information for one account. (Part 2 of 3.)

```
57      // get last name
58      public String getLastName()
59      {
60         return lastName;
61      } // end method getLastName
62
63      // set balance
64      public void setBalance( double bal )
65      {
66         balance = bal;
67      } // end method setBalance
68
69      // get balance
70      public double getBalance()
71      {
72         return balance;
73      } // end method getBalance
74   } // end class AccountRecord
```

Fig. 17.3 | AccountRecord class maintains information for one account. (Part 3 of 3.)

To compile class AccountRecord, open a command window, change directories to this chapter's fig17_03 directory (which contains AccountRecord.java), then type:

```
javac -d .. AccountRecord.java
```

This places AccountRecord.class in its package directory structure and places the package in the ch17 folder that contains all the examples for this chapter. When you compile class AccountRecord (or any other classes that will be reused in this chapter), you should place them in a common directory. When you compile or execute classes that use class AccountRecord (e.g., CreditInquiryTest in Fig. 17.6), you must specify the command-line argument -classpath to both javac and java, as in

```
javac -classpath .;c:\examples\ch17 CreditInquiryTest.java
java -classpath .;c:\examples\ch17 CreditInquiryTest
```

Note that the current directory (specified with .) is included in the classpath to ensure that the compiler can locate other classes in the same directory as the class being compiled. The path separator used in the preceding commands must be appropriate for your platform— a semicolon (;) on Windows and a colon (:) on UNIX/Linux/Mac OS X. The preceding commands assume that the package containing AccountRecord is located at in the directory C:\examples\ch17 on a Windows computer.

17.4.2 Credit-Inquiry Program

To retrieve data sequentially from a file, programs start from the beginning of the file and read all the data consecutively until the desired information is found. It might be necessary to process the file sequentially several times (from the beginning of the file) during the execution of a program. Class Scanner does not allow repositioning to the beginning of the file. If it's necessary to read the file again, the program must close the file and reopen it.

The program in Figs. 17.4–17.6 allows a credit manager to obtain lists of customers with zero balances (i.e., customers who do not owe any money), customers with credit balances (i.e., customers to whom the company owes money) and customers with debit balances (i.e., customers who owe the company money for goods and services received). A credit balance is a negative amount, a debit balance a positive amount.

MenuOption *Enumeration*

We begin by creating an enum type (Fig. 17.4) to define the different menu options the user will have. The options and their values are listed in lines 7–10. Method getValue (lines 19–22) retrieves the value of a specific enum constant.

```java
1   // Fig. 17.4: MenuOption.java
2   // Enumeration for the credit-inquiry program's options.
3
4   public enum MenuOption
5   {
6      // declare contents of enum type
7      ZERO_BALANCE( 1 ),
8      CREDIT_BALANCE( 2 ),
9      DEBIT_BALANCE( 3 ),
10     END( 4 );
11
12     private final int value; // current menu option
13
14     MenuOption( int valueOption )
15     {
16        value = valueOption;
17     } // end MenuOptions enum constructor
18
19     public int getValue()
20     {
21        return value;
22     } // end method getValue
23  } // end enum MenuOption
```

Fig. 17.4 | Enumeration for the credit-inquiry program's menu options.

CreditInquiry *Class*

Figure 17.5 contains the functionality for the credit-inquiry program, and Fig. 17.6 contains the main method that executes the program. The program displays a text menu and allows the credit manager to enter one of three options to obtain credit information. Option 1 (ZERO_BALANCE) displays accounts with zero balances. Option 2 (CREDIT_BALANCE) displays accounts with credit balances. Option 3 (DEBIT_BALANCE) displays accounts with debit balances. Option 4 (END) terminates program execution. As you study the code, notice that, unlike the examples in Section 6.19, we use exception handling here to deal with the various problems that can occur when manipulating files and obtaining user input.

```java
1   // Fig. 17.5: CreditInquiry.java
2   // This program reads a file sequentially and displays the
3   // contents based on the type of account the user requests
4   // (credit balance, debit balance or zero balance).
5   import java.io.File;
6   import java.io.FileNotFoundException;
```

Fig. 17.5 | Credit-inquiry program. (Part 1 of 4.)

```
 7   import java.lang.IllegalStateException;
 8   import java.util.NoSuchElementException;
 9   import java.util.Scanner;
10
11   import com.deitel.ch17.AccountRecord;
12
13   public class CreditInquiry
14   {
15      private MenuOption accountType;
16      private Scanner input;
17      private final static MenuOption[] choices = { MenuOption.ZERO_BALANCE,
18         MenuOption.CREDIT_BALANCE, MenuOption.DEBIT_BALANCE,
19         MenuOption.END };
20
21      // read records from file and display only records of appropriate type
22      private void readRecords()
23      {
24         // object to store data that will be written to file
25         AccountRecord record = new AccountRecord();
26
27         try // read records
28         {
29            // open file to read from beginning
30            input = new Scanner( new File( "clients.txt" ) );
31
32            while ( input.hasNext() ) // input the values from the file
33            {
34               record.setAccount( input.nextInt() ); // read account number
35               record.setFirstName( input.next() ); // read first name
36               record.setLastName( input.next() ); // read last name
37               record.setBalance( input.nextDouble() ); // read balance
38
39               // if proper acount type, display record
40               if ( shouldDisplay( record.getBalance() ) )
41                  System.out.printf( "%-10d%-12s%-12s%10.2f\n",
42                     record.getAccount(), record.getFirstName(),
43                     record.getLastName(), record.getBalance() );
44            } // end while
45         } // end try
46         catch ( NoSuchElementException elementException )
47         {
48            System.err.println( "File improperly formed." );
49            input.close();
50            System.exit( 1 );
51         } // end catch
52         catch ( IllegalStateException stateException )
53         {
54            System.err.println( "Error reading from file." );
55            System.exit( 1 );
56         } // end catch
57         catch ( FileNotFoundException fileNotFoundException )
58         {
59            System.err.println( "File cannot be found." );
```

Fig. 17.5 | Credit-inquiry program. (Part 2 of 4.)

```
60              System.exit( 1 );
61          } // end catch
62          finally
63          {
64              if ( input != null )
65                  input.close(); // close the Scanner and the file
66          } // end finally
67      } // end method readRecords
68
69      // use record type to determine if record should be displayed
70      private boolean shouldDisplay( double balance )
71      {
72          if ( ( accountType == MenuOption.CREDIT_BALANCE )
73              && ( balance < 0 ) )
74              return true;
75
76          else if ( ( accountType == MenuOption.DEBIT_BALANCE )
77              && ( balance > 0 ) )
78              return true;
79
80          else if ( ( accountType == MenuOption.ZERO_BALANCE )
81              && ( balance == 0 ) )
82              return true;
83
84          return false;
85      } // end method shouldDisplay
86
87      // obtain request from user
88      private MenuOption getRequest()
89      {
90          Scanner textIn = new Scanner( System.in );
91          int request = 1;
92
93          // display request options
94          System.out.printf( "\n%s\n%s\n%s\n%s\n%s\n",
95              "Enter request", " 1 - List accounts with zero balances",
96              " 2 - List accounts with credit balances",
97              " 3 - List accounts with debit balances", " 4 - End of run" );
98
99          try // attempt to input menu choice
100         {
101             do // input user request
102             {
103                 System.out.print( "\n? " );
104                 request = textIn.nextInt();
105             } while ( ( request < 1 ) || ( request > 4 ) );
106         } // end try
107         catch ( NoSuchElementException elementException )
108         {
109             System.err.println( "Invalid input." );
110             System.exit( 1 );
111         } // end catch
112
```

Fig. 17.5 | Credit-inquiry program. (Part 3 of 4.)

```
113          return choices[ request - 1 ]; // return enum value for option
114     } // end method getRequest
115
116     public void processRequests()
117     {
118        // get user's request (e.g., zero, credit or debit balance)
119        accountType = getRequest();
120
121        while ( accountType != MenuOption.END )
122        {
123           switch ( accountType )
124           {
125              case ZERO_BALANCE:
126                 System.out.println( "\nAccounts with zero balances:\n" );
127                 break;
128              case CREDIT_BALANCE:
129                 System.out.println( "\nAccounts with credit balances:\n" );
130                 break;
131              case DEBIT_BALANCE:
132                 System.out.println( "\nAccounts with debit balances:\n" );
133                 break;
134           } // end switch
135
136           readRecords();
137           accountType = getRequest();
138        } // end while
139     } // end method processRequests
140  } // end class CreditInquiry
```

Fig. 17.5 | Credit-inquiry program. (Part 4 of 4.)

```
1   // Fig. 17.6: CreditInquiryTest.java
2   // This program tests class CreditInquiry.
3
4   public class CreditInquiryTest
5   {
6      public static void main( String[] args )
7      {
8         CreditInquiry application = new CreditInquiry();
9         application.processRequests();
10     } // end main
11  } // end class CreditInquiryTest
```

```
Enter request
 1 - List accounts with zero balances
 2 - List accounts with credit balances
 3 - List accounts with debit balances
 4 - End of run

? 1

Accounts with zero balances:
300        Pam          White              0.00
```

Fig. 17.6 | Testing the CreditInquiry class. (Part 1 of 2.)

```
Enter request
  1 - List accounts with zero balances
  2 - List accounts with credit balances
  3 - List accounts with debit balances
  4 - End of run

? 2

Accounts with credit balances:
200         Steve        Doe            -345.67
400         Sam          Stone          -42.16

Enter request
  1 - List accounts with zero balances
  2 - List accounts with credit balances
  3 - List accounts with debit balances
  4 - End of run

? 3

Accounts with debit balances:
100         Bob          Jones           24.98
500         Sue          Rich           224.62

? 4
```

Fig. 17.6 | Testing the CreditInquiry class. (Part 2 of 2.)

The record information is collected by reading through the file and determining if each record satisfies the criteria for the selected account type. Method processRequests (lines 116–139 of Fig. 17.5) calls method getRequest to display the menu options (line 119), translates the number typed by the user into a MenuOption and stores the result in MenuOption variable accountType. Lines 121–138 loop until the user specifies that the program should terminate. Lines 123–134 display a header for the current set of records to be output to the screen. Line 136 calls method readRecords (lines 22–67), which loops through the file and reads every record.

Line 30 of method readRecords opens the file for reading with a Scanner. The file will be opened for reading with a new Scanner object each time this method is called, so that we can again read from the beginning of the file. Lines 57–61 handle the **FileNot-FoundException**, which occurs if the file cannot be opened from the specified location.

Lines 34–37 read a record. Each statement throws a **NoSuchElementException** (handled in lines 46–51) if the data is in the wrong format (e.g., a String when an int is expected) or if there is no more data to input. Also, if the Scanner was closed before the data was input, an **IllegalStateException** occurs (handled in lines 52–56).

Notice that we must read each piece of data in the record with a separate method call on the Scanner object—we read an int for the account number, two Strings for the first and last names, and a double for the balance. Unfortunately, there is no convenient way to read all four fields at once and convert them into an AccountRecord object using text-file processing. In Section 17.5, we'll show how to write and read entire objects using Java's object serialization mechanism.

Line 40 calls method shouldDisplay (lines 70–85) to determine whether the current record satisfies the account tpe requested. If shouldDisplay returns true, the program displays the account information. When the end-of-file marker is reached, the loop terminates and line 65 calls the Scanner's close method to close the Scanner and the file.

Notice that this occurs in a `finally` block, which will execute whether or not the file was successfully read. Once all the records have been read, control returns to method `process-Requests` and `getRequest` is again called (line 137) to retrieve the user's next menu option. Figure 17.6 contains method `main`, and calls method `processRequests` in line 9.

Using Method `exit` *of Class* `System`
Notice that the exception handlers in lines 46–61 each call `static` method `System.exit` and pass the value 1. This method terminates the application. An argument of 0 to method `exit` indicates successful program termination. A nonzero value, such as 1 in this example, normally indicates that an error has occurred. This value is passed to the command window that executed the program. The argument is useful if the program is executed from a **batch file** on Windows systems or a **shell script** on UNIX/Linux/Mac OS X systems. Batch files and shell scripts offer a convenient way of executing several programs in sequence. When the first program ends, the next program begins execution. It's possible to use the argument to method `exit` in a batch file or shell script to determine whether other programs should execute. For more information on batch files or shell scripts, see your operating system's documentation.

17.4.3 Updating Sequential-Access Files

The data in many sequential files cannot be modified without the risk of destroying other data in the file. For example, if the name "White" needed to be changed to "Worthington," the old name cannot simply be overwritten, because the new name requires more space. The record for `White` was written to the file as

```
300 Pam White 0.00
```

If the record is rewritten beginning at the same location in the file using the new name, the record will be

```
300 Pam Worthington 0.00
```

The new record is larger (has more characters) than the original record. The characters beyond the second "o" in "Worthington" will overwrite the beginning of the next sequential record in the file. The problem here is that fields in a text file—and hence records—can vary in size. For example, 7, 14, –117, 2074 and 27383 are all `int`s stored in the same number of bytes (4) internally, but they're different-sized fields when displayed on the screen or written to a file as text. Therefore, records in a sequential-access file are not usually updated in place. Instead, the entire file is usually rewritten. To make the preceding name change, the records before `300 Pam White 0.00` would be copied to a new file, the new record (which can be of a different size than the one it replaces) would be written and the records after `300 Pam White 0.00` would be copied to the new file. Rewriting the entire file is uneconomical to update just one record, but reasonable if a substantial number of records need to be updated.

17.5 Object Serialization

In Section 17.4, we demonstrated how to write the individual fields of an `AccountRecord` object into a file as text, and how to read those fields from a file and place their values into an `AccountRecord` object in memory. In the examples, `AccountRecord` was used to aggregate the information for one record. When the instance variables for an `AccountRecord` were output to a disk file, certain information was lost, such as the type of each value. For instance, if the value "3" is read from a file, there is no way to tell whether it came from an int, a String or a double. We have only data, not type information, on a disk. If the program that is going to read this data "knows" what object type the data corresponds to, then the data is simply read into objects of that type. For example, in Section 17.4, we know that we are inputting an int (the account number), followed by two Strings (the first and last name) and a double (the balance). We also know that these values are separated by spaces, with only one record on each line. Sometimes we'll not know exactly how the data is stored in a file. In such cases, we want to read or write an entire object from a file. Java provides such a mechanism, called **object serialization**. A so-called **serialized object** is an object represented as a sequence of bytes that includes the object's data as well as information about the object's type and the types of data stored in the object. After a serialized object has been written into a file, it can be read from the file and **deserialized**—that is, the type information and bytes that represent the object and its data can be used to recreate the object in memory.

Software Engineering Observation 17.1

The serialization mechanism makes exact copies of objects. This makes it a simple way to clone objects without having to override Object method clone.

Classes *ObjectInputStream* and *ObjectOutputStream*

Classes ObjectInputStream and ObjectOutputStream, which respectively implement the **ObjectInput** and **ObjectOutput** interfaces, enable entire objects to be read from or written to a stream (possibly a file). To use serialization with files, we initialize ObjectInputStream and ObjectOutputStream objects with stream objects that read from and write to files—objects of classes FileInputStream and FileOutputStream, respectively. Initializing stream objects with other stream objects in this manner is sometimes called **wrapping**—the new stream object being created wraps the stream object specified as a constructor argument. To wrap a FileInputStream in an ObjectInputStream, for instance, we pass the FileInputStream object to the ObjectInputStream's constructor.

Interfaces *ObjectOutput* and *ObjectInput*

The ObjectOutput interface contains method **writeObject**, which takes an Object as an argument and writes its information to an OutputStream. A class that implements interface ObjectOuput (such as ObjectOutputStream) declares this method and ensures that the object being output implements interface Serializable (discussed shortly). Correspondingly, the ObjectInput interface contains method **readObject**, which reads and returns a reference to an Object from an InputStream. After an object has been read, its reference can be cast to the object's actual type. As you'll see in Chapter 27, applications that communicate via a network, such as the Internet, can also transmit entire objects across the network.

17.5.1 Creating a Sequential-Access File Using Object Serialization

This section and Section 17.5.2 create and manipulate sequential-access files using object serialization. The object serialization we show here is performed with byte-based streams, so the sequential files created and manipulated will be binary files. Recall that binary files typically cannot be viewed in standard text editors. For this reason, we write a separate application that knows how to read and display serialized objects. We begin by creating and writing serialized objects to a sequential-access file. The example is similar to the one in Section 17.4, so we focus only on the new features.

Defining Class *AccountRecordSerializable*

Let's begin by modifying our AccountRecord class so that objects of this class can be serialized. Class AccountRecordSerializable (Fig. 17.7) implements interface **Serializable** (line 7), which allows objects of AccountRecordSerializable to be serialized and deserialized with ObjectOutputStreams and ObjectInputStreams, respectively. Interface Serializable is a tagging interface. Such an interface does not contain methods. A class that implements Serializable is tagged as being a Serializable object. This is important, because an ObjectOutputStream will not output an object unless it *is a* Serializable object, which is the case for any object of a class that implements Serializable.

```java
1  // Fig. 17.7: AccountRecordSerializable.java
2  // AccountRecordSerializable class for serializable objects.
3  package com.deitel.ch17; // packaged for reuse
4
5  import java.io.Serializable;
6
7  public class AccountRecordSerializable implements Serializable
8  {
9     private int account;
10    private String firstName;
11    private String lastName;
12    private double balance;
13
14    // no-argument constructor calls other constructor with default values
15    public AccountRecordSerializable()
16    {
17       this( 0, "", "", 0.0 );
18    } // end no-argument AccountRecordSerializable constructor
19
20    // four-argument constructor initializes a record
21    public AccountRecordSerializable(
22       int acct, String first, String last, double bal )
23    {
24       setAccount( acct );
25       setFirstName( first );
26       setLastName( last );
27       setBalance( bal );
28    } // end four-argument AccountRecordSerializable constructor
29
30    // set account number
31    public void setAccount( int acct )
32    {
33       account = acct;
34    } // end method setAccount
35
36    // get account number
37    public int getAccount()
38    {
```

Fig. 17.7 | AccountRecordSerializable class for serializable objects. (Part 1 of 2.)

```
39        return account;
40     } // end method getAccount
41
42     // set first name
43     public void setFirstName( String first )
44     {
45        firstName = first;
46     } // end method setFirstName
47
48     // get first name
49     public String getFirstName()
50     {
51        return firstName;
52     } // end method getFirstName
53
54     // set last name
55     public void setLastName( String last )
56     {
57        lastName = last;
58     } // end method setLastName
59
60     // get last name
61     public String getLastName()
62     {
63        return lastName;
64     } // end method getLastName
65
66     // set balance
67     public void setBalance( double bal )
68     {
69        balance = bal;
70     } // end method setBalance
71
72     // get balance
73     public double getBalance()
74     {
75        return balance;
76     } // end method getBalance
77  } // end class AccountRecordSerializable
```

Fig. 17.7 | AccountRecordSerializable class for serializable objects. (Part 2 of 2.)

In a class that implements Serializable, the programmer must ensure that every instance variable is a Serializable type. Otherwise, it must be declared **transient** to indicate that it's not Serializable and should be ignored during the serialization process. By default, all primitive-type variables are serializable. For reference-type variables, you must check the class's documentation (and possibly its superclasses) to ensure that the type is Serializable. For example, Strings are Serializable. By default, arrays are serializable; however, in a reference-type array, the referenced objects may or may not be serializable. Class AccountRecordSerializable contains private data members account, firstName, lastName and balance—all of which are Serializable. This class also provides public *get* and *set* methods for accessing the private fields.

Writing Serialized Objects to a Sequential-Access File

Now let's discuss the code that creates the sequential-access file (Figs. 17.8–17.9). We concentrate only on new concepts here. A program can open a file by creating an object of stream class `FileInputStream` or `FileOutputStream`. In this example, the file is to be opened for output, so the program creates a `FileOutputStream` (line 21 of Fig. 17.8). The `String` argument that is passed to the `FileOutputStream`'s constructor represents the name and path of the file to be opened. Existing files that are opened for output in this manner are truncated. Note that the `.ser` file extension is used—we use this file extension for binary files that contain serialized objects.

Common Programming Error 17.2

It's a logic error to open an existing file for output when, in fact, you wish to preserve the file. Class `FileOutputStream` provides an overloaded constructor that enables you to open a file and append data to the end of the file. This will preserve the contents of the file.

```java
1   // Fig. 17.8: CreateSequentialFile.java
2   // Writing objects sequentially to a file with class ObjectOutputStream.
3   import java.io.FileOutputStream;
4   import java.io.IOException;
5   import java.io.ObjectOutputStream;
6   import java.util.NoSuchElementException;
7   import java.util.Scanner;
8
9   import com.deitel.ch17.AccountRecordSerializable;
10
11  public class CreateSequentialFile
12  {
13     private ObjectOutputStream output; // outputs data to file
14
15     // allow user to specify file name
16     public void openFile()
17     {
18        try // open file
19        {
20           output = new ObjectOutputStream(
21              new FileOutputStream( "clients.ser" ) );
22        } // end try
23        catch ( IOException ioException )
24        {
25           System.err.println( "Error opening file." );
26        } // end catch
27     } // end method openFile
28
29     // add records to file
30     public void addRecords()
31     {
32        AccountRecordSerializable record; // object to be written to file
33        int accountNumber = 0; // account number for record object
34        String firstName; // first name for record object
35        String lastName; // last name for record object
36        double balance; // balance for record object
```

Fig. 17.8 | Sequential file created using `ObjectOutputStream`. (Part 1 of 3.)

```
37
38          Scanner input = new Scanner( System.in );
39
40          System.out.printf( "%s\n%s\n%s\n%s\n\n",
41             "To terminate input, type the end-of-file indicator ",
42             "when you are prompted to enter input.",
43             "On UNIX/Linux/Mac OS X type <ctrl> d then press Enter",
44             "On Windows type <ctrl> z then press Enter" );
45
46          System.out.printf( "%s\n%s",
47             "Enter account number (> 0), first name, last name and balance.",
48             "? " );
49
50          while ( input.hasNext() ) // loop until end-of-file indicator
51          {
52             try // output values to file
53             {
54                accountNumber = input.nextInt(); // read account number
55                firstName = input.next(); // read first name
56                lastName = input.next(); // read last name
57                balance = input.nextDouble(); // read balance
58
59                if ( accountNumber > 0 )
60                {
61                   // create new record
62                   record = new AccountRecordSerializable( accountNumber,
63                      firstName, lastName, balance );
64                   output.writeObject( record ); // output record
65                } // end if
66                else
67                {
68                   System.out.println(
69                      "Account number must be greater than 0." );
70                } // end else
71             } // end try
72             catch ( IOException ioException )
73             {
74                System.err.println( "Error writing to file." );
75                return;
76             } // end catch
77             catch ( NoSuchElementException elementException )
78             {
79                System.err.println( "Invalid input. Please try again." );
80                input.nextLine(); // discard input so user can try again
81             } // end catch
82
83             System.out.printf( "%s %s\n%s", "Enter account number (>0),",
84                "first name, last name and balance.", "? " );
85          } // end while
86       } // end method addRecords
87
88       // close file and terminate application
89       public void closeFile()
90       {
```

Fig. 17.8 | Sequential file created using `ObjectOutputStream`. (Part 2 of 3.)

```
 91            try // close file
 92            {
 93               if ( output != null )
 94                  output.close();
 95            } // end try
 96            catch ( IOException ioException )
 97            {
 98               System.err.println( "Error closing file." );
 99               System.exit( 1 );
100            } // end catch
101         } // end method closeFile
102      } // end class CreateSequentialFile
```

Fig. 17.8 | Sequential file created using `ObjectOutputStream`. (Part 3 of 3.)

```
 1   // Fig. 17.9: CreateSequentialFileTest.java
 2   // Testing class CreateSequentialFile.
 3
 4   public class CreateSequentialFileTest
 5   {
 6      public static void main( String[] args )
 7      {
 8         CreateSequentialFile application = new CreateSequentialFile();
 9
10         application.openFile();
11         application.addRecords();
12         application.closeFile();
13      } // end main
14   } // end class CreateSequentialFileTest
```

```
To terminate input, type the end-of-file indicator
when you are prompted to enter input.
On UNIX/Linux/Mac OS X type <ctrl> d then press Enter
On Windows type <ctrl> z then press Enter

Enter account number (> 0), first name, last name and balance.
? 100 Bob Jones 24.98
Enter account number (> 0), first name, last name and balance.
? 200 Steve Doe -345.67
Enter account number (> 0), first name, last name and balance.
? 300 Pam White 0.00
Enter account number (> 0), first name, last name and balance.
? 400 Sam Stone -42.16
Enter account number (> 0), first name, last name and balance.
? 500 Sue Rich 224.62
Enter account number (> 0), first name, last name and balance.
? ^Z
```

Fig. 17.9 | Testing class `CreateSequentialFile`.

Class `FileOutputStream` provides methods for writing byte arrays and individual bytes to a file, but we wish to write objects to a file. For this reason, we wrap a `FileOut-`

putStream in an ObjectOutputStream by passing the new FileOutputStream object to the ObjectOutputStream's constructor (lines 20–21). The ObjectOutputStream object uses the FileOutputStream object to write objects into the file. Lines 20–21 may throw an **IOException** if a problem occurs while opening the file (e.g., when a file is opened for writing on a drive with insufficient space or when a read-only file is opened for writing). If so, the program displays an error message (lines 23–26). If no exception occurs, the file is open, and variable output can be used to write objects to it.

This program assumes that data is input correctly and in the proper record-number order. Method addRecords (lines 30–86) performs the write operation. Lines 62–63 create an AccountRecordSerializable object from the data entered by the user. Line 64 calls ObjectOutputStream method writeObject to write the record object to the output file. Note that only one statement is required to write the entire object.

Method closeFile (lines 89–101) calls ObjectOutputStream method **close** on output to close both the ObjectOutputStream and its underlying FileOutputStream (line 94). Note that the call to method close is contained in a try block. Method close throws an IOException if the file cannot be closed properly. In this case, it's important to notify the user that the information in the file might be corrupted. When using wrapped streams, closing the outermost stream also closes the underlying file.

In the sample execution for the program in Fig. 17.9, we entered information for five accounts—the same information shown in Fig. 6.32. The program does not show how the data records actually appear in the file. Remember that now we are using binary files, which are not humanly readable. To verify that the file has been created successfully, the next section presents a program to read the file's contents.

17.5.2 Reading and Deserializing Data from a Sequential-Access File

The preceding section showed how to create a file for sequential access using object serialization. In this section, we discuss how to read serialized data sequentially from a file.

The program in Figs. 17.10–17.11 reads records from a file created by the program in Section 17.5.1 and displays the contents. The program opens the file for input by creating a FileInputStream object (line 21). The name of the file to open is specified as an argument to the FileInputStream constructor. In Fig. 17.8, we wrote objects to the file, using an ObjectOutputStream object. Data must be read from the file in the same format in which it was written. Therefore, we use an ObjectInputStream wrapped around a FileInputStream in this program (lines 20–21). If no exceptions occur when opening the file, variable input can be used to read objects from the file.

```
1   // Fig. 17.10: ReadSequentialFile.java
2   // Reading a file of objects sequentially with ObjectInputStream
3   // and displaying each record.
4   import java.io.EOFException;
5   import java.io.FileInputStream;
6   import java.io.IOException;
7   import java.io.ObjectInputStream;
8
9   import com.deitel.ch17.AccountRecordSerializable;
```

Fig. 17.10 | Reading a file of objects sequentially with ObjectInputStream and displaying each record. (Part 1 of 3.)

```
10
11   public class ReadSequentialFile
12   {
13      private ObjectInputStream input;
14
15      // enable user to select file to open
16      public void openFile()
17      {
18         try // open file
19         {
20            input = new ObjectInputStream(
21               new FileInputStream( "clients.ser" ) );
22         } // end try
23         catch ( IOException ioException )
24         {
25            System.err.println( "Error opening file." );
26         } // end catch
27      } // end method openFile
28
29      // read record from file
30      public void readRecords()
31      {
32         AccountRecordSerializable record;
33         System.out.printf( "%-10s%-12s%-12s%10s\n", "Account",
34            "First Name", "Last Name", "Balance" );
35
36         try // input the values from the file
37         {
38            while ( true )
39            {
40               record = ( AccountRecordSerializable ) input.readObject();
41
42               // display record contents
43               System.out.printf( "%-10d%-12s%-12s%10.2f\n",
44                  record.getAccount(), record.getFirstName(),
45                  record.getLastName(), record.getBalance() );
46            } // end while
47         } // end try
48         catch ( EOFException endOfFileException )
49         {
50            return; // end of file was reached
51         } // end catch
52         catch ( ClassNotFoundException classNotFoundException )
53         {
54            System.err.println( "Unable to create object." );
55         } // end catch
56         catch ( IOException ioException )
57         {
58            System.err.println( "Error during read from file." );
59         } // end catch
60      } // end method readRecords
61
```

Fig. 17.10 | Reading a file of objects sequentially with `ObjectInputStream` and displaying each record. (Part 2 of 3.)

```
62      // close file and terminate application
63      public void closeFile()
64      {
65         try // close file and exit
66         {
67            if ( input != null )
68               input.close();
69         } // end try
70         catch ( IOException ioException )
71         {
72            System.err.println( "Error closing file." );
73            System.exit( 1 );
74         } // end catch
75      } // end method closeFile
76   } // end class ReadSequentialFile
```

Fig. 17.10 | Reading a file of objects sequentially with `ObjectInputStream` and displaying each record. (Part 3 of 3.)

The program reads records from the file in method readRecords (lines 30–60). Line 40 calls ObjectInputStream method readObject to read an Object from the file. To use AccountRecordSerializable-specific methods, we downcast the returned Object to type AccountRecordSerializable. Method readObject throws an **EOFException** (processed at lines 48–51) if an attempt is made to read beyond the end of the file. Method readObject throws a ClassNotFoundException if the class for the object being read cannot be located. This may occur if the file is accessed on a computer that does not have the class. Figure 17.11 contains method main (lines 6–13), which opens the file, calls method read-Records and closes the file.

```
1    // Fig. 17.11: ReadSequentialFileTest.java
2    // Testing class ReadSequentialFile.
3
4    public class ReadSequentialFileTest
5    {
6       public static void main( String[] args )
7       {
8          ReadSequentialFile application = new ReadSequentialFile();
9
10         application.openFile();
11         application.readRecords();
12         application.closeFile();
13      } // end main
14   } // end class ReadSequentialFileTest
```

```
Account    First Name   Last Name     Balance
100        Bob          Jones           24.98
200        Steve        Doe           -345.67
300        Pam          White           0.00
400        Sam          Stone         -42.16
500        Sue          Rich          224.62
```

Fig. 17.11 | Testing class ReadSequentialFile.

17.6 Additional java.io Classes

This section overviews additional interfaces and classes (from package java.io) for byte-based input and output streams and character-based input and output streams.

17.6.1 Interfaces and Classes for Byte-Based Input and Output

InputStream and OutputStream are abstract classes that declare methods for performing byte-based input and output, respectively. We used various concrete subclasses FileInputStream InputStream and OutputStream to manipulate files in this chapter.

Pipe Streams

Pipes are synchronized communication channels between threads. We discuss threads in Chapter 26, Multithreading. Java provides **PipedOutputStream** (a subclass of OutputStream) and **PipedInputStream** (a subclass of InputStream) to establish pipes between two threads in a program. One thread sends data to another by writing to a PipedOutputStream. The target thread reads information from the pipe via a PipedInputStream.

Filter Streams

A **FilterInputStream** filters an InputStream, and a FilterOutputStream filters an OutputStream. Filtering means simply that the filter stream provides additional functionality, such as aggregating data bytes into meaningful primitive-type units. FilterInputStream and FilterOutputStream are typically extended, so some of their filtering capabilities are provided by their subclasses.

A **PrintStream** (a subclass of FilterOutputStream) performs text output to the specified stream. Actually, we've been using PrintStream output throughout the text to this point—System.out and System.err are PrintStream objects.

Data Streams

Reading data as raw bytes is fast, but crude. Usually, programs read data as aggregates of bytes that form ints, floats, doubles and so on. Java programs can use several classes to input and output data in aggregate form.

Interface DataInput describes methods for reading primitive types from an input stream. Classes **DataInputStream** and RandomAccessFile each implement this interface to read sets of bytes and view them as primitive-type values. Interface DataInput includes methods such as readBoolean, readByte, readChar, readDouble, readFloat, readFully (for byte arrays), readInt, readLong, readShort, readUnsignedByte, readUnsignedShort, readUTF (for reading Unicode characters encoded by Java—we discuss UTF encoding in Appendix L) and skipBytes.

Interface DataOutput describes a set of methods for writing primitive types to an output stream. Classes **DataOutputStream** (a subclass of FilterOutputStream) and RandomAccessFile each implement this interface to write primitive-type values as bytes. Interface DataOutput includes overloaded versions of method write (for a byte or for a byte array) and methods writeBoolean, writeByte, writeBytes, writeChar, writeChars (for Unicode Strings), writeDouble, writeFloat, writeInt, writeLong, writeShort and writeUTF (to output text modified for Unicode).

Buffered Streams

Buffering is an I/O-performance-enhancement technique. With a **BufferedOutputStream** (a subclass of class FilterOutputStream), each output statement does not necessarily result in an actual physical transfer of data to the output device (which is a slow operation compared to processor and main memory speeds). Rather, each output operation is directed to a region in memory called a **buffer** that is large enough to hold the data of many output operations. Then, actual transfer to the output device is performed in one large **physical output operation** each time the buffer fills. The output operations directed to the output buffer in memory are often called **logical output operations**. With a BufferedOutputStream, a partially filled buffer can be forced out to the device at any time by invoking the stream object's `flush` method.

Using buffering can greatly increase performance. Typical I/O operations are extremely slow compared with the speed of accessing data in computer memory. Buffering reduces the number of I/O operations by first combining smaller outputs together in memory. The number of actual physical I/O operations is small compared with the number of I/O requests issued by the program. Thus, the program that is using buffering is more efficient.

Performance Tip 17.1

Buffered I/O can yield significant performance improvements over unbuffered I/O.

With a `BufferedInputStream` (a subclass of class `FilterInputStream`), many "logical" chunks of data from a file are read as one large **physical input operation** into a memory buffer. As a program requests each new chunk of data, it's taken from the buffer. (This procedure is sometimes referred to as a **logical input operation**.) When the buffer is empty, the next actual physical input operation from the input device is performed to read in the next group of "logical" chunks of data. Thus, the number of actual physical input operations is small compared with the number of read requests issued by the program.

Memory-Based **byte** Array Steams

Java stream I/O includes capabilities for inputting from byte arrays in memory and outputting to byte arrays in memory. A `ByteArrayInputStream` (a subclass of `InputStream`) reads from a byte array in memory. A `ByteArrayOutputStream` (a subclass of `Output-Stream`) outputs to a byte array in memory. One use of byte-array I/O is data validation. A program can input an entire line at a time from the input stream into a byte array. Then a validation routine can scrutinize the contents of the byte array and correct the data if necessary. Finally, the program can proceed to input from the byte array, "knowing" that the input data is in the proper format. Outputting to a byte array is a nice way to take advantage of the powerful output-formatting capabilities of Java streams. For example, data can be stored in a byte array, using the same formatting that will be displayed at a later time, and the byte array can then be output to a file to preserve the formatting.

Sequencing Input from Multiple Streams

A `SequenceInputStream` (a subclass of `InputStream`) logically concatenates several Input-Streams—the program sees the group as one continuous `InputStream`. When the program reaches the end of a stream, that stream closes, and the next one in the sequence opens.

17.6.2 Interfaces and Classes for Character-Based Input and Output

In addition to the byte-based streams, Java provides the `Reader` and `Writer` abstract classes, which are Unicode two-byte, character-based streams. Most of the byte-based streams have corresponding character-based concrete `Reader` or `Writer` classes.

Character-Based Buffering Readers and Writers

Classes **BufferedReader** (a subclass of abstract class Reader) and **BufferedWriter** (a subclass of abstract class Writer) enable buffering for character-based streams. Remember that character-based streams use Unicode characters—such streams can process data in any language that the Unicode character set represents.

Memory-Based **char** Array Readers and Writers

Classes **CharArrayReader** and **CharArrayWriter** read characters from and write them to a char array, respectively. A **LineNumberReader** (a subclass of BufferedReader) is a buffered character stream that keeps track of the number of lines read—newlines, returns and carriage-return–line-feed combinations increment the line count. Keeping track of line numbers can be useful if the program needs to inform the reader of an error on a specific line.

Character-Based File, Pipe and String Readers and Writers

An InputStream can be converted to a Reader via class **InputStreamReader**. Similarly, an OuputStream can be converted to a Writer via class **OutputStreamWriter**. Class File-Reader (a subclass of InputStreamReader) and class FileWriter (a subclass of Output-StreamWriter) read characters from and write characters to a file, respectively. Class **PipedReader** and class **PipedWriter** implement piped-character streams for transferring data between threads. Class **StringReader** and **StringWriter** read characters from and write characters to Strings, respectively. A PrintWriter writes characters to a stream.

17.7 Opening Files with `JFileChooser`

Class `JFileChooser` displays a dialog (known as the `JFileChooser` dialog) that enables the user to easily select files or directories. To demonstrate the `JFileChooser` dialog, we enhance the example in Section 17.3, as shown in Figs. 17.12–17.13. The example now contains a graphical user interface, but still displays the same data as before. The constructor calls method `analyzePath` in line 34. This method then calls method `getFile` in line 68 to retrieve the `File` object.

Method `getFile` is defined in lines 38–62 of Fig. 17.12. Line 41 creates a `JFileChooser` and assigns its reference to `fileChooser`. Lines 42–43 call method **setFileSelectionMode** to specify what the user can select from the `fileChooser`. For this program, we use `JFileChooser` static constant **FILES_AND_DIRECTORIES** to indicate that files and directories can be selected. Other static constants include **FILES_ONLY** (the default) and **DIRECTORIES_ONLY**.

```
 1   // Fig. 17.12: FileDemonstration.java
 2   // Demonstrating JFileChooser.
 3   import java.awt.BorderLayout;
 4   import java.awt.event.ActionEvent;
 5   import java.awt.event.ActionListener;
 6   import java.io.File;
 7   import javax.swing.JFileChooser;
 8   import javax.swing.JFrame;
 9   import javax.swing.JOptionPane;
10   import javax.swing.JScrollPane;
```

Fig. 17.12 | Demonstrating `JFileChooser`. (Part 1 of 3.)

```
11   import javax.swing.JTextArea;
12   import javax.swing.JTextField;
13
14   public class FileDemonstration extends JFrame
15   {
16      private JTextArea outputArea; // used for output
17      private JScrollPane scrollPane; // used to provide scrolling to output
18
19      // set up GUI
20      public FileDemonstration()
21      {
22         super( "Testing class File" );
23
24         outputArea = new JTextArea();
25
26         // add outputArea to scrollPane
27         scrollPane = new JScrollPane( outputArea );
28
29         add( scrollPane, BorderLayout.CENTER ); // add scrollPane to GUI
30
31         setSize( 400, 400 ); // set GUI size
32         setVisible( true ); // display GUI
33
34         analyzePath(); // create and analyze File object
35      } // end FileDemonstration constructor
36
37      // allow user to specify file or directory name
38      private File getFileOrDirectory()
39      {
40         // display file dialog, so user can choose file or directory to open
41         JFileChooser fileChooser = new JFileChooser();
42         fileChooser.setFileSelectionMode(
43            JFileChooser.FILES_AND_DIRECTORIES );
44
45         int result = fileChooser.showOpenDialog( this );
46
47         // if user clicked Cancel button on dialog, return
48         if ( result == JFileChooser.CANCEL_OPTION )
49            System.exit( 1 );
50
51         File fileName = fileChooser.getSelectedFile(); // get File
52
53         // display error if invalid
54         if ( ( fileName == null ) || ( fileName.getName().equals( "" ) ) )
55         {
56            JOptionPane.showMessageDialog( this, "Invalid Name",
57               "Invalid Name", JOptionPane.ERROR_MESSAGE );
58            System.exit( 1 );
59         } // end if
60
61         return fileName;
62      } // end method getFile
63
```

Fig. 17.12 | Demonstrating JFileChooser. (Part 2 of 3.)

```
64      // display information about file or directory user specifies
65      public void analyzePath()
66      {
67         // create File object based on user input
68         File name = getFileOrDirectory();
69
70         if ( name.exists() ) // if name exists, output information about it
71         {
72            // display file (or directory) information
73            outputArea.setText( String.format(
74               "%s%s\n%s\n%s\n%s\n%s%s\n%s%s\n%s%s\n%s%s\n%s%s",
75               name.getName(), " exists",
76               ( name.isFile() ? "is a file" : "is not a file" ),
77               ( name.isDirectory() ? "is a directory" :
78                  "is not a directory" ),
79               ( name.isAbsolute( ? "is absolute path" :
80                  "is not absolute path" ), "Last modified: ",
81               name.lastModified(), "Length: ", name.length(),
82               "Path: ", name.getPath(), "Absolute path: ",
83               name.getAbsolutePath(), "Parent: ", name.getParent() ) );
84
85            if ( name.isDirectory() ) // output directory listing
86            {
87               String[] directory = name.list();
88               outputArea.append( "\n\nDirectory contents:\n" );
89
90               for ( String directoryName : directory )
91                  outputArea.append( directoryName + "\n" );
92            } // end else
93         } // end outer if
94         else // not file or directory, output error message
95         {
96            JOptionPane.showMessageDialog( this, name +
97               " does not exist.", "ERROR", JOptionPane.ERROR_MESSAGE );
98         } // end else
99      } // end method analyzePath
100 } // end class FileDemonstration
```

Fig. 17.12 | Demonstrating JFileChooser. (Part 3 of 3.)

```
1   // Fig. 17.13: FileDemonstrationTest.java
2   // Testing class FileDemonstration.
3   import javax.swing.JFrame;
4
5   public class FileDemonstrationTest
6   {
7      public static void main( String[] args )
8      {
9         FileDemonstration application = new FileDemonstration();
10        application.setDefaultCloseOperation( JFrame.EXIT_ON_CLOSE );
11     } // end main
12  } // end class FileDemonstrationTest
```

Fig. 17.13 | Testing class FileDemonstration. (Part 1 of 2.)

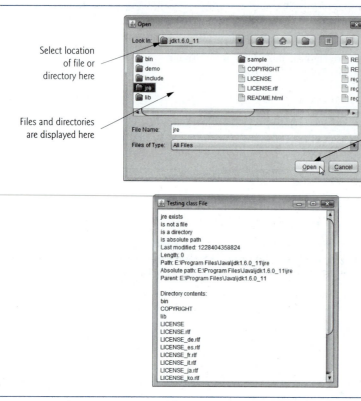

Fig. 17.13 | Testing class `FileDemonstration`. (Part 2 of 2.)

Line 45 calls method **showOpenDialog** to display the `JFileChooser` dialog titled **Open**. Argument `this` specifies the `JFileChooser` dialog's parent window, which determines the position of the dialog on the screen. If `null` is passed, the dialog is displayed in the center of the screen—otherwise, the dialog is centered over the application window (specified by the argument `this`). A `JFileChooser` dialog is a modal dialog that does not allow the user to interact with any other window in the program until the user closes the `JFileChooser` by clicking the **Open** or **Cancel** button. The user selects the drive, directory or file name, then clicks **Open**. Method `showOpenDialog` returns an integer specifying which button (**Open** or **Cancel**) the user clicked to close the dialog. Line 48 tests whether the user clicked **Cancel** by comparing the result with `static` constant **CANCEL_OPTION**. If they're equal, the program terminates. Line 51 retrieves the file the user selected by calling `JFileChooser` method **getSelectedFile**. The program then displays information about the selected file or directory.

17.8 Wrap-Up

In this chapter, you learned more about using file processing to manipulate persistent data. We compared character-based and byte-based streams, and introduced several file-processing classes provided by the `java.io` package. You used class `File` to retrieve information about a file or directory. You learned the differences between text-file processing and object serialization, and used serialization to store and retrieve entire objects. The chapter concluded with an overview of other classes provided by the java.io package, and a small example of using a JFileChooser dialog to allow users to easily select files from a GUI. In the next chapter, you'll learn the concept of recursion—methods that call themselves. Defining methods in this manner can lead to more intuitive programs.

Summary

Section 17.2 The `java.io` Package
- The java.io package includes stream classes for byte-based input from a file, for byte-based output to a file, for character-based input from a file and for character-based output to a file. Files are opened by creating objects of these stream classes.
- You can perform input and output of objects or variables of primitive data types. The data will still be stored as bytes or characters behind the scenes.
- ObjectInputStream and ObjectOutputStream objects can be used together with FileInputStream and FileOutputStream to read objects from and write objects to files.
- The complete hierarchy of classes in package java.io can be viewed in the online documentation at java.sun.com/javase/6/docs/api/java/io/package-tree.html.

Section 17.3 Class `File`
- Class File is used to obtain information about files and directories.
- Character-based input and output can be performed with classes Scanner and Formatter.
- Class Formatter enables formatted data to be output to the screen or to a file in a manner similar to System.out.printf.
- A file or directory's path specifies its location on disk.
- An absolute path contains all the directories, starting with the root directory, that lead to a specific file or directory. Every file or directory on a disk drive has the same root directory in its path.
- A relative path normally starts from the directory in which the application began executing.
- A separator character is used to separate directories and files in the path.

Section 17.4 Case Study: A Credit-Inquiry Program
- Data in many sequential files cannot be modified without destroying other data in the file. So, the entire file is usually rewritten.

Section 17.5 Object Serialization
- Java provides a mechanism called object serialization that enables entire objects to be written to or read from a stream.
- A serialized object is represented as a sequence of bytes that includes the object's data as well as information about the object's type and the types of data stored in the object.
- After a serialized object has been written into a file, it can be read from the file and deserialized to recreate the object in memory.
- Classes ObjectInputStream and ObjectOutputStream enable entire objects to be read from or written to a stream (possibly a file).
- Only classes that implement interface Serializable can be serialized and deserialized.
- ObjectOutput interface method writeObject writes an Object's information to an OutputStream. The object must be Serializable (checked by the class that implements this interface).
- ObjectInput interface method readObject reads and returns a reference to an Object from an InputStream. After an object has been read, its reference can be cast to the object's actual type.

Section 17.6 Additional `java.io` Classes

- `InputStream` and `OutputStream` are abstract classes for performing byte-based input and output.

- Pipes are synchronized communication channels between threads. One thread sends data to another via a `PipedOutputStream`. The target thread reads that information via a `PipedInputStream`.

- A filter stream provides additional functionality, such as aggregating bytes into meaningful primitive-type units. `FilterInputStream` and `FilterOutputStream` are typically extended, so some of their filtering capabilities are provided by their concrete subclasses.

- A `PrintStream` performs text output. `System.out` and `System.err` are `PrintStream` objects.

- Interface `DataInput` describes methods for reading primitive types from an input stream. Classes `DataInputStream` and `RandomAccessFile` each implement this interface.

- Interface `DataOutput` describes methods for writing primitive types to an output stream. Classes `DataOutputStream` and `RandomAccessFile` each implement this interface.

- Buffering is an I/O-performance-enhancement technique. Buffering reduces the number of I/O operations by combining smaller outputs together in memory.

- A `BufferedOutputStream` directs output operations to a buffer. Transfer to the output device is performed in one large physical output operation each time the buffer fills. A partially filled buffer can be forced out to the device at any time by invoking the stream object's `flush` method.

- With a `BufferedInputStream`, many "logical" chunks of data from a file are read as one large physical input operation into a memory buffer. As a program requests data, it's taken from the buffer. When the buffer is empty, the next actual physical input operation is performed.

- `ByteArrayInputStream` and `ByteArrayOutputStream` read from and write to a byte array.

- A `SequenceInputStream` concatenates several `InputStream`s. When the program reaches the end of an input stream, that stream closes, and the next stream in the sequence opens.

- The `Reader` and `Writer` abstract classes are Unicode character-based streams.

- Classes `BufferedReader` and `BufferedWriter` enable buffering for character-based streams.

- Classes `CharArrayReader` and `CharArrayWriter` manipulate a char array in memory.

- A `LineNumberReader` is a buffered character stream that keeps track of the number of lines read.

- Classes `FileReader` and `FileWriter` read characters from and write characters to a file.

- Class `PipedReader` and class `PipedWriter` implement piped-character streams between threads.

- Class `StringReader` and `StringWriter` read characters from and write characters to `String`s, respectively. A `PrintWriter` writes characters to a stream.

Section 17.7 Opening Files with `JFileChooser`

- A `JFileChooser` dialog enables users of a program to easily select files or directories from a GUI.

Terminology

absolute path 721
batch file 733
buffer 744
buffered I/O 743
`BufferedInputStream` class 744
`BufferedOutputStream` class 743
`BufferedReader` class 745
`BufferedWriter` class 745
`CANCEL_OPTION` constant of `JFileChooser` 748
`CharArrayReader` class 745
`CharArrayWriter` class 745

`close` method of `ObjectOutputStream` 740
`DataInputStream` class 743
`DataOutputStream` class 743
deserialize an object 734
`DIRECTORIES_ONLY` constant of `JFileChooser` 745
`EOFException` class 742
`exit` method of `System` 733
`File` class 721
`FileInputStream` class 720
`FileNotFoundException` class 732

Self-Review Exercises

17.1 Determine whether each of the following statements is *true* or *false*. If *false*, explain why.
   a) When reading data from a file using class Scanner, if you wish to read data in the file multiple times, the file must be closed and reopened to read from the beginning of the file.
   b) Method exists of class File returns true if the name specified as the argument to the File constructor is a file or directory in the specified path.
   c) An absolute path contains all the directories, starting with the root directory, that lead to a specific file or directory.

17.2 Complete the following tasks, assuming that each applies to the same program:
   a) Open file "oldmast.txt" for input—use Scanner variable inOldMaster.
   b) Open file "trans.txt" for input—use Scanner variable inTransaction.
   c) Write a statement that opens file "newmast.txt" for output (and creation)—use formatter variable outNewMaster.
   d) Read a record from the file "oldmast.txt". Use the data to create an object of class AccountRecord—use Scanner variable inOldMaster. Assume that class AccountRecord is the same as the AccountRecord class in Fig. 17.3.
   e) Read a record from the file "trans.txt". The record is an object of class TransactionRecord—use Scanner variable inTransaction. Assume that class TransactionRecord contains method setAccount (which takes an int) to set the account number and method setAmount (which takes a double) to set the amount of the transaction.
   f) Output a record to the file "newmast.txt". The record is an object of type AccountRecord—use Formatter variable outNewMaster.

17.3 Complete the following tasks, assuming that each applies to the same program:

a) Write a statement that opens file "oldmast.ser" for input—use `ObjectInputStream` variable `inOldMaster` to wrap a `FileInputStream` object.

b) Write a statement that opens file "trans.ser" for input—use `ObjectInputStream` variable `inTransaction` to wrap a `FileInputStream` object.

c) Write a statement that opens file "newmast.ser" for output (and creation)—use `ObjectOutputStream` variable `outNewMaster` to wrap a `FileOutputStream`.

d) Write a statement that reads a record from the file "oldmast.ser". The record is an object of class `AccountRecordSerializable`—use `ObjectInputStream` variable `inOld-Master`. Assume class `AccountRecordSerializable` is the same as the `AccountRecord-Serializable` class in Fig. 17.7

e) Write a statement that reads a record from the file "trans.ser". The record is an object of class `TransactionRecord`—use `ObjectInputStream` variable `inTransaction`.

f) Write a statement that outputs a record of type `AccountRecordSerializable` to the file "newmast.ser"—use `ObjectOutputStream` variable `outNewMaster`.

17.4 Find the error in each block of code and show how to correct it.

a) Assume that account, company and amount are declared.

```
ObjectOutputStream outputStream;
outputStream.writeInt( account );
outputStream.writeChars( company );
outputStream.writeDouble( amount );
```

b) The following statements should read a record from the file "payables.txt". The Scanner variable `inPayable` should be used to refer to this file.

```
Scanner inPayable = new Scanner( new File( "payables.txt" ) );
PayablesRecord record = ( PayablesRecord ) inPayable.readObject();
```

Answers to Self-Review Exercises

17.1 a) True.
  b) True.
  c) True.

17.2 a) `Scanner inOldMaster = new Scanner( new File ( "oldmast.txt" ) );`
  b) `Scanner inTransaction = new Scanner( new File( "trans.txt" ) );`
  c) `Formatter outNewMaster = new Formatter( "newmast.txt" );`
  d) `AccountRecord account = new AccountRecord();`
    `account.setAccount( inOldMaster.nextInt() );`
    `account.setFirstName( inOldMaster.next() );`
    `account.setLastName( inOldMaster.next() );`
    `account.setBalance( inOldMaster.nextDouble() );`
  e) `TransactionRecord transaction = new Transaction();`
    `transaction.setAccount( inTransaction.nextInt() );`
    `transaction.setAmount( inTransaction.nextDouble() );`
  f) `outNewMaster.format( "%d %s %s %.2f\n",`
    `account.getAccount(), account.getFirstName(),`
    `account.getLastName(), account.getBalance() );`

17.3 a) `ObjectInputStream inOldMaster = new ObjectInputStream(`
      `new FileInputStream( "oldmast.ser" ) );`
  b) `ObjectInputStream inTransaction = new ObjectInputStream(`
      `new FileInputStream( "trans.ser" ) );`
  c) `ObjectOutputStream outNewMaster = new ObjectOutputStream(`
      `new FileOutputStream( "newmast.ser" ) );`

d) `accountRecord = ( AccountRecordSerializable ) inOldMaster.readObject();`
e) `transactionRecord = ( TransactionRecord ) inTransaction.readObject();`
f) `outNewMaster.writeObject( newAccountRecord );`

17.4 a) Error: The file was not opened before the attempt to output data to the stream.
Correction: Open a file for output by creating a new `ObjectOutputStream` object that wraps a `FileOutputStream` object.
b) Error: This example uses text files with a `Scanner`; there is no object serialization. As a result, method `readObject` cannot be used to read that data from the file. Each piece of data must be read separately, then used to create a `PayablesRecord` object.
Correction: Use methods of `inPayable` to read each piece of the `PayablesRecord` object.

Exercises

17.5 Fill in the blanks in each of the following statements:
a) Computers store large amounts of data on secondary storage devices as _____.
b) A(n) _____ is composed of several fields.
c) To facilitate the retrieval of specific records from a file, one field in each record is chosen as a(n) _____.
d) Files that are created using byte-based streams are referred to as _____ files, while files created using character-based streams are referred to as _____ files.
e) The standard stream objects are _____, _____ and _____.

17.6 Determine which of the following statements are *true* and which are *false*. If *false*, explain why.
a) The impressive functions performed by computers essentially involve the manipulation of zeros and ones.
b) People specify programs and data items as characters. Computers then manipulate and process these characters as groups of zeros and ones.
c) Data items represented in computers form a data hierarchy in which data items become larger and more complex as we progress from fields to characters to bits and so on.
d) A record key identifies a record as belonging to a particular field.
e) Companies store all their information in a single file to facilitate computer processing of the information. When a program creates a file, the file is retained by the computer for future reference.

17.7 *(File Matching)* Self-Review Exercise 17.2 asked you to write a series of single statements. Actually, these statements form the core of an important type of file-processing program, namely, a file-matching program. In commercial data processing, it's common to have several files in each application system. In an accounts receivable system, for example, there is generally a master file containing detailed information about each customer, such as the customer's name, address, telephone number, outstanding balance, credit limit, discount terms, contract arrangements and possibly a condensed history of recent purchases and cash payments.

As transactions occur (i.e., sales are made and payments arrive in the mail), information about them is entered into a file. At the end of each business period (a month for some companies, a week for others, and a day in some cases), the file of transactions (called `"trans.txt"`) is applied to the master file (called `"oldmast.txt"`) to update each account's purchase and payment record. During an update, the master file is rewritten as the file `"newmast.txt"`, which is then used at the end of the next business period to begin the updating process again.

File-matching programs must deal with certain problems that do not arise in single-file programs. For example, a match does not always occur. If a customer on the master file has not made any purchases or cash payments in the current business period, no record for this customer will appear on the transaction file. Similarly, a customer who did make some purchases or cash payments could have just moved to this community, and if so, the company may not have had a chance to create a master record for this customer.

Write a complete file-matching accounts receivable program. Use the account number on each file as the record key for matching purposes. Assume that each file is a sequential text file with records stored in increasing account-number order.

a) Define class `TransactionRecord`. Objects of this class contain an account number and amount for the transaction. Provide methods to modify and retrieve these values.

b) Modify class `AccountRecord` in Fig. 17.3 to include method `combine`, which takes a `TransactionRecord` object and combines the balance of the `AccountRecord` object and the amount value of the `TransactionRecord` object.

c) Write a program to create data for testing the program. Use the sample account data in Figs. 17.14 and 17.15. Run the program to create the files `trans.txt` and `oldmast.txt`, to be used by your file-matching program.

Master file account number	Name	Balance
100	Alan Jones	348.17
300	Mary Smith	27.19
500	Sam Sharp	0.00
700	Suzy Green	–14.22

Fig. 17.14 | Sample data for master file.

Transaction file account number	Transaction amount
100	27.14
300	62.11
400	100.56
900	82.17

Fig. 17.15 | Sample data for transaction file.

d) Create class `FileMatch` to perform the file-matching functionality. The class should contain methods that read `oldmast.txt` and `trans.txt`. When a match occurs (i.e., records with the same account number appear in both the master file and the transaction file), add the dollar amount in the transaction record to the current balance in the master record, and write the `"newmast.txt"` record. (Assume that purchases are indicated by positive amounts in the transaction file and payments by negative amounts.) When there is a master record for a particular account, but no corresponding transaction record, merely write the master record to `"newmast.txt"`. When there is a transaction record, but no corresponding master record, print to a log file the message `"Unmatched transaction record for account number..."` (fill in the account number from the transaction record). The log file should be a text file named `"log.txt"`.

17.8 *(File Matching with Multiple Transactions)* It's possible (and actually common) to have several transaction records with the same record key. This situation occurs, for example, when a customer makes several purchases and cash payments during a business period. Rewrite your accounts receivable file-matching program from Exercise 17.7 to provide for the possibility of handling several transaction records with the same record key. Modify the test data of `CreateData.java` to include the additional transaction records in Fig. 17.16.

17.9 *(File Matching with Object Serialization)* Recreate your solution for Exercise 17.8 using object serialization. Use the statements from Exercise 17.3 as your basis for this program. You may

Account number	Dollar amount
300	83.89
700	80.78
700	1.53

Fig. 17.16 | Additional transaction records.

want to create applications to read the data stored in the .ser files—the code in Section 17.5.2 can be modified for this purpose.

17.10 *(Telephone-Number Word Generator)* Standard telephone keypads contain the digits zero through nine. The numbers two through nine each have three letters associated with them (Fig. 17.17). Many people find it difficult to memorize phone numbers, so they use the correspondence between digits and letters to develop seven-letter words that correspond to their phone numbers. For example, a person whose telephone number is 686-2377 might use the correspondence indicated in Fig. 17.17 to develop the seven-letter word "NUMBERS." Every seven-letter word corresponds to exactly one seven-digit telephone number. A restaurant wishing to increase its takeout business could surely do so with the number 825-3688 (i.e., "TAKEOUT").

Digit	Letters	Digit	Letters	Digit	Letters
2	A B C	5	J K L	8	T U V
3	D E F	6	M N O	9	W X Y
4	G H I	7	P R S		

Fig. 17.17 | Telephone keypad digits and letters.

Every seven-letter phone number corresponds to many different seven-letter words, but most of these words represent unrecognizable juxtapositions of letters. It's possible, however, that the owner of a barbershop would be pleased to know that the shop's telephone number, 424-7288, corresponds to "HAIRCUT." A veterinarian with the phone number 738-2273 would be pleased to know that the number corresponds to the letters "PETCARE." An automotive dealership would be pleased to know that the dealership number, 639-2277, corresponds to "NEWCARS."

Write a program that, given a seven-digit number, uses a PrintStream object to write to a file every possible seven-letter word combination corresponding to that number. There are 2,187 (3^7) such combinations. Avoid phone numbers with the digits 0 and 1.

17.11 *(Adding Object Serialization to the MyShape Drawing Application)* Modify Exercise 14.17 to allow the user to save a drawing into a file or load a prior drawing from a file using object serialization. Add buttons **Load** (to read objects from a file) and **Save** (to write objects to a file). Use an ObjectOutputStream to write to the file and an ObjectInputStream to read from the file. Write the array of MyShape objects using method writeObject (class ObjectOutputStream), and read the array using method readObject (ObjectInputStream). Note that the object-serialization mechanism can read or write entire arrays—it's not necessary to manipulate each element of the array of MyShape objects individually. It's simply required that all the shapes be Serializable. For both the **Load** and **Save** buttons, use a JFileChooser to allow the user to select the file in which the shapes will be stored or from which they'll be read. When the user first runs the program, no shapes should be displayed on the screen. The user can display shapes by opening a previously saved file or by drawing new shapes. Once there are shapes on the screen, users can save them to a file using the **Save** button.

18

Recursion

*O! thou hast damnable
iteration, and art indeed able to
corrupt a saint.*
—William Shakespeare

*It's a poor sort of memory that
only works backwards.*
—Lewis Carroll

Push on—keep moving.
—Thomas Morton

*There is a point at which
methods devour themselves.*
—Frantz Fanon

Objectives

In this chapter you'll learn:

- The concept of recursion.

- How to write and use
  recursive methods.

- How to determine the base
  case and recursion step in a
  recursive algorithm.

- How recursive method calls
  are handled by the system.

- The differences between
  recursion and iteration, and
  when to use each.

- What the geometric shapes
  called fractals are and how to
  draw them using recursion.

- What recursive backtracking
  is and why it's an effective
  problem-solving technique.

18.1 Introduction

The programs we've discussed so far are generally structured as methods that call one another in a hierarchical manner. For some problems, it's useful to have a method call itself. A method that does so is known as a **recursive method**. A recursive method can call itself either directly or indirectly through another method. Recursion is an important topic discussed at length in upper-level computer science courses. In this chapter, we consider recursion conceptually, then present several programs containing recursive methods. Figure 18.1 summarizes the recursion examples and exercises in this book.

Chapter	Recursion examples and exercises in this book
18	Factorial Method (Figs. 18.3 and 18.4) Fibonacci Method (Fig. 18.5) Towers of Hanoi (Fig. 18.11) Fractals (Figs. 18.18 and 18.19) What Does This Code Do? (Exercise 18.7, Exercise 18.12 and Exercise 18.13) Find the Error in the Following Code (Exercise 18.8) Raising an Integer to an Integer Power (Exercise 18.9) Visualizing Recursion (Exercise 18.10) Greatest Common Divisor (Exercise 18.11) Determine Whether a String Is a Palindrome (Exercise 18.14) Eight Queens (Exercise 18.15) Print an Array (Exercise 18.16) Print an Array Backward (Exercise 18.17) Minimum Value in an Array (Exercise 18.18) Star Fractal (Exercise 18.19) Maze Traversal Using Recursive Backtracking (Exercise 18.20) Generating Mazes Randomly (Exercise 18.21) Mazes of Any Size (Exercise 18.22) Time Needed to Calculate a Fibonacci Number (Exercise 18.23)
19	Merge Sort (Figs. 19.10 and 19.11) Linear Search (Exercise 19.8) Binary Search (Exercise 19.9) Quicksort (Exercise 19.10)
22	Binary-Tree Insert (Fig. 22.17) Preorder Traversal of a Binary Tree (Fig. 22.17)

Fig. 18.1 | Summary of the recursion examples and exercises in this text. (Part 1 of 2.)

Chapter	Recursion examples and exercises in this book
22 (cont.)	Inorder Traversal of a Binary Tree (Fig. 22.17)
	Postorder Traversal of a Binary Tree (Fig. 22.17)
	Print a Linked List Backward (Exercise 22.20)
	Search a Linked List (Exercise 22.21)

Fig. 18.1 | Summary of the recursion examples and exercises in this text. (Part 2 of 2.)

18.2 Recursion Concepts

Recursive problem-solving approaches have a number of elements in common. When a recursive method is called to solve a problem, it actually is capable of solving only the simplest case(s), or **base case(s)**. If the method is called with a base case, it returns a result. If the method is called with a more complex problem, it typically divides the problem into two conceptual pieces—a piece that the method knows how to do and a piece that it does not know how to do. To make recursion feasible, the latter piece must resemble the original problem, but be a slightly simpler or smaller version of it. Because this new problem looks like the original problem, the method calls a fresh copy of itself to work on the smaller problem—this is referred to as a **recursive call** and is also called the **recursion step**. The recursion step normally includes a return statement, because its result will be combined with the portion of the problem the method knew how to solve to form a result that will be passed back to the original caller. This concept of separating the problem into two smaller portions is a form of the divide-and-conquer approach introduced in Chapter 5.

The recursion step executes while the original method call is still active (i.e., it has not finished executing). It can result in many more recursive calls as the method divides each new subproblem into two conceptual pieces. For the recursion to eventually terminate, each time the method calls itself with a simpler version of the original problem, the sequence of smaller and smaller problems must converge on a base case. When the method recognizes the base case, it returns a result to the previous copy of the method. A sequence of returns ensues until the original method call returns the final result to the caller.

A recursive method may call another method, which may in turn make a call back to the recursive method. This is known as an **indirect recursive call** or **indirect recursion**. For example, method A calls method B, which makes a call back to method A. This is still recursion, because the second call to method A is made while the first call to method A is active—that is, the first call to method A has not yet finished executing (because it's waiting on method B to return a result to it) and has not returned to method A's original caller.

To better understand the concept of recursion, let's look at an example that's quite familiar to computer users—the recursive definition of a directory on a computer. A computer normally stores related files in a directory. A directory can be empty, can contain files and/or can contain other directories (usually referred to as subdirectories). Each of these subdirectories, in turn, may also contain both files and directories. If we want to list each file in a directory (including all the files in the directory's subdirectories), we need to create a method that first lists the initial directory's files, then makes recursive calls to list the files in each of that directory's subdirectories. The base case occurs when a directory is reached that does not contain any subdirectories. At this point, all the files in the original directory have been listed and no further recursion is necessary.

18.3 Example Using Recursion: Factorials

Let's write a recursive program to perform a popular mathematical calculation. Consider the factorial of a positive integer n, written $n!$ (pronounced "n factorial"), which is the product

$$n \cdot (n-1) \cdot (n-2) \cdot \ldots \cdot 1$$

with 1! equal to 1 and 0! defined to be 1. For example, 5! is the product $5 \cdot 4 \cdot 3 \cdot 2 \cdot 1$, which is equal to 120.

The factorial of integer `number` (where `number` ≥ 0) can be calculated iteratively (non-recursively) using a `for` statement as follows:

```
factorial = 1;

for ( int counter = number; counter >= 1; counter-- )
   factorial *= counter;
```

A recursive declaration of the factorial method is arrived at by observing the following relationship:

$$n! = n \cdot (n-1)!$$

For example, 5! is clearly equal to $5 \cdot 4!$, as shown by the following equations:

$$5! = 5 \cdot 4 \cdot 3 \cdot 2 \cdot 1$$
$$5! = 5 \cdot (4 \cdot 3 \cdot 2 \cdot 1)$$
$$5! = 5 \cdot (4!)$$

The evaluation of 5! would proceed as shown in Fig. 18.2. Figure 18.2(a) shows how the succession of recursive calls proceeds until 1! (the base case) is evaluated to be 1, which terminates the recursion. Figure 18.2(b) shows the values returned from each recursive call to its caller until the final value is calculated and returned.

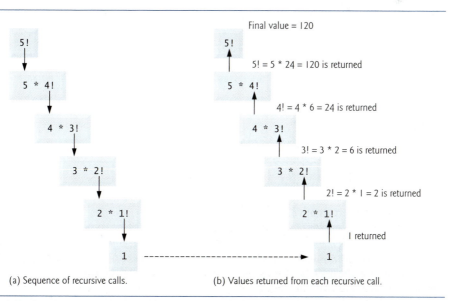

(a) Sequence of recursive calls.   (b) Values returned from each recursive call.

Fig. 18.2 | Recursive evaluation of 5!.

Figure 18.3 uses recursion to calculate and print the factorials of the integers from 0–21. The recursive method `factorial` (lines 7–13) first tests to determine whether a terminating condition (line 9) is `true`. If number is less than or equal to 1 (the base case), `factorial` returns 1, no further recursion is necessary and the method returns. If number is greater than 1, line 12 expresses the problem as the product of number and a recursive call to `factorial` evaluating the factorial of number - 1, which is a slightly smaller problem than the original calculation, `factorial( number )`.

```java
 1  // Fig. 18.3: FactorialCalculator.java
 2  // Recursive factorial method.
 3
 4  public class FactorialCalculator
 5  {
 6     // recursive method factorial (assumes its parameter is >= 0)
 7     public static long factorial( long number )
 8     {
 9        if ( number <= 1 ) // test for base case
10           return 1; // base cases: 0! = 1 and 1! = 1
11        else // recursion step
12           return number * factorial( number - 1 );
13     } // end method factorial
14
15     // output factorials for values 0-21
16     public static void main( String[] args )
17     {
18        // calculate the factorials of 0 through 21
19        for ( int counter = 0; counter <= 21; counter++ )
20           System.out.printf( "%d! = %d\n", counter, factorial( counter ) );
21     } // end main
22  } // end class FactorialCalculator
```

```
0! = 1
1! = 1
2! = 2
3! = 6
4! = 24
5! = 120
...
12! = 479001600 ——— 12! causes overflow for int variables
...
20! = 2432902008176640000
21! = -4249290049419214848 ——— 21! causes overflow for long variables
```

Fig. 18.3 | Factorial calculations with a recursive method.

Common Programming Error 18.1

Either omitting the base case or writing the recursion step incorrectly so that it does not converge on the base case can cause a logic error known as **infinite recursion**, *where recursive calls are continuously made until memory is exhausted. This error is analogous to the problem of an infinite loop in an iterative (nonrecursive) solution.*

Method main (lines 16–21) displays the factorials of 0–21. The call to the `factorial` method occurs in line 20. Method `factorial` receives a parameter of type `long` and returns a result of type long. The program's output shows that factorial values become large quickly. We use type long (which can represent relatively large integers) so the program can calculate factorials greater than 12!. Unfortunately, the factorial method produces large values so quickly that we exceed the largest long value when we attempt to calculate 21!, as you can see in the last line of the program's output.

Due to the limitations of integral types, float or double variables may ultimately be needed to calculate factorials of larger numbers. This points to a weakness in some programming languages—namely, that they're not easily extended with new types to handle unique application requirements. As we saw in Chapter 9, Java is an extensible language that allows us to create arbitrarily large integers if we wish. In fact, package java.math provides classes **BigInteger** and **BigDecimal** explicitly for arbitrary precision calculations that cannot be performed with primitive types. You can learn more about these classes at java.sun.com/javase/6/docs/api/java/math/BigInteger.html and java.sun.com/javase/6/docs/api/java/math/BigDecimal.html, respectively.

Reimplementing Class *FactorialCalculator* Using Class *BigInteger*

Figure 18.4 reimplements class FactorialCalculator using BigInteger variables. To demonstrate larger values than what long variables can store, we calculate the factorials of the numbers 0–50. Line 3 imports class BigInteger from package java.math. The new factorial method (lines 8–15) receives a BigInteger as an argument and returns a BigInteger.

Since BigInteger is not a primitive type, we can't use the arithmetic, relational and equality operators with BigIntegers; instead, we must use BigInteger methods to

```
1   // Fig. 18.4: FactorialCalculator.java
2   // Recursive factorial method.
3   import java.math.BigInteger;
4
5   public class FactorialCalculator
6   {
7      // recursive method factorial (assumes its parameter is >= 0)
8      public static BigInteger factorial( BigInteger number )
9      {
10         if ( number.compareTo( BigInteger.ONE ) <= 0 ) // test base case
11            return BigInteger.ONE; // base cases: 0! = 1 and 1! = 1
12         else // recursion step
13            return number.multiply(
14               factorial( number.subtract( BigInteger.ONE ) ) );
15      } // end method factorial
16
17      // output factorials for values 0-50
18      public static void main( String[] args )
19      {
20         // calculate the factorials of 0 through 50
21         for ( int counter = 0; counter <= 50; counter++ )
22            System.out.printf( "%d! = %d\n", counter,
23               factorial( BigInteger.valueOf( counter ) ) );
24      } // end main
25   } // end class FactorialCalculator
```

Fig. 18.4 | Factorial calculations with a recursive method. (Part 1 of 2.)

```
0! = 1
1! = 1
2! = 2
3! = 6
...
21! = 51090942171709440000    — 21! and larger values no longer cause overflow
22! = 1124000727777607680000
...
47! = 258623241511168180642964355153611979969197632389120000000000
48! = 12413915592536072670862289047373375038521486354677760000000000
49! = 608281864034267560872252163321295376887552831379210240000000000
50! = 30414093201713378043612608166064768844377641568960512000000000000
```

Fig. 18.4 | Factorial calculations with a recursive method. (Part 2 of 2.)

perform these tasks. Line 10 tests for the base case using `BigInteger` method `compareTo`. This method compares the `BigInteger` that calls the method to the method's `BigInteger` argument. The method returns -1 if the `BigIteger` that calls the method is less than the argument, 0 if they're equal or 1 if the `BigInteger` that calls the method is greater than the argument. Line 10 compares the `BigInteger` number with the `BigInteger` constant **ONE**, which represents the integer value 1. If `compareTo` returns -1 or 0, then number is less than or equal to 1 (the base case) and the method returns the constant `BigInteger.ONE`. Otherwise, lines 13–14 perform the recursion step using `BigInteger` methods **multiply** and **subtract** to implement the calculations required to multiply number by the factorial of number - 1). The program's output shows that `BigInteger` easily handles the large values produced by the factorial calculation.

18.4 Example Using Recursion: Fibonacci Series

The **Fibonacci series**,

0, 1, 1, 2, 3, 5, 8, 13, 21, ...

begins with 0 and 1 and has the property that each subsequent Fibonacci number is the sum of the previous two. This series occurs in nature and describes a form of spiral. The ratio of successive Fibonacci numbers converges on a constant value of 1.618..., a number that has been called the **golden ratio** or the **golden mean**. Humans tend to find the golden mean aesthetically pleasing. Architects often design windows, rooms and buildings whose length and width are in the ratio of the golden mean. Postcards are often designed with a golden-mean length-to-width ratio.

The Fibonacci series may be defined recursively as follows:

fibonacci(0) = 0
fibonacci(1) = 1
fibonacci(n) = fibonacci(n – 1) + fibonacci(n – 2)

Note that there are *two base cases* for the Fibonacci calculation: `fibonacci(0)` is defined to be 0, and `fibonacci(1)` to be 1. The program in Fig. 18.5 calculates the ith Fibonacci number recursively, using method `fibonacci` (lines 10–18). Method `main` (lines 21–26) tests `fibonacci`, displaying the Fibonacci values of 0–40. The variable `counter` created in the `for` header (line 23) indicates which Fibonacci number to calculate for each iteration of the loop. Fibonacci numbers tend to become large quickly (though not as quickly as factorials). Therefore, we use type `BigInteger` as the parameter type and the return type of method `fibonacci`.

```java
1   // Fig. 18.5: FibonacciCalculator.java
2   // Recursive fibonacci method.
3   import java.math.BigInteger;
4
5   public class FibonacciCalculator
6   {
7      private static BigInteger TWO = BigInteger.valueOf( 2 );
8
9      // recursive declaration of method fibonacci
10     public static BigInteger fibonacci( BigInteger number )
11     {
12        if ( number.equals( BigInteger.ZERO ) ||
13           number.equals( BigInteger.ONE ) ) // base cases
14           return number;
15        else // recursion step
16           return fibonacci( number.subtract( BigInteger.ONE ) ).add(
17              fibonacci( number.subtract( TWO ) ) );
18     } // end method fibonacci
19
20     // displays the fibonacci values from 0-40
21     public static void main( String[] args )
22     {
23        for ( int counter = 0; counter <= 40; counter++ )
24           System.out.printf( "Fibonacci of %d is: %d\n", counter,
25              fibonacci( BigInteger.valueOf( counter ) ) );
26     } // end main
27  } // end class FibonacciCalculator
```

```
Fibonacci of 0 is: 0
Fibonacci of 1 is: 1
Fibonacci of 2 is: 1
Fibonacci of 3 is: 2
Fibonacci of 4 is: 3
Fibonacci of 5 is: 5
Fibonacci of 6 is: 8
Fibonacci of 7 is: 13
Fibonacci of 8 is: 21
Fibonacci of 9 is: 34
Fibonacci of 10 is: 55
...
Fibonacci of 37 is: 24157817
Fibonacci of 38 is: 39088169
Fibonacci of 39 is: 63245986
Fibonacci of 40 is: 102334155
```

Fig. 18.5 | Fibonacci numbers generated with a recursive method.

The call to method `fibonacci` (line 25 of Fig. 18.5) from main is not a recursive call, but all subsequent calls to `fibonacci` performed from lines 16–17 of Fig. 18.5 are recursive, because at that point the calls are initiated by method `fibonacci` itself. Each time `fibonacci` is called, it immediately tests for the base cases—number equal to 0 or number equal to 1 (Fig. 18.5, lines 12–13). Note that we use `BigInteger` constants **ZERO** and ONE to represent the values 0 and 1, respectively. If the condition in lines 12–13 is true, fibonacci simply returns number, because fibonacci(0) is 0 and fibonacci(1) is 1. Interestingly, if number is greater than 1, the recursion step generates *two* recursive calls (lines 16–17), each for a slightly smaller problem than the original call to fibonacci. Lines 16–17 use BigInteger methods **add** and subtract to help implement the recursive step. We also use a constant of type BigInteger named TWO that we defined at line 7.

Analyzing the Calls to Method Fibonacci

Figure 18.6 shows how method fibonacci evaluates fibonacci(3). Note that at the bottom of the figure we are left with the values 1, 0 and 1—the results of evaluating the base cases. The first two return values (from left to right), 1 and 0, are returned as the values for the calls fibonacci(1) and fibonacci(0). The sum 1 plus 0 is returned as the value of fibonacci(2). This is added to the result (1) of the call to fibonacci(1), producing the value 2. This final value is then returned as the value of fibonacci(3).

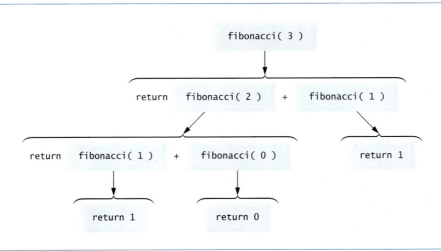

Fig. 18.6 | Set of recursive calls for fibonacci(3).

Figure 18.6 raises some interesting issues about the order in which Java compilers evaluate the operands of operators. This order is different from that in which operators are applied to their operands—namely, the order dictated by the rules of operator precedence. From Figure 18.6, it appears that while fibonacci(3) is being evaluated, two recursive calls will be made—fibonacci(2) and fibonacci(1). But in what order will they be made? The Java language specifies that the order of evaluation of the operands is from left to right. Thus, the call fibonacci(2) is made first and the call fibonacci(1) second.

A word of caution is in order about recursive programs like the one we use here to generate Fibonacci numbers. Each invocation of the fibonacci method that does not match one of the base cases (0 or 1) results in *two more recursive calls* to the fibonacci method. Hence, this set of recursive calls rapidly gets out of hand. Calculating the Fibonacci value of 20 with the program in Fig. 18.5 requires 21,891 calls to the fibonacci method; calculating the Fibonacci value of 30 requires 2,692,537 calls! As you try to calculate larger Fibonacci values, you'll notice that each consecutive Fibonacci number you use the application to calculate results in a substantial increase in calculation time and in the number of calls to the `fibonacci` method. For example, the Fibonacci value of 31 requires 4,356,617 calls, and the Fibonacci value of 32 requires 7,049,155 calls! As you can see, the number of calls to `fibonacci` increases quickly—1,664,080 additional calls between Fibonacci values of 30 and 31 and 2,692,538 additional calls between Fibonacci values of 31 and 32! The difference in the number of calls made between Fibonacci values of 31 and 32 is more than 1.5 times the difference in the number of calls for Fibonacci values between 30 and 31. Problems of this nature can humble even the world's most powerful computers. [*Note:* In the field of complexity theory, computer scientists study how hard algorithms work to complete their tasks. Complexity issues are discussed in detail in the upper-level computer science curriculum course generally called "Algorithms." We introduce various complexity issues in Chapter 19, Searching, Sorting and Big O.] In the exercises, you'll be asked to enhance the Fibonacci program of Fig. 18.5 so that it calculates the approximate amount of time required to perform the calculation. For this purpose, you'll call `static System` method `currentTimeMillis`, which takes no arguments and returns the computer's current time in milliseconds.

Performance Tip 18.1

Avoid Fibonacci-style recursive programs, because they result in an exponential "explosion" of method calls.

18.5 Recursion and the Method-Call Stack

In Chapter 5, the stack data structure was introduced in the context of understanding how Java performs method calls. We discussed both the method-call stack (also known as the program-execution stack) and activation records. In this section, we'll use these concepts to demonstrate how the program-execution stack handles recursive method calls.

Let's begin by returning to the Fibonacci example—specifically, calling method `fibonacci` with the value 3, as in Fig. 18.6. To show the order in which the method calls' activation records are placed on the stack, we've lettered the method calls in Fig. 18.7.

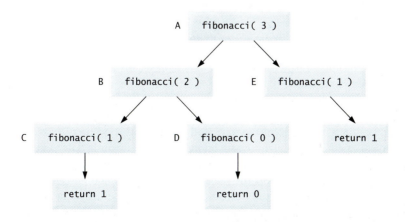

Fig. 18.7 | Method calls made within the call `fibonacci( 3 )`.

When the first method call (A) is made, an activation record containing the value of the local variable number (3, in this case) is pushed onto the program-execution stack. The program-execution stack, including the activation record for method call A, is illustrated in part (a) of Fig. 18.8. [*Note:* We use a simplified stack here. An actual program-execution stack and its activation records would be more complex than in Fig. 18.8, containing such information as where the method call is to return to when it has completed execution.]

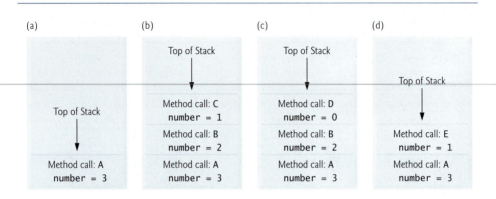

Fig. 18.8 | Method calls on the program-execution stack.

Within method call A, method calls B and E are made. The original method call has not yet completed, so its activation record remains on the stack. The first method call to be made from within A is method call B, so the activation record for method call B is pushed onto the stack on top of the one for method call A. Method call B must execute and complete before method call E is made. Within method call B, method calls C and D will be made. Method call C is made first, and its activation record is pushed onto the stack [part (b) of Fig. 18.8]. Method call B has not yet finished, and its activation record is still on the method-call stack. When method call C executes, it makes no further method calls, but simply returns the value 1. When this method returns, its activation record is popped off the top of the stack. The method call at the top of the stack is now B, which continues to execute by performing method call D. The activation record for method call D is pushed onto the stack [part (c) of Fig. 18.8]. Method call D completes without making any more method calls and returns the value 0. The activation record for this method call is then popped off the stack. Now, both method calls made from within method call B have returned. Method call B continues to execute, returning the value 1. Method call B completes, and its activation record is popped off the stack. At this point, the activation record for method call A is at the top of the stack and the method continues its execution. This method makes method call E, whose activation record is now pushed onto the stack [part (d) of Fig. 18.8]. Method call E completes and returns the value 1. The activation record for this method call is popped off the stack, and once again method call A continues to execute. At this point, method call A will not be making any other method calls and can finish its execution, returning the value 2 to A's caller (fibonacci(3) = 2). A's activation record is popped off the stack. Note that the executing method is always the one whose activation record is at the top of the stack, and the activation record for that method contains the values of its local variables.

18.6 Recursion vs. Iteration

We've studied methods `factorial` and `fibonacci`, which can easily be implemented either recursively or iteratively. In this section, we compare the two approaches and discuss why you might choose one approach over the other in a particular situation.

Both iteration and recursion are based on a control statement: Iteration uses a repetition statement (e.g., `for`, `while` or `do...while`), whereas recursion uses a selection statement (e.g., `if`, `if...else` or `switch`). Both iteration and recursion involve repetition: Iteration explicitly uses a repetition statement, whereas recursion achieves repetition through repeated method calls. Iteration and recursion each involve a termination test: Iteration terminates when the loop-continuation condition fails, whereas recursion terminates when a base case is reached. Iteration with counter-controlled repetition and recursion each gradually approach termination: Iteration keeps modifying a counter until the counter assumes a value that makes the loop-continuation condition fail, whereas recursion keeps producing smaller versions of the original problem until the base case is reached. Both iteration and recursion can occur infinitely: An infinite loop occurs with iteration if the loop-continuation test never becomes false, whereas infinite recursion occurs if the recursion step does not reduce the problem each time in a manner that converges on the base case, or if the base case is not tested.

To illustrate the differences between iteration and recursion, let's examine an iterative solution to the factorial problem (Fig. 18.9). Note that a repetition statement is used (lines 12–13) rather than the selection statement of the recursive solution (lines 9–12 of Fig. 18.3). Note that both solutions use a termination test. In the recursive solution, line 9 tests for the base case. In the iterative solution, line 12 tests the loop-continuation condition—if the test fails, the loop terminates. Finally, note that instead of producing smaller versions of the original problem, the iterative solution uses a counter that is modified until the loop-continuation condition becomes false.

```
1   // Fig. 18.9: FactorialCalculator.java
2   // Iterative factorial method.
3
4   public class FactorialCalculator
5   {
6      // recursive declaration of method factorial
7      public static long factorial( long number )
8      {
9         long result = 1;
10
11        // iterative declaration of method factorial
12        for ( long i = number; i >= 1; i-- )
13           result *= i;
14
15        return result;
16     } // end method factorial
17
18     // output factorials for values 0-10
19     public static void main( String[] args )
20     {
```

Fig. 18.9 | Iterative factorial solution. (Part 1 of 2.)

```
21          // calculate the factorials of 0 through 10
22          for ( int counter = 0; counter <= 10; counter++ )
23             System.out.printf( "%d! = %d\n", counter, factorial( counter ) );
24       } // end main
25    } // end class FactorialCalculator
```

```
 0! = 1
 1! = 1
 2! = 2
 3! = 6
 4! = 24
 5! = 120
 6! = 720
 7! = 5040
 8! = 40320
 9! = 362880
10! = 3628800
```

Fig. 18.9 | Iterative factorial solution. (Part 2 of 2.)

Recursion has many negatives. It repeatedly invokes the mechanism, and consequently the overhead, of method calls. This repetition can be expensive in terms of both processor time and memory space. Each recursive call causes another copy of the method (actually, only the method's variables, stored in the activation record) to be created—this set of copies can consume considerable memory space. Since iteration occurs within a method, repeated method calls and extra memory assignment are avoided. So why choose recursion?

Software Engineering Observation 18.1

Any problem that can be solved recursively can also be solved iteratively (nonrecursively). A recursive approach is normally preferred over an iterative approach when the recursive approach more naturally mirrors the problem and results in a program that is easier to understand and debug. A recursive approach can often be implemented with fewer lines of code. Another reason to choose a recursive approach is that an iterative one might not be apparent.

Performance Tip 18.2

Avoid using recursion in situations requiring high performance. Recursive calls take time and consume additional memory.

Common Programming Error 18.2

Accidentally having a nonrecursive method call itself either directly or indirectly through another method can cause infinite recursion.

18.7 Towers of Hanoi

Earlier in this chapter we studied methods that can be easily implemented both recursively and iteratively. Now, we present a problem whose recursive solution demonstrates the elegance of recursion, and whose iterative solution may not be as apparent.

The Towers of Hanoi is one of the classic problems every budding computer scientist must grapple with. Legend has it that in a temple in the Far East, priests are attempting to move a stack of golden disks from one diamond peg to another (Fig. 18.10). The initial stack has 64 disks threaded onto one peg and arranged from bottom to top by decreasing size. The priests are attempting to move the stack from one peg to another under the constraints that exactly one disk is moved at a time and at no time may a larger disk be placed above a smaller disk. Three pegs are provided, one being used for temporarily holding disks. Supposedly, the world will end when the priests complete their task, so there is little incentive for us to facilitate their efforts.

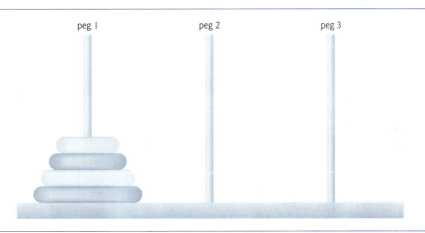

Fig. 18.10 | Towers of Hanoi for the case with four disks.

Let's assume that the priests are attempting to move the disks from peg 1 to peg 3. We wish to develop an algorithm that prints the precise sequence of peg-to-peg disk transfers.

If we try to find an iterative solution, we'll likely find ourselves hopelessly "knotted up" in managing the disks. Instead, attacking this problem recursively quickly yields a solution. Moving n disks can be viewed in terms of moving only $n - 1$ disks (hence the recursion) as follows:

1. Move $n - 1$ disks from peg 1 to peg 2, using peg 3 as a temporary holding area.

2. Move the last disk (the largest) from peg 1 to peg 3.

3. Move $n - 1$ disks from peg 2 to peg 3, using peg 1 as a temporary holding area.

The process ends when the last task involves moving $n = 1$ disk (i.e., the base case). This task is accomplished by moving the disk, without using a temporary holding area.

In Fig. 18.11, method `solveTowers` (lines 6–25) solves the Towers of Hanoi, given the total number of disks (in this case 3), the starting peg, the ending peg, and the temporary holding peg as parameters. The base case (lines 10–14) occurs when only one disk needs to be moved from the starting peg to the ending peg. In the recursion step (lines 18–24), line 18 moves `disks - 1` disks from the first peg (`sourcePeg`) to the temporary holding peg (`tempPeg`). When all but one of the disks have been moved to the temporary peg, line 21 moves the largest disk from the start peg to the destination peg. Line 24 finishes the rest of the moves by calling the method `solveTowers` to recursively move `disks - 1` disks from the temporary peg (`tempPeg`) to the destination peg (`destinationPeg`), this time using the first peg (`sourcePeg`) as the temporary peg. Line 35 in `main` calls the recursive `solveTowers` method, which outputs the steps to the command prompt.

```java
1   // Fig. 18.11: TowersOfHanoi.java
2   // Towers of Hanoi solution with a recursive method.
3   public class TowersOfHanoi
4   {
5      // recursively move disks between towers
6      public static void solveTowers( int disks, int sourcePeg,
7         int destinationPeg, int tempPeg )
8      {
9         // base case -- only one disk to move
10        if ( disks == 1 )
11        {
12           System.out.printf( "\n%d --> %d", sourcePeg, destinationPeg );
13           return;
14        } // end if
15
16        // recursion step -- move (disk - 1) disks from sourcePeg
17        // to tempPeg using destinationPeg
18        solveTowers( disks - 1, sourcePeg, tempPeg, destinationPeg );
19
20        // move last disk from sourcePeg to destinationPeg
21        System.out.printf( "\n%d --> %d", sourcePeg, destinationPeg );
22
23        // move ( disks - 1 ) disks from tempPeg to destinationPeg
24        solveTowers( disks - 1, tempPeg, destinationPeg, sourcePeg );
25     } // end method solveTowers
26
27     public static void main( String[] args )
28     {
29        int startPeg = 1; // value 1 used to indicate startPeg in output
30        int endPeg = 3; // value 3 used to indicate endPeg in output
31        int tempPeg = 2; // value 2 used to indicate tempPeg in output
32        int totalDisks = 3; // number of disks
33
34        // initial nonrecursive call: move all disks.
35        solveTowers( totalDisks, startPeg, endPeg, tempPeg );
36     } // end main
37  } // end class TowersOfHanoi
```

```
1 --> 3
1 --> 2
3 --> 2
1 --> 3
2 --> 1
2 --> 3
1 --> 3
```

Fig. 18.11 | Towers of Hanoi solution with a recursive method.

18.8 Fractals

A **fractal** is a geometric figure that can be generated from a pattern repeated recursively (Fig. 18.12). The figure is modified by applying the pattern to each segment of the original figure. We'll look at a few such approximations in this section. [*Note:* We'll refer to our geometric figures as fractals, even though they're approximations.] Although these figures had been studied before the 20th century, it was the mathematician Benoit Mandelbrot who in the 1970s introduced the term "fractal," along with the specifics of how a fractal is created and the practical applications of fractals. Mandelbrot's fractal geometry provides mathematical models for many complex forms found in nature, such as mountains, clouds and coastlines. Fractals have many uses in mathematics and science. They can be used to better understand systems or patterns that appear in nature (e.g., ecosystems), in the human body (e.g., in the folds of the brain), or in the universe (e.g., galaxy clusters). Not all fractals resemble objects in nature. Drawing fractals has become a popular art form. Fractals have a **self-similar property**—when subdivided into parts, each resembles a reduced-size copy of the whole. Many fractals yield an exact copy of the original when a portion of the fractal is magnified—such a fractal is said to be **strictly self-similar**. See our Recursion Resource Center (`www.deitel.com/recursion/`) for websites that demonstrate fractals.

As an example, let's look at the strictly self-similar **Koch Curve** fractal (Fig. 18.12). It is formed by removing the middle third of each line in the drawing and replacing it with two lines that form a point, such that if the middle third of the original line remained, an equilateral triangle would be formed. Formulas for creating fractals often involve removing all or part of the previous fractal image. This pattern has already been determined for this fractal—we focus here on how to use those formulas in a recursive solution.

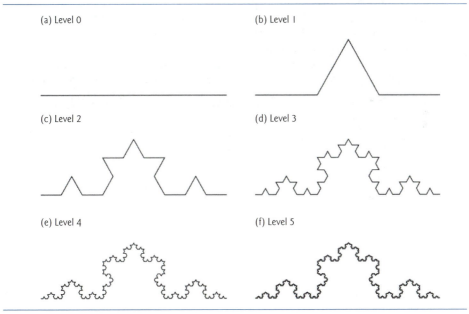

(a) Level 0   (b) Level 1

(c) Level 2   (d) Level 3

(e) Level 4   (f) Level 5

Fig. 18.12 | Koch Curve fractal.

We start with a straight line (Fig. 18.12(a)) and apply the pattern, creating a triangle from the middle third (Fig. 18.12(b)). We then apply the pattern again to each straight line, resulting in Fig. 18.12(c). Each time the pattern is applied, we say that the fractal is at a new **level**, or **depth** (sometimes the term **order** is also used). Fractals can be displayed at many levels—for instance, a fractal at level 3 has had three iterations of the pattern applied (Fig. 18.12(d)). After only a few iterations, this fractal begins to look like a portion of a snowflake (Fig. 18.12(e and f)). Since this is a strictly self-similar fractal, each portion of it contains an exact copy of the fractal. In Fig. 18.12(f), for example, we've highlighted a portion of the fractal with a dashed red box. If the image in this box were increased in size, it would look exactly like the entire fractal of part (f).

A similar fractal, the **Koch Snowflake**, is the same as the Koch Curve but begins with a triangle rather than a line. The same pattern is applied to each side of the triangle, resulting in an image that looks like an enclosed snowflake. For simplicity, we've chosen to focus on the Koch Curve. To learn more about the Koch Curve and Koch Snowflake, see the links in our Recursion Resource Center (www.deitel.com/recursion/).

The "Lo Fractal"

We now demonstrate the use of recursion to draw fractals by writing a program to create a strictly self-similar fractal. We call this the "Lo fractal," named for Sin Han Lo, a Deitel & Associates colleague who created it. The fractal will eventually resemble one-half of a feather (see the outputs in Fig. 18.19). The base case, or fractal level of 0, begins as a line between two points, A and B (Fig. 18.13). To create the next higher level, we find the midpoint (C) of the line. To calculate the location of point C, use the following formula:

```
xC = (xA + xB) / 2;
yC = (yA + yB) / 2;
```

[*Note:* The x and y to the left of each letter refer to the *x*-coordinate and *y*-coordinate of that point, respectively. For instance, xA refers to the *x*-coordinate of point A, while yC refers to the *y*-coordinate of point C. In our diagrams we denote the point by its letter, followed by two numbers representing the *x*- and *y*-coordinates.]

To create this fractal, we also must find a point D that lies left of segment AC and creates an isosceles right triangle ADC. To calculate point D's location, use the following formulas:

```
xD = xA + (xC - xA) / 2 - (yC - yA) / 2;
yD = yA + (yC - yA) / 2 + (xC - xA) / 2;
```

A (6, 5)   B (30, 5)

Origin (0, 0)

Fig. 18.13 | "Lo fractal" at level 0.

We now move from level 0 to level 1 as follows: First, add points C and D (as in Fig. 18.14). Then, remove the original line and add segments DA, DC and DB. The remaining lines will curve at an angle, causing our fractal to look like a feather. For the next level of the fractal, this algorithm is repeated on each of the three lines in level 1. For each line, the formulas above are applied, where the former point D is now considered to be point A, while the other end of each line is considered to be point B. Figure 18.15 contains the line from level 0 (now a dashed line) and the three added lines from level 1. We've changed point D to be point A, and the original points A, C and B to B1, B2 and B3, respectively. The preceding formulas have been used to find the new points C and D on each line. These points are also numbered 1–3 to keep track of which point is associated with each line. The points C1 and D1, for instance, represent points C and D associated with the line formed from points A to B1. To achieve level 2, the three lines in Fig. 18.15 are removed and replaced with new lines from the C and D points just added. Figure 18.16 shows the new lines (the lines from level 2 are shown as dashed lines for your convenience). Figure 18.17 shows level 2 without the dashed lines from level 1. Once this process has been repeated several times, the fractal created will begin to look like one-half of a feather, as shown in the output of Fig. 18.19. We'll present the code for this application shortly.

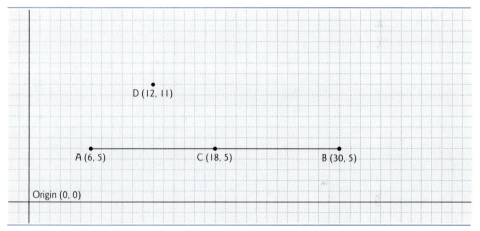

Fig. 18.14 | Determining points C and D for level 1 of the "Lo fractal."

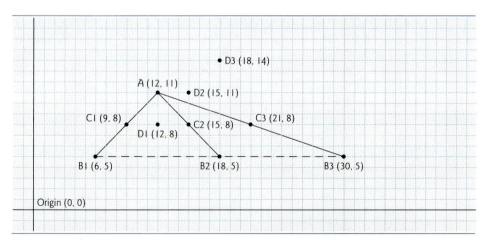

Fig. 18.15 | "Lo fractal" at level 1, with C and D points determined for level 2. [*Note:* The fractal at level 0 is included as a dashed line as a reminder of where the line was located in relation to the current fractal.]

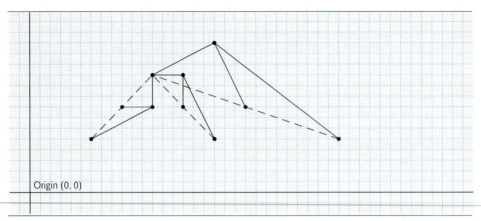

Fig. 18.16 | "Lo fractal" at level 2, with dashed lines from level 1 provided.

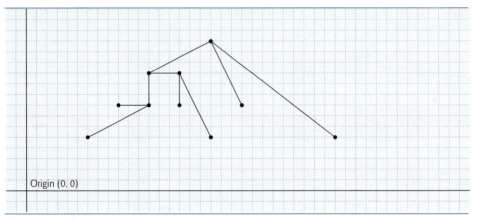

Fig. 18.17 | "Lo fractal" at level 2.

The application in Fig. 18.18 defines the user interface for drawing this fractal (shown at the end of Fig. 18.19). The interface consists of three buttons—one for the user to change the color of the fractal, one to increase the level of recursion and one to decrease the level of recursion. A `JLabel` keeps track of the current level of recursion, which is modified by calling method `setLevel`, to be discussed shortly. Lines 15–16 specify constants `WIDTH` and `HEIGHT` to be 400 and 480, respectively, for the size of the `JFrame`. The user triggers an `ActionEvent` by clicking the **Color** button. The event handler for this button is registered in lines 37–53. The method `actionPerformed` displays a `JColorChooser`. This dialog returns the selected `Color` object or blue (if the user presses **Cancel** or closes the dialog without pressing **OK**). Line 50 calls the `setColor` method in class `FractalJPanel` to update the color.

```
1   // Fig. 18.18: Fractal.java
2   // Fractal user interface.
3   import java.awt.Color;
```

Fig. 18.18 | Fractal user interface. (Part 1 of 4.)

```
 4   import java.awt.FlowLayout;
 5   import java.awt.event.ActionEvent;
 6   import java.awt.event.ActionListener;
 7   import javax.swing.JFrame;
 8   import javax.swing.JButton;
 9   import javax.swing.JLabel;
10   import javax.swing.JPanel;
11   import javax.swing.JColorChooser;
12
13   public class Fractal extends JFrame
14   {
15      private static final int WIDTH = 400;  // define width of GUI
16      private static final int HEIGHT = 480; // define height of GUI
17      private static final int MIN_LEVEL = 0, MAX_LEVEL = 15;
18
19      private JButton changeColorJButton, increaseLevelJButton,
20         decreaseLevelJButton;
21      private JLabel levelJLabel;
22      private FractalJPanel drawSpace;
23      private JPanel mainJPanel, controlJPanel;
24
25      // set up GUI
26      public Fractal()
27      {
28         super( "Fractal" );
29
30         // set up control panel
31         controlJPanel = new JPanel();
32         controlJPanel.setLayout( new FlowLayout() );
33
34         // set up color button and register listener
35         changeColorJButton = new JButton( "Color" );
36         controlJPanel.add( changeColorJButton );
37         changeColorJButton.addActionListener(
38            new ActionListener() // anonymous inner class
39            {
40               // process changeColorJButton event
41               public void actionPerformed( ActionEvent event )
42               {
43                  Color color = JColorChooser.showDialog(
44                     Fractal.this, "Choose a color", Color.BLUE );
45
46                  // set default color, if no color is returned
47                  if ( color == null )
48                     color = Color.BLUE;
49
50                  drawSpace.setColor( color );
51               } // end method actionPerformed
52            }  // end anonymous inner class
53         ); // end addActionListener
54
55         // set up decrease level button to add to control panel and
56         // register listener
57         decreaseLevelJButton = new JButton( "Decrease Level" );
```

Fig. 18.18 | Fractal user interface. (Part 2 of 4.)

```
58          controlJPanel.add( decreaseLevelJButton );
59          decreaseLevelJButton.addActionListener(
60             new ActionListener() // anonymous inner class
61             {
62                // process decreaseLevelJButton event
63                public void actionPerformed( ActionEvent event )
64                {
65                   int level = drawSpace.getLevel();
66                   --level; // decrease level by one
67
68                   // modify level if possible
69                   if ( ( level >= MIN_LEVEL ) ) &&
70                      ( level <= MAX_LEVEL ) )
71                   {
72                      levelJLabel.setText( "Level: " + level );
73                      drawSpace.setLevel( level );
74                      repaint();
75                   } // end if
76                } // end method actionPerformed
77             } // end anonymous inner class
78          ); // end addActionListener
79
80          // set up increase level button to add to control panel
81          // and register listener
82          increaseLevelJButton = new JButton( "Increase Level" );
83          controlJPanel.add( increaseLevelJButton );
84          increaseLevelJButton.addActionListener(
85             new ActionListener() // anonymous inner class
86             {
87                // process increaseLevelJButton event
88                public void actionPerformed( ActionEvent event )
89                {
90                   int level = drawSpace.getLevel();
91                   ++level; // increase level by one
92
93                   // modify level if possible
94                   if ( ( level >= MIN_LEVEL ) ) &&
95                      ( level <= MAX_LEVEL ) )
96                   {
97                      levelJLabel.setText( "Level: " + level );
98                      drawSpace.setLevel( level );
99                      repaint();
100                  } // end if
101               } // end method actionPerformed
102            } // end anonymous inner class
103         ); // end addActionListener
104
105         // set up levelJLabel to add to controlJPanel
106         levelJLabel = new JLabel( "Level: 0" );
107         controlJPanel.add( levelJLabel );
108
109         drawSpace = new FractalJPanel( 0 );
110
```

Fig. 18.18 | Fractal user interface. (Part 3 of 4.)

```
111        // create mainJPanel to contain controlJPanel and drawSpace
112        mainJPanel = new JPanel();
113        mainJPanel.add( controlJPanel );
114        mainJPanel.add( drawSpace );
115
116        add( mainJPanel ); // add JPanel to JFrame
117
118        setSize( WIDTH, HEIGHT ); // set size of JFrame
119        setVisible( true ); // display JFrame
120     } // end Fractal constructor
121
122     public static void main( String[] args )
123     {
124        Fractal demo = new Fractal();
125        demo.setDefaultCloseOperation( JFrame.EXIT_ON_CLOSE );
126     } // end main
127  } // end class Fractal
```

Fig. 18.18 | Fractal user interface. (Part 4 of 4.)

The **Decrease Level** button's event handler is registered in lines 59–78. Method
actionPerformed retrieves the current level of recursion and decrements it by 1 (lines 65–66). Lines 69–70 ensure that the level is greater than or equal to MIN_LEVEL and less than
or equal to MAX_LEVEL—the fractal is not defined for recursion levels less than MIN_LEVEL
and you can't see the additional detail above MAX_LEVEL. You can go up to any desired
level, but around level 10 and higher, the fractal rendering becomes slow due to the details
to be drawn. Lines 72–74 reset the level label to reflect the change—the new level is set
and the repaint method is called to update the image to show the fractal at the new level.

The **Increase Level** JButton works like the **Decrease Level** JButton, but the level is
incremented rather than decremented to show more details of the fractal (lines 90–91).
When the application is first executed, the level will be set to 0, which will display a blue
line between two points that were specified in the FractalJPanel class.

Class FractalJPanel (Fig. 18.19) specifies the drawing JPanel's dimensions as 400
by 400 (lines 13–14). The FractalJPanel constructor (lines 18–24) takes the current level
as a parameter and assigns it to its instance variable level. Instance variable color is set
to blue by default. Lines 22–23 change the JPanel's background color to white (so the
fractal is easy to see), and set the drawing FractalJPanel's dimensions.

```
1    // Fig. 18.19: FractalJPanel.java
2    // Drawing the "Lo fractal" using recursion.
3    import java.awt.Graphics;
4    import java.awt.Color;
5    import java.awt.Dimension;
6    import javax.swing.JPanel;
7
8    public class FractalJPanel extends JPanel
9    {
10      private Color color; // stores color used to draw fractal
11      private int level;   // stores current level of fractal
```

Fig. 18.19 | Drawing the "Lo fractal" using recursion. (Part 1 of 4.)

```
12
13      private static final int WIDTH = 400;  // defines width of JPanel
14      private static final int HEIGHT = 400; // defines height of JPanel
15
16      // set the initial fractal level to the value specified
17      // and set up JPanel specifications
18      public FractalJPanel( int currentLevel )
19      {
20         color = Color.BLUE;  // initialize drawing color to blue
21         level = currentLevel; // set initial fractal level
22         setBackground( Color.WHITE );
23         setPreferredSize( new Dimension( WIDTH, HEIGHT ) );
24      } // end FractalJPanel constructor
25
26      // draw fractal recursively
27      public void drawFractal( int level, int xA, int yA, int xB,
28         int yB, Graphics g )
29      {
30         // base case: draw a line connecting two given points
31         if ( level == 0 )
32            g.drawLine( xA, yA, xB, yB );
33         else // recursion step: determine new points, draw next level
34         {
35            // calculate midpoint between (xA, yA) and (xB, yB)
36            int xC = ( xA + xB ) / 2;
37            int yC = ( yA + yB ) / 2;
38
39            // calculate the fourth point (xD, yD) which forms an
40            // isosceles right triangle between (xA, yA) and (xC, yC)
41            // where the right angle is at (xD, yD)
42            int xD = xA + ( xC - xA ) / 2 - ( yC - yA ) / 2;
43            int yD = yA + ( yC - yA ) / 2 + ( xC - xA ) / 2;
44
45            // recursively draw the Fractal
46            drawFractal( level - 1, xD, yD, xA, yA, g );
47            drawFractal( level - 1, xD, yD, xC, yC, g );
48            drawFractal( level - 1, xD, yD, xB, yB, g );
49         } // end else
50      } // end method drawFractal
51
52      // start drawing the fractal
53      public void paintComponent( Graphics g )
54      {
55         super.paintComponent( g );
56
57         // draw fractal pattern
58         g.setColor( color );
59         drawFractal( level, 100, 90, 290, 200, g );
60      } // end method paintComponent
61
62      // set the drawing color to c
63      public void setColor( Color c )
64      {
```

Fig. 18.19 | Drawing the "Lo fractal" using recursion. (Part 2 of 4.)

```
65          color = c;
66      } // end method setColor
67
68      // set the new level of recursion
69      public void setLevel( int currentLevel )
70      {
71          level = currentLevel;
72      } // end method setLevel
73
74      // returns level of recursion
75      public int getLevel()
76      {
77          return level;
78      } // end method getLevel
79  } // end class FractalJPanel
```

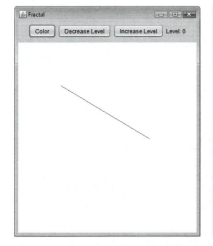

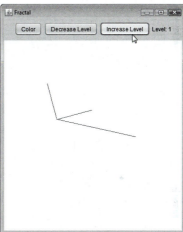

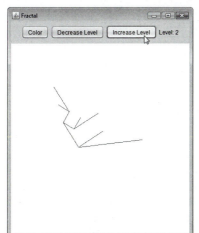

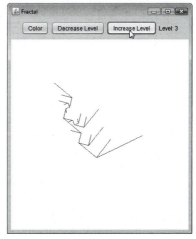

Fig. 18.19 | Drawing the "Lo fractal" using recursion. (Part 3 of 4.)

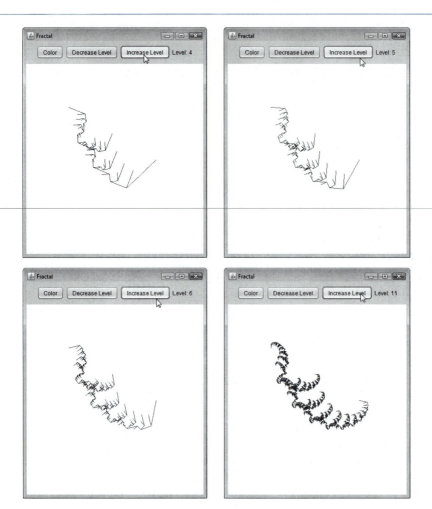

Fig. 18.19 | Drawing the "Lo fractal" using recursion. (Part 4 of 4.)

Lines 27–50 define the recursive method that creates the fractal. This method takes six parameters: the level, four integers that specify the *x*- and *y*-coordinates of two points, and the Graphics object g. The base case for this method (line 31) occurs when level equals 0, at which time a line will be drawn between the two points given as parameters. Lines 36–43 calculate (xC, yC), the midpoint between (xA, yA) and (xB, yB), and (xD, yD), the point that creates a right isosceles triangle with (xA, yA) and (xC, yC). Lines 46–48 make three recursive calls on three different sets of points.

In method paintComponent, line 59 makes the first call to method drawFractal to start the drawing. This method call is not recursive, but all subsequent calls to draw-Fractal performed from the body of drawFractal are. Since the lines will not be drawn until the base case is reached, the distance between two points decreases on each recursive call. As the level of recursion increases, the fractal becomes smoother and more detailed. The shape of this fractal stabilizes as the level approaches 11. Fractals will stabilize at different levels based on the shape and size of the fractal.

Figure 18.19 shows the development of the fractal from levels 0 to 6. The last image shows the defining shape of the fractal at level 11. If we focus on one of the arms of this fractal, it will be identical to the whole image. This property defines the fractal to be strictly self-similar. See our Recursion Resource Center at www.deitel.com/recursion/ for further resources on fractals.

18.9 Recursive Backtracking

Our recursive methods all have a similar architecture—if the base case is reached, return a result; if not, make one or more recursive calls. This section explores a more complex recursive technique that finds a path through a maze, returning true if there is a possible solution to the maze. The solution involves moving through the maze one step at a time, where moves can be made by going down, right, up or left (diagonal moves are not permitted). From the current location in the maze (starting with the entry point), the following steps are taken: For each possible direction, the move is made in that direction and a recursive call is made to solve the remainder of the maze from the new location. When a dead end is reached (i.e., we cannot take any more steps forward without hitting a wall), we back up to the previous location and try to go in a different direction. If no other direction can be taken, we back up again. This process continues until we find a point in the maze where a move *can* be made in another direction. Once such a location is found, we move in the new direction and continue with another recursive call to solve the rest of the maze.

To back up to the previous location in the maze, our recursive method simply returns false, moving up the method-call chain to the previous recursive call (which references the previous location in the maze). Using recursion to return to an earlier decision point is known as **recursive backtracking**. If one set of recursive calls does not result in a solution to the problem, the program backs up to the previous decision point and makes a different decision, often resulting in another set of recursive calls. In this example, the previous decision point is the previous location in the maze, and the decision to be made is the direction that the next move should take. One direction has led to a dead end, so the search continues with a different direction. The recursive backtracking solution to the maze problem uses recursion to return only partway up the method-call chain, then try a different direction. If the backtracking reaches the entry location of the maze and the paths in all directions have been attempted, the maze does not have a solution.

The exercises ask you to implement recursive backtracking solutions to the maze problem (Exercises 18.20–18.22) and the Eight Queens problem (Exercise 18.15), which attempts to find a way to place eight queens on an empty chessboard so that no queen is "attacking" any other (i.e., no two queens are in the same row, in the same column or along the same diagonal). See our Recursion Resource Center at www.deitel.com/recursion/ for more information on recursive backtracking.

18.10 Wrap-Up

In this chapter, you learned how to create recursive methods—i.e., methods that call themselves. You learned that recursive methods typically divide a problem into two conceptual pieces—a piece that the method knows how to do (the base case) and a piece that the method does not know how to do (the recursion step). The recursion step is a slightly smaller version of the original problem and is performed by a recursive method call. You saw some popular recursion examples, including calculating factorials and producing values in the Fibonacci series. You then learned how recursion works "under the hood," including the order in which recursive method calls are pushed on or popped off the program-execution stack. Next, you compared recursive and iterative (non-recursive) approaches. You learned how to solve more complex problems using recursion—the Towers of Hanoi and displaying fractals. The chapter concluded with an introduction to recursive backtracking, a technique for solving problems that involves backing up through recursive calls to try different possible solutions. In the next chapter, you'll learn numerous techniques for sorting lists of data and searching for an item in a list of data, and you'll explore the circumstances under which each searching and sorting technique should be used.

Summary

Section 18.1 Introduction
- A recursive method calls itself directly or indirectly through another method.

Section 18.2 Recursion Concepts
- When a recursive method is called to solve a problem, the method actually is capable of solving only the simplest case(s), or base case(s). If it's called with a base case, the method returns a result.
- If a recursive method is called with a more complex problem than a base case, it typically divides the problem into two conceptual pieces—a piece that the method knows how to do and a piece that it does not know how to do.
- To make recursion feasible, the piece that the method does not know how to do must resemble the original problem, but be a slightly simpler or smaller version of it. Because this new problem looks like the original problem, the method calls a fresh copy of itself to work on the smaller problem—this is called the recursion step.
- For recursion to eventually terminate, each time a method calls itself with a simpler version of the original problem, the sequence of smaller and smaller problems must converge on a base case. When, the method recognizes the base case, it returns a result to the previous copy of the method.
- A recursive call may be a call to another method, which in turn makes a call back to the original method. Such a process still results in a recursive call to the original method. This is known as an indirect recursive call or indirect recursion.

Section 18.3 Example Using Recursion: Factorials
- Either omitting the base case or writing the recursion step incorrectly so that it does not converge on the base case can cause infinite recursion, eventually exhausting memory. This error is analogous to the problem of an infinite loop in an iterative (nonrecursive) solution.

Section 18.4 Example Using Recursion: Fibonacci Series
- The Fibonacci series begins with 0 and 1 and has the property that each subsequent Fibonacci number is the sum of the preceding two.
- The ratio of successive Fibonacci numbers converges on a constant value of 1.618..., a number that has been called the golden ratio or the golden mean.
- Some recursive solutions, such as Fibonacci, result in an "explosion" of method calls.

Section 18.5 Recursion and the Method-Call Stack
- The executing method is always the one whose activation record is at the top of the stack, and the activation record for that method contains the values of its local variables.

Section 18.6 Recursion vs. Iteration
- Both iteration and recursion are based on a control statement: Iteration uses a repetition statement, recursion a selection statement.
- Both iteration and recursion involve repetition: Iteration explicitly uses a repetition statement, whereas recursion achieves repetition through repeated method calls.
- Iteration and recursion each involve a termination test: Iteration terminates when the loop-continuation condition fails, recursion when a base case is recognized.
- Iteration with counter-controlled repetition and recursion each gradually approach termination: Iteration keeps modifying a counter until the counter assumes a value that makes the loop-continuation condition fail, whereas recursion keeps producing simpler versions of the original problem until the base case is reached.
- Both iteration and recursion can occur infinitely: An infinite loop occurs with iteration if the loop-continuation test never becomes false, whereas infinite recursion occurs if the recursion step does not reduce the problem each time in a manner that converges on the base case.
- Recursion repeatedly invokes the mechanism, and consequently the overhead, of method calls.
- Any problem that can be solved recursively can also be solved iteratively.
- A recursive approach is normally preferred over an iterative approach when it more naturally mirrors the problem and results in a program that is easier to understand and debug.
- A recursive approach can often be implemented with few lines of code, but a corresponding iterative approach might take a large amount of code. Another reason to choose a recursive solution is that an iterative solution might not be apparent.

Section 18.8 Fractals
- A fractal is a geometric figure that is generated from a pattern repeated recursively an infinite number of times.
- Fractals have a self-similar property—subparts are reduced-size copies of the whole.

Section 18.9 Recursive Backtracking
- Using recursion to return to an earlier decision point is known as recursive backtracking. If one set of recursive calls does not result in a solution to the problem, the program backs up to the previous decision point and makes a different decision, often resulting in another set of recursive calls.

Terminology

Self-Review Exercises

18.1 State whether each of the following is *true* or *false*. If *false*, explain why.
a) A method that calls itself indirectly is not an example of recursion.
b) Recursion can be efficient in computation because of reduced memory-space usage.
c) When a recursive method is called to solve a problem, it actually is capable of solving only the simplest case(s), or base case(s).
d) To make recursion feasible, the recursion step in a recursive solution must resemble the original problem, but be a slightly larger version of it.

18.2 A _____ is needed to terminate recursion.
a) recursion step
b) break statement
c) void return type
d) base case

18.3 The first call to invoke a recursive method is _____.
a) not recursive
b) recursive
c) the recursion step
d) none of the above

18.4 Each time a fractal's pattern is applied, the fractal is said to be at a new _____.
a) width
b) height
c) level
d) volume

18.5 Iteration and recursion each involve a _____.
a) repetition statement
b) termination test
c) counter variable
d) none of the above

18.6 Fill in the blanks in each of the following statements:
a) The ratio of successive Fibonacci numbers converges on a constant value of 1.618…, a number that has been called the _____ or the _____.
b) Iteration normally uses a repetition statement, whereas recursion normally uses a(n) _____ statement.
c) Fractals have a(n) _____ property—when subdivided into parts, each is a reduced-size copy of the whole.

Answers to Self-Review Exercises

18.1 a) False. A method that calls itself in this manner is an example of indirect recursion. b) False. Recursion can be inefficient in computation because of multiple method calls and memory-space usage. c) True. d) False. To make recursion feasible, the recursion step in a recursive solution must resemble the original problem, but be a slightly *smaller* version of it.

18.2 d

18.3 a

18.4 c

18.5 b

18.6 a) golden ratio, golden mean. b) selection. c) self-similar.

Exercises

18.7   What does the following code do?

```
I   public int mystery( int a, int b )
2   {
3      if ( b == 1 )
4         return a;
5      else
6         return a + mystery( a, b - 1 );
7   } // end method mystery
```

18.8   Find the error(s) in the following recursive method, and explain how to correct it (them). This method should find the sum of the values from 0 to n.

```
I   public int sum( int n )
2   {
3      if ( n == 0 )
4         return 0;
5      else
6         return n + sum( n );
7   } // end method sum
```

18.9   *(Recursive power Method)* Write a recursive method power(base, exponent) that, when called, returns

> base ^{exponent}

For example, power(3,4) = 3 * 3 * 3 * 3. Assume that exponent is an integer greater than or equal to 1. [*Hint:* The recursion step should use the relationship

> base ^{exponent} = base · base $^{exponent - 1}$

and the terminating condition occurs when exponent is equal to 1, because

> base^1 = base

Incorporate this method into a program that enables the user to enter the base and exponent.]

18.10   *(Visualizing Recursion)* It's interesting to watch recursion "in action." Modify the factorial method in Fig. 18.3 to print its local variable and recursive-call parameter. For each recursive call, display the outputs on a separate line and add a level of indentation. Do your utmost to make the outputs clear, interesting and meaningful. Your goal here is to design and implement an output format that makes it easier to understand recursion. You may want to add such display capabilities to other recursion examples and exercises throughout the text.

18.11   *(Greatest Common Divisor)* The greatest common divisor of integers x and y is the largest integer that evenly divides into both x and y. Write a recursive method gcd that returns the greatest common divisor of x and y. The gcd of x and y is defined recursively as follows: If y is equal to 0, then gcd(x, y) is x; otherwise, gcd(x, y) is gcd(y, x % y), where % is the remainder operator. Use this method to replace the one you wrote in the application of Exercise 5.27.

18.12   What does the following program do?

```
I   // Exercise 18.12 Solution: MysteryClass.java
2   public class MysteryClass
3   {
4      public static int mystery( int[] array2, int size )
5      {
```

```
6          if ( size == 1 )
7             return array2[ 0 ];
8          else
9             return array2[ size - 1 ] + mystery( array2, size - 1 );
10      } // end method mystery
11
12      public static void main( String[] args )
13      {
14          int[] array = { 1, 2, 3, 4, 5, 6, 7, 8, 9, 10 };
15
16          int result = mystery( array, array.length );
17          System.out.printf( "Result is: %d\n", result );
18      } // end method main
19  } // end class MysteryClass
```

18.13 What does the following program do?

```
1   // Exercise 18.13 Solution: SomeClass.java
2   public class SomeClass
3   {
4       public static String someMethod( int[] array2, int x )
5       {
6           if ( x < array2.length )
7               return String.format(
8                   "%s%d ", someMethod( array2, x + 1 ), array2[ x ] );
9           else
10              return "";
11      } // end method someMethod
12
13      public static void main( String[] args )
14      {
15          int[] array = { 1, 2, 3, 4, 5, 6, 7, 8, 9, 10 };
16          String results = someMethod( array, 0 );
17          System.out.println( results );
18      } // end main
19  } // end class SomeClass
```

18.14 *(Palindromes)* A palindrome is a string that is spelled the same way forward and backward. Some examples of palindromes are "radar," "able was i ere i saw elba" and (if spaces are ignored) "a man a plan a canal panama." Write a recursive method testPalindrome that returns boolean value true if the string stored in the array is a palindrome and false otherwise. The method should ignore spaces and punctuation in the string.

18.15 *(Eight Queens)* A puzzler for chess buffs is the Eight Queens problem, which asks: Is it possible to place eight queens on an empty chessboard so that no queen is "attacking" any other (i.e., no two queens are in the same row, in the same column or along the same diagonal)? For instance, if a queen is placed in the upper-left corner of the board, no other queens could be placed in any of the marked squares shown in Fig. 18.20. Solve the problem recursively. [*Hint:* Your solution should begin with the first column and look for a location in that column where a queen can be placed—initially, place the queen in the first row. The solution should then recursively search the remaining columns. In the first few columns, there will be several locations where a queen may be placed. Take the first available location. If a column is reached with no possible location for a queen, the program should return to the previous column, and move the queen in that column to a new row. This continuous backing up and trying new alternatives is an example of recursive backtracking.]

18.16 *(Print an Array)* Write a recursive method printArray that displays all the elements in an array of integers, separated by spaces.

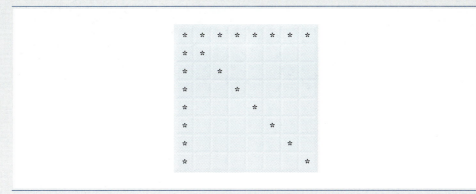

Fig. 18.20 | Squares eliminated by placing a queen in the upper-left corner of a chessboard.

18.17 *(Print an Array Backward)* Write a recursive method `stringReverse` that takes a character array containing a string as an argument and prints the string backward. [*Hint:* Use `String` method `toCharArray`, which takes no arguments, to get a `char` array containing the characters in the `String`.]

18.18 *(Find the Minimum Value in an Array)* Write a recursive method `recursiveMinimum` that determines the smallest element in an array of integers. The method should return when it receives an array of one element.

18.19 *(Fractals)* Repeat the fractal pattern in Section 18.8 to form a star. Begin with five lines (see Fig. 18.21, instead of one, where each line is a different arm of the star. Apply the "Lo fractal" pattern to each arm of the star.

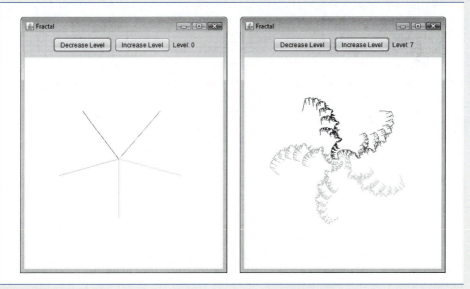

Fig. 18.21 | Sample outputs for Exercise 18.19.

18.20 *(Maze Traversal Using Recursive Backtracking)* The grid of #s and dots (.) in Fig. 18.22 is a two-dimensional array representation of a maze. The #s represent the walls of the maze, and the dots represent locations in the possible paths through the maze. Moves can be made only to a location in the array that contains a dot.

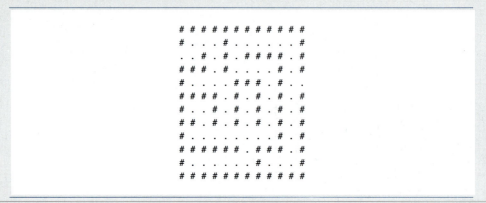

```
# # # # # # # # # # # #
#  .  .  .  #  .  .  .  .  .  .  #
.  .  #  .  #  .  #  #  #  #  .  #
#  #  #  .  #  .  .  .  .  #  .  #
#  .  .  .  .  #  #  #  .  #  .  .
#  #  #  #  .  #  .  #  .  #  .  #
#  .  .  #  .  #  .  #  .  #  .  #
#  #  .  #  .  #  .  #  .  #  .  #
#  .  .  .  .  .  .  .  .  #  .  #
#  #  #  #  #  .  #  #  #  .  #
#  .  .  .  .  .  .  #  .  .  .  #
# # # # # # # # # # # #
```

Fig. 18.22 | Two-dimensional array representation of a maze.

Write a recursive method (mazeTraversal) to walk through mazes like the one in Fig. 18.22. The method should receive as arguments a 12-by-12 character array representing the maze and the current location in the maze (the first time this method is called, the current location should be the entry point of the maze). As mazeTraversal attempts to locate the exit, it should place the character x in each square in the path. There is a simple algorithm for walking through a maze that guarantees finding the exit (assuming there is an exit). If there is no exit, you'll arrive at the starting location again. The algorithm is as follows: From the current location in the maze, try to move one space in any of the possible directions (down, right, up or left). If it's possible to move in at least one direction, call mazeTraversal recursively, passing the new spot on the maze as the current spot. If it's not possible to go in any direction, "back up" to a previous location in the maze and try a new direction for that location. Program the method to display the maze after each move so the user can watch as the maze is solved. The final output of the maze should display only the path needed to solve the maze—if going in a particular direction results in a dead end, the x's going in that direction should not be displayed. [*Hint:* To display only the final path, it may be helpful to mark off spots that result in a dead end with another character (such as '0').]

18.21 *(Generating Mazes Randomly)* Write a method mazeGenerator that takes as an argument a two-dimensional 12-by-12 character array and randomly produces a maze. The method should also provide the starting and ending locations of the maze. Test your method mazeTraversal from Exercise 18.20, using several randomly generated mazes.

18.22 *(Mazes of Any Size)* Generalize methods mazeTraversal and mazeGenerator of Exercise 18.20 and Exercise 18.21 to process mazes of any width and height.

18.23 *(Time to Calculate Fibonacci Numbers)* Enhance the Fibonacci program of Fig. 18.5 so that it calculates the approximate amount of time required to perform the calculation and the number of calls made to the recursive method. For this purpose, call static System method currentTimeMillis, which takes no arguments and returns the computer's current time in milliseconds. Call this method twice—once before and once after the call to fibonacci. Save each value and calculate the difference in the times to determine how many milliseconds were required to perform the calculation. Then, add a variable to the FibonacciCalculator class, and use this variable to determine the number of calls made to method fibonacci. Display your results.

Searching, Sorting and Big O

Objectives

In this chapter you'll learn:

- To search for a given value in an array using linear search and binary search.

- To sort arrays using the iterative selection and insertion sort algorithms.

- To sort arrays using the recursive merge sort algorithm.

- To determine the efficiency of searching and sorting algorithms.

19.1 Introduction

Searching data involves determining whether a value (referred to as the **search key**) is present in the data and, if so, finding its location. Two popular search algorithms are the simple linear search and the faster but more complex binary search. **Sorting** places data in ascending or descending order, based on one or more **sort keys**. A list of names could be sorted alphabetically, bank accounts could be sorted by account number, employee payroll records could be sorted by social security number, and so on. This chapter introduces two simple sorting algorithms, the selection sort and the insertion sort, along with the more efficient but more complex merge sort. Figure 19.1 summarizes the searching and sorting algorithms discussed in the examples and exercises of this book.

Chapter	Algorithm	Location
Searching Algorithms:		
19	Linear search	Section 19.2.1
	Binary search	Section 19.2.2
	Recursive linear search	Exercise 19.8
	Recursive binary search	Exercise 19.9
20	binarySearch method of class Collections	Fig. 20.12
22	Linear search of a List	Exercise 22.21
	Binary tree search	Exercise 22.23
Sorting Algorithms:		
19	Selection sort	Section 19.3.1
	Insertion sort	Section 19.3.2
	Recursive merge sort	Section 19.3.3
	Bubble sort	Exercises 19.5– and 19.6
	Bucket sort	Exercise 19.7
	Recursive quicksort	Exercise 19.10
20	sort method of class Collections	Figs. 20.6–20.9
	SortedSet collection	Fig. 20.17
22	Binary tree sort	Section 22.7

Fig. 19.1 | Searching and sorting algorithms in this text.

19.2 Searching Algorithms

Looking up a phone number, finding a website via a search engine and checking the definition of a word in a dictionary all involve searching large amounts of data. The next two sections discuss two common search algorithms—one that is easy to program yet relatively inefficient and one that is relatively efficient but more complex and difficult to program.

19.2.1 Linear Search

The **linear search algorithm** searches each element in an array sequentially. If the search key does not match an element in the array, the algorithm tests each element, and when the end of the array is reached, informs the user that the search key is not present. If the search key is in the array, the algorithm tests each element until it finds one that matches the search key and returns the index of that element.

As an example, consider an array containing the following values

34	56	2	10	77	51	93	30	5	52

and a program that is searching for 51. Using the linear search algorithm, the program first checks whether 34 matches the search key. It does not, so the algorithm checks whether 56 matches the search key. The program continues moving through the array sequentially, testing 2, then 10, then 77. When the program tests 51, which matches the search key, the program returns the index 5, which is the location of 51 in the array. If, after checking every array element, the program determines that the search key does not match any element in the array, it returns a sentinel value (e.g., -1).

Figure 19.2 declares the `LinearArray` class. This class has two `private` instance variables—an array of `int`s named `data`, and a `static Random` object to fill the array with randomly generated `int`s. When an object of class `LinearArray` is instantiated, the constructor (lines 13–20) creates and initializes the array `data` with random `int`s in the range 10–99. If there are duplicate values in the array, linear search returns the index of the first element in the array that matches the search key.

```
 1   // Fig. 19.2: LinearArray.java
 2   // Class that contains an array of random integers and a method
 3   // that will search that array sequentially.
 4   import java.util.Random;
 5   import java.util.Arrays;
 6
 7   public class LinearArray
 8   {
 9      private int[] data; // array of values
10      private static final Random generator = new Random();
11
12      // create array of given size and fill with random numbers
13      public LinearArray( int size )
14      {
15         data = new int[ size ]; // create space for array
16
```

Fig. 19.2 | Class that contains an array of random integers and a method that will search that array sequentially. (Part 1 of 2.)

```
17          // fill array with random ints in range 10-99
18          for ( int i = 0; i < size; i++ )
19              data[ i ] = 10 + generator.nextInt( 90 );
20      } // end LinearArray constructor
21
22      // perform a linear search on the data
23      public int linearSearch( int searchKey )
24      {
25          // loop through array sequentially
26          for ( int index = 0; index < data.length; index++ )
27              if ( data[ index ] == searchKey )
28                  return index; // return index of integer
29
30          return -1; // integer was not found
31      } // end method linearSearch
32
33      // method to output values in array
34      public String toString()
35      {
36          return Arrays.toString( data );
37      } // end method toString
38  } // end class LinearArray
```

Fig. 19.2 | Class that contains an array of random integers and a method that will search that array sequentially. (Part 2 of 2.)

Lines 23–31 perform the linear search. The search key is passed to parameter searchKey. Lines 26–28 loop through the elements in the array. Line 27 compares each with searchKey. If the values are equal, line 28 returns the index of the element. If the loop ends without finding the value, line 30 returns -1. Lines 34–37 declare method toString, which returns a String representation of the array for printing. We use Arrays static method toString to return a String representation of the array.

Figure 19.3 creates a LinearArray object containing an array of 10 ints (line 16) and allows the user to search the array. Lines 20–22 prompt the user for and store the search key. The array holds ints from 10–99 (line 18 of Fig. 19.2). Line 28 calls method linearSearch to determine whether searchInt is in the array. If it's not, linearSearch returns -1 and the program notifies the user (lines 31–32). If searchInt is in the array, linearSearch returns the position of the element, which the program outputs in lines 34–35. Lines 38–40 retrieve the next integer from the user.

```
1   // Fig. 19.3: LinearSearchTest.java
2   // Sequentially searching an array for an item.
3   import java.util.Scanner;
4
5   public class LinearSearchTest
6   {
7       public static void main( String[] args )
8       {
9           // create Scanner object to input data
10          Scanner input = new Scanner( System.in );
```

Fig. 19.3 | Sequentially searching an array for an item. (Part 1 of 2.)

```
11
12        int searchInt; // search key
13        int position; // location of search key in array
14
15        // create array and output it
16        LinearArray searchArray = new LinearArray( 10 );
17        System.out.println( searchArray + "\n" ); // print array
18
19        // get input from user
20        System.out.print(
21            "Please enter an integer value (-1 to quit): " );
22        searchInt = input.nextInt(); // read first int from user
23
24        // repeatedly input an integer; -1 terminates the program
25        while ( searchInt != -1 )
26        {
27            // perform linear search
28            position = searchArray.linearSearch( searchInt );
29
30            if ( position == -1 ) // integer was not found
31                System.out.println( "The integer " + searchInt +
32                    " was not found.\n" );
33            else // integer was found
34                System.out.println( "The integer " + searchInt +
35                    " was found in position " + position + ".\n" );
36
37            // get input from user
38            System.out.print(
39                "Please enter an integer value (-1 to quit): " );
40            searchInt = input.nextInt(); // read next int from user
41        } // end while
42    } // end main
43 } // end class LinearSearchTest
```

```
[59, 97, 34, 90, 79, 56, 24, 51, 30, 69]

Please enter an integer value (-1 to quit): 79
The integer 79 was found in position 4.

Please enter an integer value (-1 to quit): 61
The integer 61 was not found.

Please enter an integer value (-1 to quit): 51
The integer 51 was found in position 7.

Please enter an integer value (-1 to quit): -1
```

Fig. 19.3 | Sequentially searching an array for an item. (Part 2 of 2.)

Efficiency of Linear Search

Searching algorithms all accomplish the same goal—finding an element that matches a given search key, if such an element does, in fact, exist. There are, however, a number of things that differentiate search algorithms from one another. The major difference is the amount of effort they require to complete the search. One way to describe this effort is with **Big O notation**, which indicates the worst-case run time for an algorithm—that is, how hard an algorithm may have to work to solve a problem. For searching and sorting algorithms, this depends particularly on how many data elements there are.

Suppose an algorithm is designed to test whether the first element of an array is equal to the second. If the array has 10 elements, this algorithm requires one comparison. If the array has 1000 elements, it still requires one comparison. In fact, the algorithm is completely independent of the number of elements in the array. This algorithm is said to have a **constant run time**, which is represented in Big O notation as $O(1)$. An algorithm that is $O(1)$ does not necessarily require only one comparison. $O(1)$ just means that the number of comparisons is *constant*—it does not grow as the size of the array increases. An algorithm that tests whether the first element of an array is equal to any of the next three elements is still $O(1)$ even though it requires three comparisons.

An algorithm that tests whether the first array element is equal to *any* of the other array elements will require at most $n - 1$ comparisons, where n is the number of array elements. If the array has 10 elements, this algorithm requires up to nine comparisons. If the array has 1000 elements, it requires up to 999 comparisons. As n grows larger, the n part of the expression "dominates," and subtracting one becomes inconsequential. Big O is designed to highlight these dominant terms and ignore terms that become unimportant as n grows. For this reason, an algorithm that requires a total of $n - 1$ comparisons (such as the one we described earlier) is said to be $O(n)$. An $O(n)$ algorithm is referred to as having a **linear run time**. $O(n)$ is often pronounced "on the order of n" or simply "order n."

Now suppose you have an algorithm that tests whether *any* element of an array is duplicated elsewhere in the array. The first element must be compared with every other element in the array. The second element must be compared with every other element except the first (it was already compared to the first). The third element must be compared with every other element except the first two. In the end, this algorithm will end up making $(n - 1) + (n - 2) + \ldots + 2 + 1$ or $n^2/2 - n/2$ comparisons. As n increases, the n^2 term dominates and the n term becomes inconsequential. Again, Big O notation highlights the n^2 term, leaving $n^2/2$. But, as we'll soon see, constant factors are omitted in Big O notation.

Big O is concerned with how an algorithm's run time grows in relation to the number of items processed. Suppose an algorithm requires n^2 comparisons. With four elements, the algorithm requires 16 comparisons; with eight elements, 64 comparisons. With this algorithm, doubling the number of elements quadruples the number of comparisons. Consider a similar algorithm requiring $n^2/2$ comparisons. With four elements, the algorithm requires eight comparisons; with eight elements, 32 comparisons. Again, doubling the number of elements quadruples the number of comparisons. Both of these algorithms grow as the square of n, so Big O ignores the constant and both algorithms are considered to be $O(n^2)$, which is referred to as **quadratic run time** and pronounced "on the order of n-squared" or more simply "order n-squared."

When n is small, $O(n^2)$ algorithms (running on today's computers) will not noticeably affect performance. But as n grows, you'll start to notice the performance degradation. An $O(n^2)$ algorithm running on a million-element array would require a trillion "operations" (where each could actually require several machine instructions to execute). This could take several hours. A billion-element array would require a quintillion operations, a number so large that the algorithm could take decades! $O(n^2)$ algorithms, unfortunately, are easy to write, as you'll see in this chapter. You'll also see algorithms with more favorable Big O measures. These efficient algorithms often take a bit more cleverness and work to create, but their superior performance can be well worth the extra effort, especially as n gets large and as algorithms are combined into larger programs.

The linear search algorithm runs in $O(n)$ time. The worst case in this algorithm is that every element must be checked to determine whether the search item exists in the array. If the size of the array is doubled, the number of comparisons that the algorithm must perform is also doubled. Note that linear search can provide outstanding performance if the element matching the search key happens to be at or near the front of the array. But we seek algorithms that perform well, on average, across all searches, including those where the element matching the search key is near the end of the array.

Linear search is easy to program, but it can be slow compared to other search algorithms. If a program needs to perform many searches on large arrays, it's better to implement a more efficient algorithm, such as the binary search, which we present next.

Performance Tip 19.1

Sometimes the simplest algorithms perform poorly. Their virtue is that they're easy to program, test and debug. Sometimes more complex algorithms are required to realize maximum performance.

19.2.2 Binary Search

The **binary search algorithm** is more efficient than linear search, but it requires that the array be sorted. The first iteration of this algorithm tests the middle element in the array. If this matches the search key, the algorithm ends. Assuming the array is sorted in ascending order, then if the search key is less than the middle element, it cannot match any element in the second half of the array and the algorithm continues with only the first half of the array (i.e., the first element up to, but not including, the middle element). If the search key is greater than the middle element, it cannot match any element in the first half of the array and the algorithm continues with only the second half (i.e., the element after the middle element through the last element). Each iteration tests the middle value of the remaining portion of the array. If the search key does not match the element, the algorithm eliminates half of the remaining elements. The algorithm ends by either finding an element that matches the search key or reducing the subarray to zero size.

As an example consider the sorted 15-element array

2	3	5	10	27	30	34	51	56	65	77	81	82	93	99

and a search key of 65. A program implementing the binary search algorithm would first check whether 51 is the search key (because 51 is the middle element of the array). The search key (65) is larger than 51, so 51 is discarded along with the first half of the array (all elements smaller than 51) leaving

56	65	77	81	82	93	99

Next, the algorithm checks whether 81 (the middle element of the remainder of the array) matches the search key. The search key (65) is smaller than 81, so 81 is discarded along with the elements larger than 81. After just two tests, the algorithm has narrowed the number of values to check to three (56, 65 and 77). It then checks 65 (which indeed matches the search key) and returns the index of the array element containing 65. This algorithm required just three comparisons to determine whether the search key matched an element of the array. Using a linear search algorithm would have required 10 comparisons. [*Note:* In this example, we've chosen to use an array with 15 elements so that there will always be an obvious middle element in the array. With an even number of elements, the middle of the array lies between two elements. We implement the algorithm to chose the higher of those two elements.]

Binary Search Implementation

Figure 19.4 declares class BinaryArray. This class is similar to LinearArray—it has two private instance variables, a constructor, a search method (binarySearch), a remaining-Elements method and a toString method. Lines 13–22 declare the constructor. After the array has been initialized with random ints from 10–99 (lines 18–19), line 21 calls the Arrays.sort method on the array data. The **sort method** is a static method of class Arrays that sorts the elements in an array in ascending order by default; an overloaded version of this method allows you to change the sorting order. Recall that the binary search algorithm will work only on a sorted array.

```java
 1   // Fig. 19.4: BinaryArray.java
 2   // Class that contains an array of random integers and a method
 3   // that uses binary search to find an integer.
 4   import java.util.Random;
 5   import java.util.Arrays;
 6
 7   public class BinaryArray
 8   {
 9      private int[] data; // array of values
10      private static final Random generator = new Random();
11
12      // create array of given size and fill with random integers
13      public BinaryArray( int size )
14      {
15         data = new int[ size ]; // create space for array
16
17         // fill array with random ints in range 10-99
18         for ( int i = 0; i < size; i++ )
19            data[ i ] = 10 + generator.nextInt( 90 );
20
21         Arrays.sort( data );
22      } // end BinaryArray constructor
23
24      // perform a binary search on the data
25      public int binarySearch( int searchElement )
26      {
27         int low = 0; // low end of the search area
28         int high = data.length - 1; // high end of the search area
29         int middle = ( low + high + 1 ) / 2; // middle element
30         int location = -1; // return value; -1 if not found
31
32         do // loop to search for element
33         {
34            // print remaining elements of array
35            System.out.print( remainingElements( low, high ) );
```

Fig. 19.4 | Class that contains an array of random integers and a method that uses binary search to find an integer. (Part 1 of 2.)

```
36
37              // output spaces for alignment
38              for ( int i = 0; i < middle; i++ )
39                  System.out.print( "   " );
40              System.out.println( " * " ); // indicate current middle
41
42              // if the element is found at the middle
43              if ( searchElement == data[ middle ] )
44                  location = middle; // location is the current middle
45
46              // middle element is too high
47              else if ( searchElement < data[ middle ] )
48                  high = middle - 1; // eliminate the higher half
49              else  // middle element is too low
50                  low = middle + 1; // eliminate the lower half
51
52              middle = ( low + high + 1 ) / 2; // recalculate the middle
53          } while ( ( low <= high ) && ( location == -1 ) );
54
55          return location; // return location of search key
56      } // end method binarySearch
57
58      // method to output certain values in array
59      public String remainingElements( int low, int high )
60      {
61          StringBuilder temporary = new StringBuilder();
62
63          // output spaces for alignment
64          for ( int i = 0; i < low; i++ )
65              temporary.append( "   " );
66
67          // output elements left in array
68          for ( int i = low; i <= high; i++ )
69              temporary.append( data[ i ] + " " );
70
71          temporary.append( "\n" );
72          return temporary.toString();
73      } // end method remainingElements
74
75      // method to output values in array
76      public String toString()
77      {
78          return remainingElements( 0, data.length - 1 );
79      } // end method toString
80  } // end class BinaryArray
```

Fig. 19.4 | Class that contains an array of random integers and a method that uses binary search to find an integer. (Part 2 of 2.)

Lines 25–56 declare method binarySearch. The search key is passed into parameter searchElement (line 25). Lines 27–29 calculate the low end index, high end index and middle index of the portion of the array that the program is currently searching. At the beginning of the method, the low end is 0, the high end is the length of the array minus 1 and the middle is the average of these two values. Line 30 initializes the location of the element to -1—the value that will be returned if the element is not found. Lines 32–53 loop until low is greater than high (this occurs when the element is not found) or location does not equal -1 (indicating that the search key was found). Line 43 tests whether the value in the middle element is equal to searchElement. If this is true, line 44 assigns middle to location. Then the loop terminates and location is returned to the caller. Each iteration of the loop tests a single value (line 43) and eliminates half of the remaining values in the array (line 48 or 50).

Figure 19.5 performs a binary search using the search key the user enters to determine whether it matches an element in the array. The first line of output from this program is the array of ints, in increasing order. When the user instructs the program to search for 23, the program first tests the middle element, which is 42 (as indicated by *). The search key is less than 42, so the program eliminates the second half of the array and tests the middle element from the first half. The search key is smaller than 34, so the program eliminates the second half of the array, leaving only three elements. Finally, the program checks 23 (which matches the search key) and returns the index 1.

```java
1  // Fig. 19.5: BinarySearchTest.java
2  // Use binary search to locate an item in an array.
3  import java.util.Scanner;
4
5  public class BinarySearchTest
6  {
7     public static void main( String[] args )
8     {
9        // create Scanner object to input data
10       Scanner input = new Scanner( System.in );
11
12       int searchInt; // search key
13       int position; // location of search key in array
14
15       // create array and output it
16       BinaryArray searchArray = new BinaryArray( 15 );
17       System.out.println( searchArray );
18
19       // get input from user
20       System.out.print(
21          "Please enter an integer value (-1 to quit): " );
22       searchInt = input.nextInt(); // read an int from user
23       System.out.println();
24
25       // repeatedly input an integer; -1 terminates the program
26       while ( searchInt != -1 )
27       {
28          // use binary search to try to find integer
29          position = searchArray.binarySearch( searchInt );
30
31          // return value of -1 indicates integer was not found
32          if ( position == -1 )
33             System.out.println( "The integer " + searchInt +
34                " was not found.\n" );
```

Fig. 19.5 | Use binary search to locate an item in an array (* in the output marks the middle element). (Part 1 of 2.)

```
35              else
36                  System.out.println( "The integer " + searchInt +
37                      " was found in position " + position + ".\n" );
38
39              // get input from user
40              System.out.print(
41                  "Please enter an integer value (-1 to quit): " );
42              searchInt = input.nextInt(); // read an int from user
43              System.out.println();
44          } // end while
45      } // end main
46  } // end class BinarySearchTest
```

```
13 23 24 34 35 36 38 42 47 51 68 74 75 85 97

Please enter an integer value (-1 to quit): 23

13 23 24 34 35 36 38 42 47 51 68 74 75 85 97
                     *
13 23 24 34 35 36 38
         *
13 23 24
   *
The integer 23 was found in position 1.

Please enter an integer value (-1 to quit): 75

13 23 24 34 35 36 38 42 47 51 68 74 75 85 97
                     *
                     47 51 68 74 75 85 97
                              *
                              75 85 97
                                 *
                              75
                              *
The integer 75 was found in position 12.

Please enter an integer value (-1 to quit): 52

13 23 24 34 35 36 38 42 47 51 68 74 75 85 97
                     *
                     47 51 68 74 75 85 97
                              *
                     47 51 68
                        *
                              68
                              *
The integer 52 was not found.

Please enter an integer value (-1 to quit): -1
```

Fig. 19.5 | Use binary search to locate an item in an array (* in the output marks the middle element). (Part 2 of 2.)

Efficiency of Binary Search

In the worst-case scenario, searching a sorted array of 1023 elements takes only 10 comparisons when using a binary search. Repeatedly dividing 1023 by 2 (because after each comparison we can eliminate half the array) and rounding down (because we also remove the middle element) yields the values 511, 255, 127, 63, 31, 15, 7, 3, 1 and 0. The number 1023 ($2^{10} - 1$) is divided by 2 only 10 times to get the value 0, which indicates that there are no more elements to test. Dividing by 2 is equivalent to one comparison in the binary search algorithm. Thus, an array of 1,048,575 ($2^{20} - 1$) elements takes a maximum of 20 comparisons to find the key, and an array of over one billion elements takes a maximum of 30 comparisons to find the key. This is a tremendous improvement in performance over the linear search. For a one-billion-element array, this is a difference between an average of 500 million comparisons for the linear search and a maximum of only 30 comparisons for the binary search! The maximum number of comparisons needed for the binary search of any sorted array is the exponent of the first power of 2 greater than the number of elements in the array, which is represented as $\log_2 n$. All logarithms grow at roughly the same rate, so in big O notation the base can be omitted. This results in a big O of $O(\log n)$ for a binary search, which is also known as logarithmic run time.

19.3 Sorting Algorithms

Sorting data (i.e., placing the data into some particular order, such as ascending or descending) is one of the most important computing applications. A bank sorts all checks by account number so that it can prepare individual bank statements at the end of each month. Telephone companies sort their lists of accounts by last name and, further, by first name to make it easy to find phone numbers. Virtually every organization must sort some data, and often massive amounts of it. Sorting data is an intriguing, computer-intensive problem that has attracted intense research efforts.

An important item to understand about sorting is that the end result—the sorted array—will be the same no matter which algorithm you use to sort the array. The choice of algorithm affects only the run time and memory use of the program. The rest of this chapter introduces three common sorting algorithms. The first two—selection sort and insertion sort—are easy to program but inefficient. The last algorithm—merge sort—is much faster than selection sort and insertion sort but harder to program. We focus on sorting arrays of primitive-type data, namely ints. It's possible to sort arrays of class objects as well. We discuss this in Section 20.7.1.

19.3.1 Selection Sort

Selection sort is a simple, but inefficient, sorting algorithm. Its first iteration selects the smallest element in the array and swaps it with the first element. The second iteration selects the second-smallest item (which is the smallest item of the remaining elements) and swaps it with the second element. The algorithm continues until the last iteration selects the second-largest element and swaps it with the second-to-last index, leaving the largest element in the last index. After the ith iteration, the smallest i items of the array will be sorted into increasing order in the first i elements of the array.

As an example, consider the array

34	56	4	10	77	51	93	30	5	52

A program that implements selection sort first determines the smallest element (4) of this array, which is contained in index 2. The program swaps 4 with 34, resulting in

4	56	34	10	77	51	93	30	5	52

The program then determines the smallest value of the remaining elements (all elements except 4), which is 5, contained in index 8. The program swaps 5 with 56, resulting in

| 4 | 5 | 34 | 10 | 77 | 51 | 93 | 30 | 56 | 52 |

On the third iteration, the program determines the next smallest value (10) and swaps it with 34.

| 4 | 5 | 10 | 34 | 77 | 51 | 93 | 30 | 56 | 52 |

The process continues until the array is fully sorted.

| 4 | 5 | 10 | 30 | 34 | 51 | 52 | 56 | 77 | 93 |

Note that after the first iteration, the smallest element is in the first position. After the second iteration, the two smallest elements are in order in the first two positions. After the third iteration, the three smallest elements are in order in the first three positions.

Figure 19.6 declares the SelectionSort class. This class has two private instance variables—an array of ints named data, and a static Random object to generate random integers to fill the array. When an object of class SelectionSort is instantiated, the constructor (lines 13–20) creates and initializes the array data with random ints in the range 10–99.

```java
1   // Fig. 19.6: SelectionSort.java
2   // Class that creates an array filled with random integers.
3   // Provides a method to sort the array with selection sort.
4   import java.util.Arrays;
5   import java.util.Random;
6
7   public class SelectionSort
8   {
9      private int[] data; // array of values
10     private static final Random generator = new Random();
11
12     // create array of given size and fill with random integers
13     public SelectionSort( int size )
14     {
15        data = new int[ size ]; // create space for array
16
17        // fill array with random ints in range 10-99
18        for ( int i = 0; i < size; i++ )
19           data[ i ] = 10 + generator.nextInt( 90 );
20     } // end SelectionSort constructor
21
22     // sort array using selection sort
23     public void sort()
24     {
25        int smallest; // index of smallest element
26
27        // loop over data.length - 1 elements
28        for ( int i = 0; i < data.length - 1; i++ )
29        {
30           smallest = i; // first index of remaining array
```

Fig. 19.6 | Class that creates an array filled with random integers. Provides a method to sort the array with selection sort. (Part 1 of 2.)

```
31
32                // loop to find index of smallest element
33                for ( int index = i + 1; index < data.length; index++ )
34                    if ( data[ index ] < data[ smallest ] )
35                        smallest = index;
36
37                swap( i, smallest ); // swap smallest element into position
38                printPass( i + 1, smallest ); // output pass of algorithm
39            } // end outer for
40        } // end method sort
41
42        // helper method to swap values in two elements
43        public void swap( int first, int second )
44        {
45            int temporary = data[ first ]; // store first in temporary
46            data[ first ] = data[ second ]; // replace first with second
47            data[ second ] = temporary; // put temporary in second
48        } // end method swap
49
50        // print a pass of the algorithm
51        public void printPass( int pass, int index )
52        {
53            System.out.print( String.format( "after pass %2d: ", pass ) );
54
55            // output elements till selected item
56            for ( int i = 0; i < index; i++ )
57                System.out.print( data[ i ] + "   " );
58
59            System.out.print( data[ index ] + "* " ); // indicate swap
60
61            // finish outputting array
62            for ( int i = index + 1; i < data.length; i++ )
63                System.out.print( data[ i ] + "   " );
64
65            System.out.print( "\n                " ); // for alignment
66
67            // indicate amount of array that is sorted
68            for ( int j = 0; j < pass; j++ )
69                System.out.print( "--   " );
70            System.out.println( "\n" ); // add endline
71        } // end method printPass
72
73        // method to output values in array
74        public String toString()
75        {
76            return Arrays.toString( data );
77        } // end method toString
78    } // end class SelectionSort
```

Fig. 19.6 | Class that creates an array filled with random integers. Provides a method to sort the array with selection sort. (Part 2 of 2.)

Lines 23–40 declare the sort method. Line 25 declares the variable smallest, which will store the index of the smallest element in the remaining array. Lines 28–39 loop data.length - 1 times. Line 30 initializes the index of the smallest element to the current item. Lines 33–35 loop over the remaining elements in the array. For each of these elements, line 34 compares its value to the value of the smallest element. If the current element is smaller than the smallest element, line 35 assigns the current element's index to `smallest`. When this loop finishes, `smallest` will contain the index of the smallest element in the remaining array. Line 36 calls method `swap` (lines 43–48) to place the smallest remaining element in the next ordered spot in the array.

Line 9 of Fig. 19.7 creates a `SelectionSort` object with 10 elements. Line 12 outputs the unsorted object. Line 14 calls method `sort` (lines 22–39 of Fig. 19.6), which sorts the elements using selection sort. Then lines 16–17 output the sorted object. The output uses dashes (lines 67–68) to indicate the portion of the array that is sorted after each pass. An asterisk is placed next to the position of the element that was swapped with the smallest element on that pass. On each pass, the element next to the asterisk (specified at line 58) and the element above the rightmost set of dashes were swapped.

```
 1   // Fig. 19.7: SelectionSortTest.java
 2   // Testing the selection sort class.
 3
 4   public class SelectionSortTest
 5   {
 6      public static void main( String[] args )
 7      {
 8         // create object to perform selection sort
 9         SelectionSort sortArray = new SelectionSort( 10 );
10
11         System.out.println( "Unsorted array:" );
12         System.out.println( sortArray + "\n" ); // print unsorted array
13
14         sortArray.sort(); // sort array
15
16         System.out.println( "Sorted array:" );
17         System.out.println( sortArray ); // print sorted array
18      } // end main
19   } // end class SelectionSortTest
```

```
Unsorted array:
[61, 87, 80, 58, 40, 50, 20, 13, 71, 45]

after pass  1: 13  87  80  58  40  50  20  61* 71  45
               --

after pass  2: 13  20  80  58  40  50  87* 61  71  45
               --  --

after pass  3: 13  20  40  58  80* 50  87  61  71  45
               --  --  --

after pass  4: 13  20  40  45  80  50  87  61  71  58*
               --  --  --  --

after pass  5: 13  20  40  45  50  80* 87  61  71  58
               --  --  --  --  --

after pass  6: 13  20  40  45  50  58  87  61  71  80*
               --  --  --  --  --  --
```

Fig. 19.7 | Testing the selection sort class. (Part 1 of 2.)

```
after pass  6: 13  20  40  45  50  58  87  61  71  80*
               --  --  --  --  --  --

after pass  7: 13  20  40  45  50  58  61  87* 71  80
               --  --  --  --  --  --  --

after pass  8: 13  20  40  45  50  58  61  71  87* 80
               --  --  --  --  --  --  --  --

after pass  9: 13  20  40  45  50  58  61  71  80  87*
               --  --  --  --  --  --  --  --  --

Sorted array:
[13, 20, 40, 45, 50, 58, 61, 71, 80, 87]
```

Fig. 19.7 | Testing the selection sort class. (Part 2 of 2.)

Efficiency of Selection Sort

The selection sort algorithm runs in $O(n^2)$ time. The sort method in lines 23–40 of Fig. 19.6, which implements the selection sort algorithm, contains two for loops. The outer for loop (lines 28–39) iterates over the first $n - 1$ elements in the array, swapping the smallest remaining item into its sorted position. The inner for loop (lines 33–35) iterates over each item in the remaining array, searching for the smallest element. This loop executes $n - 1$ times during the first iteration of the outer loop, $n - 2$ times during the second iteration, then $n - 3$, ... , 3, 2, 1. This inner loop will iterate a total of $n(n - 1)/2$ or $(n^2 - n)/2$. In Big O notation, smaller terms drop out and constants are ignored, leaving a final Big O of $O(n^2)$.

19.3.2 Insertion Sort

Insertion sort is another simple, but inefficient, sorting algorithm. The first iteration of this algorithm takes the second element in the array and, if it's less than the first element, swaps it with the first element. The second iteration looks at the third element and inserts it into the correct position with respect to the first two, so all three elements are in order. At the ith iteration of this algorithm, the first i elements in the original array will be sorted.

Consider as an example the following array. [*Note:* This array is identical to the one used in the discussions of selection sort and merge sort.]

| 34 | 56 | 4 | 10 | 77 | 51 | 93 | 30 | 5 | 52 |

A program that implements the insertion sort algorithm will first look at the first two elements of the array, 34 and 56. These are already in order, so the program continues. (If they were out of order, the program would swap them.)

In the next iteration, the program looks at the third value, 4. This value is less than 56, so the program stores 4 in a temporary variable and moves 56 one element to the right. The program then checks and determines that 4 is less than 34, so it moves 34 one element to the right. The program has now reached the beginning of the array, so it places 4 in the zeroth element. The array now is

| 4 | 34 | 56 | 10 | 77 | 51 | 93 | 30 | 5 | 52 |

In the next iteration, the program stores 10 in a temporary variable. Then it compares 10 to 56 and moves 56 one element to the right because it's larger than 10. The program then compares 10 to 34, moving 34 right one element. When the program compares 10 to 4, it observes that 10 is larger than 4 and places 10 in element 1. The array now is

4	10	34	56	77	51	93	30	5	52

Using this algorithm, at the ith iteration, the first i elements of the original array are sorted, but they may not be in their final locations—smaller values may be located later in the array.

Figure 19.8 declares the InsertionSort class. Lines 23–47 declare the sort method. Line 25 declares the variable insert, which holds the element you are going to insert while you move the other elements. Lines 28–46 loop over data.length - 1 items in the array. In each iteration, line 31 stores in insert the value of the element that will be inserted into the sorted portion of the array. Line 34 declares and initializes the variable moveItem, which keeps track of where to insert the element. Lines 37–42 loop to locate the correct position where the element should be inserted. The loop will terminate either when the program reaches the front of the array or when it reaches an element that is less than the value to be inserted. Line 40 moves an element to the right, and line 41 decrements the position at which to insert the next element. After the loop ends, line 44 inserts the element into place. Figure 19.9 is the same as Fig. 19.7 except that it creates and uses an InsertionSort object. The output of this program uses dashes to indicate the portion of the array that is sorted after each pass. An asterisk is placed next to the element that was inserted into place on that pass.

```java
 1   // Fig. 19.8: InsertionSort.java
 2   // Class that creates an array filled with random integers.
 3   // Provides a method to sort the array with insertion sort.
 4   import java.util.Arrays;
 5   import java.util.Random;
 6
 7   public class InsertionSort
 8   {
 9      private int[] data; // array of values
10      private static final Random generator = new Random();
11
12      // create array of given size and fill with random integers
13      public InsertionSort( int size )
14      {
15         data = new int[ size ]; // create space for array
16
17         // fill array with random ints in range 10-99
18         for ( int i = 0; i < size; i++ )
19            data[ i ] = 10 + generator.nextInt( 90 );
20      } // end InsertionSort constructor
21
22      // sort array using insertion sort
23      public void sort()
24      {
25         int insert; // temporary variable to hold element to insert
```

Fig. 19.8 | Class that creates an array filled with random integers. Provides a method to sort the array with insertion sort. (Part 1 of 2.)

```
26
27          // loop over data.length - 1 elements
28          for ( int next = 1; next < data.length; next++ )
29          {
30             // store value in current element
31             insert = data[ next ];
32
33             // initialize location to place element
34             int moveItem = next;
35
36             // search for place to put current element
37             while ( moveItem > 0 && data[ moveItem - 1 ] > insert )
38             {
39                // shift element right one slot
40                data[ moveItem ] = data[ moveItem - 1 ];
41                moveItem--;
42             } // end while
43
44             data[ moveItem ] = insert; // place inserted element
45             printPass( next, moveItem ); // output pass of algorithm
46          } // end for
47       } // end method sort
48
49       // print a pass of the algorithm
50       public void printPass( int pass, int index )
51       {
52          System.out.print( String.format( "after pass %2d: ", pass ) );
53
54          // output elements till swapped item
55          for ( int i = 0; i < index; i++ )
56             System.out.print( data[ i ] + "  " );
57
58          System.out.print( data[ index ] + "* " ); // indicate swap
59
60          // finish outputting array
61          for ( int i = index + 1; i < data.length; i++ )
62             System.out.print( data[ i ] + "  " );
63
64          System.out.print( "\n                " ); // for alignment
65
66          // indicate amount of array that is sorted
67          for( int i = 0; i <= pass; i++ )
68             System.out.print( "--  " );
69          System.out.println( "\n" ); // add endline
70       } // end method printPass
71
72       // method to output values in array
73       public String toString()
74       {
75          return Arrays.toString( data );
76       } // end method toString
77    } // end class InsertionSort
```

Fig. 19.8 | Class that creates an array filled with random integers. Provides a method to sort the array with insertion sort. (Part 2 of 2.)

```
1    // Fig. 19.9: InsertionSortTest.java
2    // Testing the insertion sort class.
3
4    public class InsertionSortTest
5    {
6       public static void main( String[] args )
7       {
8          // create object to perform insertion sort
9          InsertionSort sortArray = new InsertionSort( 10 );
10
11          System.out.println( "Unsorted array:" );
12          System.out.println( sortArray + "\n" ); // print unsorted array
13
14          sortArray.sort(); // sort array
15
16          System.out.println( "Sorted array:" );
17          System.out.println( sortArray ); // print sorted array
18       } // end main
19   } // end class InsertionSortTest
```

```
Unsorted array:
[40, 17, 45, 82, 62, 32, 30, 44, 93, 10]

after pass  1: 17* 40  45  82  62  32  30  44  93  10
               --  --

after pass  2: 17  40  45* 82  62  32  30  44  93  10
               --  --  --

after pass  3: 17  40  45  82* 62  32  30  44  93  10
               --  --  --  --

after pass  4: 17  40  45  62* 82  32  30  44  93  10
               --  --  --  --  --

after pass  5: 17  32* 40  45  62  82  30  44  93  10
               --  --  --  --  --  --

after pass  6: 17  30* 32  40  45  62  82  44  93  10
               --  --  --  --  --  --  --

after pass  7: 17  30  32  40  44* 45  62  82  93  10
               --  --  --  --  --  --  --  --

after pass  8: 17  30  32  40  44  45  62  82  93* 10
               --  --  --  --  --  --  --  --  --

after pass  9: 10* 17  30  32  40  44  45  62  82  93
               --  --  --  --  --  --  --  --  --  --

Sorted array:
[10, 17, 30, 32, 40, 44, 45, 62, 82, 93]
```

Fig. 19.9 | Testing the insertion sort class.

Efficiency of Insertion Sort

The insertion sort algorithm also runs in $O(n^2)$ time. Like selection sort, the implementation of insertion sort (lines 23–47 of Fig. 19.8) contains two loops. The for loop (lines

28–46) iterates `data.length - 1` times, inserting an element into the appropriate position in the elements sorted so far. For the purposes of this application, `data.length - 1` is equivalent to $n - 1$ (as `data.length` is the size of the array). The `while` loop (lines 37–42) iterates over the preceding elements in the array. In the worst case, this `while` loop will require $n - 1$ comparisons. Each individual loop runs in $O(n)$ time. In Big O notation, nested loops mean that you must multiply the number of comparisons. For each iteration of an outer loop, there will be a certain number of iterations of the inner loop. In this algorithm, for each $O(n)$ iterations of the outer loop, there will be $O(n)$ iterations of the inner loop. Multiplying these values results in a Big O of $O(n^2)$.

19.3.3 Merge Sort

Merge sort is an efficient sorting algorithm but is conceptually more complex than selection sort and insertion sort. The merge sort algorithm sorts an array by splitting it into two equal-sized subarrays, sorting each subarray, then merging them into one larger array. With an odd number of elements, the algorithm creates the two subarrays such that one has one more element than the other.

The implementation of merge sort in this example is recursive. The base case is an array with one element, which is, of course, sorted, so the merge sort immediately returns in this case. The recursion step splits the array into two approximately equal pieces, recursively sorts them, then merges the two sorted arrays into one larger, sorted array.

Suppose the algorithm has already merged smaller arrays to create sorted arrays A:

| 4 | 10 | 34 | 56 | 77 |

and B:

| 5 | 30 | 51 | 52 | 93 |

Merge sort combines these two arrays into one larger, sorted array. The smallest element in A is 4 (located in the zeroth index of A). The smallest element in B is 5 (located in the zeroth index of B). In order to determine the smallest element in the larger array, the algorithm compares 4 and 5. The value from A is smaller, so 4 becomes the first element in the merged array. The algorithm continues by comparing 10 (the second element in A) to 5 (the first element in B). The value from B is smaller, so 5 becomes the second element in the larger array. The algorithm continues by comparing 10 to 30, with 10 becoming the third element in the array, and so on.

Lines 22–25 of Fig. 19.10 declare the `sort` method. Line 24 calls method `sortArray` with 0 and `data.length - 1` as the arguments—corresponding to the beginning and ending indices, respectively, of the array to be sorted. These values tell method `sortArray` to operate on the entire array.

Method `sortArray` is declared in lines 28–49. Line 31 tests the base case. If the size of the array is 1, the array is already sorted, so the method returns immediately. If the size of the array is greater than 1, the method splits the array in two, recursively calls method `sortArray` to sort the two subarrays, then merges them. Line 43 recursively calls method `sortArray` on the first half of the array, and line 44 recursively calls method `sortArray` on the second half. When these two method calls return, each half of the array has been sorted. Line 47 calls method `merge` (lines 52–91) on the two halves of the array to combine the two sorted arrays into one larger sorted array.

```java
 1    // Fig. 19.10: MergeSort.java
 2    // Class creates an array filled with random integers.
 3    // Provides a method to sort the array with merge sort.
 4    import java.util.Random;
 5
 6    public class MergeSort
 7    {
 8       private int[] data; // array of values
 9       private static final Random generator = new Random();
10
11       // create array of given size and fill with random integers
12       public MergeSort( int size )
13       {
14          data = new int[ size ]; // create space for array
15
16          // fill array with random ints in range 10-99
17          for ( int i = 0; i < size; i++ )
18             data[ i ] = 10 + generator.nextInt( 90 );
19       } // end MergeSort constructor
20
21       // calls recursive split method to begin merge sorting
22       public void sort()
23       {
24          sortArray( 0, data.length - 1 ); // split entire array
25       } // end method sort
26
27       // splits array, sorts subarrays and merges subarrays into sorted array
28       private void sortArray( int low, int high )
29       {
30          // test base case; size of array equals 1
31          if ( ( high - low ) >= 1 ) // if not base case
32          {
33             int middle1 = ( low + high ) / 2; // calculate middle of array
34             int middle2 = middle1 + 1; // calculate next element over
35
36             // output split step
37             System.out.println( "split:   " + subarray( low, high ) );
38             System.out.println( "         " + subarray( low, middle1 ) );
39             System.out.println( "         " + subarray( middle2, high ) );
40             System.out.println();
41
42             // split array in half; sort each half (recursive calls)
43             sortArray( low, middle1 ); // first half of array
44             sortArray( middle2, high ); // second half of array
45
46             // merge two sorted arrays after split calls return
47             merge ( low, middle1, middle2, high );
48          } // end if
49       } // end method sortArray
50
51       // merge two sorted subarrays into one sorted subarray
52       private void merge( int left, int middle1, int middle2, int right )
53       {
```

Fig. 19.10 | Class that creates an array filled with random integers. Provides a method to sort the array with merge sort. (Part 1 of 3.)

```
54          int leftIndex = left; // index into left subarray
55          int rightIndex = middle2; // index into right subarray
56          int combinedIndex = left; // index into temporary working array
57          int[] combined = new int[ data.length ]; // working array
58
59          // output two subarrays before merging
60          System.out.println( "merge:    " + subarray( left, middle1 ) );
61          System.out.println( "          " + subarray( middle2, right ) );
62
63          // merge arrays until reaching end of either
64          while ( leftIndex <= middle1 && rightIndex <= right )
65          {
66             // place smaller of two current elements into result
67             // and move to next space in arrays
68             if ( data[ leftIndex ] <= data[ rightIndex ] )
69                combined[ combinedIndex++ ] = data[ leftIndex++ ];
70             else
71                combined[ combinedIndex++ ] = data[ rightIndex++ ];
72          } // end while
73
74          // if left array is empty
75          if ( leftIndex == middle2 )
76             // copy in rest of right array
77             while ( rightIndex <= right )
78                combined[ combinedIndex++ ] = data[ rightIndex++ ];
79          else // right array is empty
80             // copy in rest of left array
81             while ( leftIndex <= middle1 )
82                combined[ combinedIndex++ ] = data[ leftIndex++ ];
83
84          // copy values back into original array
85          for ( int i = left; i <= right; i++ )
86             data[ i ] = combined[ i ];
87
88          // output merged array
89          System.out.println( "          " + subarray( left, right ) );
90          System.out.println();
91       } // end method merge
92
93       // method to output certain values in array
94       public String subarray( int low, int high )
95       {
96          StringBuilder temporary = new StringBuilder();
97
98          // output spaces for alignment
99          for ( int i = 0; i < low; i++ )
100            temporary.append( "   " );
101
102         // output elements left in array
103         for ( int i = low; i <= high; i++ )
104            temporary.append( " " + data[ i ] );
105
```

Fig. 19.10 | Class that creates an array filled with random integers. Provides a method to sort the array with merge sort. (Part 2 of 3.)

```
106                return temporary.toString();
107        } // end method subarray
108
109        // method to output values in array
110        public String toString()
111        {
112            return subarray( 0, data.length - 1 );
113        } // end method toString
114    } // end class MergeSort
```

Fig. 19.10 | Class that creates an array filled with random integers. Provides a method to sort the array with merge sort. (Part 3 of 3.)

Lines 64–72 in the merge method loop until the program reaches the end of either subarray. Line 68 tests which element at the beginning of the arrays is smaller. If the element in the left array is smaller, line 69 places it in position in the combined array. If the element in the right array is smaller, line 71 places it in position in the combined array. When the while loop has completed (line 72), one entire subarray is placed in the combined array, but the other subarray still contains data. Line 75 tests whether the left array has reached the end. If so, lines 77–78 fill the combined array with the elements of the right array. If the left array has not reached the end, then the right array must have reached the end, and lines 81–82 fill the combined array with the elements of the left array. Finally, lines 85–86 copy the combined array into the original array. Figure 19.11 creates and uses a MergeSort object. The output from this program displays the splits and merges performed by merge sort, showing the progress of the sort at each step of the algorithm. It's well worth your time to step through these outputs to fully understand this elegant sorting algorithm.

```
1    // Figure 16.11: MergeSortTest.java
2    // Testing the merge sort class.
3
4    public class MergeSortTest
5    {
6        public static void main( String[] args )
7        {
8            // create object to perform merge sort
9            MergeSort sortArray = new MergeSort( 10 );
10
11            // print unsorted array
12            System.out.println( "Unsorted:" + sortArray + "\n" );
13
14            sortArray.sort(); // sort array
15
16            // print sorted array
17            System.out.println( "Sorted:   " + sortArray );
18        } // end main
19    } // end class MergeSortTest
```

Fig. 19.11 | Testing the merge sort class. (Part 1 of 3.)

```
Unsorted: 75 56 85 90 49 26 12 48 40 47

split:    75 56 85 90 49 26 12 48 40 47
          75 56 85 90 49
                         26 12 48 40 47

split:    75 56 85 90 49
          75 56 85
                   90 49

split:    75 56 85
          75 56
                85

split:    75 56
          75
             56

merge:    75
             56
          56 75

merge:    56 75
                85
          56 75 85

split:              90 49
                    90
                       49

merge:              90
                       49
                    49 90

merge:    56 75 85
                    49 90
          49 56 75 85 90

split:                    26 12 48 40 47
                          26 12 48
                                   40 47

split:                    26 12 48
                          26 12
                                48

split:                    26 12
                          26
                             12

merge:                    26
                             12
                          12 26

merge:                    12 26
                                48
                          12 26 48

split:                            40 47
                                  40
                                     47
```

Fig. 19.11 | Testing the merge sort class. (Part 2 of 3.)

```
merge:                                  40
                                          47
                                        40 47

merge:                      12 26 48
                                        40 47
                            12 26 40 47 48

merge:       49 56 75 85 90
                            12 26 40 47 48
             12 26 40 47 48 49 56 75 85 90

Sorted:      12 26 40 47 48 49 56 75 85 90
```

Fig. 19.11 | Testing the merge sort class. (Part 3 of 3.)

Efficiency of Merge Sort

Merge sort is a far more efficient algorithm than either insertion or selection sort. Consider the first (nonrecursive) call to method sortArray. This results in two recursive calls to method sortArray with subarrays each approximately half the size of the original array, and a single call to method merge. This call to merge requires, at worst, $n - 1$ comparisons to fill the original array, which is $O(n)$. (Recall that each element in the array can be chosen by comparing one element from each of the subarrays.) The two calls to method sortArray result in four more recursive calls to method sortArray, each with a subarray approximately a quarter the size of the original array along with two calls to method merge. These two calls to method merge each require, at worst, $n/2 - 1$ comparisons, for a total number of comparisons of $O(n)$. This process continues, each call to sortArray generating two additional calls to sortArray and a call to merge, until the algorithm has split the array into one-element subarrays. At each level, $O(n)$ comparisons are required to merge the subarrays. Each level splits the size of the arrays in half, so doubling the size of the array requires one more level. Quadrupling the size of the array requires two more levels. This pattern is logarithmic and results in $\log_2 n$ levels. This results in a total efficiency of $O(n \log n)$.

Figure 19.12 summarizes the searching and sorting algorithms covered in this chapter with the Big O for each. Figure 19.13 lists the Big O values we've covered in this chapter along with a number of values for n to highlight the differences in the growth rates.

Algorithm	Location	Big O
Searching Algorithms:		
Linear search	Section 19.2.1	$O(n)$
Binary search	Section 19.2.2	$O(\log n)$
Recursive linear search	Exercise 19.8	$O(n)$
Recursive binary search	Exercise 19.9	$O(\log n)$
Sorting Algorithms:		
Selection sort	Section 19.3.1	$O(n^2)$
Insertion sort	Section 19.3.2	$O(n^2)$
Merge sort	Section 19.3.3	$O(n \log n)$
Bubble sort	Exercise 19.5 and 19.6	$O(n^2)$

Fig. 19.12 | Searching and sorting algorithms with Big O values.

$n =$	$O(\log n)$	$O(n)$	$O(n \log n)$	$O(n^2)$
1	0	1	0	1
2	1	2	2	4
3	1	3	3	9
4	1	4	4	16
5	1	5	5	25
10	1	10	10	100
100	2	100	200	10,000
1000	3	1000	3000	10^6
1,000,000	6	1,000,000	6,000,000	10^{12}
1,000,000,000	9	1,000,000,000	9,000,000,000	10^{18}

Fig. 19.13 | Number of comparisons for common Big O notations.

19.4 Wrap-Up

This chapter introduced searching and sorting. We discussed two searching algorithms—linear search and binary search—and three sorting algorithms—selection sort, insertion sort and merge sort. We introduced Big O notation, which helps you analyze the efficiency of an algorithm. The next three chapters continue our discussion of dynamic data structures that can grow or shrink at execution time. Chapter 20 presents the Java API's built-in algorithms (such as searching and sorting) and generic collections. Chapter 21 demonstrates how to use Java's generics capabilities to implement generic methods and classes. Chapter 22 discusses the details of implementing generic data structures.

Summary

Section 19.1 Introduction
- Searching involves determining if a search key is in the data and, if so, finding its location.
- Sorting involves arranging data into order.

Section 19.2 Searching Algorithms
- The linear search algorithm searches each element in the array sequentially until it finds the correct element, or until it reaches the end of the array without finding the element.
- A major difference among searching algorithms is the amount of effort they require in order to return a result.
- Big O notation describes an algorithm's efficiency in terms of the work required to solve a problem. For searching and sorting algorithms typically it depends on the number of elements in the data.
- An algorithm that is $O(1)$ does not necessarily require only one comparison. It just means that the number of comparisons does not grow as the size of the array increases.
- An $O(n)$ algorithm is referred to as having a linear run time.
- Big O is designed to highlight dominant factors and ignore terms that become unimportant with high n values.
- Big O notation is concerned with the growth rate of algorithm run times, so constants are ignored.
- The linear search algorithm runs in $O(n)$ time.

- The worst case in linear search is that every element must be checked to determine whether the search item exists. This occurs if the search key is the last element in the array or is not present.

- The binary search algorithm is more efficient than the linear search algorithm, but it requires that the array be sorted.

- The first iteration of binary search tests the middle element in the array. If this is the search key, the algorithm returns its location. If the search key is less than the middle element, the search continues with the first half of the array. If the search key is greater than the middle element, the search continues with the second half of the array. Each iteration tests the middle value of the remaining array and, if the element is not found, eliminates half of the remaining elements.

- Binary search is a more efficient searching algorithm than linear search because each comparison eliminates from consideration half of the elements in the array.

- Binary search runs in $O(\log n)$ time because each step removes half of the remaining elements.

- If the array size is doubled, binary search requires only one extra comparison.

Section 19.3 Sorting Algorithms
- Selection sort is a simple, but inefficient, sorting algorithm.

- The first iteration of selection sort selects the smallest item in the array and swaps it with the first element. The second iteration of selection sort selects the second-smallest item (which is the smallest remaining item) and swaps it with the second element. Selection sort continues until the last iteration selects the second-largest element and swaps it with the second-to-last element, leaving the largest element in the last index. At the ith iteration of selection sort, the smallest i items of the whole array are sorted into the first i indices.

- The selection sort algorithm runs in $O(n^2)$ time.

- The first iteration of insertion sort takes the second element in the array and, if it's less than the first element, swaps it with the first element. The second iteration of insertion sort looks at the third element and inserts it in the correct position with respect to the first two elements. After the ith iteration of insertion sort, the first i elements in the original array are sorted.

- The insertion sort algorithm runs in $O(n^2)$ time.

- Merge sort is a sorting algorithm that is faster, but more complex to implement, than selection sort and insertion sort.

- The merge sort algorithm sorts an array by splitting the array into two equal-sized subarrays, sorting each subarray recursively and merging the subarrays into one larger array.

- Merge sort's base case is an array with one element. A one-element array is already sorted, so merge sort immediately returns when it's called with a one-element array. The merge part of merge sort takes two sorted arrays and combines them into one larger sorted array.

- Merge sort performs the merge by looking at the first element in each array, which is also the smallest element in the array. Merge sort takes the smallest of these and places it in the first element of the larger array. If there are still elements in the subarray, merge sort looks at the second of these (which is now the smallest element remaining) and compares it to the first element in the other subarray. Merge sort continues this process until the larger array is filled.

- In the worst case, the first call to merge sort has to make $O(n)$ comparisons to fill the n slots in the final array.

- The merging portion of the merge sort algorithm is performed on two subarrays, each of approximately size $n/2$. Creating each of these subarrays requires $n/2 - 1$ comparisons for each subarray, or $O(n)$ comparisons total. This pattern continues as each level works on twice as many arrays, but each is half the size of the previous array.

- Similar to binary search, this halving results in $\log n$ levels for a total efficiency of $O(n \log n)$.

Terminology

Big O notation 793
binary search algorithm 795
constant run time 794
insertion sort algorithm 804
linear run time 794
linear search algorithm 791
logarithmic run time 800
merge sort 808
$O(1)$ 794
$O(\log n)$ 800

$O(n \log n)$ time 813
$O(n)$ time 794
$O(n^2)$ time 794
quadratic run time 794
search key 790
searching data 790
selection sort 800
sort key 790
sort method of class Arrays 796
sorting data 790

Self-Review Exercises

19.1 Fill in the blanks in each of the following statements:
  a) A selection sort application would take approximately _____ times as long to run on a 128-element array as on a 32-element array.
  b) The efficiency of merge sort is _____.

19.2 What key aspect of both the binary search and the merge sort accounts for the logarithmic portion of their respective Big Os?

19.3 In what sense is the insertion sort superior to the merge sort? In what sense is the merge sort superior to the insertion sort?

19.4 In the text, we say that after the merge sort splits the array into two subarrays, it then sorts these two subarrays and merges them. Why might someone be puzzled by our statement that "it then sorts these two subarrays"?

Answers to Self-Review Exercises

19.1 a) 16, because an $O(n^2)$ algorithm takes 16 times as long to sort four times as much information. b) $O(n \log n)$.

19.2 Both of these algorithms incorporate "halving"—somehow reducing something by half. The binary search eliminates from consideration one-half of the array after each comparison. The merge sort splits the array in half each time it's called.

19.3 The insertion sort is easier to understand and to program than the merge sort. The merge sort is far more efficient [$O(n \log n)$] than the insertion sort [$O(n^2)$].

19.4 In a sense, it does not really sort these two subarrays. It simply keeps splitting the original array in half until it provides a one-element subarray, which is, of course, sorted. It then builds up the original two subarrays by merging these one-element arrays to form larger subarrays, which are then merged, and so on.

Exercises

19.5 (*Bubble Sort*) Implement bubble sort—another simple yet inefficient sorting technique. It's called bubble sort or sinking sort because smaller values gradually "bubble" their way to the top of the array (i.e., toward the first element) like air bubbles rising in water, while the larger values sink to the bottom (end) of the array. The technique uses nested loops to make several passes through the array. Each pass compares successive pairs of elements. If a pair is in increasing order (or the values are equal), the bubble sort leaves the values as they are. If a pair is in decreasing order, the bubble sort swaps their values in the array.

The first pass compares the first two elements of the array and swaps their values if necessary. It then compares the second and third elements in the array. The end of this pass compares the last two elements in the array and swaps them if necessary. After one pass, the largest element will be in the last index. After two passes, the largest two elements will be in the last two indices. Explain why bubble sort is an $O(n^2)$ algorithm.

19.6 *(Enhanced Bubble Sort)* Make the following simple modifications to improve the performance of the bubble sort you developed in Exercise 19.5:

a) After the first pass, the largest number is guaranteed to be in the highest-numbered element of the array; after the second pass, the two highest numbers are "in place"; and so on. Instead of making nine comparisons on every pass for a ten element array, modify the bubble sort to make eight comparisons on the second pass, seven on the third pass, and so on.

b) The data in the array may already be in proper or near-proper order, so why make nine passes if fewer will suffice? Modify the sort to check at the end of each pass whether any swaps have been made. If none have been made, the data must already be in the proper order, so the program should terminate. If swaps have been made, at least one more pass is needed.

19.7 *(Bucket Sort)* A bucket sort begins with a one-dimensional array of positive integers to be sorted and a two-dimensional array of integers with rows indexed from 0 to 9 and columns indexed from 0 to $n - 1$, where n is the number of values to be sorted. Each row of the two-dimensional array is referred to as a *bucket*. Write a class named BucketSort containing a method called sort that operates as follows:

a) Place each value of the one-dimensional array into a row of the bucket array, based on the value's "ones" (rightmost) digit. For example, 97 is placed in row 7, 3 is placed in row 3 and 100 is placed in row 0. This procedure is called a *distribution pass*.

b) Loop through the bucket array row by row, and copy the values back to the original array. This procedure is called a *gathering pass*. The new order of the preceding values in the one-dimensional array is 100, 3 and 97.

c) Repeat this process for each subsequent digit position (tens, hundreds, thousands, etc.). On the second (tens digit) pass, 100 is placed in row 0, 3 is placed in row 0 (because 3 has no tens digit) and 97 is placed in row 9. After the gathering pass, the order of the values in the one-dimensional array is 100, 3 and 97. On the third (hundreds digit) pass, 100 is placed in row 1, 3 is placed in row 0 and 97 is placed in row 0 (after the 3). After this last gathering pass, the original array is in sorted order.

Note that the two-dimensional array of buckets is 10 times the length of the integer array being sorted. This sorting technique provides better performance than a bubble sort, but requires much more memory—the bubble sort requires space for only one additional element of data. This comparison is an example of the space/time trade-off: The bucket sort uses more memory than the bubble sort, but performs better. This version of the bucket sort requires copying all the data back to the original array on each pass. Another possibility is to create a second two-dimensional bucket array and repeatedly swap the data between the two bucket arrays.

19.8 *(Recursive Linear Search)* Modify Fig. 19.2 to use recursive method recursiveLinearSearch to perform a linear search of the array. The method should receive the search key and starting index as arguments. If the search key is found, return its index in the array; otherwise, return –1. Each call to the recursive method should check one index in the array.

19.9 *(Recursive Binary Search)* Modify Fig. 19.4 to use recursive method recursiveBinarySearch to perform a binary search of the array. The method should receive the search key, starting index and ending index as arguments. If the search key is found, return its index in the array. If the search key is not found, return –1.

19.10 *(Quicksort)* The recursive sorting technique called quicksort uses the following basic algorithm for a one-dimensional array of values:

    a) *Partitioning Step*: Take the first element of the unsorted array and determine its final location in the sorted array (i.e., all values to the left of the element in the array are less than the element, and all values to the right of the element in the array are greater than the element—we show how to do this below). We now have one element in its proper location and two unsorted subarrays.

    b) *Recursive Step*: Perform *Step 1* on each unsorted subarray. Each time *Step 1* is performed on a subarray, another element is placed in its final location of the sorted array, and two unsorted subarrays are created. When a subarray consists of one element, that element is in its final location (because a one-element array is already sorted).

        The basic algorithm seems simple enough, but how do we determine the final position of the first element of each subarray? As an example, consider the following set of values (the element in bold is the partitioning element—it will be placed in its final location in the sorted array):

        37 2 6 4 89 8 10 12 68 45

Starting from the rightmost element of the array, compare each element with 37 until an element less than 37 is found; then swap 37 and that element. The first element less than 37 is 12, so 37 and 12 are swapped. The new array is

        12 2 6 4 89 8 10 **37** 68 45

Element 12 is in italics to indicate that it was just swapped with 37.

        Starting from the left of the array, but beginning with the element after 12, compare each element with 37 until an element greater than 37 is found—then swap 37 and that element. The first element greater than 37 is 89, so 37 and 89 are swapped. The new array is

        12 2 6 4 **37** 8 10 *89* 68 45

Starting from the right, but beginning with the element before 89, compare each element with 37 until an element less than 37 is found—then swap 37 and that element. The first element less than 37 is 10, so 37 and 10 are swapped. The new array is

        12 2 6 4 *10* 8 **37** 89 68 45

Starting from the left, but beginning with the element after 10, compare each element with 37 until an element greater than 37 is found—then swap 37 and that element. There are no more elements greater than 37, so when we compare 37 with itself, we know that 37 has been placed in its final location in the sorted array. Every value to the left of 37 is smaller than it, and every value to the right of 37 is larger than it.

        Once the partition has been applied on the previous array, there are two unsorted subarrays. The subarray with values less than 37 contains 12, 2, 6, 4, 10 and 8. The subarray with values greater than 37 contains 89, 68 and 45. The sort continues recursively with both subarrays being partitioned in the same manner as the original array.

        Based on the preceding discussion, write recursive method `quickSortHelper` to sort a one-dimensional integer array. The method should receive as arguments a starting index and an ending index on the original array being sorted.

Generic Collections

I think this is the most extraordinary collection of talent, of human knowledge, that has ever been gathered together at the White House— with the possible exception of when Thomas Jefferson dined alone.
—John F. Kennedy

Journey over all the universe in a map.
—Miguel de Cervantes

Objectives

In this chapter you'll learn:

- What collections are.
- To use class **Arrays** for array manipulations.
- To form linked data structures using references and self-referential classes.
- The type-wrapper classes for processing primitive data values as objects.
- To use the collections framework implementations.
- To use collections framework methods to manipulate collections.
- To use interfaces to program with collections polymorphically.
- To use iterators to "walk through" a collection.
- To use persistent hash tables.
- To use synchronization and modifiability wrappers.

20.1 Introduction

In this chapter, we consider the Java **collections framework**, which contains prebuilt data structures, interfaces and methods for manipulating those data structures. Some examples of collections are the cards you hold in a card game, your favorite songs stored in your computer, the members of a sports team and the real-estate records in your local registry of deeds (which map book numbers and page numbers to property owners).

With collections, you use existing data structures, without concern for how they're implemented. This is a marvelous example of code reuse. You can code faster and can expect excellent performance, maximizing execution speed and minimizing memory consumption. In this chapter, we discuss the collections framework interfaces that declare the capabilities of each collection type, the implementation classes, the methods that process the collections, and the so-called **iterators** that "walk through" collections. This chapter provides an introduction to the collections framework. For complete details, visit `java.sun.com/javase/6/docs/technotes/guides/collections/index.html`.

The Java collections framework provides ready-to-go, reusable componentry—you do not need to write your own collection classes, but you can if you wish to. The collections are standardized so that applications can share them easily without concern for the details of their implementation. The collections framework encourages even further reusability. As new data structures and methods are developed that fit this framework, a large base of programmers will already be familiar with the interfaces and methods they implement.

20.2 Collections Overview

A **collection** is a data structure—actually, an object—that can hold references to other objects. Usually, collections contain references to objects that are all of the same type. The collections framework interfaces declare the operations to be performed generically on various types of collections. Figure 20.1 lists some of the interfaces of the collections framework. Several implementations of these interfaces are provided within the framework. You may also provide implementations specific to your own requirements.

Interface	Description
Collection	The root interface in the collections hierarchy from which interfaces Set, Queue and List are derived.
Set	A collection that does not contain duplicates.
List	An ordered collection that can contain duplicate elements.
Map	Associates keys to values and cannot contain duplicate keys.
Queue	Typically a first-in, first-out collection that models a waiting line; other orders can be specified.

Fig. 20.1 | Some collections framework interfaces.

The classes and interfaces of the collections framework are members of package java.util. In the next section, we begin our discussion by examining the collections framework capabilities for array manipulation.

In earlier versions of Java, the classes in the collections framework stored and manipulated Object references, enabling you to store *any* object in a collection. One inconvenient aspect of storing Object references occurs when retrieving them from a collection. A program normally needs to process specific types of objects. As a result, the Object references obtained from a collection typically need to be cast to an appropriate type to allow the program to process the objects correctly.

In Java SE 5, the collections framework was enhanced with the generics capabilities we introduced in Chapter 6 when discussing generic ArrayLists. This means that you can specify the exact type that will be stored in a collection. You also receive the benefits of compile-time type checking—the compiler ensures that you are using appropriate types with your collection and, if not, issues compile-time error messages. Also, once you specify the type stored in a collection, any reference you retrieve from the collection will have the specified type. This eliminates the need for explicit type casts that can throw Class-CastExceptions if the referenced object is not of the appropriate type. In addition, the generic collections are backward compatible with Java code that was written before generics were introduced in Java SE 5.

20.3 Type-Wrapper Classes for Primitive Types

Each primitive type (listed in Appendix D, Primitive Types) has a corresponding **type-wrapper class** (in package java.lang). These classes are called **Boolean**, **Byte**, **Character**, **Double**, **Float**, **Integer**, **Long** and **Short**. Each type-wrapper class enables you to manipulate primitive-type values as objects. The data structures that we reuse or develop in Chapters 20–22 manipulate and share objects—they cannot manipulate variables of primitive types. However, they can manipulate objects of the type-wrapper classes, because every class ultimately derives from Object.

Each of the numeric type-wrapper classes—Byte, Short, Integer, Long, Float and Double—extends class Number. Also, the type-wrapper classes are final classes, so you cannot extend them.

Primitive types do not have methods, so the methods related to a primitive type are located in the corresponding type-wrapper class (e.g., method `parseInt`, which converts a `String` to an `int` value, is located in class `Integer`). If you need to manipulate a primitive value in your program, first refer to the documentation for the type-wrapper classes—the method you need might already be declared.

20.4 Autoboxing and Auto-Unboxing

Prior to Java SE 5, if you wanted to insert a primitive value into a data structure, you had to create a new object of the corresponding type-wrapper class, then insert it in the collection. Similarly, if you wanted to retrieve an object of a type-wrapper class from a collection and manipulate its primitive value, you had to invoke a method on the object to obtain its corresponding primitive-type value. For example, suppose you want to add an `int` to an array that stores only references to `Integer` objects. Prior to Java SE 5, you'd be required to "wrap" an `int` value in an `Integer` object before adding the integer to the array and to "unwrap" the `int` value from the `Integer` object to retrieve the value from the array, as in

```
Integer[] integerArray = new Integer[ 5 ]; // create integerArray
// assign Integer 10 to integerArray[ 0 ]
integerArray[ 0 ] = new Integer( 10 );
// get int value of Integer
int value = integerArray[ 0 ].intValue();
```

Notice that the `int` primitive value 10 is used to initialize an `Integer` object. This achieves the desired result but requires extra code and is cumbersome. We then need to invoke method `intValue` of class `Integer` to obtain the `int` value in the `Integer` object.

Java SE 5 introduced two new conversions—the boxing conversion and the unboxing conversion—to simplify converting between primitive-type values and type-wrapper objects with no additional coding on the part of the programmer. A **boxing conversion** converts a value of a primitive type to an object of the corresponding type-wrapper class. An **unboxing conversion** converts an object of a type-wrapper class to a value of the corresponding primitive type. These conversions can be performed automatically (called **autoboxing** and **auto-unboxing**). For example, the previous statements can be rewritten as

```
Integer[] integerArray = new Integer[ 5 ]; // create integerArray
integerArray[ 0 ] = 10; // assign Integer 10 to integerArray[ 0 ]
int value = integerArray[ 0 ]; // get int value of Integer
```

In this case, autoboxing occurs when assigning an `int` value (10) to `integerArray[0]`, because `integerArray` stores references to `Integer` objects, not `int` values. Auto-unboxing occurs when assigning `integerArray[0]` to `int` variable `value`, because variable `value` stores an `int` value, not a reference to an `Integer` object. Boxing conversions also occur in conditions, which can evaluate to primitive `boolean` values or `Boolean` objects. Many of the examples in Chapters 20–22 use these conversions to store primitive values in and to retrieve them from data structures.

20.5 Interface `Collection` and Class `Collections`

Interface `Collection` is the root interface in the collection hierarchy from which interfaces `Set`, `Queue` and `List` are derived. Interface `Set` defines a collection that does not contain duplicates. Interface **Queue** defines a collection that represents a waiting line—typically, insertions are made at the back of a queue and deletions are made from the front, though other orders can be specified. We discuss Queue and Set in Sections 20.9—20.10. Interface Collection contains **bulk operations** (i.e., operations performed on an entire collection) for operations such as adding, clearing and comparing objects (or elements) in a collection. A Collection can also be converted to an array. In addition, interface Collection provides a method that returns an **Iterator** object, which allows a program to walk through the collection and remove elements from the collection during the iteration. We discuss class Iterator in Section 20.6.1. Other methods of interface Collection enable a program to determine a collection's size and whether a collection is empty.

Software Engineering Observation 20.1

Collection is used commonly as a parameter type in methods to allow polymorphic processing of all objects that implement interface Collection.

Software Engineering Observation 20.2

Most collection implementations provide a constructor that takes a Collection argument, thereby allowing a new collection to be constructed containing the elements of the specified collection.

Class **Collections** provides static methods that search, sort and perform other operations on collections. Section 20.7 discusses more about the methods that are available in class Collections. We also cover the **wrapper methods** of class Collections that enable you to treat a collection as a synchronized collection (Section 20.13) or an unmodifiable collection (Section 20.14). Such collections are useful when a client of a class needs to view the elements of a collection, but they should not be allowed to modify the collection by adding and removing elements. Synchronized collections are for use with a powerful capability called multithreading (discussed in Chapter 26). Multithreading enables programs to perform operations in parallel. When two or more threads of a program share a collection, there is the potential for problems to occur. As a brief analogy, consider a traffic intersection. We cannot allow all cars access to one intersection at the same time—if we did, accidents would occur. For this reason, traffic lights are provided to control access to the intersection. Similarly, we can synchronize access to a collection to ensure that only one thread manipulates the collection at a time. The synchronization wrapper methods of class Collections return synchronized versions of collections that can be shared among threads in a program.

20.6 Lists

A List (sometimes called a **sequence**) is an ordered Collection that can contain duplicate elements. Like array indices, List indices are zero based (i.e., the first element's index is zero). In addition to the methods inherited from Collection, List provides methods for manipulating elements via their indices, manipulating a specified range of elements, searching for elements and obtaining a **ListIterator** to access the elements.

Interface List is implemented by several classes, including classes **ArrayList**, **LinkedList** and **Vector**. Autoboxing occurs when you add primitive-type values to objects of these classes, because they store only references to objects. Class ArrayList and Vector are resizable-array implementations of List. Inserting an element between existing elements of an `ArrayList` or `Vector` is an inefficient operation—all elements after the new one must be moved out of the way, which could be an expensive operation in a collection with a large number of elements. A `LinkedList` enables efficient insertion (or removal) of elements in the middle of a collection. We discuss the architecture of linked lists in Chapter 22.

Classes `ArrayList` and `Vector` have nearly identical behaviors. The primary difference between them is that `Vector`s are synchronized by default, whereas `ArrayList`s are not. Also, class `Vector` is from Java 1.0, before the collections framework was added to Java. As such, `Vector` has several methods that are not part of interface `List` and are not implemented in class `ArrayList` but perform identical tasks. For example, `Vector` methods `addElement` and `add` both append an element to a `Vector`, but only method `add` is specified in interface `List` and implemented by `ArrayList`. Unsynchronized collections provide better performance than synchronized ones. For this reason, `ArrayList` is typically preferred over `Vector` in programs that do not share a collection among threads. Separately, the Java collections API provides so-called synchronization wrappers (Section 20.13) that can be used to add synchronization to the unsynchronized collections, and several powerful synchronized collections are available in the Java concurrency APIs.

Performance Tip 20.1

ArrayLists behave like Vectors without synchronization and therefore execute faster than Vectors because ArrayLists do not have the overhead of thread synchronization.

Software Engineering Observation 20.3

LinkedLists can be used to create stacks, queues and deques (double-ended queues, pronounced "decks"). The collections framework provides implementations of some of these data structures.

The following three subsections demonstrate the `List` and `Collection` capabilities with several examples. Section 20.6.1 focuses on removing elements from an `ArrayList` with an `Iterator`. Section 20.6.2 focuses on `ListIterator` and several `List`- and `LinkedList`-specific methods.

20.6.1 ArrayList and Iterator

Figure 20.2 uses an `ArrayList` (introduced in Section 6.13) to demonstrate several capabilities of interface `Collection`. The program places two `Color` arrays in `ArrayList`s and uses an `Iterator` to remove elements in the second `ArrayList` collection from the first `ArrayList` collection.

```
1   // Fig. 20.2: CollectionTest.java
2   // Collection interface demonstrated via an ArrayList object.
3   import java.util.List;
4   import java.util.ArrayList;
5   import java.util.Collection;
6   import java.util.Iterator;
7
8   public class CollectionTest
9   {
```

Fig. 20.2 | `Collection` interface demonstrated via an `ArrayList` object. (Part 1 of 2.)

```
10      public static void main( String[] args )
11      {
12         // add elements in colors array to list
13         String[] colors = { "MAGENTA", "RED", "WHITE", "BLUE", "CYAN" };
14         List< String > list = new ArrayList< String >();
15
16         for ( String color : colors )
17            list.add( color ); // adds color to end of list
18
19         // add elements in removeColors array to removeList
20         String[] removeColors = { "RED", "WHITE", "BLUE" };
21         List< String > removeList = new ArrayList< String >();
22
23         for ( String color : removeColors )
24            removeList.add( color );
25
26         // output list contents
27         System.out.println( "ArrayList: " );
28
29         for ( int count = 0; count < list.size(); count++ )
30            System.out.printf( "%s ", list.get( count ) );
31
32         // remove from list the colors contained in removeList
33         removeColors( list, removeList );
34
35         // output list contents
36         System.out.println( "\n\nArrayList after calling removeColors: " );
37
38         for ( String color : list )
39            System.out.printf( "%s ", color );
40      } // end main
41
42      // remove colors specified in collection2 from collection1
43      private static void removeColors( Collection< String > collection1,
44         Collection< String > collection2 )
45      {
46         // get iterator
47         Iterator< String > iterator = collection1.iterator();
48
49         // loop while collection has items
50         while ( iterator.hasNext() )
51         {
52            if ( collection2.contains( iterator.next() ) )
53               iterator.remove(); // remove current Color
54         } // end while
55      } // end method removeColors
56   } // end class CollectionTest
```

```
ArrayList:
MAGENTA RED WHITE BLUE CYAN

ArrayList after calling removeColors:
MAGENTA CYAN
```

Fig. 20.2 | Collection interface demonstrated via an ArrayList object. (Part 2 of 2.)

Lines 13 and 20 declare and initialize `String` arrays `colors` and `removeColors`. Lines 14 and 21 create `ArrayList<String>` objects and assign their references to `List<String>` variables `list` and `removeList`, respectively. Recall that `ArrayList` is a generic class, so we can specify a type argument (`String` in this case) to indicate the type of the elements in each list. Note that we refer to the `ArrayLists` in this example via `List` variables. This makes our code more flexible and easier to modify. If we later decide that `LinkedLists` would be more appropriate, we'll need to modify only lines 14 and 21 where we created the `ArrayList` objects.

Lines 16–17 populate `list` with `Strings` stored in array `colors`, and lines 23–24 populate `removeList` with `Strings` stored in array `removeColors` using **List method add**. Lines 29–30 output each element of `list`. Line 29 calls **List method size** to get the number of elements in the `ArrayList`. Line 30 uses **List method get** to retrieve individual element values. Note that lines 29–30 also could have used the enhanced for statement (which we'll demonstrate with collections in other examples).

Line 33 calls method `removeColors` (lines 43–55), passing `list` and `removeList` as arguments. Method `removeColors` deletes the `Strings` in `removeList` from the `Strings` in `list`. Lines 38–39 print `list`'s elements after `removeColors` completes its task.

Method `removeColors` declares two `Collection<String>` parameters (lines 43–44) that allow any two `Collections` containing strings to be passed as arguments to this method. The method accesses the elements of the first `Collection` (`collection1`) via an `Iterator`. Line 47 calls **Collection method iterator** to get an `Iterator` for the `Collection`. Note that interfaces `Collection` and `Iterator` are generic types. The loop-continuation condition (line 50) calls **Iterator method hasNext** to determine whether the `Collection` contains more elements. Method `hasNext` returns `true` if another element exists and `false` otherwise.

The `if` condition in line 52 calls **Iterator method next** to obtain a reference to the next element, then uses method **contains** of the second `Collection` (`collection2`) to determine whether `collection2` contains the element returned by `next`. If so, line 53 calls **Iterator method remove** to remove the element from the `Collection` `collection1`.

Common Programming Error 20.1

If a collection is modified by one of its methods after an iterator is created for that collection, the iterator immediately becomes invalid—operations performed with the iterator after this point throw ConcurrentModificationExceptions. For this reason, iterators are said to be "fail fast."

20.6.2 LinkedList

Figure 20.3 demonstrates various operations on `LinkedLists`. The program creates two `LinkedLists` of `Strings`. The elements of one `List` are added to the other. Then all the `Strings` are converted to uppercase, and a range of elements is deleted.

```
1   // Fig. 20.3: ListTest.java
2   // Lists, LinkedLists and ListIterators.
3   import java.util.List;
4   import java.util.LinkedList;
```

Fig. 20.3 | Lists, LinkedLists and ListIterators. (Part 1 of 3.)

```
5    import java.util.ListIterator;
6
7    public class ListTest
8    {
9       public static void main( String[] args )
10      {
11         // add colors elements to list1
12         String[] colors =
13            { "black", "yellow", "green", "blue", "violet", "silver" };
14         List< String > list1 = new LinkedList< String >();
15
16         for ( String color : colors )
17            list1.add( color );
18
19         // add colors2 elements to list2
20         String[] colors2 =
21            { "gold", "white", "brown", "blue", "gray", "silver" };
22         List< String > list2 = new LinkedList< String >();
23
24         for ( String color : colors2 )
25            list2.add( color );
26
27         list1.addAll( list2 ); // concatenate lists
28         list2 = null; // release resources
29         printList( list1 ); // print list1 elements
30
31         convertToUppercaseStrings( list1 ); // convert to uppercase string
32         printList( list1 ); // print list1 elements
33
34         System.out.print( "\nDeleting elements 4 to 6..." );
35         removeItems( list1, 4, 7 ); // remove items 4-6 from list
36         printList( list1 ); // print list1 elements
37         printReversedList( list1 ); // print list in reverse order
38      } // end main
39
40      // output List contents
41      private static void printList( List< String > list )
42      {
43         System.out.println( "\nlist: " );
44
45         for ( String color : list )
46            System.out.printf( "%s ", color );
47
48         System.out.println();
49      } // end method printList
50
51      // locate String objects and convert to uppercase
52      private static void convertToUppercaseStrings( List< String > list )
53      {
54         ListIterator< String > iterator = list.listIterator();
55
56         while ( iterator.hasNext() )
57         {
```

Fig. 20.3 | Lists, LinkedLists and ListIterators. (Part 2 of 3.)

```
58              String color = iterator.next(); // get item
59              iterator.set( color.toUpperCase() ); // convert to upper case
60          } // end while
61      } // end method convertToUppercaseStrings
62
63      // obtain sublist and use clear method to delete sublist items
64      private static void removeItems( List< String > list,
65          int start, int end )
66      {
67          list.subList( start, end ).clear(); // remove items
68      } // end method removeItems
69
70      // print reversed list
71      private static void printReversedList( List< String > list )
72      {
73          ListIterator< String > iterator = list.listIterator( list.size() );
74
75          System.out.println( "\nReversed List:" );
76
77          // print list in reverse order
78          while ( iterator.hasPrevious() )
79              System.out.printf( "%s ", iterator.previous() );
80      } // end method printReversedList
81  } // end class ListTest
```

```
list:
black yellow green blue violet silver gold white brown blue gray silver

list:
BLACK YELLOW GREEN BLUE VIOLET SILVER GOLD WHITE BROWN BLUE GRAY SILVER

Deleting elements 4 to 6...
list:
BLACK YELLOW GREEN BLUE WHITE BROWN BLUE GRAY SILVER

Reversed List:
SILVER GRAY BLUE BROWN WHITE BLUE GREEN YELLOW BLACK
```

Fig. 20.3 | Lists, LinkedLists and ListIterators. (Part 3 of 3.)

Lines 14 and 22 create LinkedLists list1 and list2 of type String. LinkedList is a generic class that has one type parameter for which we specify the type argument String in this example. Lines 16–17 and 24–25 call List method add to append elements from arrays colors and colors2 to the end of list1 and list2, respectively.

Line 27 calls **List method addAll** to append all elements of list2 to the end of list1. Line 28 sets list2 to null, so the LinkedList to which list2 referred can be garbage collected. Line 29 calls method printList (lines 41–49) to output list list1's contents. Line 31 calls method convertToUppercaseStrings (lines 52–61) to convert each String element to uppercase, then line 32 calls printList again to display the modified Strings. Line 35 calls method removeItems (lines 64–68) to remove the elements starting at index 4 up to, but not including, index 7 of the list. Line 37 calls method printReversedList (lines 71–80) to print the list in reverse order.

Method convertToUppercaseStrings
Method convertToUppercaseStrings (lines 52–61) changes lowercase String elements in its List argument to uppercase Strings. Line 54 calls **List method listIterator** to get the List's **bidirectional iterator** (i.e., one that can traverse a List backward or forward). ListIterator is also a generic class. In this example, the ListIterator references String objects, because method listIterator is called on a List of Strings. Line 56 calls method hasNext to determine whether the List contains another element. Line 58 gets the next String in the List. Line 59 calls **String method toUpperCase** to get an uppercase version of the String and calls **ListIterator method set** to replace the current String to which iterator refers with the String returned by method toUpperCase. Like method toUpperCase, **String method toLowerCase** returns a lowercase version of the String.

Method removeItems
Method removeItems (lines 64–68) removes a range of items from the list. Line 67 calls **List method subList** to obtain a portion of the List (called a **sublist**). This is a so-called **range-view method**, which enables the program to view a portion of the list. The sublist is simply a view into the List on which subList is called. Method subList takes as arguments the beginning and ending index for the sublist. The ending index is not part of the range of the sublist. In this example, line 35 passes 4 for the beginning index and 7 for the ending index to subList. The sublist returned is the set of elements with indices 4 through 6. Next, the program calls **List method clear** on the sublist to remove the elements of the sublist from the List. Any changes made to a sublist are also made to the original List.

Method printReversedList
Method printReversedList (lines 71–80) prints the list backward. Line 73 calls List method listIterator with the starting position as an argument (in our case, the last element in the list) to get a bidirectional iterator for the list. **List method size** returns the number of items in the List. The while condition (line 78) calls **ListIterator's hasPrevious method** to determine whether there are more elements while traversing the list backward. Line 79 calls **ListIterator's previous method** to get the previous element from the list and outputs it to the standard output stream.

Views into Collections and Arrays Method asList
An important feature of the collections framework is the ability to manipulate the elements of one collection type (such as a set) through a different collection type (such as a list), regardless of the collection's internal implementation. The set of public methods through which collections are manipulated is called a **view**.

Class Arrays provides static method **asList** to view an array (sometimes called the **backing array**) as a **List** collection. A List view allows you to manipulate the array as if it were a list. This is useful for adding the elements in an array to a collection (e.g., a LinkedList) and for sorting array elements. The next example demonstrates how to create a LinkedList with a List view of an array, because we cannot pass the array to a LinkedList constructor. Sorting array elements with a List view is demonstrated in Fig. 20.7. Any modifications made through the List view change the array, and any modifications made to the array change the List view. The only operation permitted on the view returned by asList is *set*, which changes the value of the view and the backing array. Any other attempts to change the view (such as adding or removing elements) result in an **UnsupportedOperationException**.

Viewing Arrays as Lists and Converting Lists to Arrays
Figure 20.4 uses Arrays method asList to view an array as a List and uses **List method toArray** to get an array from a LinkedList collection. The program calls method asList to create a List view of an array, which is used to initialize a LinkedList object, then adds a series of strings to the LinkedList and calls method toArray to obtain an array containing references to the Strings.

```java
1   // Fig. 20.4: UsingToArray.java
2   // Viewing arrays as Lists and converting Lists to arrays.
3   import java.util.LinkedList;
4   import java.util.Arrays;
5
6   public class UsingToArray
7   {
8      // creates a LinkedList, adds elements and converts to array
9      public static void main( String[] args )
10     {
11        String[] colors = { "black", "blue", "yellow" };
12
13        LinkedList< String > links =
14           new LinkedList< String >( Arrays.asList( colors ) );
15
16        links.addLast( "red" ); // add as last item
17        links.add( "pink" ); // add to the end
18        links.add( 3, "green" ); // add at 3rd index
19        links.addFirst( "cyan" ); // add as first item
20
21        // get LinkedList elements as an array
22        colors = links.toArray( new String[ links.size() ] );
23
24        System.out.println( "colors: " );
25
26        for ( String color : colors )
27           System.out.println( color );
28     } // end main
29  } // end class UsingToArray
```

```
colors:
cyan
black
blue
yellow
green
red
pink
```

Fig. 20.4 | Viewing arrays as Lists and converting Lists to arrays.

Lines 13–14 construct a LinkedList of Strings containing the elements of array colors. Line 14 uses Arrays method asList to return a List view of the array, then uses that to initialize the LinkedList with its constructor that receives a Collection as an argument (a List *is a* Collection). Line 16 calls **LinkedList method addLast** to add "red" to the end of links. Lines 17–18 call **LinkedList method add** to add "pink" as the last element and "green" as the element at index 3 (i.e., the fourth element). Method addLast (line 16) functions identically to method add (line 17). Line 19 calls **LinkedList method addFirst** to add "cyan" as the new first item in the LinkedList. The add operations are permitted because they operate on the LinkedList object, not the view returned by asList. [*Note:* When "cyan" is added as the first element, "green" becomes the fifth element in the LinkedList.]

Line 22 calls the List interface's toArray method to get a String array from links. The array is a copy of the list's elements—modifying the array's contents does not modify the list. The array passed to method toArray is of the same type that you'd like method toArray to return. If the number of elements in that array is greater than or equal to the number of elements in the LinkedList, toArray copies the list's elements into its array argument and returns that array. If the LinkedList has more elements than the number of elements in the array passed to toArray, toArray allocates a new array of the same type it receives as an argument, copies the list's elements into the new array and returns the new array.

> **Common Programming Error 20.2**
> *Passing an array that contains data to* toArray *can cause logic errors. If the number of elements in the array is smaller than the number of elements in the list on which* toArray *is called, a new array is allocated to store the list's elements—without preserving the array argument's elements. If the number of elements in the array is greater than the number of elements in the list, the elements of the array (starting at index zero) are overwritten with the list's elements. Array elements that are not overwritten retain their values.*

20.7 Collections Methods

Class Collections provides several high-performance algorithms for manipulating collection elements. The algorithms (Fig. 20.5) are implemented as static methods. The methods sort, binarySearch, reverse, shuffle, fill and copy operate on Lists. Methods min, max, addAll, frequency and disjoint operate on Collections.

Method	Description
sort	Sorts the elements of a List.
binarySearch	Locates an object in a List.
reverse	Reverses the elements of a List.
shuffle	Randomly orders a List's elements.
fill	Sets every List element to refer to a specified object.
copy	Copies references from one List into another.
min	Returns the smallest element in a Collection.
max	Returns the largest element in a Collection.
addAll	Appends all elements in an array to a Collection.
frequency	Calculates how many collection elements are equal to the specified element.
disjoint	Determines whether two collections have no elements in common.

Fig. 20.5 | Collections methods.

Software Engineering Observation 20.4

The collections framework methods are polymorphic. That is, each can operate on objects that implement specific interfaces, regardless of the underlying implementations.

20.7.1 Method sort

Method **sort** sorts the elements of a List, which must implement the **Comparable** interface. The order is determined by the natural order of the elements' type as implemented by a compareTo method. Method compareTo is declared in interface Comparable and is sometimes called the **natural comparison method**. The sort call may specify as a second argument a **Comparator** object that determines an alternative ordering of the elements.

Sorting in Ascending Order

Figure 20.6 uses Collections method sort to order the elements of a List in ascending order (line 17). Recall that List is a generic type and accepts one type argument that specifies the list element type—line 14 creates list as a List of Strings. Note that lines 15 and 20 each use an implicit call to the list's toString method to output the list contents in the format shown on the second and fourth lines of the output.

```java
1   // Fig. 20.6: Sort1.java
2   // Collections method sort.
3   import java.util.List;
4   import java.util.Arrays;
5   import java.util.Collections;
6
7   public class Sort1
8   {
9      public static void main( String[] args )
10     {
11        String[] suits = { "Hearts", "Diamonds", "Clubs", "Spades" };
12
13        // Create and display a list containing the suits array elements
14        List< String > list = Arrays.asList( suits ); // create List
15        System.out.printf( "Unsorted array elements: %s\n", list );
16
17        Collections.sort( list ); // sort ArrayList
18
19        // output list
20        System.out.printf( "Sorted array elements: %s\n", list );
21     } // end main
22  } // end class Sort1
```

```
Unsorted array elements: [Hearts, Diamonds, Clubs, Spades]
Sorted array elements: [Clubs, Diamonds, Hearts, Spades]
```

Fig. 20.6 | Collections method sort.

Sorting in Descending Order

Figure 20.7 sorts the same list of strings used in Fig. 20.6 in descending order. The example introduces the Comparator interface, which is used for sorting a Collection's elements in a different order. Line 18 calls Collections's method sort to order the List in descending order. The static **Collections** method **reverseOrder** returns a Comparator object that orders the collection's elements in reverse order.

```java
 1  // Fig. 20.7: Sort2.java
 2  // Using a Comparator object with method sort.
 3  import java.util.List;
 4  import java.util.Arrays;
 5  import java.util.Collections;
 6
 7  public class Sort2
 8  {
 9     public static void main( String[] args )
10     {
11        String[] suits = { "Hearts", "Diamonds", "Clubs", "Spades" };
12
13        // Create and display a list containing the suits array elements
14        List< String > list = Arrays.asList( suits ); // create List
15        System.out.printf( "Unsorted array elements: %s\n", list );
16
17        // sort in descending order using a comparator
18        Collections.sort( list, Collections.reverseOrder() );
19
20        // output List elements
21        System.out.printf( "Sorted list elements: %s\n", list );
22     } // end main
23  } // end class Sort2
```

```
Unsorted array elements: [Hearts, Diamonds, Clubs, Spades]
Sorted list elements: [Spades, Hearts, Diamonds, Clubs]
```

Fig. 20.7 | Collections method sort with a Comparator object.

Sorting with a Comparator

Figure 20.8 creates a custom Comparator class, named TimeComparator, that implements interface Comparator to compare two Time2 objects. Class Time2, declared in Fig. 8.5, represents times with hours, minutes and seconds.

```java
 1  // Fig. 20.8: TimeComparator.java
 2  // Custom Comparator class that compares two Time2 objects.
 3  import java.util.Comparator;
 4
 5  public class TimeComparator implements Comparator< Time2 >
 6  {
 7     public int compare( Time2 time1, Time2 time2 )
 8     {
 9        int hourCompare = time1.getHour() - time2.getHour(); // compare hour
10
11        // test the hour first
12        if ( hourCompare != 0 )
13           return hourCompare;
14
```

Fig. 20.8 | Custom Comparator class that compares two Time2 objects. (Part 1 of 2.)

```
15          int minuteCompare =
16              time1.getMinute() - time2.getMinute(); // compare minute
17
18          // then test the minute
19          if ( minuteCompare != 0 )
20              return minuteCompare;
21
22          int secondCompare =
23              time1.getSecond() - time2.getSecond(); // compare second
24
25          return secondCompare; // return result of comparing seconds
26       } // end method compare
27  } // end class TimeComparator
```

Fig. 20.8 | Custom Comparator class that compares two Time2 objects. (Part 2 of 2.)

Class TimeComparator implements interface Comparator, a generic type that takes one type argument (in this case Time2). A class that implements Comparator must declare a compare method that receives two arguments and returns a negative integer if the first argument is less than the second, 0 if the arguments are equal or a positive integer if the first argument is greater than the second. Method compare (lines 7–26) performs comparisons between Time2 objects. Line 9 compares the two hours of the Time2 objects. If the hours are different (line 12), then we return this value. If this value is positive, then the first hour is greater than the second and the first time is greater than the second. If this value is negative, then the first hour is less than the second and the first time is less than the second. If this value is zero, the hours are the same and we must test the minutes (and maybe the seconds) to determine which time is greater.

Figure 20.9 sorts a list using the custom Comparator class TimeComparator. Line 11 creates an ArrayList of Time2 objects. Recall that both ArrayList and List are generic types and accept a type argument that specifies the element type of the collection. Lines 13–17 create five Time2 objects and add them to this list. Line 23 calls method sort, passing it an object of our TimeComparator class (Fig. 20.8).

```
1   // Fig. 20.9: Sort3.java
2   // Collections method sort with a custom Comparator object.
3   import java.util.List;
4   import java.util.ArrayList;
5   import java.util.Collections;
6
7   public class Sort3
8   {
9      public static void main( String[] args )
10     {
11        List< Time2 > list = new ArrayList< Time2 >(); // create List
12
13        list.add( new Time2(  6, 24, 34 ) );
14        list.add( new Time2( 18, 14, 58 ) );
15        list.add( new Time2(  6, 05, 34 ) );
16        list.add( new Time2( 12, 14, 58 ) );
17        list.add( new Time2(  6, 24, 22 ) );
```

Fig. 20.9 | Collections method sort with a custom Comparator object. (Part 1 of 2.)

```
18
19          // output List elements
20          System.out.printf( "Unsorted array elements:\n%s\n", list );
21
22          // sort in order using a comparator
23          Collections.sort( list, new TimeComparator() );
24
25          // output List elements
26          System.out.printf( "Sorted list elements:\n%s\n", list );
27       } // end main
28    } // end class Sort3
```

```
Unsorted array elements:
[6:24:34 AM, 6:14:58 PM, 6:05:34 AM, 12:14:58 PM, 6:24:22 AM]
Sorted list elements:
[6:05:34 AM, 6:24:22 AM, 6:24:34 AM, 12:14:58 PM, 6:14:58 PM]
```

Fig. 20.9 | Collections method sort with a custom Comparator object. (Part 2 of 2.)

20.7.2 Method shuffle

Method shuffle randomly orders a List's elements. In Chapter 6, we presented a card shuffling and dealing simulation that used a loop to shuffle a deck of cards. In Fig. 20.10, we use method shuffle to shuffle a deck of Card objects that might be used in a card-game simulator.

Class Card (lines 8–41) represents a card in a deck of cards. Each Card has a face and a suit. Lines 10–12 declare two enum types—Face and Suit—which represent the face and the suit of the card, respectively. Method toString (lines 37–40) returns a String containing the face and suit of the Card separated by the string " of ". When an enum constant is converted to a string, the constant's identifier is used as the string representation. Normally we would use all uppercase letters for enum constants. In this example, we chose to use capital letters for only the first letter of each enum constant because we want the card to be displayed with initial capital letters for the face and the suit (e.g., "Ace of Spades").

```
1    // Fig. 20.10: DeckOfCards.java
2    // Card shuffling and dealing with Collections method shuffle.
3    import java.util.List;
4    import java.util.Arrays;
5    import java.util.Collections;
6
7    // class to represent a Card in a deck of cards
8    class Card
9    {
10       public static enum Face { Ace, Deuce, Three, Four, Five, Six,
11          Seven, Eight, Nine, Ten, Jack, Queen, King };
12       public static enum Suit { Clubs, Diamonds, Hearts, Spades };
13
14       private final Face face; // face of card
15       private final Suit suit; // suit of card
16
```

Fig. 20.10 | Card shuffling and dealing with Collections method shuffle. (Part 1 of 3.)

```
17      // two-argument constructor
18      public Card( Face cardFace, Suit cardSuit )
19      {
20          face = cardFace; // initialize face of card
21          suit = cardSuit; // initialize suit of card
22      } // end two-argument Card constructor
23
24      // return face of the card
25      public Face getFace()
26      {
27          return face;
28      } // end method getFace
29
30      // return suit of Card
31      public Suit getSuit()
32      {
33          return suit;
34      } // end method getSuit
35
36      // return String representation of Card
37      public String toString()
38      {
39          return String.format( "%s of %s", face, suit );
40      } // end method toString
41  } // end class Card
42
43  // class DeckOfCards declaration
44  public class DeckOfCards
45  {
46      private List< Card > list; // declare List that will store Cards
47
48      // set up deck of Cards and shuffle
49      public DeckOfCards()
50      {
51          Card[] deck = new Card[ 52 ];
52          int count = 0; // number of cards
53
54          // populate deck with Card objects
55          for ( Card.Suit suit : Card.Suit.values() )
56          {
57              for ( Card.Face face : Card.Face.values() )
58              {
59                  deck[ count ] = new Card( face, suit );
60                  ++count;
61              } // end for
62          } // end for
63
64          list = Arrays.asList( deck ); // get List
65          Collections.shuffle( list );  // shuffle deck
66      } // end DeckOfCards constructor
67
68      // output deck
69      public void printCards()
70      {
```

Fig. 20.10 | Card shuffling and dealing with `Collections` method `shuffle`. (Part 2 of 3.)

```
71          // display 52 cards in two columns
72          for ( int i = 0; i < list.size(); i++ )
73             System.out.printf( "%-19s%s", list.get( i ),
74                ( ( i + 1 ) % 4 == 0 ) ? "\n" : "" );
75       } // end method printCards
76
77       public static void main( String[] args )
78       {
79          DeckOfCards cards = new DeckOfCards();
80          cards.printCards();
81       } // end main
82    } // end class DeckOfCards
```

Deuce of Clubs	Six of Spades	Nine of Diamonds	Ten of Hearts
Three of Diamonds	Five of Clubs	Deuce of Diamonds	Seven of Clubs
Three of Spades	Six of Diamonds	King of Clubs	Jack of Hearts
Ten of Spades	King of Diamonds	Eight of Spades	Six of Hearts
Nine of Clubs	Ten of Diamonds	Eight of Diamonds	Eight of Hearts
Ten of Clubs	Five of Hearts	Ace of Clubs	Deuce of Hearts
Queen of Diamonds	Ace of Diamonds	Four of Clubs	Nine of Hearts
Ace of Spades	Deuce of Spades	Ace of Hearts	Jack of Diamonds
Seven of Diamonds	Three of Hearts	Four of Spades	Four of Diamonds
Seven of Spades	King of Hearts	Seven of Hearts	Five of Diamonds
Eight of Clubs	Three of Clubs	Queen of Clubs	Queen of Spades
Six of Clubs	Nine of Spades	Four of Hearts	Jack of Clubs
Five of Spades	King of Spades	Jack of Spades	Queen of Hearts

Fig. 20.10 | Card shuffling and dealing with `Collections` method `shuffle`. (Part 3 of 3.)

Lines 55–62 populate the deck array with cards that have unique face and suit combinations. Both Face and Suit are public static enum types of class Card. To use these enum types outside of class Card, you must qualify each enum's type name with the name of the class in which it resides (i.e., Card) and a dot (.) separator. Hence, lines 55 and 57 use Card.Suit and Card.Face to declare the control variables of the for statements. Recall that method values of an enum type returns an array that contains all the constants of the enum type. Lines 55–62 use enhanced for statements to construct 52 new Cards.

The shuffling occurs in line 65, which calls static method shuffle of class Collections to shuffle the elements of the array. Method shuffle requires a List argument, so we must obtain a List view of the array before we can shuffle it. Line 64 invokes static method asList of class Arrays to get a List view of the deck array.

Method printCards (lines 69–75) displays the deck of cards in four columns. In each iteration of the loop, lines 73–74 output a card left justified in a 19-character field followed by either a newline or an empty string based on the number of cards output so far. If the number of cards is divisible by 4, a newline is output; otherwise, the empty string is output.

20.7.3 Methods reverse, fill, copy, max and min

Class Collections provides methods for reversing, filling and copying Lists. **Collections method reverse** reverses the order of the elements in a List, and **method fill** overwrites elements in a List with a specified value. The fill operation is useful for re-initializing a List. Method copy takes two arguments—a destination List and a source List. Each source List element is copied to the destination List. The destination List must be at least as long as the source List; otherwise, an IndexOutOfBoundsException occurs. If the destination List is longer, the elements not overwritten are unchanged.

Each method we've seen so far operates on Lists. Methods **min** and **max** each operate on any Collection. Method min returns the smallest element in a Collection, and method max returns the largest element in a Collection. Both of these methods can be called with a Comparator object as a second argument to perform custom comparisons of objects, such as the TimeComparator in Fig. 20.9. Figure 20.11 demonstrates methods reverse, fill, copy, min and max.

```java
1   // Fig. 20.11: Algorithms1.java
2   // Collections methods reverse, fill, copy, max and min.
3   import java.util.List;
4   import java.util.Arrays;
5   import java.util.Collections;
6
7   public class Algorithms1
8   {
9      public static void main( String[] args )
10     {
11        // create and display a List< Character >
12        Character[] letters = { 'P', 'C', 'M' };
13        List< Character > list = Arrays.asList( letters ); // get List
14        System.out.println( "list contains: " );
15        output( list );
16
17        // reverse and display the List< Character >
18        Collections.reverse( list ); // reverse order the elements
19        System.out.println( "\nAfter calling reverse, list contains: " );
20        output( list );
21
22        // create copyList from an array of 3 Characters
23        Character[] lettersCopy = new Character[ 3 ];
24        List< Character > copyList = Arrays.asList( lettersCopy );
25
26        // copy the contents of list into copyList
27        Collections.copy( copyList, list );
28        System.out.println( "\nAfter copying, copyList contains: " );
29        output( copyList );
30
31        // fill list with Rs
32        Collections.fill( list, 'R' );
33        System.out.println( "\nAfter calling fill, list contains: " );
34        output( list );
35     } // end main
36
37     // output List information
38     private static void output( List< Character > listRef )
39     {
40        System.out.print( "The list is: " );
41
42        for ( Character element : listRef )
43           System.out.printf( "%s ", element );
```

Fig. 20.11 | Collections methods reverse, fill, copy, max and min. (Part 1 of 2.)

```
44
45          System.out.printf( "\nMax: %s", Collections.max( listRef ) );
46          System.out.printf( "  Min: %s\n", Collections.min( listRef ) );
47      } // end method output
48  } // end class Algorithms1
```

```
list contains:
The list is: P C M
Max: P  Min: C

After calling reverse, list contains:
The list is: M C P
Max: P  Min: C

After copying, copyList contains:
The list is: M C P
Max: P  Min: C

After calling fill, list contains:
The list is: R R R
Max: R  Min: R
```

Fig. 20.11 | Collections methods reverse, fill, copy, max and min. (Part 2 of 2.)

Line 13 creates List<Character> variable list and initializes it with a List view of the Character array letters. Lines 14–15 output the current contents of the List. Line 18 calls Collections method reverse to reverse the order of list. Method reverse takes one List argument. Since list is a List view of array letters, the array's elements are now in reverse order. The reversed contents are output in lines 19–20. Line 27 uses Collections method copy to copy list's elements into copyList. Changes to copyList do not change letters, because copyList is a separate List that is not a List view of the array letters. Method copy requires two List arguments—the destination List and the source List. Line 32 calls Collections method fill to place the character 'R' in each list element. Because list is a List view of the array letters, this operation changes each element in letters to 'R'. Method fill requires a List for the first argument and an Object for the second argument—in this case, the Object is the boxed version of the character 'R'. Lines 45–46 call Collections methods max and min to find the largest and the smallest element of a Collection, respectively. Recall that interface List extends interface Collection, so a List *is a* Collection.

20.7.4 Method binarySearch

In Section 19.2.2, we studied the high-speed binary search algorithm. This algorithm is built into the Java collections framework as a static **Collections method binarySearch**, which locates an object in a List (e.g., a LinkedList or an ArrayList). If the object is found, its index is returned. If the object is not found, binarySearch returns a negative value. Method binarySearch determines this negative value by first calculating the insertion point and making its sign negative. Then, binarySearch subtracts 1 from the insertion point to obtain the return value, which guarantees that method binarySearch returns positive numbers (>= 0) if and only if the object is found. If multiple elements in the list match the search key, there is no guarantee which one will be located first. Figure 20.12 uses method binarySearch to search for a series of strings in an ArrayList.

```java
1  // Fig. 20.12: BinarySearchTest.java
2  // Collections method binarySearch.
3  import java.util.List;
4  import java.util.Arrays;
5  import java.util.Collections;
6  import java.util.ArrayList;
7
8  public class BinarySearchTest
9  {
10     public static void main( String[] args )
11     {
12        // create an ArrayList< String > from the contents of colors array
13        String[] colors = { "red", "white", "blue", "black", "yellow",
14           "purple", "tan", "pink" };
15        List< String > list =
16           new ArrayList< String >( Arrays.asList( colors ) );
17
18        Collections.sort( list ); // sort the ArrayList
19        System.out.printf( "Sorted ArrayList: %s\n", list );
20
21        // search list for various values
22        printSearchResults( list, colors[ 3 ] ); // first item
23        printSearchResults( list, colors[ 0 ] ); // middle item
24        printSearchResults( list, colors[ 7 ] ); // last item
25        printSearchResults( list, "aqua" ); // below lowest
26        printSearchResults( list, "gray" ); // does not exist
27        printSearchResults( list, "teal" ); // does not exist
28     } // end main
29
30     // perform search and display result
31     private static void printSearchResults(
32        List< String > list, String key )
33     {
34        int result = 0;
35
36        System.out.printf( "\nSearching for: %s\n", key );
37        result = Collections.binarySearch( list, key );
38
39        if ( result >= 0 )
40           System.out.printf( "Found at index %d\n", result );
41        else
42           System.out.printf( "Not Found (%d)\n", result );
43     } // end method printSearchResults
44  } // end class BinarySearchTest
```

```
Sorted ArrayList: [black, blue, pink, purple, red, tan, white, yellow]

Searching for: black
Found at index 0

Searching for: red
Found at index 4

Searching for: pink
Found at index 2
```

Fig. 20.12 | Collections method binarySearch. (Part 1 of 2.)

```
Searching for: aqua
Not Found (-1)

Searching for: gray
Not Found (-3)

Searching for: teal
Not Found (-7)
```

Fig. 20.12 | Collections method binarySearch. (Part 2 of 2.)

Lines 15–16 initialize list with an ArrayList containing a copy of the elements in array colors. Collections method binarySearch expects its List argument's elements to be sorted in ascending order, so line 18 uses Collections method sort to sort the list. If the List argument's elements are not sorted, the result of using binarySearch is undefined. Line 19 outputs the sorted list. Lines 22–27 call method printSearchResults (lines 31–43) to perform searches and output the results. Line 37 calls Collections method binarySearch to search list for the specified key. Method binarySearch takes a List as the first argument and an Object as the second argument. Lines 39–42 output the results of the search. An overloaded version of binarySearch takes a Comparator object as its third argument, which specifies how binarySearch should compare the search key to the List's elements.

20.7.5 Methods addAll, frequency and disjoint

Class Collections also provides the methods addAll, frequency and disjoint. Collections method addAll takes two arguments—a Collection into which to insert the new element(s) and an array that provides elements to be inserted. Collections method frequency takes two arguments—a Collection to be searched and an Object to be searched for in the collection. Method frequency returns the number of times that the second argument appears in the collection. Collections method disjoint takes two Collections and returns true if they have no elements in common. Figure 20.13 demonstrates the use of methods addAll, frequency and disjoint.

```
1   // Fig. 20.13: Algorithms2.java
2   // Collections methods addAll, frequency and disjoint.
3   import java.util.ArrayList;
4   import java.util.List;
5   import java.util.Arrays;
6   import java.util.Collections;
7
8   public class Algorithms2
9   {
10     public static void main( String[] args )
11     {
12        // initialize list1 and list2
13        String[] colors = { "red", "white", "yellow", "blue" };
14        List< String > list1 = Arrays.asList( colors );
15        ArrayList< String > list2 = new ArrayList< String >();
```

Fig. 20.13 | Collections methods addAll, frequency and disjoint. (Part 1 of 2.)

```
16
17        list2.add( "black" ); // add "black" to the end of list2
18        list2.add( "red" ); // add "red" to the end of list2
19        list2.add( "green" ); // add "green" to the end of list2
20
21        System.out.print( "Before addAll, list2 contains: " );
22
23        // display elements in list2
24        for ( String s : list2 )
25           System.out.printf( "%s ", s );
26
27        Collections.addAll( list2, colors ); // add colors Strings to list2
28
29        System.out.print( "\nAfter addAll, list2 contains: " );
30
31        // display elements in list2
32        for ( String s : list2 )
33           System.out.printf( "%s ", s );
34
35        // get frequency of "red"
36        int frequency = Collections.frequency( list2, "red" );
37        System.out.printf(
38           "\nFrequency of red in list2: %d\n", frequency );
39
40        // check whether list1 and list2 have elements in common
41        boolean disjoint = Collections.disjoint( list1, list2 );
42
43        System.out.printf( "list1 and list2 %s elements in common\n",
44           ( disjoint ? "do not have" : "have" ) );
45     } // end main
46  } // end class Algorithms2
```

```
Before addAll, list2 contains: black red green
After addAll, list2 contains: black red green red white yellow blue
Frequency of red in list2: 2
list1 and list2 have elements in common
```

Fig. 20.13 | Collections methods addAll, frequency and disjoint. (Part 2 of 2.)

Line 14 initializes list1 with elements in array colors, and lines 17–19 add Strings "black", "red" and "green" to list2. Line 27 invokes method addAll to add elements in array colors to list2. Line 36 gets the frequency of String "red" in list2 using method frequency. Line 41 invokes method disjoint to test whether Collections list1 and list2 have elements in common, which they do in this example.

20.8 Stack Class of Package java.util

We introduced the concept of a stack in Section 5.6 when we discussed the method-call stack. In Chapter 22, Custom Generic Data Structures, we'll learn how to build data structures, including linked lists, stacks, queues and trees. In a world of software reuse, rather than building data structures as we need them, we can often take advantage of existing data structures. In this section, we investigate class **Stack** in the Java utilities package (java.util).

Class Stack extends class Vector to implement a stack data structure. Because class Stack extends class Vector, the entire public interface of class Vector is available to clients of class Stack. Figure 20.14 demonstrates several Stack methods. For the details of class Stack, visit java.sun.com/javase/6/docs/api/java/util/Stack.html.

Error-Prevention Tip 20.1

Because Stack extends Vector, all public Vector methods can be called on Stack objects, even if the methods do not represent conventional stack operations. For example, Vector method add can be used to insert an element anywhere in a stack—an operation that could "corrupt" the stack. When manipulating a Stack, only methods push and pop should be used to add elements to and remove elements from the Stack, respectively.

```java
1   // Fig. 20.14: StackTest.java
2   // Stack class of package java.util.
3   import java.util.Stack;
4   import java.util.EmptyStackException;
5
6   public class StackTest
7   {
8      public static void main( String[] args )
9      {
10        Stack< Number > stack = new Stack< Number >(); // create a Stack
11
12        // use push method
13        stack.push( 12L ); // push long value 12L
14        System.out.println( "Pushed 12L" );
15        printStack( stack );
16        stack.push( 34567 ); // push int value 34567
17        System.out.println( "Pushed 34567" );
18        printStack( stack );
19        stack.push( 1.0F ); // push float value 1.0F
20        System.out.println( "Pushed 1.0F" );
21        printStack( stack );
22        stack.push( 1234.5678 ); // push double value 1234.5678
23        System.out.println( "Pushed 1234.5678 " );
24        printStack( stack );
25
26        // remove items from stack
27        try
28        {
29           Number removedObject = null;
30
31           // pop elements from stack
32           while ( true )
33           {
34              removedObject = stack.pop(); // use pop method
35              System.out.printf( "Popped %s\n", removedObject );
36              printStack( stack );
37           } // end while
38        } // end try
39        catch ( EmptyStackException emptyStackException )
40        {
```

Fig. 20.14 | Stack class of package java.util. (Part 1 of 2.)

```
41              emptyStackException.printStackTrace();
42         } // end catch
43      } // end main
44
45      // display Stack contents
46      private static void printStack( Stack< Number > stack )
47      {
48         if ( stack.isEmpty() )
49            System.out.println( "stack is empty\n" ); // the stack is empty
50         else // stack is not empty
51            System.out.printf( "stack contains: %s (top)\n", stack );
52      } // end method printStack
53   } // end class StackTest
```

```
Pushed 12L
stack contains: [12] (top)
Pushed 34567
stack contains: [12, 34567] (top)
Pushed 1.0F
stack contains: [12, 34567, 1.0] (top)
Pushed 1234.5678
stack contains: [12, 34567, 1.0, 1234.5678] (top)
Popped 1234.5678
stack contains: [12, 34567, 1.0] (top)
Popped 1.0
stack contains: [12, 34567] (top)
Popped 34567
stack contains: [12] (top)
Popped 12
stack is empty

java.util.EmptyStackException
        at java.util.Stack.peek(Unknown Source)
        at java.util.Stack.pop(Unknown Source)
        at StackTest.main(StackTest.java:34)
```

Fig. 20.14 | Stack class of package java.util. (Part 2 of 2.)

Line 10 creates an empty Stack of Numbers. Class Number (in package java.lang) is the superclass of the type-wrapper classes for the primitive numeric types (e.g., Integer, Double). By creating a Stack of Numbers, objects of any class that extends Number can be pushed onto the Stack. Lines 13, 16, 19 and 22 each call Stack method **push** to add a Number object to the top of the stack. Note the literals 12L (line 13) and 1.0F (line 19). Any integer literal that has the **suffix L** is a long value. An integer literal without a suffix is an int value. Similarly, any floating-point literal that has the **suffix F** is a float value. A floating-point literal without a suffix is a double value. You can learn more about numeric literals in the *Java Language Specification* at java.sun.com/docs/books/jls/third_edition/html/expressions.html#15.8.1.

An infinite loop (lines 32–37) calls **Stack method pop** to remove the top element of the stack. The method returns a Number reference to the removed element. If there are no elements in the Stack, method pop throws an **EmptyStackException**, which terminates the loop. Class Stack also declares **method peek**. This method returns the top element of the stack without popping the element off the stack.

Method `printStack` (lines 46–52) displays the stack's contents. The current top of the stack (the last value pushed onto the stack) is the first value printed. Line 48 calls **Stack method isEmpty** (inherited by `Stack` from class `Vector`) to determine whether the stack is empty. If it's empty, the method returns `true`; otherwise, `false`.

20.9 Class `PriorityQueue` and Interface `Queue`

Recall that a queue is a collection that represents a waiting line—typically, insertions are made at the back of a queue and deletions are made from the front. In Section 22.6, we'll discuss and implement a queue data structure. In this section, we investigate Java's **Queue** interface and **PriorityQueue** class from package `java.util`. Interface `Queue` extends interface `Collection` and provides additional operations for inserting, removing and inspecting elements in a queue. `PriorityQueue`, which implements the `Queue` interface, orders elements by their natural ordering as specified by `Comparable` elements' `compareTo` method or by a `Comparator` object that is supplied to the constructor.

Class `PriorityQueue` provides functionality that enables insertions in sorted order into the underlying data structure and deletions from the front of the underlying data structure. When adding elements to a `PriorityQueue`, the elements are inserted in priority order such that the highest-priority element (i.e., the largest value) will be the first element removed from the `PriorityQueue`.

The common `PriorityQueue` operations are **offer** to insert an element at the appropriate location based on priority order, **poll** to remove the highest-priority element of the priority queue (i.e., the head of the queue), **peek** to get a reference to the highest-priority element of the priority queue (without removing that element), **clear** to remove all elements in the priority queue and **size** to get the number of elements in the priority queue. Figure 20.15 demonstrates the `PriorityQueue` class.

```
1   // Fig. 20.15: PriorityQueueTest.java
2   // PriorityQueue test program.
3   import java.util.PriorityQueue;
4
5   public class PriorityQueueTest
6   {
7      public static void main( String[] args )
8      {
9         // queue of capacity 11
10        PriorityQueue< Double > queue = new PriorityQueue< Double >();
11
12        // insert elements to queue
13        queue.offer( 3.2 );
14        queue.offer( 9.8 );
15        queue.offer( 5.4 );
16
17        System.out.print( "Polling from queue: " );
18
19        // display elements in queue
20        while ( queue.size() > 0 )
21        {
22           System.out.printf( "%.1f ", queue.peek() ); // view top element
```

Fig. 20.15 | `PriorityQueue` test program. (Part 1 of 2.)

```
23              queue.poll(); // remove top element
24          } // end while
25      } // end main
26  } // end class PriorityQueueTest
```

```
Polling from queue: 3.2 5.4 9.8
```

Fig. 20.15 | PriorityQueue test program. (Part 2 of 2.)

Line 10 creates a PriorityQueue that stores Doubles with an initial capacity of 11 elements and orders the elements according to the object's natural ordering (the defaults for a PriorityQueue). Note that PriorityQueue is a generic class and that line 10 instantiates a PriorityQueue with a type argument Double. Class PriorityQueue provides five additional constructors. One of these takes an int and a Comparator object to create a PriorityQueue with the initial capacity specified by the int and the ordering by the Comparator. Lines 13–15 use method offer to add elements to the priority queue. Method offer throws a NullPointerException if the program attempts to add a null object to the queue. The loop in lines 20–24 uses method size to determine whether the priority queue is empty (line 20). While there are more elements, line 22 uses PriorityQueue method peek to retrieve the highest-priority element in the queue for output (without actually removing the element from the queue). Line 23 removes the highest-priority element in the queue with method poll, which returns the removed element.

20.10 Sets

A **Set** is an unordered Collection of unique elements (i.e., no duplicate elements). The collections framework contains several Set implementations, including **HashSet** and **TreeSet**. HashSet stores its elements in a hash table, and TreeSet stores its elements in a tree. Hash tables are presented in Section 20.11. Trees are discussed in Section 22.7.

Figure 20.16 uses a HashSet to remove duplicate strings from a List. Recall that both List and Collection are generic types, so line 16 creates a List that contains String objects, and line 20 passes a Collection of Strings to method printNonDuplicates.

```java
1   // Fig. 20.16: SetTest.java
2   // HashSet used to remove duplicate values from array of strings.
3   import java.util.List;
4   import java.util.Arrays;
5   import java.util.HashSet;
6   import java.util.Set;
7   import java.util.Collection;
8
9   public class SetTest
10  {
11      public static void main( String[] args )
12      {
13          // create and display a List< String >
14          String[] colors = { "red", "white", "blue", "green", "gray",
15              "orange", "tan", "white", "cyan", "peach", "gray", "orange" };
```

Fig. 20.16 | HashSet used to remove duplicate values from an array of strings. (Part 1 of 2.)

```
16          List< String > list = Arrays.asList( colors );
17          System.out.printf( "List: %s\n", list );
18
19          // eliminate duplicates then print the unique values
20          printNonDuplicates( list );
21      } // end main
22
23      // create a Set from a Collection to eliminate duplicates
24      private static void printNonDuplicates( Collection< String > values )
25      {
26          // create a HashSet
27          Set< String > set = new HashSet< String >( values );
28
29          System.out.print( "\nNonduplicates are: " );
30
31          for ( String value : set )
32              System.out.printf( "%s ", value );
33
34          System.out.println();
35      } // end method printNonDuplicates
36  } // end class SetTest
```

```
List: [red, white, blue, green, gray, orange, tan, white, cyan, peach, gray,
orange]

Nonduplicates are: orange green white peach gray cyan red blue tan
```

Fig. 20.16 | HashSet used to remove duplicate values from an array of strings. (Part 2 of 2.)

Method printNonDuplicates (lines 24–35) takes a Collection argument. Line 27 constructs a HashSet<String> from the Collection<String> argument. By definition, Sets do not contain duplicates, so when the HashSet is constructed, it removes any duplicates in the Collection. Lines 31–32 output elements in the Set.

Sorted Sets
The collections framework also includes the **SortedSet interface** (which extends Set) for sets that maintain their elements in sorted order—either the elements' natural order (e.g., numbers are in ascending order) or an order specified by a Comparator. Class TreeSet implements SortedSet. The program in Fig. 20.17 places strings into a TreeSet. The strings are sorted as they're added to the TreeSet. This example also demonstrates range-view methods, which enable a program to view a portion of a collection.

```
1   // Fig. 20.17: SortedSetTest.java
2   // Using SortedSets and TreeSets.
3   import java.util.Arrays;
4   import java.util.SortedSet;
5   import java.util.TreeSet;
6
7   public class SortedSetTest
8   {
```

Fig. 20.17 | Using SortedSets and TreeSets. (Part 1 of 2.)

```
 9      public static void main( String[] args )
10      {
11         // create TreeSet from array colors
12         String[] colors = { "yellow", "green", "black", "tan", "grey",
13            "white", "orange", "red", "green" };
14         SortedSet< String > tree =
15            new TreeSet< String >( Arrays.asList( colors ) );
16
17         System.out.print( "sorted set: " );
18         printSet( tree ); // output contents of tree
19
20         // get headSet based on "orange"
21         System.out.print( "headSet (\"orange\"):   " );
22         printSet( tree.headSet( "orange" ) );
23
24         // get tailSet based upon "orange"
25         System.out.print( "tailSet (\"orange\"):   " );
26         printSet( tree.tailSet( "orange" ) );
27
28         // get first and last elements
29         System.out.printf( "first: %s\n", tree.first() );
30         System.out.printf( "last : %s\n", tree.last() );
31      } // end main
32
33      // output SortedSet using enhanced for statement
34      private static void printSet( SortedSet< String > set )
35      {
36         for ( String s : set )
37            System.out.printf( "%s ", s );
38
39         System.out.println();
40      } // end method printSet
41   } // end class SortedSetTest
```

```
sorted set: black green grey orange red tan white yellow
headSet ("orange"):   black green grey
tailSet ("orange"):   orange red tan white yellow
first: black
last : yellow
```

Fig. 20.17 | Using SortedSets and TreeSets. (Part 2 of 2.)

Lines 14–15 of create a TreeSet<String> that contains the elements of array colors, then assigns the new TreeSet<String> to SortedSet<String> variable tree. Line 18 outputs the initial set of strings using method printSet (lines 34–40), which we discuss momentarily. Line 22 calls **TreeSet method headSet** to get a subset of the TreeSet in which every element is less than "orange". The view returned from headSet is then output with printSet. If any changes are made to the subset, they'll also be made to the original TreeSet, because the subset returned by headSet is a view of the TreeSet.

Line 26 calls **TreeSet method tailSet** to get a subset in which each element is greater than or equal to "orange", then outputs the result. Any changes made through the tailSet view are made to the original TreeSet. Lines 29–30 call **SortedSet methods first and last** to get the smallest and largest elements of the set, respectively.

Method `printSet` (lines 34–40) accepts a `SortedSet` as an argument and prints it. Lines 36–37 print each element of the `SortedSet` using the enhanced `for` statement.

20.11 Maps

`Maps` associate keys to values. The keys in a `Map` must be unique, but the associated values need not be. If a `Map` contains both unique keys and unique values, it is said to implement a one-to-one mapping. If only the keys are unique, the `Map` is said to implement a many-to-one mapping—many keys can map to one value.

Maps differ from `Set`s in that Maps contain keys and values, whereas `Set`s contain only values. Three of the several classes that implement interface `Map` are `Hashtable`, `HashMap` and `TreeMap`. Hashtables and HashMaps store elements in hash tables, and TreeMaps store elements in trees. This section discusses hash tables and provides an example that uses a HashMap to store key/value pairs. Interface `SortedMap` extends `Map` and maintains its keys in sorted order—either the elements' natural order or an order specified by a `Comparator`. Class TreeMap implements `SortedMap`.

Map *Implementation with Hash Tables*

Object-oriented programming languages facilitate creating new types. When a program creates objects of new or existing types, it may need to store and retrieve them efficiently. Storing and retrieving information with arrays is efficient if some aspect of your data directly matches a numerical key value and if the keys are unique and tightly packed. If you have 100 employees with nine-digit social security numbers and you want to store and retrieve employee data by using the social security number as a key, the task will require an array with over 700 million elements because nine-digit Social Security numbers must begin with 001–733 as per the Social Security Administration's website

```
www.socialsecurity.gov/employer/stateweb.htm
```

This is impractical for virtually all applications that use social security numbers as keys. A program having an array that large could achieve high performance for both storing and retrieving employee records by simply using the social security number as the array index.

Numerous applications have this problem—namely, that either the keys are of the wrong type (e.g., not positive integers that correspond to array subscripts) or they're of the right type, but sparsely spread over a huge range. What is needed is a high-speed scheme for converting keys such as social security numbers, inventory part numbers and the like into unique array indices. Then, when an application needs to store something, the scheme could convert the application's key rapidly into an index, and the record could be stored at that slot in the array. Retrieval is accomplished the same way: Once the application has a key for which it wants to retrieve a data record, the application simply applies the conversion to the key—this produces the array index where the data is stored and retrieved.

The scheme we describe here is the basis of a technique called hashing. Why the name? When we convert a key into an array index, we literally scramble the bits, forming a kind of "mishmashed," or hashed, number. The number actually has no real significance beyond its usefulness in storing and retrieving a particular data record.

A glitch in the scheme is called a collision—this occurs when two different keys "hash into" the same cell (or element) in the array. We cannot store two values in the same space, so we need to find an alternative home for all values beyond the first that hash to a particular array index. There are many schemes for doing this. One is to "hash again" (i.e., to apply another hashing transformation to the key to provide a next candidate cell in the array). The hashing process is designed to distribute the values throughout the table, so the assumption is that an available cell will be found with just a few hashes.

Another scheme uses one hash to locate the first candidate cell. If that cell is occupied, successive cells are searched in order until an available cell is found. Retrieval works the same way: The key is hashed once to determine the initial location and check whether it contains the desired data. If it does, the search is finished. If it does not, successive cells are searched linearly until the desired data is found.

The most popular solution to hash-table collisions is to have each cell of the table be a hash "bucket," typically a linked list of all the key/value pairs that hash to that cell. This is the solution that Java's `Hashtable` and `HashMap` classes (from package `java.util`) implement. Both `Hashtable` and `HashMap` implement the `Map` interface. The primary differences between them are that `HashMap` is unsynchronized (multiple threads should not modify a `HashMap` concurrently) and allows `null` keys and `null` values.

A hash table's load factor affects the performance of hashing schemes. The load factor is the ratio of the number of occupied cells in the hash table to the total number of cells in the hash table. The closer this ratio gets to 1.0, the greater the chance of collisions.

Performance Tip 20.2

The load factor in a hash table is a classic example of a memory-space/execution-time trade-off: By increasing the load factor, we get better memory utilization, but the program runs slower, due to increased hashing collisions. By decreasing the load factor, we get better program speed, because of reduced hashing collisions, but we get poorer memory utilization, because a larger portion of the hash table remains empty.

Hash tables are complex to program. Computer science students study hashing schemes in courses called "Data Structures" and "Algorithms." Classes `Hashtable` and `HashMap` enable you to use hashing without having to implement hash-table mechanisms. This concept is profoundly important in our study of object-oriented programming. As discussed in earlier chapters, classes encapsulate and hide complexity (i.e., implementation details) and offer user-friendly interfaces. Properly crafting classes to exhibit such behavior is one of the most valued skills in the field of object-oriented programming. Figure 20.18 uses a `HashMap` to count the number of occurrences of each word in a string.

```java
1   // Fig. 20.18: WordTypeCount.java
2   // Program counts the number of occurrences of each word in a String.
3   import java.util.Map;
4   import java.util.HashMap;
5   import java.util.Set;
6   import java.util.TreeSet;
7   import java.util.Scanner;
8
9   public class WordTypeCount
10  {
11     public static void main( String[] args )
12     {
13        // create HashMap to store String keys and Integer values
14        Map< String, Integer > myMap = new HashMap< String, Integer >();
```

Fig. 20.18 | Program counts the number of occurrences of each word in a `String`. (Part 1 of 3.)

```
15
16          createMap( myMap ); // create map based on user input
17          displayMap( myMap ); // display map content
18      } // end main
19
20      // create map from user input
21      private static void createMap( Map< String, Integer > map )
22      {
23          Scanner scanner = new Scanner( System.in ); // create scanner
24          System.out.println( "Enter a string:" ); // prompt for user input
25          String input = scanner.nextLine();
26
27          // tokenize the input
28          String[] tokens = input.split( " " );
29
30          // processing input text
31          for ( String token : tokens )
32          {
33              String word = token.toLowerCase(); // get lowercase word
34
35              // if the map contains the word
36              if ( map.containsKey( word ) ) // is word in map
37              {
38                  int count = map.get( word ); // get current count
39                  map.put( word, count + 1 ); // increment count
40              } // end if
41              else
42                  map.put( word, 1 ); // add new word with a count of 1 to map
43          } // end for
44      } // end method createMap
45
46      // display map content
47      private static void displayMap( Map< String, Integer > map )
48      {
49          Set< String > keys = map.keySet(); // get keys
50
51          // sort keys
52          TreeSet< String > sortedKeys = new TreeSet< String >( keys );
53
54          System.out.println( "\nMap contains:\nKey\t\tValue" );
55
56          // generate output for each key in map
57          for ( String key : sortedKeys )
58              System.out.printf( "%-10s%10s\n", key, map.get( key ) );
59
60          System.out.printf(
61              "\nsize: %d\nisEmpty: %b\n", map.size(), map.isEmpty() );
62      } // end method displayMap
63  } // end class WordTypeCount
```

```
Enter a string:
this is a sample sentence with several words this is another sample
sentence with several different words
```

Fig. 20.18 | Program counts the number of occurrences of each word in a String. (Part 2 of 3.)

```
Map contains:
Key            Value
a              1
another        1
different      1
is             2
sample         2
sentence       2
several        2
this           2
with           2
words          2

size: 10
isEmpty: false
```

Fig. 20.18 | Program counts the number of occurrences of each word in a String. (Part 3 of 3.)

Line 14 creates an empty HashMap with a default initial capacity (16 elements) and a default load factor (0.75)—these defaults are built into the implementation of HashMap. When the number of occupied slots in the HashMap becomes greater than the capacity times the load factor, the capacity is doubled automatically. Note that HashMap is a generic class that takes two type arguments—the type of key (i.e., String) and the type of value (i.e., Integer). Recall that the type arguments passed to a generic class must be reference types, hence the second type argument is Integer, not int.

Line 16 calls method createMap (lines 21–44), which uses a map to store the number of occurrences of each word in the sentence. Line 25 obtains the user input, and line 28 tokenizes it. The loop in lines 31–43 converts the next token to lowercase letters (line 33), then calls **Map method containsKey** (line 36) to determine whether the word is in the map (and thus has occurred previously in the string). If the Map does not contain a mapping for the word, line 42 uses **Map method put** to create a new entry in the map, with the word as the key and an Integer object containing 1 as the value. Autoboxing occurs when the program passes integer 1 to method put, because the map stores the number of occurrences of the word as an Integer. If the word does exist in the map, line 38 uses **Map method get** to obtain the key's associated value (the count) in the map. Line 39 increments that value and uses put to replace the key's associated value in the map. Method put returns the key's prior associated value, or null if the key was not in the map.

Method displayMap (lines 47–62) displays all the entries in the map. It uses **HashMap method keySet** (line 49) to get a set of the keys. The keys have type String in the map, so method keySet returns a generic type Set with type parameter specified to be String. Line 52 creates a TreeSet of the keys, in which the keys are sorted. The loop in lines 57–58 accesses each key and its value in the map. Line 58 displays each key and its value using format specifier %-10s to left justify each key and format specifier %10s to right justify each value. Note that the keys are displayed in ascending order. Line 61 calls **Map method size** to get the number of key/value pairs in the Map. Line 61 also calls **Map method isEmpty**, which returns a boolean indicating whether the Map is empty.

20.12 Properties Class

A **Properties** object is a persistent Hashtable that normally stores key/value pairs of strings—assuming that you use methods **setProperty** and **getProperty** to manipulate the table rather than inherited `Hashtable` methods put and get. By "persistent," we mean that the `Properties` object can be written to an output stream (possibly a file) and read back in through an input stream. A common use of `Properties` objects in prior versions of Java was to maintain application-configuration data or user preferences for applications. [*Note:* The Preferences API (package `java.util.prefs`) is meant to replace this particular use of class `Properties` but is beyond the scope of this book. To learn more, visit java.sun.com/javase/6/docs/technotes/guides/preferences/index.html.]

Class `Properties` extends class `Hashtable`. Figure 20.19 demonstrates several methods of class `Properties`.

```java
1   // Fig. 20.19: PropertiesTest.java
2   // Demonstrates class Properties of the java.util package.
3   import java.io.FileOutputStream;
4   import java.io.FileInputStream;
5   import java.io.IOException;
6   import java.util.Properties;
7   import java.util.Set;
8
9   public class PropertiesTest
10  {
11     public static void main( String[] args )
12     {
13        Properties table = new Properties(); // create Properties table
14
15        // set properties
16        table.setProperty( "color", "blue" );
17        table.setProperty( "width", "200" );
18
19        System.out.println( "After setting properties" );
20        listProperties( table ); // display property values
21
22        // replace property value
23        table.setProperty( "color", "red" );
24
25        System.out.println( "After replacing properties" );
26        listProperties( table ); // display property values
27
28        saveProperties( table ); // save properties
29
30        table.clear(); // empty table
31
32        System.out.println( "After clearing properties" );
33        listProperties( table ); // display property values
34
35        loadProperties( table ); // load properties
36
37        // get value of property color
38        Object value = table.getProperty( "color" );
39
40        // check if value is in table
41        if ( value != null )
42           System.out.printf( "Property color's value is %s\n", value );
```

Fig. 20.19 | Properties class of package java.util. (Part 1 of 3.)

```
43          else
44              System.out.println( "Property color is not in table" );
45      } // end main
46
47      // save properties to a file
48      private static void saveProperties( Properties props )
49      {
50          // save contents of table
51          try
52          {
53              FileOutputStream output = new FileOutputStream( "props.dat" );
54              props.store( output, "Sample Properties" ); // save properties
55              output.close();
56              System.out.println( "After saving properties" );
57              listProperties( props ); // display property values
58          } // end try
59          catch ( IOException ioException )
60          {
61              ioException.printStackTrace();
62          } // end catch
63      } // end method saveProperties
64
65      // load properties from a file
66      private static void loadProperties( Properties props )
67      {
68          // load contents of table
69          try
70          {
71              FileInputStream input = new FileInputStream( "props.dat" );
72              props.load( input ); // load properties
73              input.close();
74              System.out.println( "After loading properties" );
75              listProperties( props ); // display property values
76          } // end try
77          catch ( IOException ioException )
78          {
79              ioException.printStackTrace();
80          } // end catch
81      } // end method loadProperties
82
83      // output property values
84      private static void listProperties( Properties props )
85      {
86          Set< Object > keys = props.keySet(); // get property names
87
88          // output name/value pairs
89          for ( Object key : keys )
90              System.out.printf(
91                  "%s\t%s\n", key, props.getProperty( ( String ) key ) );
92
93          System.out.println();
94      } // end method listProperties
95  } // end class PropertiesTest
```

Fig. 20.19 | Properties class of package java.util. (Part 2 of 3.)

```
After setting properties
color    blue
width    200

After replacing properties
color    red
width    200

After saving properties
color    red
width    200

After clearing properties

After loading properties
color    red
width    200

Property color's value is red
```

Fig. 20.19 | `Properties` class of package `java.util`. (Part 3 of 3.)

Line 13 uses the no-argument constructor to create an empty `Properties` table with no default properties. Class `Properties` also provides an overloaded constructor that receives a reference to a `Properties` object containing default property values. Lines 16 and 17 each call `Properties` method `setProperty` to store a value for the specified key. If the key does not exist in the `table`, `setProperty` returns `null`; otherwise, it returns the previous value for that key.

Line 38 calls `Properties` method `getProperty` to locate the value associated with the specified key. If the key is not found in this `Properties` object, `getProperty` returns `null`. An overloaded version of this method receives a second argument that specifies the default value to return if `getProperty` cannot locate the key.

Line 54 calls **`Properties` method `store`** to save the `Properties` object's contents to the `OutputStream` specified as the first argument (in this case, a `FileOutputStream`). The second argument, a `String`, is a description written into the file. **`Properties` method `list`**, which takes a `PrintStream` argument, is useful for displaying the list of properties.

Line 72 calls **`Properties` method `load`** to restore the contents of the `Properties` object from the `InputStream` specified as the first argument (in this case, a `FileInput-Stream`). Line 86 calls `Properties` method `keySet` to obtain a `Set` of the property names. Line 91 obtains the value of a property by passing a key to method `getProperty`.

20.13 Synchronized Collections

In Chapter 26, we discuss multithreading. Except for `Vector` and `Hashtable`, the collections in the collections framework are unsynchronized by default, so they can operate efficiently when multithreading is not required. Because they're unsynchronized, however, concurrent access to a `Collection` by multiple threads could cause indeterminate results or fatal errors. To prevent potential threading problems, **synchronization wrappers** are used for collections that might be accessed by multiple threads. A **wrapper** object receives method calls, adds thread synchronization (to prevent concurrent access to the collection) and delegates the calls to the wrapped collection object. The `Collections` API provides a set of `static` methods for wrapping collections as synchronized versions. Method headers for the synchronization wrappers are listed in Fig. 20.20. Details about these methods are available at java.sun.com/javase/6/docs/api/java/util/Collections.html. All these methods take a generic type and return a synchronized view of the generic type. For example, the following code creates a synchronized List (list2) that stores String objects:

```
List< String > list1 = new ArrayList< String >();
List< String > list2 = Collections.synchronizedList( list1 );
```

public static method headers

```
< T > Collection< T > synchronizedCollection( Collection< T > c )
< T > List< T > synchronizedList( List< T > aList )
< T > Set< T > synchronizedSet( Set< T > s )
< T > SortedSet< T > synchronizedSortedSet( SortedSet< T > s )
< K, V > Map< K, V > synchronizedMap( Map< K, V > m )
< K, V > SortedMap< K, V > synchronizedSortedMap( SortedMap< K, V > m )
```

Fig. 20.20 | Synchronization wrapper methods.

20.14 Unmodifiable Collections

The Collections class provides a set of static methods that create **unmodifiable wrappers** for collections. Unmodifiable wrappers throw UnsupportedOperationExceptions if attempts are made to modify the collection. Headers for these methods are listed in Fig. 20.21. Details about these methods are available at java.sun.com/javase/6/docs/api/java/util/Collections.html. All these methods take a generic type and return an unmodifiable view of the generic type. For example, the following code creates an unmodifiable List (list2) that stores String objects:

```
List< String > list1 = new ArrayList< String >();
List< String > list2 = Collections.unmodifiableList( list1 );
```

public static method headers

```
< T > Collection< T > unmodifiableCollection( Collection< T > c )
< T > List< T > unmodifiableList( List< T > aList )
< T > Set< T > unmodifiableSet( Set< T > s )
< T > SortedSet< T > unmodifiableSortedSet( SortedSet< T > s )
< K, V > Map< K, V > unmodifiableMap( Map< K, V > m )
< K, V > SortedMap< K, V > unmodifiableSortedMap( SortedMap< K, V > m )
```

Fig. 20.21 | Unmodifiable wrapper methods.

Software Engineering Observation 20.5

You can use an unmodifiable wrapper to create a collection that offers read-only access to others, while allowing read/write access to yourself. You do this simply by giving others a reference to the unmodifiable wrapper while retaining for yourself a reference to the original collection.

20.15 Abstract Implementations

The collections framework provides various abstract implementations of Collection interfaces from which you can quickly "flesh out" complete customized implementations. These abstract implementations include a thin Collection implementation called an **AbstractCollection**, a List implementation that allows random access to its elements called an **AbstractList**, a Map implementation called an **AbstractMap**, a List implementation that allows sequential access to its elements called an **AbstractSequentialList**, a Set implementation called an **AbstractSet** and a Queue implementation called **AbstractQueue**. You can learn more about these classes at java.sun.com/javase/6/docs/api/java/util/package-summary.html.

   To write a custom implementation, you can extend the abstract implementation that best meets your needs, and implement each of the class's abstract methods. Then, if your collection is to be modifiable, override any concrete methods that prevent modification.

20.16 Wrap-Up

This chapter introduced the Java collections framework. You learned the collection hierarchy and how to use the collections framework interfaces to program with collections polymorphically. You used classes ArrayList and LinkedList, which both implement the List interface. We presented Java's built-in interfaces and classes for manipulating stacks and queues. You used several predefined methods for manipulating collections. Next, you learned how to use the Set interface and class HashSet to manipulate an unordered collection of unique values. We continued our presentation of sets with the SortedSet interface and class TreeSet for manipulating a sorted collection of unique values. You then learned about Java's interfaces and classes for manipulating key/value pairs—Map, SortedMap, Hashtable, HashMap and TreeMap. We then discussed the specialized Properties class for manipulating key/value pairs of Strings that can be stored to a file and retrieved from a file. Finally, we discussed the Collections class's static methods for obtaining unmodifiable and synchronized views of collections. Chapter 21 demonstrates how to use Java's generics capabilities to implement your own generic methods and classes.

Summary

Section 20.1 Introduction
- The Java collections framework gives you access to prebuilt data structures as well as to methods for manipulating them.

Section 20.2 Collections Overview
- A collection is an object that can hold references to other objects.
- The classes and interfaces of the collections framework are in package java.util.

Section 20.3 Type-Wrapper Classes for Primitive Types
- Type-wrapper classes (e.g., Integer, Double, Boolean) enable programmers to manipulate primitive-type values as objects. Objects of these classes can be used in collections.

Section 20.4 Autoboxing and Auto-Unboxing

- Boxing converts a primitive value to an object of the corresponding type-wrapper class. Unboxing converts a type-wrapper object to the corresponding primitive value.

- Java performs boxing conversions and unboxing conversions automatically.

Section 20.5 Interface Collection and Class Collections

- Interface Collection is the root interface in the collection hierarchy. Interfaces Set and List extend Collection. Interface Collection contains operations for adding, clearing, comparing and retaining objects in a collection, and method iterator to obtain a collection's Iterator.

- Class Collections provides static methods for manipulating collections.

Section 20.6 Lists

- A List is an ordered Collection that can contain duplicate elements.

- Interface List is implemented by classes ArrayList, LinkedList and Vector. ArrayList is a resizable-array implementation of a List. LinkedList is a linked list implementation of a List.

- Iterator method hasNext determines whether a Collection contains another element. Method next returns a reference to the next object in the Collection and advances the Iterator.

- Method subList returns a view into a List. Changes made to this view are also made to the List.

- Method clear removes elements from a List.

- Method toArray returns the contents of a collection as an array.

Section 20.7 Collections Methods

- Algorithms sort, binarySearch, reverse, shuffle, fill, copy, addAll, frequency and disjoint operate on Lists. Algorithms min and max operate on Collections.

- Algorithm addAll appends all the elements in an array to a collection, frequency calculates how many elements in the collection are equal to the specified element, and disjoint determines whether two collections have elements in common.

- Algorithms min and max find the smallest and largest items in a collection.

- The Comparator interface provides a means of sorting a Collection's elements in an order other than their natural order.

- Collections method reverseOrder returns a Comparator object that can be used with sort to sort a collection's elements in reverse order.

- Algorithm shuffle randomly orders the elements of a List.

- Algorithm binarySearch locates an Object in a sorted List.

Section 20.8 Stack Class of Package java.util

- Class Stack extends Vector. Stack method push adds its argument to the top of the stack. Method pop removes the top element of the stack. Method peek returns a reference to the top element without removing it. Stack method isEmpty determines whether the stack is empty.

Section 20.9 Class PriorityQueue and Interface Queue

- Interface Queue extends interface Collection and provides additional operations for inserting, removing and inspecting elements in a queue.

- PriorityQueue implements interface Queue and orders elements by their natural ordering or by a Comparator object that is supplied to the constructor.

- PriorityQueue method offer inserts an element at the appropriate location based on priority order. Method poll removes the highest-priority element of the priority queue. Method peek gets a reference to the highest-priority element of the priority queue. Method `clear` removes all elements in the priority queue. Method `size` gets the number of elements in the priority queue.

Section 20.10 Sets

- A `Set` is an unordered `Collection` that contains no duplicate elements. `HashSet` stores its elements in a hash table. `TreeSet` stores its elements in a tree.
- Interface `SortedSet` extends `Set` and represents a set that maintains its elements in sorted order. Class `TreeSet` implements `SortedSet`.
- `TreeSet` method `headSet` gets a `TreeSet` view containing elements that are less than a specified element. Method `tailSet` gets a `TreeSet` view containing elements that are greater than or equal to a specified element. Any changes made to these views are made to the original `TreeSet`.

Section 20.11 Maps

- Maps store key/value pairs and cannot contain duplicate keys. `HashMaps` and `Hashtables` store elements in a hash table, and `TreeMaps` store elements in a tree.
- `HashMap` takes two type arguments—the type of key and the type of value.
- `HashMap` method `put` adds a key and a value into a `HashMap`. Method `get` locates the value associated with the specified key. Method `isEmpty` determines whether the map is empty.
- `HashMap` method `keySet` returns a set of the keys. `Map` method `size` returns the number of key/value pairs in the `Map`.
- Interface `SortedMap` extends `Map` and represents a map that maintains its keys in sorted order. Class `TreeMap` implements `SortedMap`.

Section 20.12 `Properties` Class

- A `Properties` object is a persistent `Hashtable` object. Class `Properties` extends `Hashtable`.
- The `Properties` no-argument constructor creates an empty `Properties` table. An overloaded constructor receives a `Properties` object containing default property values.
- `Properties` method `setProperty` specifies the value associated with its key argument. Method `getProperty` locates the value of the key specified as an argument. Method `store` saves the contents of a `Properties` object to specified `OutputStream`. Method `load` restores the contents of a `Properties` object from the specified `InputStream`.

Section 20.13 Synchronized Collections

- Collections from the collections framework are unsynchronized. Synchronization wrappers are provided for collections that can be accessed by multiple threads simultaneously.

Section 20.14 Unmodifiable Collections

- Class `Collections` provides a set of `public static` methods for converting collections to unmodifiable versions. Unmodifiable wrappers throw `UnsupportedOperationExceptions` if attempts are made to modify the collection.

Section 20.15 Abstract Implementations

- The collections framework provides various abstract implementations of collection interfaces from which you can quickly flesh out complete customized implementations.

Terminology

AbstractCollection class 857

AbstractList class 857

AbstractMap class 857

AbstractQueue class 857

AbstractSequentialList class 857

AbstractSet class 857

Self-Review Exercises

20.1 Fill in the blanks in each of the following statements:
a) A(n) _____ is used to iterate through a collection and can remove elements from the collection during the iteration.
b) An element in a List can be accessed by using the element's _____.
c) Assuming that myArray contains references to Double objects, _____ occurs when the statement "myArray[0] = 1.25;" executes.
d) Java classes _____ and _____ provide the capabilities of arraylike data structures that can resize themselves dynamically.
e) If you do not specify a capacity increment, the system will _____ the size of the Vec-tor each time additional capacity is needed.
f) You can use a(n) _____ to create a collection that offers only read-only access to oth-ers while allowing read/write access to yourself.
g) Assuming that myArray contains references to Double objects, _____ occurs when the statement "double number = myArray[0];" executes.
h) Algorithm _____ of Collections determines whether two collections have elements in common.

20.2 Determine whether each statement is *true* or *false*. If *false*, explain why.
a) Values of primitive types may be stored directly in a collection.
b) A Set can contain duplicate values.
c) A Map can contain duplicate keys.
d) A LinkedList can contain duplicate values.
e) Collections is an interface.
f) Iterators can remove elements.
g) With hashing, as the load factor increases, the chance of collisions decreases.
h) A PriorityQueue permits null elements.

Answers to Self-Review Exercises

20.1 a) Iterator. b) index. c) autoboxing. d) ArrayList, Vector. e) double. f) unmodifiable wrapper. g) auto-unboxing. h) disjoint.

20.2 a) False. Autoboxing occurs when adding a primitive type to a collection, which means the primitive type is converted to its corresponding type-wrapper class.
b) False. A Set cannot contain duplicate values.
c) False. A Map cannot contain duplicate keys.
d) True.
e) False. Collections is a class; Collection is an interface.
f) True.
g) False. As the load factor increases, fewer slots are available relative to the total number of slots, so the chance of a collision increases.
h) False. Attempting to insert a null element causes a NullPointerException.

Execises

20.3   Define each of the following terms:
   a) Collection
   b) Collections
   c) Comparator
   d) List
   e) load factor
   f) collision
   g) space/time trade-off in hashing
   h) HashMap

20.4   Explain briefly the operation of each of the following methods of class Vector:
   a) add
   b) set
   c) remove
   d) removeAllElements
   e) removeElementAt
   f) firstElement
   g) lastElement
   h) contains
   i) indexOf
   j) size
   k) capacity

20.5   Explain why inserting additional elements into a Vector object whose current size is less than its capacity is a relatively fast operation and why inserting additional elements into a Vector object whose current size is at capacity is a relatively slow operation.

20.6   By extending class Vector, Java's designers were able to create class Stack quickly. What are the negative aspects of this use of inheritance, particularly for class Stack?

20.7   Briefly answer the following questions:
   a) What is the primary difference between a Set and a Map?
   b) What happens when you add a primitive type (e.g., double) value to a collection?
   c) Can you print all the elements in a collection without using an Iterator? If yes, how?

20.8   Explain briefly the operation of each of the following Iterator-related methods:
   a) iterator
   b) hasNext
   c) next

20.9   Explain briefly the operation of each of the following methods of class HashMap:
   a) put
   b) get
   c) isEmpty
   d) containsKey
   e) keySet

20.10   Determine whether each of the following statements is *true* or *false*. If *false*, explain why.
   a) Elements in a Collection must be sorted in ascending order before a binarySearch may be performed.
   b) Method first gets the first element in a TreeSet.
   c) A List created with Arrays method asList is resizable.

20.11   Explain the operation of each of the following methods of the Properties class:
   a) load

  b) `store`
  c) `getProperty`
  d) `list`

20.12 Rewrite lines 16–25 in Fig. 20.3 to be more concise by using the `asList` method and the `LinkedList` constructor that takes a `Collection` argument.

20.13 *(Duplicate Elimination)* Write a program that reads in a series of first names and eliminates duplicates by storing them in a `Set`. Allow the user to search for a first name.

20.14 *(Counting Letters)* Modify the program of Fig. 20.18 to count the number of occurrences of each letter rather than of each word. For example, the string `"HELLO THERE"` contains two Hs, three Es, two Ls, one O, one T and one R. Display the results.

20.15 *(Color Chooser)* Use a `HashMap` to create a reusable class for choosing one of the 13 predefined colors in class `Color`. The names of the colors should be used as keys, and the predefined `Color` objects should be used as values. Place this class in a package that can be imported into any Java program. Use your new class in an application that allows the user to select a color and draw a shape in that color.

20.16 *(Counting Duplicate Words)* Write a program that determines and prints the number of duplicate words in a sentence. Treat uppercase and lowercase letters the same. Ignore punctuation.

20.17 *(Inserting Elements in a `LinkedList` in Sorted Order)* Write a program that inserts 25 random integers from 0 to 100 in order into a `LinkedList` object. The program should sort the elements, then calculate the sum of the elements and the floating-point average of the elements.

20.18 *(Copying and Reversing `LinkedLists`)* Write a program that creates a `LinkedList` object of 10 characters, then creates a second `LinkedList` object containing a copy of the first list, but in reverse order.

20.19 *(Prime Numbers and Prime Factors)* Write a program that takes a whole number input from a user and determines whether it's prime. If the number is not prime, display its unique prime factors. Remember that a prime number's factors are only 1 and the prime number itself. Every number that is not prime has a unique prime factorization. For example, consider the number 54. The prime factors of 54 are 2, 3, 3 and 3. When the values are multiplied together, the result is 54. For the number 54, the prime factors output should be 2 and 3. Use `Set`s as part of your solution.

20.20 *(Sorting Words with a `TreeSet`)* Write a program that uses a `String` method `split` to tokenize a line of text input by the user and places each token in a `TreeSet`. Print the elements of the `TreeSet`. [*Note:* This should cause the elements to be printed in ascending sorted order.]

20.21 *(Changing a `PriorityQueue`'s Sort Order)* The output of Fig. 20.15 (`PriorityQueueTest`) shows that `PriorityQueue` orders `Double` elements in ascending order. Rewrite Fig. 20.15 so that it orders `Double` elements in descending order (i.e., 9.8 should be the highest-priority element rather than 3.2).

21

Generic Classes and Methods

Every man of genius sees the world at a different angle from his fellows.
—Havelock Ellis

…our special individuality, as distinguished from our generic humanity.
—Oliver Wendell Holmes, Sr.

Born under one law, to another bound.
—Lord Brooke

Objectives

In this chapter you'll learn:

- To create generic methods to perform identical tasks on arguments of different types.

- To create a generic **Stack** class that can store objects of any class or interface type.

- To understand how to overload generic methods with nongeneric methods or with other generic methods.

- To understand raw types and how they help achieve backward compatibility.

- To use wildcards when precise type information about a parameter is not required in the method body.

- The relationship between generics and inheritance.

21.1 Introduction

You've used existing generic methods and classes in Chapters 6 and 20. In this chapter, you'll learn how to write your own. You'll also learn the relationships between generics and other Java features, such as overloading and inheritance.

It would be nice if we could write a single `sort` method to sort the elements in an `Integer` array, a `String` array or an array of any type that supports ordering (i.e., its elements can be compared). It would also be nice if we could write a single `Stack` class that could be used as a `Stack` of integers, a `Stack` of floating-point numbers, a `Stack` of `Strings` or a `Stack` of any other type. It would be even nicer if we could detect type mismatches at compile time—known as **compile-time type safety**. For example, if a `Stack` stores only integers, attempting to push a `String` onto that `Stack` should issue a *compile-time* error.

This chapter discusses **generics**, which provide the means to create the general models mentioned above. **Generic methods** and **generic classes** (and interfaces) enable you to specify, with a single method declaration, a set of related methods, or with a single class declaration, a set of related types, respectively. Generics also provide compile-time type safety that allows you to catch invalid types at compile time.

We might write a generic method for sorting an array of objects, then invoke the generic method with `Integer` arrays, `Double` arrays, `String` arrays and so on, to sort the array elements. The compiler could perform type checking to ensure that the array passed to the sorting method contains the same type elements. We might write a single generic `Stack` class that manipulates a stack of objects, then instantiate `Stack` objects for a stack of `Integers`, a stack of `Doubles`, a stack of `Strings` and so on. The compiler could perform type checking to ensure that the `Stack` stores elements of the same type.

Software Engineering Observation 21.1

Generic methods and classes are among Java's most powerful capabilities for software reuse with compile-time type safety.

21.2 Motivation for Generic Methods

Overloaded methods are often used to perform similar operations on different types of data. To motivate generic methods, let's begin with an example (Fig. 21.1) containing overloaded `printArray` methods (lines 21–28, lines 31–38 and lines 41–48) that print the `String` representations of the elements of an `Integer` array, a `Double` array and a `Charac-`

ter array, respectively. We could have used arrays of primitive types int, double and char. We are using arrays of the type-wrapper classes to set up our generic method example, because only reference types can be used with generic methods and classes.

```java
1   // Fig. 21.1: OverloadedMethods.java
2   // Printing array elements using overloaded methods.
3   public class OverloadedMethods
4   {
5      public static void main( String[] args )
6      {
7         // create arrays of Integer, Double and Character
8         Integer[] integerArray = { 1, 2, 3, 4, 5, 6 };
9         Double[] doubleArray = { 1.1, 2.2, 3.3, 4.4, 5.5, 6.6, 7.7 };
10        Character[] characterArray = { 'H', 'E', 'L', 'L', 'O' };
11
12        System.out.println( "Array integerArray contains:" );
13        printArray( integerArray ); // pass an Integer array
14        System.out.println( "\nArray doubleArray contains:" );
15        printArray( doubleArray ); // pass a Double array
16        System.out.println( "\nArray characterArray contains:" );
17        printArray( characterArray ); // pass a Character array
18     } // end main
19
20     // method printArray to print Integer array
21     public static void printArray( Integer[] inputArray )
22     {
23        // display array elements
24        for ( Integer element : inputArray )
25           System.out.printf( "%s ", element );
26
27        System.out.println();
28     } // end method printArray
29
30     // method printArray to print Double array
31     public static void printArray( Double[] inputArray )
32     {
33        // display array elements
34        for ( Double element : inputArray )
35           System.out.printf( "%s ", element );
36
37        System.out.println();
38     } // end method printArray
39
40     // method printArray to print Character array
41     public static void printArray( Character[] inputArray )
42     {
43        // display array elements
44        for ( Character element : inputArray )
45           System.out.printf( "%s ", element );
46
47        System.out.println();
48     } // end method printArray
49  } // end class OverloadedMethods
```

Fig. 21.1 | Printing array elements using overloaded methods. (Part 1 of 2.)

```
Array integerArray contains:
1 2 3 4 5 6

Array doubleArray contains:
1.1 2.2 3.3 4.4 5.5 6.6 7.7

Array characterArray contains:
H E L L O
```

Fig. 21.1 | Printing array elements using overloaded methods. (Part 2 of 2.)

The program begins by declaring and initializing three arrays—six-element Integer array integerArray (line 8), seven-element Double array doubleArray (line 9) and five-element Character array characterArray (line 10). Then, lines 12–17 display the contents of each array.

When the compiler encounters a method call, it attempts to locate a method declaration with the same name and parameters that match the argument types in the call. In this example, each printArray call matches one of the printArray method declarations. For example, line 13 calls printArray with integerArray as its argument. The compiler determines the argument's type (i.e., Integer[]) and attempts to locate a printArray method that specifies an Integer[] parameter (lines 21–28), then sets up a call to that method. Similarly, when the compiler encounters the call at line 15, it determines the argument's type (i.e., Double[]), then attempts to locate a printArray method that specifies a Double[] parameter (lines 31–38), then sets up a call to that method. Finally, when the compiler encounters the call at line 17, it determines the argument's type (i.e., Character[]), then attempts to locate a printArray method that specifies a Character[] parameter (lines 41–48), then sets up a call to that method.

Study each printArray method. Note that the type array element type appears in each method's header (lines 21, 31 and 41) and for-statement header (lines 24, 34 and 44). If we were to replace the element types in each method with a generic name—T by convention—then all three methods would look like the one in Fig. 21.2. It appears that if we can replace the array element type in each of the three methods with a single generic type, then we should be able to declare one printArray method that can display the String representations of the elements of any array that contains objects. The method in Fig. 21.2 is similar to the generic printArray method declaration we discuss in Section 21.3.

```
1   public static void printArray( T[] inputArray )
2   {
3      // display array elements
4      for ( T element : inputArray )
5         System.out.printf( "%s ", element );
6
7      System.out.println();
8   } // end method printArray
```

Fig. 21.2 | printArray method in which actual type names are replaced by convention with the generic name T.

21.3 Generic Methods: Implementation and Compile-Time Translation

If the operations performed by several overloaded methods are identical for each argument type, the overloaded methods can be more compactly and conveniently coded using a generic method. You can write a single generic method declaration that can be called with arguments of different types. Based on the types of the arguments passed to the generic method, the compiler handles each method call appropriately.

Figure 21.3 reimplements the application of Fig. 21.1 using a generic printArray method (lines 22–29). Note that the printArray method calls in lines 14, 16 and 18 are identical to those of Fig. 21.1 (lines 14, 16 and 18) and that the outputs of the two applications are identical. This dramatically demonstrates the expressive power of generics.

```java
 1   // Fig. 21.3: GenericMethodTest.java
 2   // Printing array elements using generic method printArray.
 3
 4   public class GenericMethodTest
 5   {
 6      public static void main( String[] args )
 7      {
 8         // create arrays of Integer, Double and Character
 9         Integer[] intArray = { 1, 2, 3, 4, 5 };
10         Double[] doubleArray = { 1.1, 2.2, 3.3, 4.4, 5.5, 6.6, 7.7 };
11         Character[] charArray = { 'H', 'E', 'L', 'L', 'O' };
12
13         System.out.println( "Array integerArray contains:" );
14         printArray( integerArray ); // pass an Integer array
15         System.out.println( "\nArray doubleArray contains:" );
16         printArray( doubleArray ); // pass a Double array
17         System.out.println( "\nArray characterArray contains:" );
18         printArray( characterArray ); // pass a Character array
19      } // end main
20
21      // generic method printArray
22      public static < T > void printArray( T[] inputArray )
23      {
24         // display array elements
25         for ( T element : inputArray )
26            System.out.printf( "%s ", element );
27
28         System.out.println();
29      } // end method printArray
30   } // end class GenericMethodTest
```

```
Array integerArray contains:
1 2 3 4 5 6

Array doubleArray contains:
1.1 2.2 3.3 4.4 5.5 6.6 7.7

Array characterArray contains:
H E L L O
```

Fig. 21.3 | Printing array elements using generic method printArray.

Line 22 begins method `printArray`'s declaration. All generic method declarations have a **type-parameter section** delimited by **angle brackets** (< and >) that precedes the method's return type (< T > in this example). Each type-parameter section contains one or more **type parameters** (also called **formal type parameters**), separated by commas. A type parameter, also known as a **type variable**, is an identifier that specifies a generic type name. The type parameters can be used to declare the return type, parameter types and local variable types in a generic method declaration, and they act as placeholders for the types of the arguments passed to the generic method, which are known as **actual type arguments**. A generic method's body is declared like that of any other method. Note that type parameters can represent only reference types—not primitive types (like `int`, `double` and `char`). Note, too, that the type-parameter names throughout the method declaration must match those declared in the type-parameter section. For example, line 25 declares `element` as type T, which matches the type parameter (T) declared in line 22. Also, a type parameter can be declared only once in the type-parameter section but can appear more than once in the method's parameter list. For example, the type-parameter name T appears twice in the following method's parameter list:

```
public static < T > void printTwoArrays( T[] array1, T[] array2 )
```

Type-parameter names need not be unique among different generic methods.

Common Programming Error 21.1

When declaring a generic method, failing to place a type-parameter section before the return type of a method is a syntax error—the compiler will not understand the type-parameter names when they're encountered in the method.

Method `printArray`'s type-parameter section declares type parameter T as the placeholder for the array element type that `printArray` will output. Note that T appears in the parameter list as the array element type (line 22). The `for`-statement header (line 25) also uses T as the element type. These are the same two locations where the overloaded `printArray` methods of Fig. 21.1 specified `Integer`, `Double` or `Character` as the array element type. The remainder of `printArray` is identical to the versions presented in Fig. 21.1.

Good Programming Practice 21.1

It's recommended that type parameters be specified as individual capital letters. Typically, a type parameter that represents an array element's type (or other collection) is named T.

As in Fig. 21.1, the program begins by declaring and initializing six-element `Integer` array `integerArray` (line 9), seven-element `Double` array `doubleArray` (line 10) and five-element `Character` array `characterArray` (line 11). Then the program outputs each array by calling `printArray` (lines 14, 16 and 18)—once with argument `integerArray`, once with argument `doubleArray` and once with argument `characterArray`.

When the compiler encounters line 14, it first determines argument `integerArray`'s type (i.e., `Integer[]`) and attempts to locate a method named `printArray` that specifies a single `Integer[]` parameter. There is no such method in this example. Next, the compiler determines whether there is a generic method named `printArray` that specifies a single array parameter and uses a type parameter to represent the array element type. The compiler determines that `printArray` (lines 22–29) is a match and sets up a call to the method. The same process is repeated for the calls to method `printArray` at lines 16 and 18.

Common Programming Error 21.2

If the compiler cannot match a method call to a nongeneric or a generic method declaration, a compilation error occurs.

Common Programming Error 21.3

If the compiler does not find a method declaration that matches a method call exactly, but does find two or more generic methods that can satisfy the method call, a compilation error occurs.

In addition to setting up the method calls, the compiler also determines whether the operations in the method body can be applied to elements of the type stored in the array argument. The only operation performed on the array elements in this example is to output their `String` representation. Line 26 performs an implicit `toString` call on every element. To work with generics, every element of the array must be an object of a class or interface type. Since all objects have a `toString` method, the compiler is satisfied that line 26 performs a valid operation for any object in `printArray`'s array argument. The `toString` methods of classes `Integer`, `Double` and `Character` return the `String` representation of the underlying `int`, `double` or `char` value, respectively.

Erasure at Compilation Time

When the compiler translates generic method `printArray` into Java bytecodes, it removes the type-parameter section and replaces the type parameters with actual types. This process is known as **erasure**. By default all generic types are replaced with type `Object`. So the compiled version of method `printArray` appears as shown in Fig. 21.4—there is only one copy of this code, which is used for all `printArray` calls in the example. This is quite different from other, similar mechanisms, such as C++'s templates, in which a separate copy of the source code is generated and compiled for every type passed as an argument to the method. As you'll see in Section 21.4, the translation and compilation of generics is a bit more involved than what we've discussed in this section.

By declaring `printArray` as a generic method in Fig. 21.3, we eliminated the need for the overloaded methods of Fig. 21.1, saving 19 lines of code and creating a reusable method that can output the `String` representations of the elements in any array that contains objects. However, this particular example could have simply declared the `printArray` method as shown in Fig. 21.4, using an `Object` array as the parameter. This would have yielded the same results, because any `Object` can be output as a `String`. In a generic method, the benefits become apparent when the method also uses a type parameter as the method's return type, as we demonstrate in the next section.

```
1   public static void printArray( Object[] inputArray )
2   {
3      // display array elements
4      for ( Object element : inputArray )
5         System.out.printf( "%s ", element );
6
7      System.out.println();
8   } // end method printArray
```

Fig. 21.4 | Generic method `printArray` after erasure is performed by the compiler.

21.4 Additional Compile-Time Translation Issues: Methods That Use a Type Parameter as the Return Type

Let's consider a generic method example in which type parameters are used in the return type and in the parameter list (Fig. 21.5). The application uses a generic method `maximum` to determine and return the largest of its three arguments of the same type. Unfortunately, the relational operator > cannot be used with reference types. However, it's possible to compare two objects of the same class if that class implements the generic interface **Comparable<T>** (package `java.lang`). All the type-wrapper classes for primitive types implement this interface. Like generic classes, generic interfaces enable you to specify, with a single interface declaration, a set of related types. Comparable<T> objects have a **compareTo method**. For example, if we have two `Integer` objects, `integer1` and `integer2`, they can be compared with the expression:

```
integer1.compareTo( integer2 )
```

It's your responsibility when you declare a class that implements Comparable<T> to declare method compareTo such that it compares the contents of two objects of that class and returns the comparison results. The method must return 0 if the objects are equal, a negative integer if `object1` is less than `object2` or a positive integer if `object1` is greater than `object2`. For example, class `Integer`'s compareTo method compares the int values stored in two `Integer` objects. A benefit of implementing interface Comparable<T> is that Comparable<T> objects can be used with the sorting and searching methods of class Collections (package `java.util`). We discussed those methods in Chapter 20, Generic Collections. In this example, we'll use method compareTo in method maximum to help determine the largest value.

```java
1   // Fig. 21.5: MaximumTest.java
2   // Generic method maximum returns the largest of three objects.
3
4   public class MaximumTest
5   {
6      public static void main( String[] args )
7      {
8         System.out.printf( "Maximum of %d, %d and %d is %d\n\n", 3, 4, 5,
9            maximum( 3, 4, 5 ) );
10        System.out.printf( "Maximum of %.1f, %.1f and %.1f is %.1f\n\n",
11           6.6, 8.8, 7.7, maximum( 6.6, 8.8, 7.7 ) );
12        System.out.printf( "Maximum of %s, %s and %s is %s\n", "pear",
13           "apple", "orange", maximum( "pear", "apple", "orange" ) );
14     } // end main
15
16     // determines the largest of three Comparable objects
17     public static < T extends Comparable< T > > T maximum( T x, T y, T z )
18     {
19        T max = x; // assume x is initially the largest
20
21        if ( y.compareTo( max ) > 0 )
22           max = y; // y is the largest so far
23
```

Fig. 21.5 | Generic method `maximum` with an upper bound on its type parameter. (Part 1 of 2.)

```
24          if ( z.compareTo( max ) > 0 )
25             max = z; // z is the largest
26
27          return max; // returns the largest object
28       } // end method maximum
29    } // end class MaximumTest
```

```
Maximum of 3, 4 and 5 is 5

Maximum of 6.6, 8.8 and 7.7 is 8.8

Maximum of pear, apple and orange is pear
```

Fig. 21.5 | Generic method `maximum` with an upper bound on its type parameter. (Part 2 of 2.)

Generic Method `maximum`

Generic method `maximum` (lines 17–28) uses type parameter T as the return type of the method (line 17), as the type of method parameters x, y and z (line 17), and as the type of local variable max (line 19). The type-parameter section specifies that T extends Comparable<T>—only objects of classes that implement interface Comparable<T> can be used with this method. In this case, Comparable is known as the **upper bound** of the type parameter. By default, Object is the upper bound. Note that type-parameter declarations that bound the parameter always use keyword extends regardless of whether the type parameter extends a class or implements an interface. This type parameter is more restrictive than the one specified for printArray in Fig. 21.3, which was able to output arrays containing any type of object. The restriction of using Comparable<T> objects is important, because not all objects can be compared. However, Comparable<T> objects are guaranteed to have a compareTo method.

Method `maximum` uses the same algorithm that we used in Section 5.4 to determine the largest of its three arguments. The method assumes that its first argument (x) is the largest and assigns it to local variable max (line 19). Next, the if statement at lines 21–22 determines whether y is greater than max. The condition invokes y's compareTo method with the expression y.compareTo(max), which returns a negative integer , 0 or a positive integer, to determine y's relationship to max. If the return value of the compareTo is greater than 0, then y is greater and is assigned to variable max. Similarly, the if statement at lines 24–25 determines whether z is greater than max. If so, line 25 assigns z to max. Then line 27 returns max to the caller.

Calling Method `maximum`

In main (lines 6–14), line 9 calls maximum with the integers 3, 4 and 5. When the compiler encounters this call, it first looks for a maximum method that takes three arguments of type int. There is no such method, so the compiler looks for a generic method that can be used and finds generic method maximum. However, recall that the arguments to a generic method must be of a reference type. So the compiler autoboxes the three int values as Integer objects and specifies that the three Integer objects will be passed to maximum. Note that class Integer (package java.lang) implements the Comparable<Integer> interface such that method compareTo compares the int values in two Integer objects. Therefore, Integers are valid arguments to method maximum. When the Integer representing the maximum is returned, we attempt to output it with the %d format specifier, which outputs an int primitive-type value. So maximum's return value is output as an int value.

A similar process occurs for the three double arguments passed to maximum in line 11. Each double is autoboxed as a Double object and passed to maximum. Again, this is allowed because class Double (package java.lang) implements the Comparable<Double> interface. The Double returned by maximum is output with the format specifier %.1f, which outputs a double primitive-type value. So maximum's return value is auto-unboxed and output as a double. The call to maximum in line 13 receives three Strings, which are also Comparable<String> objects. Note that we intentionally placed the largest value in a different position in each method call (lines 9, 11 and 13) to show that the generic method always finds the maximum value, regardless of its position in the argument list.

Upper Bound of a Type Parameter

When the compiler translates generic method maximum into Java bytecodes, it uses erasure (introduced in Section 21.3) to replace the type parameters with actual types. In Fig. 21.3, all generic types were replaced with type Object. Actually, all type parameters are replaced with the so-called upper bound of the type parameter, which is specified in the type-parameter section. To indicate the upper bound, follow the type parameter's name with the keyword extends and the class or interface name that represents the upper bound, or a comma-separated list of the types that represent the upper bound. The list may contain zero or one class and zero or more interfaces. For example, in method maximum's type-parameter section (Fig. 21.5), we specified the upper bound of the type parameter T as type Comparable<T> as follows:

    T **extends** Comparable< T >

Thus, only Comparable<T> objects can be passed as arguments to maximum—anything that is not a Comparable<T> will result in compilation errors. Unless specified otherwise, Object is the default upper bound. Figure 21.6 simulates the erasure of method maximum's types by showing the method's source code after the type-parameter section is removed and type parameter T is replaced with the upper bound, Comparable, throughout the method declaration. Note that the erasure of Comparable<T> is simply Comparable.

```
 I   public static Comparable maximum(Comparable x, Comparable y, Comparable z)
 2   {
 3      Comparable max = x; // assume x is initially the largest
 4
 5      if ( y.compareTo( max ) > 0 )
 6         max = y; // y is the largest so far
 7
 8      if ( z.compareTo( max ) > 0 )
 9         max = z; // z is the largest
10
11      return max; // returns the largest object
12   } // end method maximum
```

Fig. 21.6 | Generic method maximum after erasure is performed by the compiler.

After erasure, the compiled version of method maximum specifies that it returns type Comparable. However, the calling method does not expect to receive a Comparable. It expects to receive an object of the same type that was passed to maximum as an argument—Integer, Double or String in this example. When the compiler replaces the type-parameter information with the upper-bound type in the method declaration, it also inserts explicit cast operations in front of each method call to ensure that the returned value is of the type expected by the caller. Thus, the call to maximum in line 9 (Fig. 21.5) is preceded by an Integer cast, as in

```
(Integer) maximum( 3, 4, 5 )
```

the call to maximum in line 11 is preceded by a Double cast, as in

```
(Double) maximum( 6.6, 8.8, 7.7 )
```

and the call to maximum in line 13 is preceded by a String cast, as in

```
(String) maximum( "pear", "apple", "orange" )
```

In each case, the type of the cast for the return value is inferred from the types of the method arguments in the particular method call, because, according to the method declaration, the return type and the argument types match.

Possible *ClassCastExceptions*
In this example, you cannot use a method that accepts Objects, because class Object provides only an equality comparison. Also, without generics, you'd be responsible for implementing the cast operation. Using generics ensures that the inserted cast will never throw a ClassCastException, assuming that generics are used throughout your code (i.e., you do not mix old code with new generics code).

21.5 Overloading Generic Methods
A generic method may be overloaded. A class can provide two or more generic methods that specify the same method name but different method parameters. For example, generic method printArray of Fig. 21.3 could be overloaded with another printArray generic method with the additional parameters lowSubscript and highSubscript to specify the portion of the array to output (see Exercise 21.5).

A generic method can also be overloaded by nongeneric methods. When the compiler encounters a method call, it searches for the method declaration that most precisely matches the method name and the argument types specified in the call. For example, generic method printArray of Fig. 21.3 could be overloaded with a version that is specific to Strings, which outputs the Strings in neat, tabular format (see Exercise 21.6).

When the compiler encounters a method call, it performs a matching process to determine which method to invoke. The compiler tries to find and use a precise match in which the method name and argument types of the method call match those of a specific method declaration. If there is no such method, the compiler attempts to find a method with compatible types or a matching generic method.

21.6 Generic Classes
The concept of a data structure, such as a stack, can be understood independently of the element type it manipulates. Generic classes provide a means for describing the concept of a stack (or any other class) in a type-independent manner. We can then instantiate type-

specific objects of the generic class. This capability provides a wonderful opportunity for software reusability.

As you saw in Chapter 20, once you have a generic class, you can use a simple, concise notation to indicate the actual type(s) that should be used in place of the class's type parameter(s). At compilation time, the Java compiler ensures the type safety of your code and uses the erasure techniques described in Sections 21.3—21.4 to enable your client code to interact with the generic class.

One generic Stack class, for example, could be the basis for creating many logical Stack classes (e.g., "Stack of Double," "Stack of Integer," "Stack of Character," "Stack of Employee"). These classes are known as **parameterized classes** or **parameterized types** because they accept one or more type parameters. Recall that type parameters represent only reference types, which means the Stack generic class cannot be instantiated with primitive types. However, we can instantiate a Stack that stores objects of Java's type-wrapper classes and allow Java to use autoboxing to convert the primitive values into objects. Recall that autoboxing occurs when a value of a primitive type (e.g., int) is pushed onto a Stack that contains wrapper-class objects (e.g., Integer). Auto-unboxing occurs when an object of the wrapper class is popped off the Stack and assigned to a primitive-type variable.

Implementing a Generic *Stack* Class
Figure 21.7 presents a generic Stack class declaration. A generic class declaration looks like a nongeneric one, but the class name is followed by a type-parameter section (line 5). In this case, type parameter T represents the element type the Stack will manipulate. As with generic methods, the type-parameter section of a generic class can have one or more type parameters separated by commas. (You'll create a generic class with two type parameters in Exercise 21.8.) Type parameter T is used throughout the Stack class declaration to represent the element type. [*Note:* This example implements a Stack as an ArrayList.]

```java
 1   // Fig. 21.7: Stack.java
 2   // Stack generic class declaration.
 3   import java.util.ArrayList;
 4
 5   public class Stack< T >
 6   {
 7      private ArrayList< T > elements; // ArrayList stores stack elements
 8
 9      // no-argument constructor creates a stack of the default size
10      public Stack()
11      {
12         this( 10 ); // default stack size
13      } // end no-argument Stack constructor
14
15      // constructor creates a stack of the specified number of elements
16      public Stack( int capacity )
17      {
18         int initCapacity = capacity > 0 ? capacity : 10; // validate
19         elements = new ArrayList< T >( initCapacity ); // create ArrayList
20      } // end one-argument Stack constructor
21
```

Fig. 21.7 | Stack generic class declaration. (Part 1 of 2.)

```
22      // push element onto stack
23      public void push( T pushValue )
24      {
25         elements.add( pushValue ); // place pushValue on Stack
26      } // end method push
27
28      // return the top element if not empty; else throw EmptyStackException
29      public T pop()
30      {
31         if ( elements.isEmpty() ) // if stack is empty
32            throw new EmptyStackException( "Stack is empty, cannot pop" );
33
34         // remove and return top element of Stack
35         return elements.remove( elements.size() - 1 );
36      } // end method pop
37   } // end class Stack< T >
```

Fig. 21.7 | Stack generic class declaration. (Part 2 of 2.)

Class Stack declares variable elements as an ArrayList<T> (line 7). This ArrayList will store the Stack's elements. As you know, an ArrayList can grow dynamically, so objects of our Stack class can also grow dynamically. The Stack class's no-argument constructor (lines 10–13) invokes the one-argument constructor (lines 16–20) to create a Stack in which the underlying ArrayList has a capacity of 10 elements. The one-argument constructor can also be called directly to create a Stack with a specified initial capacity. Line 18 validates the constructor's argument. Line 19 creates the ArrayList of the specified capacity (or 10 if the capacity was invalid).

Method push (lines 23–26) uses ArrayList method add to append the pushed item to the end of the ArrayList elements. The last element in the ArrayList represents the top of the stack.

Method pop (lines 29–36) first determines whether an attempt is being made to pop an element from an empty Stack. If so, line 32 throws an EmptyStackException (declared in Fig. 21.8). Otherwise, line 35 returns the top element of the Stack by removing the last element in the underlying ArrayList.

Class EmptyStackException (Fig. 21.8) provides a no-argument constructor and a one-argument constructor. The no-argument constructor sets the default error message, and the one-argument constructor sets a custom error message.

```
1    // Fig. 21.8: EmptyStackException.java
2    // EmptyStackException class declaration.
3    public class EmptyStackException extends RuntimeException
4    {
5       // no-argument constructor
6       public EmptyStackException()
7       {
8          this( "Stack is empty" );
9       } // end no-argument EmptyStackException constructor
10
```

Fig. 21.8 | EmptyStackException class declaration. (Part 1 of 2.)

```
11      // one-argument constructor
12      public EmptyStackException( String message )
13      {
14          super( message );
15      } // end one-argument EmptyStackException constructor
16  } // end class EmptyStackException
```

Fig. 21.8 | EmptyStackException class declaration. (Part 2 of 2.)

As with generic methods, when a generic class is compiled, the compiler performs erasure on the class's type parameters and replaces them with their upper bounds. For class Stack (Fig. 21.7), no upper bound is specified, so the default upper bound, Object, is used. The scope of a generic class's type parameter is the entire class. However, type parameters cannot be used in a class's static variable declarations.

Testing the Generic *Stack Class of Fig. 21.7*

Now, let's consider the application (Fig. 21.9) that uses the Stack generic class (Fig. 21.7). Lines 12–13 create and initialize variables of type Stack<Double> (pronounced "Stack of Double") and Stack<Integer> (pronounced "Stack of Integer"). The types Double and Integer are known as the Stack's **type arguments**. They're used by the compiler to replace the type parameters so that the compiler can perform type checking and insert cast operations as necessary. We'll discuss the cast operations in more detail shortly. Lines 12–13 instantiate doubleStack with a capacity of 5 and integerStack with a capacity of 10 (the default). Lines 16–17 and 20–21 call methods testPushDouble (lines 25–36), testPopDouble (lines 39–59), testPushInteger (lines 62–73) and testPopInteger (lines 76–96), respectively, to demonstrate the two Stacks in this example.

```
1   // Fig. 21.9: StackTest.java
2   // Stack generic class test program.
3
4   public class StackTest
5   {
6       public static void main( String[] args )
7       {
8           double[] doubleElements = { 1.1, 2.2, 3.3, 4.4, 5.5 };
9           int[] integerElements = { 1, 2, 3, 4, 5, 6, 7, 8, 9, 10 };
10
11          // Create a Stack< Double > and a Stack< Integer >
12          Stack< Double > doubleStack = new Stack< Double >( 5 );
13          Stack< Integer > integerStack = new Stack< Integer >();
14
15          // push elements of doubleElements onto doubleStack
16          testPushDouble( doubleStack, doubleElements );
17          testPopDouble( doubleStack ); // pop from doubleStack
18
19          // push elements of integerElements onto integerStack
20          testPushInteger( integerStack, integerElements );
21          testPopInteger( integerStack ); // pop from integerStack
22      } // end main
```

Fig. 21.9 | Stack generic class test program. (Part 1 of 3.)

```
23
24      // test push method with double stack
25      private static void testPushDouble(
26         Stack< Double > stack, double[] values )
27      {
28         System.out.println( "\nPushing elements onto doubleStack" );
29
30         // push elements to Stack
31         for ( double value : values )
32         {
33            System.out.printf( "%.1f ", value );
34            stack.push( value ); // push onto doubleStack
35         } // end for
36      } // end method testPushDouble
37
38      // test pop method with double stack
39      private static void testPopDouble( Stack< Double > stack )
40      {
41         // pop elements from stack
42         try
43         {
44            System.out.println( "\nPopping elements from doubleStack" );
45            double popValue; // store element removed from stack
46
47            // remove all elements from Stack
48            while ( true )
49            {
50               popValue = stack.pop(); // pop from doubleStack
51               System.out.printf( "%.1f ", popValue );
52            } // end while
53         } // end try
54         catch( EmptyStackException emptyStackException )
55         {
56            System.err.println();
57            emptyStackException.printStackTrace();
58         } // end catch EmptyStackException
59      } // end method testPopDouble
60
61      // test push method with integer stack
62      private static void testPushInteger(
63         Stack< Integer > stack, int[] values )
64      {
65         System.out.println( "\nPushing elements onto integerStack" );
66
67         // push elements to Stack
68         for ( int value : values )
69         {
70            System.out.printf( "%d ", value );
71            stack.push( value ); // push onto integerStack
72         } // end for
73      } // end method testPushInteger
74
```

Fig. 21.9 | Stack generic class test program. (Part 2 of 3.)

```
75      // test pop method with integer stack
76      private static void testPopInteger( Stack< Integer > stack )
77      {
78         // pop elements from stack
79         try
80         {
81            System.out.println( "\nPopping elements from integerStack" );
82            int popValue; // store element removed from stack
83
84            // remove all elements from Stack
85            while ( true )
86            {
87               popValue = stack.pop(); // pop from intStack
88               System.out.printf( "%d ", popValue );
89            } // end while
90         } // end try
91         catch( EmptyStackException emptyStackException )
92         {
93            System.err.println();
94            emptyStackException.printStackTrace();
95         } // end catch EmptyStackException
96      } // end method testPopInteger
97   } // end class StackTest
```

```
Pushing elements onto doubleStack
1.1 2.2 3.3 4.4 5.5
Popping elements from doubleStack
5.5 4.4 3.3 2.2 1.1
EmptyStackException: Stack is empty, cannot pop
        at Stack.pop(Stack.java:32)
        at StackTest.testPopDouble(StackTest.java:50)
        at StackTest.main(StackTest.java:17)

Pushing elements onto integerStack
1 2 3 4 5 6 7 8 9 10
Popping elements from integerStack
10 9 8 7 6 5 4 3 2 1
EmptyStackException: Stack is empty, cannot pop
        at Stack.pop(Stack.java:32)
        at StackTest.testPopInteger(StackTest.java:87)
        at StackTest.main(StackTest.java:21)
```

Fig. 21.9 | Stack generic class test program. (Part 3 of 3.)

Methods *testPushDouble* and *testPopDouble*

Method testPushDouble (lines 25–36) invokes method push (line 34) to place the double values 1.1, 2.2, 3.3, 4.4 and 5.5 from array doubleElements onto doubleStack. Note that autoboxing occurs in line 34 when the program tries to push a primitive double value onto the doubleStack, which stores only references to Double objects.

Method testPopDouble (lines 39–59) invokes Stack method pop (line 50) in an infinite while loop (lines 48–52) to remove all the values from the stack. Note in the output that the values indeed pop off in last-in, first-out order (the defining characteristic of stacks). When the loop attempts to pop a sixth value, the doubleStack is empty, so the pop throws an EmptyStackException, which causes the program to proceed to the catch block (lines 54–58) to handle the exception. The stack trace indicates the exception that occurred and shows that Stack method pop generated the exception at line 32 of the file Stack.java (Fig. 21.7). The trace also shows that method pop was called by StackTest method testPopDouble at line 50 of StackTest.java and that method testPopDouble was called from method main at line 17 of StackTest.java. This information enables you to determine the methods that were on the method-call stack at the time that the exception occurred. Because the program catches the exception, the exception is considered to have been handled and the program can continue executing.

Auto-unboxing occurs in line 50 when the program assigns the Double object popped from the stack to a double primitive variable. Recall from Section 21.4 that the compiler inserts casts to ensure that the proper types are returned from generic methods. After erasure, Stack method pop returns type Object, but the client code in testPopDouble expects to receive a double when method pop returns. So the compiler inserts a Double cast, as in

```
popValue = ( Double ) stack.pop();
```

The value assigned to popValue will be unboxed from the Double object returned by pop.

Methods testPushInteger and testPopInteger

Method testPushInteger (lines 62–73) invokes Stack method push to place values onto integerStack until it's full. Method testPopInteger (lines 76–96) invokes Stack method pop to remove values from integerStack. Once again, note that the values are popped in last-in, first-out order. During the erasure process, the compiler recognizes that the client code in method testPopInteger expects to receive an int when method pop returns. So the compiler inserts an Integer cast, as in

```
popValue = ( Integer ) stack.pop();
```

The value assigned to popValue will be unboxed from the Integer object returned by pop.

Creating Generic Methods to Test Class Stack<T>

Note that the code in methods testPushDouble and testPushInteger is almost identical for pushing values onto a Stack<Double> or a Stack<Integer>, respectively, and the code in methods testPopDouble and testPopInteger is almost identical for popping values from a Stack<Double> or a Stack<Integer>, respectively. This presents another opportunity to use generic methods. Figure 21.10 declares generic method testPush (lines 24–35) to perform the same tasks as testPushDouble and testPushInteger in Fig. 21.9—that is, push values onto a Stack<T>. Similarly, generic method testPop (lines 38–58) performs the same tasks as testPopDouble and testPopInteger in Fig. 21.9—that is, pop values off a Stack<T>. Note that the output of Fig. 21.10 precisely matches that of Fig. 21.9.

```
1  // Fig. 21.10: StackTest2.java
2  // Passing generic Stack objects to generic methods.
3  public class StackTest2
4  {
5     public static void main( String[] args )
6     {
```

Fig. 21.10 | Passing generic Stack objects to generic methods. (Part 1 of 3.)

```
7          Double[] doubleElements = { 1.1, 2.2, 3.3, 4.4, 5.5 };
8          Integer[] integerElements = { 1, 2, 3, 4, 5, 6, 7, 8, 9, 10 };
9
10         // Create a Stack< Double > and a Stack< Integer >
11         Stack< Double > doubleStack = new Stack< Double >( 5 );
12         Stack< Integer > integerStack = new Stack< Integer >();
13
14         // push elements of doubleElements onto doubleStack
15         testPush( "doubleStack", doubleStack, doubleElements );
16         testPop( "doubleStack", doubleStack ); // pop from doubleStack
17
18         // push elements of integerElements onto integerStack
19         testPush( "integerStack", integerStack, integerElements );
20         testPop( "integerStack", integerStack ); // pop from integerStack
21      } // end main
22
23      // generic method testPush pushes elements onto a Stack
24      public static < T > void testPush( String name , Stack< T > stack,
25         T[] elements )
26      {
27         System.out.printf( "\nPushing elements onto %s\n", name );
28
29         // push elements onto Stack
30         for ( T element : elements )
31         {
32            System.out.printf( "%s ", element );
33            stack.push( element ); // push element onto stack
34         } // end for
35      } // end method testPush
36
37      // generic method testPop pops elements from a Stack
38      public static < T > void testPop( String name, Stack< T > stack )
39      {
40         // pop elements from stack
41         try
42         {
43            System.out.printf( "\nPopping elements from %s\n", name );
44            T popValue; // store element removed from stack
45
46            // remove all elements from Stack
47            while ( true )
48            {
49               popValue = stack.pop();
50               System.out.printf( "%s ", popValue );
51            } // end while
52         } // end try
53         catch( EmptyStackException emptyStackException )
54         {
55            System.out.println();
56            emptyStackException.printStackTrace();
57         } // end catch EmptyStackException
58      } // end method testPop
59   } // end class StackTest2
```

Fig. 21.10 | Passing generic Stack objects to generic methods. (Part 2 of 3.)

```
Pushing elements onto doubleStack
1.1 2.2 3.3 4.4 5.5
Popping elements from doubleStack
5.5 4.4 3.3 2.2 1.1
EmptyStackException: Stack is empty, cannot pop
        at Stack.pop(Stack.java:32)
        at StackTest2.testPop(StackTest2.java:50)
        at StackTest2.main(StackTest2.java:17)

Pushing elements onto integerStack
1 2 3 4 5 6 7 8 9 10
Popping elements from integerStack
10 9 8 7 6 5 4 3 2 1
EmptyStackException: Stack is empty, cannot pop
        at Stack.pop(Stack.java:32)
        at StackTest2.testPop(StackTest2.java:50)
        at StackTest2.main(StackTest2.java:21
```

Fig. 21.10 | Passing generic Stack objects to generic methods. (Part 3 of 3.)

Lines 11–12 create the Stack<Double> and Stack<Integer> objects, respectively. Lines 15–16 and 19–20 invoke generic methods testPush and testPop to test the Stack objects. Recall that type parameters can represent only reference types. Therefore, to be able to pass arrays doubleElements and integerElements to generic method testPush, the arrays declared in lines 7–8 must be declared with the wrapper types Double and Integer. When these arrays are initialized with primitive values, the compiler autoboxes each primitive value.

Generic method testPush (lines 24–35) uses type parameter T (specified at line 24) to represent the data type stored in the Stack<T>. The generic method takes three arguments—a String that represents the name of the Stack<T> object for output purposes, a reference to an object of type Stack<T> and an array of type T—the type of elements that will be pushed onto Stack<T>. Note that the compiler enforces consistency between the type of the Stack and the elements that will be pushed onto the Stack when push is invoked, which is the real value of the generic method call. Generic method testPop (lines 38–58) takes two arguments—a String that represents the name of the Stack<T> object for output purposes and a reference to an object of type Stack<T>.

21.7 Raw Types

The test programs for generic class Stack in Section 21.6 instantiate Stacks with type arguments Double and Integer. It's also possible to instantiate generic class Stack without specifying a type argument, as follows:

```
Stack objectStack = new Stack( 5 ); // no type-argument specified
```

In this case, the objectStack is said to have a raw type, which means that the compiler implicitly uses type Object throughout the generic class for each type argument. Thus the preceding statement creates a Stack that can store objects of any type. This is important for backward compatibility with prior versions of Java. For example, the data structures of the Java Collections Framework (see Chapter 20, Generic Collections) all stored references to Objects, but are now implemented as generic types.

A raw-type Stack variable can be assigned a Stack that specifies a type argument, such as a Stack<Double> object, as follows:

```
Stack rawTypeStack2 = new Stack< Double >( 5 );
```

because type Double is a subclass of Object. This assignment is allowed because the elements in a Stack<Double> (i.e., Double objects) are certainly objects—class Double is an indirect subclass of Object.

Similarly, a Stack variable that specifies a type argument in its declaration can be assigned a raw-type Stack object, as in:

```
Stack< Integer > integerStack = new Stack( 10 );
```

Although this assignment is permitted, it's unsafe because a Stack of raw type might store types other than Integer. In this case, the compiler issues a warning message which indicates the unsafe assignment.

Using Raw Types with Generic Class Stack

The test program of Fig. 21.11 uses the notion of raw type. Line 11 instantiates generic class Stack with raw type, which indicates that rawTypeStack1 can hold objects of any type. Line 14 assigns a Stack<Double> to variable rawTypeStack2, which is declared as a Stack of raw type. Line 17 assigns a Stack of raw type to Stack<Integer> variable, which is legal but causes the compiler to issue a warning message (Fig. 21.12) indicating a potentially unsafe assignment—again, this occurs because a Stack of raw type might store types other than Integer. Also, the calls to generic methods testPush and testPop in lines 19–22 results in compiler warning messages (Fig. 21.12). These occur because rawTypeStack1 and rawTypeStack2 are declared as Stacks of raw type, but methods testPush and testPop each expect a second argument that is a Stack with a specific type argument. The warnings indicate that the compiler cannot guarantee that the types manipulated by the stacks are the correct types, since we did not supply a variable declared with a type argument. Methods testPush (lines 28–39) and testPop (lines 42–62) are the same as in Fig. 21.10.

```
1   // Fig. 21.11: RawTypeTest.java
2   // Raw type test program.
3   public class RawTypeTest
4   {
5      public static void main( String[] args )
6      {
7         Double[] doubleElements = { 1.1, 2.2, 3.3, 4.4, 5.5 };
8         Integer[] integerElements = {  1, 2, 3, 4, 5, 6, 7, 8, 9, 10 };
9
10        // Stack of raw types assigned to Stack of raw types variable
11        Stack rawTypeStack1 = new Stack( 5 );
12
13        // Stack< Double > assigned to Stack of raw types variable
14        Stack rawTypeStack2 = new Stack< Double >( 5 );
15
16        // Stack of raw types assigned to Stack< Integer > variable
17        Stack< Integer > integerStack = new Stack( 10 );
18
```

Fig. 21.11 | Raw-type test program. (Part 1 of 3.)

```
19          testPush( "rawTypeStack1", rawTypeStack1, doubleElements );
20          testPop( "rawTypeStack1", rawTypeStack1 );
21          testPush( "rawTypeStack2", rawTypeStack2, doubleElements );
22          testPop( "rawTypeStack2", rawTypeStack2 );
23          testPush( "integerStack", integerStack, integerElements );
24          testPop( "integerStack", integerStack );
25      } // end main
26
27      // generic method pushes elements onto stack
28      public static < T > void testPush( String name, Stack< T > stack,
29          T[] elements )
30      {
31          System.out.printf( "\nPushing elements onto %s\n", name );
32
33          // push elements onto Stack
34          for ( T element : elements )
35          {
36              System.out.printf( "%s ", element );
37              stack.push( element ); // push element onto stack
38          } // end for
39      } // end method testPush
40
41      // generic method testPop pops elements from stack
42      public static < T > void testPop( String name, Stack< T > stack )
43      {
44          // pop elements from stack
45          try
46          {
47              System.out.printf( "\nPopping elements from %s\n", name );
48              T popValue; // store element removed from stack
49
50              // remove elements from Stack
51              while ( true )
52              {
53                  popValue = stack.pop(); // pop from stack
54                  System.out.printf( "%s ", popValue );
55              } // end while
56          } // end try
57          catch( EmptyStackException emptyStackException )
58          {
59              System.out.println();
60              emptyStackException.printStackTrace();
61          } // end catch EmptyStackException
62      } // end method testPop
63  } // end class RawTypeTest
```

```
Pushing elements onto rawTypeStack1
1.1 2.2 3.3 4.4 5.5
Popping elements from rawTypeStack1
5.5 4.4 3.3 2.2 1.1
EmptyStackException: Stack is empty, cannot pop
        at Stack.pop(Stack.java:32)
        at RawTypeTest.testPop(RawTypeTest.java:53)
        at RawTypeTest.main(RawTypeTest.java:20)
```

Fig. 21.11 | Raw-type test program. (Part 2 of 3.)

```
Pushing elements onto rawTypeStack2
1.1 2.2 3.3 4.4 5.5
Popping elements from rawTypeStack2
5.5 4.4 3.3 2.2 1.1
EmptyStackException: Stack is empty, cannot pop
        at Stack.pop(Stack.java:32)
        at RawTypeTest.testPop(RawTypeTest.java:53)
        at RawTypeTest.main(RawTypeTest.java:22)

Pushing elements onto integerStack
1 2 3 4 5 6 7 8 9 10
Popping elements from integerStack
10 9 8 7 6 5 4 3 2 1
EmptyStackException: Stack is empty, cannot pop
        at Stack.pop(Stack.java:32)
        at RawTypeTest.testPop(RawTypeTest.java:53)
        at RawTypeTest.main(RawTypeTest.java:24)
```

Fig. 21.11 | Raw-type test program. (Part 3 of 3.)

Figure 21.12 shows the warning messages generated by the compiler when the file RawTypeTest.java (Fig. 21.11) is compiled with the -Xlint:unchecked option, which provides more information about potentially unsafe operations in code that uses generics. The first warning is generated for line 17, which assigned a raw-type Stack to a Stack<Integer> variable—the compiler cannot ensure that all objects in the Stack will be Integer objects. The next warning occurs at line 19. The compiler determines method testPush's type argument from the Double array passed as the third argument, because the second method argument is a raw-type Stack variable. In this case, Double is the type argument, so the compiler expects a Stack<Double> as the second argument. The warning occurs because the compiler cannot ensure that a raw-type Stack contains only Doubles. The warning at line 21 occurs for the same reason, even though the actual Stack that rawTypeStack2 references is a Stack<Double>. The compiler cannot guarantee that the variable will always refer to the same Stack object, so it must use the variable's declared type to perform all type checking. Lines 20 and 22 each generate warnings because method testPop expects as an argument a Stack for which a type argument has been specified. However, in each call to testPop, we pass a raw-type Stack variable. Thus, the compiler indicates a warning because it cannot check the types used in the body of the method.

```
RawTypeTest.java:17: warning: [unchecked] unchecked conversion
found    : Stack
required: Stack<java.lang.Integer>
      Stack< Integer > integerStack = new Stack( 10 );
                                          ^

RawTypeTest.java:19: warning: [unchecked] unchecked conversion
found    : Stack
required: Stack<java.lang.Double>
        testPush( "rawTypeStack1", rawTypeStack1, doubleElements );
                                          ^
```

Fig. 21.12 | Warning messages from the compiler. (Part 1 of 2.)

```
RawTypeTest.java:19: warning: [unchecked] unchecked method invocation:
<T>testPush(java.lang.String,Stack<T>,T[]) in RawTypeTest is applied to
(java.lang.String,Stack,java.lang.Double[])
      testPush( "rawTypeStack1", rawTypeStack1, doubleElements );
      ^
RawTypeTest.java:20: warning: [unchecked] unchecked conversion
found    : Stack
required: Stack<T>
      testPop( "rawTypeStack1", rawTypeStack1 );
                               ^
RawTypeTest.java:20: warning: [unchecked] unchecked method invocation:
<T>testPop(java.lang.String,Stack<T>) in RawTypeTest is applied to
(java.lang.String,Stack)
      testPop( "rawTypeStack1", rawTypeStack1 );
      ^
RawTypeTest.java:21: warning: [unchecked] unchecked conversion
found    : Stack
required: Stack<java.lang.Double>
      testPush( "rawTypeStack2", rawTypeStack2, doubleElements );
                                ^
RawTypeTest.java:21: warning: [unchecked] unchecked method invocation:
<T>testPush(java.lang.String,Stack<T>,T[]) in RawTypeTest is applied to
(java.lang.String,Stack,java.lang.Double[])
      testPush( "rawTypeStack2", rawTypeStack2, doubleElements );
      ^
RawTypeTest.java:22: warning: [unchecked] unchecked conversion
found    : Stack
required: Stack<T>
      testPop( "rawTypeStack2", rawTypeStack2 );
                               ^
RawTypeTest.java:22: warning: [unchecked] unchecked method invocation:
<T>testPop(java.lang.String,Stack<T>) in RawTypeTest is applied to
(java.lang.String,Stack)
      testPop( "rawTypeStack2", rawTypeStack2 );
      ^
9 warnings
```

Fig. 21.12 | Warning messages from the compiler. (Part 2 of 2.)

21.8 Wildcards in Methods That Accept Type Parameters

In this section, we introduce a powerful generics concept known as wildcards. For this purpose, we'll also introduce a new data structure from package java.util. In Chapter 20, we discussed the Java Collections Framework, which provides many generic data structures and algorithms that manipulate the elements of those data structures. Perhaps the simplest of these data structures is class ArrayList—a dynamically resizable, arraylike data structure. As part of this discussion, you'll learn how to create an ArrayList, add elements to it and traverse those elements using an enhanced for statement.

Before we introduce wildcards, let's consider an example that helps us motivate their use. Suppose that you'd like to implement a generic method sum that totals the numbers in a collection, such as an ArrayList. You'd begin by inserting the numbers in the collection. As you know, generic classes can be used only with class or interface types, so the numbers would be autoboxed as objects of the type-wrapper classes. For example, any int value would be autoboxed as an `Integer` object, and any `double` value would be auto-boxed as a `Double` object. We'd like to be able to total all the numbers in the `ArrayList` regardless of their type. For this reason, we'll declare the `ArrayList` with the type argument `Number`, which is the superclass of both `Integer` and `Double`. In addition, method `sum` will receive a parameter of type `ArrayList<Number>` and total its elements. Figure 21.13 demonstrates totaling the elements of an `ArrayList` of `Number`s.

```java
1   // Fig. 21.13: TotalNumbers.java
2   // Totaling the numbers in an ArrayList<Number>.
3   import java.util.ArrayList;
4
5   public class TotalNumbers
6   {
7      public static void main( String[] args )
8      {
9         // create, initialize and output ArrayList of Numbers containing
10        // both Integers and Doubles, then display total of the elements
11        Number[] numbers = { 1, 2.4, 3, 4.1 }; // Integers and Doubles
12        ArrayList< Number > numberList = new ArrayList< Number >();
13
14        for ( Number element : numbers )
15           numberList.add( element ); // place each number in numberList
16
17        System.out.printf( "numberList contains: %s\n", numberList );
18        System.out.printf( "Total of the elements in numberList: %.1f\n",
19           sum( numberList ) );
20     } // end main
21
22     // calculate total of ArrayList elements
23     public static double sum( ArrayList< Number > list )
24     {
25        double total = 0; // initialize total
26
27        // calculate sum
28        for ( Number element : list )
29           total += element.doubleValue();
30
31        return total;
32     } // end method sum
33  } // end class TotalNumbers
```

```
numberList contains: [1, 2.4, 3, 4.1]
Total of the elements in numberList: 10.5
```

Fig. 21.13 | Totaling the numbers in an `ArrayList<Number>`.

Line 11 declares and initializes an array of `Number`s. Because the initializers are prim-itive values, Java autoboxes each primitive value as an object of its corresponding wrapper type. The `int` values 1 and 3 are autoboxed as `Integer` objects, and the `double` values 2.4 and 4.1 are autoboxed as `Double` objects. Line 12 declares and creates an `ArrayList` object that stores `Number`s and assigns it to variable `numberList`. Note that we do not have to specify the size of the `ArrayList` because it will grow automatically as we insert objects.

Lines 14–15 traverse array `numbers` and place each element in `numberList`. Line 17 outputs the contents of the `ArrayList` as a `String`. This statement implicitly invokes the `ArrayList`'s `toString` method, which returns a `String` of the form `"[`*elements*`]"` in which *elements* is a comma-separated list of the elements' `String` representations. Lines 18–19 display the sum of the elements that is returned by the call to method `sum`.

Method `sum` (lines 23–32) receives an `ArrayList` of `Number`s and calculates the total of the `Number`s in the collection. The method uses `double` values to perform the calculations and returns the result as a `double`. Lines 28–29 use the enhanced `for` statement, which is designed to work with both arrays and the collections of the Collections Framework, to total the elements of the `ArrayList`. The `for` statement assigns each `Number` in the `ArrayList` to variable `element`, then uses **Number method `doubleValue`** to obtain the `Number`'s underlying primitive value as a `double` value. The result is added to `total`. When the loop terminates, the method returns the `total`.

Implementing Method *sum* With a Wildcard Type Argument in Its Parameter

Recall that the purpose of method `sum` in Fig. 21.13 was to total any type of `Number`s stored in an `ArrayList`. We created an `ArrayList` of `Number`s that contained both `Integer` and `Double` objects. The output of Fig. 21.13 demonstrates that method `sum` worked properly. Given that method `sum` can total the elements of an `ArrayList` of `Number`s, you might expect that the method would also work for `ArrayList`s that contain elements of only one numeric type, such as `ArrayList<Integer>`. So we modified class `TotalNumbers` to create an `ArrayList` of `Integer`s and pass it to method `sum`. When we compile the program, the compiler issues the following error message:

```
sum(java.util.ArrayList<java.lang.Number>) in TotalNumbersErrors
cannot be applied to (java.util.ArrayList<java.lang.Integer>)
```

Although `Number` is the superclass of `Integer`, the compiler does not consider the parameterized type `ArrayList<Number>` to be a superclass of `ArrayList<Integer>`. If it were, then every operation we could perform on `ArrayList<Number>` would also work on an `ArrayList<Integer>`. Consider the fact that you can add a `Double` object to an `ArrayList<Number>` because a `Double` *is a* `Number`, but you cannot add a `Double` object to an `ArrayList<Integer>` because a `Double` *is not an* `Integer`. Thus, the subtype relationship does not hold.

How do we create a more flexible version of the `sum` method that can total the elements of any `ArrayList` containing elements of any subclass of `Number`? This is where **wildcard-type arguments** are important. Wildcards enable you to specify method parameters, return values, variables or fields, and so on, that act as supertypes or subtypes of parameterized types. In Fig. 21.14, method `sum`'s parameter is declared in line 50 with the type:

```
ArrayList< ? extends Number >
```

A wildcard-type argument is denoted by a question mark (**?**), which by itself represents an "unknown type." In this case, the wildcard extends class `Number`, which means that the wildcard has an upper bound of `Number`. Thus, the unknown-type argument must be either `Number` or a subclass of `Number`. With the parameter type shown here, method `sum` can receive an `ArrayList` argument that contains any type of `Number`, such as `ArrayList<Integer>` (line 20), `ArrayList<Double>` (line 33) or `ArrayList<Number>` (line 46).

```java
 1  // Fig. 21.14: WildcardTest.java
 2  // Wildcard test program.
 3  import java.util.ArrayList;
 4
 5  public class WildcardTest
 6  {
 7     public static void main( String[] args )
 8     {
 9        // create, initialize and output ArrayList of Integers, then
10        // display total of the elements
11        Integer[] integers = { 1, 2, 3, 4, 5 };
12        ArrayList< Integer > integerList = new ArrayList< Integer >();
13
14        // insert elements in integerList
15        for ( Integer element : integers )
16           integerList.add( element );
17
18        System.out.printf( "integerList contains: %s\n", integerList );
19        System.out.printf( "Total of the elements in integerList: %.0f\n\n",
20           sum( integerList ) );
21
22        // create, initialize and output ArrayList of Doubles, then
23        // display total of the elements
24        Double[] doubles = { 1.1, 3.3, 5.5 };
25        ArrayList< Double > doubleList = new ArrayList< Double >();
26
27        // insert elements in doubleList
28        for ( Double element : doubles )
29           doubleList.add( element );
30
31        System.out.printf( "doubleList contains: %s\n", doubleList );
32        System.out.printf( "Total of the elements in doubleList: %.1f\n\n",
33           sum( doubleList ) );
34
35        // create, initialize and output ArrayList of Numbers containing
36        // both Integers and Doubles, then display total of the elements
37        Number[] numbers = { 1, 2.4, 3, 4.1 }; // Integers and Doubles
38        ArrayList< Number > numberList = new ArrayList< Number >();
39
40        // insert elements in numberList
41        for ( Number element : numbers )
42           numberList.add( element );
43
44        System.out.printf( "numberList contains: %s\n", numberList );
45        System.out.printf( "Total of the elements in numberList: %.1f\n",
46           sum( numberList ) );
47     } // end main
48
49     // total the elements; using a wildcard in the ArrayList parameter
50     public static double sum( ArrayList< ? extends Number > list )
51     {
52        double total = 0; // initialize total
53
```

Fig. 21.14 | Generic wildcard test program. (Part 1 of 2.)

```
54              // calculate sum
55              for ( Number element : list )
56                  total += element.doubleValue();
57
58              return total;
59      } // end method sum
60  } // end class WildcardTest
```

```
integerList contains: [1, 2, 3, 4, 5]
Total of the elements in integerList: 15

doubleList contains: [1.1, 3.3, 5.5]
Total of the elements in doubleList: 9.9

numberList contains: [1, 2.4, 3, 4.1]
Total of the elements in numberList: 10.5
```

Fig. 21.14 | Generic wildcard test program. (Part 2 of 2.)

Lines 11–20 create and initialize an ArrayList<Integer>, output its elements and total its elements by calling method sum (line 20). Lines 24–33 perform the same operations for an ArrayList<Double>. Lines 37–46 perform the same operations for an ArrayList<Number> that contains Integers and Doubles.

In method sum (lines 50–59), although the ArrayList argument's element types are not directly known by the method, they're known to be at least of type Number, because the wildcard was specified with the upper bound Number. For this reason line 56 is allowed, because all Number objects have a doubleValue method.

Although wildcards provide flexibility when passing parameterized types to a method, they also have some disadvantages. Because the wildcard (?) in the method's header (line 50) does not specify a type-parameter name, you cannot use it as a type name throughout the method's body (i.e., you cannot replace Number with ? in line 55). You could, however, declare method sum as follows:

public static <T **extends** Number> **double** sum(ArrayList< T > list)

which allows the method to receive an ArrayList that contains elements of any Number subclass. You could then use the type parameter T throughout the method body.

If the wildcard is specified without an upper bound, then only the methods of type Object can be invoked on values of the wildcard type. Also, methods that use wildcards in their parameter's type arguments cannot be used to add elements to a collection referenced by the parameter.

Common Programming Error 21.4

Using a wildcard in a method's type-parameter section or using a wildcard as an explicit type of a variable in the method body is a syntax error.

21.9 Generics and Inheritance: Notes

Generics can be used with inheritance in several ways:

- A generic class can be derived from a nongeneric class. For example, the Object class is a direct or indirect superclass of every generic class.

- A generic class can be derived from another generic class. For example, generic class Stack (in package java.util) is a subclass of generic class Vector (in package java.util). We discussed these classes in Chapter 20.

- A nongeneric class can be derived from a generic class. For example, nongeneric class Properties (in package java.util) is a subclass of generic class Hashtable (in package java.util). We also discussed these classes in Chapter 20.

- Finally, a generic method in a subclass can override a generic method in a superclass if both methods have the same signatures.

21.10 Wrap-Up

This chapter introduced generics. You learned how to declare generic methods and classes. We discussed how backward compatibility is achieved via raw types. You also learned how to use wildcards in a generic method or a generic class. In Chapter 22, you'll learn how to implement your own custom dynamic data structures that can grow or shrink at execution time. In particular, you'll implement these data structures using the generics capabilities you learned in this chapter. For more information on generics, please visit our Java Resource Center at www.deitel.com/Java/ and click the topic **Java Generics** under the heading **Resource Center Contents**.

Summary

Section 21.1 Introduction
- Generic methods enable you to specify, with one method declaration, a set of related methods.
- Generic classes and interfaces enable you to specify sets of related types.

Section 21.2 Motivation for Generic Methods
- Overloaded methods are often used to perform similar operations on different types of data.
- When the compiler encounters a method call, it attempts to locate a method declaration that has the same method name and parameters that are compatible with the argument types in the method call.

Section 21.3 Generic Methods: Implementation and Compile-Time Translation
- If the operations performed by several overloaded methods are identical for each argument type, they can be more compactly and conveniently coded using a generic method. A single generic method declaration can be called with arguments of different data types. Based on the types of the arguments passed to a generic method, the compiler handles each method call appropriately.

- All generic method declarations have a type-parameter section delimited by angle brackets (< and >) that precedes the method's return type.

- A type-parameter section contains one or more type parameters separated by commas.

- A type parameter is an identifier that specifies a generic type name. Type parameters can be used as the return type, parameter types and local variable types in a generic method declaration, and they act as placeholders for the types of the arguments passed to the generic method, which are known as actual type arguments. Type parameters can represent only reference types.

- Type-parameter names used throughout a method declaration must match those declared in the type-parameter section. A type-parameter name can be declared only once in the type-parameter section but can appear more than once in the method's parameter list.

- When the compiler encounters a method call, it determines the argument types and attempts to locate a method with the same name and parameters that match the argument types. If there is no such method, the compiler searches for methods with the same name and compatible parameters and for matching generic methods.

- Objects of a class that implements generic interface `Comparable` can be compared with method `compareTo`, which returns 0 if the objects are equal, a negative integer if the first object is less than the second or a positive integer if the first object is greater than the second.

- All the type-wrapper classes for primitive types implement `Comparable`.

- `Comparable` objects can be used with the sorting and searching methods of class `Collections`.

- When a generic method is compiled, the compiler removes the type-parameter section and replaces the type parameters with actual types. This process is known as erasure. By default each type parameter is replaced with its upper bound, which is `Object` unless specified otherwise.

Section 21.4 Additional Compile-Time Translation Issues: Methods That Use a Type Parameter as the Return Type

- When erasure is performed on a method that returns a type variable, explicit casts are inserted in front of each method call to ensure that the returned value has the type expected by the caller.

Section 21.5 Overloading Generic Methods

- A generic method may be overloaded with other generic methods or with nongeneric methods.

Section 21.6 Generic Classes

- Generic classes provide a means for describing a class in a type-independent manner. We can then instantiate type-specific objects of the generic class.

- A generic class declaration looks like a nongeneric class declaration, except that the class name is followed by a type-parameter section. The type-parameter section of a generic class can have one or more type parameters separated by commas.

- When a generic class is compiled, the compiler performs erasure on the class's type parameters and replaces them with their upper bounds.

- Type parameters cannot be used in a class's `static` declarations.

- When instantiating an object of a generic class, the types specified in angle brackets after the class name are known as type arguments. The compiler uses them to replace the type parameters so that it can perform type checking and insert cast operations as necessary.

Section 21.7 Raw Types

- It's possible to instantiate a generic class without specifying a type argument. In this case, the new object of the class is said to have a raw type—the compiler implicitly uses type `Object` (or the type parameter's upper bound) throughout the generic class for each type argument.

Section 21.8 Wildcards in Methods That Accept Type Parameters

- Class `Number` is the superclass of both `Integer` and `Double`.

- `Number` method `doubleValue` obtains the `Number`'s underlying primitive value as a `double` value.

- Wildcard-type arguments enable you to specify method parameters, return values, variables, and so on. that act as supertypes of parameterized types. A wildcard-type argument is denoted by the question mark (?), which represents an "unknown type." A wildcard can also have an upper bound.

- Because a wildcard (?) is not a type-parameter name, you cannot use it as a type name throughout a method's body.

- If a wildcard is specified without an upper bound, then only the methods of type `Object` can be invoked on values of the wildcard type.

- Methods that use wildcards as type arguments cannot be used to add elements to a collection referenced by the parameter.

Section 21.9 Generics and Inheritance: Notes

- A generic class can be derived from a nongeneric class. For example, `Object` is a direct or indirect superclass of every generic class.

- A generic class can be derived from another generic class.

- A nongeneric class can be derived from a generic class.

- A generic method in a subclass can override a generic method in a superclass if both methods have the same signatures.

Terminology

? (wildcard type argument) 888
actual type arguments 869
angle brackets (< and >) 869
`Comparable<T>` interface 871
`compareTo` method of `Comparable<T>` 871
compile-time type safety 865
`doubleValue` method of `Number` 888
erasure 870
formal type parameter 869
generic classes 865
generic interface 871
generic method 865

generics 865
parameterized class 875
parameterized type 875
raw type 882
type argument 877
type parameter 869
type parameter section 869
type variable 869
upper bound of a type parameter 872
wildcard in a generic type parameter 886
wildcard type argument 888

Self-Review Exercises

21.1 State whether each of the following is *true* or *false*. If *false*, explain why.
   a) A generic method cannot have the same method name as a nongeneric method.
   b) All generic method declarations have a type-parameter section that immediately precedes the method name.
   c) A generic method can be overloaded by another generic method with the same method name but different method parameters.
   d) A type parameter can be declared only once in the type-parameter section but can appear more than once in the method's parameter list.
   e) Type-parameter names among different generic methods must be unique.
   f) The scope of a generic class's type parameter is the entire class except its `static` members.

21.2 Fill in the blanks in each of the following:
   a) _____ and _____ enable you to specify, with a single method declaration, a set of related methods, or with a single class declaration, a set of related types, respectively.
   b) A type-parameter section is delimited by _____.
   c) A generic method's _____ can be used to specify the method's argument types, to specify the method's return type and to declare variables within the method.
   d) The statement `"Stack objectStack = new Stack();"` indicates that `objectStack` stores
      _____.
   e) In a generic class declaration, the class name is followed by a(n) _____.
   f) The syntax _____ specifies that the upper bound of a wildcard is type `T`.

Answers to Self-Review Exercises

21.1   a)   False. Generic and nongeneric methods can have the same method name. A generic method can overload another generic method with the same method name but different method parameters. A generic method also can be overloaded by providing nongeneric methods with the same method name and number of arguments. b) False. All generic method declarations have a type-parameter section that immediately precedes the method's return type. c) True. d) True. e) False. Type-parameter names among different generic methods need not be unique. f) True.

21.2   a)   Generic methods, generic classes. b) angle brackets (< and >). c) type parameters. d) a raw type. e) type-parameter section. f) ? extends T.

Exercises

21.3   Explain the use of the following notation in a Java program:

```
public class Array< T > { }
```

21.4   Write a generic method selectionSort based on the sort program of Figs. 19.6–19.7. Write a test program that inputs, sorts and outputs an Integer array and a Float array. [*Hint:* Use <T extends Comparable<T> > in the type-parameter section for method selectionSort, so that you can use method compareTo to compare the objects of the type that T represents.]

21.5   Overload generic method printArray of Fig. 21.3 so that it takes two additional integer arguments, lowSubscript and highSubscript. A call to this method prints only the designated portion of the array. Validate lowSubscript and highSubscript. If either is out of range, the overloaded printArray method should throw an InvalidSubscriptException; otherwise, printArray should return the number of elements printed. Then modify main to exercise both versions of printArray on arrays integerArray, doubleArray and characterArray. Test all capabilities of both versions of printArray.

21.6   Overload generic method printArray of Fig. 21.3 with a nongeneric version that specifically prints an array of Strings in neat, tabular format, as shown in the sample output that follows:

```
Array stringArray contains:
one      two      three    four
five     six      seven    eight
```

21.7   Write a simple generic version of method isEqualTo that compares its two arguments with the equals method and returns true if they're equal and false otherwise. Use this generic method in a program that calls isEqualTo with a variety of built-in types, such as Object or Integer. What result do you get when you attempt to run this program?

21.8   Write a generic class Pair which has two type parameters—F and S—each representing the type of the first and second element of the pair, respectively. Add *get* and *set* methods for the first and second elements of the pair. [*Hint:* The class header should be public class Pair<F, S>.]

21.9   How can generic methods be overloaded?

21.10   The compiler performs a matching process to determine which method to call when a method is invoked. Under what circumstances does an attempt to make a match result in a compile-time error?

21.11   Explain why a Java program might use the statement

```
ArrayList< Employee > workerList = new ArrayList< Employee >();
```

Custom Generic Data Structures

22

Much that I bound, I could not free;
Much that I freed returned to me.
—Lee Wilson Dodd

'Will you walk a little faster?'
said a whiting to a snail,
'There's a porpoise close behind
us, and he's treading on my tail.'
—Lewis Carroll

There is always room at the top.
—Daniel Webster

Push on—keep moving.
—Thomas Morton

I'll turn over a new leaf.
—Miguel de Cervantes

Objectives

In this chapter you'll learn:

- To form linked data structures using references, self-referential classes, recursion and generics.

- To create and manipulate dynamic data structures, such as linked lists, queues, stacks and binary trees.

- Various important applications of linked data structures.

- How to create reusable data structures with classes, inheritance and composition.

22.1 Introduction

This chapter shows how to build dynamic data structures that grow and shrink at execution time. Linked lists are collections of data items "linked up in a chain"; insertions and deletions can be made anywhere in a linked list. Stacks are important in compilers and operating systems; insertions and deletions are made only at one end of a stack—its top. Queues represent waiting lines; insertions are made at the back (also referred to as the tail) of a queue and deletions are made from the front (also referred to as the head). Binary trees facilitate high-speed searching and sorting of data, eliminating duplicate data items efficiently, representing file-system directories, compiling expressions into machine language and many other interesting applications.

We discuss each of these major data-structure types and implement programs that create and manipulate them. We use classes, inheritance and composition to create and package them for reusability and maintainability. In general, you'd use one of the predefined collection classes that we discussed in Chapter 20. However, the techniques we present here can be used if you ever need to build your own custom collections.

For simplicity, this chapter's examples manipulate primitive values. However, the data-structure implementations in this chapter can store objects of most types. (The binary tree example requires objects that implement the Comparable<T> interface.)

If you feel ambitious, you might want to attempt the major project described in the special section entitled Building Your Own Compiler, which we've posted online at www.deitel.com/books/jhtp8LOV/. You've been using a Java compiler to translate your Java programs to bytecodes so that you could execute these programs. In this project, you'll actually build your own compiler. It will read statements written in a simple, yet powerful high-level language similar to early versions of the popular language BASIC and translate these statements into Simpletron Machine Language (SML) instructions—SML is the language you learned in the Chapter 6 special section, Building Your Own Computer. Your Simpletron Simulator program will then execute the SML program produced by your compiler! Implementing this project by using an object-oriented approach will give you a wonderful opportunity to exercise most of what you've learned in this book. The special section carefully walks you through the specifications of the high-level language and describes the algorithms you'll need to convert each high-level language statement into machine-language instructions. If you enjoy being challenged, you might attempt the many enhancements to both the compiler and the Simpletron Simulator suggested in the exercises.

22.2 Self-Referential Classes

A self-referential class contains an instance variable that refers to another object of the same class type. For example, the generic class declaration

```
class Node< T >
{
    private T data;
    private Node< T > nextNode; // reference to next linked node

    public Node( T data ) { /* constructor body */ }
    public void setData( T data ) { /* method body */ }
    public T getData() { /* method body */ }
    public void setNext( Node< T > next ) { /* method body */ }
    public Node< T > getNext() { /* method body */ }
} // end class Node< T >
```

declares class Node, which has two private instance variables—data (of the generic type T) and Node<T> variable nextNode. Variable nextNode references a Node<T> object, an object of the same class being declared here—hence, the term "self-referential class." Field nextNode is a link—it "links" an object of type Node<T> to another object of the same type. Type Node<T> also has five methods: a constructor that receives a value to initialize data, a setData method to set the value of data, a getData method to return the value of data, a setNext method to set the value of nextNode and a getNext method to return a reference to the next node.

Programs can link self-referential objects together to form such useful data structures as lists, queues, stacks and trees. Figure 22.1 illustrates two self-referential objects linked together to form a list. A backslash—representing a null reference—is placed in the link member of the second self-referential object to indicate that the link does not refer to another object. Note that the backslash is illustrative; it does not correspond to the backslash character in Java. We use the null reference to indicate the end of a data structure.

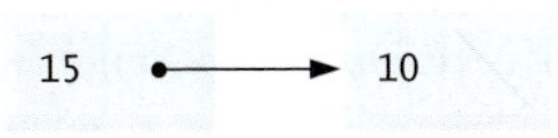

Fig. 22.1 | Self-referential-class objects linked together.

22.3 Dynamic Memory Allocation

Creating and maintaining dynamic data structures requires dynamic memory allocation—allowing a program to obtain more memory space at execution time to hold new nodes and to release space no longer needed. Remember that Java programs do not explicitly release dynamically allocated memory. Rather, Java performs automatic garbage collection of objects that are no longer referenced in a program.

The limit for dynamic memory allocation can be as large as the amount of available physical memory in the computer or the amount of available disk space in a virtual-memory system. Often the limits are much smaller, because the computer's available memory must be shared among many applications.

The declaration and class-instance-creation expression

```
// 10 is nodeToAdd's data
Node< Integer > nodeToAdd = new Node< Integer >( 10 );
```

allocates the memory to store a Node<Integer> object and returns a reference to the object, which is assigned to nodeToAdd. If insufficient memory is available, the expression throws an OutOfMemoryError.

The following sections discuss lists, stacks, queues and trees that all use dynamic memory allocation and self-referential classes to create dynamic data structures.

22.4 Linked Lists

A linked list is a linear collection (i.e., a sequence) of self-referential-class objects, called **nodes**, connected by reference links—hence, the term "linked" list. Typically, a program accesses a linked list via a reference to its first node. The program accesses each subsequent node via the link reference stored in the previous node. By convention, the link reference in the last node of the list is set to `null`. Data is stored in a linked list dynamically—the program creates each node as necessary. Stacks and queues are also linear data structures and, as we'll see, are constrained versions of linked lists. Trees are nonlinear data structures.

Lists of data can be stored in arrays, but linked lists provide several advantages. A linked list is appropriate when the number of data elements to be represented in the data structure is unpredictable. Linked lists are dynamic, so the length of a list can increase or decrease as necessary, whereas the size of a "conventional" Java array cannot be altered—it is fixed when the program creates the array. "Conventional" arrays can become full. Linked lists become full only when the system has insufficient memory to satisfy dynamic storage allocation requests. Package `java.util` contains class `LinkedList` (discussed in Chapter 20) for implementing and manipulating linked lists that grow and shrink during program execution.

Performance Tip 22.1

An array can be declared to contain more elements than the number of items expected, but this wastes memory. In these situations, linked lists provide better memory utilization allowing the program to adapt to storage needs at runtime.

Performance Tip 22.2

Insertion into a linked list is fast—only two references have to be modified (after locating the insertion point). All existing node objects remain at their current locations in memory.

Linked lists can be maintained in sorted order simply by inserting each new element at the proper point in the list. (It does, of course, take time to locate the proper insertion point.) Existing list elements do not need to be moved.

Performance Tip 22.3

Insertion and deletion in a sorted array can be time consuming—all the elements following the inserted or deleted element must be shifted appropriately.

Singly Linked Lists

Linked list nodes normally are not stored contiguously in memory. Rather, they're logically contiguous. Figure 22.2 illustrates a linked list with several nodes. This diagram presents a **singly linked list**—each node contains one reference to the next node in the list. Often, linked lists are implemented as doubly linked lists—each node contains a reference to the next node in the list and a reference to the proceding one. Java's `LinkedList` class is a doubly linked list implementation.

Fig. 22.2 | Linked-list graphical representation.

Performance Tip 22.4

Normally, the elements of an array are contiguous in memory. This allows immediate access to any array element, because its address can be calculated directly as its offset from the beginning of the array. Linked lists do not afford such immediate access—an element can be accessed only by traversing the list from the front (or from the back in a doubly linked list).

Implementing a Generic **List** *Class*

The program of Figs. 22.3–22.5 uses an object of our generic List class to manipulate a list of miscellaneous objects. The program consists of four classes—ListNode (Fig. 22.3, lines 6–37), List (Fig. 22.3, lines 40–147), EmptyListException (Fig. 22.4) and List-Test (Fig. 22.5). The List, ListNode and EmptyListException classes are placed in package com.deitel.ch22, so they can be reused throughout this chapter. Encapsulated in each List object is a linked list of ListNode objects. [*Note:* Many of the classes in this chapter are declared in the package com.deitel.ch22. Each such class should be compiled with the -d command-line option to javac. When compiling the classes that are not in this package and when running the programs, be sure to use the option -classpath with javac and java, respectively.]

```java
1   // Fig. 22.3: List.java
2   // ListNode and List class declarations.
3   package com.deitel.ch22;
4
5   // class to represent one node in a list
6   class ListNode< T >
7   {
8      // package access members; List can access these directly
9      T data; // data for this node
10     ListNode< T > nextNode; // reference to the next node in the list
11
12     // constructor creates a ListNode that refers to object
13     ListNode( T object )
14     {
15        this( object, null );
16     } // end ListNode one-argument constructor
17
```

Fig. 22.3 | ListNode and List class declarations. (Part 1 of 4.)

```
18      // constructor creates ListNode that refers to the specified
19      // object and to the next ListNode
20      ListNode( T object, ListNode< T > node )
21      {
22         data = object;
23         nextNode = node;
24      } // end ListNode two-argument constructor
25
26      // return reference to data in node
27      T getData()
28      {
29         return data; // return item in this node
30      } // end method getData
31
32      // return reference to next node in list
33      ListNode< T > getNext()
34      {
35         return nextNode; // get next node
36      } // end method getNext
37   } // end class ListNode< T >
38
39   // class List definition
40   public class List< T >
41   {
42      private ListNode< T > firstNode;
43      private ListNode< T > lastNode;
44      private String name; // string like "list" used in printing
45
46      // constructor creates empty List with "list" as the name
47      public List()
48      {
49         this( "list" );
50      } // end List no-argument constructor
51
52      // constructor creates an empty List with a name
53      public List( String listName )
54      {
55         name = listName;
56         firstNode = lastNode = null;
57      } // end List one-argument constructor
58
59      // insert item at front of List
60      public void insertAtFront( T insertItem )
61      {
62         if ( isEmpty() ) // firstNode and lastNode refer to same object
63            firstNode = lastNode = new ListNode< T >( insertItem );
64         else // firstNode refers to new node
65            firstNode = new ListNode< T >( insertItem, firstNode );
66      } // end method insertAtFront
67
68      // insert item at end of List
69      public void insertAtBack( T insertItem )
70      {
```

Fig. 22.3 | ListNode and List class declarations. (Part 2 of 4.)

```
71          if ( isEmpty() ) // firstNode and lastNode refer to same object
72             firstNode = lastNode = new ListNode< T >( insertItem );
73          else // lastNode's nextNode refers to new node
74             lastNode = lastNode.nextNode = new ListNode< T >( insertItem );
75       } // end method insertAtBack
76
77       // remove first node from List
78       public T removeFromFront() throws EmptyListException
79       {
80          if ( isEmpty() ) // throw exception if List is empty
81             throw new EmptyListException( name );
82
83          T removedItem = firstNode.data; // retrieve data being removed
84
85          // update references firstNode and lastNode
86          if ( firstNode == lastNode )
87             firstNode = lastNode = null;
88          else
89             firstNode = firstNode.nextNode;
90
91          return removedItem; // return removed node data
92       } // end method removeFromFront
93
94       // remove last node from List
95       public T removeFromBack() throws EmptyListException
96       {
97          if ( isEmpty() ) // throw exception if List is empty
98             throw new EmptyListException( name );
99
100         T removedItem = lastNode.data; // retrieve data being removed
101
102         // update references firstNode and lastNode
103         if ( firstNode == lastNode )
104            firstNode = lastNode = null;
105         else // locate new last node
106         {
107            ListNode< T > current = firstNode;
108
109            // loop while current node does not refer to lastNode
110            while ( current.nextNode != lastNode )
111               current = current.nextNode;
112
113            lastNode = current; // current is new lastNode
114            current.nextNode = null;
115         } // end else
116
117         return removedItem; // return removed node data
118      } // end method removeFromBack
119
120      // determine whether list is empty
121      public boolean isEmpty()
122      {
123         return firstNode == null; // return true if list is empty
124      } // end method isEmpty
```

Fig. 22.3 | ListNode and List class declarations. (Part 3 of 4.)

```
125
126        // output list contents
127        public void print()
128        {
129           if ( isEmpty() )
130           {
131              System.out.printf( "Empty %s\n", name );
132              return;
133           } // end if
134
135           System.out.printf( "The %s is: ", name );
136           ListNode< T > current = firstNode;
137
138           // while not at end of list, output current node's data
139           while ( current != null )
140           {
141              System.out.printf( "%s ", current.data );
142              current = current.nextNode;
143           } // end while
144
145           System.out.println( "\n" );
146        } // end method print
147  } // end class List< T >
```

Fig. 22.3 | ListNode and List class declarations. (Part 4 of 4.)

```
 1   // Fig. 22.4: EmptyListException.java
 2   // Class EmptyListException declaration.
 3   package com.deitel.ch22;
 4
 5   public class EmptyListException extends RuntimeException
 6   {
 7      // no-argument constructor
 8      public EmptyListException()
 9      {
10         this( "List" ); // call other EmptyListException constructor
11      } // end EmptyListException no-argument constructor
12
13      // one-argument constructor
14      public EmptyListException( String name )
15      {
16         super( name + " is empty" ); // call superclass constructor
17      } // end EmptyListException one-argument constructor
18   } // end class EmptyListException
```

Fig. 22.4 | EmptyListException class declaration.

```
 1   // Fig. 22.5: ListTest.java
 2   // ListTest class to demonstrate List capabilities.
 3   import com.deitel.ch22.List;
 4   import com.deitel.ch22.EmptyListException;
 5
```

Fig. 22.5 | ListTest class to demonstrate List capabilities. (Part 1 of 3.)

```
 6   public class ListTest
 7   {
 8      public static void main( String[] args )
 9      {
10         List< Integer > list = new List< Integer >(); // create a List
11
12         // insert integers in list
13         list.insertAtFront( -1 );
14         list.print();
15         list.insertAtFront( 0 );
16         list.print();
17         list.insertAtBack( 1 );
18         list.print();
19         list.insertAtBack( 5 );
20         list.print();
21
22         // remove objects from list; print after each removal
23         try
24         {
25            int removedItem = list.removeFromFront();
26            System.out.printf( "\n%d removed\n", removedItem );
27            list.print();
28
29            removedItem = list.removeFromFront();
30            System.out.printf( "\n%d removed\n", removedItem );
31            list.print();
32
33            removedItem = list.removeFromBack();
34            System.out.printf( "\n%d removed\n", removedItem );
35            list.print();
36
37            removedItem = list.removeFromBack();
38            System.out.printf( "\n%d removed\n", removedItem );
39            list.print();
40         } // end try
41         catch ( EmptyListException emptyListException )
42         {
43            emptyListException.printStackTrace();
44         } // end catch
45      } // end main
46   } // end class ListTest
```

```
The list is: -1
The list is: 0 -1
The list is: 0 -1 1
The list is: 0 -1 1 5

0 removed
The list is: -1 1 5

-1 removed
The list is: 1 5                                    (continued...)
```

Fig. 22.5 | ListTest class to demonstrate List capabilities. (Part 2 of 3.)

```
5 removed
The list is: 1

1 removed
Empty list
```

Fig. 22.5 | ListTest class to demonstrate List capabilities. (Part 3 of 3.)

Generic Classes *ListNode and* List

Generic class ListNode (Fig. 22.3, lines 6–37) declares package-access fields data and nextNode. The data field is a reference of type T, so its type will be determined when the client code creates the corresponding List object. Variable nextNode stores a reference to the next ListNode object in the linked list (or null if the node is the last one in the list).

Lines 42–43 of class List (Fig. 22.3, lines 40–47) declare references to the first and last ListNodes in a List (firstNode and lastNode, respectively). The constructors (lines 47–50 and 53–57) initialize both references to null. The most important methods of class List are insertAtFront (lines 60–66), insertAtBack (lines 69–75), removeFromFront (lines 78–92) and removeFromBack (lines 95–118). Method isEmpty (lines 121–124) is a *predicate method* that determines whether the list is empty (i.e., the reference to the first node of the list is null). Predicate methods typically test a condition and do not modify the object on which they're called. If the list is empty, method isEmpty returns true; otherwise, it returns false. Method print (lines 127–146) displays the list's contents. We discuss class List's methods in more detail after we discuss class ListTest.

Class *ListTest*

Method main of class ListTest (Fig. 22.5) creates a List<Integer> object (line 10), then inserts objects at the beginning of the list using method insertAtFront, inserts objects at the end of the list using method insertAtBack, deletes objects from the front of the list using method removeFromFront and deletes objects from the end of the list using method removeFromBack. After each insert and remove operation, ListTest calls List method print to display the current list contents. If an attempt is made to remove an item from an empty list, an EmptyListException (Fig. 22.4) is thrown, so the method calls to removeFromFront and removeFromBack are placed in a try block that is followed by an appropriate exception handler. Notice in lines 13, 15, 17 and 19 that the application passes literal primitive int values to methods insertAtFront and insertAtBack. Each of these methods was declared with a parameter of the generic type T (Fig. 22.3, lines 60 and 69). Since this example manipulates a List<Integer>, the type T represents the type-wrapper class Integer. In this case, the JVM autoboxes each literal value in an Integer object, and that object is actually inserted into the list.

List *Method* insertAtFront

Now we discuss each method of class List (Fig. 22.3) in detail and provide diagrams showing the reference manipulations performed by methods insertAtFront, insertAtBack, removeFromFront and removeFromBack. Method insertAtFront (lines 60–66 of Fig. 22.3) places a new node at the front of the list. The steps are:

1. Call isEmpty to determine whether the list is empty (line 62).

2. If the list is empty, assign to firstNode and lastNode the new ListNode that was initialized with insertItem (line 63). (Recall that assignment operators evaluate

right to left.) The ListNode constructor at lines 13–16 calls the ListNode constructor at lines 20–24 to set instance variable data to refer to the insertItem passed as an argument and to set reference nextNode to null, because this is the first and last node in the list.

3. If the list is not empty, the new node is "linked" into the list by setting firstNode to a new ListNode object and initializing that object with insertItem and firstNode (line 65). When the ListNode constructor (lines 20–24) executes, it sets instance variable data to refer to the insertItem passed as an argument and performs the insertion by setting the nextNode reference of the new node to the ListNode passed as an argument, which previously was the first node.

In Fig. 22.6, part (a) shows a list and a new node during the insertAtFront operation and before the program links the new node into the list. The dotted arrows in part (b) illustrate *Step 3* of the insertAtFront operation that enables the node containing 12 to become the new first node in the list.

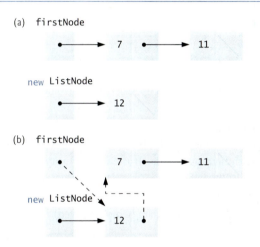

Fig. 22.6 | Graphical representation of operation insertAtFront.

List Method insertAtBack
Method insertAtBack (lines 69–75 of Fig. 22.3) places a new node at the back of the list. The steps are:

1. Call isEmpty to determine whether the list is empty (line 71).

2. If the list is empty, assign to firstNode and lastNode the new ListNode that was initialized with insertItem (line 72). The ListNode constructor at lines 13–16 calls the constructor at lines 20–24 to set instance variable data to refer to the insertItem passed as an argument and to set reference nextNode to null.

3. If the list is not empty, line 74 links the new node into the list by assigning to lastNode and lastNode.nextNode the reference to the new ListNode that was initialized with insertItem. ListNode's constructor (lines 13–16) sets instance variable data to refer to the insertItem passed as an argument and sets reference nextNode to null, because this is the last node in the list.

In Fig. 22.7, part (a) shows a list and a new node during the `insertAtBack` operation and before linking the new node into the list. The dotted arrows in part (b) illustrate *Step 3* of method `insertAtBack`, which adds the new node to the end of a list that is not empty.

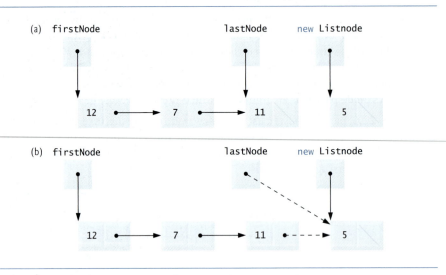

Fig. 22.7 | Graphical representation of operation `insertAtBack`.

List *Method* removeFromFront
Method `removeFromFront` (lines 78–92 of Fig. 22.3) removes the first node of the list and returns a reference to the removed data. If the list is empty when the program calls this method, the method throws an `EmptyListException` (lines 80–81). Otherwise, the method returns a reference to the removed data. The steps are:

1. Assign `firstNode.data` (the data being removed) to `removedItem` (line 83).

2. If `firstNode` and `lastNode` refer to the same object (line 86), the list has only one element at this time. So, the method sets `firstNode` and `lastNode` to `null` (line 87) to remove the node from the list (leaving the list empty).

3. If the list has more than one node, then the method leaves reference `lastNode` as is and assigns the value of `firstNode.nextNode` to `firstNode` (line 89). Thus, `firstNode` references the node that was previously the second node in the list.

4. Return the `removedItem` reference (line 91).

In Fig. 22.8, part (a) illustrates the list before the removal operation. The dashed lines and arrows in part (b) show the reference manipulations.

List *Method* removeFromBack
Method `removeFromBack` (lines 95–118 of Fig. 22.3) removes the last node of a list and returns a reference to the removed data. The method throws an `EmptyListException` (lines 97–98) if the list is empty when the program calls this method. The steps are:

1. Assign `lastNode.data` (the data being removed from the list) to `removedItem` (line 100).

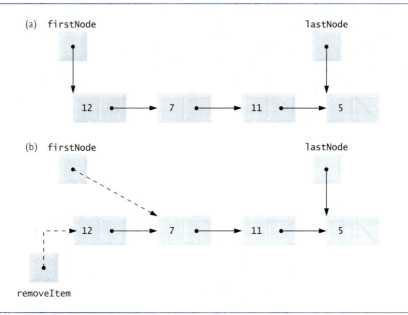

(a) firstNode   lastNode

12 → 7 → 11 → 5

(b) firstNode   lastNode

12 → 7 → 11 → 5

removeItem

Fig. 22.8 | Graphical representation of operation `removeFromFront`.

2. If the `firstNode` and `lastNode` refer to the same object (line 103), the list has only one element at this time. So, line 104 sets `firstNode` and `lastNode` to `null` to remove that node from the list (leaving the list empty).

3. If the list has more than one node, create the `ListNode` reference `current` and assign it `firstNode` (line 107).

4. Now "walk the list" with `current` until it references the node before the last node. The `while` loop (lines 110–111) assigns `current.nextNode` to `current` as long as `current.nextNode` (the next node in the list) is not `lastNode`.

5. After locating the second-to-last node, assign `current` to `lastNode` (line 113) to update which node is last in the list.

6. Set the `current.nextNode` to `null` (line 114) to remove the last node from the list and terminate the list at the current node.

7. Return the `removedItem` reference (line 117).

In Fig. 22.9, part (a) illustrates the list before the removal operation. The dashed lines and arrows in part (b) show the reference manipulations.

List *Method* print

Method `print` (lines 127–146) first determines whether the list is empty (lines 129–133). If so, `print` displays a message indicating that the list is empty and returns control to the calling method. Otherwise, `print` outputs the list's data. Line 136 creates `ListNode` current and initializes it with `firstNode`. While `current` is not `null`, there are more items in the list. Therefore, line 141 outputs a string representation of `current.data`. Line 142 moves to the next node in the list by assigning the value of reference `current.nextNode` to `current`. This printing algorithm is identical for linked lists, stacks and queues.

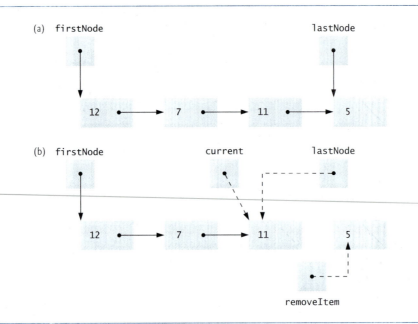

Fig. 22.9 | Graphical representation of operation removeFromBack.

22.5 Stacks

A stack is a constrained version of a list—new nodes can be added to and removed from a stack only at the top. For this reason, a stack is referred to as a **last-in, first-out (LIFO)** data structure. The link member in the bottom node is set to null to indicate the bottom of the stack. Note that a stack is not required to be implemented as a linked list—it can also be implemented using an array.

The primary methods for manipulating a stack are **push** and **pop**, which add a new node to the top of the stack and remove a node from the top of the stack, respectively. Method pop also returns the data from the popped node.

Stacks have many interesting applications. For example, when a program calls a method, the called method must know how to return to its caller, so the return address of the calling method is pushed onto the program-execution stack (discussed in Section 5.6). If a series of method calls occurs, the successive return addresses are pushed onto the stack in last-in, first-out order so that each method can return to its caller. Stacks support recursive method calls in the same manner as they do conventional nonrecursive method calls.

The program-execution stack also contains the memory for local variables on each invocation of a method during a program's execution. When the method returns to its caller, the memory for that method's local variables is popped off the stack, and those variables are no longer known to the program. If the local variable is a reference and the object to which it referred has no other variables referring to it, the object can be garbage collected.

Compilers use stacks to evaluate arithmetic expressions and generate machine-language code to process them. The exercises in this chapter explore several applications of stacks, including using them to develop a complete working compiler. Also, package java.util contains class Stack (see Chapter 20) for implementing and manipulating stacks that can grow and shrink during program execution.

In this section, we take advantage of the close relationship between lists and stacks to implement a stack class by reusing the List<T> class of Fig. 22.3. We demonstrate two different forms of reusability. First, we implement the stack class by extending class List. Then we implement an identically performing stack class through composition by including a reference to a List object as a private instance variable. The list, stack and queue data structures in this chapter are implemented to store references to objects of any type to encourage further reusability.

Stack Class That Inherits from List<T>
Figures 22.10 and 22.11 create and manipulate a stack class that extends the List<T> class of Fig. 22.3. We want the stack to have methods push, pop, isEmpty and print. Essentially, these are the List<T> methods insertAtFront, removeFromFront, isEmpty and print. Of course, class List<T> contains other methods (such as insertAtBack and removeFromBack) that we would rather not make accessible through the public interface to the stack class. It's important to remember that all methods in List<T>'s public interface class also are public methods of the subclass StackInheritance<T> (Fig. 22.10). Each method of StackInheritance<T> calls the appropriate List<T> method—for example, method push calls insertAtFront and method pop calls removeFromFront. StackInheritance<T> clients can call methods isEmpty and print because they're inherited from List<T>. Class StackInheritance<T> is declared in package com.deitel.ch22 (line 3) for reuse. Note that StackInheritance<T> does not import List<T>—the classes are in the same package.

```java
1   // Fig. 22.10: StackInheritance.java
2   // StackInheritance extends class List.
3   package com.deitel.ch22;
4
5   public class StackInheritance< T > extends List< T >
6   {
7      // no-argument constructor
8      public StackInheritance()
9      {
10        super( "stack" );
11     } // end StackInheritance no-argument constructor
12
13     // add object to stack
14     public void push( T object )
15     {
16        insertAtFront( object );
17     } // end method push
18
19     // remove object from stack
20     public T pop() throws EmptyListException
21     {
22        return removeFromFront();
23     } // end method pop
24  } // end class StackInheritance
```

Fig. 22.10 | StackInheritance extends class List.

Class `StackInheritanceTest`'s method main (Fig. 22.11) creates an object of class `StackInheritance<T>` called stack (lines 10–11). The program pushes integers onto the stack (lines 14, 16, 18 and 20). Autoboxing is used here to insert `Integer` objects into the data structure. Lines 28–33 pop the objects from the stack in an infinite while loop. If method pop is invoked on an empty stack, the method throws an `EmptyListException`. In this case, the program displays the exception's stack trace, which shows the methods on the program-execution stack at the time the exception occurred. Note that the program uses method print (inherited from `List`) to output the contents of the stack.

```java
1   // Fig. 22.11: StackInheritanceTest.java
2   // Stack manipulation program.
3   import com.deitel.ch22.StackInheritance;
4   import com.deitel.ch22.EmptyListException;
5
6   public class StackInheritanceTest
7   {
8      public static void main( String[] args )
9      {
10        StackInheritance< Integer > stack =
11           new StackInheritance< Integer >();
12
13        // use push method
14        stack.push( -1 );
15        stack.print();
16        stack.push( 0 );
17        stack.print();
18        stack.push( 1 );
19        stack.print();
20        stack.push( 5 );
21        stack.print();
22
23        // remove items from stack
24        try
25        {
26           int removedItem;
27
28           while ( true )
29           {
30              removedItem = stack.pop(); // use pop method
31              System.out.printf( "\n%d popped\n", removedItem );
32              stack.print();
33           } // end while
34        } // end try
35        catch ( EmptyListException emptyListException )
36        {
37           emptyListException.printStackTrace();
38        } // end catch
39     } // end main
40  } // end class StackInheritanceTest
```

```
The stack is: -1
The stack is: 0 -1                                            (continued...)
```

Fig. 22.11 | Stack manipulation program. (Part 1 of 2.)

```
The stack is: 1  0 -1
The stack is: 5  1  0 -1

5 popped
The stack is: 1 0 -1

1 popped
The stack is: 0 -1

0 popped
The stack is: -1

-1 popped
Empty stack
com.deitel.ch22.EmptyListException: stack is empty
        at com.deitel.ch22.List.removeFromFront(List.java:81)
        at com.deitel.ch22.StackInheritance.pop(StackInheritance.java:22)
        at StackInheritanceTest.main(StackInheritanceTest.java:30)
```

Fig. 22.11 | Stack manipulation program. (Part 2 of 2.)

Stack Class That Contains a Reference to a List

You can also implement a class by reusing a list class through composition. Figure 22.12 uses a private List<T> (line 7) in class StackComposition<T>'s declaration. Composition enables us to hide the List<T> methods that should not be in our stack's public interface. We provide public interface methods that use only the required List<T> methods. Implementing each stack method as a call to a List<T> method is called delegation—the stack method invoked delegates the call to the appropriate List<T> method. In particular, StackComposition<T> delegates calls to List<T> methods insertAtFront, removeFromFront, isEmpty and print. In this example, we do not show class StackCompositionTest, because the only difference is that we change the type of the stack from StackInheritance to StackComposition (lines 3 and 10–11 of Fig. 22.11).

```
1   // Fig. 22.12: StackComposition.java
2   // StackComposition uses a composed List object.
3   package com.deitel.ch22;
4
5   public class StackComposition< T >
6   {
7       private List< T > stackList;
8
9       // no-argument constructor
10      public StackComposition()
11      {
12          stackList = new List< T >( "stack" );
13      } // end StackComposition no-argument constructor
14
15      // add object to stack
16      public void push( T object )
17      {
```

Fig. 22.12 | StackComposition uses a composed List object. (Part 1 of 2.)

```
18              stackList.insertAtFront( object );
19          } // end method push
20
21          // remove object from stack
22          public T pop() throws EmptyListException
23          {
24              return stackList.removeFromFront();
25          } // end method pop
26
27          // determine if stack is empty
28          public boolean isEmpty()
29          {
30              return stackList.isEmpty();
31          } // end method isEmpty
32
33          // output stack contents
34          public void print()
35          {
36              stackList.print();
37          } // end method print
38      } // end class StackComposition
```

Fig. 22.12 | StackComposition uses a composed List object. (Part 2 of 2.)

22.6 Queues

Another commonly used data structure is the queue. A queue is similar to a checkout line in a supermarket—the cashier services the person at the beginning of the line first. Other customers enter the line only at the end and wait for service. Queue nodes are removed only from the head (or front) of the queue and are inserted only at the tail (or end). For this reason, a queue is a **first-in, first-out** (**FIFO**) data structure. The insert and remove operations are known as **enqueue** and **dequeue**.

Queues have many uses in computer systems. Each CPU in a computer can service only one application at a time. Each application requiring processor time is placed in a queue. The application at the front of the queue is the next to receive service. Each application gradually advances to the front as the applications before it receive service.

Queues are also used to support **print spooling**. For example, a single printer might be shared by all users of a network. Many users can send print jobs to the printer, even when the printer is already busy. These print jobs are placed in a queue until the printer becomes available. A program called a **spooler** manages the queue to ensure that, as each print job completes, the next print job is sent to the printer.

Information packets also wait in queues in computer networks. Each time a packet arrives at a network node, it must be routed to the next node along the path to the packet's final destination. The routing node routes one packet at a time, so additional packets are enqueued until the router can route them.

A file server in a computer network handles file-access requests from many clients throughout the network. Servers have a limited capacity to service requests from clients. When that capacity is exceeded, client requests wait in queues.

Figure 22.13 creates a Queue<T> class that contains a List<T> (Fig. 22.3) object and provides methods enqueue, dequeue, isEmpty and print. Class List<T> contains some methods (e.g., insertAtFront and removeFromBack) that we'd rather not make accessible through Queue<T>'s public interface. Using composition enables us to hide class List<T>'s other public methods from clients of class Queue<T>. Each Queue<T> method calls an appropriate List<T> method—method enqueue calls List<T> method insertAt-Back, method dequeue calls List<T> method removeFromFront, method isEmpty calls List<T> method isEmpty and method print calls List<T> method print. For reuse, class Queue<T> is declared in package com.deitel.ch22.

```java
 1  // Fig. 22.13: Queue.java
 2  // Queue uses class List.
 3  package com.deitel.ch22;
 4
 5  public class Queue
 6  {
 7     private List< T > queueList;
 8
 9     // no-argument constructor
10     public Queue()
11     {
12        queueList = new List< T >( "queue" );
13     } // end Queue no-argument constructor
14
15     // add object to queue
16     public void enqueue( T object )
17     {
18        queueList.insertAtBack( object );
19     } // end method enqueue
20
21     // remove object from queue
22     public T dequeue() throws EmptyListException
23     {
24        return queueList.removeFromFront();
25     } // end method dequeue
26
27     // determine if queue is empty
28     public boolean isEmpty()
29     {
30        return queueList.isEmpty();
31     } // end method isEmpty
32
33     // output queue contents
34     public void print()
35     {
36        queueList.print();
37     } // end method print
38  } // end class Queue
```

Fig. 22.13 | Queue uses class List.

Class QueueTest's (Fig. 22.14) main method creates and initializes Queue<T> variable queue (line 10). Lines 13, 15, 17 and 19 enqueue four integers, taking advantage of auto-boxing to insert Integer objects into the queue. Lines 27–32 use an infinite loop to dequeue the objects in first-in, first-out order. When the queue is empty, method dequeue throws an EmptyListException, and the program displays the exception's stack trace.

```java
 1   // Fig. 22.14: QueueTest.java
 2   // Class QueueTest.
 3   import com.deitel.ch22.Queue;
 4   import com.deitel.ch22.EmptyListException;
 5
 6   public class QueueTest
 7   {
 8      public static void main( String[] args )
 9      {
10         Queue< Integer > queue = new Queue< Integer >();
11
12         // use enqueue method
13         queue.enqueue( -1 );
14         queue.print();
15         queue.enqueue( 0 );
16         queue.print();
17         queue.enqueue( 1 );
18         queue.print();
19         queue.enqueue( 5 );
20         queue.print();
21
22         // remove objects from queue
23         try
24         {
25            int removedItem;
26
27            while ( true )
28            {
29               removedItem = queue.dequeue(); // use dequeue method
30               System.out.printf( "\n%d dequeued\n", removedItem );
31               queue.print();
32            } // end while
33         } // end try
34         catch ( EmptyListException emptyListException )
35         {
36            emptyListException.printStackTrace();
37         } // end catch
38      } // end main
39   } // end class QueueTest
```

```
The queue is: -1
The queue is: -1 0
The queue is: -1 0 1
The queue is: -1 0 1 5

-1 dequeued
The queue is: 0 1 5

0 dequeued
The queue is: 1 5

1 dequeued
The queue is: 5                                          (continued...)
```

Fig. 22.14 | Queue processing program. (Part 1 of 2.)

```
5 dequeued
Empty queue
com.deitel.ch22.EmptyListException: queue is empty
        at com.deitel.ch22.List.removeFromFront(List.java:81)
        at com.deitel.ch22.Queue.dequeue(Queue.java:24)
        at QueueTest.main(QueueTest.java:29)
```

Fig. 22.14 | Queue processing program. (Part 2 of 2.)

22.7 Trees

Lists, stacks and queues are **linear data structures** (i.e., **sequences**). A tree is a nonlinear, two-dimensional data structure with special properties. Tree nodes contain two or more links. This section discusses binary trees (Fig. 22.15)—trees whose nodes each contain two links (one or both of which may be null). The **root node** is the first node in a tree. Each link in the root node refers to a **child**. The **left child** is the first node in the **left subtree** (also known as the root node of the left subtree), and the **right child** is the first node in the **right subtree** (also known as the root node of the right subtree). The children of a specific node are called **siblings**. A node with no children is called a **leaf node**. Computer scientists normally draw trees from the root node down—the opposite of the way most trees grow in nature.

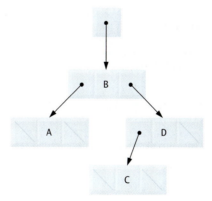

Fig. 22.15 | Binary tree graphical representation.

In our example, we create a special binary tree called a **binary search tree**. A binary search tree (with no duplicate node values) has the characteristic that the values in any left subtree are less than the value in that subtree's parent node, and the values in any right subtree are greater than the value in that subtree's parent node. Figure 22.16 illustrates a binary search tree with 12 integer values. Note that the shape of the binary search tree that corresponds to a set of data can vary, depending on the order in which the values are inserted into the tree.

Figures 22.17 and 22.18 create a generic binary search tree class and use it to manipulate a tree of integers. The application in Fig. 22.18 traverses the tree (i.e., walks through all its nodes) three ways—using recursive **inorder**, **preorder** and **postorder traversals**. The program generates 10 random numbers and inserts each into the tree. Class Tree<T> is declared in package com.deitel.ch22 for reuse.

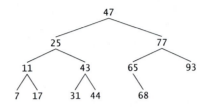

Fig. 22.16 | Binary search tree containing 12 values.

```java
1   // Fig. 22.17: Tree.java
2   // TreeNode and Tree class declarations for a binary search tree.
3   package com.deitel.ch22;
4
5   // class TreeNode definition
6   class TreeNode< T extends Comparable< T > >
7   {
8      // package access members
9      TreeNode< T > leftNode; // left node
10     T data; // node value
11     TreeNode< T > rightNode; // right node
12
13     // constructor initializes data and makes this a leaf node
14     public TreeNode( T nodeData )
15     {
16        data = nodeData;
17        leftNode = rightNode = null; // node has no children
18     } // end TreeNode constructor
19
20     // locate insertion point and insert new node; ignore duplicate values
21     public void insert( T insertValue )
22     {
23        // insert in left subtree
24        if ( insertValue.compareTo( data ) < 0 )
25        {
26           // insert new TreeNode
27           if ( leftNode == null )
28              leftNode = new TreeNode< T >( insertValue );
29           else // continue traversing left subtree recursively
30              leftNode.insert( insertValue );
31        } // end if
32        // insert in right subtree
33        else if ( insertValue.compareTo( data ) > 0 )
34        {
35           // insert new TreeNode
36           if ( rightNode == null )
37              rightNode = new TreeNode< T >( insertValue );
```

Fig. 22.17 | TreeNode and Tree class declarations for a binary search tree. (Part 1 of 3.)

```
38                else // continue traversing right subtree recursively
39                    rightNode.insert( insertValue );
40          } // end else if
41       } // end method insert
42   } // end class TreeNode
43
44   // class Tree definition
45   public class Tree< T extends Comparable< T > >
46   {
47       private TreeNode< T > root;
48
49       // constructor initializes an empty Tree of integers
50       public Tree()
51       {
52           root = null;
53       } // end Tree no-argument constructor
54
55       // insert a new node in the binary search tree
56       public void insertNode( T insertValue )
57       {
58           if ( root == null )
59               root = new TreeNode< T >( insertValue ); // create root node
60           else
61               root.insert( insertValue ); // call the insert method
62       } // end method insertNode
63
64       // begin preorder traversal
65       public void preorderTraversal()
66       {
67           preorderHelper( root );
68       } // end method preorderTraversal
69
70       // recursive method to perform preorder traversal
71       private void preorderHelper( TreeNode< T > node )
72       {
73           if ( node == null )
74               return;
75
76           System.out.printf( "%s ", node.data ); // output node data
77           preorderHelper( node.leftNode );      // traverse left subtree
78           preorderHelper( node.rightNode );     // traverse right subtree
79       } // end method preorderHelper
80
81       // begin inorder traversal
82       public void inorderTraversal()
83       {
84           inorderHelper( root );
85       } // end method inorderTraversal
86
87       // recursive method to perform inorder traversal
88       private void inorderHelper( TreeNode< T > node )
89       {
90           if ( node == null )
91               return;
```

Fig. 22.17 | TreeNode and Tree class declarations for a binary search tree. (Part 2 of 3.)

```
92
93        inorderHelper( node.leftNode );        // traverse left subtree
94        System.out.printf( "%s ", node.data ); // output node data
95        inorderHelper( node.rightNode );       // traverse right subtree
96     } // end method inorderHelper
97
98     // begin postorder traversal
99     public void postorderTraversal()
100    {
101       postorderHelper( root );
102    } // end method postorderTraversal
103
104    // recursive method to perform postorder traversal
105    private void postorderHelper( TreeNode< T > node )
106    {
107       if ( node == null )
108          return;
109
110       postorderHelper( node.leftNode );        // traverse left subtree
111       postorderHelper( node.rightNode );       // traverse right subtree
112       System.out.printf( "%s ", node.data ); // output node data
113    } // end method postorderHelper
114 } // end class Tree
```

Fig. 22.17 | TreeNode and Tree class declarations for a binary search tree. (Part 3 of 3.)

```
1   // Fig. 22.18: TreeTest.java
2   // Binary tree test program.
3   import java.util.Random;
4   import com.deitel.ch22.Tree;
5
6   public class TreeTest
7   {
8      public static void main( String[] args )
9      {
10        Tree< Integer > tree = new Tree< Integer >();
11        int value;
12        Random randomNumber = new Random();
13
14        System.out.println( "Inserting the following values: " );
15
16        // insert 10 random integers from 0-99 in tree
17        for ( int i = 1; i <= 10; i++ )
18        {
19           value = randomNumber.nextInt( 100 );
20           System.out.printf( "%d ", value );
21           tree.insertNode( value );
22        } // end for
23
24        System.out.println ( "\n\nPreorder traversal" );
25        tree.preorderTraversal(); // perform preorder traversal of tree
26
27        System.out.println ( "\n\nInorder traversal" );
```

Fig. 22.18 | Binary tree test program. (Part 1 of 2.)

```
28          tree.inorderTraversal(); // perform inorder traversal of tree
29
30          System.out.println ( "\n\nPostorder traversal" );
31          tree.postorderTraversal(); // perform postorder traversal of tree
32          System.out.println();
33       } // end main
34    } // end class TreeTest
```

```
Inserting the following values:
49 64 14 34 85 64 46 14 37 55

Preorder traversal
49 14 34 46 37 64 55 85

Inorder traversal
14 34 37 46 49 55 64 85

Postorder traversal
37 46 34 14 55 85 64 49
```

Fig. 22.18 | Binary tree test program. (Part 2 of 2.)

Let's walk through the binary tree program. Method `main` of class `TreeTest` (Fig. 22.18) begins by instantiating an empty `Tree<T>` object and assigning its reference to variable `tree` (line 10). Lines 17–22 randomly generate 10 integers, each of which is inserted into the binary tree by calling method `insertNode` (line 21). The program then performs preorder, inorder and postorder traversals (these will be explained shortly) of `tree` (lines 25, 28 and 31, respectively).

Overview of Class *Tree*

Class `Tree` (Fig. 22.17, lines 45–114) requires its type argument to implement interface `Comparable`, so that each value inserted in the tree can be compared with the existing values to determine the insertion point. The class has `private` field `root` (line 47)—a `TreeNode` reference to the root node of the tree. Tree's constructor (lines 50–53) initializes `root` to `null` to indicate that the tree is empty. The class contains method `insertNode` (lines 56–62) to insert a new node in the tree and methods `preorderTraversal` (lines 65–68), `inorderTraversal` (lines 82–85) and `postorderTraversal` (lines 99–102) to begin traversals of the tree. Each of these methods calls a recursive utility method to perform the traversal operations on the internal representation of the tree. (We discussed recursion in Chapter 18.)

Tree *Method* insertNode

Class `Tree`'s method `insertNode` (lines 56–62) first determines whether the tree is empty. If so, line 59 allocates a new `TreeNode`, initializes the node with the value being inserted in the tree and assigns the new node to reference `root`. If the tree is not empty, line 61 calls `TreeNode` method `insert` (lines 21–41). This method uses recursion to determine the location for the new node in the tree and inserts the node at that location. A node can be inserted only as a leaf node in a binary search tree.

TreeNode *Method* insert

`TreeNode` method `insert` compares the value to insert with the `data` value in the root node. If the insert value is less than the root node data (line 24), the program determines if the left subtree is empty (line 27). If so, line 28 allocates a new TreeNode, initializes it with the value being inserted and assigns the new node to reference leftNode. Otherwise, line 30 recursively calls insert for the left subtree to insert the value into the left subtree. If the insert value is greater than the root node data (line 33), the program determines if the right subtree is empty (line 36). If so, line 37 allocates a new TreeNode, initializes it with the value being inserted and assigns the new node to reference rightNode. Otherwise, line 39 recursively calls insert for the right subtree to insert the value in the right subtree. If the insertValue is already in the tree, it's simply ignored.

Tree Methods **inorderTraversal,** **preorderTraversal** *and* **postorderTraversal**
Methods inorderTraversal, preorderTraversal and postorderTraversal call Tree helper methods inorderHelper (lines 88–96), preorderHelper (lines 71–79) and postorderHelper (lines 105–113), respectively, to traverse the tree and print the node values. The helper methods in class Tree enable you to start a traversal without having to pass the root node to the method. Reference root is an implementation detail that a programmer should not be able to access. Methods inorderTraversal, preorderTraversal and postorderTraversal simply take the private root reference and pass it to the appropriate helper method to initiate a traversal of the tree. The base case for each helper method determines whether the reference it receives is null and, if so, returns immediately.

Method inorderHelper (lines 88–96) defines the steps for an inorder traversal:

1. Traverse the left subtree with a call to inorderHelper (line 93).

2. Process the value in the node (line 94).

3. Traverse the right subtree with a call to inorderHelper (line 95).

The inorder traversal does not process the value in a node until the values in that node's left subtree are processed. The inorder traversal of the tree in Fig. 22.19 is

```
6 13 17 27 33 42 48
```

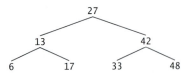

Fig. 22.19 | Binary search tree with seven values.

Note that the inorder traversal of a binary search tree prints the node values in ascending order. The process of creating a binary search tree actually sorts the data; thus, it's called the **binary tree sort.**

Method preorderHelper (lines 71–79) defines the steps for a preorder traversal:

1. Process the value in the node (line 76).

2. Traverse the left subtree with a call to preorderHelper (line 77).

3. Traverse the right subtree with a call to preorderHelper (line 78).

The preorder traversal processes the value in each node as the node is visited. After processing the value in a particular node, the preorder traversal processes the values in the left subtree, then processes the values in the right subtree. The preorder traversal of the tree in Fig. 22.19 is

```
27 13 6 17 42 33 48
```

Method `postorderHelper` (lines 105–113) defines the steps for a postorder traversal:

1. Traverse the left subtree with a call to `postorderHelper` (line 110).

2. Traverse the right subtree with a call to `postorderHelper` (line 111).

3. Process the value in the node (line 112).

The postorder traversal processes the value in each node after the values of all that node's children are processed. The `postorderTraversal` of the tree in Fig. 22.19 is

```
6 17 13 33 48 42 27
```

The binary search tree facilitates **duplicate elimination**. While building a tree, the insertion operation recognizes attempts to insert a duplicate value, because a duplicate follows the same "go left" or "go right" decisions on each comparison as the original value did. Thus, the insertion operation eventually compares the duplicate with a node containing the same value. At this point, the insertion operation can decide to discard the duplicate value (as we do in this example).

Searching a binary tree for a value that matches a key value is fast, especially for **tightly packed (or balanced) trees**. In a tightly packed tree, each level contains about twice as many elements as the previous level. Figure 22.19 is a tightly packed binary tree. A tightly packed binary search tree with n elements has $\log_2 n$ levels. Thus, at most $\log_2 n$ comparisons are required either to find a match or to determine that no match exists. Searching a (tightly packed) 1000-element binary search tree requires at most 10 comparisons, because $2^{10} > 1000$. Searching a (tightly packed) 1,000,000-element binary search tree requires at most 20 comparisons, because $2^{20} > 1,000,000$.

The chapter exercises present algorithms for several other binary tree operations, such as deleting an item from a binary tree, printing a binary tree in a two-dimensional tree format and performing a **level-order traversal of a binary tree**. The level-order traversal visits the nodes of the tree row by row, starting at the root node level. On each level of the tree, a level-order traversal visits the nodes from left to right. Other binary tree exercises include allowing a binary search tree to contain duplicate values, inserting string values in a binary tree and determining how many levels are contained in a binary tree.

22.8 Wrap-Up

This chapter completes our presentation of data structures. We began in Chapter 20 with an introduction to the built-in collections of the Java Collections Framework and continued in Chapter 21 by showing you how to implement generic methods and collections. In this chapter, you learned to build generic dynamic data structures that grow and shrink at execution time. You learned that linked lists are collections of data items that are "linked up in a chain." You also saw that an application can perform insertions and deletions at the beginning and end of a linked list. You learned that the stack and queue data structures are constrained versions of lists. For stacks, you saw that insertions and deletions are made only at the top. For queues that represent waiting lines, you saw that insertions are made at the tail and deletions are made from the head. You also learned the binary tree data structure. You saw a binary search tree that facilitated high-speed searching and sorting of data and eliminating duplicate data items efficiently. Throughout the chapter, you learned how to create and package these data structures for reusability and maintainability.

Next, we introduce Java applets—Java programs that typically execute in a browser. We overview the JDK's sample applets, then show you how to write and execute your own applets. We then introduce the Java Web Start capabilities for launching an applet and installing a desktop shortcut to relaunch the applet in the future without having to revisit the applet's website.

Summary

Section 22.1 Introduction
- Dynamic data structures can grow and shrink at execution time.
- Linked lists are collections of data items "linked up in a chain"—insertions and deletions can be made anywhere in a linked list.
- Stacks are important in compilers and operating systems—insertions and deletions are made only at the top of a stack.
- In a queue, insertions are made at the tail and deletions are made from the head.
- Binary trees facilitate high-speed searching and sorting of data, eliminating duplicate data items efficiently, representing file-system directories and compiling expressions into machine language.

Section 22.2 Self-Referential Classes
- A self-referential class contains a reference that refers to another object of the same class type. Self-referential objects can be linked together to form dynamic data structures.

Section 22.3 Dynamic Memory Allocation
- The limit for dynamic memory allocation can be as large as the available physical memory in the computer or the available disk space in a virtual-memory system. Often the limits are much smaller, because the computer's available memory must be shared among many users.
- If no memory is available, an `OutOfMemoryError` is thrown.

Section 22.4 Linked Lists
- A linked list is accessed via a reference to the first node of the list. Each subsequent node is accessed via the link-reference member stored in the previous node.
- By convention, the link reference in the last node of a list is set to `null` to mark the end of the list.
- A node can contain data of any type, including objects of other classes.
- A linked list is appropriate when the number of data elements to be stored is unpredictable. Linked lists are dynamic, so the length of a list can increase or decrease as necessary.
- The size of a "conventional" Java array cannot be altered—it's fixed at creation time.
- List nodes normally are not stored in contiguous memory. Rather, they're logically contiguous.

Section 22.5 Stacks
- A stack is a last-in, first-out (LIFO) data structure. The primary methods used to manipulate a stack are `push` and `pop`, which add a new node to the top of the stack and remove a node from the top of the stack, respectively. Method `pop` returns the removed node's data.
- When a method call is made, the called method must know how to return to its caller, so the return address is pushed onto the program-execution stack. If a series of method calls occurs, the successive return values are pushed onto the stack in last-in, first-out order so that each method can return to its caller.

- The program-execution stack contains the space created for local variables on each invocation of a method. When the method returns to its caller, the space for that method's local variables is popped off the stack, and those variables are no longer available to the program.

- Stacks are used by compilers to evaluate arithmetic expressions and generate machine-language code to process the expressions.

- The technique of implementing each stack method as a call to a `List` method is called delegation—the stack method invoked delegates the call to the appropriate `List` method.

Section 22.6 Queues

- A queue is similar to a checkout line in a supermarket—the first person in line is serviced first, and other customers enter the line only at the end and wait to be serviced.

- Queue nodes are removed only from the head of the queue and are inserted only at the tail. For this reason, a queue is referred to as a first-in, first-out (FIFO) data structure.

- The insert and remove operations for a queue are known as enqueue and dequeue.

- Queues have many uses in computer systems. Most computers have only a single processor, so only one application at a time can be serviced. Entries for the other applications are placed in a queue. The entry at the front of the queue is the next to receive service. Each entry gradually advances to the front of the queue as applications receive service.

Section 22.7 Trees

- A tree is a nonlinear, two-dimensional data structure. Tree nodes contain two or more links.

- A binary tree is a tree whose nodes all contain two links. The root node is the first node in a tree.

- Each link in the root node refers to a child. The left child is the first node in the left subtree, and the right child is the first node in the right subtree.

- The children of a node are called siblings. A node with no children is called a leaf node.

- In a binary search tree with no duplicate values, the values in any left subtree are less than the value in the subtree's parent node, and the values in any right subtree are greater than the value in the subtree's parent node. A node can be inserted only as a leaf node in a binary search tree.

- An inorder traversal of a binary search tree processes the node values in ascending order.

- In a preorder traversal, the value in each node is processed as the node is visited. Then the values in the left subtree are processed, then the values in the right subtree.

- In a postorder traversal, the value in each node is processed after the values of its children.

- The binary search tree facilitates duplicate elimination. As the tree is created, attempts to insert a duplicate value are recognized, because a duplicate follows the same "go left" or "go right" decisions on each comparison as the original value did. Thus, the duplicate eventually is compared with a node containing the same value. The duplicate value can be discarded at this point.

- In a tightly packed tree, each level contains about twice as many elements as the previous one. So a tightly packed binary search tree with n elements has $\log_2 n$ levels, and thus at most $\log_2 n$ comparisons would have to be made either to find a match or to determine that no match exists. Searching a (tightly packed) 1000-element binary search tree requires at most 10 comparisons, because $2^{10} > 1000$. Searching a (tightly packed) 1,000,000-element binary search tree requires at most 20 comparisons, because $2^{20} > 1,000,000$.

Terminology

Self-Review Exercises

22.1   Fill in the blanks in each of the following statements:

a) A self-_____ class is used to form dynamic data structures that can grow and shrink at execution time.

b) A(n) _____ is a constrained version of a linked list in which nodes can be inserted and deleted only from the start of the list.

c) A method that does not alter a linked list, but simply looks at it to determine whether it's empty, is referred to as a(n) _____ method.

d) A queue is referred to as a(n) _____ data structure because the first nodes inserted are the first ones removed.

e) The reference to the next node in a linked list is referred to as a(n) _____.

f) Automatically reclaiming dynamically allocated memory in Java is called _____.

g) A(n) _____ is a constrained version of a linked list in which nodes can be inserted only at the end of the list and deleted only from the start of the list.

h) A(n) _____ is a nonlinear, two-dimensional data structure that contains nodes with two or more links.

i) A stack is referred to as a(n) _____ data structure because the last node inserted is the first node removed.

j) The nodes of a(n) _____ tree contain two link members.

k) The first node of a tree is the _____ node.

l) Each link in a tree node refers to a(n) _____ or _____ of that node.

m) A tree node that has no children is called a(n) _____ node.

n) The three traversal algorithms we mentioned in the text for binary search trees are _____, _____ and _____.

22.2   What are the differences between a linked list and a stack?

22.3   What are the differences between a stack and a queue?

22.4   Perhaps a more appropriate title for this chapter would have been Reusable Data Structures. Comment on how each of the following entities or concepts contributes to the reusability of data structures:

a) classes

b) inheritance

c) composition

22.5 Manually provide the inorder, preorder and postorder traversals of the binary search tree of Fig. 22.20.

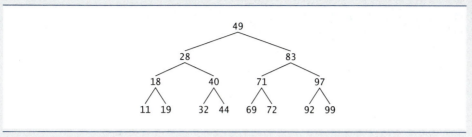

Fig. 22.20 | Binary search tree with 15 nodes.

Answers to Self-Review Exercises

22.1 a) referential. b) stack. c) predicate. d) first-in, first-out (FIFO). e) link. f) garbage collection. g) queue. h) tree i) last-in, first-out (LIFO). j) binary. k) root. l) child or subtree. m) leaf. n) inorder, preorder, postorder.

22.2 It's possible to insert a node anywhere in a linked list and remove a node from anywhere in a linked list. Nodes in a stack may be inserted only at the top of the stack and removed only from the top.

22.3 A queue is a FIFO data structure that has references to both its head and its tail, so that nodes may be inserted at the tail and deleted from the head. A stack is a LIFO data structure that has a single reference to the stack's top, where both insertion and deletion of nodes are performed.

22.4 a) Classes allow us to instantiate as many data structure objects of a certain type (i.e., class) as we wish.
   b) Inheritance enables a subclass to reuse the functionality from a superclass. Public and protected methods of a superclass can be accessed through a subclass to eliminate duplicate logic.
   c) Composition enables a class to reuse code by storing a reference to an instance of another class in a field. Public methods of the instance can be called by methods in the class that contains the reference.

22.5 The inorder traversal is

    11 18 19 28 32 40 44 49 69 71 72 83 92 97 99

The preorder traversal is

    49 28 18 11 19 40 32 44 83 71 69 72 97 92 99

The postorder traversal is

    11 19 18 32 44 40 28 69 72 71 92 99 97 83 49

Exercises

22.6 *(Concatenating Lists)* Write a program that concatenates two linked list objects of characters. Class `ListConcatenate` should include a `static` method `concatenate` that takes references to both list objects as arguments and concatenates the second list to the first list.

22.7 *(Inserting into an Ordered List)* Write a program that inserts 25 random integers from 0 to 100 in order into a linked-list object. For this exercise, you'll need to modify the `List<T>` class (Fig. 22.3) to maintain an ordered list. Name the new version of the class `SortedList`.

22.8 *(Merging Ordered Lists)* Modify the SortedList class from Exercise 22.7 to include a merge method that can merge the SortedList it receives as an argument with the SortedList that calls the method. Write an application to test method merge.

22.9 *(Copying a List Backwards)* Write a static method reverseCopy that receives a List<T> as an argument and returns a copy of that List<T> with its elements reversed. Test this method in an application.

22.10 *(Printing a Sentence in Reverse Using a Stack)* Write a program that inputs a line of text and uses a stack to display the words of the line in reverse order.

22.11 *(Palindrome Tester)* Write a program that uses a stack to determine whether a string is a palindrome (i.e., the string is spelled identically backward and forward). The program should ignore spaces and punctuation.

22.12 *(Infix-to-Postfix Converter)* Stacks are used by compilers to help in the process of evaluating expressions and generating machine-language code. In this and the next exercise, we investigate how compilers evaluate arithmetic expressions consisting only of constants, operators and parentheses.

Humans generally write expressions like 3 + 4 and 7 / 9 in which the operator (+ or / here) is written between its operands—this is called *infix notation*. Computers "prefer" *postfix notation*, in which the operator is written to the right of its two operands. The preceding infix expressions would appear in postfix notation as 3 4 + and 7 9 /, respectively.

To evaluate a complex infix expression, a compiler would first convert the expression to postfix notation and evaluate the postfix version. Each of these algorithms requires only a single left-to-right pass of the expression. Each algorithm uses a stack object in support of its operation, but each uses the stack for a different purpose.

In this exercise, you'll write a Java version of the infix-to-postfix conversion algorithm. In the next exercise, you'll write a Java version of the postfix expression evaluation algorithm. In a later exercise, you'll discover that code you write in this exercise can help you implement a complete working compiler.

Write class InfixToPostfixConverter to convert an ordinary infix arithmetic expression (assume a valid expression is entered) with single-digit integers such as

```
(6 + 2) * 5 - 8 / 4
```

to a postfix expression. The postfix version of the preceding infix expression is (note that no parentheses are needed)

```
6 2 + 5 * 8 4 / -
```

The program should read the expression into StringBuffer infix and use one of the stack classes implemented in this chapter to help create the postfix expression in StringBuffer postfix. The algorithm for creating a postfix expression is as follows:

    a) Push a left parenthesis '(' on the stack.
    b) Append a right parenthesis ')' to the end of infix.
    c) While the stack is not empty, read infix from left to right and do the following:
        If the current character in infix is a digit, append it to postfix.
        If the current character in infix is a left parenthesis, push it onto the stack.
        If the current character in infix is an operator:
            Pop operators (if there are any) at the top of the stack while they have equal or higher precedence than the current operator, and append the popped operators to postfix.
        Push the current character in infix onto the stack.
        If the current character in infix is a right parenthesis:
            Pop operators from the top of the stack and append them to postfix until a left parenthesis is at the top of the stack.
        Pop (and discard) the left parenthesis from the stack.

The following arithmetic operations are allowed in an expression:

+ addition
- subtraction
* multiplication
/ division
^ exponentiation
% remainder

The stack should be maintained with stack nodes that each contain an instance variable and a reference to the next stack node. Some of the methods you may want to provide are as follows:

a) Method `convertToPostfix`, which converts the infix expression to postfix notation.

b) Method `isOperator`, which determines whether c is an operator.

c) Method `precedence`, which determines whether the precedence of `operator1` (from the infix expression) is less than, equal to or greater than that of `operator2` (from the stack). The method returns `true` if `operator1` has lower precedence than `operator2`. Otherwise, `false` is returned.

d) Method `peek` (this should be added to the stack class), which returns the top value of the stack without popping the stack.

22.13 *(Postfix Evaluator)* Write class `PostfixEvaluator` that evaluates a postfix expression such as

```
6 2 + 5 * 8 4 / -
```

The program should read a postfix expression consisting of digits and operators into a `StringBuffer`. Using modified versions of the stack methods implemented earlier in this chapter, the program should scan the expression and evaluate it (assume it's valid). The algorithm is as follows:

a) Append a right parenthesis `')'` to the end of the postfix expression. When the right-parenthesis character is encountered, no further processing is necessary.

b) When the right-parenthesis character has not been encountered, read the expression from left to right.

   If the current character is a digit, do the following:

   Push its integer value on the stack (the integer value of a digit character is its value in the Unicode character set minus the value of `'0'` in Unicode).

   Otherwise, if the current character is an *operator*:

   Pop the two top elements of the stack into variables x and y.

   Calculate y *operator* x.

   Push the result of the calculation onto the stack.

c) When the right parenthesis is encountered in the expression, pop the top value of the stack. This is the result of the postfix expression.

[*Note:* In b) above (based on the sample expression at the beginning of this exercise), if the operator is `'/'`, the top of the stack is 4 and the next element in the stack is 40, then pop 4 into x, pop 40 into y, evaluate 40 / 4 and push the result, 10, back on the stack. This note also applies to operator `'-'`.] The arithmetic operations allowed in an expression are:

+ addition
- subtraction
* multiplication
/ division
^ exponentiation
% remainder

The stack should be maintained with one of the stack classes introduced in this chapter. You may want to provide the following methods:

a) Method `evaluatePostfixExpression`, which evaluates the postfix expression.

b) Method `calculate`, which evaluates the expression op1 operator op2.

22.14 *(Postfix Evaluator Modification)* Modify the postfix evaluator program of Exercise 22.13 so that it can process integer operands larger than 9.

22.15 *(Supermarket Simulation)* Write a program that simulates a checkout line at a supermarket. The line is a queue object. Customers (i.e., customer objects) arrive in random integer intervals of from 1 to 4 minutes. Also, each customer is serviced in random integer intervals of from 1 to 4 minutes. Obviously, the rates need to be balanced. If the average arrival rate is larger than the average service rate, the queue will grow infinitely. Even with "balanced" rates, randomness can still cause long lines. Run the supermarket simulation for a 12-hour day (720 minutes), using the following algorithm:

    a) Choose a random integer between 1 and 4 to determine the minute at which the first customer arrives.

    b) At the first customer's arrival time, do the following:
       Determine customer's service time (random integer from 1 to 4).
       Begin servicing the customer.
       Schedule arrival time of next customer (random integer 1 to 4 added to the current time).

    c) For each simulated minute of the day, consider the following:
       If the next customer arrives, proceed as follows:
         Say so.
         Enqueue the customer.
         Schedule the arrival time of the next customer.
       If service was completed for the last customer, do the following:
         Say so.
         Dequeue next customer to be serviced.
         Determine customer's service completion time (random integer from 1 to 4 added to the current time).

Now run your simulation for 720 minutes and answer each of the following:

    a) What is the maximum number of customers in the queue at any time?

    b) What is the longest wait any one customer experiences?

    c) What happens if the arrival interval is changed from 1 to 4 minutes to 1 to 3 minutes?

22.16 *(Allowing Duplicates in a Binary Tree)* Modify Figs. 22.17 and 22.18 to allow the binary tree to contain duplicates.

22.17 *(Processing a Binary Search Tree of Strings)* Write a program based on the program of Figs. 22.17 and 22.18 that inputs a line of text, tokenizes the sentence into separate words, inserts the words in a binary search tree and prints the inorder, preorder and postorder traversals of the tree.

22.18 *(Duplicate Elimination)* In this chapter, we saw that duplicate elimination is straightforward when creating a binary search tree. Describe how you'd perform duplicate elimination when using only a one-dimensional array. Compare the performance of array-based duplicate elimination with the performance of binary-search-tree-based duplicate elimination.

22.19 *(Depth of a Binary Tree)* Modify Figs. 22.17 and 22.18 so the Tree class provides a method getDepth that determines how many levels are in the tree. Test the method in an application that inserts 20 random integers in a Tree.

22.20 *(Recursively Print a List Backward)* Modify the List<T> class of Fig. 22.3 to include method printListBackward that recursively outputs the items in a linked-list object in reverse order. Write a test program that creates a list of integers and prints the list in reverse order.

22.21 *(Recursively Search a List)* Modify the List<T> class of Fig. 22.3 to include method search that recursively searches a linked-list object for a specified value. The method should return a reference to the value if it's found; otherwise, it should return null. Use your method in a test program that creates a list of integers. The program should prompt the user for a value to locate in the list.

22.22 *(Binary Tree Delete)* In this exercise, we discuss deleting items from binary search trees. The deletion algorithm is not as straightforward as the insertion algorithm. Three cases are encountered when deleting an item—the item is contained in a leaf node (i.e., it has no children), or in a node that has one child or in a node that has two children.

If the item to be deleted is contained in a leaf node, the node is deleted and the reference in the parent node is set to null.

If the item to be deleted is contained in a node with one child, the reference in the parent node is set to reference the child node and the node containing the data item is deleted. This causes the child node to take the place of the deleted node in the tree.

The last case is the most difficult. When a node with two children is deleted, another node in the tree must take its place. However, the reference in the parent node cannot simply be assigned to reference one of the children of the node to be deleted. In most cases, the resulting binary search tree would not embody the following characteristic of binary search trees (with no duplicate values): *The values in any left subtree are less than the value in the parent node, and the values in any right subtree are greater than the value in the parent node.*

Which node is used as a *replacement node* to maintain this characteristic? It's either the node containing the largest value in the tree less than the value in the node being deleted, or the node containing the smallest value in the tree greater than the value in the node being deleted. Let's consider the node with the smaller value. In a binary search tree, the largest value less than a parent's value is located in the left subtree of the parent node and is guaranteed to be contained in the rightmost node of the subtree. This node is located by walking down the left subtree to the right until the reference to the right child of the current node is null. We are now referencing the replacement node, which is either a leaf node or a node with one child to its left. If the replacement node is a leaf node, the steps to perform the deletion are as follows:

a) Store the reference to the node to be deleted in a temporary reference variable.
b) Set the reference in the parent of the node being deleted to reference the replacement node.
c) Set the reference in the parent of the replacement node to null.
d) Set the reference to the right subtree in the replacement node to reference the right subtree of the node to be deleted.
e) Set the reference to the left subtree in the replacement node to reference the left subtree of the node to be deleted.

The deletion steps for a replacement node with a left child are similar to those for a replacement node with no children, but the algorithm also must move the child into the replacement node's position in the tree. If the replacement node is a node with a left child, the steps to perform the deletion are as follows:

a) Store the reference to the node to be deleted in a temporary reference variable.
b) Set the reference in the parent of the node being deleted to reference the replacement node.
c) Set the reference in the parent of the replacement node to reference the left child of the replacement node.
d) Set the reference to the right subtree in the replacement node to reference the right subtree of the node to be deleted.
e) Set the reference to the left subtree in the replacement node to reference the left subtree of the node to be deleted.

Write method deleteNode, which takes as its argument the value to delete. Method delete-Node should locate in the tree the node containing the value to delete and use the algorithms discussed here to delete the node. If the value is not found in the tree, the method should display a message saying so. Modify the program of Figs. 22.17 and 22.18 to use this method. After deleting an item, call the methods inorderTraversal, preorderTraversal and postorderTraversal to confirm that the delete operation was performed correctly.

22.23 (*Binary Tree Search*) Modify class Tree of Fig. 22.17 to include method contains, which attempts to locate a specified value in a binary-search-tree object. The method should take as an argument a search key to locate. If the node containing the search key is found, the method should return a reference to that node's data; otherwise, it should return `null`.

22.24 (*Level-Order Binary Tree Traversal*) The program of Figs. 22.17 and 22.18 illustrated three recursive methods of traversing a binary tree—inorder, preorder and postorder traversals. This exercise presents the *level-order traversal* of a binary tree, in which the node values are printed level by level, starting at the root node level. The nodes on each level are printed from left to right. The level-order traversal is not a recursive algorithm. It uses a queue object to control the output of the nodes. The algorithm is as follows:

    a) Insert the root node in the queue.
    b) While there are nodes left in the queue, do the following:
        Get the next node in the queue.
        Print the node's value.
        If the reference to the left child of the node is not null:
            Insert the left child node in the queue.
        If the reference to the right child of the node is not null:
            Insert the right child node in the queue.

    Write method `levelOrder` to perform a level-order traversal of a binary tree object. Modify the program of Figs. 22.17 and 22.18 to use this method. [*Note:* You'll also need to use the queue-processing methods of Fig. 22.13 in this program.]

22.25 (*Printing Trees*) Modify class `Tree` of Fig. 22.17 to include a recursive `outputTree` method to display a binary tree object. The method should output the tree row by row, with the top of the tree at the left of the screen and the bottom of the tree toward the right. Each row is output vertically. For example, the binary tree illustrated in Fig. 22.20 is output as shown in Fig. 22.21.

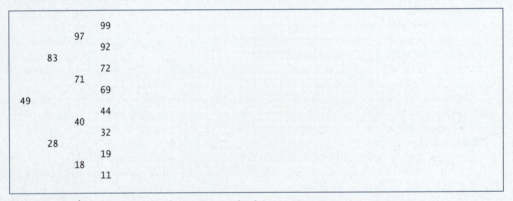

Fig. 22.21 | Sample output of recursive method `outputTree`.

    The rightmost leaf node appears at the top of the output in the rightmost column and the root node appears at the left of the output. Each column starts five spaces to the right of the preceding column. Method `outputTree` should receive an argument `totalSpaces` representing the number of spaces preceding the value to be output. (This variable should start at zero so that the root node is output at the left of the screen.) The method uses a modified inorder traversal to output the tree—it starts at the rightmost node in the tree and works back to the left. The algorithm is as follows:

    While the reference to the current node is not null, perform the following:
        Recursively call `outputTree` with the right subtree of the current node and
            `totalSpaces + 5`.
        Use a `for` statement to count from 1 to `totalSpaces` and output spaces.
        Output the value in the current node.
        Set the reference to the current node to refer to the left subtree of the current node.
        Increment `totalSpaces` by 5.

22.26 *(Insert/Delete Anywhere in a Linked List)* Our linked list class allowed insertions and deletions at only the front and the back of the linked list. These capabilities were convenient for us when we used inheritance or composition to produce a stack class and a queue class with a minimal amount of code simply by reusing the list class. Linked lists are normally more general than those we provided. Modify the linked list class we developed in this chapter to handle insertions and deletions anywhere in the list.

22.27 *(Lists and Queues without Tail References)* Our implementation of a linked list (Fig. 22.3) used both a firstNode and a lastNode. The lastNode was useful for the insertAtBack and remove-FromBack methods of the List class. The insertAtBack method corresponds to the enqueue method of the Queue class.

Rewrite the List class so that it does not use a lastNode. Thus, any operations on the tail of a list must begin searching the list from the front. Does this affect our implementation of the Queue class (Fig. 22.13)?

22.28 *(Performance of Binary Tree Sorting and Searching)* One problem with the binary tree sort is that the order in which the data is inserted affects the shape of the tree—for the same collection of data, different orderings can yield binary trees of dramatically different shapes. The performance of the binary tree sorting and searching algorithms is sensitive to the shape of the binary tree. What shape would a binary tree have if its data were inserted in increasing order? in decreasing order? What shape should the tree have to achieve maximal searching performance?

22.29 *(Indexed Lists)* As presented in the text, linked lists must be searched sequentially. For large lists, this can result in poor performance. A common technique for improving list-searching performance is to create and maintain an index to the list. An index is a set of references to key places in the list. For example, an application that searches a large list of names could improve performance by creating an index with 26 entries—one for each letter of the alphabet. A search operation for a last name beginning with 'Y' would then first search the index to determine where the 'Y' entries began, then "jump into" the list at that point and search linearly until the desired name was found. This would be much faster than searching the linked list from the beginning. Use the List class of Fig. 22.3 as the basis of an IndexedList class.

Write a program that demonstrates the operation of indexed lists. Be sure to include methods insertInIndexedList, searchIndexedList and deleteFromIndexedList.

22.30 *(Queue Class that Inherits from a List class)* In Section 22.5, we created a stack class from class List with inheritance (Fig. 22.10) and with composition (Fig. 22.12). In Section 22.6 we created a queue class from class List with composition (Fig. 22.13). Create a queue class by inheriting from class List. What are the differences between this class and the one we created with composition?

Special Section: Building Your Own Compiler

In Exercises 6.30–6.32, we introduced Simpletron Machine Language (SML), and you implemented a Simpletron computer simulator to execute SML programs. In Exercises 22.31–22.35, we build a compiler that converts programs written in a high-level programming language to SML. This section "ties" together the entire programming process. You'll write programs in this new high-level language, compile them on the compiler you build and run them on the simulator you built in Exercise 6.31. You should make every effort to implement your compiler in an object-oriented manner. [*Note:* Due to the size of the descriptions for Exercises 22.31–22.35, we've posted them in a PDF document located at www.deitel.com/books/jhtp8LOV/.]

23

Applets and Java Web Start

Observe due measure, for right timing is in all things the most important factor.
—Hesiod

Painting is only a bridge linking the painter's mind with that of the viewer.
—Eugene Delacroix

The direction in which education starts a man will determine his future in life.
—Plato

Objectives

In this chapter you'll learn:

- What applets are and how they're used in web pages.

- To observe some of Java's exciting capabilities via the JDK's demonstration applets.

- To write simple applets.

- To write a simple XHTML document to load an applet into an applet container and execute the applet.

- Five methods that are called by an applet container during an applet's life cycle.

- What the sandbox security model is and how it enables you to run downloaded code safely.

- What Java Web Start is and how to use it to download, install and run applets outside of the web browser.

23.1 Introduction

[*Note:* This chapter is intentionally small and simple for readers who wish to study applets after reading only the book's first few chapters. We present more complex applets in Chapter 24, Multimedia: Applets and Applications, and Chapter 27, Networking. Also, the examples in this chapter require some knowledge of XHTML to create a web page that loads an applet. With each example we supply sample XHTML documents that you can modify for your own purposes. To learn more about XHTML, visit the **XMTML Tutorials** link in our XHTML Resource Center (`www.deitel.com/xhtml/`).]

This chapter introduces **applets**—Java programs that are typically embedded in **XHTML (Extensible HyperText Markup Language) documents**—also called web pages. When a Java-enabled web browser loads a web page containing an applet, the applet downloads into the browser and executes.

Applet Containers

The application in which an applet executes is known as the **applet container.** It is the applet container's responsibility to load the applet's class(es), create an instance of the applet and manage its life cycle (which we discuss in more detail in Section 23.4). The Java Development Kit (JDK) includes one called the **appletviewer** for testing applets as you develop them and before you embed them in web pages. We demonstrate applets using both the appletviewer and web browsers, which execute Java applets via the **Java Plug-In.** Some browsers don't come with the plug-in by default. You can visit java.com to determine whether your browser is ready to execute Java applets. If not, you can click the **Free Java Download** button to install Java for your browser. Several popular browsers are supported. We tested our applets in Mozilla's Firefox 3, Microsoft's Internet Explorer 7, Google's Chrome, Opera 9 and Apple's Safari 3.

Java Web Start and the Java Network Launch Protocol (JNLP)

This chapter concludes with an introduction to Java Web Start and the Java Network Launch Protocol (JNLP). Together, these enable you to package your applets and applications so that they can be installed onto the user's desktop. As you'll learn in Chapter 24, Java Web Start also enables you to give the user control over whether an applet or application downloaded from the web can have limited access to resources on the local file system. For example, if you create a downloadable text-editor program in Java, users would probably want to store their documents on their own computers.

23.2 Sample Applets Provided with the JDK

Before we discuss our own applets, let's consider several demonstration applets provided with the JDK. Each sample applet comes with its source code. Some programmers find it interesting to read this source code to learn exciting Java features.

The demonstration programs provided with the JDK are located in a directory called demo. For Windows, the default location of the JDK 6.0's demo directory is

```
C:\Program Files\Java\jdk1.6.0_##\demo
```

where _## represents the JDK update number. On UNIX/Linux, the default location is the directory in which you install the JDK followed by jdk1.6.0_##/demo—for example,

```
/usr/local/jdk1.6.0_##/demo
```

For other platforms, there will be a similar directory (or folder) structure. This chapter assumes that the JDK is installed in C:\Program Files\Java\jdk1.6.0_11 on Windows or in your home directory in ~/jdk1.6.0_11 on UNIX/Linux. You may need to update the locations specified here to reflect your chosen installation directory and disk drive, or a different version of the JDK.

If you are using a Java development tool that does not come with the Sun Java demos, you can download the current JDK from java.sun.com/javase/downloads/index.jsp. Mac OS X users should visit developer.apple.com/java for information about Java on the Mac, or use virtualization software to run the Windows or Linux versions of Java in a virtual machine.

Overview of the Demonstration Applets

Open a command window and use the cd command to change directories to the JDK's demo directory. The demo directory contains several subdirectories. You can list them by issuing the dir command on Windows or the ls command on UNIX/Linux/Max OS X. We discuss sample programs in the applets and jfc subdirectories. The applets directory contains demonstration applets. The jfc (Java Foundation Classes) directory contains applets and applications that demonstrate Java's powerful graphics and GUI capabilities.

Change to the applets directory and list its contents to see the directory names for the demonstration applets. Figure 23.1 provides a brief description of each. If your browser supports Java, you can test an applet by opening the XHTML document for it in the applet's directory. We'll demonstrate three of these applets by using the appletviewer command in a command window.

Example	Description
Animator	Performs one of four separate animations.
ArcTest	Demonstrates drawing arcs. You can interact with the applet to change attributes of the arc that is displayed.
BarChart	Draws a simple bar chart.

Fig. 23.1 | The examples from the applets directory. (Part 1 of 2.)

Example	Description
Blink	Displays blinking text in different colors.
CardTest	Demonstrates several GUI components and layouts.
Clock	Draws a clock with rotating hands, the current date and the current time. The clock updates once per second.
DitherTest	Demonstrates drawing with a graphics technique known as dithering that allows gradual transformation from one color to another.
DrawTest	Allows the user mouse to draw lines and points in different colors by dragging the mouse.
Fractal	Draws a fractal. Fractals typically require complex calculations to determine how they're displayed. We discuss fractals in Section 18.8.
GraphicsTest	Draws shapes to illustrate graphics capabilities.
GraphLayout	Draws a graph consisting of many nodes (represented as rectangles) connected by lines. Drag a node to see the other nodes in the graph adjust on the screen and demonstrate complex graphical interactions.
ImageMap	Demonstrates an image with hot spots. Positioning the mouse pointer over certain areas of the image highlights the area and displays a message in the lower-left corner of the applet container window. Position over the mouth in the image to hear the applet say "hi."
JumpingBox	Moves a rectangle randomly around the screen. Try to catch it by clicking it with the mouse!
MoleculeViewer	Presents a three-dimensional view of several chemical molecules. Drag the mouse to view the molecule from different angles.
NervousText	Draws text that jumps around the applet.
SimpleGraph	Draws a complex curve.
SortDemo	Compares three sorting techniques. Sorting (described in Chapter 19) arranges information in order—like alphabetizing words. When you execute this example with the appletviewer, three windows appear. When you execute it in a browser, the three demos appear side by side. Click in each demo to start the sort. Note that the sorts all operate at different speeds.
SpreadSheet	Demonstrates a simple spreadsheet of rows and columns.
TicTacToe	Allows the user to play Tic-Tac-Toe against the computer.
WireFrame	Draws a three-dimensional shape as a wire frame. Drag the mouse to view the shape from different angles.

Fig. 23.1 | The examples from the applets directory. (Part 2 of 2.)

TicTacToe *Applet*

This TicTacToe demonstration applet allows you to play Tic-Tac-Toe against the computer. Change directories to subdirectory TicTacToe, where you'll find the file example1.html that loads the applet. In the command window, type the command

```
appletviewer example1.html
```

and press *Enter*. This executes the appletviewer applet container, which loads the XHT-ML document example1.html specified as its command-line argument. The appletviewer determines from the document which applet to load and executes it. Figure 23.2 shows several screen captures of playing Tic-Tac-Toe with this applet. You can open the XHTML document in your browser to execute the applet in the browser.

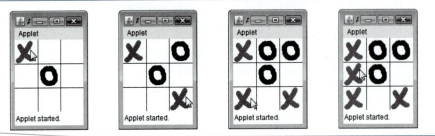

Fig. 23.2 | `TicTacToe` applet sample execution.

You are player **X**. To interact with the applet, point the mouse at the square where you want to place an **X** and click the mouse button. The applet plays a sound and places an **X** in the square if it is open. If the square is occupied, this is an invalid move, and the applet plays a different sound, indicating that you cannot make the specified move. After you make a valid move, the applet responds by making its own move.

To play again, click the `appletviewer`'s **Applet** menu and select the **Reload** menu item (Fig. 23.3), or click the applet again when the game is over. To terminate the `appletviewer`, click the `appletviewer`'s **Applet** menu and select the **Quit** menu item.

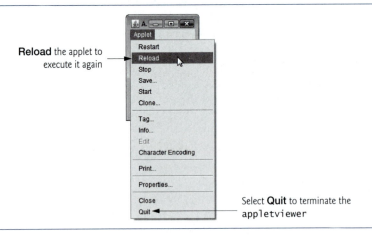

Fig. 23.3 | **Applet** menu in the `appletviewer`.

DrawTest *Applet*

The `DrawTest` applet allows you to draw lines and points in different colors. In the command window, change directories to directory `applets`, then to subdirectory `DrawTest`. You can move up the directory tree incrementally toward `demo` by issuing the command "`cd ..`" in the command window. The `DrawTest` directory contains the `example1.html` document that is used to execute the applet. In the command window, type the command

```
appletviewer example1.html
```

and press *Enter*. The appletviewer loads example1.html, determines from the document which applet to load and executes it. Figure 23.4 shows a screen capture after some lines and points have been drawn.

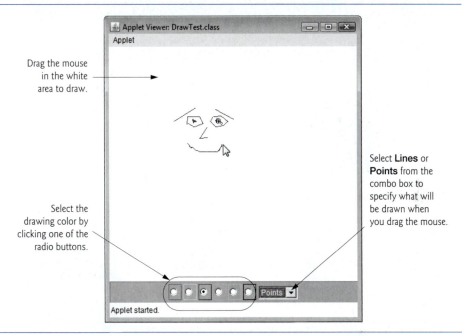

Drag the mouse in the white area to draw.

Select **Lines** or **Points** from the combo box to specify what will be drawn when you drag the mouse.

Select the drawing color by clicking one of the radio buttons.

Fig. 23.4 | DrawTest applet sample execution.

By default the applet allows you to draw black lines by dragging the mouse across the applet. When you drag the mouse, note that the line's start point always remains in the same place and its endpoint follows the mouse pointer around the applet. The line is not permanent until you release the mouse button.

Select a color by clicking one of the radio buttons at the bottom of the applet. You can select from red, green, blue, pink, orange and black. Change the shape to draw from **Lines** to **Points** by selecting **Points** from the combo box. To start a new drawing, select **Reload** from the appletviewer's **Applet** menu.

Java2D *Applet*

The Java2D applet demonstrates many features of the Java 2D API (which we introduced in Chapter 15). Change directories to the jfc directory in the JDK's demo directory, then change to the Java2D directory. In the command window, type the command

```
appletviewer Java2Demo.html
```

and press *Enter*. The appletviewer loads Java2Demo.html, determines from the document which applet to load and executes it. Figure 23.5 shows a screen capture of one of this applet's many demonstrations of Java's two-dimensional graphics capabilities.

At the top of the applet are tabs that look like file folders in a filing cabinet. This demo provides 12 tabs, each demonstrating Java 2D API features. To change to a different part of the demo, simply click a different tab. Also, try changing the options in the upper-right

Click a tab to select a
two-dimensional graphics demo.

Try changing the options to see
their effect on the demonstration.

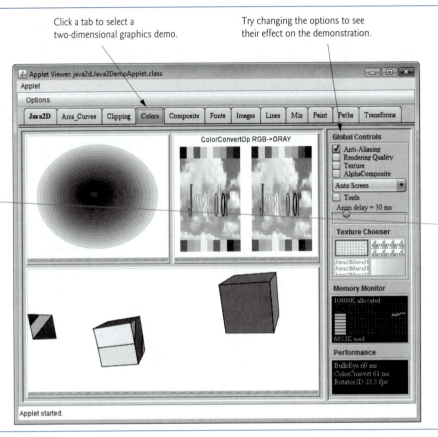

Fig. 23.5 | Java2D applet sample execution.

corner of the applet. Some of these affect the speed with which the applet draws the graphics. For example, click the checkbox to the left of the word **Anti-Aliasing** to turn off antialiasing (a graphics technique for producing smoother on-screen graphics in which the edges are blurred). Shapes that are not antialiased are less complex to draw. Accordingly, when the antialiasing feature is turned off, the animation speed increases for the animated shapes at the bottom of the demo (Fig. 23.5).

23.3 Simple Java Applet: Drawing a String

Every Java applet is a graphical user interface on which you can place GUI components using the techniques introduced in Chapter 14 or draw using the techniques demonstrated in Chapter 15. In this chapter, we'll demonstrate drawing on an applet. Examples in Chapters 24 and 27 demonstrate building an applet's graphical user interface.

Now let's build an applet of our own. We begin with a simple applet (Fig. 23.6) that draws "Welcome to Java Programming!" on the applet. We show this applet executing in two applet containers—the appletviewer and the Mozilla Firefox web browser. At the end of this section, you'll learn how to execute the applet in a web browser.

```
1  // Fig. 23.6: WelcomeApplet.java
2  // Applet that draws a String.
3  import java.awt.Graphics;   // program uses class Graphics
4  import javax.swing.JApplet; // program uses class JApplet
5
6  public class WelcomeApplet extends JApplet
7  {
8     // draw text on applet's background
9     public void paint( Graphics g )
10    {
11       // call superclass version of method paint
12       super.paint( g );
13
14       // draw a String at x-coordinate 25 and y-coordinate 25
15       g.drawString( "Welcome to Java Programming!", 25, 25 );
16    } // end method paint
17 } // end class WelcomeApplet
```

`WelcomeApplet` executing in the `appletviewer`

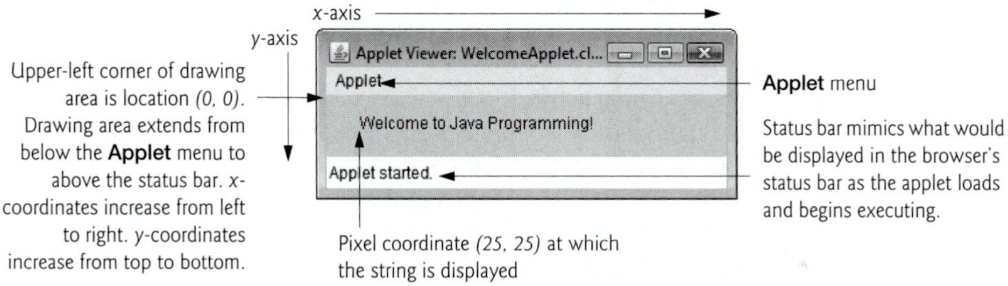
x-axis
y-axis
Applet Viewer: WelcomeApplet.cl...
Applet
Welcome to Java Programming!
Applet started.
Upper-left corner of drawing area is location (0, 0). Drawing area extends from below the Applet menu to above the status bar. x-coordinates increase from left to right. y-coordinates increase from top to bottom.
Applet menu
Status bar mimics what would be displayed in the browser's status bar as the applet loads and begins executing.
Pixel coordinate (25, 25) at which the string is displayed

`WelcomeApplet` executing in Mozilla Firefox

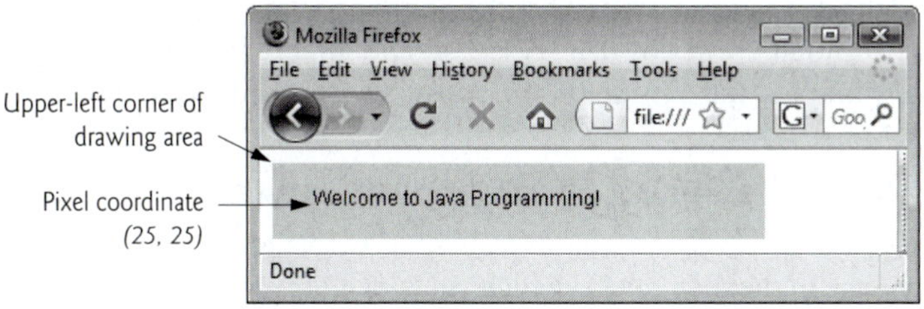
Mozilla Firefox
File Edit View History Bookmarks Tools Help
file:///
Welcome to Java Programming!
Done
Upper-left corner of drawing area
Pixel coordinate (25, 25)

Fig. 23.6 | Applet that draws a `String`.

Creating the Applet Class

Line 3 imports class `Graphics` to enable the applet to draw graphics, such as lines, rectangles, ovals and strings of characters. Class **`JApplet`** (imported at line 4) from package `javax.swing` is used to create applets. As with applications, every Java applet contains at least one `public` class declaration. An applet container can create only objects of classes that are `public` and extend `JApplet` (or its superclass `Applet`). For this reason, class `WelcomeApplet` (lines 6–17) extends `JApplet`.

An applet container expects every Java applet to have methods named **`init`**, **`start`**, **`paint`**, **`stop`** and **`destroy`**, each of which is declared in class `JApplet`. Each new applet class you create inherits default implementations of these methods from class `JApplet`. These methods can be overridden (redefined) to perform tasks that are specific to your applet. Section 23.4 discusses each of these methods in more detail.

When an applet container loads class `WelcomeApplet`, the container creates a `WelcomeApplet` object, then calls its methods `init`, `start` and `paint` in sequence. If you do not declare these methods in your applet, the applet container calls the inherited versions. The superclass methods `init` and `start` have empty bodies, so they do not perform any tasks. The superclass method `paint` does not draw anything on the applet.

You might wonder why it's necessary to inherit methods `init`, `start` and `paint` if their default implementations do not perform tasks. Some applets do not use all three of these methods. However, the applet container does not know that. Thus, it expects every applet to have these methods, so that it can provide a consistent start-up sequence. This is similar to applications' always starting execution with `main`. Inheriting the "default" versions of these methods guarantees that the applet container can execute each applet uniformly. Also, inheriting default implementations of these methods allows the programmer to concentrate on defining only the methods required for a particular applet.

Overriding Method *paint* for Drawing

To enable our applet to draw, class `WelcomeApplet` overrides method `paint` (lines 9–16) by placing statements in the body of `paint` that draw a message on the screen. Method `paint` receives a parameter of type `Graphics` (called g by convention), which is used to draw graphics on the applet. You do not call method `paint` explicitly in an applet. Rather, the applet container calls `paint` to tell the applet when to draw, and the applet container is responsible for passing a `Graphics` object as an argument.

Line 12 calls the superclass version of method `paint` that was inherited from `JApplet`. This should be the first statement in every applet's `paint` method. Omitting it can cause subtle drawing errors in applets that combine drawing and GUI components.

Line 15 uses `Graphics` method `drawString` to draw `Welcome to Java Programming!` on the applet. The method receives as arguments the `String` to draw and the *x-y* coordinates at which the bottom-left corner of the `String` should appear in the drawing area. When line 15 executes, it draws the `String` on the applet at the coordinates 25 and 25.

23.3.1 Executing `WelcomeApplet` in the `appletviewer`

After creating class `WelcomeApplet` and saving it in the file `WelcomeApplet.java`, open a command window, change to the directory in which you saved the applet class declaration and compile class `WelcomeApplet`.

Recall that applets are embedded in web pages for execution in an applet container (`appletviewer` or a browser). Before you can execute the applet, you must create an XHTML document that specifies which applet to execute in the applet container. Typically, an XHTML document ends with an `.html` or `.htm` file-name extension. Figure 23.7 shows a simple XHTML document—`WelcomeApplet.html`—that loads the applet defined in Fig. 23.6 into an applet container.

Most XHTML elements are delimited by pairs of **tags**—e.g., lines 1 and 6 delimit the XHTML document's beginning and end, respectively. Each tag is enclosed in angle brackets (< and >). Lines 2–5 specify the **body element** element of the document—this represents the elements that will be displayed in the web page. Lines 3–4 specify an **applet element** that tells the applet container to load a specific applet and defines the size of its display area (its width and height in pixels) in the applet container.

```
1  <html>
2  <body>
3  <applet code = "WelcomeApplet.class" width = "300" height = "45">
4  </applet>
5  </body>
6  </html>
```

Fig. 23.7 | `WelcomeApplet.html` loads `WelcomeApplet` (Fig. 23.6) into an applet container.

The applet and its corresponding XHTML document are normally stored in the same directory on disk. Typically, a browser loads an XHTML document from a computer (other than your own) connected to the Internet. However, XHTML documents also can reside on your computer (as in Section 23.2). When an applet container encounters an `applet` element in an XHTML document, it loads the applet's `.class` file (or files) from the same location that contains the XHTML document.

The `applet` element has several **attributes**. The first attribute in line 3, `code = "WelcomeApplet.class"`, indicates that the file `WelcomeApplet.class` contains the compiled applet class. The second and third attributes in line 3 indicate the **width** (300) and the **height** (45) of the applet in pixels. The `</applet>` tag (line 4) terminates the `applet` element that began at line 2. The `</html>` tag (line 6) terminates the XHTML document.

Look-and-Feel Observation 23.1

An applet should generally be less than 1024 pixels wide and 768 pixels tall—dimensions supported by most computer screens.

Common Programming Error 23.1

Forgetting the ending `</applet>` tag prevents the applet from executing in some applet containers. The `appletviewer` terminates without indicating an error. Some web browsers simply ignore the incomplete `applet` element.

Error-Prevention Tip 23.1

If you receive a `MissingResourceException` error message when loading an applet into the `appletviewer` or a browser, check the `<applet>` tag in the XHTML document carefully for syntax errors, such as commas (,) between the attributes.

The `appletviewer` understands only the `<applet>` and `</applet>` XHTML tags and ignores all other tags in the document. The `appletviewer` is an ideal place to test an applet and ensure that it executes properly. Once the applet's execution is verified, you can add its XHTML tags to a web page that others can view in their web browsers.

To execute `WelcomeApplet` in the `appletviewer`, open a command window, change to the directory containing your applet and XHTML document, then type

```
appletviewer WelcomeApplet.html
```

Error-Prevention Tip 23.2

Test your applets in the `appletviewer` before executing them in a web browser. Browsers often save a copy of an applet in memory until all the browser's windows are closed. If you change an applet, recompile it, then reload it in your browser, the browser may still execute the original version of the applet.

Error-Prevention Tip 23.3

Test your applets in every web browser in which they'll execute to ensure that they operate correctly.

23.3.2 Executing an Applet in a Web Browser

The sample program executions in Fig. 23.6 demonstrate `WelcomeApplet` executing in the `appletviewer` and in the Mozilla Firefox web browser. To execute an applet in Firefox, perform the following steps:

1. Select **Open File...** from the **File** menu.

2. In the dialog box that appears, locate the directory containing the XHTML document for the applet you wish to execute.

3. Select the XHTML document.

4. Click the **Open** button.

The steps for executing applets in other web browsers are similar. In most browsers, you can simply type *Ctrl + O* to open a dialog that enables you to select an XHTML document from your local hard disk.

Error-Prevention Tip 23.4

*If your applet executes in the `appletviewer`, but does not execute in your web browser, Java may not be installed and configured for your browser. In this case, visit the website `java.com` and click the **Free Java Download** button to install Java for your browser.*

23.4 Applet Life-Cycle Methods

Now that you've created an applet, let's consider the five applet methods that are called by the applet container from the time the applet is loaded into the browser to the time it's terminated by the browser. These methods correspond to various aspects of an applet's life cycle. Figure 23.8 lists these methods, which are inherited into your applet classes from class `JApplet`. The table specifies when each method gets called and explains its purpose. Other than method `paint`, these methods have empty bodies by default. If you'd like to declare any of them in your applets and have the applet container call them, you must use the method headers shown in Fig. 23.8.

Method	Description
`public void init()`	
	Called once by the applet container when an applet is loaded for execution. This method initializes an applet. Typical actions performed here are initializing fields, creating GUI components, loading sounds to play, loading images to display (see Chapter 24) and creating threads (see Chapter 26).

Fig. 23.8 | `JApplet` life-cycle methods that are called by an applet container during an applet's execution. (Part 1 of 2.)

Method	Description
`public void` `start()`	Called by the applet container after method `init` completes execution. In addition, if the user browses to another website and later returns to the applet's XHTML page, method `start` is called again. The method performs any tasks that must be completed when the applet is loaded for the first time and that must be performed every time the applet's XHTML page is revisited. Actions performed here might include starting an animation or starting other threads of execution.
`public void` `paint( Graphics g )`	Called by the applet container after methods `init` and `start`. Method `paint` is also called when the applet needs to be repainted. For example, if the user covers the applet with another open window on the screen and later uncovers it, the `paint` method is called. Typical actions performed here involve drawing with the `Graphics` object g that is passed to the `paint` method by the applet container.
`public void` `stop()`	This method is called by the applet container when the user leaves the applet's web page by browsing to another web page. Since it's possible that the user might return to the web page containing the applet, method `stop` performs tasks that might be required to suspend the applet's execution, so that the applet does not use computer processing time when it's not displayed on the screen. Typical actions performed here would stop the execution of animations and threads.
`public void` `destroy()`	This method is called by the applet container when the applet is being removed from memory. This occurs when the user exits the browsing session by closing all the browser windows and may also occur at the browser's discretion when the user has browsed to other web pages. The method performs any tasks that are required to clean up resources allocated to the applet.

Fig. 23.8 │ `JApplet` life-cycle methods that are called by an applet container during an applet's execution. (Part 2 of 2.)

 Common Programming Error 23.2
Declaring methods `init`, `start`, `paint`, `stop` or `destroy` with method headers that differ from those shown in Fig. 23.8 results in methods that will not be called by the applet container. The code specified in your versions of the methods will not execute. The `@Override` annotation can be applied to each method to prevent this problem.

23.5 Initializing an Instance Variable with Method `init`

Our next applet (Fig. 23.9) computes the sum of two values entered into input dialogs by the user and displays the result by drawing a `String` inside a rectangle on the applet. The sum is stored in an instance variable of the `AdditionApplet` class, so it can be used in both the `init` method and the `paint` method. The XHTML document that you can use to load this applet into an applet container (i.e., the `appletviewer` or a web browser) is shown in Fig. 23.10.

```
1   // Fig. 23.9: AdditionApplet.java
2   // Applet that adds two double values entered via input dialogs.
3   import java.awt.Graphics;      // program uses class Graphics
4   import javax.swing.JApplet;    // program uses class JApplet
5   import javax.swing.JOptionPane; // program uses class JOptionPane
6
7   public class AdditionApplet extends JApplet
8   {
9      private double sum; // sum of values entered by user
10
11     // initialize applet by obtaining values from user
12     public void init()
13     {
14        // obtain first number from user
15        String firstNumber = JOptionPane.showInputDialog(
16           "Enter first floating-point value" );
17
18        // obtain second number from user
19        String secondNumber = JOptionPane.showInputDialog(
20           "Enter second floating-point value" );
21
22        // convert numbers from type String to type double
23        double number1 = Double.parseDouble( firstNumber );
24        double number2 = Double.parseDouble( secondNumber );
25
26        sum = number1 + number2; // add numbers
27     } // end method init
28
29     // draw results in a rectangle on applet's background
30     public void paint( Graphics g )
31     {
32        super.paint( g ); // call superclass version of method paint
33
34        // draw rectangle starting from (15, 10) that is 270
35        // pixels wide and 20 pixels tall
36        g.drawRect( 15, 10, 270, 20 );
37
38        // draw results as a String at (25, 25)
39        g.drawString( "The sum is " + sum, 25, 25 );
40     } // end method paint
41  } // end class AdditionApplet
```

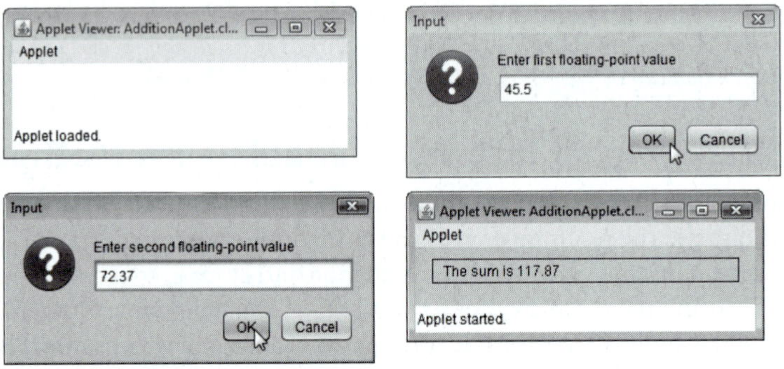

Fig. 23.9 | Applet that adds two `double` values entered via input dialogs.

```
1    <html>
2    <body>
3    <applet code = "AdditionApplet.class" width = "300" height = "50">
4    </applet>
5    </body>
6    </html>
```

Fig. 23.10 | `AdditionApplet.html` loads class `AdditionApplet` of Fig. 23.9 into an applet container.

The applet requests that the user enter two floating-point numbers. In Fig. 23.9, line 9 declares instance variable `sum` of type `double`. The applet contains two methods—`init` (lines 12–27) and `paint` (lines 30–40). When an applet container loads this applet, the container creates an instance of class `AdditionApplet` and calls its `init` method—this occurs only once during an applet's execution. Method `init` normally initializes the applet's fields (if they need to be initialized to values other than their defaults) and performs other tasks that should occur only once when the applet begins execution. The first line of `init` always appears as shown in line 12, which indicates that `init` is a `public` method that receives no arguments and returns no information when it completes.

Lines 15–24 declare variables to store the values entered by the user, obtain the user input and convert the `String`s entered by the user to `double` values. Line 26 adds the values stored in variables `number1` and `number2`, and assigns the result to instance variable `sum`. At this point, the applet's `init` method returns program control to the applet container, which then calls the applet's `start` method. We did not declare `start` in this applet, so the one inherited from class `JApplet` is called here.

Next, the applet container calls the applet's `paint` method, which draws a rectangle (line 36) where the addition result will appear. Line 39 calls the `Graphics` object's `drawString` method to display the results. The statement concatenates the value of instance variable `sum` to the `String` "The sum is " and displays the concatenated `String`.

Software Engineering Observation 23.1

The only statements that should be placed in an applet's `init` method are those that should execute only once when the applet is initialized.

23.6 Sandbox Security Model

For security reasons, it's generally considered dangerous to allow applets or any other program that you execute from a web browser to access your local computer. So, you must decide whether *you trust the source*. For example, if you choose to download a new version of the Firefox web browser from Mozilla's `firefox.com` website, you must decide whether you trust Mozilla. After all, their installer program is going to modify your system and place the files to execute Firefox on your computer. Once it's installed, Firefox will be able to access files and other local resources. Most of what you do with your web browsers—such as shopping, browsing the web and downloading software—requires you to trust the sites you visit and to trust the organizations that maintain those sites. If you are not careful, a malicious downloaded program could gain control of your computer, access personal information stored there, corrupt your data and possibly even be used to attack other computers on the Internet—as so often happens with computer viruses today.

Preventing Malicious Applets

Applets are typically downloaded from the Internet. What would happen if you downloaded a malicious applet? Consider the fact that a browser downloads and executes a Java applet automatically—the user *is not asked for approval*. In fact, an applet typically downloads *without the user's knowledge*—it's just another element of the web page the user happens to be visiting.

The designers of Java considered this issue thoroughly, since Java was intended for use in networked environments. To combat malicious code, the Java platform uses a so-called **sandbox security model** that provides a mechanism for executing downloaded code safely. Such code executes in the "sandbox" and is not allowed to "play outside the sandbox." By default, downloaded code cannot access local system resources, and an applet can interact only with the server from which the applet was downloaded.

Digitally Signed Applets

Unfortunately, executing in a sandbox makes it difficult for applets to perform useful tasks. It's possible, however, for an organization that wishes to create applets with access to the local system to obtain a security certificate (also called a digital certificate) from one of several certificate authorities (see en.wikipedia.org/wiki/Certificate_Authority for a list of authorities and more information about certificate authorities). The organization can then use tools provided with the JDK to "digitally sign" an applet that requires access to local system resources. When a user downloads a digitally signed applet, a dialog prompts the user asking whether he or she trusts the applet's source. In that dialog, the user can view the organization's security certificate and see which certificate authority issued it. If the user indicates that he/she trusts the source, only then will the applet be able to access to the local computer's resources.

In the next section, we introduce Java Web Start and the Java Network Launch Protocol (JNLP). These technologies enable applets or applications to interact with the user to request access to specific local system resources. With the user's permission, this enables Java programmers to extend the sandbox, but it does not give their programs access to all of the user's local resources—so the sandbox principles are still in effect. For example, it would be useful for a downloadable text editor program to store the user's files in a folder on the user's computer. The text editor can prompt the user to ask for permission to do this. If the user grants permission for a specific directory on disk, the program can then access only that local directory and its subdirectories.

For more information on digitally signed applets, visit java.sun.com/developer/ onlineTraining/Programming/JDCBook/signed.html. For information on the Java Platform security model, visit java.sun.com/javase/6/docs/technotes/guides/security/.

23.7 Java Web Start and the Java Network Launch Protocol (JNLP)

Java Web Start is a framework for running downloaded applets and applications outside the browser. Typically, such programs are stored on a web server for access via the Internet, but they can also be stored on an organization's network for internal distribution, or even on CDs, DVDs or other media. As you'll learn in Chapter 24, Java Web Start enables you to ask the user if a downloaded program can have access to the resources of the user's computer.

Java Web Start Features
Some key Java Web Start features include:

- *Desktop integration:* Users can launch robust applets and applications by clicking a hyperlink in a web page, and can quickly and easily install the programs on their computers. Java Web Start can be configured to ask the user if a desktop icon should be created so the user can launch the program directly from the desktop. Downloaded programs can also have an "offline mode" for execution when the computer is not connected to the Internet.

- *Automatic updating:* When you execute a program via Java Web Start, the program is downloaded and cached (stored) on the user's computer. The next time the user executes that program, Java Web Start launches it from the cache. If the program has been updated since it was last launched, Java Web Start can automatically download the updates, so a user always has the most up-to-date version. This makes installation and updating software simple and seamless to the user.

- *Draggable applets:* This is a new feature as of Java SE 6 Update 10. With a small change to the `applet` element that invokes an applet from an XHTML document, you can allow users to execute an applet in its own window by holding the *Alt* key and dragging the applet out of the web browser. The applet continues to execute even after the web browser closes.

Java Network Launch Protocol (JNLP)
A **Java Network Launch Protocol (JNLP)** document provides the information that Java Web Start needs in order to download and run a program. Also, you must package your program in one or more Java archive (JAR) files that contain the program's code and resources (e.g., images, media files, text files).

By default, programs launched via Java Web Start execute using the sandbox security model. If the user gives permission, such programs can access the local file system, the clipboard and other services via the JNLP APIs of package `javax.jnlp`. We discuss some of these features in Chapter 24. Digitally signed programs can gain greater access to the local system if the user trusts the source.

23.7.1 Packaging the DrawTest Applet for Use with Java Web Start
Let's package the JDK's `DrawTest` demonstration applet (discussed in Section 23.2) so that you can execute it via Java Web Start. To do so, you must first wrap the applet's `.class` files and the resources it uses (if any) into a Java archive (JAR) file. In a command window, change to the `DrawTest` directory, as you did in Section 23.2. Once in that folder, execute the following command:

```
jar cvf DrawTest.jar *.class
```

which creates a JAR file in the current directory named `DrawTest.jar` containing the applet's `.class` files—`DrawControls.class`, `DrawPanel.class` and `DrawTest.class`. If the program had other resources, you'd simply add the file names or the folder names in which those resources are stored to the end of the preceding command. The letters `cvf` are command-line options to the **jar command**. The **c option** indicates that the command should create a new JAR file. The **v option** indicates that the command should produce verbose output so you can see the list of files and directories being included in the JAR file. The **f**

option indicates that the next argument in the command line (DrawTest.jar) is the new JAR file's name. Figure 23.11 shows the preceding command's verbose output, which shows the files that were placed into the JAR.

```
added manifest
adding: DrawControls.class(in = 2611) (out= 1488)(deflated 43%)
adding: DrawPanel.class(in = 2703) (out= 1406)(deflated 47%)
adding: DrawTest.class(in = 1170) (out= 706)(deflated 39%)
```

Fig. 23.11 | Output of the jar command.

23.7.2 JNLP Document for the DrawTest Applet

Next, you must create a JNLP document that describes the contents of the JAR file and specifies which file in the JAR is the so-called **main-class** that begins the program's execution. For an applet, the main-class is the one that extends JApplet (i.e., DrawTest in this example). For an application, the main-class is the one that contains the main method. A basic JNLP document for the DrawTest applet is shown in Fig. 23.12. We describe this document's elements momentarily.

```
1   <?xml version="1.0" encoding="UTF-8"?>
2   <jnlp
3      codebase=PathToJNLPFile
4      href="DrawTest.jnlp">
5
6      <information>
7         <title>DrawTest Applet</title>
8         <vendor>Sun Microsystems, Inc.</vendor>
9         <shortcut>
10           <desktop/>
11        </shortcut>
12        <offline-allowed/>
13     </information>
14
15     <resources>
16        <java version="1.6+"/>
17        <jar href="DrawTest.jar" main="true"/>
18     </resources>
19
20     <applet-desc
21        name="DrawTest"
22        main-class="DrawTest"
23        width="400"
24        height="400">
25     </applet-desc>
26  </jnlp>
```

Fig. 23.12 | DrawTest.jnlp document for launching the DrawTest applet.

Overview of XML

JNLP documents are written in **Extensible Markup Language (XML)**—a widely supported standard for describing data. XML is commonly used to exchange data between applications over the Internet, and many applications now use XML to specify configuration information as well—as is the case with JNLP documents for Java Web Start. XML permits you to create markup for virtually any type of information. This enables you to create entirely new markup languages for describing any type of data, such as mathematical formulas, software-configuration instructions, chemical molecular structures, music, news, recipes and financial reports. XML describes data in a way that both humans and computers can understand. JNLP is a so-called XML vocabulary that describes the information Java Web Start needs to launch a program.

XML documents contain **elements** that specify the document's structure, such as `title` (line 7), and text that represents content (i.e., data), such as `DrawTest Applet` (line 7). XML documents delimit elements with **start tags** and **end tags**. A start tag consists of the element name in **angle brackets** (e.g., `<title>` and `<vendor>` in lines 7 and 8). Start tags may also contain attributes of the form *name=value*—for example, the `jnlp` start tag contains the attribute `href="DrawTest.jnlp"`. An end tag consists of the element name preceded by a **forward slash** (/) in angle brackets (e.g., `</title>` and `</vendor>` in lines 7 and 8). An element's start and end tags enclose text that represents a piece of data (e.g., the vendor of the program—`Sun Microsystems, Inc.`—in line 8, which is enclosed by the `<vendor>` start tag and `</vendor>` end tag) or other elements (e.g., the `title`, `vendor`, `shortcut` and `offline-allowed` elements in the `information` element of lines 6–13). Every XML document must have exactly one **root element** that contains all the other elements. In Fig. 23.12, the **`jnlp` element** (lines 2–26) is the root element.

JNLP Document: `jnlp` Element

The `jnlp` element's start tag (lines 2–4) has two attributes—`codebase` and `href`. The `codebase` attribute's value is a URL that specifies the path where the JNLP document and the JAR file are stored—this is specified in Fig. 23.12 as *PathToJNLPFile*, since this value depends on the location from which the applet is loaded. The `href` attribute specifies the JNLP file that launches the program. We saved the JNLP file and the JAR file in the Draw-Test demonstration applet's directory within the JDK's directory structure. We used the following local file system URL as the `codebase`:

```
file:.
```

which indicates that the code is in the current directory (`.`). Typically, the `codebase` references a directory on a web server with an `http://` URL. If you'd like to serve your applet or application from a web server so users can access it online, you'll need to configure your web server correctly, as described at `java.sun.com/javase/6/docs/technotes/guides/javaws/developersguide/setup.html`.

JNLP Document: `information` Element

The **`information` element** (lines 6–13) provides details about the program. The **`title`** element specifies a title for the program. The **`vendor` element** specifies who created the program. The values of these elements appear in Java Web Start's security warnings and errors that are presented to the user. The `title`'s value also appears in the title bar of the window in which the program executes.

The **`desktop` element** that is nested in the **`shortcut` element** (lines 9–11) tells Java Web Start to ask whether the user wishes to install a desktop shortcut. If the user accepts, an icon will appear on the desktop. The user can then launch the program in its own window by double-clicking the desktop icon. Note the syntax of the `<desktop/>` element—a so-called empty XML element. When nothing appears between an element's start and end tags, the element can be written using one tag that ends with />.

The **offline-allowed** element (line 12) indicates that once the program is installed on the user's computer, it can be launched via Java Web Start—even when the computer is not connected to the Internet. This is particularly useful for any program that can be used with files stored on the user's computer.

JNLP Document: **resources** Element

The **resources** element (lines 15–18) contains two nested elements. The **java element** lists the minimum version of Java required to execute the program (line 16) and the **jar element** (line 17) specifies the location of the JAR file that contains the program and whether that JAR file contains the class that launches the program. There can be multiple jar elements, as you'll see in the next chapter.

JNLP Document: **applet-desc** Element

The **applet-desc** element (lines 20–25) is similar to the applet element in XHTML. The name attribute specifies the applet's name. The main-class attribute specifies the main applet class (the one that extends JApplet). The width and height attributes specify the width and height in pixels, respectively, of the window in which the applet will execute. Chapter 24 discusses a similar element for applications—application-desc.

Launching the Applet with Java Web Start

You're now ready to launch the applet via Java Web Start. There are several ways to do this. You can use the **javaws command** in a command window from the folder that contains the JNLP document, as in

```
javaws DrawTest.jnlp
```

You can also use your operating system's file manager to locate the JNLP on your computer and double click its file name. Normally, the JNLP file is referenced from a web page via a hyperlink. The DrawTestWebPage.html document in Fig. 23.13 (which was saved in the same directory as the JNLP file) contains an anchor (a) element (line 4), which links to the DrawTest.jnlp file. Clicking this hyperlink in the web page downloads the JNLP file (in this case, it's loaded from the local file system) and executes the corresponding applet.

```
1   <html>
2      <head><title>DrawTest Launcher Page</title></head>
3      <body>
4         <a href="DrawTest.jnlp">Launch DrawTest via Java Web Start</a>
5      </body>
6   </html>
```

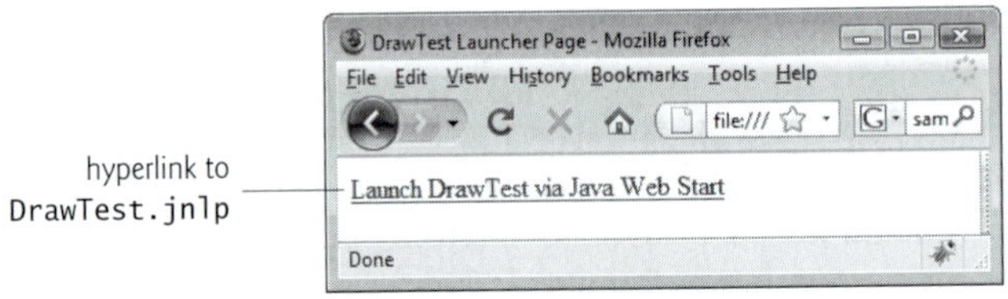

hyperlink to
DrawTest.jnlp

Fig. 23.13 | XHTML document that launches the DrawTest applet when the user clicks the link.

When you run the applet via Java Web Start the first time, you'll be presented with the dialog in Fig. 23.14. This dialog enables the user to decide if a desktop icon will be installed. If the user clicks **OK**, a new icon labeled with the title specified in the JNLP document appears on the user's desktop. The applet is also cached for future use. After the user clicks **OK** or **Skip** in this dialog, the program executes (Fig. 23.15).

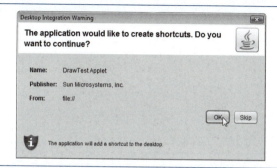

Fig. 23.14 | Dialog asking whether the user wishes to install a desktop shortcut.

Fig. 23.15 | `DrawTest` applet running with Java Web Start.

Viewing the Installed Java Web Start Programs

You can view the installed Java Web Start programs in the **Java Cache Viewer** by typing the following command in a command window:

```
javaws -viewer
```

This displays the window in Fig. 23.16. The **Java Cache Viewer** enables you to manage the Java Web Start programs on your system. You can run a selected program, create a desktop shortcut for a program (if there is not one already), delete installed programs, and more.

For more information on Java Web Start, visit `java.sun.com/javase/6/docs/tech-notes/guides/javaws/`. This site provides an overview of Java Web Start and includes links to the Developer's Guide, an FAQ, the JNLP Specification and the API documentation for the `javax.jnlp` package.

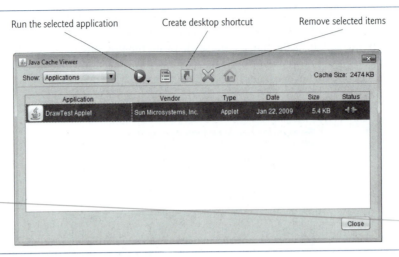

Run the selected application   Create desktop shortcut   Remove selected items

Fig. 23.16 | Viewing installed Java Web Start programs in the **Java Cache Viewer**.

23.8 Wrap-Up

In this chapter, you learned the fundamentals of Java applets and Java Web Start. You leaned basic XHTML concepts for embedding an applet in a web page and executing it in an applet container such as the appletviewer or a web browser. In addition, we discussed the five methods that are called automatically by the applet container during an applet's life cycle. We discussed Java's sandbox security model for executing downloaded code. Then we introduced Java Web Start and the Java Network Launch Protocol (JNLP). You learned how to package a program into a JAR file so that it could be executed via Java Web Start. We also discussed the basic elements of a JNLP document. In the next chapter, you'll see several additional applets as we present basic multimedia capabilities. You'll also learn more features of Java Web Start and JNLP. In Chapter 27, we demonstrate how to customize an applet via parameters that are specified in an applet XHTML element.

Summary

Section 23.1 Introduction
- Applets are Java programs that are typically embedded in XHTML (Extensible HyperText Markup Language) documents—also called web pages. When a Java-enabled web browser loads a web page containing an applet, the applet downloads into the browser and executes.
- The application in which an applet executes is known as the applet container. It is the applet container's responsibility to load the applet's class(es), create an instance of the applet and manage its life cycle. The JDK includes an applet container called the appletviewer for testing applets as you develop them and before you embed them in web pages.
- Web browsers execute Java applets via the Java Plug-In.

Section 23.2 Sample Applets Provided with the JDK
- To re-execute an applet in the appletviewer, click the appletviewer's **Applet** menu and select the **Reload** menu item.
- To terminate the appletviewer, select **Quit** from the appletviewer's **Applet** menu.

Section 23.3 Simple Java Applet: Drawing a String

- Every Java applet is a graphical user interface on which you can place GUI components or draw.

- Class JApplet from package javax.swing is used to create applets.

- An applet container can create only objects of classes that are public and extend JApplet (or the Applet class from early versions of Java).

- An applet container expects every Java applet to have methods named init, start, paint, stop and destroy, each of which is declared in class JApplet. Each new applet class you create inherits default implementations of these methods from class JApplet.

- When an applet container loads an applet, it creates an object of the applet's type, then calls the applet's init, start and paint methods. If you do not declare these methods in your applet, the applet container calls the inherited versions.

- The superclass methods init and start have empty bodies, so they do not perform any tasks. The superclass method paint does not draw anything on the applet.

- To enable an applet to draw, override its method paint. You do not call method paint explicitly in an applet. Rather, the applet container calls paint to tell the applet when to draw, and the container is responsible for passing a Graphics object as an argument.

- The first statement in method paint should be a call to the superclass method paint. Omitting this can cause subtle drawing errors in applets that combine drawing and GUI components.

- Before you can execute an applet, you must create an XHTML (Extensible HyperText Markup Language) document that specifies which applet to execute in the applet container. Typically, an XHTML document ends with an ".html" or ".htm" file-name extension.

- Most XHTML elements are delimited by pairs of tags. All XHTML tags begin with a left angle bracket, <, and end with a right angle bracket, >.

- An applet element tells the applet container to load a specific applet and defines the size of its display area (its width and height in pixels) in the applet container.

- Normally, an applet and its corresponding XHTML document are stored in the same directory.

- When an applet container encounters an XHTML document that contains an applet, the container automatically loads the applet's .class file(s) from the same directory on the computer in which the XHTML document resides.

- The appletviewer understands only the <applet> and </applet> XHTML tags and ignores all other tags in the document.

Section 23.4 Applet Life-Cycle Methods

- Five applet life-cycle methods are called by the applet container from the time the applet is loaded into the browser to the time it is terminated by the browser.

- Method init is called once by the applet container to initialize an applet when it's loaded.

- Method start is called by the applet container after method init completes execution. In addition, if the user browses to another website and later returns to the applet's XHTML page, method start is called again.

- Method paint is called by the applet container after methods init and start. Method paint is also called when the applet needs to be repainted.

- Method stop is called by the applet container when the user leaves the applet's web page by browsing to another web page.

- Method destroy is called by the applet container when the applet is being removed from memory. This occurs when the user exits the browsing session by closing all the browser windows and may also occur at the browser's discretion when the user has browsed to other web pages.

Section 23.5 Initializing an Instance Variable with Method `init`
- `Graphics` method `drawString` draws a `String` at a specified location.
- `Graphics` method `drawRect` draws a rectangle at the specified upper-left corner, width and height.

Section 23.6 Sandbox Security Model
- It's considered dangerous to allow applets or other programs that you execute from a web browser to access your local computer. You must decide whether *you trust the source*.
- A browser downloads an applet *without the user's knowledge*—it's just another element of the web page the user happens to be visiting.
- To combat malicious code, the Java platform uses a sandbox security model that provides a mechanism for executing downloaded code safely. Downloaded code cannot access local system resources, and an applet can interact only with the server from which it was downloaded.
- You can "digitally sign" an applet that requires access to local system resources. If the user indicates that he/she trusts the applet's source, only then will the applet be able to access the local computer's resources.

Section 23.7 Java Web Start and the Java Network Launch Protocol (JNLP)
- Java Web Start is a framework for running downloaded programs outside of the browser. Typically, such programs are stored on a web server, but they can also be stored on an organization's network for internal distribution, or even on CDs, DVDs or other media.
- Users can launch robust applets and applications by clicking a hyperlink in a web page, and can quickly and easily install the programs on their computers.
- Java Web Start can be configured to ask the user if a desktop icon should be created so the user can launch the program directly from the desktop. Downloaded programs can also have an "off-line mode" for execution when the computer is not connected to the Internet.
- When you execute a program via Java Web Start, the program is downloaded and cached (stored) on the user's computer. The next time the user executes that program, Java Web Start launches it from the cache.
- If the program has been updated since it was last lauched, Java Web Start can automatically download the new version, so a user always has the most up-to-date version.
- A Java Network Launch Protocol (JNLP) document provides the information that Java Web Start needs to download and run a program.
- Programs launched via Java Web Start execute using the sandbox security model. The user can permit access to the local file system, the clipboard and other services via the JNLP APIs.

Section 23.7.1 Packaging the **DrawTest** Applet for Use with Java Web Start
- The `jar` command is used to create JAR files. Option `c` indicates that the command should create a new JAR file. Option `v` indicates that the command should produce verbose output. Option `f` indicates that the next argument in the command line is the new JAR file's name.

Section 23.7.2 JNLP Document for the **DrawTest** Applet
- A JNLP document describes the contents of the JAR file and specifies which file in the JAR is the so-called `main-class` that begins the program's execution.
- JNLP documents are written in Extensible Markup Language (XML)—a widely supported standard for describing data.
- JNLP is a so-called XML vocabulary that describes the information Java Web Start needs to launch a program.

- XML documents contain elements that specify the document's structure. XML documents delimit elements with start tags and end tags. A start tag consists of the element name in angle brackets. Start tags may also contain attributes of the form *name=value*. An end tag consists of the element name preceded by a forward slash (/) in angle brackets.

- An element's start and end tags enclose text that represents a piece of data or other elements.

- Every XML document must have exactly one root element that contains all the other elements.

- The jnlp element's codebase attribute specifies the path where the JNLP document and the JAR file are stored. The href attribute specifies the JNLP file that launches the program.

- Typically, the codebase references a directory on a web server with an http:// URL.

- The information element provides details about the program.

- The title element specifies a title for the program.

- The vendor element specifies who created the program.

- The desktop element nested in the shortcut element tells Java Web Start to ask users whether they wish to install a desktop shortcut.

- The offline-allowed element indicates that a program can be launched via Java Web Start even when the computer is not connected to the Internet.

- The resources element contains a java element that lists the minimum version of Java required to execute the program and a jar element that specifies the location of the JAR file.

- The applet-desc element's name attribute specifies the applet's name. The main-class attribute specifies the main applet class. The width and height attributes specify the width and height in pixels, respectively, of the window in which the applet will execute.

- To launch the applet via Java Web Start you can use the javaws command. You can also use your operating system's file manager to locate the JNLP on your computer and double click its file name. Normally, a JNLP file is referenced from a web page via a hyperlink.

- When you run an applet via Java Web Start the first time and the JNLP document specifies that a desktop icon should be installed, you'll be presented with a dialog that enables you to decide whether to install the desktop icon. If you click **OK**, a new icon labeled with the title specified in the JNLP document appears on the desktop.

- You can view the installed Java Web Start programs in the **Java Cache Viewer** by typing the command javaws -viewer in a command window:

- The **Java Cache Viewer** enables you to manage the installed Java Web Start programs. You can run a selected program, create a desktop shortcut, delete installed programs, and more.

Terminology

Self-Review Exercise

23.1 Fill in the blanks in each of the following:

a) Java applets begin execution with a series of three method calls: _____, _____ and _____.

b) The _____ method is invoked for an applet each time a browser's user leaves an XHTML page on which the applet resides.

c) Every applet should extend class _____.

d) The _____ or a browser can be used to execute a Java applet.

e) The _____ method is called each time the user of a browser revisits the XHTML page on which an applet resides.

f) To load an applet into a browser, you must first define a(n) _____ file.

g) Method _____ is called once when an applet begins execution.

h) Method _____ is invoked to draw on an applet.

i) Method _____ is invoked for an applet when the browser removes it from memory.

j) The _____ and _____ XHTML tags specify that an applet should be loaded into an applet container and executed.

k) _____ is a framework for running downloaded programs outside the browser.

l) A(n) _____ document provides the information that Java Web Start needs to download and run a program.

m) The _____ enables you to manage the Java Web Start programs on your system.

Answers to Self-Review Exercise

23.1 a) init, start, paint. b) stop. c) JApplet (or Applet). d) appletviewer. e) start. f) XHTML. g) init. h) paint. i) destroy. j) <applet>, </applet>. k) Java Web Start. l) Java Network Launch Protocol (JNLP). m) **Java Cache Viewer**.

Exercises

23.2 Write an applet that asks the user to enter two floating-point numbers, obtains the two numbers from the user and draws their sum, product (multiplication), difference and quotient (division). Use the techniques shown in Fig. 23.9.

23.3 Write an applet that asks the user to enter two floating-point numbers, obtains the numbers from the user and displays the two numbers, then displays the larger number followed by the words "is larger" as a string on the applet. If the numbers are equal, the applet should print the message "These numbers are equal." Use the techniques shown in Fig. 23.9.

23.4 Write an applet that inputs three floating-point numbers from the user and displays the sum, average, product, smallest and largest of these numbers as strings on the applet. Use the techniques shown in Fig. 23.9.

23.5   Write an applet that asks the user to input the radius of a circle as a floating-point number and draws the circle's diameter, circumference and area. Use the value 3.14159 for π. Use the techniques shown in Fig. 23.9. [*Note:* You may also use the predefined constant Math.PI for the value of π. This constant is more precise than the value 3.14159. Class Math is defined in the java.lang package, so you do not need to import it.] Use the following formulas (*r* is the radius):

$$diameter = 2r$$
$$circumference = 2\pi r$$
$$area = \pi r^2$$

23.6   Write an applet that reads five integers, determines which are the largest and smallest integers in the group and prints them. Draw the results on the applet.

23.7   Write an applet that draws a checkerboard pattern as follows:

```
* * * * * * *
 * * * * * * *
* * * * * * *
 * * * * * * *
* * * * * * *
 * * * * * * *
* * * * * * *
 * * * * * * *
```

23.8   Write an applet that draws rectangles of different sizes and locations.

23.9   Write an applet that allows the user to input values for the arguments required by method drawRect, then draws a rectangle using the four input values.

23.10   Class Graphics contains method drawOval, which takes as arguments the same four arguments as method drawRect. The arguments for method drawOval specify the "bounding box" for the oval—the sides of the bounding box are the boundaries of the oval. Write a Java applet that draws an oval and a rectangle with the same four arguments. The oval will touch the rectangle at the center of each side.

23.11   Modify the solution to Exercise 23.10 to output ovals of different shapes and sizes.

23.12   Write an applet that allows the user to input the four arguments required by method drawOval, then draws an oval using the four input values.

23.13   Package the TicTacToe demonstration applet from the JDK (discussed in Section 23.2) for use with Java Web Start, then copy the JNLP document in Fig. 23.12 and modify it so that it launches the TicTacToe applet.

24

Multimedia: Applets and Applications

The wheel that squeaks the loudest ... gets the grease.
—John Billings (Henry Wheeler Shaw)

We'll use a signal I have tried and found far-reaching and easy to yell. Waa-hoo!
—Zane Grey

There is a natural hootchy-kootchy motion to a goldfish.
—Walt Disney

Between the motion and the act falls the shadow.
—Thomas Stearns Eliot

Objectives

In this chapter you'll learn:

- How to get, display and scale images.
- How to create animations from sequences of images.
- How to create image maps.
- How to get, play, loop and stop sounds using an `AudioClip`.
- How to play video using interface `Player`.

24.1 Introduction

Multimedia—using sound, images, graphics, animation and video—makes applications "come alive." Although most multimedia in Java applications is two-dimensional, you can use the Java 3D API to create 3D graphics applications (java.sun.com/javase/technologies/desktop/java3d/).

Most new computers sold today are "multimedia ready," with DVD drives, audio and video capabilities. Economical desktop and laptop computers are so powerful that they can store and play DVD-quality (and often, HD-quality) sound and video.

Among users who want graphics, many now want three-dimensional, high-resolution, color graphics. True three-dimensional imaging is already available. We expect high-resolution, "theater-in-the-round," three-dimensional television to eventually become common. Sporting and entertainment events will seem to take place on your living room floor! Medical students worldwide will see operations being performed thousands of miles away, as if they were occurring in the same room. People will learn how to drive with incredibly realistic driving simulators in their homes before they get behind the wheel. The possibilities are endless and exciting.

Multimedia demands extraordinary computing power. Until recently, affordable computers with that kind of power were not widely available. Today's ultrapowerful processors make effective multimedia economical. Users are eager to own faster processors, larger memories and wider communications channels that support demanding multimedia applications. Ironically, these enhanced capabilities may not cost more—fierce competition keeps driving prices down.

The Java APIs provide multimedia facilities that enable you to start developing powerful multimedia applications immediately. This chapter presents several examples, including:

1. the basics of manipulating images.

2. creating smooth animations.

3. playing audio files with the AudioClip interface.

4. creating image maps that can sense when the cursor is over them, even without a mouse click.

5. playing video files using the Player interface.

The chapter also introduces additional JNLP features that, with the user's permission, enable an applet or application to access files on the user's local computer. The exercises suggest dozens of challenging and interesting projects. When we were writing these, the ideas just kept flowing. Multimedia leverages creativity in ways that we did not experience with "conventional" computer capabilities. [*Note:* Java's multimedia capabilities go far beyond those presented in this chapter. They include the **Java Media Framework (JMF) API** (for adding audio and video media to an application), **Java Sound API** (for playing, recording and modifying audio), Java 3D API (for creating and modifying 3D graphics), **Java Advanced Imaging API** (for image-processing capabilities, such as cropping and scaling), **Java Speech API** (for inputting voice commands from the user or outputting voice commands to the user), Java 2D API (for creating and modifying 2D graphics, covered in Chapter 15) and **Java Image I/O API** (for reading images from and outputting images to files). Section 24.8 provides web links for these APIs.]

24.2 Loading, Displaying and Scaling Images

We begin our discussion with images. We'll use several different images in this chapter. You can create your own images with software such as Adobe® Photoshop®, Corel® Paint Shop Pro®, Microsoft® Paint and G.I.M.P. (gimp.org).

The applet of Fig. 24.1 uses Java Web Start and the JNLP **FileOpenService** (package javax.jnlp) to allow the user to select an image, then displays that image and allows the user to scale it. After the user selects an image, the applet gets the bytes from the file, then passes them to the ImageIcon (package javax.swing) constructor to create the image that will be displayed. Class ImageIcon's constructors can receive arguments of several different formats, including a byte array containing the bytes of an image, an **Image** (package java.awt) already loaded in memory, or a String or a URL representing the image's location. Java supports various image formats, including **Graphics Interchange Format (GIF)**, **Joint Photographic Experts Group (JPEG)** and **Portable Network Graphics (PNG)**. File names for these types typically end with **.gif**, **.jpg** (or **.jpeg**) and **.png**, respectively.

```
1   // Fig. 24.1: LoadImageAndScale.java
2   // Loading, displaying and scaling an image in an applet
3   import java.awt.BorderLayout;
4   import java.awt.Graphics;
5   import java.awt.event.ActionEvent;
6   import java.awt.event.ActionListener;
7   import javax.jnlp.FileContents;
8   import javax.jnlp.FileOpenService;
9   import javax.jnlp.ServiceManager;
10  import javax.swing.ImageIcon;
11  import javax.swing.JApplet;
12  import javax.swing.JButton;
13  import javax.swing.JFrame;
14  import javax.swing.JLabel;
15  import javax.swing.JOptionPane;
16  import javax.swing.JPanel;
17  import javax.swing.JTextField;
18
19  public class LoadImageAndScale extends JApplet
20  {
21     private ImageIcon image; // references image to display
22     private JPanel scaleJPanel; // JPanel containing the scale-selector
```

Fig. 24.1 | Loading, displaying and scaling an image in an applet. (Part I of 4.)

```
23      private JLabel percentJLabel; // label for JTextField
24      private JTextField scaleInputJTextField; // obtains user's input
25      private JButton scaleChangeJButton; // initiates scaling of image
26      private double scaleValue = 1.0;  //scale percentage for image
27
28      // load image when applet is loaded
29      public void init()
30      {
31         scaleJPanel = new JPanel();
32         percentJLabel = new JLabel( "scale percent:" );
33         scaleInputJTextField = new JTextField( "100" );
34         scaleChangeJButton = new JButton( "Set Scale" );
35
36         // add components and place scaleJPanel in applet's NORTH region
37         scaleJPanel.add( percentJLabel );
38         scaleJPanel.add( scaleInputJTextField );
39         scaleJPanel.add( scaleChangeJButton );
40         add( scaleJPanel, BorderLayout.NORTH );
41
42         // register event handler for scaleChangeJButton
43         scaleChangeJButton.addActionListener(
44            new ActionListener()
45            {
46               // when the JButton is pressed, set scaleValue and repaint
47               public void actionPerformed( ActionEvent e )
48               {
49                  scaleValue = Double.parseDouble(
50                     scaleInputJTextField.getText() ) / 100.0;
51                  repaint(); // causes image to be redisplyed at new scale
52               } // end method actionPerformed
53            } // end anonymous inner class
54         ); // end call to addActionListener
55
56         // use JNLP services to open an image file that the user selects
57         try
58         {
59            // get a reference to the FileOpenService
60            FileOpenService fileOpenService =
61               (FileOpenService) ServiceManager.lookup(
62                  "javax.jnlp.FileOpenService" );
63
64            // get file's contents from the FileOpenService
65            FileContents contents =
66               fileOpenService.openFileDialog( null, null );
67
68            // byte array to store image's data
69            byte[] imageData = new byte[ (int) contents.getLength() ];
70            contents.getInputStream().read( imageData ); // read image bytes
71            image = new ImageIcon( imageData ); // create the image
72
73            // if image successfully loaded, create and add DrawJPanel
74            add( new DrawJPanel(), BorderLayout.CENTER );
75         } // end try
```

Fig. 24.1 | Loading, displaying and scaling an image in an applet. (Part 2 of 4.)

```
76          catch( Exception e )
77          {
78             e.printStackTrace();
79          } // end catch
80       } // end method init
81
82       // DrawJPanel used to display loaded image
83       private class DrawJPanel extends JPanel
84       {
85          // display image
86          public void paintComponent( Graphics g )
87          {
88             super.paintComponent( g );
89
90             // the following values are used to center the image
91             double spareWidth =
92                getWidth() - scaleValue * image.getIconWidth();
93             double spareHeight =
94                getHeight() - scaleValue * image.getIconHeight();
95
96             // draw image with scaled width and height
97             g.drawImage( image.getImage(),
98                (int) ( spareWidth ) / 2, (int) ( spareHeight ) / 2,
99                (int) ( image.getIconWidth() * scaleValue ),
100               (int) ( image.getIconHeight() * scaleValue ), this );
101         } // end method paint
102      } // end class DrawJPanel
103  } // end class LoadImageAndScale
```

(a) Java Web Start security dialog that appears because this applet is requesting access to a file on the local computer.

(b) **Open** dialog that appears if the user clicks **OK** in the security dialog.

Fig. 24.1 | Loading, displaying and scaling an image in an applet. (Part 3 of 4.)

(c) Scaling the image.

Fig. 24.1 | Loading, displaying and scaling an image in an applet. (Part 4 of 4.)

Configuring the GUI and the JButton's Event Handler

The applet's init method (lines 29–80) configures the GUI and an event handler. It also uses JNLP services to enable the user to select an image to display from the local computer. Line 31 creates the JPanel that will contain the JLabel, JTextField and JButton created in lines 32–34. Lines 37–39 add these components to the JPanel's default FlowLayout. Line 40 places this JPanel in the NORTH region of the JApplet's default BorderLayout.

Lines 43–54 create the event handler for the scaleChangeJButton. When the user clicks this JButton, lines 49–50 obtain the user's input from the scaleInputJTextField, divide it by 100.0 to calculate the scale percentage and assign the result to scaleValue. This value will be used in later calculations to scale the image. For example, if the user enters 50, the scale value will be 0.5 and the image will be displayed at half its original size. Line 51 then repaints the applet to display the image at its new scale.

Opening the Image File Using JNLP's FileOpenService

As we mentioned in Section 23.7, with the user's permission, Java Web Start programs can access the local file system via the JNLP APIs of package javax.jnlp. In this example, we'd like the user to select an image from the local computer to display in the applet. (We've provided two images in this example's directory with the source code.) You can use JNLP's FileOpenService to request limited access to the local file system.

Lines 7–9 import the interfaces and class we need to use the FileOpenService. Lines 60–62 use the JNLP **ServiceManager** class's static **lookup** method to obtain a reference to the FileOpenService. JNLP provides several services, so this method returns an Object reference, which you must cast to the appropriate type. Next, lines 65–66 use the FileOpenService's **openFileDialog** method to display a file-selection dialog. Java Web Start prompts the user (Fig. 24.1(a)) to approve the applet's request for local file-system access. If the user gives permission, the **Open** dialog (Fig. 24.1(b)) is displayed. The open-FileDialog method has two parameters—a String to suggest a directory to open and a String array of acceptable file extensions (such as "png" and "jpg"). For simplicity, this program does not make use of either parameter, instead passing null values, which displays an open dialog open to the user's default directory and allows any file type to be selected.

When the user selects an image file and clicks the **Open** button in the dialog, method openFileDialog returns a FileContents object, which for security reasons does not give the program access to the file's exact location on disk. Instead, the program can get an InputStream and read the file's bytes. Line 69 creates a byte array in which the image's data will be stored. FileContents method **getLength** returns the number of bytes (as a long) in the file. Line 70 obtains the InputStream, then invokes its **read** method to fill the imageData byte array. Line 71 creates an ImageIcon using the byte array as the source of the image's data. Finally, line 74 adds a new DrawJPanel to the CENTER of the applet's BorderLayout. When the applet is displayed, its components' paintComponent methods are called, which causes the DrawJPanel to display the image. You can learn more about the JNLP APIs at java.sun.com/javase/6/docs/jre/api/javaws/jnlp.

Displaying the Image with Class DrawJPanel's paintComponent Method

To separate the GUI from the area in which the image is displayed, we use a subclass of JPanel named DrawJPanel (lines 83–102). Its paintComponent method (lines 86–101) displays the image. We'd like to center the image in the DrawJPanel, so lines 91–94 calculate the difference between the width of the DrawJPanel and that of the scaled image, then the height of the DrawJPanel and that of the scaled image. DrawJPanel's **getWidth** and **getHeight** methods (inherited indirectly from class Component) return the DrawJPanel's width and height, respectively. The ImageIcon's **getIconWidth** and **getIconHeight** methods return the image's width and height, respectively. The scaleValue is set to 1.0 by default (line 26), and is changed when the user clicks the **Set Scale** JButton.

Lines 97–100 use one of class Graphics's overloaded **drawImage** methods to display a scaled version of the ImageIcon. The first argument invokes the ImageIcon's **getImage** method to obtain the Image to draw. The second and third arguments represent the upper-left corner coordinates of the Image with respect to the DrawJPanel's upper-left corner. The fourth and fifth arguments specify the Image's scaled width and height, respectively. Line 99 scales the image's width by invoking the ImageIcon's getIconWidth method and multiplying its return value by scaleValue. Similarly, line 100 scales the image's height by invoking class ImageIcon's getIconHeight method and multiplying its return value by scaleValue. The last argument is a reference to an **ImageObserver**—an interface implemented by class Component. Since class DrawJPanel indirectly extends Component, a DrawJPanel *is an* ImageObserver. This argument is important when displaying large images that require a long time to load (or download from the Internet). It's possible that a program will attempt to display the image before it has completely loaded (or downloaded). As the Image loads, the ImageObserver receives notifications and updates the image on the screen as necessary. In this example, the images are being loaded from the user's computer, so it's likely that entire image will be displayed immediately.

Compiling the Applet

Compiling and running this applet requires the jnlp.jar file that contains the JNLP APIs. This file can be found in your JDK installation directory under the directories

```
sample
    jnlp
        servlet
```

To compile the applet, use the following command:

```
javac -classpath PathToJnlpJarFile LoadImageAndScale.java
```

where *PathToJnlpJarFile* includes both the path and the file name jnlp.jar. For example, on our Windows Vista computer, the *PathToJnlpJarFile* is

```
"C:\Program Files\Java\jdk1.6.0_11\sample\jnlp\servlet\jnlp.jar"
```

Packaging the Applet for Use with Java Web Start

To package the applet for use with Java Web Start, you must create a JAR file that contains the applet's code and the jnlp.jar file. To do so, use the command

```
jar cvf LoadImageAndScale.jar *.class PathToJnlpJarFile
```

where *PathToJnlpJarFile* includes both the path and the file name jnlp.jar. This will place all the .class files for the applet and a copy of the jnlp.jar file in the new JAR file LoadImageAndScale.jar.

JNLP Document for LoadImageAndScale Applet

The JNLP document in Fig. 24.2 is similar to the one introduced in Fig. 23.12. The only new feature in this document is that the resources element (lines 10–14) contains a second jar element (line 13) that references the jnlp.jar file, which is embedded in the file LoadImageAndScale.jar.

```
 1   <?xml version="1.0" encoding="UTF-8"?>
 2   <jnlp codebase="file:." href="LoadImageAndScale.jnlp">
 3
 4      <information>
 5         <title>LoadImageAndScale Applet</title>
 6         <vendor>Deitel</vendor>
 7         <offline-allowed/>
 8      </information>
 9
10      <resources>
11         <java version="1.6+"/>
12         <jar href="LoadImageAndScale.jar" main="true"/>
13         <jar href="jnlp.jar"/>
14      </resources>
15
16      <applet-desc
17         name="LoadImageAndScale"
18         main-class="LoadImageAndScale"
19         width="400"
20         height="300">
21      </applet-desc>
22   </jnlp>
```

Fig. 24.2 | JNLP document for the LoadImageAndScale applet.

Making the Applet Draggable Outside the Browser Window

The XHTML document in Fig. 24.3 loads the applet into a web browser. In this example, we use an applet element to specify the applet's class and provide two param elements between the applet element's tags. The first (line 4) specifies that this applet should be **draggable**. That is, the user can hold the *Alt* key and use the mouse to drag the applet outside the browser window. The applet will then continue executing, even if the browser is closed. Clicking the close box on the applet when it is executing outside the browser causes the applet to move back into the browser window if it is still open, or to terminate otherwise. The second `param` element shows an alternate way to specify the JNLP file that launches an applet. We discuss applet parameters in more detail in Section 27.2.

```
1   <html>
2   <body>
3   <applet code="LoadImageAndScale.class" width="400" height="300">
4       <param name="draggable" value="true">
5       <param name="jnlp_href" value="LoadImageAndScale.jnlp">
6   </applet>
7   </body>
8   </html>
```

Fig. 24.3 | XHTML document to load the `LoadImageAndScale` applet and make it draggable outside the browser window.

24.3 Animating a Series of Images

Next, we animate a series of images that are stored in an array of `ImageIcons`. In this example, we use the JNLP `FileOpenService` to enable the user to choose a group of images that will be animated by displaying one image at a time at 50-millisecond intervals. The animation presented in Figs. 24.4–24.5 is implemented using a subclass of `JPanel` called `LogoAnimatorJPanel` (Fig. 24.4) that can be attached to an application window or a `JApplet`. Class `LogoAnimator` (Fig. 24.5) declares a `main` method (lines 8–20 of Fig. 24.5) to execute the animation as an application. Method `main` declares an instance of class `JFrame` and attaches a `LogoAnimatorJPanel` object to the `JFrame` to display the animation.

```
1   // Fig. 24.4: LogoAnimatorJPanel.java
2   // Animating a series of images.
3   import java.awt.Dimension;
4   import java.awt.event.ActionEvent;
5   import java.awt.event.ActionListener;
6   import java.awt.Graphics;
7   import javax.jnlp.FileContents;
8   import javax.jnlp.FileOpenService;
9   import javax.jnlp.ServiceManager;
10  import javax.swing.ImageIcon;
11  import javax.swing.JPanel;
12  import javax.swing.Timer;
13
14  public class LogoAnimatorJPanel extends JPanel
15  {
16      protected ImageIcon images[]; // array of images
17      private int currentImage = 0; // current image index
18      private final int ANIMATION_DELAY = 50; // millisecond delay
19      private int width; // image width
20      private int height; // image height
21
22      private Timer animationTimer; // Timer drives animation
23
```

Fig. 24.4 | Animating a series of images. (Part 1 of 3.)

```
24      // constructor initializes LogoAnimatorJPanel by loading images
25      public LogoAnimatorJPanel()
26      {
27         try
28         {
29            // get reference to FileOpenService
30            FileOpenService fileOpenService =
31               (FileOpenService) ServiceManager.lookup(
32                  "javax.jnlp.FileOpenService" );
33
34            // display dialog that allows user to select multiple files
35            FileContents[] contents =
36               fileOpenService.openMultiFileDialog( null, null );
37
38            // create array to store ImageIcon references
39            images = new ImageIcon[ contents.length ];
40
41            // load the selected images
42            for ( int count = 0; count < images.length; count++ )
43            {
44               // create byte array to store an image's data
45               byte[] imageData =
46                  new byte[ (int) contents[ count ].getLength() ];
47
48               // get image's data and create image
49               contents[ count ].getInputStream().read( imageData );
50               images[ count ] = new ImageIcon( imageData );
51            } // end for
52
53            // this example assumes all images have the same width and height
54            width = images[ 0 ].getIconWidth();    // get icon width
55            height = images[ 0 ].getIconHeight(); // get icon height
56         } // end try
57         catch( Exception e )
58         {
59            e.printStackTrace();
60         } // end catch
61      } // end LogoAnimatorJPanel constructor
62
63      // display current image
64      public void paintComponent( Graphics g )
65      {
66         super.paintComponent( g ); // call superclass paintComponent
67
68         images[ currentImage ].paintIcon( this, g, 0, 0 );
69
70         // set next image to be drawn only if Timer is running
71         if ( animationTimer.isRunning() )
72            currentImage = ( currentImage + 1 ) % images.length;
73      } // end method paintComponent
74
75      // start animation, or restart if window is redisplayed
76      public void startAnimation()
77      {
```

Fig. 24.4 | Animating a series of images. (Part 2 of 3.)

```
78          if ( animationTimer == null )
79          {
80             currentImage = 0; // display first image
81
82             // create timer
83             animationTimer =
84                new Timer( ANIMATION_DELAY, new TimerHandler() );
85
86             animationTimer.start(); // start Timer
87          } // end if
88          else // animationTimer already exists, restart animation
89          {
90             if ( ! animationTimer.isRunning() )
91                animationTimer.restart();
92          } // end else
93       } // end method startAnimation
94
95       // stop animation Timer
96       public void stopAnimation()
97       {
98          animationTimer.stop();
99       } // end method stopAnimation
100
101      // return minimum size of animation
102      public Dimension getMinimumSize()
103      {
104         return getPreferredSize();
105      } // end method getMinimumSize
106
107      // return preferred size of animation
108      public Dimension getPreferredSize()
109      {
110         return new Dimension( width, height );
111      } // end method getPreferredSize
112
113      // inner class to handle action events from Timer
114      private class TimerHandler implements ActionListener
115      {
116         // respond to Timer's event
117         public void actionPerformed( ActionEvent actionEvent )
118         {
119            repaint(); // repaint animator
120         } // end method actionPerformed
121      } // end class TimerHandler
122   } // end class LogoAnimatorJPanel
```

Fig. 24.4 | Animating a series of images. (Part 3 of 3.)

```
1   // Fig. 24.5: LogoAnimator.java
2   // Displaying animated images on a JFrame.
3   import javax.swing.JFrame;
4
```

Fig. 24.5 | Displaying animated images on a JFrame. (Part 1 of 2.)

```
5    public class LogoAnimator
6    {
7       // execute animation in a JFrame
8       public static void main( String args[] )
9       {
10          LogoAnimatorJPanel animation = new LogoAnimatorJPanel();
11
12          JFrame window = new JFrame( "Animator test" ); // set up window
13          window.setDefaultCloseOperation( JFrame.EXIT_ON_CLOSE );
14          window.add( animation ); // add panel to frame
15
16          window.pack();  // make window just large enough for its GUI
17          window.setVisible( true );   // display window
18
19          animation.startAnimation();  // begin animation
20       } // end main
21    } // end class LogoAnimator
```

Fig. 24.5 | Displaying animated images on a JFrame. (Part 2 of 2.)

Class *LogoAnimatorPanel*

Class LogoAnimatorJPanel (Fig. 24.4) maintains an array of ImageIcons (declared at line 16) that are loaded in the constructor (lines 25–61). The constructor begins by using the JNLP FileOpenService's **openMultiFileDialog** method to display a file-selection dialog that allows the user to select multiple files at once. We named our sample images such that they all have the same base name ("deitel") followed by a two-digit number from 00–29. This ensures that our images are in the proper order for the animation. As in this chapter's first example, first the user is prompted to give permission, then the **Open** dialog appears if permission is granted. FileOpenService method openMultiFileDialog takes the same arguments as method openFileDialog but returns an array of FileContents objects representing the set of files selected by the user. When you run this application, navigate to a folder containing the images you wish to use and select the images. If you wish, you can use the 30 images we provide in this example's subdirectory named images.

Line 39 creates the array of ImageIcons, then lines 42–51 populate the array by creating a byte array (lines 45–46) for the current image's data, reading the bytes of the image into the array (line 49) and creating an ImageIcon object from the byte array. Lines 54–55 determine the width and height of the animation from the size of the first image in array images—we assume that all the images have the same width and height.

Method *startAnimation*

After the LogoAnimatorJPanel constructor loads the images, method main of Fig. 24.5 sets up the window in which the animation will appear (lines 12–17), and line 19 calls the LogoAnimatorJPanel's startAnimation method (declared at lines 76–93 of Fig. 24.4). This method starts the program's animation for the first time or restarts the animation that the program stopped previously. The animation is driven by an instance of class **Timer** (from package java.swing).

When the program is first run, method startAnimation is called to begin the animation. Although we provide the functionality for this method to restart the animation if it has been stopped, the example does not call the method for this purpose. We've added the functionality, however, should the reader choose to add GUI components that enable the user to start and stop the animation.

A Timer generates ActionEvents at a fixed interval in milliseconds (normally specified as an argument to the Timer's constructor) and notifies all its ActionListeners each time an ActionEvent occurs. Line 78 determines whether the Timer reference animationTimer is null. If it is, method startAnimation is being called for the first time, and a Timer needs to be created so that the animation can begin. Line 80 sets currentImage to 0, which indicates that the animation should begin with the first element of array images. Lines 83–84 assign a new Timer object to animationTimer. The Timer constructor receives two arguments—the delay in milliseconds (ANIMATION_DELAY is 50, as specified in line 18) and the ActionListener that will respond to the Timer's ActionEvents. For the second argument, an object of class TimerHandler is created. This class, which implements ActionListener, is declared in lines 114–121. Line 86 calls the Timer object's **start** method to start the Timer. Once started, animationTimer will generate an ActionEvent every 50 milliseconds and call the Timer's event handler actionPerformed (lines 117–120). Line 119 calls LogoAnimatorJPanel's repaint method to schedule a call to LogoAnimatorJPanel's paintComponent method (lines 64–73). Remember that any subclass of JComponent that draws should do so in its paintComponent method. Recall that the first statement in any paintComponent method should be a call to the superclass's paintComponent method, to ensure that Swing components are displayed correctly.

If the animation started earlier, then our Timer was created and the condition in line 78 evaluates to false. The program continues with lines 90–91, which restarts the animation that the program stopped previously. The if condition at line 90 uses Timer method **isRunning** to determine whether the Timer is running (i.e., generating events). If it's not running, line 91 calls Timer method **restart** to indicate that the Timer should start generating events again. Once this occurs, method actionPerformed (the Timer's event handler) is again called at regular intervals.

Method *paintComponent*

Line 68 calls the ImageIcon's **paintIcon** method to display the image stored at element currentImage in the array. The arguments represent the Component on which to draw (this), the Graphics object that performs the drawing (g) and the coordinates of the image's upper-left corner. Lines 71–72 determine whether the animationTimer is running and, if so, prepare for the next image to be displayed by incrementing currentImage by 1. The remainder calculation ensures that the value of currentImage is set to 0 (to repeat the animation sequence) when it's incremented past the last element index in the array. The if statement ensures that the same image will be displayed if paintComponent is called while the Timer is stopped. This can be useful if a GUI is provided that enables the user to start and stop the animation. For example, if the animation is stopped and the user covers it with another window, then uncovers it, method paintComponent will be called. In this case, we do not want the animation to show the next image (because the animation has been stopped). We simply want the window to display the same image until the animation is restarted.

Method `stopAnimation`

Method `stopAnimation` (lines 96–99) stops the animation by calling `Timer` method `stop` to indicate that the `Timer` should stop generating events. This prevents `actionPerformed` from calling `repaint` to initiate the painting of the next image in the array. Just as with restarting the animation, this example defines but does not use method `stopAnimation`. We've provided this method for demonstration purposes, or to allow the user to modify this example to stop and restart the animation.

Software Engineering Observation 24.1

When creating an animation for use in an applet, provide a mechanism for disabling the animation when the user browses a new web page different from the one on which the animation applet resides.

Methods `getPreferredSize` *and* `getMinimumSize`

By extending class `JPanel`, we're creating a new GUI component. So, we must ensure that it works like other components for layout purposes. Layout managers often use a component's **`getPreferredSize`** method (inherited from class `java.awt.Component`) to determine the component's preferred width and height. If a new component has a preferred width and height, it should override method `getPreferredSize` (lines 108–111) to return that width and height as an object of class **`Dimension`** (package `java.awt`). The `Dimension` class represents the width and height of a GUI component. In this example, the images we provide are 160 pixels wide and 80 pixels tall, so method `getPreferredSize` would return a `Dimension` object containing the numbers 160 and 80 (if you use these images).

Look-and-Feel Observation 24.1

The default size of a JPanel object is 10 pixels wide and 10 pixels tall.

Look-and-Feel Observation 24.2

When subclassing JPanel (or any other JComponent), override method getPreferred-Size if the new component is to have a specific preferred width and height.

Lines 102–105 override method **`getMinimumSize`**. This method determines the minimum width and height of the component. As with method `getPreferredSize`, new components should override method `getMinimumSize` (also inherited from class `Component`). Method `getMinimumSize` simply calls `getPreferredSize` (a common programming practice) to indicate that the minimum size and preferred size are the same. Some layout managers ignore the dimensions specified by these methods. For example, a `BorderLayout`'s NORTH and SOUTH regions use only the component's preferred height.

Look-and-Feel Observation 24.3

If a new GUI component has a minimum width and height (i.e., smaller dimensions would render the component ineffective on the display), override method getMinimumSize to return the minimum width and height as an instance of class Dimension.

Look-and-Feel Observation 24.4

For many GUI components, method getMinimumSize is implemented to return the result of a call to the component's getPreferredSize method.

Compiling the Application
Compiling and running this application requires the jnlp.jar file that contains the JNLP APIs. To compile the application use the following command:

```
javac -classpath PathToJnlpJarFile *.java
```

where *PathToJnlpJarFile* includes both the path and the file name jnlp.jar.

Packaging the Application for Use with Java Web Start
To package the application for use with Java Web Start, you must create a JAR file that contains the applet's code and the jnlp.jar file. To do so, use the command

```
jar cvf LogoAnimator.jar *.class PathToJnlpJarFile
```

where *PathToJnlpJarFile* includes both the path and the file name jnlp.jar.

*JNLP Document for **LoadImageAndScale** Applet*
The JNLP document in Fig. 24.6 is similar to the one in Fig. 24.2. The only new feature in this document is the application-desc element (lines 16–19), which specifies the name of the application and its main class. To run this application, use the command

```
javaws LogoAnimator.jnlp
```

Recall that you can also run Java Web Start applications via a link in a web page, as we showed in Fig. 23.13.

```
 1  <?xml version="1.0" encoding="UTF-8"?>
 2  <jnlp codebase="file:." href="LogoAnimator.jnlp">
 3
 4     <information>
 5        <title>LogoAnimator</title>
 6        <vendor>Deitel</vendor>
 7        <offline-allowed/>
 8     </information>
 9
10     <resources>
11        <java version="1.6+"/>
12        <jar href="LogoAnimator.jar" main="true"/>
13        <jar href="jnlp.jar"/>
14     </resources>
15
16     <application-desc
17        name="LogoAnimator"
18        main-class="LogoAnimator">
19     </application-desc>
20  </jnlp>
```

Fig. 24.6 | JNLP document for the LoadImageAndScale applet.

24.4 Image Maps

Image maps are commonly used to create interactive web pages. An image map is an image with **hot areas** that the user can click to accomplish a task, such as loading a different web page into a browser. When the user positions the mouse pointer over a hot area, normally a descriptive message appears in the status area of the browser or in a tool tip.

Figure 24.7 loads an image containing several of the programming-tip icons used in this book. The program allows the user to position the mouse pointer over an icon to display a descriptive message associated with it. Event handler mouseMoved (lines 39–43) takes the mouse coordinates and passes them to method translateLocation (lines 58–69). Method translateLocation tests the coordinates to determine the icon over which the mouse was positioned when the mouseMoved event occurred—the method then returns a message indicating what the icon represents. This message is displayed in the applet container's status bar using method **showStatus** of class Applet.

```
1   // Fig. 24.7: ImageMap.java
2   // Image map.
3   import java.awt.event.MouseAdapter;
4   import java.awt.event.MouseEvent;
5   import java.awt.event.MouseMotionAdapter;
6   import java.awt.Graphics;
7   import javax.swing.ImageIcon;
8   import javax.swing.JApplet;
9
10  public class ImageMap extends JApplet
11  {
12     private ImageIcon mapImage;
13
14     private static final String captions[] = { "Common Programming Error",
15        "Good Programming Practice", "Look-and-Feel Observation",
16        "Performance Tip", "Portability Tip",
17        "Software Engineering Observation", "Error-Prevention Tip" };
18
19     // sets up mouse listeners
20     public void init()
21     {
22        addMouseListener(
23
24           new MouseAdapter() // anonymous inner class
25           {
26              // indicate when mouse pointer exits applet area
27              public void mouseExited( MouseEvent event )
28              {
29                 showStatus( "Pointer outside applet" );
30              } // end method mouseExited
31           } // end anonymous inner class
32        ); // end call to addMouseListener
33
34        addMouseMotionListener(
35
36           new MouseMotionAdapter() // anonymous inner class
37           {
38              // determine icon over which mouse appears
39              public void mouseMoved( MouseEvent event )
40              {
```

Fig. 24.7 | Image map. (Part 1 of 3.)

```
41                    showStatus( translateLocation(
42                       event.getX(), event.getY() ) );
43            } // end method mouseMoved
44         } // end anonymous inner class
45      ); // end call to addMouseMotionListener
46
47      mapImage = new ImageIcon( "icons.png" ); // get image
48   } // end method init
49
50   // display mapImage
51   public void paint( Graphics g )
52   {
53      super.paint( g );
54      mapImage.paintIcon( this, g, 0, 0 );
55   } // end method paint
56
57   // return tip caption based on mouse coordinates
58   public String translateLocation( int x, int y )
59   {
60      // if coordinates outside image, return immediately
61      if ( x >= mapImage.getIconWidth() || y >= mapImage.getIconHeight() )
62         return "";
63
64      // determine icon number (0 - 6)
65      double iconWidth = ( double ) mapImage.getIconWidth() / 7.0;
66      int iconNumber = ( int )( ( double ) x / iconWidth );
67
68      return captions[ iconNumber ]; // return appropriate icon caption
69   } // end method translateLocation
70 } // end class ImageMap
```

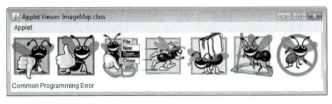

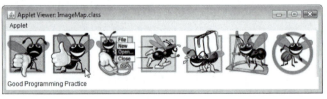

Fig. 24.7 | Image map. (Part 2 of 3.)

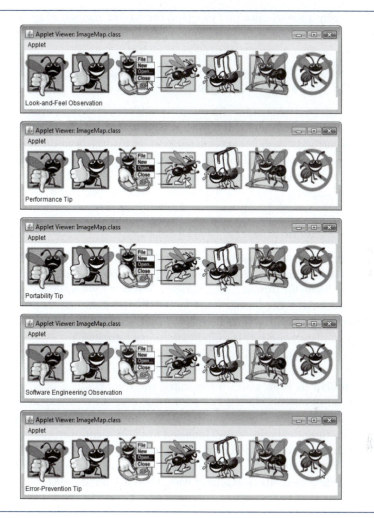

Fig. 24.7 | Image map. (Part 3 of 3.)

Clicking in the applet of Fig. 24.7 will not cause any action. In Chapter 27, Networking, we discuss the techniques for loading another web page into a browser via URLs and the `AppletContext` interface. Using those techniques, this applet could associate each icon with a URL that the browser would display when the user clicks the icon.

24.5 Loading and Playing Audio Clips

Java programs can manipulate and play **audio clips**. Users can capture their own audio clips, and many clips are available in software products and over the Internet. Your system needs to be equipped with audio hardware (speakers and a sound card) to be able to play the audio clips.

Java provides several mechanisms for playing sounds in an applet. The two simplest are the `Applet`'s **play** method and the **play** method of the **AudioClip** interface. Additional audio capabilities are available in the Java Media Framework and Java Sound APIs. If you'd like to play a sound once in a program, the `Applet` method `play` loads the sound and plays it once, then the sound can be garbage collected. The `Applet` method `play` has two versions:

```
public void play( URL location, String soundFileName );
public void play( URL soundURL );
```

The first version loads the audio clip stored in file `soundFileName` from `location` and plays the sound. The first argument is normally a call to the applet's `getDocumentBase` or **getCodeBase** method. Method `getDocumentBase` returns the location of the HTML file that loaded the applet. (If the applet is in a package, the method returns the location of the package or the JAR file containing the package.) Method `getCodeBase` indicates the location of the applet's `.class` file. The second version of method `play` takes a URL that contains the location and the file name of the audio clip. The statement

```
play( getDocumentBase(), "hi.au" );
```

loads the audio clip in file `hi.au` and plays the clip once.

The **sound engine** that plays the audio clips supports several audio file formats, including **Sun Audio file format** (`.au` extension), **Windows Wave file format** (`.wav` extension), **Macintosh AIFF file format** (`.aif` or `.aiff` extensions) and **Musical Instrument Digital Interface (MIDI) file format** (`.mid` or `.rmi` extensions). The Java Media Framework (JMF) and Java Sound APIs support additional formats.

The program of Fig. 24.8 demonstrates loading and playing an `AudioClip` (package `java.applet`). This technique is more flexible than `Applet` method `play`. An applet can use an `AudioClip` to store audio for repeated use throughout a program's execution. `Applet` method **getAudioClip** has two forms that take the same arguments as method `play` described previously. Method `getAudioClip` returns a reference to an `AudioClip`. An `AudioClip` has three methods—`play`, `loop` and `stop`. As mentioned earlier, method `play` plays the audio clip once. Method **loop** continuously loops through the audio clip in the background. Method **stop** terminates an audio clip that is currently playing. In the program, each of these methods is associated with a button on the applet.

```
1   // Fig. 24.8: LoadAudioAndPlay.java
2   // Loading and playing an AudioClip.
3   import java.applet.AudioClip;
4   import java.awt.event.ItemListener;
5   import java.awt.event.ItemEvent;
6   import java.awt.event.ActionListener;
7   import java.awt.event.ActionEvent;
8   import java.awt.FlowLayout;
9   import javax.swing.JApplet;
10  import javax.swing.JButton;
11  import javax.swing.JComboBox;
12
13  public class LoadAudioAndPlay extends JApplet
14  {
15      private AudioClip sound1, sound2, currentSound;
16      private JButton playJButton, loopJButton, stopJButton;
17      private JComboBox soundJComboBox;
```

Fig. 24.8 | Loading and playing an `AudioClip`. (Part 1 of 3.)

```
18
19      // load the audio when the applet begins executing
20      public void init()
21      {
22         setLayout( new FlowLayout() );
23
24         String choices[] = { "Welcome", "Hi" };
25         soundJComboBox = new JComboBox( choices ); // create JComboBox
26
27         soundJComboBox.addItemListener(
28
29            new ItemListener() // anonymous inner class
30            {
31               // stop sound and change sound to user's selection
32               public void itemStateChanged( ItemEvent e )
33               {
34                  currentSound.stop();
35                  currentSound = soundJComboBox.getSelectedIndex() == 0 ?
36                     sound1 : sound2;
37               } // end method itemStateChanged
38            } // end anonymous inner class
39         ); // end addItemListener method call
40
41         add( soundJComboBox ); // add JComboBox to applet
42
43         // set up button event handler and buttons
44         ButtonHandler handler = new ButtonHandler();
45
46         // create Play JButton
47         playJButton = new JButton( "Play" );
48         playJButton.addActionListener( handler );
49         add( playJButton );
50
51         // create Loop JButton
52         loopJButton = new JButton( "Loop" );
53         loopJButton.addActionListener( handler );
54         add( loopJButton );
55
56         // create Stop JButton
57         stopJButton = new JButton( "Stop" );
58         stopJButton.addActionListener( handler );
59         add( stopJButton );
60
61         // load sounds and set currentSound
62         sound1 = getAudioClip( getDocumentBase(), "welcome.wav" );
63         sound2 = getAudioClip( getDocumentBase(), "hi.au" );
64         currentSound = sound1;
65      } // end method init
66
67      // stop the sound when the user switches web pages
68      public void stop()
69      {
70         currentSound.stop(); // stop AudioClip
71      } // end method stop
```

Fig. 24.8 | Loading and playing an AudioClip. (Part 2 of 3.)

```
72
73      // private inner class to handle button events
74      private class ButtonHandler implements ActionListener
75      {
76          // process play, loop and stop button events
77          public void actionPerformed( ActionEvent actionEvent )
78          {
79              if ( actionEvent.getSource() == playJButton )
80                  currentSound.play(); // play AudioClip once
81              else if ( actionEvent.getSource() == loopJButton )
82                  currentSound.loop(); // play AudioClip continuously
83              else if ( actionEvent.getSource() == stopJButton )
84                  currentSound.stop(); // stop AudioClip
85          } // end method actionPerformed
86      } // end class ButtonHandler
87  } // end class LoadAudioAndPlay
```

Fig. 24.8 | Loading and playing an `AudioClip`. (Part 3 of 3.)

Lines 62–63 in the applet's `init` method use `getAudioClip` to load two audio files—a Windows Wave file (`welcome.wav`) and a Sun Audio file (`hi.au`). The user can select which audio clip to play from the `JComboBox` `soundJComboBox`. Note that the applet's `stop` method is overridden at lines 68–71. When the user switches web pages, the applet container calls the applet's `stop` method. This enables the applet to stop playing the audio clip. Otherwise, it continues to play in the background—even if the applet is not displayed in the browser. This is not necessarily a problem, but it can be annoying to the user if the audio clip is looping. The `stop` method is provided here as a convenience to the user.

Look-and-Feel Observation 24.5

When playing audio clips in an applet or application, provide a mechanism for the user to disable the audio.

24.6 Playing Video and Other Media with Java Media Framework

A simple video can concisely and effectively convey a great deal of information. Recognizing the value of bringing extensible multimedia capabilities to Java, Sun Microsystems, Intel and Silicon Graphics worked together to produce the Java Media Framework (JMF). Using the JMF API, programmers can create Java applications that play, edit, stream and capture many popular media types. The features of JMF are quite extensive. This section briefly introduces some popular media formats and demonstrates playing video using the JMF API.

IBM and Sun developed the latest JMF specification—version 2.0. Sun also provides a reference implementation of the JMF specification—JMF 2.1.1e—that supports media file types such as **Microsoft Audio/Video Interleave** (**.avi**), **Macromedia Flash movies** (**.swf**), **Future Splash** (**.spl**), **MPEG Layer 3 Audio** (**.mp3**), Musical Instrument Digital Interface (MIDI; .mid or .rmi extensions), **MPEG-1 videos** (**.mpeg**, **.mpg**), **QuickTime** (**.mov**), Sun Audio file format (.au extension), and Macintosh AIFF file format (.aif or .aiff extensions). You've already seen some of these file types.

Currently, JMF is available as an extension separate from the Java 2 Software Development Kit. The most recent JMF implementation (2.1.1e) can be downloaded from:

```
java.sun.com/javase/technologies/desktop/media/jmf/2.1.1/
   download.html
```

[*Note:* Keep track of where you install the Java Media Framework on your computer. To compile and run this application, you must include in the class path the jmf.jar file that is installed with the Java Media Framework. Recall that you can specify the class path with both the javac and java commands via the -classpath command-line option.]

The JMF website provides versions of the JMF that take advantage of the performance features of certain platforms. For example, the JMF Windows Performance Pack provides extensive media and device support for Java programs running on Microsoft Windows platforms. The JMF's website (java.sun.com/javase/technologies/desktop/media/jmf/) provides information and resources for JMF programmers.

Creating a Simple Media Player

The JMF offers several mechanisms for playing media. The simplest is using objects that implement interface **Player** declared in package **javax.media**. Package javax.media and its subpackages contain the classes that compose the Java Media Framework. To play a media clip, you must first create a URL object that refers to it. Then pass the URL as an argument to static method **createRealizedPlayer** of class Manager to obtain a Player for the media clip. Class **Manager** declares utility methods for accessing system resources to play and to manipulate media. Figure 24.9 declares a JPanel that demonstrates some of these methods.

```java
1   // Fig. 24.9: MediaPanel.java
2   // JPanel that plays a media file from a URL.
3   import java.awt.BorderLayout;
4   import java.awt.Component;
5   import java.io.IOException;
6   import java.net.URL;
7   import javax.media.CannotRealizeException;
8   import javax.media.Manager;
9   import javax.media.NoPlayerException;
10  import javax.media.Player;
11  import javax.swing.JPanel;
12
13  public class MediaPanel extends JPanel
14  {
15     public MediaPanel( URL mediaURL )
16     {
17        setLayout( new BorderLayout() ); // use a BorderLayout
18
```

Fig. 24.9 | JPanel that plays a media file from a URL. (Part 1 of 2.)

```
19        // Use lightweight components for Swing compatibility
20        Manager.setHint( Manager.LIGHTWEIGHT_RENDERER, true );
21
22        try
23        {
24            // create a player to play the media specified in the URL
25            Player mediaPlayer = Manager.createRealizedPlayer( mediaURL );
26
27            // get the components for the video and the playback controls
28            Component video = mediaPlayer.getVisualComponent();
29            Component controls = mediaPlayer.getControlPanelComponent();
30
31            if ( video != null )
32                add( video, BorderLayout.CENTER ); // add video component
33
34            if ( controls != null )
35                add( controls, BorderLayout.SOUTH ); // add controls
36
37            mediaPlayer.start(); // start playing the media clip
38        } // end try
39        catch ( NoPlayerException noPlayerException )
40        {
41            System.err.println( "No media player found" );
42        } // end catch
43        catch ( CannotRealizeException cannotRealizeException )
44        {
45            System.err.println( "Could not realize media player" );
46        } // end catch
47        catch ( IOException iOException )
48        {
49            System.err.println( "Error reading from the source" );
50        } // end catch
51    } // end MediaPanel constructor
52 } // end class MediaPanel
```

Fig. 24.9 | JPanel that plays a media file from a URL. (Part 2 of 2.)

The constructor (lines 15–51) sets up the JPanel to play the media file specified by the constructor's URL parameter. MediaPanel uses a BorderLayout (line 17). Line 20 invokes static method **setHint** to set the flag **Manager.LIGHTWEIGHT_RENDERER** to true. This instructs the Manager to use a lightweight renderer that is compatible with lightweight Swing components, as opposed to the default heavyweight renderer. Inside the try block (lines 22–38), line 25 invokes static method createRealizedPlayer of class Manager to create and realize a Player that plays the media file. When a Player realizes, it identifies the system resources it needs to play the media. Depending on the file, realizing can be a resource-consuming and time-consuming process. Method createRealized-Player throws three checked exceptions, **NoPlayerException**, **CannotRealizeException** and IOException. A NoPlayerException indicates that the system could not find a player that can play the file format. A CannotRealizeException indicates that the system could not properly identify the resources a media file needs. An IOException indicates that there was an error while reading the file. These exceptions are handled in the catch block in lines 39–50.

Line 28 invokes method **getVisualComponent** of Player to get a Component that displays the visual (generally video) aspect of the media file. Line 29 invokes method **getControlPanelComponent** of Player to get a Component that provides playback and media controls. These components are assigned to local variables video and controls, respectively. The if statements in lines 31–32 and lines 34–35 add the video and the controls if they exist. The video Component is added to the CENTER region (line 32), so it fills any available space on the JPanel. The controls Component, which is added to the SOUTH region, typically provides the following controls:

1. A positioning slider to jump to certain points in the media clip.

2. A pause button.

3. A volume button that provides volume control by right clicking and a mute function by left clicking.

4. A media properties button that provides detailed media information by left clicking and frame-rate control by right clicking.

Line 37 calls Player method **start** to begin playing the media file. Lines 39–50 handle the various exceptions that createRealizedPlayer throws.

The application in Fig. 24.10 displays a JFileChooser dialog for the user to choose a media file. It then creates a MediaPanel that plays the selected file and creates a JFrame to display the MediaPanel.

```java
1  // Fig. 24.10: MediaTest.java
2  // Test application that creates a MediaPanel from a user-selected file.
3  import java.io.File;
4  import java.net.MalformedURLException;
5  import java.net.URL;
6  import javax.swing.JFileChooser;
7  import javax.swing.JFrame;
8
9  public class MediaTest
10 {
11    // launch the application
12    public static void main( String args[] )
13    {
14       // create a file chooser
15       JFileChooser fileChooser = new JFileChooser();
16
17       // show open file dialog
18       int result = fileChooser.showOpenDialog( null );
19
20       if ( result == JFileChooser.APPROVE_OPTION ) // user chose a file
21       {
22          URL mediaURL = null;
23
24          try
25          {
26             // get the file as URL
27             mediaURL = fileChooser.getSelectedFile().toURI().toURL();
28          } // end try
```

Fig. 24.10 | Test application that creates a MediaPanel from a user-selected file. (Part 1 of 2.)

```
29              catch ( MalformedURLException malformedURLException )
30              {
31                 System.err.println( "Could not create URL for the file" );
32              } // end catch
33
34              if ( mediaURL != null ) // only display if there is a valid URL
35              {
36                 JFrame mediaTest = new JFrame( "Media Tester" );
37                 mediaTest.setDefaultCloseOperation( JFrame.EXIT_ON_CLOSE );
38
39                 MediaPanel mediaPanel = new MediaPanel( mediaURL );
40                 mediaTest.add( mediaPanel );
41
42                 mediaTest.setSize( 300, 300 );
43                 mediaTest.setVisible( true );
44              } // end inner if
45          } // end outer if
46      } // end main
47  } // end class MediaTest
```

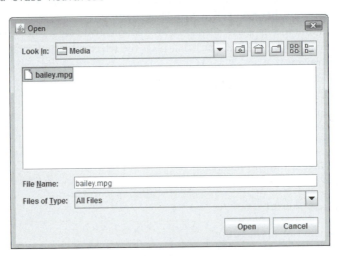

Fig. 24.10 | Test application that creates a MediaPanel from a user-selected file. (Part 2 of 2.)

Method `main` (lines 12–46) assigns a new `JFileChooser` to local variable `fileChooser` (line 15), shows an open-file dialog (line 18) and assigns the return value to `result`. Line 20 checks `result` to determine whether the user chose a file. To create a `Player` to play the selected media file, you must convert the `File` object returned by `JFileChooser` to a URL object. Method **toURI** of class `File` returns a URI that points to the `File` on the system. We then invoke method **toURL** of class URI to get the file's URL. The `try` statement (lines 24–32) creates a URL for the selected file and assigns it to `mediaURL`. The `if` statement in lines 34–44 checks that `mediaURL` is not `null` and creates the GUI components to play the media.

24.7 Wrap-Up

In this chapter, you learned how to make applications more exciting by including sound, images, graphics and video. We introduced Java's multimedia capabilities, including the Java Media Framework API and Java Sound API. You used class `ImageIcon` to display and manipulate images stored in files, and you learned about the different image formats supported by Java. You used the JNLP `FileOpenService` to enable the user of a Java Web Start application to select files from the local file system, then used streams to load the contents of those files for use in your programs. You created animation by displaying a series of images in a specific order. You used image maps to make an application more interactive. You then learned how to load audio clips and how to play them either once or in a continuous loop. The chapter concluded with a demonstration of loading and playing video. In the next chapter, you'll continue your study of GUI concepts, building on the techniques you learned in Chapter 14.

24.8 Web Resources

www.nasa.gov/multimedia/highlights/index.html
The *NASA Multimedia Gallery* contains a wide variety of images, audio clips and video clips that you can download and use to test your Java multimedia programs.

commons.wikimedia.org/wiki/Main_Page
The *Wikimedia Commons* site provides access to millions of media files.

www.anbg.gov.au/anbg/index.html
The *Australian National Botanic Gardens* website provides links to the sounds of many animals. Try, for example, the *Common Birds* link under the "Animals in the Gardens" section.

www.thefreesite.com
This site has links to free sounds and clip art.

www.soundcentral.com
SoundCentral provides audio clips in WAV, AU, AIFF and MIDI formats.

www.animationfactory.com
The *Animation Factory* provides thousands of free GIF animations for personal use.

www.clipart.com
This site is a subscription-based service for images and sounds.

java.sun.com/developer/techDocs/hi/repository/
The *Java look-and-feel Graphics Repository* provides images designed for use in a Swing GUI, including toolbar button images.

www.freebyte.com/graphicprograms/
This guide contains links to several free graphics software programs. The software can be used to modify images and draw graphics.

graphicssoft.about.com/od/pixelbasedfreewin/
This site provides links to free graphics programs designed for use on Windows machines.

Java Multimedia API References

java.sun.com/javase/technologies/desktop/media/
The online home of the Java Media APIs.

java.sun.com/products/java-media/sound/
The *Java Sound API* home page. Java Sound provides capabilities for playing and recording audio.

java3d.dev.java.net/
The *Java 3D API* home page. This API can be used to produce three-dimensional images typical of today's video games.

java.sun.com/products/java-media/speech/
The *Java Speech API* enables programs to perform speech synthesis and speech recognition.

freetts.sourceforge.net/docs/index.php
FreeTTS is an implementation of the Java Speech API.

Summary

Section 24.2 Loading, Displaying and Scaling Images

- Class ImageIcon's constructors can receive arguments of several different formats, including a byte array containing the bytes of an image, an Image (package java.awt) already loaded in memory, or a String or a URL representing the image's location.

- Java supports several image formats, including Graphics Interchange Format (GIF), Joint Photographic Experts Group (JPEG) and Portable Network Graphics (PNG). The file names for these types typically end with .gif, .jpg (or .jpeg) and .png, respectively.

- Java Web Start programs can access the local file system via the JNLP APIs of package javax.jnlp. You can use JNLP's FileOpenService to request limited access to the local file system.

- The JNLP ServiceManager class's static lookup method obtains a reference to the FileOpenService. Since other services are provided by JNLP, this method returns an Object reference, which you must cast to the appropriate type.

- FileOpenService method openFileDialog method displays a file-selection dialog. This causes Java Web Start to prompt the user to approve the program's request local file-system access. If the user gives permission, the **Open** dialog is displayed. The openFileDialog method has two parameters—a String to suggest a directory to open and a String array of acceptable file extensions.

- When the user selects an image file and clicks the Open button in the dialog, method openFileDialog returns a FileContents object, which for security reasons does not give the program access to the file's exact location on disk. Instead, the program can get an InputStream and read the file's bytes.

- FileContents method getLength returns the number of bytes in the file.

- Component methods getWidth and getHeight return the width and height of a Component, respectively.

- ImageIcon methods getIconWidth and getIconHeight return the width and height of an image, respectively.

- Class Graphics provides overloaded drawImage methods, one of which displays a scaled version of an Image. The first argument is the Image to draw. The second and third arguments represent the upper-left corner coordinates of the Image. The fourth and fifth arguments specify the Image's scaled width and height, respectively. The last argument is a reference to an ImageObserver—an interface implemented by class Component.

- It's possible that a program will attempt to display an image before it has completely loaded (or downloaded). As an Image loads, the ImageObserver receives notifications and updates the image on the screen as necessary.

- A draggable applet can be dragged outside the browser window by holding the *Alt* key and dragging the applet with the mouse. The applet will then continue executing, even if the browser is closed. Clicking the close box on the applet when it is executing outside the browser causes the applet to move back into the browser window if it is still open, or to terminate otherwise.

Section 24.3 Animating a Series of Images

- The FileOpenService's openMultiFileDialog method displays a file-selection dialog that allows the user to select multiple files at once. FileOpenService method openMultiFileDialog takes the same arguments as method openFileDialog, but returns an array of FileContents objects representing the set of files selected by the user.

- Timer objects generate ActionEvents at fixed millisecond intervals. The Timer constructor receives a delay in milliseconds and an ActionListener. Timer method start starts the Timer. Method stop indicates that the Timer should stop generating events. Method restart indicates that the Timer should start generating events again.

- ImageIcon method paintIcon displays the ImageIcon's image. The method requires four arguments—a reference to the Component on which the image will be displayed, a reference to the Graphics object used to render the image, the *x*-coordinate of the upper-left corner of the image and the *y*-coordinate of the upper-left corner of the image.

Section 24.4 Image Maps

- An image map is an image that has hot areas that the user can click to accomplish a task, such as loading a different web page into a browser.

Section 24.5 Loading and Playing Audio Clips

- Applet method play has two forms:

```
public void play( URL location, String soundFileName );
public void play( URL soundURL );
```

  One version loads the audio clip stored in file soundFileName from location and plays the sound. The other version takes a URL that contains the location and the file name of the audio clip.

- Applet method getDocumentBase indicates the location of the HTML file that loaded the applet. Method getCodeBase indicates where the .class file for an applet is located.

- The sound engine that plays audio clips supports several audio file formats, including Sun Audio file format (.au extension), Windows Wave file format (.wav extension), Macintosh AIFF file format (.aif or .aiff extensions) and Musical Instrument Digital Interface (MIDI) file format (.mid or .rmi extensions). The Java Media Framework (JMF) supports additional formats.

- Applet method getAudioClip has two forms that take the same arguments as the play method. Method getAudioClip returns a reference to an AudioClip. AudioClips have three methods—play, loop and stop. Method play plays the audio clip once. Method loop continuously loops the audio clip. Method stop terminates an audio clip that is currently playing.

Section 24.6 Playing Video and Other Media with Java Media Framework

- Sun Microsystems, Intel and Silicon Graphics worked together to produce the Java Media Framework (JMF).

- Package javax.media and its subpackages contain the Java Media Framework classes.

- Class Manager declares methods for accessing system resources to play and to manipulate media.

- Method toURI of class File returns a URI that points to the File on the system.

Terminology

Self-Review Exercises

24.1 Fill in the blanks in each of the following statements:

a) `Graphics` method _____ displays an image on an applet.

b) Java provides two mechanisms for playing sounds in an applet—the `Applet`'s `play` method and the `play` method of the _____ interface.

c) A(n) _____ is an image that has hot areas that the user can click to accomplish a task such as loading a web page.

d) Method _____ of class `ImageIcon` displays the `ImageIcon`'s image.

e) Java supports several image formats, including _____, _____ and _____.

f) The JNLP _____ class's `static` `lookup` method obtains a reference to the `FileOpenService`.

24.2 Determine whether each of the following statements is *true* or *false*. If *false*, explain why.

a) A sound is marked for garbage collection after it plays via the play method of class `Applet`.

b) Class `ImageIcon` provides constructors that allow an `ImageIcon` object to be initialized only with an image from the local computer.

c) Method `play` of class `AudioClip` continuously loops an audio clip.

d) The Java Image I/O API is used for adding 3D graphics to a Java application.

e) `Applet` method `getDocumentBase` returns, as an object of class `URL`, the location on the Internet of the HTML file that invoked the applet.

f) `FileOpenService` methods `openFileDialog` and `openMultiFileDialog` return a `FileContents` object and an array of `FileContents` objects, respectively.

Answers to Self-Review Exercises

24.1 a) `drawImage`. b) `AudioClip`. c) image map. d) `paintIcon`. e) Graphics Interchange Format (GIF), Joint Photographic Experts Group (JPEG), Portable Network Graphics (PNG). f) `ServiceManager`.

24.2 a) True. b) False. `ImageIcon` can load images from the Internet as well. c) False. Method `play` of class `AudioClip` plays an audio clip once. Method `loop` of class `AudioClip` continuously loops an audio clip. d) False. The Java 3D API is used for creating and modifying 3D graphics. The Java Image I/O API is used for reading from and outputting images to files. e) True. f) True.

Exercises

24.3 Describe how to make an animation "browser friendly."

24.4 Describe the Java methods for playing and manipulating audio clips.

24.5 Explain how image maps are used. List several examples of their use.

24.6 *(Randomly Erasing an Image)* Suppose an image is displayed in a rectangular screen area. One way to erase the image is simply to set every pixel to the same color immediately, but the visual effect is dull. Write a Java program that displays an image, then erases it by using random-number generation to select individual pixels to erase. After most of the image is erased, erase all the remaining pixels at once. You can draw individual pixels as a line that starts and ends at the same coordinates. You might try several variants of this problem. For example, you might display lines randomly or display shapes randomly to erase regions of the screen.

24.7 *(Text Flasher)* Create a Java program that repeatedly flashes text on the screen. Do this by alternating the text with a plain background-color image. Allow the user to control the "blink speed" and the background color or pattern. You'll need to use methods **getDelay** and **setDelay** of class `Timer`. These methods are used to retrieve and set the interval in milliseconds between ActionEvents, respectively

24.8 *(Image Flasher)* Create a Java program that repeatedly flashes an image on the screen. Do this by alternating the image with a plain background-color image.

24.9 *(Digital Clock)* Implement a program that displays a digital clock on the screen.

24.10 *(Calling Attention to an Image)* If you want to emphasize an image, you might place a row of simulated light bulbs around it. You can let the light bulbs flash in unison or fire on and off in sequence one after the other.

24.11 *(Image Zooming)* Create a program that enables you to zoom in on or out from an image.

24.12 *(LoadImageAndScale Modification)* Modify applet `LoadImageAndScale` (Fig. 24.1) to provide a second button that enables the user to choose a new image. The button's event handler should use the JNLP `FileOpenService` to display an **Open** dialog, so that the user can select a new image.

24.13 *(Image Viewer)* Using the JNLP techniques you learned in Sections 24.2—24.3, create an image viewer application that enables the user to select a group of images to display. The application should display a `JList` containing the names of the selected files. You can obtain the name of the file represented by a `FileContents` object by calling its `getName` method. When the user clicks the name of an image in the `JList`, the application should display the image in the window.

Special Section: Challenging Multimedia Projects

The preceding exercises are keyed to the text and designed to test your understanding of fundamental multimedia concepts. This section includes a collection of advanced multimedia projects. You should find these problems challenging, yet entertaining. The problems vary in difficulty. Some require an hour or two of program writing and implementation. Others are useful for lab assignments that might require two or three weeks of study and implementation. Some are challenging term projects. [*Note to Instructors:* Solutions are *not* provided for these exercises.]

24.14 *(Animation)* Create a general-purpose Java animation program. It should allow the user to specify the sequence of frames to be displayed, the speed at which the images are displayed, audios to be played while the animation is running and so on.

24.15 *(Limericks)* Modify the limerick-writing program you wrote in Exercise 16.3 to sing the limericks your program creates.

24.16 *(Random Interimage Transition)* This provides a nice visual effect. If you're displaying one image in a given area on the screen and you'd like to transition to another image in the same area, store the new screen image in an off-screen buffer and randomly copy pixels from it to the display area, overlaying the pixels already at those locations. When the vast majority of the pixels have been copied, copy the entire new image to the display area to be sure you are displaying the complete new image. To implement this program, you may need to use the `PixelGrabber` and `MemoryImageSource` classes (see the Java API documentation for descriptions of these classes). You might try several variants of this problem. For example, select all the pixels in a randomly chosen straight line or shape in the new image and overlay them above the corresponding positions of the old image.

24.17 *(Background Audio)* Add background audio to one of your favorite applications by using the `loop` method of class `AudioClip` to play the sound in the background while you interact with your application in the normal way.

24.18 *(Scrolling Marquee Sign)* Create a program that scrolls dotted characters from right to left (or from left to right if that is appropriate for your language) across a marquee-like display sign. As an option, display the text in a continuous loop, so that after the text disappears at one end, it reappears at the other.

24.19 *(Scrolling Image Marquee)* Create a program that scrolls an image across a marquee screen.

24.20 *(Analog Clock)* Create a program that displays an analog clock with hour, minute and second hands that move appropriately as the time changes.

24.21   *(Dynamic Audio and Graphical Kaleidoscope)* Write a kaleidoscope program that displays reflected graphics to simulate the popular children's toy. Incorporate audio effects that "mirror" your program's dynamically changing graphics.

24.22   *(Automatic Jigsaw Puzzle Generator)* Create a jigsaw puzzle generator and manipulator. The user specifies an image. Your program loads and displays the image, then breaks it into randomly selected shapes and shuffles them. The user then uses the mouse to move the pieces around to solve the puzzle. Add appropriate audio sounds as the pieces are moved around and snapped back into place. You might keep tabs on each piece and where it really belongs—then use audio effects to help the user get the pieces into the correct positions.

24.23   *(Maze Generator and Walker)* Develop a multimedia-based maze generator and traverser program based on the maze programs you wrote in Exercises 18.20–18.22. Let the user customize the maze by specifying the number of rows and columns and by indicating the level of difficulty. Have an animated mouse walk the maze. Use audio to dramatize the movement of your mouse character.

24.24   *(One-Armed Bandit)* Develop a multimedia simulation of a "one-armed bandit." Have three spinning wheels. Place symbols and images of various fruits on each wheel. Use random-number generation to simulate the spinning of each wheel and the stopping of each wheel on a symbol.

24.25   *(Horse Race)* Create a simulation of a horse race. Have multiple contenders. Use audios for a race announcer. Play the appropriate audios to indicate the correct status of each contender throughout the race. Use audios to announce the final results. You might try to simulate the kinds of horse-racing games that are often played at carnivals. The players take turns at the mouse and have to perform some skill-oriented manipulation with it to advance their horses.

24.26   *(Shuffleboard)* Develop a multimedia-based simulation of the game of shuffleboard. Use appropriate audio and visual effects.

24.27   *(Game of Pool)* Create a multimedia-based simulation of the game of pool. Each player takes turns using the mouse to position a pool cue and hit it against the ball at the appropriate angle to try to make other balls fall into the pockets. Your program should keep score.

24.28   *(Artist)* Design an art program that will give an artist a great variety of capabilities to draw, use images and use animations to create a dynamic multimedia art display.

24.29   *(Fireworks Designer)* Create a Java program that someone might use to create a fireworks display. Create a variety of fireworks demonstrations. Then orchestrate the firing of the fireworks for maximum effect.

24.30   *(Floor Planner)* Develop a program that will help someone arrange furniture in a home. Add features that enable the person to achieve the best possible arrangement.

24.31   *(Crossword)* Crossword puzzles are among the most popular pastimes. Develop a multimedia-based crossword-puzzle program. Your program should enable the player to place and erase words easily. Tie your program to a large computerized dictionary. Your program also should be able to suggest words on which letters have already been filled in. Provide other features that will make the crossword-puzzle enthusiast's job easier.

24.32   *(15 Puzzle)* Write a multimedia-based program that enables the user to play the game of 15. The game is played on a 4-by-4 board having a total of 16 slots. One slot is empty, the others are occupied by 15 tiles numbered 1 through 15. The user can move any tile next to the currently empty slot into that slot by clicking on the tile. Your program should create the board with the tiles in random order. The goal is to arrange the tiles into sequential order, row by row.

24.33   *(Reaction Time/Reaction Precision Tester)* Create a program that moves a randomly created shape around the screen. The user moves the mouse to catch and click on the shape. The shape's speed and size can be varied. Keep statistics on how long the user typically takes to catch a shape of a given size. The user will probably have more difficulty catching faster-moving, smaller shapes.

24.34 *(Calendar/Tickler File)* Using both audio and images, create a general-purpose calendar and "tickler" file. For example, the program should sing "Happy Birthday" when you use it on your birthday. Have the program display images and play audios associated with important events. Also, have it remind you in advance of these important events. It would be nice, for example, to have the program give you a week's notice so you can pick up an appropriate greeting card for that special person.

24.35 *(Rotating Images)* Create a program that lets you rotate an image through some number of degrees (out of a maximum of 360 degrees). The program should let you specify that you want to spin the image continuously. It should let you adjust the spin speed dynamically.

24.36 *(Coloring Black-and-White Photographs and Images)* Create a program that lets you paint a black-and-white photograph with color. Provide a color palette for selecting colors. Your program should let you apply different colors to different regions of the image.

24.37 *(Multimedia-Based Simpletron Simulator)* Modify the Simpletron simulator that you developed in the exercises in earlier chapters (Exercises 6.30–6.32) to include multimedia features. Add computer-like sounds to indicate that the Simpletron is executing instructions. Add a breaking-glass sound when a fatal error occurs. Use flashing lights to indicate which cells of memory or which registers are currently being manipulated. Use other multimedia techniques, as appropriate, to make your Simpletron simulator more valuable to its users as an educational tool.

Making a Difference

24.38 *(Accessibility Project: Speech Synthesis)* Computers can help people who are blind or have low vision by speaking web pages, e-mails and other documents using text-to-speech (TTS) or speech-synthesis "engines." Similarly, to help people who have difficulty interacting with a computer via the mouse and keyboard, speech-recognition engines enable computers to recognize spoken commands. With speech synthesis and speech recognition, users can "talk" with computers. In this exercise, you'll research and explore speech synthesis with the Java Speech API (java.sun.com/products/java-media/speech/). Download and install the open-source FreeTTS speech synthesizer (freetts.sourceforge.net/docs/index.php). Explore the FreeTTS documentation, then implement an application in which the user can enter text in a JTextArea. When the user clicks a **Speak** JButton, the program should use FreeTTS to speak the text aloud.

24.39 *(Accessibility Project: Speech Recognition)* In this exercise, you'll research and explore speech recognition with the Java Speech API. Download and install the open-source Sphinx-4 speech-recognition engine (cmusphinx.sourceforge.net/sphinx4/). Write a program that enables a user to speak to the computer. Use the speech-recognition capabilities to display what the user says in a JTextArea. Enable the user to save the contents of the JTextArea to a file on disk by speaking the command "save".

24.40 *(Project: Simbad Robotics Simulator)* Robotics holds tremendous promise for handling jobs that are dangerous for humans, such as mining coal; mining and farming the depths of the ocean and exploring deep space. Simbad (simbad.sourceforge.net) is an open-source Java-based 3D robotics simulator. According to the project's web page, it supports single- and multi-robot simulations; vision, range and contact sensors; and more. You can download Simbad from simbad.sourceforge.net/index.php#download. You'll also need to download and install Java 3D — instructions are provided on this site for Mac OS X, Windows and Linux.

Once you've downloaded Simbad and installed Java 3D, you can try the simple example provided at simbad.sourceforge.net/example1.php. After getting this running, read the Simbad Programming Guide at simbad.sourceforge.net/guide.php and try modifying the simple example to perform some different tasks. If you're interested in exploring robotics further, study the API documentation at simbad.sourceforge.net/doc/ and create your own robot simulation program using Simbad. For example, create a simulation of a robot vacuum cleaner that travels in the direction it's facing until it encounters an obstacle, then randomly chooses another direction.

GUI Components: Part 2

An actor entering through the door, you've got nothing. But if he enters through the window, you've got a situation.
—Billy Wilder

...the force of events wakes slumberous talents.
—Edward Hoagland

You and I would see more interesting photography if they would stop worrying, and instead, apply horse-sense to the problem of recording the look and feel of their own era.
—Jessie Tarbox Beals

Objectives

In this chapter you'll learn:

- To create and manipulate sliders, menus, pop-up menus and windows.

- To programatically change the look-and-feel of a GUI, using Swing's pluggable look-and-feel.

- To create a multiple-document interface with `JDesktopPane` and `JInternalFrame`.

- To use additional layout managers.

25.1 Introduction

In this chapter, we continue our study of GUIs. We discuss additional components and layout managers and lay the groundwork for building more complex GUIs.

We begin our discussion with sliders that enable you to select from a range of integer values. Next, we discuss some additional details of windows. You'll learn to use menus that enable the user to effectively perform tasks in the program. The look-and-feel of a Swing GUI can be uniform across all platforms on which a Java program executes, or the GUI can be customized by using Swing's **pluggable look-and-feel** (**PLAF**). We provide an example that illustrates how to change between Swing's default metal look-and-feel (which looks and behaves the same across platforms), the new Nimbus look-and-feel (introduced in Chapter 14), a look-and-feel that simulates **Motif** (a popular UNIX look-and-feel) and one that simulates Microsoft's Windows look-and-feel.

Many of today's applications use a multiple-document interface (MDI)—a main window (often called the parent window) containing other windows (often called child windows) to manage several open documents in parallel. For example, many e-mail programs allow you to have several e-mail windows open at the same time so that you can compose or read multiple e-mail messages. We demonstrate Swing's classes for creating multiple-document interfaces. The chapter finishes with a series of examples discussing additional layout managers for organizing graphical user interfaces.

Swing is a large and complex topic. There are many more GUI components and capabilities than can be presented here. Several more Swing GUI components are introduced in the remaining chapters of this book as they're needed.

25.2 JSlider

JSliders enable a user to select from a range of integer values. Class JSlider inherits from JComponent. Figure 25.1 shows a horizontal JSlider with **tick marks** and the **thumb** that allows a user to select a value. JSliders can be customized to display major tick marks, minor tick marks and labels for the tick marks. They also support **snap-to ticks**, which cause the thumb, when positioned between two tick marks, to snap to the closest one.

Thumb ——— Tick mark

Fig. 25.1 | JSlider component with horizontal orientation.

Most Swing GUI components support user interactions through the mouse and the keyboard. For example, if a JSlider has the focus (i.e., it's the currently selected GUI component in the user interface), the left arrow key and right arrow key cause the thumb of the JSlider to decrease or increase by 1, respectively. The down arrow key and up arrow key also cause the thumb of the JSlider to decrease or increase by 1 tick, respectively. The *PgDn* (page down) *key* and *PgUp* (page up) *key* cause the thumb of the JSlider to decrease or increase by block increments of one-tenth of the range of values, respectively. The *Home key* moves the thumb to the minimum value of the JSlider, and the *End key* moves the thumb to the maximum value of the JSlider.

JSliders have either a horizontal orientation or a vertical orientation. For a horizontal JSlider, the minimum value is at the left end of the JSlider and the maximum is at the right end. For a vertical JSlider, the minimum value is at the bottom and the maximum is at the top. The minimum and maximum value positions on a JSlider can be reversed by invoking JSlider method **setInverted** with boolean argument true. The relative position of the thumb indicates the current value of the JSlider.

The program in Figs. 25.2–25.4 allows the user to size a circle drawn on a subclass of JPanel called OvalPanel (Fig. 25.2). The user specifies the circle's diameter with a horizontal JSlider. Class OvalPanel knows how to draw a circle on itself, using its own instance variable diameter to determine the diameter of the circle—the diameter is used as the width and height of the bounding box in which the circle is displayed. The diameter value is set when the user interacts with the JSlider. The event handler calls method set-Diameter in class OvalPanel to set the diameter and calls repaint to draw the new circle. The repaint call results in a call to OvalPanel's paintComponent method.

```java
1   // Fig. 25.2: OvalPanel.java
2   // A customized JPanel class.
3   import java.awt.Graphics;
4   import java.awt.Dimension;
5   import javax.swing.JPanel;
6
7   public class OvalPanel extends JPanel
8   {
9      private int diameter = 10; // default diameter of 10
10
11     // draw an oval of the specified diameter
12     public void paintComponent( Graphics g )
13     {
14        super.paintComponent( g );
15
16        g.fillOval( 10, 10, diameter, diameter ); // draw circle
17     } // end method paintComponent
18
19     // validate and set diameter, then repaint
20     public void setDiameter( int newDiameter )
21     {
22        // if diameter invalid, default to 10
23        diameter = ( newDiameter >= 0 ? newDiameter : 10 );
24        repaint(); // repaint panel
25     } // end method setDiameter
```

Fig. 25.2 | JPanel subclass for drawing circles of a specified diameter. (Part 1 of 2.)

```
26
27      // used by layout manager to determine preferred size
28      public Dimension getPreferredSize()
29      {
30         return new Dimension( 200, 200 );
31      } // end method getPreferredSize
32
33      // used by layout manager to determine minimum size
34      public Dimension getMinimumSize()
35      {
36         return getPreferredSize();
37      } // end method getMinimumSize
38   } // end class OvalPanel
```

Fig. 25.2 | JPanel subclass for drawing circles of a specified diameter. (Part 2 of 2.)

```
1    // Fig. 25.3: SliderFrame.java
2    // Using JSliders to size an oval.
3    import java.awt.BorderLayout;
4    import java.awt.Color;
5    import javax.swing.JFrame;
6    import javax.swing.JSlider;
7    import javax.swing.SwingConstants;
8    import javax.swing.event.ChangeListener;
9    import javax.swing.event.ChangeEvent;
10
11   public class SliderFrame extends JFrame
12   {
13      private JSlider diameterJSlider; // slider to select diameter
14      private OvalPanel myPanel; // panel to draw circle
15
16      // no-argument constructor
17      public SliderFrame()
18      {
19         super( "Slider Demo" );
20
21         myPanel = new OvalPanel(); // create panel to draw circle
22         myPanel.setBackground( Color.YELLOW ); // set background to yellow
23
24         // set up JSlider to control diameter value
25         diameterJSlider =
26            new JSlider( SwingConstants.HORIZONTAL, 0, 200, 10 );
27         diameterJSlider.setMajorTickSpacing( 10 ); // create tick every 10
28         diameterJSlider.setPaintTicks( true ); // paint ticks on slider
29
30         // register JSlider event listener
31         diameterJSlider.addChangeListener(
32
33            new ChangeListener() // anonymous inner class
34            {
35               // handle change in slider value
36               public void stateChanged( ChangeEvent e )
37               {
```

Fig. 25.3 | JSlider value used to determine the diameter of a circle. (Part 1 of 2.)

```
38                      myPanel.setDiameter( diameterJSlider.getValue() );
39                  } // end method stateChanged
40              } // end anonymous inner class
41          ); // end call to addChangeListener
42
43          add( diameterJSlider, BorderLayout.SOUTH ); // add slider to frame
44          add( myPanel, BorderLayout.CENTER ); // add panel to frame
45      } // end SliderFrame constructor
46  } // end class SliderFrame
```

Fig. 25.3 | JSlider value used to determine the diameter of a circle. (Part 2 of 2.)

```
 1  // Fig. 25.4: SliderDemo.java
 2  // Testing SliderFrame.
 3  import javax.swing.JFrame;
 4
 5  public class SliderDemo
 6  {
 7      public static void main( String[] args )
 8      {
 9          SliderFrame sliderFrame = new SliderFrame();
10          sliderFrame.setDefaultCloseOperation( JFrame.EXIT_ON_CLOSE );
11          sliderFrame.setSize( 220, 270 ); // set frame size
12          sliderFrame.setVisible( true ); // display frame
13      } // end main
14  } // end class SliderDemo
```

Fig. 25.4 | Test class for SliderFrame.

Class OvalPanel (Fig. 25.2) contains a paintComponent method (lines 12–17) that draws a filled oval (a circle in this example), a setDiameter method (lines 20–25) that changes the circle's diameter and repaints the OvalPanel, a getPreferredSize method (lines 28–31) that returns the preferred width and height of an OvalPanel and a getMinimumSize method (lines 34–37) that returns an OvalPanel's minimum width and height. Section 24.3 introduced getPreferredSize and getMinimumSize, which are used by some layout managers to determine the size of a component.

Class SliderFrame (Fig. 25.3) creates the JSlider that controls the diameter of the circle. Class SliderFrame's constructor (lines 17–45) creates OvalPanel object myPanel (line 21) and sets its background color (line 22). Lines 25–26 create JSlider object diameterSlider to control the diameter of the circle drawn on the OvalPanel. The JSlider constructor takes four arguments. The first argument specifies the orientation of diameterSlider, which is HORIZONTAL (a constant in interface SwingConstants). The second and third arguments indicate the minimum and maximum integer values in the range of values for this JSlider. The last argument indicates that the initial value of the JSlider (i.e., where the thumb is displayed) should be 10.

Lines 27–28 customize the appearance of the JSlider. Method **setMajorTick-Spacing** indicates that each major tick mark represents 10 values in the range of values supported by the JSlider. Method **setPaintTicks** with a true argument indicates that the tick marks should be displayed (they're not displayed by default). For other methods that are used to customize a JSlider's appearance, see the JSlider on-line documentation (java.sun.com/javase/6/docs/api/javax/swing/JSlider.html).

JSliders generate **ChangeEvents** (package javax.swing.event) in response to user interactions. An object of a class that implements interface **ChangeListener** (package javax.swing.event) and declares method **stateChanged** can respond to ChangeEvents. Lines 31–41 register a ChangeListener to handle diameterSlider's events. When method stateChanged (lines 36–39) is called in response to a user interaction, line 38 calls myPanel's setDiameter method and passes the current value of the JSlider as an argument. JSlider method **getValue** returns the current thumb position.

25.3 Windows: Additional Notes

A JFrame is a **window** with a **title bar** and a **border**. Class JFrame is a subclass of Frame (package java.awt), which is a subclass of Window (package java.awt). As such, JFrame is one of the heavyweight Swing GUI components. When you display a window from a Java program, the window is provided by the local platform's windowing toolkit, and therefore the window will look like every other window displayed on that platform. When a Java application executes on a Macintosh and displays a window, the window's title bar and borders will look like those of other Macintosh applications. When a Java application executes on a Microsoft Windows system and displays a window, the window's title bar and borders will look like those of other Microsoft Windows applications. And when a Java application executes on a UNIX platform and displays a window, the window's title bar and borders will look like other UNIX applications on that platform.

By default, when the user closes a JFrame window, it is hidden (i.e., removed from the screen), but you can control this with JFrame method **setDefaultCloseOperation**. Interface **WindowConstants** (package javax.swing), which class JFrame implements, declares three constants—DISPOSE_ON_CLOSE, DO_NOTHING_ON_CLOSE and HIDE_ON_CLOSE (the default)—for use with this method. Some platforms allow only a limited number of windows to be displayed on the screen. Thus, a window is a valuable resource that should be given back to the system when it's no longer needed. Class Window (an indirect superclass of JFrame) declares method **dispose** for this purpose. When a Window is no longer needed in an application, you should explicitly dispose of it. This can be done by calling the Window's dispose method or by calling method setDefaultCloseOperation with the argument WindowConstants.DISPOSE_ON_CLOSE. Terminating an application also returns window resources to the system. Using DO_NOTHING_ON_CLOSE indicates that the program will determine what to do when the user attempts to close the window. For example, the program might want to ask whether to save a file's changes before closing a window.

Performance Tip 25.1

A window is an expensive system resource. Return it to the system by calling its dispose method when the window is no longer needed.

By default, a window is not displayed on the screen until the program invokes the window's setVisible method (inherited from class java.awt.Component) with a true argument. A window's size should be set with a call to method setSize (inherited from class java.awt.Component). The position of a window when it appears on the screen is specified with method **setLocation** (inherited from class java.awt.Component).

Common Programming Error 25.1

Forgetting to call method setVisible on a window is a runtime logic error—the window is not displayed.

Common Programming Error 25.2

Forgetting to call the setSize method on a window is a runtime logic error—only the title bar appears.

When the user manipulates the window, this action generates **window events**. Event listeners are registered for window events with Window method **addWindowListener**. Interface **WindowListener** provides seven window-event-handling methods—**windowActivated** (called when the user makes a window the active window), **windowClosed** (called after the window is closed), **windowClosing** (called when the user initiates closing of the window), **windowDeactivated** (called when the user makes another window the active window), **windowDeiconified** (called when the user restores a window from being minimized), **windowIconified** (called when the user minimizes a window) and **windowOpened** (called when a program first displays a window on the screen).

25.4 Using Menus with Frames

Menus are an integral part of GUIs. They allow the user to perform actions without unnecessarily cluttering a GUI with extra components. In Swing GUIs, menus can be attached only to objects of the classes that provide method **setJMenuBar**. Two such classes are JFrame and JApplet. The classes used to declare menus are JMenuBar, JMenu, JMenuItem, JCheckBoxMenuItem and class JRadioButtonMenuItem.

Look-and-Feel Observation 25.1

Menus simplify GUIs because components can be hidden within them. These components will be visible only when the user looks for them by selecting the menu.

Overview of Several Menu-Related Components

Class **JMenuBar** (a subclass of JComponent) contains the methods necessary to manage a **menu bar**, which is a container for menus. Class **JMenu** (a subclass of javax.swing.JMenuItem) contains the methods necessary for managing menus. Menus contain menu items and are added to menu bars or to other menus as submenus. When a menu is clicked, it expands to show its list of menu items.

Class **JMenuItem** (a subclass of javax.swing.AbstractButton) contains the methods necessary to manage **menu items**. A menu item is a GUI component inside a menu that, when selected, causes an action event. A menu item can be used to initiate an action, or it can be a **submenu** that provides more menu items from which the user can select. Submenus are useful for grouping related menu items in a menu.

Class **JCheckBoxMenuItem** (a subclass of javax.swing.JMenuItem) contains the methods necessary to manage menu items that can be toggled on or off. When a JCheck-BoxMenuItem is selected, a check appears to the left of the menu item. When the JCheck-BoxMenuItem is selected again, the check is removed.

Class **JRadioButtonMenuItem** (a subclass of javax.swing.JMenuItem) contains the methods necessary to manage menu items that can be toggled on or off like JCheckBox-MenuItems. When multiple JRadioButtonMenuItems are maintained as part of a Button-Group, only one item in the group can be selected at a given time. When a JRadioButtonMenuItem is selected, a filled circle appears to the left of the menu item. When another JRadioButtonMenuItem is selected, the filled circle of the previously selected menu item is removed.

Using Menus in an Application

Figures 25.5–25.6 demonstrate various menu items and how to specify special characters called **mnemonics** that can provide quick access to a menu or menu item from the keyboard. Mnemonics can be used with all subclasses of javax.swing.AbstractButton. Class MenuFrame (Fig. 25.5) creates the GUI and handles the menu-item events. Most of the code in this application appears in the class's constructor (lines 34–151).

```java
1   // Fig. 25.5: MenuFrame.java
2   // Demonstrating menus.
3   import java.awt.Color;
4   import java.awt.Font;
5   import java.awt.BorderLayout;
6   import java.awt.event.ActionListener;
7   import java.awt.event.ActionEvent;
8   import java.awt.event.ItemListener;
9   import java.awt.event.ItemEvent;
10  import javax.swing.JFrame;
11  import javax.swing.JRadioButtonMenuItem;
12  import javax.swing.JCheckBoxMenuItem;
13  import javax.swing.JOptionPane;
14  import javax.swing.JLabel;
15  import javax.swing.SwingConstants;
16  import javax.swing.ButtonGroup;
17  import javax.swing.JMenu;
18  import javax.swing.JMenuItem;
19  import javax.swing.JMenuBar;
20
21  public class MenuFrame extends JFrame
22  {
23     private final Color[] colorValues =
24        { Color.BLACK, Color.BLUE, Color.RED, Color.GREEN };
25     private JRadioButtonMenuItem[] colorItems; // color menu items
26     private JRadioButtonMenuItem[] fonts; // font menu items
27     private JCheckBoxMenuItem[] styleItems; // font style menu items
28     private JLabel displayJLabel; // displays sample text
```

Fig. 25.5 | JMenus and mnemonics. (Part 1 of 5.)

```
29        private ButtonGroup fontButtonGroup; // manages font menu items
30        private ButtonGroup colorButtonGroup; // manages color menu items
31        private int style; // used to create style for font
32
33        // no-argument constructor set up GUI
34        public MenuFrame()
35        {
36            super( "Using JMenus" );
37
38            JMenu fileMenu = new JMenu( "File" ); // create file menu
39            fileMenu.setMnemonic( 'F' ); // set mnemonic to F
40
41            // create About... menu item
42            JMenuItem aboutItem = new JMenuItem( "About..." );
43            aboutItem.setMnemonic( 'A' ); // set mnemonic to A
44            fileMenu.add( aboutItem ); // add about item to file menu
45            aboutItem.addActionListener(
46
47                new ActionListener() // anonymous inner class
48                {
49                    // display message dialog when user selects About...
50                    public void actionPerformed( ActionEvent event )
51                    {
52                        JOptionPane.showMessageDialog( MenuFrame.this,
53                            "This is an example\nof using menus",
54                            "About", JOptionPane.PLAIN_MESSAGE );
55                    } // end method actionPerformed
56                } // end anonymous inner class
57            ); // end call to addActionListener
58
59            JMenuItem exitItem = new JMenuItem( "Exit" ); // create exit item
60            exitItem.setMnemonic( 'x' ); // set mnemonic to x
61            fileMenu.add( exitItem ); // add exit item to file menu
62            exitItem.addActionListener(
63
64                new ActionListener() // anonymous inner class
65                {
66                    // terminate application when user clicks exitItem
67                    public void actionPerformed( ActionEvent event )
68                    {
69                        System.exit( 0 ); // exit application
70                    } // end method actionPerformed
71                } // end anonymous inner class
72            ); // end call to addActionListener
73
74            JMenuBar bar = new JMenuBar(); // create menu bar
75            setJMenuBar( bar ); // add menu bar to application
76            bar.add( fileMenu ); // add file menu to menu bar
77
78            JMenu formatMenu = new JMenu( "Format" ); // create format menu
79            formatMenu.setMnemonic( 'r' ); // set mnemonic to r
80
81            // array listing string colors
82            String[] colors = { "Black", "Blue", "Red", "Green" };
```

Fig. 25.5 | JMenus and mnemonics. (Part 2 of 5.)

```
83
84        JMenu colorMenu = new JMenu( "Color" ); // create color menu
85        colorMenu.setMnemonic( 'C' ); // set mnemonic to C
86
87        // create radio button menu items for colors
88        colorItems = new JRadioButtonMenuItem[ colors.length ];
89        colorButtonGroup = new ButtonGroup(); // manages colors
90        ItemHandler itemHandler = new ItemHandler(); // handler for colors
91
92        // create color radio button menu items
93        for ( int count = 0; count < colors.length; count++ )
94        {
95           colorItems[ count ] =
96              new JRadioButtonMenuItem( colors[ count ] ); // create item
97           colorMenu.add( colorItems[ count ] ); // add item to color menu
98           colorButtonGroup.add( colorItems[ count ] ); // add to group
99           colorItems[ count ].addActionListener( itemHandler );
100       } // end for
101
102       colorItems[ 0 ].setSelected( true ); // select first Color item
103
104       formatMenu.add( colorMenu ); // add color menu to format menu
105       formatMenu.addSeparator(); // add separator in menu
106
107       // array listing font names
108       String[] fontNames = { "Serif", "Monospaced", "SansSerif" };
109       JMenu fontMenu = new JMenu( "Font" ); // create font menu
110       fontMenu.setMnemonic( 'n' ); // set mnemonic to n
111
112       // create radio button menu items for font names
113       fonts = new JRadioButtonMenuItem[ fontNames.length ];
114       fontButtonGroup = new ButtonGroup(); // manages font names
115
116       // create Font radio button menu items
117       for ( int count = 0; count < fonts.length; count++ )
118       {
119          fonts[ count ] = new JRadioButtonMenuItem( fontNames[ count ] );
120          fontMenu.add( fonts[ count ] ); // add font to font menu
121          fontButtonGroup.add( fonts[ count ] ); // add to button group
122          fonts[ count ].addActionListener( itemHandler ); // add handler
123       } // end for
124
125       fonts[ 0 ].setSelected( true ); // select first Font menu item
126       fontMenu.addSeparator(); // add separator bar to font menu
127
128       String[] styleNames = { "Bold", "Italic" }; // names of styles
129       styleItems = new JCheckBoxMenuItem[ styleNames.length ];
130       StyleHandler styleHandler = new StyleHandler(); // style handler
131
132       // create style checkbox menu items
133       for ( int count = 0; count < styleNames.length; count++ )
134       {
135          styleItems[ count ] =
136             new JCheckBoxMenuItem( styleNames[ count ] ); // for style
```

Fig. 25.5 | JMenus and mnemonics. (Part 3 of 5.)

```
137              fontMenu.add( styleItems[ count ] ); // add to font menu
138              styleItems[ count ].addItemListener( styleHandler ); // handler
139          } // end for
140
141          formatMenu.add( fontMenu ); // add Font menu to Format menu
142          bar.add( formatMenu ); // add Format menu to menu bar
143
144          // set up label to display text
145          displayJLabel = new JLabel( "Sample Text", SwingConstants.CENTER );
146          displayJLabel.setForeground( colorValues[ 0 ] );
147          displayJLabel.setFont( new Font( "Serif", Font.PLAIN, 72 ) );
148
149          getContentPane().setBackground( Color.CYAN ); // set background
150          add( displayJLabel, BorderLayout.CENTER ); // add displayJLabel
151      } // end MenuFrame constructor
152
153      // inner class to handle action events from menu items
154      private class ItemHandler implements ActionListener
155      {
156          // process color and font selections
157          public void actionPerformed( ActionEvent event )
158          {
159              // process color selection
160              for ( int count = 0; count < colorItems.length; count++ )
161              {
162                  if ( colorItems[ count ].isSelected() )
163                  {
164                      displayJLabel.setForeground( colorValues[ count ] );
165                      break;
166                  } // end if
167              } // end for
168
169              // process font selection
170              for ( int count = 0; count < fonts.length; count++ )
171              {
172                  if ( event.getSource() == fonts[ count ] )
173                  {
174                      displayJLabel.setFont(
175                          new Font( fonts[ count ].getText(), style, 72 ) );
176                  } // end if
177              } // end for
178
179              repaint(); // redraw application
180          } // end method actionPerformed
181      } // end class ItemHandler
182
183      // inner class to handle item events from checkbox menu items
184      private class StyleHandler implements ItemListener
185      {
186          // process font style selections
187          public void itemStateChanged( ItemEvent e )
188          {
189              String name = displayJLabel.getFont().getName(); // current Font
190              Font font; // new font based on user selections
```

Fig. 25.5 | JMenus and mnemonics. (Part 4 of 5.)

```
191
192            // determine which items are checked and create Font
193            if ( styleItems[ 0 ].isSelected() &&
194                 styleItems[ 1 ].isSelected() )
195               font = new Font( name, Font.BOLD + Font.ITALIC, 72 );
196            else if ( styleItems[ 0 ].isSelected() )
197               font = new Font( name, Font.BOLD, 72 );
198            else if ( styleItems[ 1 ].isSelected() )
199               font = new Font( name, Font.ITALIC, 72 );
200            else
201               font = new Font( name, Font.PLAIN, 72 );
202
203            displayJLabel.setFont( font );
204            repaint(); // redraw application
205         } // end method itemStateChanged
206      } // end class StyleHandler
207   } // end class MenuFrame
```

Fig. 25.5 | JMenus and mnemonics. (Part 5 of 5.)

```
 1   // Fig. 25.6: MenuTest.java
 2   // Testing MenuFrame.
 3   import javax.swing.JFrame;
 4
 5   public class MenuTest
 6   {
 7      public static void main( String[] args )
 8      {
 9         MenuFrame menuFrame = new MenuFrame(); // create MenuFrame
10         menuFrame.setDefaultCloseOperation( JFrame.EXIT_ON_CLOSE );
11         menuFrame.setSize( 500, 200 ); // set frame size
12         menuFrame.setVisible( true ); // display frame
13      } // end main
14   } // end class MenuTest
```

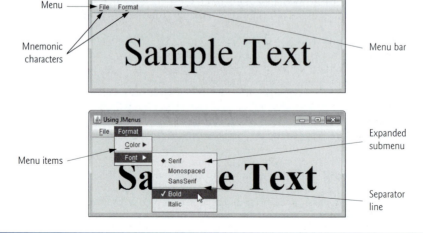

Fig. 25.6 | Test class for MenuFrame.

Setting Up the File Menu

Lines 38–76 set up the **File** menu and attach it to the menu bar. The **File** menu contains an **About...** menu item that displays a message dialog when the menu item is selected and an **Exit** menu item that can be selected to terminate the application.

Line 38 creates a JMenu and passes to the constructor the string "File" as the name of the menu. Line 39 uses JMenu method **setMnemonic** (inherited from class AbstractButton) to indicate that F is the mnemonic for this menu. Pressing the *Alt* key and the letter *F* opens the menu, just as clicking the menu name with the mouse would. In the GUI, the mnemonic character in the menu's name is displayed with an underline. (See the screen captures in Fig. 25.6.)

Look-and-Feel Observation 25.2

Mnemonics provide quick access to menu commands and button commands through the keyboard.

Look-and-Feel Observation 25.3

Different mnemonics should be used for each button or menu item. Normally, the first letter in the label on the menu item or button is used as the mnemonic. If several buttons or menu items start with the same letter, choose the next most prominent letter in the name (e.g., x is commonly chosen for an Exit button or menu item). Mnemonics are case insensitive.

Lines 42–43 create JMenuItem aboutItem with the text "About..." and set its mnemonic to the letter A. This menu item is added to fileMenu at line 44 with JMenu method **add**. To access the **About...** menu item through the keyboard, press the *Alt* key and letter *F* to open the **File** menu, then press *A* to select the **About...** menu item. Lines 47–56 create an ActionListener to process aboutItem's action event. Lines 52–54 display a message dialog box. In most prior uses of showMessageDialog, the first argument was null. The purpose of the first argument is to specify the **parent window** that helps determine where the dialog box will be displayed. If the parent window is specified as null, the dialog box appears in the center of the screen. Otherwise, it appears centered over the specified parent window. In this example, the program specifies the parent window with MenuFrame.this—the this reference of the MenuFrame object. When using the this reference in an inner class, specifying this by itself refers to the inner-class object. To reference the outer-class object's this reference, qualify this with the outer-class name and a dot (.).

Dialog boxes are typically modal. A modal dialog box does not allow any other window in the application to be accessed until the dialog box is dismissed. The dialogs displayed with class JOptionPane are modal dialogs. Class **JDialog** can be used to create your own modal or nonmodal dialogs.

Lines 59–72 create menu item exitItem, set its mnemonic to x, add it to fileMenu and register an ActionListener that terminates the program when the user selects exitItem.

Lines 74–76 create the JMenuBar, attach it to the window with JFrame method setJMenuBar and use JMenuBar method **add** to attach the fileMenu to the JMenuBar.

Common Programming Error 25.3

Forgetting to set the menu bar with JFrame method setJMenuBar prevents the menu bar from displaying in the JFrame.

Look-and-Feel Observation 25.4

Menus appear left to right in the order that they're added to a JMenuBar.

Setting Up the Format Menu

Lines 78–79 create menu formatMenu and set its mnemonic to r. (F is not used because that is the **File** menu's mnemonic.)

Lines 84–85 create menu colorMenu (this will be a submenu in the **Format** menu) and set its mnemonic to C. Line 88 creates JRadioButtonMenuItem array colorItems, which refers to the menu items in colorMenu. Line 89 creates ButtonGroup colorButtonGroup, which will ensure that only one of the menu items in the **Color** submenu is selected at a time. Line 90 creates an instance of inner class ItemHandler (declared at lines 154–181) that responds to selections from the **Color** and **Font** submenus (discussed shortly). The for statement at lines 93–100 creates each JRadioButtonMenuItem in array colorItems, adds each menu item to colorMenu and to colorButtonGroup and registers the ActionListener for each menu item.

Line 102 invokes AbstractButton method **setSelected** to select the first element in array colorItems. Line 104 adds colorMenu as a submenu of formatMenu. Line 105 invokes JMenu method **addSeparator** to add a horizontal **separator** line to the menu.

Look-and-Feel Observation 25.5

A submenu is created by adding a menu as a menu item in another menu. When the mouse is positioned over a submenu (or the submenu's mnemonic is pressed), the submenu expands to show its menu items.

Look-and-Feel Observation 25.6

Separators can be added to a menu to group menu items logically.

Look-and-Feel Observation 25.7

Any lightweight GUI component (i.e., a component that is a subclass of JComponent) can be added to a JMenu or to a JMenuBar.

Lines 108–126 create the **Font** submenu and several JRadioButtonMenuItems and select the first element of JRadioButtonMenuItem array fonts. Line 129 creates a JCheckBoxMenuItem array to represent the menu items for specifying bold and italic styles for the fonts. Line 130 creates an instance of inner class StyleHandler (declared at lines 184–206) to respond to the JCheckBoxMenuItem events. The for statement at lines 133–139 creates each JCheckBoxMenuItem, adds each menu item to fontMenu and registers the ItemListener for each menu item. Line 141 adds fontMenu as a submenu of formatMenu. Line 142 adds the formatMenu to bar (the menu bar).

Creating the Rest of the GUI and Defining the Event Handlers

Lines 145–147 create a JLabel for which the **Format** menu items control the font, font color and font style. The initial foreground color is set to the first element of array colorValues (Color.BLACK) by invoking JComponent method **setForeground**. The initial font is set to Serif with PLAIN style and 72-point size. Line 149 sets the background color of the window's content pane to cyan, and line 150 attaches the JLabel to the CENTER of the content pane's BorderLayout.

ItemHandler method actionPerformed (lines 157–180) uses two for statements to determine which font or color menu item generated the event and sets the font or color of the JLabel displayLabel, respectively. The if condition at line 162 uses Abstract-Button method **isSelected** to determine the selected JRadioButtonMenuItem. The if condition at line 172 invokes the event object's getSource method to get a reference to the JRadioButtonMenuItem that generated the event. Line 175 invokes AbstractButton method getText to obtain the name of the font from the menu item.

StyleHandler method itemStateChanged (lines 187–205) is called if the user selects a JCheckBoxMenuItem in the fontMenu. Lines 193–201 determine which JCheckBoxMenu-Items are selected and use their combined state to determine the new font style.

25.5 JPopupMenu

Many of today's computer applications provide so-called context-sensitive pop-up menus. In Swing, such menus are created with class **JPopupMenu** (a subclass of JCompo-nent). These menus provide options that are specific to the component for which the pop-up trigger event was generated. On most systems, the pop-up trigger event occurs when the user presses and releases the right mouse button.

Look-and-Feel Observation 25.8

The pop-up trigger event is platform specific. On most platforms that use a mouse with multiple buttons, the pop-up trigger event occurs when the user clicks the right mouse button on a component that supports a pop-up menu.

The application in Figs. 25.7–25.8 creates a JPopupMenu that allows the user to select one of three colors and change the background color of the window. When the user clicks the right mouse button on the PopupFrame window's background, a JPopupMenu con-taining colors appears. If the user clicks a JRadioButtonMenuItem for a color, ItemHandler method actionPerformed changes the background color of the window's content pane.

Line 25 of the PopupFrame constructor (Fig. 25.7, lines 21–69) creates an instance of class ItemHandler (declared in lines 72–87) that will process the item events from the menu items in the pop-up menu. Line 29 creates the JPopupMenu. The for statement (lines 33–39) creates a JRadioButtonMenuItem object (line 35), adds it to popupMenu (line 36), adds it to ButtonGroup colorGroup (line 37) to maintain one selected JRadioBut-tonMenuItem at a time and registers its ActionListener (line 38). Line 41 sets the initial background to white by invoking method setBackground.

```
1   // Fig. 25.7: PopupFrame.java
2   // Demonstrating JPopupMenus.
3   import java.awt.Color;
4   import java.awt.event.MouseAdapter;
5   import java.awt.event.MouseEvent;
6   import java.awt.event.ActionListener;
7   import java.awt.event.ActionEvent;
8   import javax.swing.JFrame;
```

Fig. 25.7 | JPopupMenu for selecting colors. (Part I of 3.)

```
9  import javax.swing.JRadioButtonMenuItem;
10 import javax.swing.JPopupMenu;
11 import javax.swing.ButtonGroup;
12
13 public class PopupFrame extends JFrame
14 {
15    private JRadioButtonMenuItem[] items; // holds items for colors
16    private final Color[] colorValues =
17       { Color.BLUE, Color.YELLOW, Color.RED }; // colors to be used
18    private JPopupMenu popupMenu; // allows user to select color
19
20    // no-argument constructor sets up GUI
21    public PopupFrame()
22    {
23       super( "Using JPopupMenus" );
24
25       ItemHandler handler = new ItemHandler(); // handler for menu items
26       String[] colors = { "Blue", "Yellow", "Red" }; // array of colors
27
28       ButtonGroup colorGroup = new ButtonGroup(); // manages color items
29       popupMenu = new JPopupMenu(); // create pop-up menu
30       items = new JRadioButtonMenuItem[ colors.length ]; // color items
31
32       // construct menu item, add to pop-up menu, enable event handling
33       for ( int count = 0; count < items.length; count++ )
34       {
35          items[ count ] = new JRadioButtonMenuItem( colors[ count ] );
36          popupMenu.add( items[ count ] ); // add item to pop-up menu
37          colorGroup.add( items[ count ] ); // add item to button group
38          items[ count ].addActionListener( handler ); // add handler
39       } // end for
40
41       setBackground( Color.WHITE ); // set background to white
42
43       // declare a MouseListener for the window to display pop-up menu
44       addMouseListener(
45
46          new MouseAdapter() // anonymous inner class
47          {
48             // handle mouse press event
49             public void mousePressed( MouseEvent event )
50             {
51                checkForTriggerEvent( event ); // check for trigger
52             } // end method mousePressed
53
54             // handle mouse release event
55             public void mouseReleased( MouseEvent event )
56             {
57                checkForTriggerEvent( event ); // check for trigger
58             } // end method mouseReleased
59
60             // determine whether event should trigger pop-up menu
61             private void checkForTriggerEvent( MouseEvent event )
62             {
```

Fig. 25.7 | JPopupMenu for selecting colors. (Part 2 of 3.)

```
63                    if ( event.isPopupTrigger() )
64                        popupMenu.show(
65                            event.getComponent(), event.getX(), event.getY() );
66                } // end method checkForTriggerEvent
67            } // end anonymous inner class
68        ); // end call to addMouseListener
69    } // end PopupFrame constructor
70
71    // private inner class to handle menu item events
72    private class ItemHandler implements ActionListener
73    {
74        // process menu item selections
75        public void actionPerformed( ActionEvent event )
76        {
77            // determine which menu item was selected
78            for ( int i = 0; i < items.length; i++ )
79            {
80                if ( event.getSource() == items[ i ] )
81                {
82                    getContentPane().setBackground( colorValues[ i ] );
83                    return;
84                } // end if
85            } // end for
86        } // end method actionPerformed
87    } // end private inner class ItemHandler
88 } // end class PopupFrame
```

Fig. 25.7 | JPopupMenu for selecting colors. (Part 3 of 3.)

```
 1  // Fig. 25.8: PopupTest.java
 2  // Testing PopupFrame.
 3  import javax.swing.JFrame;
 4
 5  public class PopupTest
 6  {
 7     public static void main( String[] args )
 8     {
 9        PopupFrame popupFrame = new PopupFrame(); // create PopupFrame
10        popupFrame.setDefaultCloseOperation( JFrame.EXIT_ON_CLOSE );
11        popupFrame.setSize( 300, 200 ); // set frame size
12        popupFrame.setVisible( true ); // display frame
13     } // end main
14  } // end class PopupTest
```

Fig. 25.8 | Test class for PopupFrame.

Lines 44–68 register a MouseListener to handle the mouse events of the application window. Methods mousePressed (lines 49–52) and mouseReleased (lines 55–58) check for the pop-up trigger event. Each method calls private utility method checkForTriggerEvent (lines 61–66) to determine whether the pop-up trigger event occurred. If it did, MouseEvent method **isPopupTrigger** returns true, and JPopupMenu method **show** displays the JPopupMenu. The first argument to method show specifies the **origin component**, whose position helps determine where the JPopupMenu will appear on the screen. The last two arguments are the *x-y* coordinates (measured from the origin component's upper-left corner) at which the JPopupMenu is to appear.

Look-and-Feel Observation 25.9

Displaying a JPopupMenu for the pop-up trigger event of multiple GUI components requires registering mouse-event handlers for each of those GUI components.

When the user selects a menu item from the pop-up menu, class ItemHandler's method actionPerformed (lines 75–86) determines which JRadioButtonMenuItem the user selected and sets the background color of the window's content pane.

25.6 Pluggable Look-and-Feel

A program that uses Java's AWT GUI components (package java.awt) takes on the look-and-feel of the platform on which the program executes. A Java application running on a Mac OS X looks like other Mac OS X applications. One running on Microsoft Windows looks like other Windows applications. One running on a UNIX platform looks like other applications on that UNIX platform. This is sometimes desirable, because it allows users of the application on each platform to use GUI components with which they're already familiar. However, it also introduces interesting portability issues.

Portability Tip 25.1

GUI components look different on different platforms and may require different amounts of space to display. This could change their layout and alignments.

Portability Tip 25.2

GUI components on different platforms have different default functionality (e.g., some platforms allow a button with the focus to be "pressed" with the space bar, and some don't).

Swing's lightweight GUI components eliminate many of these issues by providing uniform functionality across platforms and by defining a uniform cross-platform look-and-feel. As of Java SE 6 Update 10, this is the Nimbus look-and-feel that we discussed in Section 14.2. Earlier versions of Java used the **metal look-and-feel**, which is still the default. Swing also provides the flexibility to customize the look-and-feel to appear as a Microsoft Windows-style look-and-feel (only on Window systems), a Motif-style (UNIX) look-and-feel (across all platforms) or a Macintosh look-and-feel (only on Mac systems).

Figures 25.9–25.10 demonstrate a way to change the look-and-feel of a Swing GUI. It creates several GUI components, so you can see the change in their look-and-feel at the same time. The output windows show the Metal, Nimbus, CDE/Motif, Windows and Windows Classic look-and-feels that are available on Windows systems. The installed look-and-feels will vary by platform.

```
1   // Fig. 25.9: LookAndFeelFrame.java
2   // Changing the look-and-feel.
3   import java.awt.GridLayout;
4   import java.awt.BorderLayout;
5   import java.awt.event.ItemListener;
6   import java.awt.event.ItemEvent;
7   import javax.swing.JFrame;
8   import javax.swing.UIManager;
9   import javax.swing.JRadioButton;
10  import javax.swing.ButtonGroup;
11  import javax.swing.JButton;
12  import javax.swing.JLabel;
13  import javax.swing.JComboBox;
14  import javax.swing.JPanel;
15  import javax.swing.SwingConstants;
16  import javax.swing.SwingUtilities;
17
18  public class LookAndFeelFrame extends JFrame
19  {
20     private UIManager.LookAndFeelInfo[] looks; // look and feels
21     private String[] lookNames; // names of look and feels
22     private JRadioButton[] radio; // radio buttons to select look-and-feel
23     private ButtonGroup group; // group for radio buttons
24     private JButton button; // displays look of button
25     private JLabel label; // displays look of label
26     private JComboBox comboBox; // displays look of combo box
27
28     // set up GUI
29     public LookAndFeelFrame()
30     {
31        super( "Look and Feel Demo" );
32
33        // get installed look-and-feel information
34        looks = UIManager.getInstalledLookAndFeels();
35        lookNames = new String[ looks.length ];
36
37        // get names of installed look-and-feels
38        for ( int i = 0; i < looks.length; i++ )
39           lookNames[ i ] = looks[ i ].getName();
40
41        JPanel northPanel = new JPanel(); // create north panel
42        northPanel.setLayout( new GridLayout( 3, 1, 0, 5 ) );
43
44        label = new JLabel( "This is a " + lookNames[0] + " look-and-feel",
45           SwingConstants.CENTER ); // create label
46        northPanel.add( label ); // add label to panel
47
48        button = new JButton( "JButton" ); // create button
49        northPanel.add( button ); // add button to panel
50
51        comboBox = new JComboBox( lookNames ); // create combobox
52        northPanel.add( comboBox ); // add combobox to panel
53
```

Fig. 25.9 | Look-and-feel of a Swing-based GUI. (Part 1 of 3.)

```
54          // create array for radio buttons
55          radio = new JRadioButton[ looks.length ];
56
57          JPanel southPanel = new JPanel(); // create south panel
58
59          // use a GridLayout with 3 buttons in each row
60          int rows = (int) Math.ceil( radio.length / 3.0 );
61          southPanel.setLayout( new GridLayout( rows, 3 ) );
62
63          group = new ButtonGroup(); // button group for looks-and-feels
64          ItemHandler handler = new ItemHandler(); // look-and-feel handler
65
66          for ( int count = 0; count < radio.length; count++ )
67          {
68             radio[ count ] = new JRadioButton( lookNames[ count ] );
69             radio[ count ].addItemListener( handler ); // add handler
70             group.add( radio[ count ] ); // add radio button to group
71             southPanel.add( radio[ count ] ); // add radio button to panel
72          } // end for
73
74          add( northPanel, BorderLayout.NORTH ); // add north panel
75          add( southPanel, BorderLayout.SOUTH ); // add south panel
76
77          radio[ 0 ].setSelected( true ); // set default selection
78       } // end LookAndFeelFrame constructor
79
80       // use UIManager to change look-and-feel of GUI
81       private void changeTheLookAndFeel( int value )
82       {
83          try // change look-and-feel
84          {
85             // set look-and-feel for this application
86             UIManager.setLookAndFeel( looks[ value ].getClassName() );
87
88             // update components in this application
89             SwingUtilities.updateComponentTreeUI( this );
90          } // end try
91          catch ( Exception exception )
92          {
93             exception.printStackTrace();
94          } // end catch
95       } // end method changeTheLookAndFeel
96
97       // private inner class to handle radio button events
98       private class ItemHandler implements ItemListener
99       {
100         // process user's look-and-feel selection
101         public void itemStateChanged( ItemEvent event )
102         {
103            for ( int count = 0; count < radio.length; count++ )
104            {
105               if ( radio[ count ].isSelected() )
106               {
```

Fig. 25.9 | Look-and-feel of a Swing-based GUI. (Part 2 of 3.)

```
107                      label.setText( String.format(
108                         "This is a %s look-and-feel", lookNames[ count ] ) );
109                      comboBox.setSelectedIndex( count ); // set combobox index
110                      changeTheLookAndFeel( count ); // change look-and-feel
111                   } // end if
112                } // end for
113             } // end method itemStateChanged
114          } // end private inner class ItemHandler
115 } // end class LookAndFeelFrame
```

Fig. 25.9 | Look-and-feel of a Swing-based GUI. (Part 3 of 3.)

```
1  // Fig. 25.10: LookAndFeelDemo.java
2  // Changing the look-and-feel.
3  import javax.swing.JFrame;
4
5  public class LookAndFeelDemo
6  {
7     public static void main( String[] args )
8     {
9        LookAndFeelFrame lookAndFeelFrame = new LookAndFeelFrame();
10       lookAndFeelFrame.setDefaultCloseOperation( JFrame.EXIT_ON_CLOSE );
11       lookAndFeelFrame.setSize( 400, 220 ); // set frame size
12       lookAndFeelFrame.setVisible( true ); // display frame
13    } // end main
14 } // end class LookAndFeelDemo
```

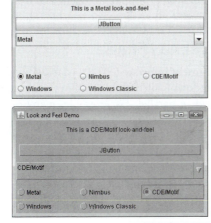
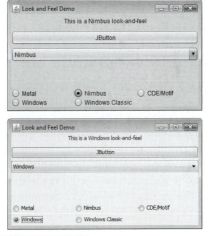

Fig. 25.10 | Test class for LookAndFeelFrame.

We've covered the GUI components and event-handling concepts in this example previously, so we focus here on the mechanism for changing the look-and-feel. Class **UIManager** (package javax.swing) contains nested class **LookAndFeelInfo** (a public static class) that maintains information about a look-and-feel. Line 20 declares an array of type UIManager.LookAndFeelInfo (note the syntax used to identify the static inner class LookAndFeelInfo). Line 34 uses UIManager static method **getInstalledLookAndFeels** to get the array of UIManager.LookAndFeelInfo objects that describe each look-and-feel available on your system.

> **Performance Tip 25.2**
> *Each look-and-feel is represented by a Java class. UIManager method getInstalled-LookAndFeels does not load each class. Rather, it provides the names of the available look-and-feel classes so that a choice can be made (presumably once at program start-up). This reduces the overhead of having to load all the look-and-feel classes even if the program will not use some of them.*

Our utility method changeTheLookAndFeel (lines 81–95) is called by the event handler for the JRadioButtons at the bottom of the user interface. The event handler (declared in private inner class ItemHandler at lines 98–114) passes an integer representing the element in array looks that should be used to change the look-and-feel. Line 86 invokes static method **setLookAndFeel** of UIManager to change the look-and-feel. Method **getClassName** of class UIManager.LookAndFeelInfo determines the name of the look-and-feel class that corresponds to the UIManager.LookAndFeelInfo object. If the look-and-feel class is not already loaded, it will be loaded as part of the call to setLookAndFeel. Line 89 invokes static method **updateComponentTreeUI** of class **SwingUtilities** (package javax.swing) to change the look-and-feel of every GUI component attached to its argument (this instance of our application class LookAndFeelFrame) to the new look-and-feel.

25.7 JDesktopPane and JInternalFrame

Many of today's applications use a **multiple-document interface** (MDI)—a main window (called the **parent window**) containing other windows (called **child windows**), to manage several open documents that are being processed in parallel. For example, many e-mail programs allow you to have several windows open at the same time, so you can compose or read multiple e-mail messages simultaneously. Similarly, many word processors allow the user to open multiple documents in separate windows within a main window, making it possible to switch between them without having to close one to open another. The application in Figs. 25.11–25.12 demonstrates Swing's **JDesktopPane** and **JInternalFrame** classes for implementing multiple-document interfaces.

```
1   // Fig. 25.11: DesktopFrame.java
2   // Demonstrating JDesktopPane.
3   import java.awt.BorderLayout;
4   import java.awt.Dimension;
5   import java.awt.Graphics;
6   import java.awt.event.ActionListener;
7   import java.awt.event.ActionEvent;
```

Fig. 25.11 | Multiple-document interface. (Part 1 of 3.)

```
 8    import java.util.Random;
 9    import javax.swing.JFrame;
10    import javax.swing.JDesktopPane;
11    import javax.swing.JMenuBar;
12    import javax.swing.JMenu;
13    import javax.swing.JMenuItem;
14    import javax.swing.JInternalFrame;
15    import javax.swing.JPanel;
16    import javax.swing.ImageIcon;
17
18    public class DesktopFrame extends JFrame
19    {
20       private JDesktopPane theDesktop;
21
22       // set up GUI
23       public DesktopFrame()
24       {
25          super( "Using a JDesktopPane" );
26
27          JMenuBar bar = new JMenuBar(); // create menu bar
28          JMenu addMenu = new JMenu( "Add" ); // create Add menu
29          JMenuItem newFrame = new JMenuItem( "Internal Frame" );
30
31          addMenu.add( newFrame ); // add new frame item to Add menu
32          bar.add( addMenu ); // add Add menu to menu bar
33          setJMenuBar( bar ); // set menu bar for this application
34
35          theDesktop = new JDesktopPane(); // create desktop pane
36          add( theDesktop ); // add desktop pane to frame
37
38          // set up listener for newFrame menu item
39          newFrame.addActionListener(
40
41             new ActionListener() // anonymous inner class
42             {
43                // display new internal window
44                public void actionPerformed( ActionEvent event )
45                {
46                   // create internal frame
47                   JInternalFrame frame = new JInternalFrame(
48                      "Internal Frame", true, true, true, true );
49
50                   MyJPanel panel = new MyJPanel(); // create new panel
51                   frame.add( panel, BorderLayout.CENTER ); // add panel
52                   frame.pack(); // set internal frame to size of contents
53
54                   theDesktop.add( frame ); // attach internal frame
55                   frame.setVisible( true ); // show internal frame
56                } // end method actionPerformed
57             } // end anonymous inner class
58          ); // end call to addActionListener
59       } // end DesktopFrame constructor
60    } // end class DesktopFrame
61
```

Fig. 25.11 | Multiple-document interface. (Part 2 of 3.)

```
62    // class to display an ImageIcon on a panel
63    class MyJPanel extends JPanel
64    {
65       private static Random generator = new Random();
66       private ImageIcon picture; // image to be displayed
67       private final static String[] images = { "yellowflowers.png",
68          "purpleflowers.png", "redflowers.png", "redflowers2.png",
69          "lavenderflowers.png" };
70
71       // load image
72       public MyJPanel()
73       {
74          int randomNumber = generator.nextInt( images.length );
75          picture = new ImageIcon( images[ randomNumber ] ); // set icon
76       } // end MyJPanel constructor
77
78       // display imageIcon on panel
79       public void paintComponent( Graphics g )
80       {
81          super.paintComponent( g );
82          picture.paintIcon( this, g, 0, 0 ); // display icon
83       } // end method paintComponent
84
85       // return image dimensions
86       public Dimension getPreferredSize()
87       {
88          return new Dimension( picture.getIconWidth(),
89             picture.getIconHeight() );
90       } // end method getPreferredSize
91    } // end class MyJPanel
```

Fig. 25.11 | Multiple-document interface. (Part 3 of 3.)

Lines 27–33 create a JMenuBar, a JMenu and a JMenuItem, add the JMenuItem to the JMenu, add the JMenu to the JMenuBar and set the JMenuBar for the application window. When the user selects the JMenuItem newFrame, the application creates and displays a new JInternalFrame object containing an image.

Line 35 assigns JDesktopPane (package javax.swing) variable theDesktop a new JDesktopPane object that will be used to manage the JInternalFrame child windows. Line 36 adds the JDesktopPane to the JFrame. By default, the JDesktopPane is added to the center of the content pane's BorderLayout, so the JDesktopPane expands to fill the entire application window.

Lines 39–58 register an ActionListener to handle the event when the user selects the newFrame menu item. When the event occurs, method actionPerformed (lines 44–56) creates a JInternalFrame object in lines 47–48. The JInternalFrame constructor used here takes five arguments—a String for the title bar of the internal window, a boolean indicating whether the internal frame can be resized by the user, a boolean indicating whether the internal frame can be closed by the user, a boolean indicating whether the internal frame can be maximized by the user and a boolean indicating whether the internal frame can be minimized by the user. For each of the boolean arguments, a true value indicates that the operation should be allowed (as is the case here).

```
1   // Fig. 25.12: DesktopTest.java
2   // Demonstrating JDesktopPane.
3   import javax.swing.JFrame;
4
5   public class DesktopTest
6   {
7      public static void main( String[] args )
8      {
9         DesktopFrame desktopFrame = new DesktopFrame();
10        desktopFrame.setDefaultCloseOperation( JFrame.EXIT_ON_CLOSE );
11        desktopFrame.setSize( 600, 480 ); // set frame size
12        desktopFrame.setVisible( true ); // display frame
13     } // end main
14  } // end class DesktopTest
```

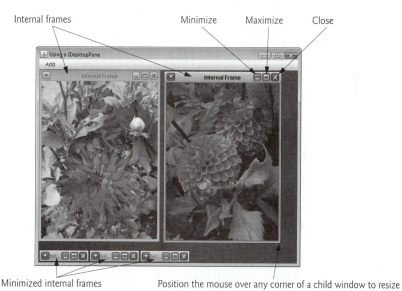

Internal frames   Minimize   Maximize   Close

Minimized internal frames   Position the mouse over any corner of a child window to resize the window (if resizing is allowed).

Maximized internal frame

Fig. 25.12 | Test class for DeskTopFrame.

As with JFrames and JApplets, a JInternalFrame has a content pane to which GUI components can be attached. Line 50 (Fig. 25.11) creates an instance of our class MyJPanel (declared at lines 63–91) that is added to the JInternalFrame at line 51.

Line 52 uses JInternalFrame method **pack** to set the size of the child window. Method pack uses the preferred sizes of the components to determine the window's size. Class MyJPanel declares method getPreferredSize (lines 86–90) to specify the panel's preferred size for use by the pack method. Line 54 adds the JInternalFrame to the JDesktopPane, and line 55 displays the JInternalFrame.

Classes JInternalFrame and JDesktopPane provide many methods for managing child windows. See the JInternalFrame and JDesktopPane online API documentation for complete lists of these methods:

```
java.sun.com/javase/6/docs/api/javax/swing/JInternalFrame.html
java.sun.com/javase/6/docs/api/javax/swing/JDesktopPane.html
```

25.8 JTabbedPane

A **JTabbedPane** arranges GUI components into layers, of which only one is visible at a time. Users access each layer via a tab—similar to folders in a file cabinet. When the user clicks a tab, the appropriate layer is displayed. The tabs appear at the top by default but also can be positioned at the left, right or bottom of the JTabbedPane. Any component can be placed on a tab. If the component is a container, such as a panel, it can use any layout manager to lay out several components on the tab. Class JTabbedPane is a subclass of JComponent. The application in Figs. 25.13–25.14 creates one tabbed pane with three tabs. Each tab displays one of the JPanels—panel1, panel2 or panel3.

```
1   // Fig. 25.13: JTabbedPaneFrame.java
2   // Demonstrating JTabbedPane.
3   import java.awt.BorderLayout;
4   import java.awt.Color;
5   import javax.swing.JFrame;
6   import javax.swing.JTabbedPane;
7   import javax.swing.JLabel;
8   import javax.swing.JPanel;
9   import javax.swing.JButton;
10  import javax.swing.SwingConstants;
11
12  public class JTabbedPaneFrame extends JFrame
13  {
14     // set up GUI
15     public JTabbedPaneFrame()
16     {
17        super( "JTabbedPane Demo " );
18
19        JTabbedPane tabbedPane = new JTabbedPane(); // create JTabbedPane
20
21        // set up panel1 and add it to JTabbedPane
22        JLabel label1 = new JLabel( "panel one", SwingConstants.CENTER );
23        JPanel panel1 = new JPanel(); // create first panel
24        panel1.add( label1 ); // add label to panel
```

Fig. 25.13 | JTabbedPane used to organize GUI components. (Part 1 of 2.)

```
25        tabbedPane.addTab( "Tab One", null, panel1, "First Panel" );
26
27        // set up panel2 and add it to JTabbedPane
28        JLabel label2 = new JLabel( "panel two", SwingConstants.CENTER );
29        JPanel panel2 = new JPanel(); // create second panel
30        panel2.setBackground( Color.YELLOW ); // set background to yellow
31        panel2.add( label2 ); // add label to panel
32        tabbedPane.addTab( "Tab Two", null, panel2, "Second Panel" );
33
34        // set up panel3 and add it to JTabbedPane
35        JLabel label3 = new JLabel( "panel three" );
36        JPanel panel3 = new JPanel(); // create third panel
37        panel3.setLayout( new BorderLayout() ); // use borderlayout
38        panel3.add( new JButton( "North" ), BorderLayout.NORTH );
39        panel3.add( new JButton( "West" ), BorderLayout.WEST );
40        panel3.add( new JButton( "East" ), BorderLayout.EAST );
41        panel3.add( new JButton( "South" ), BorderLayout.SOUTH );
42        panel3.add( label3, BorderLayout.CENTER );
43        tabbedPane.addTab( "Tab Three", null, panel3, "Third Panel" );
44
45        add( tabbedPane ); // add JTabbedPane to frame
46    } // end JTabbedPaneFrame constructor
47 } // end class JTabbedPaneFrame
```

Fig. 25.13 | JTabbedPane used to organize GUI components. (Part 2 of 2.)

```
1   // Fig. 25.14: JTabbedPaneDemo.java
2   // Demonstrating JTabbedPane.
3   import javax.swing.JFrame;
4
5   public class JTabbedPaneDemo
6   {
7      public static void main( String[] args )
8      {
9         JTabbedPaneFrame tabbedPaneFrame = new JTabbedPaneFrame();
10        tabbedPaneFrame.setDefaultCloseOperation( JFrame.EXIT_ON_CLOSE );
11        tabbedPaneFrame.setSize( 250, 200 ); // set frame size
12        tabbedPaneFrame.setVisible( true ); // display frame
13     } // end main
14  } // end class JTabbedPaneDemo
```

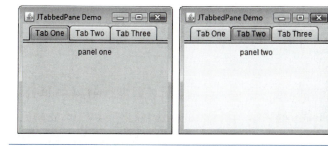

Fig. 25.14 | Test class for JTabbedPaneFrame.

The constructor (lines 15–46) builds the GUI. Line 19 creates an empty JTabbedPane with default settings—that is, tabs across the top. If the tabs do not fit on one line, they'll wrap to form additional lines of tabs. Next the constructor creates the JPanels panel1, panel2 and panel3 and their GUI components. As we set up each panel, we add it to tabbedPane, using JTabbedPane method **addTab** with four arguments. The first argument is a String that specifies the title of the tab. The second argument is an Icon reference that specifies an icon to display on the tab. If the Icon is a null reference, no image is displayed. The third argument is a Component reference that represents the GUI component to display when the user clicks the tab. The last argument is a String that specifies the tool tip for the tab. For example, line 25 adds JPanel panel1 to tabbedPane with title "Tab One" and the tool tip "First Panel". JPanels panel2 and panel3 are added to tabbedPane at lines 32 and 43. To view a tab, click it with the mouse or use the arrow keys to cycle through the tabs.

25.9 Layout Managers: BoxLayout and GridBagLayout

In Chapter 14, we introduced three layout managers—FlowLayout, BorderLayout and GridLayout. This section presents two additional layout managers (summarized in Fig. 25.15). We discuss these layout managers in the examples that follow.

Layout manager	Description
BoxLayout	A layout manager that allows GUI components to be arranged left-to-right or top-to-bottom in a container. Class Box declares a container with BoxLayout as its default layout manager and provides static methods to create a Box with a horizontal or vertical BoxLayout.
GridBagLayout	A layout manager similar to GridLayout, but the components can vary in size and can be added in any order.

Fig. 25.15 | Additional layout managers.

BoxLayout Layout Manager

The BoxLayout layout manager (in package javax.swing) arranges GUI components horizontally along a container's *x*-axis or vertically along its *y*-axis. The application in Figs. 25.16–25.17 demonstrates BoxLayout and the container class Box that uses BoxLayout as its default layout manager.

```
1   // Fig. 25.16: BoxLayoutFrame.java
2   // Demonstrating BoxLayout.
3   import java.awt.Dimension;
4   import javax.swing.JFrame;
5   import javax.swing.Box;
6   import javax.swing.JButton;
7   import javax.swing.BoxLayout;
8   import javax.swing.JPanel;
9   import javax.swing.JTabbedPane;
10
```

Fig. 25.16 | BoxLayout layout manager. (Part 1 of 3.)

```
11   public class BoxLayoutFrame extends JFrame
12   {
13      // set up GUI
14      public BoxLayoutFrame()
15      {
16         super( "Demonstrating BoxLayout" );
17
18         // create Box containers with BoxLayout
19         Box horizontal1 = Box.createHorizontalBox();
20         Box vertical1 = Box.createVerticalBox();
21         Box horizontal2 = Box.createHorizontalBox();
22         Box vertical2 = Box.createVerticalBox();
23
24         final int SIZE = 3; // number of buttons on each Box
25
26         // add buttons to Box horizontal1
27         for ( int count = 0; count < SIZE; count++ )
28            horizontal1.add( new JButton( "Button " + count ) );
29
30         // create strut and add buttons to Box vertical1
31         for ( int count = 0; count < SIZE; count++ )
32         {
33            vertical1.add( Box.createVerticalStrut( 25 ) );
34            vertical1.add( new JButton( "Button " + count ) );
35         } // end for
36
37         // create horizontal glue and add buttons to Box horizontal2
38         for ( int count = 0; count < SIZE; count++ )
39         {
40            horizontal2.add( Box.createHorizontalGlue() );
41            horizontal2.add( new JButton( "Button " + count ) );
42         } // end for
43
44         // create rigid area and add buttons to Box vertical2
45         for ( int count = 0; count < SIZE; count++ )
46         {
47            vertical2.add( Box.createRigidArea( new Dimension( 12, 8 ) ) );
48            vertical2.add( new JButton( "Button " + count ) );
49         } // end for
50
51         // create vertical glue and add buttons to panel
52         JPanel panel = new JPanel();
53         panel.setLayout( new BoxLayout( panel, BoxLayout.Y_AXIS ) );
54
55         for ( int count = 0; count < SIZE; count++ )
56         {
57            panel.add( Box.createGlue() );
58            panel.add( new JButton( "Button " + count ) );
59         } // end for
60
61         // create a JTabbedPane
62         JTabbedPane tabs = new JTabbedPane(
63            JTabbedPane.TOP, JTabbedPane.SCROLL_TAB_LAYOUT );
64
```

Fig. 25.16 | BoxLayout layout manager. (Part 2 of 3.)

```
65        // place each container on tabbed pane
66        tabs.addTab( "Horizontal Box", horizontal1 );
67        tabs.addTab( "Vertical Box with Struts", vertical1 );
68        tabs.addTab( "Horizontal Box with Glue", horizontal2 );
69        tabs.addTab( "Vertical Box with Rigid Areas", vertical2 );
70        tabs.addTab( "Vertical Box with Glue", panel );
71
72        add( tabs ); // place tabbed pane on frame
73     } // end BoxLayoutFrame constructor
74  } // end class BoxLayoutFrame
```

Fig. 25.16 | BoxLayout layout manager. (Part 3 of 3.)

```
1   // Fig. 25.17: BoxLayoutDemo.java
2   // Demonstrating BoxLayout.
3   import javax.swing.JFrame;
4
5   public class BoxLayoutDemo
6   {
7      public static void main( String[] args )
8      {
9         BoxLayoutFrame boxLayoutFrame = new BoxLayoutFrame();
10        boxLayoutFrame.setDefaultCloseOperation( JFrame.EXIT_ON_CLOSE );
11        boxLayoutFrame.setSize( 400, 220 ); // set frame size
12        boxLayoutFrame.setVisible( true ); // display frame
13     } // end main
14  } // end class BoxLayoutDemo
```

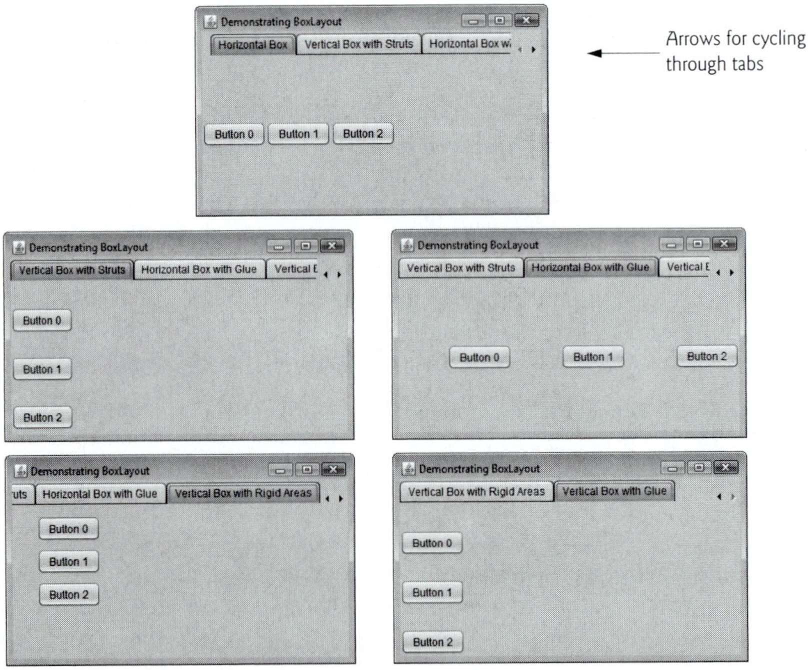

Arrows for cycling through tabs

Fig. 25.17 | Test class for BoxLayoutFrame.

Lines 19–22 create Box containers. References horizontal1 and horizontal2 are initialized with static Box method createHorizontalBox, which returns a Box container with a horizontal BoxLayout in which GUI components are arranged left-to-right. Variables vertical1 and vertical2 are initialized with static Box method **createVerticalBox**, which returns references to Box containers with a vertical BoxLayout in which GUI components are arranged top-to-bottom.

The loop at lines 27–28 adds three JButtons to horizontal1. The for statement at lines 31–35 adds three JButtons to vertical1. Before adding each button, line 33 adds a vertical strut to the container with static Box method **createVerticalStrut**. A vertical strut is an invisible GUI component that has a fixed pixel height and is used to guarantee a fixed amount of space between GUI components. The int argument to method createVerticalStrut determines the height of the strut in pixels. When the container is resized, the distance between GUI components separated by struts does not change. Class Box also declares method **createHorizontalStrut** for horizontal BoxLayouts.

The for statement at lines 38–42 adds three JButtons to horizontal2. Before adding each button, line 40 adds horizontal glue to the container with static Box method **createHorizontalGlue**. Horizontal glue is an invisible GUI component that can be used between fixed-size GUI components to occupy additional space. Normally, extra space appears to the right of the last horizontal GUI component or below the last vertical one in a BoxLayout. Glue allows the extra space to be placed between GUI components. When the container is resized, components separated by glue components remain the same size, but the glue stretches or contracts to occupy the space between them. Class Box also declares method **createVerticalGlue** for vertical BoxLayouts.

The for statement at lines 45–49 adds three JButtons to vertical2. Before each button is added, line 47 adds a rigid area to the container with static Box method **createRigidArea**. A rigid area is an invisible GUI component that always has a fixed pixel width and height. The argument to method createRigidArea is a Dimension object that specifies the area's width and height.

Lines 52–53 create a JPanel object and set its layout to a BoxLayout in the conventional manner, using Container method setLayout. The BoxLayout constructor receives a reference to the container for which it controls the layout and a constant indicating whether the layout is horizontal (**BoxLayout.X_AXIS**) or vertical (**BoxLayout.Y_AXIS**).

The for statement at lines 55–59 adds three JButtons to panel. Before adding each button, line 57 adds a glue component to the container with static Box method **createGlue**. This component expands or contracts based on the size of the Box.

Lines 62–63 create a JTabbedPane to display the five containers in this program. The argument **JTabbedPane.TOP** sent to the constructor indicates that the tabs should appear at the top of the JTabbedPane. The argument **JTabbedPane.SCROLL_TAB_LAYOUT** specifies that the tabs should wrap to a new line if there are too many to fit on one line.

The Box containers and the JPanel are attached to the JTabbedPane at lines 66–70. Try executing the application. When the window appears, resize the window to see how the glue components, strut components and rigid area affect the layout on each tab.

GridBagLayout Layout Manager

One of the most powerful predefined layout managers is **GridBagLayout** (in package java.awt). This layout is similar to GridLayout in that it arranges components in a grid. However, GridBagLayout is more flexible. The components can vary in size (i.e., they can occupy multiple rows and columns) and can be added in any order.

The first step in using GridBagLayout is determining the appearance of the GUI. For this step you need only a piece of paper. Draw the GUI, then draw a grid over it, dividing the components into rows and columns. The initial row and column numbers should be 0, so that the GridBagLayout layout manager can use the row and column numbers to properly place the components in the grid. Figure 25.18 demonstrates drawing the lines for the rows and columns over a GUI.

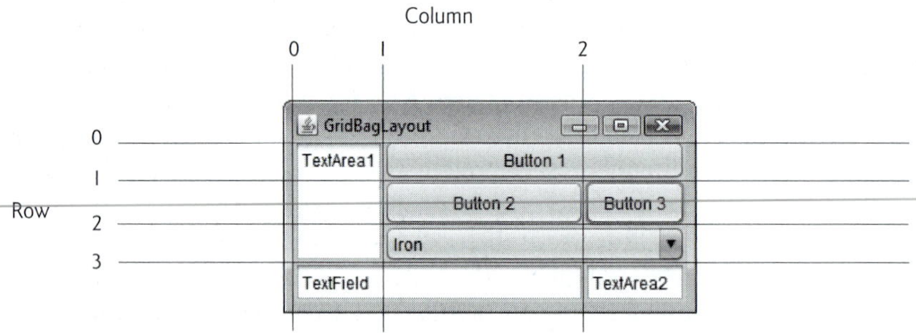

Fig. 25.18 | Designing a GUI that will use GridBagLayout.

A **GridBagConstraints** object describes how a component is placed in a Grid-BagLayout. Several GridBagConstraints fields are summarized in Fig. 25.19.

Field	Description
anchor	Specifies the relative position (NORTH, NORTHEAST, EAST, SOUTHEAST, SOUTH, SOUTHWEST, WEST, NORTHWEST, CENTER) of the component in an area that it does not fill.
fill	Resizes the component in the specified direction (NONE, HORIZONTAL, VERTICAL, BOTH) when the display area is larger than the component.
gridx	The column in which the component will be placed.
gridy	The row in which the component will be placed.
gridwidth	The number of columns the component occupies.
gridheight	The number of rows the component occupies.
weightx	The amount of extra space to allocate horizontally. The grid slot can become wider when extra space is available.
weighty	The amount of extra space to allocate vertically. The grid slot can become taller when extra space is available.

Fig. 25.19 | GridBagConstraints fields.

GridBagConstraints field **anchor** specifies the relative position of the component in an area that it does not fill. The variable anchor is assigned one of the following GridBag-Constraints constants: **NORTH, NORTHEAST, EAST, SOUTHEAST, SOUTH, SOUTHWEST, WEST, NORTHWEST** or **CENTER**. The default value is CENTER.

`GridBagConstraints` field `fill` defines how the component grows if the area in which it can be displayed is larger than the component. The variable `fill` is assigned one of the following `GridBagConstraints` constants: `NONE`, `VERTICAL`, `HORIZONTAL` or `BOTH`. The default value is `NONE`, which indicates that the component will not grow in either direction. `VERTICAL` indicates that it will grow vertically. `HORIZONTAL` indicates that it will grow horizontally. `BOTH` indicates that it will grow in both directions.

Variables `gridx` and `gridy` specify where the upper-left corner of the component is placed in the grid. Variable `gridx` corresponds to the column, and variable `gridy` corresponds to the row. In Fig. 25.18, the `JComboBox` (displaying "`Iron`") has a `gridx` value of 1 and a `gridy` value of 2.

Variable `gridwidth` specifies the number of columns a component occupies. The `JComboBox` occupies two columns. Variable `gridheight` specifies the number of rows a component occupies. The `JTextArea` on the left side of Fig. 25.18 occupies three rows.

Variable `weightx` specifies how to distribute extra horizontal space to grid slots in a `GridBagLayout` when the container is resized. A zero value indicates that the grid slot does not grow horizontally on its own. However, if the component spans a column containing a component with nonzero `weightx` value, the component with zero `weightx` value will grow horizontally in the same proportion as the other component(s) in that column. This is because each component must be maintained in the same row and column in which it was originally placed.

Variable `weighty` specifies how to distribute extra vertical space to grid slots in a `Grid-BagLayout` when the container is resized. A zero value indicates that the grid slot does not grow vertically on its own. However, if the component spans a row containing a component with nonzero `weighty` value, the component with zero `weighty` value grows vertically in the same proportion as the other component(s) in the same row.

In Fig. 25.18, the effects of `weighty` and `weightx` cannot easily be seen until the container is resized and additional space becomes available. Components with larger weight values occupy more of the additional space than those with smaller weight values.

Components should be given nonzero positive weight values—otherwise they'll "huddle" together in the middle of the container. Figure 25.20 shows the GUI of Fig. 25.18 with all weights set to zero.

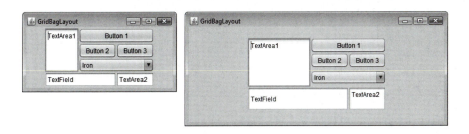

Fig. 25.20 | `GridBagLayout` with the weights set to zero.

The application in Figs. 25.21–25.22 uses the `GridBagLayout` layout manager to arrange the components of the GUI in Fig. 25.18. The application does nothing except demonstrate how to use `GridBagLayout`.

```
 1    // Fig. 25.21: GridBagFrame.java
 2    // Demonstrating GridBagLayout.
 3    import java.awt.GridBagLayout;
 4    import java.awt.GridBagConstraints;
 5    import java.awt.Component;
 6    import javax.swing.JFrame;
 7    import javax.swing.JTextArea;
 8    import javax.swing.JTextField;
 9    import javax.swing.JButton;
10    import javax.swing.JComboBox;
11
12    public class GridBagFrame extends JFrame
13    {
14       private GridBagLayout layout; // layout of this frame
15       private GridBagConstraints constraints; // constraints of this layout
16
17       // set up GUI
18       public GridBagFrame()
19       {
20          super( "GridBagLayout" );
21          layout = new GridBagLayout();
22          setLayout( layout ); // set frame layout
23          constraints = new GridBagConstraints(); // instantiate constraints
24
25          // create GUI components
26          JTextArea textArea1 = new JTextArea( "TextArea1", 5, 10 );
27          JTextArea textArea2 = new JTextArea( "TextArea2", 2, 2 );
28
29          String[] names = { "Iron", "Steel", "Brass" };
30          JComboBox comboBox = new JComboBox( names );
31
32          JTextField textField = new JTextField( "TextField" );
33          JButton button1 = new JButton( "Button 1" );
34          JButton button2 = new JButton( "Button 2" );
35          JButton button3 = new JButton( "Button 3" );
36
37          // weightx and weighty for textArea1 are both 0: the default
38          // anchor for all components is CENTER: the default
39          constraints.fill = GridBagConstraints.BOTH;
40          addComponent( textArea1, 0, 0, 1, 3 );
41
42          // weightx and weighty for button1 are both 0: the default
43          constraints.fill = GridBagConstraints.HORIZONTAL;
44          addComponent( button1, 0, 1, 2, 1 );
45
46          // weightx and weighty for comboBox are both 0: the default
47          // fill is HORIZONTAL
48          addComponent( comboBox, 2, 1, 2, 1 );
49
50          // button2
51          constraints.weightx = 1000;  // can grow wider
52          constraints.weighty = 1;       // can grow taller
53          constraints.fill = GridBagConstraints.BOTH;
54          addComponent( button2, 1, 1, 1, 1 );
```

Fig. 25.21 | GridBagLayout layout manager. (Part 1 of 2.)

```
55
56        // fill is BOTH for button3
57        constraints.weightx = 0;
58        constraints.weighty = 0;
59        addComponent( button3, 1, 2, 1, 1 );
60
61        // weightx and weighty for textField are both 0, fill is BOTH
62        addComponent( textField, 3, 0, 2, 1 );
63
64        // weightx and weighty for textArea2 are both 0, fill is BOTH
65        addComponent( textArea2, 3, 2, 1, 1 );
66     } // end GridBagFrame constructor
67
68     // method to set constraints on
69     private void addComponent( Component component,
70        int row, int column, int width, int height )
71     {
72        constraints.gridx = column; // set gridx
73        constraints.gridy = row; // set gridy
74        constraints.gridwidth = width; // set gridwidth
75        constraints.gridheight = height; // set gridheight
76        layout.setConstraints( component, constraints ); // set constraints
77        add( component ); // add component
78     } // end method addComponent
79  } // end class GridBagFrame
```

Fig. 25.21 | GridBagLayout layout manager. (Part 2 of 2.)

```
1   // Fig. 25.22: GridBagDemo.java
2   // Demonstrating GridBagLayout.
3   import javax.swing.JFrame;
4
5   public class GridBagDemo
6   {
7      public static void main( String[] args )
8      {
9         GridBagFrame gridBagFrame = new GridBagFrame();
10        gridBagFrame.setDefaultCloseOperation( JFrame.EXIT_ON_CLOSE );
11        gridBagFrame.setSize( 300, 150 ); // set frame size
12        gridBagFrame.setVisible( true ); // display frame
13     } // end main
14  } // end class GridBagDemo
```

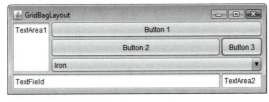

Fig. 25.22 | Test class for GridBagFrame. (Part 1 of 2.)

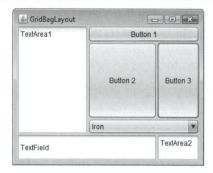

Fig. 25.22 | Test class for `GridBagFrame`. (Part 2 of 2.)

The GUI contains three `JButton`s, two `JTextArea`s, a `JComboBox` and a `JTextField`. The layout manager is `GridBagLayout`. Lines 21–22 create the `GridBagLayout` object and set the layout manager for the `JFrame` to `layout`. Line 23 creates the `GridBagConstraints` object used to determine the location and size of each component in the grid. Lines 26–35 create each GUI component that will be added to the content pane.

Lines 39–40 configure `JTextArea` `textArea1` and add it to the content pane. The values for `weightx` and `weighty` values are not specified in `constraints`, so each has the value zero by default. Thus, the `JTextArea` will not resize itself even if space is available. However, it spans multiple rows, so the vertical size is subject to the `weighty` values of `JButton`s `button2` and `button3`. When either button is resized vertically based on its `weighty` value, the `JTextArea` is also resized.

Line 39 sets variable `fill` in `constraints` to `GridBagConstraints.BOTH`, causing the `JTextArea` to always fill its entire allocated area in the grid. An `anchor` value is not specified in `constraints`, so the default `CENTER` is used. We do not use variable `anchor` in this application, so all the components will use the default. Line 40 calls our utility method `addComponent` (declared at lines 69–78). The `JTextArea` object, the row, the column, the number of columns to span and the number of rows to span are passed as arguments.

`JButton` `button1` is the next component added (lines 43–44). By default, the `weightx` and `weighty` values are still zero. The `fill` variable is set to `HORIZONTAL`—the component will always fill its area in the horizontal direction. The vertical direction is not filled. The `weighty` value is zero, so the button will become taller only if another component in the same row has a nonzero `weighty` value. `JButton` `button1` is located at row 0, column 1. One row and two columns are occupied.

`JComboBox` `comboBox` is the next component added (line 48). By default, the `weightx` and `weighty` values are zero, and the `fill` variable is set to `HORIZONTAL`. The `JComboBox` button will grow only in the horizontal direction. Note that the `weightx`, `weighty` and `fill` variables retain the values set in `constraints` until they're changed. The `JComboBox` button is placed at row 2, column 1. One row and two columns are occupied.

`JButton` `button2` is the next component added (lines 51–54). It's given a `weightx` value of 1000 and a `weighty` value of 1. The area occupied by the button is capable of growing in the vertical and horizontal directions. The `fill` variable is set to `BOTH`, which specifies that the button will always fill the entire area. When the window is resized, `button2` will grow. The button is placed at row 1, column 1. One row and one column are occupied.

JButton button3 is added next (lines 57–59). Both the weightx value and weighty value are set to zero, and the value of fill is BOTH. JButton button3 will grow if the window is resized—it's affected by the weight values of button2. Note that the weightx value for button2 is much larger than that for button3. When resizing occurs, button2 will occupy a larger percentage of the new space. The button is placed at row 1, column 2. One row and one column are occupied.

Both the JTextField textField (line 62) and JTextArea textArea2 (line 65) have a weightx value of 0 and a weighty value of 0. The value of fill is BOTH. The JTextField is placed at row 3, column 0, and the JTextArea at row 3, column 2. The JTextField occupies one row and two columns, the JTextArea one row and one column.

Method addComponent's parameters are a Component reference component and integers row, column, width and height. Lines 72–73 set the GridBagConstraints variables gridx and gridy. The gridx variable is assigned the column in which the Component will be placed, and the gridy value is assigned the row in which the Component will be placed. Lines 74–75 set the GridBagConstraints variables gridwidth and gridheight. The gridwidth variable specifies the number of columns the Component will span in the grid, and the gridheight variable specifies the number of rows the Component will span in the grid. Line 76 sets the GridBagConstraints for a component in the GridBagLayout. Method **setConstraints** of class GridBagLayout takes a Component argument and a GridBagConstraints argument. Line 77 adds the component to the JFrame.

When you execute this application, try resizing the window to see how the constraints for each GUI component affect its position and size in the window.

GridBagConstraints *Constants RELATIVE and REMAINDER*

Instead of gridx and gridy, a variation of GridBagLayout uses GridBagConstraints constants **RELATIVE** and **REMAINDER**. RELATIVE specifies that the next-to-last component in a particular row should be placed to the right of the previous component in the row. REMAINDER specifies that a component is the last component in a row. Any component that is not the second-to-last or last component on a row must specify values for GridbagConstraints variables gridwidth and gridheight. The application in Figs. 25.23–25.24 arranges components in GridBagLayout, using these constants.

```
 1  // Fig. 25.23: GridBagFrame2.java
 2  // Demonstrating GridBagLayout constants.
 3  import java.awt.GridBagLayout;
 4  import java.awt.GridBagConstraints;
 5  import java.awt.Component;
 6  import javax.swing.JFrame;
 7  import javax.swing.JComboBox;
 8  import javax.swing.JTextField;
 9  import javax.swing.JList;
10  import javax.swing.JButton;
11
12  public class GridBagFrame2 extends JFrame
13  {
14     private GridBagLayout layout; // layout of this frame
15     private GridBagConstraints constraints; // constraints of this layout
16
```

Fig. 25.23 | GridBagConstraints constants RELATIVE and REMAINDER. (Part 1 of 3.)

```
17      // set up GUI
18      public GridBagFrame2()
19      {
20          super( "GridBagLayout" );
21          layout = new GridBagLayout();
22          setLayout( layout ); // set frame layout
23          constraints = new GridBagConstraints(); // instantiate constraints
24
25          // create GUI components
26          String[] metals = { "Copper", "Aluminum", "Silver" };
27          JComboBox comboBox = new JComboBox( metals );
28
29          JTextField textField = new JTextField( "TextField" );
30
31          String[] fonts = { "Serif", "Monospaced" };
32          JList list = new JList( fonts );
33
34          String[] names = { "zero", "one", "two", "three", "four" };
35          JButton[] buttons = new JButton[ names.length ];
36
37          for ( int count = 0; count < buttons.length; count++ )
38              buttons[ count ] = new JButton( names[ count ] );
39
40          // define GUI component constraints for textField
41          constraints.weightx = 1;
42          constraints.weighty = 1;
43          constraints.fill = GridBagConstraints.BOTH;
44          constraints.gridwidth = GridBagConstraints.REMAINDER;
45          addComponent( textField );
46
47          // buttons[0] -- weightx and weighty are 1: fill is BOTH
48          constraints.gridwidth = 1;
49          addComponent( buttons[ 0 ] );
50
51          // buttons[1] -- weightx and weighty are 1: fill is BOTH
52          constraints.gridwidth = GridBagConstraints.RELATIVE;
53          addComponent( buttons[ 1 ] );
54
55          // buttons[2] -- weightx and weighty are 1: fill is BOTH
56          constraints.gridwidth = GridBagConstraints.REMAINDER;
57          addComponent( buttons[ 2 ] );
58
59          // comboBox -- weightx is 1: fill is BOTH
60          constraints.weighty = 0;
61          constraints.gridwidth = GridBagConstraints.REMAINDER;
62          addComponent( comboBox );
63
64          // buttons[3] -- weightx is 1: fill is BOTH
65          constraints.weighty = 1;
66          constraints.gridwidth = GridBagConstraints.REMAINDER;
67          addComponent( buttons[ 3 ] );
68
69          // buttons[4] -- weightx and weighty are 1: fill is BOTH
70          constraints.gridwidth = GridBagConstraints.RELATIVE;
```

Fig. 25.23 | GridBagConstraints constants RELATIVE and REMAINDER. (Part 2 of 3.)

```
71         addComponent( buttons[ 4 ] );
72
73         // list -- weightx and weighty are 1: fill is BOTH
74         constraints.gridwidth = GridBagConstraints.REMAINDER;
75         addComponent( list );
76      } // end GridBagFrame2 constructor
77
78      // add a component to the container
79      private void addComponent( Component component )
80      {
81         layout.setConstraints( component, constraints );
82         add( component ); // add component
83      } // end method addComponent
84   } // end class GridBagFrame2
```

Fig. 25.23 | GridBagConstraints constants RELATIVE and REMAINDER. (Part 3 of 3.)

```
 1   // Fig. 25.24: GridBagDemo2.java
 2   // Demonstrating GridBagLayout constants.
 3   import javax.swing.JFrame;
 4
 5   public class GridBagDemo2
 6   {
 7      public static void main( String[] args )
 8      {
 9         GridBagFrame2 gridBagFrame = new GridBagFrame2();
10         gridBagFrame.setDefaultCloseOperation( JFrame.EXIT_ON_CLOSE );
11         gridBagFrame.setSize( 300, 200 ); // set frame size
12         gridBagFrame.setVisible( true ); // display frame
13      } // end main
14   } // end class GridBagDemo2
```

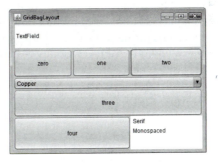

Fig. 25.24 | Test class for GridBagDemo2.

Lines 21–22 create a GridBagLayout and use it to set the JFrame's layout manager. The components that are placed in GridBagLayout are created in lines 27–38—they are a JComboBox, a JTextField, a JList and five JButtons.

The JTextField is added first (lines 41–45). The weightx and weighty values are set to 1. The fill variable is set to BOTH. Line 44 specifies that the JTextField is the last component on the line. The JTextField is added to the content pane with a call to our utility method addComponent (declared at lines 79–83). Method addComponent takes a Component argument and uses GridBagLayout method setConstraints to set the constraints for the Component. Method add attaches the component to the content pane.

JButton buttons[0] (lines 48–49) has weightx and weighty values of 1. The fill variable is BOTH. Because buttons[0] is not one of the last two components on the row, it's given a gridwidth of 1 and so will occupy one column. The JButton is added to the content pane with a call to utility method addComponent.

JButton buttons[1] (lines 52–53) has weightx and weighty values of 1. The fill variable is BOTH. Line 52 specifies that the JButton is to be placed relative to the previous component. The Button is added to the JFrame with a call to addComponent.

JButton buttons[2] (lines 56–57) has weightx and weighty values of 1. The fill variable is BOTH. This JButton is the last component on the line, so REMAINDER is used. The JButton is added to the content pane with a call to addComponent.

The JComboBox (lines 60–62) has a weightx of 1 and a weighty of 0. The JComboBox will not grow vertically. The JComboBox is the only component on the line, so REMAINDER is used. The JComboBox is added to the content pane with a call to addComponent.

JButton buttons[3] (lines 65–67) has weightx and weighty values of 1. The fill variable is BOTH. This JButton is the only component on the line, so REMAINDER is used. The JButton is added to the content pane with a call to addComponent.

JButton buttons[4] (lines 70–71) has weightx and weighty values of 1. The fill variable is BOTH. This JButton is the next-to-last component on the line, so RELATIVE is used. The JButton is added to the content pane with a call to addComponent.

The JList (lines 74–75) has weightx and weighty values of 1. The fill variable is BOTH. The JList is added to the content pane with a call to addComponent.

25.10 Wrap-Up

This chapter completes our introduction to GUIs. In this chapter, we discussed additional GUI topics, such as menus, sliders, pop-up menus, multiple-document interfaces, tabbed panes and Java's pluggable look-and-feel. All these components can be added to existing applications to make them easier to use and understand. We also presented additional layout managers for organizing and sizing GUI components. In the next chapter, you'll learn about multithreading, a powerful capability that allows applications to use threads to perform multiple tasks at once.

Summary

Section 25.2 JSlider

- JSliders enable the user to select from a range of integer values. JSliders can display major tick marks, minor tick marks and labels for the tick marks. They also support snap-to ticks, where positioning the thumb between two tick marks causes the thumb to snap to the closest tick mark.

- If a JSlider has the focus, the left and right arrow keys cause the thumb of the JSlider to decrease or increase by 1. The down and up arrow keys also cause the thumb of the JSlider to decrease or increase by 1, respectively. The *PgDn (page down) key* and *PgUp (page up) key* cause the thumb to decrease or increase by block increments of one-tenth of the range of values, respectively. The *Home key* moves the thumb to the minimum value, and the *End key* moves it to the maximum value.

- JSliders have either horizontal or vertical orientation. For a horizontal JSlider, the minimum value is at the extreme left and the maximum value at the extreme right. For a vertical JSlider, the minimum value is at the extreme bottom and the maximum value at the extreme top. The position of the thumb indicates the current value of the JSlider. Method getValue of class J-Slider returns the current thumb position.

- JSlider method setMajorTickSpacing sets the spacing for tick marks on a JSlider. Method setPaintTicks with a true argument indicates that the tick marks should be displayed.

- JSliders generate ChangeEvents when the user interacts with a JSlider. A ChangeListener declares method stateChanged that can respond to ChangeEvents.

Section 25.3 Windows: Additional Notes
- Every window generates window events when the user manipulates it. Interface WindowListener provides seven window-event-handling methods—windowActivated, windowClosed, windowClosing, windowDeactivated, windowDeiconified, windowIconified and windowOpened.

Section 25.4 Using Menus with Frames
- Menus are an integral part of GUIs that allow users to perform actions without unnecessarily cluttering a GUI with extra components. In Swing GUIs, menus can be attached only to objects of classes with method setJMenuBar (e.g., JFrame and JApplet).

- Classes used to build menus are JMenuBar, JMenuItem, JMenu, JCheckBoxMenuItem and JRadioButtonMenuItem.

- A JMenuBar is a container for menus. A JMenuItem appears in a menu that, when selected, causes an action to be performed. A JMenu contains menu items and can be added to a JMenuBar or to other JMenus as submenus.

- When a menu is clicked, it expands to show its list of menu items. JMenu method addSeparator adds a separator line to a menu.

- When a JCheckBoxMenuItem is selected, a check appears to the left of the menu item. When the JCheckBoxMenuItem is selected again, the check is removed.

- When multiple JRadioButtonMenuItems are maintained as part of a ButtonGroup, only one can be selected at a time. When one is selected, a filled circle appears to its left. When another is selected, the filled circle to the left of the previously selected item is removed.

- AbstractButton method setMnemonic specifies the mnemonic for an AbstractButton. Mnemonic characters are normally displayed with an underline.

- A modal dialog box does not allow access to any other window in the application until the dialog is dismissed. The dialogs displayed with class JOptionPane are modal dialogs. Class JDialog can be used to create your own modal or nonmodal dialogs.

Section 25.5 JPopupMenu
- Context-sensitive pop-up menus are created with class JPopupMenu. The pop-up trigger event occurs normally when the user presses and releases the right mouse button. MouseEvent method isPopupTrigger returns true if the pop-up trigger event occurred.

- JPopupMenu method show displays a JPopupMenu. The first argument specifies the origin component, which helps determine where the JPopupMenu will appear. The last two arguments are the coordinates from the origin component's upper-left corner, at which the JPopupMenu appears.

Section 25.6 Pluggable Look-and-Feel
- Class UIManager.LookAndFeelInfo maintains information about a look-and-feel.

- UIManager static method getInstalledLookAndFeels returns an array of UIManager.LookAndFeelInfo objects that describe the available look-and-feels.

- UIManager static method setLookAndFeel changes the look-and-feel. SwingUtilities static method updateComponentTreeUI changes the look-and-feel of every component attached to its Component argument to the new look-and-feel.

Section 25.7 *JDesktopPane and JInternalFrame*

- Many of today's applications use a multiple-document interface (MDI) to manage several open documents that are being processed in parallel. Swing's JDesktopPane and JInternalFrame classes provide support for creating multiple-document interfaces.

Section 25.8 *JTabbedPane*

- A JTabbedPane arranges GUI components into layers, of which only one is visible at a time. Users access each layer by clicking its tab.

Section 25.9 *Layout Managers: BoxLayout and GridBagLayout*

- BoxLayout arranges GUI components left-to-right or top-to-bottom in a container.

- Class Box represents a container with BoxLayout as its default layout manager and provides static methods to create a Box with a horizontal or vertical BoxLayout.

- GridBagLayout is similar to GridLayout, but each component size can vary and components can be added in any order.

- A GridBagConstraints object specifies how a component is placed in a GridBagLayout. GridBagLayout method setConstraints takes a Component argument and a GridBagConstraints argument and sets the constraints of the Component.

Terminology

Self-Review Exercises

25.1   Fill in the blanks in each of the following statements:

   a) The _____ class is used to create a menu object.

   b) The _____ method of class JMenu places a separator bar in a menu.

   c) JSlider events are handled by the _____ method of interface _____.

   d) The GridBagConstraints instance variable _____ is set to CENTER by default.

25.2 State whether each of the following is *true* or *false*. If *false*, explain why.

a) When the programmer creates a JFrame, a minimum of one menu must be created and added to the JFrame.

b) The variable fill belongs to the GridBagLayout class.

c) Drawing on a GUI component is performed with respect to the (0, 0) upper-left corner coordinate of the component.

d) The default layout for a Box is BoxLayout.

25.3 Find the error(s) in each of the following and explain how to correct the error(s).

a) JMenubar b;

b) mySlider = JSlider(1000, 222, 100, 450);

c) gbc.fill = GridBagConstraints.NORTHWEST;   // set fill

d) // override to paint on a customized Swing component
```
public void paintcomponent( Graphics g )
{
    g.drawString( "HELLO", 50, 50 );
} // end method paintComponent
```

e) // create a JFrame and display it
```
JFrame f = new JFrame( "A Window" );
f.setVisible( true );
```

Answers to Self-Review Exercises

25.1 a) JMenu. b) addSeparator. c) stateChanged, ChangeListener. d) anchor.

25.2 a) False. A JFrame does not require any menus.

b) False. The variable fill belongs to the GridBagConstraints class.

c) True.

d) True.

25.3 a) JMenubar should be JMenuBar.

b) The first argument to the constructor should be either SwingConstants.HORIZONTAL or SwingConstants.VERTICAL, and the keyword new must be used after the = operator. Also, the minimum value should be less than the maximum and the initial value should be in range.

c) The constant should be either BOTH, HORIZONTAL, VERTICAL or NONE.

d) paintcomponent should be paintComponent, and the method should call super.paint-Component(g) as its first statement.

e) The JFrame's setSize method must also be called to establish the size of the window.

Exercises

25.4 Fill in the blanks in each of the following statements:

a) A JMenuItem that is a JMenu is called a(n) _____

b) Method _____ attaches a JMenuBar to a JFrame.

c) Container class _____ has a default BoxLayout.

d) A(n) _____ manages a set of child windows declared with class JInternalFrame.

25.5 State whether each of the following is *true* or *false*. If *false*, explain why.

a) Menus require a JMenuBar object so they can be attached to a JFrame.

b) BoxLayout is the default layout manager for a JFrame.

c) JApplets can contain menus.

25.6 Find the error(s) in each of the following. Explain how to correct the error(s).

a) x.add(new JMenuItem("Submenu Color")); // create submenu

b) container.setLayout(new GridbagLayout());

25.7   Write a program that displays a circle of random size and calculates and displays the area, radius, diameter and circumference. Use the following equations: *diameter* = 2 × *radius*, *area* = π × *radius*², *circumference* = 2 × π × *radius*. Use the constant Math.PI for pi (π). All drawing should be done on a subclass of JPanel, and the results of the calculations should be displayed in a read-only JTextArea.

25.8   Enhance the program in Exercise 25.7 by allowing the user to alter the radius with a JSlider. The program should work for all radii in the range from 100 to 200. As the radius changes, the diameter, area and circumference should be updated and displayed. The initial radius should be 150. Use the equations from Exercise 25.7. All drawing should be done on a subclass of JPanel, and the results of the calculations should be displayed in a read-only JTextArea.

25.9   Explore the effects of varying the weightx and weighty values of the program in Fig. 25.21. What happens when a slot has a nonzero weight but is not allowed to fill the whole area (i.e., the fill value is not BOTH)?

25.10   Write a program that uses the paintComponent method to draw the current value of a JSlider on a subclass of JPanel. In addition, provide a JTextField where a specific value can be entered. The JTextField should display the current value of the JSlider at all times. Changing the value in the JTextField should also update the JSlider. A JLabel should be used to identify the JTextField. The JSlider methods setValue and getValue should be used. [*Note:* The setValue method is a public method that does not return a value and takes one integer argument, the JSlider value, which determines the position of the thumb.]

25.11   Declare a subclass of JPanel called MyColorChooser that provides three JSlider objects and three JTextField objects. Each JSlider represents the values from 0 to 255 for the red, green and blue parts of a color. Use these values as the arguments to the Color constructor to create a new Color object. Display the current value of each JSlider in the corresponding JTextField. When the user changes the value of the JSlider, the JTextField should be changed accordingly. Use your new GUI component as part of an application that displays the current Color value by drawing a filled rectangle.

25.12   Modify the MyColorChooser class of Exercise 25.11 to allow the user to enter an integer value into a JTextField to set the red, green or blue value. When the user presses *Enter* in the JTextField, the corresponding JSlider should be set to the appropriate value.

25.13   Modify the application in Exercise 25.12 to draw the current color as a rectangle on an instance of a subclass of JPanel which provides its own paintComponent method to draw the rectangle and provides *set* methods to set the red, green and blue values for the current color. When any *set* method is invoked, the drawing panel should automatically repaint itself.

25.14   Modify the application in Exercise 25.13 to allow the user to drag the mouse across the drawing panel (a subclass of JPanel) to draw a shape in the current color. Enable the user to choose what shape to draw.

25.15   Modify the application in Exercise 25.14 to provide the user with the ability to terminate the application by clicking the close box on the window that is displayed and by selecting Exit from a File menu. Use the techniques shown in Fig. 25.5.

25.16   *(Complete Drawing Application)* Using the techniques developed in this chapter and Chapter 14, create a complete drawing application. The program should use the GUI components from Chapter 14 and Chapter 25 to enable the user to select the shape, color and fill characteristics. Each shape should be stored in an array of MyShape objects, where MyShape is the superclass in your hierarchy of shape classes. Use a JDesktopPane and JInternalFrames to allow the user to create multiple separate drawings in separate child windows. Create the user interface as a separate child window containing all the GUI components that allow the user to determine the characteristics of the shape to be drawn. The user can then click in any JInternalFrame to draw the shape.

Chapters on the Web

The following chapters are available as PDF documents from this book's Companion Website (www.pearsonhighered.com/deitel/):

- Chapter 26, Multithreading
- Chapter 27, Networking
- Chapter 28, Accessing Databases with JDBC
- Chapter 29, JavaServer™ Faces Web Applications
- Chapter 30, Ajax-Enabled JavaServer™ Faces Web Applications
- Chapter 31, Web Services

These files can be viewed in Adobe® Reader® (get.adobe.com/reader). The index entries for these chapters have uppercase Roman numeral page numbers.

New copies of this book come with a Companion Website access code that is located on the card inside the book's front cover. If the access code is visible or there is no card, you purchased a used book or an edition that does not come with an access code. In this case, you can purchase access directly from the Companion Website.

A

Operator Precedence Chart

Operators are shown in decreasing order of precedence from top to bottom (Fig. A.1).

Operator	Description	Associativity
++ --	unary postfix increment unary postfix decrement	right to left
++ -- + - ! ~ (*type*)	unary prefix increment unary prefix decrement unary plus unary minus unary logical negation unary bitwise complement unary cast	right to left
* / %	multiplication division remainder	left to right
+ -	addition or string concatenation subtraction	left to right
<< >> >>>	left shift signed right shift unsigned right shift	left to right
< <= > >= instanceof	less than less than or equal to greater than greater than or equal to type comparison	left to right

Fig. A.1 | Operator precedence chart. (Part 1 of 2.)

Operator	Description	Associativity
== !=	is equal to is not equal to	left to right
&	bitwise AND boolean logical AND	left to right
^	bitwise exclusive OR boolean logical exclusive OR	left to right
|	bitwise inclusive OR boolean logical inclusive OR	left to right
&&	conditional AND	left to right
||	conditional OR	left to right
?:	conditional	right to left
= += -= *= /= %= &= ^= |= <<= >>= >>>=	assignment addition assignment subtraction assignment multiplication assignment division assignment remainder assignment bitwise AND assignment bitwise exclusive OR assignment bitwise inclusive OR assignment bitwise left-shift assignment bitwise signed-right-shift assignment bitwise unsigned-right-shift assignment	right to left

Fig. A.1 | Operator precedence chart. (Part 2 of 2.)

ASCII Character Set

	0	1	2	3	4	5	6	7	8	9
0	nul	soh	stx	etx	eot	enq	ack	bel	bs	ht
1	nl	vt	ff	cr	so	si	dle	dc1	dc2	dc3
2	dc4	nak	syn	etb	can	em	sub	esc	fs	gs
3	rs	us	sp	!	"	#	$	%	&	'
4	(	)	*	+	,	-	.	/	0	1
5	2	3	4	5	6	7	8	9	:	;
6	<	=	>	?	@	A	B	C	D	E
7	F	G	H	I	J	K	L	M	N	O
8	P	Q	R	S	T	U	V	W	X	Y
9	Z	[	\	]	^	_	'	a	b	c
10	d	e	f	g	h	i	j	k	l	m
11	n	o	p	q	r	s	t	u	v	w
12	x	y	z	{			}	~	del		

Fig. B.1 | ASCII character set.

The digits at the left of the table are the left digits of the decimal equivalents (0–127) of the character codes, and the digits at the top of the table are the right digits of the character codes. For example, the character code for "F" is 70, and the character code for "&" is 38.

Most users of this book are interested in the ASCII character set used to represent English characters on many computers. The ASCII character set is a subset of the Unicode character set used by Java to represent characters from most of the world's languages. For more information on the Unicode character set, see the web bonus Appendix L.

C

Keywords and Reserved Words

Java Keywords				
abstract	assert	boolean	break	byte
case	catch	char	class	continue
default	do	double	else	enum
extends	final	finally	float	for
if	implements	import	instanceof	int
interface	long	native	new	package
private	protected	public	return	short
static	strictfp	super	switch	synchronized
this	throw	throws	transient	try
void	volatile	while		
Keywords that are not currently used				
const	goto			

Fig. C.1 | Java keywords.

Java also contains the reserved words true and false, which are boolean literals, and null, which is the literal that represents a reference to nothing. Like keywords, these reserved words cannot be used as identifiers.

Primitive Types

Type	Size in bits	Values	Standard
boolean		true or false	

[*Note:* A **boolean**'s representation is specific to the Java Virtual Machine on each platform.]

Type	Size in bits	Values	Standard
char	16	'\u0000' to '\uFFFF' (0 to 65535)	(ISO Unicode character set)
byte	8	-128 to $+127$ (-2^7 to $2^7 - 1$)	
short	16	$-32,768$ to $+32,767$ (-2^{15} to $2^{15} - 1$)	
int	32	$-2,147,483,648$ to $+2,147,483,647$ (-2^{31} to $2^{31} - 1$)	
long	64	$-9,223,372,036,854,775,808$ to $+9,223,372,036,854,775,807$ (-2^{63} to $2^{63} - 1$)	
float	32	*Negative range:* $-3.4028234663852886E+38$ to $-1.40129846432481707e-45$ *Positive range:* $1.40129846432481707e-45$ to $3.4028234663852886E+38$	(IEEE 754 floating point)
double	64	*Negative range:* $-1.7976931348623157E+308$ to $-4.94065645841246544e-324$ *Positive range:* $4.94065645841246544e-324$ to $1.7976931348623157E+308$	(IEEE 754 floating point)

Fig. D.1 | Java primitive types.

For more information on IEEE 754 visit grouper.ieee.org/groups/754/. For more information on Unicode, see Appendix L, Unicode®.

Using the Java API Documentation

E.1 Introduction

The Java class library contains thousands of predefined classes and interfaces that programmers can use to write their own applications. These classes are grouped into packages based on their functionality. For example, the classes and interfaces used for file processing are grouped into the java.io package, and the classes and interfaces for networking applications are grouped into the java.net package. The **Java API documentation** lists the public and protected members of each class and the public members of each interface in the Java class library. The documentation overviews all the classes and interfaces, summarizes their members (i.e., the fields, constructors and methods of classes, and the fields and methods of interfaces) and provides detailed descriptions of each member. Most Java programmers rely on this documentation when writing programs. Normally, programmers would search the API to find the following:

1. The package that contains a particular class or interface.

2. Relationships between a particular class or interface and other classes and interfaces.

3. Class or interface constants—normally declared as public static final fields.

4. Constructors to determine how an object of the class can be initialized.

5. The methods of a class to determine whether they're static or non-static, the number and types of the arguments you need to pass, the return types and any exceptions that might be thrown from the method.

In addition, programmers often rely on the documentation to discover classes and interfaces that they have not used before. For this reason, we demonstrate the documentation with classes you know and classes you may not have studied yet. We show how to use the documentation to locate the information you need to use a class or interface effectively.

E.2 Navigating the Java API

The Java API documentation can be downloaded to your local hard disk or viewed online. To download the Java API documentation, go to java.sun.com/javase/downloads/ scroll down to the **Additional Resources** section and click the **Download** button to the right of **Java SE 6 Documentation**. You'll be asked to accept a license agreement. To do this, click **Accept**, then click **Continue**. Check the checkbox next to **Java SE Development Kit Documentation 6** then click the jdk-6u10-docs.zip link just below the checkbox. After downloading the file, you can use a program such as WinZip (www.winzip.com) to extract the files. If you are using Windows, extract the contents to your JDK's installation directory. To view the API documentation on your local hard disk in Microsoft Windows, open C:\Program Files\Java*YourJDKVersion*\docs\api\index.html page in your browser. To view the API documentation online, go to java.sun.com/javase/6/docs/api/index.html (Fig. E.1).

Upper-left frame lists all packages in alphabetical order.

Tree link displays the hierarchy of all packages and classes.

Deprecated link lists portions of the API that should no longer be used.

Index link lists fields, methods, classes and interfaces.

Help link describes how the API is organized.

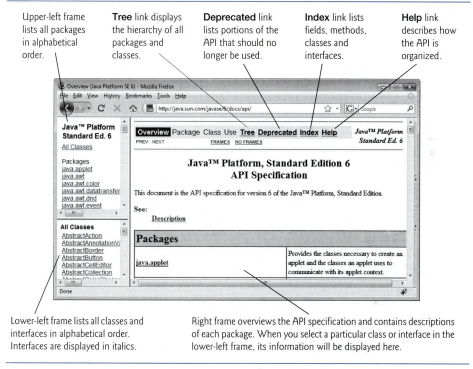

Lower-left frame lists all classes and interfaces in alphabetical order. Interfaces are displayed in italics.

Right frame overviews the API specification and contains descriptions of each package. When you select a particular class or interface in the lower-left frame, its information will be displayed here.

Fig. E.1 | Java API overview. (Courtesy of Sun Microsystems, Inc.)

Frames in the API Documentation's `index.html` Page

The API documentation is divided into three frames (see Fig. E.1). The upper-left frame lists all of the Java API's packages in alphabetical order. The lower-left frame initially lists the Java API's classes and interfaces in alphabetical order. Interface names are displayed in italic. When you click a specific package in the upper-left frame, the lower-left frame lists the classes and interfaces of the selected package. The right frame initially provides a brief description of each package of the Java API specification—read this overview to become familiar wth the general capabilities of the Java APIs. If you select a class or interface in the lower-left frame, the right frame displays information about that class or interface.

Important Links in the `index.html` Page

At the top of the right frame (Fig. E.1), there are four links—**Tree, Deprecated, Index** and **Help**. The **Tree** link displays the hierarchy of all packages, classes and interfaces in a tree structure. The **Deprecated** link displays interfaces, classes, exceptions, fields, constructors and methods that should no longer be used. The **Index** link displays classes, interfaces, fields, constructors and methods in alphabetical order. The **Help** link describes how the API documentation is organized. You should probably begin by reading the **Help** page.

Viewing the Index Page

If you do not know the name of the class you are looking for, but you do know the name of a method or field, you can use the documentation's index to locate the class. The **Index** link is located near the upper-right corner of the right frame. The index page (Fig. E.2) displays fields, constructors, methods, interfaces and classes in alphabetical order. For example, if you are looking for `Scanner` method `hasNextInt`, but do not know the class name, you can click the **H** link to go to the alphabetical listing of all items in the Java API that begin with "h". Scroll to method `hasNextInt` (Fig. E.3). Once there, each method named `hasNextInt` is listed with the package name and class to which the method belongs. From there, you can click the class name to view the class's complete details, or you can click the method name to view the method's details.

Classes, interfaces and their members are listed in alphabetical order. Click a letter to view all fields, constructors, methods, interfaces and classes that start with that letter.

Click the **Index** link to display the documentation's index.

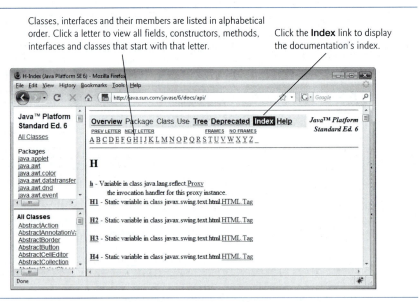

Fig. E.2 | Viewing the **Index** page. (Courtesy of Sun Microsystems, Inc.)

Click the method name to view the method's details.

Click the class name to view the class's complete details.

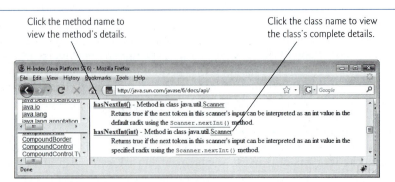

Fig. E.3 | Scroll to method `hasNextInt`. (Courtesy of Sun Microsystems, Inc.)

Viewing a Specific Package

When you click the package name in the upper-left frame, all classes and interfaces from that package are displayed in the lower-left frame and are divided into five subsections—**Interfaces**, **Classes**, **Enums**, **Exceptions** and **Errors**—each listed alphabetically. For example, the contents of package javax.swing are displayed in the lower-left frame (Fig. E.4) when you click javax.swing in the upper-left frame. You can click the package name in the lower-left frame to get an overview of the package. If you think that a package contains several classes that could be useful in your application, the package overview can be especially helpful.

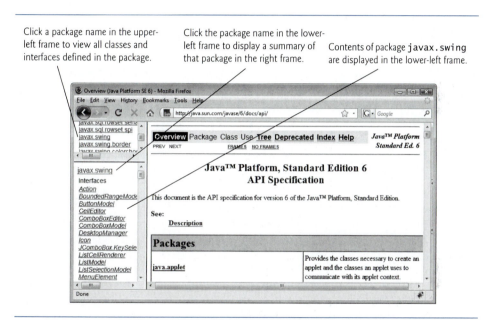

Click a package name in the upper-left frame to view all classes and interfaces defined in the package.

Click the package name in the lower-left frame to display a summary of that package in the right frame.

Contents of package javax.swing are displayed in the lower-left frame.

Fig. E.4 | Clicking a package name in the upper-left frame to view all classes and interfaces declared in this package. (Courtesy of Sun Microsystems, Inc.)

Viewing the Details of a Class

When you click a class name or interface name in the lower-left frame, the right frame displays the details of that class or interface. First you'll see the class's package name followed by a hierarchy that shows the class's relationship to other classes. You'll also see a list of the interfaces implemented by the class and the class's known subclasses. Figure E.5 shows the beginning of the documentation page for class JButton from the javax.swing package. The page first shows the package name in which the class appears. This is followed by the class hierarchy that leads to class JButton, the interfaces class JButton implements and the subclasses of class JButton. The bottom of the right frame shows the beginning of class JButton's description. Note that when you look at the documentation for an interface, the right frame does not display a hierarchy for that interface. Instead, the right frame lists the interface's superinterfaces, known subinterfaces and known implementing classes.

Click the class name to view detailed information about the class.

Detailed information about the class is displayed in the right frame.

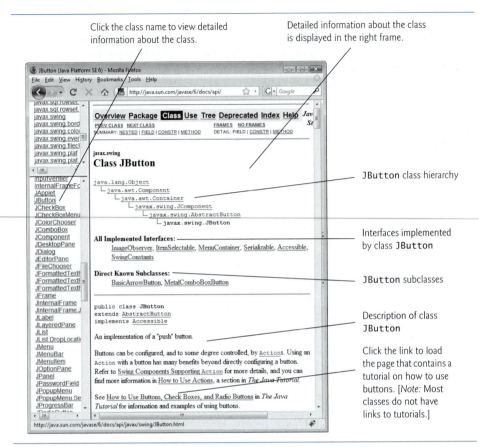

JButton class hierarchy

Interfaces implemented by class JButton

JButton subclasses

Description of class JButton

Click the link to load the page that contains a tutorial on how to use buttons. [*Note:* Most classes do not have links to tutorials.]

Fig. E.5 | Clicking a class name to view detailed information about the class. (Courtesy of Sun Microsystems, Inc.)

Summary Sections in a Class's Documentation Page

Other parts of each API page are listed below. Each part is presented only if the class contains or inherits the items specified. Class members shown in the summary sections are public unless they're explicitly marked as protected. A class's private members are not shown in the documentation, because they cannot be used directly in your programs.

1. The **Nested Class Summary** section summarizes the class's public and protected nested classes—i.e., classes that are defined inside the class. Unless explicitly specified, these classes are public and non-static.

2. The **Field Summary** section summarizes the class's public and protected fields. Unless explicitly specified, these fields are public and non-static. Figure E.6 shows the **Field Summary** section of class Color.

3. The **Constructor Summary** section summarizes the class's constructors. Constructors are not inherited, so this section appears in the documentation for a class only if the class declares one or more constructors. Figure E.7 shows the **Constructor Summary** section of class JButton.

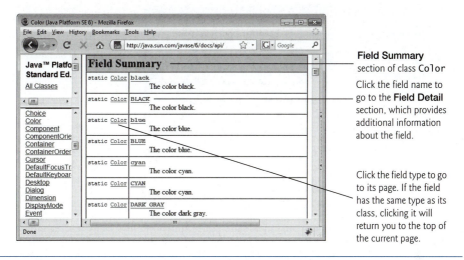

Fig. E.6 | **Field Summary** section of class `Color`. (Courtesy of Sun Microsystems, Inc.)

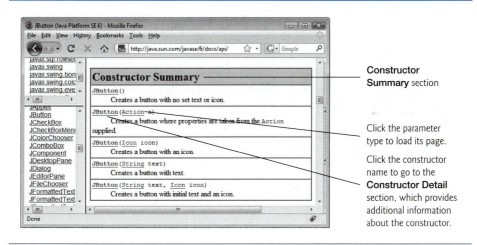

Fig. E.7 | **Constructor Summary** section of class `JButton`. (Courtesy of Sun Microsystems, Inc.)

4. The **Method Summary** section summarizes the class's `public` and `protected` methods. Unless explicitly specified, these methods are `public` and non-`static`. Figure E.8 shows the **Method Summary** section of class `BufferedInputStream`.

Note that the summary sections typically provide only a one-sentence description of a class member. Additional details are presented in the detail sections discussed next.

Detail Sections in a Class's Documentation Page

After the summary sections are detail sections that normally provide more discussion of particular class members. There is not a detail section for nested classes. When you click

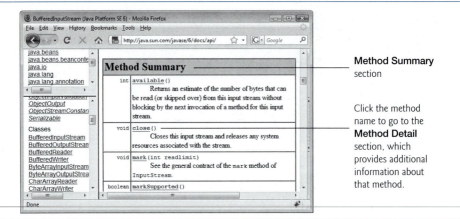

Fig. E.8 | Method Summary section of class `BufferedInputStream`. (Courtesy of Sun Microsystems, Inc.)

the link in the **Nested Class Summary** for a particular nested class, a documentation page describing that nested class is displayed. The detail sections are described below.

1. The **Field Detail** section provides the declaration of each field. It also discusses each field, including the field's modifiers and meaning. Figure E.9 shows the **Field Detail** section of class `Color`.

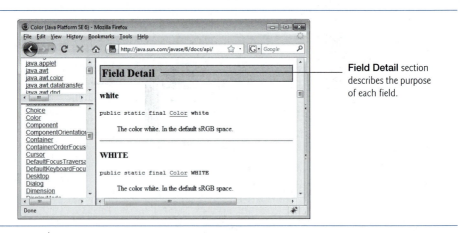

Fig. E.9 | Field Detail section of class `Color`. (Courtesy of Sun Microsystems, Inc.)

2. The **Constructor Detail** section provides the first line of each constructor's declaration and discusses the constructors. The discussion includes the modifiers of each constructor, a description of each constructor, each constructor's parameters and any exceptions thrown by each constructor. Figure E.10 shows the **Constructor Detail** section of class `JButton`.

3. The **Method Detail** section provides the first line of each method. The discussion of each method includes its modifiers, a more complete method description, the method's parameters, the method's return type and any exceptions thrown by the

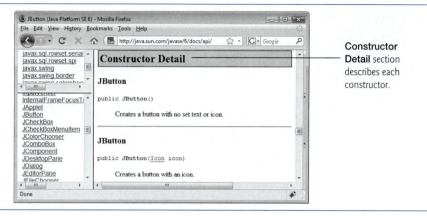

Fig. E.10 | Constructor Detail section of class JButton. (Courtesy of Sun Microsystems, Inc.)

method. Figure E.11 shows class BufferedInputStream's **Method Detail** section. The method details show you other methods that might be of interest (labeled as **See Also**). If the method overrides a method of the superclass, the name of the superclass method and the name of the superclass are provided so you can link to the method or superclass for more information.

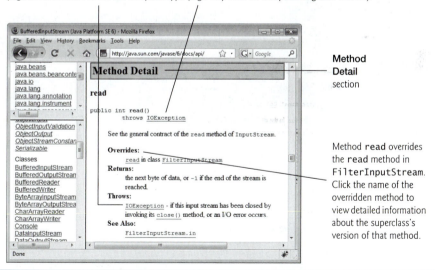

Fig. E.11 | Method Detail section of class BufferedInputStream. (Courtesy of Sun Microsystems, Inc.)

As you look through the documentation, you'll notice that there are often links to other fields, methods, nested-classes and top-level classes. These links enable you to jump from the class you are looking at to another relevant portion of the documentation.

F

Using the Debugger

*We are built to make mistakes,
coded for error.*
—Lewis Thomas

*What we anticipate seldom
occurs; what we least expect
generally happens.*
—Benjamin Disraeli

*It is one thing to show a man
that he is in error, and another
to put him in possession of
truth.*
—John Locke

Objectives

In this appendix you'll learn:

- To set breakpoints to debug applications.
- To use the `run` command to execute in debug mode.
- To use the `stop` command to set a breakpoint.
- To use the `cont` command to continue execution.
- To use the `print` command to evaluate expressions.
- To use the `set` command to change variable values during program execution.
- To use the `step`, `step up` and `next` commands to control execution.
- To use the `watch` command to see how a field is modified during program execution.
- To use the `clear` command to list breakpoints or remove a breakpoint.

F.1 Introduction

In Chapter 2, you learned that there are two types of errors—syntax errors and logic errors—and you learned how to eliminate syntax errors from your code. Logic errors do not prevent the application from compiling successfully, but they do cause an application to produce erroneous results when it runs. The JDK includes software called a **debugger** that allows you to monitor the execution of your applications so you can locate and remove logic errors. The debugger will be one of your most important application development tools. Many IDEs provide their own debuggers similar to the one included in the JDK or provide a graphical user interface to the JDK's debugger.

This appendix demonstrates key features of the JDK's debugger using command-line applications that receive no input from the user. The same debugger features discussed here can be used to debug applications that take user input, but debugging such applications requires a slightly more complex setup. To focus on the debugger features, we've opted to demonstrate the debugger with simple command-line applications involving no user input. You can also find more information on the Java debugger at java.sun.com/javase/6/docs/technotes/tools/windows/jdb.html.

F.2 Breakpoints and the run, stop, cont and print Commands

We begin our study of the debugger by investigating **breakpoints**, which are markers that can be set at any executable line of code. When application execution reaches a breakpoint, execution pauses, allowing you to examine the values of variables to help determine whether logic errors exist. For example, you can examine the value of a variable that stores the result of a calculation to determine whether the calculation was performed correctly. Note that setting a breakpoint at a line of code that is not executable (such as a comment) causes the debugger to display an error message.

To illustrate the features of the debugger, we use application AccountTest (Fig. F.1), which creates and manipulates an object of class Account (Fig. 7.7). Execution of AccountTest begins in main (lines 7–24). Line 9 creates an Account object with an initial balance of $50.00. Recall that Account's constructor accepts one argument, which specifies the Account's initial balance. Lines 12–13 output the initial account balance using Account method getBalance. Line 15 declares and initializes a local variable depositAmount. Lines 17–19 then print depositAmount and add it to the Account's balance using its credit method. Finally, lines 22–23 display the new balance. [*Note:* The Appendix F examples directory contains a copy of Account.java identical to the one in Fig. 7.7.]

```
 1   // Fig. F.1: AccountTest.java
 2   // Create and manipulate an Account object.
 3
 4   public class AccountTest
 5   {
 6      // main method begins execution
 7      public static void main( String[] args )
 8      {
 9         Account account = new Account( 50.00 ); // create Account object
10
11         // display initial balance of Account object
12         System.out.printf( "initial account balance: $%.2f\n",
13            account.getBalance() );
14
15         double depositAmount = 25.0; // deposit amount
16
17         System.out.printf( "\nadding %.2f to account balance\n\n",
18            depositAmount );
19         account.credit( depositAmount ); // add to account balance
20
21         // display new balance
22         System.out.printf( "new account balance: $%.2f\n",
23            account.getBalance() );
24      } // end main
25
26   } // end class AccountTest
```

```
initial account balance: $50.00

adding 25.00 to account balance

new account balance: $75.00
```

Fig. F.1 | AccountTest class creates and manipulates an Account object.

In the following steps, you'll use breakpoints and various debugger commands to examine the value of the variable depositAmount declared in AccountTest (Fig. F.1).

1. *Opening the* Command Prompt *window and changing directories.* Open the Command Prompt window by selecting Start > Programs > Accessories > Command Prompt. Change to the directory containing the Appendix F examples by typing cd C:\examples\debugger [*Note:* If your examples are in a different directory, use that directory here.]

2. *Compiling the application for debugging.* The Java debugger works only with .class files that were compiled with the **-g** compiler option, which generates information that is used by the debugger to help you debug your applications. Compile the application with the -g command-line option by typing javac -g AccountTest.java Account.java. Recall from Chapter 7 that this command compiles both AccountTest.java and Account.java. The command java -g *.java compiles all of the working directory's .java files for debugging.

3. ***Starting the debugger.*** In the **Command Prompt**, type **jdb** (Fig. F.2). This command will start the Java debugger and enable you to use its features. [*Note:* We modified the colors of our **Command Prompt** window for readability.]

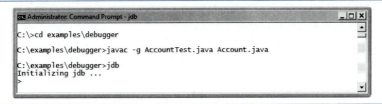

Fig. F.2 | Starting the Java debugger.

4. ***Running an application in the debugger.*** Run the AccountTest application through the debugger by typing **run** AccountTest (Fig. F.3). If you do not set any breakpoints before running your application in the debugger, the application will run just as it would using the java command.

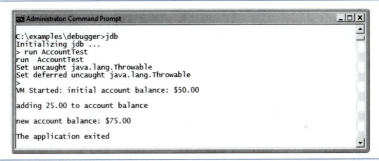

Fig. F.3 | Running the AccountTest application through the debugger.

5. ***Restarting the debugger.*** To make proper use of the debugger, you must set at least one breakpoint before running the application. Restart the debugger by typing jdb.

6. ***Inserting breakpoints in Java.*** You set a breakpoint at a specific line of code in your application. The line numbers used in these steps are from the source code in Fig. F.1. Set a breakpoint at line 12 in the source code by typing stop at AccountTest:12 (Fig. F.4). The **stop command** inserts a breakpoint at the line number specified after the command. You can set as many breakpoints as necessary. Set another breakpoint at line 19 by typing stop at AccountTest:19 (Fig. F.4). When the application runs, it suspends execution at any line that contains a breakpoint. The application is said to be in **break mode** when the debugger pauses the application's execution. Breakpoints can be set even after the debugging process has begun. Note that the debugger command stop in, followed by a class name, a period and a method name (e.g., stop in Account.credit) instructs the debugger to set a breakpoint at the first executable statement in the specified method. The debugger pauses execution when program control enters the method.

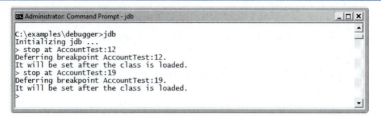

Fig. F.4 | Setting breakpoints at lines 12 and 19.

7. ***Running the application and beginning the debugging process.*** Type run AccountTest to execute the application and begin the debugging process (Fig. F.5). The debugger prints text indicating that breakpoints were set at lines 12 and 19. It calls each breakpoint a "deferred breakpoint" because each was set before the application began running in the debugger. The application pauses when execution reaches the breakpoint on line 12. At this point, the debugger notifies you that a breakpoint has been reached and it displays the source code at that line (12). That line of code is the next statement that will execute.

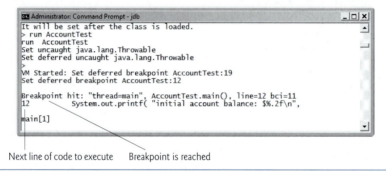

Next line of code to execute   Breakpoint is reached

Fig. F.5 | Restarting the AccountTest application.

8. ***Using the cont command to resume execution.*** Type cont. The **cont command** causes the application to continue running until the next breakpoint is reached (line 19), at which point the debugger notifies you (Fig. F.6). Note that Account-Test's normal output appears between messages from the debugger.

Another breakpoint is reached

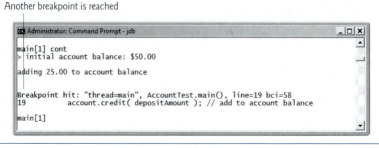

Fig. F.6 | Execution reaches the second breakpoint.

9. *Examining a variable's value.* Type print depositAmount to display the current value stored in the depositAmount variable (Fig. F.7). The **print command** allows you to peek inside the computer at the value of one of your variables. This command will help you find and eliminate logic errors in your code. Note that the value displayed is 25.0—the value assigned to depositAmount in line 15 of Fig. F.1.

Fig. F.7 | Examining the value of variable depositAmount.

10. *Continuing application execution.* Type cont to continue the application's execution. There are no more breakpoints, so the application is no longer in break mode. The application continues executing and eventually terminates (Fig. F.8). The debugger will stop when the application ends.

Fig. F.8 | Continuing application execution and exiting the debugger.

In this section, you learned how to enable the debugger and set breakpoints so that you can examine variables with the print command while an application is running. You also learned how to use the cont command to continue execution after a breakpoint is reached.

F.3 The print and set Commands

In the preceding section, you learned how to use the debugger's print command to examine the value of a variable during program execution. In this section, you'll learn how to use the print command to examine the value of more complex expressions. You'll also learn the **set command**, which allows the programmer to assign new values to variables.

For this section, we assume that you've followed *Step 1* and *Step 2* in Section F.2 to open the **Command Prompt** window, change to the directory containing the Appendix F examples (e.g., C:\examples\debugger) and compile the AccountTest application (and class Account) for debugging.

1. *Starting debugging.* In the **Command Prompt**, type jdb to start the Java debugger.

2. *Inserting a breakpoint.* Set a breakpoint at line 19 in the source code by typing stop at AccountTest:19.

3. *Running the application and reaching a breakpoint.* Type run AccountTest to begin the debugging process (Fig. F.9). This will cause AccountTest's main to execute until the breakpoint at line 19 is reached. This suspends application execu-

tion and switches the application into break mode. At this point, the statements in lines 9–13 created an Account object and printed the initial balance of the Account obtained by calling its getBalance method. The statement in line 15 (Fig. F.1) declared and initialized local variable depositAmount to 25.0. The statement in line 19 is the next statement that will execute.

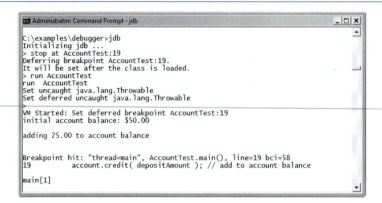

Fig. F.9 | Application execution suspended when debugger reaches the breakpoint at line 19.

4. *Evaluating arithmetic and boolean expressions.* Recall from Section F.2 that once the application has entered break mode, you can explore the values of the application's variables using the debugger's print command. You can also use the print command to evaluate arithmetic and boolean expressions. In the **Command Prompt** window, type print depositAmount - 2.0. Note that the print command returns the value 23.0 (Fig. F.10). However, this command does not actually change the value of depositAmount. In the **Command Prompt** window, type print depositAmount == 23.0. Expressions containing the == symbol are treated as boolean expressions. The value returned is false (Fig. F.10) because depositAmount does not currently contain the value 23.0—depositAmount is still 25.0.

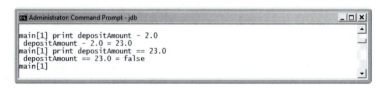

Fig. F.10 | Examining the values of an arithmetic and boolean expression.

5. *Modifying values.* The debugger allows you to change the values of variables during the application's execution. This can be valuable for experimenting with different values and for locating logic errors in applications. You can use the debugger's set command to change the value of a variable. Type set depositAmount = 75.0. The debugger changes the value of depositAmount and displays its new value (Fig. F.11).

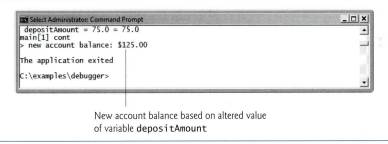

Fig. F.11 | Modifying values.

6. *Viewing the application result.* Type cont to continue application execution. Line 19 of AccountTest (Fig. F.1) executes, passing depositAmount to Account method credit. Method main then displays the new balance. Note that the result is $125.00 (Fig. F.12). This shows that the preceding step changed the value of depositAmount from its initial value (25.0) to 75.0.

New account balance based on altered value
of variable depositAmount

Fig. F.12 | Output displayed after the debugging process.

In this section, you learned how to use the debugger's print command to evaluate arithmetic and boolean expressions. You also learned how to use the set command to modify the value of a variable during your application's execution.

F.4 Controlling Execution Using the step, step up and next Commands

Sometimes you'll need to execute an application line by line to find and fix errors. Walking through a portion of your application this way can help you verify that a method's code executes correctly. In this section, you'll learn how to use the debugger for this task. The commands you learn in this section allow you to execute a method line by line, execute all the statements of a method at once or execute only the remaining statements of a method (if you've already executed some statements within the method).

Once again, we assume you are working in the directory containing the Appendix F examples and have compiled for debugging with the -g compiler option.

1. *Starting the debugger.* Start the debugger by typing jdb.

2. *Setting a breakpoint.* Type stop at AccountTest:19 to set a breakpoint at line 19.

3. *Running the application.* Run the application by typing run AccountTest. After the application displays its two output messages, the debugger indicates that the breakpoint has been reached and displays the code at line 19 (Fig. F.13). The debugger and application then pause and wait for the next command to be entered.

```
Administrator: Command Prompt - jdb                                    _ □ X
C:\examples\debugger>jdb
Initializing jdb ...
> stop at AccountTest:19
Deferring breakpoint AccountTest:19.
It will be set after the class is loaded.
> run AccountTest
run  AccountTest
Set uncaught java.lang.Throwable
Set deferred uncaught java.lang.Throwable
>
VM Started: Set deferred breakpoint AccountTest:19
initial account balance: $50.00

adding 25.00 to account balance


Breakpoint hit: "thread=main", AccountTest.main(), line=19 bci=58
19            account.credit( depositAmount ); // add to account balance

main[1]
```

Fig. F.13 | Reaching the breakpoint in the AccountTest application.

4. *Using the step command.* The **step command** executes the next statement in the application. If the next statement to execute is a method call, control transfers to the called method. The step command enables you to enter a method and study the individual statements of that method. For instance, you can use the print and set commands to view and modify the variables within the method. You'll now use the step command to enter the credit method of class Account (Fig. 7.7) by typing step (Fig. F.14). The debugger indicates that the step has been completed and displays the next executable statement—in this case, line 21 of class Account (Fig. 7.7).

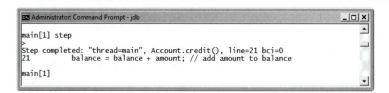

```
Administrator: Command Prompt - jdb                                    _ □ X
main[1] step
>
Step completed: "thread=main", Account.credit(), line=21 bci=0
21            balance = balance + amount; // add amount to balance

main[1]
```

Fig. F.14 | Stepping into the credit method.

5. *Using the step up command.* After you've stepped into the credit method, type **step up.** This command executes the remaining statements in the method and returns control to the place where the method was called. The credit method contains only one statement to add the method's parameter amount to instance variable balance. The step up command executes this statement, then pauses before line 22 in AccountTest. Thus, the next action to occur will be to print the new account balance (Fig. F.15). In lengthy methods, you may want to look at a few key lines of code, then continue debugging the caller's code. The step up command is useful for situations in which you do not want to continue stepping through the entire method line by line.

6. *Using the cont command to continue execution.* Enter the cont command (Fig. F.16) to continue execution. The statement at lines 22–23 executes, displaying the new balance, then the application and the debugger terminate.

```
Administrator: Command Prompt - jdb                         _ □ ×
main[1] step up
>
Step completed: "thread=main", AccountTest.main(), line=22 bci=63
22              System.out.printf( "new account balance: $%.2f\n",

main[1]
```

Fig. F.15 | Stepping out of a method.

```
Administrator: Command Prompt                              _ □ ×
main[1] cont
> new account balance: $75.00

The application exited

C:\examples\debugger>
```

Fig. F.16 | Continuing execution of the `AccountTest` application.

7. ***Restarting the debugger.*** Restart the debugger by typing `jdb`.

8. ***Setting a breakpoint.*** Breakpoints persist only until the end of the debugging session in which they're set—once the debugger exits, all breakpoints are removed. (In Section F.6, you'll learn how to manually clear a breakpoint before the end of the debugging session.) Thus, the breakpoint set for line 19 in *Step 2* no longer exists upon restarting the debugger in *Step 7*. To reset the breakpoint at line 19, once again type `stop at AccountTest:19`.

9. ***Running the application.*** Type `run AccountTest` to run the application. As in *Step 3*, `AccountTest` runs until the breakpoint at line 19 is reached, then the debugger pauses and waits for the next command (Fig. F.17).

```
Administrator: Command Prompt - jdb                         _ □ ×
C:\examples\debugger>jdb
Initializing jdb ...
> stop at AccountTest:19
Deferring breakpoint AccountTest:19.
It will be set after the class is loaded.
> run AccountTest
run  AccountTest
Set uncaught java.lang.Throwable
Set deferred uncaught java.lang.Throwable
>
VM Started: Set deferred breakpoint AccountTest:19
initial account balance: $50.00

adding 25.00 to account balance

Breakpoint hit: "thread=main", AccountTest.main(), line=19 bci=58
19              account.credit( depositAmount ); // add to account balance

main[1]
```

Fig. F.17 | Reaching the breakpoint in the `AccountTest` application.

10. ***Using the next command.*** Type `next`. This command behaves like the `step` command, except when the next statement to execute contains a method call. In that case, the called method executes in its entirety and the application advances to the

next executable line after the method call (Fig. F.18). Recall from *Step 4* that the step command would enter the called method. In this example, the next command causes Account method credit to execute, then the debugger pauses at line 22 in AccountTest.

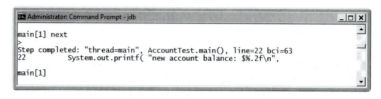

Fig. F.18 | Stepping over a method call.

11. *Using the exit command.* Use the **exit command** to end the debugging session (Fig. F.19). This command causes the AccountTest application to immediately terminate rather than execute the remaining statements in main. Note that when debugging some types of applications (e.g., GUI applications), the application continues to execute even after the debugging session ends.

Fig. F.19 | Exiting the debugger.

In this section, you learned how to use the debugger's step and step up commands to debug methods called during your application's execution. You saw how the next command can be used to step over a method call. You also learned that the exit command ends a debugging session.

F.5 The watch Command

In this section, we present the **watch command**, which tells the debugger to watch a field. When that field is about to change, the debugger will notify you. In this section, you'll learn how to use the watch command to see how the Account object's field balance is modified during the execution of the AccountTest application.

As in the preceding two sections, we assume that you've followed *Step 1* and *Step 2* in Section F.2 to open the **Command Prompt**, change to the correct examples directory and compile classes AccountTest and Account for debugging (i.e., with the -g compiler option).

1. *Starting the debugger.* Start the debugger by typing jdb.

2. *Watching a class's field.* Set a watch on Account's balance field by typing watch Account.balance (Fig. F.20). You can set a watch on any field during execution of the debugger. Whenever the value in a field is about to change, the debugger enters break mode and notifies you that the value will change. Watches can be placed only on fields, not on local variables.

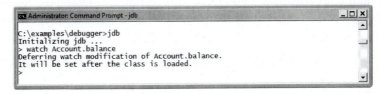

Fig. F.20 | Setting a watch on Account's balance field.

3. *Running the application.* Run the application with the command run Account-Test. The debugger will now notify you that field balance's value will change (Fig. F.21). When the application begins, an instance of Account is created with an initial balance of $50.00 and a reference to the Account object is assigned to the local variable account (line 9, Fig. F.1). Recall from Fig. 7.7 that when the constructor for this object runs, if parameter initialBalance is greater than 0.0, instance variable balance is assigned the value of parameter initialBalance. The debugger notifies you that the value of balance will be set to 50.0.

```
Administrator: Command Prompt - jdb                                    _ □ ×
It will be set after the class is loaded.
> run AccountTest
run  AccountTest
Set uncaught java.lang.Throwable
Set deferred uncaught java.lang.Throwable
>
VM Started: Set deferred watch modification of Account.balance

Field (Account.balance) is 0.0, will be 50.0: "thread=main", Account.<init>(), l
ine=15 bci=12
15            balance = initialBalance;

main[1]
```

Fig. F.21 | AccountTest application stops when account is created and its balance field will be modified.

4. *Adding money to the account.* Type cont to continue executing the application. The application executes normally before reaching the code on line 19 of Fig. F.1 that calls Account method credit to raise the Account object's balance by a specified amount. The debugger notifies you that instance variable balance will change (Fig. F.22). Note that although line 19 of class AccountTest calls method credit, line 21 in Account's method credit actually changes the value of balance.

```
Administrator: Command Prompt - jdb                                    _ □ ×
main[1] cont
> initial account balance: $50.00

addi
ng 25.00 to account balance

Field (Account.balance) is 50.0, will be 75.0: "thread=main", Account.credit(),
line=21 bci=7
21            balance = balance + amount; // add amount to balance

main[1]
```

Fig. F.22 | Changing the value of balance by calling Account method credit.

5. *Continuing execution.* Type cont—the application will finish executing because the application does not attempt any additional changes to balance (Fig. F.23).

Fig. F.23 | Continuing execution of AccountTest.

6. *Restarting the debugger and resetting the watch on the variable.* Type jdb to restart the debugger. Once again, set a watch on the Account instance variable balance by typing the watch Account.balance, then type run AccountTest to run the application (Fig. F.24).

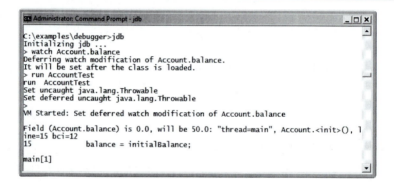

Fig. F.24 | Restarting the debugger and resetting the watch on the variable balance.

7. *Removing the watch on the field.* Suppose you want to watch a field for only part of a program's execution. You can remove the debugger's watch on variable balance by typing **unwatch** Account.balance (Fig. F.25). Type cont—the application will finish executing without reentering break mode.

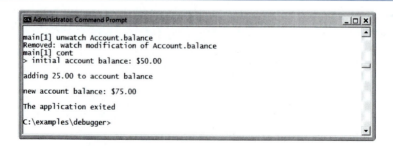

Fig. F.25 | Removing the watch on variable balance.

8. *Closing the Command Prompt window.* Close the **Command Prompt** window by clicking its close button.

In this section, you learned how to use the watch command to enable the debugger to notify you of changes to the value of a field throughout the life of an application. You also learned how to use the unwatch command to remove a watch on a field before the end of the application.

F.6 The clear Command

In the preceding section, you learned to use the unwatch command to remove a watch on a field. The debugger also provides the clear command to remove a breakpoint from an application. You'll often need to debug applications containing repetitive actions, such as a loop. You may want to examine the values of variables during several, but possibly not all, of the loop's iterations. If you set a breakpoint in the body of a loop, the debugger will pause before each execution of the line containing a breakpoint. After determining that the loop is working properly, you may want to remove the breakpoint and allow the remaining iterations to proceed normally. In this section, we use the compound interest application in Fig. 4.6 to demonstrate how the debugger behaves when you set a breakpoint in the body of a for statement and how to remove a breakpoint in the middle of a debugging session.

1. *Opening the Command Prompt window, changing directories and compiling the application for debugging.* Open the **Command Prompt** window, then change to the directory containing the Appendix F examples. For your convenience, we've provided a copy of the Interest.java file in this directory. Compile the application for debugging by typing javac -g Interest.java.

2. *Starting the debugger and setting breakpoints.* Start the debugger by typing jdb. Set breakpoints at lines 13 and 22 of class Interest by typing stop at Interest:13, then stop at Interest:22 (Fig. F.26).

```
Administrator: Command Prompt - jdb
C:\examples\debugger>javac -g Interest.java

C:\examples\debugger>jdb
Initializing jdb ...
> stop at Interest:13
Deferring breakpoint Interest:13.
It will be set after the class is loaded.
> stop at Interest:22
Deferring breakpoint Interest:22.
It will be set after the class is loaded.
>
```

Fig. F.26 | Setting breakpoints in the Interest application.

3. *Running the application.* Run the application by typing run Interest. The application executes until reaching the breakpoint at line 13 (Fig. F.27).

4. *Continuing execution.* Type cont to continue—the application executes line 13, printing the column headings "Year" and "Amount on deposit". Note that line 13 appears before the for statement at lines 16–23 in Interest (Fig. 4.6) and thus executes only once. Execution continues past line 13 until the breakpoint at line 22 is reached during the first iteration of the for statement (Fig. F.28).

```
Administrator: Command Prompt - jdb
It will be set after the class is loaded.
> run Interest
run  Interest
Set uncaught java.lang.Throwable
Set deferred uncaught java.lang.Throwable
>
VM Started: Set deferred breakpoint Interest:22
Set deferred breakpoint Interest:13

Breakpoint hit: "thread=main", Interest.main(), line=13 bci=9
13           System.out.printf( "%s%20s\n", "Year", "Amount on deposit" );

main[1]
```

Fig. F.27 | Reaching the breakpoint at line 13 in the `Interest` application.

```
Administrator: Command Prompt - jdb

main[1] cont
> Year    Amount on deposit

Breakpoint hit: "thread=main", Interest.main(), line=22 bci=55
22              System.out.printf( "%4d%,20.2f\n", year, amount );

main[1]
```

Fig. F.28 | Reaching the breakpoint at line 22 in the `Interest` application.

5. ***Examining variable values.*** Type `print year` to examine the current value of variable `year` (i.e., the `for`'s control variable). Print the value of variable `amount` too (Fig. F.29).

```
Administrator: Command Prompt - jdb

main[1] print year
 year = 1
main[1] print amount
 amount = 1050.0
main[1]
```

Fig. F.29 | Printing `year` and `amount` during the first iteration of `Interest`'s `for`.

6. ***Continuing execution.*** Type `cont` to continue execution. Line 22 executes and prints the current values of `year` and `amount`. After the `for` enters its second iteration, the debugger notifies you that the breakpoint at line 22 has been reached a second time. Note that the debugger pauses each time a line where a breakpoint has been set is about to execute—when the breakpoint appears in a loop, the debugger pauses during each iteration. Print the values of variables `year` and `amount` again to see how the values have changed since the first iteration of the `for` (Fig. F.30).

```
Administrator: Command Prompt - jdb
>    1           1,050.00

Breakpoint hit: "thread=main", Interest.main(), line=22 bci=55
22              System.out.printf( "%4d%,20.2f\n", year, amount );

main[1] print year
 year = 2
main[1] print amount
 amount = 1102.5
main[1]
```

Fig. F.30 | Printing `year` and `amount` during the second iteration of `Interest`'s `for`.

7. ***Removing a breakpoint.*** You can display a list of all of the breakpoints in the application by typing `clear` (Fig. F.31). Suppose you are satisfied that the `Interest` application's `for` statement is working properly, so you want to remove the breakpoint at line 22 and allow the remaining iterations of the loop to proceed normally. You can remove the breakpoint at line 22 by typing `clear Interest:22`. Now type `clear` to list the remaining breakpoints in the application. The debugger should indicate that only the breakpoint at line 13 remains (Fig. F.31). Note that this breakpoint has already been reached and thus will no longer affect execution.

```
Administrator: Command Prompt - jdb
 amount = 1102.5
main[1] clear
Breakpoints set:
        breakpoint Interest:13
        breakpoint Interest:22
main[1] clear Interest:22
Removed: breakpoint Interest:22
main[1] clear
Breakpoints set:
        breakpoint Interest:13
main[1]
```

Fig. F.31 | Removing the breakpoint at line 22.

8. ***Continuing execution after removing a breakpoint.*** Type `cont` to continue execution. Recall that execution last paused before the `printf` statement in line 22. If the breakpoint at line 22 was removed successfully, continuing the application will produce the correct output for the current and remaining iterations of the `for` statement without the application halting (Fig. F.32).

```
Administrator: Command Prompt
        breakpoint Interest:13
main[1] cont
>   2          1,102.50
   3          1,157.63
   4          1,215.51
   5          1,276.28
   6          1,340.10
   7          1,407.10
   8          1,477.46
   9          1,551.33
  10          1,628.89

The application exited

C:\examples\debugger>
```

Fig. F.32 | Application executes without a breakpoint set at line 22.

In this section, you learned how to use the `clear` command to list all the breakpoints set for an application and remove a breakpoint.

F.7 Wrap-Up

In this appendix, you learned how to insert and remove breakpoints in the debugger. Breakpoints allow you to pause application execution so you can examine variable values with the debugger's `print` command. This capability will help you locate and fix logic errors in your applications. You saw how to use the `print` command to examine the value of an expression and how to use the `set` command to change the value of a variable. You also learned debugger commands (including the `step`, `step up` and `next` commands) that can be used to determine whether a method is executing correctly. You learned how to use the watch command to keep track of a field throughout the life of an application. Finally, you learned how to use the clear command to list all the breakpoints set for an application or remove individual breakpoints to continue execution without breakpoints.

Self-Review Exercises

F.1 Fill in the blanks in each of the following statements:
a) A breakpoint cannot be set at a(n) _____.
b) You can examine the value of an expression by using the debugger's _____ command.
c) You can modify the value of a variable by using the debugger's _____ command.
d) During debugging, the _____ command executes the remaining statements in the current method and returns program control to the place where the method was called.
e) The debugger's _____ command behaves like the step command when the next statement to execute does not contain a method call.
f) The watch debugger command allows you to view all changes to a(n) _____.

F.2 State whether each of the following is *true* or *false*. If *false*, explain why.
a) When application execution suspends at a breakpoint, the next statement to be executed is the statement after the breakpoint.
b) Watches can be removed using the debugger's clear command.
c) The -g compiler option must be used when compiling classes for debugging.
d) When a breakpoint appears in a loop, the debugger pauses only the first time that the breakpoint is encountered.

Answers to Self-Review Exercises

F.1 a) comment. b) print. c) set. d) step up. e) next. f) field.

F.2 a) False. When application execution suspends at a breakpoint, the next statement to be executed is the statement at the breakpoint. b) False. Watches can be removed using the debugger's unwatch command. c) True. d) False. When a breakpoint appears in a loop, the debugger pauses during each iteration.

Formatted Output

G

All the news that's fit to print.
—Adolph S. Ochs

What mad pursuit? What struggle to escape?
—John Keats

Remove not the landmark on the boundary of the fields.
—Amenehope

Objectives

In this appendix you'll learn:

- To understand input and output streams.
- To use **printf** formatting.
- To print with field widths and precisions.
- To use formatting flags in the **printf** format string.
- To print with an argument index.
- To output literals and escape sequences.
- To format output with class **Formatter**.

G.1 Introduction

In this appendix, we discuss the formatting features of method `printf` and class `Formatter` (package `java.util`). Class **Formatter** formats and outputs data to a specified destination, such as a string or a file output stream. Many features of `printf` were discussed earlier in the text. This appendix summarizes those features and introduces others, such as displaying date and time data in various formats, reordering output based on the index of the argument and displaying numbers and strings with various flags.

G.2 Streams

Input and output are usually performed with streams, which are sequences of bytes. In input operations, the bytes flow from a device (e.g., a keyboard, a disk drive, a network connection) to main memory. In output operations, bytes flow from main memory to a device (e.g., a display screen, a printer, a disk drive, a network connection).

When program execution begins, three streams are created. The standard input stream typically reads bytes from the keyboard, and the standard output stream typically outputs characters to a command window. A third stream, the **standard error stream** (`System.err`), typically outputs characters to a command window and is used to output error messages so they can be viewed immediately. Operating systems typically allow these streams to be redirected to other devices. Streams are discussed in detail in Chapter 17, Files, Streams and Object Serialization, and Chapter 27, Networking.

G.3 Formatting Output with `printf`

Precise output formatting is accomplished with `printf`. Java SE 5 borrowed (and enhanced) this feature from the C programming language. Method `printf` can perform the following formatting capabilities, each of which is discussed in this appendix:

1. Rounding floating-point values to an indicated number of decimal places.

2. Aligning a column of numbers with decimal points appearing one above the other.

3. Right justification and left justification of outputs.

4. Inserting literal characters at precise locations in a line of output.

5. Representing floating-point numbers in exponential format.

6. Representing integers in octal and hexadecimal format.

7. Displaying all types of data with fixed-size field widths and precisions.

8. Displaying dates and times in various formats.

Every call to printf supplies as the first argument a **format string** that describes the output format. The format string may consist of **fixed text** and **format specifiers**. Fixed text is output by printf just as it would be output by System.out methods print or println. Each format specifier is a placeholder for a value and specifies the type of data to output. Format specifiers also may include optional formatting information.

In the simplest form, each format specifier begins with a percent sign (%) and is followed by a **conversion character** that represents the data type of the value to output. For example, the format specifier %s is a placeholder for a string, and the format specifier %d is a placeholder for an int value. The optional formatting information, such as an argument index, flags, field width and precision, is specified between the percent sign and the conversion character. We demonstrate each of these capabilities.

G.4 Printing Integers

Figure G.1 describes the **integer conversion characters**. (See Appendix H for an overview of the binary, octal, decimal and hexadecimal number systems.) Figure G.2 uses each to print an integer. In lines 9–10, note that the plus sign is not displayed by default, but the minus sign is. Later in this appendix (Fig. G.14) we'll see how to force plus signs to print.

Conversion character	Description
d	Display a decimal (base 10) integer.
o	Display an octal (base 8) integer.
x or X	Display a hexadecimal (base 16) integer. X uses uppercase letters.

Fig. G.1 | Integer conversion characters.

```
1   // Fig. G.2: IntegerConversionTest.java
2   // Using the integer conversion characters.
3
4   public class IntegerConversionTest
5   {
6      public static void main( String[] args )
7      {
8         System.out.printf( "%d\n", 26 );
9         System.out.printf( "%d\n", +26 );
10        System.out.printf( "%d\n", -26 );
11        System.out.printf( "%o\n", 26 );
12        System.out.printf( "%x\n", 26 );
13        System.out.printf( "%X\n", 26 );
14     } // end main
15  } // end class IntegerConversionTest
```

Fig. G.2 | Using the integer conversion characters. (Part 1 of 2.)

```
26
26
-26
32
1a
1A
```

Fig. G.2 | Using the integer conversion characters. (Part 2 of 2.)

The printf method has the form

```
printf( format-string, argument-list );
```

where *format-string* describes the output format, and the optional *argument-list* contains the values that correspond to each format specifier in *format-string*. There can be many format specifiers in one format string.

Each format string in lines 8–10 specifies that printf should output a decimal integer (%d) followed by a newline character. At the format specifier's position, printf substitutes the value of the first argument after the format string. If the format string contains multiple format specifiers, at each subsequent format specifier's position printf substitutes the value of the next argument in the argument list. The %o format specifier in line 11 outputs the integer in octal format. The %x format specifier in line 12 outputs the integer in hexadecimal format. The %X format specifier in line 13 outputs the integer in hexadecimal format with capital letters.

G.5 Printing Floating-Point Numbers

Figure G.3 describes the floating-point conversions. The **conversion characters e** and **E** display floating-point values in **computerized scientific notation** (also called **exponential notation**). Exponential notation is the computer equivalent of the scientific notation used in mathematics. For example, the value 150.4582 is represented in scientific notation in mathematics as

$$1.504582 \times 10^2$$

and is represented in exponential notation as

```
1.504582e+02
```

in Java. This notation indicates that 1.504582 is multiplied by 10 raised to the second power (e+02). The e stands for "exponent."

Values printed with the conversion characters e, E and f are output with six digits of precision to the right of the decimal point by default (e.g., 1.045921)—other precisions

Conversion character	Description
e or E	Display a floating-point value in exponential notation. Conversion character E displays the output in uppercase letters.
f	Display a floating-point value in decimal format.

Fig. G.3 | Floating-point conversion characters. (Part 1 of 2.)

Conversion character	Description
g or G	Display a floating-point value in either the floating-point format f or the exponential format e based on the magnitude of the value. If the magnitude is less than 10^{-3}, or greater than or equal to 10^7, the floating-point value is printed with e (or E). Otherwise, the value is printed in format f. When conversion character G is used, the output is displayed in uppercase letters.
a or A	Display a floating-point number in hexadecimal format. Conversion character A displays the output in uppercase letters.

Fig. G.3 | Floating-point conversion characters. (Part 2 of 2.)

must be specified explicitly. For values printed with the conversion character g, the precision represents the total number of digits displayed, excluding the exponent. The default is six digits (e.g., 12345678.9 is displayed as 1.23457e+07). **Conversion character f** always prints at least one digit to the left of the decimal point. Conversion characters e and E print lowercase e and uppercase E preceding the exponent and always print exactly one digit to the left of the decimal point. Rounding occurs if the value being formatted has more significant digits than the precision.

Conversion character **g** (or **G**) prints in either e (E) or f format, depending on the floating-point value. For example, the values 0.0000875, 87500000.0, 8.75, 87.50 and 875.0 are printed as 8.750000e-05, 8.750000e+07, 8.750000, 87.500000 and 875.000000 with the conversion character g. The value 0.0000875 uses e notation because the magnitude is less than 10-3. The value 87500000.0 uses e notation because the magnitude is greater than 10^7. Figure G.4 demonstrates the floating-point conversion characters.

```
 1   // Fig. G.4: FloatingNumberTest.java
 2   // Using floating-point conversion characters.
 3
 4   public class FloatingNumberTest
 5   {
 6      public static void main( String[] args )
 7      {
 8         System.out.printf( "%e\n", 12345678.9 );
 9         System.out.printf( "%e\n", +12345678.9 );
10         System.out.printf( "%e\n", -12345678.9 );
11         System.out.printf( "%E\n", 12345678.9 );
12         System.out.printf( "%f\n", 12345678.9 );
13         System.out.printf( "%g\n", 12345678.9 );
14         System.out.printf( "%G\n", 12345678.9 );
15      } // end main
16   } // end class FloatingNumberTest
```

```
1.234568e+07
1.234568e+07
-1.234568e+07                                        (continued...)
```

Fig. G.4 | Using floating-point conversion characters. (Part 1 of 2.)

```
1.234568E+07
12345678.900000
1.23457e+07
1.23457E+07
```

Fig. G.4 | Using floating-point conversion characters. (Part 2 of 2.)

G.6 Printing Strings and Characters

The c and s conversion characters print individual characters and strings, respectively. **Conversion characters c and C require a char argument. Conversion characters s and S** can take a String or any Object as an argument. When conversion characters C and S are used, the output is displayed in uppercase letters. Figure G.5 displays characters, strings and objects with conversion characters c and s. Note that autoboxing occurs at line 9 when an int constant is assigned to an Integer object. Line 15 outputs an Integer argument with the conversion character s, which implicitly invokes the toString method to get the integer value. Note that you can also output an Integer object using the %d format specifier. In this case, the int value in the Integer object will be unboxed and output.

Common Programming Error G.1

Using %c to print a String causes an IllegalFormatConversionException—a String cannot be converted to a character.

```java
1   // Fig. G.5: CharStringConversion.java
2   // Using character and string conversion characters.
3   public class CharStringConversion
4   {
5      public static void main( String[] args )
6      {
7         char character = 'A';  // initialize char
8         String string = "This is also a string";  // String object
9         Integer integer = 1234;  // initialize integer (autoboxing)
10
11        System.out.printf( "%c\n", character );
12        System.out.printf( "%s\n", "This is a string" );
13        System.out.printf( "%s\n", string );
14        System.out.printf( "%S\n", string );
15        System.out.printf( "%s\n", integer ); // implicit call to toString
16     } // end main
17  } // end class CharStringConversion
```

```
A
This is a string
This is also a string
THIS IS ALSO A STRING
1234
```

Fig. G.5 | Using character and string conversion characters.

G.7 Printing Dates and Times

The **conversion character t** (or T) is used to print dates and times in various formats. It is always followed by a **conversion suffix character** that specifies the date and/or time format. When conversion character T is used, the output is displayed in uppercase letters. Figure G.6 lists the common conversion suffix characters for formatting **date and time compositions** that display both the date and the time. Figure G.7 lists the common conversion suffix characters for formatting dates. Figure G.8 lists the common conversion suffix characters for formatting times. For the complete list of conversion suffix characters, visit java.sun.com/javase/6/docs/api/java/util/Formatter.html.

Conversion suffix character	Description
c	Display date and time formatted as day month date hour:minute:second time-zone year with three characters for day and month, two digits for date, hour, minute and second and four digits for year—for example, Wed Mar 03 16:30:25 GMT-05:00 2004. The 24-hour clock is used. GMT-05:00 is the time zone.
F	Display date formatted as year-month-date with four digits for the year and two digits each for the month and date (e.g., 2004-05-04).
D	Display date formatted as month/day/year with two digits each for the month, day and year (e.g., 03/03/04).
r	Display time in 12-hour format as hour:minute:second AM|PM with two digits each for the hour, minute and second (e.g., 04:30:25 PM).
R	Display time formatted as hour:minute with two digits each for the hour and minute (e.g., 16:30). The 24-hour clock is used.
T	Display time as hour:minute:second with two digits for the hour, minute and second (e.g., 16:30:25). The 24-hour clock is used.

Fig. G.6 | Date and time composition conversion suffix characters.

Conversion suffix character	Description
A	Display full name of the day of the week (e.g., Wednesday).
a	Display the three-character name of the day of the week (e.g., Wed).
B	Display full name of the month (e.g., March).
b	Display the three-character short name of the month (e.g., Mar).
d	Display the day of the month with two digits, padding with leading zeros as necessary (e.g., 03).
m	Display the month with two digits, padding with leading zeros as necessary (e.g., 07).
e	Display the day of month without leading zeros (e.g., 3).

Fig. G.7 | Date formatting conversion suffix characters. (Part 1 of 2.)

Conversion suffix character	Description
Y	Display the year with four digits (e.g., 2004).
y	Display the last two digits of the year with leading zeros (e.g., 04).
j	Display the day of the year with three digits, padding with leading zeros as necessary (e.g., 016).

Fig. G.7 | Date formatting conversion suffix characters. (Part 2 of 2.)

Conversion suffix character	Description
H	Display hour in 24-hour clock with a leading zero as necessary (e.g., 16).
I	Display hour in 12-hour clock with a leading zero as necessary (e.g., 04).
k	Display hour in 24-hour clock without leading zeros (e.g., 16).
l	Display hour in 12-hour clock without leading zeros (e.g., 4).
M	Display minute with a leading zero as necessary (e.g., 06).
S	Display second with a leading zero as necessary (e.g., 05).
Z	Display the abbreviation for the time zone (e.g., EST, stands for Eastern Standard Time, which is 5 hours behind Greenwich Mean Time).
p	Display morning or afternoon marker in lowercase (e.g., pm).
P	Display morning or afternoon marker in uppercase (e.g., PM).

Fig. G.8 | Time formatting conversion suffix characters.

Figure G.9 uses the conversion characters t and T with the conversion suffix characters to display dates and times in various formats. Conversion character t requires the corresponding argument to be a date or time of type long, Long, **Calendar** (package java.util) or **Date** (package java.util)—objects of each of these classes can represent dates and times. Class Calendar is preferred for this purpose because some constructors and methods in class Date are replaced by those in class Calendar. Line 10 invokes static method **getInstance** of Calendar to obtain a calendar with the current date and time. Lines 13–17, 20–22 and 25–26 use this Calendar object in printf statements as the value to be formatted with conversion character t. Note that lines 20–22 and 25–26 use the optional **argument index** ("1$") to indicate that all format specifiers in the format string use the first argument after the format string in the argument list. You'll learn more about argument indices in Section G.11. Using the argument index eliminates the need to repeatedly list the same argument.

```
1   // Fig. G.9: DateTimeTest.java
2   // Formatting dates and times with conversion characters t and T.
3   import java.util.Calendar;
4
```

Fig. G.9 | Formatting dates and times with conversion characters t and T. (Part 1 of 2.)

```
5   public class DateTimeTest
6   {
7       public static void main( String[] args )
8       {
9           // get current date and time
10          Calendar dateTime = Calendar.getInstance();
11
12          // printing with conversion characters for date/time compositions
13          System.out.printf( "%tc\n", dateTime );
14          System.out.printf( "%tF\n", dateTime );
15          System.out.printf( "%tD\n", dateTime );
16          System.out.printf( "%tr\n", dateTime );
17          System.out.printf( "%tT\n", dateTime );
18
19          // printing with conversion characters for date
20          System.out.printf( "%1$tA, %1$tB %1$td, %1$tY\n", dateTime );
21          System.out.printf( "%1$TA, %1$TB %1$Td, %1$TY\n", dateTime );
22          System.out.printf( "%1$ta, %1$tb %1$te, %1$ty\n", dateTime );
23
24          // printing with conversion characters for time
25          System.out.printf( "%1$tH:%1$tM:%1$tS\n", dateTime );
26          System.out.printf( "%1$tZ %1$tI:%1$tM:%1$tS %tP", dateTime );
27      } // end main
28  } // end class DateTimeTest
```

```
Wed Feb 25 15:00:22 EST 2009
2009-02-25
02/25/09
03:00:22 PM
15:00:22
Wednesday, February 25, 2009
WEDNESDAY, FEBRUARY 25, 2009
Wed, Feb 25, 09
15:00:22
EST 03:00:22 PM
```

Fig. G.9 | Formatting dates and times with conversion characters t and T. (Part 2 of 2.)

G.8 Other Conversion Characters

The remaining conversion characters are b, B, h, H, % and n. These are described in Fig. G.10. Lines 9–10 of Fig. G.11 use %b to print the value of boolean (or Boolean) values false and true. Line 11 associates a String to %b, which returns true because it's not null. Line 12 associates a null object to %B, which displays FALSE because test is null. Lines 13–14 use %h to print the string representations of the hash-code values for strings "hello" and "Hello". These values could be used to store or locate the strings in a Hashtable or HashMap (both discussed in Chapter 20, Generic Collections). Note that the hash-code values for these two strings differ, because one string starts with a lowercase letter and the other with an uppercase letter. Line 15 uses %H to print null in uppercase letters. The last two printf statements (lines 16–17) use %% to print the % character in a string and %n to print a platform-specific line separator.

Conversion character	Description
b or B	Print "true" or "false" for the value of a boolean or Boolean. These conversion characters can also format the value of any reference. If the reference is non-null, "true" is output; otherwise, "false". When conversion character B is used, the output is displayed in uppercase letters.
h or H	Print the string representation of an object's hash-code value in hexadecimal format. If the corresponding argument is null, "null" is printed. When conversion character H is used, the output is displayed in uppercase letters.
%	Print the percent character.
n	Print the platform-specific line separator (e.g., \r\n on Windows or \n on UNIX/LINUX).

Fig. G.10 | Other conversion characters.

```
1   // Fig. G.11: OtherConversion.java
2   // Using the b, B, h, H, % and n conversion characters.
3
4   public class OtherConversion
5   {
6      public static void main( String[] args )
7      {
8         Object test = null;
9         System.out.printf( "%b\n", false );
10        System.out.printf( "%b\n", true );
11        System.out.printf( "%b\n", "Test" );
12        System.out.printf( "%B\n", test );
13        System.out.printf( "Hashcode of \"hello\" is %h\n", "hello" );
14        System.out.printf( "Hashcode of \"Hello\" is %h\n", "Hello" );
15        System.out.printf( "Hashcode of null is %H\n", test );
16        System.out.printf( "Printing a %% in a format string\n" );
17        System.out.printf( "Printing a new line %nnext line starts here" );
18     } // end main
19  } // end class OtherConversion
```

```
false
true
true
FALSE
Hashcode of "hello" is 5e918d2
Hashcode of "Hello" is 42628b2
Hashcode of null is NULL
Printing a % in a format string
Printing a new line
next line starts here
```

Fig. G.11 | Using the b, B, h, H, % and n conversion characters.

Common Programming Error G.2

Trying to print a literal percent character using % rather than %% in the format string might cause a difficult-to-detect logic error. When % appears in a format string, it must be followed by a conversion character in the string. The single percent could accidentally be followed by a legitimate conversion character, thus causing a logic error.

G.9 Printing with Field Widths and Precisions

The size of a field in which data is printed is specified by a **field width**. If the field width is larger than the data being printed, the data is right justified in that field by default. We discuss left justification in Section G.10. You insert an integer representing the field width between the % and the conversion character (e.g., %4d) in the format specifier. Figure G.12 prints two groups of five numbers each, right justifying those numbers that contain fewer digits than the field width. Note that the field width is increased to print values wider than the field and that the minus sign for a negative value uses one character position in the field. Also, if no field width is specified, the data prints in exactly as many positions as it needs. Field widths can be used with all format specifiers except the line separator (%n).

```
1   // Fig. G.12: FieldWidthTest.java
2   // Right justifying integers in fields.
3
4   public class FieldWidthTest
5   {
6      public static void main( String[] args )
7      {
8         System.out.printf( "%4d\n", 1 );
9         System.out.printf( "%4d\n", 12 );
10        System.out.printf( "%4d\n", 123 );
11        System.out.printf( "%4d\n", 1234 );
12        System.out.printf( "%4d\n\n", 12345 ); // data too large
13
14        System.out.printf( "%4d\n", -1 );
15        System.out.printf( "%4d\n", -12 );
16        System.out.printf( "%4d\n", -123 );
17        System.out.printf( "%4d\n", -1234 ); // data too large
18        System.out.printf( "%4d\n", -12345 ); // data too large
19     } // end main
20  } // end class RightJustifyTest
```

```
   1
  12
 123
1234
12345

  -1
 -12
-123
-1234
-12345
```

Fig. G.12 | Right justifying integers in fields.

Common Programming Error G.3

Not providing a sufficiently large field width to handle a value to be printed can offset other data being printed and produce confusing outputs. Know your data!

Method `printf` also provides the ability to specify the precision with which data is printed. Precision has different meanings for different types. When used with floating-point conversion characters e and f, the precision is the number of digits that appear after the decimal point. When used with conversion characters g, a or A, the precision is the maximum number of significant digits to be printed. When used with conversion character s, the precision is the maximum number of characters to be written from the string. To use precision, place between the percent sign and the conversion specifier a decimal point (.) followed by an integer representing the precision. Figure G.13 demonstrates the use of precision in format strings. Note that when a floating-point value is printed with a precision smaller than the original number of decimal places in the value, the value is rounded. Also note that the format specifier `%.3g` indicates that the total number of digits used to display the floating-point value is 3. Because the value has three digits to the left of the decimal point, the value is rounded to the ones position.

The field width and the precision can be combined by placing the field width, followed by a decimal point, followed by a precision between the percent sign and the conversion character, as in the statement

```
printf( "%9.3f", 123.456789 );
```

which displays `123.457` with three digits to the right of the decimal point right justified in a nine-digit field—this number will be preceded in its field by two blanks.

```
1   // Fig. G.13: PrecisionTest.java
2   // Using precision for floating-point numbers and strings.
3   public class PrecisionTest
4   {
5      public static void main( String[] args )
6      {
7         double f = 123.94536;
8         String s = "Happy Birthday";
9
10        System.out.printf( "Using precision for floating-point numbers\n" );
11        System.out.printf( "\t%.3f\n\t%.3e\n\t%.3g\n\n", f, f, f );
12
13        System.out.printf( "Using precision for strings\n" );
14        System.out.printf( "\t%.11s\n", s );
15     } // end main
16  } // end class PrecisionTest
```

```
Using precision for floating-point numbers
        123.945
        1.239e+02
        124

Using precision for strings
        Happy Birth
```

Fig. G.13 | Using precision for floating-point numbers and strings.

G.10 Using Flags in the `printf` Format String

Various flags may be used with method `printf` to supplement its output formatting capabilities. Seven flags are available for use in format strings (Fig. G.14).

Flag	Description
- (minus sign)	Left justify the output within the specified field.
+ (plus sign)	Display a plus sign preceding positive values and a minus sign preceding negative values.
space	Print a space before a positive value not printed with the + flag.
#	Prefix 0 to the output value when used with the octal conversion character o. Prefix 0x to the output value when used with the hexadecimal conversion character x.
0 (zero)	Pad a field with leading zeros.
, (comma)	Use the locale-specific thousands separator (i.e., ',' for U.S. locale) to display decimal and floating-point numbers.
(	Enclose negative numbers in parentheses.

Fig. G.14 | Format string flags.

To use a flag in a format string, place it immediately to the right of the percent sign. Several flags may be used in the same format specifier. Figure G.15 demonstrates right justification and left justification of a string, an integer, a character and a floating-point number. Note that line 9 serves as a counting mechanism for the screen output.

```java
1  // Fig. G.15: MinusFlagTest.java
2  // Right justifying and left justifying values.
3
4  public class MinusFlagTest
5  {
6     public static void main( String[] args )
7     {
8        System.out.println( "Columns:" );
9        System.out.println( "0123456789012345678901234567890123456789\n" );
10       System.out.printf( "%10s%10d%10c%10f\n\n", "hello", 7, 'a', 1.23 );
11       System.out.printf(
12          "%-10s%-10d%-10c%-10f\n", "hello", 7, 'a', 1.23 );
13    } // end main
14 } // end class MinusFlagTest
```

```
Columns:
0123456789012345678901234567890123456789

     hello         7         a  1.230000
hello     7         a         1.230000
```

Fig. G.15 | Right justifying and left justifying values.

Figure G.16 prints a positive number and a negative number, each with and without the + flag. Note that the minus sign is displayed in both cases, the plus sign only when the + flag is used.

```
 1   // Fig. G.16: PlusFlagTest.java
 2   // Printing numbers with and without the + flag.
 3
 4   public class PlusFlagTest
 5   {
 6      public static void main( String[] args )
 7      {
 8         System.out.printf( "%d\t%d\n", 786, -786 );
 9         System.out.printf( "%+d\t%+d\n", 786, -786 );
10      } // end main
11   } // end class PlusFlagTest
```

```
786        -786
+786       -786
```

Fig. G.16 | Printing numbers with and without the + flag.

Figure G.17 prefixes a space to the positive number with the space flag. This is useful for aligning positive and negative numbers with the same number of digits. Note that the value -547 is not preceded by a space in the output because of its minus sign. Figure G.18 uses the # flag to prefix 0 to the octal value and 0x to the hexadecimal value.

```
 1   // Fig. G.17: SpaceFlagTest.java
 2   // Printing a space before non-negative values.
 3
 4   public class SpaceFlagTest
 5   {
 6      public static void main( String[] args )
 7      {
 8         System.out.printf( "% d\n% d\n", 547, -547 );
 9      } // end main
10   } // end class SpaceFlagTest
```

```
 547
-547
```

Fig. G.17 | Printing a space before nonnegative values.

```
 1   // Fig. G.18: PoundFlagTest.java
 2   // Using the # flag with conversion characters o and x.
 3
 4   public class PoundFlagTest
 5   {
 6      public static void main( String[] args )
 7      {
```

Fig. G.18 | Using the # flag with conversion characters o and x. (Part 1 of 2.)

```
 8          int c = 31;       // initialize c
 9
10          System.out.printf( "%#o\n", c );
11          System.out.printf( "%#x\n", c );
12       } // end main
13    } // end class PoundFlagTest
```

```
037
0x1f
```

Fig. G.18 | Using the # flag with conversion characters o and x. (Part 2 of 2.)

Figure G.19 combines the + flag the **0 flag** and the space flag to print 452 in a field of width 9 with a + sign and leading zeros, next prints 452 in a field of width 9 using only the 0 flag, then prints 452 in a field of width 9 using only the space flag.

```
 1    // Fig. G.19: ZeroFlagTest.java
 2    // Printing with the 0 (zero) flag fills in leading zeros.
 3
 4    public class ZeroFlagTest
 5    {
 6       public static void main( String[] args )
 7       {
 8          System.out.printf( "%+09d\n", 452 );
 9          System.out.printf( "%09d\n", 452 );
10          System.out.printf( "% 9d\n", 452 );
11       } // end main
12    } // end class ZeroFlagTest
```

```
+00000452
000000452
      452
```

Fig. G.19 | Printing with the 0 (zero) flag fills in leading zeros.

Figure G.20 uses the comma (,) flag to display a decimal and a floating-point number with the thousands separator. Figure G.21 encloses negative numbers in parentheses using the (flag. Note that the value 50 is not enclosed in parentheses in the output because it's a positive number.

```
 1    // Fig. G.20: CommaFlagTest.java
 2    // Using the comma (,) flag to display numbers with thousands separator.
 3
 4    public class CommaFlagTest
 5    {
 6       public static void main( String[] args )
 7       {
```

Fig. G.20 | Using the comma (,) flag to display numbers with the thousands separator. (Part 1 of 2.)

```
8          System.out.printf( "%,d\n", 58625 );
9          System.out.printf( "%,.2f", 58625.21 );
10         System.out.printf( "%,.2f", 12345678.9 );
11      } // end main
12   } // end class CommaFlagTest
```

```
58,625
58,625.21
12,345,678.90
```

Fig. G.20 | Using the comma (,) flag to display numbers with the thousands separator. (Part 2 of 2.)

```
1    // Fig. G.21: ParenthesesFlagTest.java
2    // Using the ( flag to place parentheses around negative numbers.
3
4    public class ParenthesesFlagTest
5    {
6       public static void main( String[] args )
7       {
8          System.out.printf( "%(d\n", 50 );
9          System.out.printf( "%(d\n", -50 );
10         System.out.printf( "%(.1e\n", -50.0 );
11      } // end main
12   } // end class ParenthesesFlagTest
```

```
50
(50)
(5.0e+01)
```

Fig. G.21 | Using the (flag to place parentheses around negative numbers.

G.11 Printing with Argument Indices

An **argument index** is an optional integer followed by a $ sign that indicates the argument's position in the argument list. For example, lines 20–22 and 25–26 in Fig. G.9 use argument index "1$" to indicate that all format specifiers use the first argument in the argument list. Argument indices enable programmers to reorder the output so that the arguments in the argument list are not necessarily in the order of their corresponding format specifiers. Argument indices also help avoid duplicating arguments. Figure G.22 prints arguments in the argument list in reverse order using the argument index.

```
1    // Fig. G.22: ArgumentIndexTest
2    // Reordering output with argument indices.
3
4    public class ArgumentIndexTest
5    {
```

Fig. G.22 | Reordering output with argument indices. (Part 1 of 2.)

```
6    public static void main( String[] args )
7    {
8       System.out.printf(
9          "Parameter list without reordering: %s %s %s %s\n",
10         "first", "second", "third", "fourth" );
11      System.out.printf(
12         "Parameter list after reordering: %4$s %3$s %2$s %1$s\n",
13         "first", "second", "third", "fourth" );
14   } // end main
15 } // end class ArgumentIndexTest
```

```
Parameter list without reordering: first second third fourth
Parameter list after reordering: fourth third second first
```

Fig. G.22 | Reordering output with argument indices. (Part 2 of 2.)

G.12 Printing Literals and Escape Sequences

Most literal characters to be printed in a `printf` statement can simply be included in the format string. However, there are several "problem" characters, such as the quotation mark (") that delimits the format string itself. Various control characters, such as newline and tab, must be represented by escape sequences. An escape sequence is represented by a backslash (\), followed by an escape character. Figure G.23 lists the escape sequences and the actions they cause.

Common Programming Error G.4

Attempting to print as literal data in a `printf` statement a double quote or backslash character without preceding that character with a backslash to form a proper escape sequence might result in a syntax error.

Escape sequence	Description
\' (single quote)	Output the single quote (') character.
\" (double quote)	Output the double quote (") character.
\\ (backslash)	Output the backslash (\) character.
\b (backspace)	Move the cursor back one position on the current line.
\f (new page or form feed)	Move the cursor to the start of the next logical page.
\n (newline)	Move the cursor to the beginning of the next line.
\r (carriage return)	Move the cursor to the beginning of the current line.
\t (horizontal tab)	Move the cursor to the next horizontal tab position.

Fig. G.23 | Escape sequences.

G.13 Formatting Output with Class `Formatter`

So far, we've discussed displaying formatted output to the standard output stream. What should we do if we want to send formatted outputs to other output streams or devices, such as a JTextArea or a file? The solution relies on class Formatter (in package java.util), which provides the same formatting capabilities as printf. Formatter is a utility class that enables programmers to output formatted data to a specified destination, such as a file on disk. By default, a Formatter creates a string in memory. Figure G.24 demonstrates how to use a Formatter to build a formatted string, which is then displayed in a message dialog.

```
1   // Fig. Fig. G.24: FormatterTest.java
2   // Formatting output with class Formatter.
3   import java.util.Formatter;
4   import javax.swing.JOptionPane;
5
6   public class FormatterTest
7   {
8      public static void main( String[] args )
9      {
10        // create Formatter and format output
11        Formatter formatter = new Formatter();
12        formatter.format( "%d = %o = %#X", 10, 10, 10 );
13
14        // display output in JOptionPane
15        JOptionPane.showMessageDialog( null, formatter.toString() );
16     } // end main
17  } // end class FormatterTest
```

Fig. G.24 | Formatting output with class Formatter.

Line 11 creates a Formatter object using the default constructor, so this object will build a string in memory. Other constructors are provided to allow you to specify the destination to which the formatted data should be output. For details, see java.sun.com/javase/6/docs/api/java/util/Formatter.html.

Line 12 invokes method **format** to format the output. Like printf, method format takes a format string and an argument list. The difference is that printf sends the formatted output directly to the standard output stream, while format sends the formatted output to the destination specified by its constructor (a string in memory in this program). Line 15 invokes the Formatter's toString method to get the formatted data as a string, which is then displayed in a message dialog.

Note that class String also provides a static convenience method named format that enables you to create a string in memory without the need to first create a Formatter object. Lines 11–12 and line 15 in Fig. G.24 could have been replaced by

```
String s = String.format( "%d = %#o = %#x", 10, 10, 10 );
JOptionPane.showMessageDialog( null, s );
```

G.14 Wrap-Up

This appendix summarized how to display formatted output with various format characters and flags. We displayed decimal numbers using format characters d, o, x and X; floating-point numbers using format characters e, E, f, g and G; and dates and times in various format using format characters t and T and their conversion suffix characters. You learned how to display output with field widths and precisions. We introduced the flags +, -, space, #, 0, comma and (that are used together with the format characters to produce output. We also demonstrated how to format output with class Formatter.

Summary

Section G.2 Streams
- Input and output are usually performed with streams, which are sequences of bytes.
- Normally, the standard input stream is connected to the keyboard, and the standard output stream is connected to the computer screen.

Section G.3 Formatting Output with printf
- The printf format string describes the formats in which the output values appear. The format specifier consists of argument index, flags, field widths, precisions and conversion characters.

Section G.4 Printing Integers
- Integers are printed with the conversion characters d for decimal integers, o for integers in octal form and x (or X) for integers in hexadecimal form. X displays uppercase letters.

Section G.5 Printing Floating-Point Numbers
- Floating-point values are printed with the conversion characters e (or E) for exponential notation, f for regular floating-point notation, and g (or G) for either e (or E) notation or f notation. For the g conversion specifier, the e conversion character is used if the value is less than 10^{-3} or greater than or equal to 10^7; otherwise, the f conversion character is used.

Section G.6 Printing Strings and Characters
- The conversion character c prints a character.
- The conversion character s (or S) prints a string of characters. Conversion character S displays the output in uppercase letters.

Section G.7 Printing Dates and Times
- The conversion character t (or T) followed by a conversion suffix character prints the date and time in various forms. Conversion character T displays the output in uppercase letters.
- Conversion character t (or T) requires the argument to be of type long, Long, Calendar or Date.

Section G.8 Other Conversion Characters
- Conversion character b (or B) outputs the string representation of a boolean or Boolean. These conversion characters also output "true" for non-null references and "false" for null references. Conversion character B outputs uppercase letters.
- Conversion character h (or H) returns null for a null reference and a String representation of the hash-code value (in base 16) of an object . Hash codes are used to store and retrieve objects in Hashtables and HashMaps. Conversion character H outputs uppercase letters.

- The conversion character n prints the platform-specific line separator.

- The conversion character % is used to display a literal %.

Section G.9 Printing with Field Widths and Precisions

- If the field width is larger than the object being printed, the object is right justified in the field.

- Field widths can be used with all conversion characters except the line-separator conversion.

- Precision used with floating-point conversion characters e and f indicates the number of digits that appear after the decimal point. Precision used with floating-point conversion character g indicates the number of significant digits to appear.

- Precision used with conversion character s indicates the number of characters to be printed.

- The field width and the precision can be combined by placing the field width, followed by a decimal point, followed by the precision between the percent sign and the conversion character.

Section G.10 Using Flags in the **printf** *Format String*

- The - flag left justifies its argument in a field.

- The + flag prints a plus sign for positive values and a minus sign for negative values.

- The space flag prints a space preceding a positive value. The space flag and the + flag cannot be used together in an integer conversion character.

- The # flag prefixes 0 to octal values and 0x to hexadecimal values.

- The 0 flag prints leading zeros for a value that does not occupy its entire field.

- The comma (,) flag uses the locale-specific thousands separator to display integer and floating-point numbers.

- The (flag encloses a negative number in parentheses.

Section G.11 Printing with Argument Indices

- An argument index is an optional decimal integer followed by a $ sign that indicates the position of the argument in the argument list.

- Argument indices enable programmers to reorder the output so that the arguments in the argument list are not necessarily in the order of their corresponding format specifiers. Argument indices also help avoid duplicating arguments.

Section G.13 Formatting Output with Class **Formatter**

- Class Formatter (in package java.util) provides the same formatting capabilities as printf. Formatter is a utility class that enables programmers to print formatted output to various destinations, including GUI components, files and other output streams.

- Formatter method format outputs formatted data to the destination specified by the Formatter constructor.

- String static method format formats data and returns the formatted data as a String.

Terminology

Self-Review Exercises

G.1   Fill in the blanks in each of the following:
a) All input and output is dealt with in the form of _____.
b) The _____ stream is normally connected to the keyboard.
c) The _____ stream is normally connected to the computer screen.
d) System.out's _____ method can be used to format text that is displayed on the standard output.
e) The conversion character _____ may be used to output a decimal integer.
f) The conversion characters _____ and _____ are used to display integers in octal and hexadecimal form, respectively.
g) The conversion character _____ is used to display a floating-point value in exponential notation.
h) The conversion characters e and f are displayed with _____ digits of precision to the right of the decimal point if no precision is specified.
i) The conversion characters _____ and _____ are used to print strings and characters, respectively.
j) The conversion character _____ and conversion suffix character _____ are used to print time for the 24-hour clock as hour:minute:second.
k) The _____ flag causes output to be left justified in a field.
l) The _____ flag causes values to be displayed with either a plus sign or a minus sign.
m) The argument index _____ corresponds to the second argument in the argument list.
n) Class _____ has the same capability as printf, but allows programmers to print formatted output to various destinations besides the standard output stream.

G.2 Find the error in each of the following and explain how it can be corrected.

a) The following statement should print the character `'c'`.
```
System.out.printf( "%c\n", "c" );
```

b) The following statement should print 9.375%.
```
System.out.printf( "%.3f%", 9.375 );
```

c) The following statement should print the third argument in the argument list.
```
System.out.printf( "%2$s\n", "Mon", "Tue", "Wed", "Thu", "Fri" );
```

d) `System.out.printf( ""A string in quotes"" );`

e) `System.out.printf( %d %d, 12, 20 );`

f) `System.out.printf( "%s\n", 'Richard' );`

G.3 Write a statement for each of the following:

a) Print 1234 right justified in a 10-digit field.

b) Print 123.456789 in exponential notation with a sign (+ or -) and 3 digits of precision.

c) Print 100 in octal form preceded by 0.

d) Given a `Calendar` object `calendar`, print a date formatted as month/day/year (each with two digits).

e) Given a `Calendar` object `calendar`, print a time for the 24-hour clock as hour:minute:second (each with two digits) using argument index and conversion suffix characters for formatting time.

f) Print 3.333333 with a sign (+ or -) in a field of 20 characters with a precision of 3.

Answers to Self-Review Exercises

G.1 a) Streams. b) Standard input. c) Standard output. d) `printf`. e) d. f) o, x or X. g) e or E. h) 6. i) s or S, c or C. j) t, T. k) - (minus). l) + (plus). m) 2$. n) `Formatter`.

G.2 a) Error: Conversion character c expects an argument of primitive type `char`.
Correction: To print the character `'c'`, change "c" to 'c'.

b) Error: Trying to print the literal character % without using the format specifier %%.
Correction: Use %% to print a literal % character.

c) Error: Argument index does not start with 0; e.g., the first argument is 1$.
Correction: To print the third argument use 3$.

d) Error: Trying to print the literal character " without using the \" escape sequence.
Correction: Replace each quote in the inner set of quotes with \".

e) Error: The format string is not enclosed in double quotes.
Correction: Enclose %d %d in double quotes.

f) Error: The string to be printed is enclosed in single quotes.
Correction: Use double quotes instead of single quotes to represent a string.

G.3 a) `System.out.printf( "%10d\n", 1234 );`
b) `System.out.printf( "%+.3e\n", 123.456789 );`
c) `System.out.printf( "%#o\n", 100 );`
d) `System.out.printf( "%tD\n", calendar );`
e) `System.out.printf( "%1$tH:%1$tM:%1$tS\n", calendar );`
f) `System.out.printf( "%+20.3f\n", 3.333333 );`

Exercises

G.4 Write statement(s) for each of the following:

a) Print integer 40000 right justified in a 15-digit field.

b) Print 200 with and without a sign.

c) Print 100 in hexadecimal form preceded by 0x.

d) Print 1.234 with three digits of precision in a 9-digit field with preceding zeros.

G.5 Show what is printed by each of the following statements. If a statement is incorrect, indicate why.

a) `System.out.printf( "%-10d\n", 10000 );`

b) `System.out.printf( "%c\n", "This is a string" );`

c) `System.out.printf( "%8.3f\n", 1024.987654 );`

d) `System.out.printf( "%#o\n%#X\n", 17, 17 );`

e) `System.out.printf( "% d\n%+d\n", 1000000, 1000000 );`

f) `System.out.printf( "%10.2e\n", 444.93738 );`

g) `System.out.printf( "%d\n", 10.987 );`

G.6 Find the error(s) in each of the following program segments. Show the corrected statement.

a) `System.out.printf( "%s\n", 'Happy Birthday' );`

b) `System.out.printf( "%c\n", 'Hello' );`

c) `System.out.printf( "%c\n", "This is a string" );`

d) The following statement should print "Bon Voyage" with the double quotes:

`System.out.printf( ""%s"", "Bon Voyage" );`

e) The following statement should print "Today is Friday":

`System.out.printf( "Today is %s\n", "Monday", "Friday" );`

f) `System.out.printf( 'Enter your name: ' );`

g) `System.out.printf( %f, 123.456 );`

h) The following statement should print the current time in the format "hh:mm:ss":

`Calendar dateTime = Calendar.getInstance();`

`System.out.printf( "%1$tk:1$%tl:%1$tS\n", dateTime );`

G.7 *(Printing Dates and Times)* Write a program that prints dates and times in the following forms:

```
GMT-05:00 04/30/04 09:55:09 AM
GMT-05:00 April 30 2004 09:55:09
2004-04-30 day-of-the-month:30
2004-04-30 day-of-the-year:121
Fri Apr 30 09:55:09 GMT-05:00 2004
```

[*Note:* Depending on your location, you may get a time zone other than GMT-05:00.]

G.8 Write a program to test the results of printing the integer value 12345 and the floating-point value 1.2345 in fields of various sizes.

G.9 *(Rounding Numbers)* Write a program that prints the value 100.453627 rounded to the nearest digit, tenth, hundredth, thousandth and ten-thousandth.

G.10 Write a program that inputs a word from the keyboard and determines its length. Print the word using twice the length as the field width.

G.11 *(Converting Fahrenheit Temperature to Celsius)* Write a program that converts integer Fahrenheit temperatures from 0 to 212 degrees to floating-point Celsius temperatures with three digits of precision. Use the formula

`celsius = 5.0 / 9.0 * ( fahrenheit - 32 );`

to perform the calculation. The output should be printed in two right-justified columns of 10 characters each, and the Celsius temperatures should be preceded by a sign for both positive and negative values.

G.12 Write a program to test all the escape sequences in Fig. G.23. For those that move the cursor, print a character before and after the escape sequence so that it's clear where the cursor has moved.

G.13 Write a program that uses the conversion character g to output the value 9876.12345. Print the value with precisions ranging from 1 to 9.

Appendices on the Web

The following appendices are available as PDF documents from this book's Companion Website (www.pearsonhighered.com/deitel/):

- Appendix H, Number Systems
- Appendix I, GroupLayout
- Appendix J, Java Desktop Integration Components (JDIC)
- Appendix K, Mashups
- Appendix L, Unicode®
- Appendix M, Creating Documentation with javadoc
- Appendix N, Bit Manipulation
- Appendix O, Labeled break and continue Statements
- Appendix P, UML 2: Additional Diagram Types
- Appendix Q, Design Patterns

These files can be viewed in Adobe® Reader® (get.adobe.com/reader). The index entries for these appendices have uppercase Roman numeral page numbers.

New copies of this book come with a Companion Website access code that is located on the card inside the book's front cover. If the access code is visible or there is no card, you purchased a used book or an edition that does not come with an access code. In this case, you can purchase access directly from the Companion Website.

Index

[*Note:* Page references for defining occurrences of terms appear in **bold blue**. Page references for web-based chapters and appendices are listed in uppercase roman numerals.]

End User License Agreement

Prentice Hall License Agreement and Limited Warranty

READ THE FOLLOWING TERMS AND CONDITIONS CAREFULLY BEFORE OPENING THIS SOFTWARE PACKAGE. THIS LEGAL DOCUMENT IS AN AGREEMENT BETWEEN YOU AND PRENTICE-HALL, INC. (THE "COMPANY"). BY OPENING THIS SEALED SOFT-WARE PACKAGE, YOU ARE AGREEING TO BE BOUND BY THESE TERMS AND CONDI-TIONS. IF YOU DO NOT AGREE WITH THESE TERMS AND CONDITIONS, DO NOT OPEN THE SOFTWARE PACKAGE. PROMPTLY RETURN THE UNOPENED SOFTWARE PACKAGE AND ALL ACCOMPANYING ITEMS TO THE PLACE YOU OBTAINED THEM FOR A FULL REFUND OF ANY SUMS YOU HAVE PAID.

1.GRANT OF LICENSE: In consideration of your purchase of this book, and your agreement to abide by the terms and conditions of this Agreement, the Company grants to you a nonexclusive right to use and display the copy of the enclosed software program (hereinafter the "SOFTWARE") on a single computer (i.e., with a single CPU) at a single location so long as you comply with the terms of this Agreement. The Company reserves all rights not expressly granted to you under this Agreement.

2.OWNERSHIP OF SOFTWARE: You own only the magnetic or physical media (the enclosed media) on which the SOFTWARE is recorded or fixed, but the Company and the software developers retain all the rights, title, and ownership to the SOFTWARE recorded on the original media copy(ies) and all subsequent copies of the SOFTWARE, regardless of the form or media on which the original or other copies may exist. This license is not a sale of the original SOFTWARE or any copy to you.

3.COPY RESTRICTIONS: This SOFTWARE and the accompanying printed materials and user manual (the "Documentation") are the subject of copyright. The individual programs on the media are copyrighted by the authors of each program. Some of the programs on the media include separate licensing agreements. If you intend to use one of these programs, you must read and follow its accompa-nying license agreement. You may not copy the Documentation or the SOFTWARE, except that you may make a single copy of the SOFTWARE for backup or archival purposes only. You may be held legally responsible for any copying or copyright infringement which is caused or encouraged by your failure to abide by the terms of this restriction.

4.USE RESTRICTIONS: You may not network the SOFTWARE or otherwise use it on more than one computer or computer terminal at the same time. You may physically transfer the SOFTWARE from one computer to another provided that the SOFTWARE is used on only one computer at a time. You may not distribute copies of the SOFTWARE or Documentation to others. You may not reverse engi-neer, disassemble, decompile, modify, adapt, translate, or create derivative works based on the SOFT-WARE or the Documentation without the prior written consent of the Company.

5. TRANSFER RESTRICTIONS: The enclosed SOFTWARE is licensed only to you and may not be transferred to any one else without the prior written consent of the Company. Any unauthorized transfer of the SOFTWARE shall result in the immediate termination of this Agreement.

6. TERMINATION: This license is effective until terminated. This license will terminate automat-ically without notice from the Company and become null and void if you fail to comply with any provi-sions or limitations of this license. Upon termination, you shall destroy the Documentation and all copies of the SOFTWARE. All provisions of this Agreement as to warranties, limitation of liability, remedies or damages, and our ownership rights shall survive termination.

7. MISCELLANEOUS: This Agreement shall be construed in accordance with the laws of the United States of America and the State of New York and shall benefit the Company, its affiliates, and assignees.

8.LIMITED WARRANTY AND DISCLAIMER OF WARRANTY: The Company warrants that the SOFTWARE, when properly used in accordance with the Documentation, will operate in substantial conformity with the description of the SOFTWARE set forth in the Documentation. The Company does not warrant that the SOFTWARE will meet your requirements or that the operation of the SOFTWARE will be uninterrupted or error-free. The Company warrants that the media on which the SOFTWARE is delivered shall be free from defects in materials and workmanship under normal use for a period of thirty

(30) days from the date of your purchase. Your only remedy and the Company's only obligation under these limited warranties is, at the Company's option, return of the warranted item for a refund of any amounts paid by you or replacement of the item. Any replacement of SOFTWARE or media under the warranties shall not extend the original warranty period. The limited warranty set forth above shall not apply to any SOFTWARE which the Company determines in good faith has been subject to misuse, neglect, improper installation, repair, alteration, or damage by you. EXCEPT FOR THE EXPRESSED WARRANTIES SET FORTH ABOVE, THE COMPANY DISCLAIMS ALL WARRANTIES, EXPRESS OR IMPLIED, INCLUDING WITHOUT LIMITATION, THE IMPLIED WARRANTIES OF MERCHANTABILITY AND FITNESS FOR A PARTICULAR PURPOSE. EXCEPT FOR THE EXPRESS WARRANTY SET FORTH ABOVE, THE COMPANY DOES NOT WARRANT, GUARANTEE, OR MAKE ANY REPRESENTATION REGARDING THE USE OR THE RESULTS OF THE USE OF THE SOFTWARE IN TERMS OF ITS CORRECTNESS, ACCURACY, RELIABILITY, CURRENTNESS, OR OTHERWISE.

IN NO EVENT, SHALL THE COMPANY OR ITS EMPLOYEES, AGENTS, SUPPLIERS, OR CONTRACTORS BE LIABLE FOR ANY INCIDENTAL, INDIRECT, SPECIAL, OR CONSEQUENTIAL DAMAGES ARISING OUT OF OR IN CONNECTION WITH THE LICENSE GRANTED UNDER THIS AGREEMENT, OR FOR LOSS OF USE, LOSS OF DATA, LOSS OF INCOME OR PROFIT, OR OTHER LOSSES, SUSTAINED AS A RESULT OF INJURY TO ANY PERSON, OR LOSS OF OR DAMAGE TO PROPERTY, OR CLAIMS OF THIRD PARTIES, EVEN IF THE COMPANY OR AN AUTHORIZED REPRESENTATIVE OF THE COMPANY HAS BEEN ADVISED OF THE POSSIBILITY OF SUCH DAMAGES. IN NO EVENT SHALL LIABILITY OF THE COMPANY FOR DAMAGES WITH RESPECT TO THE SOFTWARE EXCEED THE AMOUNTS ACTUALLY PAID BY YOU, IF ANY, FOR THE SOFTWARE.

SOME JURISDICTIONS DO NOT ALLOW THE LIMITATION OF IMPLIED WARRANTIES OR LIABILITY FOR INCIDENTAL, INDIRECT, SPECIAL, OR CONSEQUENTIAL DAMAGES, SO THE ABOVE LIMITATIONS MAY NOT ALWAYS APPLY. THE WARRANTIES IN THIS AGREEMENT GIVE YOU SPECIFIC LEGAL RIGHTS AND YOU MAY ALSO HAVE OTHER RIGHTS WHICH VARY IN ACCORDANCE WITH LOCAL LAW.

ACKNOWLEDGMENT

YOU ACKNOWLEDGE THAT YOU HAVE READ THIS AGREEMENT, UNDERSTAND IT, AND AGREE TO BE BOUND BY ITS TERMS AND CONDITIONS. YOU ALSO AGREE THAT THIS AGREEMENT IS THE COMPLETE AND EXCLUSIVE STATEMENT OF THE AGREEMENT BETWEEN YOU AND THE COMPANY AND SUPERSEDES ALL PROPOSALS OR PRIOR AGREEMENTS, ORAL, OR WRITTEN, AND ANY OTHER COMMUNICATIONS BETWEEN YOU AND THE COMPANY OR ANY REPRESENTATIVE OF THE COMPANY RELATING TO THE SUBJECT MATTER OF THIS AGREEMENT.

Should you have any questions concerning this Agreement or if you wish to contact the Company for any reason, please contact in writing at the address below.

Robin Short
Prentice Hall PTR
One Lake Street
Upper Saddle River, New Jersey 07458

License Agreement and Limited Warranty

Using the CDs

The interface to the contents of the Microsoft® Windows® CD is designed to start automatically through the AUTORUN.EXE file. If a startup screen does not pop up automatically when you insert the CD into your computer, double click on the welcome.htm file to launch the Student CD or refer to the file readme.txt on the CD.

Software and Hardware System Requirements

- 800 MHz (minimum) Pentium III or faster processor
- Windows Vista or Windows XP (with Service Pack 2)
- Minimum of 512 MB of RAM; 1 GB is recommended
- Minimum of 1.5 GB of hard disk space
- CD-ROM drive
- Internet connection
- Web browser, Adobe® Reader® and a zip decompression utility